The Roots of Reconstruction

by

ROUSAS JOHN RUSHDOONY

ROSS HOUSE BOOKS
VALLECITO, CALIFORNIA 95251
1991

ISBN 1-879998-00-9

Ross House Books
P. O. Box 67
Vallecito, California 95251

Table of Contents

INTRODUCTION

The essays in this volume include all my Chalcedon Report articles, except for book reviews, from the first issue in 1965 into almost middle 1989. In the early years, I was the only writer, except for two or three numbers written by someone else at my invitation. (Missing numbers in the early reports mean that I contributed nothing.) All these articles are exactly as originally written except that in three different articles a single word was added in each to clarify a point, and one brief sentence was added in a fourth report where the meaning was unclear. None of this altered the contents.

The first report in 1965 announced my concern, the need for *Christian reconstruction*, and the term was there first used. It was much criticized at the time, and by some still is. The term, however, sets forth the purpose of Chalcedon, to apply God's word to every area of life and thought and to summon the redeemed to God to their responsibilities in Christ our King. The irrelevance of too many churchmen to the dominion mandate has made the church irrelevant to our time.

A great change is now under way. In 1961, in one of my earliest books, *Intellectual Schizophrenia*, I concluded the last chapter, on "The End of an Age," with this paragraph:

> The end of an age is always a time of turmoil, war, economic catastrophe, cynicism, lawlessness, and distress. But it is also an era of heightened challenge and creativity, of issues, and their world-wide scope, never has an era faced a more demanding and exciting crisis. This then above all else is the great and glorious era to live in, a time of opportunity, one requiring fresh and vigorous thinking, indeed a glorious time to be alive. (p. 113f.)

It was not an easy time for me then when I wrote those words, nor is it now, 29 years later, but I feel even more strongly that it is a privilege to live in a time when serving the Lord can be so telling and important. I love my calling; to serve the triune God in any capacity is a joy and a blessing, whatever the problems, hostilities, and malice one encounters. I am *not* saying that I enjoy my troubles! Far from it! I am as prone to complaining to God as anyone, but I try also to be faithful in expressing my gratitude for the redemption and the calling which He has given me.

Rousas John Rushdoony
June 14, 1989

CONFLICT WITH THE STATE: A CHALCEDON POSITION PAPER

In recent years, under the influences of humanism on the one hand and pietism on the other, the church has withdrawn from many of its historic and basic functions. As the church begins to revive and resume its required ministry, the result is **conflict** with the humanistic state. It is important therefore to examine some of the historic and necessary duties of the Christian Church.

The *church* can be understood in part by the Biblical words used to describe it in the Bible. The basic word in the New Testament Greek is *ecclesia*, assembly, or congregation, which in the Old Testament was *qahal* and *edah*. The church is also described in James 2:2 as a *synagoge*, or synagogue. In the Old Testament, the government of the synagogue was by *elders* or *presbyters*; this office continues in the Christian synagogue, with the same basic requirements for the office (I Tim. 3:1-13, etc.) as required by the synagogue. The Old Testament pattern was so carefully preserved by the church that the English word *priest* is an abridgment of *presbyter*, and the College of Cardinals for centuries was a lay council of 70 (Num. 11:16), like the Sanhedrin, with the pope, like the Jewish high priest as the 71st. Jesus created a ruling-serving body of 70 also, a kind of diaconate, (Matt. 10:1, 17) as the "Sanhedrin" of the church, which called itself "the Israel of God" (Gal. 6:16).

The Old Testament clergy was divided into two classes, priests and Levites. The work of the priests was hieratic, sacrifice and offerings being its essential function. For Christians, this aspect of the Old Testament ministry ended with Christ. Even those communions who call their clergy *priests* do so with a difference, so that the Old Testament priesthood is seen as finished. The function of the Levitical ministry was instruction (Deut. 33:10). As a result, education was basic to the life of the synagogue and the Levitical ministry. The well-known Hebrew proverb declares that a man who did not teach his son the Torah (i.e., the Old Testament) and a trade taught him to be a thief. Hence, Israel was unique in antiquity because of its well-nigh universal education as the ministry of the synagogue.

Josephus declared that the origin of Hebrew schools was with Moses. (Josephus: *Antiquities of the Jews*, 4.8.12.) In *Against Apion* (2025), Josephus said of Moses, "He commanded to instruct the children in the elements of knowledge, to teach them to walk according to the laws, and to know the deeds of their fathers. The latter, that they might imitate them; the former, that growing up with the laws, they might not transgress them, nor have the excuse of ignorance." While most scholars would be skeptical of a Mosaic origin for the schools, it is clear that Deuteronomy is largely concerned with *instruction*, of both adults and children.

The influence of this standard was great. Hillel held, "an ignorant man (i.e., one ignorant of the Torah) cannot be truly pious...The more teaching of the Law, the more life; the more school, the more wisdom; the more counsel, the more reasonable action " (*Sayings of the Fathers*, 2:5; 2:7) This educational standard, noted Barclay, "has left its mark deeply upon the world, because in the last analysis it aims to educate the child in order to fit him to be a servant of God; it is an education of children for God." (William Barclay: *Train Up a Child, Educational Ideals in the Ancient World*, 48. [1959]).

The early church, the medieval church, the Reformation church, and the contemporary fundamentalist and orthodox churches, seek to continue this ancient mandate of education. The church is, as E. Schweizer, in *Church Order in The New Testament* (7b, 92), pointed out, "the realm of dominion in which the risen Lord continues to work." (Cited in Colin Brown, editor, *The New International Dictionary of New Testament Theology*, vol. 1, p. 300. [1967, 1975].)

The early church came into conflict with Rome, which sought to license, regulate, control, and tax all religions because the church refused to submit to controls. Its resistance was based on the lordship or sovereignty of Christ: Christ's domain cannot be under the dominion of Caesar. Caesar is under Christ the creator and lord, not Christ under Caesar. The church thus engaged in several unlicensed activities:

1. It held meetings which were instructional and worship meetings, without permits.
2. It collected abandoned babies (as part of its opposition to abortion), gave them to various church families, reared and instructed them; orphanages were maintained also.
3. Because of the Levitical nature of the church, i.e., a center of instruction, libraries and schools began to be built very early. Later, Cathedral schools developed, and universities.

The doctrine of academic freedom is a relic of the day when the academy was a part of the church and its functions, and hence entitled to the immunities thereof. How seriously this aspect was seen as basic to the church's life is apparent from the fact that, as soon as churches were built (not possible for the first two centuries), libraries (and schools) were a part of them. Joseph Bingham, in *The Antiquities of the Christian Church* (1850), wrote, "there were such places anciently adjoining to many churches, from the time that churches began to be erected among Christians." (Bk. VIII, ch. VII, sect. 12.) Bingham cited some of the ancient references to these schools and libraries: (Euseb. *lib*. 6, c.20; Hieron. [Jerome] *Catalog Sireptor. Eccles*. c.TS; *Gesta Purgat, ad calcem Optati*, p. 267; Augustine, *de. Haeres*. c.80; Basil, *Ep*. 82.t. 3., p. 152; Hospinian, *de Templis*, lib. 3,c.7., p. 101, etc.) Bingham referred also to a canon attributed to the Sixth Ecumenical Council, in Constantinople, 680-681 A.D., which required that presbyters in country towns and villages maintain schools for all children. He added, summing up all the evidences, "we may conclude, that schools were anciently very common appendants both of cathedral and country churches" (Bk VIII, ch. VII, sect. 12). Fault can only be found with Bingham's statement on the ground that they were not "appendants" but a basic aspect of the life of the church, whether separate from the church or within it. Bingham's high church tendencies led him to stress the liturgical rather than educational life of the church. Many critical scholars would deny that schools existed at so early a date; too often their premise is to assume a rootless church, i.e., a church without the fact of the synagogue and the Levite in the background as its origin, and in the present as a rival and reminder. Moreover, it must not be forgotten that Christianity is the religion of the book, the Bible. Literacy and education were thus natural concomitants to conversion. But this is not all. Being the religion of the Book meant that translations were made into various tongues, and, to make the translation readable, education was stressed. In Armenia, an alphabet was created for the Bible translation, and a new culture developed as a result of the new learning in that new alphabet of the Bible. Granted that invasions, wars, the backwardness of many of the newly converted peoples (as in northern Europe) made the development of schools and learning at times a slow process, but it is clear that (1) Christianity saw education or instruction as basic to its life and a necessary function of the church, and (2) education in the Western world is a unique development in history and a child of the church.

Moreover, we must remember that, in the early church, the service was Levitical or instructional. At the conclusion of the instruction (or sermon), there were questions designed to enable the hearers to clarify misunderstood or difficult points. Since not all who attended were believers, but were sometimes visitors or the unbelieving husband or wife of a believer, questions could be at times contentious. Women were forbidden to engage in this debating or in challenging the pastor or teacher. Paul says

> 34. Let your women keep silence in the churches: for it is not permitted unto them to speak; but they are commanded to be under obedience, as also saith the law.
> 35. And if they will learn any thing, let them ask their husbands at home: for it is a shame for women to speak in the church. (I Cor. 14:34-35)

The point is that the church itself in the New Testament was more a school than a temple. The Reformation, and later the Puritans, restored this instructional emphasis to church meetings. This historic emphasis is again coming to the forefront. At a few morning services in the U.S., the question and answer format has been revived; it is more common at evening services.

Even more, churches are establishing, whether as parochial or separate bodies, schools as basic to the life of the church. These are often grade and high schools, Bible colleges, in two or more cases in 1978, seminaries, and so on. These are not seen as innovations nor as activities alien to the church but as central to it. Whenever and wherever there is or has been a deepening of the Old Testament foundations of the Christian faith, together with a revived emphasis on the lordship or sovereignty of Jesus Christ, there has been a corresponding and necessary development of the *Levitical* nature of the ministry. Education then becomes essential to the ministry. The warning of Jeremiah 10:2, "Thus saith the LORD, Learn not the way of the heathen," is taken seriously.

Another factor is also stressed. Baptism, depending on the church communion, involves an explicit or implicit vow that the baptized, under penalty of curse, is the property of Jesus Christ. He and his children must be instructed in the word of the Lord. It was once commonplace to require all baptized Christians to place their children in church schools. That mandate is again returning, because of the faith that a child who is the property of Christ by virtue of his baptism, or the parent's baptism, cannot be placed in a humanistic school. The Christian School movement is the result.

The German historian, Ethelbert Stauffer, in his important study of *Christ and the Caesars* (1952 in Germany: 1955, U.S.), showed clearly that the roots of the ancient conflict between church and state are religious. Where the state claims to be god walking on earth, the state will claim sovereignty and will seek to control every area of life and thought. A free society becomes impossible. The Christian claim is not that the church is sovereign over the world, for it is not; lordship or sovereignty is an attribute of God, not man. But the Christian insistence is on the freedom of the church, "the realm of dominion in which the risen Lord continues to work" (E. Schweizer), from the controls of the state or any other agency.

It involves, moreover, a denial of the doctrine of state sovereignty. The very word sovereignty is absent from the U.S. Constitution because of the theological context of those times. The historian, A. F. Pollard, wrote:

> The colonies had been as anxious to get rid of James II in 1688 as they were to be free from Parliament in 1776. Their fundamental objection was to any sovereignty vested in any State whatsoever, even in their own. Americans may be defined as that part of the English-speaking world which has instinctively revolted against the doctrine of the sovereignty of the State and has, not quite successfully, striven to maintain that attitude from the time of the Pilgrim Fathers to the present day...It is this denial of all sovereignty which gives its profound and permanent interest to the American Revolution. The Pilgrim Fathers crossed the Atlantic to escape from sovereign power;

> Washington called it a "monster"; the professor of American History at Oxford calls it a "bugaboo"...and Mr. Lansing writes of the Peace Conference that "nine-tenths of all international difficulties arise out of the problem of sovereignty and the so-called sovereign state." (A. F. Pollard: *Factors in American History*, p. 31f. [1925]).

This statement is all the more of interest because Pollard was an English scholar and a great authority of his day on constitutionalism. Since Pollard's day, of course, the U.S. Federal government and the states have steadily advanced claims of sovereignty. At the same time, they have become increasingly humanistic in their view of law and have firmly established humanism as the religion of the "public" or state schools.

The novelty in the present conflict is not that the church or the Christian Schools are claiming new, and historically novel, immunities, but that the various American states are claiming a jurisdiction never before exercised or existing. *The novelty is on the part of the state.* It is a product of its claim to sovereignty. This claim places the state on a collision course with the church, and even more, with God, the only Sovereign. On April 30, 1839, on "The Jubilee of the Constitution," John Quincy Adams attacked the new doctrine of state sovereignty. As against parliamentary omnipotence and sovereignty, the colonists in 1776 appealed to the omnipotence and sovereignty of God. Adams declared:

> There is the Declaration of Independence, and there is the Constitution of the United States--let them speak for themselves. The grossly immoral and dishonest doctrine of despotic state sovereignty, the exclusive judge of its own obligations, and responsible to no power on earth or in heaven, for the violation of them, is not there. The Declaration says it is not in me. The Constitution says it is not in me. (S. H. Peabody, editor; *American Patriotism, Speeches, Letters, and other Papers*, etc., p. 321. 1880).

The conflict is the same religious conflict which saw Rome and the early church in bitter war, and with many Christians martyred. It is Christ versus Caesar. For the Christian, there can be no compromise. What is at stake is not his property, concern, or income, but Christ's dominion, "the realm of dominion in which the risen Lord continues to work." (January, 1979)

IN THE NAME OF JESUS CHRIST, OR, IN THE NAME OF CAESAR?

Chalcedon Position Paper No. 2

The meaning of names is largely irrelevant in our day. We name our children in terms of names that please us, whatever they may mean. In the Bible, especially in the Old Testament, names are definitions, and a man's name changed as his faith and character changed. We do not know Abraham's name before his calling; we do know that God first named him Abram, and then Abraham, to signify his place in God's plan; it was a name Abraham had to use by faith, because, humanly speaking, he was not the father of a great multitude.

Because names have become meaningless to us, we assume that they are so with God as well. Far from being the case, one of God's basic laws concerns His name: "Thou shalt not take the name of the LORD thy God in vain: for the Lord will not hold him guiltless that taketh his name in vain" (Ex. 20:7, Deut. 5:11). Proverbs 18:10 tells us, "The name of the LORD is a strong tower: the righteous runneth into it, and is safe." Paul declares, in Colossians 3:17, "And whatsoever ye do in word or deed, do all in the name of the Lord Jesus, giving thanks to God and the Father by him."

In Hebrew, name is *Shem*, it appears some 770 times; in Greek, it is *onoma*. The *name* sets forth and defines the person named. Hence, when Moses asked what God's name is, God made clear that He was beyond definition, so that His "Name" is simply I AM THAT I AM, or He Who Is, Jehovah or Yahweh. Then the Lord declares Himself to be the God of Abraham, Isaac, and Jacob (Ex. 3:13-15). Because God is infinite, omnipotent, and omniscient, He cannot be limited or described by any definition: He is the Eternal God, the One who creates and defines all things but is Himself beyond definition. He is, however, knowable in His revelation to Abraham and others, and in His word. The Name of God is thus I AM THAT I AM.

But names not only set forth the meaning and definition of a person, they also set forth his *power, dominion, and authority*. Hence, the commandments are given in the name of God. The authority, power, and dominion of Jesus Christ are so total "that at the name of Jesus every knee should bow, of things in heaven, and things in earth, and things under the earth" (Phil. 2:10).

Now, practically, what does this mean? It means, *first*, that we have seriously erred in limiting the Third Commandment to verbal profanity. To be profane, means literally to be outside the temple, outside the Lord. In its true meaning, profanity is any and every word, thought, and action which is outside the triune God, which is apart from His word and government. To be bearers of the Name, i.e., to be called Christian, means that we are totally under Christ's rule and dominion.

Very briefly, salvation, sovereignty, and government cannot be separated. Only a totally sovereign God who controls all things can save us. Such a God is totally the Lord over all creation: the government of all things is upon His shoulders (Isa. 9:6-7; Ps. 2). There is not a moment of time nor an atom or corner of all the universe which is outside the power and government of the triune God, of Christ the King. As a result, it is profanity to assume that any area can be outside of God and His law. A very common question asked of us these days is this: "I agree that homosexuals have no place in the pulpit or in a Christian School, but how can we bar them from a neutral realm like the public school or the civil service?" The answer is that there are no neutral realms: God is God over all things, and to exempt any realm from His government and law-word is profanity and a violation of the Third Commandment. "The LORD will not hold him guiltless that taketh his name in vain."

Second, throughout the Bible the lives and actions of God's people were conducted in the Name of the Lord, which, we are told, "is a strong tower: the righteous runneth into it, and is safe" (Prov. 18:10). Of this verse, Franz Delitzsch wrote, "The name of Jahve is the Revelation of God, and the God of Revelation Himself...His name is His nature representing itself...His free and all-powerful government in grace and truth...This name, which is afterwards interwoven in the name of Jesus is (Ps. 1xi:4), a strong high tower bidding defiance to every hostile assault."

However, not only is the Lord's name our defense, but also our strength in overcoming the enemy. Thus, *third*, the Lord's name is the name of power in overcoming all enemies and in subduing all things to Jesus Christ (Phil. 2:9-11). He is the Lord, and all things shall be placed under His feet (Ps. 2; Heb. 2:8).

Fourth, we must therefore, if we would not profane God's Name, do *all* things, whether in the area of thought, education, or learning, or in the area of action or deeds, in the name of the Lord Jesus (Col. 3:17). This means that our lives, homes, churches, schools, civil governments, arts and sciences, and all things else must be done in the Name, that is, under the kingship, dominion, authority, power, and the word of the Lord. Anything else is profanity and practical unbelief.

In whose name does our world operate now? The old-fashioned order, "Halt, in the name of the law," summoned up the authority of the state. That state authority was once to a degree in the Name of the Lord. Today, the state, its courts and law, and its schools are profane. They are outside of Christ and in contempt of Him.

The war of the early church against Rome was *a war of names*. Which name was the name of power, of ultimate authority, the name of Christ, or the name of Caesar? Rome's position was expressed in its fundamental law: "The health (or, welfare) of the people is the highest law." Rome's approach to the early church was thus in the name of the general welfare of the people, and the Roman Empire was the expression of that concern, and the source of authority. The approach of Rome thus was to deny that it sought to suppress freedom of religion. Rather, it sought to protect the health and general welfare of the people by requiring certain submissions of all religious groups. Implicit in this position, however, was the belief that, *first*, the state or Caesar is the best judge of the health or welfare of the people. This meant that the word of truth and wisdom was not the word of God but the word of the state. Sound social order and health thus was held to require that Caesar's word prevail and govern.

Second, the governing word is the word of power, and Rome held that Caesar's word is the word of power. But Caesar's word could not save Rome, and Caesar's coercive power could kill, but it could neither redeem nor save. The more emphatically imperial Rome asserted its word and law, the greater became the decay and the decline of Rome.

Third, "the highest law" is not the health of the people but the law-word of God, and, as a result, Roman law and society, like our own, had a false and rotting center. The more Rome developed the fundamental premises of its law, the more it hastened its decay and collapse, even as the world today increases the extent of its crisis with its remedial effort, because all its remedies have a false premise, humanism.

Fourth, the conflict then and now is a war of names. Which is the name of power, Christ or Caesar?

All too many churchmen are radically profane and blasphemous. They are either silent in the face of, or agreeable to, the state's usurpation of one area of life after another to its humanistic authority. These churchmen withdraw into a sanctimonious surrender and do nothing to stop the growing profanity whereby one area of life after another is withdrawn from the government of Christ the King and placed into the hands of Caesar. Again, all over the world, "the chief priests" of our day, like those of old, are declaring, "We have no king but Caesar" (John 19:15). If for a moment we allow humanism any title or right to any area of creation, we are profane, and we deny Christ to affirm Caesar.

Again and again, the summons of Scripture is to "believe on the name of Jesus Christ." This means to ground the totality of our lives, thinking, institutions, and world, including church, state, and school on the Name of Christ the King, *under* His authority, power, law-word, and government. This is clear from II Timothy 2:19: "Nevertheless, the foundation of God standeth sure, having this seal, The Lord knoweth them that are his. And, let every one that nameth the name of Jesus Christ depart from iniquity." Paul was condemning "profane and vain babblers" who wrongly divided the word of truth. God's foundation or reign is not affected by their profanity. God knows His own. Those who *name* the Lord are those who depart from iniquity, or injustice, unrighteousness (*adikia*). Iniquity is that condition where man opposes to God's right or righteousness, to God's order and justice, his own humanistic doctrine of order, right, or justice. Iniquity can be a physical act of lawlessness; it can also be a faith, philosophy, or order to society which sets up a law, institution, state, or order outside of God and His law-word. It is not under the Name and authority of God: it does not serve or obey Him.

It was a strong emphasis of Christian teaching and preaching for centuries that the state must serve the Lord. The New England Puritan, Charles Turner, pastor at Duxbury, in a sermon before Governor Thomas Hutchinson and the House of Representatives of the Massachusetts Bay Province, May 26, 1773, declared:

> Rulers are, at once, *ministers* of God, and *servants of society*; as Gospel ministers are servants of Christ, and of the Churches. And, if God has given to the community a right to appoint its servants, it is but rational and consistent to suppose, that the community should have a right to take effectual care, that their servants should not counteract and disappoint the great purpose for which they were distinguished from their fellow-creatures; and if, in any case, it may be seen necessary for the public salvation, to give the servants of society a dismission.

In other words, as surely as the church must dismiss ungodly pastors as false ministers, so too it must dismiss all state officers who will not serve the Lord as being ungodly ministers of state. To fail to do so is to partake in their sin and to become ourselves profane. We are today a profane society, and our cities and countryside are spotted by profane churches which take the Lord's Name in vain.

The encroachments of humanism into church, state, school, and every other realm must cease. We must cease from all personal and corporate profanity, or face God's judgment as traitors and rebels. A piety which concerns itself only with man's soul and leaves the world to the devil is a profane piety. God's warning is clear: "Cease ye from man, whose breath is in his nostrils: for wherein is he to be accounted of?" (Isa. 2:22). To be profane is to be outside of God's grace and mercy. Isaiah lived in a generation that professed the Name of the Lord, but were "a people of unclean lips" (Isa. 6:5), because their lives and politics were profane. Are we not far worse? Is there any remedy other than total submission to Christ the King, doing all things, in every area of life, thought, and action, in the Name, or power, authority, and government of the Lord? "Who is on the LORD's side?" (Ex. 32:26). Let him stand in the Name of the King. (February, 1979)

CAN WE TITHE OUR CHILDREN?

Scripture requires us to tithe our income. God requires His tithe, a modest amount as compared to the modern state's demands. But, in all things else, God requires the totality of our allegiance, our service, and our lives. We cannot tithe our children, nor ourselves. We cannot give our tenth child only to the Lord and to Christian schools, while sending all others to the state school. Neither can we give our children to the Lord one day in seven or in ten, and to the state the rest of the time.

We and all that we have are God's possession. Children are described as a "gift" or "heritage" from the Lord, and also as a "reward", "boon", or "blessing" (Ps. 127:3). To misuse God's gifts and blessings is to incur His wrath. It is only "every one that feareth the LORD; that walketh in his ways" who is "blessed" (Ps. 128:1).

The first and basic premise of paganism, socialism, and Molech worship is its claim that the state owns the child. The basic premise of the public schools is this claim of ownership, a fact some parents are encountering in the courts. It is the essence of paganism to claim first the lives of the children, then the properties of the people.

For too long most professing Christians have been practicing pagans who have honored God falsely: they "with their lips do honour me, but have removed their heart from me, and their fear toward me is taught by the precept of men" (Isa. 29:13). On all such, God's judgment is assured, and God's judgment on our age is in increasing evidence. Judgment is neither averted nor moderated by much crying or bemoaning but only by a renewed heart, by faith and obedience. How can we expect God to honor us, or bless us, when we give our children to the state schools and surrender their minds daily to the teachings of humanism? It is sin and madness to believe so, and those who try to justify their sin only increase it.

The true believer will, like Hannah (I Sam. 1:27f.), see children as a gift from the Lord, to be given to the Lord as long as they live. (February, 1979)

THE LIMITATIONS OF LAW
Chalcedon Position Paper No. 3

We fail to understand God's law unless we realize how carefully it limits man. God's law prevents man from placing too much trust in law, and from becoming a tyrant, by limiting man's powers of enforcement.

An obvious limitation on the courts of law is the requirements of corroboration: one witness alone cannot convict (Num. 35:30, Deut. 17:6; 19:15). However, a more basic limitation is that many offenses, some very serious, have no penalties which any man or court can impose. For example, tithing is God's tax; failure to pay the tithe is theft; it is robbing God (Mal. 3:7-12). God Himself imposes very severe penalties on this kind of theft, but He does not call for any man-imposed penalty. Another example: Deut. 22:5 forbids transvestite dress, i.e., the wearing of clothing belonging to the opposite sex, and I Timothy 2:9 requires modest apparel of women, but no penalties for disobedience are cited.

God's law covers every area of life: the family, the church, the state, our vocation, our relationships one to another, the use of the earth, sanitation, sexuality, warfare, boundaries, weights and measures, and all things else. The Lord makes very clear the curses and blessings He places on disobedience (Deut. 28, Lev. 26, etc.). His government is total: we can never, for a moment step outside of God's law and government. There is not a neutral corner or atom in all of creation. God is totally God, and His government and law are total, covering all things. At every point in our lives, we are face to face with the living God, in all things accountable to Him, and totally His creatures and servants.

Man, however, is not God, nor can he play god without being guilty of the great temptation of the evil one. Original sin is precisely this fact, the desire to be as God, to determine for ourselves what constitutes good and evil, and to rule all things totally. Among Nietzsche's manuscripts, after his death, was found a slip of paper on which he had written these words: "Since the old God has been abolished, I am prepared to rule the world." This is the meaning of humanism's inescapable totalitarianism. Total government is a necessity, and everything in man requires it. If there is no God to provide it, then man must supply it. More accurately, when man rebels against God's total sovereignty and government, he replaces it with his own claim to total sovereignty and government.

Thus, the present totalitarian claims and trends of virtually every civil government in the world are aspects of their humanism and their explicit or implicit denial of God. Humanism says of God, our law and government provide a better way than God's, and ours is the way, the truth and the life. In the United States, the efforts of federal and state governments to control churches and Christian Schools are the logical results of their humanism. There must be sovereignty and law, and it must be man's, not God's, is their faith. Clearly, we are in the basic religious war, and there can be no compromise nor negotiation in this war. Humanism seeks to abolish the God of Scripture and rule the world.

Humanism thus will permit no independent realm to exist outside its government. Every area must be controlled and ruled by humanistic law and sovereign power. The result is a growing statist tyranny everywhere, and the death of freedom is in sight all over the world.

The record of the church, while not as deadly as that of the modern state, is also none too good. The church too has often played god on earth and sought to exercise total government in the name of God. Protestants and Catholics alike have been guilty of going beyond God's law and usurping judgments which Biblical law reserves to God alone. Humanists are very prone to exaggerating the evils of the church's record, and Protestants and Catholics too often dearly love to believe the worst and tell the worst about one another. Granted, that humanistic historians have not done justice to the history of the church, the errors there are still real.

The problem can be illustrated by the history of a large evangelical church of the 1930s. It sought to be strictly fundamental, a commendable goal, but, in the process, it usurped God's prerogatives. For example, in terms of I Corinthians 11:1-15, it held that Scripture has a requirement that women's hair be "long." Well and good, but Scripture neither sets a length nor attaches penalties; it gives to no man, nor to the church, any such power. This church, however, decided to legislate against "bobbed hair," and it specified a length in terms of inches; anything shorter meant an appearance before the church court. Next, they specified the length of skirts, and so on and on. The results were devastating.

First, the central emphasis in the life of this once strong church became externals, with everyone overly conscious of appearances. Women eyed one another to see who was flirting with the limits of the law, and everyone began to develop censoriousness. *Second*, the youth became rebellious. The gospel was now reduced to compliance with externals, and they readily rebelled as soon as they went off to college. It was very difficult to talk with any of the youth about matters of faith and doctrine. For them, the church and Christianity represented not faith and life in Christ but a multitude of petty rules and regulations. *Third*, the church began to associate the purity of its faith more and more with its observance of forms, and less and less with a solid knowledge of Biblical doctrine. Faith was giving way to form. Rules lead to more rules, and the yoke of Pharisaic laws came to be rivalled.

Much more could be added, but, suffice it to say that finally a rebellion set in, but a sorry one. The antithesis to Pharisaic legalism and to playing God was seen as being more *loving*, and a neo-evangelical emphasis on love was the next stage in the slide of this church into modernism, and, finally, the social gospel, with the state now becoming the universal rule and law-maker in their sorry "gospel."

God's law, by reserving, in one area after another, the right of enforcement to God alone, severely limits the power of all human forms of government. Neither church, nor state, nor any other human agency is empowered to play God. Moreover, we do not gain in holiness by becoming "stricter" than God: we gain only in presumptuous sin. God alone is God: He does not delegate His throne nor His sovereign law-making power to any human being or agency. To become "stricter" than God's law, as one pastor boasted to me of being, is to imply a moral defect in God and is blasphemy.

God's law thus allows man many areas of freedom to obey or disobey without man-imposed penalties. The result is a great freedom for man to sin or to obey than most man-made institutions believe is wise. Certainly, church and state have alike worked to limit the freedom God allows.

One critic of Biblical law has declared to me that any strict adherence in every realm to God's order would be "disastrous," *first*, because in a few areas God's law is marked by an "undue severity," as witness the death penalty for adultery. (The family being God's basic institution, treason in the Bible is adultery; there is no treason with respect to the state.) Second, in most areas, Biblical law would produce "anarchy," because no penalties can be enforced by man in any strict reading thereof.

From the standpoint of Scripture, God's rule is not anarchy but justice and freedom. Redemption is not by rules and regulation; salvation is not by law. It is by God's sovereign grace through Jesus Christ. The redeemed man, lives a life of faith and obedience in the Spirit and in terms of the enscriptured word. Our liberty in Christ is from the bondage or slavery of sin and the penalty of death, and it is a deliverance also from fallen man's way of salvation, a total government by the words of law, man-made law.

If we take any law of God and alter it, or go beyond it, we too become humanistic. We "correct" God as gods over God, and we limit and finally destroy man's freedom under God.

One of the more frequently repeated declarations of Scripture is, "Vengeance is mine; I will repay, saith the Lord" (Rom. 12:19; Deut. 32:35,41,43; Ps. 94:1, etc.). Again, in Hebrews 10:30, we read, "Vengeance belongeth unto me, I will recompense, saith the Lord. And again, the Lord shall judge his people." In certain specified areas, and within carefully circumscribed limits, God gives to men and to courts of law the power to judge and convict. The word vengeance is in the Greek text *ekdikesis*, that which proceeds out of justice, *dike* being justice. God declares that He alone is the judge and Law-maker. No man can go beyond His law-word, for to do so is not that which proceeds out of justice but out of presumption and sin. Thus, when the Lord declares, "Vengeance (or, the enforcement of justice) is Mine," He bars man from playing God, from adding or subtracting from God's law-word, or from attempting to rule over men in any way which exceeds God's word. Only as men stand in terms of this faith are they protected from being enslaved by, or enslaving, other men. The law-word of God is man's only charter of liberty, and man's defense against the tyrannies of state, church, and man. The redeemed of the Lord will stand in His word as free men. (May, 1979)

SALVATION: BY WHOSE WORKS?

No man can be saved by his works, his salvation is the work of God, not man. This is a fundamental doctrine of the Christian faith, affirmed on all sides and dishonored widely. Our Lord, citing Isaiah 29:13, declares, "Ye hypocrites, well did Esaias prophesy of you, saying, This people draweth nigh unto me with their mouth, and honoureth me with their lips; but their heart is far from me. But in vain do they worship me, teaching for doctrines the commandments of men" (Matt. 15:7-9).

To believe that salvation is by grace and not by works means that all of man's works outside of Christ are futile to commend him to God and to effect his salvation.

Now Augustine made clear that for a state or civil government to be built on any other foundation than the Lord and His word is to build nothing more than a band of robbers. "Except the LORD build the house, they labour in vain that build it: except the LORD keep the city, the watchman waketh but in vain" (Ps. 127:1). How then can we imagine that any law, school, church, state, or any other thing can be a good thing or a good work when it is outside of Christ and has no place for Him? How can we imagine that a state or school which neglects or despises the basic fact of all being, our Lord and His sovereignty, can be anything but an abomination to Him?

Today, however, we have indignant churchmen waging war against pastors and Christians who work for Christian Schools; these people defend the godless state schools and seek to drive away from the church all who criticize them. To defend statist education is to defend a humanistic plan of salvation which seeks to save the world by man's educational work.

The same is true of the state. The modern humanistic state offers a cradle to grave plan of salvation. It is at war with Christ the Lord and denies His plan of redemption for its own. The state issues its own decrees of predestination, election, and salvation. Today, the Internal Revenue Service is seeking to break all who will not conform to "public policy", i.e., to the statist plan of salvation. Its doctrine of sanctification means compliance with the state and its doctrines of social justice. To be a Christian today requires that we stand against the great false doctrine of works of our time, salvation by the works of the humanistic state.

The Bible does not give us museum piece doctrines. When it condemns unregenerate man's works, it condemns not merely the Pharisees but the statist educators, the humanistic statists, the Republicans, Democrats, Socialists, Communists, and others, the male and female "chauvinists" and all others who see a hope of salvation outside of the Lord and His law-word.

By its own do-nothing, antinomian ways, the church today approves the works of humanistic educators and statists. The Bible did not merely condemn theological formulations of salvation by works; it declares false every effort by man to save himself by his own works. The Judaizers of Paul's day were wrong; so too are all organized bands of thieves who call themselves a civil government, and so too are all their schools.

Paul declares, "For by grace are ye saved through faith; and that not of yourselves: it is the gift of God: Not of works, lest any man should boast" (Eph. 2:8-9). "Cease ye from man, whose breath is in his nostrils: for wherein is he to be accounted of?" (Isa. 2:22). Salvation is the work of God, not man. (May, 1979)

THE ESCHATOLOGY OF DEATH
Chalcedon Position Paper No. 4

The dying have no future, and they know it. They speak of, and limit their vision to, the present and its sufferings. The future of the dying is a very limited one, and, usually, they do not go beyond a few days, or more than a month, in their thinking. Theirs is the eschatology of death, and men without faith have no other eschatology. Death and the certainty of death blots out all other considerations or else governs them all.

The same is true of cultures. Death comes upon them rapidly when the faith of the culture collapses or wanes. The confidence which once enabled them as a small minority to dominate their world melts away, and they cannot set their own house in order nor control it. Dying cultures block out tomorrow, having no confidence in their ability to cope with growth and the problems of growth. Dying Greece and dying Rome both saw themselves as overpopulated and as overwhelmed with peoples and problems, and so too does our modern, dying statist humanism feel. It talks desperately about zero population growth and zero economic growth, because behind such thinking is a zero future, an intellectual and religious bankruptcy.

The father of modern humanistic economics, Lord Keynes, when asked about the consequences of his economic theories "in the long run," answered simply, "In the long run, we are all dead." The growing disaster of Keynesian economics, and a world practicing it, should not surprise us. It was born without a future, and it was a product of an age which, like the dying, lived for the moment and with no thought of the future.

The dying live for the moment, because they have no future. Converted into a formal philosophy, the name of such a state of anticipated death is existentialism. For the existentialist philosopher, Jean-Paul Sartre, man is a futile passion who wills to be a god but is faced only with the certainty of death.

In one area after another, the eschatology of death governs our world. Yesterday, a letter came from a young man in Alaska which read in part as follows:

> I'm a surveyor, but I'm not registered by the state because I haven't passed a test, but I can't take the test because I haven't worked for a registered surveyor for eight years...At this time...there is no chance of employment for a registered land surveyor. I have to turn down work, because I can't sign for it. I have an education in land surveying and I feel that I could Pass the test...The registered land surveyors have legislated themselves a monopoly.

Alaska may call itself the last frontier, or a new frontier, but it was born dead, with an eschatology of death. Like dying New York City, it strangles itself with its own ungodly laws.

This situation is not unusual but commonplace. In some cities and states, no young man can qualify to be a plumber, or a carpenter, or in various other callings, unless his father is an important person in the union. The dying legislate against the future.

This eschatology of death is common to all ages and classes. The old are very prone to damning the younger generations, but one of the menaces of our time is the growing demands on public funds by the aging. With the decline in the birth rate, the United States may face a crisis in not too many years when each gainfully employed person will be supporting two persons on social security, and other forms of aid. Such a situation will not occur only because disaster will first overtake any society which works itself into such a predicament.

The younger generations are no better, of course. They seek statist solutions for all problems: totalitarianism in the economic sphere (and therefore in the political as well), and total permissiveness in the moral sphere. This is irresponsibility, and irresponsibility is an urgent invitation to disaster and death.

Not surprisingly, humanistic education is dominated by the eschatology of death. It creates a demand for instant results and instant gratification. It teaches children to play at being a state senate, or a congress, and to legislate feelings, as though "good" wishes can determine reality. The child matures physically but remains a child, demanding instant results and gratification, utopia now without either work or faith. Education for permanent childhood means a society of incompetents, of all ages, whose politics becomes a demand politics. Because a demand politics produces disasters, the politicians who feed or gratify this demand are readily and angrily made the scapegoats for a graceless and irresponsible citizenry.

In *Speech and Reality* (1970), Eugen Rosenstock-Huessy wrote of the social dangers and evils confronting modern civilization. These are, he said, *first*, anarchy. In anarchy, people and classes "do not care to come to an agreement." Instead of ties uniting men, there are now divisions only, with each pursuing his own interest. *Second*, decadence is a very great evil. Decadence is manifested at a critical point: parents do not have "the stamina of converting the next generation to their own aims and ends. Decadence is the disease of liberalism today." The consequence is the barbarization of the younger generation. Since they are not made heirs of the past and its faith, they become the barbarians of the present. (The modern family, like the modern school, is a school for barbarians.) "The only energy that can fight this evil is faith. Faith, properly speaking, never is a belief in things of the past, but of the future. Lack of faith is a synonym for decadence," Rosenstock-Huessy held.

Third, in his list of evils is revolution, which is a consequence of anarchy and decadence. The old and the past are liquidated or eliminated as meaningless and irrelevant, which indeed they have made themselves to be, by their lack of faith and their destructive education of the young. *Fourth* in the list of evils is war. War is a sign of impotence. A system or philosophy of life which has no power to convert becomes imperialistic. For the zeal and faith of peaceful missionary work it substitutes brutal terror. A failing faith resorts to war, because it lacks the contagion of faith and conviction and can only force men into its own system. War is the resort of those who lack true power and are declining.

In brief, Rosenstock-Huessy said, anarchy is a crisis created by a lack of unity and community. Decadence is the collapse of faith. Revolution means a lack of respect, indeed, a contempt, for the past and present. War is an indication of a loss of power and a resort to force to perpetuate or advance a system.

All of these things are aspects of the eschatology of death. But there is still another aspect. Because the modern taboo is death, people are prissy and hesitant about the plain facts of dying. It is often assumed, out of fear, that most deaths are costly, long, and lingering, which in most cases is not true. Death often comes quickly. It is also assumed that death comes to a bland man, again not true. It comes to Christians and to unbelievers, and with many shades of difference. Death among some of the ungodly who die a lingering death unleashes a radical hatred of the living. One man, a life-long reprobate and adulterer, abandoned his wife as "too old" and moved in with a younger widow, whom he enriched to a degree. When terminally ill, he was ordered out by his mistress, and only his wife would have him. Instead of gratitude, he daily showered her and their children with hatred, profanity, and abuse, hating them for their faith and health, "wasted" on them, he would shout, because they "didn't know how to live." This is an aspect of the eschatology of death, its hatred for life and the living, and its will to destroy them. At the heart of this is what Wisdom long ago declared: "But he that sinneth against me wrongeth his own soul; all they that hate me love death" (Prov. 8:36).

We are surrounded today by dying men whose eschatology is death and whose politics, religion, economics, education and daily lives manifest what Samuel Warner has called "the urge to mass destruction." Of this world system, Revelation 18:4 declares, "Come out of her, my people, that ye be not partakers of her sins, and that ye receive not of her plagues." In spite of this, all too many professing Christians not only refuse to separate themselves but are insistent on the morality of sending their children to humanistic state schools, an act of anarchy.

We have described the nature of the dying. What about the dead? The dead cannot wage war nor revolution, nor manifest hatred. The dead have their place, and they remain within it. No corpse can outgrow its coffin, nor conquer an inch of ground beyond that which it occupies. The dead stay in their coffins.

All too often the church is like a coffin. Instead of being a training ground and an armory for the army of the Lord, it is a repository for the dead. The people within have not the life and power to occupy any other ground, to establish Christian Schools, to conquer in the realm of politics and economics to "occupy" in Christ's name even one area of life and thought and to bring it into "captivity" to Jesus Christ (Luke 19:13; II Cor. 10:5). Where Christianity is confined to the church, it is dead, and it is only a corpse claiming that name but having none of the life nor the power thereof (II Tim. 3:5).

Christianity cannot be caged into a church and confined there like a zoo animal. "It is the power of God unto salvation to every one that believeth" (Romans 1:16). Power commands; it exercises dominion, and it reaches out "to every creature" (Mark 16:15) with the good news of Christ's redemption and lordship. It works to bring all things under the dominion of Christ, who is "King of kings, and Lord of lords" (Rev. 19:16). Jesus began and ended His ministry "preaching the gospel of the Kingdom of God" (Mark 1:14f). That Kingdom begins with our redemption through His atonement and continues with our exercise of dominion with knowledge, righteousness, and holiness over every area of life and thought.

Coffin churches have no such gospel. Instead, they summon the living dead to enter the safety of their particular casket, far removed from the problems and battles of life. They encourage their people to gush about the peace within the coffin, and to embellish the coffin with their time and effort. Coffin churches have no ministry to a dying world.

When our Lord declared, "ALL POWER is given unto me in heaven and in earth" (Matt. 28:18), He did not limit that total power which He as King of Creation exercises to the narrow confines of man's soul. Christ's "all power" is over all things in heaven and in earth in their every aspect, and over every atom, moment, and possibility in all of creation. He is the Lord, lord over all. To limit His lordship and power to the church is as absurd as limiting the sun to shining over Europe, or selected portions thereof. Even less than we can limit the sun to one continent or one country can we limit Christ the King to one sphere or institution. To do so is a denial of His deity and is practical atheism.

Because "all power" is His, the Lord of Creation sends His elect messengers out to "teach all nations, baptizing them in the name of the Father, and of the Son, and of the Holy Ghost: Teaching them to observe all things whatsoever I have commanded you: and, lo, I am with you always, even unto the end of the world" (Matt. 28:20). All nations are to be summoned to bow before their King, both as individuals and in every aspect of their lives, civil, ecclesiastical, educational, familial, vocational, and all things else. An eschatology of life and victory allows us to exempt nothing from Christ's dominion and lordship.

A sickly term in Reformed theological circles refers to God's "well-meant offer of the Gospel;" the image of God it invokes is a false one. God's word is never a "well-meant offer" but always the command word, the word of power which redeems and regenerates, or reprobates. To be "well-meant" smacks of impotence and failure, and it speaks of men whose powers are frail, fallible, sinful, and dying. It belongs to eschatologies of death. God's word is the command word, the word of power, the word of life and death because it is the omnipotent word. Only of Him can it be truly said, "The LORD killeth, and maketh alive: he bringeth down to the grave, and bringeth up" (I Sam. 2:6). Apart from the Lord, man has no future. In every area of life and thought, "Except the LORD build the house, they labour in vain that build it" (Ps. 127:1).

Education in its essence is always the transmission of the basic faith and values of a culture to its young. Education is thus in essence always a religious concern.

In many cultures, the basic values have been non-verbal and non-literary, so that education then has not been concerned with literacy but with other skills. A few cultures only have been concerned with literacy, Biblical faith and culture in particular, because of the insistence on the knowledge of the Scriptures. Modern humanism (as against classical humanism) under-rates verbal and literary skills.

Thus, not only is education a totally religious subject, but the curriculum, its contents, and its methods are all religious, in that they reflect the faith and values of a culture.

To allow our children to be in humanistic schools is to be unequally yoked and to serve two masters. (June, 1979)

ACCREDITATION AND CERTIFICATION
Chalcedon Position Paper No. 5

The word "accreditation" comes from "credo," I believe, and certification comes from a Latin word meaning "certain" and means to verify. Both words have an inescapably religious connotation. They imply a verification, a declaring that a thing is true, by the religious lord of those who seek accreditation and certification. To seek these things from the state is to declare the state to be our lord.

Is the state God's appointed agency of accreditation and certification? Is there any warrant in Scripture for contesting the state's claim to accredit and certify a church or Christian School? The answer to this question is urgently important. Today the U.S. Internal Revenue Service, and a variety of other federal and state agencies, claim precisely that right. It is held that a church has no valid status as a church, nor a Christian School any standing or legal status as a school, until some statist agency renders its decision and gives its stamp of approval. The same is held to be true of Christian School teachers. Our answer is very important: we will either offend and anger a powerful humanistic state, or we will anger and offend the sovereign and almighty God. It can also be added that, with either decision, we will offend many men.

What say the Scriptures? When we turn to the Bible, it immediately becomes apparent that our present practice reverses God's order. In Scripture, it is the prophetic ministry of God's law-word which accredits or certifies, or denounces and places under a ban, all officers of state, and entire nations as well. The sovereign prerogative of accreditation and certification of both church and state is the Lord's, and it is the calling of all God's faithful ministers to apply the rule or canon of the accrediting, certifying law-word to all men, institutions and nations.

The ministry of all God's faithful servants in every age has had this focus. Elijah denied certification to Ahab, and accreditation to Israel and its people, in terms of God's holy law. Athanasius denounced the Roman Empire and a compromising church in terms of that law-word.

The Biblical origin of the Christian ministry is the Levite. The Levites were a teaching ministry (Deut. 33:10), and the Christian pastor continues the Levitical calling, because the priestly order and sacrifice is ended. The Levites collected the tithe (Num. 18:21-28) of which one-tenth went to the priests. The rest provided for instruction, the care of the sanctuary, music, health, and, with the second tithe, welfare. The Levites taught the Law throughout the nation under Jehoshaphat (II Chron. 17:7ff.), served as judges (II Chron. 19:8ff.), and performed other services for society in general.

But the Christian ministry has another source in addition to the Levites, the prophets. The inspired, predictive role of the prophet ended in Christ; the duty of the prophet to proclaim God's word to church, state, and all of life remains. It was the duty of God's prophets and Levites to declare God's word to all men, to reprove kings and governors, and to "accredit" or refuse to certify in terms of God's law-word, the things of this world, including the state.

Civil government was strictly barred from invading God's house, as witness the case of Uzziah (II Chron. 26:16-23). It was the duty of civil authorities to protect and build up God's House, but never to claim powers in or over it. Rulers thus called for reform, but the reformation was then entrusted to God's chosen ministry.

Thus, in every area of life, accreditation and certification were by the word of God, not by state, church, or man. The law-word, not man's will, is the standard. It is a usurpation of God's prerogative when the state claims the right to accredit and to certify either a church or a Christian School. It becomes a claim to be god on earth. Those who accept such an accreditation and certification are like the 400 false prophets who served Ahab (I Kings 22:6-7). As Jehoshaphat rightly saw, these men were not prophets of the Lord.

Rome, of course, was ready to accredit all churches who would come before the authorities and confess that "Caesar is Lord." The early church refused accreditation, licensure, permits, and controls, because it confessed Jesus Christ, not Caesar, as Lord.

The Puritans, of course, had election sermons on every Sunday preceding an election in civil government. Accreditation was the purpose of these sermons. Because no area of life or creation exists outside its Creator's law, that word must be declared, in all its binding power, to every area. The election sermon was thus an accreditation sermon: it set forth the word of God as it bore upon the issues of the day. It certified that which is righteous or just in terms of God's word.

There is a law-word thus in terms of which all things are judged, and there is a bar before which all things must stand. It is God's law, and it is God's throne, and the government is on none other shoulders than that of the Lord (Isa. 9:6). For any human agency to attempt to replace God's law and God's accreditation with its own is to sin, and to play god. Its test then becomes that of Ahab concerning God's prophet, Micaiah: "I hate him; for he doth not prophesy good concerning me, but evil" (I Kings 22:8). The servants of the word of God are always hated by the humanists, in every age.

But, in the final analysis, and on the last day, no man stands apart from that word and the grace it proclaims, and no man has that grace who denies the law-word of the Lord of all grace.

The redeemed of God are those who, standing in grace, believe and obey God's every word (Matt. 4:4). That law-word is in their hands and in their hearts. As Scripture declares:

> I delight to do thy will, 0 my God: yea, thy law is within my heart. (Ps. 40:8).
>
> But this shall be the covenant that I will make with the house of Israel; After those days, saith the LORD, I will put my law in their inward parts, and write it in their hearts; and will be their God, and they shall be my people. (Jer. 31:33).
>
> And I will give them one heart, and I will put a new spirit within you; and I will take the stony heart out of their flesh, and will give them a heart of flesh. (Ezek. 11:19).
>
> A new heart also will I give you: and a new spirit will I put within you: and I will take away the stony heart out of your flesh and I will give you a heart of flesh. (Ezek. 36:26).
>
> For this is the covenant that I will make with the house of Israel after those days, saith the Lord; I will put my laws into their mind, and write them in their hearts; and I will be to them a God, and they shall be to me a people. (Heb. 8:10).

John Calvin, in a famous passage, declared that "the law is a silent magistrate, and a magistrate a speaking law" (*Institutes of the Christian*

Religion, Bk IV, ch. XX, sect. XIV). However, as the doctrine of the priesthood of all believers (Ex. 19:6; Isa. 61:6; Rev. 1:8; I Peter 2:9, etc.) makes clear, every man is called to be God's walking law. The law of God is the way of holiness for the redeemed; it is written on the tables of their hearts, and it governs their being. It is only when this is so that we can love and serve the Lord with all our heart, soul, mind, strength, and being, and love our neighbor as ourselves (Mark 12:29-31; Matt. 22:37-40; Deut. 6:5, 10:12; 30:6; Luke 10:27, etc.).

The Christian is the manifest grace of God, and is called to be the walking law of and witness to his Lord. This places a great responsibility upon covenant man.

God's law assigns various duties to institutions. Civil government is thus called to be a ministry of justice, of God's righteousness or justice (Rom. 13:1ff.), and the church is called to be the ministry of the word, and of God's grace and righteousness. It is a serious error to limit the doctrine of ordination and calling to institutions. St. Paul declares, "For we are his (God's) workmanship, created in Christ Jesus unto good works, which God hath before ordained that we should walk in them" (Eph. 2:10). We are redeemed so "that the righteousness of the law might be fulfilled in us" (Rom. 8:4).

The law in terms of which the redeemed of the Lord move is thus God's law. Only this law can accredit and certify the believer. The state may legalize abortion, homosexuality, fornication, and more, but the redeemed cannot be party to such practices nor recognize any validity in such laws. "For conscience' sake" (Rom. 13:5) the believer, in obedience to God, avoids rebellion, but for conscience' sake he also obeys God rather than men (Acts 5:29).

Least of all can the redeemed allow men to control that which belongs to the Lord. The church and the Christian School are not the property of the state, nor are they the property of the congregation: they are the Lord's, and can be surrendered to no man. The pagan principle that the state is God walking on earth has a major revival in our time. In old Russia, the Tatar invaders held that all were obliged to serve the state. Later, the tsars held to the same doctrine. A confidant of Alexander I (1801-1825) said of him, "In a word, he would willingly have agreed that every man should be free, on the condition that he should do only what the Emperor wished." Communist Russia has carried the pagan doctrine of the supremacy of the state to this logical conclusion.

In the West, however, the same doctrine has been very prevalent also, earlier in the divine right of kings, now in the doctrine of the general will and its incarnation in the state. In England, Henry VIII was part of a process going back at least to the Synod of Whitby in 664 A.D. His confiscation of church properties, and his use thereof, was an act of arrogation and blasphemy. The step preceding this act was a royal commission which indicted the church and denied it "accreditation" as the preliminary step towards confiscation. This was no new step; every tyrant who seized as much as one church first of all claimed the authority to deny that church its credentials.

The modern, 20th century attack on the church and the Christian School uses the same ploy. The Russian Revolution promoted the idea of corruption in the Russian Church, but it loved and used the corrupt and compromising, and persecuted the faithful, as it still does.

The situation is no different in the United States. The attack is on the faithful and the uncompromising, on those who declare unequivocally, "Jesus Christ is Lord," and who will not sacrifice what is the Lord's to Caesar. The Rev. Levi Whisner, and Dr. Lester Roloff, and others, have been ready to surrender their freedom, and have gone to jail at no small cost to themselves, but they have refused to surrender what belongs to Jesus Christ to American caesars.

The compromising clergy are, of course, full of "good" reasons why their way is "the path of reason." But reason is not our Lord: Jesus Christ is. These compromising clergymen cannot say with Paul, "But I certify you brethren, that the gospel which was preached of me is not after men" (Gal. 1:11). The word Paul uses is *gnorizo*, meaning to certify, declare, know, understand. Paul declared that he had been faithful, not to men, but to the Lord, and he had paid a price for that faithfulness. He understood that God's word cannot be compromised; no man can claim rights over God, or the power to judge and accredit God's realm.

To be a walking law means above all to be governed and to live, as our Lord declares, "by every word that proceedeth out of the mouth of God" (Matt. 4:4; Deut. 8:3; Luke 4:4). It means to be, like Elijah, "very jealous for the LORD God of hosts" (I Kings 19:10), to guard God's realm from the covetous hands of ungodly men. It means, as prophets and disciples saw, being "brought before governors and kings for my sake, for a testimony against them" (Matt. 10:18). It means knowing the whole of God's counsel, His law word, in all our being; living and obeying it, and bringing men and nations into conformity to it in Christ. We accredit ourselves by the Lord's sovereign word, and we require all things to be accredited by it. It means denouncing the Ahabs of our day, in church, state, and school, and declaring the Lordship of Jesus Christ over all things. It means, in brief, proclaiming the crown rights of Christ the King. (July, 1979)

THE REASON FOR THE ATTACKS

One of the problems facing Christian School men, and churches, under fire from the state is the attacks from other churchmen. No matter how flagrant the attack, excuses are made for the state. When I told someone of the demands made by the I.R.S. on a newly formed Bible Church, which included giving power of attorney to the I.R.S., the response was, "There must be a reason."

I have given copies of the Christian Law Association Defender, and Chalcedon materials, to many, and met with a similar response, or been told that these and other lawyers are trying to make money.

There is a reason for these attitudes: it is compromise, and it is sin. No man has the right to surrender anything which belongs to Jesus Christ to Caesar. There cannot be two masters over Christ's domain.

Even more, instead of surrendering Christ's realm, we must enlarge it. In the trial of a Michigan state trooper for refusing to obey an order contrary to his Christian convictions, one witness reminded the trial board that, in terms of Scripture, they are ministers of God, and will be judged as such by Him. He witnessed to the necessity for recognizing the total claims of Christ the Lord. Anything short of that is sin. (July, 1979)

THE HERESY OF DEMOCRACY WITH GOD
Chalcedon Position Paper No. 6

A young woman, mother of a girl of six years, described conditions in the grade school (K-6) across from their church. One teacher is openly a lesbian. Some boys regularly drag screaming girls into the boys' toilets to expose themselves to the girls, and nothing is done about it. The leading church officer had an answer to her call for a Christian School: he did not believe in spiritual isolationism for Christians, and this is what Christian Schools represent. Unusual? On the contrary, all too common an attitude.

In Chalcedon Position Paper no. 2, I wrote on "Can We Tithe our Children?", I quoted Psalm 128:1, "Blessed is every one that feareth the LORD; that walketh in his ways." This fell into the hands of a minister, who was apparently very upset by it. He *corrected* the word of God, and wrote to declare, "I do not like the word **feareth**, Rather LOVETH the Lord." Unusual? No, all too common.

A pastor, planning to speak on Biblical *authority* had the word "authority" altered in the church bulletin by members to read "leadership." A prominent church publication spoke with ridicule and hatred of all who would believe in anything so "primitive" as Biblical law. Another pastor, planning to discipline a seriously sinning member, was attacked by his fellow pastors at a church meeting; somehow, it is unloving to deal with sin as God's word requires it.

Is it necessary to give further examples? More pastors lose pulpits for their faithfulness to Scripture than for any other reason. Trifling excuses are found to make possible the dissolution of a pastoral relationship. Open sin is condoned, and simple faithfulness is despised. The telephone rings regularly to bring reports of fresh instances of churches in revolt against God and His word. Gary North is right. Humanism's accomplices are in the church. (*Christian Reconstruction*, III, 2.)

Much of this stems from one of the great heresies of our day, the belief in democracy. At the beginning of the century, some churchmen began talking about the democracy of God, i.e., that God wants a universe where He and His creatures can work and plan together in a democratic way. Of course, if our relationship with God is a democratic one, we can correct the Bible where it displeases us, eliminate what we cannot correct, and use other standards and tests for the church and the clergy than God's enscriptured word. Then, logically, our word is as good as God's word, and as authoritative as God's.

In his important study, *The Heresy of Democracy* (1955), Lord Percy of Newcastle declared of democracy that it is a "philosophy which is nothing less than a new religion" (p. 16). The justification for all things is not to be found in the triune God but in the people. Virtue means meeting people's needs, and the democratic state, church, and God have one function, to supply human wants. State, school, church, and God become chaplains to man, called upon to bow down before man's authority. In fact, Lord Percy said of state schools, "This is, indeed, democracy's characteristic Mark of the Beast...of all means of assimilation, the most essential to democracy is a uniform State-controlled education" (p. 13). To challenge that system is to shake democracy's structure, including its state and church. Earlier, Fichte saw statist education in messianic terms: "Progress is that perfection of education by which the Nation is made Man."

Within the church, the modernists first advocated the state as God's voice and instrument. Wellhausen, the German leader of the higher criticism of the Old Testament, declared: "We must acknowledge that the Nation is more certainly created by God than the Church, and that God works more powerfully in the history of nations than in Church history."

Behind all this is the question of authority: is it from God, or from man? If God is the sovereign authority over all things, then His law-word alone can govern all things. Religion, politics, economics, science, education, law and all things else must be under God, or they are in revolt.

If the ultimate authority is man, then all things must serve man and bow down before man's authority. As T. Robert Ingram has so clearly pointed out in *What's Wrong with Human Rights* (1979), the doctrine of human rights is the humanistic replacement for Biblical law. Man now being regarded as sovereign, his rights have replaced God's law as the binding force and authority over man and his world.

The cultural effects of this change have been far-reaching. In a remarkably brilliant and telling study, Ann Douglas, in *The Feminization of American*

Culture (1977), has shown the effects of Unitarianism and religious liberalism on American culture. From a God-centered emphasis (not necessarily consistent or thorough in application), a man-centered focus emerged. The new justification of women became the cult of motherhood (a humanistic, man-centered focus), and for men and women alike, "doing good" for one's fellow men. With this new emphasis, men left the church, or regarded it as peripheral to their lives, and the liberal clergy developed the fundamentals of what we have today as soap-opera religion. In Ann Douglas' delightfully incisive wording, "It is hardly accidental that soap opera, an increasing specialty of nineteenth-century liberal Protestantism, is a phenomenon which we associate with the special needs of feminine subculture" (p. 48). Liberal religion feminized the clergy, made women and Christianity irrelevant to life, and created a spineless, gutless clergy for whom the faith is sentimental talk and not the power of God unto salvation. To quote Dr. Douglas again, "The liberal minister who abandoned theology lost his right to start from the 'facts' of the Bible as his predecessors understood them: that God made man, man sinned against him, and God had and has the right to assign any punishment he judges fit for the offenses" (p. 200).

This humanistic soap-opera religion conquered other areas of the church. Arminianism quickly adopted it, as did much of Calvinism, as their emphases shifted from God's sovereign act of salvation to man's ostensible choice, or man's experience, and from the centrality and authority of the word, to an emotional, experientially governed "heart-religion."

In this humanist parody of Christianity, man's experience has priority over God's word. One "Christian worker" told me that it was unwise for people to read the Bible without the guidance of a "real" experience of "Spirit-filled" heart religion. Of course, for him the Spirit freed him from the word, a heretical opinion. One pastor, who announced a series of sermons on authority, i.e., the authority of God, of His word, authority under God, etc., was told bluntly that he should preach on "fellowship" with God, not God's authority. When churchmen are hostile to God's authority they are not Christians. Fellowship with God through Christ is on His terms and under His grace and authority. "If we say we have fellowship with him, and walk in darkness, we lie, and do not the truth" (I John 1:6).

A church which denies God's authority will be in no position to resist the state's authority. It will look to authorities other than the Lord's for its justification, and, in yielding to the state, it will do so in the spirit of cooperation, not compromise, because its true fellowship is with man and the state, not the Lord. Ambrose, in 385 A.D., resisted the state's requisition of a church in Milan, declaring, "What belongs to God is outside the emperor's power." Ambrose said further, in his Sermon Against Auxentius, "We pay to Caesar what is Caesar's, and to God what is God's. Tribute is due to Caesar, we do not deny it. The Church belongs to God, therefore it ought not to be assigned to Caesar. For the temple of God cannot be Caesar's by right." The emperor, he added, could be *in* the church by faith, but never *above* or over it.

Chrysostom, in dealing also with conflict with Caesar warned his people, In "Concerning the Statutes," Homily III, 19:

"This certainly I foretell and testify, that although this cloud should pass away, and we yet remain in the same condition of listlessness, we shall again have to suffer much heavier evils than those we are now dreading; for I do not so much fear the wrath of the Emperor, as your own listlessness."

Here Chrysostom put his finger on the heart of the matter: the threat was less the emperor and more a listless and indifferent church. The same problem confronts us today. The greater majority of church members do not feel that Christianity is worth fighting for, let alone dying for. They only want the freedom to be irrelevant, and to emit pious gush as a substitute for faithfulness and obedience. In soap opera religion, life is without dominion; instead, it is a forever-abounding mess, met with a sensitive and bleeding heart. Soap opera religion is the faith of the castrated, of the impotent, and the irrelevant. The devotees of soap opera religion are full of impotent self-pity and rage over the human predicament, but are devoid of any constructive action; only destruction and negation become them.

The heresy of democracy leads to the triumph of sentimental religion. Dr. Douglas defines sentimentalism thus: "Sentimentalism is a cluster of ostensibly private feelings which always attains public and conspicuous expression" (p. 307). The focus in sentimental religion shifts from God's word to man's feelings, and from basic doctrine to psychology and human needs. The doctrine of the sovereignty of man means the sovereignty of the total man, and all his feelings. We have a generation now whose concern is themselves, whose self-love blots out reality and truth.

So great is this self-absorption that, in any office, faculty, church group, or other fellowship, there are commonly persons who give their momentous personal communiques on purely private matters: "I didn't sleep well last night...I'm so tired today...Nothing I eat agrees with me lately, and I'm always gassy...I saw that film and used oodles of Kleenex...The color green always upsets me...I can't bear to have children around..." and so on and on. Purely private feelings are announced as though the world should react, be concerned, and be governed by them.

Even worse, God is approached with a similar endless gush of private feelings, as though God should be concerned and upset when an egomaniac is distressed. Few people pray, asking, "Lord, what wilt thou have me to do?" (Acts 9:6). Rather, they pray with a list of demands on God, for Him to supply. Now Paul declares that God will supply all our needs "according to his riches in glory by Christ Jesus" (Phil. 4:19), but that promise is preceded by an epistle which speaks at length of God's requirements of us, and also calls for contentment on our part with our God-decreed lot (Phil. 4:11).

Basic also to the heresy of democracy in the church is its belief, not only in man's needs as against God's requirements, but its belief in the irrelevance of God's law. If man is Sovereign, God's law cannot bind man, and both hell and justice fade away. God then is allowed only one approach to man, love. He is portrayed as needing, yearning for, and calling for man's love. Man is in the driver's seat, to accept or reject that plea.

Lord Percy stated it succinctly: "A mere breaker of law...may always be saved; but there is no salvation for the deniers of law" (p. 108). They have denied God's sovereignty and His power to save. Their only logical relationship to God then is not by salvation but by man- ordained fellowship. Then, too, what man has ordained, man can destroy, so there is no efficacious salvation, and no perseverance of the saints.

This brings us to the conclusion of sovereign man. On both sides of the "iron curtain," politicians trumpet the claim that theirs is *the free world.* "The free world" is a curious and popular term in the twentieth century, so commonly used that its meaning is hardly considered. What is the free world free from? First of all, it means freedom from the other side. The enemy represents bondage, "our side" freedom, although all the while freedom decreases in the West, even as its relics grow fewer behind the Iron Curtain. The less free we become, the more we are told of the virtues of our freedom. But, second, the whole world is not free in its more basic sense, "free" from God. For the Marxists, religion, Biblical faith in particular, is the opium of the masses. For democratic thinkers like John Dewey and James Bryant Conant, Christianity and the family are anti-democratic and aristocratic and hence incompatible with democracy. (See R. J. Rushdoony: *Messianic Character of American Education.*) The Death of God School of a few years ago did not say that God is dead in Himself, but that God is dead for us, because, they declared, we find Him "non-historical" and irrelevant to our purposes in this world. Only that which meets man's needs and purposes is alive for man, and therefore man wants to be free from the sovereign God.

The man who did not believe in "spiritual isolationism," of which he accused the Christian Schools, was emphatic on one point: we must obey the powers that be, the state, because God ordains it. Peter's words, "We ought to obey God rather than men" (Acts 3:29), brought little response from him. Obedience to many other things in Scripture, such as tithing, bring no similar strong demand for obedience, but all such are ready to call their compromise with Caesar a faithfulness to God.

But to *obey* in the Hebrew Scripture means essentially to hear the word of God, to believe it, and to act on it. Therefore W. A. Whitehouse said that the word *obey* has "the closest possible association with 'believe'" (A. Richardson, editor: *A Theological Word Book of the Bible*, p. 160.)

Contrary to the humanistic, democratic mood in religious thought today, Christianity is an authoritative faith. It is held, throughout all Scripture, that all human authority is derived or conferred (or falsely claimed) and is always subject to the sovereign and absolute authority of God and is always subject to the terms of His law-word.

We have an age that wants, if it has anything to do with God, only His fellowship, on man's terms, and without His sovereignty and lordship. It dares to correct and amend God's word; it refuses to hear Him but offers rather to love Him. (One Hollywood "Christian" leader of a few years back spoke of God as "a living doll.") It wants a universe in which man plays sovereign and creator, endeavoring to create a brave new world out of sinful man, or out of self-centered churchmen, and it produces a fair facsimile of hell. Such a world is begging for judgment, and then as now "judgment must begin at the house of God" (I Peter 4:17). As always, judgment precedes salvation. (August, 1979)

JURISDICTION: BY CHRIST OR BY CAESAR?
Chalcedon Position Paper No. 7

Words reveal our faith, tell us about our world, and manifest our presuppositions. A particularly important word is jurisdiction. It comes from two Latin words, *jus*, law, and *dico*, say. The one who has jurisdiction is the one who declares the law, whose word is the binding, authoritative word for that area or sphere of life and thought.

Jurisdiction is an essentially religious fact: it tells us who is the god over a particular sphere or area; it reveals to us who declares the law for that domain. In other words, it shows us who is lord.

The whole premise and affirmation of Scripture is that the earth is the Lord's, that, because He made all things, ordained and orders all things, God the Lord is the only Lord and lawgiver over all heaven and earth, over every aspect of creation (Ex. 9:29; Deut. 10:12-14; Ps. 24:1; I Cor. 10:26). All creation thus is under God's jurisdiction, Who declares, "I am the LORD: that is my name: and my glory will I not give to another, neither my praise to graven images" (Isa. 42:8). God's jurisdiction is total, and He shares it with none. Men can only exercise valid authority and dominion under God, in faithfulness to His law, and in terms of God's sovereignty and Kingdom. He alone is the Lord. (The most used term for Jesus Christ in the New Testament is in fact *Lord*).

It was the essence of paganism that it reserved sovereignty to man and this world. The gods were powerful spirits who could be used, had to be placated, and could be abandoned if they failed man. For the pagan, the gods were powers to deal with, but the sovereignty, and the choice of gods, remained with man. The state reserved to itself the right to recognize or to abolish gods. The Roman senate thus could make gods at will by acts of senate. Thus, even the gods were under the jurisdiction of the state, and their legal or licit existence depended upon the state.

It was for this reason that conflict between Christ and the Caesars was inescapable, between the church and the pagan doctrine of the state. It was a conflict waged in Asia, Africa, and Europe. The doctrines of Scripture required and require Christians to declare that Caesar is under Christ's jurisdiction, not Christ under Caesar's.

It is a serious error on the part of scholars that leads them to view the situation in Europe after the fall of Rome as a collapse. It was indeed a collapse of Roman statism, but not of civilization. Rather, it was a movement towards a new foundation. How radical that movement was is apparent in many and virtually all areas. To cite one alone, the family had been under statist law to a far-reaching degree, as Carle Z. Zimmerman, in *Family and Civilization* (1947), showed clearly. With the fall of Rome, and the breaking up of European forms of barbarian paganism, a different pattern emerged. As Jean-Louis Flandrin has pointed out, "Christianity seems to have brought about the disappearance of the powers of the State over the child, and thereby increased the responsibilities of the parents as regards their maintenance and education. These responsibilities were, at the same time, shared between the father and the mother" (*Families in Former Times: Kinship, Household and Sexuality in Early Modern France*, p. 176. Cambridge University Press, 1979).

Today, of course, the state claims increasing powers over the family. The children must be state controlled and educated, according to many. The parents must be under state controls, and some even suggest the state licensing of births, and legislation towards this goal has been proposed in two state legislatures. Whereas laws against non-marital sexual relations are relaxed or abolished, current legislation reaches into the marital bedroom to govern ostensible rape by a husband.

In one area after another, the state advances its claims to total jurisdiction. In Florida, a literacy test required of all high school students in order to get a diploma was ruled out by the courts as discriminatory (it discriminated against illiteracy!) and thus unconstitutional. A federal judge in Detroit, Michigan, in July, 1979, ruled that school districts, in teaching English, must recognize the existence of a child's "home language," or ghetto English. Of course, courts have ruled on the length of hair, the kind of clothing students wear, and much, much more.

Clearly, the state increasingly manifests the fact that its fundamental faith is that no limits exist on the jurisdiction of the state other than self-imposed ones. The self-discipline meanwhile grows less and less as the state grows more and more total, or totalitarian, in its claimed jurisdiction. Jeff A. Schnepper, a tax lawyer and professor, gives fearful examples of this totalitarian jurisdiction in *Inside the IRS, How Internal Revenue Works (You Over)*, (Stein and Day, 1978).

Because all heaven and earth are God's creation, and because man is created in God's image, God is the great and inescapable fact; the knowledge of God is inescapable knowledge. When men in unrighteousness or injustice suppress or deny that knowledge, they cannot evade the necessity of God, and so they declare or create new gods in their image, or in terms of their imagination (Rom. 1:18-25). The most powerful, and most deadly, of these new or false gods has, through the centuries, been the state. The state, as a false god, claims total jurisdiction, and it declares itself sovereign or god: it is, in terms of ancient paganism, Hegel, and modern political thought, god walking on earth. Men, having denied the true God, cannot escape having a god, and the modern state is the great Baal (or Lord) of modern man. The cry of modern man is a political cry, "O Baal, hear us" and save us (I Kings 18:26). Here is idolatry, and too long the church has been silent in the face of it, or has urged its people to submit to Baal in the name of Jesus Christ: to its idolatry, it has added blasphemy.

The question of jurisdiction is thus not only an urgently important one, but a religious one. Before World War I, in *Ruling Case Law*, vol. 7, (1915), the editors, working on humanistic premises but with a more conservative bent than the law has today, admitted that perhaps no more difficult question exists in law than the question of the jurisdiction of courts. They grounded the source of jurisdiction in the constitutional form of government in the three departments, legislative, executive, and judicial, plus "certain inherent powers which of right belong to all courts." Thus, law as it emanates from the state is the source of all jurisdiction.

From such a premise, the death of God is a logical conclusion, and the exclusion of all claims by Christians to any freedom from the state in terms of God's word is a necessary consequence. The humanistic state excludes God from any and all jurisdiction. Any and all liberties permitted to the church, to the Christian School, and to the Christian himself are at the sovereign grace of the state.

Thus, the Internal Revenue Service claims the right to establish, by its rules and regulations, what constitutes a valid church or Christian School. Such a claim is an assertion of jurisdiction; it is an aspect of the totalitarian claims of the modern state.

In one area or another, men claim humanistic "rights" or jurisdiction. The abortionists claim that a woman has sovereign rights over her body and her unborn child; the homosexual claims that, where his action with other consenting persons is at issue, he alone has jurisdiction. In one area after another, modern man, in defiance of God, claims an independent jurisdiction.

The result is both moral anarchy and impotence. With more and more individuals demanding a moral jurisdiction in defiance of God's law, the social scene becomes increasingly lawless; the family declines, vocations lose their discipline, schools do not educate, churches confirm sinners in their sins, and men are at war one with another. The state gains thereby a strong argument for asserting a protecting jurisdiction over a lawless scene as the working god of society.

But the state's claims to any jurisdiction apart from God are lawless claims, and its laws are godless, lawless laws. As Augustine pointed out, in *The City of God*, without faith in the Lord, the state becomes no more than a larger band of robbers, a super-Mafia. A refugee from the Soviet Union, Yuri Brokhin, in *Hustling on Gorky Street*, dealt with the question, Is there a Soviet Mafia?, thus: "There certainly is a Soviet Mafia. And it's organized a hell of a lot better than the American mafia. But is has another name. It's called the Communist Party. We wouldn't dream of trying to compete with it."

If God is dead, what is wrong with a Mafia, and its claims to jurisdiction? If God is dead, then we are beyond good and evil, as Nietzsche held, and no one has any moral basis for anything, and thus the state can claim any and all jurisdiction it pleases. This, of course, is exactly what the state is doing. It calls itself "sovereign," or lord, and few object. It claims more and broader jurisdiction daily, and the protests are few, and the resisters are condemned.

All too many churchmen believe that submission to the state's idolatrous claims is a virtue. Chalcedon's leaflet, "Can we tithe our children?", fell into the hands of one man who reacted with amazement to the statement that the state does not own the child, and that any such claim is paganism. How could any minister think that way? He wrote, "What's this? Another cult?"

Such a reaction is not surprising. God's jurisdiction has been handed over to the world by all too many churchmen, and any idea that Jesus Christ has crown rights over all things, over every area of life and thought, sounds strange in their ears. Christ's jurisdiction is limited to the church, and to the soul of man, and very feebly in both places.

But Jesus Christ is Lord (Phil. 2:9-11); He alone is sovereign: there are no limits to His jurisdiction nor to His law word. His law and jurisdiction stand as long as heaven and earth (Matt. 5:17-19); indeed, "it is easier for heaven and earth to pass, than one tittle of the law to fail" (Luke 16:17), because the triune God is the eternal, the everlasting One, and there is no end to His deity, life, and jurisdiction. To limit the Lord's jurisdiction is to limit Him, which means to deny that He is God.

To believe in the Lord thus requires us to assert His crown rights over all things and the total jurisdiction of His law word. Our Lord declares, "All power is given unto me in heaven and in earth" (Matt. 28:18). The word translated as power is *exousia*, the right to act, the rightful power, dominion, authority, and rule over all things, i.e., jurisdiction. This power in Christ is absolute and unrestricted; men can only have delegated power, subject entirely to God and His word. The Lord does not exempt from His jurisdiction any man, any state, nor any area. For us to do so is to deny Him. Indeed, one Greek lexicon gives, as basic to the meaning of *exousia*, the word *jurisdiction*. Our Lord thus says, "All jurisdiction is given unto me in heaven and in earth."

Then, He commands, "Go ye therefore, and teach all nations, baptizing them in the name of the Father, and of the Son, and of the Holy Ghost: Teaching them to observe all things whatsoever I have commanded you; and, lo, I am with you always, even unto the end of the world. Amen" (Matt. 28:19-20). Our calling thus is not only to resist any and all usurpations of Christ's jurisdiction, but to go forth and bring all men and nations, every area and sphere of life and thought, into captivity to Jesus Christ as Lord, as Sovereign. All things in heaven and earth must be placed under His jurisdiction. This includes China, Russia, Britain, and the United States. It also includes you and me. We have no independent life nor jurisdiction. "For who maketh thee to differ from another? and what hast thou that thou didst not receive? now if thou didst receive it, why dost thou glory, as if thou hadst not received it?" (I Cor. 4:7).

The assured word is this: "The kingdoms of this world are become the Kingdoms of our Lord, and of his Christ; and he shall reign for ever and ever" (Rev. 11:15). (September, 1979)

STANDARDS

A few ministers wrote recently to express limited appreciation for our stand against state control over Christian Schools and churches. However, they advocated "limited" state standards in order to "insure" quality education and to eliminate fraudulent groups. After all, one man asked, do you want another Jim Jones case? This is a statement repeatedly made, other men tell me. State controls are needed to prevent the kind of thing Jim Jones and the People's Temple represented.

The sad fact is that Jim Jones had his work licensed at every needed point, child care, everything! He was a friend of powerful political figures and a believer in state controls. If any state-controlled and cooperating church has existed in California, it was the People's Temple. It produced religion of about the same level and quality as the education in state schools!

The goal of state standards is not quality. It is, *first* of all, state control. In trial after trial, it has been shown that the "uncontrolled" Christian Schools are superior, and their students test out far in advance of public school pupils.

Second, the goal of state standards is religious, i.e., the imposition of another religion on Christian Schools, the religion of humanity or humanism. Those "Christian" Schools which submit to state imposed standards soon become inferior schools educationally and religiously.

The fight against statist controls is thus both a theological battle (To God alone belongs dominion), and a struggle for quality education.

If state standards are so good, why are the state schools so bad? If state standards are so beneficial, why not ask the state to provide standards for the church? Should Jesus Christ have applied for a license before preaching and teaching? Would any Sanhedrin then or now provide an acceptable standard? (September, 1979)

THE FAMILY
Chalcedon Position Paper No. 8

The modern age has created a new view of law. Law is seen as confronting two realms; the one realm, the public sphere, belongs to the state and its law and jurisdiction. The other sphere is the private realm, which is outside the law of the state. The distinction is a modern fiction, created by the statists. Moreover, the right to define the extent of the public realm is reserved to the state. Naturally, the state has steadily increased its claims to the detriment of the private sphere, which has grown steadily smaller.

Furthermore the state feels free to redefine what is public, and what is private. Abortion was until recently in the public sphere, and legislated; now, it is more or less transferred to the private sphere, and a matter of opinion and private choice, not legislation. Homosexuality has been largely transferred from the public sphere, and legislative control, to the private sphere, and free choice. Attempts are under way to make a similar transfer from public to private with prostitution, incest, and bestiality.

At the same time, other areas are being moved from the private to the public sphere: the family, especially children; the church and Christian School; medical practice, and much, much more.

At the heart of the evil of this current definition of law is the arrogant claim of the state to be the sole source of public law, and the only definer thereof. This claim is as old as paganism, and yet it is fairly new in Christendom and is a product of the humanism of the modern age. Christian civilization has recognized several realms of public law, and the most notable of these has been family law. Other spheres of public law have included church law, (Christian) school law (as in the medieval university and since), merchant law, and more. The state held one sphere of public law among several, and it had no legitimate claim over other spheres.

The triumph of Christianity was also the triumph over the ancient pagan equation of the state with all public law. It was the fundamental principle of the pagan state that it was the sole public sphere, and its right to govern all of life, including the private, was full and free. Plato's *Republic* presupposes the right of the state to govern everything; this claim was not new to Plato; it was only his form of it that was different.

The early church resisted this claim at every turn. It rejected the claim of Caesar over the church, family, school, and more. The rapid change of Europe after the fall of Rome was due more to faith than to collapse. Europe moved from the centralization and the totalitarianism of Rome to a decentralized society. Flandrin has observed, "Christianity seems to have brought about the disappearance of the powers of the State over the child, and thereby increased the responsibilities of the parents as regards their maintenance and their education. These responsibilities were, at the same time, shared between the father and the mother." Jean-Louis Flandrin: *Families in Former Times, Kinship, Household and Sexuality in Early Modern France*, p. 176. Cambridge University Press, New York, 1979.) Step by step, society was altered to conform to the Biblical pattern, to become the Kingdom of God. This conformity was never more than dimly or at best moderately approximated at any point, but the benefits are with us still. In particular, the family became the central public sphere.

In Scripture, the family is the basic institution of society, to whom all the most basic powers are given, save one: the death penalty. (Hence, the death penalty could not be executed on Cain.) The family is man's basic government, his best school, and his best church. The decay of the family is the decay of civilization.

To review briefly the basic powers which Scripture gives to the family, the *first* is the control of children. The control of children is the control of the future. This power belongs neither to church nor state, nor to the school, but only to the family. This power is in the modern era, from the early 1800s, increasingly claimed by the state and its schools. Flandrin cited the disappearance of all statist powers over the child with the triumph of Christianity; today, with the retreat of Christianity into pietism, we see the increasing power of the state over both the child and the parents. Nothing will affect the disappearance of that power except a revival of Biblical faith.

Second, power over property is given in Scripture to the family. Modern man is used to thinking of two kinds of property control, private ownership and state ownership. The Bible affirms that "The earth is the LORD'S," and God gives control of property into the hands of the family, not the state, nor the individual. We have survivals of this form of property control in various community property laws, which mean family property. Community here has the older sense of family. Here too, however, the state claims vast powers: to tax, confiscate, control, and in various other ways to play god over property. Community property laws are all too often simply a relic: the man sees the property as his, but as legally his wife's only because of a legal necessity, not because his thinking is familistic.

Third, inheritance in Scripture is exclusively a family power, governed by God's law. The eldest son gains a double portion, unless he is godless and or incompetent. The godly seed are blessed by an inheritance, and God's Kingdom flourishes as a result. Now, however, the state claims prior right to the estate as the true elder son, offers to care for the surviving parent by means of welfare (which is usually needed, when the state claims its share), and makes itself the real executor of the estate. It supplants God's laws of inheritance with its own.

Fourth, welfare is the responsibility of the family, beginning with the care of its own. Paul says plainly, "But if any provide not for his own, and specially for those of his own house, *he hath denied the faith, and is worse than an infidel*" (I Tim. 5:8). The family's duties towards fellow believers, strangers, widows, orphans, etc., are all strongly stressed in God's law. However much neglected by the modern church, they are basic to Scripture. Paul declares, of all who do not care for their own, that such have "denied the faith." Again, the state has moved into the area of welfare, not because of any godly or humanitarianism concern for people, but to gain power over man and society.

Fifth, education, a basic power, is given by God to the family as its power and responsibility. The modern state claims the right to control and provide education, and it challenges the powers of the family in this area also. Education in the modern age is statist predominantly. Statist education in the U.S. has led to the highest illiteracy rate in its history.

Today, the attack on the family is being stepped up. Humanistic statism sees control of the child and the family as basic to its drive towards totalitarianism. Every revolutionary movement sees control over the family and the child as central to its goal. This goal was set forth by Fidel Castro as the creation of a new man, a fundamentally humanistic, altruistic man, a perfectible man. The family must give way to the Family of Man. In a speech on July 26, 1960, Castro said: "In a Communist society, man will have succeeded in achieving just as much understanding, closeness, and brotherhood as he has on occasion achieved within the narrow circle of his own family. To live in a Communist society is to live without selfishness, to live among the people and with the people, as if every one of our fellow citizens were really our dearest brother." (Cited in Marvin Leiner: *Children Are the Revolution, Day Care in Cuba*, p. 16. New York, Viking Press, 1974.) As Leiner noted, "The Cuban early-childhood education program, therefore, is only the first step on the road to educating the entire population" (p. 6).

Various groups in the U.S. and Europe have been producing manifesto after manifesto, setting forth "Children's Rights," "Youth Rights," "A Child's Bill of Rights," and like pretentious documents. These are presented as the last word in liberalism and radicalism. They are, in fact, reactionary, going back to the worst in paganism and in decaying cultures and civilizations. These set forth the supposed right of the child or children to sexual freedom, which often means the "right" to be exploited by others; the right to political power, i.e., voting, office-holding, etc.; the right to divorce themselves from their parents, and so on.

These plans must be taken seriously. With the International Year of the Child, every state save one is issuing pronouncements which strike at the heart of the Biblical doctrine of the family. The one exception is Alabama, where a superior governor, who believes that Christian faith means profession with action, has turned to Christians for the state's guidelines with respect to the child. What these revolutionary plans on the part of the enemies of the family call for is really the end of Biblical laws governing the family, the abolition of the family, and a "new man" created by humanism and in terms of humanism's goals.

The sexual revolution was in large measure a revolt against God's laws concerning sexuality and the family. Its goal was far less love and more obviously hatred, hatred of God and man alike. It called for the depersonalization of sex in order to depersonalize man, i.e., to dehumanize man in the name of humanism. Very early in the sexual freedom movement, one prominent advocate called for the same freedom demanded by the Cynics of ancient Greece, to copulate openly in public like dogs.

When the state claims totally the public realm and denies any of it to the family and the church, it destroys man in the process. By obliterating all other claims, it reduces man to a creature of the state, under the public law of the state. Man becomes then public man, even in his copulation!

But man is created in God's image (Gen. 1:26-28), and neither man nor the state can alter that fact. Efforts to do so destroy those who attempt it. History is littered with civilizations which undermined the family. The family is God's ordained life for man, and it endures. (December, 1979)

ANTINOMIANISM VERSUS DOMINION
Chalcedon Position Paper No. 9

A contemporary historian raises the question, with respect to the early church, "Why were the Christians persecuted?" The Romans pretended that the Christians were refusing to obey minor and trifling rules and regulations out of perversity and rebelliousness. The real issue, Gilles Quispel points out, "was an implicit recognition of the divinity of the state."

Our Lord did not allow the church to forget this fact. In His letter to the church in Pergamos (Rev. 2:12-17), our Lord reminds the church in Pergamos that they dwelled "even where Satan's seat is...where Satan dwelleth." These are strong words; they come, moreover, from Jesus Christ, the Second Person of the Trinity. Pergamos was a center of emperor worship, of state worship. The Roman state was seen as the divine order; peace on earth meant the prevalence of Roman law and power. "The good life" meant the state-controlled life, a life governed from cradle to grave by the Roman state. Law was not seen as given by God but given by Rome.

Jesus Christ says, to the church in Pergamos, "These things saith he which hath the sharp sword with two edges." For us today the point of this statement is easily missed: our Lord refers to the Roman sword and declares that He, not Rome, carries true authority. The two-edged sword of Rome was a symbol of Roman power and authority, but Jesus Christ calls Pergamos, the center of Roman power in Asia, "Satan's seat...where Satan dwelleth," and declares that true power and authority are in His hands. Rome, or Satan, has a sword in its hands, and is able to kill, but Christ can slay man, empire, Rome, and Satan with the sword or power in His hand.

Our Lord therefore condemns all who hold to "the doctrine of Balaam," the false prophet who taught compromise and led Israel into idolatry and fornication. To be a Balaam is to be one who obeys Caesar rather than Jesus Christ.

About the time of our Lord's birth, Rome's cynicism began to triumph. The old religions of Rome gave way to the open deification of the state and the emperor. Its plan of salvation became statist power. In 9 B.C., Augustus Caesar dedicated the altar of peace (*ara pacis*) on the Field of Mars, the God of war. The only peace Rome could imagine or secure was by military force, by means of the subjugation of the peoples at home and abroad. This "peace" meant the suppression and death of all who resisted Rome's power. Roman salvation thus came to mean submission to the "divine" coercion of Rome. Rome forced the imperial cult on all the empire, and even on its allies. Roman salvation came to mean obliteration by Roman power.

In this situation, real resistance came from only one source, the Christians. The Christians were prepared, and believed in terms of Scripture, that they were required to be obedient to all human authorities *in the Lord*, i.e., in terms of His law-word and His prior authority. Thus, parents, masters, authorities, and rulers are to be obeyed and honored in their discharge of their God-given duties.

What if the state ceases to be God's ministry of justice? What if it becomes a terror to good works, rather than to the evil? (Rom. 13:1-5). Their obedience had to be "for conscience sake" (Rom. 13:5), i.e., in obedience to God, because of His word, for "We ought to obey God rather than men" (Acts 5:29). As a result, Christians who are faithful to Scripture have been throughout history the greatest source of principled obedience and principled disobedience, because they act in terms of faithfulness to God in both. Christians move in the certain faith that God's word is true when it declares, "Be not deceived: God is not mocked: for what soever a man soweth, that shall he also reap" (Gal. 6:7). This is not merely a hope or a general promise but God's law word. We can count on it. If we render a false obedience, or a false word in anything, we shall inescapably reap a harvest of judgment. Rome reaped such a harvest, as will the nations of our time also, unless they repent. World history is world judgment from the world King, Jesus Christ.

In our day, as humanism more and more governs the nations of the world, the nations seek increasingly to play god. Now it is the prerogative of God, and of God alone, to have all things under His jurisdiction. In the Bible, throughout the history of Israel, church and state were kept separate but together under God. Both church and state must serve the Lord, but each in its place, one as the ministry of grace, and the other as the ministry of justice. For either to claim powers and jurisdiction beyond its sphere is a sin. All things must be under the Lord, not under the church nor the state. Many of the evils of history have had their origin in the attempt of church and state to play god over man.

The modern state is dedicated to this goal, to be god walking on earth. A god has total jurisdiction and grants bounties, gratuities, or grace to those under his sway. The state increasingly claims that every area is under its jurisdiction, and any freedom the church, Christian School, family, college, press, or other agency may possess is dependent on a revocable act of grace by the state. Thus, in 1957, the California State Supreme Court held:

"It is fundamental that the payment of taxes has been and is a uniform if not a universal demand of government, and that there is an obligation on the part of the owner of property to pay a tax legally assessed. An exemption from taxation is the exception and the unusual. To provide for it under the laws of this state requires constitutional or constitutionally authorized statutory authority. It is a bounty of gratuity on the part of the sovereign and when once granted may be withdrawn. *It may be granted with or without conditions but where reasonable conditions are imposed they must be complied with.*

"A church organization is in no different position initially than any other owner of property with reference to its obligations to assist in the support of government by the payment of taxes. Church organizations, however, throughout the history of state, have been made special beneficiaries by way of exemptions..."

The state not only claims total jurisdiction, but it often demands unquestioning obedience. In a case in Georgia, a state official, in dealing with a church which stood in terms of its God-given freedom as well as the plain wording of state law, cited Romans 13:1-5 as his " justification." Pastor

John Weaver reminded the state officer of Acts 4:29, and cited the following examples of obedience to God rather than man from Scripture:

> 1. The midwives refused to obey Pharaoh (Ex. 1:15-22; 2:1-10). Would it have been better for the midwives to have murdered and thus obeyed Pharaoh or disobey Pharaoh and obey God?
> 2. Rahab refused to obey the king's order and would not deliver up the spies (Joshua 2; Heb. 11:31). God commends Rahab for her "disobedience" and lists her in the hall of the faithful (Heb. 11).
> 3. Daniel refused to obey the king's order and God blessed him greatly (Daniel 1).
> 4. The three Hebrew children refused to obey the king's command and were thrown into a fiery furnace (Dan. 3).
> 5. The Apostles refused to obey "the law" that forbade them from preaching the Gospel and were persecuted, beaten, imprisoned and killed (Acts 4-6).

In recent years, all too many churchmen have stressed total obedience to the state, while pursuing a radical antinomianism or lawlessness in relation to God and His law. It is not surprising therefore that humanism has taken over the reins of power. Antinomianism in effect says of the Lord, "We will not have this man to reign over us" (Luke 19:14), while saying to the state, It is our principle and religious faith that we obey your law rather than God's.

Man in all his being, because He is God's creation, is a law-creature. His life runs on required patterns of food and sleep, work and rest, and his being requires an ordered, patterned life, a law-life. Death is beyond law and structure; the life of a creature is inseparable from it. The only question with respect to the relationship of man to the law is, what law will man live under and obey? Fallen man has chosen humanistic law. Every non-Christian state will have some form of humanistic law.

Humanism believes in salvation by man, and by man's works and laws. Is there a problem? The answer of humanism is another law, another bureaucratic agency, psychiatry, humanistic reforms, and the like. All involve one or another form of censorship, an external coercion and control, as the means of educating, changing, and/or brain-washing men. But censorship in all its forms does not work, because it cannot change man's heart. For example, in early America, virtually no laws existed with respect to pornography; the laws have come with the rise of pornography. The earlier absence of legislation did not create pornography any more than the more recent laws have been able to suppress it. The answer to the problem is regeneration and sanctification, not humanistic legislation.

The more we rely on statist legislation to "remedy" a problem, the more power we give to the state, and the less we trust in God's saving power and His sanctifying laws. When we trust the state, we become dependent upon legislative, bureaucratic, or judicial grace, rather than on the grace of God.

Gaines Post, in *Studies in Medieval Legal Thought, Public Law and the State, 1100-1322* (1964), showed that expressions such as public or common utility, welfare, emergency, necessity, and "necessity knows no law," as well as reasons of state or public welfare had their origin in Roman law. Their use was to justify extraordinary power and authority. This was in opposition to another belief which held that "The State itself had no rights *sui generis*," that the state itself is under law. Similar developments took place in private law to justify necessity, such as using hunger to justify theft. The use of the necessity argument gave private man and the state both a priority over God's law and a freedom from restraint. The limited exemption given by necessity to private man has been steadily replaced by the necessities of the state. The argument from necessity was to its core humanistic; it held that man's necessity, as viewed by man, and the state's necessity, as viewed by the state, over-rule all law and all other jurisdictions. The U.S. Federal Register gives us volumes of "necessary" powers for state-determined emergencies.

This should not surprise us. When men see as the "necessary" answer to a problem statist law and coercion rather than God's saving power and sanctifying law, the state will be the ministry of continuing necessity and emergencies, world without end.

Both church and state, and man in his every sphere, must be bound, however, by the necessity of God's total word. The word of God has ceased to be the necessary and compelling law-word of God for most churchmen. Our emergencies are not seen as *sins*, the remedy for which is God's grace and law, but as *needs*, and the state becomes the purveyor of statist bounty and grace to man in his need. Because we have a non-Biblical view of sin, we have a non-Biblical and statist view of grace.

We are all of necessity nomians, advocates of law and antinomians, anti-law. The only question is, whose law do we advocate, and whose law do we oppose? All too many today live by the state's law and grace, and shall perish from it, instead of looking to the Lord and His grace and law.

Grace and law are inseparable. Our salvation in Christ is an act of law: it is Christ's satisfaction by His atonement of the law and justice of the triune God. As our substitute and representative man, as Head of the new humanity, Jesus Christ pays our death penalty from the law. He frees us from the *penalty* of the law, from the law as an indictment and death sentence, to free us to a way of holiness, the very law of God now written on our hearts and an aspect of our new nature.

As fallen men, we sought salvation by our works. We believed that man, as his own god, could determine, in his private, social, and statist life, good and evil, or establish law, for himself. This was our depravity, and our original sin, our sin in Adam and as members of his humanity or race.

In Jesus Christ, we know by grace that we have been freed from that hostility to the Lord and His law, from antinomianism in relationship to God. We are now antinomians with respect to Satan's program (Gen. 3:5), and every church or state which seeks to promote and develop Adam's rebellion against God. The early church, knowing that grace, refused to submit to Caesar's licensure, regulation, taxation, or control. They grounded their resistance on obedience to God: "We ought to obey God rather than men." For them, Caesar was an antinomian, in rebellion against Christ, King of Kings and Lord of Lords. They prayed for Caesar, sought to convert him, obeyed him wherever God's word permitted, but they rendered obedience "for conscience sake" only, in terms of God's word, never in violation of God's word and sovereignty.

The same issue is with us today. The modern state can no more defy Christ the King and survive than could Rome, and the same is true of the church.

Howard Ahmanson has aptly called the 1980s "The Dominion Decade", because of the rising interest in Christian dominion and reconstruction. Christ the King always has dominion. Let us exercise dominion under Him and In Him, to His praise and glory. (January, 1980)

THE QUESTION OF AUTHORITY
Chalcedon Position Paper No. 10

A major challenge confronts American churches and Christians with the January, 1980, proposal by President Carter that a military draft registration be instituted, perhaps for both men and women, a question he left open. Our first duty is to protest such a registration, if framed into law and, then, if instituted, to give serious consideration to resistance.

However, it is important, before reacting to any measure, to know what Scripture teaches. *First* of all, war in the Bible was to be waged only if in defense of justice and to effect godly order. In terms of this, such warfare was called the wars of the Lord (Num. 21:14) and required religious preparation and dedication (Josh. 3:5). *Second* the soldiers drafted were no younger than twenty (Num. 1:2, 3, 18, 20, 45; 26:2, 3), and it was a selective calling of all such, in some cases, a very limited one (Num. 31:4). *Third*, exemption was for the newly married (Deut. 24:5), the Levites, or clergy, teachers (Num. 1:48, 49), and for those who had newly built a house, or planted a field (Deut. 24:5), the principle being that production and continuity take priority over defense. *Fourth*, total war was forbidden (Deut. 20:19, 10). *Fifth*, defensive warfare was alone legitimate, and, hence, the number of horses (used in military offensives) was severely restricted (Deut. 17:16). More could be added, but, for our purposes, the relevant laws are these. They restrict warfare to a defensive purpose, and *the family* has priority. The basic defense of a country is the protection of the family.

This fact was echoed in the U.S. Constitution, Article I, Section 8, which limits the calling of the militia (the older term for a drafted army) to three purposes only: (1) to execute the laws of the union, (2) to suppress insurrection, and (3) to repel invasion. As John W. Burgess pointed out, fifty years ago, foreign wars were not included, and Wilson's draft in World War I violated the Constitution. (John W. Burgess: *Recent Changes in American Constitutional Theory*, pp. 59ff.) Since then, interventionism has been the U.S. policy, intervention in foreign affairs, and intervention in domestic affairs (into the life of the family, the church, economics, etc.). World War I, supposedly a war to make the world safe for democracy, and a war to end all wars, led instead to the bloodiest and most murderous of centuries. Each instance of interventionism since has left the world even worse off. The state is not an instrument of salvation.

The family is God's basic institution. It was established in Eden, and it is prior to both church and state. It is under neither of them but is a separate government which is directly under God.

Moreover, God's basic plan of government in church and state is based on the family, and the head of the household, the man. This is the system of elders (also called captains, bishops, presbyters), first as rulers of the family, then as the rulers in all of society (Deut. 1:13-15). Thus, instead of church or state ruling the family, the family based leadership is to rule church and state (as well as the school).

But the modern humanistic statism is both anti-God and anti-family. The family is a very powerful institution, with a capacity for survival and revival which has outlasted empires. Nations which work to destroy the family succeed thereby in destroying themselves. The state then perishes, and the family revives.

The state prefers atomism, and encourages social atomism, because an atomistic society may be a more violent and rebellious one, but it is a less successfully resistent one by far. The freedom of the family is thus anathema to the modern state.

However, long before the modern state began its attacks on the family, men had begun a rebellion against the family and the responsibilities thereof. The double standard was a product of this revolt. Scripture makes very clear that, the greater the responsibility, the greater the culpability. The sins of a man are thus more fearful in God's sight than the sins of a woman, because God has given primary authority to the man. Thus, God declares to the men of Israel, "I will not punish your daughters when they commit whoredom, nor your spouses when they commit adultery: for themselves are separated with whores, and they sacrifice with harlots: therefore the people that doth not understand shall fall" (Hosea 4:14). Moreover, our Lord says plainly, "For unto whomsoever much is given, of him shall be much required:

and to whom men have committed much, of him they will ask the more" (Luke 12:48). This means that, *first*, God requires more of any and all who hold positions of privilege and power. Status increases accountability; it does not give exemption from it. God being the source of all power and authority (Rom. 13:1), all such positions require a greater faithfulness to His law, a closer and more conscientious life and morality, and a greater culpability. The sins of a pastor or president are more culpable before God than the sins of a doorman. *Second*, the sins of a man are more culpable before God than the sins of his wife or daughters. His headship is not ordained for irresponsibility but for responsibility. *Third*, not only God but men live by this rule, for "to whom men have committed much, of him they will ask the more" (Luke 12:48). This is an obvious fact in the political sphere: politicians are rightly judged more severely by the populace than are ordinary citizens.

But men have long been in revolt against the responsibilities and authority of manhood. They have left the training of children, matters of religion, and the government of the family to their wives. By means of the double standard, they for long exempted themselves from the sexual morality they required of their wives. Sexual faithfulness was seen by all such as a necessity for women, not for men. This was the creed of the men's liberation movement.

Not surprisingly, in time women began to make the same demands, as set forth in the women's liberation movement. All the immaturity, irresponsibility, and freedom to sin long exercised by the modern male was now exercised or demanded by the women. Women's lib was men's lib coming home to roost! Before we condemn women's lib, let us remember that God, faced with a like movement in Israel, condemned rather the irresponsible men, and declared judgment on the whole culture (Hosea 4:14).

Of course, this movement has not stopped with the women. What men practice, their families will readily learn. Women's lib is being logically followed by children's lib. The culmination of such a course is the tyranny of children. Isaiah 3:12 declares, "As for my people, children are their oppressors, and women rule over them." As Pastor Gene Breed of Georgia has pointed out, we have a fulfillment of this prophecy in the present occupant of the White House, and, we can add, in all too many other childish leaders of the nation.

What we fear and love most are often closely related. Thus, today many men fear an economic collapse more than anything else; all too often, at the root of such a fear is a love of money, which money an economic collapse would endanger. It is thus important for us to ask what it is that the United States loves and fears on the world scene, and what it desires to protect.

Certainly, it is not Christianity which the U.S. loves and seeks to protect! The U.S. has in recent years done more for Red China and the Soviet Union than for Christianity. When Carter speaks of "human rights," he means humanistic rights; the persecuted Christians of Red China and the Soviet Empire mean as little to him as do the persecuted Christian Schools and churches of the U.S.A. He has been indifferent to the jailing in recent years of men like the Rev. Levi Whisner and Rev. Lester Roloff. The Afghans, in their treatment of themselves and others, have not been any better than the Soviet Union. Whatever the sins of the Shah, Iran still had a better life under him than at any other time in recent centuries. If it is oil we want, why are we selling Alaskan oil abroad? However we add up the foreign policy scene, we cannot see anything but ugly humanistic policies which are designed to further humanistic statism and its power politics.

Moreover, every modern state has demonstrated that its enmity with foreign powers is a transitory and changing thing. Yesterday's and tomorrow's enemies are today's friends, and future friends as well. Each and every modern state has one abiding enemy against whom perpetual warfare is waged, under the facade of concern and "welfare." That abiding enemy of the modern state is its own people, against whom perpetual war is waged in the name of perpetual concern. The foreign enemy is often real, but it is the domestic enemy which is constant.

This should not surprise us. The humanistic state is at war with God. For God's law, it substitutes the state's fiat law. Because the humanistic state is at war with God, it will be at war with every faithful Christian. Even more, it will be at war with man as such, because man is God's image-bearer. Therefore, the state seeks to remake man and to obliterate God's image.

Igor Shafarevich, in Alexander Solzhenitsyn's *From Under the Rubble*, writes on the goal of socialism as not only the withering away of the state but also "the withering away of all mankind, and its death" (p. 61). It works for The death of the family, the faith, the freedom of man, and all things else, because it seeks a universal destruction, like the Marquis de Sade, who described the death of God, the sun, and of all creation, as the great and most to be desired crime.

God asks, "Can two walk together, except they be agreed?" (Amos 3:3). Hence, He commands through Paul, "Be not ye unequally yoked together with unbelievers: for what fellowship hath righteousness with unrighteousness? and what communion hath light with darkness?" (II Cor. 6:14). In terms of this, God's law forbids mixed marriages, i.e., marriages with unbelievers (Deut. 7:3; Ex. 34:12-16). It also prohibits alliances with ungodly nations (Ex. 23:31-33; Deut. 7:1-4; Ex. 34:12-16). For a Christian to cooperate with a humanistic state in its humanistic goals is to be unequally and sinfully yoked.

Now, Deuteronomy 22:5 forbids a woman from certain assumptions of male life and declares it to be an "abomination unto the LORD" to do so. In *The Institutes of Biblical Law* (pp. 434ff.), I pointed out that earlier commentators had called attention to the fact that the reference in the Hebrew is not to clothes alone but is general: it refers to things, apparatus, implements, and *weapons*. Thus, Deut. 22:5 clearly is against the drafting of women and the registration of women for such a military draft. Such a draft, has as its practical consequence the destruction of God's order, and of the family.

Not surprisingly, within hours of President Carter's address, many Christians were resolving to resist such a registration on Biblical grounds. Quite rightly, they saw it as an evil; it involved, *first*, a plain violation of Deut. 22:5. *Second*, it involved an ungodly yoking of Christians to a humanistic state and its law. Nothing could have been clearer to President Carter than that such a measure would be offensive to countless Christians, but he gave priority to non-Christian considerations and left the matter an open question. *Third*, such a registration and draft require submission to an ungodly yoking of men and women.

A significant precedent for opposition was established in a mid-western state by a state trooper in 1979. Ordered to serve in a patrol car with a female trooper, he refused on Biblical grounds, and won. The hearing was a most significant one. It was admitted that the trooper was one of the most able and honest of all men in the force, a man with an excellent record. The opposition to him from his superiors was motivated, not so much by a pro-feminist perspective on their part, but by their hostility to the idea that any officer would place God's law above their own orders and regulations. Thus, the tacit issue was this: Does a man have a requirement to obey his superior officers rather than God, or shall we, must we not rather say with Peter and the other apostles, "We ought to obey God rather than men" (Acts 5:9)?

This is one of the key issues of our time. We may be spared the necessity for a decision with respect to registration and the draft, but we are not spared from the issue itself. Who has the command word over us, God or the state? Which of the two must we at all times obey?

The church has long had the luxury of a narrow and limited view of separation. It has been limited to separation from modernist churches. Modernism, of course, is humanism, and at issue is our separation from it also in school and state. The "separated church" which is separated from the modernist church down the street, but is not separated from the humanistic state schools, and from humanistic statism, is not separated to the Lord but to compromise, or to Phariseeism.

It is of the world's humanistic civil order that Revelation 18:4 commands, "Come out of her, my people, that ye be not partakers of her sins, and that ye receive not her plagues." At issue is God's authority and law. (March, 1980)

COVENANT, LAW, GRACE, AND ANTINOMIANISM
Chalcedon Position Paper No. 11

The Bible is a covenant book, and, basic to the understanding of all its teachings, is the doctrine of the covenant.

A covenant is a treaty, marriage, or bond between two parties, either individuals or groups. Covenants can be divided into two classes. *First*, we have covenants between relative "equals," or between "unequal" parties of a comparable nature. All covenants between people, or between nations, fall into this class. *Second*, a covenant can be between a great and transcendental power, a god, and a people whom he chooses; here, there is no comparable nature, nor any common level of communication. Such a covenant, on the initiative of the superior power, is a covenant of grace.

The covenant of Scripture, between the triune God and a chosen people, is a covenant of grace. For God the Lord to enter into a treaty or relationship with His creatures, and to bind Himself to faithfulness thereto, is an act of sovereign grace. Thus, from beginning to end, the Bible gives us God's covenant of grace. God's relationship to Adam, to Noah, Moses, David, and to us is an act of grace. God does not need man's aid, and, to bind Himself to a treaty with man is pure grace on His part.

A covenant, however, is also always a matter of law. To speak of a covenant is to speak of law. In covenants, two parties agree to abide by a common law and justice (or righteousness). This means a common faith or religion. Hence, God forbids all alliances by a covenant nation with ungodly powers (Ex. 23:31-33; Ex. 34:12-16; Deut. 7:1-4). Similarly, all mixed marriages, of believers and unbelievers, are forbidden as violations of God's covenant. As Amos asks of all such unequal yoking, "Can two walk together, except they be agreed?" (Amos 3:3). Paul summarizes the doctrine thus: "Be ye not unequally yoked together with unbelievers: for what fellowship hath righteousness with unrighteousness? and what communion hath light with darkness?" (II Cor. 6:14). A covenant with an unbelieving person or nation means being yoked to an ungodly doctrine of justice or righteousness, and bound by a law which is evil in God's sight.

In a covenant, the superior power gives the law to the lesser power; in human covenants, there is often some trading with regard to the legal requirements. In God's covenant with man, there is a unilateral declaration of law: the law of the covenant is God's law only. Where there is no law, there is no covenant, for a covenant imposes a law on all concerned, and the penalty for violation of covenant law is death.

Hence, a covenant is not made: it is cut, and it requires the shedding of blood to indicate the penalty for all violations of the covenant and its law. But a covenant also requires an eating, a common meal, to indicate communion and community. The covenant members are now one family. In

God's covenant with man, we are by His sovereign grace made members of His family by adoption.

God's covenant with man is all of grace, and yet it is also law. For God to give His law to man is an act of grace, a covenant act, for law is the bond of community. Law sets forth the common righteousness or justice which governs the family members. To oppose law, grace, and covenant is to deny all three; they are not opposing concepts but rather different aspects of the same fact of a relationship to the Throne of God.

Scripture repeatedly equates breaking God's law with breaking His covenant. Hosea 8:1 tells us, "Set thy trumpet to thy mouth. He shall come as an eagle to the house of the LORD, because they have transgressed my covenant, and trespassed against my law." Psalm 78:10 reads, "They kept not the covenant of God, and refused to walk in his law." To be in covenant with the Lord requires keeping His law (II Kings 23:3,24). According to Isaiah 24:5, "The earth also is defiled under the inhabitants thereof; because they have transgressed the laws, changed the ordinance, broken the everlasting covenant." Again and again, Scripture indicts all who break God's law as covenant-breakers.

Antinomianism thus is more than covenant-breaking. It is the denial of the covenant and of covenant justice or righteousness. God's covenant, grace, and law are inseparable. Antinomians, however, seek to separate grace from law, and then finally from the covenant as well. The end result is no grace at all. An unrighteous and lawless grace is not grace but sin.

Phariseeism commits the opposite sin, legalism. It denies grace in favor of works and thereby seeks to reduce the covenant to the human level, i.e., two parties of more or less equal standing, able to give something one to another. The covenant law is then altered, as in Phariseeism, to make it by re-interpretation man's tradition and law. The result is again the destruction of God's covenant, and a denial of law as well as grace.

The product of the covenant is peace, peace between God and man, and between covenant men. To violate God's covenant is to violate His peace as well. The lack of peace today is evidence of a violated covenant.

Again, basic to every covenant is an oath, a blood oath (Ex. 24:6-8), whereby each party pledged themselves ready to die for the other, or to die if they violated the covenant law. We cannot understand the constitutional requirement for an oath of office in the United States apart from this fact. An oath had only one meaning to the framers of the U.S. Constitution, a covenant oath. Hence, the oath was taken (and still is) on a Bible, at one time opened to Deut. 28. The oath signified a nation and its officers in covenant with God, invoking covenant blessings and curses on themselves in terms of their faithfulness or disobedience.

Christ's death can only be understood in terms of the covenant. God's people had broken His covenant, and the penalty was death. Christ came, as very God, to manifest God's faithfulness to His own. Christ, as very man, took upon Himself the covenant sentence of death for His remnant. The unbelieving covenant people perished, and the redeemed remnant became the nucleus of a continuing and renewed covenant of the people of God's calling and choosing.

Just as the Hebrew speaks of cutting a covenant, so it speaks of cutting an oath (Deut. 29:12). The covenant and its oath both witness to the shedding of blood for the violation of God's covenant. To violate God's law is to despise His grace and covenant, and vice versa.

Marriage is a form of covenant, and every covenant, like marriage, requires a commitment to a common life. It means that we are not our own, "For ye are bought with a price," the price of Christ's atonement (I Cor. 6:20). No more than love in marriage is antinomian and lawless is covenant love antinomian or lawless. The covenant is totally grace, law, and love.

Basic to understanding God's covenant is the fact that, in Adam, the covenant was with all mankind. Again, with Noah (Gen. 9:1-17), it was with all men, with Noah and all his descendants. Thus, the covenant is misread if seen in purely national or ecclesiastical terms. The covenant is with mankind; hence, all men are either covenant-keepers or covenant-breakers. In Jesus Christ, God creates a new humanity as His covenant people, and the Lord of the covenant sends out His people into all the world, to bring all men and nations into His covenant and under His law and grace (Matt. 28:18-20). The covenant law thus makes a claim upon all men everywhere.

The covenant requires all men to be God's people, to live in His grace by His law. The covenant alone gives peace with God, and, in Him, between men. The covenant is a brotherly covenant, or a covenant of brotherhood between covenant men (Amos 1:9). It is a covenant of peace (Num. 25:12), and of "peace and prosperity" (Deut. 23:6). In Deuteronomy 28, all the blessings and curses of the covenant, for faithfulness and for unfaithfulness, are plainly set forth; they tell us much about the calamities of our time.

Because the covenant is the mark of God's peace, certain covenant signs set forth that peace and rest in God's covenant grace. The rainbow is a witness to God's covenant (Gen. 9:17), but, even more, the Sabbath is the regular and recurring witness to the covenant and its peace. Faithfulness to the Sabbath in all its fullness of meaning thus means true rest and peace in the covenant of grace. (Circumcision and then baptism mark covenant faith as well.) In Deut. 31:9-13, the public reading of the covenant law every seventh year set forth symbolically that the law of God is His peace treaty with us in Christ, in that His law shows to covenant man the life of righteousness and peace, i.e., how to walk with the Lord.

Law is the definer of relationships; it is enacted morality and is a theological concern. All men give allegiance to one form of law, while denying other kinds of law. Law can be statist, humanistic, Buddhist, Islamic, anarchistic (every man his own law), or what have you, but law of some kind is inescapable. Any kind of law we affirm will be a religious affirmation. Men today are commonly antinomian in relationship to God's law, but they are dedicated to their own law, whatever it may be.

The crisis of our age can be seen as a crisis of law. Our age is passionately concerned with law and justice of a humanistic sort, and the result is a growing lawlessness and injustice, because humanistic doctrines of law and justice are not based on God's reality. Moreover, the more "democratic" justice becomes, the more it exalts every man's desire to be his own law, and the more the will of man takes priority over the law of God. As a result, we have what John Lukacs, in *The Passing of the Modern Age* (1970), called "the democratization of violence" (p. 48).

The Bible equates antinomianism with practical atheism. The theme verse of Judges states: "In those days there was no King in Israel (that is, God the King and law-giver had been rejected by Israel): every man did that which was right in his own eyes" (Judges 21:25; cf. 17:6,18:1,19:1). The first half of this statement calls attention to the fact that, whatever the Israelites may have professed, they had actually or implicitly denied God as their Lord and law-giver. As a result, original sin, the principle of the Fall, had become operative: "ye shall be as gods, knowing good and evil," i.e., determining for yourself what constitutes good and evil, or law (Gen. 3:5). Law and morality today are do-it-yourself projects. Basic to statist education is a pragmatic view of truth and morality. For progressive education, truth became the will of the democratic majority, and the Great Community, the incarnation of truth. Facts in themselves, it was held, are not true: they are instruments, and truth is their pragmatic application to fulfill the democratic consensus. Values then are personal goals which permit self-realization in a social context without harm to others. (The doctrine of consenting adults as validation for any act has its source in this concept.) Value or morality is not obedience to God given laws but the pursuit of personal goals without social violence. Morality was thus taught as an anti-authoritarian and purely personal standard according to which all men can do as they please, provided other persons as individuals, the group, or society were not coerced or hurt.

The practical implication was that a new and very dangerous authority was introduced, society and or the state. God's entire body of laws is comprehended in one average-sized book: it is readily understandable by all men, and its commandments easily obeyed. The laws of the state give us an ever-expanding, ever-changing body of rules. The laws governing any man, city, county, state, federal, and those of all regulatory agencies at each level, are greater by far than any man can know. Even lawyers must research each case in terms of the jungle of applicable laws. Daily, new laws and recent court decisions expand this body of laws. There are enough laws to enable the state to find any and every man guilty of some violation or other. Moreover, the body of laws applicable to each man is so great that, if he sought to have a copy of each law, to know them, he would have to have a library building greater than his house, to hold them.

Society as a standard is no better. Social judgments on good and evil have varied dramatically in my life-time, with respect to abortion, sexual laws, war (pacificism, militarism, isolationism, interventionism, etc.), and much more. The weather-vane is a fitting symbol of socially determined values and morality.

Thus, humanism begins by becoming antinomian with respect to God's law. It creates in time such social chaos that its own children become antinomian with respect to humanistic law and regard "the Establishment" anti-law as itself the cause of disorder and the enemy.

The world's present course points to disaster. "Now therefore why speak ye not a word of bringing the king back?" (II Kings 19:10). God the Lord is always King. However, if He is not our Savior and law-giver, then as King He is our judge and our enemy. The harvest of antinomianism is judgment and destruction. (April, 1980)

RELIGIOUS LIBERTY
Chalcedon Position Paper No. 12

One of the great moments of history occurred at the time of the Reformation, but its significance was too little appreciated then, and its implications were not developed. Frederick III, or, Frederick the Wise (1463-1525), was Elector of Saxony (1486-1525). He founded the university, Wittenberg, where both Martin Luther and Melancthon taught. Luther and the Elector may never have met. Although Frederick gradually came to accept certain Lutheran doctrines, he remained a Catholic to the end. His long protection of Luther was not motivated by agreement. What were his motives?

At this distance, it is not easy to say. Certainly, if we limit it to self-interest, we are distorting history. True, there were problems of jurisdiction. The Elector's area, Thuringia and Saxony, was a domain one ninth the size of England. In it were a hundred different monasteries, and parts of six different bishoprics. Five of the bishops lived outside the Elector's realm. Thus, a different law prevailed for these ecclesiastical domains. It would be easy to conclude that self-interest led Frederick the Wise to defend Luther: he could then control the church as easily as the state if his were a unified realm.

Such a conclusion presupposes a desire by Frederick to control Luther, something he did not do. Luther was more ready for a magisterial power in the church than was Frederick. Frederick protected Luther; he did not seek to control him. This point is all the more important when we recognize their religious differences.

The protection, however, went both ways. In a letter of 1522, cited by Eugen Rosenstock-Huessy, in *Out of Revolution, Autobiography of Western Man*, Luther, at a critical point, offered the Elector his protection. He wrote:

> "This is written to Your Grace that Your Grace may know I am coming to Wittenberg under a much higher protection than the Prince-Elector's. I have no mind to ask for Your Grace's protection; nay, I hold that I could protect Your Grace more than he could protect me. Moreover, if I knew that Your Grace could and would protect me, I would not come. In this, no sword can direct nor help; God alone must act in this matter, without all care and seeking.
>
> "Therefore he who believes most will protect most; and because I feel that Your Grace is still weak in the faith, I cannot by any means think of Your Grace as the man who could protect or save me."

"Protection" was thus made a theological fact. In terms of Deut. 28, it was grounded in God's blessing on faith and obedience. As Rosenstock-Huessy noted so incisively, "Thomas Paine offering George Washington his protection would seem ridiculous." Both the protection and the freedom which concerned Frederick III and Luther had become theological facts. A Catholic prince and a Protestant reformer had come together to establish an important Christian relationship, one with deep Biblical roots, and long strands in church history, which established a fact too little appreciated in the days that followed.

In the United States, the First Amendment to the Constitution represents a development of this faith. This amendment was added at the insistence of the clergy. The amendment reads: "Congress shall make no law respecting an establishment of religion, or prohibiting the free exercise thereof; or abridging the freedom of speech, or of the press; or the right of the people peaceably to assemble, and to petition for a redress of grievances." We miss the point of this law if we fail to note that each of the original ten amendments, as well as subsequent ones, is a single body of thought and law, a unified whole, a single subject. We are not talking about three, four, or five things here (freedom of religion, speech, press, assembly, or petition), nor one (freedom). After all, other amendments deal with freedom as well, and, if freedom were the key legal concept, the first five amendments could have been made one amendment.

The unifying fact in the First Amendment is a man's immunity in his faith and beliefs: the freedom to express his beliefs in religious worship, in speech, press, assembly, and petition. This law was framed by colonial men for whom these things were matters of faith and principle. There was therefore for them a necessary unity in this statement: instead of five rights they saw one fact. Their separation today means their diminution. It means also the steady decline of freedom in every aspect of the First Amendment.

Thus, the purpose of the First Amendment was to bar the state from entrance into, or powers over, the principled or religious stand and expressions of law-abiding men in worship, instruction, speech, publication, assembly, and petition. When Protestant Luther said to Catholic Elector-Prince Frederick III that he, Luther, was Frederick's protection in his (Luther's) free and independent move and expression of faith, and Frederick accepted that fact, and acted on it, a major step was taken. Freedom of religion was then not a privilege created and granted by the state, but rather something radically different. It meant rather the protection of the state by the freedom of faith. The stronger and more faithful that free exercise of faith, the greater the protection of the state. As Luther audaciously declared, "he who believes most will protect most." The stronger that free faith is, the stronger the state and society.

This freedom of religion, as earlier Americans understood it, meant that the ministry of grace had a Levitical or instructional duty to set forth the counsel of God for every area of life. The church was separate from the state, but not religion. Through the ministry of instruction, God's law-word concerning every area of life and thought was to be set forth.

Decline set in when the church limited the scope of God's word to the church, and when the state began to extend its powers over the family, the school, economics, and more. Today, current court cases see claims by state agencies which would entirely eliminate the First Amendment immunities for religion.

The dereliction of the press in this situation is particularly distressing. The press itself has been the target of various court decisions which seriously curtail or limit the freedom of the press, or, at the very least, place it under a cloud. Of course, all these decisions have a "good" purpose; every restriction placed upon freedom claims a good cause, to curtail or restrain abuses. All serve rather as restraints upon good motives, not evil ones. Evil places no value on, nor attention to, restraints; criminal codes already provide a legitimate recourse against the evil misuse of freedom. Attempts to restrain pornography and libel have had minimal results; the law-breaker is a specialist in circumventing the law, whereas the legitimate publication feels the restraints which the law-breaker is impervious to.

Moreover, laws seldom are limited to the purpose of the legislators. As Charles Curtis noted in *A Better Theory of Legal Interpretation*, "Language, at any rate in legal documents, does not fix meaning. It circumscribes meaning. Legal interpretation is concerned, not with the meaning of words, but only with their boundaries." Those boundaries are almost always extended to unrecognizable limits. As a result, attempts to eliminate "abuses" in religion or press wind up creating new and worse abuses of power by the state.

The press has been defending itself from the encroachments of statism, but on weak and limited grounds. It limits its First Amendment concern too often to four words thereof, and it neglects the portion which cites free exercise of religion. All over the United States, churches, Christian Schools, and parents and children have been on trial. The attacks have come from a variety of state agencies, especially departments of education, zoning, welfare, and the like. Federal attacks have come from the Internal Revenue Service, the Labor Department, the National Labor Relations Board, the White House, and more. The press has given minimal attention to these things, although they represent a major reversal of American policy. The press has become a commercial enterprise as part of large conglomerate enterprises reaching into a variety of manufacturing areas, all valid efforts, but, in the process, it has forgotten the religious nature of its immunity. The freedom it has enjoyed has not been a federal grant but a religious principle. The change in its status is due to a shift of faith.

If man's faith is in the state, then the state is the protector of man's freedom, and the author thereof. Then, in every area, we are dependent upon the state: the state giveth, and the state taketh away: Blessed be the name of the state!

The national favorite of the United States, "America," still celebrates in song an older and theocratic faith. The last stanza of Rev. Samuel Smith's song (1832), declares

> Our father's God, to Thee,
> Author of liberty,
> to Thee we sing.
> Long may our land be bright
> With freedom's holy light;
> Protect us by Thy might,
> Great God, our King.

Protection, in this theocratic perspective, is not by state controls, but by the might of the "Great God" who is "our King." The brightness of the land is not in regulatory agencies but in "freedom's holy light." This phrase is an echo of the premise which undergirds the First Amendment, the relationship of freedom to faith.

But this is not all. Article II, Section One, of the U.S. Constitution requires an oath of office from the president. Such an oath is now a meaningless and even blasphemous fact. However, to the framers of the Constitution, an oath was a Biblical fact. To them, an oath was, *first* a covenant fact, i.e., of a covenant between the state and God, and, *second*, a theocratic fact, an oath of loyalty to the sovereign. In the Constitutional Convention, an objection was actually made to adding anything to the oath such as "and will to the best of my ability, preserve, protect and defend the Constitution of the United States." The fact of an oath, Wilson held, made this addition unnecessary; it was, however, still retained. *Third*, an oath invoked the covenant blessings for obedience, and curses for disobedience, as declared in Deuteronomy 28 and Leviticus 26. An oath thus invokes a judgment from God rather than man as the basic judgment. It sees God, not the state, as the Author of all blessings, including liberty.

Today, we are in a time of judgment, because men have sought, all over the world, both freedom and blessings from the state rather than from God our King. As a result, they have gained slavery and curses.

In the humanistic, statist conception of things, freedom is not a privilege and a blessing from and under God, but either a human right, or a state grant. Man the sinner, however, is a slave, and his freedom is in essence a freedom to sin. The love of slavery has more clearly marked human history than the love of freedom. Mankind has largely been in chains throughout history, because men have preferred security to freedom. Men have often rebelled against the limitations imposed by slavery, but even more against the responsibilities imposed by freedom.

Freedom is not a natural fact but a religious principle, and the decline of freedom is an aspect of the rise of false faiths, false forms of "Christianity," as well as other varieties of faith.

This century has seen, moreover, the divorce of freedom from faith, with great damage and decay on both sides.

When Luther offered his protection to the Elector Frederick, he had just come out of hiding at the peril of his life. His re-appearance was an act of faith, and one which Frederick matched.

For all too long, those who have believed the most have been Marxists, Keynesians, fascists, and humanists generally. Their "freedom" has been slavery, for "the tender mercies of the wicked are cruel" (Prov. 12:10). Now, however, as the faith of Christians strengthens, battles are under way for the freedom of Christian Schools, churches, and families. Religious liberty is only a product of religious understanding, growth, and faith. If Christians lose their freedom, they will only have themselves to blame, and their indifference to the Author of true liberty, the Lord our King. (May, 1980)

THE DREAM OF REASON
Chalcedon Position Paper No. 13

Western Europe, since the beginning of the Enlightenment, has been given to one cultural fad after another. For example, the Deists, with their myth of a natural religion, common to all men, and humanistic in nature, saw old China as the actual embodiment of such a faith. The result was a long-standing delight in things Chinese for reasons unrelated to the actual life of China.

One of the most enduring and curious of these cultural fads was the interest and delight in things Turkish. Even Turkish furniture became very popular for a time, however great the discomfort; we have a relic of this fad in the continuing use of the term "ottoman" for a type of backless chair or sofa.

Historians also have been a part of the adulation, very often. The Turkish armies were inferior to Western ones, and, when strong resistance was made, hastily assembled and poorly equipped armies in the fifteenth century under Hunyadi, Skanderbeg, and Stephen of Moldavia defeated major Turkish armies. Usually, the European forces were divided; some were ready to see the Turks defeat their enemies, and others were indifferent. The Turks usually overwhelmed their enemies with dramatically larger forces and a prodigal use of men.

The Turks could usually count on most Europeans to be their friends. The father of Abdul-Hamid II ("the Damned") once ordered his son to kiss the hand of an elderly Christian visitor. When the young boy refused something he found "absolutely revolting," his father angrily declared, "Do you know who this gentleman is? It is the English Ambassador, the best friend of my house and my country, and the English, although not belonging to our faith, are our most faithful allies." According to Abdul-Hamid, "Upon this I reverently kissed the old gentleman's hand. It was the Boyuk Eltchi, Lord Stratford Canning." The reason for the English position was power politics, which made them not pro-Turkish but pro-English, as Abdul-Hamid later found out.

All the same, there was a cultural predisposition to work with the Turks. Western romantics had long idealized the Turks, and musicians loved to title various pseudo-oriental compositions as Turkish Marches, and the like. Marx too shared in this favorable view of the Turks. As Nathaniel Weyl points out, "Marx's comments concerning the Christian peoples of the Balkans were invariably harsh, contemptuous, caustic and unkind. But when he came to the Turks, he viewed them with a benevolent eye (when, that is, he wasn't including them as subjects of Oriental despotism)." (N. Weyl: *Karl Marx, Racist*, p. 128.)

Since 1918, because of the Armenian massacres, the old Turkish order is not as openly idealized, or else its last days are seen as a "decline." This is done despite the fact that the Young Turks and Kemal Attaturk were more bloody by far than Abdul-Hamid II.

Why is there so much dishonest history with respect to the Turk? Why is the old Turkey still seen through rose-colored historical glasses, despite the fact that its long history had been a vicious one? A further question is necessary; why did some late 19th and even a few early 20th century liberals view Abdul-Hamid II as a great liberal? An example of a very kindly view can be found in the two-volume memoirs of Arminius Vambery, professor of Oriental languages in the University of Budapest, *The Story of My Struggles* (1904). By 1904, the Sultan had come to dislike Western liberals and to regard himself as more enlightened than they. Vambery gave a portrait of an unfortunate and suffering monarch: "Indeed, the man had deserved a better fate. He is not nearly such a profligate as he is represented to be. He is more fit than many of his predecessors; he wants to benefit his land, but the means he has used were bound to have a contrary effect. I have received from Sultan Abdul Hamid many tokens of his favour and kindness, and I owe him an everlasting debt of gratitude. It grieves me, here, where I am speaking of my personal relations with him, to have to express opinions which may be displeasing to him" (vol. II, p. 389f).

However, for the truly great love of Turkey, we need to turn to the earlier regimes to find the reason for Turcophilia. In 1952, a Harvard scholar made observations on Mohammed II, the conqueror on May 29,1453, of Byzantium and Constantinople, which give us the key: "As a result of the innovations introduced by Mohammed II, the structure of the Ottoman state almost conformed to Plato's ideal republic" (Myron P. Gilmore: *The World of Humanism*, 1453-1517, p. 7; 1952; 1962).

In old Turkey, we see our futures as some would have it. A rigid educational system was set up, to produce a class of military and administrative guardians to run the state. The sultan or philosopher-king was at the top. He himself, however, was expendable. To prevent wars of succession, brothers and relatives of the succeeding ruler were killed off, or else held in prison, in reserve, if the reigning philosopher-king should prove incompetent. The incompetent ruler was then executed and replaced.

To provide for the guardians, Turkish and Christian children were taken. The Christian children were taken at an early age, brought up as Mohammedans, and trained for the Turkish state. A regular levy of children was the required tribute of the subject Christian peoples every five years.

Most of the tribute boys were trained for military purposes. These were the famous Janizaries, the main and core group of the Turkish army. The Janizaries were kept separate from other peoples and lived for one purpose, the service of the Turkish state. They were under the very strictest of discipline, and were brought up to regard themselves as an elite corps. Their prestige was so great, that by 1600 Turks were bribing their way into the Janizaries. In the 17th century, membership became hereditary, and the Janizaries declined into an unruly group. In 1826, they were dissolved by a standard Turkish practice, total massacre.

The ruling class and bureaucracy were similarly formed. A palace school was created to train superior children for the service of the state. These children again were from subject peoples and had been forcibly taken from their parents at an early age. Native Turks or Osmanlis had no more part in their civil government than did subject Christians, although as Moslems the Turks had a favored place before the law.

The free Moslem families provided the recruits for the learned classes, scholars, priests, teachers, and juriconsults.

The life of the Turkish state was everything; the life of the subject peoples was as fuel for the state. The lives of Turks were not more highly regarded, on the whole, and even the life of the sultan was expendable by execution if he were an impediment. The sultan could be as abominable personally as he chose, but he could not be a detriment to the empire without risking execution.

Now we come to the heart of the matter: The Turkish Empire was constructed to be a rational order, on the order of Plato's so-called republic. Its rule was to be the rule of reason, and all peoples, from sultans to subjects, were to be put in their place in terms of a governing order. Even at the top, the dreaded execution by strangulation with a bowstring was accepted as a horrible but necessary resolution of problems. The ruled and the rulers were alike subservient to the state.

Abdul-Hamid II saw himself as an enlightened and rational ruler. The rational solution to problems was to eliminate the problem: hence the systematic massacre and deportation of Armenians, begun under him, and completed by his successors. When Abdul-Hamid was deposed, he expected to be executed: it was the logical solution. His execution did not occur because his successors recognized that too drastic a break at that point was unwise.

The Platonic and Turkish ideal of a rational state has long been a dream of Western man. The French Revolution was a classic example of it: the revolutionaries debated as to what would be an ideal population for France, and then began to exterminate people to reduce France to the desired status. Unwanted peoples and classes were similarly executed.

The Russian Revolution gives us the same ideal. From top to bottom, men are expendable at the altar of the ideal order. Classes are liquidated; Christianity is made the target of obliteration, and mass murders made a policy of state. A number of writers have given us an account of this dream of order, notably of late Alexander I. Solzhenitsyn in the three volumes of *The Gulag Archipelago*, and in the essays edited by him on *From Under the Rubble*. Much earlier, Dostoyevsky had depicted the same dream or nightmare in *The Possessed*. All things are to be destroyed, to make way for the "rational" and planned society.

This same goal is very much with us. It is basic to the thinking of virtually every modern state. For this reason, the modern state is at total war with its peoples: they are its real enemies, who must be re-made, and, if they refuse, destroyed in one way or another, economically, if not physically.

The means to the goal are two-fold. The older version, as in the Soviet Union and Red China, holds to total terror as the main instrument in attaining the dream of the golden age of Reason. The more "advanced" humanists of the West have an improved version of the dream, and the classic demonstration model of this new order is Sweden. The Swedish model is in force virtually everywhere in the non-Marxist world. Instead of total terror, this new model relies on the control of education, economics, and technology. The great study of this new model is Roland Huntford's *The New Totalitarians* (1972). Sweden's planners regard the Russian effort as a failure (p. 85). Huntford noted: "It is probably correct to say that Sweden has been dechristianized more efficiently than any other country, Russian not excepted" (p. 219).

In this dream efficiency requires that the slaves of the philosopher-kings be educated to love their slavery and to regard it as freedom. (George Orwell, in 1984, saw this as a goal of the new order.) Man must become a happy cog in the machinery of the state, and reason, with its tools of technology, must rule over all men. Solzhenitsyn, in *Gulag*, III (pp. 522, 525) calls attention to what has become of law in the Soviet Union. The law has ceased to be a transcendent standard of justice: it has been made a tool of state policy. Hence, he declares, "There is no law." In Sweden, this change is openly set forth as an advantage. Carl Lidbom, formerly a judge of appeal, a Cabinet minister, and a Social Democrat theoretician, has said: "The purpose of the law is to realize official policy...It is one of the instruments of changing society." A legal official told Huntford, "it seems natural to me that the law is there to put the intentions of the bureaucracy into practice." (Huntford, p. 122)

If this sounds familiar to Americans, Canadians, and others, it is with good reason so. It is all a part of the same rationalistic dream of a scientifically planned order by philosopher-kings. These philosophers now have added science and behaviorism to their repertoire; they have moved from a rigidly planned to an existentially planning order, but their goal is the same. The methodology has been refined.

Instead of a regular five-year draft of a limited number of boys for the Janizaries and the bureaucracy, we now have an annual call-up of all five-year-old boys and girls for the state school system and its humanistic indoctrination. Military service for all is in the offing. All this is done in the name of the public welfare and as a manifestation of the general benevolence of the state. Christian social deviants who insist on educating their own children in Christian Schools are made the targets of civil and criminal charges. The state being the rational and the good order by presupposition (The Great Community), the church, Christian School, and Christian family become the obstructionist, evil, and irrational elements in society. (We have now forgotten what a radical and revolutionary step the French Revolution made in recruiting by law all its citizens for its armed forces, as its janizaries.)

Justice has now become, not the righteousness and law of God, but the law and interests of the modern and humanistic state. As Huntford said of the Swedish judiciary, "Justice to them means upholding the interests of the State, not primarily guaranteeing fair play to the citizen" (p. 123). This is increasingly true of every modern state. The triumph of Plato and Turkey is everywhere near!

This course of events should not surprise us. When men despise God's law and its requirement of very severely limited civil and human powers, they will create their own dreams of order. If we deny God's law, we will choose man's law; if we deny God's predestination or plan, we will substitute a man-made plan or decree of predestination. The dream of reason, a nightmare reality, will be with us as long as we deny God's law and government.

The words of Joshua still stand: "choose ye this day whom ye will serve... but as for me and my house, we will serve the LORD" (Joshua 24:15). (June, 1980)

THE NEW RACISM
Chalcedon Position Paper No. 14

Racism is a relatively new fact on the world scene. In earlier eras, not race but religion was the basis of discrimination. Although religious history has been marred by ugly violence against other religious groups, and the history of the Christian Church is no exception to this, there is a notable fact which is often forgotten. Missionary faiths, and supremely Christianity, normally seek to win other groups, not oppress them, and this missionary impulse has also provided, in many eras, a favorable cause for a friendly approach.

In the modern era, as Christianity's influence receded, and science began to govern together with humanism, biology came to predominate over theology. The differences between men were seen increasingly as biological and racial rather than religious. The earlier physical anthropologists made very precise and detailed physical studies of all peoples in order to establish the physical differences between races.

The theory of evolution fueled this developing scientific racism and added still another important factor. Many theories began to hold to a multiple origin for the human race. Whereas in Scripture all men are descendents of Adam, in evolutionary thought, all men are possibly descendents of very differing evolutionary sources. Common descent in Adam meant a common creation, nature, and responsibility under God. The idea of multiple origins proved divisive. The human race was no longer the human race! It was a collection of possibly human races, a very different doctrine.

It is important to recognize that racism was in origin a scientific doctrine. Whenever a scientific doctrine is discarded, as witness the idea of the acquired inheritance of environmental influences, the old scientific doctrine, as it lingers on in popular thought, is blamed on religion or popular superstition! The origins of racism are in very highly respectable scientific theorists. The fact that men like Houston Stewart Chamberlain (1855-1927), a British admiral's son and son-in-law of Richard Wagner, took this scientific literature to develop what became the foundation of Nazi thought does not eliminate its scientific origins.

The defeat of the Nazis did not end racism. Instead, it has again become respectable and widespread. We must remember that studies of Hitler's Germany indicate that his support came from liberals, democrats, socialists, and the intellectual community. Scholars like Erik von Kuehnelt-Leddihn have ably exposed the myth of a conservative or rightist origin for Hitler's support. The fact of Hitler's antipathy to Christianity helped enlist support for him.

The new racism is widespread and common to many peoples and to every continent. It has now become a part also of the religious vocabulary of many churchmen. Thus, in almost every seminary today, pompous professors rail against a missions program which would export "the white mentality" and European modes of thought. What is the white mentality, and what is the European mode of thought, as against the human, common to all men? If it is specifically white and European, it must be common to the pre-Christian European as a racial factor. The pre-Christian Saxons, for example, practiced human sacrifice, and more. Much more could be said about pre-Christian Europeans, but I have no desire to be flooded with angry letters (which I will discard without answer). No race born of Adam has a good history: this is the Biblical fact, and the historical fact.

The Western mind, common to Europe and the Americas, is a product, not of race, but of culture, religious culture. Elements of it, none too good, go back to the barbarian peoples of Europe. Other aspects are from Greek philosophy, again none too good. (The Greeks described all non-Greeks as barbarians on cultural, not racist, grounds. They gave brilliant and inventive slaves a Greek name and status.) The Western mind and culture, in all its advances, is a product of Biblical religion. It is a religious, not a racial, product.

A generation ago, a pope with humane intentions said, "Spiritually, we are all Semites." Despite his humane intentions, he was wrong. Arabs are Semites, and we are not Arabic in our faith and culture. He would have been equally wrong had he said Hebrews or Jews. The culture of the West is not the property of any race or people in its origin. It is Biblical. True, much sin is present in Western culture. True, such sin needs to be condemned. But the mind of the West bears the imprint of the Bible. It is not understandable on any other terms.

Today, however, men speak of the white mentality, the Asiatic soul, and the African mind. Some educators are insistent on the need to recognize and give status in the schools to what they call "black English."

Implicit in all of this is a racist view of man. Races are seen as the sources of varying kinds of logic and reason. To deny the validity of the concept of a white mind, an African mind, or an Asiatic mind is seen as reactionary, imperialistic, and evil.

The mentality of a people, however, is not a product of race but of religion, and the culture of that religion. The key factor is always religion. There is a hidden but insane pride among those who oppose exporting the white mentality. Although such men would never dare say it explicitly, or even think it, what they are saying implicitly is that other races are not up to comprehending the white mentality. (One brilliant black student told me, with wry humor, that he could always count on a high grade for minimum work from a white liberal professor. The man would regard him as inferior, but would never have the courage to admit as much, and would accordingly give him a good grade!) All talk of differing mentalities has a patronizing perspective; it also says that race, not sin, is the problem of other peoples and their cultures.

Because of the new racism, we now have a growing body of religious literature, aimed at the seminary student, pastor, and missionary, which talks about *contextualization*. Supposedly, the only way to communicate the Gospel to other races is by giving priority to the context over Biblical faith and confessional statements. The impetus for contextualization has come from the Theological Education Fund, set up in 1957 by the Rockefeller Foundation. Contextualization calls also for an emphasis on the struggle for justice in terms of "liberation theology" (a form of Marxism) and existentialistic responses to the historical moment in the Third World. Contextualization places a heavy emphasis on human need rather than God's infallible word. Its mission is thus contemporary and social, not theological and supernatural. Contextualists of all theological stripes shift their language from that of Scripture to the jargon spawned by the Theological Education Fund.

Closely related to this in the area of Bible translations is the dynamic equivalence theory, now common to most Bible societies and translation groups. This doctrine, of which Eugene A. Nida is an exponent, "translates" the Bible into a culture and its ideas. This can mean giving an historical account a psychoanalytic or mythological meaning. Instead of reshaping the culture, the Bible is "translated" into the culture. (Such a doctrine makes the culture in effect the unerring word, not the Bible. The culture thus corrects or amends the Bible, not the Bible culture.) As Jakob Van Bruggen, in *The Future of the Bible*, points out, "the dynamic equivalence translation theory owes its influence and effect to the blending of modern theological prejudices regarding the Bible with data borrowed from communication theory, cultural anthropology, and modern sociology rather than to insights from linguistics" (p. 151; publ. by Thomas Nelson, Inc., 1978.)

The implications of this new racism are far-reaching. Instead of working to change a people, we have a static and racist view of a people and their culture. It is the Bible and the mission which must change, not the people! We must teach a "black English" if any at all, and a black, brown, or yellow Christianity, if any at all. It takes only a brief excursion into "liberation theology," contextualization, and like doctrines to realize that it is not Christianity at all which is taught, but a counterfeit. Relevance is sought, not to the Lord and His word, but to fallen man and his racial heritage. Such is not the Gospel; it is the new racism.

The new racism passes, however, for vital, relevant Christianity. It is widely promoted by seminaries and missionary organizations. It encourages races, like individuals, to trumpet the existentialist (and hippie) slogan, "I want to be me!" The historical goal is racial realization! Providentially, the early missionaries to Europe, coming from North Africa, Asia Minor, and the Mediterranean world generally, had no such regard for the European mind. They regarded it as unregenerate and in need of being broken and redeemed. All the plagues and evils of "the European mind" are products of the fallen man and the relics of barbarian cultures, not of Christ and His word. All that is good in "the European mind" is a result of Christian culture, not of race.

The words of Paul are a sharp rebuke to all who want men to glory in their blood, race, or history: "For who maketh thee to differ from another? and what hast thou that didst not receive? now if thou didst receive it, why dost thou glory, as if thou hadst not received it?" (I Cor. 4:7). (July, 1980)

THE MEANING OF THEOCRACY
Chalcedon Position Paper No. 15

Few things are more commonly misunderstood than the nature and meaning of theocracy. It is commonly assumed to be a dictatorial rule by self-appointed men who claim to rule for God. In reality, theocracy in Biblical law is the closest thing to a radical libertarianism that can be had.

In Biblical law, the only civil tax was the head or poll tax, the same for all males twenty years of age and older (Ex. 30:16). This tax provided an atonement or covering for people, i.e., the covering of civil protection by the state as a ministry of justice (Rom. 13:1-4). This very limited tax was continued by the Jews after the fall of Jerusalem, and, from 768-900 A.D., helped make the Jewish princedom of Narbonne (in France) and other areas a very important and powerful realm (see Arthur J. Zuckerman: *A Jewish Princedom in Feudal France 768-900*; New York, N.Y.: Columbia University Press, 1965,1972). This tax was limited to half a sheckel of silver per man.

All other functions of government were financed by the tithe. Health, education, welfare, worship, etc., were all provided for by tithes and offerings. Of this tithe, one tenth (i.e., one percent of one's income) went to the priests, for worship. Perhaps an equal amount went for music, and for the care of the sanctuary. The tithe was God's tax, to provide for basic government in God's way. The second and the third tithes provided for welfare, and for the family's rest and rejoicing before the Lord (see E.A. Powell and R.J. Rushdoony: *Tithing and Dominion*: Ross House Books, P. 0. Box 67, Vallecito, California 95251).

What we today fail to see, and must recapture, is the fact that the basic *government* is the self-government of covenant man; then the family is the central governing *institution* of Scripture. The school is a governmental agency, and so too is the church. Our vocation also governs us, and our society. Civil government must be one form of government among many, and a minor one. Paganism (and Baal worship in all its forms) made the state and its rulers into a god or gods walking on earth, and gave them total over-rule in all spheres. The prophets denounced all such idolatry, and the apostles held, "We ought to obey God rather than men" (Acts 5:29).

From the days of the Caesars to the heads of democratic states and Marxist empires, the ungodly have seen what Christians too often fail to see, namely, that Biblical faith requires and creates a rival government to the humanistic state. Defective faith seeks to reduce Biblical faith to a man-centered minimum, salvation. Now salvation, our regeneration, is the absolutely essential starting point of the Christian life, but, if it is made the sum total thereof, it is in effect denied. Salvation is then made into a man-centered and egotistical thing, when it is in fact God-centered and requires the death, not the enthronement, of our sinful and self-centered ego. We are saved for God's purposes, saved to serve, not in time only, but eternally (Rev. 22:3). To be saved is to be members of a new creation and God's Kingdom, and to be working members of that realm.

In a theocracy, therefore, God and His law rule. The state ceases to be the over-lord and ruler of man. God's tax, the tithe, is used by godly men to create schools, hospitals, welfare agencies, counsellors, and more. It provides, as it did in Scripture, for music and more. All the basic social financing, other than the head tax of Ex. 30-16, was provided for by tithes and offerings or gifts. An offering or gift was that which was given above and over a tithe.

Since none of the tithe agencies have any coercive power to collect funds, none can exist beyond their useful service to God and man. For the modern state, uselessness and corruption are no problem; they do not limit its power to collect more taxes. Indeed, the state increases its taxing power because it is more corrupt and more useless, because its growing bureaucracy demands it.

California State Senator H. L. "Bill" Richardson has repeatedly called attention to the fact that, once elected, public officials respond only under pressure to their voters but more to their peer group and their superiors. Lacking faith, they are governed by power.

People may complain about the unresponsiveness of their elected officials, and their subservience to their peers and superiors, but nothing will alter this fact other than a change in the faith of the electorate and the elected. Men will respond to and obey the dominant power in their lives, faith, and perspective. If that dominant power or god in their lives is the state, they will react to it. If it is man, or their own ego, they will be governed by it. If, however, it is the triune God of Scripture who rules them, then men will respond to and obey His law-word. Men will obey their gods.

One of the more important books of this century was Albert Jay Nock's *Our Enemy, The State* (Caxton Printers, Caldwell, Idaho, 1935ff.). Without agreeing with Nock in all things, it is necessary to agree with him that the modern state is man's new church and saving institution. The state, however, is an antisocial institution, determined to suppress and destroy all the historic and religiously grounded powers of society. With F.D. Roosevelt and The New Deal, the goal of the statists became openly "the complete extinction of social power through absorption by the State" (p. 21). This will continue in its suicidal course, until there is not enough social power left to finance the State's plans (as became the case in Rome). The State's intervention into every realm is financed by the productivity of the non-statist and economic sector: "Intervention retards production; then the resulting stringency and inconvenience enable further intervention, which in turn still further retards production; and this process goes on until, as in Rome, in the third century, production ceases entirely, and the source of payment dries up" (p. 151f). It is true that crime needs suppression, but, instead of suppressing crime, the State safeguards its own monopoly of crime.

We can add that the solution to crime and injustice is not more power to the state, but God's law and a regenerate man. The best safeguard against crime is godly men and a godly society. Furthermore, God's law, in dealing with crime, requires restitution, and, with habitual criminals, the death penalty (see R. J. Rushdoony: *Institutes of Biblical Law*).

One more important point from Nock: he called attention to the fact that "social power" once took care of all emergencies, reliefs, and disasters. When the Johnstown flood occurred, all relief and aid was the result of a great outpouring of "private" giving. "Its abundance, measured by money alone, was so great that when everything was finally put in order, something like a million dollars remained" (p. 6).

This was once the only way such crises were met. Can it happen again? The fact is that it is happening again. Today, between 20-30% of all school children, K through 12, are in non-statist schools, and the percentage is likely to pass 50% by 1990 if Christians defend their schools from statist interventionism. More and more Christians are recognizing their duties for the care of their parents; churches are again assuming, in many cases, the care of elderly members. Homes for elderly people, and also for delinquent children are being established. (One of the more famous of these, under the leadership of Lester Roloff, is under attack by the state, which refuses to recognize sin as the basic problem with delinquents, and regeneration and sanctification as the answer.) Christians are moving into the areas of radio and television, not only to preach salvation but to apply Scripture to political, economic, and other issues.

Moreover, everywhere Christians are asking themselves the question, What must I do, now that I am saved? Answers take a variety of forms: textbook publishing for Christian Schools; periodicals, and more. The need to revive and extend Christian hospitals is being recognized, and much, much more.

Isaiah 9:6-7 tells us that, when Christ was born, the government was to be on His shoulders, and that "Of the increase of his government and peace there shall be no end." By means of their tithing and actions, believers are in increasing numbers submitting to Christ's government and re-ordering life and society in terms of it.

The essence of humanism, from Francis Bacon to the present, has been this creed: to be human, man must be in control (Jeremy Rifkin with Ted Howard: *The Emerging Order*, p. 27.). This is an indirect way of saying that man is not man unless the government of all things is upon his shoulders, unless he is himself god. It is the expression of the tempter's program of revolt against God (Gen. 3:5). John Locke developed this faith by insisting that Christianity is a private concern, not a public matter. Christianity thus could not be the basis of public activity but only a private faith. The foundation of the state and of public life was for Locke in reason.

But reason, separated from Christian faith and presupposition, became man's will, or, better, man's will in radical independence from God. The state then began to claim one area of life after another as public domain and hence under the state as reason incarnate. One of the first things claimed by Locke's philosophy and "reason" was man himself! Man, instead of being a sinner, was, at least in the human and public realm, morally neutral; he was a blank piece of paper, and what he became was a product of education and experience. It thus was held necessary for the state, the incarnate voice of "reason," to control education in order to produce the desired kind of man.

The state claimed the public realm. The public realm had belonged, in terms of Christian faith, to God, like all things else, and to a free society under God. The church was scarcely dislodged from its claims over the public realm when the state came in to claim it with even more total powers.

But this was not all. The state enlarged the public realm by new definitions, so that steadily, one sphere after another fell into the hands of the state. Education was claimed, and control over economics, a control which is now destroying money and decreasing social and economic productivity. The arts and sciences are subsidized and controlled, and are begging for more. Marriage and the family are controlled; the White House Conference on the Family views the family as a public and hence statist realm, one the state must invade and control.

Ancient Rome regarded religion itself as a public domain and hence licensed and controlled it. (The very word *liturgy*, Greek in origin, means public service. Religion is indeed a public concern, more so than the state, but not thereby a matter for statist control.) Rome, like all ancient pagan states, equated the public domain with the state's domain, and it saw all things as aspects of the state's domain.

For any one institution to see itself as the public domain is totalitarianism. All things public and private are in the religious domain and under God. No institution, neither church nor state, can equate itself with God and claim control of the public (or private) domain. Every sphere of life is interdependent with other spheres and alike under God. No more than mathematics has the "right" to control biology do church or state have the "right" to control one another, or anything beyond their severely limited sphere of government.

There are thus a variety of spheres of government under God. These spheres are limited, interdependent, and under God's sovereign government and law-word. They cannot legitimately exceed their sphere. The legitimate financial powers of all are limited. The state has a small head tax. The tithe finances all other spheres.

The tithe, it must be emphasized, is to the Lord, not to the church, a difference some churchmen choose to miss or overlook. This robs the individual believer of all right to complain about things; by the godly use of his tithe, he can create new agencies, churches, schools, and institutions to further God's Kingdom in every area of life and thought. Holiness comes not by our abilities to whine and bewail the things that are, but by our faithful use of the tithe and the power God gives us to remake all things according to His word.

Tithing and godly action, these are the keys to dominion. We are called to dominion (Gen. 1:26-28; 9:1-17; Joshua 1:1-9; Matt. 28:18-20; etc.). The creation mandate is our covenant mandate; restoration into the covenant through Christ's atonement restores us into the mandate to exercise dominion and gives us the power to effect it.

Aspects of that mandate can be exercised through institutions, and sometimes must be, but the mandate can never be surrendered to them. The mandate precedes all institutions, and it is to man personally as man (Gen. 1:28). This is the heart of theocracy as the Bible sets it forth. Dictionaries to the contrary, theocracy is not a government by the state but a government over every institution by God and His Law, and through the activities of the free man in Christ to bring every area of life and thought under Christ's Kingship. (August, 1980)

THE FREEDOM OF THE CHURCH
Chalcedon Position Paper No. 16

We are today being subjected to a steady attack on churches, Christian Schools, and other Christian activities. With this assault goes an attack on the First Amendment. At the same time, when evangelical ministers and church groups call attention to serious moral problems in our political affairs, or oppose abortion or homosexuality, for example, they are widely attacked for violating the First Amendment.

It is important therefore to understand a basic purpose of the First Amendment. Let us remind ourselves of the text of that law:

> Congress shall make no law respecting an establishment of religion, or prohibiting the free exercise thereof; or abridging the freedom of speech, or of the press; or the right of the people peaceably to assemble, and to petition the government for a redress of grievances.

First of all, there is no mention of the separation of church and state. This amendment did in fact separate the *federal* government and the church, but not the various states and the church. In the years that followed, separation became a fact gradually in every state. This separation is a fact which I believe we must welcome. It was a necessary consequence of the amendment, but it was not its stated and primary purpose.

Second, this amendment does *not* separate *religion* and the state. Such a separation is impossible. Every law is an expression of morality or procedural thereto. Laws express moral concern. All morality is an aspect of religion. We have Buddhist morality and law, Islamic morality and law, humanistic morality and law, and so on. Every law order is an establishment of religion. What we are seeing is the progressive attempt to disestablish *Christianity* and to establish *humanism*. Our state schools are the religious establishments of humanism, and our courts, television, films, and press reflect humanism. We must avoid a *church* establishment, but we cannot escape a *religious* establishment or foundation in this country or in any country.

Third, the First Amendment, in speaking of "an establishment of religion," was using the language of its day: it meant an established church. Robert Allen Rutland, in his study, *The Birth of the Bill of Rights, 1776-1791* (1955), called attention to the fact that the clergy of the day demanded this amendment. They were not alone.

Thus, the focus of the First Amendment is on the disestablishment of *the* church. We cannot understand their thinking unless we realize that the colonists, whether British, German, Dutch, Swedish, French, or anything else, had a European background. They usually had a horror of a state-imposed church. They saw serious problems in any such church. A state church easily becomes a *controlled church*: it is the voice of the crown rather than the voice of God. In England, first the monarch, beginning with Henry VIII, and then parliament, was the head of the church. Americans wanted no such church.

As a matter of fact, Carl Bridenbaugh, in *Mitre and Sceptre, Transatlantic Faiths, Ideas, Personalities, and Politics, 1689-1775* (1962), held that a fundamental cause of the War of Independence was the American fear of a forthcoming plan to force the Church of England and crown-appointed bishops on all the colonies. This led to war, and also to the First Amendment.

Moreover, the colonists knew that a *controlled church* is very readily a *corrupt church*. The English church was suffering then, and had for some years, from political bishops, men whose only qualification for office was their service to the Crown, not the Lord. Only the rise of competition in the form of Methodism produced a measure of reform in the English Church.

However, the key factor was something more. A corrupt church is a *silent church*. The colonists were very much accustomed to a vocal church, plain-spoken in its criticism of moral and political trends. More than a few scholars have seen the origin of the War of Independence in the Great Awakening. The alarms sounded by the colonial clergy were a major factor in arousing a moral resistance among colonists. Both from the pulpit and in print, the colonial clergy played a central role in the events which led to 1776.

The British knew this. Hence their readiness during the war to burn American churches, to burn Bibles, hymnals, and church records. The colonies, one Tory said, had run off with "an American parson," i.e., had been "seduced" by the clergy.

The purpose of the First Amendment, in requiring that the churches be disestablished, or, rather, never established in the new country, had as its purpose the protection of the freedom of the church and the school. The colonists distrusted a powerful central government. To create a federal government and to give it power to create a state church represented tyranny to them. To ensure that free religious and moral voice of judgment against all evils in state and society, they demanded the First Amendment. They wanted the *prophetic* voice of the church to be free to judge the federal government in terms of the word of God. The role the prophets fulfilled in the Old Testament the church must fulfill now.

Thus, those churchmen who speak out concerning our national life and political morality are *not* violating the First Amendment. Instead, they are doing precisely what the founding fathers and Americans of 1781 wanted to see done, the Christian voice freely and powerfully raised against sin in high places.

George Washington, in his Farewell Address, issued on September 17, 1796, with the evils of the French Revolution in mind, warned against the idea of a secular state. There could be, he held, no separation of religion and political order, nor of religion and morality. The freedom of the church and the school (and only Christian Schools existed then) were basic to his perspective.

The First Amendment is being subjected not only to misrepresentation but attack. Since World War II, the Internal Revenue Service has been actively claiming the right to establish religion. A church is supposedly not a church, unless the I.R.S. approves. For the I.R.S. to define and approve a church is to make itself the agency for the establishment of religion.

Moreover, recent efforts by state and federal agencies have implicit or explicit in them a very dangerous definition of the church. The Christian School, the Sunday School, and the sermon are *educational* and hence not *religious*. They are thus said to be outside the First Amendment protection, as are the church nursery, women's guilds, and the like. The meaning of the church, and its First Amendment immunity is reduced to a liturgical service.

It is also held that the Sixteenth Amendment has nullified the First Amendment and that churches are liable to income and other taxes. Instead of a constitutional immunity, only a statutory immunity exists, revocable at any time.

The church, however, must oppose all such efforts to limit its freedom, because they are really controls on Christ our King, and His infallible and sovereign word. The church is an educational institution, proclaiming and teaching the word of God. The Old Testament ministry was priestly (sacrificial), and levitical (instructional, Deut. 33:10). The New Testament ministry is a continuation of the levitical, and instruction of every kind is basic to its life.

It has been pointed out that the clergy of the day led in the demand for the First Amendment. They had come to see that the lordship of Jesus Christ requires a church free of all statist controls. The church must be able to speak freely and boldly in terms of the law-word of God.

All attempts to silence the Christian voice must be seen as a denial of

God's crown rights over all men. Those who try to silence the church in the name of the First Amendment are not ready to silence pornography, or anything else, save God's word.

The First Amendment requires freedom of speech, freedom of press, assembly, and petition. All these are related to freedom of religion. Most publications then were Christian; the church was the meeting-house, the place of assembly, petition, and free speech. It was not accidental that all five factors are linked together in the First Amendment: they were linked together in life.

They still are, in that all presuppose a faith and a conviction which demands expression and acts upon its convictions. The church cannot be silent without sin. It must speak write, assemble, and petition in terms of the Crown Rights of Jesus Christ. His lordship is total and cosmic. Not only the church, but every man, every state, every school, and every aspect of life must either serve Him, or be judged by Him. He is the Lord. (September, 1980)

THE CRISIS

There is an old folk tale about a man on board an old sailing vessel who was asked to go to the other end of the ship and give help. The ship had sprung a leak, and men were needed to man the pump and do emergency work. The man refused, saying, It wasn't his end of the ship, and besides, he didn't think much of the people down there, anyway!

That kind of stupidity and blindness is very much with us today. The First Amendment immunities of the church and Christian School are being breached and denied. Court cases are being used to establish new legal precedents to spell the destruction of Christian institutions. In the face of this, there is an unwillingness on the part of many to get involved because they disagree with the persecuted group. However, if a court case destroys the First Amendment's meaning, all religious groups are involved. Whether the case involves a Christian or a non-Christian group, or, an orthodox or an heretical group, if it sets a legal precedent to serve the needs of our humanistic statists, all of us will suffer.

Yet, too often, Protestants and Catholics will not work together; Arminians and Calvinists will not help one another; neither will work with Charismatic churches, who are also divided; none will work together with heretics, or non-Christian groups.

No such action means ecumenism; it simply means a common legal threat, and action against it. It means an affirmation that freedom and conversion, not tyranny and coercion, are basic to our faith.

It does not involve any approval of the "Moonies" to oppose their kidnapping and de-programming. To give assent to such de-programming is to open the door to the de-programming of converts to Christ, and there are hints of this already.

In the face of this common threat to all, the threat of totalitarian humanism, it is distressing to see the narrow-mindedness of some. I have been a witness at a number of trials. It has been amazing to me to receive letters denouncing me for appearing in behalf of a person or group, because they were supposedly the "wrong" kind of Baptist! Even worse are those "spiritually-minded" people who favor surrender to resistance and insist on calling it holiness.

It has been heartening in a few cases to see diverse groups work together. None of this led to ecumenicism; it only led to a wiser defense.

Moreover, too often churchmen assume that the Biblical requirement of separation means separation from Christians who disagree with us. In Scripture, we are told not to be unequally yoked with *unbelievers* (II Cor. 6:14-18), a very different thing. What is condemned by Paul is an unequal or subservient yoking, and a belief that there is a common ground between believers and unbelievers, in themselves. To face an enemy on the shores of our country, or in our courts, does not uphold a common religious faith but simply deals with a threat to one and all. (September, 1980)

ADIAPHORISM AND TOTALITARIANISM
Chalcedon Position Paper No. 17

One of the more important but neglected controversies of church history has been the struggle over adiaphorism, i.e., over "things indifferent." Essentially, the controversy has been over the realm of things which stand outside the word of God, over what is and is not legislated. Obviously, at the heart of this concept of adiaphora is a doctrine of God, and the nature and extent of His government and law. However, for most theological traditions, the argument over adiaphora is an old and settled one, and the issue is not seen as a very lively one in our time.

On closer examination, however, it becomes apparent that the issue is far from settled, and that the concept of adiaphora is anything but Biblical. The *concept* in fact comes from the ancient Cynic and Stoic philosophers, and its presence in church history is evidence of a pagan infiltration .

It is thus important to review briefly the Cynic and Stoic views. For the Cynics and Stoics, man existed in an essentially meaningless material cosmos. Value, meaning, and morality had no meaning in that material world; they were, rather, personal and spiritual or mental concerns and concepts. In brief, value and meaning are derived from the self and are virtually identical with it. The moral goal is thus self-sufficiency, and the wise and moral man is absolutely self-sufficient and recognizes that the material world is a world of morally indifferent things. In such a view, which Diogenes held in dramatic form, there is no law nor meaning outside of man; all things physical are indifferent. Only man's mind makes the difference in its attitudes, which are the source of values.

This view first entered the church as a heresy. Carpocrates and his followers saw nothing evil by nature (or, for that matter, good), with the only values being *faith and love*, attitudes of the self. The Nicolaites were very precise in stating the extent of things indifferent: adultery was for them a matter of indifference.[1] Of the doctrines of Carpocrates, Irenaeus reported that he held that "We are saved, indeed, by means of faith and love; but all other things, while in their nature indifferent, are reckoned by the opinions of men--some good, and some evil, there being nothing really evil by nature."[2]

Very early too these Hellenic ideas of adiaphorism entered into the apparently orthodox tradition of Christian thought. Clement of Alexandria held, "Fit objects for admiration are the Stoics, who say that the soul is not affected by the body, either to vice by disease, or to virtue by health; but both these things, they say, are indifferent."[3] Clement's point here is not an attack on environmentalism but an assertion of the separate beings of mind and body, and the necessity to cultivate the independence of the mind or soul from the morally indifferent realm of matter. For Clement, "a good life is happiness, and...the man who is adorned in his soul with virtue is happy." For Clement, virtue is to be defined in Hellenic terms; Greek philosophy for him paved the way, and Christianity simply added to that structure the incarnate truth, the Son of God:

> Although at one time philosophy justified the Greeks, not conducting them to that entire righteousness to which it is ascertained to cooperate, as the first and second flight of steps help you in your ascent to the upper room, and the grammarian helps the philosopher. Not as if by its abstraction, the perfect Word would be rendered incomplete,

---

[1] Bernard J. Verkamp: *The Indifferent Mean, Adiaphorism in the English Reformation to 1554*, p. 21f. Athens, Ohio: Ohio University Press, 1977.

[2] Irenaeus, "Against Heresies," Bk. I. ch. xxv, 5, in *Ante-Nicene Christian Library*, vol. V, The Writings of Irenaeus, vol. I, p. 96. Edinburgh, Scotland: T. & T. Clark, 1874.

[3] Clement of Alexandria, "The Miscellanies, in *ibid.*, vol. XII, Clement of Alexandria, vol. II, p. 148.

> or truth perish; since also sight, hearing, and the voice contribute to truth, but it is the mind which is the appropriate faculty for knowing it. But of those things which cooperate, some contribute a greater amount of power; some, a less. Perspicuity accordingly aids in the communication of truth, and logic in preventing us from falling under the heresies by which we are assailed. But the teaching, which is according to the Savior, is complete in itself and without defect, being "the power and wisdom of God;" (I Cor. i. 24) and the Hellenic philosophy does not, by its approach, make the truth more powerful; but rendering powerless the assault of sophistry against it, and frustrating the treacherous plots laid against the truth, is said to be the proper "fence and wall of the vineyard."[4]

For Clement, the true and Christian gnostic withdraws from the indifferent world of material things to commune with God and to approximate God's impassibility by his own indifference to external things:

> When, therefore, he who partakes gnostically of this holy quality devotes himself to contemplation, communing in purity with the divine, he enters more nearly into the state of impassible identity, so as no longer to have science and possess knowledge, but to be science and knowledge.[5]

Given such a perspective, it is easy to see why the church moved, *first*, into asceticism. An indifference to material things was seen as a mark of morality. The material world itself was now, in Cynic fashion, seen as adiaphora, as a thing of indifference to true religion and morality. *Second*, the Old Testament was no longer seen as on the same plane as the New, and the New Testament was viewed in Hellenic terms and as the "spiritual" book in contrast to the "materialism" of the Old. The apostolic preaching had been from Old Testament texts, which were viewed as more "alive" and relevant than ever with the coming of Christ. Now, the Old Testament was regarded as a lesser, more primitive, and hence materialistic revelation. God's law was thus seen as belonging to a lower era of revelation and hence now less relevant if at all so. This view then and now has led to antinomianism. *Third*, as with the Cynics, morality was now reduced also to a mental attitude. Since things material are morally indifferent, then only man's spiritual states can be moral. Logically, the Cynics, and also Carpocrates and the Nicolaites, saw now evil in material acts, in adultery, homosexuality, and the like. On the whole, despite periodic lapses, the church worked to avoid such a conclusion, however logical. This opinion did remain as an undercurrent, as Boccaccio witnessed. In the concluding

---

[4] *Ibid.*, Bk. I, XX; in *ibid.*, vol. I. p. 419f. of vol. IV in series.

[5] *Ibid.*, Bk. IV, ch. 6, in Clement, vol. II, p. 157.

paragraph of his Decameron, he states flatly that he was writing the truth about friars (and others). In the Seventh Story of the Third Day, a lover tells a married woman, whose refusal earlier had driven him into exile, "For a woman to have converse with a man is a sin of nature; but to rob him or slay him or drive him into exile proceedeth from malignity of mind."[6] In other words, adultery is a lesser sin than deliberately depriving a lover, because sins of the mind are more important than sins of the flesh. In the Eighth Story of the Third Day, an abbot convinces a woman that adultery with him is not a serious matter:

> The lady, hearing this, was all aghast and answered, 'Alack, father mine, what is this you ask? Me thought you were a saint. Doth it beseem holy men to require women, who come to them for counsel, of such things?' 'Fair my soul,' rejoined the abbot, 'marvel not, for that sanctity nowise abateth by this, seeing it hath its seat in the soul and that which I ask of you is a sin of the body.'[7]

This is a mild form of an opinion which has in the 20th century become more common among Protestant antinomians and modernists. It was in the early 1940s when I first encountered a pastor of some prominence who held that *any* sexual relationship, as long as it was *truly personal and loving*, was valid and moral. He was quite insistent that this was "the true spirit of the Gospel" and that my perspective was legalistic and unloving.

Peter Abelard was a strong champion of adiaphorism. According to Verkamp, he "suggested that apart from the intention of all human actions, considered in themselves, are indifferent."[8]

The problem of adiaphora became confused in church history because it represents an alien religious premise transposed into a Biblical faith. The concept of adiaphora presupposes, *first*, a dialectical and/or a dualistic world view. It assumes that there are two kinds of being, matter on the one hand, and spirit, mind, or Idea on the other. Of these two, matter is seen as either morally indifferent or relatively far less important. Such a view of being is clearly anti-Biblical. Scripture sees mind and matter as alike one kind of being, created being. The contrast is rather to the uncreated Being of God. *Second*, the universe of the Cynics and of adiaphorism is explicitly or implicitly a meaningless realm of brute, or meaningless and unrelated,

---

[6]Giovanni Boccaccio: *The Decameron*, p. 163. John Payne trans. (New York, N.Y.: Triangle Books, 1940).

[7]*Ibid.*, p. 171.

[8]Verkamp, *op. cit.*, p. 23.

factuality. There is no god whose eternal decree gives total meaning to all things. Adiaphorism presupposes an area or realm of indifferentism and neutrality.

The arguments used to defend this realm of neutrality go something like this: no morality is involved in a simple walk through the countryside, or a pleasure drive in one's automobile on a Saturday afternoon. The answer is that, because this is totally God's creation and a moral universe, we can never step outside the moral realm into an indifferent one. Our driving is either responsible and hence moral, or it involves a contempt for the life and property of others, a moral fact. Our walk can be an enjoyment of life and the world around us, a moral fact, or it can involve trespassing, playing the Peeping Tom, discarding paper trash, and so on, all moral facts. In one presbytery, in an argument in favor of adiaphorism, a pastor declared, "Paul probably travelled at times by ox-cart. Are we bound to do the same?" The *means* are thus indifferent, he held; we can travel by cart or car without any moral connotation involved. But is travel morally indifferent? A young man, a student, who answered an advertisement offering a free ride from coast to coast in return for driving, found himself in a vehicle with two thieves and two prostitutes, more or less a captive, and having reason to believe that the car was a stolen one. We can never step into a morally neutral realm. To assume that, because no problems arise, a situation is therefore morally neutral is a serious fallacy.

Third, adiaphorism presupposes that morality is only a mental outlook, i.e., that it is essentially a matter of love. Feminists have argued (as have others) that a wife's sexual relations with her husband can be moral or immoral, depending on whether or not it is a loving act or a reluctant duty; the same is held to be true of any other sexual relationship, adulterous or homosexual: its morality is determined by the presence of love.

Fourth, as is already apparent, the universe being totally God's creation, nothing is outside His government and law. There is nothing thus which is morally indifferent. The classic text used by adiaphorism is Titus 1:15, "Unto the pure all things are pure: but unto them that are defiled and unbelieving is nothing pure; but even their mind and conscience is defiled." Supposedly, this verse reduces morality to a mental state. On the contrary, it does not presuppose the morally neutral world, and meaningless universe, of the Cynics, but God's creation, which is totally good in origin (Gen. 1:31). Fallen man perverts even the pure things to make them impure. If "all things are pure" and good, then nothing can be called adiaphora, and if to "them that are defiled and unbelieving is nothing pure," again we have excluded adiaphora. *Since all things are made by God, there is no neutral relationship to anything.*

However, adiaphorism in church history has presupposed a universe belonging to the Cynics rather than created by God.

Not only so, but adiaphorism has been a catch-all for several kinds of problems in church history. *First*, with respect especially to the forms, of worship and church order, the argument has been between those who declare that only that which is specifically required and permitted is binding, and those who hold that whatever is not forbidden is permitted. This argument has been further confused by the fact that usually both sides have gone only to the New Testament, or mainly so, to determine what is permitted. Augustine early complained that the yoke of the Pharisees was being surpassed by church traditions, which were legislating in areas of supposed permission.[9]

Second, as already indicated, the question was, What is the scope of the binding word? Is it the whole word of God, the Old and New Testaments alike, the law, prophets, and gospel, or is it only "the law of Christ," something supposedly abstracted from the New Testament?

Third, there was the developmental view, as in Joachim of Flora, and at the Reformation in Sebastian Franck. From this perspective, the Old and New Testaments alike spoke to babes, and to the infancy of mankind. Such Spiritualists held that forms, sacraments, and law represented outworn and weak elements, useful for the infancy of the faith but due to be discarded in the age of the Spirit. All dependence on such materialistic externals was termed by Franck as a reliance on "the dregs of Satan," the inference being dualistic, i.e., that the realm of law, forms, and matter belong to Satan, and that God seeks to wean us from it.[10]

Fourth, still another problem was incorporated into the issue of adiaphora, the problem of the weak and the strong. The Pauline argument was thus again altered. The strong were now seen as those who knew that the things which troubled the weak were indifferent things. As with Titus 1:15, the presupposition imported into Romans 14:1-15:4, I Corinthians 8:1-13; 10:25-33 is of a morally neutral universe. Paul, however, tells the weak and the strong that "the earth is the Lord's, and the fullness thereof" (I Cor. 10:28), an entirely different presupposition.

It should be clear now that adiaphorism is a concept which has no place in Christian thought. Unhappily, the concept is used, and, in some works, Christian morality is discussed, not from the perspective of God's infallible law-word, but from the perspective of adiaphorism.[11]

The problem, moreover, is not simply an antiquarian one, but of very

---

[9]Philip Schaff, editor: *Nicene and Post-Nicene Fathers*, Second Series, vol. I, Letters LIV, LV; pp. 300-316. (Grand Rapids, Michigan: Eerdmans, 1956).

[10]See Verkamp, *op. cit.*, pp. 79ff., 163.

[11]Theodore Graebner: *The Borderland of Right and Wrong*. (St. Louis, MO.: Concordia, (1938), 1954).

great significance for church and state. Church and state alike cannot be confined to their God-given realms and limited spheres unless adiaphorism is dropped. *First*, because adiaphorism holds to a morally indifferent universe, or, in modified forms, to areas of moral indifference, the sovereign power of God is limited, and the powers of man (or of man's agencies, such as church and state) are accordingly extended. Man then has areas of life wherein he can legislate and act independently of God and His word. At certain points, life and the universe become open to man's imperialism, to man's legislation and freedom. Sunday morning religion is a natural outcome of adiaphorism. God's legitimate concerns are in practice limited by Sunday morning religion to a limited spiritual realm. Churches which teach adiaphorism have no legitimate ground for complaining that their members limit the scope and jurisdiction of their faith. Adiaphorism is a denial of the sovereignty of God and an affirmation that, in given areas at least, man is a free agent and his own law-maker.

Second, as Augustine pointed out, the church very early created a burden of laws and traditions as rigid and more so than the yoke of the Pharisees. Adiaphorism gives vast powers to the church. Both Protestantism and Roman Catholicism have used the concept of adiaphora to enlarge ecclesiastical powers; both have seen the "evils" of one another but not the fundamental issue. If any area is morally indifferent in terms of Scripture, it can then be an area of moral indifference to men, *or an area of legislation by man, or by church and state*. It is a "free" area for man's imperialism, a place where supposedly God has no jurisdiction, or exercises none, and man is free to do so. Thus, some years ago, I was charged with a fearful offense, namely, teaching the Bible outside the church on the Lord's Day without permission. I asked where, apart from presbytery's will, this was forbidden, demanding Biblical warrant. The answer given was that I Corinthians 14:40, "Let all things be done decently and in order," was a warrant from God to the church to govern in such areas in order to ensure that all things be done decently and in order! Paul's sentence, however, is not a general warrant for any kind of ordering but specifically a summation requiring that his precise requirements for the order of particular meetings be kept. Paul was speaking against, not in favor of, any independent powers on the part of a church or congregation to order its worship and or affairs.

Third, adiaphorism not only hands the church vast powers uncontrolled by Scripture, but the state also. The state thus sees itself as its own law-maker, and hence its own god, because law-making is the prerogative of a god; it is an attribute of sovereignty and deity. The church having declared that Biblical law is now a matter of adiaphora, the state (as well as the church) is free to play god walking on earth and to legislate at will. The modern state is the result of adiaphorism. As long as the doctrine of adiaphora is retained, man will have a problem with totalitarianism in church and state.

It will allow the modern state every freedom to expand its powers, because adiaphorism withdraws the sovereign claims, powers, and government of God from one area after another, leaving finally very little to the Kingdom of God other than a weak and simpering love, an antinomian religion of love.

Adiaphorism is at the roots of antinomianism, and it is basic to the decline of the power of Christianity. True, the doctrine is an old and venerable one; but then the tempter's doctrine (Gen. 3:1-5) has even greater venerability! Long ago, Jerome stated the thesis of the doctrine in its ecclesiastical form: "That is indifferent which is neither good nor evil; so that, whether you do it or do it not, you are never the more just or unjust thereby."[12] Using the freedom granted by this concept, Rome justified the mass and images, and Protestantism justified a variety of church rules, while each condemned the other! This is not surprising. Once the premise of adiaphorism is accepted, men are free to define for themselves the realm of the indifferent. God's powers of definition and law-making become then the prerogatives of men, and we have Catholic, Reformed, Lutheran, and Anglican doctrines of adiaphorism, and now no less the statist doctrines as well. After all, the U.S. Supreme Court transferred abortion to the realm of adiaphora. The Soviet Union and Red China have done even better! Adiaphorism means that, for vast areas, the rule which governs is simply this: Let man's will prevail. (November, 1980)

THE HUMANISTIC DOCTRINE OF INFALLIBILITY

In my study of *Infallibility, An Inescapable Doctrine*, I pointed out that every system of thought has, if not an open, at least a hidden and implicit doctrine of infallibility. The locale of infallibility will vary; it can be man's autonomous reason, the aesthetic experience, the state, a ruler, and/or a variety of other things. Men may ridicule an alien doctrine of infallibility, but it will be only to vindicate their own.

In the modern era, the most popular doctrine of infallibility comes to us from Rousseau through Kant and Hegel. Infallibility rests in man, not individual man, but in the general will of all men, which is held to be by nature unerring and good. This general will is not ascertained by majority vote, but by its expression in the elite rulers of the state, who embody or incarnate the general will. Over the years, this infallible general will has had a variety of names and incarnations. Two popular ones of recent years have

---

[12]The Second Helvetic Confession, chapter. XXVII, "*Of Rites, Ceremonies, and Things Indifferent.*"

been the dictatorship of the proletariat, and the democratic consensus. The new name is public policy.

In the name of *public policy*, a variety of evils are being promoted today. Increasingly, in the name of equality and rights, freedom of speech is being denied to Christians, because Biblical faith requires that sin be condemned, whereas humanism increasingly insists on equal rights for sin. Thus, a very prominent and forthright Texas pastor has been denied the freedom to continue broadcasting his Sunday morning sermons on television. In a sermon he condemned homosexuality as a sin; this was seen as against public policy, and his freedom to preach was curtailed. In California, sixty three churches have lost their tax exempt status and face sale of their properties for refusal to pay taxes; their troubles began when a stand was made against homosexuality. To speak out against this and like matters is now against *public policy*, the new "law."

Similarly, many courts are assuming that a children's "bill of rights" like Sweden's has been made law here because of "public policy." Christian parents, routinely administering either discipline or chastisement to their children, have been taken to court.

Moreover, *public policy* is redefining the family, as the recent White House Conference made clear. The Biblical definition of the family has been rejected. The true family is now seen as "the voluntary family." This can be a group of homosexuals, runaway youths, or a sexual commune. *Public policy* seeks to give it the protection once given the covenant family.

These trends are becoming known to more and more people, but the reaction is too often one of religious idiocy: the idea is to pass a law to correct these evils. These evils, however, are not so much a product of legislation as of a religious faith in the state and its saving power. To turn to the state for relief is to aggravate that very evil.

Moreover, there is a grim fact too seldom appreciated by "reformers." Virtually all new laws, whether good or bad, have as their consequence the increase of the state's bureaucracy. Thus, the one usual and predictable result of a new law is greater power for the bureaucracy, and an increased growth. Reform laws are hence seldom a problem to a bureaucracy; the reformers legislate new laws, appropriate money for their enforcement, and the rest is up to the bureaucracy.

But this is not all. No law is likely to mean in execution and in results what it meant in purpose and passage. When a new law is enacted, its meaning and enforcement become the province of the bureaucracy and the courts. Since legislators, good and bad alike, are not at the same time in law enforcement, they cannot predict or foresee all the practical problems which the application of law creates. This very real and important function the bureaucracy and the courts discharge. The predictable result is the growth of the bureaucracy.

Add to that bureaucracy (and to the courts) the doctrine of *public policy*, and the law is immediately subject to a radically different meaning. The U.S. Constitution thus, has been "amended" and altered more often by the varying faith and expectation of the American people than by Congress and the States. The Constitution today means, not what the framers meant, but what public policy today dictates.

A key tenet of this humanistic public policy doctrine is the "equality" of good and evil. In fact, however, no such equality exists. If evil cannot be condemned, then righteousness is condemned. If a Christian pastor cannot speak out on television against homosexuality, it means that homosexuality has the freedom to condemn and silence Christianity. Such a doctrine of equality is another name for the suppression of the freedom of Christianity.

Public policy today is another name for humanistic morality and its mandatory status. Humanistic morality governs our bureaucracies, our state schools, the press, films, television, and more, and it is promoted from Washington, D.C. down. Public policy is beginning to declare that free speech by the church must be punished. Is the Catholic Church against abortion? Move to revoke its freedom and tax-exempt status. Have Protestant Churches spoken out against homosexuality? Their tax exemption must be revoked, and their freedom curtailed.

Public policy today means humanistic policy. For this reason, every attempt by evangelical pastors and churches to revive a concern for social order among their congregations, to encourage them to vote *as Christians*, and to seek to command the political processes for Christ's cause, is greeted with hypocritical wails of dismay; supposedly all this represents a revival of Nazi faith. But it is these public policy advocates who are the architects of our new fascism, an economic and political fascism which retains the forms of freedom but uses them as a facade for state socialism. These people see themselves as the incarnation of the general will and the infallible voices of today and tomorrow. They identify their will with public policy, and the rest of us with evil. Theirs is a false faith. The only answer to it is the Biblical faith, and its application to every area of life and thought. (November, 1980)

THE FUTURE IS THE LORD'S
Chalcedon Position Paper No. 18

Peter F. Drucker, in *Managing in Turbulent Times* (Harper & Row, 1980), calls attention to some very significant facts about the Soviet Union. He believes that only a bold man will predict that the U.S.S.R. will still be in existence by the year 2000. European Russia has the world's lowest birthrate, whereas Asiatic Russia has a very high one and will have a population predominance.

Other sources have added to this forecast. Asiatic Russia is predominantly

Moslem, and, very soon, the Soviet Union will be the world's major Moslem power. There will be internal problems by 1985, as the army faces the consequences of the low birthrate among European Russians. The draftees will begin to be more and more Islamic; getting them to obey European officers will be a problem.

Alexandre A. Bennigsen and S. Enders Wimbush, in *Muslim National Communism in the Soviet Union, A Revolutionary Strategy for the Colonial World* (University of Chicago Press, 1979), trace the history of Muslim communism. From the days of Lenin, the Muslim communists were nationalists and strongly (in most cases) Islamic. They saw Marxism as a means of dealing "a death blow to Europe." Many religious leaders among the Moslems agreed with this. The end of European supremacy could be effected by means of Marxism, and the Muslim nations freed to pursue their course. "A significant number of Muslim leaders did lend their support to the revolutionary forces during the Civil War" (p. 31). These nationalistic Muslim communists were suppressed by Lenin and his successors, but their population increase, and the decline of the European Russian birthrate, have revived new currents of Muslim hope for the overthrow of Europe, including Soviet Russia. An often heard warning from Asiatic Soviet Muslims to Russians in the streets of Central Asia is, "Wait until the Chinese come. They will show you!" The Russian leadership of the Soviet Union is aging, and approaching senility. Population trends are destroying the Russian character of the Soviet Union and giving it a Turkic and Muslim character. After World War I, Turkey strongly promoted Pan-Turanian ideas, i.e., a union of all the Turkic peoples to create a great world power. This is an alternate theme to a pan-Islamic power. The Armenian massacres were an aspect of this Pan-Turanian dream.

Add to this factor within the Soviet Union an external factor, the rise of Muslim nationalism and Marxism outside of the Soviet Union, in Asia, the Near East, and North Africa, and you have all the ingredients for social turbulence, war, and revolution.

There is, however, a grim nemesis to Muslim hopes in the very nature of their faith. Bennigsen and Wimbush mention in passing "the 'past-centered awareness' which is common to most Muslims (in contrast to Christian awareness which projects a 'Golden Age' in the future," p. 98f.). Iran is good evidence of this fact. The revolutionists in Iran dream of a golden age, in the mythical Islam of Ali, a time long-gone and more a product of imagination than reality. Moreover, their concern has been more with "the sins of the Shah" than with current and pressing problems. This past-bound nature of Muslim faith and thought gives it a proneness to hope and denunciation where work and action are needed.

But this is not all. Not only is Islam past bound, but, we must add, paralyzed because its concept of power and progress is a bureaucrat's dream.

Islam sees unity and government from the top down. Mohammed was strongly drawn to the Biblical doctrine of the Kingdom of God, of God's rule over the world, and this is what Islam purports to be. However, from the beginning this kingdom was seen as coming by imposition from above, by military conquest, centralized rule, and concentrated authority. The result was a caliph, or powerful Moslem rulers, who concentrated all power in their hands. In Turkey, Baghdad, Iran, and elsewhere, it meant autocratic rule. Whereas in the Christian world, the revolutionary direction of history was to challenge centralized power in church and state, and to base the faith in the heart of man, the Islamic tendency was and is to equate strength with centralized power.

The triumph of Christian theological development, as it appeared in the West, was to formulate the creed into an intensely personal form, "I believe in God, the Father Almighty, etc." Whether recited with two or three, or with thousands, each believer in the Western tradition says, "I believe." It is personal. This is in line with Scripture, where the first required confession began with the personal pronoun: "A Syrian ready to perish was *my* father," or "*My* father was a wandering Aramean" (Deut. 26:5). This confession concluded, "And now, behold, I have brought the firstfruits of the land, which thou, O LORD, has given me" (Deut. 26:10). The emphasis is particular and personal in Scripture.

"Progress" in paganism, and in Islam, was spasmodic and superficial; it depended on a superior ruler, and it usually ended with his death. It had no roots in the life of the people. The Muslim revolution thus has no future, because it is too past bound, and too authoritarian.

Having said this, however, it is necessary to add that our world today is reproducing this same evil. The answers of statism are sterile and rootless, seeking to remake man from the top down. Eugene Rosenstock-Huessy spoke of John Dewey and his philosophy as the Chinafication of America, i.e., as the reproduction of all the evils of old China and its radical relativism. We can similarly speak of the growing centralization and bureaucratization of the Western nations as a reproduction of the narrow and decadent world of old Turkey, of the harem world and the intriguing eunuchs who ran the empire.

To command the future and to exercise dominion in the Lord's Name, it is urgently necessary for Christians to recognize the essential nature of Christian self-government to freedom, the function of the tithe in godly reconstruction, and the necessity for the Christian dominion man to take back government from the state.

Marxism has no future, nor does Islam. Similarly, humanistic statism is declining and perishing. The Marxist Muslims are right in seeing its days as numbered. The Christian must separate himself from humanistic statism, its schools and ways. The summons is, "Come out of her my people, that ye be not partakers of her sins, and that ye receive not of her plagues" (Rev. 18:4). The future is the Lord's and only ours in Him. (Decmber, 1980)

SOVEREIGNTY
Chalcedon Position Paper No. 19

In the Ten Commandments, immediately after the command, "Thou shalt have no other gods before Me," is the prohibition of all graven images. Few commandments are more badly interpreted. All too many read it as a total ban on any religious art. This is clearly not true. God Himself required a variety of carvings in the tabernacle, on the ark, and on various furnishings (but not on the altar), and He Himself called and inspired men to do the work (Ex. 31:1-6, etc.). While depictions of God were forbidden, more is in this law than is often recognized. No graven images, or any forms or likenesses, are permitted as objects to use for worship in the sense of bowing down to them, or serving them. "Thou shalt not bow down thyself to them, nor serve them" (Ex. 20:4): these words are the key, and their meaning must be understood in order to obey this commandment.

Paul had this commandment and more in mind when he cried out against the worship the people of Lystra gave him and Barnabas after the healing of a cripple (Acts 14:8-18). The priest of Jupiter was ready to serve them, and the people to bow down to them.

To bow down and to serve is an ancient sign and symbol of the recognition of sovereignty. Because the pagan kings of antiquity claimed lordship or sovereignty, they required all men to acknowledge it on coming into their presence. This meant bowing down before them, sometimes prostrating themselves completely. It also commonly meant bringing gifts, a token of service. Thus, the wise men came seeking the Christ child, the newly born king, whom they knew to be the great Messiah or God-King. They demonstrated this faith by falling down before the child, and worshipping Him; they then presented their gifts, gold, frankincense, and myrrh, as tokens of their service to Him as Lord and King (Matt. 2:11).

Thus, the law, when it reads, "Thou shalt not bow down to them, nor serve them," has reference to two related facts: *first* the recognition of lordship or sovereignty; the one to whom we bow is he whom we acknowledge as our lord; *second*, he whom we serve is the one to whom we pay our tax or tithe, and to whom we bring gifts. (Hence, God requires both tithes and offerings, the tax and gifts above the tax, as evidence of our service and love.)

In the Christian era, monarchs revived the pagan doctrine of kingship. They claimed lordship or sovereignty. They promoted the doctrine of their divine rights. In the 18th century, both Protestant and Catholic kings disapproved of the use of Mary's *Magnificat* in churches, because of the sentence, "He hath put down the mighty from their seats, and exalted them of low degree" (Luke 1:52). They wanted no Lord Christ who could put them down and scatter them.

The modern state is even worse, far worse. It does not hesitate to claim sovereignty; it presents itself, after Hegel, as God walking on earth. It claims jurisdiction over Christ's church and school as lord, and it demands that we bow down and serve it as sovereign.

This is the meaning of the law: no graven images means no representations of sovereignty or lordship. Neither a man nor an image can represent sovereignty, nor can a church nor a state. God alone is the lord. "I am the LORD, and there is none else, there is no God beside me" (Isa. 45:5). All too many churchmen are balking at a cross over the church (a symbol of Christ's triumph over sin and death), while bowing the knee to Caesar, and serving Him. Alan Stang rightfully and wisely titled his studies of the statist persecutions of the church, *Thou Shalt Have No Other Gods Before Me - Including the State.*

The Bible is emphatic that Christians are to render obedience to whom obedience is due. Again and again, this duty of obedience to, and prayers for, all those in civil authority is stressed. Moreover, because the godly way is regeneration, not revolution, Christians are warned against being humanistic social revolutionists (I Cor. 7:20-23), but they are at the same time to work lawfully to avoid being a slave people, i.e., "the servants of men."

At the same time, the nature of civil (and other) authorities is at all times and in all things limited by the word of God. Civil authorities are specifically spoken of as *ministers* of God, and the word translated as "minister" is in the Greek our English word "deacon," meaning servant. "Rulers" are thus to be servants under God, not lords or sovereigns. When the civil authorities divorce themselves from God and His law-word, they become self-styled lords and lawless as well. As Augustine pointed out, godless civil rulers are no more than bands of robbers, a more powerful Mafia, and a more dangerous one. Being lawless in relation to God, they are lawless and predatory in relation to men.

There is an important aspect to this commandment which is commonly neglected. Of the Ten Commandments, one other contains the promise of particular judgment, and one other of particular blessing. Honoring parents has the promise of life: "Honor thy father and thy mother: that thy days may be long upon the land which the LORD thy God giveth thee" (Ex. 20:12). The promise of judgment is given in Exodus 20:7, "Thou shalt not take the Name of the LORD thy God in vain: for the LORD will not hold him guiltless that taketh his name in vain" (See Chalcedon Position Paper no. 2, "In the Name of Jesus Christ, or, In the Name of Caesar?")

Here, in this law, we have the longest promise, and it is of both judgment and blessing: "Thou shalt not make unto thee any graven image, or any likeness of any thing that is in heaven above, or that is in the earth beneath, or that is in the water under the earth: Thou shalt not bow down thyself to them, nor serve them: for I the LORD thy God am a jealous God, visiting the iniquity of the fathers upon the children unto the third and fourth generation of them that hate me; And shewing mercy unto thousands of them that love me, and keep my commandments" (Ex. 20:4-6).

The judgment here promised is a lingering one: sin has social consequences. Where a false doctrine of sovereignty prevails, there is a radical social disorientation, and all life is warped and placed on false premises. A generation which asserts a humanistic doctrine of sovereignty will so alter life and society, and all the institutions thereof, that the evil consequences will persist for three and four generations. On the other hand, a true doctrine of sovereignty will affect the lives of thousands who do not share it, because it will keep society on a godly foundation.

The prohibition is against any form of idolatry, i.e., any alien or ungodly doctrine of sovereignty. Sovereignty or lordship cannot be located on earth, in the heavens, or in the seas: it is in God alone. Covetousness, indeed sin in any form, is idolatry (Colossians 3:5), because sin asserts our will as primary, and our will replaces God's law in all sin.

Sovereignty or lordship is the source of judgment and grace, either directly or by delegation. In Scripture, parents, pastors, civil authorities, employers, and others are instructed as to how to judge and reward faithful obedience and service. Their powers are under God; they are strictly delegated. The Bible recognizes no power independent of God, "For there is no power but of God: the powers that be are ordained of God" (Rom. 13:1). For any of these delegated spheres of authority to speak of themselves as powers which are independent from God is rebellion and sin. For courts, the Internal Revenue Service, and other civil agencies to speak of allowing us so many "days of grace" is blasphemy .

Today, however, autonomy is claimed by virtually every civil government, autonomy from God. All see themselves as sovereign, and hence their own source of law and power. We live in an age of statist idolatry, and we have become so blind that we do not see this obvious fact. All too many churchmen will quibble about trifles but fail to see themselves surrounded and ruled by the enemies of God, humanists, and their idol and false lord, the state.

We are ready to entertain the rule of other gods when we ourselves have openly or quietly rejected the true God, or are secretly in quest of "freedom" from the living God. It is a very comforting illusion to tell ourselves that evil men did this to us, or that a conspiracy is responsible for our captivity to false lords or sovereigns. Every conspiracy begins, however, in the human heart as a conspiracy against God. The conspiracies of history, including our time, are all too real, but they make it convenient for all too many of us to forget our own sins. All over the country, I find men retreating into Phariseeism rather than advancing into dominion, and their excuse is a false holiness. No church is good enough for them; granted, the church scene is a sad picture, but will withdrawal improve it? Moreover, are we so holy that we cannot afford to associate with other sinners saved by grace? Again, many refuse to vote, failing to recognize that voting is a means of exercising dominion. Given the faults of all candidates, there is still a choice, *and a duty*. Paul, in writing to the Corinthians that they should discipline and excommunicate a fornicator, warned them against trying to require a like standard of the world, "for then must ye needs go out of this world" (I Cor. 5 :10). They are not to leave the world but to conquer it. "Super-holiness" exalts us, not the Lord.

The law says, "Thou shalt have no other gods before me" (Ex. 20:3), including ourselves. It is not our will and law but the Lord's which must govern. "Before me" means "beside me," sharing to any degree lordship or sovereignty with Me. The relationship with God can only be exclusive.

Moreover, the modern reading of the prohibition of graven images or idolatry in any form is seriously misread if its meaning is limited to worship, or the place of worship. There are all too many today whose idol is Caesar who have no images, symbols, or signs in their plain churches. To have no other gods beside Me, beside the Lord God, means that no other lord has sovereignty over us in any and every area of life. It means that our total way of life is governed exclusively by God the Lord. To limit the scope of the law to what goes on in a church building is to deny the sovereignty or lordship of the living God. The Lord God and His law-word must govern, control, dominate, inform, and regulate every atom of our being and every sphere of life and the world. Anything short of this is idolatry.

There can be no substitute for God in any sphere. Moreover, since any and every created representation of God is banned, it is clear that God cannot be absorbed into or identified with this world and its aspects. He is the eternal God, the Creator, not an item in an already existing universe. The creation cannot define Him: He creates and defines all creation. Man seeks to define and understand all things in terms of his experience, reason, and life; this is at the heart of all idolatry, whether simplistic and primitive, or rational and philosophical. By means of this law, God rejects all man-made efforts to define Him, or comprehend Him. He is to be known only in terms of His revelation. He also makes clear that the scope of His jurisdiction is total: There can be no other gods beside Him in any sphere of life and thought.

An hour ago, I talked with a pastor whose church rebels against any application of Christ's lordship to anything outside the church, especially to anything in the sphere of the state. I was reminded of one well-known country where, at least until recently if not now, a husband's adultery gives the wife no actionable ground for complaint unless the act or acts of adultery occur in the family home! All too many churchmen have a like view of idolatry: if it does not occur in Sunday morning or evening worship, it does not count.

The key to idolatry comes to the surface in Exodus 20:7, "Thou shalt not take the Name of the LORD thy God in vain." Umberto Cassuto rendered it thus: "You shall not take up the name of the Lord your God for unreality." To take God's Name for a valueless purpose is to treat God as unreality, rather than as Lord and Creator. To limit God's sovereignty and law to the church, and to the inner life and to the "private" morality of man, is to deny His lordship and to treat Him as an unreality. When we treat God as an unreality, we will prostrate ourselves before false gods, including and especially the state, and we will serve them. Man is a religious creature; if he rejects the living God, he will serve other gods. And this God will not tolerate.

The jealousy of God (Ex. 20:5) is grounded in His absoluteness and His universal dominion. The "gods" of paganism were not jealous, because they were not universal. Their jurisdictions were limited to one nation, state, or people, and to a particular sphere within that realm. They were simply powerful "spirits" seeking to control the weather, or the sea, love, the family, or some like limited sphere. Even within those limits, their powers were faulty and uncertain. Such "gods" could not afford the luxury of claiming a broader sphere: they had enough problems minding their own shop! The God of Scripture is a jealous God, because He has total jurisdiction over all things. "I am the LORD: that is my Name: and my glory will I not give to another, neither my praise to graven images" (Isa. 42:8). No other religion has anything comparable to this law prohibiting idolatry.

Gerhard von Rad, in commenting on this same law as it appears in Deuteronomy 5:8-10, noted: "This prohibition of idols must be understood with the purpose of the idols in mind, namely to manifest the deity." (*Deuteronomy*, p.57). God reserves the power to manifest Himself to Himself. I John 3:8 declares that Jesus Christ is God manifest, and I Timothy 3:16 tells us also that "God was manifest in the flesh" in Jesus Christ. In all idolatry, physical, philosophical, or institutional, man seeks to determine what God's manifestation shall be. Wherever there is any talk of sovereignty, there is a claim to the manifestation of lordship, or deity.

Paul gives us some telling insights into idolatry. For example, in I Corinthians 10:7, he writes: "Neither be ye idolaters, as were some of them; as it is written, The people sat down to eat and drink, and rose up to play." Paul's reference is to the golden calf incident of the Exodus journey; there were, clearly, fertility cult practices on that occasion; he refers to these in the next verse: "Neither let us commit fornication, as some of them committed..." (I Cor. 10:8). Thus, Paul separates two kinds of acts on that day; the simple eating and playing, and the fertility cult sexual acts. The word *play* in the Greek text is *paizo*, children's play, harmless play, as it were. Paul's point is that even those who abstained from the fertility cult practices were guilty of idolatry because they agreed with the general dismissal of God and Moses; they were "moral" idolaters. They shared the general feeling, "for as for this man Moses, the man that brought us up out of the land of Egypt, we wot not what is become of him" (Ex. 32:1). The feasting and playing was in the Name of the LORD (Ex. 32:5), but it was in contempt of Him and His authority. In brief, Paul's meaning is that any aspect of life outside of God is idolatry. "Whatsoever is not of faith is sin" (Rom. 14:23). George Bush was right when in 1841 he wrote of this law that its meaning and spirit are "plainly exceedingly broad." (*Exodus*, I, 263). Churchmen have limited its scope in order to lessen sin.

The time has come for us to confess, in the words of Isaiah 26:13, "O LORD our God, other lords beside thee have had dominion over us: but by thee only will we make mention of thy name."

We must renounce and war against all statist and other doctrines of lordship or sovereignty in the Name of the LORD. The great baptismal confession of the early church, that "Jesus Christ is Lord," must be our confession and banner now. Jesus Christ is LORD: He is King of kings, and Lord of lords (Rev. 19:16). Let the nations tremble before Him.

Sovereignty in Action - Today

In the modern world, sovereignty or lordship has ceased to be the attribute of God and has become the attribute of either man or the state, or shared by both. Even those theologians who talk much about God's sovereignty tend to limit it to salvation, the church, and theology, which means in effect to deny God's sovereignty.

In our world today, the state has delusions of deity, and it sees itself as god walking on earth. As the concomitant of this fact, the state implicitly claims infallibility. (With the Marxists, the dictatorship of the proletariat is the incarnation of the general will and is infallible.) As a result, nothing is more difficult, in dealings with agencies of state, than to get an admission of error. Have human lives been endangered, or lost, or have "private" parties been seriously maligned or damaged by an agency of the state? The state will go to any and all lengths to evade any admission of guilt or error. Is a statist regulation absurd, inappropriate, or irrelevant? No true bureaucrat will admit such a possibility. Near Echo Summit, on U.S. Highway 50, in California, the Vern Sproch family, entirely on their own, developed the Sierra Ski Ranch. In 1978, a day lodge was built on the top of the mountain, it is a model of "advanced" construction ideas, with solar heating panels, and a windmill-powered generator as an alternate energy source. The Sprochs ran afoul of the state law requiring wheel-chair adapted toilets for the handicapped in all public places. The bureaucrats refused to consider the fact that the Lodge can only be reached by skiing, not an activity for those confined to wheelchairs! Vern Sproch was compelled to add two wheel-chair toilets at a cost of $400 each! (*Inquiry*, December 8, 1980, p. 2.) The sad part of the story is that it is not unusual; such nonsense is commonplace. In another instance, a small guest ranch hired as employees a couple, the wife as cook, the husband to handle the horses; they shared a small apartment. The "law" required the owners to provide *separate* bathroom facilities for each of them under the requirement that male and female restroom facilities be separate! The sovereign state refuses to recognize the claims of common sense: all wisdom is incarnate in the state as the new god.

Individuals are no less exempt from this madness. If one is sovereign, then all things are possible. According to Theodore Roszak, "A prominent psychotherapist remarks to me over lunch that people sleep and die only because they have been mistakenly 'programmed' to believe they have to... and goes on to suggest how this erroneous programming might be therapeutically undone" (*Harper's*, January, 1981, p. 56). Anyone who is a good listener will hear like madness roll out of the mouths of today's products of humanistic education.

All these people, however, have a reason for such beliefs. They are humanists. For them, sovereignty is an attribute of man or the state. The logic of their position leads them to such conclusions, unless they are under the influence of a Christian hangover. What can we say about the folly of those who are churchmen, ministers, and theologians, but who insist on the sovereignty of the state? They not only do so, but they insist on claiming Biblical warrant for their sin. They bleat piously about rendering unto Caesar the things that are Caesar's, but they will not render unto God the absolute lordship or sovereignty which is His (Matt. 22:21; Mark 12:17; Luke 20:25). If we render to God the things which are His, then Caesar's only place is in submission to the Lord: Caesar will not be in submission to the Lord if we are not.

Even Bertrand Russell, a militant humanist, understood what Jesus said: "The advice of Jesus to give unto Caesar what is Caesar's and unto God what is God's, is a typical example of this Jewish recalcitrance. Though on the face of it a compromise, it is nevertheless a refusal to recognize the identity of God and Emperor" (*Wisdom of the West*, p. 129). Precisely. I render unto Caesar, unto my neighbor, unto my wife and children, as to all men, whatever is their due under God, but never that which must be rendered unto God.

Very simply defined, sovereignty means a monopoly of power and law.

The two are inseparable: power and law are attributes of sovereignty. Hence, Christ as Lord and King of Creation, declares, "All power is given unto me in heaven and in earth." In terms of this sovereignty, the Lord orders the discipling of "all nations," "teaching them to observe all things whatsoever I have commanded you" (Matt. 28:18-20). The word used for "commanded" in the Greek is *entello* (noun, *entole*), meaning to order, to command. *Entole* was once in a while used as equivalent to *torah*, as in the Septuagint of Deut. 17:19, "all the words of the *law*." Thus, Christ sets forth, as basic to His royal requirement, that the disciples recognize that all power is His, and it is His law which must be taught to all, and obeyed by all who are redeemed and baptized "in the name of the Father, and of the Son, and the Holy Ghost." This is a very plain declaration of sovereignty; it made inescapable the conflict between the church and Rome, between Christ and Caesar. There cannot be two Lords.

Every social order is a system of power in application and in interrelationships; a social order is a power structure and faith in operation. The lord of the social order is the source of power in the system. The ability and authority to dominate men and institutions depends on the faith in a sovereign power. When faith in that lord or sovereign declines, the social order begins to decay and collapse. (Egon Friedell, in his (*Cultural History of the Modern Age*, saw the Black Death as the beginning of the collapse of faith in the "medieval" order, and World War I as the terminal point of confidence in the modern culture.) Today, humanism's concepts of sovereignty are decaying; it is mandatory for Christians to set forth Christ's sovereignty and His crown rights.

One of these is His law, Biblical law. Law is a statement of causation and of necessity; it describes the order of being. In natural laws, scientists seek to determine that which uniformly and of necessity occurs. God's law gives God's order of causality and necessity, as witness Deuteronomy 28. Humanism has eroded the doctrines of causality and necessity, and therefore of law; it is thus in disintegration. In the process, God's law, power, and sovereignty are being openly vindicated.

Form and Reality

The death of a culture, its civilization, and its law can be seen as very near when form replaces reality. As the end approaches, various groups begin to sense the coming collapse, and calls resound for a "return" to something. Demands for a return to reason are not uncommon; reason, however, cannot always be equated with reality, and, in a world of Hegelian thought, reason and reality are two very different things. Another common call is for a return to "religion," but the term "religion" can cover a multitude of sins. The decay may well be due to both faulty religion and faulty reason. In other words, these hoped-for returns to our various roots are not necessarily a return to reality.

When form replaces reality, there is a radical departure from the mainstays of life. It is like being content with and preferring pictures of food to food itself. The churches led the way into this retreat from life, from reality to form. By way of illustration, we can focus on the retreat from reality to form in the doctrine of communion. The church has long been divided on its view of this doctrine: closed communion or open communion; transubstantiation, consubstantiation, or memorial; and so on and on. In the process, the reality which alone gives life and meaning to the form (and prevents it from becoming blasphemous) is forgotten or neglected.

The reality behind the "symbols" has two facets. *First* and paramount is the doctrine of Christ's atonement for sin. The sacrament has behind it an historical event, Christ's atoning death and resurrection, and a legal fact, our deliverance from sin by Christ's substitution and our justification. *Second*, because, with our salvation, we are also made Christ's new humanity and members one of another, we are now a family and a Kingdom. As members of one another, we care for one another. This is the meaning of the Parable of Judgment, Matthew 25:31-46. *All* who present themselves before the King call Him "Lord;" they have been outwardly "members" of Him, no doubt faithful at worship and in participation in the sacrament. The King's test, however, is this: "Inasmuch as ye did it not to one of the least of these, ye did it not to me" (Matt. 25:45). (Many who have turned their back on men like Lester Roloff, when on trial, will hear this sentence.)

In other words, our Lord's test question is, what about reality? All facing the King in this parable call Him Lord; all are apparently agreed on "sound" doctrine as far as the forms are concerned: our Lord indicts none on these matters. All have the form of godliness but lack the power and the reality thereof (II Tim. 3:5). In the living church, people are members of one another, not wolves tearing at the flock, or false shepherds, deserting it.

In a dying world, form replaces reality, the theater replaces life, and the actor or entertainer becomes the real person. The more commanding figures of our day are actors and entertainers. Their movements, words, and affairs are momentous matters to millions. Their deaths, as with the cases of Elvis Presley and John Lennon, are front-page stories for days and of world-wide concern. (The death of John Lennon was mourned in both dying Moscow and dying New York, as well as elsewhere, and fittingly so: let the dead bury the dead, Matt. 8:22.)

In politics, we see the rapid and disproportionate increase of the bureaucracy all over the world. The modern state, when confronted with a problem, creates a bureaucracy whose province is that problem. No bureaucracy works itself out of a job! The form of a solution, a law and a bureaucracy, replaces reality. When the people grow weary of the politics of the hour, another group takes over, to substitute new forms for old ones. Meanwhile, realities like inflation, lawlessness, and social conflict increase and abound on all sides.

At the same time, the candidates and elected officials become more and more geared to presenting a good act before the cameras and press. Politics becomes a form of theater, and legislation a type of theatrical presentation. The public itself seeks new legislation, not by means of reasoned arguments and data presented before legislation committees, but by demonstrations, confrontations, and actions created for the theater of politics. Whatever route taken to influence and shape legislation and administration, a governing principle is that it must be good theater. The nature of what constitutes good theater varies from year to year, but not the essential fact that form has replaced reality.

All reality begins and ends with the triune God and His law word. Apart from that, men walk in darkness (Isa. 8:20). C. S. Lewis portrayed the inhabitants of hell as living in a deep and dark world, but insisting that it was merely the grey before the dawn! They had forever forsaken reality.

When men replace reality with forms, they desecrate and dishonor what often are otherwise good and necessary forms, because they cheapen their meaning. A Russian legend of the very early days of Christianization tells us of a lonely priest in a church when pagan Poles invaded the area. One of the Polish warriors invaded the church, dragging a captive woman. The warrior seized an image of the Virgin, threw the captive woman on top of it, and raped her. The priest, from his hiding-place, saw this, and he cried out in prayer to God to avenge the desecration of His church, and the violation of the woman. God answered the priest, saying, this sinner will in his time be punished. But why should his sin be worse in My eyes than your sins, your casualness about your calling, and your complacency before Me? The priest, in other words, had been faithful to the forms, but he had forgotten the reality of the faith, and his sin was greater.

Judgment begins at the House of God (I Peter 4:17); so too must reformation. (January, 1981)

THE MEANING OF THE SABBATH
Chalcedon Position Paper No. 20

Men commonly sin even in their professed obedience to God by reducing God's law to the lowest common denominator or to its minimal meaning. The law, "Thou shalt not steal" (Ex. 20:15), covers every form of theft: robbing another man, robbing God of His tithes and offerings (Malachi 3:8-12), the debasement of coinage and inflation (Isa. 1:22), and much, much more. Men find it convenience to limit the law to simple theft: this means that a man who produces or sells shoddy merchandise under false pretenses, or a man who does not work to earn his pay but rather does as little as possible, can claim they are not thieves. In God's sight, however, and in His court, the full meaning of the law prevails.

A key mistreated law is the Sabbath law: "Remember the sabbath day, to keep it holy. Six days shalt thou labour, and do all thy work: But the seventh day is the sabbath of the LORD thy God: in it thou shalt not do any work, thou, nor thy son, nor thy daughter, thy manservant, nor thy maidservant, nor thy cattle, nor thy stranger that is within thy gates: For in six days the LORD made heaven and earth, the sea, and all that in them is, and rested the seventh day: wherefore the LORD blessed the sabbath day, and hallowed it" (Ex. 20:8-11).

Before beginning a study of these words, two things need to be understood: *first*, the commandment is to rest, not worship. Worship is to be a continuous fact, as well as a weekly one, but the central aspect of the Sabbath observance is rest. *Second*, many have limited this observance of rest to their definitions. The Pharisees strictly limited the number of feet a man could walk on the Sabbath and had precise rules of limitation on every activity. On the other hand, many today see the Sabbath as a day for their personal relaxation and leisure. Neither is right.

To understand the Sabbath, we must see first what it involves. It means a weekly day of rest, one day in seven. The Hebrew Sabbath began on sundown of the night before, and it continued until dawn of the next day. Many Puritans observed a like Sabbath. The Sabbath rest included the work animals and also the earth, which, with man, had to rest one year in seven. The faculties of universities still are allowed a sabbatical year, but, for the most part, this observance has fallen into disuse. We need to work for its restoration. The fiftieth year was also a Sabbath, the Jubilee.

Now consider the meaning of all this as it relates to time: every seventh day, every seventh year, and every half century another year, were set aside for rest! The implications of this were far more radical in those days than now. Except for works of necessity (i.e where continuous operation was required as in milking; or works of mercy), rest was mandatory. Since production of food was then more marginal than now, it was far more difficult to store up sufficient food reserves for a sabbatical year. There was a further aspect to the Sabbath, a rest from debt. Debts had to be for a six-year term only, or a fraction thereof, if the Sabbath year were closer.

An obvious fact now appears: a society observing the sabbath had to be provident, and it could not be inflationary. To earn enough, and to produce enough, to make work unnecessary eight years out of fifty, and on over 2,000 weekly Sabbath days as well (almost six years more in aggregate, making almost fourteen out of fifty years given to the waking, Sabbath rest), required a future-oriented and provident people. Such a people must be willing, able, and productive workers. They must be able to plan and use widely their time and wealth. To observe the Sabbath was a mark of character, and more.

Even further, a society in which debt is limited to six years (Deut. 15:1-6) is a society which is anti-inflationary. Add to this the requirement of just monetary weights (Lev. 19:35-36), and inflation is virtually impossible. The result is social stability and prosperity. A society thus which observes the Sabbath can truly rest in the Lord: its todays and tomorrows are circumscribed by God's law and therefore God's blessing and providential care.

Furthermore, such a society is free from anxiety. With most men, today and tomorrow are matters of anxiety. Their failure to be provident, their participation in a lawless society, and the uncertainty of their future lead to a neurotic and anxious frame of mind. It is foolishness to believe that counselling or spiritual exercises can remove an anxiety which is the product of lawlessness. A lawless people will always be an anxious people. We are confronted today with a constant flow of books aimed at relieving anxiety, and psychotherapy is a big business, but few work at the root problem of anxiety: sin and guilt before God, and a failure to trust in His law and government.

Basic to the Sabbath and its rest is *liberation from work*. The root of this liberation is faith, faith in the Lord and His covenant salvation. To cease from our labors to so great an extent as the law requires, requires on the one hand a provident and diligent life, and, on the other, a deep trust in God's work. The Lord, having given us His covenant salvation, is able to give His covenant care. The nation, to have God's blessing, must observe this covenant sign, which means that the goal is not only a weekly observance, but the observance of the sabbatical year of rest so that all God's people may rest and rejoice in Him. This is a legal, national duty and requirement.

When we cease from our labors, we rest in the Lord's accomplished work of salvation and His ongoing work of providential care. It is a rest in which we commit ourselves and all our being into God's hands. David says, "Rest in the LORD, and wait patiently for him: fret not thyself because of him who prospereth in his way, because of the man who bringeth wicked devices to pass" (Ps. 37:7). In terms of this resting in the Lord, William Whiting Borden (1887-1913) wrote in his notebook in his freshman year at Yale, "Lord Jesus, I take hands off, as far as my life is concerned. I put Thee on the throne in my heart" (Mrs. Howard Taylor: *Borden of Yale '09*, p. 123.).

The Sabbath is liberation because it frees us from ourselves and our work in the confidence of God's superior government and work. It is liberation from history as the determining agent, because it affirms God's determination of all things. The opposite of the Sabbath is the Hindu doctrine of Karma; according to this doctrine, man is a captive of his past, of his history, and he is inescapably bound to the past. Only through a long series of many, many reincarnations can he free himself from history into death. The Sabbath does not deny causality, but, whereas Karma says causality is essentially historical, the Sabbath and its rest are a triumphant witness to the fact that causality is primarily supernatural.

The Sabbath is blessed and hallowed by God above all other days and years as a witness to its liberating character and its witness to His supernatural government and providence. The Sabbath is separated from other days, and thus we too must separate ourselves from all our other days and activities. When we reduce, as is so commonly done, the day to a church Sabbath, we deny the necessity for the separation of the whole of man and his society to the Lord. This is why the Sabbath applies to all things: ourselves, our land, the aliens in our midst, church, state, and all things. For the state to deny the Sabbath is to deny God. Biblical law separates (while making them interdependent) church and state; it does not separate the Sabbath and the state.

There is, however, a further and basic meaning to the Sabbath. As we have seen, it requires both faith and providence on the part of man: man must live so that he can rest in the seventh year without an income. He must rest (apart from works of necessity) and must do so without anxiety. Clearly, covenant man must be future oriented and provident.

He must, however, be also present-oriented. The Sabbath is a celebration of God's present order, and His ever-present help. Psalm 46 gives us this kind of faith. In the midst of cataclysmic earthquakes, floods, and desolations, the word for faith is, "Be still, and know that I am God: I will be exalted among the heathen. I will be exalted in the earth" (Ps. 46:10). It is knowing that the "Lord of hosts is with us" (Ps. 46:11), and that it is His righteous judgment that shakes our world. The things that are, are being shaken, so that only those things which cannot be shaken may remain (Heb. 12:27). It means knowing that all things work together for good to them that love God, to them who are the called according to His purpose (Rom. 8:28).

Psalm 118:24 declares, "This is the day which the LORD hath made: we will rejoice and be glad in it." The commandment orders us to keep the Sabbath because "in six days the LORD made heaven and earth, the sea and all that in them is" (Ex. 20:11). God, having created all things, has no problem in the government of all things. In the midst of our world's miseries, which are His judgments, we can rest in His government. The Sabbath is a celebration of the present day, in the face of all things, in the certain knowledge that it is God's ordained day, and we are members of His covenant. Therefore, rejoice.

Karma and the Sabbath

The world of Karma is a world without God, and without rest. Hinduism has no Sabbath, and no naturalistic faith can have a true Sabbath. In a naturalistic world, man is caught in tension between two conflicting facts. *First*, if there is no God, everything depends upon man. If everything depends on man, then man must be at the command post of his life continuously, night and day, awake and asleep. The psychological implications of this are enormous: rest is precluded, and humanistic man is plagued with insomnia, an inability to rest while seeking it with intensity, and a nightmare-haunted life with things threatening to go out of control. Life is lonely at the top, especially if we live in a dead universe, and if we are all alone in our heart's concerns.

Second, if man is alone in a dead universe, a world without God, he faces the relentless and blind workings of that universe. Things happen because they must happen, without any source in mind, reason, or purpose. This means that man's purposes work against a world of total purposelessness. It means moreover that an unrelenting and blind causality works against him. Hinduism calls this Karma; others have varying names for it. The sum total of a blind world's forces and past work against us, and govern us. Heredity, the environment, our sins, the stars, our id, ego, superego, our primordial past, and much, much more controls us. Instead of being in control, we are controlled.

Thus, a naturalistic world-view or faith tells us to be the captains of our souls and fate, but also tells us that we are the creatures of nature, Karma, or what have you. The result is *no rest.*

The Sabbath can only flourish with a living faith. It means knowing that the government of all things is on the Lord's shoulders, not ours (Isa. 9:6-7). We can therefore rest in His government, providence, and care. We can also work in the magnificent assurance that our labor is not vain or futile in the Lord (I Cor. 15:58; Rom. 8:28). If there is no God, there can be no rest. "The wicked are like the troubled sea, when it cannot rest, whose waters cast up mire and dirt. There is no peace, saith my God, to the wicked" (Isa. 57:20-21).

If we have peace and rest, we communicate it. We are then at all times a Sabbath people. If we do not have rest, then we are a restless and a warring people. We are at war with God, with our neighbor, and with ourselves. We become a center of unrest, and we radiate disturbance. We then create conflicts and try to justify them in the name of our principles.

Men without a Sabbath rest as the principle of their lives are men without Christ, who is our true Sabbath (Heb. 4:9-16). We rest in Him who declares, "Peace I leave with you, my peace I give unto you: not as the world giveth, give I unto you. Let not your heart be troubled, neither let it be afraid" (John 14:27).

The Sabbath is thus much more than a day. It is the Lord, a faith, and a faithfulness. It is resting in Him, and also living and working in Him.

Are you living under Karma, or in the terms of the Sabbath? (Feb., 1981)

TAXATION
Chalcedon Position Paper No. 21

One of the most prevalent of myths is that vast properties across the land escape taxation because they are church-owned. The tales are endlessly repeated as fact: church-owned businesses, farms, and properties which by subterfuge are removed from the tax roles. As one critic of tax exemption for churches said, ominously, a few days ago: "Nobody knows just how extensive this kind of thing is." The fact is that any and every business activity, whether privately, corporately, or church owned, is taxed, and the tax men are eager always to ferret out and tax new sources of revenue. If any such activity is untaxed, we can be sure of this: it is, like Jim Jones' Peoples' Church, a tacitly established "church," receiving state or federal funds, and serving some statist purpose. It is not true of legitimate churches.

There are, of course, vast untaxed lands, as much as 90% in at least one Western state. These lands are often exploited. In at least one state, one of the country's most powerful publishers long had, and may still have, very extensive grazing rights therein, while owning very little land himself; he is thus a cattle baron at minimal cost. Small ranchers get no such preferential treatment. These vast untaxed lands are federal and state lands. The myth holds that only such lands as the civil government holds can be protected from exploitation and abuse. The fact is that the much abused lumber "barons" take far better care of the forests they own than do the federal or state governments; if they did not, they would soon be out of business.

By what right is the state entitled to hold vast properties, and to hold them tax exempt? The answer to this question is a religious one: we are told, "The state is sovereign," i.e., the state is lord. Who made the state into a god or lord, and gave it the right to play sovereign over man? According to Scripture, "The earth is the LORD'S, and the fullness thereof; the world, and they that dwell therein" (Ps. 24:1; Ex. 9:29; Job 4:1 I; Ps. 50:12; 1 Cor. 10:26; etc.). On this fact rests God's right *to govern, to legislate, and to tax.* The Sovereign or Lord is the source of government, law, and taxation. The prophecy concerning Christ was that "the government shall be upon his shoulder" (Isa. 9:6), and the most common title applied to Jesus in the New Testament is Lord, or Sovereign. *The tithe is simply the confession that the Lord is indeed our Lord.* The state in Scripture is allowed only the head tax, and no more (Ex. 30:11-16; see Arthur J. Zuckerman: *A Jewish Princedom in Feudal France, 768-900*, Columbia University Press, 1972, for a later history of this tax.) *To refuse to tithe is to deny Christ's lordship, government, and law.*

For this reason, the early church refused to pay taxes to Rome or any other power, or to allow any licensure, regulation or control. The church as

Christ's realm cannot allow any other power to claim the right of legislation, taxation, and government over it. To do so is to deny the Lord.

For this reason too, as the church gained freedom from persecution, it encouraged the accumulation of land and properties for Christ's Kingdom; this included also the subjugation and development of new areas. The amount of land held by church agencies in the medieval era is commonly and greatly exaggerated; humanistic propaganda colors our picture of these properties and greatly distorts it. The fact is that these properties were governing agencies. Their receipts or production provided for the care of the poor, for health services and hospitals, and for education. All the basic social services were thus cared for.

When Henry VIII seized church properties and gave some of them to his henchmen, and used the rest to fatten the crown, one immediate result was a social crisis. There was no longer any agency to care for the basic needs of society. Some years later, Thomas Lever, in his St. Paul's sermons (1550), dealt with this problem. The rich had become richer, and the poor had become destitute, because of the impropriations of church properties. Here was a strong Puritan attack on impropriations, and a remedy proposed shortly. A great outpouring of funds to set up foundations and charities to revive what Henry VIII had ended soon followed. Quite naturally, the Tudor monarchs, with their claims to be sovereign, heads of the church, and with divine rights, were militantly hostile to this revival of "medievalism." The Puritans, they felt, had to be suppressed. (No accurate history of the Puritans can omit the impropriations issue.)

By 1660, however, both the Reformation, and the Counter-Reformation, had been defeated and controlled by the monarchs of Europe. The monarchs could resume the course of pagan statism, of the various medieval monarchs, and of the Holy Roman Empire, i.e., the assertion of state sovereignty or lordship. With Hegel, the state was plainly defined as god walking on earth. The present and working god of society had become the state; the God of Scripture was exiled to heaven.

The government, said the modern state, is upon our shoulders; sovereignty is the prerogative of the state. The state alone is lord, and hence the taxing, governing, and law-making power.

In terms of this lordship, the state said, the earth is the state's, and the fullness thereof, the world and they that dwell therein. Earlier, the papacy had, in Christ's name, rightly or wrongly, divided the newly discovered American continents among the nations. Now the nations claimed the earth for themselves. Previously, it had been church lands that were tax-exempt; now, those lands were steadily limited, and state lands gained the privileges of lordship.

There was a very grave difference, however. Church lands paid no taxes, but they provided a vast variety of social services. The lands were productive, and they were usually productively used. These, together with tithes and offerings, provided a growing and important government for Christ's people. True, there were abuses, but these were pale compared to current statist abuses. When Henry VIII seized church properties, he justified it by indicting relics, and by charges of immorality leveled against the monks, more than a little of it invented. Not even Henry VIII could deny the validity of their charitable works and ministries.

The states, having seized the church lands, and the whole earth, ostensibly for the general welfare, made no such use of these properties, except as national or state parks. Instead, it turned on the people, to tax them with ever-increasing taxes, to take care of needs once provided for by the tithe and by church lands. Today, taxation has become expropriation, and the greedy power state, owning most of the earth, hurls charges of special privilege against the meager church properties, almost exclusively limited now to churches and schools.

To add insult to in jury, the claim is now openly and loudly made that tax-exemption is a subsidy from the state! Nothing could be a more flagrant and blasphemous lie. The conflict with Rome by the early church was over this issue: who is the lord, Christ or Caesar? If Christ is the Lord, He cannot pay taxes to, or be controlled by, Caesar.

The church fought for and gained exemption from taxation as a *paroikia*, a foreign power, an embassy of the King of Kings. Christians are ambassadors of Christ (II Cor. 5:20; Eph. 6:20). Our English words *parish*, and *parochial*, come from *paroikia*. The church is an embassy whose duty it is to conquer the whole world, and to make all nations, peoples, tribes, tongues, vocations, and areas of life aspects of Christ's parish. The embassy is under God's sovereignty, law, and taxation. The early church, as a part of its mission, took in the abandoned babies of the pagans. (If a woman could not, in those days, abort her baby successfully, she had it abandoned at birth. In Rome, the babies were abandoned under the bridges, where wild dogs could speedily dispose of them. The Christians collected these abandoned babies, passed them around among church members, and reared them in the faith, as a step in the Christian conquest.) Another aspect of the early church's mission was the care of the sick, aged, and needy in its own midst, and, as far as possible, among their pagan neighbors. These ministries were resented by Rome, which regarded them rightly as a form of government.

Rome saw the early church as a revolutionary and tax-dodging organization. Tax-dodging is in the eyes of the state a most serious offense; money is the life-blood of the state, and, to threaten the state's source of taxes is to threaten its life. Everything was done to defame these "tax-dodgers:" they were called cannibals and sacrificers of human beings. (The communion service, the slander held, involved eating the flesh of the babies the Christians rescued, and drinking their blood.) They were accused of the sexual crimes which actually marked the Romans. (The Christians obviously loved one another, and the Romans could not dissociate love from lust, and they hence concluded that sexual rites marked the life of the church.) On and on, the defamation went, seeking to discredit the church and its work.

Today we have the same process at work. The churches, we are told, are rich, and the pastors rolling in money. The fact is that, in 1980, the average pay of church pastors in the United States was $10,348 a year. (In 1976, federal authorities called everything below $15,000 poverty.) Fourteen percent of all pastors earned less that $6,000 and had to support themselves through other jobs; only five percent earned more than $15,000. In the same year, truck drivers averaged $18,300, electricians $18,000, lawyers $25,000, and dentists over $40,000. The "rich" clergy is not so rich! (Because many are provident and thrifty, they are mistaken for rich because they make a little go a long way.) But what of the rich television and radio preachers? *Penthouse*, *Playboy*, and like publications have been outspoken in their attacks on all this "wealth." Little is said, however, of the high costs of such communications, and the normally very careful use of all funds received. The abusers are few, and, as compared with misuse of public funds by statist officers and agencies, a comparative rarity.

Charges of financial abuse, however, are commonplace. It is the stock in trade of various statist agencies and their running dogs in the press to accuse any enemy of tax fraud, financial manipulations, and the like. It is a usually successful way of discrediting churchmen, and of drying up their funds. Who wants to give to a cause charged with fraud?

The modern power state is also hostile to critics in its own ranks. When Senators Edward V. Long and Joseph Montoya began investigations of the Internal Revenue Service, the I.R.S. leaked data to the press to imply dishonesty on their part; this was enough to defeat them at the polls. (*Saturday Review*, May, 1980, Blake Fleetwood, "The Tax Police, Trampling Citizens' Rights," pp. 33-36.) Congressman George Hansen had like treatment, but was able to get re-elected. (George Hansen and Larrey Anderson: *To Harass our People*, pp. 27-35.) J. A. Schnepper has given us a long chronicle of such tyranny and oppression (J.A. Schnepper: *Inside the I.R.S.*, Stein and Day, 1978.) It is not, however, simply the IRS; it is the whole apparatus of the supposedly sovereign state. To claim sovereignty is to claim lordship, divinity, prior and ultimate right and power over all things. Although the U.S. Constitution deliberately avoided all claims to sovereignty, the modern United States claims it, and seeks to exercise it. Sovereignty by the state is assumed by every bureaucrat and agency; it occurs to none of them, however much some may claim to be Christian, that only God is sovereign. "I am the LORD, and there is none else, there is no God beside me:" thus saith the Lord God to the modern state.

To single out one agency of the federal government as the offender is to miss the point. The offender is the state in the totality of its being.

The issue is coming into focus today because of federal claims to the power to determine what is or is not properly a part of the church and its ministry (i.e., a Christian School, a ministry to delinquent children, etc.), and its claim to be granting a subsidy with the "grant" of a tax-exempt status. In the first instance, for the state to claim the power to declare what is or is not a church is to claim the right to establish religion. This is a violation of the First Amendment. Prior to World War II, no such power was claimed, and abuses were rare. Is it not time to examine the question as to why the entrance of the state into an area seems to lead to abuses in that area? In the second instance, a tax exempt status is not a subsidy from the state but a recognition by the state of its limited jurisdiction. Only if we accept the premise that the state is sovereign or lord, god walking on earth, and that the state has total jurisdiction over every area of life and thought, can we call any area of exemption or abstention a subsidy or a grant. In his own day King Canute wisely ridiculed the idea that he had total jurisdiction: he commanded the waves, which paid no attention to him! Canute thereby illustrated the limitations of his power and jurisdiction. The modern states (and NASA) show no such humility.

We must not forget that the word Baal simply means lord, owner. Baal worship was any and every kind of human activity and religion which acknowledged a lord other than the God of Abraham, Isaac, and Jacob. The modern state is simply a modern Baal. Molech worship was king worship, Molech, Melek, or Milcolm meaning king. Modern statism is Baalism.

Tax exemption is thus not a gift of the state; it rests on Christ's sovereignty or lordship. Moreover, the state itself must be no more than what God decrees that it should be, a diaconate or ministry of justice (Rom. 13:4,6). For the state to claim to be more is to claim to be god.

The tax-dodge allegation is thus a fraud; it rests on a false and blasphemous claim to lordship or sovereignty, and it denies the Lordship of Jesus Christ. This is not to deny that tax-dodging is not commonplace: it is. Every man who does not tithe to the only true Lord and God is a tax-dodger and is therefore liable to far more severe penalties than the state can impose (Malachi 3:8-12).

Moreover, such tax-dodgers cannot complain if the Baal-state whom they worship oppresses them. People having rejected God's tax now pay 40% of their income to the state, and they cry vainly for relief, because it is relief rather than the Lord they want (I Sam. 8:10-18).

The very status granted to the church as a tax-exempt organization is insulting. It is classified, when exempted, as a 501(c)(3) operation. This is a classification for a wide variety of charitable trusts. It can include a humane society, and a pet cemetery, a lodge, or a local charity. The federal government claims increasingly the right to govern all these 501(c)(3) agencies as public trusts which are to be required to conform to public policy and to use all funds, assets, and properties for the general public. The federal and state governments are steadily claiming jurisdiction over all 501(c)(3) organizations; the assumption is that they are creatures of the state, and their lives are totally under the governance of the state .

The claim of Scripture is that all of life is religious. Because God the Lord is maker of heaven and earth and all things therein, all things are under the triune God. All things live, and move, and have their being in Him (Acts 17:28), and, therefore, all things are under His jurisdiction, His government and law. For this reason, all life is religious. The Kingdom of God cannot be reduced to meat or drink (Rom. 14:17), nor can it be reduced to purely spiritual concerns: it is total in its jurisdiction. Paul could therefore say, "Whether therefore ye eat, or drink, *or whatsoever ye do*, do all to the glory of God" (I Cor. 10:31).

The present attitude of the statist-humanists is that all of life is political and hence under the jurisdiction of the state. Supposedly, it is the state in whom we live, and move, and have our being; certainly, it is the goal of the modern state to bring this to pass. The state seeks to govern our eating and drinking, and to control our families, vocations, and the totality of our lives.

The state holds that it is the focal point of power and intelligence in history, and therefore it must govern all things. The intellectuals, being humanists, agree, and hence they seek to control the state. Groups like the Council on Foreign Relations, the Trilateral Commission, and others have certain common premises. *First*, they by-pass or reject Christianity as the means to the good society; implicitly or explicitly, they are all humanists. *Second*, they hold to the perfectibility of man by man. Their presuppositions are derived from the Enlightenment and from Rousseau, not from Scripture. Man's problem is not sin and the fall, but a failure in problem-solving. *Third*, a true world order is possible on statist premises. The modern states, working together, can solve all of earth's problems. This may mean a world state, or it can mean an informal interlocking by means of money and commerce. By uniting the world economically, there can be an implicit political unity. Such a step, however, requires the prior subordination to political goals. Present-day departments of state are thus deeply involved in international politico-economic goals. Foreign loans and politically governed foreign trade become basic tools for this goal of a humanistic and statist world order.

Fourth, the architects of this new order are philosopher-kings and more. To Plato's dream another element has been added: the banker and the industrialist. The student revolts of the 1960s were in part directed against this interlocking Establishment of the state, the university, the banks, and industry, with Big Labor as sometimes a very minor partner. (Charles Levinson, in his thorough study, *Vodka Cola* does not deal with the role of labor.) The modern university, state or private, is today subsidized by the federal government and is an ally in the state's claims to and exercise of the prerogatives of sovereignty. Elitism is basic to the new world order dream, in Marxist and non-Marxist versions. There is infighting as to which of these elitists are to take priority, but all four groups tend to agree on elitism. Neither a democracy nor a republic are to their taste: the form is honored, not the substance. Lip service is paid to equality, but elitism prevails.

Fifth, the facade of benevolence is maintained. Human good and human rights are the professed goals. The elite rulers bring together tax funds and large foundation funds for their use; all men thus tithe to them as the new lords of creation, and the Lord's tithe as an agency of non-statist government is never considered. The reason is obvious. The tithe creates a non-coercive, grass-roots government under God; the state tax, with big foundation money, creates a statist rule from the top down.

Yet we are asked to believe that the church represents vast wealth which goes untaxed! The state owns more land than perhaps all the people combined, pays no taxes, grows fat off the people, and it asks us to regard the church as a rich tax evader! As we have seen, the average pay for 1980 for the American clergy was $10,348. The average pay for Christian School teachers was (and is) dramatically lower. All too many Christian School teachers can only survive if the wife teaches school also, and one or both hold summer or night jobs. The burden on these Christian Schools and teachers is increased by the cost of litigation, because they are now an especial target of the statist tyrants. (A *tyrant*, let us remember, in its ancient and original meaning is anyone who rules without God. Whether or not the people like him makes no difference; a tyrant is one who rules without God, and tyranny is godless rule in any area of life. The word *tyrant*, Greek in origin, means, like *Baal*, lord, or sovereign. A tyrant or a Baal is some human agency or person who claims lordship or sovereignty. In our very use of the word *tyrant* we witness to God! Apart from Him, all rule is evil.) We live in an age of tyranny, an era in which the modern state declares, I am the lord or sovereign, and the earth is mine, and the fullness thereof.

Theology has been replaced by political doctrines, which are the new theology. The gospel of humanistic statism is seen as man's hope rather than the gospel of the Lord Jesus Christ.

When Moses asked God for His name, he was asking God to define Himself. Names in the Bible classify and define. Adam's calling to name the animals (Gen. 2:19) was a scientific task: he was asked to understand the animals in terms of God's order and to classify them. The command and the guidelines came from God, the Creator. Because God is the Creator of all things, He is the only source of all true definition and interpretation. Since God is the Creator and definer, He Himself is beyond definition. A definition limits; it calls attention to boundaries. God declared to Moses that He was beyond definition: "I AM THAT I AM," or I am He Who Is (Ex.

3:14). He is knowable, not by man's definition, but by self-revelation. He is "the God of Abraham, the God of Isaac, and the God of Jacob" (Ex. 3:15f). All things are to be defined in terms of Him and His revelation.

Now, however, newspaper stories tell us of federal efforts "to define religious activity," or to define the church, and so on. All these attempts by statists at definition have a common purpose. They seek, *first*, to make religion a creature of the state. If the state is god, then this is a most logical step, and a necessary step. Otherwise, it is a dangerous and tyrannical activity.

Second, the purpose of these efforts at definition are tax-oriented. The money-hungry state wants to increase its taxing power and its tax resources. A greedy and evil people assent to this. "Tax the rich" has become a reality, but now the income and inheritance taxes hurt virtually all the people, perhaps least of all the very rich. Envy is a great weapon, used over the centuries, to enslave men; if envy can be used to create laws to harm those we resent, then the same laws can be used to harm us, and will be so used. Let us remember that, when the Sixteenth Amendment was under consideration, the idea that the income tax would ever be applied to any but millionaires was ridiculed as impossible in a free country. Those who today want to see the churches taxed are forging the chains and bars for their own enslavement. The death of the First Amendment is not too far distant, if the present trend continues. It will also be the death of freedom.

Slaves see freedom as license; free men see freedom as responsibility. The less free Greece and Rome became, the more they granted sexual license. The fools of the day believed themselves to be free because license had been granted, explicitly or implicitly, to a wide variety of sexual sins. Then as now, for all too many, freedom means the right to he irresponsible, and the right to penalize, tax, and harass the responsible. Romans grumbled about the growing powers of the state, but they saw themselves as more free because sin was favored and even subsidized.

St. Paul in I Corinthians 6:1-8, as B. T. Viviano, in *Study as Worship* (1978), has shown, argued for Christian courts and Christian judges and lawyers to handle cases involving Christians. Because Jesus Christ is Lord, Christians are to live in terms of His government and law, and create courts and agencies to adjudicate and govern their problems.

Through God's tax, the tithe, they are to establish God's reign in every area of life and thought. (See E. A. Powell and R. J. Rushdoony: *Tithing and Dominion*, Ross House Books, Vallecito, California 95251.) Through their self-government under the Lord, they are to become a walking law-sphere and government. The family, as God's basic institution, is fundamental to God's free society and realm.

Only by the self-government of the Christian man under God and His law can the forces of the tyrant state be pushed back and overcome. Only by

God's tax, the tithe, can we finance God's Kingdom. Everyday, in every way, we choose whom we will serve. This choice cannot be a matter of words only. It is a matter of faith and life, of action and money. You have made a choice already. Is it Christ or Caesar? (May, 1981)

"FAITH WITHOUT WORKS"

James, the brother of our Lord, tells us very emphatically that "faith without works is dead" (James 2:26). I thought of this recently when I heard an older man speak of the "old days" when silver dollars were the only kind of money in circulation in this area, and good men refused to take paper dollars in change. Such paper money was despised as "funny money" and as likely sooner or later to lose value. This attitude was commonplace when I was a boy; farmers, ranchers, and miners carried deep leather pouch purses in their jeans to hold "decent" money, silver change and silver dollars.

Then I asked my one and only question of the old man: did you save some of those silver dollars? His answer was brief: "Nope, Sure wish I had. They're worth a lot of money these days." He went on to say that he had known all along that silver dollars were real money, and paper money would "belly up."

But did he? I thought of him two nights later, as I read James 2:26. His "faith" in silver was worthless, and his paper assets are steadily depreciating; he was grumbling about how much harder it is to make ends meet financially. Scripture is right: faith without works is dead and worthless.

To say we believe in the Lord, and to continue living as though the world is governed by statism, money, or evil, is to profess a dead faith. Too many people who profess to believe in the Lord act as though the living God does not govern the world, or that He is not both Savior and Lord.

A faith *with* works moves in terms of Joshua 1:2-9. In the confidence of God's word and victory, it moves out to possess the land for the Lord, in the bold confidence that His word is true, when He says, "I will never leave thee, nor forsake thee. So that we may boldly say, The Lord is my helper, and I will not fear what man shall do unto me" (Heb. 13:5-6). (May, 1981)

KARMA, DEBT, AND THE SABBATH
Chalcedon Position paper No. 22

The doctrine of *Karma* is one of the most important religious doctrines invented by man. Its origins are Brahmanic, but its great development is Buddhist. Perhaps no other non-Biblical doctrine is more important and more perceptive, however deadly. Karma is the law of cause and effect as it regulates the present and future life of man. Karma says that what a man sows, that shall he also reap; every man inherits his own burden of sin and guilt, and no man can inherit the good or evil acts of another man. Karma holds that sin cannot be destroyed by sacrifice, penance, or repentance, but only by self-expiation. A man thus spends his life (and future reincarnations, according to this doctrine) working out the atonement for sin. The important fact about Karma is that this doctrine does justice to the reality of cause and effect; it recognizes the reality of sin in man, and the burden which sin imposes on the present and the future. Modern humanism is unable to cope with this fact of causality and chooses to ignore it. It does not escape causality thereby and only compounds its problem.

According to Karma, the past determines the present and the future. Man's sin most surely finds him out and will not let him go.

The karma faiths have no savior, but they are at least aware of the reality of sin and its demand for expiation. Their doctrines of self-atonement are ineffectual, but their realism as to man's condition make them wiser than those moderns who choose to deny causality.

The doctrine of karma was current in the world of the Bible, especially the New Testament era. The Bible speaks emphatically of causality, and the consequences of sin (Gen. 2:17; 3:7). Moses declares, "ye have sinned against the LORD; and be sure your sin will find you out" (Num. 32:23). Paul warns, "Be not deceived; God is not mocked, for whatsoever a man soweth, that shall he also reap" (Gal. 6:7). However, rather than an abstract world of causality, for the Bible the cosmos is the creation of the personal God. This fact creates a vast gulf between the Bible and the doctrine of Karma.

But Karma does stress a fact that the modern world chooses to forget: causality. It is this fact that Keynesian economists choose to forget. Keynes himself, when asked about the long-run consequences of his economics, replied, "In the long run, we are all dead." Because of its disregard for causality, Keynesianism creates an inflationary economy; long-term consequences are dismissed in favor of short-term benefits.

The average American and European is not familiar with Keynesian as a body of economic thought; they are familiar with it as a way of life, their own way of life. In Keynesian terms, all sin is assessed in terms of present benefits, not in terms of long-term consequences. As a result, debt living has become a way of life. From a moral liability at the beginning of the century, debt has become now an asset, and the word credit, which once meant reliability, now means the ability to contract debt. The world's monetary systems are no longer based on the gold standard but on debt; paper money represents debt, not wealth.

The modern Keynesian world is a rejection of the triune God and His law-word, which prohibits debt beyond a six-year limit, and then for necessities only, which requires covetous-free living, and which regards debt as a form of slavery. Between 1945 and 1980, many fortunes were built (and many lost) by pyramiding debt.

But debt, like sin, has its consequences. Karma holds that past sins govern our present and future lives. With its concomitant doctrine of re-incarnation, Karma holds that thousands of generations or re-incarnations may be necessary in some cases to work out the self-expiation necessary. The burden of sin and guilt is not lightly discarded simply because man wills it. Causality rules all things unrelentingly.

This brings us to the deadly aspect of the doctrine of Karma. Because of its unrelenting doctrine of causality, the past rules the present and the future. Only insofar as we have a better past or Karma can we have a better future. The world of Karma is a past-oriented world.

The same is true of the world of debt. For those who are in debt, the past governs the present. The first claimant on their monthly check is the past: the house payment, and other debts have a fixed claim on their income before either they or God can touch it. One of the most common questions I encounter with respect to the tithe is this: "How can I tithe, and still meet my payments on my debts?" The house is on "the never-never plan;" the car and furniture get old and shabby before they are paid for, and man's days are dominated by the past.

Modern man may not believe in Karma, but he has created a new world of Karma in debt.

The same is true in politics. Cause and effect in politics has brought the world's many nations to the raw edge of judgment. In politics, this has brought some vaguely conservative parties and administrations to power. All are looking for cosmetic solutions and avoiding the long and ugly chain of causality which has led to the present crisis. The Karma of modern politics threatens them like a crumbling cliff over a cottage, and all are offering a more modest table fare as the solution.

All around us a host of things have created a vast chain of causes and effects which threaten our world: debt, the minimum wage law, statist education and the new illiteracy, welfarism, and much, much more. The world may say, Let us eat, drink, and be merry, for tomorrow we die, but God says, Tomorrow the judgment. (One is reminded of the cartoon, picturing a sad-faced man carrying a sign on a busy street, reading: "We are all doomed: the world will not end!" Man has no escape from his sins in any way of his own devising.)

When the past governs the present, it has a paralyzing effect on it. As J. Estlin Carpenter pointed out many years ago, the doctrine of Karma froze society and led to the caste system. Basic to the dogma was this principle: "a man is born into the world that he has made." The present is read in terms of the past.

Our current Karma culture is also seeing a like stratification. Despite the talk of equality, the premise of welfarism and more is the incapacity of vast numbers of peoples. The ghettos of America have seen successive waves of immigrants come and go as they worked their way into more advanced positions. Now we have, as a policy of state, an assumption that a permanent ghetto resident is a fact of life. (Of course, because of environmentalism, we now seem to hold that a man is born into the world others made for him.)

The two principles of Karma are, *first*, "A man is born into the world that he has made," and *second*, "The Deed does not perish," i.e., consequences continue until they are fully expiated. Karma cannot be destroyed, neither by fire, flood, wind, or the gods. It must proceed unrelentingly and unerringly to its results. A man might briefly postpone the workings of his Karma, but he could never frustrate nor destroy them. All else passes, but acts and their consequences remain. Destiny, Karma, reigns and rules. The word *deva* is gods, and *daiva*, derived from it, means destiny, and, for the Buddhist, destiny is simply *past acts*, according to L. de la Vallee Poussin. Since Karma includes in its unrelenting causality mental acts as well, man's waking thoughts as well as his dreams in sleep govern his life and add to his Karma. Only through good acts can man expiate his past sins, and "the good act has three roots: the absence of lust, of hatred, and of error" (Poussin). Thus, we have a negative idea of good, so that its essential function is to diminish the retribution for the vast accumulation of past acts.

The very clear fact which emerges from this is that, in the world of Karma, there can be passivity and withdrawal, but definitely not rest. The Biblical doctrine of the Sabbath is thus unique. We are commanded to observe the Sabbath in Deuteronomy and to "remember that thou wast a servant in the land of Egypt, and that the LORD thy God brought thee out thence through a mighty hand and by a stretched out arm: therefore the LORD thy God commanded thee to keep the Sabbath Day" (Deut. 5:15). Redeemed man can *rest* because he knows that the Lord has saved him. The meaning of the cross is not that the consequences of our sin are simply overlooked, but that Jesus Christ makes full expiation for our sins. The causality is worked out on the cross; atonement is made for our sins, and we are free from the guilt and the burden of sin. Where men deny the causality of sin, they deny also the atonement, and they become antinomians.

But only Christ's atonement can free man from sin and death and give him rest. The answer to the doctrine of Karma is the atonement and the Sabbath rest which the atonement creates. The Sabbath law follows the Passover event, and it sets forth the salvation-rest of the Old Israel. The Christian Sabbath follows the atonement and the resurrection, the first day of the week, and it celebrates the salvation-rest of the New Israel of God.

The redeemed in Christ now are governed, not by the past, not by their sins, nor by Karma, but by the Lord, who is the same, yesterday, today, and forever (Heb. 13:8). They are to live righteously, to render to all their due honor, to love their neighbor as themselves, and, as a normal practice, to owe no man anything, save to love one another (Rom. 7-10).

The true Sabbath enables us to rest, because, *first* it is Christ's finished work of atonement and continuing work of providence that is our life, not our deeds and past acts. *Second*, we can rest, because we are not past-bound and past-oppressed and haunted. We can say with David, "I will both lay me down in peace, and sleep: for thou, LORD, only makest me dwell in safety" (Ps. 4:8). We have the blessedness of restful, trusting, sleep. Instead of a burden, the past has become an asset in the Lord, who makes all things work together for good to them that love Him, to them who are the called according to His purpose. (The converse of this is that all things work together for evil for those who hate God, Obadiah 15; Jeremiah 50:29; Lamentations 1:22.)

Third, because we are now future oriented, we become Dominion Men, working for godly reconstruction in every area of life and thought. Our lives are dominated, not by past burdens but by present responsibilities and the assurance of power (John 1:12). Together with Joshua (and the apostles, Matt. 28:18-20), we have the assurance: "Every place that the sole of your foot shall tread upon, that have I given unto you...There shall not any man be able to stand before thee all the days of thy life: as I was with Moses, so I will be with thee: I will not fail thee, nor forsake thee" (Joshua 1:3,5).

The sad fact today is that many church members profess Christ but live in the world of Karma. To illustrate, one church officer, an able and talented man but a despiser of God's law, has twice been bankrupt, several times a failure in business because of lawless policies and debts, and is a sour and critical leader whose ways are oppressive to many. There is no Sabbath in his life, nor any freedom and power; he has the aura of a hunted man, and, in his work, is a "plunger," one who prefers risks to sound practices. We have all too many pastors whose sermons are trumpets always sounding defeat, and echoing with the oppressiveness of sin, not the freedom and joy of victory and redemption. Their sermons echo the death of the tomb, not the triumph of the resurrection.

To all such we must say with Paul, "Awake, thou that sleepest, and arise from the dead, and Christ shall give thee light" (Eph. 5:14). (June, 1981)

The Congregation of the Dead

According to Solomon, "The man that wandereth out of the way of understanding shall remain (or, find rest, or end up) in the congregation of the dead" (Prov. 21:16).

To wander out of "the way of understanding" is to wander away from Jesus Christ and His every word, the whole of Scripture. It means trusting in our own understanding rather than in the Lord (Prov. 3:5).

Practically, what does this involve? When we come to the church and demand that it meet our needs and our desires rather than the Lord's purposes, we have forsaken understanding. We have then become humanists as well: we want the church to please man, not God.

The great answer of Dr. John Henry Jowett, sixty or more years ago, still remains the telling one. When a foolish woman asked him what he thought about God, he answered quietly, "Madam, I think the question is, What does God think about me?"

The important thing thus is not what we think about Christ's church, nor, about God, but what the Lord thinks about us. Remember, the congregation of the dead is made up of those who lean on their own understanding. (June, 1981)

THE ATTACK AGAINST THE FAMILY
Chalcedon Position Paper No. 23

Earlier this year (1981), I was a witness in the trial of some fathers for having their children in a Christian School which refused to submit to state controls. Some of the fathers were prominent citizens of that county. The charges against them were criminal charges. The state's attorney general granted immunity to their wives, who were then compelled to take the stand and testify against their husbands or face contempt of court charges.

At two points, this step meant a radical break with Biblical law. *First*, according to Scripture, husband and wife are "one flesh," a community of life, and members one of another (Gen. 2:24, Matt. 19:5-6; Eph. 5:22-33). As a result, the one cannot testify against the other; spousal testimony for the prosecution is thus barred. *Second*, the testimony must come from two or more witnesses (Deut. 17:6; Heb. 10:28; Num. 35:30; Deut. 19:15; 11 Cor. 13:1; I Tim. 5:19; John 8:17). Confession in itself is not enough to convict; there has to be corroborating evidence, as in Achan's case (Josh. 9:20-23). As a result, enforced confession is rendered meaningless, because corroboration and witnesses are required.

As a result of these laws, very early, despite abuses, justice reached a remarkably high level in Israel. Torture had no place in the law, and the burden of proof was placed on witnesses and the court. This Biblical principle had difficulty establishing itself in barbarian Europe. Legal processes were much simpler, given the "right" to use spousal testimony, or the "right" to torture. Historians for many years treated all victims of such legal procedures as necessarily innocent. Now, some scholars are finding that the evidences indicate a high rate of guilt. Then as now, a high percentage of those arrested were guilty men; because conviction was held to be desirable, ungodly and evil means were used to secure it, i.e., torture, enforced confessions, and spousal testimony.

The Fifth Amendment, and the legal bars against spousal testimony, represent one of the slowest yet most important victories in legal history. That victory is now being compromised, and the door opened to legal terrorism.

Many Americans were delighted, a few years ago, when members of criminal syndicates were brought before congressional committees, granted immunity, and ordered to testify. To have testified meant death for these men from their cohorts; to refuse to testify meant jail for contempt of court. A clever ploy, that, most Americans thought, failing to realize that the same tactics could be used against them. Moreover, few realized that the horrors of Tudor and Stuart England, and such instruments of tyranny as the Star Chamber proceedings, now have their revival in the arbitrary powers of congressional committees and bureaucratic agencies. Congress and the bureaucracy are the old tyrant writ large.

Moreover, at the same time, several states are relaxing the laws against spousal testimony. The stage is set for the kind of tyranny which prevails in the Soviet Union. It is dangerous there for a husband and wife to know too much about each other: it can be forced out of them. As a result, there is little exchange of confidence, in many cases, and yet, even with that, coerced false testimonies.

Even worse, some very foolish churchmen refuse to see that a problem exists. Legal convictions are more important to them than the doctrine of Christian marriage, and the moral value of freedom. It is important to remember that the goal of the law is not conviction but justice, and, in Biblical law, justice is not only a matter of righteousness in life and society but also in all procedures of law. God's law specifies the laws of evidence, hearings, and more, because justice is basic to every step of the conduct of the agencies of law, in church and state alike.

Moreover, to endanger the family is to endanger the basic institution of society according to Biblical law. The family is under attack. *First*, as we have seen, the unity of the twain as one flesh is being attacked by the weakening of the laws against spousal testimony. Such a step reduces marriage to a matter of sexual and economic convenience rather than the basic God-ordained unit of society. It is an anarchistic and atomistic step.

Second, abortion legalizes murder in the life of the family at the option of the mother, so that the cradle of life becomes a place of death. God gives to the family all the basic powers in society (control of children, property, inheritance, welfare, and education) save one, the death penalty. This is the reason why Cain was not executed for murder; all those then living were his immediate family. Ancient paganism, as in Rome, gave the father the power to destroy his own children. Our modern paganism, humanism, is even worse: it gives this power to the mother, so that the very womb or matrix of life becomes also the place of murder. (Will the children of mothers who aborted a brother or sister as readily espouse euthanasia for their parents in the days ahead?) Abortion goes hand in hand with a contempt for the Biblical doctrine of the family. As Kent Kelly (*Abortion, The American Holocaust*, 1981, Calvary Press, 400 South Bennett Street, Southern Pines, North Carolina 28387; $2.95) points out, abortion has taken more lives than all the wars in our history, which, from 1775 to 1975, took 1,205,291 lives, whereas deaths by abortion are c. 8,000,000.

Third, the family is under attack because its Biblical legal powers are being replaced by statist powers over the family. The Biblical family is the basic law order, so that it is more than a sexual arrangement. If the family is not more than a sexual arrangement, then any and all sexual arrangements can claim equivalent privileges, as they are now doing. The Bible, however, sees the union of man and woman as the basic law order and the fundamental unit of society. Marriage creates a new unit: the twain become one flesh. As such, they have powers and responsibilities possessed by no other element of society. The family is the matrix of the future, and as a result God entrusts the control of the future to the family, not to the church, nor to the state. Both church and state have a duty to protect the family, not to control it. Biblical law, by giving control over children, property, inheritance, welfare, and education to the family ensures that it will be the matrix of the future. (See Chalcedon Position Paper No. 8, "The Family.")

Because the state is given the power of the death penalty, it is the most dangerous agency of all for man to entrust any planning to; the state plans by means of coercion, so that its planning for the future inescapably involves repressive legislation, taxation, controls, regulations, and, sooner or later, the death penalty. For the state to be made the agency for planning and future development is a form of social suicide: the hangman has one solution to social problems, and it is a swinging one. Without agreeing with all that he meant by it, we can echo Martin Luther's comment that the prince or the state is God's hangman. To make the hangman our caretaker and planner is the height of stupidity, but it is also a folly that modern man is very much addicted to.

Fourth, the family as the basic unit is being replaced in some circles by the atomistic individual. The rise of this social atomism has preceded much of what we are describing. The Playboy philosophy and mentality is an example of this atomism. The ultimate arbiter of all things becomes the atomistic and anarchistic individual. Early in the 1970s, Dorothy and I met a young woman in her mid-twenties; her's was a remarkable and startling beauty, and her two little daughters shared her beauty. Her husband had left her; he said frankly that he had no complaints: she was "tops" in every department, but he was "bored" with living with one woman and supporting a household. He wanted freedom to use his money as he saw fit, and to do as he pleased without a "guilt-trip." Such moral anarchism is widespread and increasingly vocal. It is simply original sin, the desire of man to be his own god and law, determining for himself what constitutes good and evil. (Gen. 3:5).

Such moral anarchists talk much about the separation of church and state. For them it means freedom *from* religion, and the enforced silence of Christians on all matters of law and morality. (See Frank Brady on the

Playboy position in *Hefner*, p. 219f.; 1974.) Such people want to abolish religious freedom in favor of religious toleration. Toleration was the position of ancient Rome: a religion was tolerated if it submitted to licensure, regulation, taxation, controls, and certification, and, with all this, was silent where Rome wanted religion to be silent.

It was apparent, after the November, 1980, U.S. election, that great segments of the press and U.S. federal government want to abolish religious freedom in favor of religious toleration. This is clearly the policy of the U.S. Internal Revenue Service (and not even as *outwardly* tolerant as the Turkey of the murderous Sultans).

No small contributing factor to the rise of this atomism has been the rise of pietism in the modern era. Christianity was reduced to the experience of the individual soul. Now certainly the conversion of the individual is the starting point, but it is the starting point, not the sum total, of Christian faith and life. To so limit Christianity, as pietism has done, is comparable to limiting all literature to the alphabet and abolishing all poetry, history, law, and more, in the name of the purity of the alphabet.

We began with a court case, and the compelling of spousal testimony. People who fail to see the far-reaching implications of that case have retreated from the world-encompassing scope of our Lord's word, power, and government to a small-scale god and religion. They may love their family, but they fail to see its meaning under God.

This is the key: all things must be viewed, not from the perspective of the state, nor the individual, but in terms of God and His law-word. "For with thee is the fountain of life: in thy light shall we see light" (Ps. 36:9). This is as true of the family as all things else.

The modern age is given to absurd humanistic platitudes to justify its moral idiocy. Isadora Duncan, for example, once said, very self-righteously, "Nudity is truth...Therefore, it can never be vulgar; it can never be immoral." This she said in Boston, from the stage of Symphony Hall, whereupon she tore her tunic down and bared one of her breasts. What her sententious spoutings failed to say was that *people* can be vulgar, and *people* can be immoral, and Isadora Duncan was both vulgar and immoral.

The world is full of such nonsense in all quarters. Cotton Mather, who should have known better, wrote, in *Manuductio ad Ministerium* (1726), "My Son, I advise you to consider yourself as a *Dying Person*...I move you, I press you, *To remember how short your time is*..." What he should have said was, Remember, you are a living person under God, accountable for all your talents and days. If you are faithful and responsible in life, you have nothing to fear from death. The best preparation for death is life, and the God-ordained matrix and locale for life is *the family*. Therefore, rejoice in the wife of thy youth (Prov. 5:15-21); praise God our Savior, and serve Him in all things with all your heart, mind, and being. (August, 1981)

THE GREAT FEAR AND THE GREAT FAITH
Chalcedon Position Paper No. 24

Otto J. Scott, in *Robespierre, The Voice of Virtue*, calls attention to all important phenomenon of the French Revolution, *The Great Fear*. At a certain point, as corrosion began to destroy all forms of social order, wild rumors circulated through all of France. Fears of invasion, of disintegration, and chaos "destroyed the sense of stability and security essential to civilized patterns and orderly ways." Evil seemed to have become incarnate and dominant over history. "There was a general, unexpressed sense that a true diabolism had appeared, an evil that sent a shudder through the land. Men who had long forgotten God began to believe the Devil was real" (p. 69f.; Ross House Books, $9.50).

The Bastille fell on July 14, 1789; for the rest of that summer, the French people also fell, in their case into The Great Fear, *La Grande Peur*. None of the fears were true, but their content, Eugen Rosenstock-Huessy pointed out, was not the significant fact: "it was this complete paralysis of will and reason, the deep insight that one was no longer safe on land" (*Out of Revolution*, p. 131; Argo Books). It was the sign of disintegration: evil and madness took over, because there was despair concerning any good. France went into the Reign of Terror subsequently, but the terror first began in men's minds with the Great Fear.

According to Rosenstock-Huessy, every revolution begins with a Great Fear; it appeared before the Peasants' Revolt of Luther's day, and it again appeared in Germany in the year 1930, preceding Hitler. Frederick II in 1227 described the Great Fear in his day; so intense was it that he said "the power of love itself, by which heaven and earth are governed, seems now to be troubled, not in its later flowing, but at the very *source*."

The Great Fear marks first the break-up of man's inner being. His way of life is shattered. Man in such eras and now live on borrowed capital, on the inheritance of the past. They assume old religious standards and values without really believing in them. The old faith of society declines from a religious imperative to a convention and an accepted custom. Then the surface begins to crack, and men are suddenly without the religious resources for crisis. They become fearful and guilt-ridden, and they start at shadows.

The inner break-up precedes the outer break-up. The collapse begins in man's soul and rapidly extends into his society, which begins to disintegrate and go up in flames. Indeed, the flames of destruction become then the only active and potent social force.

In Britain's 1981 summer riots, the rock music groups had a major part in preparing the youth for the enactment of destruction and break-up. Significantly, Johnny Rotten of the Sex Pistols has summed up the "hard rock" view on life: "We are the future: no future" (Christopher Makos: *White Trash*, 1977). Modern youth culture, with its love of rock music and drugs, is determined that there be no future.

The older generation sees this with horror and without faith. The war against the Establishment is more than that: it is a war against yesterday, today, and tomorrow, against past, present, and future. Youth sings of belonging "to the blank generation," to a world without meaning or direction.

The Bible also speaks of the end and of the results of the Great Fear: it is death (Prov. 8:36). Our Lord declares that the times shall come when men shall say to the mountains, "Fall on us; and to the hills, Cover us," (Luke 23:30), as they seek vainly to escape God's judgment. In Revelation 6:16, we are again given the cry of men in the grips of the Great Fear; they say to the mountains and rocks, "Fall on us, and hide us from the face of him that sitteth on the throne, and from the wrath of the Lamb." Again, in Revelation 9:6, we read, "And in those days shall men seek death, and shall not find it; and shall desire to die, and death shall flee from them."

The Great Fear begins, as Rosenstock-Huessy saw, in the conscience of man. It is a religious fact, and it is a manifestation of man's spiritual state. As our Lord said, "Men's hearts shall fail them for fear" (Luke 21:26).

There is reason enough for that fear. By their unbelief, men have destroyed the foundations of social order. Their world is crumbling because its moral base is gone; to admit this fully means to repent and to turn to the Lord, which men will not do. As a result, they seek to provide a political, economic, or military justification for their fears. It is usually true that the political scene is an evil one, the economic sphere a decaying one, and the military situation deplorable. To stress these factors can mean covering up the religious break-up behind them. Evading this religious issue, the collapse of man's faith for living, leads to quackery: easy solutions which deal with the surface sores of the deeply-rooted cancer, or, very popular today, how to profit from world disaster. (Quick! Invest in coffins and cemetery lots! There is a lot of death ahead, and big profits in death-related industries!)

The Great Fear is creeping upon us, and it is in evidence in embryo form on all sides. Occultism and an interest in the demonic are precursors of it. So too, and especially so, is unbelief, and lukewarm religion. The Great Fear means a wild and irrational proneness to believe in anything. This is common to a rationalistic and irreligious age. When men believe nothing they are then most susceptible to believe anything and everything. To believe in God and His infallible word is to limit all possibilities and beliefs in terms of God and His word. If we believe in a world of chance, then we believe in a world of total irrationality and in every kind of irrational possibility. The triumph of humanism, science, and anti-God thinking has always marked the rise of superstition and illogical beliefs. In Greece, Rome, the late "Middle

Ages," and now, this is true. If God's predestined and absolute order is denied, then man can only believe in a radically irrational and illogical world in which anything goes, except God's order. And man, when he sees himself as a chance product of a blind world of chance occurrences, is on the verge of the Great Fear.

We are on the verge of another and the most extensive Great Fear in history. The corrosive forces of humanism are world-wide in their influence.

The only thing that can counteract and overcome the deadly personal and social effects of the Great Fear is the Great Faith. Faith today has been reduced to easy believism, to a mere assent to doctrine, and to a verbal profession. In fact, one church today is, as it has been for several years, hounding an able theologian whose only offense is to agree with Scripture that, "Even so faith, if it hath not works, is dead, being alone" (James 2:17). And why not? Let such a text and position stand, and churchmen might be expected to manifest their Christianity in action!

The Great Faith manifests the power of God in history (John 1:12). It declares, "For whosoever is born of God overcometh the world: and this is the victory that overcometh the world, even our faith" (I John 5:4). The Great Faith declares, "If God be for us who can be against us?" (Rom. 8:31). Nay, in all these things we are more than conquerors through him that loved us" (Rom. 8:37). The Great Faith is not shopping for Rapture Robes but putting on the whole armor of God (Eph. 6:10-18).

The Great Fear is preceded, not only by the general meaninglessness of life, but also by escapism. This takes various forms. Certainly alcoholism and drugs are obvious forms of this escapism which is the forerunner and accompaniment of the end. The end of any age is the death of the faith of that age, and, without faith, man cannot live in either poverty or luxury. The emptiness of life overwhelms him wherever he is and whatever his station.

Empty man tries to find meaning in empty goals and short-term interests. A few years back, a slightly drunk man approached me to unload his random thoughts. (I later learned that he was a man of some means, with a beautiful home in the hills, an alcoholic, and a homosexual.) Life in Berkeley, California (his home) was incredibly dull, he said, enough to drive one to suicide. The only thing that made life bearable for him was the realization that, when things were impossible, he could escape to San Francisco for the week-end. I suggested, then why not move to San Francisco? He looked at me as though I were an idiot and said, before moving on, If I lived in San Francisco, when I got bored, I would have no place fit to go to, and no choice but to commit suicide. Life for him meant having a small goal ahead and no more. But limited and petty goals grow empty also, when man is empty and his world dead of all meaning. This is the prelude to the Great Fear.

It has been said, with some evidence, that the Great Fear was created by conspiracy. Adrien Duport of the Club Breton devised the scheme to demoralize France. Rumors were started all over France to announce the approach of Austrians and English to massacre the people. The result was the breakdown of law and order. The point, however, is that people were ready to believe in anything. There was no hard common sense, not any strong faith, by means of which data could be assessed. One of the most obvious facts of the French Revolution was the sorry performance of the clergy, Catholic and Protestant (Huguenot). Both groups were heavily influenced by the modernism of the day, or too wrapped up in pietism, to be relevant. There was no backbone of faith to resist anarchy. Had Adrien Duport never existed, the Great Fear would have still occurred: it was the product of the break-up of the inner man; his world was collapsing, and he too had collapsed.

Earlier, I cited the words of Johnny Rotten of the Sex Pistols: "We are the future: no future." Rock music openly declares the death of all meaning: it celebrates death, contempt for purposes, and a resolute refusal to be other than suicidal. The war against life and meaning began with the sexual revolution, or, rather came out into the open then. Henry Miller set the tone in *Tropic of Cancer* when he declared his book to be "a prolonged insult, a gob of spit in the face of Art, a kick in the pants to God, Man, Destiny, Time, Love, Beauty.... what you will". With the Marquis de Sade, the modern age says, not, "Let there be light," but, Let there be universal and cosmic darkness. Now the age has nothing left ahead of itself except the Great Fear. The popular culture around us is empty and suicidal. It is geared to the existentialist moment, because, for all the modern minds, nothing else is real. Man, said Jean-Paul Sartre, is a futile passion, and he well described the existentialist mind. Modern youth is passionate, and it is also futile; its passion is death-oriented; towards life and work, its reaction is one of boredom and retreat.

It is an interesting and revealing fact that in England Oliver Cromwell and the Puritans are in disrepute. Cromwell's regime, whatever its faults, was England's last experience with a commanding Great Faith. One thing has since been clear: England has been more ready to honor the likes of the Beatles than Oliver Cromwell. As a result, the land of Cromwell is a very central part of the world-wide break-up of the inner man and the outer society.

The Great Faith must be Biblical. It must know and apply God's law-word to the totality of life and thought. God is Lord, not only over the church and man's soul, but over all of life. If He has no word for education, politics, the arts and sciences, and all things else, then He is not God but one of the many limited and local spirits called gods by the pagans of old.

The Bible speaks to all of life. The premise of Scripture and God's law is that "The earth is the LORD'S, and the fullness thereof; the world, and they that dwell therein" (Ps. 24:1). As Creator of all, the Lord God is the Ruler of all, and His word speaks to all things.

The Great Faith lives by the every word of God (Matt. 4:4), and it applies God's total word to all of life. (September, 1981)

THE IMAGE OF GOD IN MAN

The Westminster Shorter Catechism, Q. 10, asks, "How did God create man?" and answers, "God created man male and female, after His own image, in knowledge, righteousness, and holiness, with dominion over the creatures" (Gen. 1:27f.; Col. 3:10; Eph. 4:24).

Centuries earlier, the Jewish commentator, Joseph Kimhi (1105?-1170?), had written: "Image is dominion and likeness is rulership, not a physical image." This interpretation goes back at least to Saadia Gaon's translation of the Torah and is the ancient understanding of the meaning of the image of God.

Fallen man, of course, seeks an ungodly dominion and rule, one in defiance of God and His law. However, the obvious implication of regeneration is that the man in Christ is renewed in godly dominion and into rule under God. For him to fail to exercise such dominion is a sin.

The ancient interpretation of the creation of man is that Genesis 1:26 says, "And God said, Let us make man in our image (i.e., dominion), after our likeness (rulership): and let them have dominion." Dominion is thus a requirement God makes of us in our very creation. In our regeneration, this requirement is again in force. Just as the judgment of God fell on Adam for a false concept of dominion, so it will fall on us if we deny the dominion mandate.

Our Lord requires it in the Great Commission: we must disciple all nations, "teaching them to observe all things whatsoever I have commanded you: and, lo, I am with you always, even unto the end of the world." In this task, we serve the Lord to whom "all power is given...in heaven and in earth" (Matt. 28:18-20).

We cannot reject dominion and rule without rejecting our Lord's calling. (September, 1981)

THE TROUBLE WITH SOCIAL SECURITY
Chalcedon Position Paper No. 25

The social security system can be criticized on both economic and moral grounds.

Economically, the system is cruelly unfair. Thus, if a man pays in $75,000 to social security between the ages of 18 and 65, the likelihood of getting his money back is poor. His life expectancy after 65 makes it unlikely that he will get back all or half the amount he paid in for 47 years. If he dies, his widow's benefits again are too small to add up to any significant return on his "investment." The combined amount paid in by the employer and employee adds up to a very considerable sum, and the returns on it are small. The only real gainer from social security is the federal government. In 1969, Edward J. Van Allen, in *The Trouble With Social Security*, pointed out that a young worker who began paying into social security at age 18 and retired at 65 would have to live to be 111 years old to break even. If any insurance company or pension plan gave as poor returns, or misused funds as does Social Security, the managers thereof would quickly find themselves in prison!

The social security system, according to the federal courts, is not an insurance or pension plan but a tax. It gives us no claims nor rights; Congress can alter the benefits at will, or cut us out of them, and, for some, this has happened. Moreover, because the federal government uses the funds as they come in, instead of saving them, we must pay interest (in the form of extra taxes) on the federal bonds which have replaced our payments.

Moreover, the social security system promotes insecurity. It limits our ability to save; it prevents us from investing in sound pension plans, and it fuels inflation. If, instead of a federally operated system, the law required free-market insurance and pension plans to provide the benefits, we would then have a sound and stable system.

There is, however, another aspect to social security, the moral and religious factor. A simple historical fact tells us much at this point. Some years after the War of Independence, the U.S. Congress passed a pension plan for all veterans of that war. All veterans desiring a pension were to apply at designated places, submit evidence of their military status, and dictate to a court clerk their memories of the war. Those brief memoirs give us sometimes vivid glimpses of George Washington, Putnam, and other leaders of that era. The stories, however, come as a shock to any Christian reader. Were there no Christians in the Continental Army? Almost uniformly, the veterans showed no interest in the faith or the church in their mature years.

The answer to that question is a very simple one. No Christian veteran applied for a federal pension, and the churches were united in their opposition to any such application. They believed that Christian participation in a state or federal pension plan was morally wrong. They based their stand on many texts in Scripture, from the Old Testament and the New, and they saw their position as summed up and required by I Timothy 5:8, "But if any provide not for his own, and specially for those of his own house, he hath denied the faith and is worse than an infidel." From the days of the early church until this century, and definitely through the first half of the last, Christians saw this as a binding duty and law. For them it meant, *first*, that every Christian has a duty before God to care for his own family, especially those in his own household or under his roof. This did not apply to those who, like the Prodigal Son, had denied the faith and separated themselves. The family is more than a blood institution in Scripture: it is a faith bond. Indeed, where a son is an incorrigible and habitual delinquent, the family must witness for the faith and against the son by denouncing him to the authorities (Deut. 21:18-21). On the other hand, all believing members must be cared for. Our Lord denounces all who refused to provide for their parents and felt that the money for parental support could be better used by the Temple, or God's ministry. He equates this with cursing one's parents, which the law says requires the death penalty (Mark 7:9-13). Very clearly, failure to provide for one's needy kin is a fearful offense in the sight of God. The social security system is a welcome fact for all such sinners, who are readier to see this tax increase than to care for their parents.

Second, the "family" of which Paul speaks in I Timothy 5:8 includes our fellow believers. Very early, following Old Testament practices, the disciples took steps to provide for the needy widows and other like persons in the church. In Acts 6:1-3, we do not have the institution of such a practice; it was already a "daily ministration." Rather, what we have is the organization of a diaconate to provide an efficient and well organized ministry in this area. The work of the early church in this area was remarkable. No charity beyond one day was given to able-bodied men, but work was found for them, or work was made for them on subsistence wages. Indeed, one of the telling "advertisements" for the early church throughout the Roman Empire was their care one for another. Hence the saying, "Behold, how these Christians love one another!" To be a Christian meant to be a responsible person and a member of a larger family. This is one aspect of what Paul means when he says, "we are members one of another" (Eph. 4:25). It was not a light thing to be a Christian: it meant joining, or rather, being adopted into, the family of Jesus Christ as a working, obedient, and responsible member.

We cannot appreciate the significance of all this unless we realize that the New Testament was written, and the early church lived, in the context of the Roman Empire. Until our time, Rome provided the world's most massive social security and welfare system in history. It was "bread and circuses," i.e., food, housing, and entertainment. As in our day, the state was seen as god walking on earth, the source of providence and providing. Rome resented the Christian insistence that Jesus, not Caesar, is Lord, and the Christians' care one for another. Such care meant that the government of another ruler than Caesar was determining the lives of man, and that a god other than Caesar was the provider.

Third, the early church was mindful of the poor outside the fold. As early as in the days of the twelve disciples, there was a treasury for the care of such poor. We have a reference to this in John 12:1-6, and to the fact that this fund was in Judas' care, and he was a thief. What people have not bothered to note is that funds were obviously being given to our Lord, i.e., tithes and offerings. These were apparently apportioned for various purposes, the care of our Lord's ministry and its expenses, perhaps the support of the disciples' families at home, as well as the poor. There were thus perhaps several treasurers, one for each cause.

We do know that one of the great conflicts of the early church with Rome was over abortion. Not only did the church strongly oppose abortion, but it did more. Abortion was then crude and primitive and not always successful. Unwanted babies were then abandoned, in Rome itself under the bridges, where wild dogs consumed them. Christians quickly began to collect all such abandoned new-born babies and then passed them around to member families. This added to the rapid growth of the Christian population. It also embarrassed Romans, who spread stories saying that the babies were collected to be eaten in the communion services, and their blood drunk.

Much more can be said. Hospitals began as an outgrowth of the Christian ministry, and, until fairly recent generations, all hospitals were Christian. Schooling goes back to the Levite schools (Deut. 33:10), and statist education is a recent, humanistic, and socialistic step. All welfare was once Christian, and so on and on. The Bible provides for the world's only sound social security system, spiritually and materially, and Christians once applied it. It begins with salvation, and it continues with being members one of another. The Lord requires it of us.

Social Insecurity

One of the ironies of history is the fact that every age which has sought social security has produced instead dramatic insecurity. This is not to say that security is not an important and worthy consideration. To live securely in one's home, to be in safety on the streets, to have protection from assault and theft, and to have a stable monetary and economic order is clearly a positive and obvious good. It is an aspect of the Messiah's world peace that men convert their weapons into productive tools, and live peacefully, "every man under his vine, and under his fig tree; and none shall make them afraid" (Micah 4:3, 4). The desire for security is a religious and a godly goal. To condemn it is clearly wrong.

The trouble begins when security is detached from its moral and religious context. When we regard security as a product of man's order rather than God's order, we undercut the very foundations of security. I repeatedly have heard statements like this, from people in very good housing as well as in "depressed" areas: My neighbor's boys are on drugs, and they act like animals. We are afraid to leave the house empty, because they vandalize it.

Because we have a statist school system which denies God's word and law, we have produced a lawless generation and dramatic social insecurity. (Not a few social security checks fall into the hands of these new vandals, as they rob the elderly.)

The psalmist thus sees the essence of social security in godly faith and order. Unless the society is God's construction, based on His law-word, it is "vain" or futile:

> Except the LORD build the house, they labour in vain that build it: except the LORD keep the city, the watchman waketh but in vain. It is vain for you to rise up early, to sit up late, to eat the bread of sorrows: for so he giveth his beloved sleep. (Ps. 127:1, 2)

Our society is very insecure. Recently, a very liberal gun control man, after some serious episodes, bought hand-guns for himself and his wife. Such incidents are becoming commonplace. However, such a step gives only a limited although real protection. The society of our time is in decay; the lawlessness is increasing, and counter-measures do not alter the developing anarchy around us.

Moreover, most people, including churchmen, too commonly see the threat as from one direction only, i.e., from lawless peoples. The even greater threat is from Almighty God, from the triune God. It is His law which is broken, His word which is despised, His Name which is blasphemed, and His Person that is by-passed and neglected. Nothing can produce greater social insecurity than the judgment of God!

Unhappily, the very word *security* has been debased in our day by being given, in its primary sense, a limited meaning. It has come to mean, *first*, an insurance against economic hazards and dangers. Its meaning is in this sense economic. The social security system, according to one definition, "conveys the assurance of freedom from the dangers of a penniless old age, unemployment without compensation, etc." (*Dictionary of Sociology*). *Second*, security has come to mean also a psychological stability from fears and neuroses. The hunger for this psychological security has made various forms of psychotherapy one of the great growth "industries" of the 20th century. The intense concern about both these forms of security witnesses to the intense insecurity of modern man. They also witness to his very limited view of security.

God's promise to the faithful is very plain: "There shall no evil befall thee" (Ps. 91:10). Note that the promise does not say, no trouble shall befall thee, but rather no evil; there is a difference. In an age certainly not lacking in problems, Thomas Aquinas defined security as freedom from evil in this Biblical sense.

There is another meaning to *security* which seems at first glance peripheral but is actually basic. *Security* in this sense is a deposit to secure the payment of a debt, or the performance of a contract. In this sense, our security is a theological fact. The Lord God, having already given us His only-begotten Son to effect our redemption at the price of His blood, finds it surely a small thing by comparison to care for us. He is in every sense of the word our security.

In a fallen and sinful world, to expect the kind of security politicians too often promise is fallacious, illusory, and dangerous. It leads people to an avoidance of the basic source of insecurity, the sin of man. Man's depravity is the root of evils in every sphere, marital, political, economic, and so on. No political system can side step the implications of man's nature. Man's sin manifests itself in the family, in the spheres of capital and labor, in politics and education, as well as in open criminality. Man's nature is not changed by his choice of a profession or calling. Being a clergyman, politician, bureaucrat, capitalist, or union man sanctifies no one. Only God who made man can remake him. An age which looks to man's way rather than God's for the dynamics of social change can only increase its disorder and insecurity. (October, 1981)

WEALTH
Chalcedon Position Paper No. 26

The modern attitude towards wealth is a most ambivalent one. Man's materialistic bent makes him desire wealth and hunger passionately for it. Modern advertising appeals to this lust for wealth, and much of current selling and buying is motivated by the urge to appear wealthy, while appearing unconcerned about wealth. To be wealthy is seen as a reproach by the very people who hunger for wealth. In their envy, they try to make wealth into the great sin of the times. Wealth is presented as the product of exploitation; it is depicted as evidence of unconcern for the poor and needy and as something to feel guilty about. Modern man has a love-hate relationship and attitude towards wealth.

The matter is even more complex than that. The contemporary view of wealth has no awareness of the fact that wealth in different areas has meant different things. A man with many (and godly) children and grandchildren can and commonly has felt very rich, although having relatively little money. Moreover, money has not always been an evidence of wealth; more often, land has been the index of wealth, and sometimes position. Then too people can sometimes be rich and feel poor. A few years ago, one of America's wealthiest women married one of America's wealthier men. Both had jealous regards for their money, and they agreed, before their wedding, to share equally all living costs. The marriage foundered, because the bridegroom, worried about the high cost of honeymoons, tried to make his bride share the cost of their honeymoon, beginning with their first breakfast! Despite all his wealth, he was in the true sense of the word, a very poor man.

Mental and religious attitudes thus are thoroughly intertwined with our ideas of wealth. What we believe can make our wealth a blessing or a curse in our eyes, and in the eyes of others. We can feel that wealth gives us a privilege and responsibility, or we can regard it as something to apologize for, as though we had some unfair advantage because of it. Wealth can be a blessing in a godly era, and a burden in an age of envy.

It is important to recognize that the main word for *wealth* in the Hebrew, *chayil*, means *strength*. Another word means *substance*, another, *good*; still others mean *power*; *things laid up*; *fullness*; *rest*; *prosperity*. Clearly, the Bible does not see wealth as the problem, but the problem is what men do with it, and what the possessors of wealth themselves are. At times, some very harsh things are said about rich men, but wealth itself is seen as a blessing (Deut. 8:18). It is trust in wealth which is strongly condemned (Ps 49:6-8). The love of wealth can lead men into grave injustices towards their poorer covenant brothers (Isa. 5:8-10). It is not money but "the love of money" which "is the root of all evil" (I Tim. 6:10).

The idea of wealth has changed from age to age, and the concept of poverty also. Philippe Aries, in *The Hour of Our Death* (Knopf, New York, 1981; $20), notes that, in the Middle Ages, wealth was not seen as the possession of things; rather, it was identified with power over men, whereas poverty was identified with solitude (p. 136). Each concept of wealth creates its own culture, and its own advantages and problems.

Later, wealth was identified with cultivated lands and houses, and the wealthy families of Europe were not necessarily rich in money but in land and in castles or manor houses. Whatever gold or silver they acquired went into furthering their landed wealth. This attitude carried over into Colonial America, and, as rapidly as possible, bullion wealth, gold and silver, which was in excess of current needs, was turned into utensils. Much of Paul Revere's work in silver represented such assets, made for his contemporaries. In times of need, the silver teapots, trays, and other items were simply melted down into bullion for monetary use.

The Industrial Revolution redefined wealth. Capital wealth was less and less land and houses and more and more the means of production. It meant mines, ships, railroads, looms and mills, and the like. The social standard was still the older one, and the new capitalists, as they grew wealthy, bought country estates and married their children to the older families in order to gain status. Wealthy Americans bought English estates in order to feel truly rich! In time, however, the older doctrine of wealth began to decline. Both wealth and power were now industrial in orientation, and the future was defined, not in terms of land and houses, but in terms of industrial production. Thus, Henry Ford hated horses and worked to mechanize farming; he saw man's products as superior and promoted "soybean milk" and synthetic foods (John Cote Dahlinger and Frances Spatz Leighton: *The*

Secret Life of Henry Ford, pp. 170-177. Indianapolis, Indiana: Bobbs-Merrill, 1978; $10.95). As a part of this same temper, for years oleomargarine was promoted as a better and healthier food than butter. At World Fairs, the wonderful world of plastics was presented as a great hope for man and as the new road to cheap wealth for all. Manufactured products as the key to popular wealth, and the means of production as the instrument of great wealth, played an important part in the development of the twentieth century and its technology. Few doctrines of wealth have had a more revolutionary impact on the world.

This new idea of wealth meant a more fluid and liquid conception of riches, and it moved quietly and steadily to another concept, one to which the market investor and speculator, while playing an important part in the development of industrial wealth, contributed greatly. The new wealth was *monetary*. It meant, not simply the ownership of the means of production, but money, millions and even billions of dollars in money. The idea of money as wealth was being separated from the production which created it.

Less and less in the popular imagination was the really rich man the producer and more and more the non-working investor and playboy. Since World War II, we have seen the rapid development of an anti-capitalist mentality. Ludwig von Mises has written with especial effectiveness about the implications of this phenomenon in *The Anti-Capitalist Mentality* (1956). At the same time, an unprecedented number of people have become "investors" in the stock market; large numbers of these new "investors" have a hostility to the free market and demand regulations of industry. They seem to regard the stock exchange as something like Las Vegas and a slot-machine, or, better, like a race track and horse-betting. The idea of money has for many separated itself from the means of production.

The consequences of this have been far-reaching. Wealth has come to mean money, not land, houses, and the means of production. The idea of wealth has become highly liquid, and the new money is equally liquid. It is fiat money, paper money.

A society which separates wealth from the realities of land, houses, and the means of production on the one hand, and the capital of work and thrift on the other, will soon have a money which is inflated, because its idea of wealth is inflated; it has no substance.

At the same time, the doctrine of wealth will shift from a production orientation to a consumer orientation. Service industries begin to predominate over production industries. The social structure stresses wealth while producing less and less of it.

At the same time, a change takes place in the uses of wealth. We have already noted the prevalence of the consumer mentality in an inflationary culture. There is, however, always another use of wealth, for *benevolence*. Men in every age have in varying degrees shared their wealth with others; in particular, this has been a basic aspect of every culture which to any degree has been influenced by Christianity. Philanthropy becomes a major social force.

The care of the poor, the sick, and the hungry was in the Middle Ages the function of Christian foundations. Monasteries provided for a variety of social needs, and, whatever other criticisms were made of the church, a lack of charity was rarely charged or valid.

However, charity, like wealth, can be variously defined and often has radically different motivations. Helmut Schoeck, in *Envy* (1966), has shown that, in many cultures, not only is envy the basis of law but also of charity. To avoid the destructive forces of envy, the men who accumulate riches regularly divest themselves of all that they possess. Because, as Schoeck demonstrates, "the envious man is, by definition, the negation of the basis of any society" (p.26), "charity" in such a society is counter-productive and is socially destructive. Prince Kropotkin in *Mutual Aid* chose to see such "charity" as evidence of a universal moral character in men, and in this he followed Darwin's suggestion in his *Descent of Man*. However, as Schoeck shows, the desire for an equalitarian society comes from envy, not from any noble motive, and, as a result, the private and statist "charity" created by envy is socially ruinous.

In Buddhism, charity has in large measure a contempt for life. A very popular tale among the Buddhist peasantry is that of King Sivi, who gave away his eyes, and Vessantra, who gave away his kingdom, all his possessions, and even his wife and children. Many of the classic tales of Buddhist charity have a strongly suicidal character.

This suicidal motive is an important fact. Whenever and wherever envy becomes a governing force in charitable giving, suicide becomes a ruling factor. In the United States, for example, many heirs to great fortunes are so heavily influenced by the politics of guilt, pity and envy, that their charities had a strongly suicidal element. Such persons seek to absolve themselves of guilt and to escape from envy by becoming advocates of radical politics and instruments of charities designed to allay envy. Such charities do not stifle envy; rather, they feed and justify it.

In this there is a relationship to Hindu charity, which, as A.S. Geden showed, has a religious motive, "the desire to secure personal advantages and reward in the future life" (James Hastings: *Encyclopedia of Religion and Ethics*, III, 388). Not generosity but a desire to escape from Karma and the cycle of reincarnation governs such charity. The goal of society and of charity is thus not community and love but an escape from this world. The rich give to expiate past sins and to improve their karma and their future reincarnations.

The goal in these various forms of non-Biblical charity is thus man-centered. Man seeks by his giving to gain a personal advantage:

deliverance from guilt, social approval, a mitigation of Karmic burdens and an improvement of future lives, and so on.

In other words, many of these charities are past-oriented, and others are death-oriented. In past-oriented charities, the donor is seeking to make atonement for past sins and guilt, by himself or by his parents. The present world is essentially a place wherein atonement is made for the past. The inheritance of wealth is seen as a burden which must be expiated and justified by a course of guilt-governed charitable giving. Much of modern humanistic giving has such a motive. Great fortunes lead to great foundations whose function is to rehabilitate a bad conscience or a "bad name." The giving of such foundations is thus essentially on a false basis.

Other charities are death-oriented. There is a link between wealth and death; the old saying has it that "you can't take it with you," but death-oriented giving seeks to evade the force of that fact. Death-oriented charities seek to build up points for the after-life, either by their effect on the after-life, or by their effect on one's name and reputation here on earth. In many cases, charities and foundations are both past-oriented and death-oriented.

Biblical wealth and charity have as their focus the Kingdom of God and His righteousness (Matt. 6:33). Both acquisition and dispersion are governed by God's law and justice. Their function is to capitalize the present and the future under God and to further covenant life. When a man gives to justify or to atone for his wealth, his giving is self-serving and counter-productive. When he acquires wealth and gives of it in terms of God's calling and Kingdom, his activity furthers community. He then functions as a member of a covenant community, and his relationship to all who are outside the covenant is one of justice and mercy.

In such a perspective, wealth is not seen as power over men, nor as lands and houses (however desirable), nor as the means of production, and certainly not as fiat money. What a man has is the blessing of the Lord, and to be used in terms of God's law-word. All that we are and have is of the providence of God and to be used in terms of His calling, justice, and law. St. Paul states the matter simply and bluntly: "For who maketh thee to differ from another? and what hast thou that thou didst not receive? now if thou didst receive it, why dost thou glory, as if thou hadst not received it?" (I Cor. 4:7).

The wealth we have received from God may be material or intellectual; it can be money, lands, graces, aptitudes, and callings. This wealth can be accompanied by money or come without it. In any and in every case, we all have a common obligation to use it to God's glory and purpose. "The blessing of the LORD, it maketh rich, and he added no sorrow with it" (Proverbs 10:22). Note that it is not money nor land that makes us rich in the Biblical sense but "the blessing of the LORD." We cannot have that blessing or richness if we see only money as wealth, nor if we are eaten by envy. What we have, we must give. Our Lord is emphatic on this: "freely ye have received, freely give" (Matt. 10:8). If not, we are very poor indeed, poor in our very being. Rich man or poor man, which are you? (November, 1981)

WEALTH AND HEIRSHIP
Chalcedon Position Paper No. 27

One of the most powerful, corrosive, and destructive forces in all of history is very much at work today in all the world: envy. Envy is, in terms of Biblical faith, very clearly a sin, but, in the modern age, it comes disguised as a virtue. The motive force in much of the equalitarianism of our day is not a sense of brotherhood but an envy which seeks to level all things. Envy also masks itself as a concern, very commonly, for social justice, and it lays claims to saintly character while promoting hatred, revolution and murder.

Envy wars against status, but every revolution in the modern age has promoted a new elitism and established a social order more static, fixed, and class-conscious than those orders it displaces. Envy claims to promote equality, justice, and democracy, while in practice working to destroy all three of these things. Envy capitalizes on issues, not on principles. The world being a sinful and fallen order, the best of societies have glaring defects in need of correction, but envy capitalizes on these defects while avoiding principles. Envy does not correct: it destroys.

Because envy is sin, it wars against virtue and character. While capitalizing on the weaknesses of, let us say, the middle class, the doctors, technicians, press, clergy, and so on, it seeks in reality to suppress and destroy their character and strength. It says in effect, let none be better than myself. (Some years ago, as a young man, I saw in a particular church an evil family champion a pastor of bad character. In one incident, I learned that they liked him for his sins, because it "justified" them, whereas every godly man was slandered and resented by them.) The unwritten law in the hearts of envious men is, Let no man be better than myself.

Because envy is evil, it resents the good and is hence very destructive socially. It reduces church, state, and society to the lowest common denominator. Aristides the Just (C. 468 B.C.), an Athenian statesman and general was ostracized from the city in part because many people were resentful of hearing him called "the Just." Then and now, many people prefer a corrupt politician to a good and honest man: They resent excellence and superiority.

The role of envy in many spheres and with respect to many things could be cited at length, but our concern now is with a key area for envy: wealth and heirship. It is commonly said that we live in a very materialistic age; Pitrim Sorokin called it also a sensate culture. The lust for wealth, or at least the appearance of wealth, is commonplace. A variety of things, such as furniture, automobiles, and clothing, sell less for their durability and more for their utility in creating the proper image, the image of careless and assumed wealth.

Together with this lust for material and monetary wealth goes a resentment for the wealthy. The tacit premise is that, Let no man be wealthy if we cannot all be wealthy. Hence, the revolutionary urge is to destroy wealth and then try to recreate it for all, an illusory hope. The result instead is a wealthy group of social planners who will not allow any man to transcend their control or status.

At the same time, there is an intense envy and resentment of heirs. How dare anyone inherit wealth! Over the years, from professors, students, and a wide range of peoples, I have heard expressed a radical hostility to heirship. Our estate and inheritance taxes witness to this hatred, and today this uncontrolled envy of heirs has made the robbing of widows and orphans a matter of state policy. The estate of the father may be a limited one and of consequence only because of inflation, but envy strikes increasingly lower and lower, from the upper class to the middle class, and now increasingly lower on the economic scale. The income tax is similarly a consequence of envy.

Many churchmen are very much a part of this world of envy, and they promote it as gospel. The word "rich" (by which they mean richer than I) is for many the ultimate insult. Our Chalcedon mailing list friends report some examples of this. One clergyman said that it was immoral for any man to have an income in excess of $20,000 a year; another, several hundred miles away, said that an annual income of over $40,000 was unchristian and a sin. (It takes little imagination to guess what their own salaries were!)

If a goodly income is a sin, how much more so an inheritance in the eyes of these men! An heir receives money he has not earned, we are told, and therefore does not deserve. Such money should be taken from heirs and given to "the needy." In practice, taking money from the rich means giving it to an even richer state, not to the needy. Moreover, if failure to earn the money is the heir's problem, then why is it proper to give this money either to the state or to the needy, neither of whom have earned it? We have, in all envy and its social programs, a double standard.

There is one point, and a necessary point, which we must grant, and, in fact, we must insist on granting: the heir's money is unearned. This is a crucial point theologically, as we shall see. However, before proceeding to that fact, let us stop briefly to stress an important distinction. There is a very great difference between unearned wealth and unjustly gained wealth. My father left me no money, being a poor pastor, but he left me some books, (a very important form of wealth for me). I have a personal library of 25-30,000 books, many of which I inherited from my father, and from two other pastors, (and many of which I bought). I did not earn many of those books, (although many I did). Am I unjustly the owner of the unearned books? They were given to me as acts of love and grace, and I am happily and gratefully their present possessor. My books are a form of wealth for me, and they have been so also for friends and associates who have used them in their research. Only if I were to have some stolen books in my library would these be an illegitimate form of wealth. The distinction between legitimate and illegitimate wealth must not be obscured.

Now we are ready to deal with the key question, the unearned nature of wealth which is inherited. The modern world, being anti-Christian, is very hostile to heirship, whereas the Christian must regard it as central to his faith. There are far-reaching theological implications here. Very centrally, the doctrine of grace is involved.

The language of "rights" is basic to our humanistic age, which at the same time is the most murderous era in all history, very often in the name of the rights of man. Modern man assumes that he has a right to many things, and, with each decade, the catalogue of rights is increased, as is the scale of oppression and totalitarianism in the name of rights.

Theologically, however, man has no rights as he stands before God. All that he has is of grace, sovereign grace. Both man and his world are the creation of the triune God. No man is born into an empty world; we are all born heirs of our history, and we inherit the riches and the devastations of our forbears. We are what we are by the grace and the providence of God. St. Paul, in a key verse, struck at the pretensions of man, saying, "For who maketh thee to differ from another? and what hast thou that thou didst not receive? now if thou didst receive it, why dost thou glory, as if thou hadst not received it?" (I Cor. 4:7).

St. Peter says that life itself is a grace, a gift of God (I Peter 3:7). We are not the authors of life, nor the determiners of the conditions thereof. Life is a grace, a gift from God, and, for better or worse, we are all heirs. Our inheritance is often a marred one because of sin, but, all the same, we are heirs, redeemed or unredeemed. If we fail to recognize God's grace and purpose, or bow before His sovereignty, we are judged and disinherited.

But, if we are the redeemed, we are heirs of the Kingdom of God, confirmed heirs, heirs together with Christ, we are repeatedly told (Rom. 8:17; Gal. 3:29, 4:7; Eph. 3:6; Heb. 6:7; James 2:5, etc.).

The Bible requires that we recognize the fact of grace and heirship. They are essential to the doctrine of salvation, and also to the Biblical way of life. What we are, we have received, and we are not our own (I Cor. 6:19). "Therefore let no man glory in men" (I Cor. 3:21) for any reason, neither in other men nor especially in ourselves. We are not only created by the Lord but also bought back and redeemed at the price of Christ's blood (I Cor. 6:20).

The envious man of today refuses to see all this. The world is a product of chance, and, in that realm of chance, man has struggled, fought, survived, and advanced himself. He has come so far that he can now self-consciously control and direct his future evolution. We have here the most radical doctrine of works in all history. The works involved are "red in tooth and claw." And man evolves by destroying lesser forms, including the abortion of unwanted and also potentially defective unborn babies, he believes.

This envious humanistic man feels justified also in striking at the born, heirs especially, in order to further his concept of social advance and justice. Because he is at war with God, this humanistic man rejects radically the idea of grace and heirship in any and every realm, from the theological to the societal. He does more than reject it: he wars against it, and it is a total war.

Some scholars write as though Social Darwinism were a thing of the past. Their works are simply a fraud. What has passed away is the Social Darwinism of the men of Carnegie's day and class, i.e., the Social Darwinism of the powerful and largely non-Christian or anti-Christian industrialists who believed in the manipulation of the state for their purposes. In their place, we have the Social Darwinism of socialism and modern democracies, a disguised form thereof but real all the same. Behind the facade of benevolence, the modern state applies a legal guillotine to all whom it deems unfit to serve.

In such a situation, more than ever, it is imperative for Christians to revive the Biblical doctrines of grace and heirship. In a world of grace, we are all heirs: we have received unearned wealth without any work or works on our part. Heirship imposes upon us a major task of stewardship. The whole of the law gives us the pattern of stewardship for the heirs of grace. Our Lord sums it all up in six words: "freely ye have received, freely give" (Matt. 10:8).

This commandment was given to the disciples, and to us. It applies to all, whether rich or poor according to man's reckoning. We are all too prone today to assume that the duty to give freely or generously belongs to the rich, and the rest of us have the duty of receiving! It is, in fact, basic to envy that it demands that the envied give and the envier either receive or determine the disposition of that which is given. We have seen a great variety of peoples see themselves as the necessary recipients. The various minority groups believe that they have a right to gifts. So too do the elderly, and, along with the state school personnel, they constitute our most powerful lobby. Of course, industry, agriculture, and labor all seek subsidies or gifts. Envy leads to the world of coercion.

The Bible, however, says that all men begin with the grace of life. The redeemed are doubly the recipients of grace, and they are the heirs-designate of all things in Christ. They have received freely, and they must give freely.

The Christian position is thus founded on heirship and grace. We must recognize that we have received freely and that the Lord requires us to work for the reconstruction of all things in terms of God's law-word. This reconstruction requires that we give our lives, time, thought, effort, and money to that end. When James speaks of us as heirs (James 2:5), and as joint heirs with Christ the King, princes of grace, he summons us to fulfill or keep the royal law, "Thou shalt love thy neighbor as thyself" (James 2:8).

We are told, "thou shalt remember the LORD thy God: for it is he that giveth thee power to get wealth" (Deut. 8:18). We are told, "Thou shalt open thine hand wide unto thy brother, to thy poor, and to thy needy, in thy land" (Deut. 15:11).

Envy is divisive and destructive. It creates a world of conflict and hatred. Hatred of the rich is as much a sin as hatred of the poor. When we are commanded by God to love our neighbor, no qualifications are made exempting us from loving him if he is rich or poor, black or white. We are to fulfill, i.e., keep the law in relation to him by respecting the sanctity of his marriage, life, property, and reputation, in word, thought, and deed (Rom. 13:8-10), and to see him as our God-given neighbor.

Some neighbors will indeed be problems, of that there is no question! However, we must remember that in this world of grace and heirship, among the things we often inherit are problems. We have them because God intended them, not for us to complain about but to meet in His grace and by His law-word. We must face them in the confidence of Romans 8:28, that indeed all things do work together for good to them who love God and are the called according to His purpose. But to be called of God means that we are fulfilling His calling.

If all is of grace, there is no place for envy. We are heirs by the adoption of grace in order that we might give of that which we have received in order to be faithful citizens and members of the Kingdom of God.

Let us leave the world of envy for the wealth of grace and heirship.
(December, 1981)

WEALTH AND THE CITY
Chalcedon Position Paper No. 28

The word *society* comes from *socius*, an associate. A society is a family group in some sense, a community of people who feel some kinship. Historically, the binding tie in a society is a common faith, and obedience to the law of that faith. All who deny that faith and law have been in the past called *outlaws*.

The locale of a society has historically been a city, not the city as a civil structure but the city as a faith center. In the ancient world, in the "middle ages," in the Puritan village, and elsewhere, the center of the city has been the temple, cathedral, or church.

The city as the faith-center for an area has thus also been the wealth-center. A people's life, wealth, and faith are closely linked. As our Lord says, "Where your treasure is, there will your heart be also" (Matt. 6:21). If a people's treasure is their faith and in society in faith, then their hearts and their material wealth will be there also, in the same locale.

For ages, that center of faith, society, and wealth was also walled, to protect the concentration of treasures in the forms of faith, lives, society, and material wealth. The walled city was thus a symbol of a common faith and life, and also of security. (When the Huguenots lost their walled cities, it was the beginning of the end for them.) At the same time, the walled city became a target for every enemy, and every thief. The strength and wealth of the city attracted the attention of the lawless.

Faith, wealth, family, land, and the city have often been associated as means of strength and security. Thus, Proverbs 10:15 reads, "The rich man's wealth is his strong city: the destruction of the poor is their poverty." As R. V. Whybray, in *The Book of Proverbs*, noted, "wealth protects a man from misfortune just as a strongly fortified capital protects a king from his enemies." On the other hand, Proverbs 18:10-11 tells us that there are two different ways to obtain security in life: to trust in God, or to trust in wealth. The separation of wealth from faith is the destruction of man and finally of wealth. The same is true of the walled city: "except the LORD keep the city, the watchman waketh but in vain" (Ps. 127:1). Apart from the LORD and faith in Him, the city can be a death trap, and the country-side too.

A city gives men proximity one to another, but without the moral bond of a common faith, the city and its government become aliens and then oppressors of the people. In the ancient city, citizens were all who partook of the lustrations or whatever other rite of atonement they adhered to. In other words, atonement made the city and the citizen. Hence, to attempt to change faiths (and atonements) was an act of revolution. The new faith had to be either incorporated with the current one, or destroyed. Hence the persecution of the early church. Its Lord was not Caesar but Jesus Christ, and its atonement was not from the civil religion but the cross.

Modern man has worked self-consciously to throw off the shackles of the past, most notably to discard Biblical faith and all its restraints. The modern city is to be the work of man. No less than the builders of the Tower of Babel sought to build a social order without God, the builders of the modern city, and the modern state, have sought a non-theistic order. The modern state and the modern city united to assert a neutrality and an autonomy from God. Neutrality commended itself as a restraint upon the clamor of various churches to be established. Under the merits of anti-establishmentarianism, a separation from Christianity was effected. This supposed neutrality with respect to the claims of all religions served to mask an allegiance to another religion, humanism, which is the new established religion of states, courts, and state schools of the modern age.

At the same time, the claim to autonomy was advanced. The city and the state are supposedly independent of God; they constitute a free zone where God's power and law do not extend, and where man as man is his own god and law. The autonomous city sees itself as the free city, free to plan and chart its course in terms of purely humanistic considerations. The modern city was determined to be the City of Man, not the City of God.

A fundamental assumption of this new faith has been at worst the moral neutrality of man, or at best the goodness of man. All the centuries of slow and painstaking work to civilize the barbarian peoples by means of faith, and to order their lives by means of God's law, were viewed as a great aberration. Man will be most good when most natural, it was declared. As against the redeemed, twice-born man, the once-born man was championed. As against supernatural man, natural man was seen as the hope of the world.

Men like Horace Mann were enthusiastic about the prospects of mankind. The natural man, re-educated out of the superstitions of the past, would produce a crime-free, poverty-free world in which man would be his own lord. Disagreements were prevalent in the 19th and early 20th centuries as to the best means to this golden age of man. Some believed revolution and massive destruction were needed; others advocated democracy and mass education as the way to the great City of Man, the Great Community of John Dewey and others.

But a problem arose, however unacknowledged. Whether in the U.S. or the U.S.S.R., Europe, Asia, Africa, the Americas, or elsewhere, man remained, not what the ideologists and theoreticians said he was, but what God says man is, a sinner.

The new City of Man was to be a product of humanistic education, the new technology, and autonomous wealth. Humanistic education has produced a new barbarian, and mass illiteracy. The liberal Jonathan Kozol, in *Prisoners of Silence* (1980), cites federal data which reveals that 54 to 64 million Americans are not truly literate, and of these 23 million are illiterate. Natural man, moreover, was not only now increasingly illiterate but also immoral and lawless. The city was becoming a dangerous place, and more and more parents feared their own children. In perhaps the safest of America's very largest cities, over 60,000 homes were robbed in 1981. The city was now breeding its own destruction.

Wealth without faith was proving to be wealth without principles, immoral and arrogant, even as the poor had also become, and a derelict middle class as well. Technology has indeed been creating marvels, but the people who dwell among them, and use them, are increasingly like marauding barbarians in an ancient city. Neither technology nor the bobby pin have served to make man one whit a better man in any moral sense.

The new humanistic man is a parasite. Whether farmer, manufacturer, worker, or unemployed, he wants subsidies. The modern city is a subsidy center. The earlier mercantilism worked to create the humanistic, producing, urban center by means of protectionism and tariffs. A new kind of wall surrounds the city. The ancient city was walled against thieves and enemies. The modern city is walled against competition and the free market.

The United States, in its earliest years, faced a choice here. It could become the great supplier to the world of food, minerals, and other resources. It chose, however, to follow the very European pattern it had in part fought against, protectionism aimed at subsidizing industry and the city. Given the virtues of industry and commerce, protectionism all the same perverts them and renders them a source of continuing problems. Thomas Jefferson protested against these policies until he became president, whereupon he and his followers became Federalists and protectionists. The protectionism became a major contributing cause of the conflict between the North and the South, and of war in 1860.

Protectionism and subsidies do not stop. It was a natural development of this premise that led, step by step, to welfarism, to medicare, to cradle-to-grave subsidies for all. How dare one class complain about subsidies to another class when all are increasingly becoming beneficiaries?

Thus, we have the grand climax of the modern age. Having destroyed the city as a faith center, it has converted the city into a welfare center. It is routine now for our major cities to have a welfare population of a million or more. These are simply the recipients of actual welfare checks. Others receive subsidies, and some are heavily penalized to provide subsidies to others. The subsidy-program now extends into all the world in terms of foreign aid to nations. It includes subsidies to foreign industries by restraints upon U.S. producers (i.e., in oil, cattle, etc.) which handicap them. The faith-city has been supplanted by the welfare city, a lawless and selfish place.

The result is a debauchery of men and money. Protectionism must be paid for, and it is paid for by deficit financing, mortgaging the future to pay for the present. Inflation and debt are basic to the modern city. (If only the debt-free buildings and homes were to remain in our big cities, and all others suddenly disappeared, our cities would suddenly become small towns.)

Men too are debauched. Helmut Thielicke, in *Nihilism* (1961), wrote on the fact that atheistic states always become totalitarian. The premise of atheism is that "without God, everything is lawful," and men then act on this, and no man can trust another. The state becomes a police state, because the people can only be held in check by stronger and stronger controls, and by terror. (Also, the state begins to play god.) Law then becomes what the state says it is, and the result is the breakdown of law, because it has no roots in the nature of being. The city then begins to resemble a nightmare.

Past history gives us many examples of the sacking of cities by invaders. One of the worst instances was the sack of Rome by the armies of Spain. These sacks were prompted by war and by enmity. Now we have a different kind of sacking, one by the people of the city, the poor, minority groups, youths, and college and university students. The second half of the 20th century has seen more cities sacked than centuries before. The modern city is indeed a wealth center, but it is not a society, and it is being sacked by its own children.

When Rome was first sacked by the barbarians, many people, when the hordes passed, went back to life as usual. The rich villas of southern Gaul continued to be the locale of gay parties, music, poetry, and fox hunts by the wealthy, literate, and cultured old Romans, but, little by little, their lights went out, only to be relit out of the ruins and among the barbarians by Christianity.

What had happened was that the City of Rome, the wealth-center, had become the poverty-center. This was physically true in that welfare mobs ruled the city, to the point that emperors found it much more expedient to live elsewhere. For Roman emperors, Rome had become an unsafe place, a place of assassinations, riots, and unruly mobs.

Well before that, however, Rome had become, morally and religiously, a poverty-center. The old Roman faith and virtue had given way to degeneracy and perversion. In time, as Rome's intangible wealth began to disappear, so too its tangible wealth followed and waned.

The wealth of a city begins and ends with its faith. If the city is not a faith-center, it will cease to be a society and will become a conflict and poverty center.

One key form of wealth which has left the modern city is justice and vengeance, godly vengeance. One of the key facts of Scripture is God's declaration, "To me belongeth vengeance, and recompense" (Deut. 32:35; Ps. 99:8; Isa. 34:8; Jer. 50:15; Ezek. 24:25; Nahum 1:2; 1 Thess. 1:8; Ps. 94:1; etc.). We are commanded not to avenge ourselves, for "Vengeance is mine: I will repay, saith the Lord" (Rom. 12:19).

The Greek text of the New Testament is as clear as to the meaning of vengeance as the church is confused. The word is *ekdikesis*, very literally (that which proceeds) out of justice. When God says that vengeance belongs to Him, He is very plainly declaring that only His law is justice, and no other law can be used to attain justice. When He forbids us to avenge ourselves, God is saying that we can have no law nor justice other than His own, and through His appointed means. This is the plain meaning of the statement in Scripture.

Clearly, justice is gone out of the city, the state, the church, and man. Humanistic doctrines of justice and the enforcement of justice prevail, because the city is not a faith-center, nor a justice center as Biblical faith requires it to be, but a man-center.

For a city to be a faith-center means that it must be a justice-center. Justice is a key form of wealth. (One Hebrew word for wealth is a *good thing.*) The modern city is thus an impoverished place and a poverty-center in every sense of the word. Not until the pulpits of the word of God again become central to a city, and the Bible its word of justice and vengeance or that which proceeds out of justice, will the city again be a center of true wealth.

That restoration is under way, slowly but surely. The humanistic city still has its worst days ahead probably. However, out of its decay, the City of God will emerge. We are beginning to see the stirrings of a strong faith, among minority and majority groups alike. We are seeing the rise of Christian Schools and agencies, manifesting a renewed literacy, and a greater Christian compassion than we have seen for years. We are witnessing on all sides the growth of Christian reconstruction, and the applications of God's law-word to every area of life and thought.

We live in an exciting era. True, it is a time of conflict and of stress, a bloody and murderous age. An old "order," humanism, is in decay, and its strongholds are crumbling and collapsing. It is a time for building in the certainty of our Lord's triumph. "Therefore, my beloved brethren, be ye steadfast, unmovable, always abounding in the work of the Lord, forasmuch as ye know that your labour is not in vain in the Lord" (I Cor. 15:58). (January, 1982)

WEALTH, TIME, and HISTORY
Chalcedon Position Paper No. 29

Theft is a crime which increasingly creates a general uneasiness among people. Its prevalence is frightening to many. One woman, a political liberal, reacted emotionally to the sight of a burglarized home on her return: "I felt personally violated." This is a very common reaction. The privacy and safety of a home once broken leaves a psychic uneasiness and fear. Theft is all too common a fact of life in our time.

This uneasiness has had dramatic consequences in many directions. One of these is in city life. Until recently, the elite lived at the center of the city. Around the central plaza were clustered the main church, court or palace, and the great homes of the rich and powerful families. The central city was the place of freedom and security. The poor lived in the outskirts or suburb of the city. Look at almost any city and the evidences of the closeness of the great homes to the center is in evidence, except that now those great homes are either offices or slum dwellings. Taxes and lawlessness have robbed the city of its ancient character.

Theft, however, is not of material goods alone. It can involve a theft of time and history. As bad as the rise of common criminality has been, the theft of time and history has been far greater, and much more devastating. It began with the philosophers and historians, and it was put into harsh practice by statist educators.

Edward Gibbon (1737-1794) is a landmark figure in this development. His *History of the Decline and Fall of the Roman Empire* (1776-1788), reflected the spirit of the French *philosophies*, and he regarded them as his teachers. The *philosophies* mocked Christianity and regarded the past as a long night out of which reason had delivered them. They laid down a fundamental premise of modern thought which has ever since distorted historiography. Everything in the past must be viewed with cynicism, and every evil in the past must be magnified, made to be a product of Christianity, Christianity must be equated with superstition, and reason and modernity exalted. As a result, today, if anything in the past is exalted, it is usually because it was hostile to Christianity. Voltaire is an example of this. As a writer and thinker, he was of little consequence and usually dishonest in his presentation of facts. This, however, is precisely why Voltaire is seen as important: he was a successful enemy of Christianity.

Gibbon took this premise of the *philosophies* and applied it rigorously to history. He venerated Roman antiquity only to denigrate Christianity. The importance of Gibbon and his work is that he worked seriously, and methodically (unlike the French *philosophies*), to reconstruct history and the past in radically non-Christian terms. Man was now to be explained and understood in terms of man only, not God. The stage was set for a "scientific" view of man in purely naturalistic terms, as supplied about 75 years later by Darwin.

Gibbon was still very much a product of a Christian past. He viewed history moralistically, in terms of good and evil. A humanistic moralism was the result, leading to the 19th century liberal fervor to right all wrongs. The new temper also led to a new joy in discovery, the discovery of non-Christian pasts. All over the world, funds, energy and zeal were poured into archaeological and other research into the pagan past. Egypt, India, China, and the Americas saw intense research into a past "innocent" of Christianity and the Biblical God. The 19th century saw the monumental research and publication of such literature as the "sacred" books of the East.

Humanism, however, continued its logical development. Max Stirner very early saw that all morality, all ideas of good and evil, represented a hang-over from a Biblical past. Nietzsche called for life beyond good and evil, and, in the 1970s, Walter Kaufmann logically attacked the ideas of guilt and justice as relics of the Bible and called the tempter's premise of Genesis 3:1-5 the true basis for human life.

Historians reflected the same development. They began to speak of the meaninglessness of history. Providential history was not even a possible option for them. The world or universe had arisen out of a meaningless nothingness; it had no purpose nor direction, and its destiny is universal death. Such men found a Christian declaration of total meaning a particularly offensive fact. (At one collegiate conference, a professor from a major university graduate school was deeply offended and horrified because in my address, I spoke of the total rationality of creation and history, because it is the handiwork of the totally rational God. He held that the universe had in it only a thin and temporary edge of rationality in the mind of man.)

Thus, for modern man, because the world and the past are meaningless, so too are the present and the future. This attitude has infiltrated the modern mind through the state school's social studies program and its radical relativism.

The result is the great theft, the grand heist, of all history: modern man finds life robbed of meaning. Instead of a universe created, governed, and filled by the triune God, and peopled with God's heavenly hosts and guardian angels, it is an empty world. No robbed householder, returning to find his home stripped of its valuables, finds a more empty dwelling than modern man. By the time he finishes his schooling, the world is for him an empty room. Even in a crowded place, he is surrounded, not by men and women created in the image of God and under His government, but empty faces and empty minds. Life is full of sound and fury, signifying nothing.

Modern man thus, although he has inherited a great technological history and development, is very poor. He has no meaningful and purposive history. The uneasiness felt by people whose house has been robbed is an example of the disquiet modern man feels as he views life, time, and history. It is the feeling which once marked the dying of Greece and of Rome, and it expressed itself in the old proverb, Let us eat and drink, for tomorrow we die.

The Christian today is commonly infected by this same temper. The spirit of the age has a widespread contamination. The contemporary Christian may believe in God, and in the Bible from cover to cover, but the Lord seems far away, the communists and the I.R.S. very near, and what is a man to do? The real presence of the Lord is not very meaningful to him; it is the real presence of the devil which seems to be most important to all too many Christians.

Early in this century, Hollbrook Jackson, in *The Eighteen Nineties* (1913), ably characterized the new spirit. The whole attitude of the new decadence he saw contained in Ernest Dowson's famous poem on Cynara. He called it "that insatiate demand of a soul surfeited with the food that nourishes not, and finding what relief it can in a rapture of desolation." In the same era, Oscar Wilde expressed the modern will to perversity in his life and in his epigrams. One such epigram is very revealing: "I don't like novels that end happily. They depress me so much." And why not? If life has no happy endings because it is meaningless, why should a novel have one? In my student days, a professor took some time to rail against happy endings as unrealistic and not true to life; his own life manifested a wilful destruction of every possibility of happiness.

We see the consequences in modern literature. It is a long war against meaning, an assault on morality as a myth, and a declaration of war against all who hold to Biblical faith. Modern literature manifests a hatred of progress and industry, of patriotism, fidelity, and love as against sexuality. The new frontier for literature was now the moral underground and underground man. In 1871, Edward Goncourt manifested the new temper in his comment: "The riff-raff have for me the particular attraction of races unknown and undiscovered, something of that exotic quality which travellers seek in far-off lands at the cost of many hardships." Other men were still excited by ancient Troy, Egypt, India, and China, but the artist and the writer now had a new world to explore, the world of the underground. Hence, for Jean-Paul Sartre, Jean Genet became Saint Genet. Norman Mailer lionized a convict, secured his release, and the result was a killing. The moral underground has become holy ground to modern writers, and the only thing that stirs their wrath is Biblical faith and morality.

The empty world was made even more empty by the poets and writers who began to insist that meaning was anathema to a work of art. Symbolism began to be popular, greatly reinforced by Freudianism and the doctrine of the unconscious. Rational and coherent meaning had to give way to vague expressions of underground impulses and intentions. Not only was the world emptied, but now the mind also! Mallarme's Herodias said, "I await a thing unknown," an expressive line, because modern man continually awaits the unknown, never the sure hand of God. Arthur Rimbaud, in a letter to Paul Demeny, May 15, 1871, wrote, "The poet makes himself a seer by a long, intensive, and reasoned disordering of all the senses." The goal of much literature since has been to produce the same disordering in all of us.

The result of all this has been the impoverishing of man. Man's greatest and surest wealth lies in the religious realm, in the meaning which Biblical faith provides. The Bible tells man that the world witnesses to the glory of God (Ps. 19). The rainbow is a reminder to men who will see it that God will preserve this world and finally renew it into an eternal glory. The rainbow signifies God's providential peace towards the very inanimate creation.

The Sabbath requires rest one day in seven, and one year in seven. It is a sign that the future essentially rests, not on man's shoulders, but on God's government and grace. Thus, man's future is not man-made but either God-blessed or God-cursed; in either case, the handiwork of God. The Sabbath thus calls on man to leave the government on God's shoulders and to recognize that the Lord governs and rules man's own life better than man can ever dream of doing. God's signs tell us that God the Lord is closer to us than we are to ourselves. We are not alone, nor in an empty universe. Francis Thompson (1859-1907), in his wonderful poem, "The Kingdom of God, In No Strange Land," expressed this beautifully. In the second stanza, he wrote:

Does the fish soar to find the ocean,
The eagle plunge to find the air--
That we ask of the stars in motion
If they have rumor of Thee there?

The poverty of modern man is thus very great. He lives in a dead and empty world, he believes, but the deadness and the emptiness are in his own soul.

The Psalmist tells us, concerning Israel in the wilderness, that "They soon forgat His (God's) works: they waited not for His counsel: but lusted exceedingly in the wilderness, and tempted God in the desert. And He gave them their request: but sent leanness into their souls" (Ps. 106:13-15).

Leanness is very much in the souls of modern men, however fat their bodies. But now, inexorably, the consequences of their apostasy are beginning to come home to them. The economics of humanism lead always to disaster. Fiat money is sooner or later no money at all, and the inflation created wealth deflates into disaster. The economic chickens are coming home to roost with a vengeance. We will see more inflation, and more dislocation as well. Today, more and more Americans are unable to buy either houses or cars, because the price is too high. The humanists are trying to solve the problem with more inflation, which will only increase the gap between affordability and purchase price. This gap will set in, not only with respect to automobiles and houses, but other things as well. As a consequence of this gap, one segment of the economy after another will cease to be affordable to more people, and unemployment will increase.

The emptiness which humanism has brought to time and history will become an emptiness in the pocketbook and at the dinner table.

Modern man is singularly unprepared for trouble. He has too meager a reserve of inner strength to cope with problems. On top of that, he is at every turn harried by his new god, the state. When the state fails him, as it most certainly shall, and his money fails him also and becomes very cheap paper, the poverty of modern man will be very great, and it will be an evil poverty. The treasures of humanism are corruptible ones, and they are now steadily appearing for what they are. We are summoned to do otherwise: "Lay up for yourselves treasures in heaven, where neither moth nor rust doth corrupt, and where thieves do not break through nor steal: For where your treasure is, there will your heart be also" (Matt. 6:20-21). Our greatest and surest treasure is God the Lord, His grace and government. We are not alone. We are the people of the King of Kings, and Lord of Lords (Rev. 19:16). We have been called to victory, knowing that "whatsoever is born of God overcometh the world, even our faith" (I John 5:4).

God's victory requires the destruction of the present world order, and He will destroy it. God laughs at the plans and conspirings of His enemies: "the LORD shall have them in derision" (Ps. 2:4). His victory is sure and inevitable, and His presence and government fills all heaven and earth and transcends all things. (February, 1982)

WEALTH AND THE STATE
Chalcedon Position Paper No. 30

A key aspect of idolatry is that an often otherwise legitimate aspect of this world is made absolute. Very commonly, the state, which has a very limited but lawful status under God is made into an idol and becomes, in Hegel's terms, God walking on earth. This is idolatry. However, it is equally false to see the state as absolute evil and the source of sin. It is the heart of man which is the source of sin, and the state reflects our sins and our envious desires.

The same is true of wealth. It is not in and of itself good nor is it evil. It is man who makes wealth either a good or an evil. Wealth can be a blessing from God, and a means whereby we can bless others, or it can be a witness to our lust for power and a curse to others. Private wealth can capitalize a society, as it has in Christendom, or it can decapitalize a society, as in old India, where the vast wealth of the rajahs served only their pleasures.

Attempts therefore to think of wealth in isolation from God and His purposes lead us readily into idolatry. Wealth is made into an ultimate good or an ultimate evil, and the latter is becoming all too common in our day. For some churchmen, the ultimate evil is to be rich, especially a rich Christian in a hungry world. Some pastors actually declare that it is a sin for any man to be paid more than $20,000 a year, or, as another holds, more then $40,000 a year, which may be his way of saying it is a sin to make more than I do!

Wealth, like all things else, must be understood in terms of God's purposes. Any consideration apart from that is not faithful to Scripture. Again and again, the Bible speaks of God's concern for the poor, and we are told that the poor man is our brother, but it would be absurd to conclude that poverty is seen as a happy goal for man! Rather, we are told, if God's people are faithful to His law, "there shall be no poor among you: for the LORD shall greatly bless thee in the land which the LORD thy God giveth thee for an inheritance to possess it: Only if thou carefully harken unto the voice of the LORD thy God, to observe to do all these commandments which I command thee this day" (Deut. 15:4-5). God thus designates the abolition of poverty as the goal of His law-word. To avoid the force of Deut. 15:4-5, all too many will cite Matthew 26:11, "For ye have the poor always with you; but me ye have not always." All this means is that the Lord told the disciples that, during their lifetime, they would always have opportunities to minister to the poor, but not to His physical person and presence.

Over and over again, the Bible stresses the fact that the godly seed must inherit the wealth, and that God's purpose in time is that all the world's wealth pour into the Kingdom of God: "ye shall eat the riches of the Gentiles, and in their glory shall ye boast yourselves" (Isa. 61:6). God's purpose is that wealth capitalize the godly, and through them, His Kingdom. This capitalization of the Kingdom of God means conversion, knowledge, technology, and godly progress in every area of life and thought.

The modern world, however, is deeply committed to decapitalization because of the reign of envy. Envy says, if I cannot be rich, let no other man be rich. Modern politics and economics is governed by envy, and envy cloaks itself in the name of the welfare of the poor.

The world is now seeing the economic consequences of decapitalization. Through taxation and inflation, men's assets have been watered down and decapitalized. We hear much talk about the wealth of the "big" corporations, and too little about their precarious existence. Martin D. Weiss, in *The Great Money Panic* (1981), points out that in 1973 General Motors and its subsidiaries had an interest cost of 36 cents of every dollar of net profits. In 1979, interest costs were 93 cents of every dollar of net profit. The cost of borrowed money was almost equal to the money earned. The situation since has grown worse. In varying degrees all of the 500 major corporations in the United States save one are in the same predicament. Probably the largest of all American corporations is General Motors. How "big" is it? The press, the university, the pulpit, and the media promote the idea of gigantism, as though our major corporations are rivals in size and wealth to the United States. However, as Michael Novak, in *Toward a Theology of the Corporation* (1981), has pointed out, "Running a multinational corporation in the *Fortune 500* is, in most instances, about equivalent to running a major university." The smallest of the 500 has only 529 employees; the largest, General Motors, has no more than 14,000 employees in Michigan; add to this its over 200 units in over 177 congressional districts, and General Motors still does not equal in size and wealth the University of California. The problem with the corporations has not been their size and power but their cowardice in the face of federal power and their too frequent compliance.

The corporations have been decapitalized by controls, taxation, and inflation, and the people also. As long as inflation and fiat money continue, this decapitalization will continue. Each succeeding presidency has furthered this decapitalization in the name of remedying it. To rob the people, every political scoundrel pleads a great concern for the poor and the needy while never giving to any need out of their own often considerable wealth.

The central guilt, however, belongs to the church. There is scarcely a seminary where liberation theology, a sentimental form of Marxism, is not taught. Catholic and Protestant seminaries and missionary agencies are too often cesspools of liberation theology.

The pulpit too is radically delinquent. Where do we hear sermons on

Matthew 23:14, "Woe unto you, Scribes and Pharisees, hypocrites! for ye devour widows' houses, and for a pretence make long prayer: therefore ye shall receive the greater damnation." Our Lord here thunders out against an evil which was small compared to what is commonplace today, our confiscation by estate and inheritance taxes of the properties rightfully belonging to widows and orphans. It is easy, in such contemporary instances, to feel a rage against the Internal Revenue Service, but this is to miss the point. The I.R.S. is the agency of the voters' envy. Through Congress, we enact envy into law, and now that envy reaches into our pockets, we are angry. This is not to say that the I.R.S. is without guilt, but that the primary guilt rests with Congress and the people. The fact is that the majority of the people want out of envy to see their superiors hurt, even if it means their own hurt. A friend, while in a country in Europe, was discussing the confiscatory taxation of that nation and called attention to its destructiveness. His hosts defended the taxation, while agreeing as to its threat. Their reason? It's good to see the high and mighty humbled.

Octavio Paz, in *The Labyrinth of Solitude* (1961) said, "Marx wrote that all radicalism is a form of humanism, since man is the root of both reason and society. Thus every revolution tries to create a world in which man, free at last from the trammels of the old regime, can express himself truly and fulfill his human condition. Man is a being who can realize himself, and *be* himself, only in a revolutionary society."

This revolutionary society is the goal of every humanistic state. Some hope to achieve it by violence, others by democratic change. In either case, the goal is the same, man as god or, more specifically, the humanistic state as god. Since one attribute of God is creation, the modern state seeks to create wealth, cradle to grave or womb to tomb security, and also to create money. Modern money, fiat, paper money is the result. It is state created money which is used to erode all traditional forms of wealth, and to place all wealth under the control of the state. We see today small family farms, in the same family for generations or from the colonial era, being sold because of taxes. This disaster is also taking place in Britain and elsewhere.

Godly wealth in Scripture is in terms of the faithful development of potentialities under God. God created the world, and He created the possibility of wealth through its natural resources, the earth's fertility, and the mind of man. Creation and all its ingredients are the handiwork of the triune God and none other. It is His law therefore which is the only true ground for godly wealth. The Lord condemns all *trust* in wealth as a form of humanism, as a kind of worship of the creation of our own hands rather than the Creator of all.

This, however, is the kind of wealth the modern state regards as alone acceptable, a state-created, humanistic wealth. Instead of being defined in terms of some God-given aspect of creation, gold, silver, land, or other assets, all wealth is to be reduced to state-created paper. Now the value of money is its liquidity which makes for its ready and easy use. When the modern hyper-taxing state creates a paper money inflation, it thereby requires every other form of wealth to be equally liquid. The family farm is no longer an inheritance from the past to the future generations; it is converted from a stable form of wealth to a highly unstable and liquid form by paper money, inflation and taxation. In the years of limited state power, the tax on a family farm in many areas was a few dollars at most. After World War II, many farmers were shocked when their taxes hit $25 and then $50; now they run into the thousands of dollars. At present, a growing number of American farmers are in serious trouble because of the combination of high taxes and debts they cannot repay. In the United States, every economic crisis has been preceded by a farm crisis.

Decapitalization is a world-wide fact today. In the Soviet Union, it is far gone, and not for the first time. In 1939, Stalin's Russia was bankrupt; by means of World War II, it recapitalized itself through an act of piracy approved by Roosevelt and Churchill. The Soviet Union was allowed to seize Central Europe, cannibalize East Germany and Poland, and more. Since then, the Soviet Union has been recapitalized annually by aid from the United States, and from American and European banks. These loans have been even more profitable than the seizure of Central Europe perhaps. However, both by its foreign and its domestic policies, the United States has been decapitalizing itself. A socialistic economy is a parasitic one: its continued life depends on the life of the host. Both the U.S.S.R. *and* the U.S. are today parasites living off the American people. There is no future for the American people until they rid themselves of the parasites, which means a radical change of perspective with regard to the nature of civil government.

Unless we have freedom under God and in obedience to Him, our definition of wealth is born of hunger, not of bounty. One American, long a prisoner in the Soviet Union, saw wealth as one potato, and two potatoes as undreamed of wealth. A refugee couple from Cambodia celebrated their wedding anniversary in the Cambodian jungle with an unexpected and welcome gift in their hunger, a rat's skin shared with them, to boil into a broth. A decapitalized (and unfree) society redefines wealth in pathetic terms. To each according to his needs, Marx held, and the Marxists have reduced the level of needs to beggarly dimensions. They have redefined wealth to make it the legitimate possession of the state and none other.

Redefinition has occurred in many areas. Students are routinely taught that there is an economic distinction between consumption and investment. Franklin W. Ryan, and Dr. Elgin Groseclose, in his excellent *America's Money Machine: The Story of the Federal Reserve System*, show otherwise. (The family is called by them the greatest production enterprise in society, and yet we are today at war against the family.) If I feed myself and my family, I am investing in our future; if I use junk food, I am making a poor investment. Whatever money I spend on the family is either a good or bad investment or consumption. To indict the idea of consumption is absurd; there is good consumption and unsound consumption.

The point of it all is that we are seeing an assault on and an erosion of the Biblical doctrine of wealth and stewardship. In its place, the state as the new god wants to remake man and society, and it believes that it can also create wealth by legislation, taxation, redistribution, and controls. What the modern state is accomplishing instead is the erosion of true wealth, and morality as well. The modern state has become history's great devourer of widows' houses, while it talks piously of a love for the poor, and the church is largely silent in the face of this growing evil. The sure promise of God to all such is judgement, unless men separate themselves from these evil ones to the Lord, Who says to us today as Moses did when Israel worshipped the golden calf, "Who is on the LORD'S side? Let him come unto me" (Ex. 32:26). (March, 1982)

RELIGIOUS LIBERTY versus RELIGIOUS TOLERATION
Chalcedon Position Paper No. 31

One of the areas of profound ignorance today is religious liberty and the meaning thereof. The common pattern throughout history, including in the Roman Empire, has been religious toleration, *a very different thing*.

In religious toleration, the state is paramount, and, in every sphere, its powers are totalitarian. The state is the sovereign or lord, the supreme religious entity and power. The state decrees what and who can exist, and it establishes the terms of existence. The state reserves the power to license and tolerate one or more religions upon its own conditions and subject to state controls, regulation, and supervision.

The Roman Empire believed in religious toleration. It regarded religion as good for public morale and morals, and it therefore had a system of licensure and regulation. New religions were ordered to appear before a magistrate, affirm the lordship or sovereignty of Caesar, and walk away with a license to post in their meeting-place.

The early church refused licensure, because it meant the lordship of Caesar over Christ and His church. The early church refused toleration, because it denied the right of the state to say whether or not Christ's church could exist, or to set the conditions of its existence. *The early church rejected religious toleration for religious liberty.*

Over the centuries, both Catholics and then Protestants often fought for religious liberty. Over the centuries also, the churches too often capitulated to religious toleration, with very evil results. Toleration was productive of fearful evils. *First*, one church was tolerated and established *by the state*, not by Christ, as the "privileged" or state-tolerated institution. This "privilege" called for concessions to the state.

These took a variety of forms. It could mean that the state appointed or controlled the bishops (Protestant or Catholic). It meant that only the state could give permission for a meeting of the church's national convocation or general assembly. In a variety of ways, establishment meant an establishment under the state's control. At its best, the church was turned into a privileged house-slave; at its worst, the church was simply a part of the bureaucracy, and the working pastors were rare and alone. Sooner or later, an establishment meant subservience and bondage to the state.

*S*econd, the tolerated church became a parasite, because it was dependent too often on state aid to collect its tithes and dues. It lived, not because of the faith of the people, but because of the state's subsidy. As a result, the state church served the state, not the Lord, nor the Lord's people. (When the states turned humanistic and, losing interest in their captive churches, began to cut their "privileges" and subsidies, revivals broke out in many established churches as a result!)

Third, the tolerated or established church became a persecuting church. It could not compete with its now illegal rivals in faith, and so it used the state to persecute its competitors. Both Catholic and Protestant establishments built up an ugly record in this respect. Meanwhile, their humanist foes could criticize their intolerance and speak of this inhumanity as a necessary aspect of Christianity!

Fourth, religious toleration leads to intolerance, as it should now be apparent. Toleration is licensure; it is a state subsidy, and those possessing it want a monopoly. Hence, intoleration of competitors results, and the church becomes blind to all issues save monopoly. In 17th century England, for example, the blindness of the Church of England under Archbishop Laud, as he fought the Puritans, was staggering. However, when Cromwell came to power, the Presbyterians became a one-issue party, the issue being the control and possession of the Church of England. Had they triumphed, the evils of Laud would have been reproduced. Cromwell balked them; later, the Presbyterians undermined the Commonwealth and helped bring in the depraved Charles II, who quickly ejected them from the Church of England.

In Colonial America, uneasy semi-establishments existed. Technically, the Church of England was the established church for all the crown realms, including Catholic Ireland. (Ireland was never more Catholic than *after* England imposed an alien church on the land!) Carl Bridenbaugh, in *Mitre and Sceptre* (1962), showed how the fear and threat of a full-scale establishment with American bishops alarmed Americans and led to the War of Independence. Meanwhile, in the colonies, men began to oppose religious toleration in favor of religious liberty. Here, the Baptists were most important, especially Isaac Backus.

Backus declared, "We view it to be our incumbent duty to render unto Caesar the things that are his but also that *it is of as much importance not to render unto him anything that belongs only to God, who is to be obeyed rather than any man*. And as it is evident that God always claimed it as his sole prerogative to determine by his own laws what his worship shall be, who shall minister in it, and how they shall be supported, so it is evident that this prerogative has been, and still is, encroached upon in our land." (Wm. J. McLoughlin, editor: *Isaac Backus on Church, State, and Calvinism, Pamphlets, 1754-1789*, p. 317. Harvard University Press, 1965.) The defenders of establishment or toleration became, Backus said, "Caesar's friend," citing the Pharisees who said to Rome's magistrates about Jesus, "If thou let this man go, thou art not Caesar's friend" (John 19:12). We cannot make the state the definer of man's duty to God, as the establishment-toleration position does. This position, Backus held, takes matters of faith from the conscience of man to the councils of state and thus undermines true faith. Backus saw that the new country would have no unity if establishment and toleration became lawful in the Federal Union. Backus quoted Cotton Mather, who said, "Violences may bring the erroneous to be hypocrites, but they will never bring them to be believers." The heart of Backus' position was this: "Religion (meaning Biblical religion) was prior to all states and kingdoms in the world and therefore could not in its nature be subject to human laws" (p. 432).

The First Amendment to the U.S. Constitution, replacing religious toleration and establishment with religious liberty, was the result of the work of Backus and many other churchmen. It represented a great and key victory in church history.

Now, however, religious liberty is dead in the United States. It only exists if you confine it to the area between your two ears. Instead of religious liberty, we have religious toleration. Now, religious toleration is the reality of the situation in Red China and Red Russia. In both cases, the toleration is very, very limited. In the United States, the toleration is still extensive, and most churchmen fail to recognize that the states and the federal government are insisting that only toleration, not liberty, exists, and the limits of that toleration are being narrowed steadily.

Thus, Senator Ernest F. Hollings of South Carolina has given expression to the position of the regulators and tolerationists, writing (2-19-82), "Tax exemption is a privilege, not a right. It is not only proper but Constitutional that the government condition that privilege on the Constitutional requirement of nondiscrimination. Religious freedom is a priceless heritage that must be jealously guarded. But when religious belief is contrary to the law of the land then it is the law, not religion, that must be sustained. The 1964 Civil Rights Act provided there be no discrimination in institutions receiving Federal financial assistance and the courts have interpreted this to mean that no public monies be appropriated directly or indirectly through tax exemption to those institutions that discriminate" (Letter by Hollings, re: the Reagan bill S2024, to control Christian Schools).

Sen. Hollings has, with many, many other members of Congress, *first*, replaced religious liberty with state toleration. Tax exemption originally meant no jurisdiction by the state over the church, because the power to tax is the power to control and destroy. Now, these humanistic statists tell us it is a subsidy! Tax exemption is called "Federal financial assistance," and the courts hold that controls must follow assistance from the civil treasury. This means a mandate to control churches, and every facet of their existence, including Christian Schools, colleges, seminaries, employees, etc., in the name of controlling federal grants!

Second, Hollings (and others, including many judges) hold that this means that the Civil Rights Act of 1964 must take priority over the First Amendment. The Civil Rights laws forbid discrimination in terms of race, and also a number of other things, *including creed*. The evidence is accumulating that federal authorities believe that they have now the legal *right* to require churches to ordain women, and homosexuals; on January 26, 1982, to a group of us meeting with Edwin Meese and 8 or 10 Justice Department lawyers in the White House, Meese (a Lutheran layman!) said flatly that this was within the legitimate power of the federal government. This means that the church, in terms of the same laws, can be forbidden to discriminate with respect to creed! This would mean equal time for all creeds, including humanism and atheism, in every church. In the World-wide Church of God case, the court held that a church and its assets belongs, not to the members thereof, but to all people, all citizens!

Third, the position of Hollings; Reagan; before him, Carter; the Justice Department; the Internal Revenue Service; the Labor Department; the Treasury Department; and the several states is that the only "freedom" tha the church can have is that activity which the state chooses to tolerate Toleration on any and all activities is subject to regulation, controls, an oversight.

This is, of course, totalitarianism. The fact is that religious liberty is dea and buried; it needs to be resurrected. We *cannot* begin to cope with ou present crisis until we recognize that religious liberty has been replaced wit religious toleration. The limits of that toleration are being steadily narrowe If Christians are silent today, the Lord will not be silent towards them whe they face the judgment of His Supreme Court. There is a war agains Biblical faith, against the Lord, and the men waging that war masquerade behind the facade of non-discrimination, subsidies, legitimate public interes and so on.

All this is done in the name of one of the most evil doctrines of our tim *public policy*. Nothing contrary to public policy should have tax exemptio and, some hold, *any* right to exist. Today, public policy includes homosexual "rights," abortion, an established humanism, and much, much more. The implication is plain, and, with some, it is a manifesto: No one opposing public policy has any rights. The public policy doctrine is the new face of totalitarianism. It has all the echoes of tyrannies old and new, and with more muscles .

What is increasingly apparent is that the triune God of Scripture, the Bible itself, and all faith grounded thereon, are contrary to public policy. Christianity has no place in our state schools and universities; it does not inform the councils of state; every effort by Christians to affect the political process is called a violation of the First Amendment and "the separation of church and state." Our freedom of religion is something to be tolerated only if we keep it between our two ears. A war has been declared against us, and we had better know it, and we had better stand and fight before it is too late.

We may be able to live under religious toleration, but it will beget all the ancient evils of compromise, hypocrisy, and a purely or largely public religion. It will replace conscience with a state license, and freedom with a state-endowed cell of narrow limits. This is the *best* that toleration may afford us in the days ahead.

But the Lord alone is God, and He does not share His throne with the state. If we surrender to Caesar, we will share in Caesar's judgment and fall. If we stand with the Lord, we shall stand in His Spirit and power. "Stand fast therefore in the liberty wherewith Christ hath made us free, and be not entangled again with the yoke of bondage" (Gal. 5:1). At the heart of that yoke of bondage is the belief and fear that the powers of man (and the state) are greater than the power of God. It is bondage to believe that man can prevail, or that man can frustrate God's sovereign and holy purpose. The only real question is this: will we be a part of the world's defeat and judgment, or a part of the Lord's Kingdom and victory? (June, 1982)

ON GIVING TO THE RICH, THE MIDDLE CLASS, AND THE LOWER CLASS
Chalcedon Position Paper No. 32

The idea explicit in our title is hardly a popular one. In an age which propagates and exploits class conflict, it is clearly not popular to speak of giving to anyone. The popular reaction will be something like this: what do the rich need, that we should give them? The middle class is self-righteous, smug, and censorious: what does it deserve but contempt? As for the lower class, what should those lazy good-for-nothings get? They are already milking us for hand-outs, welfare, or grossly higher wages! So runs the popular reaction.

This should not surprise us. The modern Darwinian world view rests on the concept of a lawless nature, the struggle for survival, and conflict in all areas. Class conflict, as Karl Marx saw, is a necessary development of such a faith. Hence, all areas of human life view all others with suspicion. The conflict of interests view of society pits classes against one another and makes for the politics of confrontation. The origins of this view go back to Hegel, to his view of life as conflict leading to synthesis, and then conflict afresh leading to another brief synthesis.

In *The Secret Six*, Otto J. Scott has shown how this view led to war in 1860. (It was first termed "a civil war" by a Virginian.) In the North, the abolitionists worked, not for peaceful solutions, but confrontation, war, and devastation as the answer. In the South, where only a very small minority owned slaves, and the majority hated slavery, extremists also worked for confrontation and conflict. In 1858, these extremists sought to re-open the slave trade, make very cheap slaves available in great numbers, and thereby include nonslave-owning citizens in their cause. In both North and South, extremists who believed in the social value of conflict set the temper of political discourse and overwhelmed the uninvolved peoples.

There is a second factor in the conflict of interests faith. Not only does it create social warfare but inner, psychological warfare. As a result, modern man is, more so than men of other eras, at war with himself. Not only does he hate other social classes, but he is consumed with self-hate.

As a result, most heirs of wealth have problems with themselves. The world of Darwin rather than Romans 8:28 governs their psychology. They see themselves as guilty because they are rich, and all too often use their wealth to try to atone for their affluence. They will be suspicious of others and given to hating themselves.

The middle class is no better off. All too many younger members of it can only speak of their parents with venom. For them, the ultimate and unforgivable sin is to be content with a good suburban home, a good income, and good friends, and virtue is equated with feeling guilty and miserable about the plight of man.

The lower class is no different. It sees those above it as in conspiracy against the poor, and poverty is somehow a creation of others, of society, of the system, or something else, in short. For example, one "inner city" young man delighted in throwing paper towels on restroom floors to mess up things, and candy wrappers, cigarette butts, and the like on the neatly manicured lawns of the well-to-do to express his hatred of their concern for cleanliness. In all three classes, class hatred and self-hatred go hand in hand.

Why then talk about giving to all three classes as a duty? Why bring up a subject which is apparently so remotely possible of attainment?

One of the great evils of humanism and the modern age is its equation of things as they are with norms. The Kinsey studies of human sexuality marked the social triumph of this faith. For Kinsey, whatever occurred in nature was hence natural and therefore normal. This meant that child molestation and homosexuality were normal and simply a variation in normal human behavior. Lamar and Corinne Strickland, of the Strickland Christian School, tell of a well-to-do mother who transferred her superior daughter to a depraved state school situation because the child supposedly needed to learn to live with reality. What the mother was in effect saying was that the Lord God is not real but that drugs, illicit sex, and humanism are real.

To live with reality is to live with the God of Scripture and His law word. Any other way of life is living with illusions and with evil. God declares, "I am the LORD, and there is none else, there is no God beside me" (Isa. 45:5). To try to live without Him, or in contempt of Him and His law, is to invoke His judgment. Because we are God's creation and servants, we have a total obligation to obey Him, and to meet His requirements towards one another. We have a commandment of love towards one another, which means keeping the law, which is love in action (Romans 13:8).

What can we give to the rich? Like men of all estates, they need to know and obey the Lord. With respect to their persons, it will not do for us to set ourselves up as judges over men, and to judge them as a class. Every class has its own characteristics; the sins of others are always more offensive to us than our own sins, which to us are "understandable" and even lovable sins. The rich are not ipso facto knaves. They are often able, useful, and very capable men. Many of them are active in Christian reconstruction in their own ways. They are carrying on, quietly and often anonymously, effective work among minority groups, the poor, and the unsaved. Like all of us, they need respect, understanding, and appreciation, nor for their checkbooks, but for themselves as persons. Like the rest of us, the rich need friends, not parasites. The rich need a sense of mission, not a "bite" on them. They need respect and help when they have a sense of mission, not attempts to get on "the gravy train." Above all else, the rich need from us the love God requires us to show to all men. To see them as targets of class conflict and hatred is to sin against both God and man.

The middle class is often the target of hatred because of the widely fomented hostility towards "the Protestant work ethic," now in the United States the common property of Catholics and Protestants. It is an ironic fact that wealth, great or small, earned in sports or entertainment, is seen as legitimate, but, if earned in industry or business, is somehow illegitimate! Because 19th Century radicals associated Christianity with the middle class, much of the hatred of the middle class is still in part a hatred of Christianity, even though the association is no longer valid. The middle class includes most of our modern population. Efforts to destroy it are thus equivalent to efforts to destroy our social order, not to remake it. To despise the middle class is to despise work and thrift, and most of the people of our time. The middle class needs to be respected and appreciated, not only as an economic and socially stabilizing force historically, but as people who, like all others, are created in God's image. We are to love all men, and God exempts none from His commandment of love. We are to love them by loving His law and keeping it, and by being true neighbors one to another (Leviticus 19:18).

The lower class is not exempt from the law of love. Some may lack the opportunity to better themselves and have the ability to do so. Others may simply have less than mediocre abilities and goals, and to be so does not make any man an object of contempt. The Bible makes sin the line of division, not class, social, or economic status. However much modern man may prattle on about social and economic "justice" for the poor, he is more comfortable around a homosexual with social status than a poor man with none. The line of division is now social and economic status and education, not faith; sin is not objectionable, but a low status is. One reason why so many today are full of verbal and political concerns for the poor is to mask their personal aversion for them. There is no social or economic cut-off line for either sin or God's grace, nor can there be for our love and friendship.

In brief, the graces and virtues that God requires of us are to be manifested towards all men. The line of demarcation is sin, and sin is to be dealt with only in terms of God's law word, with His judgment applied, and also His salvation proferred. No man is our possession, and therefore no man is ours to judge in terms of our human distinctions. "The earth is the LORD'S, and the fullness thereof; the world, and they that dwell therein" (Ps. 24:1). Therefore the world and all men can only be viewed, judged, governed, and received in terms of God's word and will, not our own.

This brings us to a cardinal sin of the modern age. Humanism and evolution posit an original nothingness, a primeval chaos. Out of this impersonal void, the cosmos evolved. Consciousness and personality are late-comers in a "universe" of supposedly billions of years in age, and both are likely in time to disappear, in terms of this view.

This means that material forces, mindless and lawless, govern the life of man, not a personal God. Ultimacy is thus impersonal, not personal; mindless, not mindful. The intellectual and scientific attitude calls for dealing with reality therefore in abstract terms. Thus, sociology deals with impersonal trends, social forces, and the like, not God and man in a totally personal universe. "Capital" deals with a labor force, not persons, and unions negotiate with "management" and "capital," not persons. Each depersonalizes the other and then wonders why there is no communication, or why a credibility gap exists. (If a man refuses to treat me like a person, how much credibility will he have with me? If someone tries merely to use me, however correct his outward demeanor, I will soon resent him.) We have depersonalized one another, and we do not understand why others have no liking for us. We like an impersonal world, because it enables us to avoid *personal* responsibilities for others, and we wonder why "alienation," conflict, and social warfare prevail. We reduce persons to members of classes, and we wonder why there is class conflict. Do any of us, except the self-conscious revolutionary, think of ourselves as essentially a member of a class rather than a person? For that matter, does God pigeonhole us as members of a particular class, or by income, social status, or race?

We must see ourselves and one another as God sees us, not as our contemporary world does. The Lord God sees us as creatures made in His image (Genesis 1:26-28), and we dare not view ourselves and our fellow men any differently. Because God is no respecter of persons, we cannot respect persons in our judgment either; we must view them in terms of His law word (Deut. 1:17), and His criterion is Himself and His law. Even then, God is patient, and, up to a point, sends His rain and sun to the just and the unjust (Matt. 5:45; Deut. 28:12, 23, 24).

The extent of our departure from the Lord is seen in the extent to which we allow human distinctions, however real, to be our determining premise in judgment, rather than God Himself. What social classes are now giving one to another is hatred and warfare. In judging one another, they are insisting on playing God and in setting up their own criteria as a new law for man.

The modern age makes much of "the common good" and "the general welfare." We forget that these terms go back into medieval law and practice. Their meaning at times was defective and Hellenic; at other times, it was Biblical. A common statement was, in Wyclif's words, "every common good is better than any private one." The great line of demarcation has been the meaning of "every common good." It has had two meanings. *First*, it has often meant and now commonly means the humanistic, statist general welfare as defined by man. In this tradition, the rulers, philosopher-kings, or elitist planners of the state define the common good and thus play god. The state then becomes a god walking on earth. We are suffering greatly today from this false, deadly, and heretical view of "the common good." In effect, it means the common tyranny.

The *second* meaning of "the common good" is that common moral law and requirement made by God for all men. The common good then is the Kingdom of God, and the reign of God's justice in the lives of all men. It means the grace of God in the life of man, applied in all our relationships, so that we manifest the Holy Spirit in human action. The common good in this sense rests on common prayer, on common faith, and on a common life in Christ. We will then be "members one of another" (Eph. 4:25), and not of a social class. (July, 1982)

THE OPPOSITE OF SIN
Chalcedon Position Paper No. 33

Sometimes the best way to understand the meaning of an idea or concept is to know its opposite. Thus, the opposite of night is day, which tells us something about both night and day. The opposite of life is death, but if we say it is freedom, we reveal a suicidal disposition. Some psychologists have used this matter of antonyms, opposites in words, to understand the mental state of patients.

This means of understanding has other uses, including philosophical and theological ones. Our concern here is Biblical and theological. Ask yourself this question: what is the opposite of sin? The answer is not a new one; it goes back to the Bible, and Proverbs especially sets opposites together to help us understand what God means. This teaching method was used in Israel, and it still continues to a degree in Jewish educational forms. The church once used it but has abandoned it.

To return to our question, what is the opposite of sin? The Old Testament Hebrew has several words for sin, *chatha, 'aven, pesha, 'avah*, and more. (The New Testament Greek uses especially *hamartia*, and *anomia*.) These words mean failure, blame-worthiness, iniquity, rebellion or transgression, and crooked. They have reference to a wrong done to God or to man in violation of God's law. The Westminster Shorter Catechism summarized it thus: "Sin is any want of conformity unto, or transgression of, the law of God" (I John 3:4).

The opposite of sin is a commandment obeyed in faithfulness, or, in terms of current Hebrew, a *mitzvah*. A *mitzvah* is, in its primary sense, a commandment of God as set forth in His word. In its secondary sense, it means our faithfulness to God's law, our act of faith and obedience whereby we manifest the grace and righteousness of God. To "do a mitzvah" was thus to obey the Lord. (One folk proverb said, "one *mitzvah* leads to another.")

In origin, the word mitzvah is derived from a Hebrew root meaning "to command" or "to ordain." It has reference to God's law-word. (Most people are familiar with the word "mitzvah" from the rite of bar-mitzvah, when boys, at the age of 13 plus one day, and girls in the bat-mitzvah, at the age of 12 plus one day, publicly acknowledge their duty to keep the commandments of God. This rite in some form is very ancient, and it was continued in the church in the rite of confirmation. It is very regrettable that confirmation is becoming a less and less educational process, or, in some churches, has been dropped entirely. A study is long overdue on the purpose and place given to a child by the bar/bat mitzvah and by confirmation. Here we have a cultural fact of great importance which has been ignored by historians.)

The opposite of sin is a commandment by God, the whole of God's law-word. As we have seen, sin is any want of conformity to, or transgression of, the law of God. Saving righteousness, justifying righteousness, or justice, is the faithfulness of Jesus Christ to the every word of God, and His atoning death and resurrection, as our vicarious substitute and head. Sanctifying righteousness is our faithfulness to the law-word of God.

The child, from its earliest days, is taught that certain things are forbidden, and certain acts required. The world is governed by "thou shalt nots," and also by requirements, "this shall ye do, and live." By chastisement and by discipline, the child is taught the right way, and barred from the wrong, while being told that one's only justifying righteousness before God is in and through our redeemer, Jesus Christ.

Then, with Christian schooling, and in some form a mature confirmation of the faith in his own life and experience, the young man or woman is now ready for adult life, for maturity, "to do a mitzvah," to use the old phrase.

It is at this point that the church, like the synagogue before it, has failed. College and university graduates are regularly told that their real schooling is just beginning. More correctly, they should be told, it should now begin, but, for the most part, they settle into the routines of their life and learn as little as possible thereafter. The same is true in the church. One pastor, who visited a former charge after more than 25 years, found it a joy to see old friends, but, religiously, a discouraging experience. Despite the many years, there were too few evidences of growth in Christian faith, knowledge, and action. In the intervening time, they had been served by pastors who were able teachers, but they had been content to remain babes in Christ.

If the opposite of sin is the commandment or law-word of God, and doing His will, this means that Christian action in the world is the antonym of sin. The Christian community has a world responsibility (Matt. 28:18-20).

We have forgotten what was once a very important doctrine, *vocation*. It means seeing our life *and* work as a calling from God to serve and obey Him. A famous poem by George Herbert set forth this doctrine:

Teach me, my God and King,
In all things Thee to see;
And what I do in anything,
To do it as for Thee!

A man that looks on glass,
On it may stay his eye;
Or if he pleaseth, through it pass,
And then the heaven espy.

All may of Thee partake;
Nothing can be so mean,
Which with this tincture, "for Thy sake,"
Will not grow bright and clean.

A servant with this clause
Makes drudgery divine:
Who sweeps a room, as for Thy laws,
Makes that and the action fine.

This is that famous stone
That turneth all to gold;
For that which God doth touch and own
Cannot for less be told.

W. R. Forrester, in *Christian Vocation* (1953), called attention to the fact, "in language after language the same word is used for toil and childbearing, e.g., 'labour' and 'travail'" (p. 129). Both are burned with the curse of the Fall (Gen. 3:16-19), but the two are the essential key to any possible future for man. Both are the purpose of God for man, and, with man's redemption, become man's blessing (Ps. 127). Our Lord says, "My meat is to do the will of Him that sent Me and to finish His work" (John 4:34). By this He says that for a man's soul a calling is the sustaining thing, as food is for the body.

Luther said, "What you do in your house is worth as much as if you did it up in heaven for our Lord God...Therefore we should accustom ourselves to think of our position and work as sacred and well-pleasing to God, not on account of the position and the work, but on account of the word and faith from which the obedience and the work flow. No Christian should despise his position and life if he is living in accordance with the word of God, but should say, 'I believe in Jesus Christ, and do as the ten commandments teach, and pray that our dear Lord God may help me thus to do.'"

Calvin, in his *Institutes* (III, X, 6), spoke of "the boiling restlessness of the human mind," and our need of a calling. This calling is of God's appointing, not our day-dreaming. "Every man's mode of life, therefore, is a kind of station assigned him by the Lord, that he may not be always driven about at random. So necessary is this distinction, that all our actions are thereby estimated in his sight, and often in a very different way from that in which human reason or philosophy would estimate them...in everything the call of the Lord is the foundation and beginning of right action."

This calling, doing God's will and living in terms of His law-word or commandments, is life to the faithful. One of the sharpest and clearest comments about this came from James Chalmers, missionary to New Guinea in the very earliest days of that mission: "Don't send us men who talk of self-sacrifice." We must say with Christ, "Lo, I come to do thy will, O God" (Heb. 10:9), because life apart from our calling of faithfulness, of obedience, is not life for us.

The psalmist knew what it was "to do a mitzvah"; he sang about it: "Thy statutes have been my songs in the house of my pilgrimage. I have remembered thy name, O LORD, in the night, and have kept thy law" (Ps. 119:54-55). Again, "O how I love thy law! It is my meditation all the day" (Ps. 119:97).

To have a calling without faith in God and obedience to His commandments is evil and even demonic. Oswald Spengler, in *The Decline of the West*, saw the decline and destruction of the West in the rise of ambitious men with purely secular callings. He saw the socialists of the future as the arch-imperialists of history, and, of Cecil Rhodes he said, "Rhodes is to be regarded as the first precursor of a Western type of Caesars, whose day is to come though yet distant" (I, 37).

The demonic Titanism which Spengler, writing in 1914-1918, saw in the world's future, came much earlier than he had predicted. Socialism, both national and international, has become imperialistic. Fascism and Naziism, and especially the Soviet Union, Cuba, Libya, and other Marxist states, have been history's bloodiest powers. Since 1975, in its brief history, Marxist Cambodia (or Kampuchea) has executed half of its population. At the same time, as Carroll Quigley has shown in *The Anglo-American Establishment* (Books in Focus, 1981), the heirs and followers of Rhodes have devastated the rest of the world with their sickly idealism. If our calling, our *mitzvah* is not to do the will of Him that sent us, and to finish His work (John 4:34), we are faithless to our Lord and dangerous to society. To have a calling without and apart from God's law-word is to be a deadly menace to other men and to society.

The opposite of sin is to do the commandments in faith, to *confirm* our faith in action. This means the Great Commission, the conversion of all the world, the discipling of all nations, the application of God's law to every area of life, and the recognition by every sphere of the Lordship of Christ.

Forrester called attention to the difference between vocation and ambition. Vocation allies itself with the Lord and places itself under the every word of God (Matt. 4:4). A vocation is the result of regeneration and faithful obedience. It sees freedom as obedience to the Lord. Ambition is marked by a lust for power and preeminence. The ambitious man seeks to use God and man to gain his own ends.

The ambitious man assents to the great temptation and says, I shall be my own god, determining or establishing for myself, in terms of my will, what constitutes good and evil (Gen. 3:5). The man with a calling says with our Lord, "It is written, Man shall not live by bread alone, but by every word that proceedeth out of the mouth of God" (Matt. 4:4).

The ambitious man, because power is his god, will slaughter kulaks, persecute Jews, capitalists, whites, blacks, or workers, exploit all men, treat youth as cannon fodder, and generally dedicate himself to what, in terms of God's law-word, is sin and only sin, however noble a cause he may ascribe to his actions. (Most sins come labelled with a noble rationale; sinning is usually called liberation; and murders in the cause of sin are usually called victories over the enemies of the people, the state, or the Great Cause).

As against this, our Lord says, "Thou shalt love the Lord thy God with all thy heart, and with all thy soul, and with all thy mind. This is the first and great commandment. And the second is like unto it. Thou shalt love thy neighbor as thyself. On these two commandments hang all the law and the prophets" (Matt. 22:37-40). On these two also hang the future of society. For the man with a godly vocation, this is the way of life.

The doctrine of the priesthood of all believers is inseparable from the facts of confirmation (and doing a mitzvah), and vocation. A work of some years ago, on confirmation, spoke of the training for, and the rite of, confirmation as having this goal, "the professing of the faith" in all one's life and actions.

Thomas Wilson (1663-1755), bishop of Sodor and Man, in his *Sacra Privata*, wrote, "He lives to no purpose who is not glorifying God." We glorify God when we keep His commandments, do His will, and rejoice in our calling in Him.

The opposite of sin is doing the commandments in faithfulness. "Faith without works is dead" (James 2:14-26). Our Lord speaks clearly on this: "Not every one that saith unto me, Lord, Lord, shall enter into the kingdom of heaven; but he that doeth the will of my Father which is in heaven" (Matt. 7:21). (August, 1982)

SIN, CONFESSION, AND DOMINION
Chalcedon Position Paper No. 34

By early summer of 1982, it was clear that the feminist equal rights amendment to the U.S. Constitution was dead. The movement perished in part because of its own excesses. These excesses were born out of the mythology of modern man and man's view of himself as a victim rather than a sinner. Of course, ever since Adam and Eve, people have chosen to plead an innocence born of environmental premises. Adam and Eve both pleaded victimization; their own hearts were good, but the environment led them astray. When the women's liberation movement made half the human race into victims and the other half into oppressors, it pushed the myth too far. One woman, in an impassioned book, portrayed all men at heart as rapists. Sadly some clergymen, in reviewing the work, praised it; one wonders at their mentality, and certainly their womenfolk should! In another highly praised book, another feminist wrote, "When a female child is passed from lap to lap so that all the males in the room (father, brother, acquaintance) can get a hard-on, it is the helpless mother standing there and looking on that creates the sense of shame and guilt in the child." Prestigious publications praised this garbage, but attitudes like this have helped weaken the old foundations of humanistic thought which has made us all into victims and also all into oppressors. If we are male or female, we victimize sometime. If we are parents we warp children. If we are rich, middle class, or poor, we somehow are responsible for the evils of our time.

Responsibility, denied by environmentalism, has a habit of reappearing! We may be victims of our environment, but, because we are someone else's environment, we are guilty, not for our own sins, but for someone else's sins! This places us in an ugly predicament; our own sins, we can do something about, but we cannot do much about the sins of a man down the road.

The doctrine of the conflict of interests (and Darwinism) has greatly increased the problem. Class (or race, or religious, or social) warfare is assumed to be basic to the human situation. The "superior" group is then by definition the oppressing group. If you are rich, you are by common assumption the oppressor of the poor. If you are white, you are racist; if you are a male, you are guilty of sexism, and so on and on.

But sin is common to all of us. Marx portrayed the capitalist as the oppressor of the workingman, and the debaucher of the working-girl. Of course, this did not keep Marx, the socialist, from debauching his wife's maid, nor modern socialists from doing the same. Women executives can be as guilty of sexism as men, and as zealous in their pursuit of underlings.

Moreover, the plain fact is that maids have often seduced their masters or their master's son, no less than masters have seduced maids. Sin is not a property belonging to any race or class, nor is virtue.

We have long been subjected to the myth of the innocent or oppressed class. Films and television have treated us ad nauseam with tales of whores with hearts of gold. For film writers, it would seem that the one qualification for virtue is to have no virtue. We are shown a world of sorry victims who are the casualties of life, having been exploited by someone.

It is at this point that modern thought is meeting with disaster. It denies the Biblical doctrine of sin for a concept of an evil environment. We are all victims, but, because we are all somebody's environment, we are all an evil force which needs bull-dozing out of the way. Out of such an impasse, men see no escape.

For some years now, we have seen a growing disaffection and distaste for modern thought on the part of the very children of our modern leaders. The student rebels of the 1960s came largely from liberal and permissive homes; they were indeed the children of the establishment.

The rebellion of the 1960s has given way to cynicism and indifference. There is a dropping out into drugs, liquor, or simple existence without relevance. I talked briefly in the past year or so with the son of a prominent father, whose mother is also a part of the intellectual community. His parents were both dismayed, he said, because he had quit the university, after less than two years, to take a job. When I asked him why, he described the university as "just plain s--t. All they do is to lay a guilt trip on you." This young man was very much a part of the modern culture in his habits and tastes, but he had broken with the essence of modernism, its doctrine of man as victim. When he saw his parents, he loved to offend them, by his own admission, by ridiculing their belief in the innocence of minority groups, unions, or anything else he could think of, not out of conviction but out of contempt for the modern myth.

The homosexuals and the feminists have both exploited the myth, and both are beginning to see the hints of its decline and even backlash.

David, in Psalm 8:4, asks the question of God, "What is man, that thou art mindful of him?" To be *mindful* in Hebrew means to think well of, to consider favorably. In essence, mindfulness has a religious root. God is *mindful* of man, because, *first*, man is His creation, made in His own image, for righteousness, knowledge, holiness, and dominion. *Second*, God is mindful of man, because He has given man a great calling, the task of subduing the earth, and of exercising dominion over it (Gen. 1:26-28). For the performance of this task, God has crowned man "with glory and honour" (Ps. 3:8) and has placed all things implicitly under man.

At least from Nietzsche to Stalin and the present, a major strand of humanism has seen man merely as manure for the creation of the future superman or communistic man, or the Great Society. Virtually all humanism has seen man as either good or as neutral in his moral nature, and hence as a victim of God or the environment. This view of man is now in decay. Freud rightly saw his role as critical in the destruction of the Enlightenment's optimistic view of man. Man for Freud is a product of his unconscious, and the unconscious is made up of the *id*, the anarchistic pleasure principle, man's will to live; of the *ego*, the reality principle and the will to death; and the *superego*, the teachings and effects of the immediate environment. The *id* and *ego* represent the past environment. Freud saw little hope for man in escaping from his past. While some of Freud's ideas are now under attack, his doctrine of man essentially remains in force, and it is contributing to the decay of the world of humanism.

In answer to the question, "What is man, that thou art mindful of him," the modern world is answering that it is mindful of ideal man, the man of its imagined future. It is not mindful of independent man, Christian man, resisting man, or any man who refuses to bow down to the state. The modern state says, in effect, be a victim, and we will love you, and care for you.

But man today is seeing only the breakdown of the humanist order. In a play of 1967, *The Hawk*, a product of the experimental theater, the "Hawk" is a heroin peddler with an insatiable lust for victims. The Hawk's litany is a simple one: he is an animal; he "kills" because he is hungry; whatever happens has no moral meaning; we do what by nature we are impelled to do.

The world of *The Hawk* is beyond good and evil, beyond morality. It is a world in which all men are victims of their own nature, and their nature is a product of the past. In 1970, Michael Novak, in *The Experience of Nothingness*, said that the fundamental human question is, "Granted that I must die, how shall I live?" (p. 48). To this question, the modern mind has no answer. In fact, at that time Novak himself could only say that there is no self over and apart from the world, only a self in tension with the world and a part of it, so that, better than speaking of the self, we should speak instead of "a conscious world" or "a horizon" (p. 55). Ethics, instead of being God's commandment, was for Novak at that time simply man's "invention" or "creation", man's "possibility" (p. 79).

For such opinions, men pay a price, or, in Seon Manley's apt sentence, "we pay for dreams." And dreams are broken by reality.

"What is man, that thou art mindful of him?" has been answered increasingly with a rejection of mindfulness. Men are not even mindful of themselves, and suicidal habits are prevalent. To blunt one's mind with drugs or marijuana is certainly a blatant example of unmindfulness. Man as victim cannot confess sin; he can only indulge in self-pity.

On the other hand, in the Bible we have a different view. In Joshua 7:19, Joshua tells Achan, the sinner, "My son, give, I pray thee, glory unto the LORD God of Israel, and make confession unto him." The word *confession* in the Hebrew is *toda*, which means confession and praise. Thus, when Joshua asks Achan to confess his sins, which carried a death penalty, he was also asking him to praise God. This gives us a glimpse into a radically different world than that of 20th century man, for whom confession means essentially self-abasement and humiliation. In the Bible, the confession of sin is a major step in the restoration of order, God's order, and it is thus a means toward praising God. The church of our day has lost the meaning of confession.

A victim cannot make confession. A man created to be a priest, prophet, and king in Christ finds in confession his restoration into a royal estate and a great calling.

"Sin is any want of conformity unto, or transgression of, the law of God," according to the Westminster Shorter Catechism. Confession is the first step towards restoration into our God-appointed status and dominion. It is the recognition that we are not victims but sinners, and we are sinners because we have departed from and rebelled against God's mandate and calling.

There are indications that, in earlier centuries of the Christian era, monarchs, before their coronation, had to make confession. However falsely done by many kings, its purpose was to remind them that all men are judged by God's law and the praise of God begins with our confession of sins, and our submission to God's law order. It is God's law order which alone can exalt human society and make it joyful and triumphant.

David, after asking, "What is man, that thou art mindful of him?" goes on to say: "Thou madest him to have dominion over the works of thy hands: thou hast put all things under his feet" (Ps. 8:6). The conclusion of true confession is dominion. The restored man as king exercises dominion over every area of life and thought and brings all things into captivity to the obedience of Christ (II Cor. 10:5).

The myth of victimization is being shattered. Its own advocates, by pushing it to its logical limits, have exposed its absurdities. It is a myth that has failed, and it is now dying.

This, however, is not enough. Clearing the ground of a tottering structure is a need, but it does not erect a new building. What is now needed is a strong and forthright emphasis on Christian reconstruction, on dominion man and his mandate to conquer every area of life and thought for Christ, and on the certainty of victory. For victims, there is no victory. For confessors of the Name, victory is inescapable, because God the Lord remains forever King over all creation. Then let us be joyful, let the earth be glad "before the LORD: for he cometh, for he cometh to judge the earth: he shall judge the world with righteousness, and the people with his truth" (Ps. 96:13). (October, 1982)

THE LOVE OF DEATH
Chalcedon Position Paper No. 35

One of the most telling sentences in Scripture is Proverbs 8:36: "But he that sinneth against me wrongeth his own soul: all they that hate me love death." This means that the love of death marks every person and culture which is in sin against God: they are suicidal. This fact, stated so clearly by Solomon, has not lacked confirmation over the generations. In this century Sigmund Freud, on non-Biblical grounds, held that the will-to-death is the basic and governing fact in the lives of all men, and he accordingly had dim hopes for the future of civilization.

The Bible tells us that there is an inseparable link between sin and death. Sin separates from God, the Creator and giver of life: it is rebellion against God's law and government. The consequence of this separation from the Source of all life is death, and all sin means a love of and addiction to death. Jesus Christ says, "I am the resurrection and the life: he that believeth in me, though he were dead, yet shall he live: And whosoever liveth and believeth in me shall never die" (John 11:25-26). To accept Christ's atonement and His lordship means that we separate ourselves from sin and death to life and righteousness or justice, and eternal life begins at once for us, so that the power of death is broken (I Cor. 15:55-57)

Meanwhile, all around us, the world is marked by a will to and a love of death. Every day the world economic scene shows more clearly this will to death. Inflation is the planned destruction of money and of the economy.

In recent years, some people have acted as though one relatively mildly destructive habit was newly found to be harmful, i.e., smoking tobacco. But people knew that more than a generation ago, when Dr. Pearl's studies were released. Before Dr. Pearl's day, even the erring schoolboys knew it and called cigarettes "coffin nails!" It was definitely not a lack of knowledge. The same is true in the economic sphere. Very clearly, when Keynes was asked about the consequences of his economics, he said, "In the long run, we are all dead." Suicidal men demand suicidal economics, and the same kind of politics.

President Reagan's campaign speeches spelled out the consequences of deficit financing, unsound money, financing and aiding world Marxism, and more--all things he is presently doing and defending. The politics of death prevails in Washington, D.C., and all the world capitols. The dying do not plan for tomorrow or next year, and the politics of death thinks only in terms of today.

George Orwell, in *1984*, depicted clearly the consequences of the politics of death. However, not being a man of Biblical faith, he failed to see the roots thereof. Modern man has denied the triune God and has insisted that the universe is a product of chance and accident. Instead of a cosmic and total meaning, his universe is one of absolute meaninglessness. If the only rationality in the universe is in the mind of man, and if the mind of man, since Freud, is simply the irrational product of man's unconscious, then meaninglessness is absolute and total. Then to hunger for truth and meaning is a sign of foolishness and irrationality. Greco-Roman paganism saw this cosmic emptiness as grounds for hedonism: "Let us eat, drink, and be merry, for tomorrow we die." The greatest celebration and most loved event of the Roman Empire was the "circus" with its gladiators battling to death, Christians thrown to the lions, and death in various other ways made into a spectator sport. The cry of the gladiators on entering the arena, "Hail, Caesar! We who are about to die salute you!", epitomized the spirit of Rome. Death was a game, and all courted it in their own way, and glorified it in the arena. As the Lord declares, "All they that hate me love death."

Statist education is increasingly education for death, national death. Jonathan Kozol, in *Prisoners of Silence*, and the *U.S. News and World Report*, May 17, 1982, pp. 53-56, "Ahead A Nation of Illiterates?" document the sorry plight of the United States. The economy is requiring more and more educated and skilled workers, and the state schools are producing illiterates who cannot hold such jobs. The illiterate and near-illiterate (or, functionally illiterate) number between 57 and 63 million. This illiteracy (and joblessness) constitutes "a form of social dynamite." The situation grows worse annually, and the attacks on Christian Schools for providing an alternative and superior education grows more intense. To criticize the state schools is in many circles the mark of fascism, superstition, religious bigotry, and more! The lovers of death resent the possibility of life and a future for any segment of the republic.

On every side, the death wish is with us, organized into intense campaigns and movements: Zero Population Growth, Zero Economic Growth, and so on. Note the passion with which the antinuclear weapons movement exaggerates the potential of such weapons, its readiness to believe in the total destruction of the world (and to relish a film depicting it), while at the same time pursuing policies of disarmament which will invite war.

Within the church, it is amazing to see the passion with which men defend eschatologies of death. History, such men insist, cannot end in the Lord's victory and the rule of the saints from pole to pole, but only in defeat. Things will only go from bad to worse, such men declare, until the end of the world. Somehow, they see it as unspiritual and un-Christian to believe in an eschatology of victory. Instead of a joyful and triumphant faith, such men manifest a sour and retreatist faith.

The love of death is very clear in the abortionist movement. Its advocates are suicidal in a number of ways. While I have no way of verifying this, a few persons familiar with abortion "clinics" tell me that there is a high rate of the use of narcotics and an over-use of alcohol among staff members.

It is important to note that the Ten Commandments, in the word or law concerning life, reads, "Thou shalt not kill." Some translate it as "murder", but there is another Hebrew word, as in Psalm 10:8 for murder, *harag*, to smite or kill with deadly intent. In Exodus 20:13, the word is *ratsack*, from a root, to dash in pieces, kill, to put to death; this word *can* mean murder also, but it is somewhat more general. The meaning of "Thou shalt not kill" is that all killing is forbidden except where permitted by God's word, i.e., in the execution of lawfully condemned men, in self-defense in defensive warfare, in eliminating those animals and pests which hinder farming, ranching, etc., in killing for food, and the like. In other words, all life is created by God, and the taking of any life must be subject to God's law-word. Because we are not our own, but are God's creation and property, we cannot take our own lives, because we are God's possession.

One of the marks of a sound faith is a love of life and the godly use thereof, whereas a suicidal and a destructive use of our lives and of the lives of other men and creatures manifests an alien foundation.

Suicide is thus normally a religious fact. This qualification, "normally" is necessary these days, because many medically administered drugs have deadly side-effects, and, when more than one is taken, produce deadly and frightening results.

Many religions have taken a favorable view of suicide and have even exalted it as the path of honor and dignity. In some cultures, when the king died, wives and retainers competed for the privilege of being buried alive with their monarch. H. J. Rose, in his survey of suicide among non-Christian religions (Hasting's *Encyclopedia of Religion and Ethics*, vol. XII, p. 23), held "Probably the chief, if not the only, reason for this (religious opposition to suicide) among primitive races is simply the dread of the ghost. The self-destroyer must have been greatly wronged or troubled in some way, or he would not have acted as he did, therefore his ghost will be an unusually troublesome and revengeful spirit." However, the fact is that in these cultures all the spirits of the dead are feared as hostile. Life is seen as a realm of hostilities and suspicion, and death may even aggravate that fact. Hence, such religions manifest a fear of life as such, and they see no escape even in death from the cosmic hostilities. The cosmos is a realm of the wars of the gods, men, and spirits.

Not too long ago, I wrote Position Paper no. 25, "The Trouble with Social Security." It was reprinted in various newsletters and magazines, and the reprints brought in some interesting mail. At present, Social Security is both morally and economically bankrupt. Arlo Sederberg commented recently, "With the graying of America, one of the ticking time bombs in the money war is the Social Security system which could make the troubles of Chrysler or International Harvester seem like child's play" (Arlo Sederberg, "Moneyline", in *Los Angeles Herald Examiner*, Tuesday, August 31, 1982, p. A-8). The system is economically unsound, but, with retired persons accounting for about 20% of all voters, nothing constructive is being done. It is easy to see why. The people who wrote to me were elderly persons on Social Security; facts meant nothing to them. They saw any "tampering" with Social Security as "un-Christian". Social Security has pushed France into an economic sickness and socialism, and, if the present trend continues here, will lead to an American debacle as well. No one is ready to discuss the economic issues, nor the moral ones. Any and every refusal to face the fullness of reality, however, is suicidal.

The love of death is a cultural and personal fact. Where men do not have true atonement, they seek self-atonement, which means sado-masochistic activities. The result is that the culture is death rather than life oriented. However, there is no honesty in this orientation. Typical of this fact was a young man, an artist with wasted abilities, who liked nothing more than to rant against the churches and Christians for their supposed lack of any love or enjoyment of life. He refused to see his own death wish and love of death, as evidenced in his part in the sex revolution, drug culture, and his living in flagrant contempt of common sense. He was dead before thirty, and, to the last, insisting that he was a champion of life and freedom.

On the other hand, the love of God is the love of life. Obedience to God is obedience to the laws of life. To seek to live without law, God's law, is to seek death. The dead in a graveyard are integrated with the natural world. Those who are alive in the triune God exercise dominion over that world in terms of God's law-word. They do not conform either to the culture of this world or to "natural" impulses, because, having been created in the image of God, it is to God's image they must conform themselves. The image of God, in its narrow sense, is defined thus by the Westminister Shorter Catechism, no. 10: "God created man male and female, after his own image, in knowledge, righteousness, and holiness, with dominion over the creatures" (Gen. 1:26-28; Col. 3:10; Eph. 4:24). In its broader sense, the image of God includes more: His revelation in Scripture is a manifestation of His image, of His knowledge, righteousness (or, justice), holiness, dominion, glory, law, grace, judgment, and more.

Thus, to conform ourselves to God's image rather than to the tempter's plan to be our own god (Gen. 3:5), means to live by every word that proceeds out of the mouth of God (Matt. 4:4). There is no true life by bread alone, but rather by God's sovereign grace through Christ, and faithfulness then to His word. Jesus Christ is declared to be "the Word of life" (I John 1:1). It is He who shows us "the path of life" (Ps. 16:11), and this is set forth in the totality of His word. We cannot claim to love life and neglect the Lord and Giver of life, and His word which sets forth the way of life.

The path of life, and the love of live, means a God-ordained way in every area of life and thought. The essence of the modern perspective is that man claims to be autonomous and to seek his freedom from the triune God. All too many churchmen profess an adherence to the Lord of life while affirming an autonomous way in most things. This is antinomianism; it is also the love of death.

"Now therefore hearken unto me, O ye children, for blessed are they that keep My ways. Hear instruction, and be wise, and refuse it not. Blessed is the man that heareth Me, watching daily at My gates, waiting at the posts of My doors. For whoso findeth Me findeth life, and shall obtain favour of the LORD" (Prov. 8:32-35). (December, 1982)

THE FAILURE OF MEN
Chalcedon Position Paper No. 36

The roots of every cultural crisis rest in personal crises. The failure of a culture is the failure of the men in it. A society cannot be vital and possessed of an on-going vigor if the men therein are marked by a loss of faith, a retreat from responsibility, and an unwillingness to cope with personal problems. A culture loses its will to live and to conquer if its members manifest a spirit of retreat and surrender.

In the cultural crisis of our time, the role of men is particularly significant. When we say "men" in this context we mean males, not humanity as a whole. How little true masculinity they in general possess is manifested in their predilection for role-playing. The macho image is cultivated in dress, speech, and behavior; the facade of a man replaces a man. Role-playing is basic to our times; people play a part, they act out a role, because the reality of their being is far less important than their public image. The roots of role-playing go deep into the modern mentality.

The foundations of modern philosophy are in Descartes. His thinking made the individual consciousness the world's basic reality and the starting point of all philosophy. Man's ego, the "I", took precedence over God and the world. Not surprisingly, the logic of this led to Hume, who dispensed with God and the world as epiphenoma, and even the mind was eroded to the point that it was only momentary states of consciousness rather than a reality. Immanuel Kant went a step further; things in themselves, i.e., realities, are unknowable and only phenomena can be known. The real world is thus not a valid area of knowledge, because we can only know appearances. As Schopenhauer put it, the world is will and idea.

Philosophy thus set the stage for the substitution of role-playing, i.e., phenomena, for the real man, the thing in itself, reality. It could thus be said that clothes make the man (or woman), and that a good front is essential; appearances become everything.

Appearances began to replace reality in personal relations as well as in national policy, both domestic and foreign. The results have been devastating. Role playing in the theater ends commonly in a curtain call and a pay check. In real life, politics, role playing leads instead to disaster.

The result is the failure of men, of males. Early in the modern era (only in the 19th century in the United States), men abandoned the family and its responsibilities to their wives, and religion was similarly relegated to women as their concern. Men chose irresponsibility, and the double standard became a way of life. Of course, men insisted on all the Biblical authority given to a man while denying its responsibilities, forgetting that all human authority in Scripture is conditional upon obedience to God. No absolute authority is given to man in any sphere, and all authority has service to God and man as its purpose, not self-promotion or aggrandizement.

The women's liberation movement is simply the attempt by women to claim the irresponsibilities which today constitute male rights, for themselves. The purpose of the children's liberation movement is to claim like privileges of irresponsibility for children.

Logically, men who cannot govern themselves will not be able to govern successfully their families, vocations, or nations. The most famous American president of the 20th century could not handle his money nor his own affairs, but he sought to rule the world. More than a few presidents have been like him. Of another man, twice a candidate for president, his ex-wife wrote a poem to the effect that men who cannot rule their nanny, wife, children, or nurse, are prone to seek to rule the universe! Not surprisingly, our world-wide cultural crisis is rooted in the failure of men. The remarkable fact of our era is not that we have had an at times aggressive women's liberation movement but that the vast majority of women have patiently endured the willful immaturity of men.

As a high school student, I was interested in athletics and earned two or three "letters" on the team of one sport; as a university student, I had no time to watch a single game. Since then, I have had an occasional interest in some sports. What amazes me is that men who never played while in school, nor showed much or any interest in sports then, will now show a startling devotion to televised sports. It almost seems as though any refuge from maturity and reality is desired, and spectator sports are a good substitute for the real world and its problems.

The pleasures of maturity and reality are to be found in family and work, in worship and in growth in the faith. If maturity and reality are not desired and seen as fulfillment, then role-playing which stresses a public image and perpetual youth (or immaturity) will be basic to man's way of life. (For the Chalcedon Reports since September, 1965, one of the ugliest and most hostile reactions I have received was to a one-sentence reference about the pathetic absurdity of a woman over 80 dressed in a bikini! I was told that it was evil for me to question her "right" to play the role of a teenager!)

Although role playing is common to men, women, and children, it is the failure of men because of their role-playing which has the deepest roots and the most tragic consequences. The abdication of men from their responsibilities as husbands and fathers is having sad results in family life.

This abdication does not end in the family. Again and again, all over the country. I have heard men say that they welcome union rules which prevent or make difficult the firing of any man. The responsibility of telling a man that he lacks competency is something they do not want. Some have closed down a particular department and laid off two or three good men to get rid of one incompetent one. An engineer in a plant dealing with federal contracts said that hiring was on a wholesale basis with new contracts; it would quickly become apparent that many of the engineers were only paper shufflers, but nothing would be done, because the contract would terminate in a year! At the end of the year, another plant with a new contract would hire the same unchallenged incompetents; no man ever had a bad record follow him. Whether in business, the academic community, or in civil government, nothing is done that is decisive. Presidential candidates promise cuts and clean-ups and as president do nothing. Being role-playing men, they are good candidates and very poor executives.

The Madison Avenue approach has triumphed; advertising an appearance and playing a role have replaced reality. Manhood is now a front, not a reality, to our culture in its popular manifestations. Manhood is popularly defined, not in terms of God, calling, and family, but in terms of money and status, i.e., in terms of ability to present the right public image.

The church has done much to further this trend. Instead of an unswerving insistence on the unity of faith and works, profession and action, it has been ready to stress pious gush and surface instead of the reality of faith. As a result, pulpit and pew are given to role-playing. Now role-playing by churchmen is first of all an attempt to con God, the supreme act of arrogance. It has long been known that "con" men are most readily victimized by other "con" men. This is no less true in the church. The old proverb is true, like priest, like people, and also, like people, like priest. The role players find one another, or, to cite another good bit of proverbial wisdom, birds of a feather flock together.

Our Lord says, "By their fruits ye shall know them" (Matt. 7:20), a sentence constantly evaded as excuse makers try to offer a profession of faith (role playing) for the reality thereof. Labels replace reality. If a man labels himself Christian, we are told we must take him for one. If man calls himself a Christian lawyer, or a Christian politician, we are told it is wrong to call attention to the discrepancy between his profession and his actions. To do so is "judgmental" and a sin, it is held; the practical consequence is that those who are judged are they who expose sin, not those who commit it!

The result is a strange religious climate of surface faith. The church is full of millions who profess this surface faith, whom Paul describes as "having a form of godliness, but denying the power thereof" (I Timothy 3:5). We thus have people who want no tampering with their religion, while they refuse to allow their religion to tamper with them! One of the most obvious facts about God, however, is that He does more than tamper with us! He breaks us to remake us.

Our cultural crisis rests in the retreat of males from the responsibilities and duties of manhood. The faith has been sentimentalized, and a sentimental faith is unable to produce more than pious gush. The richness of life's spheres and all the varieties of institutional responsibilities have been eroded. Men do not see themselves as priests, prophets, and kings under God. Biblical law emphasizes the local and personal origins of government. All men are to be elders, rulers, under God, rulers over families, vocations, and the institutions of which they are a part. Over every ten families, there is to be an elder over ten, then over fifty, a hundred, thousands and so on up. The *hundreds* were once a basic unit of law and court structures. All men had to be men or pay a price for their refusal. In Scripture, the man who chose to live by subsidy had to have his ears pierced as a public witness to his rejection of a man's responsibility and freedom in favor of security.

The ironic fact is that when men cease to be men they commonly pretend to be men, the macho role, or, more often they seek to play God. Man's original sin is to try to be as God, every man his own god, knowing or determining for himself what is good and evil (Gen. 3:5). Some scientists have tried to use science to gain this goal. Dr. Joshua Lederberg holds that we shall enter a post-human age, one in which science will, through genetic engineering, create super-human men, man-gods, who will have none of the infirmities of present-day men. Science will be able to regrow defective organs such as a liver or a heart, a uterus will be implanted in a male body to produce a child, and so on and on. Because of the respect for the status of such scientists, their fantasies are not subjected to the ridicule they deserve.

Let us assume for a moment that these mad dreams are possible. Will the human predicament be any better? Will man's moral dereliction be solved, or will it not rather be enhanced to produce a demonic world order?

Moreover, will the men who do these things, and the men to whom they are done, be more responsible men? It is clear that our scientific community shows no advantage over the rest of the population in integrity, responsibility, and a capacity to function as a husband and father! The dreams of these scientists solve no problems; they evade them.

One reason for the uneasiness of many men at the feminist challenge is that the indictment strikes home. However, conceding to the feminists is no substitute for responsibility but a further abdication.

Margaret Wade Labarge, in her study of *Henry V* (b. 1387), comments on the state of things in that era. Religion had become a superstructure, taken for granted by all. Everyone was given to conventional religious practices with neither commitment nor much concern. The clergy was dedicated to a "decent formalism." Henry V perhaps took his faith a bit more seriously than most, and, as an administrator, he sought to keep all things functioning in their proper order and place. One would have to say that he functioned better than most heads of state today and that society had a better focus on justice then than now.

There was, however, a silent and growing erosion, the erosion of faith and therefore of men. The crisis in English society was deferred, not resolved.

In our time, the crisis is past deferment. The time has come for men to ground themselves in the whole counsel of God, to be responsible, mature, and venturesome. There can be no resolution of our world crisis without a resolution of the crisis in male responsibility. To blame conspiracies, however real some may be, special problems, the past, and more, are all evasions if men do not assume their responsibilities today as a privilege and a duty under God. (January, 1983)

BAPTISM AND CITIZENSHIP
Chalcedon Position Paper No. 37

Churchmen have long discussed, debated, and analyzed the meaning of baptism in terms of the church. They have called attention to its meaning in terms of regeneration, purification, and more. All these emphases are important, and it is not our intention to displace or downgrade them in calling attention to another and central meaning.

Baptism is an act of citizenship. In the early church, it was not only an act of citizenship in Christ's Kingdom, but it involved what was in the eyes of the Roman Empire a treasonable affirmation. The New Testament tells us that baptism is "in the Name of the Lord Jesus" (Acts 19:5;1 Cor. 6:11; Acts 8:16). *The Name* stands for the person, authority, and power, so that baptism in the Name of the Lord Jesus is into citizenship or membership in His Person, authority, and power, and hence Christians face the world as citizens of the Kingdom of God and as ambassadors thereof.

In the early church, Christians faced the requirement of Rome to be a licensed religion, with an imperial certificate in their meeting place. To gain that certificate meant an affirmation of subjection to the Empire; the required confession was, "Caesar is Lord." As Polycarp faced martyrdom for refusing that confession, the imperial magistrate, doing his best to persuade the aged Christian, asked him, "What harm is there in saying Caesar is Lord?" As the historian J.N.D. Kelly commented, "The acclamation *Kurios Kaiser* would seem to have been a popular one in the civic cult of the Roman empire, and Christians were no doubt conscious of the implicit denial of it contained in their own *Kurios Iesous*" (*Early Christian Creeds*, p. 15). In fact, the confession, Jesus Christ is Lord, was the baptismal confession of the early church (Acts 8:36-38; Phil. 2:9-11).

Rome boasted of being the conqueror of the world, and its emperors were gods. The early church countered this. I John 4:15 declares, "Whosoever shall confess that Jesus is the Son of God, God dwelleth in him, and he in God." Every believer was given a higher status than the emperor! As against the emperor as the world conqueror, John declares, "Who is he that overcometh the world, but he that believeth that Jesus is the Son of God?" (I John 5:5). Since one meaning of Lord is *God*, the implications of the baptismal confession are obvious. Every believer confessed a greater and higher citizenship in a kingdom which would overcome and outlast all others. In terms of his faith, he held, "The Kingdoms of this world are become the Kingdoms of our Lord, and of his Christ: and he shall reign for ever and ever" (Rev. 11:15). The joy of Pentecost is inseparable from this faith. So intense was this faith in the Lord and subjection to the great King of kings, that Ignatius wrote in a letter (Trall. 9), "Be deaf when anyone speaks to you apart from Jesus Christ." The horror of Rome in facing these Christians can be seen in part by the irritation of modern statists as they face American Christians on trial for refusing statist controls.

Rome recognized no power and no loyalty beyond itself. Even the gods of Rome were made gods by resolution of the Senate and were thus subordinate to the empire. The idea of a power greater than and over the

Roman Empire was anathema. This, however, was precisely the faith of the early church. Jesus Christ, they held, is the King of kings and Lord of lords (I Tim. 6:15). It is difficult to imagine a faith which was more an affront to Rome. Christians declared to one and all that Jesus Christ is the universal and cosmic Lord. He is Lord not only over the church, the individual, and the family, but over the state, the arts and sciences, economics, education, and all things else. All things must either serve Christ the Lord or be judged by Him. So great is His over-lordship, that He will not only judge all things in time as Lord and Ruler, but, at the last, in the general resurrection of the dead, "he will judge the world" (Acts 17:31). When Paul spoke of this, the Athenians on Mars' Hill turned away; the idea of such a lord was too much for them.

It should be now apparent what baptism meant to the early church, and to Rome. It was an act of membership, of citizenship, in the Lord Jesus Christ. It was the public declaration of a higher loyalty and a higher obedience. It was baptism into Christ and His Kingdom, of which the local church was a visible outpost. It is thus a seriously misplaced emphasis to speak of being baptized into the church; this is a secondary aspect. Baptism is essentially into Christ and His Kingdom. After baptism, a person was regarded as being "in Christ", or "in the Lord."

Citizenship in the Roman Empire, in the New Testament era, was a privilege highly prized; most people were subjects, not citizens. When the Roman chief captain in Jerusalem learned that Paul was a Roman citizen he said, "With a great sum obtained I this freedom" (i.e., Roman citizenship), and Paul answered, "But I was freeborn" (i.e., born a citizen Acts 22:28). To lay hands on a Roman citizen could be dangerous: he was a privileged person. But now these Christians were claiming a higher citizenship, with greater powers, and one which is open to every man!

Paul in Philippians 3:20 declares, "For our conversation is in heaven: from whence also we look for the Saviour, the Lord Jesus Christ." The word *conversation* is a translation for the Greek *politeuma* which means *citizenship* or *commonwealth*. The word *conversation* is an aspect of its meaning. Members of a family have a common life, conversation, and citizenship. To be a citizen of heaven and the Kingdom of God is to have a conversation with the Lord and with fellow members in him, to be members of Him and of one another, and to be together a commonwealth and Kingdom and citizens thereof.

Hence, the call to baptism is a call to regeneration and to citizenship in Christ and His Kingdom. Peter in Acts 2:38 declares, "Repent, and be baptized every one of you in the Name of Jesus Christ..." *Name* means person. To be baptized into the Name of Jesus means to be baptized into His Body, His Life, into citizenship and membership in His Kingdom.

This tells us too what it meant to confess "Caesar is Lord," *Kurios Kaisar*

It meant confessing that Caesar is god, and that our highest allegiance is to Caesar. This is a confession which some pastors and churches are making; in so doing, they are implicitly denying that Jesus Christ is their Lord. Then, and until recently, the invocation of a Name was the invocation of one's lord. We have an echo of this in the old expression, "Open, in the name of the law," i.e., in the name of the ruling power. To invoke the Name was to swear allegiance to one's king and Lord. It also invoked aid and protection, and the king's servants could claim the immunities of the king by declaring that they acted in the Name of the king. Hence, the Christian prays in Jesus' Name, the Name of power at the throne; he calls himself a Christian and so claims the protection of the Name and citizenship in the Lord's Kingdom.

Truly to say that "Jesus Christ is Lord," is to reveal our faithfulness and obedience to Him. It means that our conversation or citizenship is manifest in all our being in words, thought, and deed. Moreover, as Paul makes clear, "No man can say that Jesus is the Lord, but by the Holy Ghost" (I Cor. 12:3); it is the revelation of the power of the Kingdom in and through him. The life of all such is a manifestation of the Lord, and they are like men "having (the Lamb's) Father's name written in their foreheads" (Rev.14:1). The baptized confessed their citizenship in the Name, in the Lord, in all their being.

Citizenship requires allegiance and loyalty, faithfulness to the Lord of the realm, who in turn confesses, knows, and protects them. Paul thus says, "Nevertheless, the foundation of God standeth sure, having this seal, The Lord knoweth them that are his. And, Let every one that nameth the name of Christ depart from iniquity" (II Tim. 2:19). *The Didache*, before giving instructions about baptism, spoke at length of the two ways, the way of obedience to the every word of God (Matt. 4:4), the way of life, as against the way of death, and then said: "Now concerning baptism: Baptize as follows, *when you have rehearsed the aforesaid teaching*." In other words, baptism is into a way of life as set forth in the Person of Christ and the righteousness of God, His law. Peter speaks of this in I Peter 3:21, when he writes, baptism is "not the putting away of the filth of the flesh", i.e., not merely an external cleansing of the body like a bath, but a new life in Christ, "the answer of a good conscience toward God, by the resurrection of Jesus Christ." Christ having made atonement for us, gives us also the new life of the resurrection; therefore, as the faithful and obedient people of the Lord, we have a good conscience, because we manifest God's righteousness as set forth in his law-word and thereby follow Christ as members of His new humanity.

The old humanity of the first Adam has a common life, conversation, and citizenship in sin and death. The new humanity of the last Adam has a common life, conversation, and citizenship in Jesus Christ. The rulers of the old humanity recognize only one loyalty and one citizenship, to themselves.

All men, says John, are summoned by this old world power to acknowledge its power and to be marked or branded as the possession of this humanistic power. This old power seeks total control over humanity, an exclusive control, to the point that "no man might buy or sell," or have a church or Christian School, except under its control (Rev. 12:16-18).

However, the early church saw all men as God's creation and therefore under God and His law, and hence under God's judgment. For them, the word of God was clear on this matter: "The Kingdoms of this world are become the kingdoms of our Lord, and of his Christ: and he shall reign for ever and ever" (Rev. 11:15). Hence, says John, the rejoicing in heaven: the triumph of the Lord is assured.

This means that all Christians are by baptism members of Christ and citizens of the Kingdom of God; they are therefore "more than conquerors" in Christ (Rom. 8:37).

In antiquity, men wore the garb of their rank, i.e., their clothing was a badge indicating who they were, and what their status was. Sumptuary laws required the same kind of identification well into the modern era and made it illegal for a man or woman to dress above his rank. St. Paul has an amazing reference to this practice. In Galatians 3:27, he writes, "For as many of you have been baptized into Christ have put on Christ." This means we wear the marks of membership, citizenship, in the royal household of the King of kings and Lord of lords! The parable of the wedding feast tells us the same thing (Matt. 22:1-14). No man has any place in the royal court unless he is one who puts on the raiment of the king, i.e., is a member of the family of the king in word, thought, and deed. Baptism is thus the act of citizenship, of membership.

As citizens of the great Kingdom of God, we pay our tax, the tithe, to the King and His work, and, above and over the tax, we bring our gifts and offerings. Because we belong to the King, our children too must be offered to Him, as His to take and use with us, and this is the true meaning of infant circumcision and then baptism. As citizens of the Lord's realm, we place all other allegiances under our duty to the Lord. Thus, we obey rulers in civil government, not because they require it, but because the Lord requires it and only as far as His word permits. Our obedience is thus not for the state's sake, but "for conscience sake" (Rom. 13:5), as a part of our baptismal requirement of obedience unto "a good conscience toward God" (I Peter 3:21).

As we have seen, in antiquity, very few men were citizens of a country. Only a privileged few had that status, and the power and wealth that marked citizenship. Paul tells us that the mark of baptism is the gift of the Spirit and all the wealth and power which the King gives to the royal family. "For by one spirit are we all baptized into one body, whether we be Jews or Gentiles" (I Cor. 12:13). So great was the early Christian sense of wealth, power, and joy in their Savior-King that Paul could say to King Agrippa, "I would to God, that not only thou, but also all that hear me this day, were both almost, and altogether such as I am, except these bonds" or chains (Acts 26:29)! It was this recognition of power that made the early Christians "more than conquerors." Only the same faith and citizenship can triumph today. (February, 1983)

STATE INTEREST VERSUS PUBLIC INTEREST
Chalcedon Position Paper No. 38

In a recent trial in a federal court, questions by the state attorney gave me an opportunity to enter into the records some thoughts which would otherwise have been objected to by the state. Constant reference had been made about the "compelling state interest" which ostensibly made state intervention into the life of the church and its schools a necessity. The most compelling state interest should be *freedom with justice*. As a matter of fact, in my earliest school days, this was stressed. The climax of the Pledge of Allegiance states the purpose of the United States, of the federal union, as "liberty and justice for all."

Now, however, a "compelling state interest" means *controls*. The obvious fact in these trials is that Christian Schools are providing markedly superior teaching in both moral training and in academic disciplines. The state schools are usually a nightmare of lawlessness and ignorance and have given the United States its highest rate of illiteracy in its history. The "compelling state interest" of which the state attorneys speak is the power to control. A century ago in France, Leon Gambetta made it clear that equality was more important to the state than freedom, and that both equality and liberty had to give way to fraternity, which for him was force. He said, "Force is an indivisible element in the grandeur of races." Basic to fraternity and force for him were state schools. For him too morality was to be derived from the politics of the state, not the church. (E. M. Acomb: *The French Laic Laws*, 1879-1889; New York: Octagon Books, 1967.)

This was nothing new. When Diocletian further centralized power *over* the people, and began the savage persecution of Christians, he spoke about power *to* the people. The publicity theme of his coinage was "Genii Populi Romani," i.e., he deified the Roman people even as he enslaved them! The cult of Rome and the Roman people went hand in hand with the enslavement of Rome and of all the people (Michael Grant: *The Climax of Rome*; Boston, Massachusetts: Little, Brown, 1968.)

The state has long had a habit also of using every occasion to do a little good as an opportunity to advance a great deal of evil. Thus, in late 18th century Austria, Joseph II used the same goals as the French Revolution to centralize his power. The serfs were freed to break the feudal power and strengthen the monarchy. As Beloff noted, "Both liberty and equality were devices by which the State could be strengthened." Instead of various levels of feudal power, all citizens were made *equally subordinate* to a central power and bureaucracy and equally taxable. The age of the French Revolution saw in France and elsewhere temporary or illusory freedoms accompanied by great increases of centralized state power. The illusion was that increased state powers would eliminate ancient evils, when in reality they created greater ones. As a result, the "age of absolutism" ended only to see the beginnings of a new and greater one in the twentieth century. (Max Beloff: *The Age of Absolutism 1660-1815*, p. 127, etc. New York: Harper, 1962.)

For a time, the free market extended liberties, but the growing powers of the central state in time suppressed these freedoms. The state as the new god was asserting its sovereign powers. This had religious consequences.

Bismarck in Germany made the state paramount over all things. He was pragmatically a conservative and a liberal, whichever served the state best at the moment. Theodor Fontane, who described himself as Bismarck's greatest admirer, once said, in another context, "Bismarck was the greatest despiser of principle that ever existed." (Fritz Stern: *Gold and Iron, Bismarck, Bleichroder, and the Building of the German Empire*, p. 280. New York: Knopf, 1977.) For Bismarck, the state interest could not be subordinated to any other interest. This is the mark of the statist, whether he calls himself a liberal, conservative, fascist, or radical. All things must be subordinated to the interest of the state. Our rising American fascism clearly manifests this premise in its attack on the freedom of religion. Even Theodor Mommsen was an exponent of such statism. He appealed to deracinated Jews to join the church because, he explained, the nation-state hates all vestiges of particularism. Much later, the Nazis added to this hatred not only the Jews but all churches. Rosenberg, in the *Myth of the Twentieth Century* (1931), declared "All German education must be based on the recognition of the fact that it is not Christianity that has brought us morality, but Christianity that owes its enduring values to the German character." The churches were therefore attacked for opposing the compelling state interest. The Catholic Bishop of Berlin, von Preysing, held to the contrary, "Justice is not derived from the will of the society...There is an eternal right outside man's will and guaranteed by God." By the end of 1938, however, the Nazis had suppressed all church schools in Bavaria, Wurttenberg, Baden, Saxony, Thuringia, Oldenberg, the Saar, and large parts of Prussia and Austria. Religious publications were also suppressed (in the U.S. in 1983, not only are Christian Schools under attack, but also religious publishing houses, as witness the case of the Presbyterian and Reformed Publishing Company.) In Germany in the 1930s, it was declared that children are to be trained "as though they had never heard of Christianity." (M. Searle Bates: *Religious*

Liberty, An Inquiry, p. 31. New York: Da Capo Press, 1972.) In the United States, such education has long been the reality of statist education, with humanism as the established religion of the state schools. Now the attack has been launched against Christian Schools.

The Nazi goal was uniformity. Hence, all particularism was attacked and suppressed: Jews, Christians, Gypsies, all alike were anathema. The Jews were identified with hated causes, i.e., communism and capitalism, and the same applied to the churches at the time.

The same has been even more true, and with unequalled barbarism and savagery, in the Soviet Union. There, the old revolutionary ideal of liberty, fraternity and equality is mocked by reality. There is neither fraternity nor liberty, and the only equality is in slavery. The statist road to the old liberal goals has proven to be the road to hell.

The state has insisted upon identifying the state interest with public interest. This means that the state is equated with the people. Such an identification ensures totalitarianism, because the state then is the voice and even the incarnation of the people. To oppose the state means to oppose the people, and dissenters are classified as "enemies of the people." No private concern nor any public concern can then exist. To oppose the state interest is to oppose the will of the people. Because the state interest is at the same time identified with justice and moral concern, a most arrogant phariseeism ensues.

This is presently the position of most bureaucracies the world over. It is certainly the stance in the U. S. of state and federal attorneys as they confront churches and their functions. It is they who speak as the voice of justice and morality, as the guardians of the "public interest." All too often, as history makes clear, the state interest has been the enemy of the public interest.

The statists see a compelling state interest in the control of the spheres of education, economics, religion, and more. Once having assumed the sovereignty or lordship of the state, there is then logically no limitation on either the jurisdiction or the power of the state. Sovereignty or lordship means total and ultimate authority. Those who acknowledge the lordship of Jesus Christ can then withhold no area of life and thought from His dominion. Given the sovereignty or lordship of the triune God, it follows of necessity that law must proceed from God, because law-making is an attribute of sovereignty. Antinomianism is a denial of God's sovereignty and an implicit affirmation of the state's lordship.

Sovereignty has been very briefly defined as "complete power." Clearly, complete power can only be an attribute of the triune God. Every state claiming sovereignty, however, logically seeks to gain complete power over all things, especially the mind and bodies of men. Such an effort leads to totalitarianism and tyranny. To gain surface compliance to its claim to sovereignty, such a state resorts to measures designed to subjugate man. To this, there are two approaches. The *first*, so ably described by Roland Huntsford in *The New Totalitarians* is by controlling education. Only state-controlled and state-approved instruction which meets the state's needs for conformity is approved. Since the church is a teaching ministry, this means control of the churches in all aspects of their ministry. The New Totalitarians are consummate hypocrites in their war against Biblical faith. They mask it with a multitude of bureaucratic concerns: zoning regulations, the need for supervision and regulation, the compelling state interest in all such matters, and so on and on. The Marxists openly persecute Biblical faith; the New Totalitarians do it by indirection.

Second, Marxist totalitarianism relies only secondarily on education and primarily on total terror. By means of torture, slave labor camps, fear, and suppression, the Marxist dictators strive for the total compliance of their peoples.

The Psalmist (Ps. 115:3) tells us that God the Lord is unlike all false gods: "Our God is in the heavens: he hath done whatsoever he hath pleased." God's sovereignty is undivided: "Hear, O Israel: The LORD our GOD is one LORD" (Deut. 6:4). God therefore requires an undivided allegiance: "And thou shalt love the Lord thy God with all thine heart, and with all thy soul, and with all thy might" (Deut. 6:5). These words by Moses are the mandate for obedience to God's law. Because He is the Lord, the sovereign, the ultimate One, He must be totally obeyed with all our love in all our being. Our Lord, in repeating these words of Deuteronomy 6:5, thereby reconfirmed the sole sovereignty of God and the full authority of His law (Luke 10:27).

Significantly, Mohammed, while departing from the Biblical premises at many points, retains this one, the sovereignty of God: "There is no god but God." It was this premise which gave Islam power.

Religions which deny the sovereignty of their "god" become polytheistic. It is logically impossible to ascribe sovereignty to any being other than God and still retain a god in one's system. The transfer of sovereignty to the state means that law-making and lordship are transferred to the state. The power to make laws is the power to declare things to be good and evil. Since Aristotle's state, in his *Politics*, is the source of law, his state was also the source of morality. Nazi Germany was emphatic that morality came from the state, not from the Bible. The state schools of America (and other countries) also see morality as a man-created or state-created thing. Value-education is established by these educators on humanistic, statist foundations.

All over the world, "sovereign" states are manifesting their tyrannies. The great tyranny, Soviet Russia, brutally and ruthlessly manifests its tyrant power against Christianity and against all dissent in any form. The Western democracies are, in varying degrees, replacing the God of Scripture with themselves and are, in many instances infringing on or suppressing Christian liberties. Israel, indignant at Arab hostility, is repressive of Arab and Christian dissent, while the Arabs are repressive towards Jews and Christians. All self-righteously assert their right to do as they please in terms of compelling state interests.

Compelling state interests are essentially and ultimately hostile to God as their rival and to man as a dissenter. We must assert that there is a compelling theological interest in freedom. To acknowledge the sovereignty of and predestination by the triune God is to deny the sovereignty of the state and predestination (i.e., total planning and control) by the state. Sovereignty and predestination are exclusive attributes. If God is the Lord, if there is no god but God, then neither man nor the state can be the sovereign or lord. If essential and ultimate determination, planning, and control belong to God alone, then no man nor state can assume such a prerogative unto itself. Men and nations then must acknowledge God's sovereignty, and men and nations must seek to know their place and calling in God's plan. There is then a compelling public interest to know, obey, and serve God, for "Man's chief end is to glorify God, and to serve him forever." (March, 1983)

BOX THEOLOGY
Chalcedon Position Paper No. 39

In the presidential address to the Economic History Association September 12, 1980, Richard A. Easterlin commented on the fact that the modern era began with the rejection of the medieval church (and, one can add, Christianity,) and "humanity ultimately took up a new 'religion of knowledge,' whose churches are the schools and universities of the world, whose priests are its teachers, and whose creed is belief in science and the power of rational inquiry, and in the ultimate capacity of humanity to shape its own destiny" (*The Journal of Economic History*, vol. XLI, no. 1, March, 1981, p. 17). We can add that the great agency of this new religion is the modern humanistic state.

If a religion is not catholic, universal in its faith, jurisdiction, and scope, it will quickly fail. Religion by its very nature either speaks to all of life, or it in time speaks to none. Man by his nature has boundaries to his life and activities; they are inescapable for man. There are boundaries to my property, my abilities, and my authority. By definition, no god nor religion can have boundaries and limitations to its sway without self-destruction. A god is either sovereign and total in his jurisdiction, or else he is soon no god at all; something else bests him and replaces him. All the false gods of history until recently were false gods because the men who made them also placed limits upon them. This was especially clear with the gods of Rome; they were created by men, the Roman Senate specifically, and hence men always had priority over the gods. The gods in time became more and more obviously tools and a department of state for the Roman Empire, which claimed catholic or universal sway and sovereignty for itself.

In the modern world, the humanistic state claims this sovereignty: it is the modern god walking upon earth. The modern state claims sovereignty and catholicity; the United Nations is the attempt of humanistic statism to attain true and full universality and catholicity.

Meanwhile, the Christian Church is busily departing from the doctrine of God's sovereignty and His necessary catholic jurisdiction. Christianity is increasingly limited to a "spiritual" realm (of which it now concedes vast areas to psychology and psychiatry), and the rest of the world is granted to the state.

The result is *box theology*. To understand what box theology is, let us compare the universe to the Empire State Building, a great, modern, skyscraper office building. In box theology, the church claims one small office among hundreds for Christianity. All the rest of the building is given over to the jurisdiction of the state and the sciences. One area after another is deemed non-religious and is surrendered. This is done despite the fact that God is the Creator and Lord of the whole universe and therefore has total and absolute jurisdiction over all things. God's law-word, jurisdiction, and authority must govern all things. "All things were made by him; and without him was not any thing made that was made" (John 1:3).

The jurisdiction of the *church* is a limited one, but the jurisdiction of the triune God, of Christ our King, and of the Bible, God's law-word, cannot be limited. Every area of life and thought must be under the dominion of the Lord: He alone is truly sovereign. To limit the jurisdiction of Christ is to posit a limited god, one who cannot survive because a limited god is a contradiction and is no god at all. If God is God, if He truly is the Lord or Sovereign, everything must serve Him and be under His dominion, the state, schools, arts, sciences, the church, and all things else. To limit the jurisdiction of the God of Scripture to the soul of man and to the church is to deny Him. A limited god cannot save man, because he is not in control of all things; what he does today can be undone tomorrow, and his "salvation" is at best temporary.

Box theology limits the church, moreover, and destroys it. If the church and its word is limited, to return to our image, to one room and none other in the Empire State Building, then its only legitimate area of concern is the church, and to a degree, the soul of man. There can then be no dealing with the problems of the age, because they lie outside the jurisdiction of the church.

The results are both deplorable and revolting. The "world" of the church is then no larger than the church; it is boxed into its narrow little room. All its battles then are waged within that "world," the church. This means that the world of the church in box theology becomes a realm of continual civil war, Protestants and Catholics against one another, Arminians and Calvinists in opposition to one another, and so on. This does not mean that the issues between these groups are inconsequential. It does mean that subordinate issues are made the only ones. The crown rights of Christ our King over the whole world are then neglected or forgotten. The necessity of bringing politics, economics, the arts and sciences, education, the family, all peoples, tongues, tribes, and nations under the dominion of Christ the Lord is truncated or shortcircuited.

Box theology believes it is strict because it is narrow in its scope, whereas a true strictness claims all things for Christ the King. This false strictness leads to phariseeism and to censoriousness. (One such pathetic little group of box theology advocates rails at all other Christians in issue after issue. One recent publication actually declared that John Whitehead "scorns the cross" because he disagrees with their view, and held that I believe in the Inquisition, arriving at this by a wild misreading of one of my books! These are the pathetic dead, revelling in their narrow coffin box.)

Box theology men battle against their fellow Christians continually, while the world claims more and more of Christ's realm. Because box theology allows the state to be sovereign or lord, it offers no resistance to statist controls. As a result, in state after state, where attempts to control the church are in process, many advocates of box theology insist on surrender to the state and sometimes go to court to witness for the state against the resisting churches.

Box theology is implicit polytheism. It says in effect that there is one God over the church, but other gods over every other realm, or else, that all realms other than the church are neutral realms. These "neutral" realms are not under the mandate of Scripture but are free to follow the dictates of natural (fallen) reason wherever it leads them.

This idea of neutrality is, of course, a myth. If the God of Scripture is the true and living God, there can be no realm of neutral facts and neutral jurisdiction. All things are under God's sovereignty and law, and nothing can exist apart from Him, nor can any law be valid other than His law. To claim neutrality for any realm is to deny that God created it, and to posit neutrality is to cease to be a Christian.

Because God is God, His jurisdiction is total, and His sovereignty absolute and indivisible. No human institution, neither church nor state, can claim any jurisdiction beyond its limited sphere. Thus, while the church has a limited sphere of authority under God, the word it must proclaim is the word of the total God for the totality of life and thought. The word proclaimed by the church cannot be limited to the church, because, if it is Scripture, it is not the word of the church, but the word of God. The word judges all things, governs all things, and offers hope in Christ to all men and all areas of life.

Box theology is dead theology, with a god too small to speak to anything more than the church. In its own way, box theology proclaims the death of God, because a limited God ceases to be God. The forces of humanistic statism have advanced only through default. Churchmen have retreated from and abandoned one area after another to the humanists, and many continue to retreat. Sigmund Freud saw the inner world of man as the last domain of Biblical religion; all other spheres had been captured.

By converting psychology (the word concerning the soul) from a theological to a scientific discipline, and guilt from a theological fact to a scientific concern, Freud hoped to make religion totally irrelevant (See R.J. Rushdoony: *Freud*). Even more than Freud, the pietists have been remarkable in their enforced limitations upon Biblical faith.

Ironically, the bankruptcy of humanism has increased as its sway and power have been broadened. When the Enlightenment triumphed over the Reformation and Counter-Reformation, it brought into sharp focus a development which had previously marked the Renaissance era, the rift between classes. There had previously been very serious problems between the rich and the poor, but the fact of a common faith and a common life in the church had provided a bond and a basis for community, a hope for the potential solution to problems. Christian faith had stressed a necessary harmony of interests.

With the Enlightenment, the common faith gave way to a widening gulf and to hostilities. Leon Garfield, in *The House of Hanover* (1976), called attention to the fact that, with the first Hanover ruler in England, the first Riot Act was passed. The foreign king, George I, was a fitting symbol of the fact that rulers and the people were now foreigners one to another. The people, said Garfield, were prone to rioting. Silk-weavers, coal-heavers, sailors, powdered foot-men, gaol-birds, and ex-soldiers, all were rioting. Ex-soldiers from Marlborough's foreign wars turned highwaymen, and the modern age came with the affirmation of Reason, and with riots.

The number of offenses which received the death penalty grew steadily, but so too did crime. Today too we have many who believe that stricter laws and penalties will solve the problem of crime, but they did not then, nor will they now. All such men have their own version of box theology or box philosophy. Hanging children for stealing a loaf of bread did not stop crime or juvenile delinquency in 18th century England; the evangelical awakening, a partial return of Puritanism, did much to alter the situation.

Moreover, law and order have various meanings in the Soviet Union, Red China, Sweden, and the United States, but they are all variations of humanism. Only Biblical law and order, coupled with the regenerating power of Jesus Christ, can alter a society.

Ultimately, any faith which does not have the triune God of Scripture and Jesus Christ as its alpha and omega is a box philosophy or theology, and this is clearly true of our new imitation catholicism, the modern humanistic state. However totalitarian its claims, its faith fails to be universal or true, because it boxes itself in to insulate itself from God and His law-word. It is thus dead to life and to truth, and it is doomed to collapse and the grave.

The law of the modern state is the law of death. In both the United States and Canada, for example, pornography trials have as their premise "community standards." Whether it be adult or child pornography, the legal test of its legality is the community standard. This is the legal enactment of Genesis 3:5, every man as his own god, knowing, or determining for himself, what is good and evil. Such a "community standard" as law means that, if the community favors abortion, theft, murder, rape, or incest, these things can become legal.

A box theology or philosophy is finally no bigger than man, whether man's pietism or man's sin, but, in any case, it is no bigger than man. God's sentence upon it is the sentence already pronounced on all the sons of Adam, and upon all their institutions, philosophies, and theologies, ---death. There is no escaping this sentence apart from Jesus Christ, who is the Lord or Sovereign over all men and all creation.

To acknowledge Jesus Christ as Lord is to bring ourselves, our every thought, every action and word, all spheres of life, and all institutions, under His jurisdiction and law-word. Box theologies and philosophies are finally allotted a narrow box by God; its name is Hell. The glorious liberty of the sons of God is to be a new creation in and through Jesus Christ, to work for the fullness of that new creation, and to dwell therein eternally in the great consummation by Him who makes all things new. (April, 1983)

THE LAW, THE STATE, AND THE PEOPLE
Chalcedon Position Paper No. 40

The nature and the meaning of law have changed from one culture to another. *First* of all, all law is religious in its presuppositions, because it is an expression of basic and ultimate values. Laws protect those values most important to a society and prescribe those regarded as alien and evil. Every legal system embodies a concept of ultimate concern, of religion and ethics. *Second*, laws, beside protecting *values*, also protect *men*. The men protected in contemporary states can be, theoretically, all men within the society, the state and its agents, or one class of men, such as the proletariat. It is not our concern at the moment whether or not the protection is theoretical or actual. In antiquity, the law was commonly royal law; even more, it was often the law of an ostensibly divine-human King whose word was law. In some sense, the law is always *partial*; it protects those whom the law deems just and prosecutes those suspected of injustice. Where the partiality of the law is determined by men, all who differ from the law-makers can be judged illicit and criminal. There is thus no freedom for capitalists in the Soviet Union, and there are limitations at times on the freedom of communists in some democracies. Where laws come from men, men will determine the limits of the law's protection.

The law thus always has an *interest*; law protects and punishes in terms of pre-theoretical presuppositions which are in essence religious. The important question to ask of law is the nature of its *interest* or concern. The interest can be royal, democratic, fascist, racist, and so on. In every case, it is an expression of values.

Historically, law, which we like to see as the expression of justice, has been very commonly seen as injustice. The royal law in India for centuries was exploitive of the peoples and seen as oppressive. One aging missionary who had a contact with elderly Chinese who had seen the rules of the empress, the "republic", and the communists, asked them about the difference from one regime to another as they affected them, the peasants. Their answer was that all things were essentially the same: "All masters want their will and our work." Theoreticians of the law like to see it as equivalent to justice. During most of history, men have seen it as the oppressive will of the masters.

Ancient Israel was an exception to this. Law-making was recognized in times of faithfulness as God's prerogative, not man's, and God had revealed His covenant law through Moses. This law was defended and expounded by the prophets, and it was binding for the King and the people. Nathan's indictment of King David, one of a long series of such confrontations, was without parallel in antiquity. A law beyond man and from God judged both kings and peoples, indeed, all men and nations.

For our purposes here, a few limited aspects of Biblical law must be noted. *First*, every system of law imposes certain restraints on some for the freedom of others. Outside of Biblical law, these restraints are on one segment of men for the freedom of another, sometimes only a few. In Plato's *Republic*, the free are very few; they are the philosopher-Kings. In other systems, other elites are free and the rest restrained. *Second*, not only is freedom in a social order selective, but it is also both positive and negative. Thus, in Soviet Russia, there is a freedom *from* capitalism, and a freedom *for* the state to control its citizenry. A man who exercises the freedom to sin thereby ensures freedom from virtue and its many blessings. No stand or act has a single consequence; we are at all times in a nexus of events, past, present, and future. Biblical law gives us freedom from men and from the state, but not from God. The social order created by Biblical law distrusts man as a sinner and thus minimizes his controls while stressing his responsibility.

This means, *third*, that Biblical law leads to a minimal state. The king or judge in Israel had less power than is now routine for the higher officials of state bureaucracies. The stress of Biblical law is on man's responsibility to God and to his fellow men under God. Man must distrust himself, his fellow men, and his rulers. In Isaiah's words, "Cease ye from man, whose breath is in his nostrils: for wherein is he to be accounted of?" (Isa. 2:22). Power and authority are not to be accorded to men apart from God's word and law. At the same time, we are commanded to remember always that "we are members one of another" (Eph. 4:25).

Much more can be said of Biblical law, but, for our present purposes, this suffices. With the progressive conversion of the Western world to Christ, the canon of society and the states became God's law-word, so that a new element was introduced into the life of the law. Rome early saw the far-reaching implications of Christianity and therefore resisted it. Two rival doctrines of sovereignty and law were at war one with another, the sovereignty of God and His law versus the sovereignty of man, the state, and man-made law. From the days of Rome to the present, history has been witness to this continuing battle.

In any system of thought, the sovereign is the law-maker and thus the de facto god. Sovereignty, or lordship, and law-making are inseparable. The power to make laws is a manifestation of ultimacy and sovereignty in a society and over a society. It is a religious fact,and it manifests the god of that system.

Because of this, the conflict of Christianity with various forces, most notably the state, has been a continuing fact of Western history. The periodic prevalence of the Christian perspective has meant the freeing of man from statist controls. It has also meant that Western history has been marked by a freedom unknown to other areas of the world, and the result has been a vitality in the West of unequalled dimensions.

Instead of a monolithic society dominated by a monolithic state, we have seen both conflict and freedom. However faulty the Christian community has usually been, its presence has been productive of social energies and progress unequalled in all of history. Any study of the history of the West which is separated from theology is an exercise in evasion and futility. To chronicle events is not to understand history.

As a result of this Christian factor, the *interest* of a social order is a divided one. It is popular now with statists to speak of the *state interest* and to equate it with the *public interest*. This identification was basic to ancient tyrannies and is now a commonplace with our newer ones. Its modern origins are in Jean-Jacques Rousseau, who identified the state as the voice of the people's general will. This identification has made possible the tyrannies of modern Marxism and National Socialism. Rousseau held that the public "must be taught to know what it is that it wills." In the *Social Contract*, Rousseau held that while the will of the people may not correspond to the general will, "The general will is always right and tends always to the public good; but it does not follow that the deliberations of the people always have the same rectitude...There is often a great difference between the will of all and the general will." This identification of the *true* will of the people as the general will, and the general will with the state, led to a revival of the ancient pagan state. After Hegel, the state was indeed a god walking on earth.

The French Revolution began the idealization of the state to a degree previously unknown in the Western world. It also rationalized tyranny in the name of the people. The recognition that the public interest and the state interest could be very different had grown slowly and steadily. Now, with the secularization of society and the idealization of the state, that distinction began to be set aside.

In the English-speaking world, that distinction had become especially strong. A long tradition of courageous men defended the public interest against the powers of the crown. Step by step, that distinction was stressed and expanded. The unlimited powers of crown commissions were checked, and the areas of freedom expanded. The statement of James Otis in New England, that a man's house is his castle, was in this tradition, which goes back to the Middle Ages, Thomas Becket, the Magna Carta, and more. The papacy had a role in this, a major one, in challenging the controls various monarchs sought to place on the church. Freedom was a long battle, or, rather, a war with many battles, some still to be fought.

We must now turn to a key factor in all this. As we have seen, this Christian development led slowly to a recognition of the difference between the state interest and the public interest. David's indictment by the prophet Nathan is an important example of this in Old Testament history. European, English, and American histories give us many more examples of this.

The fact which made possible this differentiation and more was law, God's law. Unlike all other laws, God's law was not identified with any class, race, or people; it judged the Hebrews, and later, the Jews, even more harshly than other peoples, so that it gave them no exemptions and was emphatic about precluding this.

God's law is not identified with the state interest nor with the public interest. It stresses their differences, but it does not favor either. Rather, the law of God speaks from beyond history to judge and govern all within history. In II Samuel 12, the prophet Nathan says to David, "Thou are the man," and then pronounces God's judgment upon him. God's law judges both the public interest and the private interest because it transcends both.

All man-made laws reflect a particular human interest. At this point, humanistic legal theories and systems have been vulnerable to the Marxist critique. According to Marxism, laws are not objective systems of transcendental truth but class products. As class products, the legal systems defend their creating and sponsoring class. Accepting this premise, Marxists hold that the workers must be the dominant and controlling class, and the laws must reflect their class interest. Here too, however, an elite group expresses the supposed will of the people, but not with the consent of the people or workers.

Moreover, while Marxism has seen the partiality of the law, it has not solved the problem but has aggravated it by insisting on a rigid and total class partiality to replace the older limited one. As a result, it has replaced the mixed society with its frequent injustices with a totalitarian state dedicated to unremitting and total injustice.

Clearly, the state is not god; it cannot escape, on its humanistic premises, confusing the state interest with the public interest and from insisting that its will is the law. Because of this identification, there is a steady loss of religious freedom, and personal and family freedom. The loss in other realms, economic, educational, cultural, and so on, is also considerable. The state increasingly identifies its concerns with justice.

In the United States, there is a steady movement by regulation and by law to enforce a "public social policy" doctrine on all churches. This would give the federal government the power to regulate, control, or eliminate any and all groups whose stands conflict with "public policy." Since "public policy" currently favors such things as homosexuality and abortion, this means that churches opposed to either have the option of surrendering their faith or submitting to the state on these and other issues. Such a trend spells the death of freedom.

Whenever and wherever law has been seen as the voice of the people or the voice of the state, this totalitarian faith has prevailed. Either law is transcendental, or it is the product of some human agency. If law is the product of a human agency, it cannot judge that agency. When the state makes laws, it cannot be taken to court without its own consent, and then in its own courts. In every humanistic social order, justice becomes the will of the state, and freedom becomes a luxury reserved for the state and its agents.

Because we are today witnessing the long consequences of a deeply entrenched departure from the transcendental nature of law, from God's law, we witness on all sides an attack on Christian liberty.

At the same time, we see the rise of another kind of freedom, the freedom of slaves, the freedom of irresponsibility. What we often forget is that one of the worst factors in slavery has always been the intangible one, the diminution of responsibility. Nothing is more devastating to man and society. Abortion, the sexual revolution, homosexuality, and more are all evidences of slave freedom, not responsible freedom.

Those who despise God's law are thus railing against responsibility, justice, and responsible freedom. Freedom under God makes us members of, not lords over, one another. It delivers us from bondage into a calling under

God. The law of God is justice; man's law-making leads to injustice. The starting point of freedom and justice is Jesus Christ and His regenerating power: "If the Son therefore shall make you free, ye shall be free indeed" (John 8:36). (May, 1983)

COMMUNION AND COMMUNICATIONS
Chalcedon Position Paper No. 41

We are not accustomed to associating *communion* and *communications* with one another. For us, communion is a sacrament or an ordinance of the church, whereas "communications" refers to the media, to the exchange of ideas between peoples, to telephones, radio, television, and the like. The fact remains that the two words have a common root in the Latin and are closely related. *Communication* comes from *communicatio*, a making common, an imparting, sometimes a consulting of the hearers. *Communion* comes from the Latin *communio*, a community, mutual participation, or fellowship. Interestingly, *communio* or *conmunio*, depending on the context, can also mean to fortify, make sure, strengthen, or secure. One can perhaps say that communion and communication thus are not only means of sharing but also a fortifying and strengthening as well of all those who are involved.

It is common, in our day for men to speak of the communications gap. This gap exists in various quarters. The generation gap is one example, the inability of the old and the young to communicate in certain segments of our world. The gap exists also between the rulers and the ruled in almost every country; the high and the mighty, it is said, do not "speak the same language" as the rest of us, because their power places them on a different level of communication. In one area of life after another, the communication gap exists. Men may live and work close together and yet be worlds apart in this essential lives.

The simple fact is that there can be no communication where there is no communion. Proximity and a common background are not the answers. Husband and wife, and parent and children, can co-exist in the same house and have no communication of any significant sort. In one such family, a member remarked once to me that occasional efforts at intimacy were painful, because they called attention to the very serious gaps and differences between them; living without communication was easier.

As a result, a fact of modern life is man's readiness to live in isolation from close fellowship with others, because such a life of community means problems and also responsibilities. Many church members are ready to give for missions afar off rather than minister to needs close by. There are "valid" reasons for this: all people are born sinners and, even when converted, are far from perfected in grace. As a result, close contacts with people are close contacts with sin. Of course, we all find our own sins to be lovable ones, and the sins of others are for us intolerable! Hence, a retreat from community becomes very appealing to modern man.

At the same time, this retreat exacts penalties. Man was made by God to have community with God and with man. To retreat from community is thus to retreat from life as God ordained it. We have the paradox thus of men avoiding community while complaining of the communications gap.

Meanwhile, modern education, because it is humanistic, has lost the capacity to further or to create community. By teaching the radical ultimacy of man, the humanistic school isolates the individual from God and society. The statist school, normally a great instrument for communication and community, has been highly destructive thereof.

An historic communications function of the school has now broken down: *communication with the past*. The student who reads Shakespeare, Milton, Tolstoy, Dostoyevsky, Augustine, Anselm, Fielding, and others enters into communication with the past and is challenged, informed, enriched, or stimulated by it. Communication with the past is an essential part of the schooling of man, not only in the formal school, but in the family, the church, and the community. Family life should link the past to the present and the future. Where parents leave the care and the teaching of children to others, a vital link is broken. Similarly, the church's faith has deep roots into the past, and is the "Faith of our Fathers, living still." It cannot live if the past is untaught and ignored. That basic past is the Bible and its history, and it is alone the church's future. If the Bible is simply mined for salvation purposes (and salvation by such people is rather fire and life insurance from the J. C. Agency), then most of the Bible is ignored. At the same time, the language of the basic translations of the Western world, (the King James Version in English), is a language which also opens the doors to our past. Children brought up on the King James Version can read the literature of the past with an ease other children lack. The "community" of our day has lost its sense of the value of historic celebration of a nation's past; this is in part due to the modern state's evil ways, and men's shrinking from the old loyalties.

The various modern art forms have also often ceased to be means of communication. Expression rather than communication is their motif, and the expression is too often contempt, hatred, envy, and rage. As a result, art, historically one of the great means of communication, is ceasing to communicate. "Successful" and critically approved art is now elitist and increasingly restricted in its audience. To communicate easily and widely, i.e., to be readily understandable, is regarded as philistinism and bad art. Thus, modern art, by its very criteria, excludes the basic purpose and function of art, to communicate. A new school of art drops its style and changes rapidly as soon as it becomes popular, because such a dawning awareness of community is anathema to the artists. Basic to avant garde art is a hostility to all real communication with the greater part of the people. Nicanor Parra's *Anti-Poems* (1960) tells the story in its title. Instead of communicating, modern art has become exclusive and esoteric, which is another way of saying that it has ceased to be art. In fact, the esoteric and exclusive character of modern art is a denial of the very meaning of art. Marcel Duchamp was an "artist" who accepted and promoted this denial.

We have a communications problem, and we have a decline of art, because we have a decline in communion, and we have a decline in communion as a relationship, because we have a decline in the centrality of communion as a sacrament. At the heart of the church's life is the celebration of communion, the celebration of the great and central fact of history, the atonement by Jesus Christ. Man, created by God for communion with Him, and to work under God as His vice-gerunt over the earth, rebelled against God and sought to be his own god, establishing and determining his own laws and his own ideas of good and evil (Gen. 3:5). Man's fall meant a broken communion with God; it meant instead that man's communion was now with sin and death, and with himself in preference to God. This fallen man sought to create his own form of communion by means of a humanistic world order, a Tower of Babel, but the verdict of God and the requirement of his own fallen nature bring that hope to confusion and destruction. Throughout history to the present, men have tried to build their Towers of Babel, with consistently drastic consequences. Virtually all modern nations are Babels, and they have thus an anciently ordained predictable future. Fallen man has a communications gap, with God, with other men, and with himself. There is no solution to his problem apart from Jesus Christ.

The Lord, by His atonement, re-establishes us into communion with the triune God. We have peace with God through Christ, and we therefore have the principle of peace with other men and with ourselves in Christ our Lord.

As man grows in grace, he moves from the world of sin and death, and the isolation thereof, into the world of communion. Hell is the consummation of isolation, of every man as his own god and universe, living in total separation from all other men. Heaven, on the other hand, is the consummation of communion and community, of life in peace and perfect communion with God, man, nature, and ourselves.

The rite of communion thus celebrates a future perfection, and it is a feeding for the present task of developing that community here and now. Communion thus is, when it is truly communion, a triumphant present and future fact. It declares that we are *one body* in Christ. This means that we seek to be governed, not by our will, but by His. The Kingdom we are members of and serve is not of this world but of the Lord: it is the Kingdom of God.

We are therefore summoned in communion to die to ourselves, to our old man, and to live in Christ, "And that ye put on the new man, which after

God is created in righteousness and true holiness. Wherefore putting away Lying, speak every man truth with his neighbor: for we are members one of another" (Eph. 4:24-25). We move from the law of our fallen being into the law of God, now written in all our being by His grace.

Communion thus celebrates the fact of the growth of new life and new power, the purpose of which is to bring all things into captivity to Christ and their new creation in Him. The goal is summed up in the heavenly proclamation: "The kingdoms of this world are become the Kingdoms of our Lord, and of his Christ; and he shall reign for ever and ever" (Rev. 11:15). To partake faithfully of the Lord's Table is thus to partake of life, growth, power, and victory. It means that we become a part of the great army of God, and our purpose is the conquest of all things for Christ our King. All peoples, cultures, spheres of life and thought, and all time must be brought under His dominion.

It means also that communion ends the communications problem. St. Paul says, "Faith cometh by hearing, and hearing by the word of God" (Rom. 10:17). All things were created by the Lord's fiat word (John 1:3), and all things were made to hear and obey that sovereign law-word. God's word therefore is the word that penetrates to the heart of every man. It is the only word that can get under the skin and into the blood and the bones of unregenerate men. It is the word of power, and the Holy Spirit works with it always.

We are plainly told that, "Except the LORD build the house, they labour in vain that build it" (Ps. 127:1). Apart from Him, there is no communion, community, nor communication. The foundations of our political and economic orders must thus be in His law-word. Education apart from Him ceases to communicate anything but sin and death, and our statist education today gives abundant evidences of the devastation wrought by humanism.

In a society without communion, sin and death are the governing factors in every area of life, including the family, the arts, and the sciences. All too many scientists today treat man as an experimental animal; being governed by sin and death, they can produce little else. Abortion and homosexuality are fitting symbols for twentieth century man, and for the century of world wars, drugs, and suicide. Having lost communion, men lose the ability to communicate, and, finally, the will to live. Suicides, personal and cultural, give evidence of the failure and *the refusal* to communicate with God and man; they are, simply, the rejection of life because the Lord of life is first of all rejected. (I do not here include the "suicides" of persons given mind-deranging drugs by prescription: these come closer to murder.)

The modern age is dying because it has no communion. It has abandoned faith in the Lord who alone is Life and the source of life, and it has chosen death (Prov. 8:36) rather than life. For us, the living, it is thus most urgently a time for communion, growth and reconstruction.

"This is the day which the LORD hath made; we will rejoice and be glad in it" (Ps. 118:24). (July, 1983)

ATONEMENT AND AUTHORITY
Chalcedon Position Paper No. 42

One of the recurring facts of history has been "the revolt of the masses," the intense, unorganized rebellion of peasants, slaves, and serfs against the tyranny of their overlords. In various eras, the tyranny has been very real and very ugly. Basic to this has been a radical contempt for all physical work, for "menial work," and for all those who are engaged in it. The examples of this from various cultures are legion. To cite but one, from 17th century England, Viscount Conway said, "We eat and drink and rise up to play and this is to live like a gentleman, for what is a gentleman but his pleasure?" James Barbary: *Puritan and Cavalier, The English Civil War*, p. 37.) The royalists looted with such abandon (even plundering their own friends), that the orders of Puritan leaders Sir Thomas Fairfax and Oliver Cromwell that Commonwealth plunderers would be shot swung sentiment to their side. Among the nobility and the Cavaliers, imprudence and improvidence became virtues. When Elizabeth Cavendish (1527-1608), widow of Sir William, died, she left to each of her grandsons 2,000 marks to buy land and establish estates. When one prudent youth put his share into land, Sir Charles said contemptuously, "If any son of mine put money into land before he was twenty, I'd disinherit him." (Geoffery Trease: *Portrait of a Cavalier, William Cavendish, First Duke of Newcastle*, p. 27.) To be provident indicated a non-noble and middle class outlook!

This evil outlook was carried into the South by many settlers who sought to be a like aristocracy and had a like contempt for the practical and the provident act. The problem at Jamestown, Virginia, was that too many of the colonists were either "gentlemen" or would-be gentlemen, people who "never did know what a days work was," according to Captain John Smith. As a result, they expected to get rich without working! Trouble was thus inevitable, and slavery "answered" their social problem some years later. (Edmund S. Morgan, "The Labor Problem at Jamestown, 1607-18," in *American Historical Review*, vol. 76, no. 3, June, 1971, pp. 597, 606.) Meanwhile, in Jamestown the results were "idleness and hunger."

This element in the South believed in slavery because it believed in itself as an aristocracy in control of the lower classes. It was marked by pride of blood, pride of place, and a contempt for all menial work and workers, whether black or white. During the war, President Jefferson Davis and his cabinet were treated with disrespect, because they were the newly rich, not the old aristocracy. It took the Yankees to make Jefferson Davis popular with their mistreatment of him!

Historians fail to appreciate the Baptist social revolution in the South after 1865. My first awareness of this came years ago, as a student. A professor from the South, in a passing and extraneous reference to Southern Baptists, treated them as a joke, and he called them "unSouthern" and "low class." By this he meant, of course, that they did not represent "the true South," the old aristocracy. The fact is that power and leadership was passing into new and resented hands in the South, and the older element hated it. The Baptists now defined and led the South, not the older element, whose popularity was now in New York City and its high society. (William Stadiem: *A Class By Themselves, The Untold Story of the Great Southern Families*.)

We have touched only on *mild* examples of the arrogance of position in order to keep the emphasis on an *attitude*, not the long history of oppression. The same attitude now prevails among liberals and intellectuals, a new, self-appointed nobility and elite. The fact is that, all over the world, from pagan antiquity to the communist imperial states of this century, rulers have seen the masses of peoples as there merely for their use. The Cavaliers bewailed the death of "merrie olde England," meaning an England in which the common man existed to please his superiors and to bow and scrape before him. Christopher Hill, in *The World Turned Upside Down* (1972), shows us the explosive and radical thinking of the common man which found expression when the Puritan regime removed censorship. In 1642, preachers were quoting the battle cry of peasant revolts in an earlier century: "When Adam delved and Eve span, Who was then the gentleman?"

In the modern age, revolutions in the name of the common man (but led by others usually) began to succeed. No more than in earlier revolutions, such as the Mazdakite triumph of the fifth century A.D., were the results good. They were, in fact, more tyrannical and unjust.

History gives abundant illustrations of the fact that no class has ever ruled wisely or well. History has to a considerable degree been a long trail of tears and a bloody tale of exploitation. Each class in turn has seen itself as the locale of wisdom and authority and manifested with clarity the fact of total depravity, i.e., the infection of sin in every aspect of man's being. Isaiah's judgment stands vindicated: "Cease ye from man, whose breath is in his nostrils: for wherein is he to be accounted of?" or to be valued (Isa. 2:22).

Whatever his class, or pride of birth and place, man is a sinner, a fallen and depraved creature who is at war with God, with truth, and with reality. At the core of his life is a lie, his belief that he is his own god, able to determine and to establish good and evil for himself (Gen. 3:5). The political, economical, social, and religious orders created by such a man reflect his nature and evil. History cannot escape from this necessary connection between a man's moral nature and his life and society. Every effort by men to devise a social order which will negate this fact has been a failure. Man cannot change himself from an evil to a good man, nor can he give to his social order a character he has not.

This is the reason why the atonement is not only a religious but a political and social fact. The atonement restores communion between God and man, and man is recreated by God's sovereign grace. This fact of communion makes possible community. It does not eliminate social problems, because redeemed men are by no means fully sanctified men. It does mean that there is now a possibility of a solution.

Meanwhile, the problem has grown more complex. As we have noted, throughout the centuries, we have had self-appointed elites lording it over other men, and, at the same time, the revolt of enslaved masses. To complicate and aggravate this tension, in the past two centuries two movements have arisen and made powerful and insistent claims to rulership. On the one hand, we have a new and arrogant elite, the scientific--academic--intellectual establishment, which sees itself as the channel of truth, science, and reason. On the other hand, we have equalitarianism, which was earlier fostered by the new elite, is still given lip service, but is at the same time a threat. The new elite seeks a disguised but still essentially totalitarian authority. The equalitarian spirit challenges all authority.

A few days ago, a public school teacher told me of a disastrous school battle in which she was a trial witness. This large school had eight teachers with administrative credentials, all of whom felt that their own ideas would best govern the school. (Some other teachers felt that they too knew better than the principal.) As a result, the school became a shambles, and education gave way to a power struggle.

This situation is a familiar one. The equalitarian impulse moves people to question authority and to demand that their will be done. The elitist authoritarian impulse leads others to using people to advance themselves and to enhance their own power. The age-old battle for power thus has a newer and more deadly character.

Our Lord called attention to the power-struggle and the love of the powerful for exercising authority over men. However, He ordered, "But it shall not be so among you: but whosoever will be great among you, let him be your minister: And whosoever will be chief among you, let him be your servant: Even as the Son of Man came not to be ministered unto, but to minister, and to give his life as a ransom for many" (Matt. 20:25-28). The fact of the atonement made Christ the great Servant. The great Head and Adam of the new humanity made Himself a servant using His power and authority to minister to His people in terms of God's covenant, covenant law, and Kingdom. Authority in the new creation must be an exercise of grace and service, and so too must be submission. Paul, in stressing this same pattern, says, "for we are members one of another" (Eph. 4:25). The community and communion of Christ's Body and Kingdom are broken by both those "above" and "below" when they insist, "my will be done." All authority is from God, and is conditional upon our prior obedience to Him, and all submission must be under God and in terms of our trust in and obedience to Him.

The invasion of the Christian community by elitist and equalitarian motives is creating critical problems and is moving the community from the Kingdom of God to the Kingdom of Man.

The theme verse of the Book of Judges, as stated more than once, is "In those days there was no King in Israel (i.e., God was not recognized as King):every man did that which was right in his own eyes" (Judges 21:25). Apart from the Lord, men in authority and under authority will try to do that which is "right" in their own eyes. The result is anarchy.

A Biblical doctrine of authority and community does not become a reality by affirmation or by negation. We cannot fight it or gain it by demands: we must live it. When Paul says, "Let every man abide in the same calling wherein he was called" (I Cor. 7:20), he was not advocating passivity but rather ordering believers away from futile and destructive activity. The Kingdom of God comes, not by revolution but by regeneration, and as regenerated men remake every area of their lives in terms of God's law-word.

Not only authority but community and reconstruction come out of the atonement. The modern world seeks community by means of revolution, statist legislation, and the appropriation of tax funds. It creates instead a conflict society. Neither revolutionary violence nor legislation can convert vultures into canaries, but it is the essence of humanistic statism to attempt to do so.

The atonement restores man into community with God in terms of God's covenant and covenant law. The atonement is a covenant fact. It is the essence of a covenant that both parties bind themselves into a law-treaty. Each agrees to be totally faithful to the other, and to be ready to die in faithfulness to the covenant. Man broke the covenant by his sin and rebellion, but God, who in grace gave man a status in His covenant and in grace gave man the covenant law, added the culminating act of grace. God the Son in His incarnation gave His life on the cross to restore man into the covenant, even though, for his rebellion, man deserved to die. The God-man Jesus Christ paid the death penalty for us as very man of very man, and, as very God of very God, revealed the amazing grace of our covenant God.

At the same time, the pattern of covenant authority was set forth by the Son. It was manifested practically and typically by the Son in the foot-washing episode which followed the covenant Supper (John 13:1-16). He declared, "I have given you an example, that ye should do as I have done to you" (John 13:15).

Too often, however, modern authority is "Gentile" and lordly, humanistic and non-Christian. Similarly, those in more subordinate positions are rebellious, proud, and critical. Both pay lip service to Christ, and actual service to their own evil being. Both see the mote in the other's eye, but not the beam in their own eye. Our Lord has a summary judgment concerning all such people: "Thou hypocrite!" (Matt. 7:1-5).

The world daily moves deeper into revolution and tyranny. This is the destiny of an arrogant people. The only alternative is Jesus Christ, His atonement, and the authority which flows from that fact. (August, 1983)

GUILT, ATONEMENT AND FREEDOM
Chalcedon Position Paper No. 43

Shakespeare's *Hamlet,* in his famous soliloquy, says at one point, "Conscience does make cowards of us all." In this sentence, Shakespeare summed up an ancient awareness of the corrosive effects of a bad conscience. Guilty men pay a price: they lose the power to be free. Being enslaved to sin, they become outwardly slaves as well. As our Lord says, "Whosoever committeth sin is the servant (or, slave) of sin." However, "If the Son therefore shall make you free, ye shall be free indeed." (John 8:34, 36).

When the Russian Revolution began, only a very small minority of the people favored the Bolsheviks. The Bolsheviks, however, led by Lenin, preached envy and hatred on every possible occasion. When their takeover began, many millions were ready to exploit the situation to loot shops and homes. Having done this, they were guilty partners to the revolution and thus had little moral grounds to fight the Bolshevik power. Many years later, an older man said sadly, We brought judgment upon ourselves.

With World War II, Stalin, fearing more than anything else his own subjects, encouraged the most vicious behavior by his advancing troops. Everything was done to incite them to rape, murder, and looting. The Germans were provoked to brutality in every possible way. As Nikolai Tolstoy says, in *Stalin's Secret War* (1982), "Stalin went out of his way to invite Nazi ill-treatment and later extermination of Russian prisoners-of-war" (p. 261). He knew that the reaction to this would be greater brutality by the Soviet troops.

By so doing, Stalin demoralized his own men. How could they, after the war, fight against the horrors of Stalin and communism when they themselves had been guilty of like brutalities? How could they stand against Stalin's evil when they themselves had been so readily and brutally evil? A bad conscience had disarmed them.

Guilt has always been a useful and basic tool of tyranny and false power. Over the years, I have encountered situations where a husband or wife try secretly and covertly to push their spouse into adultery. The purpose is to give them a bad conscience which will enable the manipulator to dominate the erring partner. In one case, a wife, failing to push her husband into adultery, became violent and mentally unstable because she had been unable to use guilt to control him.

This power is well known to evil politicians. A guilty people are a more readily controlled people. Hence, such politicians are prone to creating guilt. We have heard much in the past generation about hunger in America, even to "statistics" on the number of the hungry. That this is a myth has been shown more than once, to no avail. We are given horror stories about how exploitive we are, in order to make us more readily exploitable. The purpose of a vast amount of political oratory is to create guilt in the people at large and all who oppose them. Too many "liberals" are people who feel guilty for things they never did while feeling no guilt for unhappy things done.

It is very difficult for a Christian to speak before certain types of audiences without being indicted for things totally unrelated to his subject. To cite one example, one questioner (or indicter) declared that no Christian had a right to speak, given the treatment of the Indians! The fact is that, very often, the only friends the Indians had were Christians. Most of the men on the frontier were lawless men, runaways from the law and from a disciplined society. They were godless men. Does it make sense to blame contemporary atheists for the sins of past atheists? More than a few of the traders and agents who exploited the Indians were Masons. This gives us no moral right to condemn current Masons for anything other than their own sins.

When men are found guilty and convicted, they may or may not face a physical prison, but they most certainly face an inner prison. Their conscience convicts them first of all, and their conscience imprisons them in the barless but far stronger prison of guilt.

Those who work to lay a "guilt trip" on us are simply trying to imprison us and to take away our freedom in order to have the freedom to work their own evil will.

At the least, they seek to put godly men on the defensive, trying to vindicate their innocence rather than to do their work. The answer thus to the question about the mistreatment of the Indians is a counter-charge: If you believe this country was stolen from the Indians, as a few million of you do, sell all you have, give your money and land to the Indians, and migrate back to Europe. Until you do that, believing what you do, are you not a hypocrite?

Guilt is the enemy of freedom. It disturbs rest and sleep, and it hinders our work and functioning. Most important, it is a precondition for the enslavement of a people. As I pointed out in *The Politics of Guilt and Pity* (1970), enslavement by guilt is an essential aspect of modern politics. If we are rich, we should feel guilty; if we are middle class, again, we are guilty; if we are lower class, we are somehow sub-human and responsible for it. If we are Christians, we should feel guilty. If we have had a good education, shame on us. If we enjoy our work, or our play, our family, or our friends, we are somehow guilty of neglecting "the big picture" and are vile creatures. Politics has become the art of creating and manipulating guilt in order to increase the powers of the state.

The Bible too tells us that we are guilty men, that "there is none righteous, no, not one" (Rom. 3:10), "For all have sinned, and come short of the glory of God" (Rom. 3:23). For Scripture, however, the recognition and confession of sin and guilt is the first step towards absolution. We are told emphatically that sin and death are causally related: death is the consequence of sin and guilt. The whole point of Scripture is that redemption and freedom from sin, guilt, and death are to be had through Christ's atonement. Not only does Christ become our sin-bearer and vicarious atonement, but He remakes us so that we are a new creation. To be free from sin, guilt, and death is to be a new man with a renewed nature. The purpose of salvation is to make us a free people: "Ye shall know the truth (Jesus Christ), and the truth shall make you free" (John 8:32). Only a free people can create a free world.

Thus, the release from sin and guilt before God is the necessary prelude to human freedom.

This is why atonement is so essential to political freedom. In the ancient world, men were aware of the dangers of guilt. Hence, they sought to be free by requiring atonement for all citizens. In Rome, all citizens (except soldiers on duty) had to be present for the annual lustrations, to be washed of their sins. Freedom from guilt was essential to the status of a freeman. All such efforts were futile of course, because the Roman lustrations provided no atonement. It should be noted, however, that Rome did see in its early years the relationship between a clear conscience before the gods and freedom.

Now the recognition is of the power of a bad conscience and guilt in enslaving people. A few years ago, one man told me that he no longer subscribed to a daily paper, because the input from the "news" was, "If I don't save the world before lunch, I'm a dirty, rotten bastard." More than a few businessmen have withdrawn from social responsibility in a sick disgust: both politicians and their modernist pastors do little more than to "lay a guilt trip" on all businessmen, and they are weary of it. But they are impotent in the face of it without faith. No man escapes from slavery merely by resenting it.

We have spoken of the role of politicians in fostering guilt. It is very necessary to speak also of the role of the clergy. I can never forget the friend who told me of her father, a life-long member of a fundamentalist church. Every pastor he had ever had was an expert at congregational control through guilt. Every Sunday that poor man went home feeling wretched because he had "failed" God; he was a miserable sinner, and so on. Instead of empowering the congregation to go forth in the power of the Lord to serve Christ's Kingdom in every area of life and thought, the pastor made one and all feel how sinful they were, and how they had to do more for and give more to their church to be "right" with the Lord.

This is preaching for enslavement, and it is very popular with both fundamentalist and modernist churches. It goes hand in hand with over-government. The guilt-laying church no less than the guilt-laying state wants to control people. A church that is very "strict" in church government is not necessarily any more godly than one which is very lax. Many a "strict" church prides itself on its godly severity when what it is really saying is that it does not believe in the power of the Holy Spirit. (Not without reason, Milton wrote, "New presbyter is but old priest writ large.")

Over-government allows no room for freedom nor for growth. It allows for one voice in the church, and none other. It furthers centralization of power in both church and state. In brief, over-government distrusts the power of God in the life of man. Some of the religious over-governors seem to believe that, while they were created in the image of God, the residue of men were only created in a partial image and hence need the dictatorship of the elite element. These non-elite ones are to he kept in line with a bad conscience.

Revelation 6:16 tells us of the guilty, as they face God's judgment, that they cry out to the mountains and rocks, "Falls on us, and hide us from the face of him that sitteth on the throne, and from the wrath of the Lamb."

Earlier, we cited the use by Stalin of guilt as a means of enslaving and governing his subject peoples. It must be added that Stalin himself was governed by guilt. He demanded the most fulsome adulation and praise to conceal the truth of his nature; he wanted pictures of himself to mirror his ideal image and had several portrait painters shot for falling short of his demands. "The desire to humiliate and terrify extended even to his own family" (N. Tolstoy, p. 23), and, with it, an intense fear of all men, including his own carefully selected guards. He had an obsessive belief in the omnipresence of his enemies and went to extreme lengths to protect himself. The one constant factor in Stalin's policy, according to Tolstoy (p. 50), was fear, a total fear that warped all his being. He had made slaves of all the people, but he himself was the continually haunted slave of his bad conscience and his fear of the people.

Since Stalin's day, there has been no essential change in the rulers of the Soviet System. Slave labor is still the lifeblood of the economy, and total surveillance and total fear prevail. The same extreme precautions are taken to protect the present leaders from the people. There is no real or substantial difference between Stalin and Andropov: both represent the enthronement of evil and of evil power. The cowardice of Stalin stemmed from a bad conscience; the same bad conscience governs in the Kremlin today.

Although not to the same degree, the same bad conscience governs most Western heads of states. They wage war, usually covertly, against God and man in terms of a humanistic ideal. They see other men as no more than manure to fertilize the ground of a planned future. They sacrifice men in wars they do not plan to win, and they treat people as instruments to be manipulated .

Like a volcanic ash which covers the entire earth, colors the sun, and becomes a part of the air men breathe, so too a bad conscience is a part of the spiritual air of the 20th century. It colors the life and thought of most men: it makes cowards and slaves of them.

The world's great and overwhelming need is for freedom, but men reject freedom when they reject Christ. "Ye shall know the truth, and the truth shall make you free" (John 8:32). That truth is Jesus Christ, who declares "If the Son therefore shall make you free, ye shall be tree indeed" (John 8:36). This is a political and psychological fact and premise, and even more, it is the religious premise for all things. (October, 1983)

NO GOD, NO LAW
Chalcedon Position Paper No. 44

The German, Carl Schurz, came to the United States after the failure of the revolution of 1848. He found the nature of the United States to be dramatically different from Europe: "Here in America you can see how slightly a people needs to be governed. In fact, the thing that is not named in Europe without a shudder, anarchy, exists here in full bloom." (David Tyack and Elizabeth Hansot: *Managers of Virtue*, p. 19.) What Schurz meant was that civil government was at a minimum, especially on the state and federal levels. There was almost no government other than the self-government of the Christian man.

Now, in 1983, the powers of the state are vastly increased. Only in the most nominal sense does the United States have the same kind of civil government it had then. From an almost non-existent civil government, the United States has moved to a highly centralized, omnipresent power state. From a free republic and a loose federation of states, it has become an increasingly fascist order. (Fascism is that form of socialism which maintains the facade of private ownership and the free market while controlling all things with regulations so as to socialize all things.)

At the same time, "laws" have also increased at a phenomenal rate, man-made laws replacing the rule of God's law. The increase of laws has not led to any increased order. The increase of lawlessness and crime has been phenomenal.

At the same time, the modern state has become humanistic and hence determined to play God. This has meant that its goal has become more and more power and total control. Because the state sees itself as absolute, it recognizes no superior law and no superior Being as having any binding power over it. Lin Piao, the Chinese revolutionary leader, expressed the faith of the modern state very bluntly: "Political power is an instrument by which one class oppresses another. It is exactly the same with revolution and with counter-revolution. As I see it, *political power is the power to oppress others*." (Paul Johnson: *Modern Times*, p. 556). When we read the writings of Marxist and Fascist leaders, it becomes apparent that George Orwell's vision in 1984 was not inaccurate when he described the goal of the humanistic state as power, and the purpose of that power as "a boot stamping on a human race forever."

In such a society, there can be no law. Law assumes a higher order, a justice above and over man and the state which both must serve. Walter Kaufmann, in *Without Guilt and Justice* (1973), was logical: by denying the God of Scripture, he denied also guilt or innocence, and justice or injustice, as invalid; they were simply implications and aspects of faith in God and His higher order. Humanistic man must be beyond good and evil. This means also that humanistic man is beyond law. There can be no higher law governing or binding man.

As Paul Johnson noted, there is no Marxist philosophy of law. Evgeny Pashukanis, a Soviet legal theoretician, pursued the issue logically and declared that in a true socialist society "Law would be replaced by Plan." (Paul Johnson: *Modern Times*, p. 679). During the 1930s, the Plan led to, among other things, the death of Pashukanis.

He was, however, right. Soviet society is governed, not by law, but by plans. The same is increasingly true in the rest of the world. Most "laws" today are bureaucratic regulations, created by some federal, state, county, or city agency or planning commission. The number of laws enacted by representative legislative bodies is small by comparison. Power is moving from the legislative bodies to the planning agencies which they created.

This leads to a curious fact. The number of lawyers is proliferating, but the traditional practice of law is giving way to bureaucratic law. Law is ceasing to be law in any historic sense.

Recently, the American Bar Association expressed dismay at the bad image lawyers have with the public. That bad image is not unique to lawyers. Politicians are commonly despised; bankers are distrusted; so too are doctors; the clergy are in disrepute; and so on. Virtually every calling is held in contempt or viewed at least with suspicion. Since all have become infected with relativism, all are viewed with distrust.

In law, irrelevant technicalities of form over-rule the substantive claims of justice, a condition not limited to law, although especially deadly where justice is the issue.

The Plan is replacing Law, and the Plan is a humanistic concept. It represents man's *ad hoc* concept of order, and the Plan allows no disagreement, because no higher law exists, it is believed, to judge the Plan. As one of Stalin's economists, S. G. Shumilin said, "Our task is not to study economics but to change it. We are bound by no laws" (Johnson, p. 267).

The word *law* in its origin and its still current meaning is that which is *laid*, set, or fixed; it has reference to an established standard. But it is no longer true of law that it gives us a fixed standard; it is at its best a rubber yardstick. Early in the 1970s, a lawyer remarked with disgust that too often he did not know what the law was until he went to court and heard the judge give the law a new meaning. Men no longer seek to conform themselves and their societies to God's higher Law rather, they conform the law to society's demands.

Such an attitude is not new. It has been the goal of tyranny for many centuries. Let us remember that the root meaning of *tyranny* is rule by man's law. W.P.M. Kennedy noted, of Queen Elizabeth I, "The Elizabethan ideal in religion was national unity" (*Studies in Tudor History*, p. 233). Tudor despotism brought even family devotions in private under the spying supervision of Tudor agents. Homes were regularly searched for the slightest evidences of Catholic piety; later, the same interest was shown in discovering Puritan piety. Both Catholics and Puritans refused to recognize the monarch's headship over the church. In Kennedy's words, "It was a dangerous experiment to scorn her Governorship of the Church. She was in a very real sense what Lord North described her, 'Our God on earth,' and a Puritan appeal to Scripture was, in her eyes, political heresy, as it dishonoured the National Church of which she was Supreme Governor. The insult was an insult to the throne--and the throne was a Tudor throne" (p. 242f.). One can add that law was also to a large degree Tudor law.

The problem was not new. It was an attitude common to pagan antiquity. Darius of Persia at least qualified his power, declaring, "by the grace of Ahuramazda, I am king," but the Roman emperors made no such qualification as imperial theology developed. Rome's central cult "was the worship of Rome itself" (Michael Grant: *The Climax of Rome*, p. 164).

The persistent tendency of political theology over the centuries has been to make the state absolute (God walking on earth) and the source of law. This objective has never had more eager and more philosophical justification than in the modern era. Especially since the French Revolution, it has become basic to the modern age. It is worthy of note that two basic concepts of this era are totally lacking in the U.S. Constitution. Neither the words *sovereignty* nor *nation* appear in that document.

Sovereignty was held to be an attribute of God alone, and the nation-state was not seen as the standard. Rather, the prevailing concept of the American framers was of a freedom and justice state. Today the U.S. Constitution has a radically different meaning, and it has been re-interpreted and re-written in effect to include federal sovereignty and nationhood.

At the same time, life has been politicized. To live under the rule of law is one thing, but to live under the rule of politics and planning emphatically something else. John Lukacs has summed it up very clearly: "The administrator rather than the producer has become the typical (and respected) American occupation" (John Lukacs: *A New History of the Cold War*, p. 295). The triumph of the administrator is a triumph in every sphere, in politics, industry, the church, education, and elsewhere. It is the triumph of planning over law, because the administrator's goal is not a given order but the control of all factors in terms of his plan.

So far has this emphasis on man-made planning gone that Nobel laureate Sir Francis Crick has said that man's planning should establish what is human: "no newborn infant should be declared human until it has passed certain tests regarding its genetic endowment and...if it fails these tests it forfeits the right to live" (T. Howard and J. Rifkin: *Who Should Play God?*, p. 81). Crick is not alone in this opinion: it is shared by others. One aspect of it is abortion. The champions of abortion refuse to recognize any law of God over them. For them, the essential question is whether or not the unborn baby fits into their plan.

We have state planning because we have personal planning which is in defiance of God's law. Where men can choose their forms of sexual expression in defiance of God's law, take the lives of unborn babies at will, and assume the prerogative of directing their lives without God, there will be no hesitation to apply the same principles of humanistic planning in the realm of the state. Law gives way to planning.

The tragic fact in this process is that lawyers, who should be champions of the law, have become extensively advocates of planning. Charles Moraze traced this change back to the era before the French Revolution. The old regime badly needed accountants, "while what she had was lawyers," not lawyers with any real sense of law but lawyers whose heads were full of plans. They talked therefore of the rights of man and proceeded to execute men to achieve their planned society (Charles Moraze: *The Triumph of the Middle Class*, p. 113ff.). The plans could be described as "good intentions," but the good intentions of fallen, sinful men have a crippling and evil effect on social order.

The great superstition of the modern age is a political superstition: it is the belief that more power in the hands of the state can lead to a better Plan and to man's triumph under the Plan. In terms of this superstition, man will eliminate poverty, prejudice, war, and a host of other evils by means of the Plan. Hence, more power to the State!

The Plan supplants law, God's law. The Plan denies justice or righteousness. It recognizes only the supremacy of the power state and the philosopher-kings (or "scientific" planners) thereof. Because justice, God's justice, stands always above and over man and man's plan, the Plan works to exclude God's law or justice, and it therefore wages war against Biblical faith. If there is no God, there is no Law, only man's Plan.

The Plan, in fact, must work to disassociate itself from justice because it seeks to separate itself from God. Kaufmann derided the concept of justice as a Biblical hangover. Albert Camus said, "Since God claims all that is good in man, it is necessary to deride what is good and choose what is evil" (*The Rebel*, p. 47).

The modern humanistic state has done exactly that. Its course is self-consciously humanistic. The U.S. Supreme Court legalized abortion and, in the process, avoided any consideration of a Biblical position. All kinds of premises were examined but not that of God's Law: no transcendent law order was given any attention. Law was replaced by the humanistic Plan.

Elections, however important, cannot change the mind and heart of man. Law is in essence a religious question. When even churches are indifferent to God's law, the state will be also. But to be indifferent to God's law is to deny that God is God, and that His law-word alone is sovereign, like Himself. But, if there is no God, then there is no law, and no justice. (November, 1983)

KENOSIS: THE GREAT MODERN HERESY
Chalcedon Position Paper No. 45

The Doctrine of Kenosis is something rarely mentioned in our time, but its evil influence is overwhelmingly pervasive in this century. The doctrine has deep roots in Eastern Orthodox churches, especially Russian. In the 19th century, it became influential in Lutheranism through the writings of Sartorius (1832, 1834), of Konig (1844), and of Thomasius (1845). It then moved into English and American theological thought. Its supposed foundation is in Philippians 2:6-8, where Paul speaks of Christ's great step from the Godhead into the incarnation. This the kenotic thinkers interpreted to mean that Christ emptied Himself of all power and thereby set a pattern for self-abasement by all His followers.

Nadejda Gorodetzky, in *The Humiliated Christ in Modern Russian Thought* (1938), wrote of the "Kenotic mind, mood, or character" of Russian religion and its emphasis on self-abasement, poverty, non-resistance and the submissive acceptance of suffering and death. Gorodetzky commented, "It even seems to us that the main importance of Russian 'kenoticism' lies precisely in the fact that there was no 'doctrine' about it." It had become the true way of piety and life. The life of the redeemed, according to this belief, is one of self-humiliation and self-abasement. The goal is a world without rich men, superiors, or success. The ideal of the medieval begging friars is held out as the goal of all true Christianity. Only of those who are "abandoned by all in poverty and sickness" can it be said "they alone are sons of Christ and have full right to beg in His almighty name."

As in pre-Marxist Russia, so today in Western Europe and the United States the doctrine of Kenosis is no longer a formal doctrine but is equated with the Christian life. The popular assumption is that a Christian should be, as one unbeliever summed it up, "the All-American patsy," sucker, or victim. Some years ago, a woman whose life had been dedicated to destroying people, first as a beauty and then as a manipulator, turned on me when I blocked her evil ways, declaring I was obviously not a Christian. Why? Because "A Christian is someone who never hurts anyone's feelings." The Christian is expected to be the victim, the ready pacifist in every situation who believes in peace at any price.

This doctrine has penetrated far and wide and has become a part of Western culture, Christian and non-Christian. Its tenets are basic to the so-called peace movement, and they undergird the thinking of R. J. Sider and others like him. The Russian doctrine of Kenosis, as it moved westward, found a congenial soil in Western Protestant and Catholic pietism. Certainly John Wesley, especially in his marital life, displayed the symptoms of kenotic surrender and self-abasement.

The direction of this way of life revealed itself all too clearly in some of the Russian mystical and heretical sects such as the Khlysty and the Skoptsy. The Skoptsy carried the required self-humiliation to the point of castration. Moreover, just as the Sicarii of ancient Judea, if anyone expressed interest in their beliefs, would kidnap him and forcibly circumcise him, so the Skoptsy would kidnap and perform more radical surgery on anyone who appeared friendly, and sometimes on others as well. (Frederick C. Conybeare: *Russian Dissenters*, p. 369, 1921).

These extreme cases serve as an indicator of the direction of kenotic thinking: it is suicidal. Whereas Christ identifies Himself as "life" (John 14:6), and declares, "I am come that they might have life, and that they might have it more abundantly" (John 10:10), Kenosis offers a retreat from life which is implicitly suicide .

Given the saturation of the Western world by kenotic thought, it should not surprise us that we have today the politics and economics of suicide. Vast sums of money are appropriated by the United States, and loaned by U.S. and European banks to "Third World" Countries. These funds do not reach the peoples; they prop up corrupt and evil regimes. They hinder growth and production in those countries, and these funds are creating a world-wide inflation which is destroying economics, money, men, and nations. The press gives us many reports of this world-wide crisis. The result? Suicide! This is the prescription of the sons of Kenosis.

Whether in the sphere of economics, politics, international conflicts, or more, this suicidal faith is undergirded by popular religion. Many atheists, modernists, and fundamentalists may disagree extensively on a wide variety of ideas and issues, but they are agreed on one essential point, the need for self-abasement, non-resistance, poverty, and the acceptance of suffering and death.

Indeed, much pastoral counselling of troubled and afflicted people is kenotic. Its one "wisdom" is submission to evil. Is your husband beating you, or is he guilty of incest? Is your wife or husband flagrantly unfaithful? "Your problem is your anger or grief over this. Go back and be more loving and submissive." So runs the counsel of defeat, of surrender to evil.

Suicide is, after all, a form of surrender, and surrender has been ennobled by kenotic thought into a higher way of life. The "real" Christian is someone who lies down to be walked over; the "real" liberal is someone whose trumpet always sounds retreat.

Leo Tolstoi, a great exponent of the kenotic way of life, had a major convert in Gandhi. Gandhi found the doctrine an admirable way of playing on the weakness of the West. He shed his top hat and suit for a loin cloth and pacifism to shame Western liberals with their own tacit religion. It should be remembered, however, that Gandhi also said, "Where there is only a choice between cowardice and violence, I would advise violence." (Cited by Arthur Waskow: *The Freedom Seder*, p. 52, 1969).

Western civilization has so deeply identified itself with Kenosis as a way of life that it gives aid, technology, and food to nations bent on its destruction, and does so with a glow of virtue. It rejoices at every opportunity for preparing its own funeral!

The great Russian novelist of the last century, Turgenev, in his *Poems in Prose*, described his stop in a humble village church. Although not a believer, he spoke of having a "vision" of Christ, and Christ looked like a peasant and had "a face like that of all others. "The apostle John, however, tells us that, when he saw in vision the ascended Christ, in awe he "fell at his feet as dead" (Rev. 1:17). He was not looking at an ordinary peasant face! It is, however, customary now to portray Christ as a very ordinary person, somewhat more effeminate than most men. All this is forgetting that He is very God of very God; the visual depictions of Christ have for some generations been kenotic. He is not shown as the Lord of Glory but as a plaintive beseecher who wants us to love Him.

The "ideal" kenotic Christian life was sought by St. Tykhon, Bishop of Voronezh (Timofey S. Sokolov, 1724-83, canonized in 1861). St. Tykhon represented the ideal which Dostoevsky tried to portray in his novels, and Dostoevsky was not alone among Russian writers in his admiration of St. Tykhon. That Tykhon was concerned with the plight of the poor, sold the silk, velvet, and furs belonging to him as a bishop to give to the poor, lived very, very simply and helped generously, indeed marked him as a Christian man of grace and charity. But St. Tykhon went further. In an argument with a landlord, the landlord, in place of any good response, struck St. Tykhon on the face. Bishop Tykhon fell on his knees, prostrated himself before the landlord, and asked his pardon for having induced him into temptation!

(Gorodetsky, p. 102). Such behavior, in a kenotic culture, gains great admiration; however, it does not change men nor abolish slums.

Moreover, St. Tykhon said, "Christ is begging through the poor" (p. 105). This is a common identification in contemporary liberation theology. *The Body of Christ is identified with the poor, not with the faithful.* The result is a profoundly false distortion of Christianity. That Scripture requires us to be mindful of the poor is very clear; that God regards widows and orphans, find our treatment of them, as a barometer, is obvious. That Christ in the parable of judgment (Matt. 25:31-46) identifies Himself with His poor, imprisoned, and needy members is most emphatically true, but He does not say that he identifies Himself with poverty as such, or with the poor as such, nor with a masochistic self-abasement.

In approaching men and nations, the spirit of kenotic faith has certain emphases. *First*, there must be a self-abasement. As with St. Tykhon and the landlord, we must see ourselves as in the wrong, and the other person as right. There is a pharisaical pride and virtue in self-abasement. Thus, we and our nation must always be seen as the offenders.

Second, this kenotic submissiveness to evil requires us to downgrade the sins of men and nations. As the Russian leader, "Father John" (John Iliytch Sergieff, the predecessor to Rasputin in the Russian court), said, "Love every man in spite of his falling into sin. Never mind the sins..." (John Iliytch Sergieff, *My Life in Christ*, p. 95. 1897). Or, as a pastor said to a wife whose husband was, to cite his lesser sin, flagrantly adulterous, "Never mind your husband's sins. Let's concentrate on your duty to love him and to be submissive." Neither should we concentrate on or discuss the sins of Soviet Russia; we should only concern ourselves with our own sins. Kenotic submissiveness requires a self-blinding to reality.

Third, again to cite Father John, "Never mind the sins, but remember that the foundation of the man is the same--the image of God" (*idem*). A common humanity is to be stressed, not the fact of sin, nor how to deal with the problems it creates. However, when men obscure the sin, they also obscure the answer. It is sin which is the barrier between men and God, and between men and men. Kenosis depreciates everything it touches, as do all false doctrines.

Moreover, Kenosis creates a false antithesis. Every erroneous faith presents men with a false antithesis. We have seen Gandhi's view of the antithesis, cowardice vs. violence. The problem is that each produces the other. Moreover, the antithesis to cowardice is courage, not violence! It is a strange mind that sees it as violence, but it is a mind too much in evidence today.

The kenotic advocates of a nuclear freeze and unilateral disarmament present us also with a false antithesis; on the one hand is peace, seen as pacifism and surrender, and, on the other, world destruction. A false antithesis is one which creates false alternatives in order to compel us to choose a pre-ordained course. Such an antithesis fails to note that a large variety of options exist between surrender and world destruction. To see the options as only "Better Red than Dead," or "Better Dead than Red," is an insanity, and a common one.

Kenosis involves a radical and childish solution to the problems of life. Instead of faith, the works of faith, patience, a slow development over the generations, and the use of as many instruments as possible to solve man's problems, Kenosis wants an instant solution by means of surrender, defeat, abasement, and self-inflicted poverty. Faith and work are replaced by dramatic gestures and postures, and intelligence is supplanted by picket slogans.

As the doctrine of Kenosis came Westward, it merged commonly with Protestant and Catholic pietism. These had prepared the way for Kenosis with their emphasis on a mindless religion. In France, Madame Guyon (1648-1717) had been a major source of Quietism. She believed that the essence of true faith is an act of resignation and submission to God in which the believer is without words, without actions, and without any will of his own, and then thereby without sin. The role of such thinking in preparing the way for the French Revolution deserves exploring. An atmosphere of surrender and submission was created precisely in those circles where a strong moral will and resistance were most needed. Certainly, Louis XVI was amazingly derelict in manifesting a stance of unresisting submission to the progressive demolition of France.

Kenosis, as we have seen, is a way of life common to churchmen and to unbelievers, it is common to a variety of religions in the modern world. Its advocates take various Bible verses out of context to justify their position, but they are substantially and essentially at odds with Scripture. Kenosis has so thoroughly permeated our time that it has ceased to exist as a known doctrine. It is now a part of the intellectual air which all men breathe. That air, however, is deadly, because the kenotic mind-set is suicidal. The kenotic plan of salvation by works of Kenosis is a way of death. As Solomon said, setting forth the word of the Lord: "He that sinneth against me wrongeth his own soul: all they that hate me love death" (Prov. 8:36). God's true antithesis still stands: "See, I have set before thee this day life and good, and death and evil...Therefore choose life, that both thou and thy seed may live" (Deut. 30:15,19). (December, 1983)

THE ULTIMATE PORNOGRAPHY
Chalcedon Position Paper No. 46

In these days, some people who are normally the most asleep to the world around them are actually stirring and showing signs of life and even indignation! I am referring to parents of children in state schools. Normally unaware of the radical subversion of their children by humanism, these parents are in growing numbers being shocked out of their indifference by the kind of "literature" assigned to their children.

Meanwhile, films and television give us a fare which, when not repulsive, is too stupid and painfully bad to watch. The film and television audience has been decreasing in recent years with good reason. Too much of even the "culture" fare is insulting in its implications and rests on a contempt for man.

A recent "educational" television film was about wild horses. About forty years ago, I lived in wild horse country. In their natural state, these wild horses were runty, diseased, and, with occasional exceptions, poor specimens of their kind. At that time, they were often rounded up to be sold for dog food. In recent years, special national range areas have enabled the breed to improve. To cut down on the surplus and to prevent a destruction of the range, many of the excess horses have been corralled to be sold as riding horses. The result? Indignation by our sentimentalists over the horses' "loss of freedom". It does not occur to these people that these are "welfare" horses, not truly wild but protected and cared for. At the same time, these sentimentalists, who would never allow the killing of excess horses, and have blocked efforts to kill off California's very prolific population of wild burros, are pro-abortion where human beings are concerned. Neither the millions of Marxist victims of slave labor camps, nor the growing millions of unborn babies slaughtered annually, distress or disturb them. This is pornography indeed.

At the same time, a preserve is being established in Southern California to protect the California condor, an "endangered" bird. Now this condor is plentiful in Mexico and Latin America. The condor is a vulture. Its future in the United States is a bleak one, not because of the "press of population" but because the conditions in the U.S. are unfavorable to its diet. After all, how many dead bodies do Americans leave lying about, of animals or men, for vultures to feed on? Even a dog hit by an automobile is quickly removed and buried in most cases. What do they plan to feed the condors? The million and half aborted fetuses each year? After all, more concern is expressed in some circles for the condors than for unborn babies. Is this not a form of ultimate pornography?

Pornographic films, books, and magazines, however bad they are, represent only the superficial and surface manifestation of a deep-seated cancer. We have today a radical inversion of values and a studied hatred of Biblical faith, law, and norms, because the triune God of Scripture is seen as the ultimate enemy. The more alien something is to the word of God, the more highly it is prized. One recent "educational" television film, in approaching a "primitive" tribal people, declared that the people and their culture should be taken "at absolute face value." This is the way every such "primitive" group is approached. No such absoluteness, of course, is ever ascribed to Scripture, to Christianity, or to the life of an unborn child! The unborn child is seen as merely a part of the woman's body, *her property*, which, as someone has pointed out, is exactly how slaves were once viewed, as *property*.

The ultimate pornography is very simply described in Proverbs 8:36, "But he that sinneth against Me wrongeth his own soul: all they that hate Me love death." The hatred of life and the love of death is the ultimate pornography. Every particular form of pornography is simply an exemplification of this fact.

In Genesis 6:5 we are told of the world before the Flood, "And God saw that the wickedness of man was great in the earth, and that every imagination of the thoughts of his heart was only evil continually." Pornography is the triumph of this evil imagination; it sees people, not as they really are, but in terms of an imagination which uses people to serve a man-god. Sexual pornography makes all the world the slave of the pornographic imagination; women, for example, only exist to please the would-be god and to coo in delight at the "privilege."

This pornographic evil imagination is not limited to the sexual sphere. An even more popular area is the politico-economic realm. One of the most influential and evil works of pornography ever produced was Plato's *Republic*, which reduced the great mass of humanity to the status of tools for the philosopher-kings. The respect accorded to Plato is evidence of the diseased character of the academy.

Igor Shafarevich, the Soviet Russian mathematician, has described socialism as the organized love of death. The socialist ideal is equality in death. It calls for the destruction of hierarchy, of private property, of religion, of the family, and, finally, of life itself (In Alexandr Solzhenitsin: *From Under the Rubble*). Its governing force is hatred, the attempt to be god, and the savage hostility to all that is of the true and living God. The socialist imagination refuses to recognize God's existence, nor man's existence apart from its own power and control. Just as the pornographic tales of the Marquis de Sade created impossible people who could not exist in life, so too the socialist imagination calls for the creation of a like people. When people refused to conform to de Sade's imagination, he sought to force them to do so; the socialist imagination uses coercion also to bend living men into its evil mold.

This is, of course, the appeal of abortion. In the early days of its civil legalization, many avant garde women, single and married, became pregnant in order to have an abortion. It provided good table talk, the ability to boast of in effect playing god over human life. We fail to understand abortion unless we see this aspect as central to it.

Bernard N. Nathanson, M.D., a former abortionist, reports in *Aborting*

America (1979), on the pleasure expressed by one administrator at the number of abortions performed.

If the pro-abortionists were logical, they would speak of the supposed need for abortions with regrets and dismay as a sorry fact and "necessity." In reality, they speak of it as a right and a freedom. A freedom to kill? They are not honest enough to say so, but this is their motivation, the love of death, for others and for themselves.

According to Scripture, the unforgivable sin is blasphemy against the Holy Ghost (Matt. 12:31-32). This has been seen as the inversion of the moral order to the point where a man makes evil his good, and God's good his evil. All forms of pornography flirt with, advocate, or whole-heartedly embrace this inversion. This is why any involvement with this inversion of the moral order is so deadly dangerous.

In my study of *The Politics of Pornography* (1974), I called attention to the fact that the new sexual pornography is radically different from the older forms. The earlier forms of sexual pornography were self-consciously written as "dirty books"; they were playing with sin and crime and knew it. The new pornography is written as the new health, the new freedom, as a witness to the truly good life. It presents us therefore with an inversion of the moral order lacking in the older works. It exemplifies the sin against the Holy Ghost in its motivation.

Dr. Lewis A. Tambs, of Arizona State University, in writing on "World War II -- The Final Phase" (in *Christian Statesman*, November-December, 1983, 422 7th Avenue, Beaver Falls, Pennsylvania 15010; editor, Ray Joseph, a Chalcedon friend, $2 a year) cites 1946 to 1975 as the first stage, Containment. The second stage, Detente, 1960 to 1979, has been succeeded by the third stage, Double Encirclement, 1964-1985. This is "the Tartarian tactics of choke-point control and tribute collection." The goal is not to destroy but to control, work, and exploit, to make the West, and especially the United States, a satellite or slave state. The Soviet Union, while professing to work for the freedom of man, has become history's greatest slave state, together with Red China. Both talk of liberation while working for total enslavement. Those who love death see slavery as a major step in the right direction.

Because the whole world outside of Christ loves death rather than Christ who is life (John 14:6), every man outside of Christ is at heart an ally of the forces of enslavement and death. As a result, the parties of the right and left in the "free" world are ready and willing to serve the needs of Marxist states. Foreign aid programs do more for Marxism around the world than domestic programs do for the citizenry.

What then is our hope? Apart from Christ, there is no hope. The redeeming power of Jesus Christ alone can save men. The law-word of God alone gives the guidelines for freedom and prosperity.

Men and states, however, prefer their own fiat word and law to God's, because, in rebelling against God, they rebel against life. They are dedicated priests of death.

To love Christ is to love life. Life is full of the unexpected (including guests) and the untidy. Too many people want showcase living in showcase houses, where everything is hostile to life and to children. To be truly against abortion means to love life and children, and children mean dirty diapers, messy rooms, toys strewn about, noise, and more. These are all things alien to the prim, prissy, and proper pro-abortionists. They prefer houses as neat and trim as a cemetery. (This primness has in my lifetime reached the cemeteries! Upright headstones are banned in the newer ones in favor of ground-level markers in order to give a neat, easily maintained death-park. The desire of many today is the legend, "Untouched by human hands." All too many people want a life untouched by other human beings. This is the love of death; it is pornography.)

The love of Christ is the love of life. It is the love which motivated Lester Roloff and motivates Mother Teresa. It is the love of children and family in Christ, the love of children's growth, and of their joy and laughter. It is the love of a man and a woman which creates a family in Christ, and which erects therein a realm of dominion under God.

There is a fundamental disorderliness about life because the present is not the final order. My library, where I am writing this, is a very disorderly place, with books piled here and there, stacks of papers, and manuscripts, letters and more, because *work is in progress*. To bring my library of 30,000 books to a final order is to walk out of it and die! The passionate purpose of my life and all that I have is God's final order, and the subordination of all things to that realm. It is pornography for me to impose an order of my imagination or desire on that purpose, or to supplant it.

Where sexual pornography, abortion, socialism, and more are involved, I do not seek to impose *personal* standards on others, because what is at stake is not a personal preference but God's law, God's order, *life* itself. Neither I nor any other man has the right to say, "My will be done." God's will alone is right.

Jesus Christ is the way, the truth, and the life (John 14:6). His working and power through the Holy Spirit is an overwhelming flood of grace, authority, and regenerating power which overturns and shatters the things which are so that only those things which are unshakable may remain (Heb. 12:27). Against this force, the death-sayers are helpless. Therefore choose life and live. It is our calling to reconstruct all things in terms of God's sovereign law-word, to bring all men, nations, and every sphere of life and thought into captivity to Christ our King, into freedom from sin and death and captivity to life and justice. Our King shall in due time make even the cemetery dead alive in Him! (January, 1984)

THE PLACE OF WOMEN
Chalcedon Position Paper No. 47

One of the chronic problems of men is that too often they react instead of acting. The terms and nature of the problems of life are set by their opposition rather than by themselves, and the reactions are foolish.

This has all too often been true of the reactions of men, Christian and non-Christian, to the women's liberation movement. The results are sometimes painful. Two examples will suffice. In one church, some of the women came together to study Scripture. The women were of varying ages but with a common need to know the Bible better in its application to their everyday problems. The church ordered the meetings ended, although no problem had arisen. The concerns of the study were not ecclesiastical, and the meetings were not a part of the church's work nor limited to church members. By no stretch of the imagination can any text of Scripture be made to forbid women to study Scripture together.

In at least several other churches, the women are held in an unbiblical subjection which treats them as children, not adults. The Bible declares Sarah to be the model wife in her obedience and subjection (I Peter 3:1-7). We cannot understand the meaning of that without recognizing the fact that, on occasion, Sarah, confident in the godliness of her position, gave Abraham an ultimatum (Gen. 16:5; 21:9-13), and God declared, "in all that Sarah hath said unto thee, hearken unto her voice" (Gen. 9:12), a sentence men rarely if ever use as a sermon text!

Moreover, as Charles Hodge said, with respect to Ephesians 5:22, the authority of the husband (or any human authority) is not unlimited. "It extends over all departments, *but is limited in all*; first, by the nature of the relation; and secondly, by the higher authority of God. No superior, whether master, parent, husband or magistrate, can make it obligatory on us either to do what God forbids, or not to do what God commands" (Charles Hodge: *Commentary on the Epistle to the Ephesians*, p. 314f).

But this is not all. The stupidity of all too many men is nowhere more apparent than in the assumption that subordination means inferiority. Most of us have at some time or other, and, usually, most of the time, been subordinate to very inferior men. In a fallen world, this is routine. The world commonly appraises a man's position in terms of very limited criteria, such as wealth, birth, education, and the like. The natural aristocracy of talent and character usually does not prevail in a sinful society! To assume that pre-eminence in position and power is pre-eminence in intelligence, character, and ability is to assume that the men who rule in Washington, D.C., and in the Kremlin, are the cream of history! Such a perspective would be sheer idiocy, but it is a kind of idiocy all too many men have in relationship to women.

One aspect of this idiocy, proudly taught as gospel by some such churches and pastors is the blasphemous assumption that the husband is the mediator between God and the wife. Scripture tells us that the husband is the head of the family, not a mediator, nor a little Christ. In relationship to the Lord, husband and wife are declared to be "heirs together of the grace of life" (I Peter 3:7); the husband is not declared to be the central heir, nor the recipient of greater grace or wisdom. We are not told that the wife's prayers are hindered or void if she fails to pray through a mediator-husband. Too many men want a lovely and charming wife to serve them and then to be a silent zombie the rest of the time! Peter tells us that the prayers of a husband and a wife are hindered if either is false with respect to their duties under God.

Some churches give men a cheap and false religion which justifies keeping a wife in line while the man is free to be his fallen self. Men find such a religion very palatable!

When God ordained marriage, He also gave us a sentence to set forth its meaning: "Therefore shall a man leave his father and his mother, and shall cleave unto his wife: and they shall be one flesh" (Gen. 2:24). This is the opposite of what too many see in marriage: the woman is viewed as leaving her parents and cleaving, or adhering to, her husband. That she does so is true enough, but the Bible stresses the *requirement* that the man make a break and cleave to his wife. Moreover, Jesus Christ declares that this is God's own statement (Matt. 19:5). Why then are commentaries and preachers silent about its meaning? It is clear that headship is given to the husband. Is it not here equally clear that a particular and very great centrality is given to the woman, who is "the mother of all living" (Gen. 3:20)?

Man is made of the bones and flesh of his father and mother, as C. A. Simpson has pointed out in *The Interpreter's Bible*, to become, in the act of marriage, one flesh, one community of life, with his wife. In the Hebrew, the word "cleave" means to cling close together, to be joined together, stick, or follow closely after. Given this meaning, it is most significant that it is the man whom God in particular requires this of. Since headship is given to the man, the human expectation would be that woman must adhere to the man and cling to him. God, however, places another requirement on marriage: the man must be joined to, cling to, or cleave unto his wife.

Man, it should be noted. is given dominion over the earth, over the fish, birds, and animals, and he shares the exercise of that dominion with his wife

(Gen. 1:26-28). Man's headship is in the exercise of that dominion. When Sarah called Abraham "lord" (I Peter 3:1-7), it was because Abraham was the head in the exercise of their dominion under God's covenant. In other words, a man is given headship over his wife in the exercise of dominion, not dominion over her.

A man's relationship to his parents is a blood relationship. He is genetically bone of their bones, and flesh of their flesh. This, however, is the relationship he must "leave" to "cleave" unto his wife, a non-blood relationship. This new non-genetic relationship must still become bone of his bone, and flesh of his flesh (Gen. 2:23-24).

It would be dangerous and false to push the point too far, or to see it as more than an important Biblical analogy, but the analogy to circumcision is there. In circumcision, the organ of generation is made the covenant mark by its circumcised status, signifying that man's hope is not in generation but in regeneration, a new life in the Lord. Circumcision, as Gerhardus Vos, in *Biblical Theology* (1948), pointed out, "stands for justification and regeneration, plus sanctification" (Rom. 4:9-12; Col. 2:11-13) (p. 105).

In some sense, marriage is also comparable to a new life. The twain become "one flesh," a new community of life. In terms of this unity, Paul uses marriage as a type of the unity of Christ and His church (Eph. 5:21-33). By this analogy. we are told that husbands must love their wives as Christ also loved the church, "and gave himself for it." This, plainly, calls for sacrificial service to the new entity or life, the family. The headship of the husband is one of a comparable radical love and sacrificial service, not a tyrannical power. Headship in Scripture means, our Lord makes clear, service: "He that is greatest among you shall be your servant" (Matt. 23:11). In the foot-washing episode, our Lord says, "I have given you an example, that ye should do as I have done to you" (John 13:15). For men to seek the blessings of Christian marriage with pagan doctrines of headship is blasphemous.

The family thus creates a new entity: the twain becomes one flesh. Two blood-lines and faith-lines come together to create a new union, one which unites two heritages. Eugen Rosenstock-Heuessy, in *The Multiformity of Man* (1936), called attention to the fact that, in the old days, a bride went from her father's house to a new house with a unity of faith and heritage. "She was not exposed to any other man's doctrine or ideals or values." This is now completely changed by public or statist education. The state imposes many fathers on a family's sons and daughters; these teach creeds and values antagonistic to those of the pupils' families. The result said Rosenstock-Huessy, is a polytheistic education. "Thus, a modern man is not marrying one man's daughter, but many men's pupil," and the same polytheistic education is true for the young man.

The result is that, instead of marriage creating a new entity, it creates another carbon copy of a machine-stamped factory assembled, statist model. With the teaching of sex education in these "public" schools, carbon copy techniques are carried to the marriage bed, where performance is by the book-model, and in terms of the most recent sexological research! That problems result should not surprise us.

One of the reasons for Christian Schools is to preserve the priority of the family in the life of the child. The state school undercuts the Christian family and is anti-familistic and thus is the poorest kind of training ground for marriage.

The Biblical family is by nature future oriented. Because it requires that there be a continuity of faith and honor, it maintains its roots in the past. "Honour thy father and thy mother: that thy days may be long upon the land which the LORD thy God giveth thee" (Exodus 20:12). This "honor" means continuity and love. At the same time, there must be a departure: leaving father and mother to cleave unto one's wife. Past, present, and future, are from God and under God.

A statist world is different. The goal of the state is control and the restriction of change to the state. Instead of the individual or family as the source of innovation, change, and entrepreneurship, we then have the state in control of all these things. The state, however, when it becomes this powerful, becomes a vast bureaucracy, and it gives us a frozen, pre-arranged world, not a future.

The family is the true wellspring of the future, not the state, and the woman is the key to it. The statist school is a citizen-producing factory designed to manufacture people whose every loyalty is eroded. No family ties bind the well-taught statist school product. Thus, all competing institutions or loyalties of family, faith, and heritage are eliminated. The result is a mass man; such a man is easily a rebel, a malcontent, or a drone, but he is not capable of anything but a statist answer to problems, because for him no other agency has any stature or viability. He is a factory product with standardized reactions and responses.

The Biblical family, however, is future oriented. It begins under God as an act of faith, not a trial experiment in living. It is governed by a faith and by a way of life that ties the past to the present and to the future. The grandparents and the parents alike share a concern for the children's future, and for a continuity of faith and life. At the same time, they have a concern that there be progress for the children.

Some economists have somberly predicted that the current and coming generation will be the first in American history whose standard of living will be lower than that of their parents. If statist controls continue and increase this may well be true, because statism seeks a frozen pre-arranged world order, not a free one.

Scripture orders a man to cleave or adhere to his wife because the godly woman is the mother of life. To cleave to one's wife means that one clings to, or follows closely after, not his parents but his wife. To cleave to one's wife means that a man sees the future with her and in terms of her, not in terms of his past, *nor in terms of the state*. We are definitely not told to cleave to or follow closely after the state, our president, governor, or prime minister. All too many men are more married to the state and its promises than to their wives, and the result is what can be called orgasmic politics. The future hope is then political, not personal.

Marriage is a personal act between two persons creating a very personal "one flesh" under the very personal God of Scripture. The future created by the family in Christ is not the impersonal monster-world of statist planners but a free society in the Lord.

The dominion mandate of Genesis 1:26-28 is followed by the institution of marriage, Genesis 2:20-24. These are not unrelated. The second implements the first.

The headship of men does not mean the shelving of women. The Pauline epistles tell us plainly how real and extensive the role of women was in the New Testament church. Men who seek to make a woman the mere adjunct of themselves are stupid, foolish, and unchristian. They pass up the wealth of God's way for the poverty of their ego. The churches which relegate women to a limbo of irrevelance are guilty before God. Subordination does not mean irrelevance nor incompetence. If this were true, every corporation would be better off if all the staff and employees were fired, and only the chairman of the board remained! It would commonly mean the departure of intelligence.

In terms of Scripture, the women's liberation movement is nonsense, but so too is the position of all too many churchmen. Genesis 2:24 tells us something we dare not forget. Beginning with the first couple, Adam and Eve, God requires a leaving and a cleaving. There is a natural and happy cleaving by women to their husbands, to godly husbands. But there is the cleaving which is central, is commanded by God, and is at the heart of true marriage; it is by the husband to his wife. (February, 1984)

KENOTICISM, THE "GOSPEL" OF DEFEAT
Chalcedon Paper No. 48

The doctrine of Kenosis (see Position Paper no. 45) is one of the great hidden influences of our time. It is a hidden influence because it has become so much a part of the intellectual atmosphere that it is commonly taken for granted, as we take the sun, the air, and the ground beneath our feet for granted.

Its immediate Western origins were in old Russia, but its original home was in the Far East. It came westward through Greco-Roman thinkers, but also later it came directly from the Orient. Buddhism in particular has been a fertile ground for such influences as well as Hindu religions. Some illustrations of such thinking which have passed into Western thought will tell us much.

A Buddhist sect tells of a Bodhisattva, a perfected man, who manifested perfect love and knowledge. On seeing a hungry mother tiger with unfed and hungry cubs, the Bodhisattva threw himself down the cliff to provide food for the hungry tigers. This act of self-sacrifice is seen as exemplifying holiness. (Marxism, especially in China, is full of like tales to promote its cause.)

Another story, as retold by the chaplain of a "Christian" mental hospital: an old Buddhist holy man, seeing a scorpion about to be swept away by a flooding river current, worked to save the scorpion, but the scorpion only kept poisoning the holy man's hands with his sting, which promised death. When rebuked for his efforts, the holy man said, "because it is the scorpion's nature to sting, why should I give up my nature to care?" The chaplain then compared the holy man to God, who "keeps trying," even when we respond like the scorpion (See my *Institutes of Biblical Law, Vol. II, Law and Society*, p. 478f.).

Unitarianism was a major source and influence in the introduction of Kenosis into the United States. Moncure Daniel Conway in *My Pilgrimage to the Wise Men of the East*, promoted much of this in the latter half of the 19th century. Conway was particularly impressed by the example of Kwanyin, the Chinese goddess of mercy. Conway wrote, "She is the woman who refused to enter paradise so long as any human is excluded. 'Never will I receive individual salvation,' she said, and still remains outside the gates of heaven" (p. 71).

Kenotic thinking prepared the way for the ready reception of Buddhist and other Eastern religions in the West. The philosophical premise of these religions is world and life negation. The ultimacy of non-being and defeat is presupposed, and an essential pacifism and non-resistance to problems, challenges, crises, and evils results. Kenosis and Eastern religions program a man for the acceptance of defeat.

As a result, eschatologies of defeat have become popular. Men program themselves to be losers, to be defeated, and to live with evil rather than to overcome it. As a result, the Western world, despite its marked advantages, is faltering and retreating. The lions are turning cowards before mice.

The basic thrust of Kenosis is: submit. The basic faith of Scripture is, that "Jesus Christ is Lord" (Phil. 2:11) and Savior, (John 3:16) and, in His Name, we must "occupy" till He comes (Luke 19:13). The occasional superficial resemblances between kenotic faith and the Bible cannot overcome the vast gulf between the two faiths.

According to the strict form of Kenosis in "Christian" theology, Christ in His incarnation laid aside His divine self-consciousness; only gradually and dimly at times was He aware of His divine Being. This is plainly contradicted by many texts, such as John 1:14-18; it was His "fullness" that "all we received." His divinity was plainly manifested in His every word, thought, and deed. As for the cross, it was not a kenotic act, but atonement, a very different thing.

Kenosis does not produce a godly morality. (It is of interest that a leading American preacher of Kenosis was the famous and notorious Henry Ward Beecher.) Kenosis places the emphasis on a pacifistic submission rather than on faith, and obedience to the every word of God (Matt. 4:4).

Kenotic faith places very great emphasis on *humiliation*. Because Christ's incarnation is seen as a humiliation of His deity, humiliation is seen as the model for Christian morality and behavior. The fallacy of such thinking is that we are not gods, and to be Christian is for us not a humiliation but our glory. The word of God is a command word, and it is God's plan and law for victory, not defeat. We are required to believe and obey the Lord, not to be humiliated. One very prominent pastor of some years ago, and a very well paid one, constantly courted humiliation. Although having a good wardrobe, he appeared at banquets poorly dressed to the point of being an embarrassment.

There is an affinity between Kenosis and psychological masochism. Masochism seeks self-abasement and punishment as ways of making atonement. The masochist does not find his freedom in Christ's atonement; he seeks to pay for his own sins by a variety of actions which bring punishment, shame, and defeat upon himself.

This is closely related to kenotic theory, which often sees victory as meaning defeat. This is apparent in Ronald J. Sider and Richard K. Taylor, *Nuclear Holocaust and Christian Hope* (1982). It is very much in evidence in the Vietnamese classic, *The Tale of Kieu*, written in the early 1800s by Nguyen Du. It pictures a society of victims, punished for crimes and sins they did not commit. The thesis of the tale is that all things in the universe work together for evil, the exact reverse of Romans 8:28. *The Tale of Kieu* is a kind of popular handbook in Vietnam, and it tells us much about that country. The poem tells us that the root of good lies in man, but God is mean and cruel. Basic to its perspective is the doctrine of reincarnation. If people in some previous life committed sins, they must expiate their guilt now. Hence, punishment now must be seen as our fate, and we must undergo humiliation and many horrors to escape the cycle of Karma. We have a "debt of grief to fate."

Here we see the religious roots of Kenosis, in reincarnation, a radically anti-Biblical doctrine. The illogical self-humiliation and self-abasement which underlies kenotic thinking has its origin in a non-Christian belief in self-atonement through self-punishment. Believers in *The Tale of Kieu* are programmed for defeat. The infiltration of kenotic thinking into Christendom is also a program for defeat. It is born of defective Christian thinking, and it erodes the life of faith in favor of a life of defeat.

Defeatism is all too much a part of the modern mentality. Some years ago, in a very important study, Samuel J. Warner described *The Urge to Mass Destruction* (1957). His perspective was not Christian, but his work fits best into a Christian context in its implications. Warner noted that many of the living hate all life and seek to destroy all life. Nietzsche was for him a classic example of this. Such people have an essential nihilism, and they promote and counsel courses of action which are absurd and which lead to disaster and death. They seek defeat for themselves and for others and advocate courses which will promote it. Their goal is frustration, humiliation and defeat, all things Nietzsche invited while professing something else. Such people work against life-preserving values in favor of life-defeating and destroying ones. They may profess a doctrine of love or of power, but they manifest hatred and self-defeat.

Indeed, said Warner, such people seek "victory through defeat," i.e., they seek to equate defeat and destruction with a "moral" victory. What they in fact manifest is an "urge to mass destruction."

Warner's analysis was psychological, not theological. All the same, his study was telling and important. All too commonly, morality and virtue are ascribed to masochistic tendencies and programs which promise only destruction for the West. These programs include inflation, foreign aid, foreign loans by major banks, and much, much more.

Behind all these trends is the doctrine of Kenosis, which sees morality, not in terms of obedience to God's word, but as a self-emptying.

Awhile back, c. 1967, a godly friend guided a dedicated pastor and his wife in the investment of their limited savings. His counsel was particularly astute and well-informed. In a few years, before they realized what had happened, their assets increased very dramatically. Instead of being glad, the couple was badly shaken and upset. They had expected something only slightly better than bank interest as their returns. Their response? They divested themselves of all their holdings and gave away all their profits in order to regain their kenotic "purity." They thought it shameful and unbecoming to be other than either poor or only modestly well-off. They were insistent to an absurd degree that virtue requires a self-emptying and deprivation. They could not see that the Bible equates virtue with faithfulness to the Lord and His law-word, not self-deprivation.

Kenosis is a recent heresy in the West. Older theological works make no mention of it, because it did not then exist in Western Europe nor in the United States. Pietism and Quietism were in fact providing the seed-bed for the receptivity to Kenosis when it moved into Germany c. 1830 and then into other countries. The Rev. Charles Buck (1771-1815) in his *Theological Dictionary*, has no mention of Kenosis. More than a generation later, William Smith and Samuel Cheetham did not list it in their *Dictionary of Christian Antiquities*. After that, however, it was not only known but all too readily accepted.

One of the reasons for the ready acceptance of Kenosis was the rise of the higher criticism and modernism. The adherents in the church of this new critical thinking found the orthodox Chalcedonian doctrine of Christ much too strong to reconcile with their growing unbelief. A Christ who did not know Himself to be God, having been "emptied" of divinity in His incarnation, was easier for them to accept. Such a Christ had a gradually dawning awareness of His role as He grew in His human self-consciousness. Modernism thus encouraged Kenoticism.

There was another facet. In England, Bishop Gore and other high churchmen adopted a form of Kenoticism which held that God the Son voluntarily surrendered certain prerogatives and attributes of God while retaining the ethical properties of truth, holiness, and love. The surrendered attributes were those most commonly linked exclusively with the deity; the retained ones can be shared by all men. Thus, Christians are to stress truth, holiness, and love, while emptying themselves of power, wealth, victory, and other conquering factors. At the same time that Gore and others emptied Christ, they sought to increase the power of the church. However, in emptying Christ of deity, they also hindered His church and His people. They furthered Christian ritual but not power. To lower Christ's status is also to lower man and the church.

Kenoticism tells us that evil is power and Christ is helplessness and humiliation. Karl Barth said, in *Dogmatics in Outline* (1947), "the man who calls 'the Almighty' God misses God in the most terrible way. For the 'Almighty' is bad, as 'power in itself' is bad. The 'Almighty' means Chaos, Evil, the Devil" (p. 48).

Given such a perspective, with echoes of it in Roman Catholic, Protestant modernist, fundamentalist, and 'Reformed' thought, is it any wonder that the church is helpless? It has sought helplessness as though it were a virtue. It has lusted after an unholy impotence as a higher way of life. It has courted defeat as though this were a virtue.

Hymns which speak of victory have been slighted and criticized. Back in my student days, I heard one such ancient hymn of victory ridiculed, a hymn ascribed to St. Andrew of Crete, 660-732, "Christian, dost thou see them?" After all, St. Andrew's hymn has such lines as "Christian, up and smite them," and "Peace shall follow battle, Night shall end in day." Such militant language was held to be in poor taste! The same was true of Isaac Smith's hymn (c.1770), "Soldiers of Christ, arise, And put your armour on, Strong in the strength which God supplies, Thro' his eternal Son." Smith's hymn goes on to say, "From strength to strength go on, Wrestle, and fight, and pray: Tread all the powers of darkness down, And win the well-fought day." Winning? A kenotic church wants no such songs! Thus, Smith's great hymn is not a common one now.

However, as Isaac Watts' better known hymn (c 1724) "Am I a soldier of the cross?" says, in a verse often omitted, "Sure I must fight if I would reign; Increase my courage, Lord: I'll bear the cross, endure the pain, Supported by Thy word."

George J. Webb, in "Stand up, Stand up, for Jesus" (1837), declared, "From victory unto victory, His army shall He lead, Till every foe is vanquished, and Christ is Lord indeed."

When the church forsakes Kenoticism for Christ, the church too will know victory. (March, 1984)

DOCETISM AND THE MANDATE FOR DOMINION
Chalcedon Position Paper No. 49

Heresies often disappear in church history to return as false orthodoxies. One such example is Docetism. This concept, a form of Gnosticism, refused to accept the incarnation and union (without confusion) of the human and the divine in Jesus Christ. For the Docetists, Jesus was a spiritual being, a kind of phantom, who had only the appearance of flesh. By means of this doctrine, in Neander's words, "the connection of Christ's appearance with nature and with history" was broken. Christ was "real" only in that He was fully visible and present, but not as actual flesh and blood but as pure spirit. Such a view meant, as Neander saw, the "evaporation" of Christianity.

We have in John a very clear insistence on a total separation from this view in its earliest forms: "Hereby know ye the Spirit of God: Every spirit that confesseth that Jesus Christ is come in the flesh is of God: And every spirit that confesseth not that Jesus Christ is come in the flesh is not of God: *and this is that spirit of antichrist* whereof ye have heard that it should come; and even now already is it in the world" (I John 4:2-3). Docetism is thus on apostolic authority declared to be of antichrist; it is antichristian to the core.

In the Epistle of Ignatius to the Smyrnaeans, we have an attack on the Docetists: "They who would make nothing but a spectre of Christ are themselves like spectres--spectral men." Such a doctrine made a material and personal stand for the faith unnecessary: "But if these things were done by our Lord only in appearance, then am I only in appearance bound. And why have I surrendered myself to death, to the fire, to the sword, to wild beasts?"

Tertullian also attacked the Docetists, saying, "How is it, that you make the half of Christ a lie? He was all truth." Again he said, "You are offended when the child is nourished and fondled in the uncleanness of its swaddling-clothes. This reverence shown to nature you despise--and how were you born yourself? Christ, at least, loved man in this condition. For his sake, he came down from above; for his sake, he submitted to every sort of degradation, to death itself. In loving man, he loved even his birth, even his flesh."

This "reverence shown to nature" by our Lord, of which Tertullian wrote, was lacking in the Docetists. For them, the world was divided between two alien and contradictory substances, spirit and matter, a Hellenic division. Salvation for Docetism was essentially from materialism, from matter, into spirituality. For Docetism, the goal of holiness was separation from material things, and their Christ thus could not be truly incarnate, because to be made flesh would make Jesus Christ sinful. For all forms of Gnosticism, the fall of man was essentially a fall into flesh, into matter or materialism, and hence salvation meant becoming spiritual.

However, then as now, whenever men seek this false salvation, their sin increases. When men become "spiritual" by seeking to forsake materiality and flesh, they fall into many material or physical sins. On all sides of the church front, charismatic and non-charismatic, holiness groups and "main-line" churches, wherever people seek a "spiritual" way of life as against a materially relevant one, they fall readily into fleshly sins.

There is a reason for this. Salvation is not from flesh or matter but from sin, a very different thing! God created all things, and He created all things "very good" (Gen. 1:31). To blame what God created for man's fall is morally wrong. To seek salvation from God's creation is sin, and an indictment of God. Sin is not matter, nor is it spirit. "Sin is any want of conformity unto, or transgression of, the law of God," according to the Shorter Catechism, no. 14. "Sin," says I John 3:14, "is the transgression of the law."

Satan is a purely spiritual being and yet totally evil; his evil nature is not due to his spirituality but to his moral choice. Adam was created a flesh and blood man; his fall was not due to his materiality but to his moral decision, his desire to be his own god, determining what is good and evil for himself (Gen. 3:5). In both cases sin, not flesh nor spirit, was responsible for their fall. To see spirit as necessarily good is not Scriptural, nor to see matter as necessarily bad. Both are God's creation; sin is an ethical, not a metaphysical fact, a matter of moral choice, not of being either spiritual or material.

Docetic and Gnostic thinking has become a part of the religious life of the church. People assume spirituality to be good per se: I John 4:2-3 tells us it can be demonic. People assume materiality to be bad, which it can be, but it can also be holy. It is sin which renders spirit or matter bad; it is sin, not an aspect of God's creation which is bad.

One consequence of Docetic thinking in the church has been to undermine the mandate for dominion (Gen. 1:26-28). Psalms 72:8 tells us of Christ, "He shall have dominion also from sea to sea, and from the river unto the ends of the earth:" Isaiah 64:25 tells us that, *before* the end of the world, man's longevity will be greatly extended. I Corinthians 15:24-27 tells us that, before the end of the world and Christ's second coming, all Christ's enemies shall be put under His feet, as well as "all rule and all authority and power." We are also told that there shall be world peace; "nation shall not lift up sword against nation, neither shall they learn war any more" (Isa. 2:4). No man nor nation shall stand against the Lord: "they shall be as nothing; and they that strive against thee shall perish" (Isa. 41:11). In fact, "*the nation and kingdom that will not serve thee shall perish; those nations shall be utterly wasted*" (Isa. 60:12). Such verses cannot be "spiritualized" away, as Docetism seeks to do. Their meaning is too clear.

The mandate for dominion is, *first*, required by the fact of creation. God having made all things, governs all things and requires His covenant man to rule all things by God's law word. God did not create any part of the universe or earth to be ruled by His enemies. On the contrary, He gives His covenant law to His redeemed people as the instrument for dominion. Law is the key instrument for government. To be antinomian is to be against government by, for, and under God. Docetism wants a separation from matter, law and government, and in so doing separates itself from the Lord. All forms of Gnosticism do this same thing, from Valentinian to Karl Barth and the "spiritual" evangelicals. The fall was the consequence of sin, of moral dereliction, and salvation is our restoration into moral responsibility, materially and spiritually. The law of God is the way of holiness, the instrument and means for exercising moral responsibility. The law of God is thus the way of dominion whereby redeemed men can subdue the earth and rule it under God.

Second, the mandate for dominion is clearly set forth in the incarnation. God the Son became incarnate; He took upon Himself all the being of man. Had the purpose of His coming been to pull people out of a material world, He would not have been made flesh; He would have come as a Docetic phantom. Jesus Christ is the last and great Adam (I Cor. 15:45-47); the first Adam fell into sin and could not exercise dominion; the last Adam came to destroy the power of sin and death, and to send forth His people to command all nations for Him (Matt. 28:18-20). The incarnation tells us that the triune God is working to bring God's creation under God's total government, and hence God in the flesh enters time, history and matter to redeem it. The incarnation is a material fact. We cannot be Christian and deny the incarnation. John says, "Whosoever shall confess that Jesus is the Son of God, God dwelleth in him, and he in God" (I John 4:15). We must affirm that the totally human Jesus is also totally the son of God; only those who make this confession are "in God", John makes clear. Without the incarnation, there is no Christianity.

Third, the atonement is an anti-Docetic mandate for dominion. It is anti-Docetic because it has to do with the satisfaction of God's law, and Docetism is antinomian because law, God's law, is concerned with the government and dominion over our very material world. Government and law are forms of dominion, and there can be no dominion without government and law. The atonement tells us that God is the supreme Governor and the only true law-maker. It is the requirement of His law and rule or government which requires atonement, or propitiation and satisfaction. This atonement does not have as its purpose the abandonment of His law but its restoration as our way of life. As a death sentence on sin, the law is a way of death to the unredeemed. When we die to the law as a death penalty, we are then alive in it as the way of life and justice (Rom. 8:4), and as the way of dominion. The atonement frees us from slavery to sin (John 8:24) to make us more than conquerors in Christ (Rom. 8:37), and to be a conqueror is to exercise dominion. There is no dominion in Docetism, because there is no true atonement and no law. Docetic salvation is from matter, not sin. The redeemed in Christ know that the difference between holiness and sin in the realm of sexuality is faithfulness to the law of God. "Marriage is honourable in all, and the bed undefiled: but whoremongers and adulterers God will judge" (Heb. 13:4). The atonement and the life of faithfulness make the difference, not a Docetic spirituality. Because of their false spirituality, Docetists and Gnostics are very prone to sexual sins; they seek salvation from their materiality and in spiritual experiences rather than through Jesus Christ and His atoning blood.

Fourth, the doctrine of the resurrection is a mandate for dominion. Our Lord conquered the power of sin and death over His new humanity. The Apostles' Creed declares that Jesus Christ, who "was crucified, dead, and buried...rose again from the dead." It also sets forth as an article of faith "the resurrection of the body, and the life everlasting;" it is our bodies which shall be resurrected, because Christ is risen from the dead (I Cor. 15:12-20). Christ rose from the dead as our Adam, "For since by man came death, by man came also the resurrection of the dead. For as in Adam all die, even so in Christ shall all be made alive" (I Cor. 15:21-22). Where Adam failed to exercise dominion (Gen. 1:26-28), and his fallen heirs only worked out the implications of sin and death, we in Christ are required to exercise dominion over ourselves and the world. In the place of the outworkings of sin and death, we have the development in and through us of righteousness, of justice, and life. We are called to be the dominion people, and all things must be brought into a captivity to Christ. His dominion must be from sea to sea, beginning with us.

Dennis Peacocke recently reminded me of the fact that *proletarian* is a word having as its root *proles*, children; the proletariat are the breeders of children whose function it is to breed for the state and to be the tools of the state, its children. The Christian is not called to be a proletarian, but *Christ's dominion man*. The modern state seeks to proletarianize man; we must make of a man a new creation in Christ by being the instruments of His word and Spirit. The battle lines are now being drawn between proletarian men, the children of the State, and dominion men, the sons of God in Christ by the adoption of grace.

In this battle, the Docetist is irrelevant. He regards interest or activity in politics as materialistic and tainted, and the same is true of economics. He is content to allow the humanistic state schools to educate his children, because he regards Christian Schools as too materialistic an activity, and his faith is purely "spiritual" in its concerns. The Docetist deserts Christ for his own spirituality, and he seeks to bring others into his "higher" and "spiritual" way.

The Docetists are often kindly and well-meaning people. They promote their antinomianism and anti-dominionism as the true gospel, which requires them to relegate most of the Bible to some meaningless category. The modern Docetists do not say that Jesus did not come in the flesh; they have sophisticated the argument, as did all the heretics of the early church. For them, Christ came supposedly to make us "spiritual": whereas Scripture tells us that He came and died for us to make us righteous or just before God. John tells us that all such falsity is of antichrist (I John 4:1-3); it turns a man into a false prophet.

But we have men and nations to conquer for Christ, who is the "only Potentate, the King of kings, the Lord of lords" (I Tim. 6:15). He must reign in and through us, until all his enemies are put under His feet, and all rule and all authority and powers acknowledge and obey Him (I Cor. 15:24-26). Only then shall the end come, and the last enemy, death, be destroyed. Before then, the Docetists, the apostles of irrelevancy, will all be gone.

INCORPORATION
Chalcedon Position Paper No. 50

One of history's most important doctrines is today widely subject to abuse, neglect, and attack. This is the concept of the corporation. In any truly strict definition of the term, no corporation existed outside of the Biblical revelation nor apart from Scriptures doctrine of a people created by God's covenant. Some Roman developments had a resemblance to the corporation but cannot be identified with it.

The word "corporation" tells us much. It is from the Latin, and is related to the term common in medieval faith, "De corpore et sanguine Domini," "the body and blood of the Lord." In its original sense, the corporation, which means a body which does not die with the death of its members, has reference to the body of Christ, His Church. This corporation, Christ's Body, has as its origin covenant Israel; the calling of twelve disciples to replace the twelve patriarchs of Israel had as its purpose to set forth the continuity of the corporate covenant community. The church is the new Israel of God; it used that term, "Israel of God" (Gal. 6:16), to distinguish itself from the Israel of blood.

The church thus, as the original and true corporation, has an earthly as well as a supernatural life. It is here in history, but it is also "the heavenly Jerusalem;" it is "an innumerable company of angels," and the "general assembly and church of the firstborn" (Heb. 12:22-23). Paul says that Christians are "one body in Christ" (Rom. 12:5), i.e., a corporate entity in and of Him. We are all "baptized into one body" (I Cor. 12:12-20), wherein there are "many members, yet one body." The texts which stress this fact are too many to cite in so small a compass as this. The church saw itself from the beginning as a "corporation," a body whose life and continuity did not depend on the life of its members.

It is amazing that there is so little to be found on the significance to society of the doctrine of the church as Christ's corporation. It is one of history's most revolutionary doctrines, and it has influenced many areas of life and thought. A key sphere of influence has been, for better or worse, the state. One of the problems of the non-Christian world was long the lack of any concept of continuity. The office or person of a king might be sacred, but rule was personal, i.e., non-institutional. Subordinate rulers swore loyalty, not to a civil government, but to a man, a ruler. The death of that ruler dissolved the ties, and his successor had to regain loyalties through demonstrable power to compel it. The result was that civil authority was purely personal in most cases, and very erratic as a result. This was a problem Rome tried to solve, but not very successfully. With the rise of Christendom, this problem lingered. The Holy Roman Empire continued in the old pattern, and, as a result, alternated between great power and virtual non-existence as an effective force.

Not surprisingly, the doctrine of the church as Christ's corporation began to influence society. It should be added that the church was not the only corporation set forth in Scripture: the family is another. When a man dies, the Bible tells us he is "gathered unto his people" or his fathers (Gen. 49:33), or, with some analogous term, stresses the family's corporate unity. Naboth's refusal to sell the vineyard to Ahab was due to this corporate fact: it was the property of his father before him (I Kings 21:3), and of his descendents after him. This strong sense of the family as a corporate religious entity has been the reason for the survival of the Jews; with the rise of humanism, the Jewish family is now disintegrating. Within Christendom, many of the problems created by men in their false sense of dominion, and women with their feminist rights movements, have been due to a failure to recognize the corporate nature of the family in Biblical law. That corporate nature, and its relationship to the doctrine of the church, is very forcefully set forth in Ephesians 5:21-33.

Ernst H. Kantorowicz, in *The King's Two Bodies* (1957), set forth the statist use of this concept and its many perversions, in the medieval and early modern developments of the doctrine. The Crown became a corporation; hence, it could be said, when a king died, "The King is dead; long live the king," because the monarchy did not die with the death of one monarch. The state indeed went so far as to see itself as the mystical body of Christ and as the true and central Christian corporation. The consequences of this and other perversions are very much with us, and in well developed forms. The fact that, since Hegel, a pantheistic theology undergirds the doctrine of the state does not alter the fact that the modern state sees itself as the true church or kingdom under whom all things subsist. The state sees itself as god walking on earth and as the great corporation of which all men are members.

The Bible tells us that there are two great bodies or corporations, with all other bodies as aspects of the one or the other. These two are the humanity, body, or corporation of the old or first Adam, and that of the new or last Adam, Jesus Christ (I Cor. 15:45-50). The modern state sees itself as the super-corporation, embracing both. St. Augustine saw the two humanities as the Kingdom or City of God (in Christ) or the City of Man, in the fallen Adam. The state without Christ is in the City of Man and is no different in character than a band of robbers; it is an evil, criminal agency oppressing man. Augustine did not counsel revolt, because he knew that the key to change is regeneration in Christ, not revolution.

The influence of the concept or doctrine of incorporation or the corporation went beyond the state into the world of commerce. The business corporation echoes, whether or not it knows it, the Biblical doctrine of the church.

Two things may be said at this point. *First*, it goes without question that the doctrine of the corporation has, in humanistic hands, been greatly abused and misused. However, this should not lead us into overlooking a *second* fact, namely, that the concept of the corporation has given continuity to man's activities in one sphere after another. Medieval and modern institutions have a continuity and history unlike anything in the non-Christian world.

What the corporation doctrine has enabled men to do is to transcend the limitations of their time and life-span. Men can create and develop a business, a school, or an agency whose functions live beyond themselves. This has been a very revolutionary and Biblical fact. The Bible tells us that man is earth-bound, and, because of his sin, will return to earth, "for dust thou art, and unto dust shalt thou return" (Gen. 3:19). However, this is not the whole story. We are also told, "Blessed are the dead which die in the Lord from henceforth: Yea, saith the Spirit, that they may rest from their labours: and their works do follow them" (Rev. 14:13). That a man's works can survive him on earth is obvious; we are told that they follow him beyond the grave. Such a faith gives a great confidence in both time and eternity. Men can work knowing that their "Labour is not in vain in the Lord" (I Cor. 15:58).

Granted that corporations are not necessarily good (nor necessarily bad), it still remains true that the concept of the corporation has been important in history by giving continuity to the works of men. Among other things, the original corporation, the church, has given a new meaning to time. Time is now time in terms of Christ, B.C., Before Christ, or A.D., Anno Domini, the year of our Lord, in Christ. Previously, time was commonly dated in terms of the accession of the current ruler, i.e., in the first year of Mithradates, or the eighth year of Antiochus, and so on. There was no continuity, only an endless beginning and ending. Now all time is in Christ, and His Body is the great corporation. That pattern gives continuity to all of life, so that human activities now have a life span beyond that of their founders. Moreover, all that the ungodly accumulate shall flow into God's Kingdom, so that its continuity will prosper His people (Isa. 61:6, 54:3, etc.). The continuity serves Christ, and us in Him.

The development of corporations in Western history has been very important. Many Christian corporations were established during the medieval era to carry on specific Biblical duties and to organize people for common action to meet a specific Christian need or function. Attempts at statist control were also common. In the reign of James I of England, that monarch held that corporations could only be created by the fiat of the state. This meant that neither a Christian calling nor vocation could create a corporation but only the crown.

In the United States, virtually total freedom existed for generations for all kinds of corporations. The incorporation of a church or Christian agency of any kind was simply a legal formality notifying the state of the existence of such a body and its immunity from statist controls. In recent years, the statists have turned that notification into a form of licensure and control. The matter can be compared to filing a birth certificate. When the birth of Sarah Jones is recorded by her parents and doctor, permission for Sarah Jones to exist is definitely not requested; rather, a fact is legally recorded. Similarly, in American law religious trusts, foundations, or trusts did not apply for the right to exist but recorded their certificate of birth, their incorporation. The current Internal Revenue Service doctrine is that the filing is a petition for the right to exist. This turns the historic position, and the First Amendment, upside down. It asserts for the federal government the "right" to establish religion and to control the exercise thereof. As a result, a major conflict of church and state is under way.

At the same time, many abuses of the concept of a church corporation prevail. Some organizations sell "ordinations" as pastors and priests to enable men in the evasion of income taxes. This kind of abuse does not invalidate the integrity of a true church, nor is it a legitimate reason for the entrance of the state into the life of valid churches.

Then too, because of the intrusion of the federal and state governments into the sphere of church incorporation, some are advocating disincorporation by churches. Given the vulnerability of the church as an incorporated legal entity to statist controls, we should not forget the total vulnerability with disincorporation. In some court cases, the results are proving to be especially disastrous. If our weapons against an enemy prove to be somewhat defective, does it make sense to throw away those weapons and to disarm ourselves?

Not only should the church fight for the freedom of incorporated existence, but Christians need to establish a wide variety of Christian foundations to meet their wide-flung responsibilities in Christ. Educational foundations to further the promotion of Biblical faith and knowledge are needed. Christian charitable trusts to minister to the needs of the poor, prisoners, the sick, delinquents, and more are urgently needed. Hospitals are a product of Christian corporate activity to minister to human need; they were once all Christian. There is a need to reclaim this ministry which, in humanistic hands, has become increasingly a problem.

Christian corporations or foundations were once the ministries in the spheres of health, education, and welfare, and there is a growing return to responsibilities in these areas. These agencies use God's tax, the tithe, to exercise government in key spheres of life in the name of Christ. They are outside the sphere of statist taxation and control, because they are areas of Christ's Kingdom and government.

We have a weak doctrine of corporation today because we have a weak doctrine of the Body of our Lord, and of communion. If we limit the doctrine of corporation to the institutional church, we limit the scope of Christ's work in the world. To incorporate means to give body to something; we need to incorporate our faith into the total context of our world and to minister and govern in our various spheres in Christ's name and power. (May, 1984)

THE MANICHAEAN HERESY TODAY
Chalcedon Position Paper No. 51

In its origin, Manichaeanism was not a heresy but a rival religion. The religion of Mani arose in the middle east in the 3rd century A. D. and spread throughout the Roman Empire. The central teaching of Manichaeanism, a religion akin to Zoroastrianism, is that two rival gods exist, the god of light and spirit, and the god of darkness and matter. The identification of light and spirit, and of darkness and matter may not have been present or fixed in the thought of Mani, but, in time, this was the dualism of Manichaean faith. What is of especial concern to us is that the contrast in Manichaeanism is not between good and evil as moral positions but as metaphysical ones. What this means is that a state of being became the religious goal rather than a state of faith and its moral requirements. A simple illustration will suffice to explain this in part. If a man is born black or white, he cannot change his racial past: it is his state of being. A man can, however, be transformed morally from an evil to a good man. Having said this, we must concede that dualism does permit some degree of change, by forsaking as much of material things as possible, and by becoming as spiritual as possible. This is not, however, a moral change but an attempt to suppress one side of our being, the material, for the other side, the spiritual. This emphasis marked the many medieval Manichaean heresies or cults, such as the Albigensians. Under the facade of a seeming Christianity, these peoples found salvation, not in Christ, but in forsaking fleshly things for spiritual things. By giving one aspect of their being pre-eminence over the other, they were supposedly saved.

For Biblical faith, salvation is by Christ's atonement and by His regenerating work in us. From being rebels against God, we become members of Christ's new humanity. This conversion makes us a new creation in the moral, not the metaphysical sense.

For Manichaeanism, we have the substance of two rival gods in ourselves, one a good, the other a bad god. Our "salvation" is to side with the one god or substance in our being.

It is clear that Manichaeanism was related to Gnosticism and its various forms of expression such as Docetism and Kenosis. Old Russia, the origin of Kenotic thinking in our time, was also the home of many Manichaean cults. The one best known to Americans (because of the Canadian colony) is the Dukhobors, whom Tolstoy befriended and shared some ideas with, in a rationalistic fashion. Among other things, the Dukhobors believe in the transmigration of souls to pure spirit; they deny that Jesus was of real flesh and blood, and they see the human soul as the image of the true god. As Frederich C. Conybeare, in *Russian Dissenters* (1921), reported, they believe and say, "there is a God, He is Spirit. He is in us, *we are god*." In their spiritual being, men are of one substance with God. Those who forsake the flesh thus concentrate on the good being or nature in them.

This is Manichaeanism as a religion, as a rival to Christianity. It has, however, largely disappeared in the western world as a rival religion and has re-appeared as a heresy within the ranks of Christianity as well as humanism.

The defining mark of Manichaeanism as a heresy is that it defines the issues confronting man, not as a moral antithesis, but as an antithesis of being. If the antithesis is moral, someone clearly needs changing. Christianity thus insists on the necessity of conversion. When a man is born again, he is not another being; he is the same man but with a new heart, with a spirit of faith and obedience, not of rebellion and disobedience.

If the antithesis is one of being, then the prescription for a cure is death, the destruction of all evil being. This prescription is basic to modern Manichaeanism.

A classic example of this faith is Jean-Jacques Rousseau. For Rousseau the antithesis of being is between the natural man who is good, and civilization, which is evil. This means that "over-civilized" men are hopelessly evil. By changing the nature of the antithesis of good and evil from morality to being, Rousseau ushered in the age of revolution. In terms of Rousseau, and beginning with the French Revolution, men began to dismantle civilization and to exalt salvation by death, the guillotine.

Another example of this faith is Karl Marx. For him, humanity was divided into two classes, one good, the other bad. His solution was revolution and death, and his followers such as Trotsky, Lenin and Stalin became great advocates of total terror, i.e., death for the "enemies" of the working class. This Manichaean heresy solves no problems; rather, it aggravates them. Having once liquidated the old "ruling class," it continually finds new evidences of this irredeemable evil in its own ranks in all who disagree. The Marxist prescription is not conversion but the slave labor camp and death.

Racism provides another instance of modern Manichaeanism. Evil is seen as incarnate in a particular race, black, white or yellow; in Jews, or in Gentiles; in their group, not ours. In the liberal version of racism, all men are naturally good (except Christians), and it is the environment of religion and the family which is evil. Much more than a few adherents of Anglo-Israelism are convinced that all who are not members of the "chosen" tribes are "the seed of the Serpent," demonic. This is Manichaeanism.

Because of Manichaeanism, the problems of modern man cannot be solved without a return to Biblical faith. If my enemy can be converted, I can pray for him, be patient with him, and do all that is morally possible to work peaceably with him. I do not make myself his victim, but I do work to evangelize him. However, if a man views reality with implicitly Manichaean premises, as most men now do, not conversion but suppression and death become the solution. For many of our humanistic statists, the evil is Christianity; hence, they work to suppress and destroy it. At the same time, whatever their differences, they sense their essential identity with Marxists and are ready to work with them. For Manichaeanism, peace is a highly selective practice; it is applied only towards those who are on the side of true spirituality or intelligence.

It should be easy for Christians to confront, expose, and convert these Manichaeans. All the weapons in their Biblical arsenal provide them with the most effective means of bringing a saving knowledge of Christ to these peoples. The problem, however, is that too many churchmen are themselves infected by this implicit Manichaeanism.

Within the church, the covert Manichaeanism of modern man takes another form, an older one. Instead of a moral antithesis between faith and obedience to Jesus Christ, ("by their fruits ye shall know them." Matt. 7:20), on the one hand, and man's rebellion against God, and his attempt to be his own god (Gen. 3:5), on the other, these churchmen have another antithesis. This false antithesis is between spirituality and materialism. Many churchmen will object to a doctrinal clarity of faith; they prefer to be general and vague on matters like infallibility and inerrancy, the atonement, and the incarnation, and silent on such things as six-day creationism, predestination, and God's law. They are at the same time very vocal about the need for more "spirituality," a vague term which often means being more church oriented.

In the church today, the word "spiritual" covers a multitude of sins. In some churches, very strong and active members are considered "unspiritual" because they do not attend one of several prayer groups or meetings, but too often these prayer meetings are dominated by pious hypocrites whose long-winded prayers bar newcomers from participation. (Our Lord spoke of such Pharisees in Matt. 6:5). In his day, Moody put one such person in his place during a public meeting in England.

These "spiritual" Christians are often of no earthly good in dealing with needs among brethren, or in their community, but they are devotees of the forms of religion. I recall one man who could never count on having a meal on time; or clean clothing, because his wife spent so much time at the church; she, in turn, regarded him as very "un-spiritual" because he complained!

Much more can be said. The church today is so involved in this Manichaean emphasis on spirituality that it forgets that the Christian calling is to be faithful. Biblical religion is intensely practical. Cotton Mather is very much abused in our day, but that old Puritan summed up the Christian life in the title of one of his books, *Essays To Do Good*. William Wilberforce in his study, *A Practical View of the Prevailing Religious Systems of Professed Christians Contrasted With Real Christianity* (1797), denied that religious observances were the sufficient marks of faith. How real a person's faith is becomes evident, Wilberforce said, in how seriously they view the education of their children in the faith. "It cannot be expected, that they who are so little attentive to this great object in the education of their children, should be more so in other parts of their conduct, where less strongly stimulated by affection, and less obviously loaded with responsibility." If in this key area, the family, we do not take our Christian duties seriously, our pretenses at spirituality elsewhere are evil. It is a significant but suppressed fact that one of the most powerful evangelical leaders of this century, who died some years ago, was thoroughly detested by his godly family.

Another form of this false spirituality is a solemn and dour countenance and manner, as though spirituality means a pompous demeanor. The answer to this kind of behavior was beautifully set forth in an old hymn, "Why should the children of a King go mourning all their days?"

What Scripture presents us with is not two gods in endless and eternal conflict, but the one true God who made all things, and made them very good (Gen. 1:31). Things are out of joint, not because matter is evil but because man has sinned. If matter is the problem, there is no remedy for it, because we live material lives all our days, and face the resurrection of our bodies at the end of history. If spirituality is the answer, Christ's coming was not necessary, because many religions stressed the need for spirituality. (Socrates and Plato both stressed spirituality and were both homosexuals who saw their vice as a spiritual love).

Manichaeanism has been a governing undercurrent in the Western world. Its influence both within the church and outside of it has been enormous. Denis de Rougemont, in *Love In The Western World* (1939), traced its influence on the idea of romantic love. Because Manichaeanism sees man as being of two substances, the one good and the other evil, for Manichaeanism there is no real solution to man's problem. However "spiritual" he becomes, he still remains a material, a physical being. The result is frustration. Mario Praz called it, in his book of that title, *The Romantic Agony*.

Our Manichaean culture and nations are thus in the grips of an ideology of perpetual war. The deeper the nations become involved in the conflict of interests faith, the deeper they fall into the morass of continual battle in a war that cannot end. Manichaeanism posits an irreconcilable conflict of interests. In this conflict, from a Manichaean perspective, suppression and death are both a necessity and a futility. For over half a century, the Soviet Union has been killing off "class enemies," but they seem to arise as fast as they are worked to death in slave labor camps. The Manichaean solution is suppression and death, but it is an unsuccessful solution, because the "enemy" is an equally essential part of being.

The Christian solution is conversion. What we need is a purging of all elements of this covert Manichaeanism from the thinking of the church. Then the power of God unto salvation will be clearly manifest. (June, 1984)

THE MONTANIST OUTLOOK
Chalcedon Position Paper No. 52

One of the sadder movements in the early church was Montanism. It was not in purpose a heresy, although it became one in time. Montanism began as a demand for stricter discipline in the church. It wanted a return to the earlier years of Spirit-created acts and utterances; it emphasized spirituality as against "carnal" Christians, and it stressed the belief that the Second Coming would very soon occur. Almost every emphasis made by Montanism was rapidly carried to dangerous extremes.

The founder, Montanus, had himself a background which did not favor his cause. He is said to have been a castrated Phrygian ex-priest of Cybele who was much given to trances and visions. His physical lack of wholeness, according to Leviticus 21:17-23, should have disqualified him from leadership.

The Montanists called themselves "spiritual" Christians; for them, the existing churches were full of "carnal" Christians. The time was the latter half of the second century. The young church had many new converts and thus many problems, since these new Christians were not without their lingering pagan traits. This was no less true of Montanus, and his two prophetesses Priscilla and Maximilla, who left their husbands to proclaim the "true faith."

A strong emphasis by St. Paul in his first letter to Timothy is that a novice or someone young in the faith was not to be ordained as an elder (I Tim. 5:22). The testing of time and experience is necessary; every faith must be tested.

Montanism substituted zeal for testing and experience. The Montanists, as a result, soon had many churches in an uproar. They believed that their faith gave them instant wisdom. By stressing the *experience* of the Holy Spirit, they assumed that this experience gave them the *wisdom* of the Spirit. A true experience of the Spirit increases grace and humility; the Montanist experience increased pride and judgement all too often. The great man in the Montanist movement was Tertullian, who was clearly and strongly orthodox. Montanism in the main was faithful to Biblical faith, but it was guilty of the error of "instant wisdom" on the part of novices in the faith, many of whom were fanatical women and ignorant men.

The Montanists believed and stressed the priesthood of every believer: "There is neither Jew nor Greek, there is neither bond nor free, there is neither male nor female: for ye are all one in Christ Jesus" (Gal. 3:28). This means that we are equally priests before God the Father and have direct access to Him through Christ, whose members we are. This, *however*, does not alter our status among men and in institutions. Status in a family, or in a church, is not altered by our priesthood before God. The Montanist emphasis on the Spirit in the life of man tended to be erosive of authority. This, combined with their belief in the continuation of the Pentecost gifts, made Montanists a problem rather than an asset to the churches.

But this was not all. Montanism was intensely given to stressing the immediate return of Christ. Maximilla said, "After me there is no more prophecy, but only the end of the world." Our Lord in teaching His disciples to pray, taught them to say, "Thy Kingdom come. Thy will be done in earth, as it is in heaven" (Matt. 6:10). This was seen as a mandate to convert the world and to bring it under the dominion of Christ and His law-word. It was a part of the Christian commission to bring all things into captivity to Christ. Now, in the hand of the Montanists, it became simply a prayer for the end of the world.

The results were ironic. Montanism had criticized the church for its lack of zeal, but now Montanism directed Christian zeal into a narrow channel and tended to reduce it to a hope for the end of the world. The result was a stifling of the momentum of the Christian calling to exercise dominion and to subdue the earth.

The Montanists distinguished between "spiritual" and "carnal" Christians, a distinction which has been revived in modern times. They did more. They saw four stages in the development of religion. They did so, not in terms of Scripture, but by analogy to development in the natural world. Thus, despite their zeal, they imported Greco-Roman naturalism into the faith. They held, *first*, to natural religion and the innate idea of God. *Second*, there was the Old Testament revelation of a "legal" religion, of law. *Third*, the Gospel of Christ came as the word of grace. *Fourth*, with Pentecost, there was the revelation of the Spirit, His gifts, and the rise of "spiritual" religion. This scheme bears real similarities to Joachim of Fiore and his three age thinking. Joachim, the medieval abbot, divided history into three ages: the age of law, the Old Testament; the age of grace, the New Testament; and the final age, the age of the Spirit and of love. We do not know of any influence of Montanism on Joachim; both had, however, a common assumption, a belief in an evolutionary development of religion and of God's way towards men. Where the analogy of nature is applied to God, God develops and changes like His own creation.

Montanism also tended to deny the validity of authorities in the church and to reduce authority to God-possessed utterances by its prophets. The Montanists claimed for their prophets an authority denied to the rulers of the church. Authority was now, to a considerable degree, self-proclaimed as various persons gave utterances to visions. The Montanists condemned the distinction between the clergy and the laity as authoritarian, but they created a new authoritarian aristocracy of visionaries who were above both the clergy and the laity.

The Montanist prophecies had four concerns. *First*, they proclaimed the immediate return of Christ. They had added many beliefs to the Biblical doctrine of the second coming as well. *Second*, they prophesied persecutions, which were very real, and only increased. *Third*, they required as law within the church a variety of ascetic practices and fastings to separate the "spiritual" from the "carnal" Christian. *Fourth*, their visions created new distinctions between the various sins.

Tertullian saw the law of God as abolished by Christ. He held it to be wrong that the church saw the Old Testament law and the Gospels as a unity. He said categorically, "the old law has ceased" ("An Answer to the Jews." chapt. VI). In his "On Prescription Against Heretics," Tertullian made his famous statement, "What indeed has Athens to do with Jerusalem? What concord is there between the Academy and the Church? What between heretics and Christians?" (Chapt. VII). The Montanist Jerusalem, however, was not the Jerusalem of the Bible; their new Jerusalem was to come down on the village of Pepuza in Phrygia. New revelations were creating a new "gospel." Tertullian, in his treatise on "Modesty," listed seven mortal sins, which, if committed after baptism, were unpardonable.

The result was a new legalism. Where men neglect God's law, they do not thereby evade the fact of law. Law is a necessity of life. Nothing can live without, apart from, or outside of law in God's universe. Men deny God's law only to create their own. Montanism became a fertile source of legalism, as it developed rules (from new revelations) to replace God's law.

Tertullian's treatise on "Fasting" is evidence of this. Fasting had become a new law for "spiritual" Christians, and Tertullian had to answer the "carnal" Christian's use of the Bible against Montanism. Tertullian admitted that these people drew their defense of limited or no fasting from Scripture. Tertullian held to very strict ascetic practices concerning fasting, and more. In the course of his argument, Tertullian showed that "appetite," not sin, was for him the evil, the "undermining" cause of spiritual decline. As against the charge of being in violation of Galatians 4:10, etc., of Galaticizing the church, Tertullian said that Paul spoke only of the end of the old ceremonies, not those of the New Testament. In brief, a new legalism had replaced Biblical faith.

The Montanists also courted martyrdom; it was a sign of spirituality to *want* to die for Christ.

Second marriages were condemned; the spiritual life meant even lifelong continence. While Montanism was opposed to Gnosticism, it had imbibed the Gnostic view of the material world. The same spirit undergirded its millennialism; Montanism wanted to see the end of a material order which it regarded as a hindrance to spirituality.

Much more can be said about the errors of Montanism. The Montanists were mainly orthodox in their doctrines of God, the incarnation, and most basic doctrines. Indeed, Tertullian is important in the history of Christian doctrine. Their basic error lay in their implicit denial of history. The Montanists had a doctrine of historical development, but its essential thesis was that the ages now had their culmination, and it was the end time. There was in their view no room nor time for further development. Hence, their demand on *perfection now*. Christian growth and sanctification were replaced by an insistence on the fullness of holiness now. This belief in the end time led to a down-grading of marriage. Tertullian, who had written earlier in praise of godly marriage, came to an ugly hostility to it. Virginity and continence were prescriptions for all, since the end was near.

Moreover, since the Montanists saw their era as the last days of history, they were disinterested in the various Christian efforts to change the world around them and to conquer it for Christ. Tertullian and others were ready to "prove" that the world had to end soon because it was "over-populated," its natural resources over-used, and so on. With their end-time mentality, it was easy for them to locate "evidences" to prove that the world had to end.

But the demand for "perfection now" does not create instant perfection among church members, only instant hypocrisy. Both in Montanist, and, later Donatist circles, hypocrisy proliferated because there was little patience with weak and sinning fellow believers. Only strength was tolerated. Where growth is denied in favor of instant perfection, weakness only increases under the hypocritical front of strength. In a moment of wisdom, H.G. Wells once said, "Brave men are men who do the things they are afraid to do." We can say that strong men in Christ are men who know their weakness and increasingly rely on the Lord, not themselves.

What Montanism gave to church history was a recurring demand for instant perfection together with a belief that the end time is now. Throughout the medieval era, the Reformation, and to the present, a great deal of Christian zeal and energy has been deflected into sterile channels by this mind-set. Instead of furthering Christ's Kingdom, too often the Montanist temper hinders it.

A pathetic example of this was cited in 1877 by Daniel Steele, in *A Substitute for Holiness, or Antinomianism Revived, or The Theology of the So Called Plymouth Brethren Examined and Refuted*. Steele reported that some of the followers of John Darby (the source for C.I. Scofield), had gone to Jerusalem to await the Second Coming: "A handful of Americans, fragments of families, possessed by this infantile interpretation of Scripture, are eking out an existence in Jerusalem. They have adopted and are called by the name of 'The American Colony.' They are determined to be at the head of the line of office-seekers when the new administration comes in."

Then and now, the Montanist perspective has commanded countless numbers of Christians. Some, like Tertullian, have been and are great and good men. All have been sure, from 171 A. D. to the present, that theirs is the end time of history, and they have had charts and computations to prove it. What they have instead demonstrated is their own irrelevance.

Christ our Lord "is the blessed and only Potentate, The King of kings and Lord of lords" (I Tim. 6:16). For a Christian to make his faith and his Lord irrelevant to his age and history is to sin surely. No one is more relevant to all things than Christ the Lord, and only the faithful and active Christian can be a relevant man. (July, 1984)

THE CHANGED MEANING OF LIBERTY
Chalcedon Position Paper No. 53

Words change their meanings, and people who assume that older meanings still prevail invite deception thereby. It is part of current Marxist ideology to give a new content and an alien meaning to such familiar words as peace, freedom, republic, law, and so on.

New meanings precede revolutions, because the content of human hopes is altered dramatically, and the existing order finds that it cannot satisfy the new meanings. Before the French Revolution, the idea of liberty had taken on a new meaning, a very different one than had previously prevailed. As Frank E. Manuel, in *The Prophets of Paris* (1962), pointed out, "The very term liberty lost its medieval connotation of a privilege and became the right to bring into being what had not existed before" (p. 24). Liberty as a privilege had reference to a religious fact of immunity from civil controls and regulations. Thus, the ancient privilege of the church is its freedom from the state because it is Christ's personal domain and body and hence subject to no controls but those of His law word. Similarly, the privileges of the family exempted it from various controls. Each area of life had its privileges. We still use the word *privilege* in this older sense when we speak of "privileged communication." A privileged communication, as for example between a priest or pastor and a parishioner making a confession or seeking counsel, or between a doctor and a patient, or a lawyer and a client, is free from the controls or knowledge of the state or of other men and agencies. This freedom and immunity is, moreover, a religious fact. Thus, the older definition of liberty as a privilege and as a religious immunity rested firmly and clearly on a Christian culture. As long as the education and culture of the Western World was clearly Christian, liberty or freedom remained a Christian privilege.

This older meaning survived in the United States as recently as 1868, when the Fourteenth Amendment to the Constitution declared, "No state shall make or enforce any law which shall abridge the privileges or immunities of citizens of the United States." Unhappily, the Federal Government did not bar itself from any such infringement of the people's "privileges or immunities." The annotated edition of the Constitution published by the federal government says of this, "Unique among constitutional provisions, the privileges and immunities clause of the Fourteenth Amendment enjoys the distinction of having been rendered a nullity by a single decision of the Supreme Court issued within five years after its ratification" in the Slaughter-House Cases. The Court at that time began also to redefine the term "privileges and immunities" by declaring them to be, not religiously grounded, but owing their existence to the grace of the Federal Government. The state had begun to usurp the place of God!

It was the Enlightenment thinkers and the French "philosophes" who began the redefinition of liberty and its separation from the religious foundation which liberty as privilege had enjoyed. The French Revolution greatly advanced the new meaning. Its slogan was "Liberty, Fraternity, and Equality," and it soon became apparent that all three had new, ugly, and murderous meaning. Not without reason, as Madame Roland in 1793 went to the guillotine, that new symbol of freedom, she cried out, "O Liberty, what crimes are committed in thy name." All French landlords had to paint on their walls, "Unite, indivisibilite de la Republica, Liberte, Egalite, Fraternite ou la Mort!" Death came quickly for many, and for lesser reasons than failing to paint this slogan.

The Declaration of Rights of the French Revolution set forth the new meaning of freedom: "Liberty consists in being allowed to do whatever does not injure other people." If this definition sounds familiar, it is because it has been the premise behind the sexual revolution, homosexual arguments, abortion, and a variety of so-called "victimless" crimes.

Liberty has come far from its earlier meaning of a religious privilege or immunity. The meaning of liberty has changed because the culture has changed, so that it is a part of a vast panorama of new meanings. Liberty, as someone told me last year with all the solemnity of a prophet revealing new truth, means that I can do as I please as long as I do not hurt another person. It was soon obvious that we had differing definitions also of the meaning of "hurt." We also differed on what constitutes a "person." For him, it did include a Soviet KGB officer (as it must for me, since he is like myself a creature made in God's image), but not a Nazi, perhaps not a South African white, not a white racist or anti-Semite, not an unborn child, and possibly not some terminally ill elderly people. Because he was a humanist and I am a Christian, our meanings differed at every point. Each of us had a different principle of definition because we had different religions.

Karl Marx in 1848, in the *Communist Manifesto*, gave a differing humanistic interpretation of liberty. For him, economic equality was the prior goal and virtue. His doctrine of "from each according to his ability, to each according to his needs," called for the satisfaction of all the economic needs before the hunger for liberty is satisfied. However, his plan meant also that a dictatorship defined every man's needs as well as the abilities and the productive responsibility of each man! In such a system, the needed food for a man as well as his needed freedom became a statist decision by elite planners.

When freedom lost its Christian definition, man became the new definer. Previously, God's law and sovereignty set boundaries on man's power. Man was not free from flagrant sins and breaches of liberty prior to the Enlightenment, but he knew that in all these things he was a sinner. Now, with humanism, he was a new god finding and expressing himself in his autonomous powers. The modern state, as the collective expression of these powers, was "liberated" to be humanity's new god walking on earth.

Artists began to give expression to this new world and life view. In France, Giullaume Appollinaire (1880-1918), an influential writer of the avant-garde, worked for total liberation from Christianity. Like the decadents and Andre Gide, he sought it in the gratuitous act, "l'acte gratuit," as the example of consistent human freedom. Since the free act, liberty, meant liberation from Christianity, only an inversion of morality could make men free. This meant the evil act, *unmotivated evil*, evil for its own sake. It meant "the liberating power of wickedness." (Roger Shattuck: *The Banquet Years*, p. 304, 1955). The purity of the acts of liberation rested in the gratuitousness of their evil.

Within a generation or so after Apollinaire, Lindner, an American, wrote on *Rebels Without a Cause*, a study of juvenile criminals and their purposeless crimes. The assault, murder, and mutilation of innocent persons totally unacquainted with the criminal became increasingly commonplace after 1960. The new doctrine of liberty was being enacted on the streets.

The French Revolution had declared any act legitimate if it did not hurt or injure another person. The French revolutionary leaders quickly saw their enemies as non-persons and proceeded to kill them. Where God's definition of man is despised, soon man himself is despised and readily killed or victimized. Apollinaire in a novel, had put a prophecy into the mouth of one man: "On my arrival on earth, I found humanity on its last legs, devoted to fetishes, bigoted, barely capable of distinguishing good from evil -- and I shall leave it intelligent, enlightened, regenerated, knowing there is neither good nor evil nor God nor devil nor spirit nor matter in distinct separateness" (Shattuck, p. 253).

When all values are denied except man, every man is free to define his own values and to act accordingly. The state, having greater power, has greater freedom to enforce its own values, and, as a result, the new freedom of humanism ends up in history's most malevolent tyranny and slavery. The new liberty is the old slavery writ large.

The modern world is far removed from the older world of liberty as a religious privilege which required responsibility and accountability to God. Sinning now passes as the new freedom, and the more perverted the sin the higher ostensibly the manifestation of liberty.

The saddest aspect of all this is the failure of so many churchmen and conservatives to see that, when politicians make promises using the old language of privilege and immunity, they have in mind the newer and revolutionary meanings. William Blake, himself a revolutionary, called attention to the fact that he and his opponents, reading the same thing, read differently: one read black where the other read white. Their presuppositions differed, and hence their reading.

The presupposition of the humanistic doctrine of liberty are anti-God and anti-man. For humanism, the great evil is deprivation. Man is seen as entitled to the fullest liberty to express himself, to gratify himself, and to reach true personhood in self-expression.

An old hymn, once popular, celebrates Christ as King of all creation, and of all things therein. The last two verses read:

"The government of earth and seas
Upon his shoulders shall be laid:
His wide dominions shall increase,
And honours to His name be paid.
Jesus, the holy child, shall sit,
High on His father David's throne;--
Shall crush his foes beneath His feet,
And reign to ages yet unknown."

When Christians ceased to work in terms of this assured victory, the humanists began to do so. In terms of their plan, it is Christ and his people who are to be crushed beneath the feet of history and humanistic man. Their current power witnesses to the church's default. Wars are not won when men refuse to fight, nor can armies move against an enemy they refuse to recognize exists! Now that the long sleep of the church is ending, the battle begins.

The decline of true Christian liberty began when the enlightenment ideas of natural religion infiltrated the church and replaced the Biblical doctrine with the new ideas of "natural liberty." Previously, theology had, like Thomas Boston in his study of man's *Fourfold State*, distinguished between man's moral abilities in the state of innocence, the state of depravity, the state of grace, and the eternal state. Our Lord, in John 8:33-36, makes clear that true freedom comes from Him alone; it is an act of sovereign, saving grace. It gives us powers and immunities, and it restores us to our calling to exercise dominion and to subdue the earth (Matt. 28:18-20). Our freedom is a privilege and an immunity.

God's act of creation and His providential government establish Him as Sovereign or Lord. His law sets boundaries on man's will and thus gives us privileges and immunities which men and civil governments are forbidden to violate.

At one time, men spoke of their freedom as "ancient privileges and immunities." What was urgently needed was the development of this premise. The concept of sphere laws was early set forth in the church's struggle for freedom from the state. The Puritans, with their affirmation of covenanted spheres of life, advanced this doctrine. Abraham Kuyper, who admired the Puritans, formulated this concept philosophically and theologically.

On this foundation, the Christian community must revive the doctrine of liberty as a religious privilege and immunity. The claims of the state to be the source of freedom are false and evil. The American patriotic song is clearer on the issue when it hymns God as the "Author of Liberty." Those words are no longer sung in most public schools. Both God and liberty are now denied by the humanists. For this bit of honesty, we can thank them, as we work to undo their legacy of slavery. (August, 1984)

DONATISM
Chalcedon Position Paper No. 54

Some heresies begin with very noble motives but end in evil; this was certainly true of Donatism. Church historians usually classify Donatism as a schismatic movement rather than a heresy, but there are weighty reasons for seeing it as a heresy despite an outward orthodoxy.

During the times of persecution, especially that of Diocletian (245-313 A.D.), there were varying responses from the church. Some men virtually welcomed martyrdom; others accepted it as a necessary consequence of the battle between Christ and Caesar. Still others took prudent or temporizing steps, and others compromised or abjured the faith. When the persecutions ended, there were bitter feelings between those survivors who had not compromised and had endured persecution and those who had compromised.

The Donatists, named after their leader, called Donatus the Great, wanted no part of the compromisers. They demanded a pure church. They appealed to Constantine, who ruled against them, and they subsequently became bitter enemies of the state. Constantine insisted on liberty of faith and worship, and the Donatists were not touched by him. In a church council of 330 A.D., the Donatists had 270 bishops present. In 411 A.D., at another council, the Donatists bishops present numbered 279, the Catholic bishops, 286.

Donatism was no small movement.

The Donatists were separatists who demanded a pure church. The church had to be the community of regenerate saints. In the process of seeking this holy church, the Donatists forgot what the Catholic party knew, that saints can sin, and sinners can repent. Time proved that there was no lack of sin among the Donatists, but there was less ability to face it and cope with it. The issue was at root the doctrine of the church: was it a school for holiness, or the congregation of the holy? The Donatists were often stern in church action against sinners, less effective as a missionary church.

More important, Donatism strongly opposed the restoration of pastors who had proven to be cowardly under persecution, who had either surrendered church records, or, worse, denied the faith. Such unholy priests were held to be incapable of restoration, and their actions as pastors, and the sacraments administered, *invalid*. The donatists held that holiness cannot be communicated by the unholy, nor faith received from a faithless man. Such a pastor gave guilt, not faith. As a result, the Donatists held Catholic baptism to be *invalid*.

The results of this position were deadly. If a pastor's acts are only valid if he is personally holy, then no man can be sure if his baptism and communion are valid until the priest dies without falling out of the true faith! This raised other questions also: if a pastor strayed from the faith, and the baptisms he performed were invalid, were the marriages invalid also? The whole Christian life was plunged into uncertainty, and assurance was denied. The Donatist Petilian said, "He who receives the faith from a faithless priest, receives not faith but guilt."

St. Augustine, the great adversary of the Donatists, said, "But Christ is not unfaithful, from whom I receive faith, not guilt...My origin is Christ, my root is Christ, my head is Christ. The seed, of which I was born, is the word of God, which I must obey even though the preacher himself practices not what he preaches. I believe not in the minister by whom I am baptized, but in Christ, who alone justifies the sinner and can forgive guilt." With respect to baptism, Augustine said also, "To my mind it is abundantly clear that in the matter of baptism we have to consider not who he is that gives it, but what it is that he gives; not who it is that receives, but what it is that receives."

The Donatists, in their zeal for purity, had come to give too great a role to the pastor and the church. The validity of the faith was made to depend on the validity of the church. Paul, in Romans 10:17, says "faith cometh by hearing, and hearing by the word of God."

The issue was sovereign grace. It is not the church nor the pastor that saves us, but the Lord. In their zeal and passion for the purity of the church, the Donatists had exalted the church to a position far in excess of its appointed place. Salvation was in effect made to depend upon the holiness of men rather than the holiness of God. We are not saved because our pastor is holy and gracious but because God is.

It is not surprising that, ever since then, separatist churches, often rebelling against very great evils and unfaithfulness in their mother church, readily fall into a phariseeism. They stress the rightness of their church rather than the grace and mercy of God. It is because of this over-emphasis on the holiness of the church that they fall into heresy and slight the sovereign grace of God. Only the church which stresses sovereign grace can avoid this peril.

It is easy to understand the Donatist hostility to church members and leaders who had proved weak under persecution. It is understandable that questions were raised about their restoration to membership or office. Such questions had to be raised. However, it was no solution to bar them permanently from their place in the church. This step placed the validity of church ordinances and of the church itself upon men rather than in Christ. It is not surprising that in time Donatism was under suspicion of Pelagianism. Its doctrines placed an undue reliance on man rather than the Lord.

After some generations, Donatism disappeared as an organized movement and church, but as a faith, temper, and disposition, it lingered, and it had been a problem for all segments of the church. It has been most a problem where men became most zealous for the purity of the church. The path of Donatism leads from a passion for the faith to an undue trust in men and in institutions. In its results, it becomes a form of humanism.

Donatism as a temper in history has been applied far beyond the boundaries of the church. I am regularly asked by modern Donatists who have never heard of Donatism if they are not freed from any duty to obey the state since the state allows abortion, homosexuality, and more. Their zeal for reform in these areas is wonderful; such people are often the activists whose work is of central importance to more than a few causes. (Some, however, react by a pharisaic separation from all reform action.)

Many medieval scholars held that a state could be placed outside the pale and its ruler a legitimate target for "execution." They failed to see that murder cannot restore a civil government to a godly function: much more is needed!

Indeed, we must say that the revolutions of our era are a product of a modern version of Donatism. A great deal of current historiography is modern Donatism: it seeks to justify the destruction of one order after another on the grounds that only a strict and destructive separatism can unleash justice. The church Donatists held that separation would ensure grace; the political Donatists hold that it will ensure justice.

The word *revolution* gained its modern meaning from Copernicus and his work on *De Revolutionibus Orbium Coelestium*. Just as Copernicus radically altered man's view of the universe, political revolutionists believe that justice requires the destruction of old orders in favor of their idea of justice. The ruling class must be overthrown and replaced; existing social institutions must be scrapped and only approved ones allowed to exist. The goal is to create "a truly human order" in which man remakes man in terms of a revolutionary goal.

Otto J. Scott, in *The Secret Six* as well as in *Robespierre, The Voice of Virtue*, gives us accounts of the destructive nature of revolutionary men, men who were by nature Donatists.

Job answered Zophar at one point with bitter irony, saying, "No doubt but ye are the people, and wisdom shall die with you" (Job 12:2). This is a telling summation of a temperament common to many people, and certainly to the Donatists. They believe that wisdom was born with them and will die with them. Rather than manifesting grace, they manifest judgment. As St. Augustine pointed out, in *On Baptism, Against the Donatists* (c. 400 A.D.), the Donatists began to separate from one another and to quarrel in their own ranks. Men whose forte is condemnation cannot be the blessed peacemakers! Augustine said, "We exhort them to come to the soundness of peace and Christian charity." Here was a critical weakness of Donatism, the lack of charity. What began as an honest zeal for purity became before long a censorious and uncharitable spirit.

Purity is indeed a legitimate goal of the Christian Church. Holiness too is basic to God's nature, and to the image of God in man (Ephesians 4:24). Priority, however, belongs to grace, to sovereign grace. Every reform movement which does not give priority to grace fails to gain either purity or holiness.

The Donatists held to a theory of purism, and, in the name of purity, fought with the Catholics and then with one another. Had they begun with grace, they would have made a great and lasting contribution to the church. In the name of purity, they became persecutors! In the process, Augustine charged, they distorted Scripture, the word of grace, to become a Donatist word. They had, charged Augustine, become not only schismatics but heretics.

This was not all. Because the Donatists stressed purity and holiness more than grace and forgiveness, they were ready to believe in compulsion. Our political Donatists who want the perfect society now seek by revolution and then by means of revolutionary regimes to compel men to believe, to be "good," and to be loyal.

By their demand for what Augustine felt was an absolute purity of all priests the Donatists guaranteed two things, first, phariseeism, and, second, censoriousness.

We have today many Donatist movements in the church and in politics. That reform is commonly necessary in both realms goes without saying. We must rejoice that many are dedicated to reform if their dedication is marked by grace, charity, and patience. If these are lacking, such people are a major hindrance to their own cause.

Because of this warped emphasis, the Donatist temper believes with Job's sorry friends that wisdom was born with them and will die with them. The Donatist is harsh, arrogant, censorious, and impatient. He rejoices in the sins and short-comings of his opponents and responds to them with condemnation, not with grace.

The key issue is grace, sovereign grace. Apart from that, nothing can change. The Kingdom of God comes, not by our nagging, condemnation, nor efforts, but by the sovereign grace of God. That grace God communicates to us through His word, not ours (Rom. 10:17). Isaiah 52:7 tells us, "How beautiful upon the mountains are the feet of him that bringest good tidings, that publisheth peace; that bringeth good tidings of good, that publisheth salvation, that saith unto Zion, Thy God reigneth!"

If our God reigns, we are not sour Donatists; we are sovereign grace men bringing good tidings of peace and grace, of salvation and victory through our Lord and Savior, Christ the King. (September, 1984)

NATURAL LAW AND CANON LAW
Chalcedon Position Paper No. 55

Words change their meanings with time, and it is a mistake to assume that an older or "original" meaning still governs the word. Thus, the word "silly" once meant good or blessed; "farm" meant a tax, and a "farmer" was a tax collector; "vote" could mean either a plea or prayer, or a determination, or an expression of will, which is closer to its present meaning. These and other words have changed in meaning, and it is important, in using writings of the past, to understand each change of meaning in the term.

One such very changed term is "natural law." It comes from the ancient Greeks, who meant something very different by it than many recognize. First of all, for the Greek thinkers nature was not fallen; second, the material world was divided into two substances, matter and ideas. The ideas or patterns were universals which good reasoning could discover, so that the philosophers, in their reasoning, assumed that their rational conclusions, where correct, represented natural law. Aristotle and Plato thus assumed that their political reasoning grasped the universals of life and thus represented true order and natural law. The distinction was between "man-made law" (what unreasoning men legislated) and "natural law" (what the philosophers saw as the logos or reason of being). Natural law thus claimed to set forth the true order in nature. We can say that Marx, in describing the inevitable historical process and its conclusion, echoed natural law in this sense.

The medieval era had a different concept at first, although never entirely free from the Greek inheritance. Gratian (c. 1148) wrote, "mankind is ruled in two ways: namely, by natural law and by customs. The law of nature is that contained in the law and the Gospels" (Decretum pt. I, distinction 1). In subsequent passages, the Greek influence is apparent, but for most men of his day, Biblical law was seen as natural law, the law of the Creator by which all things are governed.

In Aquinas, the Greek revival was strong. Natural law was seen as something pertaining to right reason. God and man share a common being, and "all beings other than God are not their own being, but are beings by participation" (*Summa Theologica*, I, Q 44, A 1); this represented a shift from creation to participation, a Greek concept. It meant that "the intellectual principle which we call the human soul is incorruptible" (Q 75, A 6). The rational creature therefore "shares in the eternal reason...and such participation of the rational creature in the eternal law is called natural law" (Q 91, A 2). Nicholas of Cusa (c. 1400-1464) also held to this: "since natural law is naturally in the reason, every law is known to man in its root."

Such thinking by-passed the doctrine of creation, and it made void the doctrine of the fall. Evil became metaphysical instead of moral and was equated with non-being. All being was good, because all being by participation was continuous with God's Being. The revival of Aristotle made the Enlightenment inevitable, because the Enlightenment simply took over these concepts of right reason and natural law and carried them to their logical conclusion. Christianity and the church were very quickly seen to be excess baggage.

If right reason is expressive of natural law, then the rational state, i.e., that order established by philosopher kings, is the true state and expressive of natural law. The theory of the divine right of kings held to the royal manifestation of natural power and law.

The two great enemies of the divine right of kings were the Jesuits and the Calvinists. The Jesuits upheld the power of the papacy to govern all things spiritual and to declare God's will for rulers; the Calvinists insisted on the sovereignty of God over church and state.

The divine right of kings was a curious doctrine. It held to the claim that the king's power came directly from God to the king. Some exponents of this theory attached the divine right to the *office* rather than the person, but this limitation was rejected by men like James I of England. The right was natural and hereditary as well as divine. Like the private succession of land under feudal law, divine right was a natural hereditary possession belonging to a royal line and its rightful heirs. Hence, care was given to establish the legitimate order of succession. The power of divine right "included nothing less than the complete disposal of his subjects' persons and property." (Charles Howard McIlwain, editor: *The Political Works of James I*, p. xxxiii f. Cambridge, Mass.: Harvard University Press, 1918.) Kings were thus little gods, according to James I.

No supernatural law could take priority over, or be cited against, this natural succession. As a result, there was an increasing de-emphasis of Biblical law and super-naturalism in favor of natural law and right reason. One consequence, very early, was Deism. Another, later on, was Romanticism. Nature became the new source of law, learning, and revelation. William Wordsworth, in "The Tables Turned," said,

"One impulse from a vernal wood
May teach you more of man,
Of moral evil and of good,
Than all the sages can."

Plato and Aristotle held that persons or things were only rightly employed when used according to their nature. The Stoic morality summed up the matter in the precept, "Follow Nature."

Jeremy Bentham, in *Principles of Morals and Legislation* (1789), saw all standards of right and wrong determined by *pleasure and pain*. Darwin added to this triumph of natural law the thesis of a struggle for survival, and Herbert Spencer identified the right with what is conducive to survival.

The moral content, a Biblical content, of natural law in Gratian had been reduced to zero. ("If it feels good, do it!") By making nature normative, natural law advocates had made sin normative, and the pro-abortion, homosexual "rights" movements and like causes are the logical outcomes of this fact.

At a recent meeting of Christian leaders, a natural law advocate was challenged to define or name an agreed upon content of natural law. The theologian making the challenge called attention to the fact that the concept is contentless (unless borrowings are made from Scripture). Two political leaders asked, "What does natural law have to say about adultery and fornication?" The answer: "That question is irrelevant."

Natural law thinking, where pursued consistently, ends up in antinomianism and Arminianism. Gratian's meaning (which he did not consistently maintain) is best maintained by seeing God's law as over nature, not inherent in it. When Paul speaks of the inescapable knowledge of God in Romans 1:20, he does not say that this knowledge is seen in creation but "*from* the creation of the world." This is a clearly different meaning.

The fact that many natural law advocates, Catholic and Protestant, have been fine men does not alter the fact that the concept has been a confused one. It has readily lent itself to misuse because it begins with a false premise. The venerable antiquity of a concept does not give it truth. After all, the premise of sin, Genesis 3:5, every man as his own god and law-maker, goes back to the Garden of Eden! Whatever usefulness the doctrine may have had has long since been lost Even more, why cling to so nebulous a concept of natural law when we have the clear and written law of God, the Bible? It seems that the abiding value of natural law is to give men a chance to puff themselves up as the discoverers of law.

At this point, it is necessary to contrast natural law and canon law. Ask almost anyone what canon law is and most will tell you it is ecclesiastical or church law, a mistake made even by *The Catholic Encyclopedia* of 1910 because they defined it, not historically, but in terms of today. The word "canon" means a rule, a straight line or measure. Paul uses the word in II Corinthians 10:13 (canonos) and 16 (canoni), as well as Galatians 6:16 (canoni). The early church used the term extensively. Irenaeus called the baptismal creed "the canon of truth;" others spoke of "the canon of faith." As the early councils faced problems, they set forth canons or truths and laws in terms of Scripture. True canon law is Biblical law. Canon law most certainly applied and applies to the church, but we miss a critical fact of history if we fail to see that Christians have always held that canon law applies also to nations. Two current examples of this application to nations are Gods laws, or the rule or canons concerning, abortion and homosexuality. During most of the church's history, the church has seen God's rule or canon as applicable to all men, institutions, and states. In fact, the justice pagans recognized in old Rome in the canon law led them to go to church courts with their cases. So much of the litigation by 300 A.D. was in the hands of the church courts that Constantine, on gaining power, gave all bishops the status of Roman magistrates in order to give official status to the governing courts! To this day, bishops wear the garb and carry the insignia of Roman magistrates. For some centuries after the fall of Rome, canon or Biblical law was the only law of Europe. (Biblical law was the essential law of American colonies and the early republic.)

Recently, several nominal Catholics denied the relevance of God's law to the state, insisting on consensus and private choice. These persons, Gov. Mario Cuomo, Sen. Edward Kennedy, and Rep. Geraldine Ferraro (all bucking for the status of Heretic, First Class), were reminded by columnist John Lofton (Calvinist, First Class), "Canon 21 of the Council of Trent's sixth session decree...says this: 'If anyone says that Jesus Christ was given by God to men as a redeemer in whom to trust, and not also as a legislator whom to obey, let him be anathema'" (*Washington Times*, Friday, September 21, 1984, p. 3A).

Canon or Biblical law was restricted to the church by the rise of natural law. The natural law advocates, in turning to the old Greco-Roman concept, did not realize what they were doing. Ostensibly they found classical support for Biblical faith; in reality, they undermined it.

The natural sphere could now claim to be a source of law. The church was seen as the voice of the supernatural kingdom and realm, and the state as the voice and head of the natural sphere and realm. This freed the monarchs from the constraints of canon law; each could now claim to be his own law sphere. The church was to limit itself to the "spiritual" sphere, and the state was to rule the "natural" sphere. This meant that the church was to keep out of that law sphere which belonged to the state, and its canons might be valid for the believer's private life, but not in civil life. (Of late, Governor Cuomo of New York, and vice-presidential candidate Geraldine Ferraro have echoed this argument.)

The results have been deadly. The state, with its independent law sphere, now recognizes no canon or rule other than its will. Both in Protestant and Catholic countries, there is a wide gap between the canon professed "within the church" and the canon professed by the same persons "within the state." Where there is no universal canon, there is hypocrisy and social decay.

A significant legal term is "the rule of law," i.e., the canon of law. The primary meaning of the rule of law is its supremacy over all things, its application to all classes and groups, and the exclusion of all exemptions from its province. In other words, the rule of law means the catholicity or universality of law. The significant part of the rule of law concept is that it has reference to the state's law, not God's. The law of the state has become the new canon law because the state claims sovereignty or lordship. It is the natural order in its full power, and it recognizes no other canon or rule, least of all now from and by God.

A good many years ago, when I was somewhat younger, I listened in silence to an informal discussion on natural law by Christian and non-Christian advocates of it. They had dismissed their differences, in response to a woman's statement that natural law did not seem to affirm any clear-cut content, by saying that this was true of the Bible too, because interpretations differed. Where, asked the woman, are your Ten Commandments? We may differ in their numbering, but the words are the same for all Christians. They had no real answer. Esau sold his birthright for a mess of pottage; at that, he got more than those who abandoned God's canon for that of fallen nature. (October, 1984)

THE WAY
Chalcedon Position Paper No. 56

If we begin our thinking with a false premise, we will work our way to a false conclusion, or, at best, a faulty one. A persistent problem which has plagued the church has been the influence of Greek philosophy. So many of the Greco-Roman converts were men of learning and ability, that their entrance into the church meant also the entrance of alien presuppositions. An important example of this was Origen (185/6-253); Origen was apparently a most appealing figure as well as a scholar of note, but he brought into the church some strange opinions. With respect to Scripture, Origen held to the belief that Scripture's plain sense could not be accepted. No man of intelligence, he said, could believe, with respect to Genesis 1, that the first, second and third days of creation were literal and normal days without the sun, moon, or stars. Also, he held it was "silly" to believe, in terms of Genesis 2, that God, like a farmer, "planted a paradise eastward in Eden." The Bible gave us, Origen believed, "figurative expressions which indicate certain mysteries through a semblance of history and not through actual events" (*On First Principles*, Chapter III).

For such men, the "truth" of the Bible was not in its material content but in the ideas or principles set forth in the "history" and behind the "history." For Greek philosophy, there were two kinds of being, matter and ideas; the wise men worked through the material husk to grasp the ideas or principles, the universals.

In the Eastern Church, this approach was very strong. St. Gregory of Nyssa (c. 331-c. 396), the younger brother of Basil the Great, wrote *The Life of Moses* in terms of this. The law of God through Moses was ignored as too materialistic. Now Gregory's premise was, "the law does not instruct us how to eat," because "Nature...is a sufficient lawgiver with regard to these things." As a result, even the Passover was seen in terms of a hidden meaning. Gregory was a leader in the kind of interpretation still popular in some evangelical circles; the law was ignored, but hidden meanings were seen in the tabernacle colors and the colors of the priest's vestments. Gregory always sought "the hidden meaning" of the Bible's history, the spiritual truth behind the material dross. Like a good Greek, his trust was in "guiding reason." Even the Egyptian army in pursuit of Israel was reduced to "the various passions of the soul by which man is enslaved."

Gregory's *Life of Moses* tells us little about Moses or God's word. It tells us much about a Greek view of the spiritual life. The Bible became an arcane book which philosophers alone could interpret. It was a book which revealed hidden meanings which only the elite minds could penetrate.

Western, Latin Christianity was less infected by such thinking and grew rapidly and vigorously. However, the revival of Greek thought affected the West in time. From 1100 to 1517, according to scholars, we see the emergence of lay spirituality in the west. Ideas previously limited to some monastic groups now became popular, and doctrine gave way to "spiritual religion." The new piety, according to Caroline Walker Bynum, in *Jesus as*

Mother, Studies in the Spirituality of the High Middle Ages (University of California Press, 1982), now located the fundamental religious drama and battle not on the cross, but within man's self. Religious faith became experiential and revivalistic. Christ's propitiation was replaced by the individual's experiential approach to God. By the 13th century, some women were preaching, hearing confessions from nuns under them, and bestowing blessings, and some nuns claimed priestly powers. Experience gave authority, it was held, i.e., religious experiences. Gertrude of Helfta spoke to fellow nuns, in the late 13th century, of God as "She," saying that God is a mother. The spirituality of the day became feminized, and, Bynum says, it was held that "in the eucharist, God gives to the soul power over himself." In Gertrude's writings, Bynum noted, there is "no reference to a cosmic war between good and evil, little attention to the devil, and little sense of an ontological rift in the universe created by the fall and knit up in some way by the resurrection."

The medieval church was destroyed in part by spiritual religion, by a shift from Christ and His finished work to man and his spiritual experiences. The Bible had become a book for scholars and pietists, in which levels of hidden meaning were found.

The Reformation stressed the Bible in its historical and doctrinal meaning, and the results were explosive. However, all too soon, the Greek influence was revived. In England, the Puritan power was quickly undermined by the Cambridge Platonists and their spiritual religion. The Anglican, William Gurnall, in *The Christian in Complete Armour*, saw life as a perpetual inner struggle and inner quest for experience. Gurnall lived and died in a critical period of history without ever making a stand for anything. He was irrelevant to his times, and thus to the faith.

What passes for Protestantism today very often has closer ties to Gregory of Nyssa than to the reformers.

Of late, many fine persons speak eloquently of restoring "the principled approach" to education, the Bible, and politics. They are echoing Origen and Gregory of Nyssa. *Principles are abstractions*. They are ideas we see as "basic" to something and which we formulate, as though the goal of thinking is an abstraction. However well intentioned, this method is anti-Christian. The focus of Scripture is on Jesus Christ: He is not an abstraction nor a principle but God incarnate. Our focus cannot be principles or ideas, abstractions, but incarnation. Our calling is to incarnate God's law-word in all our being, our education, politics, family life, economics, arts and sciences, and all things else. "The principled approach" is a retreat, not an advance; it overlooks the incarnation instead of building on it. It returns to a Greek universalism instead of seeing the unity of the universal and the particular in Jesus Christ and the triune God.

History requires the incarnation, because history is God's handiwork. History moved to Christ's incarnation, now moves to our incarnating His law-word in our lives, and in all the world, and to His coming again.

Because God's history requires the incarnation and its mandate for us, when Christians turn aside from their task, others assume it. And for Christians, with the wealth of God's law-word and the power of the Holy Spirit to go after the (purely spiritual) Greek fleshpots is insanity. The result has been antinomianism and irrelevance on the part of the Greeks in our pulpits.

Others have assumed the task of incarnational work. In 1935, David Friedrich Strauss published in Germany his work, *The Life of Jesus*. Its effect was revolutionary in more ways than one. Strauss divided the Jesus of history from the Christ of faith. The Jesus of history was a Palestinian peasant of whom we know little or nothing, except that He made such an impression on His time and place that all kinds of sayings, miracles and events were attached to Him, and He was called divine, although the real Jesus was none of these things. Thus far, Strauss had no new statement of great importance. What was important was that Strauss gave expression to a Hegelian philosophy which he related to the idea of Christ. As Marilyn Chapin Massey, in *Christ Unmasked, The Meaning of The Life of Jesus in German Politics* (1983), points out, European intellectuals for over a century had been affirming that Humanity should replace Christ as the true divinity. Strauss saw the Jesus of history as a primitive forerunner of this idea of the true Christ, the human species, so that "Humanity is the union of the two natures -- God become man." This "God" was Hegel's Spirit in nature, working blindly to find expression in an evolving culture.

For Strauss, the Biblical history was not true, nor was it important. It is the ideas or principles behind that history which are true. Taken literally, Bible history is offensive because it is supernatural. If things happen in the Biblical manner, which Strauss did not believe, they could not be divine, because the truly divine is the truly natural, working in the evolving natural process.

For Strauss, in differing editions of his book, there were two possible incarnations of this evolving god. First, he could become identical with Humanity, with people as a whole, so that true democracy would express the voice of God. Second, this natural god could incarnate himself in an elite group of Philosopher-Kings who rule over lesser men. Both these forms of incarnationism are very much with us today.

Unhappily, some churchmen have nothing to offer a world in the grips of a savage war of evil against God but homilies on the colors of the tabernacle furnishings! Origen is alive and well in all too many pulpits. Origen is well known as a man who castrated himself to avoid lust; it did not work!

Antinomians have cut themselves off from the power of God and think they have gained thereby.

Origen said, "who will dare to say that the Word of God is of no use and contributes in no way to salvation, but does no more than tell of events that happened in the past and have no relation to us?" Here was the key: everything had to have a "relation to us," i.e., to our spiritual experience! Now, the many chapters on the construction of the tabernacle (Ex. 24-40) deal with the past, but not our present situation or experience. For the sons of Origen, these chapters on the tabernacle must be spiritualized, and books have been written and many sermons preached on their esoteric meaning. But what does the Bible tell us in Exodus 25-40? It tells us that the living God, the God with whom we have to do, is so precise in His requirements that He permits no creative or innovative designing in His House. This should scare these addlepated "spiritual" leaders. The God who is so exacting and precise about His House will never permit innovative ethics, symbolic theology, or creative churchmanship. This is no God to trifle with by using our imagination to come up with new meanings.

David saw that he could not fight God's battle in Saul's armor, nor can we.

Gregory of Nyssa, in his account of Joshua and the spies, cites the bunch of grapes brought back by the spies and suspended on wood as typical of Christ on the cross, and His blood as the "saving drink for those who believe." Gregory excelled in this kind of imaginative symbolism, and he brought no small intellectual power to the task. But, while Gregory wrote, Rome was dying. Unlike Salvian, he was little aware of that fact. He wrote *The Life of Moses* in the early 390s, when Rome had not long to live. Not surprisingly, he wrote for monks who had withdrawn from the world. He believed in Aristotle's doctrine of virtue as the mean, not Scripture's view of virtue as faithful obedience to the law-word of God. His greatest debt was to Plato, with whom he sought truth in abstractions.

But Jesus Christ declares, "I am the way, the truth, and the life: no man cometh unto the Father but by me" (John 14:6). Jesus Christ is a person, not an abstraction, a principle, or an idea, and He declares that truth is a person, Himself. We cannot seek after abstractions and be faithful to Christ. He alone is the Way, the Truth, and the Life. (November, 1984)

MARCIONISM
Chalcedon Position Paper No. 57

Marcion of Sinope was a heretic whose era was near the middle of* ^T^U(second century A.D. Few men have left a more deadly and lasting influence on the church. Marcion had a background of involvement in Stoicism and Gnosticism. His decisive teacher was Cerdon, a gnostic.

In a general way, Marcion's thinking was this: the Old Testament was the product of a God who was largely evil. This creator God is the source of law, justice, and hate. The Messiah this God promised the Jews did not come, but another and good God sent His Son, Jesus Christ, into the world. The purpose of this Son was to free men from the world of matter and from the law, in fact, to free them from creation. Since the material world is evil, compromise with it was evil to Marcion. Marriage is one such form of compromise, and Marcion refused to baptize married people because he held it to be a sin to propagate a race which is in subjection to the bad Creator God. Naturally, the Marcionites denied the resurrection of the body.

Given his hatred of the law, Marcion saw the enemies of the Creator God and His law as the true saints of the Old Testament. According to Marcion, Jesus descended into hell to rescue God's prisoners, men like Cain, Esau, Korah, Dathan, and Abiram.

Besides rejecting the Old Testament, Marcion rejected much of the New as well, because it revealed the old God and His law. He allowed only one Gospel, Luke, in an edited version which, among other things, excluded the first four chapters. He only allowed some of Paul's epistles after he had edited and expurgated them to allow only those texts which fitted in with his new dispensation.

For Marcion, the attack on Jesus by the Jews was motivated by the evil God of law. As a result, he cut all references by Jesus to the Creator as His Father. The two dispensations had to be separated totally.

Marcion's father, a bishop, excommunicated his son and refused ever to see him again.

Fundamental to Marcion's position was the separation of law from the gospel and from grace. At this point, Marcion was more logical than many of his followers. He saw clearly that if law and grace come from the same God there can be no contradiction between them. All that a perfect God expresses must be in perfect harmony: God's law, justice, mercy, grace, love, forgiveness, and wrath cannot be divided in the perfect God. Hence, law had to be the product of an evil God because Marcion's presuppositions saw law and matter as evil. Marcion found the world repulsive. Could a good God make reptiles and insects? Marcion found especially repulsive the "uncleanness" of sex and childbirth, and a good God would seek to deliver a man from such a creation. Marcion applied Luke 6:43 to God, the God of the Old Testament: "For a good tree bringeth not forth corrupt fruit; neither doth a corrupt tree bring forth good fruit." The Creator God of the Old Testament had brought forth matter, law, and sex. This made Him for Marcion a corrupt tree, an evil God, and salvation had to be salvation from this evil God's world and law. Marcion felt only hostility towards the "just" and "judicial" God.

Marcion was extremely anti-Jewish; he used Paul as a means of attacking Old Testament faith. In the process of his misinterpretation of Paul, he left ideas in the church which have since colored and falsified men's perspectives on Paul. In his *Antitheses*, Marcion collected verses from the Bible to show how "ugly" the Jewish God was. He also used Christ's words in Matthew 5:17 and had them say exactly the opposite of what our Lord declares. For Marcion, Jesus said, "I am come not to fulfill the law and the prophets, but to destroy them." Marcion's perversion has since become "dispensational truth." In creating a division in the Bible, Marcion was the father of both modernist critics and of dispensationalism.

Marcion was not only against marriage, but also against eating meats (except for fish), and against wine. Thus, in his communion service, only bread was used. Baptism for the dead was sometimes practiced, and women could perform baptism. The Marcionites were quite numerous for some centuries, and were later absorbed into the Paulician movement, and the Cathars in the West.

For Marcion, his Jesus was a spiritual person, not truly man. The Jewish Messiah he regarded as political because of the Messianic concern over the Kingdom of God. For him, the true Messiah could not be materialistic and political in his concerns. There was for Marcion no real incarnation, because this would for him have ended Jesus' divinity. Man needed deliverance from his body, not a God incarnating Himself in flesh.

Quite logically, Marcion viewed the law with horror. How could a good God concern Himself with dietary laws, laws governing sex, property, and so on? How could good men read such a law without embarrassment?

Until Marcion, Christians saw the Bible as one book. Apostolic preaching and writing makes clear that what we call the Old Testament was used as totally relevant and as coming into its own in Christ. In defending the apostolic writings against Marcion, the church tended to segregate them. Because Marcion had created a false New Testament, the church, in defending the true apostolic canon, segregated it. For us to read the Bible as two books rather than as one unified word of God is to fall under Marcion's influence.

Under Appelles, a Marcionite leader, the extremes of Marcion's thinking were altered. There was for Appelles one God, but this one God had a different dispensation for the Jews than for the Gentiles. The Old Testament was thus a lower, cruder word for the Jews; there was now a better word for the Gentiles. This development broadened the influence of Marcion, and it continues to this day. It is interesting to note, and Jaroslav Pelikan, in *The*

Christian Tradition, vol. I, The Emergence of the Catholic Tradition (100-600), 1971, calls attention to the fact, Karl Barth saw "remarkable parallels" between himself and Marcion.

The Hellenic roots of so many leaders in the early church made them susceptible to a modified Marcionism. Greek philosophy downgraded the world of matter in favor of the world of ideas. As a result, churchmen who strongly condemned Marcion were still ready to agree with a modified Marcionism. Origen, in *First Principles*, ridiculed the idea of taking Genesis 1, and much else, too literally; God obviously meant something more spiritual than the Hebrew text indicated. Gregory of Nyssa allegorized the law, because he could not believe that God's law could actually be serious in telling us how to eat (Gregory of Nyssa: *The Life of Moses*, II, 105).

The result of all this was that, while Marcion was condemned, his thinking, in modified form, gained ground steadily in the church. There was, this modified, dispensational Marcionism held, one God, but He had differing dispensations, one for those primitive Hebrews, and a higher one for the Christians!

A clear result of Marcion's influence has been to limit the effectiveness of Christians and of the church. It would never have occurred to the Old Testament Prophets that they should be non-political! They confronted and indicted rulers and kings, as our Lord did in His day. The word of the Lord, they held, speaks to all men and to every condition, and not the least of these is the political sphere. The Bible is an intensely relevant book for church, state, school, family, and every other sphere of life. (Marcion held that the family was outside of God, unless husband and wife pledged themselves to refrain from sex permanently!) The basic premise of the prophets and apostles is that the world must be under God's law, and under Christ as King.

Marcionism is very much with us. The church in Christ cannot isolate itself from the problems of life but must apply God's law-word to every area of life and thought. Precisely because Christians are under grace they are under God's law as their way of life, and grace, their way of sanctification.

The consequences of Marcionism have been deadly. *First* of all, a major consequence of Marcionism has been the separation of faith from the world. Marcionism is always self-defeating because it denies the reliance of its religion to the very real problems of life. The appeal of Marcionism is its easy answers. Marcionite churches grew easily and readily. By denying the validity of Biblical law, they made their faith easy. By separating themselves from politics and the family, they separated themselves from two very prolific sources of human problems. Family life, for example, is a succession of responsibilities and problems, but the blessedness of life in Christ comes from meeting problems in terms of God's law-word and spirit and gaining a victory thereby.

Marcionism places itself on the shelf, or in limbo, by its false view of separation. Biblical faith is a prophetic faith, not a retreatist one. Paul, in speaking of the need for a disciplinary separation (upon excommunication), adds that this separation cannot be from all men who are sinners, "for them must ye needs go out of the world" (I Cor. 5:10). Marcionism, however, sought precisely that, to take people out of the world.

There was thus a radical separationism in Marcionism. Believers were to separate themselves from the God of the law and justice, from marriage, from meats, from politics, and from all materialistic concerns. Their dispensationalism left them with a very fragmentary Bible, so that their source of guidance was not God's law-word but vaguely spiritual concerns. They were too spiritual for Moses to instruct them, or for the prophets to speak to them. The result was that this dispensational separation led to a very great spiritual pride. To deny God's law means that a man now lives by his own law, the church's law, or some other form of humanistic law. The fact that this antinomian way was called "spiritual" only added to its sin and evil.

Second, as is already apparent, Marcionism changed salvation into a form of escapism. As I have pointed out in *Salvation and Godly Rule* (Ross House Books, $16.50 postpaid), salvation means deliverance into victory, health, and dominion. Jesus Christ gives us salvation by His mighty victory over sin and death. His atonement restores us into God's covenant as His faithful law-keepers, dominion men who are now empowered to be "more than conquerors through Him that loved us" (Rom. 8:37).

Marcionism separated men from God because it separated them from God's covenant law. In faithfulness to that covenant and its law, Jesus Christ came as very man of very man to pay the death penalty for our transgression of the law, and, by His atoning death and regenerating power, to restore us to faithfulness, to obedience to that covenant and its law.

By its dispensationalism, Marcionism separated men from the covenant Christ to tie them to his imagined Christ. He wanted no Christ whose office it is to be King of Creation, the ruler over men and nations. As a result, his "spiritual" Christ was no Christ at all.

Third, Marcionism destroyed the unity of God's revelation. The Old Testament is not an obsolete, lower, or inferior revelation. The Word of God is one word; the Bible is a unity, and, to the extent that its unity and its relevancy is denied, the power of the faith is diminished and harmed.

The currents of modified Marcionism within the church must be purged in order to restore the church to power. The Holy Spirit works through His word, the whole word. Will you listen? (December, 1984)

THE DEFINITION OF MAN
Chalcedon Position Paper No. 58

One of the problems of our time is the inadequacy and failure of men to be truly men under God. The popular images of masculinity are caricatures, and the "macho" idea ludicrous and absurd.

Because God created man, only God can define a man. The humanistic definitions are thus perversions which warp all who live by them.

According to the Bible, "man" was created by God in His image, and "male and female created He them" (Gen. 1:27). This tells us two things: *first*, the word "man" here is inclusive of male and female, so that, despite the difference in the time of their creation, male and female are alike comprehended as "man" and as a unity in God's purpose. *Second*, although there are differences, both male and female are created in God's image. The Shorter Catechism tells us, "God created man male and female, after His own image, in knowledge, righteousness, and holiness, with dominion over the creatures" (Gen. 1:27-28; Col. 3:10; Eph. 4:24). The Larger Catechism (no. 20) tells us also that the providence of God toward man includes responsibility, marriage, communion with Himself, the Sabbath, and the covenant of life with its requirement of "perpetual obedience." Thus, man is defined by God in terms of and in relation to Himself.

For men to seek a self-definition is a sin, and for men to define women in terms of themselves compounds the sin. In Ephesians 5:21-33, we have a much abused text concerning male and female. It is important to note that the command to love is given to the man concerning his wife, not to the wife concerning her husband. Husbands are commanded to love their wives as Christ loved the church and gave Himself for it. Even as Christ is the head of the church to protect and care for it, so too must the husband be. His headship is not a "gentile" fact, one of lording it over his wife. The general command to male and female, to all Christians in their relationships is this "submitting yourselves one to another in the fear of God." There is for both a hierarchy of authorities, first of all God, and then the community. In their human relationships, they are to be "members one of another" (Eph. 4:25), and, because of this, submit their will to the common good in Christ.

We are called and required to serve God unquestioningly. We cannot, however, serve any man so, for such an obedience would be a form of idolatry. Scripture presents Sarah as the model for wives (I Peter 3:6), and certainly Sarah spoke plainly and bluntly to Abraham (Gen. 21:9-10), but God on at least one occasion told Abraham "in all that Sarah hath said unto thee, hearken unto her voice" (Gen. 21:12). For a woman to be silent and obedient to evil is a sin; it is morally wrong, and it makes her an accessory to the evil.

Unhappily, we have too many people promoting the idea of an unquestioning and servile obedience by wives to their husbands; this is to promote idolatry in the name of faithfulness. Some wives are guilty of a super-obedience as a part of a false piety; they expect God to bless them and give them miracles if they make doormats of themselves. God created the woman to be man's help-meet in the dominion mandate (Gen. 2:18), not to be his slave, doormat, or idolatrous servitor.

Moreover, the calling of man, male and female, is to be responsible and accountable, supremely to God, but also to one another. Our Lord says, "For unto whomsoever much is given, of him shall be much required: and to whom men have committed much, of him they will ask the more" (Luke 12:48). This means that both male and female, although especially males, have very great responsibilities and an accountability one to another: they are not their own: they belong to Christ (I Cor. 6:19-20), and, after that, to one another, so that mutual consent is the premise in all things, including sexual abstinence or activity (I Cor. 7:5).

This premise, that we are not our own (I Cor. 6:19), is thus applied to all human relations, and especially to marriage. Male and female are accountable one to another in marriage; headship thus on the human level involves "submitting yourselves one to another in the fear of God" (Eph. 5:21). The greater the responsibility, the greater the accountability, and the greater the realm of accountability. The accountability of a senator is great, but not equal to that of the president. The accountability of the husband is greater than that of the wife.

Reality is hierarchical. Modern man, with his radical equalitarianism, is unwilling to see that there are gradations of authority and ability in all the world. One of the first things dropped by every equalitarian revolution, including the Russian Revolution, is the practice of equality. Equalitarian demands are usually the prelude to a new re-alignment of status and the coming to power of a new elite.

Elitism is the insistence and attempt of self-appointed leaders to assume a total power over society. Elitism is opposed to the idea of hierarchy, because hierarchy means sacred rule, i.e., authority in terms of a God-appointed order. The authority of a father and mother is God-ordained and to be used in terms of God's law: it is hierarchical. Elitism sets man-made standards and requires others to meet them; it means that man plays god and requires the world to bow down to his word.

Because man is created by God and defined by God, man's authority is hierarchical. Both male and female have a hierarchical power which is basic to life and necessary to social order.

In all authority, the primacy of God is the foundation. If God's primary and absolute authority be denied, all authority crumbles. All men then seek to do that which is right in their own eyes. If men will not be ruled by God, they lose the capacity to rule. Men who will not be ruled by God cannot rule themselves nor others. They can at best or worst be tyrants, not authorities.

Moreover, to deny God means ultimately to deny definition and meaning in every realm. The sexual chaos of our time is a logical one, for to deny God is to deny the meaning of all things, including male and female. The effort by men to define themselves apart from God is suicidal, because it substitutes an empty, humanistic perspective for the Biblical one. Because God is the creator of all things in heaven and on earth, only His order is the natural one. To depart from God's order is sin, a disturbance of the natural order of life.

Furthermore, because, as Paul says, we are members one of another in Christ, for men and women to put down one another is to put down themselves even more; because in marriage male and female become one flesh, a community of life, they cannot take advantage of one another without harming themselves. Life is not ordained by God to be lived in isolation from God and from one another. It is "not good" for man to be alone, God tells us.

But loneliness is much more than being alone. A man can be lonely in a crowd, if his life is out of focus. Loneliness is most deadly when we are out of touch with life, and to be out of touch with God is to be out of touch with life. We cannot see reality as it is unless we see all things as God's creation and of necessity understandable only in terms of God's law-word. Without faith in the triune God, our lives and vision are out of focus, and we are not in touch with reality.

Our Lord tells us, "seek ye first the kingdom of God, and his righteousness (or, justice)" (Matt. 6:33). If we seek first our will and our hopes, we warp our lives and our perspectives. Failure to live in terms of reality and an insistence that our will constitutes the real and the true is insanity, and this insanity is endemic to fallen man. It is basic to our world's problems and evils, and also to our own. Our Lord says plainly that it is God's rule and justice we must seek first, i.e., above all things else. Only then, He says, will "all these things (which you desire)...be added unto you" (Matt. 6:33). In other words, our hopes have no place in God's purposes unless His rule and justice have priority with us.

Males who seek their own will first warp every area of life which they touch. Whereas Christ, their model, "loved the church, and gave himself for it" (Eph. 5:25), such men make themselves, not their families, the center of their lives. They thus impose a warp on the lives of their families, and on all who are associated with them, or are under them. Precisely, because in God's order the family is the basic and central institution in life, to warp the family at the central point of human authority has repercussions of a radical sort. Society as a whole is then distorted and rendered ungodly.

Our calling requires us to give God the glory, and the priority in all things. David tells us, God made man "a little lower than the angels, and... crowned him with glory and honour" to have "dominion over the works" of God's hands; "thou hast put all things under his feet" (Ps. 8:5-6). When men deny God the Lord, they deny also their calling. As a result, instead of having dominion, men fall under the dominion of sin. Their moral universe is turned upside down, and their true strength denied.

Julianus Pomerius (c. 497 A.D.), in *The Contemplative Life*, wrote that "faith...is the foundation of justice." For there to be justice or righteousness in the world, there must first be faith, men of faith. Faith, and its consequence, justice make us aware that we are not our own, that we are part of a God-created order with a responsibility to God and to one another. As Julianus Pomerius added, "From justice equity also flows, which makes us call the necessities of all men our own and makes us believe we were born not for ourselves alone but also for mankind in general." "Born not for ourselves alone!" Man in his sin sees the whole world as existing for his pleasure, to be used as he wills it. But "man's chief end is to glorify God, and to enjoy Him forever." For this we were created, for this we were ordained and born. To deny our nature and calling is to destroy our true freedom and to warp our being. As God's creatures, we are also called to love one another, and to be members one of another.

Our Lord tells us that the meaning of God's law can be summarized in two commandments: "Thou shalt love the Lord thy God with all thy heart, and with all thy soul, and with all thy mind. This is the first and great commandment. And the second is like unto it, Thou shalt love thy neighbour as thyself." (Matt. 21:37-39). These two sentences tell us what all of God's law deals with; the law gives us the specific ways in which our love of God and of our neighbor is to be manifested. God's law, James 1:23 and 2:12 tells us, is "the perfect law of liberty." An attempt recently to place an animal heart in a human baby was a disaster; the human body rejected the alien heart. When man is given an alien law, any law other than God's law, an even greater rejection factor is at work. Instead of liberty, the alien law produces death. The more a society departs from God's law, the closer it is to death.

The macho male and feminist female images warp life and replace liberty with social suicide.

In this development, false theology has played a key role. As Ann Douglas, in *The Feminization of American Culture*, shows so tellingly, America's departure from Calvinism led to a feminization of both theology and culture, and also of the clergy.

Not surprisingly, the liberal clergy was regarded as effeminate, and people spoke of the three sexes, men, women, and preachers. We now see the consequences of that long and unhappy development. One of the common problems across the country is the oppression of the clergy by whining and complaining parishioners. The pastor is expected to serve the whims of sniveling men and whining women, not Christ the Lord. If he fails to do their bidding and play his sanctimonious part, the complaint is that "he is not a spiritual man." Some peoples redefine man and the church in terms of themselves. (A particularly fine pastor was recently told by a nasty old wretch, "You're not doing enough for us senior citizens;" the complainer had only one demand of the church, that it serve him, not that he serve the Lord.)

Until men define themselves in terms of the Lord, His Kingdom, law and justice, our society's troubles will only increase. Man has no right to define himself. God did that on the day of creation. (January, 1985)

DISCONTINUITY & ANTINOMIANISM
Chalcedon Position Paper No. 59

From the days of the early church to the present, a variety of heresies and opinions have contributed to the development of modern antinomianism. In our previous Position Papers, some of these have been discussed. It is important now to look at the American influences, and other modern philosophies, which have gone into the modern formulation of this concept.

In the early years of the republic, the pressures of English Deism led to a progressive de-emphasis on the Old Testament. For the Deists, the Old Testament was a primitive religious expression of the ancient Hebrews; having no love for their contemporary Jews, the Deists were not disposed to view their Hebrew forbears favorably.

The results became apparent in a lessened interest in the Old Testament. Whereas earlier the Puritans had seen the whole Bible as the binding word of God, now, as Jay Fliegelman has noted in *Prodigals and Pilgrims* (1982), "'The Bible' was slowly becoming identified with the New Testament alone." From 1777 to 1800, there were only 33 American editions of the whole Bible, but nearly 80 separate printings of the New Testament. This was a break with the Puritan love of the whole word of God.

At the same time, the Baptists were waging a dual attack on the old order. *First*, and rightly so, they fought against the establishment of any church in favor of the establishment of Christianity as the faith undergirding the social order. *Second*, because the other churches stressed the continuity between circumcision and infant baptism, the Baptists attacked the validity of this continuity by denying the continuity between the Old and the New Testaments. Instead of a renewed covenant in Christ with a new Israel of

God, a new chosen people, the Baptists insisted on two covenants of differing characteristics.

This assault was followed by a more deadly one, by the Unitarians. William Ellery Channing in 1819 preached the ordination sermon for Jared Sparks in Baltimore, Maryland. On that occasion, Channing attacked the Calvinists and declared that "the dispensation of Moses" was very different from the new one and had been "adapted to the childhood of the human race." The Bible thus represented two very different dispensations of religion.

Ralph Waldo Emerson went further. In an address to the senior class in divinity at Harvard, he attacked "the assumption that the age of inspiration is past, that the Bible is closed." He insisted that men need no mediator, and that all of us can become "bards of the Holy Ghost." In "Uses of Great Men," Emerson insisted that a "rotation" or change of dispensations "is the law of nature," and added, "nor can the Bible be closed until the last great man is born."

During this time, the idea of cultural evolution was being advanced, and, later, it was applied to biology. The influence of evolutionary thinking on dispensationalism was real, despite the fact that, at a later date, evolutionary and dispensational thought separated and clashed.

Another powerful influence was the philosopher Hegel. In Hegel's thought, a variety of ancient pagan strands re-surfaced, among them the belief in the conflict of interests as necessary to progress. Whereas Biblical faith asserts the harmony of interests because of the governing and predestinating hand of God, non-Biblical faiths see order evolving out of a conflict of interests.

These pagan ideas had long plagued Christian thought, but never so much as after Hegel, whose influence was decisive throughout Christendom, and especially so in Germany. Hegel came into Biblical studies very plainly in the work of Ferdinand Christian Baur. As Hans Conzelmann noted, in *An Outline of the Theology of The New Testament* (1969), and noted with approval, Baur "interprets Paul with the basic concepts of Hegel." What this meant was that Scripture was no longer seen as a unified whole, as the one word of God. From beginning to end, the Bible was now seen as a war of ostensibly true ideas and factors. In Paul especially, this warfare was supposedly sharpest. Flesh is for Paul by presupposition in antithesis to spirit, law is opposed to grace, mercy to judgment, love to wrath, and so on.

The Bible was now seen as a divided book, and, by implication, God was divided and in conflict with Himself. God had one plan of salvation for the Jews, another for the Christians.

Such ideas were not new. As heresies, they had long plagued the church and often influenced the orthodox. Now, however, such antinomian and dispensational ideas represented "the latest scholarship." Biblical studies began to major in dividing the word and in seeing one writer as opposed to another, or in conflict with himself.

It became "good scholarship" to see error and division in the Bible. Martin Dibelius, in *James, A Commentary* (1976), held that, because Christians "were living in expectation of the end of the world, they had neither the inclination nor the ability to initiate an ethical renewal of a world which seemed to be doomed for destruction." How a commentator on James could make such a statement is amazing. It is a witness to the triumph of scholarship over reality.

This is not all. Another and revolutionary influence which came to focus in the United States was a hostility to continuity. America was to be "the new order of the ages," a totally new dispensation. The Old Testament era was "primitive"; Europe was "backward," but America was to be the new "course of empire" and a new age in a new world. Many Deists in Europe shared this view and adored Franklin as an example of the new, free man. Jefferson was hostile to the past in the same way and believed that family and continuity were impediments. As he wrote to John Adams on October 28, 1813, he believed the human race should be scientifically bred like animals, with superior men (like himself) given harems, "not for the sake of pleasure" but to breed. For the same reason, hostility to continuity, Jefferson affirmed in another letter (September 4, 1823) his belief in perpetual revolution to destroy the past and create Jefferson's imagined paradise. He knew that so radical a revolution as he wanted was mass murder, "yet the object (or goal) is worth rivers of blood and years of desolation." (*The Adams - Jefferson Letters*) Jefferson's great hatred was reserved for Calvinism, which he called demonism.

Jefferson made respectable the belief in discontinuity. Since his Unitarianism, while suspected by some, was not public knowledge, his influence among churchmen was extensive, and he carried their votes easily. Jefferson did popularize the belief that the United States has to break with the past, and sons with their fathers. Jefferson hated the power of birth and inheritance, i.e., the ability of men to begin with an inherited advantage. John Adams said of Plato, but with an eye on Jefferson, "no man expressed so much terror of the Power of Birth. His genius could invent no remedy or precaution against it; but a Community of Wives, a confusion of Families, a total extinction of all Relations of Father, Son and Brother." It is not an accident that all radical movements, from the ancient Mazdakites to the Marxists, have tried to destroy the family.

In the United States, this Jeffersonian anti-familism has meant a hostility to sons of successful men. Is a wealthy industrialist the son of a rich founding father? Then it is assumed that the son is only successful because of his inheritance. The fact is that very often (not always) the son advances what the father began. The belief in discontinuity plus envy directed against ability leads to the hostility. To cite a very specific current example from within the church, Franky Schaeffer, son of Francis Schaeffer, is regularly the target of hostile comments in and out of print. These sanctimonious hypocrites attack Frank with a show of sadness and regret because he is supposedly not up to his father's abilities and name. The fact is that Frank Schaeffer begins where his father left off in *The Christian Manifesto* and builds logically and very ably on that foundation. His work is a step forward and in excellent continuity with his father's work. Two motives are at work against him. First, those who lacked the courage to attack his father are now piously bleating about a supposed "decline." Second, the old hostility against continuity is at work. There must be no inheritance of wealth, ability, or status for these men. The Jeffersonian hatred of continuity is very much with us.

Such a view is essential to antinomianism. Law means continuity. It means that God has an established order in all of history. The sins of the fathers have an effect on the children, and the mercy of God upon the fathers is also felt by the children. The past is not dead; it is alive in all of history, because God's law governs, ordains and uses all things. Because the wages of sin are always death, history can only change within a God-given framework of curses or blessings. Men have no other options than those given by the triune God and set forth in His law word.

The idea of revolution, of discontinuity, is to overthrow the force, power, and government of God's law, to break the bonds of God's rule (Psalm 2). The Mazdakites in 451 A.D. sought to eradicate the past by enforcing the communism of wealth, women, and land, and killing Christians, (among them a hostage, Isaac Rushdoony), but they ended by destroying their realm. Today state schools are a great weapon of discontinuity, well tooled to destroy the family. Those who resist state control of education are taken to court on *criminal* charges.

Within the church, all these currents of thought had an extensive influence. The Unitarians like Channing dismissed the Old Testament and its law as a primitive dispensation for the ancient Hebrews. They also dismissed Puritan Calvinism as an old and barbarous era, as clinging to a dispensation well left behind. The believer, in his devotional life, was encouraged to concentrate on the New Testament, and the Psalms. Alexander Campbell attacked the law and called for "New Testament Christianity." Such thinking was seeping into all churches, although Southern Presbyterians resisted it until 1869. The church was abandoning the Bible of Jesus Christ!

In 1970, Bible-believers in the U.S. numbered at least one fourth of the population, enough to command the country, but most of them did not vote and regarded politics as "a dirty business." They failed to appreciate the fact that their retreat had made it so.

Not surprisingly, the persecution of churches, Christian Schools, and home schools soon began. The god of the law was now the state, not the Lord God of Scripture. In one state, where such persecutions have taken place, a Christian attorney called attention to the dereliction and surrender of some churches; as a result, six pastors banded together in an effort to force the attorney out of town.

Newsweek (February 4, 1985) called attention to the epidemic of sexually transmitted diseases, now said to number "25 or so diseases" which infect "1 in 4 Americans between the ages of 15 and 55 at some point in his or her life." Serious as this is, it does not compare in its harm to the damage done by antinomianism. If God's law does not govern man, the state's law will, and the state's law is Genesis 3:5 writ large, every man (or civil government) as his own god, determining for himself what is good and evil.

It is time to ask churchmen plainly: Who is on the Lord's side? Let him serve the King and honor His law. (February, 1985)

THE PRIVATIZATION OF MORALITY AND SOCIAL DECAY
Chalcedon Position Paper No. 60

One of the errors of the rationalistic temper in our times and earlier has been its depreciation of both religion and history. The assumption too often has been, as with Hegel, that "the rational is the real," i.e., what a man who sees himself as rational conceives to be reasonable has at least a logical inevitability if not an historical reality. To confuse the ideal with the real leads to the brutalities of modern revolutionary history, as men force their rational "realities" onto masses of men.

A rationalistic approach is non-historical. Thus, early Protestants catalogued instances of Catholic persecutions to give a picture of Catholicism which did no justice to history, and Catholics wrote similar works on Protestants. Such approaches have little historical value: they express a bias, not an understanding.

To understand the First Amendment, we must ask why it is a product of Christendom and not of some other religion and its culture. Greco-Roman cultures did not allow the freedoms we take for granted. In antiquity, either the state, the ruler, or the office was seen as divine, as god waking on earth a la Hegel. Rome, for example, was the most "liberal" of ancient orders, but Rome saw religion as a necessary social cement and hence to be strictly controlled and regulated. All religions had to be licensed and governed by the state, and the conflict with Christianity was over this issue, the refusal of the church to submit to control. This refusal was born of Old Testament faith. God's realm is to be beyond man's control. The great victory of this faith against an alien power is set forth in Ezra 7, the agreement of the Persian monarchy to refrain from taxing, regulating, or controlling the Temple of Jerusalem, and the practitioners of its religion even to the porters and door-keepers of the Temple. Later, Rome gave to Judea substantially the same immunity, although controlling the elections of high priests. The church inherited this immunity until the Jewish-Roman War of 66-70 A.D. and fought for the totality of it thereafter.

During much of medieval history, despite the problems of dealing with newly converted barbarians, this freedom existed to a degree, but the states of Europe, and the Holy Roman Empire, sought to re-establish the pattern of control. We miss the meaning of medieval religion if we fail to see it as a long history of struggle, with the state in the main controlling and using the church.

The statist pattern from pagan antiquity through the centuries and well into the Christian era has been religious toleration. In religious toleration, the state proscribes certain faiths and establishes and regulates others. This was the goal of medieval and modern states. In legal toleration, the state determines which groups will be tolerated. Toleration is also the premise of the U.S. Internal Revenue Service, the Federal Government, and most states. Tolerance and establishment go together, because the act of defining the limits of toleration is the establishment of licit religion.

As against this, the American pattern represented a major break with past civil standards and a return to Biblical requirements. Two things in particular marked the constitutional settlement. *First*, the word *sovereignty* was completely avoided. It was held then and later that sovereignty is an attribute of God alone.

Second, the U.S. broke with the toleration-establishment pattern to place itself entirely outside the field of religion. Religion was recognized to be an independent sphere from the state, and neither church nor state are to have jurisdiction over one another in federal policy. The First Amendment thus set forth religious freedom, not toleration.

At the same time, however, Enlightenment thought held that religion and morality could be separated, and that non-religious grounds could be found for moral law. By this they really meant non-theistic grounds, i.e., rationalistic and humanistic grounds. They were thus separating *theistic* religion from morality, not humanistic religion. George Washington spoke against this opinion in his Farewell Address, saying:

> "...And let us with caution indulge the supposition, that morality can be maintained without religion. Whatever may be conceded to the

> influence of refined education on minds of peculiar structure, reason and experience both forbid us to expect, that national morality can prevail in exclusion of religious principle."

No human freedom is or can be absolute, and the same is true of religious freedom. This fact came into focus in the case of United States vs. Reynolds (98 United States Reports 145), wherein the U.S. Supreme Court said in part concerning the Mormon practice of polygamy in relation to the First Amendment:

"Congress was deprived of all legislative power over mere opinion, but was left free to reach actions which were in violation of social duties or subversive of good order...there never has been a time, in any State in the Union, when polygamy was not an offense against society, cognizable by the civil courts, and punishable...It is impossible to believe that the constitutional guarantee of religious freedom was intended to prohibit legislation in respect to this most important element in social life - marriage: while, from its nature the sacred obligation is, nevertheless, in most civilizations, a civil contract, and usually regulated by law...

"Laws are made for the government of actions, and while they cannot interfere with mere religious belief...they may with practices...Suppose one religiously believed that human sacrifices were a necessary part of religious worship, would it be seriously contended that the civil government could not interfere to prevent sacrifices? Can a man excuse his practices...because of his religious belief? To permit this would be to make the doctrines of religion superior to the law of the land; and in effect would be to permit every citizen to become a law unto himself. Government could exist only in name...It matters not that his belief was a part of his religion; it was still a belief and a belief only."

This decision recognized clearly the nature and dimensions of the problem. No civil government can exist where there is a total freedom of religion. Among the practices found in some religions are ritual prostitution, murder, human sacrifice, cannibalism, incest, bestiality, and much, much more. All these and other practices have at one time or another been *established* by some civil order, great or small. To grant total religious liberty is to deny the possibility of civil government.

On the other hand, in United States vs. Reynolds, the Supreme Court avoided the problem George Washington had called attention to, the false separation of religion and morality. The Court called monogamous marriage "the sacred obligation." But this was Reynolds' contention, that polygamy was for him a sacred obligation. On what ground could the Court limit the sacredness to monogamy? The answer is an obvious one: the court presupposed the validity of Christian morality and saw it as alone having a licit status.

Washington had called attention to an ancient bit of knowledge and wisdom which the 18th century had called into question, namely, that all law represents a moral order, and every concept of moral order is a matter of religious faith and expression. Laws proscribe certain kinds of actions to protect thereby other and licit behavior. Every law, whether it is civil, criminal, or procedural, represents a vision of moral order which the law-makers and courts seek to approximate and attain. That vision of legal-moral order is a religious vision. Every legal system is thus an establishment of religion, inescapably so. This does not mean the establishment of a church, but of a religion, a very different thing. Such an establishment does not approve of a particular form of theology but simply of the religion in question as the moral foundation of the state. It was this that Justice Joseph Story had in mind when he spoke of Christianity as the foundation of our legal and social order. He held Christianity to be a part of the common law. The sociologist, Eugen Rosenstock-Huessy, saw the common law itself as a Christian product. In 1955, John C. H. Wu, in *Fountain of Justice*, commented on this question thus:

"The question has often been asked if Christianity is a part of the common law. It depends on what you mean by Christianity. If you mean a revealed religion, a faith as defined by the Apostles' Creed, it is not a part of the common law in the sense that you are legally bound to believe in it. Christianity as a Faith comes into the courts, not as a law, but as a fact to be taken judicial notice of, on a par with other facts of common knowledge. On the other hand, if you mean by Christianity the fundamental moral precepts embodied in its teachings, it is a part of the common law in the sense that all the universal principles of justice written in the heart of every man are a part thereof."

In this sense, there is a common concern in both church and state. The political scientist, James McClellan, in *Joseph Story and the American Constitution* (1971), held, "At bottom, church and state are forever united; their total separation impossible" (p. 126). Church and state are not united in any institutional or legal sense but in a common concern on common moral premises for a particular form of moral order.

The freedom recognized by The First Amendment serves to enable both church and state to work with greater independence and vigor for that moral order. Basic to that freedom is the belief that sovereignty does not reside in the human sphere but in God alone. It follows therefore that no human agency, such as church and state, can claim exclusive or total jurisdiction. Totalitarianism is a consequence of non-theistic doctrines of sovereignty. If God alone is Lord or sovereign, God alone has total jurisdiction over all things.

The absence of a doctrine of sovereignty in the Constitution made the

First Amendment possible. The rise of the doctrine of federal sovereignty is now threatening the First Amendment. Only a true doctrine of lordship or sovereignty can turn the present drift into totalitarianism around. Only then can we counteract what Judge Robert H. Bork, in *Tradition and Morality in Constitutional Law* (1984), called "constitutional nihilism."

We must remember, however, that constitutional nihilism has its roots in moral nihilism. Gertrude Himmelfarb, in the February, 1985 *Commentary* (vol. 79, no. 2), writes on "From Clapham to Bloomsbury: A Genealogy of Morals." The Bloomsbury circle, which included the economist Keynes, Virginia Woolf, Lytton Strachey, and others derived its premises from the philosophy of G. E. Moore. Moore not only separated religion and morality but implicitly made both unnecessary, so that, as some of his followers soon saw, the problems of society were simply technical and managerial ones. The Bloomsbury group thus viewed their life style in terms of aesthetics, not morality, and they called their "liberated" homosexuality "the Higher Sodomy." For them morality was not a problem because it was irrelevant.

The influence of this circle is quite pervasive in our time. It affects our media, our legislative assemblies, and our courts. It turns the meaning of the First Amendment upside down. That document, instead of setting forth the independent sphere of religion so that it might better govern and inform public faith and morality, is now seen too often as the guarantee for every kind of immoralism and social disorder. The First Amendment was written to give freedom to the expression of religious and moral convictions in the civil sphere in terms of an historic faith that Biblical religion constitutes an independent sphere. It has now become the prop of a philosophy which insists on the irrelevance of religion and morality to social order. The consequence of this religious and moral nihilism is Constitutional nihilism.

Judge Bork wrote also of the current "privatization of morality, which requires the law of the community to practice moral relativism." It is this that leads to constitutional nihilism. Behind all this lies a moral nihilism. As a result of an emphasis on appearance which was strong in the Victorian era, people are now judged socially and aesthetically, not morally. A man may be a homosexual, a dedicated adulterer, a dishonest dealer, or more but, unless there is a public scandal connected with him, he is acceptable if well dressed, well bathed, and aesthetically "right" in his life-style, whereas a virtuous man is looked down on. This is the Bloomsbury tradition although its roots go deeper.

Until men recognize that law, morality, and religion are inseparable, and religion is basic to social order, our decay will continue. The privatization of morality is anti-Biblical and it leads to moral and social nihilism and death. (March, 1985)

HOLINESS VERSUS PERFECTIONISM
Chalcedon Position Paper No. 61

A Biblical incident rarely preached on is II Kings 5:18-19. The Syrian general Naaman, healed of his leprosy by the prophet Elisha, has made a profession of faith. He has a problem, however. The Syrian King, in his infirmity, required a man to lean on as he goes to worship in the Temple of Rimmon. Naaman is that trusted man. For a general, who could easily seize the throne, to be so trusted indicates how highly Naaman was regarded. But Naaman is troubled. When the King bows to his god, Naaman must help him to do so and himself bow in the process. Will the LORD pardon Naaman for this? Elisha's answer is affirmative: "Go in peace." Naaman was not summoned to a life of perfection but of holiness and there is a difference. Naaman was not compromising his faith but performing a minor duty in a major career.

The idea of perfection is in essence a pagan doctrine. The word *perfect* as it appears in Scripture has a different meaning than in pagan cultures. Several Greek words are used in the New Testament. In Matthew 5:48, "Be ye therefore perfect, even as your Father which in heaven is perfect," the word is "teleios," matured, reaching its appointed goal, completed; other words translated as "perfect" have related meanings. For us to be perfect in the Biblical sense means to mature in our calling, to do God's will for our lives, and to serve Him with all our heart, mind, and being. Perfection in this sense is a process. The Preamble to the U.S. Constitution uses "perfect" in this theological sense and thus speaks of forming "a more perfect union." In the modern sense, this is absurd: what can be more perfect than perfect?

Perfection in the non-Biblical sense has long been a goal in various pagan religions, and it has been essentially linked to the idea of autonomous man. To use neo-platonic terms, man must incarnate in himself the principle of being and attain perfection. This is in essence a solitary quest, because to attain true spirituality or intellectuality, to be pure mind or pure spirit, one must divorce oneself from the material world and from other people. People are a troublesome burden, endlessly concerned with their trifles, and an impediment to the realization of the principle in one's being.

This pagan concept of perfection separated the person from the world and from society. It created hermits, monks, and detached people. In one pagan faith after another, the true goal of life is detachment, a world and life negation. Eastern religions in particular have been dedicated to this goal of detachment, but its influence has been powerful in the West also. Most of the desert hermits of the early church, many monks, and much popular piety, Catholic and Protestant, have been dedicated to this ideal. In the 14th century, the monks of Athos believed that fasting plus concentration could enable them to realize the uncreated essence of God. The concentration came from navel-watching. When Barlaam opposed the "navel-souled ones" a Synod was called to condemn him.

The way of perfection is the solitary way. It is often associated with mysticism. In its forms within the church, its goal is the vision of God, or, in other forms, pietism, the perfection of one's personal piety. It is, in any case, an autonomous exercise, not a social one. In relation to the world, it seeks escape and anonymity. Perfectionism and self-absorption go hand in hand.

The doctrine of holiness is radically different. When our Lord summons us to be "perfect" or mature, i.e., to grow in terms of our God-appointed end, He is summoning us to serve God with all our being, and to be holy unto Him. "Ye shall be holy unto me; for I the LORD am holy, and have severed you from other people, that ye should be mine" (Lev. 20:26). Holiness is always unto the Lord. Moreover, as Revelation 15:4, in the great "song of Moses, the servant of God, and the song of the Lamb," declares, "Thou only art holy." God alone is holy; we are holy to the degree that we separate and dedicate ourselves to Him and to His Kingdom. To abide in Him means to bring forth fruit (John 15:2); to love God means to keep His commandments (John 15:10,14). Our goal thus is to do the will of our Father, to serve Him with all our heart, mind, and being, to love God and our neighbor.

The Reformation, and especially the Puritans, defined this work of holiness as the Kingdom of God, as a ministry in Christ's name, the goal being, "The kingdoms of this world are become the kingdoms of our Lord, and of his Christ; and he shall reign for ever and ever" (Rev. 11:15). This goal was one present from the earliest days of the church, and strong in many medieval movements, although the neoplatonic perfectionism gained an ascendancy.

The rise of Pietism again subverted this priority of holiness in the Biblical sense; perfectionism took over. With the rise of perfectionism, impracticality has often been associated with perfection and a psuedo-holiness. Modernism, even more than Catholic and Protestant orthodoxies, has been very prone to perfectionism, and it has done much damage the world over. Pacifism is one form of this perfectionism; hostility to armament in any form is another. In one seminary, it was enough to dismiss from consideration as a worthy Christian a prominent churchman for the professor to say, "He has a collection of guns and loves to hunt."

The prevalence of perfectionism in the Western World has been part and parcel of incredibly stupid foreign and domestic policies. It means moving in terms of assumptions which are unrelated to reality, because the ideal must be assumed in order to make it real. Perfectionism sees man as the creator and the world as his will and idea.

Modern education is perfectionist. It teaches students that the world can be remade if we believe men are naturally good and peace-loving, and that, if only we treat them so, they will be as hoped for. As one prominent "theologian" believes, if we surrender to the Soviet Union and greet their troops with smiling faces, love will triumph.

Churchmen equate their "good intentions" with perfection. To end poverty is good; therefore, to call for the redistribution of wealth means to favor a godly society and a perfect solution to the problem of poverty. The solution to economic and other problems is seen as political, i.e., the issuing of political fiats which will supposedly change the world.

Perfectionism believes in cheap remedies. The great perfectionist, Satan, had a simple solution. God was requiring men to learn the discipline of work, science, and dominion in the Garden of Eden as the first step towards exercising dominion over all the earth (Gen. 1:26-28). This was seen as a painfully slow process which would require centuries and much effort. How much simpler it would be if man would, like God, issue a fiat word, determine good and evil for himself, and be the creator of his own world (Gen. 3:1-5). God's way required holiness, a total dedication and obedience to God's law word, and the slow process of maturation (the Biblical meaning of perfection). The tempter offered a simpler route, perfection, not holiness, not obedience to every word that proceeds from the mouth of God (Matt. 4:4), but being one's own god and decreeing the perfect world. (So modern politics was born.)

Perfectionism also trusts in religious or devotional exercises as the way to power with God. Isaiah speaks very bluntly (as do other prophets) about the evil this can be, saying that God declares, "Is it such a fast that I have chosen? a day for a man to afflict his soul? is it to bow down his head as a bulrush, and to spread sackcloth and ashes under him? wilt thou call this a fast, and an acceptable day to the LORD? Is not this the fast that I have chosen? to loose the bands of wickedness, to undo the heavy burdens, and to let the oppressed go free, and that ye break every yoke? Is it not to deal thy bread to the hungry, and that thou bring the poor that are cast out to thy house? when thou seest the naked, that thou cover him; and that thou hide not thyself from thine own flesh? Then shall thy light break forth as the morning, and thine health shall spring forth speedily; and thy righteousness shall go before thee; and the glory of the LORD shall be thy reward. Then shalt thou call, and the LORD shall answer; thou shalt cry, and he shall say, Here I am. If thou take away from the midst of thee the yoke, the putting forth of the finger, and speaking vanity; and if thou draw out thy soul to the hungry, and satisfy the afflicted soul; then shall thy light rise in obscurity, and thy darkness be as the noonday, and the LORD shall guide thee continually" (Isa. 58:5-11).

What the Lord requires of us is holiness, but holiness is not gained by saying, Go to now, I shall be a saint. Rather, holiness comes as we seek first the Kingdom of God and His righteousness or justice (Matt. 6:33). We do not become holy by seeking holiness in and of itself. The Lord is the Holy One, and we are holy if we do His will. Christ is holy because He is the obedient Son: "For I came down from heaven, not to do mine own will, but the will of Him that sent me" (John 6:38). Twice in Hebrews we are told of our Lord that His avowed and ordained purpose was this: "Lo, I come to do thy will, 0 God" (Heb. 10:7,9). This must be our purpose too as members of His new humanity. We are not saved to retire to our own devices but to serve, glorify, and enjoy God forever. We are summoned to be holy, which means to love, serve, and obey the Lord with all our heart, mind, and being, and to love our neighbor as ourself.

Holiness is too often seen as mere negation. As one man said recently, echoing an old sentence, he had lived for years on the premise that he was a Christian because "I don't smoke, and I don't chew, and I don't go with girls that do." Holiness is not merely nor essentially negation; it requires separation, but it is false to see it merely as separation from sin. Our Lord describes false separation tellingly. A man rid himself of an unclean spirit and cleansed his life of many things, but his zeal for perfection and a negative holiness left the "house" merely "empty, swept, and garnished." As a result, "the unclean spirit returned with seven other spirits more wicked than himself" with the result that "the last state of that man is worse than the first" (Matt. 12:43-45). This parable by our Lord explains why some supposedly converted people are so great a problem.

True holiness is a dedication to the Lord's service with the totality of our being. It is not a concern with our perfection, but a concern for the Lord's work. As David says, "The zeal of thine house hath eaten me up" (Ps. 69:9) a sentence finding total expression in our Lord (John 2:17). David's sins were very real and were judged by God, but David's zeal for the Lord's work was honored and blessed by God, because David sought God's Kingdom and glory.

Remember Naaman and Elisha's word. What would some of our modern perfectionists, with their false holiness, have said to Naaman? Or to Abraham, Solomon, Peter, and many another saint richly blessed by God?

There is much talk today about holiness, but it is a warped and perfectionist doctrine which is too often stressed. The result is negation, and instead of powerful men of God, it is mousy churchmen who are the results of such teachings.

The church must be a training camp and barracks room, sending soldiers of Christ into the world, each in his or her own sphere, to exercise dominion in the name of the Lord. A good army is not trained for exhilaration and parade but for action.

Our God, who is alone holy in and of Himself, is a God of action and power. Our holiness comes in working in obedience and faithfulness to His law word. (April, 1985)

LOYALTIES
Chalcedon Position Paper No. 62

Over the years, I have repeatedly seen, and commented very often about, the evil of self-pity. Self-pity is the most deadly spiritual cancer a man can inflict upon himself. With self-pity, we wall ourselves off from the world and joy; we give a self-centered meaning to all events, and we see life, not as a gift and grace from God (I Peter 3:7), but as a conspiracy against us. We then view life and politics, not as a responsibility, but as a vast plot. That men conspire is true, and Psalm 2 tells us that the basic conspiracy of history is against God and His law. We are also told by all of Scripture that faithfulness to the Lord makes us victorious in history against all enemies and powers (Deut. 28).

Men, however, find it easier to blame others than to assume responsibility. Hence the radical absorption of many in documenting all the evils perpetrated by one group or another. Such documentation changes nothing. Men are not saved by knowing their enemies but by knowing and being strong in the Lord. We can best see where our enemies are, and who they are, when we are most in Christ.

A great deal of our bigotry comes from a concentration on the wrongs we have suffered rather than on the wrongs we inflict on other people. No lying is involved, only an emphasis on one aspect of our lives. To illustrate. and to limit the illustrations to the American experience, ever since I was young, I have had Jewish friends tell me of the bitter persecutions they endured: being called "Christ-killers," "Kikes," and more, being discriminated against in various ways, and so on. All of this is clearly true.

Again, I have heard Catholic friends express their hurt and indignation at having their church called "the whore of Babylon," at being treated as evil people because of their faith, abused for their religious practices, and so on. Some of the indignities suffered are painful to hear about. I have no doubt as to their truth.

Furthermore, many Protestants can tell like stories, all true. One girl told me of her painful experience in being the only Protestant in a business establishment with over a dozen girls, all the rest Catholic, with a Jewish boss! Only her unquestionable excellence kept her out in front; every kind of effort was made to push errors on to her. She was the target of ugly remarks about her faith, and so on and on. Only the pay and her need to work kept her going. Many, many more such tales can be told, all true.

But this is only one side of the story. More than one Catholic, Protestant, and atheist has told me of the problems of living in an old-fashioned Jewish neighborhood, and walking as a child down the street and having the Jewish old folks on their stoops spitting at them, of falling and hurting oneself badly and everyone laughing with delight, and so on.

Again, a Jewish boy in any non-Jewish neighborhood has suffered torment at the hands of Catholic, Protestant, and atheist boys in the neighborhood. I have heard more than a few stories of the cruel humor, the nasty pranks, and the like, all too routine in such cases. Each has tried to outdo the other in unkindness.

Need I say more? There is not a group in society which has not suffered some indignities and also inflicted indignities on others. Can you convince any group of their sins? They loved to major in the sins of others.

This holds true in marriage. "Men!" I heard a woman snort indignantly once, "I could tell you a lot about them, the ______!" I am sure she could have, and I am sure that men could have told me a lot about her. In marriage, men and women too often have the bad habit of concentrating on their spouse's sins and shortcomings, not their own, and feeling a great deal of self-pity. One wife, who neglected her most routine responsibilities as a wife but complained endlessly about her husband, became venomously angry when I asked her about her responsibilities. I have seen men bitterly angry because their wife has a problem; the men have assumed that only they have a right to needs and wants. We all tend to forget that the one person we can change is ourselves, and this is our God-required duty. Everyone, however, wants to reform others, especially their enemies. We forget that the greatest menace to community comes from this kind of Phariseeism. It is the essence of Phariseeism to see oneself as superior, and others as the problem people of the world. We miss the whole point of our Lord's indictment of the Pharisees if we forget that, to a very real degree, they were the best people of their day, and they knew it. Their attitude towards others reflected this. In His biting attack on the Pharisees, our Lord portrays one boasting even to God of his superiority: "God, I thank thee, that I am not as other men are, extortioners, unjust, adulterers, or even as this publican" (Luke 18:11). What the Pharisee did was to separate himself from other men in terms of his ostensibly superior religious stand. Our Lord tells us that the publican was justified before God, not the Pharisee (Luke 18:14).

Let us remember too that our Lord declares that the summation of God's law is in two commandments: "Thou shalt love the Lord thy God with all they heart and with all thy soul, and with all thy mind...And...Thou shalt love thy neighbor as thy self" (Matt. 22:37,39). Not humanistic or social criteria but the love of God must govern all our being. When we love God truly, then we can also love our neighbor as ourselves. Two things are clear in this latter commandment. *First*, it presupposes that we love ourselves. We can only respect ourselves and have a healthy self-love when we know that we are created in the image of God and redeemed by Jesus Christ. Men who cannot love themselves cannot love others. Much of the failure of various groups, Protestant, Catholic, Jewish and others to have the godly respect for groups or persons outside their fellowship that they should is due to a lack of a Biblical view of themselves under God.

God's repeated test of the integrity of a people's faith is their care for widows, orphans, and strangers, for those who are outside their normal realm of association. This is the *second* aspect of this commandment. To love our neighbor as ourselves is to show as great a concern for their welfare, rights, and reputation as for our own. To love our neighbor as ourselves means to respect our neighbor's marriage and its sanctity ("Thou shalt not commit adultery"); his life ("Thou shalt not kill"); his property ("Thou shalt not steal"); his reputation ("Thou shalt not bear false witness"); and to do this in word, thought, and deed ("Thou shalt not covet...").

What this means is very clear. Beyond a very limited sphere, judgment is the province of God. A godless state will assume more and more of the prerogatives of God and assume powers of judgment over all of life. Because we are not God, for us the decisive power in society must be the regenerating power of God and the work of the Holy Spirit in and through us. Not revolution but regeneration, not coercion but conversion, is our way of changing the world and furthering the Kingdom of God. This is the heart of Christian reconstruction. The heart of Biblical law is that it makes us the basic government of society in and through our personal and family life, through our vocations, churches, and schools. In Biblical law, civil government is a very limited and minor sphere of rule and power.

No society can be healthy if the people are not strong in their faith. A strong state means a weak people. The various civil governments of the world are all strong and over-bearing in their power because the peoples are weak in the faith. Statist power grows to fill a vacuum in government created by the irresponsibility of the people. When men say of their Lord, "We will not have this man to reign over us" (Luke 19:14), they are inviting anarchy. The Book of Judges describes such a time. Men had rejected God as their king, and, because "In those days there was no king in Israel" God having been denied, "every man did that which was right in his own eyes" (Judges 21:25).

When men do that which is right in their own eyes, when they deny Christ our King and His law-word, then their word and their group becomes the source of determination for them. Men then act humanistically and are determined by their group, not the Lord. Our governing allegiance must be to Jesus Christ and His reign, not to our Catholic or Protestant churches.

Our faith can rarely surpass our allegiance. If our allegiance is Presbyterian, Baptist, Catholic, Methodist, or what have you, we are small men indeed, and our "faith" a warped one at best. Churches like persons must be instruments in the hand of God, not the centers of our lives. We can and must respect the instruments, but we warp the faith if we are not God-centered.

The story is told of a famous evangelist of almost a century ago who encountered a drunkard who blubbered gratefully that he owed his conversion to him. The evangelist responded, "I must have converted you, because obviously the Lord didn't."

If our allegiance is to anything short of the triune God and His word, our loyalties will be humanistically oriented. We will be overly-governed by groups and institutions, however good, and insufficiently governed by God the Lord. A prominent American political leader, a man of unique independence, once told me that peer pressure governs most politicians. Before their election, they are motivated by what they and their constituency want. After their election, the peer pressure of their new group now governs them, and they are less responsive to the demands of their electorate.

Peer pressure is a most potent force in the modern world because religious faith is by contrast weak and fragile. Indeed, in one church college, group dynamics are taught as an important and worthy source of social strength.

This goes hand in hand with a major shift in man's outlook which came progressively into force with the Enlightenment. The domain belonging to religion and the church was seen as the inner world, the spiritual life of man. The domain of reason and the state was held to be the material sphere. There is no warrant in Scripture for any such division. All things were made by God the Lord, and all things are subject to His law-word and government. His church must declare God's word and its relevance to all the world, the state no less than any other sphere. For the church to be silent in any sphere, or to limit the scope of God's government, law, and rule is to sin and to deny to that degree its Lord.

We are not therefore to be governed by our parochial loyalties, nor by group dynamics, nor by peer pressure. All our churches, institutions, groups, races, nationalities and allegiances must be subject to the prior government of the triune God and His law-word. Anything short of that is idolatry.

The fundamental declaration of God's law is this: "Thou shalt have no other gods before me" (Ex. 20:3). We must remember that even very good things can be turned into idols and false gods. For many their church is an idol, or their family, their children, their race, nationality, or group. However good these things may be, they can become and often are idols when we give them priority over the love of God, and, in that love of God, our love of our neighbor. A limited good, if given too high a place in our lives, can be as destruction or more than an open and obvious evil. Remember, such a perspective led men into crucifying Christ. (May, 1985)

THE CATHARS
Chalcedon Position Paper No. 63

One of the most prominent anti-Christian groups of the medieval era, which masked itself as true Christianity, was Catharism. They were a Manichean or dualistic people whose doctrines have deeply influenced and infiltrated into Christianity. In fact, most of the underground forces which earlier and later worked to undermine and destroy Christianity were dualistic.

The *first* article of faith with the Cathari was a belief in two ultimate powers or gods. The good god for them was the source of light and spirit. Being good, he did not create matter, which was bad. The evil god, equally strong, was the creator of the material world as a means of entrapping souls in the snares of evil.

This was a denial of the doctrine of the Trinity and also of Christ's incarnation. For the Cathari, the Word could not have been made flesh without having been made sinful. Christ only took on Himself the shadow or appearance of a man, but He was never truly man.

Again, the resurrection of the body was denied. Since flesh for them was evil, God would not glorify an evil nature by resurrecting it. Salvation for them was deliverance from the flesh, not its resurrection and glorification.

The *second* article of faith for the Cathari was the rejection of Biblical law. They held that "the law of Moses was given by the prince of darkness, that is, by the malignant god, while the law of the gospel was given by the prince of light, that is, by the merciful god." So hostile to the Old Testament were the Cathari that they held that *all* the Old Testament saints, Abraham, Moses, David, and even John the Baptist were damned because they belonged to the world of the law. Justice and the law belonged for them to the world of the evil god whom Christ came to repudiate. Salvation for them was deliverance from the flesh.

In Southern France, the Cathari were called Albigenses, after their stronghold in Albi; in Eastern Europe, they were called Bogomils, Bulgari, Bugares, and Bugres, from whence our word "bugger" comes. In the Near East, they were known as Paulicians.

Because of their contempt for the flesh, the Cathari despised sexuality. Marriage was seen as particularly evil because it gave respectability to what they regarded an evil act. To show their contempt for the holiness of marriage, the Cathari sometimes were ready to practice homosexuality as a means of desecration. Well into the modern era, various revolutionary and anti-Christian groups continued this use of homosexuality as a way of desacralizing the body. In Southern France, the Albigensians started their own school systems to undermine Christian teaching.

The Cathari had many sects, but, within their circles, they had two classes of members, the *Perfecti*, and the *Credentes*, or believers. The Cathari ate vegetables and fish; they refused to kill most animals, and they may have believed in metempsychosis, the return of the souls of the dead in the bodies of animals. Being against the law, they were against capital punishment, and they were pacifists of a sort.

In some areas where they were not as strong, the Cathari masqueraded as good Catholics. Historians are usually favorable to heretics and anti-Christians, so much remains to be explored here. We do know that the Cathari despised God's law and Biblical morality, and they did so in word and in deed. We know too that some had infiltrated the Catholic Church. It is an open question to what extent these covert Cathari applied their ideas towards corrupting men, women and children while serving as monks and priests. What we call corruption some of them saw as a moral duty.

Liberals and Protestants have often seen the Cathari as good people persecuted by the medieval church. As a result, they have been unwilling to accept the facts of their doctrine. Recent studies have more than confirmed that the Cathari were what the medieval church said they were. Far from being a happy, joyful people, they were a sour, dirty, and an evil group. They were pharisaical and censorious, and intensely self-righteous. They had re-defined Christianity in terms of pagan dualism, and their Christ bore little resemblance to the Christ of Scripture. They were New Testament "Christians" who had denied all of the Old Testament and the meaning of the New.

For the Cathari, salvation was deliverance from the flesh *and* from the law. Moses and the law were an obstacle to salvation, because the law assumed that God gave the law to govern the world He made. The Cathari denied that the good god made the world or gave a law to govern it.

The Cathari had a catalogue of deadly sins; these were the possession of earthly property, associating with men of this world, war, killing animals other than reptiles, eating animal food other than fish, and sexual intercourse. Suicide was common among the Cathari. The *Perfecti*, who had received the *consolamentum*, their sacrament, could lose their salvation if they sinned after receiving it. To avoid this, they committed suicide or were sometimes put to death by their families.

The Cathari thrived as an adversary group. They were at their best in ridiculing and undermining. In Bosnia-Herzegovina, they became Moslems and worked within Islam.

They left everywhere an evil heritage. *First of all*, they had a joy in perversity. The pleasures of sex for them were in sinning against the Christian God, in polluting and desacralizing marriage. A delight in sexual sin became an undercurrent in Christendom. The pleasure was not in sex, as such, but sex as sin, as an assault of Christian faith and morals. Denis de Rougemont's *Love in the Western World* studied the influence of this aspect of Manicheanism on Western thought and, in particular, on the Romantic movement. Mario Praz' *Romantic Agony* is pertinent to the same fact although its concerns were different. Significantly too, many subversive movements made a virtual ritual out of immorality and, in particular, of homosexuality.

Second, the Cathari hated property, because the ownership of houses, land, and things meant a concern over material things. Dualistic cults, on gaining power, legislate against private property. In fact, the first communist revolution, the Mazdakite revolution in Persia in the 5th and 6th centuries, required the total communization of property, money, and women. It also required incest within families to demonstrate adherence to that dualistic faith. The Christian Armenians resisted, and among the martyrs was Isaac, Bishop of the Rushdoonys, and, in the war which followed (451 A.D.), "The Troops of the Rushdoonys" are listed as very active by the ancient chronicler Yeghisheh.

The contempt for property and for material things is contempt for God and for His creation. It is a way of despising His good gifts and the godly uses we are to make of them. It is a rejection of the dominion mandate (Gen. 1:26-28) to exercise dominion and to subdue the earth and make it God's Kingdom. Christians are all too deeply infected by this Manichean strain.

Third, pacifism was advocated by the Cathari. This great profession of being lovers of peace did not make them less active in waging war against Catholics. In the crusade against them in Southern France, they took a heavy toll of their enemies. By professing to be "peace lovers," they gained credit for pacifism while being ready to wage war. They were strong for the non-killing of all non-reptilian animals, but they were prone to suicide and murder. They had no sound perspective on human life and animal life.

Fourth, their hostility to marriage made them enemies of the basic institution in God's created order, the family. Being married and having children was for them evidence of imperfection and sin.

Europe and the churches did not follow the Cathari prescription concerning marriage, but it is strange that what was in Scripture the key institution has been until recently so little studied by scholars. Our view of culture is warped because it is not family oriented.

Fifth, Catharism placed all the emphasis in salvation on what man does, none on what God has done through Christ. The Cathari were strong "free will" advocates. For them, all men have the principle of self-salvation in themselves, their souls. Man's soul is good, and man needs only become spiritual by an act of will, by renouncing material things, and he can be saved. Christ came to make men spiritual, because for the Cathari spirituality is by definition good and matter by definition evil. For them, there was no true fall, only commingling of matter and spirit and salvation was separation from material things and from all adherence to material or physical things, such as marriage and property.

Six, the Cathari were totally antinomian; they hated and denied Biblical law and declared it to be the work of the evil god of the Old Testament, the creator god. As a result, the Cathari could not create a social order; they were a negative group. By their spirituality, they were by choice irrelevant to life's problems, battles, and victories. The law is God's justice or righteousness, His plan for establishing His Kingdom. The Cathari denied the law of God and the very idea of law because law seeks to order the historical, material world in terms of a religious faith. Our faith determines what kind of law and order will govern and direct society. Islamic faith and law give us one pattern, Hinduism another, Buddhism still another. The Biblical doctrine of order is set forth in God's law. The Cathari were by their faith hostile to all order because they rejected creation, matter, and history. Salvation for them was withdrawal from history.

In this respect, they left a deadly legacy of antinomianism and false spirituality to the church. Catholics and Protestants have often alike been infected by the Catharist retreat from history. When we strip the anti-Christian glamorization from the Cathari, we see them as a sad, retreatist group of people with no real future because of their rejection of history.

Marc Block, in *Feudal Society*, cited by Jaroslav Pelikan in *The Growth of Medieval Theology* (600-1300), said, "If I were to sum up in two words what I believe is the essential message of medieval thought, I would say: it is the spirit in which it restated tradition; and this spirit is Faith and Joy." A Catholic scholar, Friedrich Heer, in *The Medieval World*, described "the sense of great joy and inward freedom" which marked the early church and many centuries after. As the medieval era progressed, this joy gave way, Heer said, to "feelings of terror and estrangement" and a fearfulness before God. The burden of sin replaced the freedom of forgiveness.

This was not all. The leadership had left the faith. As Heer pointed out, "In the Italian cities of the twelfth and early thirteenth centuries it was tacitly accepted that highly respected noblemen and women were 'heretics'; indeed, in Italy at this time *nobile* was synonymous with 'heretic.'"

The Cathari had left an ugly inheritance. Spirituality had come to mean impracticality and retreatism. Christian thinkers were becoming irrelevant, pietistic, and mystical. The same is true again in our time, and its consequences have been deadly.

Christianity is much more than a spiritual religion. It is faith in the creator and living God, Father, Son, and Holy Ghost, who requires of us that we occupy till He come, and that all things be brought into captivity to Christ the King. The crown rights of Christ the Lord require this of us. (June, 1985)

RELIGIOUS LIBERTY AND DOMINION
Chalcedon Position Paper No. 64

When the Supreme Court, in early June, 1985, ruled against prayer in the "public" schools, even if it were silent prayer, there was much jubilation in humanistic circles and some dismay in church responses. Prayer in state schools dedicated to humanism and anti-Christianity was in itself no great advantage. Prayer in these schools for illiteracy and paganism would be inappropriate, as would be mandatory prayers in houses of prostitution. How can there be a blessing on the systematic neglect of the triune God? If faith without works is dead (James 2:14-26), so too is prayer without works. We cannot ask God to bless what is against His will, nor us if we are where we ought not to be.

Some very important issues were raised, however, by the Supreme Court's decision. Implicit in the Court's perspective and decision was what *The Stockton* (California) *Record* made explicit in an editorial, June 6,1985, "School Prayer Ruling Sound" (p. 12): "The Know-Nothings are at it already, calling the latest Supreme Court ruling on prayer in the schools 'an act of war against this nation's heritage.' The ruling, quite to the contrary, is an affirmation of this nation's religious heritage. That heritage was *religion is a private, personal matter* and that government can neither promote nor proscribe its practice."

It is emphatically true that the U.S. Constitution held "that government can neither promote or proscribe" religious practice on the federal level. In recent years, this has been extended to the states. The premise of this perspective is that God's Kingdom cannot be controlled by the state. The early church fought for this, as did the medieval and the modern church. Limits were thereby placed on the power and jurisdiction of the state, limits which the courts now treat as non-existent. If the church enjoys any immunities, it is viewed as a state grant and subject to statist change and control.

The central evil of the modern view is that "religion is a private, personal matter." This is a revolutionary idea, a product of the modern era and of revolutionary ideologies. Basic to the Western world has been the premise that, because the God of the Scriptures is the living God, the Maker of heaven and earth and all things therein, any attempt to establish man and society apart from Him and His law is suicidal. Because the triune God is the way, the truth, and the life (John 14:6), any attempt to establish anything apart from Him is a lie and a deadly venture (Ps. 127:1; Prov. 8:36). In terms of this, the free exercise of religion is a necessity in order that the wellsprings of human life be nourished, personally and socially.

To say that "religion is a private, personal matter" is to say that it is irrelevant. You and I may enjoy crossword puzzles, but such things are not public concerns, merely private ones.

On the contrary, however, the faith of a people is the most public of all concerns. In a very real sense, the life of the people depends upon its faith. What the state is, and its strength and virtue, depends upon the faith and character of the people, and the integrity of the church's witness. The state can be no stronger than its people and their faith. Our problem in the modern world is that nations confuse strength with armament and with controls over the people.

When the state limits the scope and freedom of Christianity, it limits its own strength and paves the way for its destruction. It is not an accident that the de-Christianization of schools and state since World War II have been followed by a great increase in crime, drug use, illegitimacy, sexual crimes, perversions, pornography, and more.

In this process, it must be noted, the churches have had a great part. By their growing modernism, their socialist gospel, and their faith in statist salvation, they have become gravediggers for both church and state.

Religion is both a public and a private concern. To restrict it to a personal matter is to deny its truth and to deny Christianity religious liberty. If "religion is a private, personal matter," then religious liberty has a very narrow scope; the area of religious freedom then, as attorney William Bently Ball has noted, is the distance between our two ears. If "religion is a private, personal matter" then it has *no legitimate place on the public scene*. It should then be barred, as the courts have progressively done, from the schools, the state, and all public agencies.

Of course, what is not barred is the new established religion, humanism. It is the new public faith, and its articles of faith are routinely affirmed by public figures as a public duty. The obscurantists deny that humanism exists or dominates; this does not say much for their honesty.

The Stockton Record went on to say, "It is a mis-reading of the Supreme Court's 1962 decision on organized prayer in public schools and its ruling this week to suggest the court has banned prayer in public schools. It has only prohibited government involvement in a private matter. Anyone can silently pray any time, any place and for any reason; government cannot suggest such prayer or ban it."

Again, this limits religious freedom to a purely private and personal realm. Such editorial writers are silent when Christian Home School parents, and Christian Schools, are on trial. Court ordered testing has repeatedly demonstrated the far greater scholastic achievements of such students, but the courts show no regard for their religious freedom. Do such people really believe in religious freedom for Christians? The past decade has seen the persecution and at times imprisonment of pastors and parents. The press which heralded this recent Supreme Court decision has usually been silent in these other cases. Is this not hypocrisy? And how long will the state respect freedom of the press when it destroys freedom of religion? The press, by approving the court's growing fascism, is preparing the way for its own destruction.

The Stockton Record quoted Justice John Paul Stevens (our John Paul III?) as insisting, in the majority opinion of the Court, that the school prayer violates the "established principle that the government must pursue a course of complete neutrality toward religion." The state can have such a neutrality only after the Court can negate gravity and float in space as it renders its godlike decisions! The state rests on law; all law is enacted morality and represents as such a religious foundation and a religious faith about good and evil, right and wrong. Neutral laws cannot exist. Laws against murder rest on the premise that man is created in God's image and must live by God's law.

Peter J. Ferrara, in *The Wall Street Journal* ("Reading Between the Lines of the School-Prayer Decision," Tuesday, June 11, 1985, p. 32), said: "The fact that a moment of silence is inherently neutral between prayer and other forms of meditation or contemplation should have been sufficient for the court to uphold the Alabama law. The majority's suggestion that students would somehow be bullied into praying by the history of the Alabama statute or the expressed hope by some legislators that students would use the time to pray, surpasses fantasy. Moreover, in straining so mightily to hold the statute unconstitutional, the court communicated a message to the public of hostility to religion."

In this century, we have seen a massive persecution of various religions (Buddhists in Tibet, Jews in the Soviet Union, Moslems in Albania, Bahais in Iran), but most of all of Christianity. The Marxist states have, since World War I, slaughtered millions; Turkey massacred Christian Armenians and Greeks; Africa has seen countless massacres in recent years, as has southeast Asia; Cuba has persecuted Christians, as have many other states. The Christian victims number into many tens of millions. The world press has been largely silent on these matters, and increasingly so.

In fact, many editorial writers act and write on the premise that Christians are persecuting them when they protest such treatment! This should not surprise us: a bully with a bad conscience hates and resents his victims because he knows their presence is an indictment of him. I was told of a schoolyard bully who loved to pick on and mercilessly pummel boys smaller than himself. Then, as he started to leave, he would turn on his victim, or a bystander, saying, "You don't like it, do you?", and, whatever the answer, beat up on them at once. Not even an unspoken dissent is tolerable to a bully. The bully press has a very loud voice, and it knows that its enemies have a very small one.

The new definition of religious liberty is tailor-made to destroy Christianity. By reducing its freedom to "a private, personal" realm, it is doing what the Soviet Union has done. This kind of "religious freedom" exists in the Soviet Union. Practically, it means that parents cannot speak about their faith to their children. In some states of the U.S., parents can be jailed for educating their own children, i.e., by applying their Christian faith to education. In the Soviet Union, husband and wife are often silent about their faith one to another; in a time of trouble, such knowledge can be used against them.

As the Soviet Union defines religious liberty, i.e., as a private personal matter, it can and does boast of its record of religious freedom. What faith men hold between their two ears, they are free to hold!

But Christianity cannot be so restricted. It governs our lives, our marriages, children, homes, schools, churches, civil governments, vocations, arts, sciences, and all things else. It governs them by governing us and making us instruments of God's law and order. It makes us dominion men so that God's Kingdom is manifested in and through us.

To do this, Christian faith transforms old institutions into new ones and creates new agencies for the new life. It can only do this if our faith is for us a personal and a public concern, the way of life for man and for society. If Christianity does not do this, it perishes.

This is what our Lord means when He says, "I am come to shed fire on the earth" (Luke 12:49). What He gives is not a purely private and personal matter: it is a transforming power which will destroy what needs destruction, renovate what needs renovation, and build what needs to be built and established.

The Lord declares, "Behold, I make all things new" (Rev. 21:5). Where men prefer their ways to God's justice, they will resent and wage war against God's remaking of all things. Because they see themselves as their own gods, and man as his own source of law (Gen. 3:5) they want no part of the faith. They will seek to suppress and destroy it without being honest enough to say so.

This should not surprise us. It is logical on the part of unbelievers. It has been this way all through history.

The important question is this: what will those who call themselves Christians do about this? Will they be silent "mummified" churchmen, as General William Booth described them, or will they be the Lord's dominion men? (July, 1985)

THE DEFINITION OF INSANITY
Chalcedon Position Paper No. 65

The question of insanity has not greatly troubled most people in our time. Many accept the usual psychiatric definitions with their pseudo-scientific terminology. These have been ably attacked by another psychiatrist, Dr. Thomas Szasz, who sees insanity as a game people play to evade responsibilities. Except where a physical problem exists, i.e., senility or paresis, insanity is seen by Dr. Szasz as a creation of medical and psychoanalytic practitioners rather than as an actual mental disease. Early in the history of psychiatry, the prevalent "disease" was hysteria, and hysteria became commonplace. When it was debunked, it quickly disappeared as a social problem.

The fact remains, as someone observed recently, there seem to be many insane people running loose, and not in Washington only! What is the matter with them? Treating such people is a growth industry, and our medical schools are training many psychiatric practitioners. The theories about insanity (or "mental illness") produced by these practitioners are having a major influence on our courts and legislators and are subverting criminal law, among many other things. As a result, it is necessary to think seriously about the matter. If crime is a product of mental illness, for example, the criminal is then seen as the victim, not the victimizer. If alcoholism is a mental illness, then the drunk driver who kills someone is not charged with murder, but the bartender or host is treated as legally liable to pay large sums in compensation to the dead person's family. The Biblical doctrine of responsibility ("the soul that sinneth, it shall die" Ezek. 18:4) is replaced with an environmental premise.

We must therefore insist that insanity is an evasion of responsibility. Even more, it is a flight from reality. It must follow, moreover, that since God is the absolute reality by whom all things were made, to deny the triune God is irrational and a departure from reality. Atheism is thus insane, and atheists do not think realistically because they think without God. If the Bible is true, then to deny it and to try to think and live without God is insane. To have schools without Christ, politics without the Lord, or anything without the Creator is to forsake reality and to court suicide.

This must be the foundation of our thinking, but we dare not take statist steps in dealing with the problem. This has been done, and the courts regularly confine people as "insane." In the early years of the republic, Warren Chase tells us that a Bostonian was sentenced to sixty days in prison "for publishing in his own paper that he did not believe in their orthodox God" (Warren Chase: *The Life-Line of the Lone One*, p. 23. 1881.) In 1873, Mrs. E. P. W. Packard wrote a two volume account on imprisonment in asylums for expressing disbelief in certain doctrines of the church (*Modern Persecutions, or Insane Asylums Unveiled*).

What these and other like actions revealed was a confusion of issues, and of truth and error. For these people who confined others as mad because of their unbelief, conversion had given way to coercion. Instead of relying on the Holy Spirit and the Bible, they relied on their own, humanistic, coercive power. The faith was harmed rather than served thereby. They were right in seeing unbelief and atheism as a departure from reality. They were very dangerously wrong in seeing coercion rather than conversion as the solution.

The Christian has this remarkable recourse: what man cannot do, God can do, i.e., change the heart and nature of men. Coercion is dangerous because at best it brings an outward conformity without an inward change. It produces phariseeism, not Christianity, and the consequences are evil.

Humanism does not believe in supernatural re-generation. It must therefore place its hopes on education and coercion. Its doctrine of education soon becomes a form of coercion with statist controls and regulations. Horace Mann and his successors to the contrary, state control of education has not created the hoped for humanistic millennium, the Great Community, but rather a decaying and collapsing social order. As a result, humanism's hope for change is now predominantly in statist coercion.

A key part of this coercion in the Soviet Union is psychiatry. Mental sickness is now defined as social deviation from the Marxist regime. Because Marxism is defined as the salvation of man, anyone who opposes the Marxist power is thereby seen as an enemy of man and as mentally sick. In the Soviet Union, such people are committed to prison-like hospitals; their minds are broken down with powerful drugs to make them recant. One Soviet banner in a prison read, "In a socialist state there can be no social basis for infringement of the law." The dissidents are therefore sociopaths by definition. They have taken leave of their senses and do not comprehend reality. Psychiatrists treat anti-state activity as insanity.

It must be recognized, however, that any and every humanistic society will move in the same direction as the Soviet Union because it holds to the same religion, humanism. Here in the United States, one mother, whose husband was a scientist, was called to a state school for consultation. Her son, she was told over the telephone, was manifesting "deviant behavior." This statement left her in a state of shock. She went over every kind of "deviant behavior" she could think of; she was sure her boy was not guilty on all scores. But, then, why was she called to school unless something gross and serious occurred? Arriving at school sick at heart, she learned that her son's "problem" and "deviant behavior" was an absorption in books when other children were playing! In anger and shock, she called attention to the fact that her husband was a scientist, that she had done some graduate work, and that they were surrounded by books; professors and scholars were commonly guests in their home. Her son's absorption with reading was a natural outcome of his family life; he was a happy child, doing what his aptitudes led him to do. The counselor and teacher were unmoved; for them social integration was all important. The boy showed no hostility to any race or group, and, in fact, came from a family open to a variety of peoples. This meant nothing to the statist staff members: the boy's behavior was deviant, and, for them, social integration was basic to "education."

Unusual? Not at all. In public discussions as well as in court trials, the point made over and over again by the enemies of the Christian or the Home School is that the child may do well academically, or even better, but that the child in non-state schools is "deprived" of the social integration necessary for his or her development.

The unspoken thesis is that the child who is not in touch with the state school staff and children is not being prepared to face "the real world." (This argument I heard today in a telephone conversation, and it came from a supposedly Christian woman!) For all such people, reality, the basic reality we are all supposed to keep in touch with, is the world of anti-Christianity, of humanism, and immoralism. We are not supposed to "deprive" our children of their time in the sewer.

If God is the key to all reality, then any education or living apart from Him is madness. It is education for disaster and for suicide. If God be God, to act as though He does not exist is death. It means that any godless education, politics, economics, science, entertainment, or anything else is out of touch with reality.

It is not poetry when the psalmist declares, "Except the LORD build the house, they labour in vain that build it: except the Lord keep the city, the watchman waketh but in vain" (Ps. 237:1). We are plainly told that it is futile to plan any national defense if our lives are not grounded in the triune God and His law-word.

The word we have used repeatedly is insanity, a word which, while in popular use, is decried by sociologists and anthropologists. The term they prefer is "mental disease." According to the *Dictionary of Sociology*, "The term insanity is gradually giving place to mental disease, the latter term being more accurate and less socially derogatory and humiliating." In the definition of "mental disorder," we are told: "Whether or not certain mental phenomena are to be considered 'normal' and are therefore not further complicated by social stigma and maladjustment, is largely a matter of definition of situation in terms of the current culture." In other words, the current culture defines what is a mental disease or a mental disorder.

This is a definition from an American work. It is in substance the same as the Soviet Union's definition of insanity. The difference is not in definition but in application. In the Soviet Union, dissidents are taken to prison hospitals and treated as mentally sick. This is not yet routine in the United States; instead, dissidents are treated as "extremists" who represent "the lunatic fringe" of American Life.

It is clear, thus, that the definition of insanity is not a trifling or academic matter. It is a matter of life and death.

Jesus Christ, who was most in total harmony with God the Father, and thus with reality, manifested His triumph over the tempter and the fall, when He declared "It is written, man shall not live by bread alone, but by every word that proceedeth out of the mouth of God" (Matt. 4:4). The more we live in Christ and by God's every word, the more we live in terms of reality, with sanity and wisdom as well as grace.

The Fall was an act of sin and as such insanity also. Man, the creature, decided to be his own god and law, determining good and evil for himself and being his own law-maker (Gen. 3:5). For man to declare his independence from God, and to place himself on the same level as God, was and is insanity and sin. It was and is the supreme act of irresponsibility. Ever since, the world has been under the sway of sin and death.

The remedy for this insanity of sin is not coercion but conversion. Humanism creates a coercive state because it denies supernatural regeneration in favor of statist power and control as the remedy for man's disorder.

The Christian must oppose the coercive state and stress the necessity for regeneration as man's sole hope of salvation and sanity. (August, 1985)

CATHOLICITY
Chalcedon Position Paper No. 66

In the earliest forerunners of the Apostles' Creed, we find the confession, "I believe...in the holy church." In its final form, this became, "the holy catholic church." The word "catholic" comes from two Greek words, *kata*, concerning, and *holos*, whole, meaning universal. This catholicity, universality or all-inclusiveness of the Kingdom of God was declared by Paul in Galatians 3:28: "There is neither Jew nor Greek, there is neither bond nor free, there is neither male nor female: for ye are all one in Christ Jesus." Status before the Lord does not depend upon status before men; salvation is for all peoples. The distinctions which remain are thus those required by God's law word, not those created by men.

This was the practice of the early church. An interesting example was Callistus, who became Bishop of Rome in 220. Some years earlier, Callistus, then a pagan slave, had been imprisoned for theft. As pope, Callistus I allowed the marriage of patrician girls to freedmen, something forbidden by Roman law. We do not know whether or not this contributed to Callistus' martyrdom. What we do know is that more than a few men of low estate, like Callistus, governed over Christians with an aristocratic status. What counted in the church was a person's status before the Lord rather than before men.

While the word "catholic" came into usage slowly, it did very early mark the life of the church. Catholicity means not only universal, but also universal jurisdiction. Because the Head of the church is Jesus Christ, who is "the blessed and only Potentate, the King of Kings, and Lord of lords" (I Tim. 6:15), the church is catholic or universal because our King has universal jurisdiction.

It was this fact that made the declaration, "Jesus Christ is Lord" (Phil 2:9-11), the baptismal confession of the early church.

We must not forget that Rome, the empire, saw herself as "eternal Rome" and thus as universal Rome. Its required confession of allegiance was, "Caesar is Lord," and the obvious implication was that Caesar was the catholic or universal lord.

The result was conflict. Two powers, Caesar and his empire, and Christ and His church, both claimed catholicity. Rome fought Christianity as she did no other religion. Herbert B. Workman, in *Persecution in the Early Church* (1906), stated the issue: "The Christians were not persecuted because of their creed, but because of their universal claims." Their offense was "this universality of claim, this aggressiveness of temper, this consciousness from the first of world-wide dominion -- in a word, all that in later days was summed up in the title of Catholic."

It is a sad fact that for many who call themselves "Catholics," the word is a name, not a fact, and that for many Protestants the word is something they are against, not something that describes the church, something saints died for.

When Callistus, in violation of Roman law, said that freed slaves could marry noble women, it was a radical step. Rome had all kinds of legal lines of separation. There was no equal standing before the law. A Roman citizen was a privileged person, a member of the ruling class.

In the third century, however, by an edict of Caracalla, all free inhabitants of the Roman Empire were given the status of citizens. At the same time, efforts were soon made to compel all inhabitants to observe the old Roman religion as the one universal or catholic faith. They could hold their personal religion on a local, private basis; the public faith had to be that of Rome, the imperial cult. This was the required and "catholic" faith. The result was more Christian martyrs.

The catholicity of the church had been an offense to Rome, and as a result the Roman Empire developed, re-asserted, and increased its own claim to catholicity. Catholic Rome and Catholic Church battled for supremacy and universality.

All this is very important for us to know. If we forget their meaning, forgotten past victories become present defeats. Because Rome insisted that the Empire alone was catholic or universal in its jurisdiction, all religions had to be local, limited, and personal, not public and catholic. All other religions were agreeable to such a place; Christianity alone insisted on the universal jurisdiction of Jesus Christ as Lord and Savior, and the church as Christ's catholic voice on earth.

Today we face a similar battle. The modern state sees itself as catholic, i.e., universal. Within its borders it asserts total power and jurisdiction. It sees freedom in any sphere as a state grant, not as a God given immunity. As a result, the state, its legislatures, and its courts, increasingly seek to extend the powers of the state as the logic of catholicity.

To this, all too many churchmen have agreed. We have the immoral horror of many church leaders who claim to believe the Bible from cover to cover insisting they cannot take a stand against abortion or homosexuality, for example, because it would be the "social gospel" to do so. For them, Christianity's only concern is saving souls. This would reduce Christianity to the status of Rome's mystery religions, i.e., to paganism and to a denial of Christ's catholicity of power and jurisdiction.

Antinomianism too is a denial of catholicity. God's law is His plan of government for every sphere of life. It is the expression of God's dominion as Creator and Lord or Sovereign, and it is His plan for covenant man to exercise dominion. To live under a foreign law is to be a slave, however comfortable the slavery. The laws of the nations are today humanistic laws. They are motivated by an anti-Christian faith and purpose. The society they envision and educate for is one aiming to destroy Christianity totally. Antinomianism surrenders Christ's lordship or sovereignty to the state and is the expression of a people who are in captivity and love it.

We must remember that it was the best Roman emperors who were usually the worst persecutors. As Workman pointed out, the more faithfully Roman they were, the more zealously they persecuted the church to preserve Rome's exclusive and total jurisdiction. Today also, a "good" humanist civil ruler is often a major problem to the church, because the rigors of statist claims over the church increase. Thus, to vote for a "good" humanist can mean voting in a man more dedicated than most to the idea of a catholic state.

When the word "catholic" was first used by the early church, it was to designate the church as Christ's body, open to all mankind, in order to distinguish the church from the Jewish congregations. Both originally called themselves synagogues, or assemblies. The Christian synagogue was the one summoning all mankind to Christ without the necessity of becoming Jews first.

One of the earliest uses of the word is by St. Ignatius, in "The Epistle to the Smyrnaeans," chapter 8, who said, "wherever Jesus Christ is, there is the catholic church." The word "catholic" was also used by Polycarp, according to Eusebius' *Church History*, IV, 15.

In its earliest usage, the word "catholic" meant *first*, more than Jewish; many churchmen were Jews, but the church was inclusive of all peoples. *Second*, as problems developed in the church, the word early came to mean "orthodox" as against "heretical." The catholic faith, while still persecuted, had to defend itself against a variety of false and anti-Christian doctrines which had been brought in by various peoples. Both these meanings were accurate: the true church was more than Jewish, and it was orthodox, not heretical. These were, however, subordinate meanings. Catholic means universality of scope and of jurisdiction.

To proclaim the catholic faith thus meant and means to set forth "the crown rights of Christ the King" over every area of life and thought. Indeed, "The Crown Rights of Christ the King" was a Puritan battle cry in Cromwell's day. One of the texts most used to set forth the church's catholicity has been Hebrews 12:22-24: "But ye are come unto mount Sion, and unto the city of the living God, the heavenly Jerusalem, and to an innumerable company of angels, To the general assembly and church of the first born, which are written in heaven, and to God the Judge of all, and to the spirits of just men made perfect, And to Jesus the mediator of the new covenant, and to the blood of sprinkling, that speaketh better things than that of Abel."

This tells us, *first*, that the covenant has been renewed; in Jesus Christ we are again at Mount Sion, and there the old covenant is made with a new people, now God's new Israel and chosen ones. *Second*, this realm is also "the city of the living God." "City" here means kingdom or realm, as the City of Rome. St. Augustine, in writing on *The City of God* in this sense, meant the Kingdom of God. *Third*, this realm is also "the heavenly Jerusalem," so that it is more than natural. It is a supernatural kingdom which is inclusive of all God's creation, natural and supernatural.

Fourth, this supernatural aspect and power of Christ's catholic or universal jurisdiction includes "an innumerable company of angels" who are, with us, fellow subjects and citizens of Christ's Kingdom.

Fifth, this Kingdom has the church as part of its jurisdiction, "the general assembly and church of the firstborn." Christ is the firstborn, and, as members of His Body, we are in union with the great company of heavenly powers that are part of His realm.

Sixth, these are all, ourselves included, "written in heaven" because our membership in Christ is not our doing but God's grace through Jesus Christ.

Seventh, because this catholic realm is total in its jurisdiction over all things in heaven and earth, God is "the Judge of all." All things and all peoples are accountable to Him because God's power and jurisdiction are catholic and total.

Eighth, this Kingdom includes "the spirits of just men made perfect," i.e., those saints who have died and are now with their Lord.

Ninth, supremely, it includes our Savior and mediator, through whose atoning blood we have been made members of this catholic or universal Kingdom or empire.

The modern state is a false messiah, a false savior. Its only legitimate place is under Christ, together with the church, family, school, our vocations, the arts and sciences, and all things else. The claims of the state to universal jurisdiction, to catholicity, are a lie. Do you believe and serve that lie, or is Christ your Lord? (September, 1985)

ELITISM
Chaldcedon Position Paper No. 67

It is a significant fact that Karl Marx championed equalitarianism while being an elitist. The two go together. Honest men know the limitations of all men and that equality and inequality are myths. They are essentially mathematical terms which cannot do justice to the diversity of life. You and I may excel in doing certain things and feel totally incompetent in other areas. A man can be a mathematical genius and also incompetent in simple household repairs. If we were all equal, we would all be omnicompetent and would not need each other. This is why equalitarian regimes are so murderous: they see all men as readily replaceable and readily disposable, except for the elite few, the philosopher-kings.

The great sourcebook for elitism is Plato's *Republic*. Its doctrine of justice is humanistic to the core: "Everyone ought to perform the one function in the community for which his nature best suited him. Well, I believe that principle, or some form of it, is justice." This justice means that society must be ruled by philosopher-kings. Under them are the guardians: soldiers and public officials. Most people must make up the masses; they are the slaves, and their virtue must be temperance, meaning self-restraint and obedience.

For such a "republic" to work, Plato felt that two factors which make for individualism had to go: property and the family. Private property must be abolished, and child-bearing must be regulated and strictly controlled.

But this is not all. Basic to the ideal "republic" or elitist state is the state control of all education. This means also the control of books, music, and popular entertainment .

Later elitists refined the controls. Sir Thomas More, one of the uglier figures of the renaissance era, a man who lived badly but died well, added to Plato's communism the control of money. Gold should be used only for making slave chains and chamber pots. Lenin was pleased with the latter part of this plan by More and adopted it. Much later, Edward Bellamy, in *Looking Backward* (1888), wanted state-issued credit cards to replace money. (This would enable the state to starve dissidents into submission.)

Chad Walsh, in *From Utopia to Nightmare* (1962), cited the principle articles of faith held by utopians. Four of these are of concern to us. *First*, man is basically good. The doctrine of original sin is anathema to elitists, because it places all men on common ground before God; it is perhaps the only valid form of equalitarianism. *Second*, man is plastic man; he has no fixed nature and can be readily molded to suit the goals of the philosopher-kings. The doctrine of evolution is an elitist myth which "vindicates" the elitist world view. It means that the elite can remake man and the world after their image. Much science is devoted now to such goals. *Third*, individual happiness is only possible in any true sense if society is served and flourishes; to seek happiness in separation from the goals of society is subversive and is not true joy. Hence in the Soviet state, the workman who surpasses the work goals is the happy man, because he sees his good and joy in terms of social goals. Fourth, man is a rational being who can become more systematically rational. Society will flourish as reason and science flourish. Hence, the philosopher-kings, as reason incarnate, must guide the state and the masses into the life of reason. The implication in all such elitist orders is that submission to the state and its elite is submission to pure reason, and revolt against the elite is irrationalism.

Thus, in every elitist social order, the elite holds this as a fixed premise: think as we do, and you are a sane and rational man; if you disagree with us, you are a social deviate with a serious mental problem.

Almost all nations are now ruled by elitists. When men depart from Christianity, they abandon hierarchy, which means sacred rule in terms of God's law-word, for man's rule by elitists. These elitist rulers have more in common one with another than with their own peoples. Elitists love elitists, or at the least prefer them. Our elitists in the United States have made us allies in effect of Red China and the Soviet Union, but not of the Republic of South Africa. Although the R.S.A. has many points in common with them, economic controls for one, it still smacks too much of the old order of Europe and must be destroyed. Red China has the world's most murderous abortion laws, and extensive state-created famine, but no one proposes disinvestment in Red China, except a few students. The Soviet Union has its slave labor camps and planned genocide, but where are the demands for disinvestment in the USSR?

Elitists love other elitists; they profess to love the masses and are militant equalitarians in legislation and snobs in person. The elitist loves "exclusive" places; he will patronize with delight a fine restaurant if few know about it, but, let it become too popular, and it is "spoiled." He loves out-of-the-way places to travel to and rhapsodizes over them, but let a few "common people" begin to enjoy the same place and he sees it as "commercialized" and spoiled.

The elitist hates the free market because it gives in its own way a good form of democracy. In a free market economy, most men, if they want them, can earn enough for an automobile, television, and their own house. In this way, they pass out of the servant class ("It's so hard to get good servants these days") into the middle class, and this means an independence from the elite. The great evil of Puritanism and of Cromwell to the English elite was that "Merry England" was "destroyed," since now no large class of servitors were bowing and scraping before them. For some ever since, the restoration of such an order has been a dream, whereas their ex-servitors in many cases want to hurt "the ruling class" even if it destroys the country in the process.

Elitism is common to all spheres. Its origins are commonly in Plato, for whom the true universals are abstractions, or ideas, or principles, not the concrete universal, the triune God. Recently, on a trip, one earnest person, who knew the Bible well, asked me in some bewilderment, "I know my Bible, I know Jesus Christ as my Lord and Savior, and I try to live by God's word, but what are these principles our school principal keeps talking about?" Neither Christ nor the Bible can be reduced to a *Greek* abstraction or principle: there is never anything abstract about Scripture. Theft, murder. adultery, false witness and more are forbidden, not because of some abstract principle, but because God says so. Tithing is required, the sabbath rest is mandatory, and short term debt and more is the law of God, not because of some abstract principle, but because we are God's creation and property, and He commands us. Principles lead us to another religion; faithfulness leads us to the Lord.

Elitism takes other forms as well in the church. The Bible gives us legitimate and God-ordained types and symbols which are specific and concrete: they refer to Christ, our salvation and sanctification, and the like. Biblical typology is open to all believers; it is not esoteric. Symbolic theology is elitism. Who but those scholars who know fertility cult-religions and have studied under one or two esoteric seminary professors will ever see, in the plain words of Scripture, the hidden and esoteric meanings in the conflict between Moses and Zipporah over circumcision? And what believer, reading the account of the first passover in Egypt, could even imagine that the sides of the door represented a woman's legs, the top her pubic area, and the blood of the lamb a woman's hymeneal blood on her wedding night? When the Bible tells us that Christ is God's passover lamb, what believer will look for an abstract symbol or principle?

Elitism governs the academic community of our time. In the seminaries, professors tend to look down on those students who intend to be pastors; the favored students are the potential professors. For them, religion often is something to dissect and discuss, not marching orders from the Lord God. For this reason, most seminaries tend to do their students more harm than good. It is of significance that today the fastest growing churches are those which do not require seminary training.

Colleges and universities are schools of elitists. They are hostile often to true scholars as well as to most students. The theory held by intellectuals is that their intelligence sets them apart and makes them distinctive. However, as one professor, a true scholar, once remarked to me, few places are more governed by the mores of a wolf pack than the university. It is not intelligence that makes men strong and independent, but rather faith and character.

As we have noted, elitism stresses education, but it is humanistic education. Such schooling does not breed freedom nor independence but an emphasis on the group. Peer pressure then governs people. When a child begins to attend a state school, that child very soon is governed by his peer group, the other students, and the directions given to the peer group come from the statist educators. The result is a growing breach between the child and his home.

Elitism is moreover very prone to styles, fashions, and fads. These can be with respect to clothing, foods, ideas, recreations, and more. There are continual changes in what is acceptable, because the elite want to be different, and the imitating masses want to follow their trends. It is ironic that for elitism the consent of the governed, according to Plato, is "where the desires of the inferior multitude will be controlled by the desires and wisdom of the few." Now that the elite set the trends for the masses, they long to be different, and they alter their styles and tastes to show their difference.

As we have seen, for Plato (and Socrates), justice is an elitist doctrine. It means that all people do what the elite feels is best for them to do. In Plato's words "we have laid down, as a universal principle, that everyone ought to perform the one function in the community for which his nature best suited him. Well, I believe that principle, or some form of it, is justice." Notice that Plato, the elitist, lays down a principle, a rationalistic premise. Disagree, and you go to a slave labor camp or to execution. God instead gives us commandments and laws which we are to obey. These are not ideas to discuss and try to understand but marching orders for life. God's laws are more intelligent than all the intellectualism of Plato and every elitist since then, because God's law-word sets forth the way of life, of faith, and of understanding. We are plainly told, "The fear of the LORD is the beginning of knowledge, but fools despise wisdom and instruction" (Prov. 1:7). Again, "For the LORD giveth wisdom: out of his mouth cometh knowledge and understanding" (Prov. 2:6). This not a principle: it is a fact of life. It presupposes that God made the world and all things therein, and all creation is governed and judged by Him. Elitism presupposes a self-created world; it has thrived on the myth of evolution. In that world of brute factuality, there is no law-word of God. Man therefore fashions ideas or principles with which he proposes to govern and rule the world. When Christians try to combine God and principles, they try to join what cannot be joined.

In earlier years, I felt that the Hellenic concept of ideas or principles was too deeply enmeshed in our thinking for eradication. I have since come to the conviction that it is wrong to compromise with such thinking, or attempt to use and direct it, as I did earlier. Our duty is to be faithful; the results are in the hands of God. (October, 1985)

JUSTICE AND TORTURE
Chalcedon Position Paper No. 68

An important and neglected fact of Biblical law has to do with "confession." The appearances of this word in any form are restricted to the confession of sins before God. Leviticus 5:5 requires it as a part of the trespass offering. Leviticus 16:21 tells us that Aaron confessed the sins of all Israel and laid them on the scapegoat for atonement. Leviticus 26:40 refers to the confession of apostasy. Numbers 5:7 is again about the confession of sin before atonement.

An amazing fact emerges: Biblical law gives no place to the confession of a criminal offense as a means of court trial and conviction. H.B. Clark's *Biblical Law*, an old legal study, has no entry for it. Very clearly, in Biblical law there was to be no conviction on confession.

The Bible gives us a remarkable instance of this, Achan's offense. The enormity of his crime against God and Israel is stressed; men died because of it. God required the death penalty for the offender, and He also gave to Joshua a supernatural means of discovering the offender. Joshua then appealed to Achan to "give glory to the LORD God of Israel, and make confession to him" (Joshua 7:19). Even the confession of a crime had to be primarily to God, secondarily to man.

But this is not all. Not even God's supernatural discovery of Achan, nor Achan's confession, sufficed for conviction. Only after Achan's story was confirmed by full evidences which plainly convicted him and his family was he convicted and executed. In terms of God's law, thus, even a God-established confession must have the corroboration of evidences. Clearly, confession in itself had no real standing in Biblical law. In this respect, Biblical law preserves the person of the suspect with all the respect due to one created in the image of God.

According to George Horowitz, in his influential study, *The Spirit of Jewish Law* (1953), the Mishnah spoke of confession, not in relation to court procedure, but that, on conviction and before execution, the condemned man was asked to confess his sin in order to be received of God. In fact, "a confession, of course, could never be used against a defendant to assure his punishment on earth." (Section 338; p. 641). The importance of this is very great; it meant that, because a confession was inadmissible evidence, torture was not and could not be used. This preserved the person of the accused from torture, the third degree, or any other like method of extracting a confession. It meant that justice required evidence gained by lawful means.

Thus, the whole of Biblical law worked, *first*, to protect the accused from lawless methods of compelling a confession. Since a confession in itself is not evidence in Biblical law, we have all the ingredients of what in the United States became the Fifth Amendment, the immunity of the accused from being compelled to testify. The Biblical legislation goes further than the Fifth Amendment, in fact. *Second*, Biblical law requires restitution and atonement for every offense. Thus, in Deuteronomy 21:1-9, when a murdered man's body was located in a field, the responsibility fell on the nearest town to see that justice was served. If the murderer remained unknown, then the work of restoration was the duty of that nearest town.

How remarkable it is that men choose to despise God's law and idolize or at least idealize Greek and Roman law. The Greeks used torture regularly and their methods of capital punishment included crucifixion, beheading, poison, clubbing the person to death, burial alive, stoning, hurling a man from a precipice, and more. The Romans eliminated poisoning and strangling but used torture, and they refined crucifixion.

Early Christendom more or less followed Biblical law, and the results were good. The two revivals of torture took place in the 13th century, with its effects lasting to the 19th, and again in the 20th century on a most formidable scale. It is worthy of note that in 865 A.D. Pope Nicholas I, in a letter to the Bulgars, forbad the use of torture, because confessions are not to be extracted by coercion and are forbidden as a result.

When scholars began to study Roman law, and, later, Aristotle, Greco-Roman norms began to replace Biblical ones. Whereas Biblical law required evidence, not confession, now, as Edward Peters noted in *Torture* (1985), "Confession ascended to the top of the hierarchy of proofs" and remained there (p. 44). The consequences were devastating. *First*, it simplified the work of law enforcement. The needed "evidence" was extracted by torture from the suspect. There was an analogy, Peters noted, to plea bargaining. Most suspects in plea bargaining cases are guilty; the work of the police and the court is simplified by having the suspect plead guilty to a lesser offense. Torture also simplified the legal process; a majority of the suspects may have been guilty, but, as for the rest, well, human justice could not be perfect.

Second, in Greco-Roman thought, politics or the state, as Aristotle so plainly outlined it, is the source of morality, not a religion. Such a faith shifts the whole center of the moral universe from God's word to the state's word. With the revival of Greco-Roman thought, the shift began in Europe from the centrality of the faith and the church to politics and the state. We are now reaping the consequences of that shift in our operative paganism.

Third, as a result of this shift, the rational modern state and its philosopher kings or elite became the great defenders of man. Reason, progress, and man's hope were now defined in terms of the state. The state was seen as man's savior from the evils and superstitions of Christianity and the church. To suspect the state was for the philosophers of the state like suspecting God. They held plainly that right is what the state does. Marxism holds to the infallibility of the dictatorship of the proletariat. Mussolini said, of the fascist state, "Beyond the state, nothing that is human or spiritual has any value whatsoever." In Nazi Germany, justice became racial: "The People's sound sense of justice" governed; "Law is what serves the German people. Injustice is what injures it." Some of the worst statements came from English idealist philosophers, Bosanquet, Green, and others, who identified the state with Right, after Hegel.

We have thus had a major revival of torture in our time, and the greatest mass murders as well. A higher percentage of mankind has been killed in the 20th century than ever before by mass murders, death camps, man-made famines, war, revolution, torture, and so on. The end is not yet.

So routine has man's torture of man become that in Marxism and fascism the medical profession has been routinely used in sophisticated modern forms of torture. It has taken much of this century to bring Western psychiatrists even to the point of considering the condemnation of Soviet psychiatric tortures.

This should not surprise us. As Western medical practice has departed from Christianity, it has become more and more a class of professional technicians rather than healers. The inability of medical societies to condemn and bar abortionists makes clear their moral dereliction. How can men condemn the torture of adults when they will not condemn the murder of unborn babes?

It is ironic, given the injustices of humanistic law, that men declare God's law to be "barbaric" and "primitive" and affirm the validity of modern humanistic law. Greek law was brutal towards all save the limited number of elite, and Greek society was a slave society in which the elite few regarded their will as justice. The idealization of the Greeks is by our modern elitists, who dream of a like power over the masses, i.e., over the rest of us. It is an anti-Christian dream.

The clergy, by their indifference or hostility to God's law, are thereby implicitly affirming humanistic law. For humanism, man is a product of evolution, not a person created in the image of God. For an evolutionary faith, man is expendable, because, as man controls and guides evolution, he must eliminate the unfit to create the new man of the future.

It is no longer God and His Great Assize, the Supreme Court of the universe, which is the focus of justice, but the temporal state. Because the state is now central, reasons of state have replaced the laws of God. It is significant, as Congress regularly debates tax laws, it talks about closing "loopholes." Those loopholes are the areas of freedom still left to us where our money is our own; reasons of state call what we are allowed to keep "exemptions" which the state gives and can take away.

Biblical law is not popular with men even though it limits civil government to a minimal dimension; sharply limits civil taxation to a small sum; preserves the person from torture; requires self-government; and furthers freedom. It has a great fault; it indicts all men as sinners before God, something man refuses to hear.

But hear it he shall! Scripture speaks of the Last Judgment. This was once important in church art, and in church teachings. Men were made aware that the books shall be opened on us all, and there will be a total accounting and final and full judgment. The ultimate Court will institute ultimate, full, and final justice, so that a total restitution and restoration will be effected. The Last Judgment tells us, *first*, that justice is inescapable. We live in a moral universe, God's universe, and all wrongs shall be righted. So total is this justice, our Lord tells us, that it will extend to "the uttermost farthing" (Matt. 5:26). The ungodly will vainly say to the mountains and the rocks, "Fall on us, and hide us from the face of him that sitteth on the throne, and from the wrath of the Lamb" (Rev. 6:16). Every aborted child will be there to accuse the guilty parents and doctors.

Second, the Great Judge is also our Savior and Lord, whose members we are by His atonement. Hence the magnificent promise and pledge: "And God shall wipe away all tears from their eyes; and there shall be no more death, neither sorrow, nor crying, neither shall there be any more pain: for the former things are passed away...Behold, I make all things new" (Rev. 21:4-5). This is the glorious climax of God's covenant law.

Some men say with a show of horror, "How can you go back to Biblical law?" The answer is, we haven't even come up to it yet, with its justice and freedom! Humanistic law is ancient despotism idolized afresh. It sycophants are never lacking. The Stuarts and the Tudors before them, had their choruses of lackeys praising them as saviors. Ben Jonson, in his "Irish Masque," had "wild" Irishmen turn into civilized courtiers by the divine power of King James (a homosexual). "In the presence of the King," Jonson, that lackey of lackeys, said, even "wild" Irishmen "came forth new-born creatures all!" For like insanities, consult your daily paper, your television set, the nearest university, and statists anywhere. Their hope for justice is in acts of state, and the acts of state are bringing them doom. (November, 1985)

FALSE RELIGIONS
Chalcedon Position Paper No. 69

The writer, Michael Hamburger, in his poems (*Weather and Season*, 1963), declares at one point, surveying the seeming meaninglessness as well as the evils in the world, "Amid such omens how dare we live?" In another poem, he says, "How mind abhors a circle. Let there be laws." Countless other writers in varying ways give witness to the need for a governing religious faith to provide meaning to life.

The critical problem is, what religion? Fallen man, left to himself, recognizes the need for order and meaning; he knows that a religion, a faith for living, is a necessity. Because of his fallen nature, however, man creates religions in his own image, in terms of his revolt against God and his desire to redefine justice in terms of his own will. As a result, the world is full of false religions.

Apart from the supernatural grace of God, man cannot know true religion; he will only reproduce and refine the false religion of the Fall, his desire to be his own god, knowing or determining good and evil, right and wrong, and establishing all law for himself (Gen. 3:5).

The problem is further complicated by the fact that, as converted men, we often carry unconverted areas of thinking into our lives in Christ. The theme song of many seems to be, "Partially converted, Lord, I am Thine. Heal and make me, partially Thine." Too many want all that Christ can give together with all that they want. False religions are served by this fact. We cannot say "Thy will be done, O Lord, except when I want mine." (In many churches too it can be said, Every heart is converted, but very few pocketbooks are. Ask any pastor.)

In brief, people want religion and they want salvation on their terms. We can view religion as our life-support system, or as the way to glorify God and to serve and enjoy Him forever.

Prominent among the false religions of history is *politics*. Now civil government is a Biblical concern and an area of ministry. Paul declares that all rulers are primarily and essentially "ministers" or "deacons" of God (Romans 13:4). Civil government is a ministry of justice and an important area of Christian service.

The problem arises when men see the state as the way to social salvation. The messianic state then begins to claim jurisdiction over every area of life and thought as the legitimate lawmaker and savior thereof. The modern state everywhere seeks this totalitarian (and humanistic) goal, and the result is an accelerating tyranny. In church and state cases, I am increasingly hearing judges insist that no religious freedom is at stake, merely a question of compliance or non- compliance with an act of the state, a regulation or a law. The premise of the state as justice is also increasingly prominent. The state has at times been just, but history gives more evidences of statist injustice.

Liberals and radicals see the answer to current inequities as more power to the state, and this solution is powerfully furthered by most of the media. The statist solution is seen as morally correct, so that all who challenge the growth of statist power are somehow insensitive and morally wrong. In the minds of many, a link is being forged between true morality and the increasing powers of the state.

Is the alternative the solution? Was Jefferson right in declaring that the best government is the least government? Given the growing and oppressive powers of the state, it is tempting to think so. Without all the oppressive regulating and taxing agencies, how much easier our lives would be! Or would they? I once lived for some years in an area of very minimal state policing powers, and the results were fearful. The more sinful man is, the more dangerous he is, with statism or without statism. Statism is a false religion which sees the state as god walking on earth. But to see a limited state as the answer is to forget that sin comes essentially from man, not primarily from the state! The old proverb is true: You can't make a good omelette with bad eggs. Whether you have a big omelette or a small omelette, a power state or a very limited state, bad eggs are bad eggs, and bad men are bad men. It is false religion to believe that a re-arrangement of the state apparatus will give us better men.

This is definitely not to say that it is irrelevant what kind of civil government we should have. It would be morally wrong too for us to say that civil government is not an area of Christian concern and calling. Rather, just as our place is under God and His law, so too is the place of civil government. Politics is not the means to salvation but an area where the godly can exercise dominion under God.

Another false religion of our time is economics. There are all too many who believe in economic solutions to the world's problems. This is not to deny that many of our problems are in the sphere of economics. However, no more than the fact that a man has troubles with his job means that the job is at fault, do problems in the economic sphere necessarily have an economic cause.

All too many intellectuals of the modern era have held and believed that socialism or communism is the solution to man's economic problems. The fact that every socialist state is a disaster does not trouble these people. In their view, if men would only try their brand of socialism, all would be well. In our time, economics is an area of particularly fanatical beliefs and believers.

There is here also an alternative, the free market. Very clearly, history does give us a remarkable account of the social advances brought in by the free market; it is one of history's more remarkable stories. Given the results, why have men turned against the free market? Is it possible, (perish the thought!) that MAN can be illogical? (One is tempted to say, the better our mind, the greater our capacities to be illogical! Can any equal intellectuals in bad logic? Ability magnifies all our errors.)

But men have again and again destroyed the free market and all its beneficent products. This should not surprise us. A free market requires free men, and the lovers of slavery demolish every threat of freedom. Economics cannot be free if men do not cherish and value freedom.

For me, an unforgettable recollection from the early 1960s, is the lecture by an economist to a university audience on freedom. This scholar's book on liberty is still in print. He was shocked when the first question raised by a student was this: "What's so important about freedom?" The student regarded freedom as of minimal value, and almost all the students agreed.

Let us assume for the sake of argument that most men are not hypocrites when they profess to want freedom. Freedom, like religion, is more than a matter of verbal profession; it is a characteristic of our lives. Freedom does not stand alone; it goes hand in hand with other things such as responsibility, the courage to face risks, and more. The riskless life is a slave life, and the welfare state is a slave state. A slave people will create a slave state, and no free market will be other than destroyed by them.

Thus, economics, like politics, can become a false religion if we believe that economic arrangements can create the good society. Here, as in every other sphere, there is a right and a wrong *economically*, but the success of good economics depends on good men.

Christians as free men in Christ have a calling in economics, but it is an area for dominion, not a means to salvation. A good society begins with men in a good relationship to Jesus Christ who then in terms of the Lord exercise dominion in every sphere. To neglect economics is deadly dangerous; to expect from it what only God can supply is a sin.

Moreover, we can add that the *church* is no more the exclusive sphere of religion than are politics and economics. The primary locale of religion is in the life of man. Our life and our faith must be inseparable and united. Our faith must be more than what we believe; it must also be what we live.

Neither politics nor economics have given us nor can give us world peace. Bad eggs never make good omelettes, and at the heart of our world's problems is the fallen heart of man.

Another false religion is modern *education*. Here too we encounter amazing fanaticism. Many hold that the solution to the world's problems is education. Are there sexual problems among youth? Education has the answer, we are told, and the result is sex education (Really now, the subject of sex deserves better than what statist schools are doing with it! This is no laughing matter, say the experts, so they are turning it into a crying matter!) Is crime increasing? We need to spend more money on education, and then we can solve the problem. Education has for many become the great way of salvation for man and society.

Going back to basic education is surely good, but not of itself. Phonics will again teach children to read, but is a barbarian who reads any the less a barbarian? Knowledge is clearly good, but has knowledge made our professors any better than the rest of the population? Do professors have a lower percentage of moral and mental problems than do farmers?

We cannot neglect education, and the works of a liberal, Jonathan Kozol, have given us a telling report and analysis on how bad our schools really are. But education per se is not a way of salvation; it is a marvelous tool for faith and living when governed by a sound premise, but it can be and commonly is a false religion.

Certainly for Horace Mann and his associates it was a religion, and a messianic one. Mann expected public schools to create a better man and a better world. He was confident, with all the confidence of those early New England Unitarians, that his kind of School would eliminate crime, and, in time, save the world. We live in the shambles of the world created by the Horace Manns of the past two centuries, and it is not a very pleasant prospect. Clearly, education has often been and still is a false religion.

There are so many kinds of false religions, more than we can take the space to discuss, but we should mention Art. Many are convinced that Art will civilize and elevate man, and, in many cities, the arts have become the new religion for many prominent women. How eagerly they work "to make the world a better place to live in" with their sponsorship of the arts. I once heard a woman speak of the ghetto classes in painting and dancing she and others were sponsoring; she was sure it would create better children and bring culture to the ghetto. Well, some children were no doubt entertained, and perhaps an occasional child found a calling, but cultural activities become false religions when we seek to transform society through them.

False religions all expect more of man than man can ever give; they are men at work, and their works manifest their limitations and their sin.

The meaning of true religion comes out clearly in the last question and answer of the Heidelberg Catechism: "What is the meaning of the word 'Amen'? Amen means: So shall it truly and surely be, for my prayer is much more certainly heard of God than I feel in my heart that I desire these things of Him." How intensely we sometimes desire and pray for certain things! Yet we are told that God's hearing our prayers, and His concern for us, far, far exceeds any desires on our part. Jesus Christ is God's assurance of that fact. In true religion, more power and wisdom are always at work in us and around us than we can ever fathom or imagine. (December, 1985)

LIVING IN THE PAST
Chalcedon Position Paper No. 70

Living in the past is a favorite and chosen pastime of many people everywhere. Individuals and classes, nations and races, regions and localities, all are addicted to their version of the Golden Age in the past.

This is not all. Being surrounded in many cases with the achievements and glories of the past, people assume that these things are their own accomplishments. Men without faith have lived near the cathedrals of the middle ages and other monuments of the past and acted as though this past greatness somehow accrued to them. In the United States the monuments of a Puritan culture are treated by descendents and present inhabitants as their present merit, even while they despise the Puritan faith. Throughout the Western world, we have all too many pygmies living among the ruins and relics of the past as though past greatness means their greatness too.

Europe and America are not alone in this. All over the world, some segments of various cultures look back to the past, a past they never made nor can reduplicate, and act as though the past were their accomplishment. At the same time, such people are an impediment to the development of a better today and tomorrow.

Rome in its dying days was sure that so great a past ensured an enduring future, but Rome was dead and never knew it. "The old order" in many cultures is a handicap to the very values it professes to believe in. As one American of colonial origins and long standing roots once sadly remarked to me, "Our old families act upset over what is happening here, but they themselves are the worst element, because they have power and yet they use power to conspire against our future. Every ugly power group is loaded with 'our kind' of people."

But this is not all. Again and again, those who claim to be the heirs of past greatness invent a mythical past to suit their fancies. A sad example of this is Ireland. The greatness of the early Irish Church is an exciting fact, but Irish nationalism in the late 1800s passed over this in favor of an invented past. The folklore romantics who began their work in Germany had a profound effect on some Irish romantics. An Irish past was invented, filled with little people, leprechauns, witches, hobgoblins, the evil eye, and more. Every little scrap of peasant belief was converted into a national treasure. In due time, more and more people of Irish descent became convinced that such things as "second sight" were "in their blood." Men like George Russell and William Butler Yeats created a new image of the Irish, and many since have been trying to live in terms of that image.

The Irish were by no means alone in this. What makes the Irish change so notable is that it occurred in a country so devoted to its faith. All the same, Ireland was converted from a Catholic culture towards a nationalistic one which stressed the mystical qualities of Celtic blood.

At the same time, of course, the national character of many European countries was molded into new characteristics by the folklorist and nationalist impulses.

This movement has not been lacking in the United States, a nation of immigrants. Many of the immigrants changed their names on arriving on American shores out of anger and resentment at what their native land had become. Their descendents now romanticize the country of their origin and have made a spiritual emigration to the country their ancestors renounced. At a safe distance from the poverty and oppression of the past, these heirs can fly in comfort to the places of their remote origin and talk glibly of their heritage. However, the more men live in the past, the less relevant they are to the future.

In fact, we need to see changes as opportunities sent to us by the grace of God. To cite but two examples, the American South and the American West have changed dramatically and radically since World War II. However much we may have liked the past, we need to recognize that it is gone, and that the present comes from the hand of God and is a challenge to new growth and greatness. If we are not in Christ, we are dead men, and all our todays and tomorrows will only emphasize the fact that we are dead and irrelevant.

Some years ago, when I began the studies which led to the writing of *The Messianic Character of American Education* (1963), I was greatly interested in the role of new England men in the development of the United States. In the early years, New England's Puritan faith had its impact in other colonies, in England itself, and in the formation of the United States. By the early 1800s, the New England influence had shifted from Christ to politics in terms of a new hope of salvation by political and social action. In 1830, 36 members of Congress, one eighth of that body, were born in Connecticut, and that state by population was only one forty-third part of the United States. Of these 36 Congressmen, 31 came from Western states to which they had migrated. New England men were moving west-ward to assume leadership in the states in politics, and then in education. Much of the Western radicalism was New England radicalism.

In California, New Englanders like John Swett, state superintendent of schools, 1863-1868, one of many such men to head west, left their names on many streets and institutions. They also brought Unitarianism to California as to other places. Swett's life's motto came from Horace Mann, another Unitarian: "Be ashamed to die until you have won some victory for humanity." This was now the New England god, not Christ but Humanity. Swett saw private property as the property of the state, and the children in California as "the children of the state." The sons of the Puritans were Yankees and statists.

Nothing stands still, however. William Hale Thompson Sr., a prominent descendent of a New England family, was on the staff of Admiral David G. Farragut. While on leave in 1865, he married Medora Gale, a member of a pioneer Chicago family, whose father was one of the 38 original incorporators of the town of Chicago, and whose grandfather, Theophilus Smith, was a Justice of the Illinois Supreme Court. Two notable families were thus united. Their second son, William Hale Thompson, Jr., was born on May 14 1867; he was to become Chicago's most notorious mayor.

Earlier, New Englanders had left Christ for the gospel of salvation by the state, or, for salvation by education. Now another step was taken, the quest for power as such. "Big Bill" Thompson, born into prominence and culture, vulgarized himself progressively to become "a man of the people." He was Chicago's mayor in the corrupt Al Capone era. His morality was expediency. Thus, in campaigning for Len Small for governor, he attacked Small's able opponent because he was a Jew. When Thompson's Jewish friends protested, "Big Bill" was bewildered and told them: "You know I've been a friend to Jews. Look at the record of my appointments. I'm saying what I've got to say to make Small win. That's the only thing that's important here. Len Small has got to win!" Thompson ran repeatedly on a "reform" platform; he had the churches on his side during his early years. For Thompson, politics was an invigorating game, and the meaning of his life for him was the enjoyment thereof. He introduced religious and racial bigotry into some of his campaigns, not because he personally had any such feelings but in order to exploit existing suspicions and hostilities. It is likely that, as far as Thompson was capable of having a sincere belief, he was appreciative of the American past. Certainly he was a professional patriot and flag-waver. He took America's power and success as a natural fact of life, and, like Lake Michigan, something to be used and exploited.

The history of "Big Bill" Thompson is revelatory of the history of New England, and, in miniature, of the United States, and of other countries as well. The age of faith, which established its greatness, gave way to non-Christian faith, statism, political action as salvation. New Englanders moved across the United States to mold the frontier areas while working at the same time to destroy the old South. These humanistic reformers gave way in time to the exploiters, political bosses, and men of expediency in one area after another. Boston, once the center of Puritanism, became after some generations a city better known for political corruption.

All over the world, people like the New Englanders, Englishmen, Germans, Hollanders, Frenchmen, Spaniards, Italians, Austrians, and others, sit among the disappearing relics of a great past like pygmies. They identify themselves in all their pettiness, triviality and unbelief with past greatness, as though honor and greatness are inherited with land and buildings. I have walked across the grounds of famous colleges and universities and had professors speak proudly to me of past glories as though they were a present fact, when a casual acquaintance with the school made clear its intellectual and moral bankruptcy.

Living in the past is very comforting. Its problems are gone, and only its monuments remain. In every country, men live proudly and nostalgically in terms of their past. In the United States, New Englanders, Easterners, Southerners, and even some Westerners, who have very little past, can tell you how wonderful things were before "they" came in and destroyed them. It is a superficially comforting way to live, but its promise is death. To arrest the past in any country or place is to turn it into a cemetery, or, at best, into a museum. This seems to be the goal of much of the western world. An expression of a few years ago aptly stated this frame of mind: "Stop the world. I want to get off." This is a will to suicide.

One cannot live under God without living in terms of the present and the future, albeit with a respect for the past. Some years ago, Nathan R. Wood, in *The Secret of the Universe* (1936, 1955), spoke of the movement of time from the future to the past: "Tomorrow becomes today. Today becomes yesterday. The future becomes the present. The present becomes yesterday. The future becomes the present. The present becomes the past. The future is the source, it is the reservoir of time which will some day be present, and then past...The Past issues, it proceeds, from the Future, through the Present."

This concept has been formulated by a few writers in terms of scientific theories. For us, it must be a theological fact. Given the Biblical doctrine of God and His plan of predestination, the future goal of the triune God determines the present and the past. The crucifixion, second Advent, and the New Creation determine all history back to Adam, and behind Adam to day one of creation. To live in Christ is thus to live in terms of the present and the future. The graveyards of history are the places for those living in the past. We have a future, and it comes from the Lord. (January, 1986)

THE CULT OF VICTIMIZATION
Chalcedon Position Paper No. 71

The Romantic Movement marked a major change in the world's history and fathered many revolutions. Not only was it a major intellectual force, but it was at the same time a powerful popular movement, affecting all classes. Christianity had earlier been unique in being so great a popular movement and one which reached into all segments of society. Centuries later, the witchcraft cults represented also a great popular movement, and an evil one.

Although the Enlightenment was an anti-popular movement, marked by a contempt for the common man and a depreciation of women, it set the stage for Romanticism. By making Nature a substitute for God, the Enlightenment paved the way for the Romantic exaltation of the state of Nature. It was Jean-Jacques Rousseau who brought together the various ingredients to unleash the Romantic movement. *First* of all, there was the idealization of Nature as the state of innocence, and the denigration of civilization as the Fall of man. (Karl Marx, as a Romantic, simply substituted capitalism for civilization.) Instead of being conformed to and remade by God, man to be saved now simply had to be himself. The "noble savage" and "the simple peasant" gained status as the true people. (Marx converted this into the worker class as the bearers of true humanity, needing freedom.)

Second, because man's salvation now was no longer a second birth in Christ but to recapture the "innocence" of his first birth, egoism was exalted, and the self-centered "hero" became an idol. Byron's poems exalt such men repeatedly. Romantic love has been defined as "the dream of a universe peopled by two alone, where they and time stood still." Love and marriage previously had been a relationship, not only between two persons, but between two families, and it was based on a unity of faith and life. Now, it became possession, and Faust told Mephistopheles, "Get me the girl." With every man as his own god and idol, the purpose of sex was possession, exploitation, and abandonment. The Romantic poet Shelley saw every girl he desired to possess as a goddess; afterwards, if she wanted an on-going relationship, she became a witch.

Third, because time passes, the Romantics, as would-be gods, mourned mutability, change, a constant theme in their writings, and sadness became the romantic posture. All happiness was lined with sadness, because nothing stays the same. The romantics felt perpetually thwarted. They were the innocent victims of God and time, and they hated both. As a result, people believed at times more in dying for love than living for love, because life is only frustration to the passionate ego. The same is true of love: consummated love for the Romantic begins to perish. The Romantics took a perverse pleasure in frustration. It vindicated their view of life.

Fourth, reason and logic were downgraded and even despised by some in favor of passion and feeling. William Blake expressed such sentiments most plainly. As a result, sentimentality, which had emerged earlier as a reaction against the Enlightenment, began to predominate in literature. The earlier sentimentality was still tied to moral concerns, but increasingly the focus was *feeling*. People became sensitive to their every emotion and feeling, and Western man became introspective on a pathological scale. Novelists devoted books to exploiting the sensitive souls of romantic persons, and the essence of the modern novel, film, and television story is not an intelligent content or point but the exploitation of feelings for their own sake.

Fifth, since Romanticism stressed the ego of individual man, it stressed his remarkable and "divine" uniqueness. At the same time, it stressed the uniqueness of various nationalities, their origins and folklore, and nationalism became a governing force in European life and thought. It was, moreover, a nationalism which displaced Christianity as the focal point of life. Just as for the Romantic hero, the good of the individual is paramount and takes precedence over all other considerations, so for the nation, in the Romantic faith, the good or concern of the nation is the highest good and takes precedence over Christian concerns. National self-interest went hand in hand with a belief in national superiority and self-glorification. Every nation and would-be nation saw in itself a manifest destiny in humanistic terms. In earlier eras, men felt loyal to a lord or a king, not to the nation as such; now allegiance was to a nation state, and many minorities began to agitate for what came to be seen as the only true freedom, a nation state. Napoleon was himself a figure of the Romantic faith but, in establishing a European empire, he ran counter to the stirrings of nationalism and created a full-blown nationalistic fervor in one area after another. This same impulse for "national freedom" (which is not the same as a free society) has led to the post-colonial states of Africa and Asia, and their tyrannies. In India, national freedom has led to tyrannies and mass killings undreamed of in Mogul and British eras. Thus, while Romanticism stressed at the beginning the individual, it came in time to stress the freedom of the national state, or the worker's state, or a racial state, at the cost of personal freedom.

Sixth, at the same time, the Romantic movement, by requiring impossible and egocentric hopes of men and nations, cultivated an ugly response in men, sado-masochism. Mario Praz and other scholars of the Romantic temper have documented this tradition in literature in the 19th century. History has given us the documentation in life in the 20th century. Its governing impulse is the sense of victimization. Communist revolutions are made possible by creating a sense of being victimized in the people. The result is a sadistic revolutionary destructiveness, and then the even more vicious suppression of the people in the name of the revolution, and a masochistic acceptance. Hitler's national socialism began with an appeal to this sense of victimization. The world powers, it was held, had cruelly victimized Germany, but, in their own midst, the Jews had been the conniving agents of that victimization. As a result, the Jews had to be punished; when it was over, the Germans were also victims!

The people of the Austro-Hungarian Empire saw themselves as victimized; they have now a much more thorough oppression than they had ever remotely experienced. With more and more peoples, victimization became their version of their past. Ireland was certainly long brutally oppressed by the English, but at the same time it manifested a resistance, a verve, and an inner spirit of remarkable character. With Romanticism, only the bleak aspects of its past became important.

The Jews in Europe were certainly oppressed at times, but they were also vigorous in their development and power during long eras. With Romanticism, the Jewish self-image began to shift from the Chosen People to the Victim People, and even in America, with freedom and prosperity, this self-concept remains with more than a few.

Similarly, the Armenians, with a remarkable history, and with cities which remained free to World War I, forgot their many triumphs to think instead of their defeats and massacres, real enough, but not their total history.

But this is not all. Amazingly, powerful nations like the United States, Britain, France, and Japan are not lacking in numbers of peoples who are sure that their country has been exploited and abused by other nations. Before long, at this rate, the school bully will be going to the counselor to cry about being victimized.

All over the world, men and nations wallow in self-pity and a belief that they have been victimized. The cult of victimization is perhaps the most popular religion of our time. Shortly after World War II, some psychiatrists, notably Dr. Bergler, commented on the growing trend on the part of many people to find a perverse pleasure in defeat. The world is then seen as too coarse and evil to tolerate the sensitive and pure soul, and defeat becomes a vindication of one's nobility and purity.

Criminals are prone to the same perspective. They see themselves often as the victims of society. Anyone who has done even a little work with prisoners soon finds that this self-pity and sense of victimization is very prevalent. One police officer with some experience with vice squads said that he found prostitutes and homosexuals uniformly "rotten" and full of self-pity and a sense of victimization to the core of their being.

Worst of all, too many churchmen seem to believe and teach that victimization is a proof of holiness. One could say that for them the more one is willingly victimized, the holier one becomes! I have regularly encountered persons who, while undergoing hellish abuse, found many who seemed to manifest loving concern and friendship. When, however, they took successful steps to deliver themselves from evil, these "Christian" friends turned on them! Several times lately I have heard from people who have been told to surrender to repulsive evils because they will then be suffering for Christ's sake. This is not Christianity; it is the cult of self-victimization and masochism. It produces an entirely bogus religiosity.

Such a bogus religiosity cannot produce a free people. The world has been moving into slavery because people refuse to recognize that the Biblical word, salvation, means deliverance, health, and victory.

The party of defeat is the devil's party. The devil is the one who sees himself eternally as the victim of God's arbitrary ways. In the temptation of our Lord, the three alternatives offered by Satan all presuppose man as God's victim. If you are truly a son of God, says Satan, how can you let people go hungry? By a miracle, turning stones into bread, solve the economic problem and make work unnecessary. Again, says Satan, walking by faith is painful and difficult for man; use the angels to perform a mighty public miracle so that men may walk by sight, not by faith. Finally, Satan says, worship me, not God; recognize that I am right in saying that God's plan makes man a victim, and that man is not a sinner but a victim of God's harsh ways. Our Lord does not argue: He simply says, It is written. God has spoken, and His truth prevails. It is reality, not man's self-pity.

The cult of victimization and its sense of self-pity has its immediate roots in Romanticism. Its ultimate origin is the Satanic insistence on the will of the creature rather than the Creator. With this began man's Fall, and with it continues man's misery.

Salvation is Christ, resurrection, deliverance, health, and victory. (February, 1986)

THE DOCTRINE OF DEBT
Chalcedon Position Paper No. 72

The doctrine of debt is an important and neglected emphasis of Scripture. The Lord God having created us, and redeemed us, we are totally His creation and possession, and absolutely in debt to Him. We are therefore not our own, but the Lord's (I Cor. 6:19-20). We cannot legitimately treat ourselves nor our possessions as our own. As Paul tells us, "For who maketh thee to differ from another? and what hast thou that thou didst not receive? now if thou didst receive it, why dost thou glory, as if thou hadst not received it?" (I Cor. 4:7). Our Lord makes clear that we can never put God in our debt: "So likewise ye, when ye shall have done all those things which are commanded you, say, we are unprofitable servants: we have done that which was our duty to do" (Luke 17:10).

Because we are God's property and in debt to Him for everything, God's law does not allow us to incur long-term debt to men. The seventh year must be a sabbatical from debt, among other things (Deut. 15:1-6), because debt is a form of slavery (Prov. 22:7), and we are called to be free men in Christ (John 8:36). While short-term debt (six years) is permitted as a need at times, the normal premise is to "Owe no man any thing, but to love one another" (Rom. 13:8).

If men obeyed the Biblical laws on debt, there would be no inflationary society. Debt makes men past-oriented in their work, in that a sizable portion of their income ties them to debt, past spending, decisions, or commitments. Debt-free men can command the present and the future. The economic ramifications alone of God's law concerning debt, money, interest, and other economic concerns, if applied, would give us an inflation-free and prosperous society, which is the intention of God's law. We can see all around us the economic chaos created by humanistic law.

With John Law (1671-1729), the monetary policies of nations began to change. What had previously been practiced as a form of theft now became "good" monetary policy. The repeated failures of paper money since Law's day have not changed men's minds, because Law's economics give men the opportunity to play god and to create monetary values on their fiat word. The hope of these humanists is that eventually, given enough power, they will make it work. As a result, what now stands behind paper currencies is debt, not wealth in the form of gold or silver. In the lives of the people also, debt has become a form of psuedo-wealth, and true wealth is confiscated by statist controls and policies.

In another and very much neglected area, a major change in the doctrine of wealth came into focus in the 19th century. The name Peter Lavrov (1823-1900) is little known today; he was in his time a major force in Russian thought and abroad. He was a friend of Karl Marx and Fredrich Engels, while not in full agreement with them, and his ideas on a revolutionary party formation had a decisive influence on Lenin. The Russian Revolution owed more than a little to Lavrov.

Our concern with Lavrov is in a related area, the concept of debt. In his very influential *Historical Letters* (1840, also the year of Lenin's birth), Lavrov wrote with a strong moral burden. The privileged minority, he held, owes a debt to "the people." The privileged classes owe their advantages to the exploitation of the poor. Like all socialists, Lavrov could not see wealth and technology as something created by the intelligence, character, foresight, thrift, and industry of some men, but rather purely as exploitation and expropriation. This perspective of Lavrov's *Historical Letters* now governs the world, is taught in our schools and universities, and governs the nations.

Given this "debt to the people," it followed for Lavrov and his successors that this debt must be repaid. A debt, it was held, ought to be repaid. As a result, while sociologists generally deny any moral absolutes, at this one point they are absolutists: "the debt to the people" must be repaid. It is, in fact, an article of faith from Lavrov to the present that "historical necessity" will effect the payment. A form of economic and social predestination mandates the repayment of the debt to the people.

The earlier Russian populists favored a romantic view of the people. The peasants and workers were the innocent peoples, the good ones, and the rich were bad. Later, the peasants and workers were seen as exploited fools whom the elite revolutionary cadres had to control for their own good. No change took place in the view of the capitalists: they were by definition evil.

The influence of Lavrov's *Historical Letters* was dramatic and far-reaching. A.0. Lukashevich said of its influence in 1871-1872: "The latter book, which quickly became a special sort of gospel among the young people, placed before us very vividly the thesis - which stirred us profoundly - of the *irredeemable debt* to the people owed by the Russian intelligentsia" (Peter Lavrov: *Historical Letters*, p. 49; 1967 edition).

Lavrov's thinking spread across the world as a new gospel of debt and salvation. It went hand in hand with humanism. Lavrov, in his "First Letter," held with Hegel that man was now taking a great step forward: "Man again became the center of the entire world." Given the tremendous inequity of society, and the need to repay "the debt to the people," Lavrov wrote in favor of terrorism. The use of violence to destroy evil would hasten the triumph of good.

The terrorists of our day have not heard of Lavrov, but they are his heirs and successors. They unite with their atheism and moral relativism this one 'great moral demand'; the debt to the people must be repaid, and terrorism is justified as a means of righting ancient wrongs.

The politics of the world is now the politics and morality of Lavrov. The Marxists states apply Lavrov's doctrine of the debt to the people logically and systematically. The democracies agree with Lavrov but are slower in paying the debt, and hence they are morally weaker versions of the Marxist states.

American foreign policy since World War II is infected with Lavrovian thinking. Throwing money at poorer nations is viewed as a moral necessity and a debt to be paid for being a successful nation. The intelligentsia, the press, the media, and the women's clubs for the elite treat even modest cuts in foreign aid as moral offense and as proof of evil in those who propose them. If Congress were true to its convictions, it would order a statue of Lavrov to be placed in the halls of Congress!

The churches too have adopted this doctrine of a debt to the people. The Bible tells us that we are totally in debt to the Lord God, that we owe Him as our Lord the tithe as a minimum, and our lives as living sacrifice. The new doctrine of debt turns the moral universe upside down. The poor replace God as the focus of moral concern.

Now the Bible requires that we care for the poor, for widows and orphans, the alien, and all in need. This concern is mandated for the Lord's sake, not for the poor's. It is obedience to God, our debt to the Lord, not a debt to the people, which must govern us. It is therefore God who judges us, not the poor, nor the elite revolutionaries.

Because of this shift in the doctrine of debt from God to man, there is also a shift in the nature and necessity of judgment. In Scripture, God settles all accounts, rights all wrongs, and repays all debts on Judgment Day. The books are then opened, and there is a final and full accounting. History ends in total justice, and a new heaven and earth begin.

Humanistic socialist faith also has its doctrine of judgment, and of the repayment of all debts. Its name is THE REVOLUTION. The Revolution, in every country, is a bloody affair, in that sharp and savage judgment is meted out to all the "privileged" classes. No punishment or torture is too much for them. "The moral debt to the people" requires the obliteration of all its "enemies," and it is the revolutionaries who decide who the enemies are. If you deny this doctrine of a "moral debt to the people," then you are the enemy, whether you are rich or poor. If you feel that your work entitles you to what you yourself grow, to sell or to use, then you are an enemy. The peasants of Russia, the "Kulaks" of the Ukraine, and others were poor people, but by retaining a Biblical perspective on work and debt, they became enemies and were murdered by the millions.

What about Lavrov? The academicians alone remember him. They disagree as fellow-intellectuals with him on various points, but he is treated with respect as a fellow member in the great fraternity of anti-Christian thinkers who plan a brave new world.

All over the world today, people are brutally oppressed and murdered in the name of paying a moral debt to the people. This evil doctrine of debt is one of the governing moral truisms of the twentieth century. It no longer belongs to one man, Lavrov. It has become the common property of journalists, teachers, preachers, professors, legislators, the media men, and of children. It is a part of the humanistic plan of salvation.

But God is not mocked. We either live by God's law, or we die by it; in the long run, it is death for all, and the world is marching towards a self-inflicted judgment.

Knowing about this evil doctrine is necessary, but it is not enough. We must know God's doctrine. Our debt of judgment and death is paid to God the Father by Jesus Christ in His atonement. Our debt of service must be paid all our life. Because we are now alive in Christ, we must follow the way of life, His law, and we must see ourselves as saved to serve, to love and to obey Him.

"What shall I render unto the LORD for all his benefits toward me? I will take the cup of salvation, and call upon the name of the LORD. I will pay my vows unto the LORD now in the presence of all his people" (Ps. 116:12-14). (March, 1986)

DETACHMENT
Chalcedon Position Paper No. 73

The French writer, Gide, spoke often to Georges Simenon about the writer's need to remain unattached. Gide held that the writer must not love in depth, must not have children, must not have to worry about money, and must dedicate himself to his art alone.

Gide was also the man who wrote, "Family, I hate you!" The politician Leon Blum, an architect of France's disaster in World War II, had a like view: "Bourgeois, I hate you!:" (Georges Simenon: *When I Was Old*, pp. 233, 255. 1971).

These comments are an excellent insight into the spirit of the modern age. The two poles go together, i.e., being unattached, and hating. The family, to put it mildly, requires attachment; the true family is an intense, deep, and basic relationship. The family gives birth to life, nurtures and protects it, and is very strongly protective of itself when it is a healthy and vital family unit. If a man hates attachment, he will hate the family, so that indifference becomes impossible. In fact, love furthers unity, cohesion, and life, whereas unattachment breeds distance, hatred, and death.

Dr. James J. Lynch, in *The Broken Heart, The Medical Consequences of Loneliness* (1977), describes a very interesting bit of evidence on this matter. An alcoholic, aged 54, whose life had separated him completely from everyone, had a heart attack. For fourteen days, doctors struggled to restore him to health, giving him "the most intense medical care that could be imagined." He had no visitors, and he had gone into a coma. A nurse took pity on the lonely, dying, comatose patient and held his hand. When she did, there was a decrease in the heart rate and a stabilizing of the heart rhythm. In other words, the touch of another person's hand had a marked effect for life on a comatose man. Attachment is conducive to life, and unattachment to death. How much more true this is with godly attachments.

Our modern culture is not congenial to true attachments, only to superficial ones. Modern civilization has become very urban precisely at that stage of history when the city is less needed as a concentration point. Before the era of trains, motor cars, trucks and planes, the city was built at a seaport, i.e., a good shipping point, to facilitate the movement of goods. Such vantage points were not many, and growth in production required a strategic location in terms of shipping. Now, two reasons at least makes this markedly less necessary. *First,* from the military point of view, decentralization is an important form of defense. Army and navy bases are dispersed, and so too are production centers, because concentration increases vulnerability. *Second,* hand in hand with this decentralization is a greater ease of travel and shipment. In terms of time and ease of travel, as well as convenience, Los Angeles is today "closer" to New York City than Buffalo was in 1815, and goods can be moved more readily and conveniently now from Los Angeles to New York than could be from Buffalo then.

Cities have grown phenomenally in this century for several reasons, but especially because they supply anonymity, no attachment, and a separation from the family and the small town. In the early years of this century, novelists waged increasing war against both the family and the small town. As for the farmer, once seen as the strength of America, he was now the "boob," "hick" and clod. It became intellectually fashionable to despise Christian familistic culture, and university professors held up such moral requirements as marked Biblical faith to contempt and scorn. A large number of writers made themselves famous giving vent to their hatred of Biblical doctrines of morality and attachment.

Because Biblical charity is personal, it had to be replaced, according to the humanistic intellectuals, by impersonal statist charity. The Bible requires that charity be personal in order to bind together in one community the rich and the needy. The needy are constantly referred to in Scripture as "thy brother," i.e., in family terms, with attachment, not detachment in mind.

The culture of humanistic statism has stressed impersonality and detachment. It should not surprise us that it has fostered cultural, class, and racial conflict. The rise of pornography is one of many consequences. In pornography, the person is depersonalized and rendered into something to be used. Women and children are reduced to a sexual function and are denied their status as persons created in God's image and to be seen and known only under God's law and in His mandate for love and community.

The sexual revolution was against Christian family life and also against attachments. Sex was depersonalized. In group sex, wife-swapping parties, and like activities, the cardinal sin was to express verbally or otherwise any affection for one's partner of the moment. The sexual act had to be totally depersonalized for one to be truly "liberated."

Homosexuals have been central to the realm of detachment. Not surprisingly, the "culture" of detachment produces homosexuals in great numbers. Hatred of the family, of responsibility, of deep and abiding personal and religious ties, and much more marks the homosexual. There is a studied rootlessness as well as a commonly urban orientation, or else an "arty" and rootless colony of social rebels.

Simenon himself reflected this rootlessness and a desire for a "new man" in terms of unattachment. We still see Man, he wrote, with all kinds of additions to his "natural state: education, instruction, profession, environment, nationality, etc." He did not include religion and family in his list of "additions" to man because, as a true modern, he had already ruled them out. For Simenon, man heretofore has been "clothed" man, clothed with a variety of affiliations and attachments. He felt that we were now apparently "moving towards the naked man" (p. 69). This new concept of man, he felt, was "apparent in unemployment insurance, social security, old-age pensions, and more or less free medical care, including cures at therapeutic spas and dental prosthesis" (p. 71). For him impersonal charity, detachment, was the mark of the new society for the new man. It would all lead to "a new religion, or a state religion, which amounts to the same thing" (p. 72).

Ironically, at the same time that humanistic statism de-personalizes life and man, it speaks often about "the *brotherhood* of man," a term from family life. This doctrine of brotherhood, however, is an intellectual concept and an abstraction. It has nothing to do with family-life, even though the term "the family of man" is often used. This idea of brotherhood refers to the statist integration of races, nationalities, and cultures to form a homogeneous blend in which all the distinctives of each are lost. The God-given personal identities and ways of white, black, Oriental, and other peoples are all offensive to these statists. They seek to create a humanity which has no personal identities but acts, responds, and functions in terms of social revolutionary plans. Theirs is a plan for death, and they call it life.

This goal of detachment is also stressed by scientists as a special merit on their part. The idea of scientific detachment is, of course, a myth, but it is a myth which has passionate believers. Supposedly, truth comes only by detachment, and hence to object to the experiments by fascist and Marxist tyrannies with human lives, or to object to the use of live aborted babies in experiments, is to despise science and its "necessary" detachment.

The monsters of history have always had a detachment with respect to human life. For scientific practitioners in any field, medical or non-medical, to dignify detachment is revelatory. We should not be surprised that human beings are callously used for experimental purposes. Neither should we be surprised that the figure of the mad and evil scientist has entered into popular literature and thinking. Such detachment is evil, and it is productive of cultural suicide.

Detachment at its worst appears in the life of the people. Our Chalcedon scholar, Samuel L. Blumenfeld, has been speaking from coast to coast on education. He tells his listeners that a simple way to change this country's direction is to change the thinking of the next generation of adults by giving our children a Christian schooling now. He has found, as have others of us, that people want to sit on the sidelines and do nothing. They want somebody's "exposure" of evils to effect an automatic change, as though words can make problems disappear. It makes no difference what their income level is: they say that they cannot "afford" Christian schools. This is another way of saying they cannot afford freedom and find enslavement cheaper.

This proneness of people to do nothing is a form of detachment from life; it invokes cultural death. The continual price of liberty is not only vigilance but also moral commitment and hard work.

A few years back, an able historian called attention to the fact that the old Gary Cooper film, "High Noon," was a lie. The story tells us that, when three gunmen returned to a town to control it, no man stood with the lone law man. In the frontier era, however, men everywhere stood together to establish law and order. "High Noon" better described this century than the last one. This is the era of detachment and non-involvement.

Only by the restoration of Biblical faith can we end our suicidal detachment from one another and from life. Christian reconstruction is not merely a theological concern: it is a matter of faith and life. Our detached world is a hate-filled world. This state of things will not change until men are first in communion with God through Christ, and, in Him, in communion one with another. The parable of the Good Samaritan makes very plain that life in God's family is not determined by social prominence or status but by godly love and faith in action. The humble Samaritan ranks higher before God than pharisaic churchmen and public leaders.

Symptomatic of our age is the conduct of many retired people. As they move into an area congenial to their retirement plans, they do certain things with their church life. Some refuse to join any church or "get involved" in church life and duties. They become church tramps and visit different churches. Others look for a big church with many members, reasoning that in such a congregation involvement is not necessary, except to that degree which pleases them. Still others, feeling that they must join, insist on being inactive. Very simply stated, this desire for detachment is ungodly. In

Scripture, age increases status and responsibility, whereas we insist on diminishing it. This fits in nicely with the popular view of heaven as a place without responsibility. The parable of the talents (Matt. 25:14-30) is a parable about work and responsibility. Those who are responsible "shall have abundance," but those who bury their talents and retire from responsibility and a godly attachment to others in Christ shall have even that which they have taken from them.

The detached man and church face judgment and death. (April, 1986)

GNOSTICISM
Chalcedon Position Paper No. 74

One of the most common of ancient heresies was Gnosticism, which is still very much with us. Gnosticism held that salvation is from the material or physical world, from flesh, and it comes through knowledge. Evil thus was not in man's heart but in some aspect of his world: the flesh, the environment, for many today in technology, and so on. Gnosticism was a development of Greek thought, plus far eastern influences, which infiltrated Jewish and Christian thought. Many post-Christian Jewish writings, both mystical and apocalyptic, were influenced by Gnosticism, as was the later classic of gnostic thought, the Kabala. In Christendom, the gnostic influences continued for centuries and then began to diverge. At first, gnostics like Jacob Boehme, Swedenborg, and William Blake had a Christian veneer, but subsequently gnostic thinkers broke with Christianity. In the realms of art and philosophy, the gnostics have been many. They include J. W. F. Hegel, Soren Kierkegaard, Friedrich Nietzsche, Nerval, Rilke, Yeats, Mozart, and others, according to Benjamin Walker in his *Gnosticism, Its History and Influence* (p. 186, 983).

Gnosticism was "antagonistic to the Old Testament and all that it stood for" (Walker, p. 7). This is a fact of central importance. Over the centuries, virtually all heresies have been hostile to the Old Testament, or have decreed that it is now an ended dispensation, or in one way or another have down-graded it in part or in whole. This has meant antinomianism, a hostility to Biblical law, and hence a vague and sometimes ascetic morality. Down-grading the Old Testament is a way of re-writing the New, because the meaning of the New is destroyed if the Old Testament is set aside in any fashion. As a result, the "New Testament Christianity" of such heretics winds up being no Christianity at all.

Any tampering with the full force of the Bible, either the Old or the New Testaments, in effect is intended to silence God, to diminish His spoken word. It should not surprise us that the ancient gnostics held that silence best expresses God because He is a hidden deity (*deus absconditus*) who is unknown and unknowable. Moreover, He is impassible, incapable of emotion, feeling, or passion. (This is, of course, all alien to the God of Scripture.) In fact, many gnostics held that being or existence could not be ascribed to God, who is also beyond good and evil as well as existence. The modern gnostic, Paul Tillich, held that neither being nor non-being could be ascribed to God. To all gnostics, Biblical law was and is anathema, for to hold that God requires righteousness or justice of us is to entangle God in time and history.

Because the gnostics held that God is beyond good and evil, and beyond being, they could not identify God with any one form, i.e., either good or evil, or male or female. Hence, in their writings God had to be inclusive of both male and female, Father and Mother, while transcending both. The gnostic overtones in feminism are many.

Gnosticism did not hold Adam accountable for the Fall. It was something done to Adam. Modern thought, which looks to heredity, environment, the id and ego, or some like "cause" for human failure and sin is alive with Gnosticism. (For many gnostics, the Fall was into matter. Severus, a disciple of Marcion, held that man is divine from the navel up, and the devil's creature from the navel down.) Man's being for gnostics was tripartite: body, mind, and soul.

Gnosticism has always flourished in secret societies and lodges, most of which are full of gnostic symbols, rites, and doctrines. It has also espoused secret believing, i.e., making no necessary actions in conformity to one's faith. As a result, gnostics in the church saw no harm in compromising with state demands by Rome for registration and certification of all churches. For them, the faith was purely a spiritual matter, and compromise and apostasy were routine practices with them. None felt any moral hesitation in submitting to controls and avoiding persecution. One gnostic woman "saint," a hermit who had been a prostitute, decided to make a pilgrimage to Jerusalem; she paid her way by plying her old trade as a prostitute; since her faith was a "spiritual" one, what she did with her body was immaterial. Male gnostics sometimes resorted to castration to humble the flesh. Many gnostics were strongly ascetic; others went into libertinism to show their contempt for the flesh, often committing flagrant adulteries and other lawless acts to show their contempt for the flesh and the sins thereof.

In all these and a variety of other rites and acts, many of which are fanatically ascetic or sexual, the emphasis was on what man does, not what Christ has done. This should not surprise us. Its name comes from *gnosis*, the Greek word for knowledge. Salvation comes, not from God's grace, but from man's knowing; it is thus man's doing, not God's. Gnosticism was thus a form of humanism within the church. The first statement in Humanist Manifesto I, 1933, reads, "Religious humanists regard the universe as self-existing and not created." While gnostics talked about their God (a non-being), and "emanations" from Him, their cosmos was essentially a dualistic, evolving, cyclical realm which was self-existing; a non-being God cannot create. Hence their hatred of the Old Testament. Man in his cosmos of spirit and matter has an untangling job which is primarily intellectual and secondarily action. In either case, salvation is man's doing by knowledge and then by action. This action is non-moral. There is no sin in apostasy, compromise, adultery, or any other act *provided* man moves with the knowledge that only our spiritual life matters. Moral passion is as wrong as immoral passion for Gnosticism. We must separate ourselves from all such concerns and concentrate on spiritual knowledge.

Gnostic influence spread into a variety of areas. In Hinduism, the *Bhagavad-Gita* shows gnostic thought, as does Mahayana Buddhism, and Sufism in Islam, the Hermetics, the Neoplatonists, Manicheans, Cathars, Paulicians, Messalians, the Athingani non-touching sect, the Bogomils, Albigensians, Troubadours, Goliards, and others. It has never lacked defenders, as witness G. Kruger in *The New Schaff-Herzog Encyclopedia of Religious Knowledge*. Faiths which exalt elitist man are usually very popular. Of course, theosophy and like beliefs are current manifestations of Gnosticism on one level of society.

As we have seen, the gnostic emphasis is on what man does, not on Christ's work. As a result, Gnosticism is a humanistic religion. But this is not all. The doctrine of God in gnostic religions and philosophies in effect eliminates God. The consequences of this are far-reaching.

Many groups which are not gnostic in intent have still been influenced by Gnosticism, in their view of God's law, the Old Testament, man's part in salvation, and much, much more. All this leads to a loss of God's immediacy. When I read the law of God, I hear God speak: He makes clear that my whole life, my mental and physical existence, is circumscribed and governed by His law. I cannot act nor think except within the boundaries of His law without incurring His personal wrath and judgment. At the same time, I am totally surrounded by His grace, love and providential care. Because I take God's word very seriously and literally, I realize that God is closer to me than I am to myself. He knows me better than I can ever know myself, and He loves me better than I can ever love myself.

In fact, my relationship to myself must be at all times a mediated one: I can only live my life through Christ, my mediator, and in terms of His enscriptured word. I can have no direct or one on one relationship with anyone, only and always one under God in Christ and through Him. My wife, Dorothy, once told someone very close to her, who was trying to use and exploit that closeness, "You are trying to have a one on one relationship with me, but that's impossible. I can only have a relationship that is mediated by Christ and His word." This explains the nature of modern art: it seeks a direct and autonomous experience between the artist, and the person. This experience is unmediated and unique; it is not a shared experience, nor is there a common meaning in the work of art for one and all. Immediacy is totally humanistic and autonomous.

For example, the Bible tells us that man is made in God's image, in knowledge, righteousness and holiness, and dominion (Gen. 1:26-27; Col. 3:10,; Eph. 4:24). There is thus a law against any worship of a man-made image as a representation of or a substitute for God (Ex. 20:4-6). Only God can set forth His meaning. Modern art rejects this. So John Berger said, in *Ways of Seeing*, "all images are man-made" (p. 9; 1972). The older art still saw the world as God-created not man-made. But all that is now ended, these men hold. "The art of the past no longer exists as it once did. Its authority is lost. In its place there is a language of images" (p. 33). These images are "valueless, free" (p. 32), meaning free from God and His realm of law. In terms of the canons of modern art in every sphere, a man cannot be an orthodox Christian and still an artist.

Whether in the world of art, the sexual sphere, or any other realm, modern man wants total immediacy. One writer, himself a part of this world of art, satirized the drive towards immediacy by saying that motion pictures, having attained speech ("talkies") would go on some day to develop "feelies."

Humanistic immediacy, the gnostic goal, has replaced the Biblical immediacy of God and the mediated relationship of man with all creation including other people. One result of this change is that men find the Bible's account of God's immediacy embarrassing. The God of Scripture is too close, too blunt, and too ever-present to suit modern man. One reason why the Holy Spirit is so neglected or wrongly viewed by many is because in the Spirit the immediacy of God is inescapable. In Psalm 139:7-13, David says: "Whither shalt I go from Thy Spirit? or whither shall I flee from Thy presence? If I ascend up into heaven, Thou art there: if I make my bed in hell, behold, Thou art there. If I take the wings of the morning, and dwell in the uttermost parts of the sea; even there shall Thy hand lead me, and Thy right hand shall hold me. If I say, surely the darkness shall cover me; even the night shall be light about me. Yea, the darkness hideth not from Thee; but the night shineth as the day: the darkness and the light are both alike to Thee. For Thou has possessed my reins: Thou hast covered me in my mother's womb." David praises God for what modern gnostic man rejects.

But men cannot escape the immediacy of God. They will know Him either in grace, or in judgment. (May, 1986)

TITANISM
Chalcedon Position Paper No. 75

Not all errors and heresies are clearly labelled as such. Some pass as virtues. Titanism is one of them.

The name Titanism comes from Greek religion. The Greek gods were deified men; for example, more than a few cities boasted of their association with Zeus before his death, when he took his place as a spirit god in the upper world. The twelve Titans, six males and six females, were the sons and daughters of Uranus and Gaea. The Titans, led by Cronus, deposed their father and ruled the universe. The Titans were later deposed by Zeus and condemned to Tartarus. Some of the descendants of the Titans have familiar names: Prometheus, Atlas, Hecate, Selene, and Helios. Especially with the Romantic movement, the Titans and their children came to symbolize man's heroic efforts against fate and the gods. Shelley, who said he had "a passion for reforming the world," turned to Prometheus as hero. His "Prometheus Unbound" is full of idealistic bombast against the heavens and glorifies attempts to storm the heavens and defy fate. Titanism thus means glorifying as a virtue all attempts to do the impossible.

Titanism has many faces in the modern world, within the church, in humanistic circles, and among revolutionary youth. It is a continuing source of "cannon fodder."

Our concern is the presence of Titanism within the church. Our Lord places strict limits on what we are to do. We are very clearly told that "with God all things are possible" (Matt. 19:26); we are also told that, while faith can move mountains (Matt. 21:21), there are definite limits to what we are allowed to pray for (I John 5:16). We are forbidden to receive church leaders who teach false doctrine, for to do so makes us partakers of their evil deeds (II John 9-11). We are commanded to avoid all who "cause divisions, and offenses contrary to the doctrine which ye have learned" (Rom. 16:17).

But this is not all. Our Lord forbids us to waste our time on those who will not hear, and on places where no results are forthcoming. We are to shake the dust off our feet and move on to a place which is more receptive to the Gospel (Matt. 10:11-15). This does not mean that God may not convert that person, place, city, or country in his own good time, but it does mean that we ourselves are forbidden to waste time on futile or sterile efforts. We need to remember that while God is omnipotent, we are not. God, in His work, has no limitation of time; we do. God is able "to raise up children unto Abraham" out of the stones of the field (Matt. 3:9), but we cannot regenerate a single man.

To go against God's word in these things, as all too many do, is Titanism. It may be "baptized" Titanism, but it is still sin. There are limits on what man may do, and can do, and we had better know it.

Some years ago, a very fine missionary worked for many years in a country, now Communist, without results. A brilliant Christian businessman, the missionary's friend, commanded him in Christ's name to come home. To labor in vain, he said, is wrong. Christ commands us to move on, and he cited some of the verses, such as Matthew 10:11-15, that required this. The missionary, a man ready to learn, came home.

Not all are as apt to hear. Last year, a woman told me to give her a list of all the public school textbook publishers whose books are humanistic. She declared that she "always" succeeded in converting anyone she witnessed to. Her plan was to visit each publisher, convert them to Christ, have Christian textbooks, and "solve" the public school crisis! This is Titanism; it is also kind of a moral insanity, whether in the poet Shelley or in this woman. I have had people tell me of their mission to save homosexuals, and I have heard their glowing tales of how many they have "saved." When I ask how many ceased being homosexuals, I get another story and am accused of legalism!

In other instances, where people of incredible evil are involved, I have seen like cases of Titanism. People will say, of some moral monster, "I am going to pray him into heaven." At the same time, their children may be on the road to hell, people around them in need, and their mother in a rest home, but these people want no simple everyday responsibilities, only titanic causes. They assume that, because they have assumed so great a prayer-burden, this fact somehow makes them great also! They are ready to indulge in pious gush about how heroic their prayer life is, but they are failures in routine responsibilities.

There is no modesty about Titanism. As one woman once told me, "The Lord and I have such a sweet fellowship, and together we have seen such miracles take place." Her speech was always sugar coated, and never humble. Because of her supposedly "intimate" walk with the Lord, this Titaness had felt it her duty to rebuke "sweetly" a whole succession of pastors. (One thing which Titanism is never converted to is common sense! Whether in the church or out of it, Titanism feels that it has a special calling to defy common sense.)

In this life, the Christian is still not fully sanctified. He shows the habits and failings of the old Adam, however great his growth in grace. Many years ago, I was told of a elderly priest who remarked to his congregation one Sunday that, in his many years of hearing confession, he had never heard anyone confess to being stingy, whereas experience had taught him that this was a failing common to almost all of them!

His point was well taken. No doubt, all the stingy people in his parish and others could describe their stinginess as prudence, providential money management, and so on, in any number of flattering ways. Likewise, the extravagant ones who waste their money have "good" reason for everything they do. Every man marshals more "good" reasons for his sins than he does for his virtues!

Titanism among humanists calls itself a passion for justice, social reform, peace, and so on. Sin loves to cover itself with noble causes. Basic to

Titanism, however, is the desire to play god, to be the determiner of things and to take the government out of God's hands (Gen. 3:5). The Greeks called it *hubris*, pride; they both feared it and idealized it; when successful, it made one a god, when a failure, as with the Titans, it was still heroic.

Christians very early saw it as a deadly sin. Whenever and wherever it occurred, they saw it as an evil and as a deadly, corrupting force. With the Romantic movement, Titanism became romantic, heroic, and the indication of superiority. Thus, Lord Byron's *Manfred* rejected both Christian counsel and patience, declaring:

> Patience and Patience! Hence--that word was made
> For brutes of burden, not for birds of prey:
> Preach it to mortals of a dust like thine--
> I am not of thine order.

Manfred saw himself as semi-divine and above all moral order, as a bird of prey. He despised "the herd" of common men and saw himself as a lion, or the head of wolves. Facing death, Manfred denied punishment in any future life, for that would be a crime, to punish crime by crime! Byron, Shelley, and the other humanistic practitioners of Titanism had a knack for being losers, victims, and injured. Their failures proved to them that they were so far above the common herd of humanity that few could appreciate their greatness.

Romantic Titanism has since then been endemic in Western civilization, most of all among the intellectuals, college students, and liberal politicians. It is a fine recipe for losers, because of the very fact of defeat and frustration is seen as "proof" that one is a Titan, a visionary whose greatness and cause go unappreciated. For Byron, Lucifer and Cain were heroes, and his Cain declares, "Cursed be He that invented life that leads to death!" For life to be good for humanistic Titanism, it must be on the Titan's terms, not God's.

In philosophy, of course, Titanism has held full sway. Nietzsche, with his vision of life beyond good and evil by supermen, was most vocal about it, but it has been no less prevalent in men like Bertrand Russell, Wittgenstein, and others. It has been implicit in philosophy since Descartes and his starting point, "I think, therefore I am." In the United States, the Transcendentalist-Unitarian pastor, Theodore Parker, drew a logical conclusion: "I am, therefore God is." A modestly phrased but strong Titanism was popularized by Ralph Waldo Emerson.

All of this had its influence in theological circles also, and evangelicals absorbed elements of Titanism. Instead of exalting God's sovereign grace in salvation, many began to exalt man's sovereign choice. The order of determination in the universe was reversed, and man was given priority in the order of salvation.

The effect on prayer was dramatic. Recently, I heard one evangelical pastor describe much current praying as "giving God His instructions for the day." Such praying is blasphemy. Prayer is access to the throne of grace, the government center of all creation. The ancient Persians understood the meaning of sovereignty, although they wrongly ascribed it to human monarchs. Prayers to the sovereign could have penalties. As Esther said to Mordecai, "All the King's servants, and the people of the King's provinces, do know, that whosoever, whether man or woman, shall come unto the King into the inner court, *who is not called*, there is one law of his to put him to death, except such as to whom the King shall hold out the golden sceptre, that he may live" (Esther 4:11). As Christians, we are called into the King's Presence, but our requests must be in His Name and according to His law-word. We are forbidden to make a show of prayer, or to use vain repetitions (Matt. 6:2-7), and we are also forbidden to waste our lives and time in vain or futile work (Matt. 10:14). We are not our own; we have been "bought with a price" (I Cor. 6:20), Christ's atoning death, and hence we cannot waste our lives and time in a parade of "heroic" effort that results in little or nothing. Our calling is not to Titanism but to service. (June, 1986)

ORIGINAL SIN
Chalcedon Position Paper No. 76

Sin is usually a very interesting subject to most people, provided it is not their sin which is the subject of conversation. Our concern here, however, is everybody's sin, original sin, the common inheritance of all mankind. It is described for us in a single sentence in Genesis 3:5; it is man's desire to be his own god, knowing or determining for himself what is good and evil, what is law and morality, and becoming himself the sovereign or lord over his life.

This desire to be one's own autonomous lord and governor permeates all of fallen man's being; it infects his thinking, willing, and acting. This is the meaning of total depravity. Total depravity does not mean that fallen man is incapable of doing some things which are outwardly good but rather that all man's actions are governed by his will to be the autonomous lord of his life and realm. His actions may conform outwardly to the law of God, but his reasons for acting rest in his own "autonomous" selfhood.

The fall of man was his agreement with the tempter that his program, set forth in Genesis 3:5, is the way, the truth, and the life for man, and that the tempter was right in holding that God seeks to limit and control man's own "divinity" and freedom.

It was the fall which introduced fear into the world. Man, having sinned, was now afraid of God and His judgment (Gen. 3:10). Fear is now basic to the human scene. Theodor Reik wrote somewhere that he did not know a single psychiatrist who believed in God, or know of one who was not afraid of Him! There is no escaping the fact of fear.

Many texts tell us that the fear of the Lord is the beginning of learning, life and wisdom (Prov. 1:7, 14:27, 15:33; 19:22, etc.) We are also told "The fear of man bringeth a snare: but whoso putteth his trust in the LORD shall be safe" (Prov. 29:25). The fear of God is clean and healthy, whereas the fear of man is servile. With Christ, the love of God begins to grow in us; I John 4:18 declares, "There is no fear in love; but perfect love casteth out fear." Such a perfect love will only be ours in heaven, but, as we grow in grace, so too does our love of God increase. This love of God is not and cannot be antinomian, for love is the fulfilling, the putting into force, of God's law because we now are re-made in His image (Rom. 13:8-10).

Meanwhile, fear is not only a constant element in life but a major fact of history and politics. The modern state cultivates fear in the people. The Internal Revenue Service finds that, the more people fear it, the easier their work is. Civil regimes find that guilty people are subservient to their will, and it therefore uses guilt as an instrument of power. In every modern state, because of the great multiplicity of laws, rules, and regulations, it is easy to keep most people afraid of being subject to prosecution.

Totalitarian states create a mindless terror in order to have a mindless fear among the people. If I know a simple set of laws, such as the Ten Commandments, and I know that I am not in physical violation of any, and I earnestly seek to keep them faithfully in my mind, then I have a sense of peace and freedom. I then know the law, and my status before it. If, however, laws and regulations are produced by tens of thousands each year, I cannot know them, and I am left with a vague disquiet about them. Fear can disarm people and leave them defenseless.

Fear is thus a basic instrument of government in the modern world. If men are kept in a state of fear and uncertainty, they are thereby disarmed of their courage and strength.

Paul, in speaking of love as keeping the law, mentions the need also to keep God's law concerning debt (Rom. 13:8-10). Debt, like fear, creates a paralysis of moral strength and a dependency. It limits our freedom. It is not without significance that, since World War II, the modern state has encouraged debt, and has given tax benefits to those who go into debt. In the United States, interest payments on debts gain tax deductions for the debtor. By encouraging debt, the state enables debt-slavery, moral bondage, and a paralysis of freedom to result. Combine debt with fear, and you have a greatly weakened moral fiber in the people.

The decay of the family is another concomitant, and it further weakens the freedom and moral power of men. As the family is undermined, it leaves the lonely individual with no intervening and controlling power between itself and the state.

Original sin thus divides man from man, from his own family, and it leads to fear, debt, and slavery to the state. The human condition becomes a sorry one.

Among the responses of our time to this human crisis are the various gospels of liberation by love. New Testament or Koine Greek has three words for love. *Eros* refers to sexual or erotic love. More than a few of our "love-babies" have seen this as the way of liberation. Sin for them is denying oneself of the liberation of sexuality. Henry Miller was an advocate of such a salvation, and the sexual revolution was a manifestation of it. This hope is now foundering, with its consequences including many mental and emotional wrecks, the proliferation of sexually transmitted diseases, including AIDs, and death as the result of freedom. Another Greek word is *philos*, which refers to human love, brotherly love, the love of man for his fellow men. The problem with this gospel of love has been that fallen man, being governed by original sin, is exploitive in his love. The "love-babies" who are going to save the world with this kind of love are unwilling to face up to the fact of sin, especially their own. There is a particularly obnoxious arrogance and pride about these "love-babies." They are sure that the power of their love can regenerate the world, but they are incapable of coping with the fact of man as a sinner. Their answers are superficial and their love a form of pride.

There are, of course, ostensibly "Christian love-babies" as well, people who believe that *agape*, or love as grace, is being channelled through them. They are antinomian to the core, and for them love has replaced God's law. They know all the "love texts" in the new Testament, except John 15:10, "If ye keep my commandments, ye shall abide in my love;" "Ye are my friends, if ye do whatsoever I command you" (John 15:14); and "If ye love me, keep my commandments" (John 14:15). To separate love from law is to turn it into a denial of God's word and into a form of humanism. The "love-babies" are full of themselves and their love, not Jesus Christ, nor the Holy Spirit.

Original sin is man's effort to replace God as God with man, to replace God's law with man's word, to replace the mercy, grace, and love of God with the love of man. Thus, original sin is antinomianism, and Adam and Eve were the first antinomians. They replaced God's law-word with their own will. When the tempter said, "Yea, has God said?" (Gen. 3:1), Adam and Eve agreed that, whatever God has said, man's own word should be equally valid.

Thus, original sin is man saying, my will be done. This is the governing impulse in fallen man. When our Lord, at the Mount of Olives, just prior to His arrest, trial, and crucifixion, said, "Father, if Thou be willing, remove this cup from me: nevertheless not my will, but Thine, be done" (Matt. 22:42), He, as the Adam of the new humanity (I Cor. 15:45-50), established the pattern for His people. We are the new human race in Christ in whose hearts the law is now written (Jer. 31:33), and who say in Christ, "Lo, I come to do thy will, O God" (Heb. 10:9). It is we who must say always, "not my will, but Thine be done." Antinomianism is at the heart of fallen man; it is original sin.

History has been the long attempt of men to make original sin work. Politics (in the United States, whether Republican, Democrat, or anything else) is usually the art of persuading men that a particular platform and version of original sin will solve all our problems and abolish sin itself. Most political campaigning today is like that of the tempter in the Garden of Eden: it offers sin as the way of salvation.

This brings us to the heart of the matter. Original sin is man's own plan of salvation. God had created all things, and, on earth, fenced off one area, the Garden of Eden, as a pilot project for man. Here man was to learn how to exercise dominion and to subdue the world (Gen. 1:26-28). This was an agricultural task, calling for tillage; a scientific task, because it required "naming" or classifying the animals; a technological task, because it required making tools, fencing fruits and vegetables from the animals, and so on. In a variety of ways, this calling of man to knowledge and dominion required work, very hard work. it was especially hard because Adam and Eve began with nothing. It was a sinless world, but not a perfect or mature one, and certainly not easy.

The tempter offered an easier way to dominion and wealth than work. God was seeking to repress man's powers and limit man's scope. Thus God's word was not to be trusted. The best word is man's own autonomous word, because man's enlightened self-interest will work best to further man's dominion and wealth.

Original sin was thus the denial of God's law-word in favor of man's law, word, and plan. As men develop their original sin, they develop also their Five Year Plans, their regional plans, economic plans, educational, cultural, and other plans, because for them the solution is in man's autonomous word.

The world thus sees the deepening shadows of the Fall and of the judgment of God on man's autonomy. It cannot escape judgment. As Isaiah 14:26-27 tells us, "This is the purpose that is purposed upon the whole earth: and this is the hand that is stretched out upon all the nations. For the LORD of hosts hath purposed, and who shall disannul it? And his hand is stretched out, and who shall turn it back?" God's judgment shall fall on all the nations until they know, Isaiah says, that God is the Lord and Sovereign. Man in his original sin has no hope, nor have the nations.

Our Lord requires us to pray, not in terms of our plan, but God's. Someone has observed that too many people, in their prayers, are giving God His instructions for the day. Then they wonder why they are not heard!

Our Lord requires us to seek first God's Kingdom and His justice (Matt.

6:33), and to pray thus: "Thy Kingdom come. Thy will be done in earth, as it is in heaven" (Matt. 6:10). Only then will the things we need be added to us (Matt. 6:32-33). (July, 1986)

EDUCATION AND DECADENCE
Chalcedon Position Paper No. 77

On June 19, 1986, *U.S.A. Today* carried an editorial on the "crack" epidemic. "Crack" is a form of refined cocaine which the editorial said "causes convulsions, brain seizures, heart attacks, respiratory problems and severe vitamin deficiencies. It leads to paranoia, depression, suicide and homicide." In a "sampling" of opinions from coast to coast, seven persons were quoted as to the answer to the question, "What can we do about the 'crack' epidemic?" Three of the seven called for more education of our students; three called for stricter law enforcement (one of these three called for more information to children from their parents), and the seventh felt the solution was "to have a Hands Across America to fight drugs." None mentioned Christian faith and life as the solution. All believed in the great delusion of our time, namely, that human problems can be resolved by technical means rather than by faith and character.

It can with merit be argued that our law enforcement agencies, other than the courts, are better now than fifty years ago. There is no lack of zeal on the part of the police in many areas to enforce the law. Even if the courts were as good as we would like them to be, this still would not alter the delinquent and suicidal bent of youth and adults alike. No man who takes Scripture seriously can believe so. Proverbs 8:35-36 tells us plainly: "For who so findeth me findeth life, and shall obtain favor of the LORD. But he that sinneth against me wrongeth his own soul: all they that hate me love death."

Law enforcement is a necessity in any godly society, but it protects rather than creates godliness. When the law-breakers far outnumber the police, a society is in trouble. When besides law-breakers, we have an antinomian population which pits a lawless love against God's law, we have death facing a society. Pour all the antibiotics and drugs you can into a dead man, and it will not heal him. Too often also a body without the will to live resists curative medicine but gives ground readily to a disease, because its resistance is gone. Societies too can reach a point where their sickness is more prized by the body politic than any cure. Evidence for this fact can be found on most editorial pages. Whether or not this truly represents society in the main will be determined in the next decade.

Education today is a part of the problem, not the cure. Proverbs 1:7 tells us, "The fear of the LORD is the beginning of knowledge; but fools despise wisdom and instruction." This means that the neglect of God and His word is the beginning of ignorance and death, because the fools have despised the source of wisdom. It can be asked if our state schools today are not educating for death, Christ being the way, the truth, and the life (John 14:6).

Statist education today is suicidal in its impact because of its emphasis on evolution and equalitarianism. If evolution is true, then all things are the product of chance. Instead of absolute truth and order undergirding all creation, we have chance and meaninglessness as ultimate. This means that "truth" is an evolutionary and a changing thing, and we cannot be bound by past truths as we face the future. Law is then the evolving experience of mankind, and the criminal is perhaps an evolutionary pioneer, as some have held. To further evolution, it becomes necessary to break up old forms of law and order to facilitate evolutionary growth. Such a perspective reduces past, present, and future to meaninglessness. Instead of being the great force for progress, as early evolutionists believed, the doctrine of evolution has worked to destroy the belief in progress. Reason also has come to be seen, since Freud, as another fallen idol.

Equalitarianism has been no less destructive, especially when linked with evolutionary faith. Equalitarianism cuts the ground out from under authority and obedience. Given equality as an article of faith, every man is as good as everyone else, or as bad. If we are as good as the next man, why submit to his authority? When then should we obey him? We have on all sides, in the church and out of it, a general spirit of rebelliousness, a refusal to submit to authority. In Sweden today, we see the extremes of this: it is illegal to maintain discipline and authority by spanking one's daughter, but not illegal to have sexual relations with her; the one act asserts authority and the need for obedience, the other applies equality.

Thus, we see everywhere savage disagreements and even court contests because people refuse to submit to authority where only minor matters are involved. One woman took after her husband with a butcher's knife because, seeing the sinks and drainboards piled high with dirty dishes, pots, and utensils, he dared to suggest that perhaps she ought to wash the dishes. Her statement later was, "How dare he lay down the law to me? Who does he think he is?" If no one is higher in authority than we are, how then can anyone tell us what to do?

Given this perspective, the proposed Children's Bill of Rights is logical. Children have as many "rights" as their parents! Given too the fact of evolution, the next generation must be "free" to express itself and to develop without the governance of "the dead hand of the past."

Equalitarian education is thus a training ground for social anarchy and chaos. It is a form of social suicide, since it subverts the normal order of education, the importation of the learning skills, and the faith of the past, in order to provide for stability and growth tomorrow.

Moreover, modern education, in terms of Dewey's philosophy, sees truth as pragmatic and instrumental. Truth then becomes whatever works for us.

The consequences of such a belief are far-reaching and deadly. If "truth" is a pragmatic and instrumental thing, it changes as circumstances change. There is then no fixity of good and evil. Men will not willingly die for a truth which may change tomorrow, and neither will they live for it. Men and societies then see bare survival as the only value, if a value at all; for them, nothing is important enough to make a stand for because all things are equally meaningless.

Otto Scott has wisely observed that a people are decadent when they will no longer defend themselves and their culture. Our era is cynical of the concept of decadence. Richard Gilman in *Decadence* (1975) called the concept the refuge of "the shallow, the thoughtless and imitative, the academically frozen: monkey-minds." This is a simple device to rule out all who disagree! With respect to Oscar Wilde, Gilman held that to think of him as "decadent" was very wrong; it "would be to abet the conspiracy through which our icy, unyielding moral technology maintains its power to settle things, to bring complexity to heel." Gilman agreed with Wilde's comment to a friend in a letter about his condition, which Gilman called "besieged and mysterious." Wilde had said, "I was a problem for which there was no solution."

If good and evil are equal, equally valid or invalid, then there are no solutions to any problems, whether they be Wilde's homosexuality or anything else. If there be no right nor wrong, there can be no answer to any problem, no solutions, and finally, no problems. There can then be no judgment and no answer, hence nothing worth fighting for. This is decadence, and it is very much with us.

It is also a basic part of statist education. If God's absolute authority and word do not undergird our education, then there is no solid ground for judgment. If the concepts of good and evil, of morality and immorality, of social strength and decadence, are invalid and are the refuge of "the shallow, the thoughtless,...and...monkey-minds," then children and youth in their education are open to all possibilities. Even more, they are directed against Biblical faith by the pragmatic or instrumentalist philosophies which undergird statist education today. Moral judgment is denied validity, and the student is encouraged to establish his own values, not to follow those of church and family.

Education then becomes education for decadence. To yield up one's children to state schools is to surrender them to a major source of decadence. It is noteworthy that state school teachers in so many cases have their children in Christian Schools. In fact, the ratio is twice that of the general population.

The belief that education per se is good is wrong; Nazi education and Soviet education are obvious examples of deadly and false schoolings of the child. Education can be for good or for evil; it can strengthen a society or destroy it. To believe that education can neglect the source of all wisdom, the triune God, is to believe that folly and suicide are better than wisdom and life. (August, 1986)

THE FREEDOM TO SIN
Chalcedon Position Paper No. 78

Some many years ago, a man asked me a rhetorical question, "What would you do if you were God?" he demanded, and then proceeded to answer it himself. "I know what I would do." He continued to tell us what he as god would do, and most of the men agreed. His conclusion was this: because God did NOT do these to him so obviously good things, and God is supposed to be all-good, God does not exist.

The essence of all that he said was very simple: he felt that a good God could not allow men to sin, to make mistakes, to wrong themselves and others, and so on and on. In brief, man should not have the freedom to sin. The Garden of Eden was for him no paradise, because at its very center there was a tree to tempt man and destroy him. All our lives, no matter how well-intentioned we are, and no matter how "good," we are prey to ugly consequences from simple mistakes. For this man, Darwin's struggle for survival and the survival of the fittest was at least an accurate description of life and the world. The human endeavor, he believed, should be to eliminate the problems which frustrate and trip up man by means of intelligent social planning and control. Only so could man create the world which the Biblical God refused to create.

At the heart of this man's argument was the desire to play god and to prevent man from sinning. It was implicit to his argument that mankind through the state should strive to create the great world community which God refused to create. Naturally, for him sin was not the problem: it was and is the ugly circumstances and environment which man faces.

Humanistic man has tried to save man and the world by works of statist law. I discussed the approaches used in The Chalcedon Report, nos. 161-163, January - March, 1979. As I pointed out then, the *first* step was law as a means of *reformation*, the salvation of man and society by law. A basic step in this plan was the introduction of the prison system, reformatories wherein men were to be reformed and made into useful citizens.

The *second* step was *regulation*, laws used to so control men as to make sinning impossible. In such a social order, all men are controlled by various state agencies in order to prevent any outbreak of evil. Prohibition was a major step towards this goal; gun controls is another. Regulating agencies to police capital, labor, farming, medical practice, and all other spheres of activity are now commonplace attempts to abolish sin.

The *third* step is now in process, law as a means of *redistribution*, and the Internal Revenue Service is important towards this goal. The "evils" of inequality of wealth and opportunity must be equalized, it is held, by the compulsion of taxation, confiscation, and various forms of legalized expropriation. The redistributive state wants a world beyond good and evil, beyond criticism and judgment, a world of total equality - except for the elite rulers.

By eliminating the freedom to sin, the modern state becomes progressively more coercive, and brutally so. The Gulag Archipelago is the logical conclusion of every attempt by man to play god and to eliminate the freedom of sinning. At root, our political and related problems have their source in man's desire to have a new Garden of Eden without any possible source of temptation and fall. Many of the child rearing problems which confront modern parents have a like origin. Parents want to spare their children the necessity of being tried and tested, which means that the parents believe in indulgence, not true freedom. True freedom necessitates risks, trials, and temptations. It necessitates the possibility of failure, but it also makes success possible. A risk-free, failure-free world is a world doomed to die.

Let us look at this problem a bit further, and theologically so. *First*, we have seen the statist solution; statist men say, let us prevent the possibility of sinning that grace may abound. Of course, the grace here meant is humanistic grace, a beneficent spirit on the part of all men which will create the great world community of men's dreams. In such a faith, grace is a purely negative factor; it is the absence of all opportunity for sinning. It produces an unfree, graveyard society. If such a society could be realized, men would cease to be men. Not surprisingly, some socialistic thinkers have seen this ideal world as one comparable to an anthill or a beehive. Personal consciousness will disappear, and, like the ants, all subordinate men will be like the worker ants.

Over the centuries, a *second* answer has arisen repeatedly from heretical sources. Paul summarizes this position in Romans 6:1, "Shall we continue in sin that grace may abound?" Antinomianism often flirts with this evil doctrine. Because God is all love and all grace, it has been held, sin draws God's pitying love, grace, and mercy. Before the Russian Revolution, some cults in that country showed evidences of such a belief, as have groups in other areas over the centuries. All such views manifest a mechanistic doctrine of God, as though there is an automatic reaction from God to certain conditions.

Neither the supposedly no-sinning great community of the states, nor the deliberate sinning of Manichaeans and some antinomians can produce grace: it is always the gift of God, and it is sovereign grace. Nothing man can do can produce grace. However, grace in the life of man produces faith and faithfulness, the spirit of obedience to the Lord.

Man's law seeks to create a temptation free world wherein men cannot sin, and it creates instead hell on earth. Man's law has as its goal a naturalistic grace produced by the legalistic abolition of the possibilities of temptation, trial, testing, and failure, but instead of men of grace it produces human monsters.

Quite obviously, men need testing. Adam had the freedom to sin, and to pay the price thereof. We too have a like freedom, and we too must pay a price for all of our sins.

William Blake, often the source of every heresy, at one point saw the issue clearly when he wrote, "I saw the finger of God go forth, giving a body to falsehood that it may be cast off forever." Man is made in God's image, but this does not make him a god. It gives him a very great potential for dominion under God, but it also tempts him to play god. However, as Solomon said, "The LORD hath made all things for himself: yea, even the wicked for the day of evil" (Prov. 16:4). We are not our own; we have been bought with a price, and we must therefore serve and glorify God (I Cor. 6:19-20).

What God's permission for us to sin means is that we quickly learn that we are not gods, and that "the wages of sin is death" (Rom 6:23). We rebel against this knowledge, and many suppress it, but we are not usable to the Lord until, by His grace, we accept the fact of what we are and what we must become in Christ.

I was a young man when I first read a line from the concluding portion of James Russell Lowell's poem "Under the Willows." Lowell spoke of men as "we who by shipwreck only find the shores of divine wisdom." He was right. It is not our works, nor our self-righteousness that saves us. God ship-wrecks us to makes us ready for His grace.

We live now in an age of judgment which will soon break over us. Scripture makes clear that judgment and salvation go together; the cross is the supreme example of their coincidence. It is the symbol of God's judgment upon us, and His grace unto salvation. Without judgment, we would have no hope. The world would then proceed systematically into hell.

The freedom to sin in Eden, and in the world, is God's purpose. By our sins, we know ourselves to be but men, however proud and angry, by our sinning. By His grace, we know ourselves to be His creatures, called to be His dominion men, priests, kings, and prophets in His everlasting kingdom.

A medieval popular song thanked God for the fall of Adam, concluding thus:

> "Blessed be the time that apple taken was!
> Therefore we may singen Deo Gracias." (September, 1986)

OUR WORLD TODAY
Chalcedon Position Paper No. 79

Recently, I was in an eastern state as an expert witness in a freedom of speech and freedom of religion trial. Two street preachers were on trial and had been arrested and imprisoned earlier. The judge in this case, unlike so many, was courteous and conducted the trial with dignity; however, he readily admitted hearsay evidence against the two preachers. The city brought to the trial a zeal which would have been more appropriate for a case involving rape or murder. I left at the end of the first day, having given my testimony, but the memory of the case remains, together with a sharp awareness of this country's degeneracy. Pastors and Christian School leaders, and children, are regularly on trial. Widows and orphans, whom the Lord regards as the test of a people's faith, are systematically robbed by inheritance taxes, and most people, in and out of the church, do not care and are indifferent to the evils of our times.

The other morning I was awakened by a very vivid and horrifying dream. In my dream, I was back at the courtroom (where *in fact* no local pastor came to give open support, being fearful of the hostility or disfavor of the city fathers). In my dream, three mildly friendly men unrelated to the trial offered to drive me to the airport. There was an oppressive darkness in the air and in the minds of men. All had left faith and morality behind, and the world was Christless. We stopped at an intersection; a nearly naked black girl of about 12 years ran crying to the automobile, asking help. I demanded that she be taken in. Just then, a van, going in the opposite direction, pulled alongside of us; the two men in the cab, one black, one white, demanded the girl's return. They mistook my refusal's reason, and offered to sell her, adding that they could supply any age or color, any sex, for any purpose. I demanded that the driver gun the motor and leave, and we escaped the slave-wagon. I asked the frightened girl her name, and she had none, only "girl." The three men told me the girl was my "problem;" they wanted no part of "stolen property." I realized I was in a slave world without Christ and Scripture, the law-word of God. Then I woke up with the recognition that the world I live in and the world of my dream are not very far apart.

The next day, *The Wall Street Journal* (Thursday, August 7, 1986, p. 24) gave confirmation to my dream in an article by Bruce S. Ledwitz, "The Questions Rehnquist Hasn't Had to Answer." The author called attention to the ironic fact that prominent conservatives and clergymen had strongly supported Justice William Rehnquist for chief justice of the U.S. Supreme Court. Rehnquist follows strictly in the legal footsteps of Holmes. He denies the relevancy to law of personal moral judgments, because they are "subjective" and supposedly cannot be proved.

Legal positivism governs our courts increasingly and is separating religion and morality from law. The same legal cynicism that led to Marxism and to National Socialism is now increasingly commonplace in American law.

My dream was very logical. A world not under God's law is soon a world in which only tyranny prevails. Moral order is replaced by statist order, and man ceases to be a person before the law. We should remember that John Dewey, the father of modern statist education, was skeptical about personal consciousness and conscience. For him the reality was the statist community.

Bruce S. Ledwitz called attention to the churchmen and conservatives who supported Rehnquist's nomination as chief justice by President Ronald Reagan. These men won the battle, but they continue to lose the war, because the basic issue is obscured. What we face is more than a political battle, and more than an intellectual struggle. It is a conflict of faiths, and, by supporting men like *Rehnquist*, we are aiding and abetting our own destruction. The conservatives have won many victories in recent years which have only advanced the cause of their opponents.

A key problem of our time is the failure of men to see what is at stake. A spiritual blindness marks our age. In 1924, Eileen Power wrote an interesting study entitled *Medieval People*. In 1938, she wrote an essay, later included in the 1963 (tenth edition) printing, entitled "The Precursors," which begins with a survey of "Rome in Decline." Towards the end of her essay, she commented, "The fact is that the Romans were blinded to what was happening to them by the very perfection of the material culture which they had created. All around them was solidity and comfort, a material existence which was the very antithesis of barbarism." They might have problems, but for the Romans it was unthinkable that barbarism could replace civilization. As Eileen Power grimly noted, "Their roads grew better as their statesmanship grew worse and central heating triumphed as civilization fell."

Central to Roman irresponsibility and blindness according to Professor Power, was their educational system. It was irrelevant to their problems, she noted, "and it would be difficult to imagine an education more entirely out of touch with contemporary life." The Romans were guilty of "the fatal illusion that tomorrow would be as yesterday."

Rome was full of cultured Rehnquists who were busily making Rome and its ways irrelevant to reality. Its liberals were building up statist power and destroying society. Its conservatives had impotent criticism, of which Petronius Arbiter gives us an example, in the complaint, "And it is my conviction that the schools are responsible for the gross foolishness of our young men, because, in them, they see or hear nothing at all of the affairs of everyday life." True enough, but neither Petronius Arbiter nor any of his fellow satirists could offer Rome the faith and morality needed to revitalize their world. The Romans were practical men of the variety Disraeli described in the 19th century, when he observed, "Practical men are men who practice the blunders of their predecessors."

Professor Ledwitz said of Rehnquist, "In a 1976 article, Justice Rehnquist formally set forth the ideas he has implicitly championed throughout his judicial career. In the article, he formally endorsed Justice Holme's call for 'skepticism' about moral values." From coast to coast, our press snarls with rage at those who try to apply religious and moral standards to man and society. The "good" is increasingly defined by what the state does because no God and law above the state is recognized, and the state is viewed as a god walking on earth.

Phil Donahue used a Soviet propagandist on his television show, and the man, Vladimir Posner, saw the U.S. as "bad" because it has unemployment, poverty, and homeless peoples, whereas the U.S.S.R. he said had none. Bayard Rustin, in criticizing Donahue and Posner, called attention to the fact that his black grandparents were slaves and had full employment, food, and housing, and it was not a good order for them. Remove God and His law from society and you have the moral confusion demonstrated by Posner and his friends.

Roman civilization, said Eileen Power, lost the power to reproduce itself. She gave no clear answer to this problem, but, as Christians, we can supply one. If you believe nothing, what can you transmit to your children? If you have no faith, can you give your heirs anything but cynicism as a way of life? If good and evil are myths, then how can we call life itself good? The increasing incidence of suicide among state school children is the logical conclusion of an educational system stripped of Christianity.

Modern man has no solid grounds for condemning slavery, tyranny, child abuse, sexual abuse, or anything else. Fifteen years ago, some of the avant garde leaders of the new amorality were insisting that all things between consenting adults should be legal. Now the limitation of consent is disappearing as some groups agitate for the freedom to molest children. As Dostoyevsky observed more than a century ago, if there is no God, then all things are possible.

But there is a God, the Lord God of Scripture, and He lives, and He is a consuming fire to His enemies (Heb. 12:29). All things are not possible, because God reigns. There is therefore causality and judgment in history, and God's law governs all things.

Can men make this the kind of world I dreamed about? Yes, and they are doing so. But, as the Sabbath song, Psalm 92, declares in vv. 7-8, "When the wicked spring as the grass, and when all the workers of iniquity do flourish; it is that they shall be destroyed forever: But thou, LORD, art most high for evermore." Men's Towers of Babel are always confounded and destroyed. The judges and rulers of this world will in time take notice, because none can escape the righteous judge of all creation. (October, 1986)

THE RECOVERY OF MEMORY
Chalcedon Position Paper No. 80

Memory is basic to the life of man. The loss of memory is basic to senility and is a sad fact whenever it occurs. Some years ago, I knew briefly (in his old age) a gracious gentleman whose family history went back to the colonial era; an important founding father was among his forbears. Although otherwise in good health, this man lost his memory. It was a while before people became aware of it. A cultured, widely travelled man, he could provide interesting conversation on many subjects, even when he was not sure of his name; he picked up readily on the subjects being discussed. He spoke several languages, including Mandarin Chinese, and, on one occasion while on a walk, asked a Chinese couple whom he met for directions, in Mandarin, to his one time residence in Peiping. Because he was so well schooled in good manners, courtesy, and intelligent small talk, it took time even for his wife to realize that he did not know her name or his. The loss of memory strips us of much of our life and abilities.

Most people think very little of the importance of memory, either personal or cultural. Existentialism has left us indifferent to the importance of the past to life and knowledge. Our present-oriented culture is sometimes even contemptuous of personal memory and history. But history is simply a religious memory of the past. In our history, we remember the faith, men, and events which we recognize as basic to our lives. When men despise history, they are on the road to barbarism, because to despise history is to reject Biblical faith and to reject meaning and purpose in life in favor of gratification in the moment. People who have no past have no future. They represent cultural senility.

Few have appreciated more the role of memory than the Marxists, and the liberals who are neo-Marxist. For the systematic thinkers in this tradition, it is memory that makes us human. Without agreeing with that opinion, we can recognize the deadly effects of a loss of personal memory or of a distorted social memory or history. In the 19th century, as a result of Enlightenment thinking and ground-breaking, historians began the systematic re-writing of all history. The Marxists later were especially zealous in this task. To create the new man in the Marxist model, the memory of socialist man had to be remade by rewriting all of history. In this task, the Marxists were not alone. In every country, humanistic historians began to create a new past for man, and a new past for their country. In the 1930s, many attacked Germany's Nazi education as a school for barbarians. They should have added that all humanistic educational philosophies and schools have become schools for barbarians. Their role model is "the naked ape," not God's incarnate Son, Jesus Christ.

Barbarism is thus the logical product of modern education. It is a necessary and logical consequence of humanistic schools. This barbarism will only increase until all the world is enveloped in its savagery, or until Christians see to the conversion of men, send them forth to exercise dominion, and work earnestly for the reconstruction of all things in terms of God's law word.

The greatness of the task is seldom appreciated. More people are alive today than have ever died in all of history. Most people now alive have been born since 1940. They have little or no knowledge of the world prior to that time. The social sciences have replaced and re-written history, so that our cultural memory has been warped and re-shaped. Things were bad enough before 1940, but there was a better awareness of the past and a respect for the meaning of the ritual of a Christian civilization.

The word *barbarian* has an interesting history. It comes to us through the Latin from the Greek, *barbaros*, meaning originally rude, and brutal, and *barbarismos*, a slave. The word in time came to mean even in Greek simply an alien, but its original implication of brutality and savagery has since returned. As the Greeks first used it, the word referred to anyone lacking the knowledge and culture of Greece; as it is now used, it means anyone outside of culture and civilization and destructive of it.

In this sense, we can say that not only our state schools and humanistic universities are schools for barbarians but that our humanistic press and other media train for barbarism.

Too often also the churches follow in their wake. From time to time, I hear of devout and godly pastors, who, in addition to all the regular services and study groups of their congregation, attempt to start a class in church history and doctrine. The response is often either indifference or hostility. This is barbarism.

Meanwhile, Christendom is suffering from a loss of memory, and the nations have an altered memory of their past. In the 1960s, I met an American veteran's bride, a young woman whom the veteran had met soon after the end of World War II, in the Netherlands. Living in a bombed-out city through the war years, she knew nothing of her country's history. Since I had, as a very young man, read Motley's marvelous histories of that country, I was interested in discussing them with her. I found that she knew nothing of her motherland's history. Because of the war, during the key years of her life, she had been without schooling. The bombed out schools and the life of deprivation had meant no schooling, and hence no past as a Hollander. She knew about as much of her country's history as she did of Libya's, and she frankly confessed her ignorance.

The loss of historical memory in her case was war-created. Wars have brought much dislocation and major separations from the past. One man from Central Europe told me that he had lived, without changing his location, under six flags. With each change of rule came a new version of the past.

In the United States, we must say that we have done it to ourselves. To submit to what normally is imposed by foreign conquerors, and to view it as progress, is the startling fact about American statist education.

Earlier, I cited the Marxist premise that it is memory that makes us human, and the necessary step towards remaking man and society is to reshape man's memory. Joseph Stalin was fully aware of the implications of this, and so too was George Orwell, who presented it as basic to the world of 1984 and its totalitarianism.

History is social memory, and, for this reason humanists of all varieties began early to replace history in schools with "social science," which is, *first*, the reduction of history to a naturalistic science, one purged of God and His purpose. *Second*, since history is man making himself, science is basic to this task. Man must make society into a social experiment towards attaining humanistic goals. (See R. J. Rushdoony: *The Philosophy of Christian Curriculum*. Vallecito, California: Ross House Books, 1981, 1986.)

For us as Christians history cannot be a social science because it is a theological science. It is God, not man, who is the creator and determiner of all things. We must approach all things in terms of the triune God and His word. As David tells us, "For with Thee is the fountain of life: in Thy light shall we see light" (Ps. 36:9). The French philosophers wrote about "the omnipotence of criticism," exalting themselves and their critical reasoning. For us, the determining fact is the omnipotence of the Lord God of Hosts. Therefore, hear ye Him.

Western civilization, Christendom as it once was, now suffers from amnesia, a loss of memory, from senility, which is the harbinger of decline and death. This loss of memory is far gone, and the pundits of humanism feel free therefore to make increasingly outrageous statements about the past and history. Both within the church and without, George Orwell's newspeak and double think confront us on all sides. A loss of memory means a loss of direction, and most peoples have lost their sense of direction.

A recovery of memory begins with conversion, with Jesus Christ and the Bible. Then we understand man's past and present, his fall, his depravity, and his regeneration in Jesus Christ. Then we know both the beginning and the end of man, and all man's histories are then seen in perspective and true focus.

The purpose of stripping men of their past is to reshape them into whatever form their elite rulers choose. The result, however, is not a new man, but a lost and dying man, not the new Soviet man nor the member of the Great Community of John Dewey and others, but a barbarian, a slave. Only Jesus Christ, our great Adam and our Redeemer, can restore man to his rightful place and right hand "If the Son therefore shall make you free, ye shall be free indeed" (John 8:36). (November, 1986)

THE FAMILY AS TREASURE

Matthew 6:21 declares, "For where your treasure is, there will your heart be also." This reverses our natural expectation: in fact, many people wrongly quote this verse as, where your heart is, there will be your treasure also. This renders it, if true, impossible to know what a man treasures, whereas our Lord makes clear that we know a man's heart by his works: "by their fruits ye shall know them" (Matt. 7:20).

In terms of this we know what men are, who, despising the centrality of the family in Scripture, and prizing extra money, or material advantages, insist that their wives work rather than continuing their proper duty as mother and housewife. In all too many cases, where there is no urgent need, men insist that their wives give priority to working for money to working for the family as the mother and wife. Such a perspective means placing present advantages above the enduring welfare of the family. It means that a man's treasure is in material things, not his family in Christ. (November, 1986)

THE POSSESSOR OF TRUTH
Chalcedon Position Paper No. 81

The history of the Christian church is a very remarkable one. It tells us of men of faith who carried the Gospel into all the world, transformed men who were savages and barbarians into men of God and made the peoples of northern Europe, many of whom practiced human sacrifice, into cathedral builders and architects of civilization. Despite the attacks of its enemies, the great achievements of the church are obvious and clear.

This does not mean that the church has not been guilty of great wrongs, nor that all criticism is in error. The years ahead promise us, if present trends continue, a dramatic resurgence of Christian power and culture. If Christians as individuals and as churches are going to exert the right kind of influence, and initiate the right kind of action, they must learn from the past, and this means both recognizing our sins and errors, and also re-establishing our roots in the word of God.

Our concern here is with one particular error, and with its implications. Before doing so, the connection between sin and error needs to be cited, Years ago, I heard about a man who bought his first automobile and, being a successful man, rejected the attempt of the seller to teach him a few things about its maintenance. His attitude was, when I need to have the car taken care of, I'll bring it back to you. He did, very soon, towed by horses, because of neglect by ignorance of a simple fact. He made a foolish error because in his sin he was too arrogant to bother learning a few simple facts. Sin warps our perspective, and the result is often error.

A great error of the churches over the centuries into the early years of the modern era had its roots in the doctrine of the church. The church is the body of Christ; it is a supernatural fact, created by God in Christ, and beginning its life in us with God's supernatural and regenerating grace.

Moreover, theologians have spoken of the church as Militant and Triumphant. The Church Triumphant is the church in heaven, the great assembly of the redeemed from the beginning of history until now. The Church Militant is the church in history, working to bring all things into Christ's realm and rule, to disciple all nations, and to teach them the totality of God's command word. The Church Militant cannot be severed from the Church Triumphant, but neither can it be identified with it.

The source of great error has been the belief that there can by definition be only one true church. In a very real sense, this is true. Outside of Christ, there is no salvation. Peter declares, "Neither is there salvation in any other: for there is none other name under heaven given among men, whereby we must be saved" (Acts 4:12). This fact is basic to Christianity.

The problem arises when we predicate what is true of the church in Christ for the church as an institution in history with sinful and fallible men as members and officers thereof. What is true of Christ is not true of us, and what the church is in eternity, it is not yet on earth.

The belief in "our" church as the one true church has marked east and west, Orthodox and Latin churches alike, Catholics and Protestants, as well as the Anabaptists. It has led to persecution, because if "our" church is the one true church, we cannot view with kindly eyes false churches.

Because of this belief, a gradual shift took place in church life. Earlier, men sought to formulate creeds, confessions, and theological treatises in order to correct error and further the truth. The answer to error was to deepen one's knowledge of the faith and to proclaim the truth as the corrective to error.

However, in time, as each group identified itself as the one true church, it followed that they saw themselves as the sole possessor of truth. Over the centuries, each has seen the "fallacies" in the positions of other churches while remaining confident in itself as Christ's one true body and voice.

In a very real sense, this identification had pagan roots. Paganism, like humanism today, absolutized the temporal, and this is idolatry. In terms of God's law, idolatry is a fearful offense. A particular church may be closer to the truth on certain particulars, i.e., a specific doctrine, a form of government, and some other facet of the life of the church, but no church this side of heaven can be defined as the one true church. When God says, "Thou shalt have no other gods before me" (Ex. 20:3), He does not thereby ask us to judge the other churches but to clean up our own lives and to separate ourselves from every idolatry of church, nation, race, person, and so on.

From Old Testament times, however, the covenant people have looked to themselves rather than to God in defining the true order. God through Amos (9:7) asked the people of Israel "Do you think you are more than the children of Ethiopia to me, O children of Israel?" Israel like the church stood only by God's truth.

Given this propensity to believe that one is the sole possessor of truth, it followed that each group felt that its control over a people made all the difference between eternal life and eternal damnation. According to Scripture, it is Christ, not the church, who makes the difference.

Absolutizing one's perspective, group, or powers is the constant problem of history. It is one of the marks of the apostate intelligentsia of the modern era. In the 18th century, the French philosophes believed in "the omnipotence of criticism." Our modern intellectuals use more modest language, but their beliefs are no different.

In the political sphere, men and nations are prone often to regard their nation as the bearer of civilization, so that the welfare of mankind depends on their survival and triumph. The Lord God did very well when the modern nations did not exist, and He will do better when they are gone!

Our Lord tells us, "I am the way, the truth, and the life; no man cometh unto the Father, but by me" (John 14:6). He did not say, 'the church is the truth, and no man can go to the Father apart from the church.'

When a church falls into idolatry and sees itself as the possessor of the truth, it shifts its ministry from the lordship of Christ to the lordship of the pastors, elders, bishops, deacons, or whatever its authorities may be. Such an idolatrous church then makes central to its dealings with its members not departures from Scripture but disagreements with the idle and oppressive pontificating of the church's little caesars.

St. Paul, though inspired of God and personally called to the apostleship by the revelation of Jesus Christ, still wrote humbly, "Not as though I had already attained, either were already perfect: but I follow after, if that I may apprehend that for which also I am apprehended of Christ" (Phil 3:12).

It is not we who are the truth of God, either as individuals, nor as churches. The triune God can never be contained and limited to an institution, however great.

Solomon dealt with this issue at the dedication of the Temple. The Temple had what no church has ever had, the tabernacling presence of God in the Holy of Holies. But Solomon said, "But will God indeed dwell on the earth? behold, the heaven and the heaven of heavens cannot contain Thee; how much less this house that I have builded?" (I Kings 8:27). If the Temple could not be viewed as the sole possessor of God and His truth, how can any church make such a claim? The church becomes great by serving Christ, not by exalting itself.

To scale down the claims of the church is not to scale down the truth of God, His absolute claim on us, and the exclusive truth of His revelation.

Rather, it is to recognize the servant role of churches and peoples.

We need to recognize that the more naturalistic and humanistic men and institutions are, the more they see themselves as the voice of truth. Having denied a truth over them, their only truth is, after Hegel, what is incarnated in history as the state and its elite rulers. The less Biblical we are, the more idolatrous we become. It should not surprise us that Marxism is radically idolatrous. Absolutizing the temporal is always idolatry wherever it appears.

Foolish churchmen have often seen themselves as the truth (and also as the wrath) of God. This is idolatry, and God will judge such men. Not the church, nor men, but Jesus Christ is the truth of God, and He alone is our Redeemer. (December, 1986)

THE DEATH WISH OF MODERN MAN

At our staff breakfast recently, John Saunders commented on the fact that modern humanistic man has a death wish and is suicidal. The humanists are thus destroying themselves. Otto Scott added that in the process they are surrendering the world to the Soviet Union, and us to slavery.

Proverbs 8:36 declares, "But he that sinneth against me wrongeth his own soul: all they that hate me love death." To understand our times, we must understand the importance of this verse. Life apart from the Lord is suicidal, it is a rejection of the conditions of life. Since all things were made by Him, and without Him was not anything made that was made (John 1:3), all conditions of life are God-created. God's law is a condition of life.

It is useless to look to solutions which neglect this fact. A suicidal people will vote for death, not for solutions which lead to life. This does not mean that voting is not very important, but it does mean that the heart of the matter is that people who vote, act, and live suicidally have a very serious religious problem. "Whoso findeth me findeth life" (Prov. 8:35).

We have today an international drug problem; we have abortion, homosexuality, alcoholism, a high suicide rate, and more. We have a declining birth rate, an evidence of a loss of faith in a good future, and we have a zero-expectations generation. We have occultism, Satanism, and destructive forms of music.

With all these things, to expect hope in anything else than a return to a radical faithfulness to God is illusory. Man cannot live by bread alone, only by the every word that proceeds from the mouth of God (Matt. 4:4). The redeemed in Christ will hear and obey Him. (December, 1986)

FALSE ANTINOMIES
Chalcedon Position Paper No. 82

William H. Riker, in *The Art of Political Manipulation* (1986), describes how men win by setting up a situation in such a way that people will join them, sometimes with no persuasion at all. He terms this "heresthetics," and it is "structuring the world so that you can win." Riker sees this as legitimate and is not concerned with either the immoral or unintended uses of this method but rather its legitimate usage.

However, intentionally or unintentionally, many people do structure things to give one answer, the one they want. For example, do Americans favor or oppose abortion? It all depends on whose poll you take as your authority. There are enough people "in the middle" who can be easily swayed one way or another by the nature of the questions asked to give either side their desired result.

The same is true in the realm of the church. Issues can be falsified and so presented that only one conclusion seems possible. Anyone dissenting can then be called a heretic, or any name the champions of the false antinomy choose.

The great classic example of a false antinomy is grace versus law. Are these two things to be opposed one to another? Certainly salvation is by grace, not by law, but it is not therefore salvation by lawlessness. If we are logical about this false antinomy, we must then fall into the evil Paul describes, i.e., believing that we should continue in sin that grace may abound! This is the logic of antinomianism. But the opposite of grace is not law: it is reprobation. We are saved by grace, and if we do not have grace, we are reprobate. This is the true contrast; grace versus reprobation. This alone sets forth the issue as to what is at stake, salvation.

The false antinomy of grace versus law has done much harm. It has led to the depreciation of the law and far-fetched and fantastic efforts to escape the force of our Lord's words in Matthew 5:18-20, where the requirement that the law be fulfilled or put into force is very bluntly stated.

But this is not all. This false antinomy has led men to abandon dominion, because God's law is the instrument for dominion. As a result, the church has been in steady retreat, surrendering one area of life after another to humanism. The law, as the way of sanctification, spells out the means whereby man, growing in grace by faithfulness to God's every word (Matt. 4:4), brings all things into captivity to Jesus Christ.

This false antinomy, by pitting God's grace against God's law and eliminating God's law, has put churchmen into the evil position of turning to humanistic law as the solution to the world's problems. The church thus becomes an ally of anti-Christian forces.

Another false antinomy is faith versus works. Such an antinomy is a violation of God's plain word that faith without works is dead (James 2:14-26), because faith cannot be fruitless: it has consequences and manifests itself in works. The man of faith is a good tree bearing good fruit, good works (Matt. 7:16-20), whereas an evil man has evil works. Paul, in affirming justification by the grace of God through faith, says, "Do we make void the law through faith? God forbid: yea, we establish the law" (Rom. 3:31).

When men oppose faith and works, they limit faith to one outlet, pietistic exercises. Prayer then becomes "vain repetition" and a public display to give the aura of holiness (Matt. 6:5-7), rather than talking with our heavenly Father, thanking Him, submitting ourselves and our needs to Him, and looking to Him for our help and our daily needs. The life of holiness is warped by antinomianism into a shallow form.

To condemn the works of faith is to condemn the Lord who requires them. Power in the Lord is associated with fruit-bearing, works: when we bring forth fruit, then "whatsoever ye shall ask of the Father in my name," He will give us (John 14:13,14).

Another false antinomy is love versus law. Again, this is a clear defiance of Scripture. We are told that "love is the fulfilling of the law," i.e., the keeping of God's law (Rom. 13:7-10). We do not love God if we despise His law, nor do we love our neighbor, our spouse, or our children if we break God's laws that protect them. Sin does not express love but rather hatred of both God and man. Sin means saying, "My will be done." It is the application of the tempter's program, every man as his own god and law, determining or knowing for himself what is good and evil (Gen. 3:5).

The opposite of grace is not law but reprobation. The opposite of law is lawlessness. The opposite of faith is faithlessness or unbelief, and the opposite of good works is evil works. The opposite of love is hatred, not law. These false antinomies are not only erroneous but evil. They paralyze Christian faith and action and falsify Scripture.

Heretics and heresies over the centuries have used false antinomies to break up the unity of the faith, to divide wrongly the word of truth (II Tim. 2:15). We have seen the Old and New Testaments held to be opposites rather than the one word of God. Paul is opposed to Jesus, James to Paul, and so on and on, Peter against Paul, the law versus the prophets, and every imaginable antinomy men can devise. *These all lead to evil.*

If we have a false view of what Scripture teaches, we will soon have a false doctrine of God, and the consequences of that are very serious. Walter Oetting, *The Church of the Catacombs* (1964), outlined the Roman doctrine of God: "'Deity' was usually not defined philosophically, but was seen as that which gives good things. Since Rome brought peace and justice, it was honored and praised and worshipped. But what was the symbol of imperial Rome? The person of the emperor was the obvious choice. Hence the emperor cult" (p. 98). In our time, men in effect have worshipped the modern state because it is the 'god' which gives them good things. The devil then becomes whatever works against the modern state. Marx very early held that all enemies of the socialist state should be viewed as evil and separated into a hell for such dissenters. Marx had set up a false antinomy deliberately, and it has been used to kill millions of peoples.

The theological false antinomies have been even more deadly because they deal with the issues of time and eternity. They tamper with God's revealed word and misdirect men and churches. They are a very serious form of false witness and a violation of God's law. They lead to the degradation of the faith.

Oetting's definition of the meaning of the word "god" to the Romans has been cited. This definition did not stand still. As Harold Mattingly, in *The Man in the Roman Street* (1947), pointed out, for the Greeks and Romans the word came to mean two things. *First*, god or gods could mean powers outside and over man. These could be transcendent gods or spirits, or the current emperor. *Second*, it could mean "inner" gods, a man's genius, the virtue in a man's soul, and the like. Since the great gods like Jupiter or Zeus were once man, all men of power (virtue) could become transcendent gods also (p. 86f.). By beginning with a false definition of god, the Greeks and Romans went from one error to another and thereby falsified their view of things. They then created false antinomies to compound their error. The Roman Empire had great power, but in its economic and political policies it began by positing false antinomies and thus it aggravated its problems by false solutions.

To avoid such errors, we must be rigorously Biblical, as Cornelius Van Til has always insisted. In Isaiah's words, "To the law and to the testimony: if they speak not according to this word, it is because there is no light in them" (Isa. 8:20).

Our age needs the light of God's requirement, that we believe and obey His word, not man's.

In the middle of the 16th century, Bishop Hooper found that in his diocese of Gloucester (England) a hundred and seventy clergymen could not repeat the Ten Commandments, and twenty seven were ignorant as to who was the author of the Lord's Prayer. Under Queen Mary, the situation grew worse as men were hastily ordained without qualifications. As a result of this kind of ignorance, the church was weak, both before and after Henry VIII.

This was very bad, but at least the Puritan party could point to an obvious evil and gain strength by their obvious knowledge of the faith. Today, the ignorance is of a different kind, rests in error, and is more serious because it falsifies the truth. By teaching the false antinomy of grace versus law, they obscure the fact that the opposite of grace is reprobation, and the opposite of law is lawlessness. This is a gross error and a dangerous one. It has a monumental implications for evil, and for the destruction of the church. (January, 1987)

FREEDOM AND RESPONSIBILITY
Chalcedon Position Paper No. 83

Some years ago, while at the state capitol of a Southern state, I was asked to speak at the opening session of the House. Earlier, while in the office of the Speaker of the House, that man, with some dismay, expressed his fears for the future. Until then, said this elderly man, the legislature had met briefly every two years; now, it was by law meeting annually, and in session most of the year. He felt that both on the state and federal levels a year-round legislature and Congress spelled destruction for this country and any other country adopting it. Any legislature in continuous session would be susceptible and radically vulnerable to the great evil of constant pressure from the largest lobby of all. At that time, it was commonly assumed that the largest lobby was the teachers' lobby, or the labor unions. Not so, he said; "it is the bureaucracy." They are always close at hand, always active, always full of ideas, and more numerous than all other lobbyists. I am glad, said the Speaker of the House, that I am too old to live long enough to see the full damage the bureaucracy's lobbies will do to the state and to the country.

He could have added another factor to this danger from a bureaucracy. Every bureaucracy sees itself as the answer to all possible problems. Instead of the free workings of the people, of the market-place, of the churches, families, and institutions of a society, a bureaucracy sees all solutions in terms of bureaucratic action and control. In terms of this, nothing is more dangerous to a bureaucracy than freedom, and the ideas of a bureaucracy and a free people are mutually contradictory.

Having said this, I must add that bureaucracies arise when a people and their representatives in civil government abandon responsibilities and self-government. It is very easy to rail against various bureaucracies, such as the Internal Revenue, the state tax commissions, land control agencies, and so on, but they exist because people have rejected the responsibility of freedom for license, for irresponsibility. Even more easy comes the excuse that a conspiracy is *responsible* for our plight. Conspiracies exist; they have always existed, but they only flourish when men will not govern themselves, when men seek something for nothing, and when men want a risk-free world.

The risk-free life is slavery. Freedom always means risk, and when men seek to minimize risk, this means minimizing freedom. Controlling evil is justice; controlling risk beyond a minimum means slavery.

Today, we have the moral order reversed. Evil is given status and privilege. Abortion, homosexuality, adultery, fornication, and more all have legal status, and there are demands to legalize incest and other evils. At the same time, risk is termed evil and is punishable. Doctors are required to be perfect, even though the finest surgery involves risks. Our courts are clogged with cases filed by a people who want a risk-free, accident-free world. A non-risk world is a non-free world, and bureaucracies represent the will of the majority in action, creating a world without risks.

The U.S. Congress is the U.S. people writ large (or, perhaps, small). The people delegate powers to Congress, and they then demand, not the execution of justice, but the delivery of privileges, entitlements, grants, subsidies, welfare, and more from Congress. Congress in turn delegates its powers to the bureaucracy, together with the grant of vast sums of money, to give the people what they want: Security and a risk-free life. As Ludwig von Mises noted, "delegation of power is the main instrument of modern dictatorship" (Ludwig von Mises: *Bureaucracy*, p. 5) Tax revolts treat the symptoms, not the problem. The problem is the refusal of people to govern themselves. As long as they are in slavery to sin, they cannot be free men. "Whosoever committeth sin is the servant (or, slave) of sin" (John 8:34). Only if the Son makes us free are we free indeed (John 8:36).

Freedom requires risk. It means the risk of our money, our property, and our lives. Most people when they talk about freedom, see it in radically irresponsible terms, as freedom from controls, from taxes, from moral duties and judgments, and so on and on. In effect, they are defining freedom as freedom from causality, and they believe in a fairy tale world. I recall some years ago at a college forum where I was one of the speakers, hearing a liberal "economist" speak. He had been important in three administrations as a White House advisor. In his enthusiastic scenario of a liberal agenda, he concluded that, if his vision were adopted, then "we can eat our cake, and have it too!" Such dreaming is now responsible for the world's growing economic nightmare.

To seek the elimination of risks is to eliminate freedom. At the same time that we seek freedom we must enhance responsibility. It is very important that we insist on *the inseparable link between freedom and responsibility*. This is well illustrated in Deuteronomy 22:8, which (in the Berkeley Version), reads: "When you build a new house, you must put a parapet around the roof, lest if someone falls to the ground, you bring bloodguilt upon the house." This law refers to the flat-topped roofs of houses in those days. On warm summer nights, people ate, spent their evenings, and sometimes slept on the rooftop. To have such a roof without a strong railing to prevent falling was irresponsible and incurred, religiously and civilly, blood-guilt. It was and is immoral to expose people needlessly to danger, and hence it was a punishable offense. Freedom means responsibility, not irresponsibility. However, no bureaucracy enforced the building of parapets or railings. Rather, it was the fact that a fall by a friend or guest could lead to a manslaughter charge at least, and heavy restitution, that morally controlled people and led to the routine construction of parapets. Irresponsibility was severely penalized.

In discussing the philosophy of bureaucratism, von Mises said that it leads to seeing good embodied in the State, and evil materialized in the "rugged individualism" of selfish men. The State then is always right, and the people always wrong (p. 74).

How can such a condition develop? People must have a god; if they reject the living God of the Scripture, they turn to other sources for the good, to the State, to the free market, to Reason, and so on, to a variety of false and home-made gods. When men worship false gods, they falsify their total being. The abler and the more educated they are, the more powerful and effective is the sway of evil in their lives. At this point, von Mises' insight was telling: "It is remarkable that the educated strata are more gullible than the less educated. The most enthusiastic supporters of Marxism, Nazism, and Fascism were the intellectuals, not the boors" (p. 108). The problem, however, with these gullible ones was not their education but their lack of a Biblical faith.

We are told, in Psalm 14:1, "The fool hath said in his heart, There is no God. They are corrupt, they have done abominable works, there is none that doeth good." David does not tell us that such men, infidels, do not believe there is a God. Indeed, as Paul tells us, all men know that God is, but they suppress this knowledge in their unrighteousness or injustice (Rom. 1:18-20). The fool tells himself there is no God to punish him, and, in his corruption, he then acts in contempt of God's law. All such action is *irresponsible.* To be irresponsible is to be irresponsible to the Triune God, who made us and who has given us His law to live by. Irresponsibility is towards God, and therefore towards His creation and other men also. If we deny God, we deny His law, and His moral order. We then refuse to believe there is a heaven, and certainly no hell. If there is no hell, there is no justice, *and no risk.* Hell means that there is a risk in living. People who believe in a Hell-free life are commonly prone to believing in a risk-free life. For them then, a bureaucracy is a good way of working towards a risk-free world. Bureaucracies are modern man's alternative to the providence of God. God's providence is our assurance that a moral order is basic to all creation, and that even a fallen world must move in terms of God's law. Tyrants may rise up, as did Sisera, but, as Deborah declares in her song of triumph, "They fought from heaven; the stars in their courses fought against Sisera" (Judges 5:20).

If men will not obey God's law, they will have man's law, and man's providence in the form of a bureaucracy. If men will not tithe and see themselves as responsible under God for a wide range of duties towards God, and towards their neighbor, they will have an income tax, other taxes, and welfarism. There are no easy "outs" in God's world! As Paul tells us, "Be not deceived; God is not mocked: for whatsoever a man soweth, that shall he also reap" (Gal. 6:7). Again, "the wages of sin is death" (Rom. 6:23), and, we can add, taxes also!

We cannot have our cake and eat it too. We cannot have a risk-free and tax-free life; the more we try to remove risks from life, the more we create bureaucracies to remove money from us. But, first of all, we surrender freedom for slavery.

There is one thing slaves have usually done well -- whine about their slavery. I am weary of whiners. (February, 1987)

PIECEMEAL DESTRUCTION

An instructive episode from history is the treatment by the Turkish conquerors of the Near East of their Christian populations, which some scholars have admired. In some respects, the sultans, beginning with Mehmet II, gave more powers to the patriarchal offices of the churches by making them a part of the bureaucracy, giving them administrative duties, and a role in the collection of taxes.

At key points, however, the church was very seriously undermined. Its power to acquire and hold land and estates was largely wiped out, and also the church endowments. The independence and freedom of the church was thus destroyed, and its was all the more a dependent aspect of the imperial bureaucracy.

Another very important power of the church was also almost eliminated, the freedom to maintain schools. Christians within the Turkish Empire had to travel abroad to enter Christian schools and colleges. This had the effect of freezing growth and paralyzing the intellectual and theological life of the churches.

Another deadly control was a virtual ban on the ownership of presses by the church. The Patriarch Cyril Lucaris, of the Greek Orthodox Church, was educated in Europe, in Catholic and Protestant centers. He became a Calvinist and set up a press in Constantinople in 1627 to bring the scholarship of the West into the Empire. Almost at once the Turks destroyed the press, and Cyril was subsequently murdered.

Every anti-Christian order strikes against these three areas in order to weaken and destroy the church. In the United States today, the freedom of Christian Schools is especially threatened, but there are also some restrictions on estates and on the freedom of the Christian press. (February, 1987)

THE CULTIVATION AND PROMOTION of IMPOTENCE
Chalcedon Position Paper No. 84

In her study, *The Knight in History* (1984), Frances Gies tells us of the growth of irrelevance in knighthood. Originally, the knight was an important and key figure in feudal society. However, after 1050, knights began to stress their status rather than function, and, "what had been a rank became a hereditary caste" (p. 26). In time, their lives and their tournaments became "an adjunct of theatrical productions and partook of their character" (p. 200). The same thing in time became true of royalty: it became a matter of blood and theater. Earlier, a ruler like William the Conqueror was a bastard whose mother was emphatically not royalty; later, such a king was ruled out. It was not ability that counted but blood. Royal "courts" ceased to be a place of justice and became social centers where dress prevailed in importance over character and ability.

What had happened was men preferred the facade to reality. The centers of power became centers of fashion and theater, not of justice and government, and, before long, they lost their power. When fashion and theatricals become more important to those in power than justice and social advancement, then the end is not far away.

To prefer fashion and theater to justice means that the ruling powers have lost their hold on reality. They seek admiration and envy, not results and progress. But this is not all. Art is divorced from Christianity to become a substitute for religion, and the power elite becomes linked to an art elite which is similarly out of touch with reality. Each serves to exalt the other as they go blindly into destruction. Such a direction is not limited to heads of states. It is also true of the world of commerce. Otto Scott has often commented on a revealing aspect of the life of corporations. Their founders are true entrepreneurs, men of ability, vision, and foresight. As innovators, they build a great industrial empire out of little or nothing other than their dedication and ingenuity. Such men vary in character, and their biographies reveal sometimes very real flaws, but they were builders. But there is another fact about them: often they were short and unprepossessing in their appearance. Many had character traits which today would lead to their immediate rejection by any personnel department. If they appeared today, looking for jobs with firms they established, they would be rejected! It was rare for any of these innovators to have a college degree. Today, the firms they founded take college men only, and only those over six feet, in many cases! The result is cloning an image of an advertising agency's fashion plate. Is it any wonder that the corporations are having problems?

The same problem exists in the church. Administration is often given priority over pastoral and preaching concerns. "Ministerial relations" committees handle placements in many church bodies, and these committees are more concerned often about loyalty to the church than loyalty to Christ and Scripture. Such a superficial churchmanship leads to a theatrical view of reality. Ecumenical meetings by failing churches pronounce all kinds of judgment on things they know little about. There is more concern with public relations and a good press than there is with reality.

In the world of the theater, life and death are both make believe, not reality. Reality is no longer real to some people. Theodore Shank, in his study of the *American Alternative Theater* (1982), which he found pleasing on the whole, cited one leading figure in the theater who declared, "Life, revolution, and theater are the words for the same thing: an unconditional

NO to the present society." But to equate revolution and theater with life is to have lost a hold on reality! Shanks said, of the Living Theater group, "life is theater, and theater is their life." Such a view means that a hold on reality is lost. It should not surprise us then that one performer has insisted, "Acting is not make believe but living exquisitely in the moment."

This is the avant garde theater today, and this too is much of our world; it feels that only when one is on stage, only when one is a part of a "living theater," is life real. (One man seriously told me once that to be truly alive one had to live in New York City!) Is it any wonder today that more and more of our "news" and politics is dominated by press conferences, public hearings, and television coverage than by actions and accomplishments?

On stage, life and death are make-believe, not real. So too are births, accomplishments, and victories. When men move from reality to theater, they sentence themselves to impotence.

For the living dead, there are virtues in impotence. It means none of the pains, expenses, and heartbreaks of family life, of birth and death, and the partings of ways. Impotence eliminates many of the cares and problems which are basic to life.

Our age obviously loves impotence and death. It favors homosexuality, abortion, euthanasia and more. It will not face up to the growing epidemic of AIDS, and it continues to live in its fantasy world. The Presbyter Salvian, describing the fall of Trier in the last days of the Roman Empire, tells us that men did not defend the city because they were too interested in the games at the arena. After the rape, looting, and burning of Trier, the survivors petitioned the emperor to rebuild their arena so that the games could go on and their morale improved! Salvian said of Rome, "it is dying, but continues to laugh." So too this modern age: it is dying but continues to laugh.

Impotence today is cultivated on all sides. A few years ago, at its inception, I joined a national group ostensibly dedicated to studying and implementing matters of national policy. Its members were to be Christians and conservatives. Very quickly, in only a few years, it has become theater. It is more interested in providing a forum for "big names" than in serious study. Its meetings are now expensive social events. One might say that, instead of being a training ground for war horses, it has become the gathering place to produce geldings and mules! Impotence is cultivated, and ineffectuality is the order of the day. Men must love impotence, because they spend so much money to produce it!

In 1947, in *The Abolition of Man*, C. S. Lewis began with a telling chapter on "Men Without Chests," i.e., on education as planned sterility. At the end of the chapter, he said, "In a sort of ghastly simplicity we remove the organ and demand the function. We make men without chests and expect of them virtue and enterprise. We laugh at honor and are shocked to find traitors in our midst. We castrate and bid the geldings be fruitful" (p. 16). This is true not only of education but of every area of life and thought. The culture and promotion of impotence is central to our contemporary culture.

Biblical faith is vital and demanding. It requires that we die in Christ and become a new creation in Him. It requires our total surrender. We must become Christ's creation and creatures.

The world prefers a surface religion. It was surface religion which destroyed the medieval church long before the Reformation. Margaret Wade Labarge, in her study of *Henry V* (1975), wrote of the fact that Henry took his religious duties seriously. However, with most people, religion had become conventional. "Conventional religious practice required no individual initiative and did not necessarily imply any personal commitment. A look at the hierarchy of the day provides still another impression of decent formalism" (p. 95). Before the immoralism of recent years, we too had our era of "decent formalism." It has given way to indecent immoralism and rebellion!

I have had calls from time to time from troubled pastors, all with a common problem. People visit their church to see "what's happening." They want a church where they can be spectators to much action, but they do not want to be part of *the work*. One pastor reported that one visiting couple said that they wanted a church "where things happen and miracles take place!" They did not ask for an opportunity to serve. They wanted to be spectators. This is an easy route to damnation.

Given the modern perspective, when Paul was converted on the road to Damascus, instead of asking. "Lord, what wilt Thou have me to do?" (Acts 9:6), Paul instead should have asked,"Lord, what's in it for me?"

Returning again to Henry V, Labarge's comment is of interest when she says of medieval kingship that it was associated with justice. "Justice was the prime virtue of a medieval king" (p. 187). Not all medieval kings were just, but enough of them were, and the concern for the realities of rule governed them, not theatricals. Even ungodly kings were able to retain power, because they did not lose touch with reality.

Monarchy disappeared when it became theater, when it lost touch with reality. Ludwig of Bavaria, Richard Wagner's friend and patron, was such a ruler. He was far more beneficent than many a predecessor, but his idea of a kingship was so unrealistic and so theatrical that it proved suicidal for the future of the crown. Wagner himself took Germany and much of the Western World into a land of fantasy and irrelevance. Wagner adopted the current anthropological doctrine of myth as a higher reality and thus a higher realm of truth.

The same evil doctrine is widely prevalent today, especially in seminaries, Catholic and Protestant. A myth is said to be a higher form of religious truth and not to be confused with falsehood. By "seeing" the mythological character of the Bible, we supposedly have a firmer grip on truth and reality!

How much trust can we place in a mythological bridge across a canyon? Such men may insist that these "myths" embody a higher reality, but in so speaking, they declare themselves to be, at the very least, fools, if not knaves.

Such professors turn Christianity from the truth of God into a lie called myth. They insist that theater in the form of myth is reality, and, by implication, reality is unreal.

We live in an age when men believe "life is theater and theater is their life." They insist that "acting is not make believe, but living exquisitely in the moment." This is insanity and a flight from reality. But that flight from reality is all around us. Press conferences replace action, and public relations govern the world of "living theater." The curtain always comes down on the stage; the play-acting comes to an end. But life goes on; it does not end with us, nor our children, and we cannot ring down the curtain on neat and invented endings made for an imaginary, theatrical world without birth or death.

The world of the "living theater" is not for us. We are told, "Come out of her, my people, that ye be not partakers of her sins, and that ye receive not of her plagues. For her sins have reached unto heaven, and God hath remembered her iniquities." (Rev. 18:4-5).

The impotent have no future. The cultivation and promotion of impotence is the calling of the humanists. Our Lord is the Lord of life. (March, 1987)

COVENANT VERSUS DETENTE
Chalcedon Position Paper No. 85

St. Paul, in II Corinthians 6:14, sums up a basic premise of God's law: "Be ye not unequally yoked together with unbelievers: for what fellowship hath righteousness with unrighteousness? and what communion hath light with darkness?"

In Exodus 23:31-33, all treaties and alliances with godless nations are banned, and this is restated in Exodus 34:12-16, where this ban includes inter-faith marriages. We are also told that all such unequal yoking is the prelude to idolatry (Deut. 7:3-4). Not only are treaties and marriages religious facts, but they also presuppose and require, if they are to succeed, a common morality, law, and truth. Every religion has its own doctrine of morality, of law, and of truth. If we believe in Marxism, then we believe that truth is instrumental; there is no absolute truth, and words are as surely to be used as weapons as are guns. For Marxists, law and morality are determined by the dictatorship of the proletariat, and they are thus also relativistic and instrumental, not binding. The same words thus mean different things to a Marxist and to a Christian. Failure to recognize this fact means that Christians are regularly duped. They are duped because they refuse to take God's law seriously. They are not covenantly minded.

A covenant is a treaty of law. God's covenant with man is an act of grace whereby God gives to man His saving grace and the laws of life, of holiness and righteousness or justice. Because God gives us His law as an act of grace, we cannot violate His covenant, His treaty with us in Christ, by entering into a treaty with any unbelieving nation or in marriage with an unbelieving person. To do so is to renounce God and His covenant for other gods. It is an act of apostasy and unbelief. From beginning to end, Scripture speaks plainly on this issue. It tells us that the source of detente is unbelief.

The word "detente" is relatively new to English; it comes from the French, and only in very recent years has it gained much usage. It presupposes a humanistic religious faith and mission.

Dale T. Irvin, a liberal seminary professor, has spoken of mission as "dialogue," not conversion. For a time, Irvin met regularly with a group of prison inmates, not to convert them, but to hold a dialogue with them. (Some would say that the prisoners converted him!) Irvin is dubious that "salvation comes only through one particular story, one particular history." He is happy that "a new form of mission" is now underway, and promoted by such groups as the Seminarians for Peace. This new mission is "co-existence." For the "Christian" participants in this kind of mission, i.e., such as the Seminarians for Peace, "it was clear that the categories of Western Christian thought are in their last hours." For such people, there is no exclusive truth or revelation, and traditional, orthodox Christianity must die in order to make way for "a new humanity." For Irvin, the true resurrection is to enter into a world-wide coexistence, with all the old "forms" now "integrated into the common life of humanity." (Dale T. Irvin, "Mission as Dialogue," in M.D. Bryant and H.R. Huessy, editors: *Eugen Rosenstock-Huessy, Studies in his Life and Thought*, pp. 203-216, 1986. Edwin Mellen Press.)

In this perspective, all that matters is humanity as such, not God, not truth, not justice, only the coexistence of humanity, only detente.

From China, we get a like word. *The Beijing Review*, January 12, 1987, tells us that Mao Zedon, in "Two Talks of Philosophy," wrote: "The extinction of mankind and the earth is different from the 'end of the world' preached in Christian churches. We predict that after the extinction of mankind and the earth, more progressive things will replace mankind, that is, a higher stage of development." Mao went on to say, "Marxism also has its emergence, development and extinction. This may sound strange, but since Marxism holds that everything born must die, why shouldn't this apply to Marxism itself? It is metaphysics to deny its extinction. Of course, more progressive things will replace it." In such a faith, the only thing not permissible is the belief in an absolute God, the God of Scripture, and His truth.

In another issue of the *Beijing Review* (January 5, 1987), a student, Shi Ling, confesses that he once believed in a fixed Marxism and hence found it "hard to believe our great Chairmen Mao had made such monumental mistakes." But he did believe, because the State told him so! He came to understand, and he titled his article, "What Marxism Means." It means that, "if reality changes, knowledge must change...Inflexible doctrines must be discarded." A true Marxist thus recognizes that it is change which demonstrates vitality. For this reason, "Marxism is powerful and there is hope for socialism."

In terms of this, instrumentalism is basic: people, words, truth, treaties, and all things else are valued only insofar as they can be used. There are no unchanging values. In terms of this, detente, not covenant, is man's practical course of action. One American General, in expressing his dissent with U.S. foreign policy and its dedication to detente, did so on Christian grounds. He was told that his "devil theory" of foreign policy (i.e., a belief that the issues involve good and evil) is "untenable."

The Bible tells us that our relationship to God is a covenantal one, that is, it rests on His grace and is in terms of His law-word. On both counts, it is personal. "Sin is the transgression of the law" (I John 3:4). Sin, moreover, is the transgression of the law of the totally personal God, and it is offensive to Him. In the humanistic state, law is an impersonal fact, whereas to the triune God sin is a personal affront. When the concept of "crime" replaces "sin," we depersonalize the offense. The legal charge then is the state versus the criminal, whereas in Scripture it is God versus man. Humanism also depersonalizes the relationship between the sinner and the one sinned against. Marriage becomes a legal tie, not a totally personal union which involves two persons, two families, and all society.

The covenantal relationship is under God. The humanistic relationship is ultimately atomistic and is governed by autonomous man.

To remove the covenant of God as the foundation of man's life and of law and society is to open the door to total relativism, to detente. Because of the spirit of detente, ie., peaceful coexistence, we now have a major movement to legalize sodomite and lesbian marriages. There is also a move to drop adultery as a ground for divorce, property divisions in divorce, and children's custody. The logic of detente requires us to subordinate all things to peaceful coexistence.

The poet William Blake was an early advocate of detente. He wrote of it honestly as "The Marriage of Heaven and Hell." In any such "marriage," heaven must cease to be heaven, for to coexist with hell is to turn all things into hell.

St. Paul tells us that unequal yoking is evil and forbidden; it is also a surrender, because what fellowship can righteousness or justice have with unrighteousness, or injustice? What communion, he asks, can light have with darkness? The requirements for detente with darkness is to put out the light!

It is startling, then, to find many churchmen who piously oppose mixed marriages advocate mixed politics, mixed everything, as the "common sense" perspective. There is an old saying about something or other not having a snowball's chance in hell. The point in this saying is that a snowball in hell is not in its proper context. A snowball at the North Pole has a good "life expectancy," but not at sea level at the equator. The same is true of all unequal yoking.

We have today many advocates of cultural, educational, and political conservatism who preach detente, unequal yoking, as the solution. One conservative periodical recently hailed this concept as the hope of the future, as the solution to our problems. Charles Hodge a century ago saw the fallacy in such thinking. Speaking of state education, he wrote, "he that believes most must give way to him that believes least, and then he that believes least must give way to him that believes absolutely nothing" (*Popular Lectures on Theological Themes*, p. 283f. 1887.)

At one time, both Catholics and Protestants opposed all such unequal yoking; now too often both are often avid for it. At one time, a declaration by God commonly recognized and obeyed was His word in Isaiah 42:8, "I am the LORD: that is my name: and my glory will I not give to another, neither my praise to graven images."

The Lord God is emphatic that He will not give His glory to another. The prophets repeatedly declare God's wrath and judgment on all persons and nations who practice unequal yoking, who make alliances with ungodly nations, and who believe that man's diplomacy and detente rather than God's law is the way to peace and to victory.

If the Old Testament and the New are true, then it is clear that we face a world-wide judgment for our policies of detente. We have made our peace with evil and become evil. We have had more faith in detente than in the power of our covenant God. We have done evil and called it good. The men and nations of the world have treated God and His law as irrelevant and immaterial to their problems, and now they face their greatest problem, the wrath of God. Detente is an alliance with evil to accomplish a humanistic good, and it is therefore as much under God's judgment now as in Biblical times. God who does not change, condemns all forms of detente.

Liberation theology is a form of detente. It is easy to condemn such an unequal yoking. However, does such a practice of detente become tenable and holy if we practice it? Does "our side" define what is good, or does God? The essence of injustice and evil is, "In those days there was no king in Israel (i.e., God was rejected as King): every man did that which was right in his own eyes." (Judges 21:25). The covenant requirement is, "And these words, which I command thee this day, shall be in thine heart" (Deut. 6:6) and shall govern all of life. Jesus Christ is the covenant Redeemer, come to create a new covenant people and to empower them to establish His Kingdom.

All who are brought into the covenant of God by His grace are, in terms of Scripture and the ancient laws of covenants or treaties, *vassals* of God in

Christ. The vassal cannot enter into any treaty with another power, or with anyone who is not also a vassal of the triune God. To do so is to betray the covenant and to be guilty of treason. The covenant God requires uncompromising and unswerving allegiance. Then alone is our warfare God's warfare.

The curses pronounced in Scripture are curses against covenant breaking, and the blessings pronounced are for covenant faithfulness. To be in the covenant is to be in God's power and endowed with it.

Oliver Cromwell was a strong champion, not of any particular church, but of God's covenant. In a letter to his son-in-law, Lord Fleetwood, husband of Cromwell's eldest daughter, Bridget, Cromwell wrote, on June 22, 1655: "Dear Charles, my love to thee; and to my dear Biddy, who is a joy to my heart, for what I hear of the Lord in her. Bid her be cheerful and rejoice in the Lord once again: if she know of the Covenant, she cannot but do so. For that transaction is without her; sure and steadfast, between the Father and the Mediator in His blood. Therefore, lean upon the Son, or looking to Him, thirsting after Him, and embracing Him, we are His seed; and the Covenant is sure to all His seed. The Compact is for the Seed; God is bound in faithfulness to Christ, and in Him, to us. The Covenant is without us; a transaction between God and Christ. Look up to it. God engageth in it to pardon us; to write His law in our hearts; to plant His fear so that we shall never depart from Him. We, under all our sins and infirmities, can daily offer a perfect Christ; and thus we have peace and safety, and apprehension of love, from a Father in the Covenant, who cannot deny Himself. And truly in this is all my salvation; and this helps me to bear my great burdens." (M.H. Watts: *God's Covenants*, Vol. I, p. 1Of.)

In detente, all we have is man and his folly. In the covenant, we have the power of the triune God. (April, 1987)

THE RISK-FREE LIFE
Chalcedon Position Paper No. 86

It was shortly after World War II that I encountered the demand for an end to baseball playing by grade-school children. It was too competitive, said some angry women liberals; it was also too individualistic, they complained, and a boy at bat, or catching a fly ball, had too much concentrated and isolated responsibility placed upon him. Such a game, it was said, could have traumatic consequences. The women were also against losing; defeat could be disastrous for some children.

They did not stop to think that there can be no victory where there is no possibility of defeat. It also did not occur to them that the more competitive a group game is, the more cooperation it demands for winning. As for traumatic effects, it is true that defeat can be traumatic for some, but to eliminate the possibility of victory is truly deadly. It is true that the fear of defeat can be traumatic for a coward, but why encourage the coward in us all by eliminating risks? The risk-free life is a victory-free life. It means a life-long surrender to defeat, and nothing can be more deadly for man and society.

The lust for a risk-free life is all around us. It governs politics all over the world. Its logic leads to the world of Marxism, where the removal of the risks of failure for some means failure for all. An economy guaranteed against failure is an economy ensured against success.

All too often today men want to start with a guaranteed success, not with risks. As a result, we have in increasing evidence fraudulent successes, i.e., insider trading, artificially inflated stocks, and much, much more. The goal in all these dishonest activities is success without risk.

The risk-free life, however, is a deadly illusion. Freedom always involves risks. Eliminate the risks of freedom and you thereby establish slavery and defeat. But risk is still not eliminated! If the risks of freedom are banned, the risks of tyranny are ensured. Slave-labor camps represent a higher risk in the U.S.S.R. than do the risks in a free society. But this is not all. The Soviet military intelligence, GRU, for example, has a high risk factor to ensure performance. Anyone entering the GRU knows from the beginning that, if he disobeys or fails in even minor ways, he will be cremated alive in punishment. (Viktor Suvorov: *Inside the Aquarium*, pp. 2f., 93, 162, 190, 233, 237, 239f. New York, NY: Macmillan, 1986) In every aspect of the "risk-free" life in the Soviet Union, the risks of slavery make pale by comparison those risks which freedom requires.

Unhappily, throughout the Western world, the risks of freedom are highly unpopular. It is not an accident that capitalists and unions alike love monopolies and subsidies: they fear risks. In state after state in the U.S., gerrymandering by Republicans and Democrats serves towards ensuring their control of the political machinery and eliminating risks of defeat.

In whatever the sphere of action, those in power are most opposed to risk, because it can bring about defeat for them. The establishment uses its power to lessen risk for itself as a necessary step towards retaining power. After all, revolutions are made by those out of power who are seeking power!

I was a grade-school student when I first read Shakespeare's *Julius Caesar* and memorized with delight many of the speeches. One which I cannot forget is Caesar's comment:

> "Let me have men about that are fat;
> Sleek-headed men, and such as sleep o'-nights:
> Yond Cassius has a lean and hungry look;
> He thinks too much: such men are dangerous."

In other words, power-hungry men out of power are consumed with a lust for power.

But there is more, much more. Those who have the most to lose are those least prone to risks and to bold actions. Remember that the bold, enterprising and innovative work that went into the birth of computers came from young outsiders. Most of the bold entrepreneurial action of the post-war years has come from new-comers. The major corporations have declined or stagnated, and their "gains" have come from buying out the new men. Bankers favor such loans, because banks invest usually in established success, which means that banks invest in the past.

Today, in the U.S. and elsewhere, the major political forces are made up of well-established and powerful men. These are men who have the most to lose and hence the least to venture apart from money. Given the liberal establishment of the U.S., it is not surprising that the Democrats command the most wealth in their ranks. The number of wealthy men ready to risk the wrath of the powers that be is very few, and they are under attack. Power always draws the strongest support. The Republicans, however, are no different; power is always concerned with power, not risk. The conservatives also play the same game. In order to create a movement to win the country over to their cause, conservatives create groups of powerful men, and thereby sentence themselves to impotence, because they have created an alliance, council, or organization of men who have too much to lose to be bold. The result is sterility, and such groups become as effectual on the national scene as a ladies' sewing circle. It was no accident that the major political and social impact of recent years came from student movements. These student groups were sometimes chaotic, disorganized, and highly foolish, but their total impact was remarkably great. They had little to lose and hence were ready to lose it. Their causes were far more important to them than any penalties that risks would involve.

In the U.S., since Dorr's Rebellion and the Whisky Rebellion to the present, the risk-takers have commonly been foolish and have shown a talent for courting defeat. On the other hand, the established power groups have uniformly drifted into disasters because all their efforts have gone to keeping power, not towards creating a harmonious society.

Elsewhere, the men like Cassius, men of envy, hatred, and enmity, have overthrown by revolution their hated power brokers, only to become far worse instruments of power. They have taken risks, but only for evil ends.

It is thus important to examine the full implications of a risk-free world. Risks are inescapable, and we face either the risks of freedom, or the risks of tyranny. But risks rest on a world order beyond man and society. We are born into a world of risks, because we face the risk of death from the moment of our birth. Men may imagine it, but they cannot abolish the risk of death from this world.

This is not all. There is also the fact of moral risk. From Day One of creation, man faced moral risk, and death, if he partook of the forbidden fruit (Gen. 2:17). Risk was built into paradise, and it is certainly very much a part of our fallen world.

To dream of a risk-free world is to imagine a creation without hell, and also without heaven. It means the denial of any moral antithesis in creation. If there is no good nor evil in the universe, then there can be no heaven nor hell. This involves denying the reality of justice. Justice rests on the premise that it matters to God and to the very being of creation that good prevail and that evil perish. From my earliest days, one of the resounding verses of Scripture for me has been Judges 5:20, from the Song of Deborah: "They fought from heaven; the stars in their courses fought against Sisera." Justice is written into every atom of creation, and justice is inescapable. To deny hell is to deny justice. As Emory Storrs observed years ago, "When hell drops out of religion, justice drops out of politics." One can add that, when hell is denied as a reality and place, hell reappears as world-wide injustice and evil. Earth then becomes hell because the reality and finality of justice is denied.

To deny hell is to insist that life must be without moral risks. When churches become antinomian, they quickly then downplay the fact of hell because it emphasizes the ultimacy of God's law and justice. To deny hell is to deny the reality of morality and justice and to affirm a cosmic relativism. The fact of hell is our reassurance of cosmic justice.

But there is more. If we seek to eliminate risk from life and society, and to eliminate hell from eternity, we also eliminate the Sabbath rest and heaven. The Sabbath rest is meaningless apart from salvation. The Sabbath is a covenant fact, a celebration of salvation (Hence, the Passover dates the weekly Old Testament rest, and the Resurrection the weekly New Testament rest.) If there is no salvation, there is no rest. "There is no peace, saith my God, to the wicked" (Isa. 57:21).

Paul tells us, that our "Labour is not in vain in the Lord" (I Cor. 15:58). He does not say that it is risk-free. In fact, Paul is able to catalogue the risks he took by preaching the gospel, and the penalties he suffered: imprisonment, beatings, stonings, shipwreck, and much, much more. What he does tell us is that the moral risks have their certainty of reward because God's law and justice govern all creation.

It was after the end of World War II that our child-centered, risk-free culture began to predominate. Today's newspaper carried a story about the growth of criminal activity among children under 10 years of age; one police officer expressed his dismay at the evil dispositions and vicious street knowledge of such children. This should not surprise us. Children who have been spared the trauma of punishment are taught thereby that justice does not exist. It is still true, "He that spareth his rod hateth his son: but he that loveth him chasteneth him betimes" (Prov. 13:24). We teach our children that there is no justice if we do not punish them.

The dream of a risk-free life is an evil dream, because it is in essence a denial of causality; it is an insistence that cause and effect do not exist, and it is a denial that "the wages of sin is death" (Rom. 6:23).

It is also a denial of justice, because it rejects the fact that life involves inescapable moral judgments and risks.

The dream of a risk-free life is closely related to the pornographic imagination. Pornography gives man a world which is an imaginary one, one in which moral consequences are totally absent, and a world in which all things revolve around the individual's desires. Real people are lacking in the world of pornography; the evil imagination runs riot and re-orders all things to suit itself. Risks are removed from pornography in order to satiate without limitations the evil imagination.

The only risk-free world is in the evil imaginations of men: it has no substance nor reality. It cannot exist in the real world. Those who dream of a risk-free life are sooner or later, all losers. (May, 1987)

HYPOCRISY
Chalcedon Position Paper No. 87

The word *hypocrisy* is an interesting one with a long history. Our Lord frequently called the Pharisees hypocrites for a variety of reasons.

The origin of the word is the Greek *hypokrites*, which the Septuagint twice translates as "godless." A hypocrite in Greece originally referred to an actor who wore a mask and was not in reality what he pretended to be as an actor. Today the dictionary defines hypocrisy as feigning or pretending to be what one is not, or saying or pretending to one thing while being something else.

James 2:14-17 defines hypocrisy very clearly for us: "What doth it profit, my brethren, though a man say he hath faith, and have not works? can faith save him? If a brother or sister be naked, and destitute of daily food, And one of you say unto them, Depart in peace, be ye warmed and filled; notwithstanding ye give them not those things which are needful to the body; what doth it profit? Even so faith if it hath not works, is dead, being alone." Paul says the same thing in Romans 3:31, and our Lord is emphatic that we can know men by their fruits, their works (Matt. 7:15-20).

The Bible is thus very clear. Hypocrisy is a disparity between a man's faith and his works; it is faith without works.

Hypocrisy is very much with us in all camps. Certainly it is rampant in the churches. Antinomianism is organized, arrogant, and proud hypocrisy. It denies that faith will inevitably have works or fruits. One major American seminary actually dropped from its faculty a respected theologian who insisted on the link between faith and works. He was accused of denying the orthodox doctrine of justification of creating a works religion, and much more. The vilification was intense and passionate. Hypocrisy triumphed over sound theology.

Churchmen have no monopoly on hypocrisy; we find it in every camp, and, indeed, it governs most. Take, for example, the libertarians. Much of what they have to say in economics is usually good and often especially telling. Their fellowship is usually one of well-educated and superior minds. Their weakness includes a free-market totalitarianism. They love to impress men by their dedication to the free market, and they insist on a free market equality and freedom for narcotics as well as for food, and for prostitution equally with marriage. All this gives them a Pharisaic edge in claiming superiority over others in their dedication to freedom. But where are the libertarian schools for their children? Here we have an urgent problem. A recent statement coming from the statists themselves, avers that by the year 2,000, not far off, two out of three Americans will be functionally illiterate. And where are most of the libertarians' children but in the state schools! This is hypocrisy on a grand scale.

The liberals are amazing masters of hypocrisy. Take Senator Edward M. Kennedy of Massachusetts, for example. On February 25, 1987, the press reported his "moral" stance on South Africa, calling for stricter sanctions banning South African imports. Moral indignation is hardly becoming to the senator on any subject. On his trip to South Africa, he had to cancel his speaking engagement in Soweto because of black demonstrations against him; the blacks opposed disinvestment and felt Kennedy was against their interests. Kennedy refused Mayor Sol Kreiner of Cape Town when Kreiner invited him to see that apartheid had been dismantled. Although Zulu Chief Minister Mangoseethu Buthelezi, and all the Black National African Federated Chamber of Commerce made clear their opposition to disinvestment, Kennedy, on his return, claimed he "never met a single Black person in South Africa who opposed disinvestment." Much more can be said. Kennedy's qualifications as a moral voice are dubious and hypocritical.

Having said that, it is only fair to add that he is definitely not the worst member of Congress; many are far more hypocritical and far less able than he. (Given the Massachusetts representation in both houses of Congress, would this be grounds for disinvestment in Massachusetts?) The liberals have no lack of disparity between their faith and works, between their moral profession and their moral lives and works.

What about the media? The media supposedly is the source of news, but its concern is more closely tied to commanding instant interest with opening statements which bear false witness. Misrepresentation is routine and is taken for granted. If a man offends the media, his pictures then routinely are in the worst possible form, with his mouth open, in an awkward move, and so on. Handsome and kindly men appear as ogres, and women as modern witches. (It was a shock for me to meet one senator, a mild-mannered, kindly man, soft-spoken and good-humored, who is regularly depicted as a hard, ugly man and a ranter.) But the media sees itself in a somewhat messianic role, as an elite, and most certainly as champions of the very freedom of expression they resent in others. Here again we are face to face with hypocrisy, with a faith in freedom but not the works thereof, only license.

Conservatives are no less guilty. In the United States, in this century, the conservative premise can be summed up in words, "For God and country." Unhappily, for too many of these men, God does not even come second in their thinking. He is part of a slogan, and, after that, at best an afterthought. Most of them would get more respect from God as honest atheists. To take the name of God in vain is a violation of a basic law, a transgression of the Ten Commandments. To use God's name for political purposes is a sin. We have no right to invoke God unless we, in word, thought, and deed, are radically committed to the rule of God over us and in every sphere of our world. James 2:19 tells us that the very devils believe in God, and tremble. Too many churchmen and politicians invoke God casually, and do not tremble. They are hypocrites with less faith in God than the devil himself.

Churchmen are past masters in the art of hypocrisy. The churches, mainline ones especially, are full of men who profess much and believe in little or nothing. I recall, many years ago as a student, hearing one candidate for ordination declare with laughter in the hallway, "I just affirmed all Thirty-Nine Articles of the faith, and believe none of them." Of course, he arose to high positions and honor in that church, and why not? The church of our Lord's day made clear to Him that they preferred hypocrisy to the incarnate Son of God, and they crucified Him. The Pharisees and hypocrites are with us still.

Jean-Baptiste Massillon, Bishop of Clermont in the days of Louis XIV, was a man who showed, often tellingly, a knowledge of the propensity of man's heart for self-flattery and hypocrisy. When someone complimented him on one occasion for his brilliancy, Massillon replied, "The devil has said the same thing to me already, and more eloquently than you." Massillon recognized that men are not willing to face up to what they are. He remarked, "we all wish to avoid ourselves."

In the early years of the 19th century, an American preacher whom some regarded as a national treasure was Edward Norris Kirk of Albany, New York, a Presbyterian leader in his day. Kirk knew the significance of hypocrisy. In preaching on Romans 8:7, "Man's Natural Enmity to God," Kirk declared, "All over the world, and in every period of human history, men have hated, not the fact here stated, but the declaration of that fact. Men are willing, that it shall be true that they hate God, but they are not willing to read it, nor to hear it." Men, Kirk went on to say, "generally appear to be sincere, in denying that they hate God." In fact, most people in and out of the church will deny that fact, or affirm "with perfect sincerity--No, I love Him."

But, Kirk said, man outside of Christ is in enmity to God, although he may live a good, neighborly life. All the same, his own life is central to him, not God and His Kingdom. Even when converted, this carnal or fallen, egocentric aspect of our being, while juridically dead, is not yet totally mortified.

Kirk singled out three areas as revelatory of our natural enmity to God. *First*, he said, "Man hates the character of God as a Lawgiver." The basic prerogative of God's nature for which God "will contend with the power of His throne, is that of making laws for His creatures." But basic to man's old nature is his desire for his own way, his own will and his own law. Man, however, masks his enmity towards God's law with all kinds of devices. "This is one great source of deception." Men claim to love God while hating His law. "Let the awful truth be repeated; -- man has staked his happiness against the authority of the eternal Lawgiver." Of course, men use, said Kirk, high-sounding and 'moral' reasons for setting aside God's law while professing to love Him. One way this is done is "to deny the revealed character of a law so pure, and holy, and difficult, and contradictory to our passions." Another way "is, to admit the existence of the law, but on various grounds to deny the execution of the penalty."

Second, Kirk said, "Man hates the sovereignty of God." It does not please man that all things were made by God for His own purpose and glory. "But what if the plans of a sovereign God require the abandonment of our most beloved objects? Must we then cordially submit? Yes, you must either love, or hate a sovereign God. If you love Him supremely, your chief happiness will be derived from seeing Him accomplish His sovereign will." If our personal hopes and dreams come first, "you must be the enemy of God." (Strong words, these, but it tells us something about America then that Kirk's sermons were widely read.)

It is our disposition, Kirk said, when God denies us our will, to cry out, "O, God! what have these innocent ones done, that Thou shouldest thus tear them from earth's bright prospects? What have I done, that Thou shouldest rob me of more than life?" But the world cannot be ordered for our benefit, it moves in terms of God's purposes, not ours.

Kirk's *third* premise was this: "the carnal mind hates the mercy of God." If man resents or hates God's sovereignty, why should he hate God's mercy? But mercy is more than the "direct gratification of the wants of men." The purpose of mercy is to further God's Kingdom and His sovereign purpose. God's mercy is not essentially for our but for His sake and purpose. "The Israelites were led out of Egypt in mercy; but because everything was not arranged to their wishes, the very plans and achievement and instruments of that mercy perpetually aroused their wrath. The prophets were sent in mercy; but these were stoned and sawn asunder and driven to dwell with wild beasts. At last the Son of God came, the Messenger of mercy. From the cradle to the tomb, he drew forth the rage and malice of men."

How shall we cope with this fact in ourselves? We need to recognize its reality and pray truly God's will be done, in earth and by ourselves as it is in heaven. Our conscience needs the continual renewing of the Holy Spirit. "God has no other mercy than a holy mercy; no other merciful treatment of thee than to make thee holy. If this please thee not, it is because thou hast the carnal mind, which hates God." So wrote Kirk.

Massillon said that, having known God's mercy and love, we have only one proper response: "Love is the price of love alone." This means loving and obeying God with all our heart, mind, and being, and our neighbor as ourselves. The sad fact is, Massillon declared, that "the three principles which usually bind men to each other...are fancy, cupidity, and vanity." Society is constantly in a state of war because "religion and charity unite almost nobody." There is thus, said Massillon, a brittleness to human relations. There is hypocrisy in what passes as good Christianity, because "It is not rightly loving our brethren, to love them only through fancy; it is loving one's self." Our lives as Christians are false and hypocritical, because "are Christians made to live estranged, and unconnected with each other?"

Hypocrisy is faith without works, which means really no faith at all. A variety of such hypocritical faiths contend on the human scene, and they contend for power, and for control over men.

Our Lord declares that it is the way of the peoples, the Gentiles, to exercise authority or power over other men, "But it shall not be so among you: but whosoever shall be great among you, let him be your minister; and whoever will be chief among you, let him be your servant: even as the Son of man came not to be ministered unto, but to minister, and to give his life a ransom for many" (Matt. 20:26-28).

Hypocrisy is faith without works, power and authority without performance or service. Christian faith manifests itself in works, in service to God and to man.

The works cited are Edward Norris Kirk: *Sermons on Different Subjects* (1840); and Jean Baptiste Massillon: *Sermons*, vol. I. (June, 1987)

"FIRST THE BLADE"
Chalcedon Position Paper No. 88

One of the very important and much neglected verses of Scripture is Mark 4:28: "For the earth bringeth forth fruit of herself: first the blade, then the ear, after that the full corn in the ear." Our Lord tells us (Mark 4:26-29) that the Kingdom of God, as it develops in history, has a necessary growth and development. No more than we can plant grain and then expect the harvest at once, can we expect quick or immediate results in the growth of God's Kingdom. If we plant grain, we must cultivate it, often water it, tend to the field, and, only after much labor, reap a harvest. To expect otherwise is stupidity and foolishness, whether in farming or in the work of the Kingdom. In fact, our Lord describes quick growth as false (Matt. 13:5-6, 20-21).

The expectations of most people nowadays run contrary to our Lord's words. They demand immediate results, and then wonder why their harvests never come.

Within the church, this demand for immediate and spectacular results is commonplace. We need to remember that in church history sometimes the most successful preachers over the centuries have been heretics and compromisers. Carl E. Braaten has rightly observed, "John Tetzel was surely a popular preacher. He told people what they wanted to hear and sold people what they wanted to get. He was a preacher of indulgences, and lots of peoples swarmed to hear him and bought what he had to offer." (*Currents in Theology and Missions*, vol. 14, no. 2, April 1987, p. lllf.) Today, even the *Catholic Encyclopedia* speaks of Tetzel's "unwarranted theological views."

However, we need not go back to Tetzel. Today preachers of all sorts, and laymen too, believe in and demand of God instant results: sow the seed and stand back while the harvest pops up at once! As a result, such men often do better at growing weeds than grain.

This mentality is common in all circles, modernist and fundamentalist, socialist and conservative. During the 1930s, I recall spending a futile dinner hour trying to persuade a fellow student out of quitting his university training. A passionate and devout leftist, he was convinced that, very shortly, the forces of international fascism would conquer the world. It was therefore necessary to go underground with the party of world revolution and work for world liberation. He was totally convinced that, once the forces of world fascism were broken, peace and plenty would flourish from pole to pole and sea to shining sea. I believe that on that occasion I first made serious use of Mark 4:28, but it was futile.

In the 1960s, great numbers of students all over the world fell victim to the same wild delusion. They believed that, with a little action, the full ear of corn could be reaped at once. One group held that only the reactionaries prevented the immediate dawn of an automated, work-free, and war-free world. When a reporter asked one girl in the group how a work free world could produce food, she answered with haughty contempt, "Food IS!" The student movement commanded superior minds academically, but it lacked any sense of historical development and growth. God can produce instantaneous results; He created all things out of nothing. But the Kingdom of God in history moves, our Lord tells us, in a different way, even as "the earth bringeth forth fruit of herself: first the blade, then the ear, after that the full corn in the ear" (Mark 4:28).

In the past ten years, I have been involved in many court trials defending the freedom of the church, the Christian School, home schools and families.

It regularly amazes and appalls me that so many Christians, before they have fought a court case or voted (so many still do not vote), are ready to give up hope or to think of extreme measures and flight. (In this, they resemble the students of the 1960s.) Only yesterday I talked with a fine veteran of Viet Nam whose pastor sees no alternative to total obedience to the state except revolution; since he opposes revolution, he insists on total obedience as the Christian duty. He overlooks the vast realm in between, i.e., voting, pressure on legislatures, the education of Bible believers (of whom 50% do not vote), and so on.

It is important to recognize that this inability to see the necessity of growth is a modern failing, and also to see its source. The church fathers by and large tended to neglect Mark 4:28; but Calvin noted that the parable has as its purpose to make us diligent and patient "because the fruit of...labour does not immediately appear."

It was the Enlightenment and Romanticism which produced the new mentality. According to Scripture, man's problem is himself: he is a sinner. His original sin is his desire for autonomy, to be his own god and law, determining good and evil for himself (Gen. 3:5). However, there is nothing man wants less to face than the fact that, whatever other problems he has, he, his own nature, is his main problem. In fact, man rejects radically and totally the idea that God's indictment of him is correct. He may approve of the motto, "In God we trust," but he lives in terms of the premise, "In myself I trust."

The more man develops in his sin, in his evil will-to-be-god, the more he believes that his own fiat word can make reality. If statist man says, Let there be prosperity, there should be prosperity. If he says, Let poverty, hatred, and oppression be abolished, these things should disappear.

But, the more he pursues this course as god and creator, the more the evils around him increase. As James tells us, "From whence come wars and fightings among you? Come they not hence, even of your lusts that war in your members?" (James 4:1). Men create evils and then blame God, their environment, and other men for them.

How many politicians are ready to say, "We, the people, are responsible for the mess we are in. We want something for nothing. We want to eat our cake and have it too. We have despised God's laws concerning debt, and much, much more, and we deserve the judgment God is bringing upon us."

Man himself is the primary problem, and man insists that the blame must be laid on someone or something else. As a result, his problem is compounded.

The Enlightenment and Romanticism deny the Biblical answer. According to the Enlightenment, man's Reason is the solution to the problem, whereas Romanticism locates the answer in man's will. In either case, man is the answer, not the problem.

Such thinking placed the modern age (in Europe, after c.1660 especially) in radical disagreement with orthodox Christianity. The modern era exalts man and his needs, and it is at total war against the faith that declares man to be a sinner. The epitome of a God-centered faith is the Westminster Shorter Catechism's opening statement, "Man's chief end is to glorify God, and to enjoy him for ever."

The logic of such man-centered thinking in the Enlightenment and Romanticism led to Revolution. John Locke, after Aristotle, insisted that man's mind and being is a moral blank, neutral to good and evil. The premise of modern education is Locke's assumption: education then becomes the conditioning of the morally blank child.

But what about adults who are no longer morally blank but have been conditioned into an evil outlook by Christianity, family and capitalism? (This, for modern thinkers, is the great trinity of evil, Christianity, the family, and capitalism.) How are these peoples and cultures who have been conditioned by evil going to be changed? How can they be dealt with?

Revolution is held to provide the answer. Revolution is seen as personal and cultural shock therapy. We should not be surprised that psychiatrists turned for a time to electro-shock therapy: it is a form of psychological revolution. All old patterns are supposedly destroyed in order to clear the mind of past beliefs and habits; then the new, revolutionary changes can be instilled. Such a "therapy" has proven to be a dramatic failure; the moral nature of the man remains. It is not that which comes from outside which pollutes and warps a man but that which comes from within.

Political revolutions rest on the simple-minded belief in shock therapy. The French and Russian revolutions, and the Spanish and other revolutions, have all believed that destruction will free man from the chains of bondage, but all these revolutions have only enslaved man all the more. The more modern the revolution, the more destructive and vicious it becomes. The Russian Revolution murdered priests wholesale, worked to destroy the family, and confiscated property. The murder of priests became even more savage and intense in the Spanish Revolution.

The belief has been that the murder of man's past is his liberation into a glorious future. The results have been hell on earth, but the revolutionists never blame themselves for it. It is rather the lingering mentality of the past which is to blame. Gorbachev, to "reform" the Soviet Union, has intensified the war against Christianity.

Modern man refuses to be earth-bound. The proud American boast after the first space flight showed an astronaut as a newly born baby, and his umbilical cord tying him to earth being cut. Man now was supposedly transcending the earth to enter into a "space age" of freedom. With this new, god-like status, man, some held, would guide his own evolution, clone himself, and overcome space, time, and death.

Is it any wonder that evil churchmen have neglected Mark 4:28? Our Lord is very clear: the pattern of the Kingdom of God is like that of the earth which bringeth forth fruit of itself. There is an order and a progression from the seed, to the first green shoot to emerge, to the cultivated growth, and finally the harvest. Both time and work are essential.

I still recall my pity and revulsion for a prominent American pastor who, after World War II, wanted people to spend their time praying for a speedy Second Coming of Christ. He was arrogantly contemptuous of all Kingdom building as wasteful of time and money. He agreed with another prominent preacher who dismissed all efforts at Christian Kingdom action as "polishing brass on a sinking ship." Such men do not preach on Mark 4:28.

I recall also, sadly, a very fine man, a very wealthy man, who called me to see him not too long before his death. His family and the firm's director were now fully in charge of all his wealth. About seven years earlier, I had suggested to him that, if he had as his intention turning America around to a better direction, starting Christian Schools across the country would do it. He rejected my answer sharply. Now, near death, he called me in to say that if he had spent the millions he did seeking a "quick victory" on Christian Schools instead, the country would indeed be different.

That man was the antithesis of everything revolutionary. He had funded generously a number of anti-Communist causes. He loved deeply the more simple America he had known in his youth. He loved the one-room schoolhouse of his midwestern youth, and the country church with its kindly, neighborly believers in the old-time religion. He was a simple, honest, hard-working, old-fashioned American Christian.

At the same time, although he did not know it, and would have been outraged at the suggestion, he was a revolutionist. However much old-fashioned, he had something in common with all revolutionaries, namely, the hunger for and the belief in a "quick victory."

Millions of American conservatives demonstrated, shortly after Reagan's election in 1980 that they too were believers in the myth of victory by revolution. They acted as though the millennium had arrived with Reagan's victory! Conservative political action groups saw an alarming decline in monetary contributions. Reagan was elected, the war was over, the troops were leaving to resume life as usual in their now peaceable kingdom.

The mentality of instant results is all around us. It is the mentality of the modern age, and of revolution. It is the belief that the problem is not ourselves but something outside of us which an election, revolution, money, education, or some other like measure can alter tomorrow. Meanwhile, we ourselves see no need for change where we are concerned! We can maintain our modern lifestyle and make God happy with a few dollars tossed into an offering plate.

But God says to us, as His prophet Nathan said to King David, a better man than all of us, "Thou art the man" (II Samuel 12:7). The turn-around begins with us. Then, we work in terms of God's order on earth for His Kingdom: "First the blade, then the ear, after that the full corn in the ear." (July, 1987)

THE COMMUNION OF SAINTS
Chalcedon Position Paper No. 89

Otto Scott has wisely observed that, to understand the United States, we must recognize that it is a nation of "minority" groups; it has no majority groups, unless we divide it into "whites" and "blacks." Such a division assumes a unity and harmony in such groups which is nonsense. Northern Ireland is almost all "white", but that does not make for unity!

Is the U.S. a WASP, white Anglo-Saxon Protestant country, as some have insisted? Those of English descent number only 14 percent of the population, and the next most numerous group of Americans are Germans, 13 percent; Germans may be equal to or surpass the English, since many have Anglicized their names, i.e., Mueller into Miller, Schmidt into Smith, and so on. Moreover, these groups are not united in action, outlook, faith, or politics. Germans number many Catholics, and also many Lutherans, in their midst. The Irish are, in the U.S., more Presbyterian than Catholic, and so on.

In the United States, all are members of one or more minority groups, but, in law and the media, the myth of a persecuting majority exists.

A Welshman, John Morgan, after a few years stay, wittily and wisely noted a common fact about Americans. From the first Englishmen, to at least the Vietnamese, each new group believes this was a great country, until the next group of immigrants arrived to "spoil" America!

In the 1920s and 1930s, ethnic jokes were common on radio and usually enjoyed by the ethnic group in question. We were, that is my family, in the '30s in our home town, a Swedish farm town, when a new comedian gained popularity with his ethnic humor and simulated accent, "Ole Olson." He was the endless delight of the Swedish community. In those days, ethnic humor, if not malicious, was relished. Jewish friends had an endless stock of Jewish jokes; Scots loved Scottish jokes, and so on. The difference between affectionate and malicious humor has been lost. Humor today is too often an ugly put-down.

But "racism" and "prejudice" are today the major sins in the eyes of many people. At the least, this is humanism and a theological error.

On April 3, 1987, *The Wall Street Journal* had a front-page story on campus "racism" at American universities. It showed clearly the illusions of our time. Some real incidents were cited, but a subheading told part of the story: "A Junior at MIT: 'I'm Alone'." As a university student during the

Depression, I was not alone because I had no time to be. Most students held one or more jobs to pay their way through school. A major problem for some was getting enough to eat. A social life was a peripheral fact. I am sure, of course, that many black and white students today are lonely, but can you abolish loneliness and create friends by law?

Today, however, the media is full of people who are constantly on the look-out for instances of the great modern sin, prejudice. The cases become sometimes very ludicrous.

On Thursday, April 9, 1987, *The Stockton* (California) *Record* carried a major story on pages 1 and 10, with a large photograph of an indignant Hindu spokesman. The story carried the author's by-line, Christopher Woodword. The problem? At St. Mary's High School, the principal, the Rev. John Fallon, uses a large bulletin board in front of the school to advertise school events. If there are no announcements, he throws in witty comments with a moral content. In April, he had a sentence on the board designed to ridicule bigotry and prejudice: "Sacred Cows Make Great Hamburgers." Innocent? Clever? Well, not to the Stockton Hindus! It was a slur, they held, against them and their religion! (Will they picket meat market beef sales next?) They held that the sign was offensive to their belief that "all life is sacred, especially the cow." A 'spokesman' declared, "I don't go putting up a sign saying white people make good hot dogs."

Father Fallon was naturally distressed, and he promised to have the one-liner removed. But the "horror" of this crisis did not end there. Father Fallon had gotten the sentence out of a calendar put out by a Jewish group dedicated to combatting persecution, the Anti-Defamation League! The question of the moment is this: will the Hindu 'spokesman' now demand of the Jews whether they would like a sign saying something invidious about the Jews?

Are we uniting society with all this nonsense, or are we dividing it? Many people who long wanted and even worked for an end to bigotry are now hesitant about close relations with self-styled minorities: they find them often too touchy for more than casual contacts.

But this is not all. Within each group, hyper-sensitivity is begetting an increasing isolation on all sides. I often hear remarks which, in a variety of ways, say the same thing: close fellowship is increasingly a problem because everyone is so "touchy" and easily provoked. A people with an exaggerated sense of personal rights are not capable of sound relationships with others.

A deserted island was once seen as a terrible place to live. Now for some people it is an ideal setting! If only such an island could be stocked with certain things, and people barred, it would be a paradise for many.

Fifty years ago one of John Donne's best known lines was widely used: "No man is an island." Donne also said, "The greatest misery of sickness is solitude," and, "Solitude is a torment which is not threatened in hell itself."

"In heaven," said Donne, "there are orders; of angels and armies of martyrs and in that house many mansions; in earth, families, cities, churches, colleges, all plural things; and lest either of these should not be company enough alone, there is an association of both, a communion of saints which makes the militant and triumphant church one parish; so that Christ was not out of his diocese when he was in our flesh."

Donne was speaking of the communion of saints. The antithesis of communion is solitariness, isolation. While Donne held solitude to be a torment not even threatened in hell, we must say that hell is self-chosen isolation from God and man, a realm in which every man is his own god, law, and universe (Gen. 3:5). All the Biblical images of hell stress its meaninglessness and isolation.

The communion of saints is not a natural fact. In a fallen world with sinful man, communion is a divine grace, act, and gift, a sacrament which celebrates fellowship with God in Christ, and with other men.

The goal of humanistic civil government is community. Among the names given to the envisioned world order of humanism and socialism are "The Great Society," and, "The Great Community." The goal is to attain a world order in which all men are brothers and all live together in peace and prosperity.

This Great Community is to be brought about by social and political revolution. Laws, or "works of law," education, and coercion are to bring in liberty, fraternity, and equality. Economic controls are to be used to equalize society and enhance fraternity.

There is thus a vast difference between the Great Community and the communion of saints. The communion of saints is an article of faith, affirmed in the Apostles' Creed; it is God's act, His sovereign grace, which makes us members of that communion. Our obedience then to God's law-word enables us to further that communion.

If men seek community humanistically and by acts of state, they destroy true community. They establish rather a "community" of evil, a unity only in hatred against Christianity. We should not be surprised that humanistic efforts to attain community become anti-Christian. It is held that Christianity, by its insistence on Christ alone as the Truth and the Savior, is discriminatory and hence must be controlled or destroyed.

This becomes then an insistence on a community which denies absolute truth and is beyond good and evil. Marxism is thus both more logical and more consistent than other forms of humanism because it denies all meaning which transcends man.

Humanism enthrones the ultimate bigotry and prejudice: it is against Truth because it is anti-God, and, because it is anti-God, it is of necessity anti-man, because man is created in God's image. Hence, the goal of humanism is to create a new man and efface the image of God. In every sphere, mental, sexual, political, economic, and more, man is to be remade.

Recently, *The Capsule* for January-March, 1987 (1205 West 5th St. Terr., Caneron, Missouri 64429), quoted Jeremy Rifkin as follows: "We no longer feel ourselves to be guests in someone else's home and therefore obliged to make our behavior conform with a set of pre-existing cosmic rules. It is our creation now. We make the rules. We establish the parameters of reality. We create the world, and because we do, we no longer feel beholden to outside forces. We no longer have to justify our behavior, for we are now the architects of the universe. We are responsible to nothing outside ourselves, for we are the kingdom, the power and the glory forever and ever."

This statement is simply an expansion of Genesis 3:5, "Ye shall be as God, knowing (or, determining for yourself) good and evil" in every sphere, law, sex, society, everywhere. This is original sin, fallen man's desire to be his own god. Now, however, it is not called sin: it is humanism, it is the means to true community, it is man's revolution of freedom against God.

The goal of the humanistic Great Community is the brotherhood, the fraternity, of all men. But how can you open your mouth in such a social order? After all, words are divisive; words define, delimit, and separate. The best way to get ahead, more than one person in politics, business, unions, and other groups have told me, is to keep your mouth shut and your eyes half-closed. After all, look where five little words got Father Fallon and the Anti-Defamation League! "Sacred Cows Make Good Hamburger" - this is religious and racial bigotry, something for the front pages of a daily paper!

Must we now be careful at a chicken dinner about expressing a preference for dark meat, or white meat, or any meat all! There is now a well-funded lobby, with many film and television stars as its champions, defending animal rights. After all, why should animals not have the same legal right not to be eaten as do you and I?! If this sounds outrageous, remember that it is costing cattlemen and farmers money to fight this movement!

The end is not yet. Some scientists, in India and elsewhere, are telling us that trees and vegetables feel pain when harvested! Are we in for a vegetables' rights movement? (The fruits already have a movement going.) One fool claims that the air is highly nutritious and provides sufficient food! He heads up a Breatharian movement of one.

Is that the direction of our society, millions of movements of one? But is that possible? After all, with so many people schizophrenic, how can any such a person organize himself into a movement of one?

A society, according to one political scientist of some years back, is a power structure. He was simply summing up a truism of his profession. More recently, a classical scholar, studying ancient Greece, used this same premise and added, "Power structures are rooted in brute strength" (Eva C. Keuls). Certainly history gives abundant evidence of this fact.

Because of this premise, social reformers logically assume that no Great

Community is attainable except by creating a power structure and using brute strength, unremitting social pressure and coercion. This is what our politics is all about.

The Biblical premise is radically different: "I believe...in the Communion of Saints." To believe in that communion is an act of grace, sovereign grace. It is of the Lord, not of us. He who made us remakes us into His people and community. He then requires us to live by His law, to live as "members one of another" (Eph. 4:28), and to remember that "unto whomsoever much is given, of him shall be much required" (Luke 12:48). We who have received the gift of Christ's atoning grace have received more than the world itself. Much is required of us. (August, 1987)

SIN AND EVIL
Chalcedon Position Paper No. 90

Words often tend to be dulled and cheapened with time. Careless usage, poor education, and indifference to clarity serve to blur the meaning of words, so that we often inherit words which were once sharp tools but now have dulled edges.

Two such words are sin and evil. Until recently, the dictionary definition of sin retained its Biblical focus: "sin is the transgression of the law" (I John 3:4), God's law. The Biblical orientation of the word "sin" tells us why the term is not much used outside of the church: it speaks too clearly of personal responsibility to God.

"Evil" on the other hand, has a broader definition, in the Bible and in dictionaries. It can and does include sin, but it means much more. It covers calamities, diseases, death, disasters, and the like.

Evil can be a result of sin; thus, sexually transmitted diseases are always evil, but they are not always a result of sin, if caught innocently. On the other hand, death is a result of the fall and of man's sin, but death itself is not a sin, although it is called an "enemy" (I Cor. 15:26). Sickness is an evil, but not necessarily a sin, although on occasion it can be a result of sin.

The distinction between sin and evil is a very important one. Theological errors have resulted from their confusion. Thus, Christ by His atonement redeems us from sin; He takes upon Himself the penalty for sin, the death sentence, so that we are delivered into everlasting life. By His atonement, we are made a new creation (I Cor. 5:17), and our calling is to reconstruction, to the restoration of all things and the elimination of all evils until, with Christ's coming again, "the last enemy, death," is then destroyed (I Cor. 15:25-26).

The atonement thus covers sin, not evil. The redeemed man has a duty to destroy the effect of sin in himself, i.e., to "mortify" it (Rom. 8:13; Col. 3:5). Christ must reign in the new man and through Him subjugate "all rule and all authority and power" so that only "the last enemy,...death," remains at Christ's coming (I Cor. 15:24-26). This destruction of evil comes through sanctification; it comes also through scientific work which overcomes diseases and "natural" threats of a fallen world. In every sphere, we are to work to overcome evil and enthrone Christ.

Our atonement does not sanctify us perfectly: it gives us the power to make our lives and spheres holy. Our standing before God is as innocent in Christ, but we now have the duty to develop the new life of righteousness or justice in every sphere.

In false views of the atonement, sin and evil are both seen as destroyed, not only with respect to our legal status before God, but in our psychological status, so that we are supposedly perfect in holiness and freed from evil. To be sick then becomes evidence of sin! A generation or two ago one minor cult leader was sure that the atonement had freed him from sin and death so that he would neither sin nor die. (He did both.)

In terms of such thinking, healing, instead of being a ministry of compassion, became a demand for trust or belief in the atonement.

A key difference between sin and evil is that sin is always personal, whereas evil is often impersonal. Sins are the acts of men and have no existence apart from human action, creaturely action, in transgression of the law of God. It is thus an absurdity to say we should hate the sin and love the sinner. It is an artificial distinction. Theft, adultery, murder, false witness, covetousness, idolatry, dishonoring parents, and other sins are the acts of men and are the expressions of their moral nature. The man who steals is a thief, and the man who commits murder is a murderer. The act does not occur of itself; it is the act of a sinful man, and it is an expression of his will and life. Our Lord insists on the unity of a man's life and his works; hence, "by their fruits ye shall know them" (Matt. 7:20). "Either make the tree good, and his fruit good; or else make the tree corrupt, and his fruit corrupt: for the tree is known by his fruit. O generation of vipers, how can ye, being evil, speak good things? for out of the abundance of the heart the mouth speaketh" (Matt. 12:33-34).

Sin is not an entity: it is an act of man's will, whereby he transgresses God's law because man prefers his own will and way to God's requirements. Its origins are in Genesis 3:5, man's will to be his own god.

Modern man does not like to speak of "sin." Many churches have dropped the word "sin" from their vocabulary. Pastoral psychology finds all kinds of good reasons for sins: need, loneliness, neglect, self-realization, deprivation, and much, much more. All these "reasons" have a common purpose, to diminish personal responsibility for sin. We are full of "good excuses," and we encourage them. "I didn't know what I was doing." "My intentions were good, but, before I knew what I was doing, I was in trouble." "If only my training had better prepared me, this never would have happened." Or, in

"Flip" Wilson's words, "The devil made me do it." Perhaps the most common "not guilty" plea is this: "Well, I'm only human!" In other words, God made me this way, so He is to blame.

Sin is not a popular subject for preaching these days! Many church officers and members will insist on "positive preaching" to "build up" the listeners, and the congregation's size. (For a year or two, one woman wrote me particularly vicious letters every few weeks to let me know what a hateful person I obviously was because of my writings. Particular statements would move her to fury; they obviously troubled her, and she called me every kind of ugly name. She demanded a gospel of love, told me she was praying for my salvation, and then signed her letters, "In Christian love." I have received, over the years, much hatred and venom by mail, all in the name of love! Show me a "love-baby," and I will likely be face to face with an accomplished hater!)

Modern man does not like to hear anything about sin, but he does speak freely of evil. Remember, sin is personal, very personal. If someone talks about sin in your life and mine, they are getting totally personal! However, if they talk about the evil we experience, the talk is impersonal. A disastrous storm, or a tornado, can do much evil, but it involves no guilt on your part and mine. But if you talk about my sin, you are getting very personal!

Today, because fallen men run nations, the talk is about evils, not sins. These evils are outside of us. They are things like poverty, hunger, war, sickness, and more. The "solution" to social evils is then declared to be the appropriation of more money; more power to the state; more money for education, research, and study; more social engineers and planners; and so on and on.

The cost of these legislative and bureaucratic solutions is very, very great. For one thing, it means more and more taxation. In the United States, it adds up, on all levels, to a taxation in excess of 45% of our income. In most countries, the direct and indirect taxes add up to far more. This, however, is only the taxation cost by income, sales, manufacturing, and other taxes. An even more deadly form of taxation is inflation, which steadily devours savings and capital; it also destroys the value of pensions and life insurance. There is also the cost of freedom, and we continually see our freedom diminished in the name of this war against social evils.

Meanwhile, the evils increase, because the solution is a false one and only aggravates the problem. It was man's sin that brought evil into the world, and to bypass sin is to give evil greater freedom. God declares (Deut. 28) that He diminishes evils as men believe and obey Him, and increases and intensifies them as men disobey Him.

We also aggravate our plight by insisting that sin is not sin but a social evil, not personal but impersonal. Sociologists do not call sin by its proper name; criminals are explained by heredity, or by environment. Their genes were bad, or their family environment was entirely wrong for them. This is another way of saying that criminals are "not guilty."

Drop the word "sin" from law, and in time you drop also the word "guilty." Remember, sin is personal; it is the transgression of the law of God. It is a personal act of rebellion by man against God and His word.

Dostoyevsky saw the logic of unbelief: If there were no God, all men could do as they pleased, because there would then be no sin. Nietzsche embraced this belief: the new man must live beyond good and evil because, he held, God is dead. Walter Kaufmann, in *Without Guilt and Justice* (1973), held that guilt and innocence, justice and injustice, are theological doctrines. Because man now lives beyond this belief in God, in autonomy, he can dispense with guilt and justice, because neither concept now has meaning. The last "chapter" of Kaufmann's book is his retelling of Genesis 3:15; man is now ready to be his own god and determine good and evil for himself. "Nobody knows what is good. There is no such knowledge. Once upon a time God decided, but now that he is dead it is up to you to decide. It is up to you to leave behind guilt and fear. You can be autonomous." (p. 237). (We should not be surprised at any kind of madness in Kaufmann's writings: he was a man who not only read Hegel on his honeymoon but wrote proudly of it!)

No God, no sin, no guilt -- this is the modern equation, a thoroughly suicidal one. God declares, "he that sinneth against me wrongeth his own soul: all they that hate me love death" (Prov. 8:36). The men who heralded the death of God were actually declaring the death of man.

Long before Nietzsche and Kaufmann, men were paving the way for them by subverting the moral criteria. When Milton's Satan, in *Paradise Lost*, says, "Evil be thou my good," Milton was giving us a long-current opinion through Satan. The humanist scholar, Lorenzo Valla, in *De voluptate* (1431), held that pleasure is the only authentic good of man; all goods can be reduced to pleasure. This is man's natural and hence normative goal. True, Valla could say, and his apologists use it to justify him, that glory and a contemplative life give pleasure to some. Let us remember, however, the pleasure Valla took in declaring, "courtesans and harlots are more deserving of honor from humankind than holy and chaste virgins." Some men try to tell us that Renaissance humanism meant simply the study of classical literature. It was indeed that, but it was commonly governed by a delight in classical immoralism. For too many classical scholars, sin was a form of freedom, and for some the key form.

This is still true of many circles, including the circles in which Lord Keynes, Strachey, and others, the so-called "Apostles," moved. It is basic to the "sexual revolution," to abortion, and to the homosexual agitation: sin is declared to be the new freedom. Evil is by some then defined as restriction on the freedom of man to live in defiance of God and to declare sin to be man's true freedom.

It is instructive, in this regard, to remember that this was the creed of developed and mature paganism in imperial Rome. As Donald Earl noted, in *The Age of Augustus* (1980), "Sexual freedom...was a prerogative of the Roman noble, female as well as male" (p. 192). Now, with the prevalence of the democratic spirit, this "right" to immoralism is claimed by all classes. Less than ten years ago, a raging U.C.L.A. student insisted to me that the wages of sin are not death (Rom. 6:23), but a richer and freer life.

The Westminister Larger Catechism echoes Scripture to declare, "Sin is any want of conformity unto, or transgression of any law of God, given as a rule to the reasonable creature" (no. 24). As I John 3:4 and all of Scripture makes clear, "sin is the transgression of the law," i.e., the law of God.

This brings us to the heart of our problem. When the church is antinomian and despises the law of God, what can we expect of the world? When the church bypasses the Bible's definition of sin, why should the world pay attention to it? The reformation of society must begin with the reformation of the church. (September, 1987)

AGAINST MUCH PRAYING
Chalcedon Position Paper No. 91

One of the familiar and very much neglected comments by our Lord has to do with prayer. We are commanded to pray, and to pray quietly, without ostentation, and "in secret," i.e., not to publicize our praying. "But when ye pray, use not vain repetitions, as the heathens do: for they think they shall be heard by their much speaking" (Matt.6:7). Note that repetitions are *not* forbidden, but vain repetitions are. The widow in our Lord's parable was much given to intense repetition ("Avenge me of my adversary"), but it was not *vain* repetition but rather a repeated and passionate prayer for justice (Luke 18:1-8). He condemns "much speaking" or praying which has as its purpose a desire to impress God.

This is especially a great temptation in our time. We live in what some call the democratic age; even tyrannies function in the name of the People. They hold mock elections in which everyone must vote, even though all candidates run unopposed, as in the Soviet Union. The People must all favor what has been predetermined for them. Even the Soviet Communist Party leaders, who know that the elections are a formality, go through the sanctimonious ritual of voting. It is a religious duty for the People to express their common will!

Given this mentality, now, more than ever, people are impressed by numbers. More than a few organizations add thousands of worthless names to their mailing lists because prospective donors are influenced by numbers!

In the years just after World War II, a very fine Christian layman began a small organization to stem the modernism then arising in his church. The "fellowship" was remarkably effective in its early years. Then some members agitated for an increased membership. The founder insisted on a maximum of 50 members; most insisted on thousands in order to make an impact. Those favoring a large membership won out, and, before long, the association was a model of impotence. Its stance had been compromised, its publication became moderate and conventional, and it was incapable of decisiveness.

The demand for numerical strength continues unabated, despite a world filled with examples of failures. Even worse, this mind-set has infected prayer. The assumption is that, if we can get 1 million people, or even 10,000, praying zealously for something, God will give it to us! The assumption is that God is guided, not by His knowledge and wisdom, but by our nagging.

The results are tragically evil. Devout Protestants, who view the medieval endowments for continuous prayers by monks and nuns with horror, now create "prayer towers" where for 24 hours daily, a number of people are gathered to pray for all prayer requests. One evangelist on television has said that as many as 35,000 people have tried to call his "800" number in a single hour.

Somehow, people believe that God will hear them more readily if 500 or 5,000 people are praying for them. Whatever happened to the priesthood of all believers? Must a professional praying-person pray for us before God hears us?

A good many years ago, a sick man asked me to pray for him. I knew the man well, and that he was afraid of death and admitted it. I told him to do his own praying, and to begin by confessing his very serious sins. He refused. He wanted healing, not communion with God.

Today, however, certain electronic ministries stress strongly their prayer ministries for people. They invite people to call in, and they speak of the large number of people manning telephones (or should I say womanning telephones?) to hear our prayer request and to pray for us.

One young pastor recently was left feeling very uncomfortable when someone demanded to know whether or not the church had a prayer ministry! Perhaps, very soon, we may have churches with blinking neon signs advertising 24-hour prayer ministries with no waiting!

Now, St. Paul tells us that "we are members one of another" (Eph. 4:25). We pray for our family members, our friends, and our fellow church members out of love and concern. Here at Chalcedon, we thank God for our supporters; we have come to know many of you and pray for you when we know of your problems. But do we have a department of prayer, or a formal prayer ministry? No. Much speaking carries no weight with God.

Moreover, all too often prayer ministries concern themselves with personal wants, not the Kingdom of God. How many of those prayer ministry or prayer tower groups are concerned about persecuted Christians in the Soviet's power, or with American parents persecuted in the courts for home schooling, or for sending their children to a Christian school?

Even more, how many concern themselves with God's Kingdom and justice? Yet our Lord tells us, in Matthew 6:33, "seek ye FIRST the Kingdom of God, and His righteousness," or justice. Are not unending "gimme" prayers insulting to God? Do they not become more insulting when we line up great numbers of people to nag God?

Our Lord gives us His model of prayer in Matthew 6:9-13, declaring, "After this manner therefore pray ye." We are to begin by hallowing His name. Our paramount request must be, "Thy Kingdom come. Thy will be done in earth, as it is in heaven."

God wants His Kingdom to rule and reign as fully on earth as in heaven, and we have a duty to pray for this, and to work for it. He has given us the laws of His Kingdom, and we must obey and apply them.

As we are faithful, so He too is faithful. He will give us our daily bread, and He forgives our debts "*as we forgive our debtors*." Prayer has as its companion obedience and action. The focus of prayer is wrong if it is our needs primarily rather than God's Kingdom.

If we pray essentially for ourselves rather than God's Kingdom, it will not make our prayer more effective to have 500 people unite with us in saying that "my will must be done."

In II Chronicles 7:14, God declares to Solomon, "If my people, which are called by My name, shall humble themselves, and pray, and seek my face, and turn from their wicked ways; then will I hear from heaven, and will forgive their sin, and will heal their land." The priority in prayer is clearly not our wants but God's will.

Let us look again at our Lord's words in Matthew 6:7, "But when ye pray, use not vain repetitions, as the heathen do." Clearly, our Lord is warning us against the pagan forms of prayer. E.N. Fallaize, in James Hastings' *Encyclopedia of Religion and Ethics*, defined "primitive" prayer in these words: "In its simplest and most primitive form prayer is the expression of a desire, cast in the form of a request, to influence some force or power conceived as supernatural" (vol. 10, p. 154). The word "influence" tells us all. This is "heathen" or pagan prayer, a belief that God can be influenced. This is not Christian prayer: we enter into communion with God through Christ in order to find our place in His will and Kingdom and to receive His blessings.

Too commonly, the fostering of mass prayers is to compel God's attention and to influence Him by numbers. This is paganism.

Our Lord identifies another aspect of "heathen" prayer: "vain repetition." The pagan's "vain repetition" was associated with magic. Certain repeated incantations could influence and command the spirits or gods. The "heathen" prayers our Lord refers to were really more spells, magical formulae, than prayers. They were seen as magical words of power, and they would have more power if certain persons repeated them for us, shamans, medicine men, and the like. In some instances, these spells had to be repeated at various hours of the day to be effective, and this is what our Lord also meant by "vain repetition."

The goal of such pagan "vain repetition" was to control a supernatural power by exercising and commanding a greater power. In I Kings 18, we have a classic example of pagan "prayer." The priests of Baal sought to control the powers over earth by numbers, by shouting "vain repetitions," and by mutilating themselves. Perhaps at the same time as this was happening at Mount Carmel, all the priests of Baal at the various sanctuaries may have been using "vain repetitions" to help the priests at Mount Carmel! Against all this, as James notes, "The effectual fervent prayer of a righteous man availeth much" (James 5:15). Elijah's concern was God's Kingdom and God's justice.

It is worthy of note that paganism usually has had a specialized "praying" class. To have influence with or control over the forces of nature or the spirits, an expert technician had to be used.

Among some American Indians, for example, communion with the spirits was an elitist fact, reserved to the limited number of members of a secret society. Such a power made them sometimes feared because of the damage it was believed they could do, using the spirits.

More "advanced" religions in antiquity had rituals and prayers which often are quite remarkable. They seem at times close to a Biblical emphasis. They stress penitence, a strong moral sense, and a desire for communion with the gods. There is, however, a significant difference between all such pagan rituals and prayers, and Scripture.

The stress in these "advanced" pagan religions is on self-reformation and self-commendation. The "worshipper" presents himself as one who has repented and reformed himself, and he then proceeds, with "vain repetitions," to nag the god or gods for acceptance and for his petitions. The stress is on the human initiative, the self-reformation, and the self-qualification. The man says, I am here, O god, ready to receive. How can you refuse me, and why do you? In Egyptian religion, the worshipper presented himself to the gods after death with a litany of self-praise and with a recital of all his virtues.

This was the "heathen" model against which our Lord warns us. It was present all around Him, and it is all around us today, and sometimes in us. This is why the Lord's Prayer is so important for us to use: it teaches us the true perspective in prayer. We dare not use the Lord's Name in pagan prayers.

The doctrine of the priesthood of all believers is Biblical. It rests on the premise that believers are members of God's covenant and family and therefore in faithfulness to their Lord and in communion with Him. Prayer or communion is thus a common privilege of all Christians, and of all who seek God's face in repentance and faith. (November, 1987)

FALSE MORALITY AND FALSE REFORM
Chalcedon Position Paper No. 92

One of our persistent problems today is that so much "reform," approved by Christians and non-Christians, and liberals as well as conservatives, is simply immoral. An example of such a false perspective is an article in the October, 1987, *Reader's Digest*, condensed from *The Wall Street Journal*: Patricia Bellew Gray's "Tobacco Goes on Trial."

Before someone decides to condemn me as an apologist for the tobacco companies, I shall make two things clear. *First*, I am not a smoker; I have never even tried it, and I see it as a foolish habit. *Second*, the tobacco industry does not have a good record as a moral concern! During World War I, a major tobacco corporation worked hard to protect an enemy country, Turkey, because of its contracts for Turkish tobacco; its sympathies and efforts were not with the massacred Christians but with its Turkish partner in business.

The point of Mrs. Gray's article is that people dying, apparently, of tobacco-induced lung cancer, or their families, are suing the tobacco industry for failure over the years to alert users of the dangers in smoking. The defense of the tobacco industry in the legal battles is described as "a lavishly financed and brutally aggressive defense that scares off or exhausts many plaintiffs long before their cases even get to trial." So far, the industry has not lost, but Mrs. Gray has high hopes because of two new cases, in Mississippi and New Jersey.

Let us begin by granting the *medical* case against smoking: it is a dangerous and even suicidal habit. But are the companies liable? Were people ignorant of the dangers of smoking before the warning notices were placed on cigarette packages? Is knowledge of tobacco's threat to health something new?

I am now 71 years old, I cannot recall a time when the menace was not clearly known. In the 19th century and well into the depression years of the 1930's cigarettes were known popularly as "coffin nails." Hygiene classes, athletic coaches, and other authorities regularly warned the young of the dangers of smoking. I was quite young when a Dr. Pearl studied insurance statistics and demonstrated that smokers died earlier than non-smokers. The young who started to smoke were warned, "It will stunt your growth," "It will kill you," and so on. It was impossible for anyone to grow up without endless naggings and warnings about smoking.

The young would begin smoking as an act of bravado, or to act sophisticated, or out of sheer defiance. In my home town, because the scout-master bore down heavily against smoking, all the Scouts would leave the meeting to light up cigarettes in gleeful defiance. It was their way of thumbing their noses at authority.

Now, if we say the tobacco companies are then responsible, we deny all godly morality, and we give the right to those who defy well-known facts of health to blame others for their condition. Will farmers be sued next because people who over-eat have health problems?

We can be grateful that there were no American courts and judges in the Garden of Eden. Adam and Eve might then have sued God for creating the tree of the knowledge of good and evil, and also for creating the tempter who tempted them! After all, Eve did blame the tempter, and Adam blamed Eve, and he also blamed God for having given him Eve! The suits against the tobacco industry follow the same pattern. They turn the moral universe upside down. They deny the facts of sin and responsibility.

Given this type of law-suit, what shall we expect next? Will we have suits against call girls and other prostitutes for having given a customer a sexually transmitted disease?

In Concord, California, an anti-war protest group, in violation of the law of trespass, moved in front of a train with munitions, then leaving the Concord Naval Station. One man was hit and lost both legs below the knee. The protesters wanted news and television coverage and had notified the media. They expected to be removed, arrested, and to be on the evening news. After the accident, created by their trespass, they were outraged that no charge was filed against the crew of the train (*The Stockton* [California] *Record*, Thursday, Sept. 24, 1987, p. B-2).

Protesters of various kinds have routinely destroyed and harmed individuals as their fundamental right, but they regard it as "oppression" if any consequences affect them.

Whether we are anti-war, or anti-tobacco, the moral fact remains the same: when we knowingly do something, we must be prepared to accept the consequences. We cannot shift the blame onto others. To do so is sin. No matter how just or righteous our cause may be, it cannot justify sinning on our part. If you are struggling for breath because of lung cancer, it is because you did wrong. No one forced you to smoke. When you sue the tobacco industry for your own stupidity, then you really do wrong before God: you deny your own responsibility, and you blame others for what you have done. The fact that the tobacco industry is not a model of Sunday School deportment does not alter the fact that you are wrong. The other person's sins can never justify your crimes.

The suits against the tobacco industry should not surprise us. They are a part of the spirit of an apostate age. Adam and Eve both denied their guilt: they insisted that they were *victims*. This is the stance of ungodly man: his sin is not his responsibility but a consequence of the environment. Somebody or something else is blamed: "The devil made me do it." This evasion of responsibility is basic to sinners.

In a society of sinners this means that guilt must be located elsewhere. Criminals have learned the language of psychiatry: they "explain" their offenses by calling attention to their "bad" homes, which is often a lie. Child molesters insist that they were themselves molested as children, and we are supposed to feel sympathetic and understanding as a result. Back in the 1950s, I found instances where even children under 10 years of age were excusing their conduct with terminology coming from psychologists.

All the excuses are there, so now we accept them, treat parents, capitalism, society, the church, and other agencies as guilty. The offenders are seen as victims!

Thus far, the tobacco industry has won the cases, but the outlook is not good. Our society is more and more ungodly, and it bases its "morality" on the rationalizations of the Fall, not on God nor on His Law-Word. Our laws increasingly reflect a bias against the Biblical doctrine of sin and responsibility. We should not be surprised that Christianity is increasingly attacked as the evil in society, and the sinner justified in his sin.

We come now to the most deadly implications of this present temper. According to Scripture, God through Christ's atonement justifies the sinner. Christ takes our guilt and sin upon himself and dies in our stead. The Holy Spirit regenerates us and makes us morally new men, new creations. Our justification cost Christ the cross because God's law is unchanging, and sin requires judgment and restitution. Christ righted the legal and moral balance and makes us His responsible and righteous people.

There is, however, a different doctrine of justification in these lawsuits and in much of our current "reform" legislation: *it justifies the sinner in his sin*. According to the logic of this view, the Tempter, rather than Adam and Eve, should have been at the least cast out of Eden, if not killed; the tree of the knowledge of good and evil should have been demoted and sued for creating the possibility of temptation and sin. Is this what you want?

There are two moral realms in conflict, the Kingdom of God versus the Kingdom of Man. Beware lest in your foolish sympathies you align yourself against God.

Incidentally, God created tobacco. One of these days, when we approach it as God-created, we may find a variety of healing uses in its composition which could amaze us. Remember, God made all things good (Gen. 1:32). Our misuse of things cannot alter that fact. (December, 1987)

(Note: *Daily News Digest*, August 29, 1990, reported that the anti-war protester who lost both legs when he lay down before a munitions train has received a settlement for $920,000.)

WEALTH, RESPONSIBILITY AND COWARDICE
Chalcedon Position Paper No. 93

In recent years, a very important fact with great repercussions in society has marked our society. At one time, for better or worse, men of great wealth exercised important powers and positions in society. Their gifts created charities, subsidized the arts, and governed many areas of life. In more ways than one, men of great wealth set the pace.

In this century, this has steadily become reversed. In part, this is due to the democratization which Alexis de Tocqueville feared would subvert Western civilization and lead to a barbarization of society.

But this is not all. There are other factors which are far more important which have been at work. There is a very clear religious dimension here which we must never overlook. The Bible is clear that wealth brings with it responsibilities. Our Lord sums up the meaning of the law and the prophets in these words: "*For unto whomsoever much is given, of him shall be much required: and to whom men have committed much, of him they will ask the more*" (Luke 12:48). The history of Western civilization and Christendom cannot be written apart from these words. Both the medieval church, and the Reformation churches, have unleashed vast sums of giving by their insistence on the duties of all who prosper, whether little or much, towards others. In every part of the world, such Christian giving has made an impact unequalled in all of history. It warps history to make no note of this fact.

In recent years, however, some signs of change are readily apparent. The patronage of the arts is an obvious realm in which the difference appears. The ultra-modern, avant garde art, really pretentious junk art, has a patronage perhaps unequalled in history. To gain respectability, our corporations great and small buy such junk art for their office and corridor walls, and to store in their warehouses. The corporations are the mainstay of the various purveyors of junk art. At the same time, television has on its "public" channels all kinds of programs financed by corporations.

Two things can be said. *First*, all such funding, including much funding of the Left, wins no friends for the corporations. Their money is taken, and they continue to be reviled. They in effect finance their own condemnation. *Second*, the corporations are careful to give little or nothing to Christian churches and agencies which are evangelical or reformed. Except for a few men, they act as though some kind of sin against society would be committed by such a gift. Some executives justify this, saying, our shareholders are not all Christian, so it would mean problems if we gave such gifts. But many of their shareholders are Christians: does their stand and faith count for nothing? Moreover, how many of their shareholders would favor their gifts to leftist causes?

The problem lies elsewhere. *First*, too many corporate executives are men without faith. They may belong to "mainline" churches, and, in some parts of the country, are expected to join them for public relations purposes, but they are still men without faith, often in churches without faith. Recent studies have shown that, whereas most Americans affirm a Christian faith, a very great majority of the men in the communications media do not. Moreover, many are strongly anti-Christian. It would be interesting to see if a study of corporate executives would give like results. Of course, for public relations purposes, many such executives would perhaps routinely give dishonest answers.

Second, without faith, a man finds courage drained out of his system. For him then the world is without meaning, and, in such a world, what is worth fighting for? To such a man, easy and evasive solutions are the best. Not surprisingly, cowardice has become very common among corporate executives. Nowadays, to find a courageous executive usually means that he is a believer, whether Christian or Jew. He does not evade responsibility: he assumes it as a privilege. Most, however, have much to lose and no faith, and hence, are timid and cowardly.

As a result, most corporate leaders today are supportive of power, whoever holds it. They reject any stand on the bases of beliefs and morals of a pragmatic position.

As a result of this lack of faith, and this cowardice, men of wealth have abandoned their responsibilities to society. Some such men have organized various councils to deal with a variety of social and political issues, but all these groups are models of impotence. If a problem arises, and a group or people become threatening, the "solution" is to throw money at them. Hence our foreign aid program, and hence too our insane bank loans to countries incapable of repayment. The solutions of these councils are the "solutions" of bankruptcy -- moral, intellectual, and financial.

Because of this, we have seen the rise of underground man, of the lowest elements in society. They are the new revolutionary element! They are bold, because, having nothing, they have nothing to lose. And they are bold because they can smell the fear of them by the rich, and also by the middle class.

Moreover, because the rich, *and* the middle class, are marked by a weak faith or no faith at all, they are cowardly when challenged. The underground people, sensing this, push as much as they can.

Once underground man was confronted with the challenge of the gospel of Jesus Christ. Now, money is thrown at him in the vain hope of buying him off.

Cowards find talk of conspiracies comforting. Conspiracies have always existed, but men of faith have conquered them again and again over the centuries. Now, as someone has rightly observed, the homosexuals have come out of the closet, and the Christians have entered the closet. Every kind of group grows bolder as the rich, the middle class, and the lower class show a weak faith and much cowardice. Cowardice is no respecter of class or status.

"Unto whomsoever much is given, of him shall be much required." Our generation has been given much, and the Lord requires much of us. We have been schooled to demand much of others, however, and we demand to be saved! I am regularly amazed by the fact that people who have *never* contributed a penny to Chalcedon will write to demand hours of thought and work from us at their bidding! One such person wrote twice thereafter, very indignantly, to indict us for failing to answer to his every demand! As a professor of history told me about 15 years ago, we are witnessing the death of civility.

Much is required of this generation, and the time of reckoning draws near. We have a calling to serve the Lord with all our heart, mind, and being. We have a work to do, or a judgment to face. As against all that we face, we have the power of God unto salvation (*Romans 1:16*). If we know Christ, then we know the power of His resurrection (*Philippians 3:10*), so that we are summoned, not to continue in weakness or cowardice, but in His almighty power. (January, 1988)

THE TAX REVOLT AGAINST GOD
Chalcedon Position Paper No. 94

An important fact of the current American scene is the tax revolt, primarily directed against the U. S. Federal government. No one knows how many people are involved in this, but the numbers are considerable. While not at all in agreement with this movement, I must add that it has in its ranks some of the finest and most dedicated men in the country. They recognize clearly the growing power of the state, the onset of totalitarianism, and the awesome waste of tax funds. For 50 years, the policy of "tax and spend" has governed both parties. Their occasional good resolutions when out of office turn into forgotten rhetoric when in office. The evil is clearly there. Writers like columnist Donald Lambro, in such books as *Washington, City of Scandals* (1984), document the prodigal waste of funds by Congress. As against critics who decry this waste, both parties excuse their actions by citing the needs of the poor, when in reality much of the money goes to enrich the rich even more.

We must remember, however, that Scripture gives no room for tax revolt. Judea, in our Lord's day, was deeply involved in a tax rebellion against Rome. In one instance, tax money was demanded of Jesus, who made clear His immunity from taxation as the Son of God the King, but, at the same time, He instructed Peter to pay it by means of a miracle (*Matt. 17:24-27*).

On another occasion, spies, and a "trick" question, were used in an attempt to trap Jesus. In that day, anyone opposing the tax revolt lost popular support, and was regarded as a tool or servant of Rome, by the people. On the other hand, if a well-known person advocated the tax revolt, his arrest quickly followed. The question asked of Jesus was, "Is it lawful for us to give tribute to Caesar, or no?" To answer, "yes," would mean the contempt of most Jews; to answer, "no," would mean arrest and prison. Our

Lord called attention to Caesar's image and superscription on the coin, and said, "Render therefore to Caesar the things which be Caesar's and unto God the things which be God's" (*Luke 20:20-26*).

The meaning was clear: the coin witnessed to the fact that Caesar provided them with coinage, military protection, courts, law, public works, roads, and more. By their sins, they had made Caesar their Lord or Sovereign. However, if they would render to God what God requires, in full obedience to His law, then God would again be their Lord. In other words, the tax revolt was the wrong answer; it did not alter the moral and religious fact of their apostasy. They invoked the name of the Lord, as churchmen do today, but they did not obey His law-word.

Charles Adams, in *Fight, Flight, Fraud, The Story of Taxation* (1982), gives us an excellent survey of the history of taxation. Even more, he sees the heart of the matter clearly, stating, "taxing power is the guts of sovereignty" (p. 125). This is the key fact. Whomsoever we make our sovereign has then the right to tax us: taxation is the prerogative of sovereignty. Today, the state is man's sovereign; it is Hegel's god walking in history, and hence it has unlimited powers, because a sovereign cannot be bound or controlled by any law.

According to Scripture, God is our Lord or Sovereign. The most common term applied to God the Father in the Old Testament is "Lord," and in the New Testament "Lord" is the most used term for Jesus. The triune God is our creator (*Gen. 1:1-31*). Therefore, "The earth is the LORD'S, and the fullness thereof; the world, and they that dwell therein" (*Ps. 24:1*). It is God the Lord who therefore allots funds to church and state alike. Civil government is limited to half a shekel for all males 18 years and older (*Ex. 30:10-16*) to provide an "atonement" or civil protection or covering for them. For worship, *one-tenth* of the tithe, or 1 percent of a man's increase was provided (*Num. 18:24-26*). The Levites were to use the rest of the tithe for education (*Deut. 33:10*) and a variety of other societal services. Thus, clearly, God does not allow in His law for any centers of power in church or state. Both are to be small institutions, the one a ministry or diaconate for civil protection, the other a ministry of grace (*Rom. 13:1ff*).

When the problem of a power state develops, the key is not rebellion but obedience to God the Lord. All things are under the government and the providence of God. We are in our present predicament because of our disobedience to the Almighty.

Remember, the major tax revolt is not against the modern state: it is against God. It is significant, too, that God's law makes no provision for the enforcement of the tithe *by man*. Neither church nor state have the power to require the tithe of us, not to tell us where it should be allocated, *i.e.*, whether to Christian Schools or colleges, educational foundations, missions, charities, or anything else. The tithe is to the Lord.

The fact is clear that man cannot impose rules to govern God's tax, nor require it of us. God, however, can enforce this law in His own way, and does. In Malachi 3:8-12, God tells us certain things about His tax. *First*, failure to pay it means robbing Him, robbing God! God expects not only tithes from us, but also offerings, *i.e.*, gifts above and beyond the tithe. *Second*, failure to pay God His tax means that we shall be under a curse. This curse will affect us in the realm of nature, in the realm of civil government, and in every other sphere of life. In other words, in Malachi's plain terms, God takes a tax revolt against Him far more seriously than the U.S. Internal Revenue Service does in cases of tax revolts against it. And God has far more efficient powers of enforcement! *Third*, God declares that His powers to bless us for paying His tax far exceed anything we imagine. It is the promise of life.

All God's laws carry with them curses and blessings (*Deut. 28*). The first promise in this regard, *i.e.*, first in importance, concerns the family: "Honor thy father and thy mother; that thy days may be long upon the land which the LORD thy God giveth thee" (*Ex. 20:12*). In Ephesians 6:2-3 Paul stresses the life-giving fact of obedience to this commandment. The tithe is one of these life-giving laws when obeyed.

This means that men and nations cannot expect God's blessing when they neglect His tax and laws. Why should God bless a people who disobey Him, are engaged in a tax revolt against Him, and who insist on declaring that His law has been done away with? It was because God's law is so important and unchanging that only the vicarious sacrifice of the Son of God could make atonement for us. Is the law now a trifle? Some insist that we are no longer under such laws as "Thou shalt not commit adultery...steal...kill...bear false witness," and so on, only under grace. Granted that these are extreme antinomians, but what grace is there in any neglect of God's law, of any disregard for it? Remember, our Lord declares, "Whosoever therefore shall break one of these least commandments, and shall teach men so, he shall be called the least in the kingdom of heaven" (*Matt. 5:19*). Did our Lord change His mind about this after the resurrection? If so, He neglected to say so!

The tax revolt against the U.S. Federal Government is thus really a small matter. It will not affect the fundamental course of things, nor stop the growing totalitarianism. The key problem is the tax and law revolt against God. You can be sure that He does not take it lightly. (February, 1988)

INVISIBLE RULERS
Chalcedon Position Paper No. 95

Many people like to believe that somewhere invisible rulers pull the strings which govern all of us. Such a belief denies that man is created in the image of God and is governed by two basic motives. *First*, Paul tells us, all men know the truth of God, things visible and invisible, because they are written in every atom of our being by our Creator. Men "hold" or suppress these things because of their unrighteousness or injustice. No man anywhere can escape this knowledge (*Romans 1:17-21*) For this reason all men are "without excuse." *Second*, all men everywhere, as sons and daughters of Adam, are fallen, and they seek to be their own gods, determining law, morality, and all good and evil for themselves (*Gen. 3:5*). The strings that pull us come out of our heart and mind.

In the modern age, man has reversed the historic definitions of knowledge. *First*, according to Scripture, to know, love, and fear God is the beginning and essential part of knowledge and wisdom. *Second*, according to classical Greek philosophy, knowledge is gained by ascertaining the abstract universal ideas of the totality of being. *Third*, for science, especially after the Enlightenment, it was knowing the facts. This view is still very powerful, although it has been demonstrated that our presuppositions determine what is for us a fact.

With Kant, a *fourth* view of knowledge came into dominance. Kant, in his preface to the second edition of his *Critique of Pure Reason*, stated the matter bluntly: "Hitherto it has been assumed that all our knowledge must conform to objects. But all (such) attempts...ended in failure. We must therefore make trial whether we may not have more success in the tasks of metaphysics, if we suppose that objects must conform to our knowledge." In other words, the "real" world is what our mind says it must be.

If you grasp Kant's implication, then you will understand the modern world, its religion, politics, art, education, and much, much more. The source of truth is no longer, for the modern mind, to be found in God, ideas, or facts, but in our own being, in our rationality, or in our feelings, according to some.

Hegel embraced Kant's thinking and furthered it. In his *The Phenomenology of Mind*, he wrote, "I am I in the sense that the I which is object for me is sole and only object, is all reality and all that is present." The "I...is all reality!" For Hegel, the rational is the real; reality is what our reason says it must be. With such a premise, existentialism was inevitable.

I have often called attention to the fact that modern man has a will to fiction. His basic reality is his imagination, and he lives out his life in his imagined world instead of reality. One of the most unpleasant letters I have received (and they are many, often foul-mouthed, from churchmen and atheists alike) declared me to be vicious because I was undercutting the dream world of harmless peoples.

But is it harmless to live a lie? Never before in all of history have people lived so extensively in terms of their dream worlds rather than reality. They watch television by the hours, see movies, read fiction, and they believe that the world of their imagination is better than God's reality. Communists are not what they say they are but what our imagination wants them to be. Politics is going to give us our hopes because we believe in it. Churches too often succeed by preaching smooth things and an easy "gospel." When an artist asked to have permission to paint Cromwell's portrait, Cromwell granted it on the condition of honesty, that he be painted warts and all. No portraitist is likely to hear such a demand in our time. We want to be seen as we imagine ourselves to be. The modern mood was well stated by an early Romantic poet, William Blake, who complained, "O why was I born with another face!" The "real" face of his imagination was somehow not in place.

Hegel's real world was the world of consciousness, the mind of man. This is the "real" world of too many people now, in the churches and outside of them. A simple and grim evidence of this is that pastors who have congregations of elderly people find them complaining if the pastor talks about the evils of abortion. This, they say, is of no meaning to them, since they are past the child-bearing years; they want sermons which are "personally" helpful. When I hear, as I do regularly, of such common comments in our best churches, I am sick at heart and sometimes shiver in horror at God's certain judgment. Such people seem unaware that "our God is a consuming fire" (Heb. 12:29). Too many people, I find, in their vain imagination reduce God to a Father Christmas. They use Biblical language with idolatrous purposes.

Yes, we do have invisible rulers, in a sense, in various philosophers and their ideas, but they rule over us because they please us in their insistence on man as his own god. The true ruler of all things is Christ, for the government is upon His shoulders (Isa. 9:6). He warns us against ascribing the government of things to men or to secret Satanic conspiracies. In Revelation 2:24, He condemns all who study "the deep things of Satan," i.e., Satanic conspiracies. To hold that the creature, or any combination of creatures, can take over control from God is a fearful sin. In Psalm 2, we see that God laughs at all human conspirators against Him, and at their believers.

Because we do not live by every word that proceeds out of the mouth of God (Matt. 4:4), we are the victims of our sins, and of those who choose to exploit our sins. Too many people, for example, rail against "the international bankers" without stopping to think that their debt-living creates inflation, and the kind of banking we now have. Of course, it is always more popular to talk about the sins of other peoples and not our own! The prerequisites of all blessings from God include the confession of sin, our sins, not other people's sins. The old Office of Compline, which ended the day, had a telling prayer, a general confession: "I confess to Almighty God, the Father, the Son and the Holy Ghost, and before all the company of heaven, that I have sinned, in thought, word and deed, through my fault, my own fault, my own most grievous fault: wherefore I pray

Almighty God to have mercy upon me, to forgive me all my sins, and to make clean my heart within me."

When men and nations persist in sin and avoid confession, they become self-righteous and Pharisaic. They insist in living in illusions about themselves, i.e., in living a lie, in an insistence that their private fictions are public realities. We have a world today passionately devoted to its fictions.

So deeply ingrained is this will to fiction that several friends who are monetary and market economists regularly find themselves rebuked for stating carefully documented facts: they are told, "It's people like you who create economic disasters by talking as you do." In some countries, it is now a criminal offense to cite the crime rate of any particular ethnic group, even though true. It is called racism to do so. Supposedly, if we ignore a group's sins, they will be better people, and so shall we! This is the will to fiction. It is the belief that the rational is the real; or, in Kant's terms, the real world, the "objective" world, is in our minds, not out there. Thinking will make it so, supposedly. Is this not really insanity?

There is a great chain of people involved in Kantian and Hegelian thinking. Marx was their intellectual heir; so too was John Dewey, and all political parties from the left to right are infected by Hegelian thought. Our intellectuals, our schools, pulpits, and media echo such thinking all too often. It undergirds antinomianism, because antinomianism finds the idea of God's law, "out there" governing us all, to be anathema. For Hegel, it is the spirit in the universe and man which is the source of all evolving truth.

If we do not take the fall of man and original sin seriously, we will believe that some group of invisible rulers is responsible for our problems. We will then become good Pharisees, denouncing evil in someone else. If we believe in the fall and man's original sin, his will to be his own god (Gen. 3:5), then we identify, the real problem, and we see its locale: *in all of us*. We know the remedy, Jesus Christ, and we know that His will must be done, so that His Kingdom may come. That will of the Lord is set forth in every word of the Bible. That book tells us, "Thou art the man," but it gives us the power to work, as God's new creation, to overcome the powers of darkness.

We are the invisible rulers who will not rule. We find it much easier to blame others.(March, 1988)

THE POLITICAL ILLUSION
Chalcedon Position Paper No. 96

It would be absurd to deny the importance of politics, but it is also very dangerous to over-rate it. One of the persistent problems of Christendom has been the tendency to over-rate both church and state. In Numbers 18:21-26, we see that God orders the tithe to be paid, not to the priests but to the Levites, whose varied functions included education. Thus, worship *per se* received mainly a tithe of the tithe. At the same time, the civil tax was limited to half a shekel for all males over 18, the same amount for all. As a result, both church and state in Scripture are, however important, *restricted* in size and power. The power-center is the covenant man and the family.

Michael Kammen, in *A Machine That Would Go of Itself, The Constitution in American Culture* (1986), has shown how modern men since Newton have seen their hope and salvation in machines. The universe was seen as a machine, and politics was seen also as an area where, if the proper machinery of government were once established, all would then go well. Constitutionalism was seen as such a mechanism; once properly established, it would ensure the orderly processes of government and justice. Machine imagery was used well into this century by men like Oliver Wendell Holmes, Jr., and President Franklin Delano Roosevelt. Even the critics of the U. S. Constitution used the same language, saying, "the machinery of government under which we live is hopelessly antiquated (and) should be overhauled." After World War II, as colonies were granted independence, they were also given constitutions which had no meaning in terms of their cultures and laws. Not surprisingly, these constitutions soon became meaningless. Contrary to Western expectations, constitutions guaranteed nothing when the culture of a people was unrelated to the paper rules.

In the 1930's, the New Dealers added a biological character to the "mechanism" of the Constitution. After Darwin, they held that constitutions have also an organic character and thus must evolve into more advanced forms. This mechanistic and sometimes biological theory of law and constitutionalism was the *first* and major form of American (and, often, European) faith concerning political order.

The *second*, stemming from Jean-Jacques Rousseau, held to a belief in the will of the people as embodied in the general will. Philip S. Paludan, in *A Covenant with Death, The Constitution, Law, and Equality in the Civil War Era* (1975), has shown how the popular will came to outweigh law in many minds. Davy Crockett claimed that the heart of the common man was *at least* the equal of books and the learning of judges. He boasted of having never read a law book and of having based his decisions as a justice of the peace on "common sense and honesty" and of having "relied on natural born sense and not law learning." Thus, the certainty of the "mechanism" of the Constitution was giving way for many to the natural goodness of man's will. Such advocates of man's natural wisdom held that no law or constitution could outweigh the will of man.

Many, of course, tried to combine the idea of constitutions and laws as the mechanism of justice and government with the idea of supremacy of the popular will, the majority, or the democratic consensus. As a result of this union of the two ideas, it became commonplace to use the word "democracy" instead of "republic" in describing the United States. The U.S. Constitution was re-interpreted along democratic lines, as was the British Constitution. Will and mechanism had become a unity and an instrument whereby man's problems would be solved. Salvation was now on its way by means of the democratic process in and through civil government.

Church and state have often seen themselves as man's saviors. One of the premises of the states of the ancient world was that a stateless man was no longer a man, that outside the state there was no salvation. A like belief has at times been common to some churches. The Biblical faith, of course, is that there is no salvation outside of Christ. Peter declares: "neither is there salvation in any other: for there is none other name under heaven given among men, whereby we must be saved" (*Acts 4:12*). Our Lord says plainly, "I am the way, the truth, and the life: no man cometh unto the Father, but by me" (*John 14:16*). (Ironically, I have been told by critics more than a few times that to believe in a salvation exclusively through Christ is bigotry. These same people will declare that there is neither hope nor future, no salvation, in other words, for men except through democracy. This is more than bigotry: it is pharisaic stupidity!)

Modern men believe earnestly that their hope of salvation is in and through politics, through the state. As a result, the capture of the state in order to institute their plan of salvation is an urgent matter to many men and their political parties. Some talk as though the world will come to an end if the opposition party wins the election!

Now, clearly, political parties can do some good, and much harm, but they cannot create the good society nor a new paradise on earth. Political change is coercive change, not moral transformation. Political power cannot regenerate men. All too often, politics is the art of turning a working society into a disaster. At its best, however, civil government cannot give to a people the character they do not have.

To expect social regeneration by means of politics is to believe in moral shortcuts. It is the belief that men and nations can be made new by legislation. Imperial Germany before and during World War I was very strongly socialistic; every area of life was regulated and controlled: it was an ordered society. After World War I, many liberals believed that freedom from socialist regulations would produce, automatically, a free, liberal economy and society. The result instead was the moral anarchy of the Weimar Republic: it was not productive as the liberals had hoped but was instead given to lawlessness. In voting for Hitler, many people were voting for a return to order, for a respite from lawlessness, only to find that an ordered society can be a radically lawless one.

Only a moral society can be a truly orderly one, and a moral society requires a regenerate people.

Too often, the churches have followed either one of two equally vain approaches to civil government. *First*, the social-gospel faith sees man's hope in terms of civil law. Hence, the control and use of the civil order becomes an essential step to social salvation. Instead of a personal moral commitment to charity and social responsibility, the social-gospel churches substantiated political commitment, they are now dying, because a century of social action has produced only minor goods and major ills.

Second, the pietistic churches want no involvement in either society or civil government. For them, the *essence* of the Gospel is, "Ye must be born again." They forget that this is *the starting point*, not the essence, for our Lord declares, "Seek ye first the kingdom of God and his righteousness (or, justice)" (*Matt. 6:33*). Because of this misplaced emphasis, such churches produce at best usually only babes in Christ. They forget that a baby that never grows up is an idiot. It should not surprise us that such churches are marked by social impotence. People can attend them year in and year out and hear nothing either to offend or to challenge them. In effect, such churches give assent to the savior state by their unwillingness to confront it.

Salvation by political action is the ruling religion of our time. It is a form of humanism. It will destroy us in time, if we do not replace it with Jesus Christ as Lord and Savior, and the wholeness of the word of God. We have as a people sought salvation through education, "social justice," and also politics. All have failed us. It is time to bring back the KING.
(April, 1988)

THE CHURCH AS FUNCTION
Chalcedon Position Paper No. 97

The church began its history in the Roman Empire, in the midst of a Greco-Roman culture. Jerusalem itself reflected that fact and was richly subsidized by the emperors because of its strategic importance. Keeping Judea peaceful and happy was a basic policy. Judea's failure to appreciate its "privileges" led to the intensity of Roman vengeance during and after the war of A.D. 66-70.

The church was both influenced by that Greco-Roman culture and also hostile to it. Herbert B. Workman, in *Persecution in the Early Church* (1906), noted: "By Roman theory the State was the one society which must engross every interest of its subjects, religious, social, political, humanitarian, with the one possible exception of the family. There was no room in Roman law for the existence, much less the development on its own lines of organic growth, of any corporation or society which did not recognize itself from the first as a mere department or auxiliary of the State. The State was all and in all, the one organism with a life of its own. Such a theory the Church, as the living kingdom of Jesus, could not possibly accept in either the first century or the twentieth." Many churchmen then as now tried to accommodate themselves to the sovereignty of the State or emperor rather than Christ. They were willing to confess, "Caesar is lord." The church in part was preserved from absorption by Roman persecution. The intransigent, uncompromising Christians preserved the church by their refusal to compromise.

All the same, however, some things were absorbed, *i.e.*, neoplatonism, Aristotelianism, Stoicism, asceticism, and the like. An important borrowing from Rome was organization and bureaucratization. The church was in a very real sense a continuation of the synagogue, and in the Greek text of James 2:2, the word translated as *assembly* is actually *synagogue*.

The church, unlike the synagogue, was not only an Hebraic organization but it was essentially an organic body, a corporation: the body of Christ. Now the members of a body (*i.e.*, hands, feet, etc.) do not hold offices; they have *functions*. The words translated as *office* in the New Testament make this clear. For Romans 11:13, I Timothy 3:10 and 3:13, the word used is *diakonia* in Romans and *diakoneo* in Timothy. The word, in English as *deacon*, means a servant, service; it refers to a function. In Romans 12:4, *office* in the Greek is *praxis*, function. In Timothy 3:1, it is *episkope* and its meaning is supervision or inspection to give relief or help. In Hebrews 7:5, the reference is to the Old Testament priesthood, *hierateia*, and refers to the sacerdotal function.

Thus, what we call church offices are in reality functions of the body of Christ in this world. This fact is very important. Offices lead to a bureaucracy and a ruling class, whereas functions keep a body alive.

In the early church also, we have no evidence of what is commonplace today, regular, stated bureaucratic meetings of presbyteries, synods, councils, bishops, etc. Instead, beginning with the Council of Jerusalem in Acts 15, the meetings were called to resolve a problem or meet a need. They were functional meetings, not organizational; they were aspects of the life of a body, not of a bureaucratic organization. They exercised no coercive power, but they did formulate questions and answers pertaining to faith and morals carefully and precisely.

Both Eastern and Western churches, and, in the West, Catholicism, Protestantism and Anabaptism, have developed great and powerful bureaucracies which impede the life of the church. Both church and state, and especially the state, suffer badly from bureaucratization and consequent constipation in their life. As a result, in the United States, many Protestants and Catholics have some home study groups which bring new life to their faith. In Edinburgh, Scotland, I found a remarkable charismatic church; it had purchased a large stone church closed by the Presbyterians and was the center of extensive ministries. But it had no membership list! Fearful of bureaucratic strangulation, it was keeping the church together as a faith bond in the Spirit rather than as an institution. While it is not necessary to go to such a length, clearly a corrective to emphasize function and life is urgently needed.

One of the consequences of bureaucratization in the church is the rise of the star system. This is certainly true also in other spheres, especially the state. People vote for presidents in terms of their "image" projection, not their faith and life, not their action. Most of the presidents of the earlier years of the United States would never be elected today. Lincoln is liked in retrospect. His high pitched voice, carelessness in dress, and much more, would today finish him after one television appearance.

The importance of the star system is necessary to understand. People want the star to epitomize what they want, or would like to be. They identify with the image he projects. Thus, some people feel that a prominent political leader, or a religious leader, is "entitled" to moral lapses because of his importance. In earlier times, such lapses were called the royal prerogative. The star must be the expression of the popular or common will, the general will.

In the church in the United States, the star system set in soon after churches began to move on the one hand into Unitarianism, and on the other, into Arminian revivalism. People gravitated towards powerful pulpiteers on both sides of the fence. The churches then began to take their life from the star: a star could bring in hundreds and even thousands of people, lead to a great church complex, attract people and money, and give the members the vicarious feeling of being part of a great church. This still is very, very much with us. Some people will simply say, "I want a church where the action is." By action, they mean crowds; the result is often a surrogate "Christianity," not a living faith.

The result too is spectator "Christianity," a star performing before hundreds and thousands. The mandate to believers in both numerically large churches as well as small is then reduced to being good spectators and contributors. For the surrogate "Christian," someone else expresses the faith and does the work. We have then what General William Booth called mummified church members.

The star system has had its shipwrecked stars over the centuries, men like Savanarola, Henry Ward Beecher, and others of more recent years, and the end is not yet. The star system tends to give, not life, but a form of life. As Paul says in II Timothy 3:5, some have the form of godliness but not the power thereof. Instead, what the stars usually have is the power of money.

Paul tells us that we are "the church of the living God" (*I Tim. 3:15*) Jesus Christ declares that He is "the way, the truth, and the life" (*John 14:4*) The Trinity is never identified as the Great Bureaucracy but as life, the author of life, and more. For the church to identify itself in terms of its bureaucracy is a sorry fact.

If the church indeed is the Body of Christ, it must function as if it is alive. A dead church is a non-functioning church; it is salt which has lost its savor and is fit only to be cast out and trodden under foot by men (*Matt. 5:13*)

This is a grim possibility in our time. We cannot say that in all places the church today is dead, but in too many areas it is badly arthritic and feeble. Christ, the Lord of life, commands us, saying, "I say unto thee, arise!" (May, 1988)

THE PARADISE OF WOMEN
Chalcedon Position Paper No. 98

Slander shifts its ground readily, because it is concerned with what will hurt rather than what is true. In different eras, different charges hurt the most. What in one period may be a hurtful accusation may become a compliment in another day.

This was certainly true of Calvin, and of Geneva in Calvin's day and in his time of influence. As Gillian Lewis and Roger Stauffenegger have pointed out, Calvin's Geneva came to be known as "the paradise of women." ("*Calvinism in Geneva in the Time of Calvin and of Beza* (1545-1605)," in Menna Prestwich, ed.: International Calvinism 1541-1715, p. 49. Oxford, England: Clarendon Press, [1985] 1986.) There were good reasons for this. Calvin was strongly protective of "women's rights." Under his guidance, church consistories went after wife abusers. They prosecuted guardians who had misappropriated trust funds of widows and orphans. Deserted wives were protected, and so on. Prestwich has referred to "the attraction of Calvinism for women" in that area. ("*Calvinism in France*, 1555-1629," in ibid., p. 96.)

In that era, and for centuries before, powerful and prosperous elderly men and women contracted marriages with very young women and men. The families of the young complied with these arrangements for their personal advantages. Calvin felt strongly that such marriages should not be allowed. In January, 1557, the Consistory dissolved a marriage between a woman of "more than 70" with a man of 27 or 28. (Philip E. Hughes, ed: *The Register of the Company of Pastors of Geneva in the time of Calvin*, p. 321. Grand Rapids, Michigan: Eerdmans, 1966.) Rules were published to protect both men and women in marriage. To avoid deception, many rules were established. Thus, "strangers coming from a distant country" could not be permitted to marry in Geneva until a careful investigation of their past and their family were made. (*Hughes*, p. 75.) A woman persecuted for her faith could legitimately leave her husband. (*Hughes*, p. 197.)

It would be an error to say that the pastors of Geneva were always wise in their judgments in cases involving women. What is clear is that Calvinist Geneva was seen in its day as "the paradise of women" because of the receptivity of Calvin and others to their plight and their need for justice.

There was a reason for this attitude. It was the revival of the Old Testament as an inseparable part of the Bible; the New Testament was read as an essential part of the Old Testament.

Because the Old Testament solidly links holiness with the law, and the law is concerned with everyday life, the result was what Henri Hauser called the "secularization of holiness," *i.e.*, holiness was made a matter of everyday life for all believers. Holiness now was the pursuit of all Christians. It was, in Luthy's words, an "insistence on saintly life as the duty of every believer." (Herbert Luthy, "Variations on a Theme by Max Weber," in *Prestwich*, p. 381) Calvin said of Luke 6:35, ("But love ye your enemies, and do good, and lend, hoping for nothing again; and your reward shall be great, and ye shall be the children of the Highest for he is kind unto the unthankful and the evil") that it is our duty to do good, expecting nothing; we are to exercise a royal goodness, not a mercenary one, having received grace, we should then manifest grace. (Calvin: *Harmony of the Evangelists*, I, p. 302f.)

We have a remarkable fact here in Calvin's reformation of Geneva. It was a city rightly called in its day "the paradise of women." This is an aspect of the Reformation which has been given insufficient attention. The reason is that these reforms in civil and church law which made Geneva so remarkable in its day are now associated with patriarchalism, and patriarchy is a hated word to the feminists in both skirts and trousers. It suggests visions of male oppression, domination and rule. It has become a symbol of past and present evils.

The significant fact, however, is that patriarchalism was not male-centered but faith- and family-governed. Modern men in the atomistic family often have more power, if they choose to exercise it, than did patriarchal man. The reason was a very clear one: patriarchal man was a trustee from the past to the future. In I Kings 21, we see that Naboth did not feel that he had the right to sell the family land no matter how much money King Ahab offered The land was not his except as a trust from his forefathers to the generations yet unborn.

The appeal of existential living is that it limits all right and power to the present moment. Existential man sees no responsibility to the past nor to the future, nor to anything in the moment other than his will and desire This is why, given any opportunity, existential man is always tyrannical and oppressive: he will do what he can safely do without incurring immediat judgment. Both power and "right" are limited to the moment and to his wil

Not so with patriarchal man. He is linked to responsibilities, to the family and to other people. His wife is his partner and vice-gerunt i responsibilities, and both must be future-oriented.

Feminism, like masculinism, is existentialist and present oriented. It ha no sense of community nor the harmony of interests. Both feminists an masculinists believe in a war of the sexes and are out to win in that war. A good Darwinians, they believe in the survival of the fittest in a cosmic wa for survival. Since the universe has no law nor morality in their faith, th fittest are simply the survivors, those whose radical ruthlessness an contempt for morality enables them to survive.

To all such people, patriarchy is a trap, because it presupposes, despite the Fall and man's depravity, the ultimacy and triumph of God and His law. The universe is thus a moral universe. As Deborah declares in her song, "*The stars in their courses fought against Sisera*" (Judges 5:20).

A Biblical, patriarchal culture sees the essential conflict in life as a *moral* conflict, not a personal one. As a student, I heard a professor, not in favor of patriarchalism, call its central characteristic *hospitality*, and openness to people. He cited as revelatory of patriarchalism Abraham's response to the three strangers: he invited them in to share his "salt" or life (Genesis 18).

Modern social atomism, however, sees all men as enemies and turns the world into a hostile place. Class is set against class, and race against race. Woodrow Wilson, as a student at Princeton, shared in the hatred of students for town boys, called "snobs" at Princeton, and wrote, "We will have to kill some of those snobs yet before they will learn prudence." (Jonathan Daniels, "Woodrow Wilson's Pious Young," in *The New Republic*, October 29, 1966, p. 28; vol. 155, no. 18.) Wilson, of course, had no such murderous plan, but he liked to think in such terms. Not surprisingly, he helped advance the cause of class conflict. Even as he dreamed of a one world made safe for democracy, he advanced social divisions by his thinking.

Biblical, patriarchal culture is now very much despised by those who, as humanists, hate moral solutions. For them our problems are not to be diagnosed as a rebellion against Christ and God's law but as a matter of economic conflicts, class tensions, and sociological conditionings of a regressive and sociopathic nature. Calvin is for them a symbol of bad answers, and a recent book sees Calvin as essentially a "sick" man! The book tells us more about the author than Calvin.

I have on occasion cited, in speaking, the work of the bishop, St. Charles Borromeo, whose charities included "giving marriage dowries to penniless girls whose fate would otherwise have been the streets," and, in addition to the hostel for the street people of his day, orphanages, a home for reformed prostitutes, and a home for unhappily married women. (Margaret Yeo: *Reformer: St. Charles Borromeo*, pp. 115, 228f. Milwaukee, Wisconsin: Bruce, 1938.) The reaction is sometimes a cold one. "Social" problems, many hold, should be dealt with by the state, not by "amateurs."

When we depersonalize the problems of men and women, we also depersonalize ourselves. We reduce people to mathematical ciphers whose answers lie in acts of Congress or Parliament. We deny Christianity and Christ in favor of the state and its social workers. Borromeo in Milan and Calvin in Geneva gave us another answer.

But for many today, Geneva could not have been "the paradise of women." After all, Geneva had no Equal Rights Amendment or law!

Paul tells us, however, "where the Spirit of the Lord is, there is liberty" (II Cor. 3:17), and it is the Spirit who gave us the law and the gospels.

If we do not seek our answers in the Lord and His word, we are a part of the problem. (June, 1988)

WORLD SALVATION VERSUS WORLD DOMINATION
Chalcedon Position Paper No. 99

An error common to many intelligent men is to assume that what they regard as outmoded is therefore obsolete and irrelevant to all other men. Liberals and humanists generally are very prone to this. Thus, they regard nationalism as a relic of past years, but, for better or worse, it is very much with us. All over the world, as in France among the Bretons, in Spain with the Basques, and elsewhere, nationalism is a powerful force. Both Wilson and Lenin assumed in World War I that internationalism was mankind's future, and their thinking has only created chaos and warfare. Again, people who have forsaken Christianity assume that, because God is dead for them, He is really dead, and that all men will soon attain their own humanistic "wisdom." Such illusions lead to major conflicts in history.

One of the most powerful and least known racial-nationalistic movements of the past century has been Pan-Turanism, or Pan-Turkism. It began in what is now the Soviet republic of Azerbaijan in the late years of the 19th century, among the Azeri Turks of that country. It was intensely anti-Armenian and also anti-Islamic. It dreamed of a Pan-Turan empire from Turkey to the borders of China. The Turkic people in 1920 numbered 40 million to 50 million; they may be twice that number now, no small power. Early in the 20th century, the Azeris moved against the Armenians; they attacked them for their Christian faith, and, significantly, for "the *oppression* of the Turkish *proletariat* by the Armenian *capitalists*."

Very early, the Pan-Turanists allied themselves to Lenin and the Bolsheviks, and their power enabled Lenin to triumph. Lenin then liquidated the Pan-Turanist leaders, but about 15 Soviet republics were created to be small Turkeys, and two provinces of Armenia, Karabagh and Zangezur, 90 percent Armenian in population, were given to Azerbaijan. This helped to keep the Pan-Turanists in line.

Since that time, two major forces have developed as a threat to the Soviet Empire. Pan-Turanism is alive and strong, especially in the area of its birth, Azerbaijan, and hence the murders of Armenians, and the renewed pressure. For Moscow, this is a major threat: it dare not attack so numerous a people, but to tolerate attacks on the Armenians is to invite attacks next against Russians. The other major force is Pan-Islamism among the more conservative elements in Soviet Asia. The Pan-Turanists, like many Turks in Turkey, have dropped Moslem names for ancient Turkish names. The Pan-Turans detest Arabs, Iranians, and Islam generally.

The Pan-Turanists agree with much in Marxism, especially the worst in

Soviet tyranny. Zarevand, in *United and Independent Turania* (1926, 1971), pointed out, "*The Turk, a pragmatic type, thinks, not in terms of World Salvation, but of World Domination*" (p. 48). This attitude leads to a contempt for Christianity and an affinity to Marxism. As Zarevand noted, "The Turks do not fear God, but that is because they like to play *'God of Fear'* themselves. One of their favorite boasts is: *'Biz dunyayi yilder-mishiz'* (We have terrorized the world)" (p. 62).

All the same, Pan-Turanism is essentially an anti-Russian movement; most of the Turanian peoples are under the Soviet regime. They are waiting for the day when they can kill the Russians, the Armenians, and all non-Turkish peoples and establish the Turanian state.

At the same time, the fact remains that, although most Turks in Turkey and Asia were Moslems, their leadership was rejected by Islam. The Ottoman sultans had made themselves the caliphate of Islam, but this was rejected by many groups, *i.e.*, the Moroccans, Afghans, Arabs, the Seyyidists, the Wahabis, the Durzis, and others. This has not been forgotten. Moreover, the Turks have never believed in equality before the law: no non-Turkish group could have the same status as a Turk.

Pan-Turanism, whose symbols are the horse-tail standard and the she-wolf, claims the "right" to possess all lands wherever Turks or Turanians have set foot *at any time*. This means the Middle East, much of Europe, Siberia and more.

All this is important to any understanding of what is happening in 1988 in Azerbaijan. Without understanding the Turanian nationalism, and its hostility especially to Christianity, there can be no comprehension of the problem in the province of Karabagh. To assume that this is a local conflict, limited to two peoples within a single area, is to miss its significance entirely. The problem is radically racial and religious, centuries old, and it threatens not merely the life of the Soviet Union but many other peoples. It is not a problem which will be resolved by a series of conferences within the Soviet Empire, by the use of troops, or by the presence of more KGB agents.

Men cannot solve racial problems if they deny that racism exists; outlawing racism simply drives the problem underground. Men cannot solve religious conflicts when they fail to recognize the centrality of faith and its governing force.

Even more, men cannot resolve any problem when they refuse to see man as a fallen creature whose actions are governed by his depravity, not by his professed ideals.

Remember, the Turkish contempt for "world salvation" is because they believe in "world domination," in terrorizing the world. However, the world cannot confront this evil faith because it shares it. Lenin shared it with the leaders of Pan-Turanism, and the Soviet Union continues to apply it.

In the liberal West, world domination is also the goal, despite the facade of democracy and massive foreign aid. The purpose of these liberal strategies is still a world order dominated and controlled by humanism.

Is it any wonder that the West cannot confront or deal with either Pan-Turanism or Marxism? Is it any wonder that minority and majority groups all over the world are ruthlessly victimized by the champions of world domination?

It is significant that godly man in Genesis 1:26-28 is called to exercise *dominion* (not domination) over the earth, *not other men*, to develop all things in terms of God's law-word and to make this earth into God's realm and domain. Fallen man does not seek dominion, which begins with his salvation and his ability to rule himself, but, rather, the goal of fallen man is *domination*, to control other people.

In Ephesians 5:21-33, a husband's godly dominion over his wife is compared to Christ's ministry and the sacrifice of His life to redeem the Church. It is declared to be love: "He that loveth his wife loveth himself. For no man ever yet hated his own flesh, but nourisheth and cherisheth it, even as the Lord the church." This is not domination, yet all too many husbands who call themselves Christian still insist on replacing dominion with domination.

It should not surprise us, therefore, that Christians cannot cope with an evil world given to terror and to domination. Neither should it surprise us that too often the most successful clergymen are those who exercise, not dominion but domination, because this is what the world respects.

The ways of the Turko-Tatar world are all too close to the ways of all nations, men and groups. World domination is the goal. Pan-Turanism glorifies Chenghis Khan and his conquests; its ideal is that of their great Khan, to bring "*the entire world under Mongol-Tatar domination*" (Zarevand p. 28). People with more sophisticated versions of the same dream will not be able to counteract such movements. If, on top of that, they believe in the goodness of man, themselves especially, they will see every step towards World Domination as a step towards World Liberation. This was the view of the French Minister of Public Instruction, Jules Ferry (1879-1881). In a speech on July 10, 1870, Ferry said that humanity would be truly emancipated "when humanity appears to us, no longer as a fallen race stricken with Original Sin...but as an endless procession striding on toward the light; then, we feel ourselves part of the great Being which cannot perish, Humanity, continually redeemed, developing, improving; then we have won our liberty, for we are free from the fear of death" (John McMannors, *Church and State in France, 1870-1914*, p. 49, 1972).

Whether we call it Pan-Turanism, Marxism, Humanism, or any other name, such beliefs in World Domination really mean world death. They shall not prevail. The Ruler of all nations is the Lord of life, Jesus Christ. (July 1988)

THE MILITARIZATION OF LIFE
Chalcedon Position Paper No. 100

Reality is unpleasant for fallen man because it is not his creation. "A world I never made" is what most people do not want. As a result, they prefer to live by their own myths, in terms of what they imagine reality to be, or what it should be. Because the 20th century seeks aggressively to live without God, to live profanely, it is especially prone to myths. Myths can kill you, because falsifications of reality mean the risks of disaster and death.

More and more, various states are built on myths. A common myth insists that all wealth comes from the workers, and that capitalists are parasites who contribute nothing and take almost everything. This myth is common to most nations. Thus, in the United States, when students and voters have been asked what corporate profits amount to, the answers run from 25 to 75 percent of the net. In reality, during better and freer years, they ran 4 to 6 percent, and they are now commonly 2 to 2 1/2 percent. "Excessive profits" are usually a myth.

When the Russian Revolution resulted in the Bolsheviks' triumph, and the seizure of businesses and factories, this myth led to remarkable incidents. The workers expected to find vast wealth in gold and paper in the seized offices and found nothing. They searched carefully for all the "ill-gotten wealth" supposedly seized from the workers' sweat and blood, and they found none. The Communist workers filed reports like this: "I arrived at the factory and began to exercise control. I broke open the safety vault but could take no account of the money. There was no money to be found there." (James Bunyan: *The Origin of Forced Labor in the Soviet State, 1917-1921*, p. 24. 1967.)

The communists tried to run the shops and factories, but they failed to recognize the central role of capitalization and management in production. As a result, production collapsed, and the Soviet Union was very quickly in a major crisis. They had the workers, and they had the plants, but no production.

If myths had not governed the Bolsheviks so thoroughly, they would have recognized the fallacy of their theories. This they were not ready to do. The fault could not be in Marxist theory, which, in their thinking, was reality. As a result, God's reality had to be corrected to conform to Marxism.

The problem, created by Marxism, had to be resolved, but only on Marxist terms. This was like saying that the cure for poison is more poison. Lenin by late 1919 recognized the vast dimensions of the crisis, and the growing economic collapse. He turned to Leon Trotsky, then people's commissar of war and chairman of the Military Revolutionary Council of the Republic. Trotsky came up with a plan, with 24 propositions or theses in good Kantian-Hegelian-Marxist style. The essence of Trotsky's plan was the radical militarization of all Soviet labor, urban and rural, commercial, industrial, scientific, educational and agricultural. This meant the end of the freedom to change jobs at will, an end to all strikes, and an end to any freedom for labor.

Later, of course, Stalin and Trotsky clashed, and Trotsky lost. The Soviet Union, however, never has abandoned its Trotskyite militarization of all labor: it is basic to the Soviet Union. The slave labor camps represent the ultimate in the militarization of labor. Because of Trotsky's logical development of Marxist theory, the workers' destiny in "the workers' paradise" is slavery. Of course, productivity has declined in every segment of the Soviet economy. Slavery has never been an effective form of labor, and the Soviet Union is a classic example of its incompetence and inefficiency.

The premises of Marxism, however, were not the exclusive property of Marxists; they were shared by Western liberals, such as the British Labor Party, and the followers of Woodrow Wilson in the United States.

Thus, when President Franklin Roosevelt took office during the depression, he turned at once to the military model. He also turned to an Army officer, General Hugh S. Johnson, to head up the National Recovery Act, 1933-1934. Johnson proceeded (he was a lawyer also) to lay down the law to businessmen like an occupation army chief. Very few like Walter Chrysler were ready to stand up to him. Roosevelt's military model destroyed many small businesses before the Supreme Court voided the NRA.

Faith in the military model did not die, however. Both Republican and Democratic administrations have turned to it repeatedly, and the courts now view it benignly. The military model is thus being applied to every sphere of life, business, education, religion, everything. Controls are the answer to all problems. American productivity has declined, as has American education.

This same decline, with the same cause, the militarization of national life is occurring in countries all over the world, and with the same ugly results. In no country do the politicians seem ready to recognize the stupidity of the Trotsky plan for productivity.

Ironically, the militarization of national life has gone hand in hand with the demilitarization of the military! In the Soviet Union, political commissars saturate the military with their presence and hamper military common sense.

In the West, the military has also been politicized in one country after another, in some nations to a startling degree. In the name of civilian control, the military have been politicized. In all this, only one group apparently retains power and trust: the theoreticians. Where reality has its slimmest hold, there the greatest power resides!

In all this, it is clear that, *first*, God has no place. Men are determined to play god. They believe that their theories can create a new and better reality, and they see wisdom as born with them. For freedom to militarize men and institutions more effectively, the "superstitions" of Christianity must be eliminated, they maintain. In one nation after another, the war on Christianity begins with an attack on cults, and the definition of cults is soon expanded to include Christianity. The U.S. Congress is now talking about the need to do something about "cults." If, as Congress insists, it must be "neutral" with respect to religions, why should some be labeled "cults" and singled out for national hostility?

Second, the militarization of society means a radical distrust of freedom. Almost 20 years ago, I was one of three men speaking at a well-attended forum, with a distinguished professor presiding. My subject was freedom in education. When the session ended, one state school teacher, who had not gained recognition during the question-and-answer time, came up indignantly to accuse me of quackery for talking about freedom. She said, "In the modern world, freedom is obsolete." In a scientifically governed social order, all factors had to be controlled to produce valid results, and freedom was thus an obsolete and non-valid concept. This is the faith of all too many today.

Of course, most such believers would resent the Trotskyite term of *militarization*; they prefer to use the concept of a *scientifically governed and controlled social order*. Whichever term is used, the results are the same: freedom is replaced with controls.

The controls are man-made controls; they are means whereby man seeks to create new terms and conditions for living, and to remake the world. Man's dream "reality" or utopia replaces God's creation. Instead of original sin as the problem, such men see God and His law as the problem.

In October, 1837, *The United States Magazine and Democratic Review* carried a long statement expressing the Jacksonian democratic faith. The author was probably the political editor, John O'Sullivan. He held, "Democracy is the cause of Humanity. It has faith in human nature. It believes in its essential equality and fundamental goodness." This for him was the governing principle in terms of which "All history has to be rewritten." At the same time, other theoreticians of Jacksonian democracy were asserting, as Gilbert Vale did in 1832, and again in *The Diamond* in 1841, "We find it gravely asserted, and almost uniformly acted upon, that the *majority should govern the minority*; and this is the key to all the miserable legislation in the world, and the foundation of most of the evils; this is the father of the religious and political persecutions, and the grand impediment to improvement...What is this governing majority but a subversion of all justice."

Thus, long before Trotsky, and in terms of Rousseau, men were promoting the suppression of the popular will in favor of an imaginary general will. Their ideas, from Rousseau on, called for one "logical" solution: the militarization of life and society.

The conclusion to all such efforts, however, is not life but death. It is the fool who says in his heart, "There is no God" (*Ps. 14:1*). God, who sits "in the heavens shall laugh: the LORD shall have them in derision" (*Ps. 2:4*). (August, 1988)

THE DEATH OF EMPTY FORMS
Chalcedon Position Paper No. 101

Men through the ages have commonly trusted in some political form, religious ritual, or social organization as the hope of mankind. Rome believed that simplification and centralization would solve the problems of state, and thereby Rome made the empire unwieldy and unworkable. The early centuries after Rome's fall saw a marked decentralization, the feudal era. This also created problems, while solving some; and the "solution" was sought in a strong Holy Roman Empire and a strong papacy. The Empire was to provide protection against the coming of Anti-christ. We still have the symbol of the Holy Roman Empire with us, the dollar sign, the two vertical strokes representing the Pillars of Hercules and the wavy bank a scroll. The Empire was a faith in the necessity for holy power and the mastery of nations. The papacy centralized power in itself to provide an international court of appeals for justice. For a time, both church and Empire served their purposes but became themselves the targets of reform. The conciliar movement aimed at a broader church authority, and the national states undermined imperial power. The Reformation also sought to broaden the basis of power and authority within the church.

In the Puritan Commonwealth era in the 17th century, both in church and state the desire for decentralization was strong. This was a hope strongly shared by Christians and humanists. It was basic to the Independents Presbyterians, Anabaptists, and others. One man, Henry Marten, a wealthy man who championed unpopular causes (the Irish, the Levellers, prisons fo debt, and others), said of the monarchy, "I do not think one man wis enough to govern us all." Certainly Charles I lacked that wisdom. Marten' solution was a republic, which for him meant an honest civil government His reason for this hope he clearly stated: "The People have this advantag in their choice, that they are incapable of being bribed." (C.M. Williams "The Anatomy of a Radical Gentleman, Henry Marten," in Donal Pennington and Keith Thomas, eds.: *Puritans and Revolutionaries*, pp 118-138. Oxford, England: Clarendon Press, [1978] 1982.)

Marten's faith in the people was naive. Like kings and nobles, they *coul* be bribed. In contemporary U.S. politics, votes are purchased by subsidie to virtually every group in society, corporations, labor, the "senior" citizen minority groups, and so on and on. Theories about the infallibility of th people, i.e., Rousseau's doctrine of the general will, are now appearing to b as invalid as the divine right of kings. In the late 15th century in Russia, th

Josephite Doctrine of the Tsar was developed; it held that "the Tsar was similar to humans only by nature, but by the authority of his rank similar to God; he derived his authority directly from God, and his judgment could not be overruled by that of any prelate." (Arthur Voyce, *Moscow and the Roots of Russian Culture*, p. 16. Norman, Okla.: University of Oklahoma Press, 1964.) Rousseau's thinking about the general will gave a like authority to the democratic expression, or the democratic consensus, as many call it now.

Michael Kammen has shown, in *A Machine That Would Go of Itself, the Constitution in American Culture* (1986), how Americans have commonly had a blind trust that the constitutional form would preserve freedom and justice.

No thought was given to the fact that man's depravity can turn any form, monarchy, republic, democracy, or anything else, into an instrument of tyranny. We have seen tyranny triumph repeatedly in history, whatever the legal safeguards or the forms of government. All the well devised hopes and schemes of men are destroyed by the fact that man is a sinner. Without Christ, he will corrupt any and all forms of civil and ecclesiastical polity.

This trust in forms is equally prevalent in the church. Jeremiah spoke of the false trust of Jerusalem in having "*The Temple of the Lord*" (Jer. 7:4). An apostate people trusted in the sacrificial system, i.e., in atonement as ritual rather than a faith with works, and Hosea condemned this, declaring, "*For I desired mercy, and not sacrifice; and the knowledge of God more than burnt offerings*" (Hosea 6:6); our Lord twice cites these words of Hosea (Matt. 9:13; 12:7), yet I am often assured by churchmen that their particular forms and observance of baptism and communion assure the purity of their church. They forget that their observances can also ensure their damnation (I Cor. 11:29ff). Such "celebrations" are frightening.

This does not mean that forms in civil and ecclesiastical policy, or in rituals and sacraments, are nothing. It does mean that, just as faith without works is dead (James 2:14-26), so too works, forms, rites, polities, and governments without faith are dead also. The modern faith is strongly in the forms.

One of the shapers of 20th century United States was Justice Oliver Wendell Holmes Jr. He openly questioned whether "if cosmically an idea is any more important than the bowels," or "if man is any more significant than a baboon or a grain of sand." He denied God emphatically, and man also. Of pacifism and a concern for human life, he said: "All 'isms seem to me silly - but this hyperethereal respect for human life seems perhaps the silliest of all." (Rocco J. Tresolini, *Justice and the Supreme Court*, pp. 67, 72. Philadelphia: J.B. Lippincott, 1963.)

In such a perspective, man being nothing, truth and justice are nothing. All that remains is the power state. All this is a prescription for tyranny. The best constitution in the world is worthless if justice is meaningless. The forms are no protection if men are without faith. Antinomianism is finally anti-life and pro-tyranny and death.

Repeatedly in history, as empty forms replace faith and works, and as fame takes precedence over character, every area of life and thought is affected adversely. John Pearson has called attention to the fact that the modern temper has affected the British monarchy and is "a phenomenon of immense importance to the future of the monarchy." This, he points out, has been "the virtual extinction of the cult of human greatness, which had been steadily succeeded by something rather different, the cult of the celebrity." (John Pearson, *The Selling of the Royal Family*, p. 193. New York: Simon and Schuster, 1986.) Whether in the sphere of popular music, politics, the church, or the arts, celebrity has replaced greatness. This has been very sharply in evidence in such cases as Andy Warhol, rock and roll groups, and so on.

The very word "celebrity" is a curious one. It comes from "celebrate" and "celebration," the root idea of which is in Latin a good, well-traveled road, a way to a place. Its historic reference has been extensively ritualistic, that is, to celebrate marriage, the celebration of communion, or of the mass, or of baptism, and so on. The focus is religious, communal, or ritual. *With "celebrity," however there is a radical shift from a people united in a common act to a focus on an individual.* It is now the celebration of an individual, a "celebrity." One can perhaps suggest that the modern ritual is the elevation of the individual, the celebrity, instead of the bread and wine, i.e., the body and blood of Christ. The word reveals a climax of emptiness.

When the faith is removed, the forms collapse. Institutions and constitutions then become empty and meaningless, and justice gives way to celebrities, and to political briberies. Nothing works, because our world does not depend upon mechanical forms in church and state but on a living faith a faith with works.

When so influential a judge as Holmes regarded man as worth no more than a baboon or a grain of sand, and respect for human life as the sillies of illusions, is it any wonder that murder, rape, abortion, and euthanasia are increasing? Indeed, baboons and criminals are often given a better statu before the law than godly men.

Forms have their place, but forms cannot save us. The people who truste in "The Temple of the Lord" went into captivity, even as we now are doing because our trust is in something other than the Lord of history. U.S. Justic Wiley B. Rutledge expressed his faith in 1947 in a *Declaration of Legal Fait* thus: "I believe in law. At the same time I believe in freedom. And I kno that each of these things may destroy the other. But I know too, tha without both, neither can long endure...justice too is a part of life, c evolution, of man's spiritual growth...Law, freedom, and justice - this trinit is the object of my faith." (Tresolini, *op. cit.*, p. 134). Rutledge was a kind man, and he had his moment of greatness in the Yamashita case, but h faith was a weak one; he coasted on his religious background and adde nothing to it; rather, he lived off the moral capital of his past. Rutledge earthly trinity has proven to be empty without the triune God.

Wherein is your hope, and on what ground do you stand? (September, 1988)

HYPOCRITICAL GUILT
Chalcedon Position Paper No. 102

On one occasion, Otto Scott and I met a young man who lost no time in telling us of his burden of "guilt." His forefathers had been Southern slavers, dealing in the transport and sale of black slaves. We quickly gathered that he was a sensitive soul who wore his "guilt" as a badge of nobility.

On another trip, I was told of a young white woman, about 20 years old, who had been raped by a black hoodlum. She refused to report this crime, nor to tell her parents of it. Like her father and mother, she was a liberal. To report the rape, she felt, would confirm "a racial stereotype," and this she could not do. She spoke of understanding "the suppressed rage of oppressed black men." She too was a "noble" soul who took upon herself the guilt of past generations.

Of course, all this is a false virtue which rests on a hypocritical guilt for past sins which they themselves did not commit. Neither of these two persons, nor others like them, feel any guilt for present sins in themselves. Instead, they claim a false nobility and virtue for their hypocritical guilt for the past of their people. As a student, I knew a wealthy young man who made clear that his father's business practices (whatever they were) were repugnant to him. This was his claim to a high moral ground. His immediate personal life was very bad, but he felt virtuous in condemning his father, whose money he used freely.

We have a new form of Phariseeism today which looks at the past and says, "I thank Thee, Lord, that I am not as one of those insensitive souls." When our Lord says, "*Sufficient unto the day is the evil thereof*" (Matt. 6:34), He forbids us to borrow troubles (or guilt) from both the past and the future. To borrow either problems or guilt from the past or the future is ungodly.

Even more, guilt is personal. It has to do with one's own sins of commission and omission. To confess our parents' sins, or our ancestors' sins rather than our own is Phariseeism and a claim to being spiritually sensitive at their expense. It does not deal with one's own sins!

Some people feel very virtuous in "confessing" other people's sins. They are experts in correcting everyone around them. I regularly hear from such people about myself! Now, bad as that is, I believe it is even worse to confess our forefathers' sins and not our own. It is a violation of the law requiring us to honor our father and mother.

Paul speaks of some who have their "*conscience seared with a hot iron*" (I Tim. 4:2), who claim a higher holiness than others. They refine their moral stance to give themselves a holier and higher way than others. To have one's conscience seared with a hot iron means to be insensitive to God, while sensitive to one's own will. It means that these insensitive people claim a higher sensitivity. Such people become adept at confessing other people's sins, and we see whites confessing black sins, blacks confessing the sins of whites, Orientals confessing Western sins, and so on. People love to catalogue the sins of other nations, of the United States, Japan, South Africa, Guatemala, Britain, and so on and on.

All of this means devaluing sin and changing its seriousness. It is routine now in much so-called evangelism to assure people that their sins are forgiven before they have admitted to or confessed sin. It is no wonder that such "converts" are routinely moral problems. Cheap forgiveness shows contempt for the cross. If our sin required Christ's atoning death, to treat sin and forgiveness lightly is a very serious offense against God's grace and mercy.

David understood the seriousness of sin and forgiveness. He wrote, "*I acknowledge my transgressions: and my sin is ever before me. Against thee, thee only, have I sinned, and done this evil in thy sight*" (Psalm 51:3-4).

Confessing other people's sin, the sin of our forefathers or the sin of our nation in the past, is a common evasion of responsibilities in the present. One women's club revels in hearing speakers who regale them with the sins of everyone outside their own "enlightened" circles. They know more "dirt," or fancied "dirt," about more people and groups than one can imagine! They are a happy lot of Pharisees who believe that they grow in virtue as they grow in their information about the sins of others!

Such Phariseeism is common on the right and on the left. It is very popular politics. It adds nothing, however, to the moral direction of society.

All morality rests on a religious faith, and it results in action: no action, no morality.

Today we have a world in which everybody seems eager to correct or regulate everyone else. Whenever a congress, legislature, or parliament meets, it seeks more controls over others. (The U.S. Congress, as an accomplished body of Pharisees, routinely exempts itself from the laws it passes to bind all others!) This is Phariseeism, and it is evil.

Our Lord condemns Phariseeism above all else. He accused them of shutting up the Kingdom of Heaven by their warped teaching. He declares, "*ye shall receive the greater damnation*" (Matt. 23:24).

At the same time, our Lord *requires* us to seek *first* His Kingdom and righteousness (or, justice) (Matt. 6:33); this is Christian reconstruction. The emphasis is on what the Lord would have us do, and it requires a faith with results, a faith which moves us to service and to faithfulness. When Paul was converted, his first words were, "*Lord, what wilt Thou have me to do?*" (Acts 9:6). He did not sit back to wait for heaven; he became a vineyard worker for the Lord. To be converted, to be regenerated, means to be made alive in Christ to serve and obey Him. (October, 1988)

SLAVERY
Chalcedon Position Paper No. 103

Slavery has been common to all of history and to all continents and peoples. Ownership of other people, and power over them, has been sought by individuals and by states. In the 20th century, most countries, in fact virtually all, have banned by law the *private* ownership of slaves, but *state* ownership is increasing, not only in the forms of slave labor camps and the use of prisoners, but also in the increasing statist power over all the citizenry.

Slavery has not been limited to any one people. In the age of exploration and Renaissance, trade in black slaves became common, but, in other areas, Asiatics, Europeans, and others provided the slave labor.

Although Europe in the modern era has tended to see its imperial history more readily, the truth is that Europeans have over the centuries been perhaps the major source of slaves. The very word slave comes from the name of a European people, the Slavs. Before the Mongols, and especially with the Mongols, the Slavs were treated as a slave people to be harvested regularly.

Other Europeans were also enslaved and were common in the slave markets of Greece and Rome. After the fall of Rome, Jewish merchants moved into northern Europe as traders. They exchanged goods with the barbarian tribes for furs and other valuables. Chieftains often sold some of their people in trade. Jewish law required some elementary compliance on the part of slaves with Judaism; in terms of Scripture, those who converted to Judaism became free Jews. This in time meant that most European Jews were of European stock, even as Eastern European Jews were of Asiatic origin. As Irving A. Agus, in *Urban-Civilization in Pre-Crusade Europe*, (1965) pointed out, a slave could also gain freedom by converting to Christianity according to the laws of European countries. As a result, to keep their slaves both as slaves and then as Jewish converts, the Jewish traders were "forced to assume a very warm and human attitude to their slaves" (*Vol. I, p. 96*). Excess slaves were sold to the Mediterranean slave trade which, with Islam, became a major market.

At first, because the barbarian tribes saw slavery as a normal thing, enslavement was not a problem; in fact, for some it was a step upward materially to be a slave to a Jew.

With the rise of Islam, however, Islamic slavers began to move northward up the rivers of Europe to seize slaves. France was routinely raided. At the same time, the Christianization of the tribes led to a hostility to slavery and to Moslems and Jews. But there was still the fact that slavery was Europe's "best business," to use Michael Wood's expression, in this era. The Moslems were the slavers from the South; the Vikings were the slavers from the North, and later, the Mongols on the East. The Vikings loved especially to raid on Christian holy days and take various peoples, especially the British and most of all the Irish, as slaves. Jewish and Syrian merchants in such places as Verdun processed the slaves, and many of the males were made eunuchs. Wood writes, "A frightened pilgrim in the late ninth century in Taranto saw nine thousand Italian captives being loaded onto ships, making up just one consignment to Egypt" (*In Search of the Dark Ages*, 1987, p. 169). Slave-trading was very big business indeed.

The result was a resentment towards Jews and Moslems. The early form of the Crusades was pushing the Moslem slave raider-traders out of Europe and converting and civilizing the savage Vikings.

Then, when Christian pilgrims to the Holy Land were attacked and enslaved, the Crusade was proclaimed for that area as well. At the same time, the European Christian attitude toward the Jew changed, and the hostility was directed against all, not just the slave traders. Slavery had earlier been an accepted fact of life by all; now it was seen with hostility.

With the Renaissance, and with the revival of classical humanism, the medieval view of slavery was altered to an acceptance. Thus, when a merchant returned from a long trip to find that his wife had given birth to an illegitimate son, he waited until the boy was an adolescent and then took him on his next trip and sold him as a slave. (Lucien Febvre: *Life in Renaissance France*, p. xvii. 1977). The times were congenial for a return to a massive slave trade, this time with Africans. Over the centuries, however, the major source of slaves has been Europe. Europeans prefer to remember their imperial greatness and power, which has been remarkable, but Europe has been a continent subjected to extraordinary wars, degradations, evils, and conflicts.

Europe has seen over the centuries the most sustained enslavement and also the systematic harvesting by slavers, one unequalled elsewhere except in local settings such as Aztec Mexico. It has also seen the greatest freedom. Europe has moved from a casual acceptance of slavery to a world-wide war against it.

The reason for this has been its Christianization. Those who today are hostile to Western civilization and its Christian heritage should remember that, outside the sphere of Christian culture, the two most commonplace aspects of societies have been slavery and polygamy. To abolish Christendom, as some hope, will in time restore both.

Our Lord tells us that slavery begins within man; the basic slavery is to sin: "*Whosoever committeth sin is the servant (or, slave) of sin...If the Son therefore shall make you free, ye shall be free indeed*" (John 8:34, 36). This should tell us that non-Christian politics is the politics of slavery because it denies the only valid source of freedom, Jesus Christ.

The world today is moving rapidly into slavery. We cannot be indifferent to the politics of slavery, because it is committed to anti-Christianity. Its victory will mean the enslavement of our children and of their children.

But are not the churches full of people? Are not millions in the United States professing believers? The answer to that was well stated by David E. Rockett, in his monthly newsletter, *The Faithful Steward* (July, 1988): "The lack of Holy distinctiveness neuters the potency of the Church's voice and its effectiveness in the world. We are not taken seriously by our pagan, secular, countrymen because to their eyes, we are not different from them."

We are Christ's Kingdom, His dominion men, in this world. If we are only slaves or at best by-standers in our day, we have failed Him.
(November, 1988)

BIGOTRY IN THE NAME OF TOLERANCE
Chalcedon Position Paper No. 104

Bigotry in the modern world is viewed with disfavor, and rightfully so. A bigot is defined as "An illiberal adherent of a religious creed or of any party or opinion." Bigotry is thus no respecter of persons. A bigot can be a believer or an unbeliever, a professor, scientist, politician, or anyone else who views all who disagree with him as stupid, evil, or ignorant. Many evolutionary scientists are intensely bigoted, as are many intellectuals and media men. Like Job's foolish friends, bigots tend to believe that wisdom was born with them and may well die with them (Job 12:2).

Because bigotry is so extensively condemned, when it now manifests itself, it is disguised as truth, or freedom of speech, or The First Amendment rights, and so on. In this disguised form, we are asked to tolerate bigotry or else reveal that we are bigots! Thus, we get bigotry in the name of tolerance.

A telling example of this in 1988 has been the film, *The Last Temptation of Christ*. It is for all who believe in Jesus Christ as revealed in Scripture a blasphemous and evil bit of fiction. The proponents of the film insisted that it is a deeply religious film; they accused their critics of intolerance and censorship; they charged them with bigotry.

Who is the best judge of whether or not something is offensive? Should we have asked Hitler if his anti-Jewish speeches and actions were offensive? Were not the Jews who suffered at his hands a better judge of that? Or, if a mob attacks members of some minority group, as is happening in Europe, should we ask the mob about the merits of their acts or words?

Should we justify racist films which attack various segments of the community? There is a vast difference between saying a man has the *freedom* to do something, and saying it is *morally right* for him to do so.

Anti-Christianism increasingly demands more and more freedom to attack Christ and Christianity while insisting that any attempt by Christians to protest against such bigotry is wrong. This is a morally dishonest position. It is a denial of freedom to the Christian community.

For these bigots to tell orthodox Christians that the film is a deeply reverent one compounds their sanctimonious hypocrisy. It is like telling someone, after spitting in their face, that it was really a kiss! Bigotry in the name of tolerance is doubly evil because it compounds its sin with phariseeism and hypocrisy.

Such bigotry, however, is the order of the day. Congress routinely passes law after law binding on the people and the administration while exempting itself from the applications of the law, or the criminal penalties for violations thereof. It then attacks administrators and demands their trial for doing what Congress routinely does! A good law should bind all people to compliance. Why have our various guardians of constitutionalism not challenged laws which give the freedom to commit crimes to one group? Is there any justice in such an arrangement?

For any intelligent man to deny that *The Last Temptation of Christ* was a film hostile to any except modernistic churchmen is hypocrisy; it has offended evangelicals, Calvinists, Catholics, and even some others as well. An orthodox rabbi has condemned it as defamatory. It treats an historical Person in radical contempt of history. No one connected with the film could have been so obtuse as not to recognize that it would be offensive. In fact, we can with justice ask: Was it not meant to be offensive, as surely as anti-Jewish or anti-black writings are intended to offend? Was it not meant to defame, to ridicule, and to offend? Or are these men more insensitive than KGB torturers and Nazi Storm Troopers?

A little more than a year ago, I was a witness in a trial in the South. The state's attorney charged several pastors with child abuse, not because any such actual case had come up, but because their churches in their various forms of child care, believed in spanking unruly children, with parental consent. The state's attorney declared the Bible to be a "child abuse manual." A recently published book on satanism absolved Satanists of crime but charged that "fundamentalist Christians" are the main source of child abuse in the United States.

Such persons assume, *first*, that their humanistic views of child care are "scientifically" valid, and the views of Christians are false. *Second*, they refuse to see that they are intensely anti-Christian because they identify themselves with the truth and all Christians as in error, if not evil. Anti-Christianism is the new face of phariseeism; it claims to be the objective truth, and its opponents to be evil. It is a strident bigotry which pretends to be sweet tolerance personified.

On the church side, too many people have come to believe that it is greater virtue to tolerate anti-Christianism than to recognize it for what it is and to call attention to its evil. Such people are afraid of the names they might be called, such as bigot, and they live timid and withdrawn lives. They dare not face men with the Gospel; how can they ever face God?

By the time of the Renaissance and thereafter, an interesting development took place with respect to death. Prior to that time, the tombs of the mighty stressed God's judgment and the resurrection. Now they began to stress lineage, prestige, and power, not the faith. T. S. R. Boase, in *Death in the Middle Ages* (1972) wrote that the tomb of Count Karl Adam von Lanberg, who died in 1689, has a skeleton raising the lid of the coffin, and the Count, "fully periwigged, emerges." The Cathedral tomb gives us the count's coat of arms, and various trophies. "Secularism could go no further" (p. 87).

Death for the count was to be a continuation of life in heaven with his same rank and nature. Because such men could not grasp the meaning of Christ, and of death and resurrection, they could not understand the meaning of life, nor live as godly men.

Today we have a generation of church people who believe that heaven will give them an all-expense-paid vacation where they will continue their secularized and self-centered living. Because they do not understand that Jesus Christ is *life* (*John 14:6*), they do not know how either to live or to die. They cannot cope with anti-Christianism because they do not recognize the absolute claims of the living Christ.

A very fine black pastor lost his church recently because the people rebelled against his teachings on Christian education and on the evils of welfarism. The congregation, like thousands of others, wanted the form of faith without the power thereof (II Tim 3:5). The weakness and cowardice of churchmen gives anti-Christianism a license, so that small groups can deal contemptuously with the faith of millions.

Our Lord is clear that a good tree will bear good fruit; "*wherefore by their fruits ye shall know them*" (Matt. 7:20). James, the brother of our Lord, tells us that faith without works is dead or non-existent (James 2:14-26). It is an amazing fact that churches now equate faith with easy-believism. Worship, while important, has replaced Christian faithfulness and dominion. As a result, the churches are powerless. "Powerless Christianity" is a contradictory term, because salvation means that the power of God has redeemed us, cleansed us, and is at work in and through us. No man touched by the Holy Spirit can be impotent.

The early church was faced with the same kind of bigotry from the intellectuals and rulers of their day. They were accused of incest, cannibalism, treason, of being disrupters of the peace, and more. They were also killed in great numbers. They triumphed because, in terms of God's Word, they were His Kingdom and government on earth. They preached the Word; they cared for the sick, the poor, the young, the old, and for captives. They were a kingdom within a kingdom, and it was their power which prevailed.

Demonstrations change nothing. Regeneration, not revolution, alone leads to Christian reconstruction. We face strong and vehement anti-Christianism, even within the church. It is "*the gospel of Christ*" which "*is the power of God unto salvation*" (Rom. 1:16). We face bigotry in the name of tolerance now; we face far worse things tomorrow unless we are ready to live and die for Christ. He alone is the true Lord, the only wise God and our Savior. (December, 1988)

REVOLUTION OR REGENERATION
Chalcedon Position Paper No. 105

Although the word "salvation" is usually restricted to theological discussions, it is all the same a concern of all men, i.e., how to solve problems and make society a healthy and harmonious order. A variety of solutions, or plans of salvation, have been offered: philosopher-kings, economic doctrines, sexual arrangements, and more. One of the most popular salvation doctrines of the 20th century has been education, mass education as the means of social salvation. This hope is still with us, but is fading steadily.

Basically, the difference between all these plans of salvation and Christianity is this: these non-Christian hopes believe that the problem is not in man but in something outside of him, in his environment, family, heredity, schooling, or some like external factor. Thus, to change man, you first change the world around him. The most logical and thorough-going expression of this faith is revolution. It is held that the transformation of man must begin with the radical transformation of his social order. Then man will himself be changed. Liberation theology is the application of this faith within the church: change the world, it is held, and then man can become a Christian. This is the same faith set forth by the tempter to Jesus in the wilderness (Matt. 4:1-11).

Biblical faith holds the contrary view. For Christianity, man must be changed by the sovereign grace of God through Jesus Christ. Then the changed man can change the world. Salvation cannot come to man nor to society apart from Christ's atonement and His regenerating power. The dynamics of society are from God to man to the world.

In recent years, there has been a growth within the church of revolutionary ideas. The power of God unto salvation has been abandoned in favor of the power of revolutionary action unto salvation. We have already cited liberation theology as a proponent of this anti-Christian doctrine.

Another common application of the revolutionary premise is the ta revolt, that concept so much loved by Karl Marx, who understood it meaning. The excuse is the godlessness of the state. But Jesus Christ an Paul lived under men like Tiberius and Nero; they lived in a time of unjus taxation, abortion, homosexuality, and more. Neither our Lord nor St. Pau counseled a tax revolt. Rather, as against the tax revolts of their day, the counseled tax-paying (Luke 20:19-26; Rom. 13:7). Not revolution, but regeneration is the Christian hope for man and society.

In 1988, another revolutionary ploy became the methodology of many churchmen, the demonstrations at abortion clinics designed to violate the laws of picketing and protest and ensure arrest for impeding access. It is questionable whether or not these demonstrations saved the lives of any unborn babies: the women seeking abortions simply went elsewhere. Even more, the demonstrators set a precedent in violating civil laws of various sorts. What is to prevent pro-abortion people from blocking access to churches, or even entering them to disrupt services? If we allow lawless protest to one side, we justify it for all.

No Scriptural justification is offered by these demonstrators. The closest thing to a text to justify them is Acts 5:29, the answer of Peter and the other apostles, "We ought to obey God rather than men." What does this mean, however? There is no civil government anywhere which does not disobey God at some points, and, for that matter, there are no perfect churches either. The best of churches fall short of perfect obedience. Are we then justified in obeying only when we believe God's Word is faithfully observed? Then are those around us or under us entitled to rebel against our authority whenever they feel we fall short of or neglect God's Word? Nothing in Scripture gives warrant to that. David's respect for Saul, despite Saul's sin, gives us another model.

Where freedom of God's Word in the church, its schools, its families and members is denied, then we must obey God, not the state. We do not disobey to save our money nor even our lives but where God's Word and its proclamation is at stake.

The moral anarchy which revolutionists advocate is being brought into the church by some men. Not surprisingly, they impugn the Christian character of those who criticize them, men such as Dr. Stanley, and Rev. Joseph Morecraft III.

To believe in the efficacy of violence to change society means to abandon peaceful means. Not surprisingly, peaceful, legal action is being neglected. A pro-abortion justice on the U.S. Supreme Court has said that, in a new case, abortion would lose. Such a case would require much funding and highly competent legal help. The money to do this is being spent in sending people from one end of the country to the other to take part in demonstrations, to bail them out of jail, so on.

The methodology of such demonstrations has been borrowed from non-Christian and revolutionary sources. From one end of the Bible to the other, no warrant can be found for this methodology. To use ungodly means is a way of saying that God's grace and power are insufficient resources for Christian action. It means abandoning Christ for the methods of His enemies.

Such methodology can be effective, but not for the triumph of grace. When the leaders of the people wanted to force Pilate's unwilling hand, they assembled a mob to demonstrate before Pilate and to shout down all protest, screaming, "*Crucify Him*" (Mark 15:13).

There is a long history of injustice at the hands of mobs. There is no Christian calling to create mobs and to violate laws to achieve a purpose.

The sad fact is that, once we adopt a position, the logic of that faith carries us forward. Thus, I am finding that those who approve of demonstrations, and of the violation of the properties of abortion clinics, find it easy to justify violence against the property (bombing) and against the persons who are abortionists (which means murdering them).

The power to punish murders is a civil power, not an ecclesiastical nor a personal one. Just as we must believe that the spheres of the church and of the family should not be violated by the state, so we should avoid trespassing on the state's sphere. The early church faced many evils in the civil sphere: abortion, slavery, and more. Paul spoke against a revolutionary move against slavery but counseled the use of lawful means (I Cor. 7:20-23). The early church took a strong stand against abortion and disciplined severely all who were guilty of it. It organized its deacons to rescue abandoned babies (who had not been successfully aborted earlier), and it took strong stands without ever suggesting violence.

Humanism gives priority to man and the will of man over God and His Law-Word. If we place saving babies above obedience to God, we wind up doing neither the born nor the unborn any good, and we separate ourselves from God.

It is amazing how many people on all sides of issues are so prone to violence as their first and last resorts. They believe, when they see a serious problem, in taking to the streets, getting their guns, fighting the Establishment, and so on and on, without even using the many peaceable means which are at hand. For them, violence is not a last resort when all other means have been exhausted, but a first resort. Instead of providing answers, resorts to violence mean the death of a civilization. The use of violence, whether by Christians or non-Christians, is a way of saying that voting, the law courts, mean nothing, or, that faith and the power of God are irrelevant to the problems of our time.

The resort to revolution or to revolutionary tactics is thus a confession of no faith; it means the death of a civilization because its people are dead in their sins and trespasses. They may use the name of the Lord, but they have by-passed him for "direct action." In doing so, they have forgotten that since Day 1 of creation, all the power and the direct action are only truly in God's hands. By assuming that everything depends on their action, they have denied God and His regenerating power.

And they have forgotten our Lord's requirement: "*Ye must be born again*" (John 3:7). Regeneration, not revolution, is God's way. (January, 1989)

CATHARSIS
Chalcedon Position Paper No. 106

It was Aristotle who formulated the literary theory of *catharsis*, although as scholars have admitted, there is no certainty as to what Aristotle meant by it. The Greek word *katharsis* means, literally, a purging. It is related to our meaning of a cathartic, a laxative, something to cleanse the system.

Like everything else in Aristotle, Christians over the centuries have given catharsis a moral meaning. A drama or tragedy must end in a moral resolution and an outcome which gives more meaning to life. Greek tragedy, however, shows that this was not the case; a brutal, meaningless, and blind Fate prevails. In fact, an innocent man like Oedipus is the victim of diabolical coincidences at the hands of the gods. The Greek catharsis meant usually that hatred, evil, and grim fate work out an ugly conclusion.

Despite its Christian veneer, the concept of catharsis began to revert to its pagan origins. The Renaissance saw its implications. Boccaccio argued that to deprive a person of the sexual freedom to fornicate and to commit adultery would create mental problems. Sexual "freedom" was a form of catharsis.

With the Romantic movement, this idea of catharsis became increasingly strong, and the Romantics pursued the forbidden areas of life religiously as the way of freedom. Revolution became very popular as a means of social catharsis. In time, intellectuals came to a belief that all leftist revolutions are good because of the social catharsis they provide. The violence, brutality, and the mass murders of revolutions were justified as a necessary form of social catharsis. The French Revolution applied the idea of a medical catharsis to society. As Otto Scott wrote of Robespierre, "He demanded a purge; that was his word. Knowing his precision, it must be assumed he realized it was then a medical term meaning the forced expulsion of feces; he gave it a new meaning that is with us still" (Otto Scott: *Robespierre, The Voice of Virtue*, p. 213.) Since then, the idea of a purge or social catharsis has been generally accepted as a part of revolutionary faith. The feces of society are the capitalists, propertied peoples, conservatives, and, above all, Christians, and they must be purged, it is believed.

This kind of social catharsis has made the 20th century the most brutal in history, in that a higher percentage of mankind than ever before has been purged or killed in the name of the health and welfare of the people.

The idea of catharsis found expression in many other ways. Many Satanist and occultist groups appealed to people because their ideas and rituals gave an opportunity for people to participate in a cathartic service. Not surprisingly, crimes often resulted. Like the "therapy" of some psychologists, these Satanist and occultist services were forms of psychodrama. Those participating in them were being schooled in the theory of catharsis.

Instead of replacing evil thoughts and destructive impulses with constructive and Godly purposes, the culture of the age has favored the expression of those things, not in a holy confession of sin, but in an unholy venting of evil impulses. As the concept of catharsis was stripped of its Christian accretions it became a justification for revolution, for the destructions of Christian morality, and for anarchistic freedom. The cult of violence and aggression of students and intellectuals in the 1960s was an example of cathartic expression. So too was "the theater of cruelty," the thesis of many novels and films and more. The Marquis de Sade became popular and was hailed by some as a great psychologist because of his insistence on total cathartic expression.

As E.M. Thornton has shown in *The Freudian Fallacy* (1983), the idea of catharsis was basic to Freud's thinking. Insane dreams were a form of catharsis for Freud, as were aberrations in behavior. His "therapy" was not to impose a mental or moral discipline on patients but to encourage their expression of inner drives. Catharsis or healing came through their expression. Hence Freud refused to condemn various forms of perverse sexuality: they were cathartic expressions. Christians, hence, were the sickest of people for Freud because they behaved with health and morality; obviously, he held, they had escaped a personal neurosis by embracing the cosmic neurosis, God!

Freud's greatest success was in the arts. Painters and writers found in his ideas a congruency with literary theory (Aristotelian) and with revolutionary ideologies, which also utilized the Aristotelian doctrine of catharsis. The deterioration of standards in the arts has been due to the steady assault on all impediments to cathartic expression. The result has been distortion and contortion in music, painting, literature, and elsewhere in the name of free and purgative expression. Vitality in the arts has come to mean revolutionar and cathartic expression. Robert Pielke, in *You Say You Want a Revolution* (1986), says that the vitality and the appeal of rock music is religious: i represents an alternate religiousness. It represents the essence of the current cultural revolution, which is "the rejection of America's religious heritag and its replacement with something contrary."

In the current faith in catharsis, it is held that mental and social problems are a result of repression. Hence, the way to health is to repress nothing. A kinds of slogans have justified this lawless self-expression since the 1960s: " it feels good, do it"; "Me first"; "Do your own thing"; and so on and on.

The *Shorter Westminster Catechism* begins, "What is the chief end of man Man's chief end is to glorify God, and to enjoy Him for ever." The focus God, not man. Job, after losing his children and wealth could say, "*Nake came I out of my mother's womb, and naked I shall return thither: the LOR gave, and the LORD hath taken away; blessed be the name of the LORD*" (Jo 1:21). Such a God-centered faith is the antithesis of 20th century practic Man has become the measure, and man judges God in terms of man requirements. The doctrine of catharsis, stripped of its accretions, h become the doctrine of total self-expression: "I've got to be me;" "Let it all hang out"; and so on.

E.M. Thornton saw the "permissive society" as a result of Freud's teachings. The sexual revolution, the drug culture, abortion on demand, euthanasia, and homosexuality now give evidence of Freud's results, as does "the Pill." The goal of this new culture was to be the happy world of Eros, sexual love. Herbert Marcuse brought Freud and Marx into an intellectual oleo in his teachings. It is said that one demonstration's slogan in 1968, "The riot is the social extension of the orgasm," came from Marcuse. However, as Thornton noted, "By the end of the seventies the neo-Freudians had moved on from Eros to Thanatos," from *Love to Death* (p. 252).

The 1980s have seen AIDS show what free catharsis can lead to!

Catharsis cannot save man, nor does Freudian catharsis cleanse a man. Only the grace of God unto salvation can cleanse, purify, and regenerate a man. We are told that the Lord declares, "*Behold, I make all things new*" (Rev. 21:5). Catharsis and revolution after the manner of Aristotle, Robespierre, Marx, Freud, and others produce death, not renewal and life. Thornton noted, "It is interesting that James Joyce, who suffered from Neurosyphilis, wrote the celebrated reverie in *Ulysses* under the influence of cocaine" (p. 154).

The world of catharsis is the world of self-willed death. "Wherefore come out from among them, and be ye separate, saith the LORD, and touch not the unclean thing *and I will receive you*" (II Cor. 6:17). (February, 1989)

OUR DOXOLOGY
Chalcedon Position Paper No. 107

We are very clearly told in Acts 6:7, that, in the earliest days of the church, "the word of God increased; and the number of disciples multiplied in Jerusalem greatly; and a great company of the priests were obedient to the faith." The religious control of Judea was firmly in the hands of Rome through collaborators. As a result, men of faith were routinely shelved by Rome and the Sanhedrin in favor of pragmatic men. The goal of these pragmatists was freedom for Judea, but, meanwhile, an astute policy of resistance and compromise prevailed. Until the Jewish-Roman war of A.D. 66-70, the Roman and Jewish leadership maintained an uneasy alliance.

The Christians, with their faith in Jesus Christ as the world's Messiah, and in terms of His Great Commission (Matt. 28:18-20), were outsiders to this situation. However many Jews they converted, and priests as well, the Judean goal was at odds with their purpose. Caiaphas, the high priest, had expressed clearly the national perspective: "*it is expedient for us, that one man should die for the people, and that the whole nation perish not*" (John 11:50). In Judea, as well as throughout the Roman Empire, the Christian converts were largely Israelites.

Dr. Jakob Jocz, a brilliant Jewish Christian scholar, has described Judaism as believing in man's ability to save himself, with help from God; "man only sins, but is *not sinful*." Man at birth is pure and sinless, not fallen. It is a religion of self-salvation whose essence is ethics; "the covenant of God with man is never broken." "Israel's sufferings sufficiently warrant their redemption, regardless of repentance." Righteousness is not imputed but attained. Hence, in Judaism and Christianity we have "two worlds diametrically opposed to each other." (Jakob Jocz: *The Jewish People and Jesus Christ*, pp. 264-286. Grand Rapids, Mich.: Baker Book House, [1941] 1979.)

It is easy to see why there was conflict between the two faiths; it was inescapable. The question is this: after the close of the New Testament era, was the conflict only an intellectual one, or did it continue to be one in which Jewish Christians were in a charged emotional conflict against their unconverted brethren? Did Jewish conversions dwindle after the fall of Jerusalem, or did they continue? Were only the Ebionates and a few others left of Jewish Christianity, or did the conversions continue, and the absorption into the world faith of Jewish Christians become an influence of note, or was it only the Hellenic converts who then shaped the church? Were the Jewish Christians only a remnant of Israel, or were the unbelievers the remnant? These are questions which cannot be answered with certainty, but they need to be asked, and some direction determined, if possible.

We do know that many churchmen over the centuries were converted Jews. Eusebius, in Constantine's day, gave a list of a number of Jewish bishops. Earlier, Justin's *Dialogue* made clear that Jews were very much a part of the faith and that the debate, tension, and conversion factors remained very much as in St. Paul's day. Much later, Jewish popes appear from time to time, indicating the continuing presence, zeal, and importance of Jewish Christians. Early in the 11th century, Hildebrand became pope as Gregory VII. Jewish descent has been ascribed to him; whether this is true or not, we do not know. We do know that, in a crisis, he raised an army with "the help of financially gifted Jews." (J.P. Whitney: *Hildebrandine Essays* pp. 10, 22. Cambridge University Press, 1921.)

But there are other indications of a close tie between church and synagogue. In the 12th century, we find that one of the great Armenian Church fathers, St. Nerses Shnorhali, a writer of hymns, produced hymns which link him to Rabbi Jehuda Halevi of Spain (and, briefly, Egypt). There are too many links like this to be ignored.

The great authority here in a specific area was Eric Werner, a professor of liturgical music, who in 1959 published his findings, titled *The Sacred Circle, The Interdependence of Liturgy and Music in Synagogue and Church During the First Millennium*. We know that the earliest term for the church was *synagogue*, as we see in the Greek text of James 2:2. The synagogue officers and structure were taken over by the church. But, Werner showed, so too was the liturgy and music. The use of musical instruments was dropped by the synagogue after the fall of Jerusalem. Instruments such as the organ were too joyful for a people in mourning over the fall of their city and country. The old forms were retained in the church, both of the Temple and of the synagogue. The Christian Church sought to be faithful to the Old Testament Church because it saw itself as the true continuation thereof. After Paul, the church saw itself as "*the Israel of God*" (Gal. 6:16). In its better moments, the church's call to the Jews was to come home.

This influence and faithfulness to Old Testament liturgical practices continued. Thus, in the Reformation, a notable figure was John Immanuel Tremellius (1510-1580), a converted Jew who was born in Ferarra. He became a Catholic about 1540, and his godfather was Cardinal Reginald Pole, later archbishop of Canterbury. In 1542, Tremellius became a Protestant and a Calvinist. He was then in England, in Lambeth Palace with Crammer, and also Cambridge, before going to Germany when Queen Mary's persecution began. He returned to England in 1565 and concluded his teaching career at Sedan. In England, Tremellius helped frame the Thirty Nine Articles and assisted in the formation of the Book of Common Prayer. The unification of worship sought by the English reformers meant faithfulness to Scripture and to the Biblical precedents in the worship in the Temple and the synagogue.

The ugly side of the relationship between church and synagogue is often told, i.e., enforced baptisms, compulsory Jewish attendance at times to Christian preachings, and so on. At times, the worst in hostility to the Jews were Jewish converts, or men of Jewish ancestry, such as King Ferdinand of Spain, and Tomas de Torquemada, the Grand Inquisitor. All the same, the "come home" motive was also very much a fact. When, shortly after World War II, Pope Pius XII said that spiritually we are all Semites, he was echoing a centuries-old theme.

The heretical influence of Marcion led to a division between the Old and New Testaments, to antinomianism, and to a hostility to the Jews. As against this, there was always also a belief in the unity of Scripture, plus an insistence that faith without works is dead (Matt. 7:16-20; Rom. 3:31; James 2:14-26), and an adherence to the Pauline hope and summons to "come home."

This aspect of church history is of more than academic interest. It is important to know how deep our roots are, that the church is "*the Israel of God*" (Gal. 6:16), and that our worship echoes that of Old Testament saints and is linked to the victorious song of the Church Triumphant (Rev. 15:3).

In the early church, the Greek intellectuals expressed contempt for all music which did not follow the standards of classic Greek music. They were thus not congenial to the Christian (hence strongly Hebraic) music. Many held to Pythagorean doctrines, such as the cathartic power of music; this was the theory set forth in Mozart's *The Magic Flute*, a strongly Masonic opera. Hebraic-Christian music was not men-centered; its goal was not a humanistic cathartic result but the glory of God. We can perhaps call the Doxology the epitome of truly Biblical worship and song because it centers on God, not man. Although it is trinitarian, the Doxology echoes Scripture, the Temple, and the synagogue. (See E. Werner: *The Sacred Circle*, pp. 273-213.) The spirit of the Doxology and of Hebraic, Biblical music is well summarized in the first statement of the Westminster Shorter Catechism: "Man's chief end is to glorify God and to enjoy Him forever." It is also joyfully expressed in a Christian hymn with an Old Testament root and an ancient Hebrew melody ("Leoni"), the magnificent "The God of Abraham Praise."

The church was not born with us, nor with our rebirth. Men who despise their past also despise their future. As Christians, we are the heirs of the ages, and heirs in Christ of all things (Rom. 8:17; Gal. 3:29; 4:7; Eph. 3:6; Heb. 6:17; James 2:5, etc.). We have a Doxology to sing which resounds across the centuries and is the music of eternity. (March, 1989)

INFERENCES AND COMMANDMENTS
Chalcedon Position Paper No. 108

The failure to distinguish between God's commandments and inferences made from them has, over the centuries, led to serious moral problems in Judaism and Christianity. When God gives a commandment, He speaks very plainly; there can be no mistaking what he says. His "thou shalt nots" and His "thou shalts" are blunt and unequivocal. Unhappily, too many people over the centuries have insisted on seeing commandments where there are none. They base their rules, and their determination to bind the conscience of the faithful, on inferences, sometimes wrongful ones. Not even a valid inference is a commandment.

To illustrate, our Lord, in Luke 12:48, says, "For unto whomsoever much is given, of him shall be much required: and to whom men have committed much, of him they will ask the more." In other words, the greater the responsibility a man has, the greater is his culpability and guilt. In Leviticus 4, the laws of sacrifice set forth this same premise: the sin offering of a priest or prince is a greater one than that of a commoner. God says that, in His sight, the greater our responsibilities, the greater is our sin in His sight. A logical inference is that the sins or crimes of important people deserve more punishment. Before *God*, guilt is greater, according to Leviticus 4, but this greater punishment is not a law for *man* to enforce, although it is a sound inference. Notice too that in Luke 12:48 our Lord says that, in such cases, *men* "will ask the more." While it can be done, it is not mandatory. How God enforces His law is not always what He requires of *us*.

The problem becomes even more serious where unwarranted inferences are made, I recall as a student at the university listening to an off-campus Christian speaker who laid down the "law" in unequivocal terms; the text he used for his particular "mandate" was very familiar to me, but I had never seen such a meaning in it. My immediate reaction was one of anger; then I thought that perhaps there was a meaning in the Greek text I was ignorant of; I later learned there was no such meaning, only his inference, and a wrong one.

The trouble with inferences is that, when repeated over and over again, they become a part of the meaning of the law, and people read them into the text.

There are many who resent the strange and alien ways in which the U.S. Supreme Court routinely interprets the U.S. Constitution. The U.S. Government Printing Office periodically issues a revised edition of a heavy tome entitled *The Constitution of the United States, Analysis and Interpretation*, which gives us, line by line, the Constitution with all the interpretations thereof, sometimes of a single word, made by the Supreme Court. At times, by inferences, the original meaning is turned around.

Chief Justice John Marshall was known for his ability to take a statement and make it mean what he chose. His cousin, Thomas Jefferson, said: "When conversing with Marshall I never admit anything. So sure as you admit any position to be good, no matter how remote from the conclusion he seeks to establish, you are gone. So great is his sophistry, you must never give him an affirmative answer, or you will be forced to grant his conclusion. Why, if he were to ask me whether it was daylight or not, I'd reply, "Sir, I don't know. I can't tell. "

We have many people who are vehement strict constructionists with respect to the U.S. Constitution who at the same time are looser than loose constructionists where the Bible is concerned. They erect a vast structure of inferences and call it God's law. What amazes me is that these same people are strongly hostile to theonomy, to God's law! If the law itself is no longer binding, how can strange inferences be made binding?

Operation Rescue builds its case on inferences; so too do those who oppose birth control, smoking tobacco, and interest, and so on and on. In his personal life perhaps a man can seek ways which his conscience feels are important, but can he bind the conscience of other men? God's law is very plain, so that all may understand. Inferences take us into the realm of human conclusions. Anything important enough to be a law and bind our conscience is plainly stated by God: it is not left for men to discover.

Inferences can be very, very dangerous, not only to the life of faith but to our standing before God. People who major in inferences wind up trying to be holier than God, a particularly evil state. (See Otto Scott's essay on "Easy

Virtue," pp. 7-8.) Sadly enough, the world of inferences is peopled by persons who began at times with earnestness and a sound zeal.

In the time of our Lord, the Pharisees were the result of an earnest and dedicated development of inferences. Their inferences in time became more important to them than God's law-word. Our Lord attacked them and their misinterpretation with particular intensity, because He knew how evil their methodology was.

Phariseeism not only continued as Judaism itself, virtually supplanting other parties, but, over the centuries, it has had a powerful influence in Greek Orthodoxy, Roman Catholicism, and Protestantism. Its appeal is a supposed super-piety and a super- holiness. It appears to offer a greater purity and strength.

When our Lord attacks "*the tradition of the elders*" (Matt. 15:2), He attacks the tradition of inferences. One example He gives of this brings together the law requiring that one honor his father and his mother, and the law, Thou shalt have no other gods before Me, i.e., God's absolute priority. The Pharisees said that one could cease supporting one's parents if the money were dedicated to God instead. This was a logical inference! Yet our Lord called them "hypocrites" and said:

> Ye hypocrites, well did Esaias prophesy of you, saying, This people draweth nigh unto me with their mouth and honoureth me with the lips; but their heart is far from me. But in vain do they worship me, teaching for doctrines the commandments of men (Matt. 15:7-9).

Was it wrong for the Pharisees to draw inferences, and is it right for churchmen to do so? Did it make the Pharisees hypocrites, while it makes churchmen super-faithful saints? Will the Pharisees triumph again, and destroy their civilization in the process?

Remember, God's law is always very plain, even too blunt and plain! Mark Twain was right when he said that what bothered him in the Bible was not what he could not understand, but what he did understand!

If it is not plainly written as law by God Almighty, let no man bind your conscience with it.

Our Lord said of the Pharisees of His day that they were hypocrites, because they gave as God's word that which was their own inference, and they bound men by them. Beware of the Pharisees. They are with us still. (April, 1989)

THE CARTESIAN HERESY
Chalcedon Position Paper No. 109

We are routinely influenced by men whose names we may not know but whose ideas are the axioms of almost all men. The key figure in the modern age in this respect has been Rene Descartes. The starting point of philosophy in the modern era has been Descartes' *Cogito, ergo sum*, I think, therefore I am." The autonomous human consciousness and mind were his starting point, and, with this existential premise, Descartes reasoned out to substantiate or prove the existence of the physical world and of God. For Descartes, man's mind or soul was locked up inside one of man's glands and therefore received all knowledge through the senses - second hand.

Bishop Berkeley applied Occam's razor to Descartes and discarded the physical world: all that a man has are sense impressions of such a world, sent by God. Hume was more logical: we could not know nor demonstrate the reality of either God or the physical universe. All we have is the mind of autonomous man and his impressions. All this made sense, remember, on the premise that man's mind is distinct from his physical being and has only second-hand sense impressions in his mind.

Immanuel Kant resolved this crisis by saying that knowledge is not the congruity of our mind with objects outside of us. Rather, "We must make trial whether we may not have more success in the task of metaphysics, if we suppose that objects must confirm to our knowledge." (Kant: *Critique of Pure Reason*, Preface to the Second Edition, B-xiv). Among the many who saw some of the implications of this was Karl Marx. In his "Theses on Feuerbach," he wrote, "The philosophers have only *interpreted* the world, in various ways: the point, however, is to *change* it." Hegel had said, "The rational is the real," and now Marx and others were determined to make reality become what their mind conceived to be rational. Sartre and others limited reality also to the autonomous and existential consciousness of the human mind. Instead of being one aspect of reality, man's mind had become reality.

The result is a blindness especially marked in modern man, a refusal to recognize as real whatever is objectionable to one's mind. David Klinghoffer, in "AIDS and 'Just Another Word,'" in *The Wall Street Journal* (January 20, 1989, p. A-17), wrote "Miss (Susan) Sontag wants to do to AIDS what her admirers in the semiotics department have done to literature, namely, bleed all the meaning out of it."

Reality has become what the self-consciously would-be autonomous minds of scientists, and intellectuals will it to be. A recent book by a scientist is emphatic on this point: Bruce Gregory's *Inventing Reality, Physics as Language* (1988). Physics, we are told, is simply a language. It does not give us facts about reality because physics as a language is reality. "There seems to be no already-made world, waiting to be discovered. The fabric of nature, like all fabrics, is woven by human beings for human purposes" (p. 186). Gregory, associate director of the Harvard-Smithsonian Center for Astrophysics, cites with approval Albert Einstein's comment when someone asked how he would have felt if observations failed to confirm his theory. Einstein answered, "Then I should have felt sorry for the dear Lord - the theory is correct." (p. 10). Einstein also said, "Physical concepts are free creations of the human mind, and are not, however it may seem, uniquely determined by the external world" (p. 189).

There is much more in this vein in Gregory's book. Our concern is to call attention to the fact that this same Cartesian reduction of reality to man's autonomous mind and its sense impressions and ideas also marks theology.

In theology, the Cartesian perspective replaces the Biblical history with ideas. These ideas are called "myths" and "symbols." Because myths and symbols are mental constructs, they are more real, for these thinkers, than are the God-given facts. Like Einstein, if their symbols disagree with God's revealed word, so much the worse for God!

The liturgy of the church until recently had ancient roots in the Old Testament and in the early church. Now, the old meanings of the various liturgical practices are being replaced with man-made or man-ordained meanings. The reality of the crucifixion and the atonement is replaced by the symbols of the communion. *The historical meaning is replaced by the primacy of the symbol.*

Because these theologians in speaking to "ordinary" believers, do not try to distress the faithful by denying the reality of the historical, the people do not see what has happened to the historic faith.

Karl Barth was insistent on the centrality of the Virgin Birth to the faith, but he denied that it was an actual historical event. Reinhold Niebuhr said that the resurrection was at the heart of Christianity, but not as something that occurred in the physical world in Jerusalem.

An emphasis on symbolism and the symbols of the faith in this Cartesian sense is now pervasive in all circles: Greek Orthodox, Catholic and Protestant, Fundamentalist and Modernist, Calvinist and Arminian. In one sphere after another, symbols have replaced reality and become the new reality.

Some years ago, an image of pathos and humor was the madman who believed he was Napoleon; what his mind decreed that he was became for him "reality." What in such a person was seen as insanity is now good philosophy! The world of Descartes now holds, in economics, politics, education, theology, and elsewhere that the rational is the real, that which man's mind decrees to be the valid symbols becomes thereby reality.

The roots of this are in Genesis 3:5 - man's will to be his own god, knowing or determining for himself what constitutes good and evil, reality and non-reality.

Real is a word coming from the Latin *realis*, of the thing itself. The concept once presupposed reality to be something above and beyond man. The supreme and uncreated Reality is the triune God; the universe of created things is a subsistent reality (i.e., a reality which subsists or stands under God).

Because of Descartes' presupposition and its effect on modern thought, reality now has either an existential meaning or a pragmatic one. We are told that, for pragmatism, truth or reality is what works, this should be qualified to read, it is what works for me. The ultimate criterion for Cartesianism is the autonomous mind of man.

At one time, the test of reality, truth and authenticity was, "What say the Scholastics?" or "What are the scientific facts?" or "What say the Bible?" Now, people respond,in any argument, with "Well, I think" or "In my opinion" or "I feel." Every man has become his own version of reality, and he is the test and the standard of all things.

In recent years, some academicians have declared that we are now in a post-modern era. These same people are often advocates of deconstructionist thinking. In either case, their basic position is to demolish the validity of all reality outside the mind of man. They are simply radical and abject followers of the Cartesian model.

The dualism inherent in Descartes is not Biblical. In Scripture, the mind of man, or his soul, is not a something cooped up in a gland, or anywhere else. Man was created by God "a living soul" (Gen. 2:7). He is fully mind and body, not a half-and-half product!

Descartes made man's central problem to be one of knowledge; the Bible disagrees: man's problem is primarily and essentially sin. As long as man evades his true problem, his sins will increase, and his knowledge will be blighted.

The word "heresy" means a taking for oneself, i.e., determining for oneself what to believe and accept instead of assenting to what God sets forth in His Word. Cartesianism exalts precisely this temper into a philosophy, the mind of man as the determiner of truth and reality.

At present, state schools in the United States boast of teaching values, but the values they teach are self-determined or Cartesian values. The student is taught that it is his choice, that values are to be chosen in terms of one's needs and goals. This is why our humanistic world order is in trouble and is under judgment.

Cartesian self-indulgence is also apparent in churches when people demand that the preaching please them, make them feel good, concentrate on what interests them, and so on. The emphasis is on what the people want, not what God ordains.

The world of Descartes is a dying world, and a mad world. "Wherefore come out from among them, and be ye separate, saith the Lord" (II Cor. 6:17).

Walt Whitman said, "Man...must become a law unto himself." Ralph Waldo Emerson declared, "Build therefore your own world." The result is a nightmare world. To separate ourselves from this mad world of dreams and symbols is an act of sanity and faith. (May, 1989)

MORALITY AND GROWTH
Chalcedon Position Paper No. 110

A very serious error many churchmen are guilty of is to assume that non-Christians share common moral values and standards with Christians. All that is supposedly needed is to add Christ to their lives. This means overlooking the fact that the unbeliever is at enmity with God (Rom. 8:7; James 4:4). The fact of enmity may be concealed, but it is all the same very real. "Evangelism" based on this error presents Christ as a plus, an asset to be added to one's existing life to make it complete, whereas what the Lord requires it the total remaking or regeneration of man.

A second serious error, especially important in our time, is to assume that, because we view life morally, other people see things like we do, as a conflict between good and evil, right and wrong. But the essence of modern thought is to deny that such a distinction is valid. If man's problems are environmental, educational, or inherited, morality is not the issue.

A retired American general, a man of particularly high character and ability as well as Christian faith, questioned the nature of U.S. State Department policies to some leaders there. Recognizing his Christian stand, they immediately discounted his remarks, calling them "the devil theory of politics." By this they meant that it is wrong to speak of evil political movements, like Marxism. The problem is not evil but a matter of understanding and assistance.

The classic formulation of this perspective on an international basis was the work of President John F. Kennedy, who, in terms of the thinking of Daniel Bell, declared that our national and international problems are not moral but technological ones, to be solved by scientific experts. Kennedy's presidency brought into the open, and into power, a long-developing tendency to abandon the Christian and moral perspective for a sociological one. Christians may continue to view political problems moralistically, and politicians may continue to use moral language, knowing that it appeals to the people, but, in the halls of Congress, the administration, and the courts, the moral dimension is largely gone.

We see this in foreign affairs with especial clarity. World peace is going to be attained, it is believed, by world trade and by foreign loans. By making the nations interdependent, they believe, the nations will of necessity live in peace, hence, foreign loans. Morality is no longer a consideration of state except as a means of appealing to "backward" voters who are still governed by Biblical "mythology." For these enlightened ones, Christians are about as irrelevant as the flat earthers.

We do not abolish the sun when we become blind. Neither can our unbelief abolish God or abrogate His laws. They remain as a judgment against us. One consequence of trying to abandon Biblical moral premises is hypocrisy. Because man is created by God, every atom of man's being is inescapably governed by religious and moral premises, and for man to deny this fact is to go against his own being. If man denies good and evil in life and mankind, he puts on a false front, and "hypocrisy" means a mask, a false front. One of the most telling books of recent years was by Tung Chi-Ping and Humphrey Evans, *The Thought Revolution* (London, 1967). Tung Chi-Ping's account of life in Red China gives us an Orwellian picture. He wrote, "One aspect of Communist ideology concerns the theory that human nature can be altered by changing the environment. Under the environment of the preceding social orders, people were motivated by self-interest. Under socialism, however, the individual would begin to act in response to the best 'interests of his community'" (p. 97). In brief, man's "character" is a product of economic determinism, not moral choice. In practice, however, the new economics did not change anyone. During a time of food shortages, the pigs were fed human feces to keep them alive and fatten them. University students were taken out of their classes to collect and feed the latrine contents to the pigs. This repulsive cargo was carried in a barrel slung from a pole carried on the students' shoulders. From time to time, the pole would break and the contents spill over the young man or woman carrying the barrel. What the Communist party chief wanted to hear at the testimonial sessions was hypocritical joy over the task. What Tung Chi-Ping told Mi-Mi, a girl who had a barrel's contents wash over her, was this: "On your next one (testimonial time), you must mention this incident. Make it sound as bad as you can. Then say that in the days of the previous regime, you would have been unspeakably embarrassed. Now, however, while your distress is equally great, it is due entirely to your regret that some of the people's precious pig fodder has been wasted" (p. 102).

Success was assured by this strategy, because it meant that all such persons were not thinking moralistically but pragmatically, not in terms of good or evil but rather political opportunism. It was recognized that such people were essential to the Revolution. Moral people are critical; pragmatists are subservient.

A generation ago, Harry Ironsides wrote on holiness, the true and the false. He called attention to the fact that doctrines of holiness which call for perfectionism lead to serious mental and moral problems. A pious front replaces moral strength; a pretense of holiness replaces day-by-day growth in grace. The results become either hypocrisy or mental breakdowns.

We live in a moral universe. We are converted out of a conscious or unconscious enmity to God and His Law. When we are born as infants, we must grow into maturity. When we are reborn in Christ, growth is again a necessity. For this reason, St. Paul warned against the hasty promotion into leadership of a new convert (I Tim. 3:6). A novice in the faith is not ready for leadership (I Tim. 3:6). (James Moffett's rendering of I Timothy 5:22 is very telling: "Never be in a hurry to ordain a presbyter; do not make yourself responsible for the sins of another man - keep your own life pure.")

An age which denies either the necessity of a moral perspective, or, which denies the need for moral growth, for sanctification, is in deep trouble. It has blinded itself to the light of the sun, and it insists that the sun does not exist.

We live in a moral universe, and in a realm that requires growth in every sphere. The sovereign grace of God through Jesus Christ removes us from the no-growth world of sin and death into the world of grace and growth. There are neither problems nor growth in the grave. Given our need to mature in Christ, our world of problems are a challenge to growth and to victory. We need to hear from the pulpits what parents once routinely said: "Stop complaining and grow up!"

By rejecting morality for technological standards, the world of John F. Kennedy is doomed to die. The regenerating power of Christ unto salvation gives life, and God's Law as our moral order gives us maturity or growth. (June, 1989)

MATURITY
Chalcedon Position Paper No. 111

One of the long popular hymns of the church is "Jesus, Thou Joy of Loving Hearts." It is attributed by many to St. Bernard of Clairvaux, but an 11th century manuscript attributes it to a Benedictine abbess. Most hymnals now use only five stanzas of the hymn; it was written with 54 stanzas. Many older hymns had many more stanzas than hymnals carry now.

Similarly, many popular novels of the past century had long descriptive passages at the beginning and throughout. Very recently, I reread a boy's book written in 1889 and once very popular. It began with a foreword, and then almost seven pages of description and stage-setting before a single instance of conversation; it ended with a Latin quotation. Dickens, Scott, and other popular writers are now edited to eliminate the long descriptive sections.

Another illustration: about 40 years ago, shortly after the war, I heard an Episcopal bishop from India preach: his sermons lasted two hours and 40 minutes, routine in India at the time. In Scotland, in the 1800s, preachers spoke two hours and more routinely, with 40-50 points in their sermons. During the week, parishioners could routinely recite every point in order as they discussed the sermon.

Modern man's attention span is shorter! I myself do not favor a return to long sermons, or long anything! I am interested, however, in what has happened.

People now are less attuned to words, to reading and listening, and more attuned to action and sound. It is important to understand why.

The legitimate theater was for centuries a narrow realm, limited mostly to major cities and to a limited audience. The stage requires overstatement; the actors speak to be heard in the last row: this means an element of over-acting without appearing to do so. The slow pace of life must be stepped up to tell a story in a short time. This means also a heightened emotionalism to sustain interest.

The film industry began without sound - silent films. Over-acting and action were increased to carry the meaning and story. With sound, the over-acting was simply enhanced, and new technologies made more dramatic action possible.

All of this has led to an interesting result. Films have affected life. People, shaped because they lack a strong faith, became more emotional and more prone to dramatize themselves. Both children and adults are given to emotional outbursts. What 50 and 60 years ago would have embarrassed old and young is now routine with both. The decline in reading skills because of the growing failure of statist education has also aggravated the problem.

One of the marks of maturity is self-control. A child cries when hungry; this is natural enough in a baby, but maturity begins when the child learns to conform his appetites to the family's hours; the child is also taught to control his bladder and bowels; his temper tantrums are rebuked and are gradually replaced with intelligent behavior, and so on.

What we see now with adults is all too often a continuation of infantile behavior patterns. Maturity is less and less an ideal, and more and more evaded by all too many people. In the 1970s, I wrote, in a *Chalcedon Report* article, about the absurd and painful appearance of a woman well into her 80s in a bikini bathing suit, imitating a teen-age girl. The response was amazing. Some were highly emotional as they insisted on the "right" of a woman to act as a teenager, whatever her age. Of course, I never denied her freedom to do such a thing; I did question her lack of common sense and maturity! A few years later, I referred to this incident again in the *Chalcedon Report*, and I received another angry letter!

I find such things amazing. Is no one interested in the joys of maturity any more? Is it any wonder, with the lust for perpetual youth (or, continuing infantilism, take your choice), the attention span of old and young is shorter?

Life at every stage is wonderful. St. Peter (I Peter 3:7) speaks of "the grace of life." Life can only be a grace when it is lived under God with a readiness to grow in Him. We can then enjoy each stage of life with the knowledge that each has its problems and challenges, and the goal is eternal life in Him. Romans 8:28 tells us that, in Christ, all things are made by God to work together for our eternal good. The immediate event or burden may not be felt to be good, but we know it is used by our Lord for remarkable and blessed goals.

Paul in Romans 5:1-5 tells us that our troubles or tribulations produce patience. Patience gives us a mature experience, and experience increases our hope, because our faith has matured. The Berkeley Version (Verkuyl) of Hebrews 1:11 tells us that then "faith forms a solid ground for what is hoped for, a conviction of unseen reality." Then too we are now longer children, tossed about by every wind of doctrine, and so childish that we are the pawns of men (Eph. 4:14). Maturity is something which does not come from a television set, nor from emotional outbursts. Our growth in sanctification produces maturity, something to work for an enjoy. (July, 1989)

THE HOLY SPIRIT AND FREEDOM
Chalcedon Position Paper No. 112

Life is the arena of theology. The doctrines of our faith have been and are being made plainer for us by the testings of history. There is a telling sentence in a recent study by Dr. Joel R. Beeke: "Saving faith is rich because it is the pith of doing Christian theology." (*Personal Assurances of Faith, English Puritanism and the Dutch "Nadere Reformatie": From Westminster to Alexander Comrie* (1640-1710), p. 369, 1988.) Life is a matter of "doing Christian theology." In one era of church history after another, attacks on one or more doctrines compel Christians to think more seriously of them and to deepen their understanding of Scripture.

In this century, two areas of doctrine are under especial attack: the inspiration and authority of Scripture, and the doctrine of the Holy Spirit. As in the past, heresies cluster around neglected or under-thought areas of the faith. Our concern here is the doctrine of the Spirit, not with respect to its formulation but rather its importance, and why errors here are so dangerous.

There have been recurring times and movements of error linked to this doctrine: Montanism in the early church; the many movements originating in the thinking of the Abbot Joachim of Fiora; Quakerism, and more. In part, the heresies have arisen because of the neglect of this doctrine, and in part, to free man from God in the name of God the Spirit.

Our concern here is with the meaning of Biblical thinking with respect to the Holy Spirit. There are very important implications. Life cannot exist without patterns, direction and controls. Even those who are not Christian sneak in purpose in a disguised fashion. The believers in evolution do not allow the possibility of devolution. Is it not equally logical to affirm that all things are devolving as to say they are evolving? If you deny God's order, you must posit some other order rather than to admit universal disorder and chaos.

The question is this: what is the source of order in a universe of chance? Supposedly, that realm of chance has accidentally, by chance variations, produced our remarkable universe of apparent order. Will not change capriciously destroy that order? An answer to this, in print since 1936, is V. Gordon Childe's *Man Makes Himself.* Man can now supply purpose and control to a mindless evolution. Since this was written, we have seen efforts to control man's genes, to control "outer" space, and so on.

It was Karl Marx's keenest insight that he saw the publication of Darwin's *Origin of Species* in 1859 as the assurances of the triumph of socialism. If evolution and Darwin are correct, then there is no God in control. But control, planning (for predestination), and meaning are necessary. If there is no God to supply them, then man must. Practically, this means an all-powerful state; it means cradle-to-grave controls over all of life, and it means that the state must be free from all controls in order to control its realm totally.

As against this, some posited man as the center of all controls. These thinkers, anarchists, were still moving in terms of 18th century premises. They believed that Nature represents an order, and if let alone (*laissez faire*), would provide man and society with freedom and order. This was, however, simply a watered-down belief in the Biblical God. To affirm such an order without God, and, at the same time to believe in evolution, meant that these thinkers were schizophrenic in their presuppositions.

The rise of evolution meant the rise of totalitarian statism. The modern state claims powers never imagined by the pagan tyrants of old. It is able also to achieve unprecedented kinds of control because of modern technology.

The choice is this: either we are controlled by the power of the Holy Spirit, or we are controlled by the modern pagan state. Either God's providence rules all things, or the state must do so to avert disorder and chaos. This is why the doctrine and the person of the Holy Spirit are so important to man in our time. At issue is the freedom of man. St. Paul states the issue very plainly: "where the Spirit of the Lord is, there is liberty" (II Cor. 3:17).

Where the Spirit of God is denied, then the modern state becomes a substitute spirit, and the goal then is to create out of the state the caring, providing spirit of man. It is not an accident of history that, as the leftist student movement of the 1960s collapsed, its advocates and leaders took two directions. *First*, many became functionaries and bureaucrats of the state, its schools and universities. They sought to keep alive the spirit of man in a statist network. *Second*, many others became leaders and shapers of the new charismatic movement of the 1970s on. Having lost faith in the spirit of man, they turned with intensity to the Spirit of God, the Holy Spirit. The spirit of man had been everything to them, the answer to all problems; now the Spirit of God was the answer. The mainline churches, to whom the Holy Spirit was mainly an article of the Apostles' Creed, were amazed and then shocked. Old-line Pentecostalism had become church-oriented more than

Spirit governed, and while it gained from the new movement, was often very suspicious of it.

But something had happened; the doctrine of the Holy Spirit had become a matter of importance and of life. The Holy Spirit became a matter of more than an article in the creed to many evangelical churches.

This did not end the problem, it created new ones. To illustrate, someone arguing against a friend of ours on Biblical matters insisted that she was right because "the Spirit told me." The answer she received was the Spirit and the Bible tell me differently.

The Spirit cannot be separated from His written word. The modern age places its certainties in man, so that people say, "I think," or, "I believe," or, "I know," or, "I feel," and so on and on. The spirit of man replaces the Spirit of God. This is heretical: it frees man from God to himself! You and I, apart from God's word and Spirit, can be as tyrannical as the enemies of God if we make idols of our spirit or our minds.

The Nicene Creed tells us: "And I believe in the Holy Ghost, the Lord, and Giver of Life, Who proceedeth from the Father and the Son: Who with the Father and the Son together is worshipped and glorified; Who spake by the prophets." Since He is one with the Father and the Son, to neglect Him is to neglect God Himself. To separate Him from His word is false, and to identify our spirit with Him is idolatry. It is "where the Spirit of the Lord is, (that) there is liberty," and nowhere else.

There is no good future for man and society apart from Him who is "the Lord and giver of Life." (August, 1989)

VOUCHERS, FREEDOM AND SLAVERY
Chalcedon Position Paper No. 113

In the early years of the 20th century, the Fabian Society of England came out strongly in favor of state aid to independent Christian schools. When a board member resigned in protest, George Bernard Shaw rebuked him strongly. Nothing, Shaw held, would more quickly destroy these schools than state aid; their freedom and independence would soon be compromised, and, before long, their faith. Events soon proved Shaw to be right.

In the United States, a remarkable and vigorous Christianity developed early and has had a world-wide impact, in missions, education on every continent, and its development of many charitable and reform agencies. Since World War II, a phenomenal growth of Christian and home schools has taken place which now commands 33% of all primary and secondary school children and is growing steadily each year. This movement is one of the most remarkable developments in American life in the 20th century. It now faces total disaster, not from the statist's own ranks. A growing number of well-meaning leaders are seeking Federal or state aid by various means, notably the voucher plan.

The fact is that some years ago the courts established a very firm premise, namely, that, wherever state aid goes, there state controls must follow, even if Congress by law declares against such controls. No agency of state can relinquish the necessary civil control over agencies using or receiving tax funds. To receive any state funds whatsoever is to receive state controls.

Thus, to channel statist or taxed income in any way into the hands of Christian or home schools is to surrender their freedom and to exchange it for civil controls. A variety of schemes have been proposed to circumvent such controls, but they are evasions and are not likely to be tenable in court. Many legal precedents, including the Grove City College case, make clear that a very remote "cause" is routinely used to vindicate controls. We must remember that not too many years ago federal control over a restaurant was asserted because the salt in the salt shaker was a part of interstate commerce.

On the practical side, no more inefficient use of money exists than in any statist undertaking. On the other hand, Christian and home schools are financed with usually superior economy and very cheaply. To ask for vouchers or anything else from statist sources is to ask for higher taxes. In one country, home schooling mothers have asked to be paid as state teachers! The whole drift into a socialist mentality is a startling one.

Today a remarkable and far-reaching Christian renewal is in evidence in the United States and elsewhere. If our humanists today were as shrewd as G.B. Shaw, they could abort the Christian renewal by giving it state funds.

The Lord's work requires the Lord's tithe, and gifts and offerings over and above the tithe. Nothing better reveals commitment than giving. No commitment means no giving, and little commitment means token giving.

There is a correlation between finances and commitment. In the 1950s, some American Christian schools began to provide free tuition to needy children, only soon to find that virtually all their discipline problems were within this group. When the conditions were altered, and either these needy students had to work out part of this tuition, or else their parents so worked, the discipline problems usually ended. Normally, what costs a child or a man nothing, he treats as nothing.

Christian education is an urgently necessary aspect of Christ's Kingdom and its work. Children and their schooling are the key to a people's future. To make a humanistic state the controlling force in Christian education is a tragic mistake.

But, complain many, we are over-taxed by the state, have heavy family financial burdens, must support the church, and are taxed to support the state schools. It is too much of a burden then to pay for our children's Christian schooling! Precisely! It is a burden. But remember, although deer and fish are clean animals, they could not be used in the sacrifices to God. Only those domestic animals could be used which cost a man something in labor or in money. The Lord does not make things easy for us. If we are going to re-establish a Christian society, we are going to pay for it in more ways than one. A responsible people cannot be created without cost.

It is easy to understand the voucher plan by looking at existing examples of it, such as the welfare system, food stamps, and the like. All have the same premise; in the name of need, freedom and responsibility are surrendered, and dependence is called a virtue. The Israelites in the wilderness longed for the leeks and garlic, the melons and the slavery of Egypt, because slavery removes responsibility and the problems of freedom. God sentenced that generation to die in the wilderness.

If the voucher plan succeeds, all groups, of course, will be eligible: humanists, Muslims, New Agers, any and all who want their own schools. This is legally a logical consequence. But historically it has been Christians who have most thrived under freedom. It is the Christian home school and church school which have grown most dramatically; nothing else compares with them. Christianity has done best where most free of the state and its controls. It will be a sorry day when Christian education becomes another special interest group. There are no Biblical precedents for any such step.

The law of the tithe tells us what we must do. The Levites normally received the tithe (although the tither could administer it himself), and the Levites gave 10 percent of the tithe to the priests for worship (Num. 18:25,26). Ninety percent was for levitical use. The Levites had broad functions, including the fact that they were the teachers (Deut. 33:10). When we restore God's laws of tithing, we can re-establish the Christian strength in worship, health, education, and welfare, and we will have done it in God's way. I fear that any other solution will bring God's judgment upon us. Remember that God told Samuel that Israel had rejected him in seeking man's rule and man's laws. Because of this, their sons and daughters would become servants of the state power; they would be heavily taxed, and their property would be expropriated. In time they would cry out to the Lord in their distress, but, said Samuel, "the LORD will not hear you in that day" (I Sam. 8:18).

Are we working to place ourselves in a condition where the Lord will not hear us? Are we so covetous of the state's mess of pottage that we will sell our birthright for it? Do we have money for our pleasures but not our children's schooling? Will we in time de-Christianize our home and Christian schools in order to meet federal standards? It amazes me that men who profess to hate socialism want to espouse the voucher plan! But such blindness is common. Businessmen who hate socialism demand various subsidies, as do workers and their unions,farmers, and others. Each group wants socialism for itself only, and so too do all too many churchmen now. They want vouchers to free them from financial problems, forgetting that they thereby surrender freedom. They assume that the answer to our problems lies in the state, forgetting how bankrupt morally and financially the state is!

"Arise, O LORD, let not man prevail" (Ps. 9:19). (September, 1989)

REVOLUTION, COUNTER-REVOLUTION AND CHRISTIANITY
Chalcedon Position Paper No. 114

On July 14, 1789, the French Revolution began with the storming of the Bastille. In the succeeding months and years, millions were killed to help establish the civil reign of Reason. On July 14, 1989, many heads of state gathered in Paris to honor and celebrate that event. Only one, Prime Minister Margaret Thatcher of Great Britain, called attention to the murderous nature of the French Revolution and questioned the absurd idea that human rights and freedoms originated in it.

The French Revolution quickly developed into the Reign of Terror, as have all revolutions since then. It was morally and intellectually bankrupt, but men have continued to believe that men, nations and history can only be regenerated by blood-letting, and murders continue.

The thesis of revolution is radically anti-Christian. Revolutionary man believes that the rise of Christianity was the fall of man, and that the true direction of history must be from Christ to Adam, from supernatural man to natural man. This means that Christianity is the greatest impediment humanity has ever had, and so forces of revolution seek its obliteration. The greatest holocaust of all history, and of the 20th century, has been and is the massacre of Christians. It occurs all over the world, and the media is in the main silent concerning it.

In 1989, the evil of revolutions was clearly underscored by the events in China, Russia, Poland, Bulgaria, and elsewhere in the realms of humanistic statism. None of this dimmed the determination to celebrate the French Revolution, and to extend the dominion of revolution.

But what about Counter-Revolution? Did it not finally succeed in Europe after Napoleon? It did indeed, and the successes of the Counter-Revolution revealed its bankruptcy. Its theorists were right: the Old Order, however bad, was better; they worked for a restoration.

What they failed to recognize was that the Old Order was a decayed relic of Christendom. A Christian society could not be restored without a vital Christianity. Chateaubriand could say, "Religion is the source of liberty" but this intellectual awareness did not necessarily mean a living faith (Jacques Godeshot: *The Counter-Revolution, Doctrine and Action, 1789-1804*, p.135.

Princeton University Press, 1971). To talk about "God and country" does not align God on your side, nor mean that you believe His every Word.

The failure of Counter-Revolution, put simply, was that it wanted the form of godliness but not the power thereof, the name of God but not God Himself. Men are not governed by echoes, however lovely their sound, and Counter-Revolution was an echo.

The greatest theorist of the Counter-Revolution was Edmund Burke. Burke was a good analyst of his times; he knew the strength of the Old Order; Burke saw the value of Christian premises, but reality to him was continuity, not Jesus Christ. As a result Burke's work was essentially a failure.

Other men recognized the failure of the Revolution, and of Counter-Revolution. For them, Christianity was not an option. Civilization, as they saw it, needed a new foundation. In this, they agreed with the French Revolution. Two men who were deeply concerned over this issue were Ralph Waldo Emerson and Thomas Carlyle. Both had abandoned orthodox Christianity. Emerson, in "Historic Notes of Life and Letters in New England," wrote of the new generation of men "born with knives in their brains, a tendency to introversion, self-dissection, (and) anatomizing of motives." These men with knives in their brains put the knife to Christianity. Emerson and Carlyle had seen the removal of Christianity from the center of their own being. Even among conventional Christians, faith was less and less the dominant force in their lives. God's law was giving way to the state's law.

Emerson and Carlyle were not as radical as men like Karl Marx, Max Stirner and Friedrich Nietzsche, although "Carlyle did love destruction for its own sake. the attraction was mainly esthetic" (Kenneth Marc Harris: *Carlyle and Emerson*, p. 116, Harvard University Press, 1978). As far as ideas were concerned, their premises were very radical. Man and history replaced God and Christ in their thinking. (*Ibid.*, p. 117ff.) For Carlyle, the hero and, for Emerson, the power of man and his character replaced the power of God (Robert E. Spiller and Wallace E. Williams, eds.: *The Early Lectures of Ralph Waldo Emerson*, vol. III, 1838-1842, pp 243f., 276f., etc., Harvard University Press, 1972).

As Counter-Revolution developed into conservatism, its premises, despite a sometimes pious facade, became as humanistic as those on the left. Both Revolution and Counter-Revolution, right and left, had become humanistic and explicitly or implicitly anti-Christian. Because the churches are themselves all too often infused with humanism, they have been little disturbed by these developments.

National indignation should have been aroused when it became known that, during the Reagan presidency, homosexual prostitutes and their customers were at times given private, guided tours of the White House. One wealthy homosexual in particular had much power among Republicans. (Gary Potter, in *The Wanderer*, vol. 122, no. 29, July 20, 1989, pp. 1,8, "GOP Homosexuals. The Reason Why 'Social Agenda' Gets Nowhere?") John Lofton wrote in *The Washington Times* (July 31, 1989) about another prominent Republican who had raped and sodomized a teen-aged intern, and in another case, was convicted but given a suspended prison term for a savage five-hour rape of a young woman. A prominent conservative publisher berated John Lofton for writing against a Republican! Apparently only Democratic rapes are bad.

The rot runs deep, not only in the body politic but in the churches. Too many churchmen are too busy warring against each other, or waiting for the rapture (due in 18 months, I was told today), and being generally irrelevant to know what is happening all around them.

For some years, I have been in many court trials as a witness for churches, Christian schools, home schools, families, and so on, who faced an attack for their faith and practice. I have seen a state attorney hod aloft a Bible and declare it a child-abuse manual. Several pastors were on trial for requiring the chastising of children in their schools or day-care facilities, although no parents had complained. This was in a southern Bible-belt state. No church members were in the courtroom to lend their moral support. (Neither pastors nor the lawyer have ever informed me of the outcome of the trial, a routine occurrence. So much for the calibre of our churches!)

Incidents like this are commonplace. The enemy is shooting at Christians, and the church is indifferent.

But now total war is under way, as Shelby Sharpe so telling reports it. The purpose is the obliteration of Christianity. If America's churches do not resist this attack, God will give them over to destruction and replace them with another people and other churches.

In I Peter 4:17 we read,"For the time is come that judgment must begin at the house of God: and if it first begin at us, what shall the end be of them that obey not the gospel of God?"

What will happen to churches who are blind to what is taking place? And what can we say of a political order, which, faced with crisis upon crisis, plans to convert the country to Methanol-powered automobiles, using a particularly dangerous and poisonous fuel? There is a growing blindness all around us which is a prelude to God's judgment. There is a concern with irrelevant issues which is always the mark of irrelevant man.

We are at war, but the weapons of our war are not material but Biblical and Spiritual ones, and our calling is to believe and obey the Lord, to bring people to Christ, to extend His dominion, and to establish the crown rights of our King in every area of life and thought. (October, 1989)

INFERENCES AND THE LAW
Chalcedon Position Paper No. 115

One of the "problems" with God, for many people, is that He gives His creature man too much freedom - the freedom to sin, to think, and to make decisions. As far as most people, churches, and civil governments are concerned, this is wrong. They want laws to govern every area of life and thought. I get letters from time to time written by people who question the validity of God's law because, they tell me, there is so much in the modern world which is not covered by the few pages of Biblical law (some 600 plus laws only). Such people want a totalitarian set of laws to control everything! Where God is silent, they impose laws through church or state, or in their personal domain.

But God's law has limits! Man seeks a total law, whereas God does not, even though He is the absolute Sovereign and Creator. God does not present His law as the salvation of man and society but as the way of holiness. This is a very different thing.

In understanding God's law, we must recognize, *first*, that much of it is *case law*. The classic instance of this, used by Scripture to show us its meaning, is Deuteronomy 25:4, "Thou shalt not muzzle the ox when he treadeth out the corn." This minimum example sets forth the fact that, even with an animal, the laborer is worthy of his hire (I Cor. 9:9; I Tim. 5:18). This means that especially to those who labor worthily in Christ's work double "honor" or pay should be given (I Tim. 5:17).

Another case law is found in Deuteronomy 21:18-21, the case of an incorrigible son. Those who are hostile to God's law insist on reading "son" as a baby. The age is not specified, but what is clearly intended is what we call an incorrigible and habitual criminal. The point made is that a family must side with God's law against its own flesh and blood, if necessary, and society hence must not hesitate to execute habitual criminals.

Case law give us clear statements about the *application* of God's law.

Second, God's law does not always require a man-imposed sentence. We are told that God's penalties for failure to tithe are severe (Mal. 3:8-12), but no human agency is given any right to enforce the tithe. Deuteronomy 25:4 (cited above) is very important, but, again, God reserves to Himself the power to punish as well as to bless. A very considerable percentage of the 600-plus laws of God call for no punishment by man, the church, the state, or any human agency! However, man's original sin is his desire to be his own god and to determine his own law (Gen. 3:5), and, as a result, man strives in every sphere to impose a totalitarian law. This totalitarian tendency is present in every sphere of life today, with ugly results. Men want a totally prescribed life, and the power of total prescription for themselves.

In recent years, with serious problems in the Catholic Church and in

Protestant churches, many distressed members have come together to set up organizations to recall the church to its faith, or to establish new or continuing church bodies. Very commonly, these groups have serious problems which end in their dissolution. The most common problem is a desire to over-control everyone, beginning often with compilation of voluminous by-laws which often break up the group! They want a totally prescriptive governing document and thereby in effect deny the power of the Holy Spirit. For them, safety lies in full controls, not in the Third Person of the Trinity.

Third, God's law gives us plain commandments, and our humanistic inferences cannot supplement them. In the April 1989 *Chalcedon Report*, Position Paper 108, I wrote on "Inferences and Commandments." The response was amazing and amusing. Together with my article on "Revolution or Regeneration," it aroused rage and fury in many. One man told us to "cease publication" at once! Very few were ready to cite Scripture with respect to either article in their arguments. The few who did made inferences.

Matthew 15:1-9 is the classic text against inferences and their traditions. God commands honoring father and mother, and He commands tithing, and He asks us to give gifts above and over the tithe. The Pharisees took two commandments and opposed them to one another. They held that honoring God takes priority over honoring parents, hence, by inference, money for the support of one's parents could be better used as a "gift" to God. Our Lord calls this "logical inference" hypocrisy. "Thus have ye made the commandment of God of none effect by your tradition." It is vain worship because it substitutes men's commandments for God's. Such people, He said, seem very close to God in their verbal professions, "but their heart is far from me." We are not permitted to expand on God's law by our humanistic inferences. This is how the U.S. Supreme Court treats the Constitution, but it is not how we are to treat God's Word.

Fourth, let us remember how few God's laws are. Let us remember also how limited in number are those that allow man to punish the offenders. God requires us to take His law very literally, but never to place our trust for salvation in law, least of all man's law. Beginning with Eden, God's law gives man the freedom to sin and to make a mess of his life. God obviously does not share the view of the modern state that men must be so controlled that the opportunity to sin (for men or business, or churches, or unions, or anyone) be reduced to the minimum, or to point zero. Of course, the result has been the development of an irresponsible people and the increase of crime, and welfarism has become history's most potent anti-human welfare activity. The horrors of wars and famines have usually been short-term; the destruction of man's sense of responsibility is having long-term consequences. Scripture equates true freedom with our redemption and regeneration in Christ: "If the Son therefore shall make you free, ye shall be free indeed" (John 8:36). The inescapable fact of history and Scripture is that God has given men the freedom to rebel *against* Him and His law, to create their evil empires, dream their humanistic dreams, and seek to control all things (Psalm 2). His goal is by "the law of the Spirit of life in Christ Jesus" to free us from "the law of sin and death" (Rom. 8:2) The Truth, Jesus Christ, can alone make us free (John 8:32; 14:6).

The desire to use coercion, or to compel by massive demonstrations, any redirection of human action is a humanistic methodology. A corrupt society cannot be kept more than briefly and poorly by massive coercion. The compelling force must be in the hearts of men, or society will remain corrupt. The truth of the old saying remains: "You can't make a good omelette with rotten eggs."

Some find it baffling that we, as advocates of God's law, are so hostile to some kinds of legal (or illegal) action. It is because we take God's law-Word very seriously, and the Triune God who gave the law most seriously.

Men must turn to Christ for atonement and regeneration. They must be guided by the Holy Spirit, not their anger against certain things but by their grace and power in the Spirit.

There are too many churchmen today more filled with rage than with the Spirit of God. A verse once commonly quoted seems now to be forgotten by man: "where the Spirit of the Lord is, there is liberty" (II Cor. 3:17). Only by this freedom can the power of sin and evil be broken.

In the April 1989 *Chalcedon Report*, Otto Scott wrote on "Easy Virtue" and said, "No one has ever managed to reach heaven through ridding someone else of sin," for "To correct the sins of others does not lessen one's own." Our generation seems determined to rely on coercion rather than regeneration; it prefers its way to God's way; it follows the Pharisees in replacing God's law with their inferences. Can we escape the judgment of the Pharisees by adopting their methods and calling them Christian?

Can we by a totally prescriptive law replace the work of the Holy Spirit? The goal of the totalitarian state, and too often of the church, is to so control people that they cannot have the freedom to sin. Our world today is in a shambles because of this policy of salvation by law. We may well say, of our time, "The harvest is past, the summer is ended, and we are not saved" (Jer. 8:20) - nor can we be saved by the present trust in law.

God gave man the freedom to sin, and today both church and state are earnestly trying to nullify the freedom God has given. A cartoonist recently depicted a police commando team surrounding a building, and an officer with a bull-horn declaring, "We know you're smoking in there. Come out of the bathroom and the house with your hands up!"

It does not occur to those who criticize Biblical law for not covering every conceivable sin that, *first*, God wants us to grow in holiness in His Spirit and to apply the meaning of righteousness to all of life: and, *second*, if God had given us the totally prescriptive law some people demand, men would be zealously hounding one another for tens of thousands of infractions of the law, exactly as the state is now doing, and as the church too often yearns to do. The Bible leaves such people without excuse.

The Christian and the church must learn to believe, obey, and respect not only the enscriptured Law-Word of God, but His silences also. (November, 1989)

CHALCEDON MEDICAL REPORT NO. 1
The Medical Profession as a Priestly Calling

One of the difficulties with the ancient Greek view of medicine, and of the modern view as well, has been its severe materialism. So far has this view been carried at times by some that, on one occasion, a reference was made to doctors as "glorified mechanics." In a very limited sense, this is a very remarkable mechanic, but not all mechanics are surgeons! We cannot confuse the part with the whole.

The identity and the nature of the doctor have been very much confused in our era, as indeed are most "images." It is important therefore to call attention to and revive the meaning of the doctor in the Biblical tradition. In terms of the Bible and Christian tradition, the doctor has a *priestly* role. His very area of concern, *health*, requires this. In the Hebrew-Christian heritage, the doctor, in origin a Levite, is concerned with *health*, and health is an aspect of salvation. The Latin word, *salve*, carries the same implication, and it is a fitting fact, in terms of the Bible, that our English word *salvation* has as its root the word of *health*. Salvation is total health, spiritual and material; it means in its final form the resurrection of the body, in its inception, regeneration, and, in between, growth in terms of the principle of health, God in Christ. As a result, for Biblical faith, care of the body is a religious concern, and health a godly duty and blessing. The man who ministers to the body has thus a priestly calling, as does the man who ministers to the spirit. Both doctor and pastor have a priestly calling or ministry.

According to the Biblical doctrine of the fall, the whole man fell, and the whole of man is affected by sin. This means that the spiritual is not necessarily good. After all, Satan is a purely spiritual being! It has been neoplatonism which has depreciated the physical and wrongly exalted the spiritual. The doctrine of the resurrection of the body means that total redemption is the Biblical doctrine: a new creation is the goal, in time and in eternity. *Healing* is thus religious, whether physical or spiritual in its areas of concern. The healing professions, whether medical or pastoral, are thus priestly callings.

There is thus, although almost entirely forgotten now, a religious reason for medical privileged communication. Before discussing medical privileged communication, it is important to distinguish it from another form, where a lawyer or a spouse is concerned. Talking to a lawyer is legally in effect talking to one's own self; the lawyer is your "mouthpiece." The right against self-incrimination and torture means that the agent who speaks for us and represents us in court cannot be compelled to divulge that confidence we place in him. Similarly, a husband or a wife is an extension in a sense of our person, theologically, "one flesh" with us, and a similar protection is extended. The tyranny of modern Marxist and other totalitarian states is in part their denial of this immunity against self-incrimination and the privileged communications which are a part of this immunity.

Privileged communications to a doctor, priest, or pastor are different: they are religious communications. In confessing to a pastor, we are in effect confessing to God through the medium of His servants, and we seek spiritual healing and health. In talking to a doctor, a patient is in effect confessing, opening his physical being for examination, and again the purpose is healing and health. In both cases, the purpose is religious in the Biblical sense and a part of the redemptive process. The "confession" in either case is privileged communication and is closed to other men, and to the various agencies of man and the state.

The infringement of this privileged communication by the state is religious: the state usurps the place of God and claims the right to be privy to all that goes on between man and man, and between man and God, because it claims to be the acting god of this world.

It must be thus held that statist interference with either church or medicine is a very serious matter, a religious matter, and a threat to the freedom of man.

So seriously did the early church regard the priestly vocation of the doctor that, by the fifth century A.D., it became a popular requirement that doctors, like monks, be celibates. It is significant that this requirement of sacerdotal celibacy for doctors came some six hundred years before the same requirement was made of the priests. There were, of course, mixed motives in this requirement. The influence of neoplatonism meant a depreciation of the physical life of man, and of sex, and hence an insistence on celibacy as a higher way of holiness. On the other hand, this high regard for doctors as holy and priestly men, because of their healing work, was Biblical and Hebraic to the core. Medicine was plainly seen as a holy profession.

Although the knowledge of its origins has been lost, this aspect of medicine still survives. Now, as through the centuries, the doctor hears many confessions having only a remote relationship to bodily complaints. I was told recently of a woman, in good health, who made an appointment for a check-up simply because she said, "I just need to talk to Dr.-- about my problems." This is nothing new: the over-lapping of medical and pastoral offices is of long standing. Parishioners ask pastors medical questions to gain courage to face a doctor, and they ask doctors religious questions for counsel beyond a medical prescription.

The priestly and confessional aspect of the doctor-patient relationship has been neglected, because our age has become increasingly ignorant of its religious heritage. In spite of this ignorance, the religious character of the doctor persists, because it is inherent to his calling. People expect "something more" from a doctor and a pastor by virtue of their calling.

This is why abortion is so damaging to the image of a doctor. To be a hangman is a legitimate office, and, through the centuries, there have been executioners of various kinds who have been normal, everyday members of their society. However, if a priest or pastor had ever assumed the office of an executioner, the response would have been a most justifiable shock, and a sense of horror. The religious office of priest and pastor is concerned with saving men, not killing them. Even where the clergy must strongly assent to an execution, they cannot alter the character of their calling by becoming an executioner. The office of an executioner, however, is a legitimate and necessary one in terms of Scripture and its requirement of capital punishment. Abortion, clearly, is not: it is against Biblical law (Ex. 21:22-23), and it is murder. For those whose calling is to heal, to kill is a flagrant violation of their office, and it leaves psychological scars even with those who seek abortion. (Anyone who has talked with or counselled women who believe in abortions and have had them, knows that their attitude towards their doctor is radically different from that of mothers who are against abortion. Such pro-abortion women will and do resent my views, but they view their doctors with contempt.)

The *trust* which is a doctor's necessity in his successful practice is a religious trust. A once popular painting showed a family doctor by a child's bed, *deeply concerned*. What many people forget, as they recall this painting, is that the doctor is *not* presented as having all the answers. He is very much concerned as he looks at the child, and this was seen by the artist as basic to the family doctor. He brings the children into the world, and their health is his concern. The parents regard the doctor with *trust*: he will do all that he possibly can, and no man can do more. The painter shows the doctor, not as a worker of medical miracles, but as a family friend and a medical pastor. Moreover, very clearly the appeal of this painting was due to the fact that the doctor had an *honored and loved status*. The picture has a strongly religious flavor, and it was a much loved one because the doctor was seen as a man with a calling, an essentially religious vocation.

Medicine has made some of its most important advances since that picture was painted, but there has been some loss in the position of the doctor. Much of the loss is due to the decline of Christian faith in our society, so that men now come to a doctor with pagan demands and expectations, not in terms of the historic role of the doctor in Christendom.

The growth too of non-Christian materialism has led to false and rather mechanical views of medicine. If our car needs oil or gas, we add these things to the car; if we need a new fuel pump, we replace the old one. In like manner, some people expect cure-all dosages and changes and are resentful when the doctor cannot work miracles. Their expectation, however mechanical, is still religious, but it is in essence paganism, not Biblical faith.

This, of course, is the heart of the matter. There must be a return to a

Biblical view of medicine as a *calling*, and as a priestly-pastoral calling, but there must also be a return to Christian faith on the part of the people, or false and unreasonable demands will be made of medicine.

Let us now examine another aspect of the medical profession, its general name of *doctor*. *Doctor* in Latin means *teacher*, from *docere*, to teach. This is why the great theologians are called doctor (or teachers) of the church; the doctorate at a university is that degree which ostensibly qualifies a man as an advanced teacher. Very early in church history, *doctor* meant a teacher of Christian doctrine. This usage had deep roots in Hebraic and New Testament practice. The academic degree perhaps arose in the twelfth century, but, long before that, the term was common and applied to theologians.

The earlier term for the medical doctor was *physician*, a curer or healer, a natural philosopher, one expert in physics. In the Greek sense, a physician was somewhat more close to what we call a physicist than we now realize. As the physician has developed his calling in Western civilization, it has become necessary to take the root of the word and create a new noun, physicist, to name the practitioner of what was once largely the physician's province.

Moreover, while the Yellow Pages of the telephone directory may list him as "Physician," very few people nowadays ever use that term. It is too clinical, too impersonal; it still reeks of physics and the laboratory. The popular name for the physician has come to be a very personal one, *doctor*, teacher, a word allied with "Master" and "Rabbi" in the New Testament.

The Canadian scholar (and humorist) Dr. Stephen Leacock once wrote an amusing account of his profound embarrassment because of his doctoral degree in literature. On board a ship to Europe, he was called when a medical emergency arose because he was on the passenger list as "Dr. S. Leacock." He had to explain to a surrounding group eager to see a sick passenger revived that he was not a *medical* doctor, and the incident was painful. People seemed to feel that a teacher had no right to use the title of doctor! This is indeed a very interesting and remarkable development. Popular usage has taken the title of doctor from those who are literally doctors or teachers and given it to physicians. Physicians still list themselves as physicians in the telephone directory, but virtually everyone speaks of them as doctors.

There is a long history behind this designation, and it is a Christian one. It was once commonplace in many areas to call all older pastors "Doctor." This is still true in some parts of the United States. Travelling as much as I do, I quickly became aware of this fact: as I approached fifty, I found that in certain parts of the country I "graduated" to "Dr. Rushdoony"! The term "doctor" in this tradition is very much in the tradition of the New Testament usage of "Master" or "Rabbi": it designates a respected teacher whose word brings healing. It was in this custom that one came to Jesus asking, "Good Master, what good thing shall I do, that I may have eternal life?" (Matt. 19:16). In this same custom, people approached the physician asking, "Tell me, doctor, will I get well?" The physician in the Christian world thus became a *doctor*, one on whose word and act men depended for healing.

The modern professor is losing his hold on the name of *doctor*. His word has no teaching and healing character, and the religious orientation of his office is gone to a large degree. The continuing Christian regard for the religious character of medicine has made the name of *doctor* the common one for physicians. (The Biblical tradition is equally strong in Jewish circles in this respect. Doctors and rabbis have a high standing, and one of the most coveted of callings for a Jewish boy is that he become a *doctor*.)

There is thus a remarkable history, a religious history, behind the medical practitioner. Important as the medical school may be to medicine, and as far-reaching as twentieth century advances in medicine may be, the *doctor* in the minds of Western men is more than a scientist or a scientific technician: he is a *doctor* with all that the word means in Christian tradition.

Any departure from that tradition and faith means a serious dislocation in the meaning and practice of medicine, and a major problem in public relations. The paganization of medical practice has meant a change of attitude from trust to distrust, and the rise of something out of pagan antiquity, the liability suits. These and other factors indicate that the image of the doctor has suffered to a degree. The reasons for this change are deeply rooted in the general crisis of our culture, in the humanism which so heavily governs our era.

Reconstruction thus must begin in the hearts and minds of all men. It requires a clarification of issues and a development of basic motives. Medical practice cannot, by its very nature, escape religious implications and overtones. If these are pagan, there are very serious consequences for doctors. It will be our purpose to develop the historic Biblical faith and meaning of the *doctor* in the Biblical faith.

CHALCEDON MEDICAL REPORT NO. 2
Liability Laws: Their Pagan Origin

Very commonly, historians praise ancient medical practice and declare that its corruption was the fault of Christianity. Prior to rise of Christianity, medicine was supposedly making steady progress, and it was the Christians who brought this to a halt. The decline, however, in ancient medicine began in the third century, B.C., long before the birth of the church. (J. Beaujeau, "Medicine," in Rene Taton, ed. *History of Ancient and Medieval Science, from the Beginnings to 1450*, p. 365. New York: Basic Books, 1957,1963.) According to Dr. Entralgo, it was in fact Christianity which rescued medicine from sterile presuppositions. (Pedro L. Entralgo: *Mind and Body, Psychosomatic Pathology: A Short History of the Evolution of Medieval Thought*. New York: P. J. Kennedy & Sons, n.d.)

In the pagan tradition, the doctor was a god or a semi-incarnate agent of a god, such as Asklepios. Medicine was an occult practice; medical practice in the healing tradition of the Asklepieia of the Greeks was by oracles. Asklepios was the chief Greek god of healing; he was also the first Greek god to be received into the Roman pantheon, indicating the importance of healing to the Romans.

Because paganism saw medical practice as a form of divine manifestation, it expected too much of the doctor. The gods being very powerful, it followed, that when the gods chose, they could do almost whatever they would. Thus, if an agent of the gods did not heal you, it meant ill-will on his part, because all the resources of the god were his to command. The result was the pagan doctrine of the physician's liability: *liability was seen as commensurate to power, and thus the doctrine of total liability was common to paganism*. If the patient died, it was assumed to be the doctor's fault, because his power to heal was proportionate to his god's power. A doctor who lost his patient could lose his life, or at least his right hand.

This does not mean that such executions or mutilations were commonplace, although they did occur. The ancient physician was also a good psychologist who could deflect blame and break with his patient before death.

In the 1940's, when I was for eight and a half years on an Indian Reservation, I saw this ancient method in practice. The medicine men claimed occult powers, and they never lost a patient (in those days). As astute men, they could see a patient slipping away, and they recognized the patient's awareness of his condition. They would provoke a quarrel, in which the fearful and doubting patient would be manipulated into being the aggressor, and then would terminate treatment saying, in so many words, "So you don't want me. It's the white doctor you want, is it? Well, go to him and see if he can do you any good, but don't say I didn't warn you what would happen if you doubted me and left me." The medicine man would then leave in indignation, and the hapless patient would be taken to the white man's doctor, usually to die. As a result, the white doctor acquired a poor reputation whatever his skills, and the medicine man a remarkable statistical record of no lost patients! No one could then accuse the medicine man of evil intent, and, as for the white doctor, everyone knew, who trusted in medicine men, that all white men were anti-Indian in some degree.

The ancient pagan doctor operated on the same premise: he claimed occult and semi-divine powers, and he was thus exposed to an equally great liability. His liability was not that of a man but of a semi-divine being.

Moreover, it was precisely the element of naturalism in pagan antiquity which led to this view of the physician. There was no true doctrine of a transcendent God, but only of gods who were divinized heroes, so that men could point to the grave of Zeus, for example, and various cities claimed association with him during his lifetime. The pagan doctrine was formalized in Pliny's statement: "Deity only means Nature." The hero, who through his power, or the physician who through his knowledge of medicine, commanded nature was thus in some sense a divine being and has a measure of infallibility. His liability then was not the liability of a man but of a superman, a hero, or a divine being. The result was a paradox: the more naturalistic the pagan physician became, the more he saw himself and was seen by others as a godlike being. Thus, the doctor of the Greco-Roman world, the more his practical knowledge grew, the more authoritarian he became. He readily turned also to charms and amulets, because magic was seen as a means of controlling nature. Hebrew medical history, because it did not confuse God and nature, avoided on the whole the peril of occultism and magic. Because the modern world so greatly idealizes Greek civilization, it failed to see the serious and unavoidable defects in its politics, philosophy, or medicine.

Our concern now, however, is with the liability concept. Limited liability is a modern concept, one which has become common only in the last 125 years. There are serious defects in the concept, which cannot be dealt with here. (See R. J. Rushdoony: *Politics of Guilt and Pity*, pp. 254-262; Nutley, New Jersey: The Craig Press, 1970; and R. J. Rushdoony: *The Institutes of Biblical Law*, pp. 104-106, 273f., 463-467, 627, 664-669; Nutley, New Jersey: The Craig Press, 1973.) The idea of limited liability leads to socialism in that it does not eliminate liability but simply transfers it from the individual to the group. The idea of unlimited liability, however, is of two kinds. *First*, in the Hebraic or Biblical tradition, liability is unlimited, but it is not total. Man is not a god; he cannot at any point be ascribed total responsibility for all things. To expect more of a man than a man can do, or to expect inerrancy and infallibility, is a serious error and puts an impossible burden on men and society. The human factor is thus inescapable. Men can do their best, and no more. Applied to medicine, this doctrine means that, when I choose a doctor, I cannot expect him to work miracles. Moreover, I am responsible for choosing him, so I cannot complain if his abilities are not equal to the medical problem. There is a difference between criminal action and human inadequacy. The implications of this Biblical concept were enormous. The pagan doctrine of total liability receded, and, until the recent revival of paganism, liability suits were a rarity.

Second, in the pagan tradition, total and unlimited liability falls on the doctor. Any and all failures by the doctor to heal represent criminal intent or negligence and hence require prosecution in terms of criminal law. Thus, whether it was the Code of Hammurabi, Greek law, or any other pagan tradition, the failures of the doctor had a place in criminal law. Aristotle's lectures to his students were private and esoteric, unlike his published works, and he claimed descent from Asklepios. Such a claim meant special powers and secret knowledge. Instead of magic being an early aspect of medicine, which fell by the wayside as rationalism developed, magic was a late development which arose with rationalism. L. Bourgey admits that in Greece, for example, "This magical kind of medicine was not part of the original tradition and its full development occurred very much later." (L. Bourgey, "Greek Medicine from the Beginning to the End of the Classical Period," in Rene Taton, editor: *Ancient and Medieval Science from the Beginnings to 1450*, p. 245.) Again, in the 20th century, we have seen, simultaneously, a return of magic and occultism, and also of severe malpractice suits against doctors. These malpractice suits commonly imply the pagan approach to medical liability and an ancient pagan distrust of the medical practitioner.

Because historians write from the presupposition of the myth of evolution, they discard much data. In approaching medical history, they see magic as an early phase which was later abandoned as rationalism developed. The fact is that the two grew side by side. Bourgey merely notes this fact and ignores it. Others note with surprise that Homer's *Iliad* has a sounder knowledge of medicine than the more advanced Greek civilization of later centuries, when both rationalism and magic flourished.

What was the relationship of the two, and why is it that our age, ostensibly emancipated, is turning again to magic and to a magical demand from doctors? The rationalism involved in both cases is of a particular kind. It was a naturalistic rationalism which, as Pliny later stated it, reduced God to Nature, and expert man to the status of the expression of the powers of Nature. Aristotle's esotericism and his science are inseparable. Because there was nothing beyond Nature for Aristotle, this meant that an understanding and control of Nature placed a man above the common herd. Knowledge was power to be used to control man, and to train elite man. When Alexander the Great, whose tutor Aristotle had been, heard of the publication of some lectures of Aristotle, he protested, saying, "How shall we be any better than the rest?" Aristotle assured him that the esoteric aspects of his science were still secret: "The private lessons are both published and not published. Nobody will be able to understand them except those who have had the oral instruction." (Benjamin Farrington: *Greek Science*, II, p. 15f. Penguin Books, 1944, 1949.) Alexander's self-deification is a development of the implications of the Greek and pagan traditions. An inscription under a statue of Alexander read, "I hold the earth." A similar motto could describe the Greek scientists: "I hold the sciences." Magic, whether in its sophisticated or naive and primitive forms, is the attempt by man to control man, nature, and whatever powers may be. Because *power and control* were so basic to ancient medicine, the practitioner was feared and distrusted.

Certain strands in modern psychology are in this ancient magical tradition of *power and control*, as witness the Behaviorists and B. F. Skinner's *Beyond Freedom and Dignity* (1971). There have also been elements of this in medical research, but medical practitioners, whatever their personal faith, have not been much affected by this pagan tradition.

The Biblical faith, as it entered into the mainstream of history, altered the idea of medical practice. Because *salvation* is basic to Biblical faith, and salvation means healing, physical and spiritual, a new emphasis was added. Moreover, because it is so central to Biblical faith "to know the Lord," it became important in ancient Israel as well as in the Christian tradition to acquire *knowledge* of God and all His works. Christian (and Hebraic) civilization have thus been unique on their emphasis on learning, on knowledge.

Practically, what this meant for medicine was an emphasis on *knowledge and healing*. A long struggle ensued, as medicine sought to cast off the sterile and pagan presuppositions of Greek medicine, and the result has been a remarkable one. The doctor has become, like the rabbi and the pastor, a priestly figure in this tradition, as against the godlike magical practitioner of paganism. One of the first results of this changed status of the doctor was the end of total liability and a regard for the doctor as one who sought to help men rather than to exercise power and control in and over them.

The return of paganism has seen a return of the pagan attitude towards medical liability. In 1973, some ten thousand medical malpractice cases were filed in the United States. Granted that many of these were nuisance suits filed by people ready to exert pressure on an insurance company, still it must be said that, while thirty years ago insurance companies had their share of such suits, they virtually did not exist where medical practice was concerned. Juries were not favorable to suits against doctors in those days; they are today. Then the doctor was viewed with trust, now too often with suspicion. It would be interesting to know where those suits were filed. *The Journal of the Medical Association of the State of Alabama* says that a few states account for well over half of these cases, and California for twenty five hundred pending medical malpractice cases. California is a state in which the modern mood dominates, and magic and occultism flourish. I would suggest that the other states in which medical malpractice cases flourish will be similar to California in their modernity and magic, and that the cities which show the most cases will have a like complexion. I suspect that more conservative and "churchy" areas of strong Christian faith will show the least number of such cases, or virtually none.

The claims which go to trial are only one in ten, which means that the malpractice suit is still largely a nuisance, although an ugly one. In many areas, the main function of the malpractice suit is to damage the reputation of the doctor, and of medicine in general, whether or not it goes to court, and whether or not the plaintiff loses. With all too many people, in malpractice suits, the doctor cannot win. Common observations by such people include the following: "The doctors all stick together, so you can't prove anything against a doctor because no doctor will back you up"; "Mrs. Doe has never been the same since that doctor got ahold of her, but try and prove anything against a doctor," and so on and on.

The attack on doctors is fed by a stream of statements from "medical experts" and medical school faculty members, who try to promote their goals for medicine by berating the practitioner. In the past month, I saw two newspaper articles citing medical experts on the backwardness of practicing doctors. A lawyer, Truman Hobbs, writing on "Fire, Pestilence, Flood, and Medical Malpractice Suits" in the March, 1974 *Journal of the Medical Association of the State of Alabama*, quotes Dr. Paul Howley, former Director of the American College of Surgeons, as stating:

> "One half of the surgical operations in the United States are performed by doctors who are untrained, or inadequately trained to undertake surgery."

Dr. Howley no doubt has in mind a high standard of surgical practice as his standard, so that, in terms of his ideal, half of the operations and doctors represent an unacceptable standard in his eyes. If, however, his statement were taken at face value, it would mean that a lot of butchery goes on in the name of medicine. This I refuse to believe. I am sure most doctors can point to inadequate practitioners, but such practitioners are a minority. The overwhelming majority of operations are successful and represent a practicing competence if not an ideal one.

Such statements as that of Dr. Howley have their place as an in-group nudge for improved standards and up-to-date competence. But, in an age already given to demanding perfection and total competence from doctors, it is a rather dangerous statement to make, in that it leads to highly erroneous conclusions.

Implicit in the idea of total liability is a demand for total competence to overcome all problems, and a suspicion of failure. During the years that I was a missionary and a pastor, because of my unusual situations, I had an unusually large number of hospital and sick-bed visitations to make, and more funerals in a few years than most pastors have in a lifetime, a few hundred or more in all. I talked with many, many seriously ill and dying people and was often startled by their insane (and that is the necessary word) demand for miraculous healing. Men and women in their eighties, having had a long and full life, will insist that the doctor is somehow worthless or malevolent because he does not restore them to health. I found this out, because as I tried to prepare them for death, all their hidden hatred would then spill out.

To cite another example, a woman whose family business it was to make orthopedic shoes, found, in the many years of this business with her father and then alone, that there were almost no satisfied customers. What the patients actually wanted from their doctor and from the orthopedic shoemakers was a removal of all their disabilities, and anything short of that they resented. What they hesitated to tell the doctor, they told the hard-working woman, Mrs. L. S., as she tried to help them. What they wanted, she quickly recognized, was magic, and, lacking that, they manifested and ugly and vicious disposition.

The pagan patients of old tolerated no failures. The doctor's life could be demanded for failure. The modern mood is on the same track of total liability. As a result, the demand is for more and more control over medicine, and more and more legislation to ensure that the patient gets all the benefits and the doctor all the penalties. Medical practice has never been more competent, and yet the hostility grows.

Is this an over-statement? I do not think so. The reaction of one substantial businessman (who is not on our mailing list) to our Chalcedon Medical Report No. 1 was one of the most intense anger and rage. The man, a modern irreligious individual, regarded the Report as a fraudulent attempt to prop up a group of blood-sucking leeches, and so on and on. He especially resented, with more than a little anger, the title of the Report, "The Medical Profession as a Priestly Calling." The medical profession, he held, had to be treated as civil servants, kept firmly in line and made fully liable for all their mistakes.

Doctors are today still much loved by those who, in the Hebrew-Christian tradition, see them as healers with a priestly function. Those who see the doctor in pagan terms as one whose goal is *power and control* regard the doctor with hostility.

Medical practice cannot, by its very nature, escape religious implications and overtones. It must thus recognize its religious presuppositions and develop them. It must recognize that medical practice offers more than medicine: it offers a personal and pastoral function in relationship to healing.

Over six months ago, my daughter and son-in-law moved from this area to a community over fifty miles away. They return here regularly for three reasons: to visit us, to attend church, and to see their doctor. This is not an accidental correlation. It is basic to the Biblical tradition and its concept of the doctor.

CHALCEDON MEDICAL REPORT NO. 3
The Meaning of Liability

The concept of liability is in essence a religious and theological question. Because our age is one of religious syncretism, confusion, and doubt, there is a corresponding confusion in the realm of ideas, and the doctrine of liability in particular is an area of uncertainty and doubt.

It is important to begin by differentiating between some basic varieties of liability, because the word *liability*, like the word *government*, covers a wide field of contradictory and conflicting instances.

The first kind of liability to recognize and understand is *total liability*. This is exactly what pagan thought required of the doctor, a total liability for all consequences on the assumption that the doctor was a god. As a god, therefore, the pagan doctor was totally liable for all consequences that befell a patient. Some years ago, I saw examples of this among the older generation of Indian medicine men. They claimed total responsibility for good results and only avoided liability for bad results or consequences by ascribing them to a distrust by the patient, or to outside forces working against him. In much pagan practice, not even this way out existed: the medical practitioner had total liability for all consequences of any kind. A god, it was held, has total power in a given sphere belonging to that god; therefore, anything that happens to that doctor's patient is his fault, because he is identified with the healing god.

Total liability is an untenable idea for man. It ascribes to man powers which are beyond man, and it places an impossible burden on medical practice. Unfortunately, the idea of total liability is a recurring force in our civilization.

Very different is another concept, *unlimited liability*. The idea of unlimited liability means that I am completely responsible where I have responsibilities, to the reasonable limit of human ability. Thus, if I, through my negligence, am responsible for an accident, I am fully liable for the accident I have caused. My liability does not go beyond my own failure. Unlimited liability goes hand in hand with a belief in human responsibility. The criminal is guilty of his crime, and the criminal must make restitution. The friends and relatives of the criminal, who have no complicity in his offence, have no liability in his offense, nor does his community. Unlimited liability has been basic to Christian civilization and prevailed legally until the mid-nineteenth century. It began to erode as the doctrine of responsibility began to erode, and as environmentalism began to replace it.

The result was the doctrine of *limited liability*. Responsibility does impose burdens; it makes us liable for the consequences of our acts. We reap their harvest, both good and bad, both profit and loss: this is unlimited liability. Limited liability says, however, that "society" is also responsible, so that the criminal's crime is partly society's fault, and the successful man's profit is also partly society's profit, and thus both must be shared. In the business world, it means that our liability is limited to the degree of our investment, not to the degree of our responsibility. A negligent board of directors and shareholders may wipe out a company, and in the process also ruin many suppliers and default on numerous notes, but they are only responsible to the extent of $500 or $5,000, or whatever else, they have in shares, no more. One corporation which collapsed recently wiped out thousands of people, but the owner came out a million dollars richer: his liability was limited. Limited liability, whether in the world of business, crime, or elsewhere, is a product of modern humanism.

These three concepts, *total liability, unlimited liability, and limited liability*, are the theoretical and religious presuppositions which undergird men's thinking as they come to the practical questions of legal liability, how liability is viewed in law and the courts. Very obviously, men will react differently as judges, lawyers, and plaintiffs in terms of which of these three concepts they affirm. Unless these three areas are clearly differentiated, men will be arguing and reasoning at cross purposes.

Our discussion of *legal liability* will be a simple one, not geared to the precision of law but to an elementary understanding of what we must know with respect to law.

There are thus three types of liability that concern us in this context: *tort* liability, *criminal* liability, and *contract* liability.

The premise of liability is that, when a person damages another, wilfully and intentionally, without just cause or excuse, there is ground for action, because the law presumes responsibility and liability, and also that, within the sphere of human action, where there is a wrong there is a remedy. The damage involved is damage which results from an unlawful act.

Criminal liability, while broadest in scope perhaps, is most readily understood. *Contract liability* is breach of contract, or a negligence in the performance thereof. A *tort* is any wrongful act, but not a breach of contract, for which a civil action is required rather than a criminal action; a tort liability is a civil wrong which is independent of a contract. A tort liability results when a man by act or omission disregards or fails in his duty. The three main areas of duty which fall under the law of torts are "to abstain from wilful injury, to respect the property of others, and to use diligence to avoid causing harm to others." An offense which is punishable by law but is not a ground for civil action is not a tort.

In recent years, in varying degrees, doctors have been liable for all three types of liabilities.

In California especially, medical malpractice suits have succeeded in terms of an old English tort law case and its doctrine of *res ipsa loquitur*, Latin for "the thing speaks for itself." The origin of this doctrine is from an old lawsuit in which an English customs official was hit on the head by several sacks of sugar falling out of an warehouse window. On the grounds that such an incident obviously indicated negligence, a judge remarked, "*Res ipsa loquitur*." Practically, this means that it is unnecessary to prove negligence: the thing speaks for itself. In medicine, this means that the burden of proof is shifted to the doctor, who must prove his innocence. Res ipsa loquitur ostensibly applies only when (a) an injury takes place which is only a product of negligence, (b) control of the situation was exclusively in the hands of the person from whom damages are sought, and (c) the complaining party was free of any contributory negligence. In the sacks of sugar case and others like it, this doctrine has an important place, but it is difficult to see any validity in medical malpractice cases. The patient is not accidentally in the doctor's care, nor is he without responsibility in his choice of doctors and the treatment he consents to. It is questionable as a whole whether or not tort liability has any significant place in matters of medical liability.

The same is true of contract liability. It must be emphatically denied that contract applies to medicine. The fee paid to the doctor is not a contract to heal: the doctor is not a god. Just as the going to a church whether voluntary or a requirement of membership in some cases, is not a contract for salvation, so a medical fee is not a contract to heal. (Recently, one man sued for recovery of his tithe to the church, on the ground that he had not received from God that which he had hoped to gain). Implicit in almost all medical tort cases, and explicit in all cases based on the idea of an implied contract, is the idea of total liability, the old pagan idea that the doctor is a god and therefore total in his powers within his jurisdiction as well as infallible in his knowledge and abilities therein.

It is no accident that medical malpractice suits have vastly increased precisely now when medical practice has so greatly improved. The reason is that at the same time there has been a paganization of our culture, and the medical progress has made it easier for a pagan mentality to demand perfection from physicians.

The contract mentality is very commonplace. It is normal nowadays, in our major urban areas especially, to hear people say something like this: "The surgery, hospital, and everything else cost me $2,500, and I'm hardly any better than I was before." The speaker can be someone of 75 years who should be grateful that he was kept alive. Ask them, "You didn't expect to be made young again, did you?" and the result is only resentment.

The doctor *cannot* guarantee health, nor can he guarantee healing. He cannot even guarantee to bring the best available knowledge and skill to bear on a particular illness, because no doctor is omnicompetent, and no patient can legitimately expect his doctor to be the outstanding practitioner with regard to a particular ailment.

Such unreasonable expectations have their origin in a resentment against aging and dying, and this resentment manifests itself in hostility against the clergy and against doctors.

An important factor is the intrusion of the state into medicine. A very important question, not our concern at present, is whether the state has any more jurisdiction in controlling the medical profession that it does the clergy. Is it not possible that doctors can better govern themselves that the state can? Is it not possible too that the often-repeated charge that doctors always stick together has reference to a defensive action against a growing illegitimate intervention by the state and its courts?

Such questions are relevant to still another question: The laws against quacks are many, and they vary from state to state. All the same, an important question rises: do not some of these laws imply that the failure of the quack is a contract liability? Much study is needed here, but it is at the very least open to question that laws against quackery establish in some cases dangerous implications, namely, that good medical practice is a contract obligation which the quack fails to live up to. The consequences of such legal action against quacks are alive with booby traps for legitimate medical practitioners. The attempt, in fact, in some malpractice suits is simply a move to demonstrate that the doctor is a quack because he has not healed, or because his work has not been perfect. There should thus be a careful re-evaluation of laws against pseudo-medical practitioners: are they establishing in some cases highly questionable legal precedents which can be used, or are being used, against honest doctors?

The very fact that we are now talking about "National Health Insurance" is significant. Granted that all such proposals do not mean that health is guaranteed, the very language of such proposals is implicit with such ideas, and the expectation of an increasing number of people is in line with such faulty understanding.

Our culture today is different from all others in that we have isolated people from sickness and death. There was a time, especially before World War II in the country, and before World War I in the city, when serious illnesses and deaths were seen in the home. Retarded children were less institutionalized and more often worked into the normal routine of farm or small town life. Family members, relatives, and friends helped with digging the grave, and, after the service, filling it. (I have done this more times than I can remember. At a funeral in zero weather, a turn at the shovel was a good way of keeping warm.)

Except in a few areas, this is now gone. The overwhelming majority of people have rarely seen death, have never coped with serious illness in the home, and the new pornography is any honest treatment of death. In some rest homes for the aged, no reference is ever made to death. If someone dies, the nurses and staff say that Mrs. Blank was taken to "the hospital."

As a result, death has been an "outsider" to our culture; science, it is popularly believed, will some day soon eliminate death. Hang on long enough, and someone will come up with a cure for what ails you, will reverse aging, and even overcome death. In John F. Kennedy's day, much was said about "the revolution of rising expectations." Precisely when men are gaining the most they are expecting and demanding more. In fact, they expect *everything* as their right: cradle to grave security, perfect health no matter how they live, the elimination of all human problems while they themselves become insufferable problems, and much, much more.

A very important aspect of this "revolution of rising expectations" is the refusal to take anything less than perfection, the insistence on the best of all possible worlds *now*. The doctor is a prime scapegoat in this situation. He must take his fee as a contract to heal, or else his patient assumes the right to complain and to sue. Health is assumed to be a commodity to be purchased like any other item.

It is significant that, at the same time that malpractice suits have arisen, in the 1930s, and especially since 1950, *environmentalism* has also flourished. Environmentalism holds that we are a product of our environment; if Johnny is delinquent, his home, community, church, and school are to blame. Man is assumed to be a *product rather than a producer*, and responsibility is accordingly shifted from the individual to the environment. The influence of environmentalism on religion, psychology, education, and politics has been enormous. It has weakened or eroded the ideas of sin and guilt and replaced Christianity with sociology. The basic tenets of environmentalism have been imbibed even by small children. In my study, *Intellectual Schizophrenia*, I cite an instance where a small boy, a third grader at most, was a problem to every Sunday School teacher. During a vacation school session, he pushed one very patient teacher to the point where she lost her temper and self-control. The boy, afraid that punishment was finally about to overtake him, threw up his arms defensively, covering his face, and cried out, "Don't you hit me! Don't you hit me! What I need is love and affection." The child had learned his lesson well in terms of modern thought, not individual responsibility but a radical environmentalism.

As areas of the United States most readily adopted in education and everyday life the environmentalist philosophy, they also adopted a limited liability philosophy, and a proneness to malpractice suits set in. Environmentalism means *at best* limited liability, and in its extreme, *no* liability by the individual: someone else or something else, the environment as a totality, is to blame. The more environmentalism flourishes, the more readily total liability is ascribed to the environment. In environmentalism, the environment functions as a god. In medical matters, the doctors functions as the environment, and increasing liability is transferred from the individual to the doctor.

Practically, this means a different kind of patient increasingly. Forty years ago, it was quite common for people in bad health to say, "Well I've only got myself to blame for this." Now, one hears increasingly, "You would think the doctors could come up with something to take care of me." Between the two there is a vast religious difference, a greatly different concept of liability and responsibility, and a different approach to the doctor.

The roles of heredity, responsibility, and self-control and discipline in matters of health, healing, and recuperation are now too little appreciated by the average man, especially in the more modern areas of the country. One doctor, in a city of 243,000 in a smaller state with a large percentage of foreign-speaking people, has had only two malpractice suits in over thirty years; both cases involved tourists from one of the biggest cities in the United States. In both cases, this able doctor encountered people with a radically different philosophy of life.

The solution thus does not lie within the legal realm, although the three forms of legal liability cited are very important for the doctor to understand, since they are everyday issues in our courts. The root lies elsewhere, in the philosophical premises of the liability concept.

In this realm, we have cited the three kinds of liability: total, unlimited, and limited. The idea of limited liability, as we have seen, is in varying degrees a denial of individual responsibility and can thus be a very limited liability. Ironically, limited liability and total liability are related concepts and they go together. They transfer powers from God to the created order in one area, and deny human powers in another; the environment replaces God, and man ceases to be responsible man, created in the image of God and fully accountable to God for all his acts, and to man under God for his offenses against man. The inability of people to cope with life and death makes them ready to lash out against what their current beliefs regard as the responsible agency. For the majority of those under age forty, politics is the answer and the problem. Although politicians are no worse than the average citizen and usually a little better at least, the younger citizens ascribe to the politicians an undue liability for the state of the nation. Employees who think nothing of stealing from an employer or defrauding a corporation become pharisaically indignant if a politician acts no differently. They have transferred liability for the state of the nation to the politician, and, for themselves, they operate on very limited liability.

In medical malpractice, fifty-three percent of the claimants are over age forty, although only about thirty three percent of the population is over forty. The hope of the younger element is politics; the hope of the older element is in medical miracles. Both live in a dream world, and both are destroying the real world.

However, heart attacks, once uncommon except among older people, now are increasingly in evidence among men in their forties, thirties, and even twenties. The result is that a sick expectation with respect to medical liability is growing among the younger, politically oriented citizenry. The underground press, and the porno-press, increasingly treat the doctor as an enemy. The deeply ingrained neoplatonism in our culture (discussed in my study, *The Flight from Humanity*) leads to a highly erroneous hatred of success and wealth, and a hostility therefore to any material success by a doctor. (We will, in a subsequent Report discuss the philosophy of medical fees.)

All of this has serious repercussions: ideas do have consequences. In one major city, very prone to malpractice suits, a doctor, an anesthesiologist, had to retire, because his insurance fees were beginning to approach his net income when he reached the age of fifty-two. This is an extreme case, in an extreme situation, but it is an indication of a trend in our culture. It is a product of a religious change, and it means that none of us, least of all the doctor, can be indifferent to the philosophical and theological issues of our time.

CHALCEDON MEDICAL REPORT NO. 4
The Meaning of Risk Medicine

An aspect of the current malpractice crisis which many neglect is the fact that, with some notable exceptions, it is all too often the better doctors who get sued.

But this is not all. Malpractice suits are in particular an American phenomenon to a large degree. This does not mean that Americans are more prone to litigation than other peoples by any means. In some areas, Americans are indeed more prone to litigation than are other peoples, and one of these is medical practice, but this is not true in all areas, nor is it true of all parts of the United States. For example, one California doctor has a malpractice insurance fee of $26,000, whereas an urban doctor, of comparable age and practice in another state, pays less than $400. Malpractice suits are rare in the second state, and common in California. Why? Certainly, there is no residential neurosis which turns Californians, most of whom were born in other states, into a litigation-oriented people. Since World War II began, the population of California has quadrupled because of the heavy influx of people from other states. Thus, a very high percentage of the people suing doctors are ex-residents of the East, South, and Mid-West. What is the connection then between malpractice suits and California?

In order to understand the relationship, let us remember, *first* of all, that American medicine is, on the whole, still the freest of any nation of consequence today. We can and must regret and oppose the steady encroachment of statist controls over men in every area of life, including medicine, but we cannot deny the great measures of freedom which we still enjoy. American medicine is in process of being socialized, but, as it still exists, it is the product of freedom and enjoys a measure of freedom still.

A *second* fact about American medicine is that it is the most innovative. Whether in surgery, drugs, or other fields of practice, American medicine has manifested a high degree of enterprise, initiative, and advance. American doctors who study or travel abroad find here and there examples of a high excellence and pioneering practice, but, by and large, the leadership remains with American medical practice. Many may contest this fact, but the practical situation is this: a regular stream of foreign dignitaries and personages do come quietly to the United States in order to consult a doctor or undergo surgery.

There is, moreover, an American predisposition to the innovative which is a stimulus to innovation in every area of life, thought, and activity. Americans believe in progress; they demand development and improvement. Foreigners who reside in the United States for a time are startled by the American appetite for innovation and progress. However Americans may indulge in a nostalgia for the past, or talk about a yen for simple living, when they act and spend their dollars, they demand innovation and progress.

This temper is no less true in medicine than in any other area. It is commonplace to hear Americans express the hope and belief that a new drug or a new treatment will eliminate this or that disease or condition in a few years. Americans demand progress and victory in every area of life, including medicine. A common question asked of doctors is some variation of this: "Will they have a new drug or treatment soon to take care of my condition?"

Third, this demand for innovation and progress means that American medicine is the most vulnerable of any, because it continually moves out onto a high risk frontier. People are not ignorant of the fact that new drugs often have serious side-effects. World War II stimulated a vast amount of emergency surgical and drug innovations, and it was obvious then that new drugs can cause trouble. The idea that the drug companies represent a vicious conspiracy on the public, working to foist improperly tested drugs on them for a quick profit, is a false one. This does not mean that the testing programs of the drug companies are sound ones, nor does it deny that improper testing occurs. The central fact is that Americans demand innovative medicine, including new drugs, and the drug companies cannot survive if they fail to meet this demand.

More than a few doctors have told me that many of their patients would best be served by a simple prescription: rest and sleep, and, at best, an aspirin tablet or two as well. But patients demand more. They are unwilling to believe that simple health care is the best remedy; they want a miracle pill. For example, heart patients are commonly told to lose weight and exercise, as well as to take some prescribed medicine. What such patients do most faithfully is to take the pill; the rest is gradually forgotten by many. Americans have more faith in innovative medicine that in sensible health care. Doctors did not create this condition or frame of mind. Most speak against it, but it prevails.

As a result, doctors are highly vulnerable. Most Americans, where their health is concerned, are guilty of consistent malpractice in taking care of themselves. They are totally tolerant of *their* life-time health malpractice, and yet highly intolerant of an occasional real or imagined malpractice by a doctor. They forgive every kind of health malpractice in themselves, and they forgive nothing in doctors.

Modern man wants salvation in a pill, or in a treatment. I can recall all too many occasions over the years when men, for example, have become greatly excited or hopeful because some new treatment would supposedly restore their lost potency and make them nearly young again!

Thus, this American love for innovation and progress has, on the one hand, made American medicine highly prone to advance and success, and, on the other, highly vulnerable to intense disappointment, disillusionment, untested recourses, and malpractice suits.

American medicine has a proneness to experiments, which means both dramatic advances and sometimes disappointments.

Fourth, we must turn now to California. From 1940 on to the present, a remote American state has become the most populous one. It has, during those years, experienced a great burst of prosperity. It has also been marked by an aura of confidence, optimism, and generosity. Fund raisers look to California as a prime area of giving. Workers up till now have received better pay in California, whether farm workers or hospital employees.

The newer California hospitals have tried to make their rooms have an air of restfulness and hint of a holiday rest. Californians have developed an intolerance for failure, defeat, or anything but the best. Prosperity has created a strong vein of perfectionism, and a rebellion against anything else. The readiness to innovation is greater in California than elsewhere, and hand in hand, there goes a readiness to complain and protest against anything short of the imagined perfection.

As a result, Californians make a very heavy demand on their doctors, consult them very frequently, depend on them, and also sue them.

Moreover, this mentality is not restricted to Californians; they are merely "ahead" of others in manifesting it, and action on it.

The result, of course, is that this mentality frustrates the very thing it most wants, innovative medicine. In all too many cases, where a short time ago doctors took risks and often saved lives, they now take two courses. They refer the patient to another doctor, who may himself do something as evasive. Or else, they terminate hope by taking no chances. In a short time, I have encountered several instances where doctors have simply refused to attempt risky surgeries or treatments of seriously ill patients because the dangers of failure and malpractice suits were too great.

But risk is basic to medical progress. Whether people like it or not, it is precisely the risky cases which so often prompt medical progress.

Even more, wars have been an unequaled stimulus to medical progress. During war-time, doctors in the Armed Forces have been required to perform risky surgeries, experiment with drugs and techniques, in an unprecedented way. Wars, with all their horrors, have as a beneficial by-product, medical progress. This does not justify a war; what it means is simply that *risk* medical practice is basic to medical advance. Many elderly people, as well as young, are today able to walk and function normally because of orthopedic advances made in recent wars. Doctors serving on war duty have an opportunity to see in a short span of time a variety of medical emergencies most doctors never see in a life-time. As a result, a remarkable amount of improvisation, innovation, and high-risk medical practice is routine. The world came out of World War II with worse problems that those facing it in 1939, bad as those were. Neither Korea nor Vietnam have eased our world crisis. However, we have come out of those wars with notable medical advances. Not only countless war veterans but untold numbers of civilians are alive today only because of the new developments made possible by the high risk medical practice of war-time medicine.

There is, of course, a difference between war-time and peace-time practice. A common factor remains, however. It is risk medicine which more often saves lives, and which makes medical progress possible. Where risk medicine is abolished, medical advance is also abolished.

As a result, whether by malpractice suits or by socialist controls, where risk medicine is inhibited or ended, there medical progress is also inhibited or ended.

Risk medicine is then also abolished in effect to either slave-labor camps or to prisons, and it accomplishes little in either because it is also increasingly dehumanized.

Innovative medicine does mean sometimes dangerous as well as risky medical practice. Innovative practice can lead to sometimes good and sometimes bad results. To deny the right of the one is to deny the right of the other. Criminal practice is one thing; risk medicine is radically different. Malpractice suits, the food and drug administration, some hospitals, and some medical societies, are all saying to both, whether they recognize it or not, that they are the same.

Moreover, a society which wants good innovations and *no* risks is asking for the impossible. It is denying the freedom to progress. It is saying in effect that there must be heaven only, and no possibility of hell. To deny the possibility of failure is to deny the reality of success.

This attitude is the same as that fostered by "progressive education" in many state schools, the no grading policy. Several teachers have reported to me at various times on the consequences of such a philosophy. One or two, who insisted on trying to fail or expel a student, came close to being themselves expelled and were over-ruled. The results of such a no grading policy are a lack of incentive to learn on the part of most, an inability to see the difference between right and wrong, and an indifference to standards. In such a school, only one door is open, to promotion. One teacher reported that students who are functional illiterates (but still being graduated) feel that society owes them the best of everything. Such students are the products of a no-risk philosophy. Themselves failures, they tolerate no failure in society, in politics, medicine, or elsewhere: what they want must be delivered to them.

In varying degrees, this is the philosophy of modern men everywhere. It is productive of malpractice suits, and it is also productive of revolutions. Such an attitude is in fact the product of a great cultural revolution, the rise to power of humanism in the modern world. What appears in malpractice suits is but one tip of a huge iceberg.

The result is, of course, that there are no easy answers to the malpractice crisis, unless one accepts a growing socialization and control of doctors, together with a minimum risk practice, as a solution. A minimum risk or no risk practice will solve no problems, nor will it result in contented patients. It will, in fact, harm doctors greatly in the long run.

The simple fact is that we are at a turning point in civilization. The course of Western culture shifted slowly after 1660 from a Christian to a humanistic foundation. With the French Revolution that shift became open and explicit. Since World War I, the world has been seeing the triumph of humanism, and the suicide of civilization. We are at a turning-point in the history of the world. The malpractice crisis is one facet of a world crisis and man's deep rebellion against everything that makes for order.

Very plainly, this means that there is no return to the 1930s and 1940s. Our yesterdays led to our todays. Only the suicidal can afford non-involvement in the great task of a new foundation for civilization. The foundation must not be institutional; it cannot be either church or state without unhappy consequences. It must be theological, and it must be Christian.

Because the role of a medical practitioner in the Biblical tradition is a priestly one (as against the pagan tradition, with the doctor as a god), the doctor must be directly involved in re-thinking the foundations of culture and society. Not only a man's mind but his society are involved in his well-being. As a result, the doctor cannot afford to neglect the problems of society. The problems of society not only make his patients ill, or give them ulcers, but they also infect and harm medical practice. The sickness of our society is damaging man's view of medicine and of healing.

It is also damaging the medical schools. Racial quotas are always bad, and they have never been more in evidence than now, and applied in the name of equality and tolerance. I have seen a letter from a medical school, rejecting without examination, all out-of-state applications other than those from Blacks, Mexicans, and Indians. It has been reported to me that discrimination exists in medical schools against the sons of doctors, and the report came from an authoritative source, within a school. I have seen a very superior student, a doctor's son, rejected, and a mediocre student, with an unstable recent past, accepted. This medical school trend in some respects posses a graver threat than the malpractice suits. The indications of discrimination against the sons of doctors indicates a desire to break with the past and create a new kind of doctor.

A major aspect of this problem, in the medical school, the courts, and in the minds of men, is that a new philosophy of medicine is at work. What men believe will govern what they do. There is an essential relationship between faith and action. We must not confuse this element of faith with *professions* of faith. Thus, most Americans profess to be Christians; when their articles of faith are closely examined, it becomes clear that they are instead humanists. Their actions therefore manifest their humanistic faith.

The philosophy of medicine which is increasingly in evidence has its roots in a humanistic faith. In this humanistic philosophy, the doctor in socialist states must report to the state on whatever the state wishes to know about his patients. The state claims the right of God to know everything that transpires in every area of life. The idea of a privileged communication between doctor and patient is therefore seen as an anti-social act against society and the state, and it is punishable as a crime.

For humanism, medical practice is a social or public service. The doctor, like the politician, the bureaucrat, and the mailman, is engaged in serving "the public," which in practice means the civil government. As a result, the doctor, if not actually made a part of a civil service, is still subjected to civil control. He may, indeed, lack some of the rights which civil service employees enjoy.

Medicine, it is argued by humanists, is too important to the life of the public and the welfare of the state to be uncontrolled. In order to make social justice possible, medical services and personnel must be allocated and planned, or else we have an unequal distribution of services. Like the police, doctors are a necessary social agency, it is declared, and therefore must of necessity be under state jurisdiction.

This philosophy of medicine has led, in a number of countries, to socialized medicine. There are no appreciable malpractice suits under socialism, or none at all, if the socialism is an "advanced" one. To sue a doctor would then mean suing the state, and this is rarely possible. Complaints against doctors of course abound under socialized medicine. The difficult conditions imposed by state requirements make adequate medical examination and treatment almost impossible. The state creates the problem, and the state then punishes the doctors as though they were responsible.

In the United States, the philosophy of socialized medicine is very prevalent, but we are not yet into fully socialized medicine. Some politicians and all humanists insist therefore on seeing the very fact of medicine's limited freedom as the problem. A frame of mind is created whereby medical practice and doctors are seen as a conspiracy against the public. It is in centers of liberal, humanistic faith, such as San Francisco and nearby areas, that the malpractice syndrome has flourished. Malpractice suits are a rarity, on the other hand, in Bible Belt cities: the temper of such communities is not yet congenial to such suits.

In any case, however, for doctors to seek a remedy to the malpractice crisis by going to the state is a serious error. It has been statist pressures which have led to the present degree of state control. From sources within various civil agencies, it is clear that the malpractice crisis was welcomed by the state and federal governments. Their readiness to hear the doctors' requests had all the same symptoms of the wolf's happy reception to Little Red Ridinghood. The doctors had previously dealt with the state, in every negotiation, from a position of strength. Now they were negotiating from a position of crisis and weakness. Predictably, the results have not been encouraging to doctors.

The medical schools increasingly exemplify a humanistic and statist doctrine of medicine. The state and its courts increasingly move to require it. This, more than malpractice, serious as that crisis is, represents the real problem.

For the doctors to be free, they must have a philosophy of medicine and a faith that makes for freedom. Instead, medical practice has moved in the other direction. It has been assumed that the state knows best what medical practice should be: the state licenses doctors, a civil authority passes on drugs, and so on. Are civil servants competent in such areas? If the civil authorities can govern medical practice, why not religion, and all things else? What special competence of jurisdiction does the state have in areas other than the administration of law with the respect to crime and the like?

Is it the state or God who is the over-all umbrella, under whom all things exist? Are we not returning to ancient paganism, where the only government was by the state? Are we forgetting that there are other alternatives?

It is these alternatives which we must explore. Simply to fight off attacks is a strategy of retreat: it has no future. The philosophy of medicine must be rethought if doctors are to be free.

CHALCEDON MEDICAL REPORT NO. 5
Doctors as State Property

One of our most common and more dangerous fallacies is the idea that the real and important world was born with us. Like so many historians, we read the present in terms of the present, forgetting that the past lives all around us and in us. Our legal structures have a long history; we are ourselves genetically the product of the ages. Behind every moment and event are a multitude of yesterdays. We can never understand the present without knowing first of all the past. It is therefore highly impractical to neglect the past. As Disraeli observed, "Practical men are men who repeat the blunders of their predecessors." They regard themselves as realists, because they focus on the present, and they thereby manifest their historical blinders and their proneness to blunders.

Anyone who reads legal documents will soon find more than a small hint of mustiness in the language, and with good reason. The language of law is full of ancient terms that go back to the Roman Empire, and to pagan antiquity. Take, for example, the word fee, used by both lawyers and doctors. In its remote origin in Old High German, it meant cattle, and is related to the words *fief*, and *feudal*. A fee, among other things, meant tended property held under a feudal overlord, or a payment to an overlord. The term in law is still in essence feudal, and, behind its feudal meaning stands a world of pagan religion and politics. In its usage in law today, the word *fee* has reference to the ownership of property, as *fee simple*, and that pagan world unknown to most moderns continues to exist in the laws governing their property *and themselves*.

It is important therefore for us to understand that pagan world and its faith. Basic to that faith was the belief that divinity in essence resided in the political order. The ruler, the office, or the people or state were held to be divine. Civil government was thus entirely a religious function, the central religious institution of society. The state was god walking on earth, as a modern philosopher, Hegel, restated it for modern theory. All religious allegiance and obedience went to the state and its ruler. The people and all that they owned were the property of the state.

In the Old Testament, Molech worship is very strongly condemned (Lev. 20:1-5). The word *Molech* is very simply the word for *king*. The worship of Molech meant that the state of king owned the land and the people as his property. Apparently, children were "baptized" into this faith by being passed over the fire before the king's image, to signify their total dedication to the state. If occasion demanded it, they could be sacrificed to the state. At all times, the property, families, income, children, time, and lives of the subjects were subject to the draft of the state. Molech worship, like most forms of Baal worship, was the deification of the state and its claim to sovereignty and over-lordship over man. We can understand from this why God so strongly condemns every form of this faith in His law.

Feudalism was a varied and diverse way of life. Many strands within feudalism represent ancient European paganism; others are clear manifestations of Biblical law. Serfdom, for example, began on the imperial estates of Rome and was inherited by feudalism, and was thus emphatically not original to it. Our concern here is with an unhappy and pagan heritage feudalism has passed on to us.

The terminology of property laws and of state powers is to this day feudal and pagan. This affects our lives and persons. We think of ourselves as *citizens*, which indeed we are, because we have suffrage, but we forget that, in our property and persons, we are also *subjects*. We hold our land today in *fee simple*; this is an ancient term which means that we have the right to pass our real property on to our heirs, or to sell it at will. These are the "rights" to real property which we purchase. The real title belongs to the state, whose socman or tenant we are. Our title is by free and common socage, not an absolute or allodial ownership. The state can tax, regulate, control, condemn or expropriate our land. It can govern our persons similarly. Jonathan R. T. Hughes, writing *The Government Habit*, observes rightly: "It would surprise most American landowners today, as it often does those who cannot meet their property taxes, to learn that the state owns the land outright. Owners in fee simple have possession only of rights in real estate: this phenomenon is part of what historians call the English heritage" (p. 15f).

When the American Colonies were settled, the Kings of England, like other European monarchs, alone has an absolute possession of land. All lands in their realm, or any area over the seas explored and occupied by their subjects, belonged to them. As a result, the American Colonies, and all the lands therein, were held by the colonists in fee simple as tenants under the monarch.

The colonists, it should be remembered, were strong Christians on the whole. Many were fleeing from the English religious settlement. As far as possible, they tried to introduce Biblical law, but the crown was hostile to too much of this. In effect, two gods cannot co-exist, so that the British crown was hostile to Biblical Law. When, under Cromwell, the missionary to the Indians, John Eliot, tried to reconstruct Indian Christian villages in terms of Biblical law, his effort was condemned when Charles II came to the throne. Eliot's book advocating Biblical law was ordered burned by the public hangman.

As a result of all this, the ancient legal principles of paganism, basic to European monarchies, were written into American legal documents. After the War of Independence, there was an increasing rebellion against the older concepts, so that, by the early 1800's Chancellor Kent, in his *Commentaries on American Law*, could speak of them as relics. The language remained, Kent held, but the older meaning was gone.

The language, however, was there in the law, and the law is the law. The states were the first to make use of the language. In Illinois, the state claimed the right to overlordship and thus the right to regulate commerce within the state. (In the war some few years later, between state rights and federal rights, both sides were talking an essentially pagan language. The same was true of the early anarchists who were talking about individual rights. All were making man their god, statist man, or individual man.) The Illinois case, *Munn* v. *Illinois*, finally reached the U.S. Supreme Court, and Illinois won. The decision cited the practices "in England from time immemorial" to justify its argument. The language has survived; now its meaning was fully set forth.

Why had this past returned? Why was the old concept of fee, fief, socage, tenancy, and statist ownership so clearly in focus after a lapse of perhaps fifty to seventy five years, depending on the state?

The answer is religious. As the faith of men began to change, their social order changed to match their faith. Their faith began to look more and more like the old paganism that had long held the world and even Christendom in bondage.

In terms of Biblical faith and law, the state is not the lord or overlord: God alone is Lord. The original and basic confession of faith in the early church was simply this: "Jesus is Lord" (Phil. 2:11; I Tim. 6:15, etc.). The conflict of Christianity with Rome was over lordship. Rome was ready to grant religious freedom and licensure to Christianity on two conditions. *First*, the church must confess that Caesar is lord. This meant that every area of life and thought is subject to the control and regulation of Caesar or the state as man's basic lord, authority, and power. This meant the control of religion, medical practice, trade, wages and prices, and all things else. All things were to be under the jurisdiction of Caesar or the state. Rome could choose to regulate or de-regulate at will. This was and is an assertion of the omnicompetence of the state, the belief that human wisdom and more is incarnate in the state, so that what men cannot do for themselves, the state can do. The early church refused to acknowledge Caesar as Lord and instead proclaimed Jesus Christ as Lord. Conflict was thus inescapable.

Second, Rome was ready to recognize Christianity as a licit or legal religion provided also that it would be subject to licensure and taxation. Again, the early church refused. The right of licensure and taxation meant a confession of Caesar's overlordship with respect to Christ. Caesar was a subject of Christ the King, not Christ of Caesar. The right to license meant to acknowledge that Christ's Kingdom was the property of Caesar. The word license comes from the Latin licere, to be permitted, to be for sale. The licensee would thus be the property of the licensor.

The clash was so real and intense, that, before the clash began in the form of persecution, the early church wondered whether any obedience to Caesar was possible. St. Paul's answer to this was that the Christian way is not warfare and revolution but regeneration. Hence Christians must, up to a point, obey Caesar, not in agreement, but in obedience to God. Thus, obedience is "for conscience sake" (Romans 13:5).

The state, Paul told the Romans is, *first*, "ordained of God" (Rom. 13:1). It is therefore God's creature. It is God who is the true Lord, not Caesar. The claims of Caesar are thus invalid. However, the state does have a legitimate function under God, and this must not be overlooked in the disagreement and struggle.

Second, this legitimate function of the state is to be "the minister of God... to be a terror...to the evil" (Rom. 13:3,4). The state is thus emphatically a *ministry of justice* whose function it is to punish crime and to ensure social order by protecting people from external and internal enemies.

Third, the state is thus clearly limited to one realm, justice. It has no over-lordship, no right to govern religion, health, education, welfare, and other areas of life. These and other areas are outside the competence and the jurisdiction of the state.

Fourth, the taxing power of the state, very limited in Biblical law, is thus with reference to its legitimate functions. No more that the church has a right to control the state, medicine, agriculture, or anything else, does the state have legitimate authority from God to go outside its realm. From the Biblical perspective, it is as wrong for the state to do these things as it would be for organized medicine to attempt to control law enforcement, education, marriages and family life, baseball, and art. Each sphere of life is a law sphere under God, interdependent with other spheres but never lord over them.

Fifth, basic to Biblical faith and law is the declaration, often stated and summarized in Psalm 24:1, which declares, "The earth is the LORD's and the fullness thereof; the world, and they that dwell therein." The earth and all its fullness, and all the inhabitants thereof, are the property of God, not the state. God's laws must thus govern the earth, its use, conservation, and development. If man is not subject to God, he will become the subject of Molech. If we do not follow the Lord, we cannot complain if Molech claims us: we have created him with our apostasy.

Sixth, the Biblical doctrine of vocation or calling makes clear that *all* of life as well as every kind of work or calling is in essence religious. It is either done to the glory of God or to the glory of man, usually ourselves. In either case, it will be subject to law. Man cannot live without law. His life must be circumscribed by law; he lives in a universe ruled by law, his physical being moves to laws not of his making, and he is inescapably a creature for whom life and law are almost identical and clearly inseparable. Man can only be oblivious to law in death.

Medical practice cannot exist outside a world of law. The question thus is, which world of law? The answer to this is a religious answer. If we are humanists, we cannot escape the present dilemma of medicine. It is the creature of the state, and doctors are state property. Their work is licensed by the state and subject to the regulation and examination of the state. In a Christian social order, only criminal medical practice would be within state jurisdiction.

Why should the state regulate or license medical practice? Does it have more wisdom to do so than do doctors? State control is irrational but religious: it is grounded on the faith that the state has an omnicompetence as well as a total jurisdiction. Medicine was for centuries unlicensed by the state. The state entered into the picture in the United States in part by the ostensible revelation that some medical schools were incompetent. A restudy of the data would probably show that these few schools contributed little to the actual practice of medicine as against the better schools. Certainly, we cannot say that the present and growing regulation of medical schools in terms of equalitarian principles is contributing to the welfare of medicine. The problem was created by humanism, and the humanistic remedy is compounding the problem. It should be noted that state licensure, regulation, and control can protect medicine and doctors, but in the same way that slavery protects slaves. There are benefits, but the loss is a vital one.

Hospitals were once all Christian institutions, and medical practice has a Biblical framework of faith. It had a freedom under God, because freedom is from and under God, not the state.

Modern men and modern doctors are state property. They may grumble at being sheared periodically, or sacrificed to suit the state, but, in essence, most are getting what they have asked for by their daily lives. They are statist in faith. The slave may grumble about his working conditions, but he is simply property, and he will be used as such. If he wants a real change, he must work for his freedom.

Medical practice is a vocation, either a vocation under God, or under the state. I have received reports from readers of what happens to doctors and nurses without a godly sense of vocation. I will not go into an account of these: they are a familiar story, and they will be a more common one, unless a Christian sense of vocation is restored to medicine. Meanwhile, they are a source of major concern to conscientious doctors and nurses.

They are also a concern to politicians, who use a certain type of medical "horror story" to attack all American medical standards. For an example, let us look briefly at a prominent politician's work of a few years ago, Senator Edward M. Kennedy's *In Critical Condition, the Crisis in America's Health Care* (1972).

Superficially, the book is both very convincing and very vulnerable. *First,*

Kennedy's title is hardly a fair one. The words "critical" and "crisis" set the stage for a highly selective and prejudicial argument. Senator Kennedy himself has received excellent medical attention for his own critical conditions, and he shows little appreciation for his own excellent care in his highly selective stories. In dealing with dental services, he quotes the testimony of Dr. Powell E. Bellin, first deputy commissioner of the New York City Health Department concerning the quality of dental care given to Medicaid patients in New York City. According to Dr. Bellin, "Our working statistic based upon four and a half years experience in this town is that about five to ten percent of the practitioners represent abusers" (p. 162). Let us assume that something resembling this is true of doctors. Would we be right in assuming that such men, given private practice or socialized practice, would still be of the same character? As Christians, we must hold that it is not environment that determines character, but character which determines environment. Moreover, a certain type of character is drawn to a congenial environment. Kennedy is right that some doctors are mercenary, thoughtless, and uncharitable. But does working for the federal government remedy these sins? If so, the men of the Internal Revenue Service should be notable for their unselfishness, thoughtfulness, and charity. Senator Kennedy assumes that the federal government can by legislation provide a substitute for moral character. This is the grand illusion of modern politics.

Second, Kennedy wrote of the wealth of doctors and the "enormous salaries" in the health insurance industry (pp. 13, 180). In view of Kennedy's private wealth, such an argument is an amazing example of phariseeism. Kennedy's senatorial salary alone, with all its fringe benefits considered, makes him far wealthier than almost any doctor.

Third, Kennedy's economic sense was sadly in error when he wrote, "When you go to a doctor in Great Britain, you pay nothing" (p. 222). There is no more costly means of payment than by taxation. No man ever pays more for anything than when he gets services from the state.

It would be easy to go on in this vein, and to hold Senator Kennedy's arguments up to ridicule. This is not my intention. At the critical point, Kennedy is on firm ground, basic ground and neither he nor his associates can be answered except on the same grounds. Kennedy concluded his study by declaring, "We have a choice of conscience to make in America" (p. 252). Precisely! This is the key, the choice of conscience. What are the choices? The question is one of lordship. Who is the lord? Who governs man's life, conscience, and calling?

The *first* answer is the state, the ancient god Molech. This is clearly Senator Kennedy's choice. Whatever his nominal profession, his religious faith is statism. There is no hint in him of the medieval reliance on Christian healing foundations, hospitals, and the like. For him, state action is the moral answer. Most men today agree with him. They only protest when their own ox is gored. An associate of President John F. Kennedy rightly criticized the president's critics as hypocrites, because the typical critic went to public schools, going there on a school bus on a public highway; he attended college on the G. I. bill, bought a house with an FHA loan, started a business with a loan from the Small Business Administration, retired on social security, and then sat back to criticize the welfare recipients as freeloaders. Such critics deal with issues, not principles. They stand, not on principles, but on pragmatic purposes.

The *second* answer is by anarchists, or autarchists, who hold that not the state but man is the lord. Man is the absolute and is responsible to none. Again, this view has many followers, who, as a matter of conscience, resist statist encroachment and work for what they regard as a truly free society. From a Biblical perspective, this position too is wrong. Man is a creature under God, whose true freedom is in God and God's law. But too often the only answer to statism which doctors have made is anarchism.

The *third* answer of conscience is the Biblical one. Kennedy is right: "We have a choice of conscience to make," but his choice is altogether a false one. Medical practice must again become a priestly calling under God. The source of true moral character is in God alone, not in man, and a sound conscience, which is basic to every calling, and certainly to medical practice, is a product of Christian faith and growth.

Doctors are today state property, as we all are. Some men see the answer in anarchism, in self-ownership. The Biblical answer is that we are the Lord's and no man, nor any institution, has the right to usurp God's property, nor can we alienate what is rightfully the Lord's. St. Paul's warning is especially timely: "Ye are bought with a price: be not ye the servants of men" (I Cor. 7:23).

The roots of our problem lie not only deep in the past but also deep in our own hearts.

CHALCEDON MEDICAL REPORT NO. 6
Sovereignty and Medical Practice

At first glance, the question of sovereignty seems unrelated to medical practice. Indeed, for those who view medicine as a purely technical practice of a particular type of scientific skill, the question of sovereignty is an unrelated one. The luxury of such insular thinking is, however, becoming increasingly impossible. The world, and especially the state, now leaves no man alone. The claims of humanistic statism all over the world increasingly imply that no private, restricted, or exempt domain can exist. All things are subject to the control of the state. Even in the United States, far freer than most of the world, a man in Pittsburgh, PA, had to go to court to defend his bone marrow from expropriation by a sick cousin. It apparently did not occur to the court that there are limits to the court's jurisdiction. In Ohio, a devout Christian farmer was arrested for placing his daughter in the only available Christian School, one located next to his farm. But the school is Amish, and the farmer is not, and hence his arrest! The amount of paper work required today of every kind of organization in order to meet state, federal, county, and city requirements is now past measuring, even by tons. On all sides, we are confronted by a multitude of regulations, laws, controls, agencies, bureaus, and statist employees whose business it is to govern and control us. And medical practice is no exception to this will to control.

What we are talking about is the exercise of sovereignty. Although we are all confronted at every turn by the exercise of statist sovereignty, very few people concern themselves with the meaning of sovereignty. A sovereign is one who possesses supreme authority, and sovereignty is the state of being sovereign and exercising supreme authority.

When we talk about sovereignty, we are talking about a religious fact. Another word for sovereignty is lordship. The word "lord" appears in the Bible as a designation of the triune God. In the Koine Greek, lord, or *Kurios*, means God, sovereign, or absolute property owner. In the Hebrew of the Old Testament, one of the words for "lord" is Baal, a general term used often for the Baalim, or false gods, of the Canaanites.

One of these Baalim was Molech, or Melek, also appearing as Moloch, Milcom, and Malcolm. The word simply means "king". Moloch worship was worship of the state and its ruler as god. It declared that all peoples within the state, their families, properties, possessions, and lives were the property of the state. Moloch worship apparently included a form of dedication service, whereby children were passed over a fire before an image of the king-god to indicate that they belonged to him, and, if need be, would be sacrificed to him. Such a sacrifice could be an actual human sacrifice in an emergency, or the life-long possession of the child or man by the state. The condemnation of Moloch worship in Scripture is a repeated one, and is one of the most severe condemnations of Scripture (see Lev. 20:1-5). The sovereignty of the state is thus bluntly condemned by Scripture and regarded as an extreme form of idolatry and a particularly evil one.

However, it is precisely this fact, sovereignty or lordship claimed by the modern, humanistic state which now confronts us at every turn. It is a form of ancient paganism, Moloch worship, Roman emperor and state worship, and more. The philosophy and cult of the state as sovereign, the state as god walking on earth, came into its own with Georg Wilhelm Friedrich Hegel (1770-1831). In his *Philosophy of History*, Hegel declared:

> The only thought which Philosophy brings with it to the contemplation of History, is the simple conception of *Reason*; that Reason is the Sovereign of the World; that the history of the world, therefore,

> presents us with a rational process...On the one hand, Reason is the *substance* of the Universe; viz., that by which and in which all reality has its being and subsistence. On the other hand, it is the *Infinite Energy* of the Universe...That this "Idea" or "Reason" is the *True*, the *Eternal*, the absolutely *powerful* essence; that it reveals itself in the World, and that in the World nothing else is revealed but this and its honour and glory - is the thesis which...has been proved in Philosophy, and is here regarded as demonstrated.

For Hegel, this faith in Reason was religion and philosophy. It was also his politics, because he saw reason incarnating itself in the state and exercising its sovereignty through the state.

The implications of this faith are far-reaching, and they make ancient Moloch worship look like a mild example of statism by comparison. *First*, Reason replaces the God of Scripture as lord and sovereign over all things. There is now a new god, and his name is Reason. *Second*, Reason comes into its own in elite men; hence such doctrines of elitism as the dictatorship of the proletariat, the Feuhrer principle, the democratic consensus, and other like examples of modern political theory, all born of Hegel. Thus, the revealed truth for mankind comes from elite rational man. *Third*, Reason and men of Reason find their incarnation in the state, so that the modern state is god walking on earth, and the true voice of that state is elitist rational man. *Fourth*, man's visible sovereign is not the God of Scripture but the new god of humanity, the humanistic state.

Now let us consider some of the facets of sovereignty. *First*, sovereignty means absolute and total government. The Bible is emphatic that God the Lord governs all men and things absolutely, so that not even a sparrow falls apart from His will. The very hairs of our head are all numbered (Matt. 10:29-31). We live and move and have our being entirely in God and His government (Acts 17:29). For the state to claim sovereignty or lordship means to claim the total jurisdiction of God over all our lives and activities. Whereas Scripture speaks of God the Lord as "our refuge and strength, a very present help in trouble" (Ps. 46:1), the state as lord becomes a very present oppressor, a tyrant. Remember, the original meaning of "tyrant" is one who rules without God and His law.

Second, the Bible tells us that God is the one who ordains and predestines all things (Acts 15:18; Rom. 8:30, 9:8-24). This is an aspect of lordship. Thus, the state which claims to be sovereign must therefore aim at total control and planning, i.e., the ordination and the predestination of all things by man. (I live in a county whose "big city", Angels Camp, has a population of 2,700. A "master plan" handed to the county supervisors "from above" calls for a total plan which governs still non-existent things such as city alleys! Such plans are good examples of humanistic attempts at predestination.) All over the world today, the various nations are busy playing god and trying to exercise lordship or sovereignty by their master plans.

Third, another attribute of lordship or sovereignty is omniscience; a god knows all things. Hebrews 4:13 says of God the Lord, "Neither is there any creature that is not manifest in his sight: but all things are naked and opened unto the eyes of him with whom we have to do." God's knowledge of all things is a total and absolute knowledge. When the state claims sovereignty, the logic of its position requires that a like total knowledge be acquired concerning all men and things, and the result is the inquisitive and prying state which aims at knowing all in order to govern all. God's omniscience is totally righteous and good. The state's attempts at omniscience are totally evil and corrupting.

Fourth, a fundamental principle of Biblical law, as well as of Biblical song, is that "The earth is the LORD'S, and the fullness thereof; the world, and they that dwell therein" (Ps. 24:1). We, the earth, and all things, are God's property. We cannot be used by other men or by the state as property: we are the Lord's. But the state claims us as its property when the state claims to be sovereign, and we become things to be used and resources to be exploited. We become then the property of a pretender god, a grand inquisitor and tyrant.

Fifth, God reserves to Himself the right to set the boundaries of man's rule, including man's civil tax (Ex. 30:11-16; I Sam. 8:7-18). God limits His own tax to a tithe, or tenth. When the state claims to be sovereign, it claims all and often takes all, either by open confiscation in Marxist states, or by confiscatory taxation (income taxes up to 120% in some cases). The individual has no "rights" against a sovereign state: he is simply state property.

Sixth, in Scripture God the Lord (or Sovereign) reserves to Himself the power to determine law and to regulate courts, as well as to define justice or righteousness. The modern state believes that it can make better laws than God and thus sees itself as the true god over man. (Sadly, too many churchmen believe in the state as god and prefer the state's laws to God's law.)

Enough has been said to make clear that sovereignty is a very relevant matter to medical practice, as to all things. We are confronted at every turn with the rival claims to sovereignty, the sovereignty of God verses the sovereignty of the state. How we deal with these rival claims will determine our future. The words of Elijah are still timely, more than ever so: "How long halt ye between two opinions? If the LORD be God, follow him; but if Baal, then follow him" (I Kings 18:21). Men get the God they follow.

The new god, meanwhile, is very much concerned about medical practice. It is anxious to "correct" all the "evils" therein. Now it is easy at this point to become justly indignant over statist interference and to document statist corruption as against the far lesser degree of faithlessness in medical practice. Such indignation is futile, however. It is true that the evils in medical practice are small matters when compared with the massive corruptions of the various levels of civil government. Books are not lacking to document civil, governmental corruption. In my own library, I have many such volumes. Significantly, the corruptions of twenty years ago look pallid compared to those of today. As power is concentrated in the modern state, corruption goes up proportionately. However, documenting corruption is a futile task, on the whole. Why?

First, men are not saved by a vision of evil but a vision of the good. Progress and sound change have never been achieved by means of a knowledge of corruption and evil but only by a strong knowledge of the good and a mandate, calling, and mission to assure its triumph. Muck-racking can cater to a prurient interest and lead to phariseeism. Many Americans, including doctors and ministers, gain a cheap and pharisaic sense of self-righteousness by damning Washington, D. C. The Kingdom of God, however, cometh not by denunciation but by faith and righteousness.

Second, the basic faith of our age, statist humanism, is not challenged by accounts of corruption. It is an article of faith for modern man that the truest and best government is not from God and a Christian conscience, but by Reason incarnated in the state. Thus, the common answer to corruption is more statist controls! As a result, we get more controls and less freedom. Hegel's religion is not challenged by the exposes of corruption.

Third, modern man believes in salvation by the state, not by Jesus Christ. As a result, he looks to the very agency which is oppressing him for answers to his problems! For modern man to look to the humanistic state for answers to his problems is like a bleeding victim of an assassination attempt to ask his assassin for surgery! The knife in the hand of the tyrant state is not a surgeon's knife.

The question of sovereignty is thus at heart a religious one. Who is man's lord, the triune God, or the state? There are many who reject either alternative. Their answer, humanistic to the core, is the sovereignty of individual man. This position, known by a variety of names, such as libertarianism, anarchism, autarkism, and the like, pits the sovereignty of the individual against the sovereignty of God, or of the state. Man is held to be his own god and absolute. No values exist outside the will of man. The logic of this position was pushed to its extremes by the Marquis de Sade. This faith holds that Reason is incarnate, not in the state, but in man. If there is no law outside or beyond sovereign man, this means that man is not only beyond good and evil, since all things are good and evil in terms of their relationship to him and their definition by him, but sovereign man is also beyond health or sickness. Mary Baker Eddy saw man as an aspect of cosmic mind or Reason and hence beyond sickness and death. After all, sovereignty and perfection go together. Perfection is an attribute of ultimacy and sovereignty; they thereby claimed some kind of immortality, so that the monarchy became a corporation. The king might die, but he also lived on as a continuing corporation in his heir. Hence, the ancient cry, "The King is dead. Long live the King!" In his brilliant study of political theology, the late Ernst H. Kantorowicz, in *The King's Two Bodies*, wrote:

> That the king is immortal because legally he can never die, or that he is never legally under age, are familiar stage properties. But it goes further than expected when we are told that the king "is not only incapable of *doing* wrong, but even of *thinking* wrong: he can never mean to do an improper thing: in him is no folly or weakness" (Sir William Blackstone). Moreover, that king is invisible, and, though he may never judge despite being the "Fountain of Justice," he yet has legal ubiquity: "His Majesty in the eyes of the law is always present in all his courts, though he cannot personally distribute justice" (Blackstone). (Kantorowicz, p.4)

The modern state has taken over the ancient sovereignty of kings; in doing so, it has avoided the bold language cited by Kantorowicz while still claiming all the ancient powers of sovereignty and expanding their application. The facade now is that sovereignty is exercised in the name of the people; the reality is that the modern power state exercises sovereignty *over* the people.

Sovereignty is a religious question, and our problem today with the tyrant state is at heart a theological problem. Because our perspective today is humanistic, we feed the growing tyranny of the state by our assent to a humanistic view of life.

A sovereign requires that his "arms" or agencies stand with a certain immunity. In a key text, our Lord reminds us of this fact:

> 24. And when they were come to Capernaum, they that received tribute money came to Peter, and said, Doth not your master pay tribute?
> 25. And he said, Yes. And when he was come into the house, Jesus prevented him, say, What thinkest thou, Simon? of whom do the kings of the earth take custom or tribute: of their own children, or of strangers?
> 26. Peter said unto him, Of strangers. Jesus saith unto him, Then are the children free.
> 27. Notwithstanding, lest we should offend them, go thou to the sea, and cast a hook, and take up the fish that first cometh up; and when thou hast opened his mouth, thou shalt find a piece of money: that take, and give unto them for me and thee. (Matt. 17:24-27).

Our Lord declares His immunity to taxation and control, while setting forth a temporary and expedient submission. On this, and numerous other texts, the church based its immunity to controls, taxation, licensure, and regulation. As an aspect of the King's sovereign work, it was beyond any regulation by all save the King Himself.

The immunity of the medical profession has the same foundation. Salvation in the Bible means literally health, health of life in relation to God, and also health of body, since the body is God's creation. The Biblical roots of medical practice are in the Levitical ministry. The relation between patient and pastor or doctor is immune from man's controls and intervention, because it is a facet of God's ministry to man's total life.

Where the faith which is the foundation of that immunity wanes, that immunity wanes also. This is our problem today, and we cannot alter the decline without having a reversal of faith, from faith in the sovereignty of the state to faith in the sovereignty of the triune God.

Of course, we must remember that immunity does not disappear; it is transferred to the same locale as sovereignty. Because sovereignty is now an attribute of the state, immunity now is also an attribute of the state, its courts, officers, and congresses. Immunity follows sovereignty. As our Lord notes, "Then are the children free." *Under any form of humanism, the immunity of doctors is lost and is rootless at best.* The medical profession thus has as much at stake in affirming the sovereignty of God as does the church!

Moreover, a humanistic order finds the old immunities offensive and a challenge. We have thus the numerous and rapidly increasing (but not publicized) legal trials and persecutions of Christian Schools, churches, missionary agencies, and the like. We have also the baying of the statist hounds after doctors as the great enemies of man, as bloated profiteers in human misery. The savage hostility to doctors and clergymen is a growing factor in our time. As "holdovers" of a Christian order in their immunities, they are a threat to the brave new world of humanism.

Paul Tillich, normally a poor guide, was all the same clear when he defined religion as ultimate concern. All men are inescapably religious because they are created by God and thus are religious creatures. Their lives are governed by their faith, by their ultimate concern. This can be a debased concern or a God-centered faith, but man is in any case inescapably religious. Now to talk about sovereignty is to talk about our god; this god can be the state, ourselves, or the God of Scripture. Wherever our god is, there too is sovereignty, authority, morality, and ultimacy.

Our lives are governed by our faith. A false faith gives us a false sovereign, a false morality, and a false way of life. Dr. James F. Jekel, of the Department of Epidemiology and Public Health, Yale Medical School, has had some telling things to say about this. Writing on "The Coming Revolution in Health Care" in the *Journal of the American Scientific Affiliation*, (vol. 30, no. 3, September, 1978, p. 116-123), Dr. Jekel declares:

> We are in the midst of a revolution in the assumptions, goals, and methods of health care. Assumptions seriously being questioned

> include: (1) that scientific medicine is largely responsible for our current level of health, (2) that scientific medicine will markedly extend our life expectancy beyond current levels, (3) that the biomedical model is a satisfactory guide to medical practice and research, (4) and that most health care is provided by professionals. There is increasing concern that the current approach to health care is causing physical, social, and cultural harm and that the current direction cannot continue for cost reasons alone.
>
> The Scriptures inform our current dilemma by emphasizing (1) that health is the result of a way of life and not a product that can be purchased from healers, (2) that we must be as concerned with improving the quality of life as with extending its length, and (3) that health care is best when provided in the context of the family and immediate community.

Dr. Jekel is not trying to down-grade medical practice. Rather, he is stripping it of the humanistic expectations with have led people to demand impossible things from doctors. Humanism believes that man is sovereign and is therefore capable of anything. If the doctor cannot deliver instant miracles at the demand of the humanist, he is somehow a villain. But Dr. Jekel makes clear that in Scripture "health is the result of a way of life and not a product that can be purchased from healers." That way of life, he makes clear, means not only sound rules of physical hygiene, but a sound view of life. As Solomon observed, "A merry heart doeth good like a medicine: but a broken spirit drieth the bones" (Prov. 17:22). (Dr. James J. Lynch, of the School of Medicine, the University of Maryland has written on this in *The Broken Heart, The Medical Consequences of Loneliness*, $10.95, New York: Basic Books, 1977; I am grateful to Dr. Collin E. Cooper, M.D., of La Canada, California, for calling this book to my attention.)

The humanist, because he expects man to become god in action, is disappointed wherever he turns. By the very nature of the case, all things fail him. He turns then in wrath against all whom he finds to disappoint him, and doctors are a key target.

Senator Curtis has called attention to the unreasonable hostilities against doctors, and the fact that the horror stories do not represent the truth about medical practice. In the U.S., 169 million people have surgical insurance, 48 million medicaid. Most thus are covered. Of all Americans only 8/10s of 1% during the course of a year have medical expenses of over $5,000; 87% of these are covered by medical insurance. Moreover, as of 1975, the U.S. had over one million hospital beds. Also, the total picture is one of growing improvement. Do these facts impress the humanists? The answer is an emphatic *no*. The humanistic state, as the new god, wants total jurisdiction over all things including medical practice, and it also wants perfection. But who can deliver perfection?

The sovereign state by its very nature becomes a controlling and obliterating state. The state also declares in its own way, "Thou shalt have no other gods before me," and it seeks to destroy all who stand in the way of its claim to total sovereignty.

In this struggle, if the doctor stands in terms of humanism, and in terms of a purely personal desire to be free and uncontrolled, he is religiously defenseless and easily attacked as "socially irresponsible."

If the doctor stands rather in terms of a full-orbed Biblical faith, in terms of the sovereignty of God as against the sovereignty of the state, then he gets to the heart of the matter, and he stands in strength. As John declares, "For whatsoever is born of God overcometh the world: and this is the victory that overcometh the world, even our faith (I John 5:4). Moreover, as Paul reminds us, "If God be for us, who can be against us?" (Rom. 8:31).

CHALCEDON MEDICAL REPORT NO. 7
The Principles and Practice of Quackery

At the beginning of the 1950s, I had a very searching conversation with a treasured friend. Whenever I was in his area, I stayed at his home, and we talked until one or two in the morning. He was almost twice my age; he was a surgeon of national stature, and taught at the medical school of a major university. I guided Dr. G. C.'s theological reading; he guided me in far broader fields.

One evening I spoke with great interest of a popular writer on medicine, Paul de Kruif was his name, as I recall it, and of the medical miracles he was forecasting. I then commented on the apparently remarkable results a doctor 100 miles away was getting with some of the newest wonder drugs. At first, G. smiled, but, finally, he opened up to me as a friend in need of correction. This other doctor was moving into quackery, he said flatly, and all the new wonder drugs which promised to revolutionize life in the post-World War II era were close to being quack medicines.

He asked me to recall the old-time medicine men and their quack medicines. One ad I recall seeing had a long list of ailments which it declared it could heal. The list included tuberculosis, female complaints, rheumatism, impotence, and many, many more things.

The difference between a quack doctor and a good one begins with a sense of limitation. A quack medicine and a quack doctor both promise too much. A sound medicine offers limited help for a limited and specific problem. It offers no miracles and works none. It cannot replace good hygiene, sound nutrition, and healthy habits. The wise doctor makes no large promises; he knows how limited his role is, and yet, *within those limits, very important*. The more we demand of a doctor or of a medicine, the more likely we are to fall prey to quackery.

Dr. C. expressed both skepticism and fear concerning the new "wonder drugs." At best, he held, we have only the most preliminary and cursory of reports on their results, effects, and side-effects. He was fearful that too great a trust in the new medicines, and too uncritical an attitude, would turn medical practice into the dangerous vagaries of quackery. To expect too much of doctors and medicine was to leave oneself wide open to trouble, and it was like preferring a Ponzi pyramid scheme to an old-fashioned, conservative bank.

Not too much later, another fine doctor and friend told me rather wearily one evening that he had all too many unnecessary patients. They came to him daily for "wonder drugs", when a little rest and/or an aspirin would do them more good. If he did not prescribe one of the newest "miracle" drugs, they were annoyed, and they regarded him as a doctor who was not "up" on his medical practice.

I thought of these things very much of late, as I regard various accounts of the harm wrought by a variety of "miracle" drugs, of the ugly consequences of the IUDs, and the birth control pill, and then Christopher Norwood's article, "The Hormone Babies: A Condemned Generation?" (*New York*, vol. 13, no. 20, May 19, 1980, pp. 49-55). About 10 million mothers-to-be were dosed over a period of years with human sex hormones, including DES (diethylstilbestrol). The girls born of such mothers are prone to a rare genital cancer, and the boys to genital abnormalities, including microphallus, according to Norwood and others.

The saddest fact of all is that this is but one "miracle" drug among many. Worse yet, the doctors are the sole "villains" in the story, and all doctors are equally condemned, the promiscuous "wonder" drug dosers and non-dosers alike. Even worse, the appetite is for much more quackery. On a recent trip, I sat in an airport waiting room, awaiting the announcement of my flight. Two women behind me were talking randomly and apparently drifted into a discussion of some loved one's illness. Then came a sentence which, of all the talk, alone interrupted my reading and caught my attention: "You'd think the doctors could come up with some medicine to take care of that!" People demand quacks and quackery, because of their own bad character.

As a result, we have quackery all around us, in the church, the school, and in politics. Quackery in the church is not limited to the cults; it is present wherever men offer something short of God's word as the bread of life. In the state schools, we have educators promising us the best kind of education as their stock in trade, while turning out 30 million functional illiterates in America. Politics, of course, is our most fertile ground for quackery, because it is for most people the central area of life. No old time medicine man promised as much as our quack politicians: cradle to grave security, health care for all, the abolition of unemployment, and almost anything and everything else one can think of. We live in the Golden Age of Quackery, and, instead of merely giving an Oscar to our top quacks, we have been giving them the White House with increasing frequency. Quackery is in great demand.

On a plane trip recently, I glanced through a few of the available magazines, after completing my planned reading. I encountered a hostile note concerning doctors, and a "news" report on expected break-throughs with "wonder" drugs which would in a few years solve many problems and give us longer, healthier, problem-free lives. The two items go hand in hand. If you expect miracles from doctors, you will be disappointed, and you will demand quacks, not doctors.

Dr. David Ehrenfeld, professor of Biology at Rutgers University, has described much of modern humanistic and scientific thinking as not only arrogant but as "magical." Modern man is substituting the word *magic* for *science* in his thinking and identifying the two. (David Ehrenfeld: *The Arrogance of Humanism*; New York: Oxford University Press, 1978.) As a result, he approaches every discipline with unreasonable demands and a belief in the possibilities of total control by man. I recall, shortly after the 1971 earthquake in Los Angeles, listening day after day to the comments of people in check-out lines and elsewhere. One comment was, "Why doesn't the government do something about it?", i.e., why doesn't the federal government spend enough money to learn how to eliminate all earthquakes? No doubt, the same hope prevails concerning floods, tornados, and other natural disasters!

One patient, aware that he was going to die, asked of a nurse plaintively, "Can't they do something about it?" Instant miracles are demanded by men when they need them. Thus, we live in an age of quackery.

The problem is at heart theological. The theology of all who demand humanistic miracles is that of Genesis 3:5; as sinners, they see themselves as gods, and they want life to move at their behests. The writer, Ambrose Bierce, married one of the most beautiful women in the San Francisco Bay area. In addition, Mollie Day was the daughter of one of the wealthiest men of that part of the state. Not too many years later, in 1888, he left her, after discovering that she had kept some letters from a man who loved her, although she had never been involved with him or returned his affections. Life had to be on Bierce's terms, and his wife could not have even a keepsake or thought apart from him. Later, Bierce, fearful of old age, went to Mexico to join Pancho Villa's rebels (and die), and he was never heard from again.

Life becomes an impossible burden for those who play god. Trifles become crises, and life becomes a continual problem and an unending burden. We are all familiar with people who have everything, and are miserable. We are also familiar with people who do not have everything, and are also miserable. Such people want life on their terms. If things go contrary to their will, no matter how trifling, they are miserable. They resent a world they never made, and yet the only world any man can live in is God-made, not man-made. Their attitude is, 'I do well to be miserable,' as though the world will stop in its tracks to satisfy them, when the world sees that they are offended.

Such egocentricity (or sin) is a fertile ground of quackery. These men demand impossible things and require that they be given them. It was one of the most successful of all con-men, Weil, who said that he never 'conned' any man who did not first of all have larceny in his heart, and expected to take advantage of him; they had one thing in mind, their own expectations and satisfaction, *not reality*.

The prevalence of quackery means a departure from reality into fantasy and magic. It means a denial of God's world in favor of the world of imagination. It is no accident that the prevalence of evolutionary thought has coincided with the return and prevalence of magic. Both presuppose a world of chance rather than God's sovereign creation and His laws. Magic and evolution enthrone chance and deny any meaning beyond man. If Christianity is weak or wanes, magic and quackery will prevail. Eric von Kuehnelt-Leddihn, in *The Intelligent American's Guide to Europe* (Arlington House, 1979), describes how a journalist in Iceland attacked him furiously for his religious "superstitions" such as belief in Christ's resurrection, the Virgin Birth, and so on. Half an hour later, the same man whispered to him, pointing through the window of his library: "You see that man there? Beware of him! Several weeks ago he changed himself into a bull and chased me across the fields" (p. 202). Why not? If you believe in chance, you will believe that anything is possible, except God, Who is the antithesis of chance.

The problem of quackery is thus at root a religious problem. The elimination of quackery must begin from the pulpit, and it must be carried out in every field, beginning with the church and politics. The problem, however, is more than an ecclesiastical one. The doctor himself must have a realistic perspective of his role, and that of medicine. Medical practice is a calling, and it must be practiced under God. The principles and practice of quackery are magical, although they pass as science, and Christian medical practice must avoid them.

The Return to Magic

Some years ago, in the 1920s, a liberal, non-Christian writer and editor, Kenneth Burke, predicted that the modern world would see a return to a belief in magic and occultism. He did not welcome this: he was simply setting down what he believed was inevitable.

His reasoning was clarity itself. Modern man has rejected God and the supernatural. In doing so, he has not rid himself of his hunger for miracles, for grace, and for super-human power at work in society. This hunger, Burke reasoned, will create an appetite for and lead to a revival of, occultism and magic. Men will seek grace and power from below.

Let us extend this thinking further. Men have rejected, in the 20th century, God, the Father, the Son, and the Spirit. Having denied supernatural power and authority, they seek to replace this same need by humanistic ones. The political leader in our day succeeds most who invokes a father image and has "charismatic" qualities. The result is a 20th century proneness to dictatorship, authoritarian politics, and the rule of men rather than laws. Men have transferred their religious devotion from God to their political leaders, and candidates for office set forth a salvationist politics. An atheistic or humanistic populace turns its political leaders into religious leaders, and it pins hopes on the political process which politics can never realize. The result is widespread disillusionment and cynicism. The failure of modern politics is inevitable: it can never deliver what the people demand of it. The more it tries to be what the people try to make it to be, the greater its failure and the resulting disillusionment and bitterness.

The same false expectation, disillusionment, and hostility can be found in other areas, notably medicine. One doctor's wife, weary of listening to women patient's talk about her husband with unrealistically high faith, said that at times she was tempted to answer: I think my husband is a very good doctor and a fine man, but I happen to know that he is not God! Exactly. No age is unbelieving; it may be ungodly, but its beliefs are no less intense; they are rather falsely directed. It is this false direction which predisposes people to quackery: they expect and demand from everyone, children, husbands, wives, doctors, politicians, clergymen, and scientists, more than they can honestly deliver. They want humanistic miracles.

It should not surprise us that the press and the public speak of the post-World War II medicines as "wonder" drugs. The original and basic meanings of "wonder" are (1) a prodigy, and (2) something supernatural. Both meanings underlie the popular usage of the word as applied to drugs, and they underscore the falsely religious expectation with which people approach medical aid. Similarly, "bionic man" is not only a television person but a popular belief. Few stop to think that bionic additions are inferior: they cannot replace good health and sound health practices. Eye-glasses, after all, are a "bionic" addition and definitely inferior to good eyes! So too medicine is, like eye-glasses, at times a need, but it is never a "wonder"; its true scope is limited though important.

The roots of quackery are in false religion, and in a humanistic faith in man, and man's products.

CHALCEDON MEDICAL REPORT NO. 8
Statist Medicine

An important book published recently is Alexander Podrabinek's *Punitive Medicine* (1980; Karoma Publishers, Caroline House, 236 Forest Park Place, Ottawa, Illinois 61350; xiii; 223 pp.). The author is now serving a sentence of exile in Siberia. This is a careful and documented account of the use of psychiatry for political purposes in the U.S.S.R.

Notable opponents of the communist regime are discredited by being sentenced to mental institutions, there to be drugged and tortured into submission. The psychiatrists act on orders from above. They justify this prostitution of their profession by saying that no man in his right mind would speak out, take a stand against, or contradict and challenge the state system and the official ideology. "Normalcy" and mental health to them means living with the system. To question or fight the system is for them not a normal act nor a sensible one; hence, it is a sign of mental problems.

Thus, mental health is defined by conformity to the Marxist order, not by a sound mind in relationship to God, and to men in and under God. Normalcy and mental health become whatever the state decrees and does. Such a definition is very close to that of the Western democracies and their schools; men are group directed, subject to group dynamics, and are trained to regard the behavior of those resisting the group as "deviant." (One mother of an intelligent boy, whose father was a noted scientist, was called to the public school to discuss her "deviant" son. His "problem", which brought him under suspicion, was a preference for reading over playground horseplay.) The group is the norm; society determines standards and mental health. The Marxists have simply put this humanistic standard under more disciplined direction: not the group, but the state, determines normalcy and mental health.

As a result, we have what Podrabinek calls "legalized lawlessness" (p. 99), the newer psychiatric "hospitals" are less evil (p. 34), but all grow in perversity with time, and sadism becomes the order of the day among doctors and guards (pp. 30ff). No doubt, the courage of the resisters is a reproach to them, and intensifies their sadism and evil. Added to this is the fact that orderlies use patients for sexual perversions (p. 31).

The Soviet definition of mental health as conformity leads to strange diagnoses such as these: "She is suffering from nervous exhaustion caused by justice-seeking;" "You have schizo-dissent," and so on (p. 78). "Soviet psychiatry does not allow any opportunity for conscientious refusal to adapt" (p. 77).

Very aptly, Juliana Geran Pilan calls all this "The Shame of Soviet Medicine" (*Reason Magazine*, January, 1980). The problem is not restricted to psychiatry but is common to all medicine in Marxist countries. For example, venereal diseases are dogmatically called "bourgeois." How can a bourgeois infection exist in a socialist paradise? It not only exists but is very widespread, although not acknowledged. No statistics are given on V.D.; it has supposedly been abolished. Because it has been abolished, there are no clinics to treat it. The unhappy patient must go to the "dermatology" clinics for treatment! Dermatologists visiting the Soviet Union are assumed to be specialists in venereal diseases.

The same is true of narcotics. The newspapers like to write about "The Absence of Addicts in the Soviet Union: One More Proof of the Superiority of Communism Over Capitalism." All the while, the use of drugs flourishes, and a drug culture is very real. (See Yuri Brokhin: *Hustling on Gorky Street*, pp. 74, 121).

The point is clear. Diseases and problems do not "exist" unless the Marxist state allows them an official existence or recognition. Medical training is controlled; doctors and psychiatrists are controlled; hospitals are controlled; drugs, like all medical practice, are a state monopoly. The medical profession serves the state, not the patient. Doctors are a part of a bureaucracy which has a state-controlled life and conscience.

Punitive Medicine? Of course. In cannot be otherwise. As Podrabinek notes: "Punitive medicine is a tool in the struggle against dissidents who cannot be punished by legal means" (p. 63).

The most serious mistake we can make is to treat punitive medicine as a Soviet aberration. We should instead see it as the logical conclusion of all socialized medicine.

The advocates of socialized medicine believe that such a step would bring more medical care to the poor and needy. The fact is that, at least in the United States, the poor have usually had more medical services rendered to them than any other class. The fact of their poverty has made them the recipients of free services, or subject to very nominal fees, and hence they have more readily used doctors.

But the problem goes deeper. Ostensibly, socialized medicine will serve the people. Senator Edward M. Kennedy, in his book, *In Critical Condition, The Crisis in America's Health Care* (1972), sees socialized medicine as "the choice of conscience." "The government" will supposedly have a conscience and a concern for the poor which doctors ostensibly lack. Private practitioners, whom he sees as grasping businessmen, will somehow all become Good Samaritans when the federal government controls them. His picture is a passionate, selected, and extremely partial one. It is also very unrealistic.

There is no reason to believe that socialized medicine anywhere will serve the people any better or as good as private practice. On the contrary it will serve the federal government. Let us remember, after all, that the Sixteenth Amendment (the income tax) was voted into the U.S. Constitution in the name of helping the poor! The income tax was to be limited to "soaking the rich" and distributing the wealth. It would make a freer and happier America possible. The worker would come into his own, and there would be a better America for all.

There is no reason to suppose that a socialized and federalized medicine will be any more benevolent that the Internal Revenue Service. The I.R.S., after all, was created with at least equal idealistic motives. Anyone who can think of the I.R.S. as the people's friend today does indeed have mental problems! Socialized medicine will be no better than the I.R.S., and potentially far worse. Any and everything which puts us into contact with a powerful state and its bureaucracy is dangerous, and socialized medicine will place us in a very close relationship to that power-state: at pregnancy and childbirth, in ill health and accidents, for a variety of required medical examinations, and much more. Also, as euthanasia becomes an accepted practice like abortion, the more the state knows about you, the less safe you are.

Already, of course, the hand of the state is very heavy upon all doctors. Medical schools are extensively subsidized and thereby federalized. Because of funding, the medical school looks as much to Washington, D.C., as it does to the general practitioner, or the surgeon, and their problems. Hospitals are also serving the state and are more ready to displease doctors and patients than federal authorities. What the state controls serves state purposes.

Thus, Alexander Podrabinek's *Punitive Medicine* gives us merely the avant garde aspect of the new medical practice, socialized medicine.

It is a very logical development. The state is a punitive agency or institution. Its purpose is to punish or to vindicate. Its basic and truest instruments are the courts, the police, and the military. Their purpose is to punish or to vindicate. The life of the state is geared to punitive action. St. Paul, in Romans 13:1-4, makes clear that the true function of the ministry of justice (the state) is to be a terror to evil-doers. The state is the agency of coercion. The church's function is to educate; industry's function is to produce, and the medical professions' function is to heal. To place the healing arm of society under the coercive or punitive arm is the height of folly and unreason.

No realm taken over by the state has escaped its coercive and punitive nature, to the detriment of its original function. Thus, before the states in America took over education, the United States had the world's lowest illiteracy rate and a remarkably capable populace. Today, after a century and half of Horace Mann's evil "reform," state control of education, we have our highest illiteracy rate in history. Jonathan Kozol, in *Prisoners of Silence* (1980), gives us some very alarming estimates, from federal and other sources. The Office of Education estimates that fifty seven million Americans are unequipped to carry out the most basic tasks. This means over 35% of the entire adult population. Some place the figure as high as sixty four million. Perhaps twenty three to thirty four million of these are illiterate; the rest can barely function. Illegal aliens, who may number as high as eight million, are not in these statistics at all. Kozol is a liberal, a concerned liberal. How does the teachers' bureaucracy deal with all criticisms of its incompetence? With evidences of illiteracy among teachers themselves? Typical of its reaction is an article on "New Right's Attack on

Teachers" in the *Tennessee Teacher*, April, 1980. Well, it is all an ugly conspiracy! "Since we as teachers believe in public education and in professional dignity, then surely we see the New Right as very wrong - a dangerous threat to the freedoms we inherited and continue to espouse." A bureaucracy calls itself the vessel of freedom! This is 1984 and newspeak indeed! It is also the voice of monopoly and unreason. Coercion remains in the public schools, because they are agencies of the state: compulsory attendance laws, the persecution of Christian Schools, and the like. But education is disappearing.

There is no reason to believe that socialized medicine will be any better. It will rather become *punitive medicine*.

Thus, the problem is not merely a Soviet problem: it is our problem as well.

The sphere of the state is the ministry of justice according to the Bible. Its activities are properly punitive, and its jurisdiction must be limited to those areas which are legitimately punitive. Healing is not one of these. When the state takes over all areas, coercion prevails in all areas. As a result, because no independent, uncoerced, and free voice exists, corruption prevails. Brokhin noted that the chief stimulus to labor in the Soviet Union is the bribe. Without it, the economy would collapse (p. 97). As Brokhin further observed: "There will never be a Watergate-style scandal in the Soviet Union. No party boss ever has been or ever will be brought to trial and jailed for bribery, corruption, or theft. If one corrupt high official were ever sent to jail, all the rest would have to go too, almost without exception" (p. 102). Where charges of corruption are made in the U.S.S.R., they are a facade for a personal vendetta, or for coercing dissent.

American life - and medicine - needs to be preserved from statist controls. Punitive medicine is not an agency of healing but an aspect of total terror. Those who seek it should be viewed with distrust. At the very least, they suffer from moral and intellectual myopia.

CHALCEDON MEDICAL REPORT NO. 9
The Criticism of Medical Practice By Doctors

In recent years, more than a little dissatisfaction with the medical profession has been forthcoming. More than a little of this has come from physicians themselves. True, the political criticism, from men like Senator Ted Kennedy, has been very much in evidence, but, apart from that, physicians themselves have been vocal in their criticism.

Over the years, some of the most readable books of current interest have been written by physicians. Because medical practice involves crises and drama, doctors' lives and tales make good reading. It is not an accident that, together with Westerns, detective and crime dramas, medical tales provide a high proportion of television fare. After all, it would be difficult to develop a television series around dental practice, or accounting! Medical practice lends itself to drama - and also for that very reason to more public interest and criticism. It can be argued that there are as many problems in dental practice, and more in accounting, but who is interested in critiques of dentists and accountants? (Accountants tend to favor the Internal Revenue Service in preparing your returns to avoid too many audits, and hostility to their clients, which could put an accountant out of business.) Thus, doctors get an undue amount of attention, both pro and con, because of the very nature of their calling. Like politicians, they are very much in the public eye, whether they like it of not.

The sharp criticism of medical practice by physicians is a relatively new thing, but a very important factor. Without necessarily agreeing with the criticism, we need to welcome it as a healthy development. State control over medical schools and medical licensing was a very serious step in the history of American medicine. Whatever short-term benefits these steps may have brought about, they were fateful in that the basic premise of socialized medicine was thereby granted. The state was no longer limited to the control of medical practice which had become criminal; it now controlled all of medical practice in principle. In recent years, the state has moved toward using the potential powers gained when its controls over medical schools and licensure were established. Some men, like Dr. M.R. Saxon, M.D., of Aurora, Illinois, have not only written and spoken against this trend but taken practical steps against it. There is a growing awareness among many physicians of the basic issues in state controls.

Thus, some of the medical critics are clearly in the ranks of greater freedom and self-reform. One such doctor is Robert S. Mendelssohn, M.D. (*Confessions of a Medical Heretic*, 1979), whose concern for freedom led him to be a witness for Rev. Lester Roloff, in Austin, Texas, in a trial with respect to the attempt of the state to control Roloff's ministry to delinquent children.

A very different book is by Dr. John S. Bradshaw, a British surgeon, *Doctors on Trial* (1978). Dr. Bradshaw presents his book as a simulated trial of his profession before a judge, and he presents an array of testimonies pro and con before rendering a *guilty* verdict. Bradshaw does call attention to the over-use of drugs, high technology medicine, the Tuskegee case, the Willowbrook case, and more.

Another similar work is by Keith Alan Lasko, M.D., *The Great Billion Dollar Medical Swindle* (1980). Like Bradshaw, Lasko (a California doctor), calls attention to a great deal of medical malpractice. Some of the areas he covers deal with methadone, hypoglycemia, impotence, vasectomy, mastectomy, hysterectomy, gall bladder stones, herpes, cancer, hospitals, drugs, ambulances, and more. His book is much more informative than

Bradshaw's, and is an exceptionally thorough statement of areas of serious problems. Like Bradshaw's book, it is marred by too much hostility and an element of self-righteousness. He is more honest that Bradshaw, in that he states his premises openly and plainly: "the major reform needed for the U.S. health care system is the removal of the profit motive from medicine" (p. 226). Dr. Lasko then raises the pertinent question: Can our bungling, inept, and corrupt federal government, "the same federal government that gave us Amtrack, the Postal Service, the swine flu fiasco, the Vietnam debacle, the Bay of Pigs, and the Veterans Administration, not to mention the national defense mess, the energy crisis, the 'war on poverty,' and the 'war on cancer,' give us a good national health care administration?" (p. 227). Lasko's answer is an amazing one: "if America is to survive, one has to assume that some leadership will eventually surface in Washington D.C." (p. 228).

Why does one have to assume that? On the contrary, those nations in past history who have looked to the state for salvation have perished for that very reason. Would it not make much more sense to set the doctors free from controls and allow the free market to give us good medicine?

Contrary to Dr. Lasko's belief, "The profit motive" does *not* disappear when the state takes over the economy, or aspects thereof. Profit in the form of graft and corruption then sky-rockets, even as services decline. Socialism replaces a normal and healthy profit motive with massive fraud and corruption. Many, if not most, of the evils Dr. Lasko attacks in his profession are the products of federal intervention into medicine, which have made possible the proliferation of needless (state or federally paid) surgeries he criticizes. Those of us who are not on Social Security, Medicare, medical insurance, or what have you, seem to need far less surgery or hospital care! We still belong to the old order of freedom, not subsidy.

All the same, it is necessary to call attention to a very important point made by the various medical champions of socialized medicine, the need for a higher moral standard among doctors and less surgery, prescription and practice for money's sake. Up to a point, we can and must agree with this. But let us look more closely at this objective.

The goal of the advocates of socialized medicine is that doctors become socially concerned and moral, and they believe that this can be accomplished by legislation. We are dealing with a false doctrine long condemned by orthodox Christianity, salvation by law. Its premise is anti-Christian, and its success is impossible. The idea of socialized medicine is even less workable than was Prohibition.

The hope of making doctors moral by law has in it some very seriously faulty premises. Two of these concern us at the moment. *First*, it is assumed that profit is evil, a premise we cannot accept. Moreover, it is curious that, even in Marxist countries, no successful attempt is made to eliminate the profit motive for artists and writers. The facts of quality and market control and market receptivity cause problems, very obvious ones. True, the Soviet

Union does try to subsidize subservient writers and painters, but, somehow, the better writers sometimes get published, at home or abroad, and are far more successful. Also, the independent painters build up an underground market. The controls do not militate against profit: they militate against quality. In medical practice, free choice does often reward a good "bedside manner," but it also rewards quality, and it gives the decision-making power to the consumer-patient rather than the state. The state usually rewards subservience, and its choices are less to be trusted than the individual's, as witness almost everything the state does.

Second, while we can legislate morality to a degree, i.e., we can have laws against murder, we cannot by legislation change the heart of the murderer. Legislation is legitimate if it legislates against a crime, but it is presumptuous, dangerous, and false if it legislates against the innocent man as a potential criminal. It is the murderer who must be controlled, not the innocent man. The assumption of socialized medicine is that physicians constitute a socially dangerous and/or derelict element which must be controlled.

As this point, let us look again at Dr. Bradshaw's indictment (and conviction on paper) of the medical profession. In his concluding paragraph, Bradshaw speaks of the need to create a new society. This goal requires something we now lack: "the philosophy, the religion, needed for the establishment of such a society" (p. 313). It would appear that what Dr. Bradshaw has in mind as the philosophy or religion of the future is a humanistic statism. He does bring his doctors to the bar before a British judge in New York City!

Acts 3:6 tells us of the incident before the Temple when St. Peter healed a lame man, saying, "In the name of Jesus Christ of Nazareth, rise up and walk." Today, all too many doctors and politicians, seeing the sickness within the medical profession, are trying to say, "In the name of the state, I command thee, rise up and walk, and be whole." It does not work!

Without accepting the strident critique these doctors make of their profession, we can grant them certain of their arguments. The medical profession does need healing, but healing from what?

The rise of very hostile criticisms of the medical scene, doctors, hospitals, medical schools, and more, is a fairly recent thing. It did not exist to any appreciable degree before World War II, and it has become prominent since c. 1960. We can thus say that it has risen in part at the same time as federal intervention into medicine was stepped up dramatically. In fact, it has developed together with Medicare. Very bluntly, the common opinion is that doctors fought it bitterly, but, when they found that it could be exploited financially, they did so. As some doctors have plainly said, there is truth to this charge.

An even more important issue is abortion. Travelling as I have very extensively across country, and talking to people on planes, in terminals, and at meetings, a curious fact has come to my attention. The pro-life and the pro-abortion people both have strong convictions on the question of abortion, but they are agreed on one thing. They do not trust "most doctors." It took me a while to realize this, and it came out only accidentally and/or unconsciously from pro-abortion people, but abortion has affected their view of doctors. Such a person will go to a doctor for an abortion, but can you trust a man with your life who takes life for money? A man who sees no evil in taking life? Psychologically, this has taken a fearful toll on the public image of doctors.

Let us assume that an American Clergymen's Association existed, with all clergymen in the U.S. in it, or most of them, and all members were state-licensed. Let us further assume that this ACA either declined to take a stand against abortion, homosexuality, and adultery, or approved of these things. Would not every person in this country look askance at the clergy, whether or not they approved of these things?

Here we come to the heart of the problem. Psychiatry has "dropped" homosexuality as a perversion or as evidence of some disorder. The homosexuals gained a bit from that judgment, but psychiatry lost disastrously; it gained public contempt. Medical societies recognize abortionists as physicians in good standing, and every doctor is hurt by that recognition. He who recognizes murder as legitimate is classed with the murderer.

Bradshaw is right in seeing the need for religion, although we cannot agree with his argument (before a court!) or his religion. The religion of statist humanism has been bought by too many doctors; they simply balk at the logical conclusion of their faith. Their moral dereliction can no more be cured by socialized medicine than alcoholism can be cured by a warehouse full of whiskey.

The problems raised by the medical critics of physicians, and by the political critics as well, are at heart moral problems. The state cannot minister to any of those problems. Moreover, our society as a whole is morally and religiously derelict, and it needs a truly Biblical faith to be renewed. Prescriptions for the medical profession which neglect, overlook, or sidestep this fact are dangerous. For men like some of our current senators to present themselves as the bearers of a moral solution to the problems of health care is Phariseeism of a most flagrant variety. However, in every age, Phariseeism is a most popular religion. The only effective answer to it is a truly Biblical faith.

CHALCEDON MEDICAL REPORT NO. 10
Division and Separation

Some years ago, in the mid-1950s, I visited briefly with a prominent pastor in a major city. The church of which he was the minister was probably the most important, or nearly so, in that city in terms of its membership, influence, and financial power. Its members were prominent business and professional men, and, socially, membership in the church was an asset. The witty and urbane pastor was a popular after-dinner speaker. As a serious speaker, he had a knack for raising all the right questions, and the possible answers, without coming to an open commitment to any one answer. His impressive study had a little sign, intended to be humorous, which read, "Take your troubles to God, but bring me your cash." As anyone with painful problems found out, there was more truth than humor in the sign: the man wanted no people with embarrassing problems in his congregation.

What made the supposedly humorous sign so repulsive was that the ministry is not intended by God to be profit oriented, although Scripture requires that those who labor in the ministry be very well rewarded. The motivation, however, must be the Lord's work. A priestly calling, i.e., a sacred vocation, requires a non-economic motivation. The pastor in question was a modernist of sorts, i.e., with no great convictions about what he believed and what be disbelieved in Scripture. His motivation, hence, was hardly likely to be a Biblically sound one.

Over the years, we have seen divisions and separations in the churches over the issue of faith. Within Protestantism, the line of division is quite extensive now between the modernists and the orthodox or fundamentalists. Such divisions are beginning to enter into Catholic circles; in at least one city, the telephone "classified" listings carry two classifications: "Catholic Churches, conservative," as against the liberal ones. Some laymen say the division may go further.

All this is by way of indicating that this line of separation is no longer limited to the churches. State schools versus Christian schools is another, and there are more. There are growing hints of a like division in medicine between those who see medical practice as a business and those who see it as a priestly calling and ministry.

Two illustrations will indicate the problem. One of our Chalcedon staff men suffered a very serious accident in mid-1984. Rushed to a hospital, with his life perhaps at stake, the surgeon asked first, not content with what the receptionist may have ascertained, "Before we begin, can you pay for this?"

Currently, one of our Christian School teachers has a daughter (married and in her twenties), who has suffered some kind of internal rupture, is in a very critical condition, and losing grasp of consciousness. Rushed to the hospital, she was told by a doctor, "If you can't pay, you'll have to endure the pain." And wait she must, and, we hope, surviving, until her grandfather and some of us guarantee the cost.

Nowadays, many such stories can be told. If they make you angry, remember how deeply angry and offended many fine doctors also are, often more so than the rest of us. They see such men polluting medical practice, and all too many hospitals a party to this evil.

The fact is that, never before have hospital and medical bills been more provided for in our history. By 1975, 48 million Americans had medicaid care, and 168 million had surgical insurance. The numbers have increased. Moreover, few people face large medical expenses totalling over $5,000 a year, and 87% of these will be covered by medical insurance. Moreover, by 1975, there were over one million hospital beds in the United States. Since then, the situation is even better.

It is very true that both state and federal medical aid is very slow in reaching doctors and hospitals. The same is true of private health insurance. In both statist and private spheres, endless forms must be filled out, and much red tape ensues. Papers get lost, and some doctors' secretaries grow very weary of making out fresh copies of old claims. More than a few believe that federal, state, and private insurance or aids are deliberately stalling on payments in order to hold funds longer.

Such things are minor problems, however. The real evil lies elsewhere. In the 20th century, many clergymen have simply sidestepped the requirement to believe in God's word and to take their ordination vows seriously. They seek clerical status without the responsibilities and the faith thereof. Saint Stephen called all those of false faith "betrayers and murderers" (Acts 7:52).

Now, within the ranks of physicians, a division like that within the church and education is in evidence. There have been divisions and break-ups in some clinics over these issues.

Abortion is murder, and it is murder of a particularly repulsive sort. Many nurses report on the horrors which are commonplace in the medical practice of abortionists. Any pro-life group can give us a vivid account of what these are. These horror stories, however, are not necessary when it comes to assessing these doctors.

A doctor's calling is healing and health. The word for salvation in the Latin is salve, health, and both Old and New Testaments speak of salvation as the total health and restoration of man, in all his being, into the fullness of life in the Lord.

For a doctor to become a murderer is to turn his vocation upside down. It involves, not failure or incompetence, but a reversal of all moral order. It turns his calling into a perversion.

It thereby alters the relationship of the patient to the doctor. That relationship, with all its privacy and privilege, is intended to be a healing one. It is a medical form of the confessional, and its purpose and goal is healing. A false confessor, whether in the church or in medical practice, is a great evil, and a menace to the life of the one who seeks healing.

The minister and the medical doctor are ministers of life and healing. In the absolute sense, Jesus Christ is "life" (John 14:6), and Satan is the Destroyer of life (Rev. 9:11, apollyon, meaning Destroyer). This line of division is basic to the Bible. It undergirds the meaning of creation, and

God's joy in creating. God, in answering Job's friends, speaks of His joy in all creation, in the wild ox, the grass, the wild goats, and all His handiwork. He tells us that, in the creation week, "the morning stars sang together, and all the sons of God shouted for joy" (Job 38:7). Those who go against God and His law sin against their own life or soul and reveal thereby a love of death (Prov. 8:36). True faith is a celebration of life.

When the minister and the physician are faithful to the Lord of life who is Himself absolute life, they are healers, and their work is them a ministry of healing. They are a ministry of health in the fullest sense of the word.

Our devastating social dislocations have roots in the failures of ministries. Where the man in the pulpit, and the man in the clinic or hospital, becomes a minister of death, the whole society is adversely affected. The ministries of life have then been poisoned.

Our world today is marked by a love of death and a hatred for life, and hence its anti-Christianity, and hence abortion. Igor Shafarevich, a mathematician within the Soviet Union, wrote, in Alexander Solzhenitsyn's *From Under the Rubble* (1974), on Marxism as a hatred of man, of religion, of the family, and of life itself; he documented the determined will to death of Marxist man. Earlier, an American psychotherapist, Samuel J. Warner, in *The Urge to Mass Destruction* (1957), analyzed the modern world's craving for an apocalyptic disaster and end. He saw an operational correspondence between Satan and such modern thinkers as Nietzsche. Writing in the easy years of post-World War II optimism, he saw the sickness of modern man's soul, and the crises ahead. He saw man facing two roads, the road to death, and the road to life, and our modern world as predisposed by its philosophies to death.

Warner did not envision (or speak of) abortion or euthanasia, but, very clearly, these are major milestones on the road to death.

We cannot and must not say that physicians have caused this. They reflect the false morality of our time. However, a major Biblical premise is that, the greater the responsibility, the greater the culpability and the guilt. Our Lord says, "For unto whomsoever much is given, of him shall be much required: and to who men have committed much, of him they will ask the more" (Luke 12:48). In Leviticus 4, we are told that the sin of a priest is the most serious in any society and requires a greater atoning sacrifice. No matter where the source of an infection in the life of any society may come in, ministers, teachers, and doctors, because theirs is a priestly calling, bear a greater guilt if they fail to have a ministry of life.

In recent years, the areas of strength in our society have been those areas where, in church and school, a separation and a division has taken place. This separation and division can and has taken two forms. On the one hand, it can mean breaking away to create new entities and a renewed faith. On the other hand, it can mean cleansing a body or group of all false members in order to restore health.

It should be remembered, to hark back to the two illustrations of medical malpractice cited earlier, that the problem is not money but a false faith. Saint Paul tells us, as does our Lord, and the law, that "the laborer is worthy of his reward." Moreover, those presbyters who are faithful and able, are "worthy of double honour," i.e., double pay (I Tim. 5:17-18). Nothing in the Bible can justify underpaying anyone, and, the more important the work, the better should the reward be. On the other hand, the Bible is clear that men should work in terms of their calling. A businessman has a right to his profit, and the consumer to honest goods. But, while in some callings a profit or an "increase" is a proper goal, this is not true of all. It is not money itself, but "the love of money (which) is the root of all evil" (I Tim. 6:10). There is nothing wrong with money itself, but it is the love of it which is very evil. It warps and perverts both man and society.

The Biblical linkage between the love of money, death, evil, and Satan is not an accidental one. When we serve Mammon, we cannot serve God (Matt. 6:24, Luke 16:9, 11, 13). One nurse once described abortion to me as "the biggest financial bonanza ever to hit medicine."

Morality is an issue of life and death, and inescapably so, God declares that the moral alternatives involve blessings or curses (Deut. 28). Current attempts to eliminate the moral question are particularly evil. To call abortion personal freedom, or a woman's "right" to control her own body, is to evade morality and to choose death. Doctors are no less involved in this invasion. *Newsweek*, January 14, 1985, cited a prominent obstetrician and gynecologist who now avoids most abortions, referring them to area clinics. He is increasingly reluctant to perform abortions. But, he insists, "I don't like abortions. It's not a moral question - I just have a bad feeling about it. It's always a strain" (p. 26).

This de-moralization of life is basic to the evil infecting medical practice, and all of us. To reduce a question of life and death to a matter of how we feel (do we have good feelings or bad "vibes" over it?) is to separate ourselves from God's world and its moral order. It is to choose death.

The division between life and death is a matter of reality. Death entered the world because of man's sin, his moral separation from God. When men bring death to unborn babes, they have chosen death in a particularly evil fashion. No man or society can be indifferent to the social consequences of such a choice. It is an invitation to judgement and destruction: it is social suicide.

CHALCEDON MEDICAL REPORT NO. 11
The Church and Medical Ethics

In one sense, to speak of *medical ethics* is a misnomer; morality is not a localized matter. God's law is valid in every area of life and thought, so that what is true in economics, politics, the ministry, and the family is also true in medical practice. *Right* and *wrong*, *good* and *evil*, do not change in nature from one calling to another.

In another sense, however, *medical ethics* is a necessary concern if seen as a concern to apply the one unchanging moral law of God to a particular sphere of life, medical practice. From this perspective, medical ethics has never been of more urgent concern to the church.

To begin with, both the church and medical practice have a common concern, salvation. The word *salvation* is in New Testament Greek *soteria*, which means deliverance, preservation, safety, victory, and health. When we are saved, we are rescued from the death of sin into the life and health of our new humanity in Jesus Christ. Salvation in its totality means the fullness of health, spiritually and physically. This is why it culminates, in the world to come, with our perfect sanctification, and, with the end of the world, with our resurrection bodily.

Our English word *salvation* reflects this fact. It comes from a Latin word meaning *good health*, (*salve*, the adverb; *salveo*, the verb, *salvus* the adjective; and *salus*, health, welfare, prosperity, deliverance, soundness, or preservation).

In the ministry of our Lord, both aspects of salvation are very clearly evident. Paul says, "if any man be in Christ, he is a new creature (or, creation): all things are passed away; behold, all things are become new" (II Cor. 5:17). Our Lord tells Nicodemus that a man must be born again of the Spirit (John 3:2-5). But this is not all. Our Lord tells us that He brought physical and social health and healing to men: "The blind receive their sight, and the lame walk, the lepers are cleansed, and the deaf hear, the dead are raised up, and the poor have the gospel preached to them" (Matt. 11:5).

For Christians, healing, i.e., medical practice is a religious practice and salvific activity. This means that medicine is a priestly vocation and calling. For this reason, historically the church has fought for the sanctity of the confessional. What is confessed to a pastor is a confession made with a healing of the soul in mind; the pastor hears at God's command to administer the word of God to the sick soul. This is privileged communication; it is between man and God and is related to private prayer. The same is true of all communications between a patient and a doctor: it is a form of confession for the purpose of healing. The doctor is God's agent in the process, and the communication is privileged. Because in recent years we have forgotten this religious character of doctor-patient relations, we have allowed the state to make inroads on its immunities.

Next, we must remember that, while God's moral law is the same for every man and for every calling, there are God-imposed limitations of functions in the various spheres. One example is the death penalty; it applies to all men in all callings and spheres of life, but not all men can apply it. In

Scripture, all but one of the basic powers, control of children, property, inheritance, education, and welfare, are given to the family, and the death penalty is withheld. The church has important powers, but not the death penalty. The same is true of medical practice, of *Healing*. Like the church, medical practice must concern itself with restoring and strengthening life, with fighting off death rather than execution. For the church or the doctors to embark on a program of executions is thus immoral and offensive. On the other hand, given our current situation of lawlessness and crime, for the state to restore and use the death penalty is emphatically a moral step. We can and must do as citizens things we cannot morally do as doctors, and vice versa.

All callings are under God's law and are required to obey it, but each domain or sphere has a limitation of duties and of powers. For medical practice thus to *kill* means a fundamental violation of God's moral order. This means, first, that doctors must not be executioners, killing men because they may truly deserve to be executed. This is the state's function, not the doctor's. This means, second, that what is forbidden to the state, to kill the innocent, is doubly forbidden to doctors, i.e., euthanasia and abortion, for example.

Third, for any sphere to exceed its God-appointed area is to play god. The power to kill is not given to the family; it is the realm of nurture, not of death. The same is true of the church; for the church to usurp the power of family or of state would be to deny its calling and to play god. The doctor has a related role. As we have seen, medical practice is a religious, a priestly vocation because it has to do with health. To take human life by abortion or euthanasia is a violation of the calling to heal.

But this is not all. There is a relationship too between medical practice and the family. Despite the present anti-Christian trends in medicine, the term *family doctor* still survives. Like the family itself, the family doctor has a nurturing role, to nurture life.

Medical schools seem to have forgotten this fact. Medical offices seek increasingly to be impersonal and scientific, cold in their appearance and their crisp methodology. Physicians fail to understand why their profession is often held in disrespect. *First*, the casual acceptance of murderers, i.e., abortionists, as fellow colleagues in medical associations certainly does not make for a moral regard for doctors. The old saying, "He who lies down with dogs will rise up with fleas" is a valid one. Pro-lifers and pro-abortionists may disagree as to the percentage of those in opposition to abortion and euthanasia, but, whichever figures we take, it is a very sizable body of people, many, many millions. On the whole, the moral outrage of millions of people is shared by too few doctors. This most certainly works against the entire profession.

Second, when medical offices cultivate a scientific air which is sterilized against personal kindliness, the results are hardly conducive to good "public relations." The answer on the part of some aggravates the problem. It is no remedy for a doctor to start calling patients he meets for the first time by their first name. It is a public relations ploy, and it is demeaning and condescending. Public relations ideas are no solution to a failed sense of vocation.

The sense of vocation, of a calling, is needed in medicine, and in every area of life. Here again a major problem is a false view of science. Students are given "scientific" aptitude tests. The tests tell them what they should be, not their personal goals and sense of mission, something now becoming rare. The school counselor adds insult to injury. If the student's aptitude test indicates that he is fitted by abilities for medicine or for engineering, he is then told of the job situation in his field. Does it seem over-crowed at the moment? He is urged to look towards some of his secondary aptitudes. Thus, the two prime factors or considerations are, *first*, what a supposedly scientific test tells him, and, *second*, what supposedly scientific surveys of that field say about job opportunities. Given this process, the amazing thing is that we have as many good doctors, dentists, lawyers, etc. as we do! Science has preempted the doctrine of calling with the idea of scientific determination. In the process, life has been made barren.

How important this point is was made apparent in a recent letter from Philip Spielman. A notable figure in Berkeley, California, in arguing for abortion, objected to the argument that abortion kills *persons*. The term *person*, be held, escapes definition. It is, as some hold, a verbal fiction, and the only way to know what a person is, is to define the term legally. Such a perspective means that people of any age or race can be declared non-persons and denied the right to life. Charles Rice, a professor of law, has called attention to the fact that the legal groundwork for such a step has already been laid.

In one sense, the Berkeley man was right. If we do not know God as the supreme Person, we have no grounds for defining anyone as a person. We then become simply a fortuitous concourse of atoms, coming from nowhere and going nowhere. Then too life is simply an epiphenomenon, not a reality.

There can thus be no medical ethics if there are no Biblical ethics. If we undermine God's law-word, we undermine all areas of life and thought, and every vocation. To restore and improve medical ethics, we must restore and develop Biblical ethics, God's law-word, within the realm of the church. The church is where the crisis began, and the church is where we must begin the restoration.

CHALCEDON MEDICAL REPORT NO. 12
Medicine's Mechanical Model

Every area of life and study has its presuppositions, its starting points. Whether it be science or politics, certain axioms or paradigms of thought form the premise of all life, study, and research. A false premise can become progressively more dangerous for men and nations. It is thus essential that presuppositions, paradigms or axioms be analyzed, to determine whether or not they are true or false.

The medical model of Western Culture is centuries old. Its roots are in Greco-Roman thought, in paganism, and, although Christian influences are present and at times have been strong, the pagan element is now dominant.

Dr. Magnus Verbrugge, M.D., in *Alive* (Ross House Books), has shown how costly it is for science to bypass the Biblical view of life. Scripture tells us that God created man our of "the dust of the ground," and by the miracle of His ordination, man "*became* a living soul" (Gen. 2:7). The word soul means *life* or *living being*, not the Greek idea of spirit. The key to the definition of man is not material or immaterial but life. Man is created life, and, if he separates himself from God by sin, he dies (Gen. 2:17). Our Lord says, "I am the resurrection and the life: he that believeth on Me, though he die, yet shall he live; and whosoever liveth and believeth on Me shall never die" (John 11:25-26).

Life is thus a religious fact, inescapably so. To forget this is dangerous.

The pagan, *mechanical* model does ignore this fact. In my student days, textbooks declared consciousness to be an "epiphenomenon" and dismissed it together with the fact of life as vague, imprecise, and non-scientific questions. The implications for medicine from the time of the Greeks have been very serious and are now becoming deadly.

The *mechanical* model sees the body as a material and even mechanistic thing. We all know how to deal with mechanical things to some degree. An automobile will not run without gasoline, so we add gasoline, an all is well. When it requires oil, we add oil lest the motor burn up. When mechanical parts wear out or malfunction, we exchange them for new parts.

This is the dream and concept which governs much of modern medicine. It also governs fiction and films. A few years ago, a popular television series, featured a bionic man; when his parts malfunctioned, he went to a medical "shop" to have them repaired or replaced. This is, of course, a silly dream. All of us, as we get older, become partially "bionic" as we wear spectacles or glasses to see better, or a hearing aid to hear better, or even a wig or toupee to look better! But no man in his right mind prefers his "bionic parts" to the living parts he was born with.

There is however, much, much more to the mechanical model than this. The mechanical model produces not only a distorted medical practice but a dangerous one. The idea of man being a person created in the image of God is bypassed. Life is no longer seen as a religious fact but a legal definition, as Dr. Charles Rice has pointed out. In matters of abortion, the courts now determine what constitutes a person, and an unborn child is now not legally a person: he is defined as a piece of tissue. Many millions of people affirm this, and they are logical, given the presuppositions of modern thought. Only because they are the creation of God does their conscience still trouble them.

Because of the mechanical model, euthanasia is now practiced in many parts of the world. The elderly are seen as old, worn-out models, now useless, and fit only for the human junk-pile. Given their presuppositions, i.e., the mechanical model, this idea is logical.

At the same time, medical practice is pursuing this mechanical model with intense zeal. The spare parts idea is cultivated - aborted babies are a source of raw materials and the dying are cannibalized for spare organs. Both the moral factor and the fact that the body works to reject these alien parts are sidestepped. Somehow the spare parts idea is going to be made to work. There are hints here and there that this kind of medical practice is not the wonder-working break-through that the press would have us believe. In any case, increasingly, some people feel that they have a "right" to spare parts when they need them. (On one trip, I was told of the pressures put on some heart-sick and grieving parents to sign over their child's body for parts while the child was still fighting for life. One wonders: given the contempt for life shown by some of these medical men, can they be trusted with the life of a perhaps dying child whose "parts" can be used elsewhere?)

In the Netherlands, the elderly are increasingly afraid to go to the hospital, lest they be "put to sleep," or killed. In the United States, some older people are promising their husband or wife never to send them to a hospital if they become seriously ill.

This should not surprise us. Given the mechanical model, doctors and families will alike show less and less respect for life.

What is urgently necessary, therefore, is a strictly Christian model for medical practice. This will take time and serious thought to develop. It must begin with systematically Biblical presuppositions, and with humility. We have had non-mechanical models, such as holistic medicine, but these are still alien to Scripture and heavily influenced by Oriental mysticism. It is strange that some who resent any reference to the Biblical model are still ready at times to experiment with such things as acupuncture! They prefer any answer by man rather than one by God; the ultimacy of man's word seems to be their presupposition.

Time is running out. Given the mechanical model, what is to prevent some tyrants from declaring various groups of people to be non-persons? Marxism and fascism have already done this, politically and medically. With abortion, the democracies have followed suit. Nothing is more foolish that to believe that either time or ideas will stand still. They move on, and the mechanical model in medicine means a variety of deadly possibilities. Today, most people believe in the medical model and are constantly "popping pills," taking drugs, as the answer to their problems. They believe that adding some pills to their system will be like putting gasoline in a car-tank; it will make them go. Many *demand* pills from their weary doctors in the confidence that some additive to their inner machinery will solve their problems.

Of such illusions are evils and tyrannies made!

A SPECIAL CHALCEDON ALERT NO. 1
The War Against Christ's Kingdom

The destruction and death of the Christian faith is planned and in progress by our humanistic statist establishment. This is to be a destruction by indirection, i.e., by regulation, licensure, and controls. Step by step, the controls are to be introduced and extended.

Recently, the Ohio Department of Public Welfare published a new set of "Proposed Rules Governing Licensure of Day Car Centers." These rules propose to license and control all church nurseries, Sunday Schools, Vacation Bible Schools, "church-operated" day cares, and "church-operated" preschools. These rules would make the Welfare Department the governing board over all these church activities.

Lest it be assumed that this problem is unique to Ohio, it should be added that like plans are under way in other states. In one major state, a welfare department official has stated that all Sunday Schools will have to be licensed and controlled as child care facilities if even one child attended at any time without his or her parents. (The same rule would apply to a church service.)

But this is not all. In all fifty states, child control plans are being readied, to be introduced piece-meal in some cases, which undercut the family, the church, and the Christian School. The goal of these plans is religious, i.e. humanistic in faith: the purpose is to create a new generation. This new generation is not to be created through rebirth in Christ but by separation from the old corrupt generation and family, with its pollution of Biblical faith. In one state, "health" homes are proposed for all children, the implication being that the family is an unhealthy home.

This ties in with the recent insistence on giving recognition to the "voluntary" family, i.e., any group of lesbians, homosexuals, runaway youths, or a sexual commune.

The child control plan includes a two-year national service requirement of all youth, male and female, between the ages of 17 and 19.

The obviously *fascist* direction of all this is clear. Fascism is that form of socialism which retains the forms of freedom, of private property, and the church, while totally controlling every area of life and activity to accomplish the same statist goals of socialism. We should not be fooled by the professed horror of the establishment for Hitler and Mussolini. The fact is that the real patron saint of virtually all modern states is Mussolini.

Roland Huntford, in *The New Totalitarians*, describes clearly and accurately, in terms of Sweden, what this new totalitarianism (and fascism) is. The older model of the totalitarian state is the Soviet Union, a model in sorry internal disarray and decay. Its instrument of power was *terror*, total terror. However, with respect to its more able citizenry, even the Soviet Union is using the newer model, psychiatric brainwashing and punitive medicine (See *Chalcedon Medical Report No. 8*, and my article in the January, 1981 *Chalcedon Report* on the medical model versus the moral model in law). This new totalitarianism relies on a state school system to control and brainwash the people, on the medical model of law, on the regulation and control of every area of life while maintaining the form of freedom, and so on. It is the new totalitarianism, a development of the old fascism. All over the world, it is on the march, and one of its main targets is Biblical faith.

The church is being reclassified steadily in the United States, as a part of this control, as a charitable, not a religious, trust. The position of the Internal Revenue Service, and, for example, of the California Franchise Tax Board, is that the Sixteenth (Income Tax) Amendment ended the First Amendment immunity of the church to taxation and control. There is thus, it is held, no longer a constitutional immunity from taxation, only a statutory one, revocable at will. Since the Sixteenth Amendment made no exemption for churches, an income tax can be assessed against them if the state so wills (November 5, 1979, statement of the California Franchise Tax Board to Calvary Baptist Church of Fairfield, California).

As a charitable trust, the church would be required to drop all discrimination with respect to race, color, sex, sexual preference, or creed. The church, it was held, in the case against the Worldwide Church of God, belongs to all people, and its assets, funds, and properties must be used for all the people, not just the members or believers. This will mean integration: an equal number of men and women in the pulpit and church boards; it will mean the integration of lesbians and homosexuals into the church staff and pulpit. It will also mean equal time for all creeds: the church will have to give equal time to humanism, Buddhism, Mohammedanism, occultism, and more.

This *charitable trust doctrine* goes hand in hand with another doctrine, the *public policy doctrine*. This is held by the I.R.S. and various local, state, and federal agencies. Whatever is contrary to public policy is thereby not entitled to tax exemption, nor to a free exercise of faith, i.e., to any legal existence. Thus, if abortion and homosexuality are held to be public policy, no group has a "right" to tax exemption, or to maintain its legal freedom to pursue and uphold its "discrimination," but must assent to these policies. *No better blue-print for totalitarianism has been ever devised than this public policy doctrine*. It is with us now. There is a law-suit to remove the tax-exempt status of the Roman Catholic Church in the United States for its stand against abortion.

In other words, this is total war, and we had better believe it, and make our stand.

Together with all this, there is a campaign under way to give a new meaning to the First Amendment and the separation of church and state. Almost every day, the press carries attacks on the recent role of the church on the political scene. It is plainly stated that tax exemption requires silence on the part of the church, and that separation of church and state requires no comment on anything political by the church.

The fact is that the purpose of the First Amendment was to keep the church free to exercise its prophetic role with respect to the state and other areas of life. The clergy demanded the First Amendment because they knew that an established church is a controlled church; a controlled church is a silent church, and usually a corrupt one as well. The election sermon was then a routine fact before civil elections. The church was the prophetic voice of God, spoke to every area of life, including the state, bringing God's word to bear on all things. (See Chalcedon Position Paper no. 16, "The Freedom of the Church.") For the church to be silent is a sin, and it is a denial of its calling, and a forsaking of the very purpose of the First Amendment. The freedom of the church to apply God's word, God's law and moral requirements, to the state is necessary for the health and welfare of the state and society. Today, as in ancient Israel and Judah, where evil rulers sought to silence the voice of the prophets, so now evil and anti-Christian rulers again seek to silence the prophetic word of God, and the church, the ministry of that word.

To be silent in such a time is to deny the Lord, abandon the faith, and concede to the enemy.

Another thrust of statist action against the church is to limit the scope of the First Amendment immunity of the church. It is implied or stated that only the "purely religious" activities are under First Amendment "protection." This is very narrowly defined to mean little more than the liturgy of worship. The Christian School is called "educational." So too is the Sunday School. But it does not stop there. It has been implied that the sermon too is "educational!" This would remove all of these from any immunity from control.

This is, of course, the goal: *control*. Let us remember that more people are in church on any given Sunday in the United States than have ever voted in a national election. These people are a tremendous and potential source of power. That power began to manifest itself in the 1980 U.S. election. It promises to do more in 1982. This can spell the death of humanistic statism.

But this is not all. We may not agree with all the preaching on radio and television, but we do know this, there is a great deal of it! The preaching congregation is thus far, far greater than the very considerable number who are in church. It includes millions more, and many of these listen daily. This is a frightening fact to the enemy.

It should not surprise us that the 1980 election was preceded and followed by a very extensive newspaper and magazine attack on the church. Ironically, the church was portrayed as the new fascism by these champions of fascism! Such publications as *Playboy* and *Penthouse* joined in the attack, as did former Senator McGovern.

The saddest part of the story is the role of the pietists in the church. The more serious the battle becomes, the more they avoid it. Their idea of moral courage is to attack all those who are fighting for the freedom of the faith. These men seem to believe that spiritual exercises are a substitute for the obedience of faith. They try to vindicate their position, and their flight from battle, by stressing their super-holy exercises and their refinement (not application) of doctrine. In some cases, these men will involve themselves in the battle--by appearing as witnesses against Christian brothers on trial. They do not hesitate to slander the men under fire, nor to cross over to the other side of the road (Luke 10:31,32); they want no "contamination" from the world.

The state is a religious fact. The state is, in fact, the oldest religious institution in world history. *Baal* means *lord*, or master, and Baal worship was state worship. *Molech* worship was a form of Baalism; Molech (or Moloch, Melek, Milcom, or Malcolm) means *king*; Molech worship, declared by God to be a very great abomination, is a form of state worship.

The state from antiquity has claimed to be *lord*, or *sovereign*. This is a religious claim. It is an assertion of divinity and ultimacy. For this reason, the early Christians refused to be licensed by Rome, which involved declaring that "Caesar is lord" or sovereign. Instead, they declared, Christ is lord over Caesar, not Caesar over Christ.

The conflict of church and state ever since has been over this issue. Wherever the state claims sovereignty, it claims, after Hegel, to be god walking on earth. The modern state is the heir of Rome and Baal-states in its claims to sovereignty.

The U.S. Constitution broke with European civil theologies by avoiding totally the use of the word *sovereign*. For the founding fathers, as John Quincy Adams later stated, that doctrine belongs only to the Lord God of Hosts, not to man, nor to civil government. The American civil system thus began with a religious rejection of sovereignty.

Nothing more clearly reveals the extent of apostasy and theological decline than the fact that almost no churches challenge the civil doctrine of state sovereignty as anti-Christian and blasphemous. Certainly, it is an example of the claim to be God; clearly, the attempt to control and govern the church (and to compel it to become an instrument of humanism) is something which should remind us of II Thessalonians 2:4: "he as God sitteth in the temple of God, shewing himself that he is God." Christ is Lord; He alone is head of the church; His word alone can govern and command the church. For the state to claim that right is to declare itself to be man's true savior and lord. It means arrogating to the state the prerogatives and powers of none other than Jesus Christ. For any churchmen to be silent in the face of this is a denial of Christ.

For the state to attempt to license, regulate, control, or tax the church in any of its activities is for the state to usurp the powers and office of Jesus Christ. We cannot render unto Caesar that which belongs to God alone.

We have slipped by easy stages into the compromise which has made this evil possible. The church, we have been told, must serve man; it must be "responsive to the needs of the people." The goal has been to make the church more "democratic," more people and experience oriented and less theologically and Biblically governed. More than a few churches have boasted of "serving the needs of the community." Having been long governed by man, and by man's needs, the church has trouble seeing any problem in being governed by the state.

Perhaps the most powerful (and evil) movement in the church today is "liberation theology," a form of Marxism. In the name of human need and hunger, "liberation" theologians seek to liberate the church from God and to enslave it to man and the state. Given this softening of the faith and theological mind of the church, the readiness to surrender in many quarters is understandable. Men who do not know the Lord will have no problem bowing down before, or surrendering the church to, the only lord they know, the sovereign or Baal state. Before Gideon could free Israel, he had to reject Baalism (Judges 5:25).

In the Ohio situation, the Proposed Rules to control Sunday Schools, etc., exceed the statutory authority given to the Ohio Welfare Department. The same situation prevails in numerous other states. As a witness for Christian Schools, churches, and other Christian agencies, I have seen state officials acting with little regard for, and often little knowledge of, their own department's code, as established by the state (or federal) government. Their very obvious position is this: they see their office as a blank check to exercise total power. They thereby plainly assume the sovereignty of the state. Any resistance to them is seen by them as evidence of evil intent. These officials immediately assume dark and evil motives on the part of the resisting Christians: illegal goals, financial mismanagement, abuse of trust, and so on and on. A servile press, which depends on statist news handouts for its materials, echoes these charges with impunity.

There is no way out of this solution except with the Lord. He alone can triumph. The time has come to attack the very gates of hell: they cannot prevail, or hold out, against our King (Matt. 16:18).

A SPECIAL CHALCEDON ALERT NO. 2
Humanism and Christ's Kingdom

In January, 1982, President Reagan introduced a bill into Congress to control ostensible racism in Christian Schools, and to control the churches of which these schools are a part. No more evidence of "racism" was shown than two cases out of 538 investigations by the Internal Revenue Service. All the same, many thousands of institutions were to be radically controlled by the bill.

By March, 1982, the president's bill was apparently virtually dead, but not the impetus behind it. Some states saw the introduction of similar measures, as well as other bills to place all Christian Schools under state departments of public instruction. In one major state, a bill was introduced to give the state sole and exclusive control over all instruction and all instructional programs. The state Department of Public instruction, in its analysis of the bill, stated the following: "Instruction includes teaching, educational counseling, the rendering of advice on educational matters, or any other process by which knowledge is attempted to be imparted to any person by another. 'Instruction elsewhere than school' means the instruction of any person of compulsory attendance age which regularly occurs outside of a public school and other than as authorized or provided under the auspices of a school district pursuant to statute."

Consider the implications of this measure. Any non-state approved regular teaching of children ages 5 to 18 would be illegal unless licensed, regulated, and controlled by the state department of education! This would include Sunday School; church services attended by those aged 5 to 18; nightly family Bible readings, teaching, and prayer; Christian Schools, and more. At least one other state is trying to gain most of these powers by fiat regulation; at least one or more are planning to do the same, and courts in many states are asserting the same powers.

The argument of many congressmen and senators who have defended the president's bill is (1) that tax exemption is not a privilege but a subsidy, and (2) activities contrary to public policy are not entitled to tax exemption. Both arguments are totalitarian and fascistic. The next logical step from these premises is to deny freedom to anyone who holds to opinions, or is active in matters, contrary to public policy, whether or not the activists are tax exempt.

Religious freedom is not a grant from the state but the affirmation of the sovereignty of God, not the state. We are not "one nation under God" if the state can control religion. From the days of the early church, Christians have fought for freedom from state controls because Jesus Christ is Lord or Sovereign, and Christ is Lord over Caesar, not Caesar over Christ. That victory is now in jeopardy.

It is in jeopardy from two sources, first, from the assaults of humanistic statism, and, second, from churchmen whose voices always trumpet retreat and surrender.

One prominent man is justifying surrender to state licensure on the grounds of Acts 21:40; Paul, after the mob scene in the Temple, was taken into custody by the Roman captain. Paul asked for permission to speak to the crowd, identifying himself as "a Jew of Tarsus, a city in Cilicia, a citizen of no mean city" (Acts 21:39). To be a citizen of Tarsus meant that one belonged to an old aristocracy, with full burgess rights, which were respected in Rome. (See W. K. Ramsay: *The Cities of St. Paul*, p. 174ff; 1907.) This fact would have made the captain ready to be agreeable. Paul, however, may have meant that he was a citizen of Rome, which he was, a point the captain missed, to his later dismay. (See R.C.H. Lenski: *Interpretation of the Acts of the Apostles*, pp. 896 ff.; 1944.) Then, we are told, the captain gave "license" to speak, according to the King James Version; the word translated as "license" is the Greek *epitrepo*, to allow, let, or permit; it has no reference to formal licensure, and a military captain had no such power to license. That a man of learning would offer such a "justification" for licensure and surrender indicates in him and those who follow him an amazing intellectual prostitution and cowardice. These men refuse to comment on the many texts which tell us, as Acts 5:29 does, "We ought to obey God rather than men."

Meanwhile, one of the clearest indications of God's grace to the United States is that He is raising up an increasing number of men, all over the country, who will not surrender to Caesar. More than a few have paid or are paying a price for this. On February 18. 1982, in Nebraska, District Judge Raymond Case sentenced Pastor Everett Siliven of the Faith Baptist Church, Louisville, Nebraska, to a four month prison sentence on a contempt of court hearing. Pastor Siliven had refused to allow the church's school ministry to be licensed and controlled by the state.

What we are seeing all over the world is the rise of *fascism*. Fascism is a form of socialism which retains the forms of a republic and/or a democracy while rendering those forms meaningless. Open socialism proceeds to the outright ownership, "free" elections, and like things. Benito Mussolini, the first fascist leader, was a Marxist who learned his lesson well from Lenin and his associates. The Soviet Union, more openly socialistic, all the same adopted the forms it sought to destroy. It called itself a Union of Soviet Socialist *Republics*, although none were republics. It uses the appearance of elections to ratify totalitarianism. It has a legislative body with no independent voice, unions which cannot strike, hold free meetings and elections, or do anything normal to a union, and so on and on. The Soviet Union has instituted history's perhaps greatest slave state (Red China is its rival here) in the name of freedom, and it presents itself to the world as the champion of freedom! Because all socialist states find it necessary to disguise their tyranny, they all become fascist in due time. A few Marxist journalists are belatedly waking up to this fact.

Like most modern states the world over, the United States is moving into fascism. Its excuse is the civil rights of people, the desire to further brotherhood, prevent injustice, and so on, the classic justifications for tyranny in every age. Limit freedom to gain worthy goals, say these apologists. One congressman has written, defending the president's bill, that the Federal Government must protect the "civil rights of all Americans, regardless of race, color, or creed," and hence controls are necessary. Presidential aide Edwin Meese feels that the federal government has the power to require, if it chooses, the ordination of women as pastors and priests (no discrimination), and of homosexuals as well; he does not believe this administration will take that step. To assert the priority of the civil rights act over the First Amendment means that discrimination in terms of creed can also be abolished; churches and synagogues will then be required to give equal time to all faiths, to humanism-atheism, Buddhism, Mohammedanism, and so on. In at least one court decision, this is implicit.

The New Fascism, more than the old, seeks to justify itself in terms of every humanitarian idea, in terms of social justice, brotherhood, equality, and the like. In the process, it begins by destroying freedom, and then all the goals it claims to seek.

The major beneficiary, and the one continuing beneficiary, of the New Fascism is the state, the modern power state. The champions of the New Fascism in civil government, the press and media, the university, and the pulpit are a self-styled elite who believe that their program of controls is the solution for all man's problems. They love controls, as David Lebedoff points out in *The New Elite, The Death of Democracy* (1981), because growth is free and uncontrolled. Risk, the entrepreneurial climate and necessity, is a horror to the new elite: they want a controlled world possible only in the graveyard.

Because the new elite distrusts representative government, it looks increasingly to rule by court fiats, and, as a result, the courts are more and more ruling the country. On top of this, "sweetheart suits" are increasingly used to sidestep any defense by the people. In a "sweetheart suit," one branch of the federal government, e.g., the Justice Department, sues another branch, e.g., the Internal Revenue Service, as the ostensible champion of some aspect of the non-statist sector, e.g., Christian Schools. The real defendant is kept in ignorance of the trial until a decision is rendered. All this in the name of human rights! This is the New Fascism, together with bureaucratic regulations.

Huey Long, when asked if America would ever go fascist, said, "Yes, only we'll call it antifascism." We call reaction, reform; we call slavery freedom; and so on. As Lebedoff says, "An elite is coming to power under the name of antielitism. Thus, every change in the rules was made in the name of reform. 'Openness' was the battle cry of those who closed things up. What the New Elite extols is precisely what it seeks to destroy" (p. 82).

Moreover, for the New Fascism, here as in Sweden (Roland Huntsford: *The New Totalitarians*, 1972), justice is now equated with legality. The presupposition of such a view is that the state is god walking on earth, and therefore there is no truth nor justice beyond the state, or the Great Society. What the state does is just, because there is said to be no God whose doctrines can be used to judge the state and its laws. At the foundation of the New Fascism is the denial of the God of Scripture and the assertion of the ultimacy of man (elite man, or the philosopher-kings), and man's humanistic state.

Such a view abolishes by fiat any higher law, and it denies any court higher than man's court. The denial of any law, of God, and of any court above man and the state is the foundation of tyranny. Statist fiats are then both law and justice. The vital nerve of resistance to evil, the faith in a higher good, the God of Scripture, is then cut, and darkness settles over the land.

Crime then ceases to be sin but becomes social deviation, a refusal to bow down to the modern Baal, the state. Then too the state, without God, ceases to be what St. Paul tells us God ordains it to be, a terror to evil-doers (Rom. 13:3,4), and becomes instead a terror to the godly. The state asserts and equates its control with justice, when Scripture tells us that it is God's law-word which is alone justice. St Augustine saw clearly, in *The City of God*, that a state without God, and submission to Him, is simply a larger criminal gang or syndicate.

The modern state is less and less a terror to evil-doers, more and more a threat to the godly. In Sweden, according to Huntsford (p. 336), a state legal expert has said openly, "our aim is remove all traces of Church morality from legislation." The same goal is in evidence in one country after another, and certainly in the United States. Emancipation and freedom have come to mean to humanistic statism liberation from God and His word into the world of the tempter, every man his own god, doing what he considers right in his own eyes (Gen. 3:5). This new liberation is ancient sin and tyranny.

This decade will see this battle develop with force and intensity. There is no neutrality in this war, and Christ recognizes none. There was a time when the most common painting, reference, and designation of Jesus Christ was as Christ the King. The Puritan battle cry was, "The Crown Rights of King Jesus." He is the Lord, the sovereign, and we cannot surrender that which belongs to Him without incurring His judgment. If you are indifferent to what is happening to Christ's faithful ones, what can you expect from Christ the judge? We dare not surrender to anyone that which is the crown property of the King of Kings, and Lord of Lords.

A SPECIAL CHALCEDON ALERT NO. 3
The New Sovereign or God

The most common term for God in the Old Testament is *Lord* (*Adonai* in the Hebrew), and for Jesus Christ in the New Testament is again *Lord* (*Kyrios* in the Greek). It means absolute owner, God, or sovereign. In the ancient world, the state or the ruler claimed lordship or sovereignty; the battle between Rome and the early church was over this issue. Rome was ready to recognize any religion as licit or legal and give it a license to operate if it would declare, "Caesar is lord." The answer of faithful Christians was the profession of faith in terms of Philippians 2:9-11, that "Jesus Christ is Lord." This was the beginning of a long battle between church and state which still marks European history. The European settlement was in part an uneasy compromise. The church gained many of its claimed exemptions, but the rulers of the state asserted a sovereignty under God by grace. Thus, an English half-penny of 1966 carries this inscription: "Elizabeth II - Dei Gratia Regina," Elizabeth II by the Grace of God. The coronation service stressed the covenantal nature of her throne. However, even in the days of George VI, some of the coins, in Britain and the dominions, limited "Dei Gratia" to "D.G.," while retaining "Rex" (as in a 1944 half penny). Newer coins now omit even "D.G." God and His grace have been dropped as meaningless baggage even in a country heavily wedded to tradition and forms. (Thus, in the New Penny of 1971, only "D.G." remained. In the large Australian $.20 piece of 1981, not even this truncated reference to God's grace and over-lordship remained.)

The United States, ostensibly, was to take another course. The Constitution deliberately omitted all reference to sovereignty, and the prevalent belief was, rightly, that it belongs only to God. On the Jubilee of the Constitution, April 30, 1839, John Quincy Adams declared that the War of Independence had been a revolt against "the omnipotence of Parliament" to "the omnipotence of the God of battles." Of sovereignty, Adams, a Unitarian and a liberal of his day, said: "The grossly immoral and dishonest doctrine of despotic state sovereignty, *the exclusive judge of its own obligations, and responsible to no power on earth or in heaven, for the violation of them*, is not there. The Declaration says it is not in me. The Constitution says it is not in me."

Very early, however, John Marshall introduced the doctrine of sovereignty into U.S. Supreme Court decisions. Especially in the 20th century, and since 1936, the doctrine has grown rapidly to its logical conclusion. In the Bob Jones University case, this was very clear. We may or may not agree with the inter-racial dating policy of Bob Jones University: this was a minor and peripheral issue in the court's decision. The court chose to assert unlimited federal sovereignty: public policy, not freedom, shall prevail. If public policy favors abortion and homosexuality, then these cannot be opposed. Suits are already being prepared to destroy churches opposed to abortion, homosexuality, and homosexuals and women as pastors and priests. *Public policy* is simply another word for totalitarianism: it means that the will of the state is the law, and there is no appeal against the state, the new god walking on earth.

In a subsequent decision, abortion was held to be a human right which no law can infringe. As professor of law Charles E. Rice in *Beyond Abortion, The Theory and Practice of the Secular State* (Franciscan Herald Press, 1434 West 51st Street, Chicago, Illinois 60609, 1979; $8.95), has pointed out, the courts now define a person legally, i.e., whether or not one is biologically and medically a living human being is replaced by whether or not the courts define us as a legal person. The door has been opened, not only for abortion, but for the elimination of the sick, the senile, and all hated groups as legal non-persons.

Thus, in these two areas we have seen the First Amendment wiped out by a new doctrine, the mandatory conformity to public policy (implicitly for taxed as well as tax-exempt groups), and the right of the state to kill all whom it considers to be non-persons.

INCARNATION AND HISTORY
"He Whose Right It Is"
Delivered by R. J. Rushdoony to a Chalcedon Guild Dinner
December 8, 1974

The first proclamations of the coming of Jesus Christ go back to the very beginnings of history, to the birth of time. In the Garden of Eden, as sentence is passed on mankind, the promise is given of restoration through the seed of the woman, who shalt "bruise," or literally, *crush* the Serpent's head (Gen. 3:15). The coming of the promised Son is the institution of victory.

Later, the dying Jacob prophesied concerning the coming of the Son. Again there is the note of militancy and victory. The Son is to come through the Tribe of Judah, and Judah's military power is particularly noted. The great Victor of all history is to be born of warrior's blood. "Judah is a lion's whelp," Jacob declared, one who goes up, or grows up, on prey (Gen. 49:9).

But Judah is only a custodian of power, a symbol of dominion, who holds his sway until the Great One comes, He whose right is it. "The sceptre shall not depart from Judah, nor a lawgiver from between his feet, until Shiloh come; and unto him shall the gathering of the people be" (Gen. 49:10). Power must be husbanded for the Man of Power, Shiloh. The Jewish Targums paraphrase "until Shiloh comes," with "until the time when the King Messiah comes to whom it belongeth." The sceptre of power and dominion belong to the Christ, and the source of law is the ultimate law-giver, the Christ. *Shiloh* is a name of the Messiah, and it can mean "To whom it belongs," or "he whose (right) it is."

The meaning of the name *Judah* is, "God shall be praised." Jacob began his prophecy, "Judah, thou art he whom thy brethren shall praise." In Genesis 29:35, we read that Leah "conceived again, and bare a son: and she said, Now will I praise the LORD -- therefore she called his name Judah." The hand of Judah, Jacob went on to declare, "shall be on the neck of thine enemies," and his brothers would acknowledge his authority and power. As E. W. Hengstenberg declared, Judah would be his brothers' "forechampion in the warfare against the world, and God has endowed him with conquering power against the enemies of His kingdom." But the meaning of Judah is Shiloh, and in Shiloh dominion will be realized. As Solomon declared, "All kings shall fall down before Him: all nations shall serve Him" (Ps 72:11). David was equally emphatic: "All the ends of the world shall remember and turn unto the LORD: and all the kindreds of the nations shall worship before thee" (Ps. 22:17). Again, "All nations whom thou hast made shall come and worship before thee, O Lord; and shall glorify thy name" (Ps. 86:9).

The Messiah is the one to whom all dominion, power, and authority belong: He is Shiloh, He whose right it is. The sceptre of dominion is His, and He is the law-giver and the source of all law. His coming will mark the beginning of a battle unto victory against all who arrogate dominion unto themselves.

According to Numbers 24-17, a sceptre, the sceptre of world and universal dominion, rises out of Israel in the person of the Messiah. He shall arise to wage war against and to destroy all the sons of tumult (or Sheth, Num. 24:17). The tumult of the nations shall give way to the reign of the Prince of Peace, Jesus Christ.

Unto Him shall be "the gathering" or *obedience* of the peoples (Gen. 49:10). Jesus Christ has a title to and an absolute claim on the obedience of all peoples, and He shall establish this right by overturning all things that deny, neglect, or oppose HIM. The name Shiloh, He whose right it is, is echoed in Ezekiel 21:27, wherein God declares, concerning the ancient world, "I will overturn, overturn, overturn it: and it shall be no more, until he come whose right it is; and I will give it him." The whole of the Old Testament era is a great shaking of the nations, a shattering of the conspiracies of men against God, to prepare the way for the coming of the Lord. Now that He has come, the great and final shaking is under way. Its meaning, St. Paul declared, is "the removing of those things that are shaken, as of things that are made, that those things which cannot be shaken may remain" (Heb. 12:27).

Therefore, when Christ, the Great Overturner, was born, the world in the person of King Herod struck at Him, striving to kill Him, knowing that Christ alive meant the defeat and death of the fallen world order. Earth and hell joined, in the events of His birth, temptation, trial, and crucifixion, in a grand design to overturn God's plan, to shake God's eternal decree, and to establish their own pretended right.

The issue was joined: *Who is Shiloh? The whole point of the fall was that man said, I am Shiloh, I am he whose right it is.* This is and must be a democratic universe, one in which every man has the right to be his own god, choosing or determining what constitutes good and evil for himself. There is no paradise of man possible apart from this faith. On this premise, fallen man operates, and on this premise he claims autonomy, declaring his independence from God and man, from all morality not made by man, and from all claims of authority over him. And the result, from the days of the judges to the present is the same, whenever and wherever God the Sovereign King is denied: "In those days there was no king in Israel: every man did that which was right in his own eyes" (Judges 21:25).

So too the modern state declares itself to be Shiloh, he whose right it is. The modern state acknowledges no law beyond itself, no law-giver save itself, no savior beyond man, and no binding power beyond time and history. It sometimes disguises its hatred by a show of tolerance for Christianity, but that toleration is itself a form of declaring that Biblical faith is irrelevant. If the claims of Scripture and the God of Scripture are true, then there is no way in which men and institutions can sidestep the absolute requirement of total submission to Jesus Christ as Lord. Their option is only Christ or judgment: there is no life apart from Him, nor any order possible in contempt of Him.

For the state to attempt, as 20th century states do, to establish an order apart from Christ is to say that God is not the Lord, and that the universe is open to other claims of deity and sovereignty.

At the first Christmas, the battle was joined, church (the priests), state (Herod), and fallen humanity against the Christ-child. At the crucifixion, the battle continued, with priests, Sanhedrin, and Rome united in striving to destroy the King. In virtually every capitol in the world today, the battle continues, as new sanhedrins, called parliaments, congresses, national assemblies, and like names, seek to set aside and suppress the claims of Christ as absolute Lord and only Savior. The new Herods and Pilates seek sanctimoniously to wash their hands of Him, and then to go about their own great business of creating a paradise on earth without God, and the only result is hell on earth.

Gil Elliot, in his *Twentieth Century Book of the Dead* (1972), tells us that in the 20th century, the era of the triumph of humanism, between 80 and 150 million people have died in war and revolution, and their related violences, famines, slave labor camps, and the like. His statistics err on the side of conservatism; at some points, very able historians would even double the figures. Nor does he include other forms of mass murders, such as abortions. What Elliot does point out, however, is that every attempt to call some other era more bloody is untenable: "every attempt to do so shows the twentieth century to be incomparably the more violent period." (This, of course, does not deter humanistic scholars from viewing with horror the sins of Christian rulers in the past, while seeing all the events of the present as a prelude to paradise. But, as Solzhenitsyn observes, in *The Gulag Archipelago*, "pride grows in the human heart like lard on a pig.")

To the question, *Who is Shiloh*?, the 20th century rarely answers, *Jesus Christ*. Even among those who profess to call Him Savior, too few will also acknowledge Him to be the Lord. But, if He is not our Lord, He is not our Savior. Jesus Christ is not an insurance agent, writing out an insurance policy on us, and then making no further claim on us, as long as our policy is paid up with modest sums from time to time. He is Shiloh, He whose right it is, and He will not surrender His sovereignty unto any other.

Because Jesus Christ is Shiloh, our world is under judgment for refusing to acknowledge Him Lord and Savior. These troubled times should not distress or trouble us: they are evidences that Shiloh is at work, shaking the things which can be shaken, so that the unshakeable may alone remain. He will overturn, overturn our humanistic world, shatter its pride, autonomy, and complacency, and He shall reign in both judgment and in peace. It is He and not the world who is our peace. In the troubled world of His birth, the glorious song of the heavenly host was "Glory to God in the highest, and on earth peace, good will toward men" (Luke 2:14). The meaning of this peace, our Savior-King declares, is Himself. "For he is our peace, who hath made both one, and hath broken down the middle wall of partition" between God and man (Eph. 2:14). By means of His grace and law-word, all things are to be brought into and under His peace. His strong and calming word to us is this: "Peace I leave with you, my peace I give unto you: not as the world giveth, give I unto you. Let not your heart be troubled, neither let it be afraid" (John 14:27).

Christ's Birth: The Sign of Victory

One of the magnificent and resounding prophecies concerning our Lord is Isaiah 9:6-7: "For unto us a child is born, unto us a son is given: and the government shall be upon his shoulder: and his name shall be called Wonderful, Counsellor, The mighty God, The everlasting Father, The Prince of Peace. Of the increase of his government and peace there shall be no end, upon the throne of David, and upon his kingdom, to order it, and to establish it with judgment and with justice from henceforth even for ever. The zeal of the LORD of hosts will perform this."

Prior to these words, Isaiah gives us a perspective on the world apart from and in rebellion against God. It is a view of darkness, evil, gloom, and stumbling in the darkness of sin and misery. Isaiah's day was Assyria's day of power, and Assyria's threat hung over the nations like an imminent death sentence, The evils of history seemed only to be intensifying and the darkness deepening.

The origin of this darkness was the apostasy of the covenant people. Instead of being the people of dominion, they had become instead the slaves of sin. In a world of evil, the half-hearted and hypocritical sinner is no match for the dedicated sinner, even as today the inconsistent and masquerading humanists of the West are no match for the militant and more systematic humanists of the Soviet Empire. The triflers of Israel were no match for the ruthless warriors of Assyria. They were under the rod of their oppressors, but their foremost oppressor was their own sin and apostasy.

A victory, however, was in the offing, "as in the day of Midian" (Isa. 9:4), i.e., as in the day of Gideon. Gideon's victory was emphatically supernatural. The battle was the Lord's, and the battle cry was, "The sword of the LORD, and of Gideon" (Judges 7:18). Before Gideon could go into battle he had to recognize that the victory is of the Lord, and for His glory.

This victory is to be more dramatic: instead of a Gideon, it will begin with a child, a wonder child and a miracle. God the Son will invade history! "The earth is the LORD's, and the fullness thereof: the world and they that dwell therein" (Ps. 24:1). The earth and the peoples thereof belong to the Lord; they have fallen under the dominion of sin and are in rebellion against God the Lord. As King and Sovereign, He invades the world to recapture His possession and to make it again fully His. As against the Assyrian invader, another Invader is coming, One whose power created and ordained all things.

A male child shall be born, "a Son is given," the heir-Son of David, God's only-begotten Son. On His shoulder is the government of all things, so that all creation is in the hollow of His hand. This wonder-child's name is Immanuel, God with us (Isa. 7:14), and He is virgin-born, the new Adam and the Head of a new humanity to replace the old humanity of the fallen Adam.

Isaiah describes this coming king: He is the Wonder of the Ages, and the great Counsellor, the source of all wisdom and counsel, so that His law-word is the governing and true word for all ages and all men. This Son is also the Mighty God, the Everlasting Father, and The Prince of Peace. He restores peace to the world and reigns over it in peace as the great and eternal Prince and God.

Moreover, His coming is the beginning of His reign, power, and sway, for "Of the increase of his government and peace there shall be no end." As King, He shall establish His reign with Justice, and His law shall govern all things for ever.

Magnificently, this prophecy cannot fail. "The zeal of the LORD of hosts will perform this." Men of zeal are the doers of the world; their efforts are feeble and limited when compared with the zeal of the almighty and triune God. His zeal will perform the triumph of Christ's Kingdom!

What this prophecy tells us plainly is that the Lord God is concerned with more than the redemption of our souls. His work of salvation does emphatically include our salvation, but it also includes His triumphant repossession of the whole creation. With Christ's coming, death, resurrection, and ascension, God began the shaking of all the things which are, so that only those things which cannot be shaken may remain (Hebrews 12:26-29).

History thus is a great shaking, a continual earthquake. God the King so orders all things that men cannot rest in their sins. His judgments shake and shatter the nations in their smug self-satisfaction with their sins. "There is no peace, saith my God, to the wicked" (Isa. 57:21). The present turmoil of history witnesses to the presence of God the Lord. He is shaking and dispossessing the peoples of our time for their lawlessness. He who refused to spare either Israel or Judah, no less than Assyria, will not spare today an unrepentant Russia, Europe, or America. His judgments bring us closer to our triumph in and through Him. Therefore, rejoice.

Among the most beautiful and resounding words from the liturgy of the Presanctified of the early church are these concerning the birth of our Lord:

"The Virgin, today, cometh into a cave to bring forth ineffably the Word that is before the ages. Dance, thou universe, on hearing the tidings: glory with the Angels and the Shepherds him that willed to be beheld a little Child, the God before the ages."

"Prepare thyself, O Bethlehem, Eden is open to all; make thyself ready, O Evphratha, because in the cave the tree of life hath budded from the Virgin: for truly an intellectual Paradise is her womb become, in which is the divine plant, Whereof eating we shall live, and not, as Adam, die. Christ is born to raise the image that was formerly fallen."

These early Christians believed that Christ's coming had altered history and all creation: therefore, they sang, "Dance, thou universe!" Christ's coming meant the death-knell of the Caesars and Romes of history, if they refused to submit to Christ the Lord. In terms of Scripture, these men saw themselves as "more than conquerors" (Rom. 8:37), as victors over the nations in Christ, not as victims. Only such a faith could and did conquer.

Many of the errors, sins, and shortcomings of the early church are no longer with us, but neither is their zeal, nor their assurance of victory.

Whittaker Chambers, on deserting the communists to work for the restoration of the republic, remarked sadly that he had apparently left the winning side for the losers. Too many churchmen today act as if they too joined the losers in becoming Christians. Such an attitude is a denial of the incarnation and resurrection. They surrender what cannot be surrendered, the assured Kingship of Christ, and the everlasting increase of His government and sway. They assume that, because they lack zeal for Christ's Kingdom, the Lord too lacks zeal. But Isaiah tells us, concerning Christ's Kingdom and government, "The zeal of the LORD of hosts will perform this."

By and large, the humanist believes that, with respect to history, death ends all. Some humanists with occultist tendencies hold that after death we live as spirits in some vague and neutral realm. This neutral realm is an undivided realm and hence without heaven or hell, defeat or victory. All too many Christians are little better. History is for them the arena of retreat and defeat, and the world to come a retirement home for the pious defeated ones. (This plainly denies Revelation 22:3, "and his servants shall serve him.") Having no dominion on earth, they see no dominion in the world to come.

The glory of our Lord's birth is the glory of sure and total victory. The Virgin Mary, inspired of God, saw her Son's birth as the beginning of a great overturning: "He hath put down the mighty from their seats, and exalted them of low degree" (Luke 2:52). In the modern era, the kings of Europe banned the Magnificat from churches because of that sentence! The kings are gone, and Christ remains as Lord and King.

Those churchmen who would deny or abolish the note of victory are as foolish as those crowned heads of Europe, and they will join them in the trash-heap of history. Christ is King: let the peoples tremble! Let none dare deny His sway.

The joy of the Christmas season is the joy of triumph, the joy that the King has come, and He reigns. It is "joy to the world," because "the Savior reigns." Hence the summons, "Dance, thou universe," or, as Isaac Watts said, "heaven and nature sing." Again, in Watts' words,

> Let joy around like rivers flow;
> Flow on, and still increase;
> Spread o'er the glad earth
> At Immanuel's birth--
> For heaven and earth are at peace.

History was no picnic in Watt's day, but he knew that for those who are in Christ, "heaven and earth are at peace," and, as the people of Christ, we establish that peace on earth through our faithfulness.

How then do we become the people of the Prince of Peace? He is our Peace, and we proclaim Him as the Man of Peace. In Paul's words, "But now in Christ Jesus ye who sometimes were far off are made nigh by the blood of Christ. For he is our peace, who hath made both one, and hath broken down the middle wall of partition between us" (Eph. 2:13-14), i.e., between

God and man. The reign of peace begins with peace with God through Jesus Christ.

The establishment of that peace then is the application of God's law-word to every area of life and thought. God's law teaches us how to live in peace with Him, and at peace with our neighbor. It teaches us how to be at peace with the earth, by keeping God's laws in relation to it.

Because Christ is our Sabbath rest (Hebrews 4:1-16), we are able to rest in a restless world. We have peace in a war-sick age, because "This man shall be the peace" (Micah 5:5).

We have in God's law the prescription for the ills of men and nations, and in the incarnate Son of God the healer with power, who enables men to rise up and walk in obedience to His law.

The church cannot honestly celebrate Christ's birth, Christmas, and sing the triumphant carols, and then turn its back on the mandate to exercise dominion and to be "more than conquerors."

From the early church, The Order of the Orthros, comes this prayer: "By night our spirit watcheth early unto Thee, O God, for Thy precepts are light. Teach us, O God, Thy righteousness, Thy commandments, and Thine ordinances; enlighten the eyes of our understandings, lest at any time we sleep unto death in sins; dispel all gloom from our hearts; bestow on us the Sun of Righteousness; and unassailed do thou keep our life, in the seal of Thy Holy Spirit; direct our steps into the way of peace; grant us to behold the dawn and the day in exultation, that to Thee we may send up our morning prayers. For Thine is the might, and Thine is the Kingdom, and the power, and the glory, of the Father, and of the Son, and of the Holy Spirit, now, and ever, and unto the ages of the ages. Amen."

COMMENTS IN BRIEF

Capitalization Is The Product of Work and Thrift

Capitalization is the product of *work and thrift*, the accumulation of wealth and the wise use of accumulated wealth.

This accumulated wealth is invested in effect in progress, because it is made available for the development of natural resources and the marketing of goods and produce.

The thrift which leads to the savings or accumulation of wealth to capitalization is a product of *character* (Proverbs 6:6-15).

Capitalization is a product in every era of the Puritan disposition, of the willingness to forego present pleasures to accumulate some wealth for future purposes (Proverbs 14:23). Without character, there is no capitalization but rather decapitalization, the steady depletion of wealth.

As a result, capitalism is supremely a product of Christianity, and, in particular, of puritanism which, more than any other faith, has furthered capitalization.

This means that, before decapitalization, either in the form of socialism or inflation can occur, there must be a breakdown of faith and character. Before the United States began its course of socialism and inflation, it had abandoned its historic Christian position. The people had come to see more advantage in wasting capital than in accumulating it, in enjoying superficial pleasures than living in terms of the lasting pleasures of the family, faith, and character.

When socialism and inflation get under way, having begun in the decline of faith and character, they see as their common enemy precisely those people who still have faith and character.

How are we to defend ourselves? And how can we have a return to capitalism? Capitalism can only revive if capitalization revives, and capitalization depends, in its best and clearest form, on that character produced by Biblical Christianity.

This is written by one who believes intensely in orthodox Christianity and in our historic Christian American liberties and heritage. It is my purpose to promote that basic capitalization of society, out of which all else flows, *spiritual* capital. With the spiritual capital of a God-centered and Biblical faith, we can never become spiritually and materially bankrupt (Proverbs 10:16).

Rewards and Punishments

A common opinion in recent years holds that rewards and punishments represent an unsound means of dealing with children or adults. We are told that rewards produce an unhealthy motive in those who win, and are traumatic for those who lose. It is also said that punishment is merely vengeance. On these premises some educators have eliminated grading as well as other forms of rewards and punishments. This hatred of rewards and punishment is one form of the attack on the inter-related concepts of *competition* and on *discipline*. Whether in the spiritual realm, with respect to heaven, or in the academic world for grades, or in the business world for profits, rewards and punishment (or penalties) motivate people (Psalm 19:11; 58:11; 91:8; Matthew 5:11, etc). This motivation leads to competition and the competition requires discipline, self-discipline, discipline under civil and criminal law, and discipline under God (Hebrews 12:1-11). And a result of honest competition is character.

But some people object, why not by cooperation? Isn't cooperation a superior method to competition? But as stated by Campbell, Potter, and Adam, in *Economics and Freedom*, "in a free market, voluntary cooperation and competition are names for the same economic concept". Historically, the competition of the free market has only been possible where a common culture and a common faith lead individuals to cooperate with each other.

Men compete for cooperation in the confidence that others respect quality, and they constantly improve their products and service to earn that cooperation. Cooperation dies if competition dies, because then "pull" compulsion, and force replace the free, cooperative operations of the market.

Ultimately, rewards and punishments presuppose two things. First, they presuppose God, Who has established certain returns in the form of rewards and penalties in the very nature of the universe as well as in moral law (Exodus 20:5,6; Judges 5:20). Thus, any attack on the idea of rewards and punishment is an attack on God's order. Second, rewards and punishments presuppose liberty as basic to man's condition. Man is free to strive, to compete, to work for rewards and to suffer penalties. Thus, any attack on these concepts is also an attack on liberty: it is an insistence that a levelling equality together with total controls is a better condition for man than liberty is or can be. St. Paul declared, "Where the Spirit of the Lord is, there is liberty" (II Corinthians 3:17). God and liberty are inseparable. And liberty presupposes and requires free activity: it has its striving, its rewards and punishments, its heaven and hell, its passing and its failure. These are the necessary conditions of freedom. The alternative is slavery. Slavery offers a very real form of security, but then so does death and a graveyard (Deut. 30:15-20). To respect rewards and punishment, competition, and discipline is to respect life itself, and to value character and self-discipline. It means, simply, choosing *life*: therefore choose life, that both thou and thy seed may live: (Deut. 30:19).

Love Thy Neighbor -- What Does it Mean?

A familiar Bible verse is often used by many to justify socialism and to attack the defense of property as "selfish." But does the commandment, "Thou shalt love thy neighbor as thyself," call for sharing the wealth, for welfare programs, and for one-world unity?

The main Biblical passages explaining this verse are Leviticus 19:15-18, 33-37; Matthew 19:18,19; 22:34-40, and Romans 13:8-10. What do they tell us?

First, who is thy neighbor? In Leviticus 19:33-37, Moses made it clear that our neighbor means anyone and everyone we associate with, including our enemy, and Jesus emphasized this in the parable of the Good Samaritan (Luke 10:29-37) citing the Samaritan's mercy toward an enemy, a Jew.

Second, what does the Bible mean by *love*? The word *love* today is a term concerning feeling, feeling which is stronger than the "bonds" of law. The biblical word *love* "is the fulfilling the law" (Romans 13:10). Moreover, love has reference to the fulfilling primarily of God's law; it relates to justice in the Bible, and it refers to God's law and God's court of law. The modern man who breaks either sexual or property laws in the name of love is thus lacking in love from the biblical perspective for love "is the fulfilling of the law".

Third, what laws are involved in loving your neighbor? According to Jesus (Matthew 19:18-19), and again emphasized by Paul (Romans 13:8-10), to love our neighbor means to keep the second table of the Ten Commandments in relationship to him. This means "Thou shalt not kill", or take the law into your own hands, but must respect your neighbor's God-given right to life. "Thou shalt not commit adultery", means we must respect the sanctity of our neighbor's home and family. "Thou shalt not steal" means we must respect our neighbor's (or enemy's) God-given right to property. "Thou shalt not bear false witness" means we must respect his reputation. And "Thou shalt not covet" requires an obedience to these laws in thought as well as in word and deed.

To "love thy neighbor as *thyself*" is thus the basis of true civil liberty in the western world. It requires us to respect in all men *and in ourselves* the rights of life, home, property, and reputation, in word, thought, and deed. The biblical word love has nothing to do with erotic love, which is anti-law. Biblical love "is the fulfilling of the law" in relationship to all men. It does not ask us to like all men, or to take them into our families or circles, or to share our wealth with them. The Bible simply says: love friend, enemy, and self by respecting and defending these God-given rights to life, home, property, and reputation for all. Modern "humanitarians" are thus too often guilty of breaking God's law in the name of an anarchistic love. Biblical love keeps the law.

Freedom Under God

One of the great founders of the American system was the Rev. John Cotton (1584-1652), who made basic to colonial government the premise that godly law and order means *limited powers and limited liberty*. Neither man nor his civil governments have the moral right to unlimited power or to unlimited liberty. At all times it must be power and liberty under law, and, ultimately, *under God*. (Deut. 17:14-20; Proverbs 8:15, 16; I Kings 2:1-4, etc.)

But today we have demands for both unlimited power and unlimited liberty, which are mutually contradictory ideas. We also have the growing claim that liberty is not under law and under God but *outside the law*. There are those who believe that they can only be free by denying the claims of all law, and by affirming that true rights and true liberty mean a *freedom from law*.

The Biblical faith is that true law is a gift of God, and the ground of man's freedom (Deut. 16:20). Law is the condition of man's life: just as man physically breathes air to live, so socially and personally his environment of life is law, which the grace of God enables him to have and to keep (Psalms 119; Prov. 6:23). Man can no more live without law than he can live without eating. The purpose of God's law is life; as Moses declared, "the Lord commanded us to do all these statutes...that he might preserve us alive" (Deut. 6:24). Man was created and is saved by God to live by law, for its discipline is "the way of life" (Prov. 6:23).

Here we have the great division: Americans, reared for generations in the Biblical perspective, have seen freedom as life under God's law, but many today are asserting that freedom is escape from law.

The alternatives to freedom under God, to liberty under law, were declared clearly by Karl Marx. They are twofold. First, one can have anarchism, every man a law unto himself, with no law, and a total "freedom" from any responsibility to anyone. Second, one can substitute the state for God, and the total law of the state replaces the law of God. Freedom then disappears, and total statism or communism for man's "welfare" takes its place. This is a denial of liberty as a "bourgeois" ideal and a substitution of state-planned welfare for freedom as man's truer happiness.

Every attempt therefore to remove this republic from "under God" means that either anarchism or communism will surely result, whether planned or not by those who strike at God's place in American life. It is an inescapable alternative.

To restore true liberty, we must restore true law (Isaiah 8:20). The Bible speaks of "the perfect law of liberty" (James 1:25; 2:12), because it views God's law as the very source and ground of man's liberty. We must abandon the dangerous idea that freedom means an escape from law: this can only be true if the escape is from communism, which is not true law but is *tyranny*. The word *tyranny* is an ancient Greek word with a simple meaning; it means secular or human rule instead of law, instead of true freedom under God. The American system is neither anarchy or tyranny but *freedom under God*.

Socialism and Inflation Both Decapitalize an Economy

Decapitalization means the progressive destruction of capital, so that a society has progressively less productive ability. Decapitalization is the dissipation of accumulated wealth (Prov. 14:23).

Some of the potentially wealthiest agricultural countries are importers of agricultural produce, such as Venezuela and Chile. The fishing-grounds off the Pacific Coast of South America are some of the richest known to the world, rich enough to feed the countries of that area.

> Chilean fishermen cannot market fish properly and dump marvelous catches of fish into the sea, because they have neither storage nor

transport to take their fish to the markets. Thus, there is neither a lack of labor nor a lack of markets for the fish, but necessary capitalization to provide the facilities for bringing labor, produce and market together is lacking.

Much of the world is in the same predicament: it has the labor, the natural resources, and the hungry markets for its produce, but it lacks the necessary capital to make the flow of goods possible. Socialism tries to solve this problem but only aggravates it because it furthers the poverty of all concerned. Socialism and inflation both accomplish the same purpose: they decapitalize an economy.

Inflation succeeds when people have larceny in their hearts, and the same is true of socialism. Socialism is organized larceny; like inflation, it takes from the haves to give to the have-nots. By destroying capital, it destroys progress and pushes society into disaster.

As the products of capitalization begin to wear out, new capital is lacking to replace them, and the state has no capital of its own; it only impoverishes the people further and therefore itself by trying to create capital by taxation.

Abominations

The Lord God uses strong language throughout Scripture to tell us how He views sin. We must recognize that there is a difference between strong language and profanity. Profanity is a sign of weakness and impotence; profane men cover up their inadequacies by the use of profanity; they present a pseudo-manliness in place of the realities of quiet strength. God's strong language reveals His nature, justice, and power.

One such word is *abomination*, which appears repeatedly in the King James Version. It is a translation of several Hebrew words, all similar in meaning: *shehkets* means filthy, idolatrous; *towebah* means disgusting, abhorrent, idolatrous; *taab* means to loath or detest; *piggul*, to stink; *zaam*, to be enraged, to foam at the mouth; and so on. Homosexuality (Lev. 18:22) is described as disgusting, idolatrous, (*towebah*), and Leviticus 18:30 applies this term to the entire catalog of sexual evils and to Molech worship. In Leviticus 11:10,11,12,13,20,23,41,42, the term shehkets, filthy, idolatrous, is applied to forbidden foods.

Sacrifices offered to God in a false spirit are called an abomination (*towebah*); Prov. 15:8; Isa:1:13, etc.), and lying lips and false weights are so designated in Proverbs 12:22;20:23, and elsewhere with the same word.

Two basic stresses in the words used in the Greek and Hebrew and translated as *abomination* are that an abominable thing is, *first* of all, idolatrous. It is idolatrous because it is contrary to God's law. The Greek word for abomination (Acts 10:28; I Peter 4:3) is *athemitos*, meaning unlawful (*themis* being the word for law). Another Greek word, *bdelktos*, appears in Titus 1:16 to describe men who profess to know God but deny Him by their works; such men, Paul says, "Profess that they know God; but in works they deny him, being abominable, and disobedient, and unto every good work reprobate." It is this same word, in its nominative form, which is used to describe the "abomination of desolation" (Matt. 24:15), the epitome of false religion. In Revelation 21:27, all such are barred from the Holy City, the New Creation. Thus idolatry involves despising God's law and pretending to have faith while being disobedient.

Second, the words for *abomination* also indicate that there is filth, stench, and repulsiveness inseparably connected with what God abhors. Paul says, "Whether therefore ye eat, or drink, or whatsoever ye do, do all to the glory of God" (I Cor. 10:31). We cannot do anything to God's glory if it is not in faithfulness to God's law word. Scripture asserts the unity of things physical and spiritual, so that the unity of both is apparent both in faithfulness and disobedience. That which is lawless and idolatrous is also repulsive and filthy in God's sight, and it therefore should be so in our eyes also. God, who does not change, does not call something an abomination at one time and good at another. What disgusts God should disgust us.

The word *abomination* does not describe something which is "particularly offensive to the religious feeling," as one scholar has said, but something which is totally abhorrent to God. Different cultures have had different ideas on the subject. Genesis 43:32 tells us that the Egyptians would not eat with the Hebrews, "for that is an abomination unto the Egyptians." Herodotus said, "no Egyptian man or woman will kiss a Grecian on the mouth," because it was an abomination for them to do so. Differing cultures have had varying ideas on the subject, but our view must be Biblically, not culturally, governed. It is what is an abomination to God that must govern us.

Thus, when we encounter the word abomination in Scripture, we should take warning. God is using strong language, and He expects us to take a strong stand in obedience to His word.

Mild Atheism

In a thoughtful article Donald E. Demary wrote in the summer, 1982, *Asbury Theological Seminary Herald* on "Mild Atheism." Borrowing the term from Bryon S. Lawson, he defined worry, distrust, doubt, and a weak faith as mild atheism. Perhaps a better term might be practical atheism; at any rate, the point is a good one.

The term is a very fitting one for what we see all around us today. In late 1982, Pastor Everett Siliven was very much in the news; because he refused to allow the State of Nebraska to control the teaching ministry of the church of which he is pastor, he was arrested and jailed. At the same time, similar trials were under way, or decisions pending, in several other states. I was a witness at many of these trials.

The sad fact is that many of the fellow pastors of these men on trial did not stand with them. For a variety of reasons, they chose to separate themselves and to be critical. In some instances their fears of state reprisals were most evident. Now, let us concede at once that the state is very powerful; moreover, the modern state is especially militant, not in dealing with crime, but in crushing any threat to its sovereignty. There are very good reasons for being afraid of the state!

There is, however, a more serious consideration. However much at times we may be afraid of men, we need all the more to be afraid of God. We are plainly told by God's law-word, "It is a fearful thing to fall into the hands of the living God" (Heb. 10:31). If we are more afraid of men than of God, we manifest a practical atheism. The Bible tells us plainly, "The fear of the Lord tendeth to life and he that hath it shall abide satisfied; he shall not be visited with evil" (Prov. 19:23). Again, "The fear of man bringeth a snare: but whoso putteth his trust in the Lord shall be safe" (Prov. 29:25).

Some time ago, at a meeting of scholars attended by Otto Scott, one of the speakers was Dr. Milton Friedman, the Nobel Laureate economist. Friedman described the present time as a transition era, and he saw three possibilities for the future. First, "We seem to be moving toward a limping welfare state." Second, "We may go all the way to totalitarianism." Third, the powers of the federal government, "will be either cut back or spread;" any prospect of cutting is somewhat dimmed at the present.

Let us add a fourth possibility. Either Christians will apply the law-word of God to every area of life and thought and conquer in Christ, or, as salt that has lost its savor, they will be thrown out by Christ, "to be trodden under foot of men" (Matt. 5:13). It is Christ who pronounces and who executes this word of judgment. Practical atheism pays a fearful price.

This is why Christian Reconstruction is so burning a passion and concern with us. The Lord summons us to be either the salt and the light of the world (Matt. 5:14), or be cast out by Him to be trampled underfoot by the forces of judgment. When we are ruled by the fear of men, the Lord God gives us over to that fear in a total way: "And upon them that are left alive of you I will send a faintness into their hearts in the lands of their enemies" and the sound of the shaken leaf shall chase them; and they shall flee, as fleeing from a sword: and they shall fall when none pursueth" (Lev. 26:36).

When Franky Schaeffer produced the film, *Whatever Happened to the Human Race?*, the reaction of many pastors matched the description of Leviticus 26:36. They were already in captivity to the fear of man. What hope can they expect from God without repentance? There was obviously with each of these men "no fear of God before his eyes" (Ps. 36:1).

Few of us are naturally courageous, and natural courage or boldness is not the issue here, but faith and a holy boldness. We cannot have this godly courage if we do not pray for it and cultivate it.

We will be governed by fear, either the fear of God or by the fear of man. We will stand up to and deny someone, either God or man. Most of us dislike confrontations, but God requires them, and life is a continual confrontation with problems, with evil, and with opportunities. All confrontations are opportunities if we meet them in Christ, who makes all things work together for good to them that love him, to all who are the called in Christ (Rom. 8:28).

"We Have Met the Enemy..."

A man deeply concerned about all the problems of our times, spoke to me not too long ago. He was ostensibly asking me some questions, but, in reality, during the course of twenty minutes, he did virtually all the talking. However, it was clear to me that he was a part of the problem, himself a problem in every sphere of activity, and, at the moment a pain to his wife! All too many who bewail the world's condition are a part of its evil. As a character in Pogo said many years ago, "We have met the enemy, and they are us."

I was reminded of this recently when one of our Chalcedon trustees, Howard Ahmanson, passed on a very telling bit of data to me. It was this: the American middle class gives a *lower percentage* of its income to religious and charitable causes than either the lower or the upper classes. The middle class, in this analysis, was made up of all who receive an annual income of $25,000 to $100,000.

Those below $25,000 give a higher percentage of their income! Many of these as they move into a higher income bracket, begin then to give a lower percentage. Their middle class concern becomes material self-improvement, more ambitious vacations, luxury items, and so on. Our wealthier people give generously also, and they face a serious problem. They are continually besieged by groups and causes seeking their support. However, even if our wealthier people gave all their money away, it would only slightly affect the religious and charitable scene because there are not that many wealthy people with cash. Most wealth today is in buildings, factories, offices, land and the like.

Historically, the great social force for change and growth since the Reformation has been the middle class. Because of its numerical strength, (in the U.S., most people are in the middle class), its Christian faith and giving have made the development of missions, education, Christian agencies and activities, charities, and more, possible all over the world. Our present world decline is in large measure due to the retreat of the middle class into self-indulgence and minimal giving. When the middle class, c. 85% or more of the population, becomes self-indulgent, we have no future.

God has created and ordained two kinds of ministries. The *first* is the ministry of the Word and of grace, which is to receive our tithes and offerings. This sphere of ministry includes the church, its missions and educational work, charitable work, groups such as Chalcedon which seeks to teach the meaning of God's word for our times, and much, much more in the way of ministries.

The *second* God-ordained area of ministry is civil government, the ministry of justice: we have a duty to support it. We do not have many Christian leaders here, (nor in the church, etc.), because we do not support them. More than a few Christians who have run for civil office have told me how church people treat them. They are told, "God bless you, brother; we need men like you in government: I'll pray for you." At the same time, they will not contribute to their campaign expenses! Is it any wonder so few Christians are elected?

The Lord calls civil office a ministry (Rom. 13:1-4); will He not judge us if we fail financially to support His ministers? Is not our present condition as a country a sign of His judgment?

If we have fed and nurtured you with Chalcedon's ministry, *we should have your financial support, and the Lord God will judge you for taking without giving.*

If you want, need, and expect Christians to function in civil government, *then you must support them financially or be judged by the Lord.*

We urge you to increase your support to us and to other Christian ministries.

We urge you to help finance Christian candidates and incumbents. (If you do not know where to sent such support, drop us a note, and we will send you data. Do not send us such funds, that is, for the support of candidates: we are only seeking to be helpful to you).

The Lord God did not create us for such a time as this to indulge ourselves but rather to serve Him. Will you do it?

Community and Strength

Because man is a creature, he cannot stand alone. Neither economically nor socially, can man be a hermit without serious loss of his function and development. Communion and community are essential to man's growth. It is thus all important to make sure that our community is not a harmful or empty one, and that our communion is not in trifles.

Man's being requires communion and community with the Creator, the triune God. As St. Augustine said, "Our hearts are restless till they rest in Thee." Man's strength is a result of his relationship to God.

Modern man, however, has only a slight relationship to God. His "Christianity" is by and large a matter of fire and life insurance, not a community of life with God. Men today relate more readily to their fellow men, and they are far more dependent on this community than on God. They are more concerned about what other people think of them than what God thinks of them.

All this has consequences. We have seen, in many hijackings and kidnappings, the victim identify with their captors against their own family or country. They may be brutalized by their captors, in one case raped, and yet they will side with them in all too many cases.

This should not surprise us. If men do not have an over-ruling and governing communion with God, they must have, and will have, such a relationship with men. In our humanistic age, men draw their standards and laws from men, and therefore their basic community and communion is with men. It is only such people who can be "brainwashed;" in truth, "brainwashing" is a myth. It simply means that men without faith in God are dependent on and vulnerable to men and will be shaped by them. If the Lord does not mold us, then men will.

Communion and community with the triune God is established through Jesus Christ and His atonement. The day by day means of community are maintained by obedience to God's law word, His way for our life in communion. If we follow man's law as our way of life, it is because our community is with men.

This is not to deny for a moment that community with our fellow men is essential, but not on humanistic grounds. We have today a major communications gap among peoples, problems between the generations, the social classes, within the family, between employers and employees, and so on. If men are not at peace with God, they cannot be at peace with one another. The loss of faith in the triune God is followed by a loss of community among men. The rise of antinomianism is a symptom of a changed centrality in the lives of men: man's word and law have replaced God's. The "virtues" of too many churchmen are what James Saurin two centuries or more ago called negative virtues, i.e., abstaining from evil, when we are required also to manifest positive virtues. Moreover, Saurin spoke out against "mutilated virtues," i.e., a selective obedience to God and His law where we think He is 'worth obeying' and a neglect of other commandments. True virtue he saw as "connected by the bonds of obedience to the will of God."

Our Lord said, "My meat (i.e., my strength) is to do the will of Him that sent me, and to finish His work" (John 4:34). If Christ's strength came from full obedience, will not our strength and communion come the same way also?

CHALCEDON REPORT NO. 1
October 1, 1965

In this first Newsletter, instead of a report on activity, I want to discuss the significance of what you, my supporters, are doing.

Most of us know the Renaissance as a period of great art, promoted and sponsored by wealthy patrons who were the kings, dictators, and rulers of that era. That art was the beautiful icing on the Renaissance era: the heart of it lay elsewhere.

For centuries, the church had been the major patron of arts and letters, and a Christian culture had flourished. Emperors and kings very early began to subsidize contemporary thinking with this view. There were clearly religious and philosophical trends pointing towards humanism and statism, but it was the heavy, steady, and long promotion of these things by subsidy that was responsible for the rapid spread and victory of these forces. Europe has been steadily conquered by a rapacious and brutal statism; the Renaissance was a period of showy art, but, behind that facade, it was an era of brutal terror, an era that brought monstrous men to power, some of whom made the Borgias look pale by comparison.

Our age is seeing a similar development. The major and minor foundations have been extensively captured by the forces of humanism and statism, and a new age of terror is developing all around us. Scholarship, arts, and literature are being subsidized to serve the purposes of humanism and statism, and our schools and colleges have been largely captured by these forces, as have been most publishers and periodicals.

This movement has been a long time in developing: it cannot be defeated overnight. It cannot be defeated by short-sighted people who want victory today or tomorrow, and are unwilling to support long-term battle. The future must be won, and shall be won, by a renewal and development of our historic Christian liberty, by an emphasis on the fact: the *basic government* is the self-government of the Christian man, and by a recognition that an informed faith is the mainspring of victory. History has *never* been dominated by majorities, but only by dedicated minorities who stand unconditionally on their faith.

What you are doing, in your support of me, is to sponsor a counter-measure to the prevailing trend, to promote by your support, interest, *and* study, a Christian Renaissance, to declare by these measures your belief that the answer to humanism and its statism is Christian faith and liberty. Our choice today is between two claimants to the throne of godhood and universal government: the state, which claims to be our shepherd, keeper, and savior, and the Holy Trinity, our only God and Savior. You have made your choice by both faith and action.

CHALCEDON REPORT NO. 2
October 31, 1965

During this past month, in the course of my travels, I spent several hours visiting with an outstanding conservative leader, a man who is a major force in one of our most notable anti-communist organizations. In the first few minutes, he raised the question: "Do you see any hope?" Many ask this same question. I am reminded of the question asked of Adoniram Judson (1788-1850), pioneer American Baptist missionary in Burma. Hostile forces soon succeeded in destroying Judson's mission, his converts, printing press, and his possessions. Judson himself was thrown into a filthy Burmese prison, and, with arrogant humor, asked by a captor, "How are your prospects now?" "As bright as the promises of God," responded Judson, who lived to see those promises fulfilled in the success of his mission. Our prospects are also as bright, if our confidence is in the same omnipotent God.

The revolution of our day rests on certain anti-Christian premises: First, it is held that anything goes, because there is no God. No God means no law, and no law means that nothing is a crime, and hence all acts are equally valid. Second, by "outlawing" God and declaring Him to be non-existent, the revolutionaries outlaw the idea of good and evil. They are supposedly beyond good and evil. If good is mythical, then evil is also, and man cannot be evil! Therefore, whatever the world-planners do cannot be evil, because evil does not exist: it is simply either a successful scientific experiment, or it is a failure. Third, because God is abolished as a myth, the approach to man's problems must be scientific, that is, experimental, and man is thus the prime laboratory test animal. In school, your children are to be objects of experimentation, even as you are also by means of every communication media. There is no evil in such experimentation, since there is no God, but only success or failure. Fourth, every experiment, to be valid, requires total control of all factors. Hence, the scientific society must be totalitarian to the full measure, or it will not work.

The various phases of this vast attempt to turn the world from God's creation to the scientific planners' re-creation can be documented in detail. It has been done by the volume. The answer, however, is not in facts and knowledge but in a restoration of Christian faith.

Because God is God, and because He will not allow Himself to be dethroned, the scientific planners are doomed. This judgement is a certainty because God cannot allow sin to go unpunished. All sin is either atoned for, or punished. The question is whether we will be among those judged, or among those, the saved remnant, who shall undertake even now *the task of reconstruction*.

CHALCEDON REPORT NO. 4
January 1, 1966

Recently a very fine man, who should know better, sent me a statement containing his answer to the rising tide of evil: "Let's pray about it." I believe that such statements are blasphemous. We are commanded in Scripture to pray, but prayer can never be a substitute for responsibility. If, for example, we refuse to work, and then we pray to God for food for our family, we are doubly guilty before God, guilty of improvidence and of blasphemy.

How then shall we deal with the problem of evil? Only God can change the heart of the wicked. We need to proclaim the gospel of Jesus Christ and His salvation, and to pray for the conversion of the unregenerate. Prayer here, if coupled with Christian efforts, is not only proper but absolutely necessary. But, while only God can *convert* the wicked, men have the power to *control* the wicked. And the means of control is a strict sense of law and order, of justice. But today the sentimentalism that parades as Christianity, instead of seeking to control and to convert the evil seeks instead to love it and subsidize it. The result is a destruction of civilization and harm to both the godly members of society as well as to the wicked who cause the destruction.

I was interested recently in re-reading a passage in a book I first read in 1957, and which was written a few years earlier. Felice Belliotti, in the study of *Fabulous Congo*, wrote (on p. 189):

> Like all primitives, the negro only recognizes force, and the result of a policy of gradual concession of rights is easy to foresee: as soon as he realizes clearly that no one can hang him or kill him out of hand and that the white men are incapable of casting the evil eye on him there will be no holding him back. He has no conscience, no western code of ethics to guide him in his actions, and when his heart is really free of physical punishment he will become a hopelessly intractable rebel.

The Congo is a shambles today, and the major victims are the Negroes, not because there are more evil men today but because good men have surrendered control.

Another illustration: In the 1830's, American ships began to suffer savagely at the hands of Malay pirates. One incident is especially memorable. Captain "Josh" Stevens and his bark *Aurora* from Boothbay, Maine, were becalmed and unable to sail away from the vicinity of an island. The Malay pirates attacked repeatedly, knowing the ship to be undermanned, and finally all but four men were killed. These four men, all wounded, escaped in the longboat, led by the second mate, Avery. Their only supply was a small store of water and dry biscuits. They could have rowed to a friendly island five hundred miles away. They chose instead to make for the *Polestar*, from

Rockport, Maine, under Captain "Hen" Crossley, a hundred miles away and no doubt becalmed like themselves. With only the briefest pauses, never wasting breath for speaking, the men rowed night and day until they reached the *Polestar*. Captain Crossley immediately sent men by longboat to Captain Edwards of the *Emerald*, of New Bedford, and Captain Nye of the *Southern Cross* sent 15 men, and the Emerald 10 men, to give a total of over 50 with extra weapons also loaned. The *Polestar* sailed to *Perang*, where Crossley, pretending that his ship was disabled, began "repairs," keeping most of his men hidden and his weapons concealed. The Malay pirates poured out in great numbers, happy to have another Yankee ship to loot. The climax is dramatically recounted by A. Hyatt Verrill (in *Perfumes and Spices, Including an Account of Soaps and Cosmetics*, p. 4f.):

> Onward came the Malays. Once again a helpless vessel was at their mercy. Once more they felt sure they could satiate their lust for white men's blood and white men's rum, and confident of victory, they dashed alongside the *Polestar*, leaped from their proas with savage yells, and swarmed-up the ship's sides.
>
> Not until the natives' heads appeared above the rails did Captain Crossley give the word to his impatient men. Then, with lusty shouts and curses, the fifty-three whale-men sprang up. With blazing muskets and pistols, with deadly spades and heavy lances, they and the merchant seamen fell upon the utterly astounded Malays. Turbaned heads were sliced from shoulders by the blubber spades; heavy lances were plunged through naked bodies by arms that had driven the weapons to the hearts of sperm-whales, broadaxes cut through limbs and skulls, and shot and bullets mowed down scores of the savages. Not a Malay lived to set foot upon the *Polestar's* decks. Not one who had attempted to board the ship remained uninjured to drop back to the proas. Dozens, terrified, utterly demoralized, thinking only to escape the fearsome weapons and demoniacal fury of the white men, flung themselves into the sea where they were instantly torn to pieces by the ravenous sharks attracted to the scene by the blood that flowed in crimson streams from the ship's scuppers.
>
> And when the occupants of the last two proas saw the awful carnage and heard the terror-stricken yells of their fellows, and hastily tried to turn back, Captain Hen trained his single cast-iron cannon upon them and sent a deadly hail of nails, bolts, screws, links of chain and other junk into them with terrible effectiveness. Not a single Malay ever reached the shore alive. Within ten minutes the battle was over. Without the loss of a man the Yankees had completely annihilated the natives and had exacted a terrible vengeance for the murder of Captain Stevens and his crew.
>
> As the yards were swung and the *Polestar* headed to the open sea, Captain Crossley gazed with grim satisfaction upon the carnage he had

> wrought. Spitting reflectively to leeward, he glanced at the receding bulk of Perang, at the drifting, shattered, corpse-filled proas, at the sharp black fins cutting the surface of the blood-stained water.
>
> "I calc'late that's what ye might call a good deed well done," he remarked to Mr. Avery. "Derned if I didn't say I'd learn 'em a lesson, and by glory I reckon I done so."
>
> He had. For years thereafter no Yankee ship was every again attacked by the natives of Perang. The mere sight of a weather-beaten, lofty-sparred ship would send them in terror to their jungle lairs, and for generations the islanders spoke in awed tones of the white devils who had avenged their slain countrymen.

There was no lack of evil in past years, *but* there was also no lack of control over evil. Delinquency, crime, and evil were major problems in the 19th century America, *but* the controlling forces were also vigilant. Today the rapid growth of crime (and subversion) is *basically a problem of the removal of controls*. Crime in the U.S. has risen 58% since 1958 and is increasing six times faster than the population. Significantly, in 1964, there was a deliberate assault on one out of every ten U.S. policemen, and 57 policemen were murdered. Even more significantly, 15% of the population are in the age 10-17 group, but this element of the population was responsible for 43% of all crimes against property in 1964. But this is the age group which should be almost the most easily controlled in a country *if* there is any sense of discipline.

Our problem is thus *not* evil as much as it is the *lack of control over evil* by the forces of righteousness. On the one hand, we have vast portions of "good" America talking about "love", which amounts in practice to a tolerance of and a subsidy for evil, and, on the other hand, we have other portions of "good" America whose answer to the problem is, "Let's pray about it." Because God is a righteous God, there is every reason to believe that such talk, on both sides, only angers Him and invokes His judgment.

A quick glance at the current scene easily reveals the causes of our crisis. The following item is important, with respect to the Watts "riots."

> A few Mexican-American "direct action" advocates are already saying that the way to get attention - and millions of dollars of aid - is to start a riot. So far this feeling is only in the grim-faced grumbling state. However, if all of the anti-poverty money starts flowing to Watts, another hot spell could mean trouble on the East Side. (Joyce Peterson, "Start a Riot -- Get $29 Million Aid," reprinted in Los Angeles *California Jewish Press*, Friday September 10, 1965, pp. 1, 5.)

We have two powerful forces at work to destroy law and order. First, we have subversives, who are working to destroy America by destroying its legal and moral structure. Second, and even more important, we have the vast majority of "good" Americans, who, by indulging in sentimental and unrealistic fancies, refuse to exercise the hard and necessary control over evil. And thus control must begin in the personal life, in the family, and it must be rigorously applied to every aspect of American life.

This is not a merciless attitude. True mercy can only flourish where justice prevails, whereas, in the words of Solomon, "The tender mercies of the wicked are cruel" (Proverbs 12:10). These "tender mercies of the wicked" are today cruelly destroying the fabric of American life.

We have always had evil in the world. We always will have it. The problem lies elsewhere: will it be controlled? Will godly men meet their responsibility to "occupy" in Christ's name and enforce God's law in every area? The world will either be under God's law, or under His judgment.

CHALCEDON REPORT NO. 5
February 1, 1966

One of the unhappy facts of our day is the gap between evangelical Christianity and political action. We have, on the one hand, those whose religion is politics; they expect more than justice from the political order: they expect salvation. A political cause becomes their religion. On the other hand, we have those who say that, because Christ is their Savior, they are not interested in the "dirty business" of politics. Both attitudes are clearly wrong and dangerous as well. For the Christian to separate himself from political action is to separate himself from responsibility, and to separate himself from responsibility is to separate himself from God.

What we have seen in U.S. politics is a departure from Christian American constitutionalism. In a very important speech, delivered on March 2, 1930, a prominent American declared that the Constitution gave the federal government *no right to interfere in the conduct of public utilities, of banks, of insurance, of business, of agriculture, of education, of social welfare and of a dozen other important features. In these, Washington must not be encouraged to interfere.*

He went on to condemn the idea that "master minds" or a brain-trust could be trusted with the powers of decision or regulation:

> The doctrine of regulation and legislation by "master minds" in whose judgment and will all the people may gladly and quietly acquiesce, has been too glaringly apparent at Washington during these past years. Were it possible to find "master minds" so unselfish, so willing to decide unhesitatingly against their own personal interests or private prejudices, men almost god-like in their ability to hold the scales of Justice with in even hand, such a government might be to the interest of the country, but *there are none such in our political horizon, and we*

> *cannot expect a complete reversal of all the teachings of history.* Now to bring about government by oligarchy masquerading as democracy, it is fundamentally essential that practically all authority and control be centralized in our National Government. The individual sovereignty of our States must first be destroyed, except in mere minor matters of legislation. We are safe from the danger of any such departure from the principles on which this country was founded just so long as the individual home rule of the States is scrupulously preserved and fought for whenever it seems in danger.

The Governor went on to cite the limited "powers delegated to the United States by the Constitution." They are, briefly, 1) the military power for the purposes of defense, 2) the treaty-making power, "and the sole right of intercourse with foreign States", 3) the issue of money and its protection from counterfeiting, regulation of weights and measures, foreign commerce, protection of patents and copyrights, post offices, and minor Federal tribunals in the states, and 4) the power to collect taxes, duties and imposts, to pay the debts for the common defense and general welfare of the U.S. The Governor added,

> *On such a small foundation have we erected the whole enormous fabric of Federal Government which costs us $3,500,000,000 every year, and if we do not hold this steady process of building commissions and regulatory bodies and special legislation like huge inverted pyramids over every one of the simple Constitutional provisions, we shall soon be spending many billions of dollars more.*

What was absolutely necessary, the Governor declared, was a return to basic principles:

> But what are the underlying principles on which this Government is founded? There is, first and foremost, the new thought that every citizen is entitled to live his own life in his own way as long as his conduct does not injure any of his fellow men.

Who was this speaker? It was Governor Franklin Delano Roosevelt of New York, criticizing the leftward drift of the Hoover administration!

Let us glance briefly at another speech, delivered in Austin, Texas, on May 22, 1948 by Lyndon B. Johnson:

> The civil rights program, about which you have heard so much, is a farce and a sham...an effort to set up a police state in the guise of liberty. I am opposed to that program. I fought it in the Congress. It is the province of the state to run its own elections.

Both men were right the first time. They sinned with knowledge and against knowledge. And this is not surprising. When men are without Christian character, they will choose the way of power rather than of truth and integrity. Where there is a moral disintegration, there is no assurance that an elected candidate will maintain a professed position. The number of elected conservatives who have switched sides is legion; they crumbled under pressure and under the temptations of power. There is thus little assurance that an election will gain any results, if there is no assured faith and character in the elected man. *And politics cannot produce character: Christianity must*. The decline of faith is a decline of character and a decline of character is the forerunner of political decay and collapse. Christianity has an obligation to train a people in the fundamentals of God's grace *and* law, and to make them active and able champions of true political liberty and order.

In 1776, in a letter to John Scollay, Samuel Adams wrote, "I have long been convinced that our Enemies have made it an Object, to eradicate from the Minds of the People in general a Sense of true Religion and Virtue, in hopes thereby the more easily to carry their Point of enslaving them." How much more true this is now of every subversive agency, and how tragic and desperately wicked that the churches are themselves a major force in working for this eradication of faith and character. And this eradication is basic to man's enslavement.

Am I advocating political preaching by the clergy, and is not this position too close to the social gospel attitude of political involvement? The answer on both counts is no.

Two similar questions have been received: What is the relation of clergy and politics? Should men in the pulpit speak out on social and political questions, and, if so, under what circumstances? Answer: The clergy cannot faithfully expound the Word of God without dealing with virtually every social and political question. The Bible speaks not only about salvation but about God's law with respect to the state, money, land, natural resources, just weights and measures, criminal law, and a variety of other subjects. The clergy are not to intermeddle in politics, but they must proclaim the Word of God. There is a difference: political intermeddling is a concern over partisan issues: preaching should be concerned with Biblical doctrines irrespective of persons and parties.

Too many clergymen are operating with a "shorter Bible", one limited to a fairly few passages and pages. One class of "shorter Bible" preachers are the modernists, who refuse to believe most of the Bible and limit themselves mainly to a few chapters, such as those that talk about love. The other class of "shorter Bible" preachers claim to believe all the Bible but they drop almost everything except passages dealing with the saving of souls. These men are too spiritually minded to be of much earthly good.

The excuse of this second group, who are Pietists, is that the law has been done away with by grace, and so there is no reason to preach the law of

God. This is false doctrine. The law is done away with only as an indictment against us; it stands as the righteousness of God which we must uphold. Every aspect of the Old Testament law still stands, except those aspects of the ceremonial and priestly law specifically fulfilled by the coming of Christ, and those laws specifically re-interpreted in the New Testament. We are saved from the law as an indictment *but* not to break the law freely. Is the law done away with and the Christian "free" to kill, commit adultery, or steal? Rather the Christian is saved to be able to live in and under God's law and the law now is written on the tables of his heart.

We are used to talking about the apostasy of the modernist clergy. Equally serious, if not more so, is the apostasy of the clergy who claim to believe the Bible but surrender the world to the devil, who refuse to proclaim the whole counsel of God to man.

The Bible is totally relevant to our world, and it must be so preached. Men are not given grace to despise the law but to enable them to keep the law. We have a lawless land because we have lawless preachers. The Bible speaks plainly in many passages on debt, theft (by individuals or by the state), on justice, and other matters. Is it not a contempt of God's word to neglect these passages? Salvation must be the starting point of all preaching, but, if our preaching be limited to this only, we are doing two things. First, we are, like the modernists, tossing out more of the Bible. Second, we are limiting God's word only to what concerns our own souls, a very humanistic emphasis.

An interesting aspect of colonial Puritan preaching was the election sermon, sermons on fundamental moral issues preached before every election to instruct people in the Biblical mandate. Modernistic social gospel preaching is relevant to our world, but it is anti-biblical in its perspective. What we need is relevant biblical preaching of the *whole* Bible, not only on doctrines or social issues of interest to us but on *all* that the Bible teaches.

CHALCEDON REPORT NO. 6
March 1, 1966

Recently, someone passed on to me a very interesting article. The November, 1965, *American Legion Magazine*, in an article on "The Systematic Terror of the Vietcong" by Deane and David Miller cites among the instances of terrorism; the execution of a farmer who "was 'tried' by a 'People's Court', sentenced to death, made to dig his own grave, shoved in and burned alive" (p. 11). This incident is a practical application of two major communist principles, the use of terror and the idea of making the enemy dig their own graves. The use of terror rests on both a delight in terror and a belief in its power to intimidate opposition. Making people dig their own graves is again a strategic tactic and an evidence of a vicious and incorrigible will to evil.

The question we need to ask is very simply this: Are we being misled into digging our own graves? The evidences indicate that we are and in a great many directions and ways. Our purpose now is to analyze the use made of one bulwark of liberty, whereby American indignation is turned against this bulwark to its own destruction. This is the Fifth Amendment to the U. S. Constitution:

> No person shall be held to answer for a capital or other infamous crime unless on a presentment or indictment of a Grand Jury, except in cases arising in the land or naval forces, or in the militia, when in actual service, in time of war or public danger; nor shall any person be subject, for the same offence, to be twice put in jeopardy of life or limb; nor shall be compelled, in any criminal case, to be a witness against himself; nor be deprived of life, liberty, or property, without due process of law; nor shall private property be taken for public use, without just compensation.

Our concern is particularly with the prohibition against compulsory self-incrimination. The roots of this Fifth Amendment are Biblical. Apart from Biblical law, all law has made legal the use of force to compel a witness to testify against himself. The result has been torture and terror, and the certainty of conviction, whether the victims of such compulsion were guilty or innocent. The Biblical law recognized voluntary confession, but, apart from that, conviction had to be on the basis of the testimony of two or three witnesses (Deuteronomy 19:15), and under oath (Exodus 22:10,11). An oath was a conditional curse, and the penalties for false testimony were severe, requiring restitution (Leviticus 6:1-6). A witness to a crime had an obligation to testify. "When a person sins by being adjured to testify and has seen or has learned of the matter, but fails to inform, he assumes his iniquity" (Leviticus 5:1, Berkeley Version). In other words, the witness becomes an accomplice by his failure to testify against the criminal. Two witnesses were the minimum necessary for conviction (Deuteronomy 17:6,7; 19:15). The requirement of witnesses were clear-cut: "Present no hearsay, unsupported evidence; do not cooperate with an evil-minded person to become a malicious witness. Do not follow the crowd in wrong doing, nor, when witnessing in a lawsuit, lean toward the majority to thwart justice; neither be partial to the poor man in his suit" (Exodus 23:1-3, B. V.). The place for testimony is in a court of law, not in neighborhood talk: "Practice no unfairness in a court decision; you shall neither favor the poor nor show deference to the influential; judge your neighbor with fairness. You must not go around among your people as a gossiper or take your stand against your neighbor's life. I am the LORD" (Leviticus 19:15,16). The witness had to be prepared, in a capital offense, to back his testimony by assisting in the execution (Deuteronomy 17:7). The Ninth Commandment prohibited false witness (Exodus 20:16; Deuteronomy 5:20, Leviticus 19:20). A perjured witness incurred the same punishment as that to which the defendant was liable: "ye shall do to him what he had planned to have done to his brother" (Deuteronomy 19:15-21). This was in terms of a major Biblical principle which sentimental humanism ignores "as thou hast done, it shall be done unto thee: thy reward shall return upon thine own head" (Obadiah 15; in the Berkeley Version, the latter part reads, "your doings will come back upon your own head"). In Jeremiah 50:29, we see this same principle: "according to all she hath done, do unto her." (cf. Lamentations 1:22).

The emphasis on honest testimony and the necessity for unforced evidence, i.e., not forced from the defendant but resting on the moral conscience of witnesses, was basic to the procedures of justice. The goal of justice was defined as God's order, and the true judgment is thereby the judgment of God: "You must show no partiality in your decisions. You must listen to low and high alike without being afraid in the presence of any man; for judgment belongs to God" (Deuteronomy 1:17). God's curse was upon all violators of their oath.

The establishment of these Biblical laws of justice and of testimony were basic to the American tradition and to the Constitution. The Constitution established the independence of the courts from political coercion, and of the witnesses from self-incrimination and the rule of terror and torture. We have seen the courts become major political instruments. Now the integrity of the defendant is under attack. If we are persuaded to weaken in any way the protection of the Fifth Amendment, we are being made to dig our own graves and to assist in our own destruction.

Some will immediately object, "But haven't the Communists made evil use of the Fifth Amendment? Mustn't we do something to prevent that?" Let us examine a specific case of such use of the Fifth Amendment. A minister was several times identified before a Congressional committee as a party member from the 1930's on. He had served as president of a party organization, and he had a long record of prominent membership in a variety of Communist front groups. The testimony on these things was clear-cut and telling, and it would have been impossible for the man to have denied the validity of a massive documentation. What was gained by putting this Communist on the stand? It was obvious, first, that he had no intention of confessing, and second, that he would sit there by the hour, taking the Fifth Amendment as his ground for refusing to testify. It was equally obvious that this man *wanted* to be on the stand. First, it gave him a national platform from which he could denounce the entire hearing as a "witch hunt"; he thereby took attention away from himself and the testimony against himself and centered it on the House Committee and its "persecution" of him. Second, by pleading the Fifth Amendment by the hour, he aroused the hostility of many Americans to that law, thereby contributing to the breakdown of that law.

As a result, other issues than the testimony against him became the focus of public attention.

What has happened? The courts have weakened or destroyed laws against subversion, while the Communists have made the Fifth Amendment a "dirty word" for many Americans. The answer is not to weaken or destroy the Fifth Amendment but to re-establish and enforce laws against subversive activities. Instead, such laws are progressively being destroyed, and the Fifth Amendment is under attack.

The Fifth Amendment is being breached from two directions. *First*, the Bureau of Internal Revenue requires the tax-payer to produce his records, i.e., to incriminate himself. Thus, a law which broke with the spirit of the Constitution as it was framed is now being used to destroy the citizen's liberties. *Second*, members of the criminal syndicate are being promised immunity from prosecution if they will testify against their associates (which would mean incurring death at the hands of their associates), and are being sentenced for contempt for refusing to testify. We cannot be sympathetic with criminals, or defend them, but we must defend godly law and such testimony is only technically not self-incrimination. Such a requirement weakens the force of the Fifth Amendment and paves the way for the return of torture and terror as the instruments of "law", and this certainly is a Communist goal. The courts are making it harder for law enforcement agencies to convict criminals legitimately. Are they paving the way for a demand for illegitimate demands and means? Is anarchy and disorder promoted in order to make us cry out for totalitarian force to suppress it? The defenses of the Constitution are being steadily replaced by the offenses of the totalitarian state.

The roots of this waywardness are in the religious apostasy of Americans. Their conception of law is increasingly humanistic and man-centered rather than Biblical and God-centered. As a result, they have no yardstick, no true standard of measurement, and they are easily misled. Isaiah declared of old, "To the law and to the testimony: if they speak not according to this word, it is because there is no light in them" (Isaiah 8:20).

CHALCEDON REPORT NO. 7
April 1, 1966

It is important for us to face up to the growing problem of *confiscation*, since it is an ever-threatening fact on the modern scene.

In London, England, a 10 year old girl was taken from her mother by a juvenile court. According to the Santa Barbara *New-Press*, March 4, 1966, "The child's only offense is to wipe her knife and fork with a table napkin before meals." Because the girl persisted, and the head-master barred her from "the school canteen," the mother "refused to send her to school." The child was then taken at once from the mother. Whether the child or mother were right or wrong is irrelevant: The central issue is the destruction by the state of a family. The normal procedure in such cases has been "a small fine." In this case, the state asserted its power to declare implicitly that any resistance to its will constitutes delinquency, and therefore the home must be broken. The state thus becomes the "true" parent of the child. The authority of the family is abolished by the authority of the state.

Another case: As a Los Angeles *Times* editorial for Wednesday morning, March 9, 1966, noted, "Last July the Department of Interior announced plans to offer recordable contracts to Imperial Valley farmers served by the All American Canal under which they would be required to dispose of holdings in excess of 160 acres. Now the department has asked the Department of Justice to file court action to enforce that limitation." This is the most recent development in a federal program which began in 1902. Its legal history is a tangled one. Even in terms of its own laws, the federal action is illegal. The purpose of this action is in effect "agrarian reform", the socialistic confiscation of private lands. Supposedly, the action is to favor small holdings, but no small farm is secure if the federal power to confiscate is admitted. If this step is morally valid, then the federal government also has the right to declare that a house with more than three bedrooms, or more than six rooms, cannot receive power until it is "shared" with someone else. The principle is exactly the same: it is theft by socialistic confiscation. The fact that the "law" is used to steal only makes the act more immoral.

In the Los Angeles *Times* for Thursday, March 1, 1966, President Johnson's call for "gun control" is reported. This attempt is to limit further the constitutional right to bear arms and an attack also on the right of self-defense. It is a step towards confiscation of rights as well as of arms.

The Whittier *Daily News*, March 9, 1966, reports Martin Luther King's confiscation or seizure of a building in Chicago. Assuming that the 81-year-old landlord, John B. Bender, who has been legally served notice to correct 23 building code violations, was in the wrong, King's act is still immoral. To seize a building and collect its rents is theft; what would happen if a John Birch Society leader tried to do the same? Would he be free to continue lecturing and granting interviews? But King has over 100 union leaders assisting him in his programs, and the "law" today is a respecter of persons: it discriminates against property and property owners.

The *Santa Ana Register*, January 22, 1966, "the federal government has used $188,000 of the taxpayers' money to set up a subsidized newspaper in Willow Run, Michigan, which, in the subsidized newspapers' own words, was to provide 'honest and true reporting (which) the government feels of interest'." Other plans have been announced for a federal government press. Public funds are thus being used to further statist control of communications. Freedom of the press is thus being destroyed.

Taxation is increasingly becoming confiscation. Many people who own their homes are paying what almost amounts to a rental fee in taxes. And the end is not yet near.

Confiscation, in a variety of other ways, is a political and economic fact or threat. It is inescapably so. Socialism offers people the promise of paradise on earth, but socialism cannot deliver on its promises because it is economically a bankrupt system. Instead of plenty, it leads to poverty. The Ukraine under the tsars was "the breadbasket of Europe"; today, Russia must import grain to avoid starvation. Great Britain was once a center of world commerce and a prosperous people; socialism has made the life of the average Englishman a poor one. Socialism is a parasitic economy. It must rob, it must confiscate, in order to give; it cannot create new wealth, but it destroys existing wealth.

As a result, socialism steadily begins to founder and falter and move towards total collapse. When this happens, socialism is faced with a choice: who shall survive, the people or the state? Socialism claims to seek the people's welfare, but, faced with the question of survival, it sacrifices the people. For example, inflation develops, and the state has a decision: sacrifice socialism and its money management, or sacrifice the people? Stop deficit spending, or control private spending by inflation, taxation, and regulation? The socialist choice has always been to sacrifice the people.

But no sacrifice helps to prop up socialism more than briefly. More sacrifices are needed. Instead of admitting gross error and, going out of business, socialism puts the citizens out of business. It confiscates by inflation, taxation, regulation, and finally seizure. The citizens, private property, civil liberties, all things are steadily sacrificed to make the continuation of socialism possible. The promise of plenty, which seemed possible in the earlier stages of welfarism, begins to give way to the certainties of disaster. As long as it can confiscate and live, socialism will confiscate and live. This is socialism's historic answer to its economic problems: *progressive confiscation.*

According to Psalm 24:1, "The earth is the LORD's and the fullness thereof; the world, and they that dwell therein." Socialism confiscates not only man's possessions but it strikes also at God's sovereignty over the earth. It is an attempt of men to be gods, to be the re-creators of man and the earth. And God is jealous of His honor and power. The law of God's creation is thus totally against the socialist planners, and they are therefore doomed to fail. Their "new order of the ages" is the repeated failure of the ages and the condemned order. Because socialism cannot confiscate God's sovereignty, it is inescapably doomed to failure and destined to collapse.

We are therefore clearly living at the end of an era. Socialism is finished, and no desperate remedies will keep it alive indefinitely. It has taken the world's economy past the point of no return and is thus headed for total disaster. What we face is the worst phase of socialist desperation to keep its failing order alive. There will thus be a difficult period of survival, and then the fresh air of God's free world. We must prepare for survival *and* for reconstruction. Important to such a preparation is a sound Christian faith, a trust in His grace and mercy and His providential care, a use of godly wisdom and common sense, and the confidence that, although the times are difficult, we are on God's side, the winning side. Basic to such a preparation is the creation of Christian institutions, godly schools and colleges, and a deepening of our faith. The socialistic revolutionaries of today shout, "We shall overcome!" but God, according to David, laughs and has them in derision, for the victory is God's (Psalm 2). Martin Luther commented on Psalm 2:

> "What a great measure of faith is necessary in order truly to believe this word: For who could have imagined that God laughed as Christ was suffering and the Jews exulting? So, too, when we are oppressed, how often do we still believe that those who oppose us are being derided by God, especially since it seems as if we were being oppressed and trodden under foot both by God and men?
> ...We should...fortify our hearts and look toward the invisible things and into the depths of the Word...I also shall laugh with my God."

CHALCEDON REPORT NO.8
May 2, 1966

I have been asked to discuss two subjects in this newsletter, debt and fear. There is a connection between these two things.

The world of the Bible is a very different one in many respects from the world around us, not because it represents a more "primitive" culture but because it is deliberately designed on different foundations.

Debt was as important a factor in ancient culture as it is today, and a highly developed system of commercial credit existed in the major empires. Assyria and Babylon, in fact, built their empire as Rome did later, in part on the expansion of influence and power through commercial credit. Before the Assyrian and Babylonian armies marched into an area it was usually already heavily in debt to them and its moral fibre was sapped through debt living. When the prophet Nahum wrote of Assyria that "Thou hast multiplied thy merchants above the stars of heaven" (Nahum 3:16), he used a word for merchant that meant a government agent who was a money-lender and trader.

The Bible shows no trace of any system of commercial credit because its perspective on debt is that it is to be avoided and is only a recourse for emergencies and special needs. Solomon stated the Biblical principle very briefly: "the borrower is servant (or slave) to the lender" (Proverbs 22:7).

Debt is a form of slavery; it gives another man power over us, it involves borrowing against our future, and thus it is not to be entered into lightly. To live in terms of debt is a way of life for unbelievers, but believers have no right to mortgage their futures or their children's future: their lives belong to God. Unbelievers cannot be asked to live in terms of this standard, since their way of life is different. Christians can therefore lend on long-terms to unbelievers, but, for themselves, the conditions are different.

Many passages deal with the subject of debt, but perhaps some of the central requirements are summed up most succinctly in Deuteronomy 15:1-6. In the Berkeley translation, used here for clarity and modernity of language, these principles appear:

> 1. Debts by believers are not to be extended beyond the sabbatical or seventh year and since they begin after the previous sabbatical year, are for six years in essence. "At the end of every seven years there must be a canceling of debts" (Deut. 15:1). "A foreigner you may press for payment, but whatever of yours was due from a brother (an Israelite) you shall cancel" (Deut. 15:3). Loans to fellow believers and by believers were thus limited to what could be payable within the six year spans.
> 2. The surest way to prosperity and to the abolition of poverty is the observance of God's law in this and every other regard. "Owe no man anything save to love one another" (Romans 13:8), "However, there should be no poor among you, for the LORD your God will abundantly bless You in the land He will give you to possess as a heritage, if you listen to the LORD your God and rightly observe all these commandments which today I am enjoining upon you. When the LORD your God blesses you as He promised you then you shall lend to many nations, but not borrow; you shall rule many nations, but they shall not rule over you" (Deut. 15:4-6).
> 3. It is thus clear that the Bible presupposes that the principle of blessing is not in any humanistic standard but in obedience to God. We are not to move in terms of human advantage but in terms of God's law. Thus, it is a real temptation to take advantage of inflation and buy on long terms and pay off with increasingly cheaper and more worthless money. This, of course, involves assuming that inflation will continue forever; it also involves a questionable moral premise, and, finally, it involves setting aside God's law concerning debt. A Christian moves in terms of God's law, not merely when it is convenient to do so, but at all times.

One of the reasons cited by the prophets for the Babylonian captivity was the popular disregard for these laws. As a result, when Nehemiah re-established Jerusalem, among the laws which he required the people to avoid God's judgment was the observance of the time-limit on debt (Nehemiah 10:31). (Another important rule, incidentally, was the prohibition of mixed marriages, Neh. 10:30). This law was for some time taken very seriously. In a work of Hebrew literature from the period between the Old and New Testaments, Ben Sirach wrote, "Do not be impoverished from feasting on borrowed money when you have nothing in your purse" (18:33).

The point of all this is that our lives must be lived in conformity to God and His word rather than in terms of conformity to man and man's ways. Our age is given to being group-directed, to being governed by what the group does or thinks. The Bible says, "Thou shalt not follow a multitude to do evil" (Exodus 23:2). Moreover, "The fear of man bringeth a snare: but whoso putteth his trust in the LORD shall be safe" (Proverbs 29:25). The latter part of this verse can also be translated, "whoever trusts in the LORD will be lifted up" (Berkeley Version). Moreover, our Lord declared, "Fear not them which kill the body, but are not able to kill the soul: but rather fear him which is able to destroy both soul and body in hell" (Matthew 10:28).

A great deal of nonsense is written about fear. One man has said, "We have nothing to fear but fear itself," implying that fear is an evil. Fear can be good or evil, depending on what it is that we fear. We are told that the fear of the Lord is the beginning of wisdom (Psalm 111:10, Proverbs 1:7,etc.). Solomon said, "Fear God, and keep his commandments: for this is the whole duty of man" (Ecclesiastes 12:13).

What is it that men *usually* fear? Men fear, first that which they neither understand nor can control, and which threatens their existence, or else, second, they fear out of a bad conscience, because they are afraid of the consequences of their sin.

Fear is a natural consequence of sin and of guilt. Solomon said, "The wicked flee when no man pursueth: but the righteous are bold as a lion" (Proverbs 28:1). And in the fourth century B.C. in *The Fables of Pilpay* it is observed that "Guilty consciences always make people cowards." Shakespeare in *Hamlet* (Act III, sc. i, 1. 83) wrote, "Conscience doth make cowards of us all."

The other common form of fear is in the presence of a danger which we cannot understand or control. Very clearly, our world today is seeing the rising power of evil men whose purpose it is to control us and to destroy us if we threaten their plans and control. It would be foolish understate or under-estimate that fact. On the other hand, we dare not over-estimate that fact. The world is still totally in God's hands. It is Satanism to believe that evil governs history. In the battle against evil, the casualties are often heavy, although the victory is assured. We need to ask ourselves: whom do we believe is the lord of history, God or man? The one we fear most is the one we believe to be in control.

According to the Bible the fear of man is to be overcome by faith in God. Of the man of faith, it is written, "He shall not be afraid of evil tidings: his heart is fixed, trusting in the LORD. His heart is established, he shall not be afraid, until he sees his desire upon his enemies" (Psalm 112:7.8). God knows our very real fears, but he summons us to faith, and to the confidence that He is God, the sovereign Lord of all history. In Revelation 21:8, "the fearful and unbelieving" are numbered with the most grievous sinners, "The abominable, and murderers, and whoremongers, and sorcerers, and idolaters, and all liars."

The word "fear" is *very closely* related to the word "worship", and this relationship is apparent in II Kings 17: 35,36, as well as in studies of worship. When we fear something, we are thus in effect worshipping it as either a basic or ultimate power in the universe, or as something closely related to that power. All duly constituted authorities are thus linked by the Bible to that clean fear, the fear of God and His orders of authority. Thus when we move in terms of the fear of man, we are in effect worshipping man; when we move in terms of the fear of evil, we are in effect worshipping evil. We are to exercise godly caution and protect ourselves against evil, but the object of worship must be the triune God alone. It is significant that in the Book of Acts one of the terms for Christians or believers is "one that feareth God." Those who move in terms of the holy confidence of faith are those who believe in God and obey Him. Let us believe and obey him in matters spiritual and material, monetary and personal, so that our hearts may remain firm, fully trusting in the Lord.

CHALCEDON REPORT NO. 10
July 2, 1968

Johnny Hart, in his comic strip "B.C.", had some interesting observations last November 4 on how hate can be successfully abolished from this world. The strip read:

"You know what I hate?"
"What?"
"Hatred"
"Me too!"
"Let's wipe out hatred"
"How do we do that?"
"Outlaw love!"

The reverse is equally true: if you want *to abolish love* from the world, *outlaw hate*. If a man truly loves a thing, he does not love its opposite. If a man loves his country, he will hate treason. If he loves God, he will hate evil, heresy, and all anti-Christian activities. If a man loves God's law and order, he will hate and resent all lawlessness. There is always an exclusiveness about love: love cherishes the thing loved and excludes its antithesis. Every attempt therefore to abolish hate by telling men they must love all things is an attempt to abolish love: it is a summons not to love but to hate. Universal love is an impossibility: a man cannot at one and the same time love Christ and love every evil and Satanic thing. Our Lord said, "No man can serve two masters: for either he will hate the one, and love the other; or else he will hold to the one, and despise the other. Ye cannot serve God and mammon" (Matthew 6:24). When we are asked to have this universal love for all things, we are asked to *tolerate evil*. If a man's attitude towards a criminal and towards a saint be the same, then he is saying there is no difference between the two; by his tolerance of evil he is discounting righteousness and acting intolerantly towards the claim of God that they who fear Him must depart from evil (Proverbs 3:7). The idea of world brotherhood means a world-wide tolerance of evil and a discounting of the good.

When our Lord asked us to love our enemies and our neighbors, he made clear, as Matthew 19 and Romans 13 reveal, that love is the fulfilling of the second table of the law. Love in this sense is the keeper of the law: it means respecting every man's right to life (Thou shalt not kill), home (Thou shalt not commit adultery), property (Thou shalt not steal), reputation (Thou shalt not bear false witness), and these God-given rights must be kept in thought (Thou shalt not covet) as well as word and deed. "*Love in this sense is keeping the law*, living by law. *In the modern sense, when we are asked to love, we are asked to set aside the law*.

When I was in seminary, most students were prone to use a little poem which met us on every turn. I still know the words, and most ministers, even the soundest; often err by using them. Edwin Markham's little poem reads:

> I drew a circle that shut him out,
> Heretic, rebel, a thing to flout.
> But love and I had the wit to win.
> We drew a circle that shut him in.

It is easy to confuse this sentiment with the evangelical "passion for souls," with the desire to redeem men from their sins and to make known to them the saving power of God. The Christian attitude is one of grace towards men, but a realization that, apart from Christ, they are lost sinners. Markham's attitude was that all men, as they are, irrespective of what they believe and do, must be loved. If you like Markham's idea, then invite murderers, rapists, blasphemers, traitors, and pornographers into your home. The result will be *revolution*, if practiced on a large scale, the overthrow of godly law and order and the corruption of Christian families. And *revolution* was what Markham wanted. He wrote the outstanding revolutionary poem of the 20th century, which many of us were taught in school: "The Man with the Hoe." For Markham, the worker is plundered, profaned and disinherited. Markham said that the rulers should either do something for the workers or face a worldwide revolution.

When whirlwinds of rebellion shake all shores
How will it be with kingdoms and with kings ---
With those who shaped him to the thing he is ---
When this dumb Terror shall rise to judge the world,
After the silence of the centuries?

In other words, surrender to or appease the workers, or face a world revolution in which the worker will be the world judge and "Terror!"

Where is Markham's love now? Exactly at its logical conclusion: revolution. Total love means a total tolerance of evil and a departure from God.

Then what about the verse, "Judge not, that ye be not judged. For with what measure ye judge, ye shall be judged; and with what measure ye mete, it shall be measured again" (Matthew 7:1). These words are from the Sermon on the Mount. Christ presented true righteousness as against Pharisaic self-righteousness, God's law as against man's law. We have no right to judge on purely personal terms. Scripture gives us endless laws and precepts to enable us to discern and judge between good and evil. We shall be judged, Jesus said, with "what measure ye judge." If our standard is God's law, then we have the defense and security of God's law, which has already judged, condemned, and freed us in Jesus Christ. If we judge within God's law, we have the protection of God's law; if we judge outside God's law, we have, not its protection but its wrath.

The heresy of love is a major menace of our time. "Love" is presented as another way of salvation than Jesus Christ. We are told that people are going to be made new creatures and changed if we love them enough. This is a totally humanistic plan of salvation. It makes man the savior rather than Jesus Christ. It is a departure from the faith. But the heresy of love sounds so noble and good that few see it for what it is: a demand that evil be accepted and loved and a revolution against godly law and order be promoted. The real result of these demands for universal love will be the death of love and the rise of revolution and the isolation of man into the faceless and silent proletariat of socialism.

CHALCEDON REPORT NO. 11
August 1, 1966

The August, 1966, *Farm Journal* has an important article entitled "The Wheat Shortage is Here," by Karl Hobson. Hobson begins by warning:

> The world shortage of wheat that I warned about in *Farm Journal* 2 1/2 years ago is now here and it will likely last a good many years. For seven years the world has been using more wheat than it has been raising. The has reduced world carry-over stocks by more than half. A

> year from now, these stocks will be small - and wheat prices will be still higher unless the government uses price controls.

The world production of wheat this year will be 6000 - million bushels less than the needed amount for world consumption.

> This is not a good year for wheat production. Drought is reducing output sharply in the U.S., North Africa, India, China and Australia. Poor seeding weather last fall held wheat acreage down in Europe.

But this is not all. Other reports indicate the serious nature of the feed grain shortage. More feed grains are now being used to feed cattle than has been previously raised in one year. Thus, cattle production is faced with a feed grain shortage, and, with the drought, a hay and water shortage. Cattle are being sold heavily, over-sold, because many ranchers are unable to carry them through the year. The drought in Australia is in its fifth year; the situation in China and Russia is very critical: food is a major problem.

But the nearly world-wide dry year and hot climatic conditions are not the cause: the crisis was coming already, and the hot, dry weather has only accentuated it. Hobson claims that "the population explosion is the chief cause," but this is hardly the case. The *population explosion is a myth*. Russia has not had a population explosion, for example, but it is in serious trouble. The Ukraine was, in the days of the tsars, "the bread-basket of Europe", today, it is producing poorly, and in some years has not fed itself. *The real problem is socialism.*

The correlation between hunger and socialism has been very well traced by E. Parmalee Prentice in *Hunger and History*. In an earlier work, *Farming for Famine,* Prentice in 1936 cited the four causes of famine:

> 1. The prevention of cultivation or the willful destruction of crops.
> 2. Defective agriculture caused by communistic control of land.
> 3. Governmental interference by regulation or taxation.
> 4. Currency restrictions, including debasing the coin.

All of these add up to one thing, *socialism*, and the root of all socialism and communism is *money management*, a managed currency replacing the free coinage of gold and silver. Long ago, Montesquieu in *The Spirit of Laws* (Book XVIII, chap. 3), wrote: "Countries are not cultivated in proportion to their fertility, but to their liberty." Today, as *Barron's* front page story on "The Third Horseman," December 20, 1965 stated, "Thanks to socialism, famine again stalks the earth,... Like a horse and carriage, 'socialism and hunger' inevitably go together." The picture is a grim one.

Regardless of climate and soil, socialism throughout the world has yielded bitter fruit. Since 1961, when the Soviet Union suffered the first of a series of 'non-recurring' crop failures, wheat shipments from West to East have increased from 165 million bushels to 750 million...Mao's agrarian reformers have brought Red China to the brink of starvation. Much of Eastern Europe, once a granary in its own right, lives off U. S. surpluses, while the fertile farmlands of Algeria, which produced so bountifully for the hard-working colons, have turned barren. Now the blight has spread to India. Starvation has already claimed its first victims...If present trends of population growth and farm output persist, concluded the USDA experts, India by 1970 will require fully one-half the US wheat crop to feed its teeming masses. The situation is now far worse than when these words were written last December. And it will get far, far worse before it ends.

Repeatedly in history, socialists (as far back as Plato!) have talked about birth control. The population explosion is an ancient *excuse* for socialist failure and a means of establishing total control over life, including birth itself. The persistent consequence of socialism has been *depopulation*, depopulation by two central methods. First, there is depopulation by the socialist terror, by mass liquidations. Second, there is depopulation by famine. We have seen, are seeing, and shall see more of both.

Will anything be done to prevent this? The answer is clearly *NO*. Our humanistic education has geared our generation to think in terms of a revolutionary doctrine of love, and to think well of all men, so it is impossible to shake the faith of the majority in the goodness of all men and especially of our elite planners, the philosopher-kings who will remake the world.

A telling account of our spiritual idiocy and susceptibility to evil was analyzed in *The Review of the News*, August 3, 1966, pp. 17-24. On July 13, 1966, a criminal entered an apartment inhabited by nine student nurses. Although he later displayed a revolver, he did not have it in his hand when he entered, nor when he tied up the girls one by one. Nine girls, screaming and clawing, could have routed him. The four Filipino nurses favored ganging up on the intruder, (they had time for a debate!) but the American nurses favored appeasement and won. They argued, "Maybe if we are quiet and calm, he will remain quiet and calm...We more or less have to trust him..."

Here in brief is the religion of love preached from our pulpits and the philosophy of appeasement practiced by our civil governments. As *The Review of the News* commented:

> Apparently, appeasement of criminals has now become a national characteristic of Americans, not only in dealing with the mass-killers of international Communism, but in dealing with criminals within our own society. The country has been so brainwashed, so conditioned to believe that all a criminal needs is a little love and understanding, that it has lost all sight of what the criminal mentality is all about.

Our problems are an outgrowth of humanism. Humanism is a philosophy or perspective which is dominant in our day. According to the *Dictionary of Philosophy*, humanism is "any view in which interest in human welfare is central." This is the *basic* definition, and humanitarianism is "any view in which interest in human values are central." The Merriam-Webster International Dictionary, second edition, defines "humanitarianism" in full as follows;

> 1. Theol and Ch. Hist. The distinctive tenet denying the divinity of Christ; also, the system of doctrine based upon this view of Christ.
> 2. Ethics. a. The doctrine that man's obligations are limited to, and dependent alone on, man and human relations. b. The doctrine of Saint-Simon that man's nature is perfectible through his own efforts without divine grace.
> 3. Regard for the interests of mankind; benevolence.

In all these definitions, one thing is obvious: *man* is central; man's welfare is the highest law and the only real law. Moreover, *socialism* (not only with Saint-Simon) is basically and essentially humanism applied to economics. Socialism denies economic laws; it plans to remake the world in terms of man's welfare as seen by the planners. It is a government of men, not of laws, by men, not by law, and society is placed under man, not under God.

A generation reared in humanism is bent on sacrificing law to suit the criminal, giving food to subsidize socialism; paying men not to work, appeasing criminals and Communists, and on pouring out its pity on the degenerates. Listen to this: J. Edgar Hoover wrote in *This Week Magazine* August 25, 1957:

> Recently many of you must have joined me in my feeling of sympathy for the Detroit father whose six-year old daughter was brutally slain by a sex pervert. This bereaved father said, "I can't blame the man as much as the society that produced him. It's a society that allows its young people to read and distribute the worst sort of pornography!" ("Let's Wipe Out the Schoolyard Sex Racket!")

With all due respect to Mr. Hoover for his great services to all Americans, he is here *dead wrong*. I have no sympathy for this father: he was as degenerate as that pervert. Instead of righteous indignation against a criminal who, according to God's law, deserved to die, he said, "I can't blame the man as much as the society which produced him." This is simply environmentalism, economic determinism, Marxism --- humanism. Man is not to blame --- his world must be remade to remake man. How can we defeat Marxism when fathers are so degenerate, and when the chief agent of anti-communism for the USA expresses sympathy for such a perspective? *We are far gone indeed.*

Will people ever wake up? Yes, when famine and death, economic collapse and anarchy, and the triumph of criminal anarchy drain every drop of stupid humanism and pity for evil-doers out of their veins, and *only* when they stand in terms of a world under God's law, for the rule of justice, not sentimentality.

Don't expect miracles, unless you believe in God. And if you believe in God, don't offend Him by expecting Him to bail out the very people who despise Him and war against His law and order: "ye that love the Lord, hate evil" (Psalm 97: 10). More serious than the wheat shortage is the shortage of true faith.

But, because the world is under God's law, the coming and growing economic crisis is a judgment upon world socialism and also its destruction.

CHALCEDON REPORT NO. 12
September 1966

One of the things we shall hear more and more about these days is planning. Master plans are either being developed for every community, county, state, business, and group, or else are slated for development. Hand in hand with this go plans for data banks, master files giving full information on every individual, organization, or group. Some of the statements made by the planners are alarming. Thus, Mel Scott, in proposing a metropolitan area government for Southern California, said, "One of these days there will be brought into being in this metropolitan region an urban resettlement agency...It should be the most unorthodox agency ever conceived and should be free to experiment with a great variety of services, projects, methods and legal powers." On the other hand, some planners are themselves alarmed at the potential menace in planning. Whether liberals or socialists, they believe that their planning is for the good of man, and the dangerous overtones of planning frighten them. Thus, planner Albert Mindlin has asked, "In marching courageously forward to a 1984 utopia, are we not also blindly paving the way for a possible 1984 Big Brother?"

The answer is obviously yes. Socialism rests on two foundations: *First*, managed money, counterfeit money, or paper money. Since money is the life-blood of economics, control of an economy requires control of money. When money controls begin, socialism ensues, whether it is intended or not. *Second*, planning is the next requirement. To manage an economy it is necessary to increase the controls over the economy, and this calls for ever increasing planning and finally total planning. To manage the economy, you must control and plan it, and the control begins with money and spreads to every aspect of every man's life.

Planning means several things. *First*, its goal is total control over man in order to provide man all the benefits socialism offers. For socialism to function, total control is necessary. *Second*, this means that there must be a *total plan* for man. We shall hear more and more about total planning. It is impossible to go to any corner of the United States and escape a master plan for the area, and for yourself. Socialism wants to save man, and to save man it must plan and control his life. *Third*, to plan and control man, it is necessary to have *total knowledge* about man. As a result, data banks and master files are being accumulated to provide that total knowledge about every man, community, group, vocation, and all things else.

A Marxist, Maurice Cornforth, in an important work, *Marxism and the Linguistic Philosophy* (International Publishers, 1965) has written, "The goal of socialist politics and socialist planning is, obviously, to produce an absolute abundance of goods and services, so that all that anyone can need is available to him. And, apart from obstacles of external interference, natural calamities and errors of planning, all of which are surmountable, there is no reason why this goal should not be reached" (p. 327).

In total planning, the state takes the place of God, and it gives us predestination by man, predestination by the socialist state, as the substitute for God's predestination. But, as Cornforth said, to accomplish this, the state must be free from opposition, natural disasters (which are unplanned, as droughts and floods always are), and also free from human errors. This is quite an order!

What happens in reality when the state begins to plan? The stronger the state becomes, the more extensive becomes its planning, and the more serious its penalties for non-conformity. The statistics of a state decline in accuracy to the same ratio as the state increases in power. A powerful state demands success of its bureaucracy, and it demands conformity. It gets conformity but not success. Every Five Year Plan in the Soviet Union was planned on the basis of statistics provided by every division of state and industry, and agriculture as well. The statistics were dishonest. Men were afraid to report the chaos which existed in their area, and they provided doctored statistics as a result. The Soviet planning rested therefore on erroneous statistics. When the plan ended, who wanted to report failure and go to Siberia? Everyone reported success. Thus the plan was a success; the USSR was gaining on the US,--- and people were starving when statistics reported a good harvest!

It is not necessary, however, to go to the Soviet Union for dishonest statistics. They exist everywhere and in all states. When the European powers took over Africa, they worked to civilize it. Cannibalism was outlawed. Now every good colonial administrator wanted to report success and gain promotion, and so they reported a steady decline in cannibalism and a rise in civilization. Thus they went on to a higher post after claiming a 30% decline in cannibalism. Their successors followed a similar practice, until cannibalism was statistically abolished and civilization reigned in

Africa! But the difference between statistics and reality appeared when the colonies gained independence and cannibalism revived. Nigeria was regarded as a showplace of African statehood, with extensive education, British degrees from distinguished universities abounding, and the Prime Minister, Sir Abubaker Tafaw Balewa, knighted by Queen Elizabeth. Unfortunately, on January 15, 1965, Sir Abubaker, Sir Ahmado Bello, and other dignitaries proved to be the main course at a dinner held "by local democrats and humanitarians."

U.S. statistics, as provided by the federal, state, county, and city governments are little better, and the higher up one goes, the worse they get. Statistics are *economic data*; but, when collected for state usage, they become *political facts*, and they are therefore bent, twisted, and altered to suit political purposes. A business firm must have accurate statistical data on sales, cost, and production, or it will go out of business. From start to finish, business statistics are economic facts and are governed by hard economic realities. But, from start to finish, under socialism statistics are political facts and are governed by political realities; as a result, economic reality is suppressed, and the result is continued political power for a time together with economic chaos.

This is a nemesis of socialism. Socialism cannot work, because, *first* it tries to assume the role and prerogative of God, which is impossible. And, *second*, because socialism destroys economic order by giving politics primacy and power over economics. And since political management of the economic sphere is a basic tenet of socialism, socialism is by nature involved in a contradiction and an impossibility.

How then does socialism survive at all? There are two roads for socialist survival: *First*, socialism is parasitic. It must feed on a healthy body to survive. A parasite can only live as long as it has a healthy or living body to feed on. When the host body dies, the parasite either finds another host or dies also. Today, the US is the host body for the world parasites, and it is bleeding to death. *Second* because socialism is parasitic, it is imperialistic. Every socialist state must capture ever fresh countries in order to gut their economies and survive a little longer. Whether military or otherwise, imperialism becomes a necessity for socialism. We need not be surprised then at the continual aggression of a socialistic era.

Master planning thus ends in a masterpiece of anarchy, lawlessness, and confusion. Man's plan is failing everywhere, as it of necessity must. God's plan alone remains assured, and we must move in terms of it.

CHALCEDON REPORT NO. 13
October 1, 1966

One of the most important things for us to know, in understanding our world, is that it is a world under God's law. At every point in our lives, we are governed by law. The laws of physiology, the laws of our body, are very real laws, as are laws of digestion, rest, exercise, sleep, and so on: we despise or break them at our peril. The physical world has its laws, and we live in terms of them: we cannot annul gravity because we have decided on an impulse to float upward instead of falling down. We have laws in every realm, biological, sociological, chemical, economic, religious, and so on.

In some areas, the laws are no less certain but not so quick in their consequences. Taking arsenic has a quick effect; taking narcotics is somewhat slower, and being an alcoholic is slower yet, but each course involves a violation of God's laws for the body, and the pursued course is death.

In the world of human affairs, God's laws are, as everywhere else, operative, but, by the providence of God, man is given more rope in some areas than in others and these areas become significant therefore in human history.

Politics is one such area. God's basic requirement of the political order is the recognition that sovereignty belongs, not to man, nor to the state, but to God alone. The state *cannot* be neutral towards the triune God. It *must* recognize that the triune God is the basic and ultimate lawgiver and it *must* seek to further godly law and order.

But politics is also a realm where man can assert and has repeatedly asserted his maximum defiance of God. The state has claimed sovereignty and set itself up as God and as man's savior. The state has made man's law supreme and has despised God's law. It has claimed the right to govern other law spheres, such as religion and economics, and the state has acted as though there were no absolute law in the universe, only man-made law.

This attitude is, of course, basic to *socialism* in its *every* form, Fabian, Marxist, "Christian", and so on. And many, many people are socialist without knowing it, because they either put their trust in politics, or ascribe fearfully impossible powers to politics, which are impossible in God's world.

Economics is a law-sphere. The economists have named the laws, but they operated before they were named. Gresham's Law has been true in all history: "bad money drives out good money"; no man will trade real silver and gold for counterfeit if he can avoid it, and, in the long run, the silver and gold are hoarded, and the counterfeit or debased coinage alone circulates until it collapses. Gresham did not invent this law: he simply observed a reality in God's universe.

The socialist believes that politics can successfully control economics: "Washington won't let it happen; they can't afford to politically." But Washington is not God, and Washington, D. C., having set aside economic law, will suffer the consequences of violating economic law: *economic disaster. If man can avert the consequences of God's law, then man has dethroned God.* If Washington D. C. can make its own economic laws as it goes along; and, by legislation and by administrative action, avert the consequences of its action, then causality has been abolished, law has been abolished, and the political managers are the new gods of the universe.

This, of course, is their very claim: "God is dead, long live the welfare state." They are very religious about it. One prominent scientist, in his book entitled *Man's Means to His End*, concludes with a chapter entitled "Godliness Without a God." According to Sir Robert Watson-Watt, "Man's Chief End is to glorify Man and to enjoy him forever." Man is his own god, and therefore man is his own law-giver, making his own laws as he goes along.

Now it is unpleasant to think about troubles ahead. We all tend to like our life as it is. We want the world to change without anyone's hair being mussed. But the fact of economic crisis and collapse is the certainty of God's government. Man is not permitted to re-make the world or himself after his own image. God's judgment and God's laws prevail. To believe in a *political* answer to *economic* problems is to desert belief in law for a belief in man. To hope that we can solve economic problems by political action is to succumb to the socialist temptation. Politics has a very important part in man's life *as politics*. The founding fathers and the colonial leaders of America were active in politics to limit politics, to keep its role as limited as possible. They were fearful of any politics which claimed too much ability or power for the political order.

The essential meaning of the political hope is *humanism*. The humanist worships man. His faith is in man's capacity to remake the world and man through political action, and this political action is the province of a scientific elite, a managerial and planning elite who feel no need to conform to any law beyond themselves, because they believe that no law exists outside of man.

Humanism has captured the American scene, and the real religion of the United States is no longer Christianity but humanism. The courts have replaced Christianity in education with the new established religion, humanism. Humanism has also captured the churches and is preached from the pulpit by men who are sometimes unaware of their capture. Love, man's humanistic love, is the new savior, replacing Jesus Christ, the second person of the Trinity.

The basic temptation of Satan in Eden was, "Ye shall be as God, knowing good and evil," i.e., every man will be his own god, knowing or determining what is good and evil for himself. This is the essence of humanism in its every form, pragmatism, existentialism, Marxism, Fabianism, etc. But law, God's law, is the habitat of man. The law sphere of a fish, physiologically, is water; take him out of water and put him on a table, and he dies. Man's physiological law sphere is air; place him in water, and he dies. The total law sphere of man and the universe is God: "in Him we live and move and have our being." Take man out of God's law spheres, and man dies. And this is exactly what humanistic politics has done and continues to do. The result will be death. Humanistic politics can solve no problems and prevent no economic collapse: it is itself responsible for the evils which plague it.

The Dictionary of Philosophy defines "Political Philosophy" as "That branch of philosophy which deals with political life, especially with the essence, origin and value of the state. In ancient philosophy politics also embraced what we call ethics." This is an extremely important point. As Christians, we believe that our ethics, our morality, must be derived from the only true source of law, the triune God. Our ethics are theocentric, God-centered, having reference to His word and to His judgment. But, outside of Biblical morality, all morality has been *political*, being derived from the political order and having reference to political judgment. We cannot understand what is happening in our courts, schools, and pulpits unless we recognize that American morality has been leaving Christianity for humanism, for a political orientation. We are becoming group-oriented, and the Supreme Court is defining morality for us.

A very interesting work on the new statist morality and congenial to it, is edited by Peter B. Neubauer, M.D., director of the Child Development Center in New York, and entitled *Children in Collectives, Child-Rearing Aims and Practices in the Kibbutz* (Springfield, Illinois: Charles C. Thomas, Publisher, 1965). Children in Israel's Kibbutzim are given a thoroughly socialistic, humanistic training. The Kibbutzim is their real parent. Boys and girls sleep together, four to a room, until they are eighteen; family ties are downgraded for the social tie. The children are really experimental animals. According to one of the writers, "The basically different character of the Kibbutz offers uniquely rich possibilities for research activities; beyond this, the existence of a real striving for *new conditions of life* demands from all of us the study of differences, in order that we may broaden our own views" (p. 321).

Unless God is the source of all law, including moral law, man and the state will be the source of law and of morality. And this we are seeing at an accelerated rate. But God remains the only true law-giver, and the Scripture declares that God is a very jealous God, and He does not take lightly man's usurpation of God's prerogatives. Men may dream that they control the world, that they have abolished economic law and the possibility of economic disaster, but God laughs, as He laughs at all would-be gods and law-makers: "the Lord shall have them in derision...Thou shalt break them with a rod of iron; thou shalt dash them in pieces like a potter's vessel" (Psalm 2: 4,9).

There's a war going on, and wars hurt. Either way, either side, there will be some losses and some hurt. Pick your side: God or the state? God cannot lose, and He makes "all things work together for good to them that love

God, to them who are the called according to his purpose" (Romans 8:28). The politicians of the world may say, "We will not let economic disaster happen," and God laughs. "All the nations are as nothing before Him; they are accounted as less than nothing and worthlessness" (Isaiah 40:17, Berkeley Version). This God is our God,, and He is our hope.

CHALCEDON REPORT NO. 14
November 5, 1966

An expression increasingly stressed in some conservative quarters has a rather strange history. "For God and country", we are told, sums up our cause. Now certainly the phrase calls to mind an apparently noble purpose but is it entirely a wise slogan? And how has it been used in the past?

Some years ago, a country in the midst of war summoned people to sacrifice their savings, gold and silver, time and effort, "For God and country." People loyally lined up and cooperated; for some who gave heavily, iron medals were awarded for their services.

Another crisis situation: inflation. The citizenry were summoned to rally to their country's welfare by surrendering their gold and silver including their wedding rings, "For God and country."

We can agree that these were bad uses of the phrase, especially since enemy powers were involved. Is the phrase a sound one in the right hands? To answer this question, it is necessary to examine the nature of Biblical ethics or morality.

The demand of humanism (and of its child, socialism) is for a *universal ethics*. In universal ethics we are told that, even as the family gave way to the tribe, and the tribe to the nation, so the nation must give way to a one-world order. All men must treat all other men equally. Partiality to our family, nation, or race, represents a lower morality, we are told, and must be replaced by the "higher" morality of a universal ethics.

But Biblical morality is not a universal ethics. It does *not* have one code for all men. Where mankind is concerned, Biblical morality has three separate kinds of moral requirements.

First, there is the law of God for the family. The family has a high and central position in Biblical law. There are four laws that pertain to the family in the Ten Commandments alone: "Honor thy father and thy mother, as the LORD thy God hath commanded thee; that thy days may be prolonged, and that it may go well with thee, in the land which the LORD thy God giveth thee" (Deuteronomy 5:16). The seventh commandment forbids adultery (Deut. 5:18), and the tenth, covetousness of our neighbor's wife, home and possessions (Deut. 5:21). The eighth commandment (Deut. 5:19) forbids theft and protects property, and, in Biblical law, property is seen as one of the central mainstays of family life. In the New Testament, it is emphasized that a man's first human obligation is towards his family: "But if any provide not for his own, and specially for those of his own house; he hath denied the faith, and is worse than an infidel" (I Timothy 5:8). A man's first and basic responsibility, in the realm of his relationships towards his fellow men, is towards his own family. He cannot put them on the same level as all mankind. The consequence of a universal ethics can only be communism. In a universalistic morality, all men must be given the same love, support, and consideration as we give to our family. It is impossible to do this without total communism. But Biblical morality insists that the family, which must be grounded on Christian faith, must come *first*. A man is *required* to love and support *his* wife; he is forbidden to love and support any other women. He must support and discipline his children; he cannot do this for other children. A universal ethics is a communistic ethics.

The *second* area of law in Biblical morality deals with our brethren in the faith, our relationship with true believers. We are with true believers members of a larger family, the household of Jesus Christ. We have an obligation of love to our "brethren" in the faith. The early church established the order of deacons and a deacon's fund for the care of widows (or orphans) who had no family (Acts 6:1-6). Christians share a common faith and a common destiny. They believe in the Bible and thus have in common a standard of law: they are a community. We can, very quickly, feel a sense of kinship with true believers whom we have scarcely met, because we share a common perspective, yet a neighbor, whom we see daily, is in reality a stranger to us, because his every belief is hostile to our's. God *requires* us to be partial to that which is our own. To give equal favor, support, or attention to that which is hostile to us is to destroy ourselves: it is to subsidize the opposition.

The *third* level of Biblical law deals with the rest of the world, with unbelievers. Here we are to "walk honestly toward them that are without" (Thessalonians 4:12), i.e., our behavior towards unbelievers must be honorable. We must love our neighbor and our enemy, which means giving him the God-given privileges of the second table of the law. The Bible repeatedly identifies, as in Romans 13:8-10, love of others as "the fulfilling of the laws" thou shalt not kill, i.e., respect all men's right to life; thou shalt not commit adultery, i.e. respect the sanctity of every home; thou shalt not steal, i.e., all man's property is under God's law and safeguard of law; thou shalt not bear false witness, i.e., respect all men's reputations; thou shalt not covet...i.e., respect these things in thought, as well as in word and deed. Works of mercy, in emergencies, are to be extended to all men, as the law, and the Parable of the Good Samaritan make clear. But our Christian family comes first, then our fellow believers, and, last, the world at large.

"For God and country." Where does our country come in? We serve God, not only directly in worship, but by our faithfulness in every area of our life, by our family life, our relationship to the world. We serve Him by our integrity in our vocation, and in our citizenship. We have dealt with our moral relationship to men: to family, fellow believers, and to the world. What about institutions, such as church and state? Both institutions are ministries of God. The church is the ministry of the word, the sacraments, and of true discipline. Without these, there is no true church, even though an institution may call itself a church. The state is the ministry of justice (Romans 13:1-6): its function is to provide godly law and order. The obligation of believers is to be an obedient citizen, insofar as the state does not require what is contrary to our duty to God and our responsibilities under God, for "We ought to obey God rather than men" (Acts 5:29). The citizen must pay taxes, and bear arms in his country's defense. He must be honest and industrious, and he ought to pray for those having authority. More than that cannot be required of him.

Where does the state come in? Certainly it does *not* have the same status as our family. *No man* can morally sacrifice his family to his country; this is no more than a modern form of human sacrifice to a false god. Our family *must* come before church work and before patriotic work. The moral foundations of society are in the Christian family. It cannot be sacrificed to anything else, to either church or state. If we say the country is a bigger and more important thing, and must come first, the liberal can say that the world is bigger and has priority over the nation and the family.

Then where does the state come in? Where does our country rank in moral importance? This depends on the country. *If* it is a Christian country, it has a rank placing it in the realm of our duties to our fellow believers: the state has entered into the ranks of the faithful. But if the country (or church, or school), has departed from the faith, if it has officially and practically denied God and His word, then it is a part of the world of unbelief, and honesty requires that we treat it as such.

Does this mean that we stand by and let our country go down the drain? By no means, by no means at all. All the more zealously, for the Lord's sake and for our children's sake, we need to reclaim our country. But we must have a sense of proportion. Some churches absorb so much of their members "time for the Lord" supposedly, that family life disintegrates; but family life is the first area of godly responsibility. And some patriots are ready to sacrifice their husbands and children "for the cause." But their first area of responsibility is to their husband and children. The same holds true for many men. How many, many people spend years trying to win radicals over to conservatism, and then wake up to find their children have become themselves radical! Certainly the schools have a share of the blame, but the first responsibility is parental. Should they quit their work? Again, by no means. But their work must have a sense of proportion.

If our work is truly "For God", it will be primarily constructive in every area, in the home, church, community, school, and country. To be "For God" means to establish godly homes, Christian schools, Christian study groups, godly political action, godly businesses geared to sound economics, and so on. It does not mean merely reacting to the opposition. It will be for the family, for the faith, for the country, and for the school, because it is "For God."

There is much to commend in the phrase, "For God and for Country", but there is much against it. It is a handy phrase for the enemy to use in the future, with the help of apostate churches: "For God and country", "For God and the Fatherland", or "For God and the Soviet Union" as apostate Russian churchmen say. But, as Joshua said, "choose ye this day whom ye will serve ...but as for me and my house, we will serve the LORD" (Joshua 24:15).

But even more militates against the phrase, "For God and country". With all due respect to the dedicated and fine patriots who use it, the term makes an equation where no equality exists. The phrase has a ring of truth, but it will not stand up to investigation. It joins the absolute, God, with a relative, the country. We cannot link a relative and an absolute together. We cannot call for service to "God and church" or to "God and school", because the service God requires, and the claims God has on us, far transcend the claims of church, country, or school. The essence of statism and totalitarianism is that it makes the relative absolute. It makes the state into another god; it gives to the state power and authority which rightfully belongs to God only.

The state today is claiming too much. In the United States, the purpose of the founding fathers was to limit severely the powers of the federal government by means of the Constitution. The federal union had to be strong enough to avoid impotence, but it could not claim powers which infringed on God's sovereignty and man's liberty under God. The foundation of liberty they saw in the faith. As George Washington said "Let it be simply asked, Where is the security for property, for reputation, for life, if the sense of religious obligation desert the oaths, which are the instruments of investigation in courts of justice?" Patrick Henry said that subversive and revolutionary forces from Europe were seeking to destroy "the great pillars of all government and of social life; I mean virtue, morality and religion. This is the armor, my friend, and this alone, that renders us invincible...If we lose these, we are conquered, fallen indeed!" How many men today can equal Patrick Henry's dedication to his country? But Patrick Henry was a great American because of the greatness of his faith, character, and intelligence, and because he brought a sense of proportion and dedication to all things.

Our Pledge of Allegiance says it best: "one nation, under God". This is the true perspective, one to which we must give allegiance and service as well. Let us serve family, school, church, and country under God and only *under God*. No cause can rightfully claim more of us.

CHALCEDON REPORT NO. 15
December 1, 1966

Concern about the Bill of Rights is greatly in evidence these days, and in many quarters. The Bill of Rights should particularly concern Christians, since it is a product of Biblical Christianity; the idea of a Bill of Rights is unknown in other religions and civilizations.

The State of California has now issued a book, the first printing in mimeographed form, of a "Source Book for Teachers" entitled *The Bill of Rights*. The book, copyrighted in 1966 by the California State Department of Education, has a favorable introduction by Max Rafferty, Superintendent of public Instruction. The cover of the book bears this notice: "Preliminary Printing by California Teachers Association." On page x. we are told that "The State Board of Education acknowledges with gratitude the gift of thirty thousand dollars from the Constitutional Rights Foundation of Los Angeles. This gift, used for payment of operational expenses, has made this publication possible." Two years ago Dr. Rafferty refused to help judge a Bill of Rights essay contest sponsored by this Rights Foundation because three directors of the Foundation had been named as supporters of Communist fronts in reports from the State Senate Committee on un-American Activities. No authors are listed for the Source Book, but an Advisory Panel is given.

The Source Book is very carefully researched, and very carefully written. A summary of the major sections of the Table of Contents best gives a perspective on the work:

Part One: Judicial Review, the Fourteenth Amendment and Federalism
Section A: Judicial Review
Section B: The Fourteenth Amendment and Federalism
Part Two: Equal Protection of the Law
Section A: Voting
Section B: Education
Section C: Housing
Section D: Employment
Part Three: Criminal Due Process
Section A: The Criminal Trial
Section B: Law Enforcement
Part Four: Freedom of Expression
Section A: Seditious Speech
Section B: Obscenity
Section C: Modes of Regulation of Speech
Part Five: Freedom of Religion
Section A: History
Section B: The Free Exercise of Religion
Section C: The Establishment Clause

In terms of its given purpose, the Source Book is an excellent summary of the present legal state of the Bill of Rights, as far as the Supreme Court is concerned, and as far as the Great Society is concerned. We are given a careful statement of the civil rights position with respect to voting, integration, education, and federal aid, housing, and so on. But we are given very little about the Bill of Rights as such. Instead of being a study, as the title would indicate, of the Bill of Rights, it is rather a study of the progress in law of the civil rights revolution. Had the book been titled something like *The Present Legal Status of the Civil Rights Movement*, it would have been an able and acceptable work.

But it is mistitled. It is not a study of the Bill of Rights. The Bill of Rights and the Supreme Court interpretations are two different things. A former Assistant Attorney General of the United States, Charles Warren, wrote in *The Supreme Court in United States History*, vol. III, P. 470f.: "However the Court may interpret the provisions of the Constitution, it is still the Constitution which is the law and not the decision of the Court." Another writer stated some time ago, "Any citizen whose liberty or property is at stake has an absolute constitutional right to appear before the Court and challenge its interpretation of the Constitution, no matter how often they have been promulgated, upon the ground that they are repugnant to its provisions...When the Bar of the country understands this, and respectfully but inexorably requires of the Supreme Court that it shall continually justify its decisions by the Constitution, and not by its own precedents, we shall gain a new conception of the power of our constitutional guarantees." (Everett A. Abbott: *Justice and the Modern Law*, 1913.)

It is important to know what the Court has said about the Bill of Rights, and how is has interpreted it, but it is even more important to know what the Bill of Rights has to say, and what it meant to the framers of it.

Unfortunately, however, besides giving basically a modernistic interpretation to portions of the Bill of Rights, other portions are simply bypassed as though they were non-existent. Thus, Amendment II states: "A well-regulated militia, being necessary to the security of a free State, the right of the people to keep and bear arms, shall not be infringed." This right is simply dropped out of consideration. The same is true of Amendment III, concerning the quartering of soldiers in private homes. Amendment IV - VIII are treated in part III, as a piece. Amendment IX, "The enumeration in the Constitution of certain rights, shall not be construed to deny or disparage other rights retained by the people", a very basic provision, is also bypassed. The same is true of Amendment X, "The powers not delegated to the United States by the Constitution, nor prohibited by it to the States, are reserved to the States respectively, or to the people." Amendments XIII, XIV and XV are included as part of "The Expanded Bill of Rights" and they are apparently regarded as invalidating Amendments IX and X. The Source

Book admits, however, that the intention of these amendments had exclusive reference to the ex-slaves.

The original purpose of the Bill of Rights was to protect the citizens and the states from the power of the federal government. This is obliquely noted by the Source Book: "One of the goals of the framers of the Constitution was to establish a government which was strong enough to enforce the law, yet not so strong as to threaten individual liberty." (p. III - 1.). This is true, but, more than that, the purpose of the Bill of Rights was to impose restraints on the Federal Government and to protect the citizenry in its God-given immunities. The fear was of *federal* power. The citizens of the several states were expected to protect themselves from the states through state constitutions and state bills of rights: The first ten amendments of the U.S. Constitution were imposed on the federal government by the people to protect themselves from that particular form of civil government. The one thing neither the Constitution nor the Bill of Rights even remotely envisioned was that the Federal Government and its Supreme Court would become the protectors of the people from the states and from each other. What was once the feared Big Bad Wolf has now been made the Big Good Protector. The American people in 1787 were not afraid of each other. They knew one another's frailties and injustices. This civil and criminal laws were designed to keep the people in check. But who could protect the people from Big Government? The object of the Constitution was to provide sufficiently strong civil government without creating too big a power. The Constitution and the Bill of Rights strictly limited the scope of the federal union by checks and balances, divisions of powers, separation of powers, the express powers doctrine, and prohibitions placed on civil government.

But now "the Great Society" declares that the best guardian of our liberties is the very power the Bill of Rights distrusted, and the Source Book expounds this new doctrine. "Rights" now mean equality, integration fair housing, and whatever else "the Great Society" tells us our rights are. What *are* our rights now? They are whatever the Federal Government decides is man's necessary fulfillment. And all man's "rights" in "the Great Society's" definition are things which do not interfere with the state's interest and necessity. For an example of this, notice what Justice Goldberg had to say in *Griswold* v. *Connecticut* (1965), when the Court, by a seven-to-two majority, invalidated a law prohibiting the use of contraceptives by married people. Goldberg defended the right of marital privacy, but at the same time limited it by saying, "Surely the Government, absent a showing of compelling state interest, could not decree that all husbands and wives must be sterilized after two children have been born to them." But what this implies is that, if there is "a showing of a compelling state interest", the state could decree such a sterilization. Is this what the Source Book calls "the Court's function in protecting individual liberty under the Constitution? (p. 1-15). Is this expressive of "the very nature of the Court's role in protecting individual liberty from government encroachment"? (idem).

The Bill of Rights was written because the states and citizens of the newly formed United States pointed the finger at that federal government as the threat to their liberties. Today, the federal government and the U.S. Supreme Court, far bigger than the people of 1787 ever imagined it could be, point the finger at landlords, private associations, individuals, and various small organizations as the threat. Conservatives in particular are denounced by politicians as a menace to liberty. In other words, the wolves are insisting that the Bill of Rights was written to protect them from the assault of lambs and that it therefore cannot be used by lambs.

The new textbook *Land of the Free*, by John Caughey, John Hope Franklin, and Ernest R. May, is written from this same perspective. The meaning of American history is seen as fulfilled in the civil rights movement. The heroes of American history are therefore people like these: Edward Hicks, Quack Walker, George Guess, Harriett Tubman, Mary Ann Hafen, Anthony Burns, Frederick Douglass, Kate Shelley, Arthur Goldberg, Ishi, Jacob Riis, Jane Addams, Dante Sacco and Bartolomeo Vanzetti, Charles Drew, Linda Brown, and others. But more than these persons, the real meaning of American history is in the drive towards equality and the civil rights revolution.

What is the answer to these things? Shall we continue to hope in the public schools to protect us? The state schools are socialist schools; can we expect them to teach anything other than socialism? Socialism in education means the state control of education, just as socialism in business is the state control of business, either by regulation or take-over. Can you expect the wolves to protect you against themselves?

The course of action with respect to creeping socialism is to destroy it where it can be destroyed, and to restrain it, if no more can be done at the moment.

The only logical conclusion of the present concept of civil rights is communism. It demands "full equality." And where does equality stop? Economic, political, cultural, racial, personal, and every other kind of equality is demanded. One of the logical outcomes of the demand for economic equality is socialization of industry and "agrarian reform." There are major steps in this direction already. The acreage limitation on irrigated farms, the Delta Ministry of the N.C.C., various federal policies, all point to "agrarian reform", towards the communization of agriculture. And increasing socialist controls over industry are already in evidence.

"Full equality" means that no differences can be tolerated with respect to race, color, creed, economics, and all things else. This means the planned destruction of the very elements of society who have made our civilization. The reduction of the Bill of Rights to a program of equalitarianism is to interpret the Bill of Rights as an instrument of socialistic revolution.

But the Bill of Rights rests on a Biblical foundation. Its origin is in the demand for the respect for other men's life ("Thou shalt not kill"), home ("Thou shalt not commit adultery"), property ("Thou shalt not steal"), and reputation ("Thou shalt not bear false witness"). (In Newsletter 6, we discussed the origins of various other laws, including legal procedure and the Fifth Amendment, in the Mosaic law).

Can we expect water to come out of a faucet when the reservoir is bone dry? Will a new faucet do the trick for us? To imagine such a possibility is ridiculous, but in essence this is what people are demanding today. The American reservoir *is* dry. Spiritually, we are bankrupt. The overwhelming majority of Americans are content, with occasional grumblings, to remain in churches which are clearly apostate. They sit under pastors who know less Bible and doctrine than they do, which isn't much, and whose politics is the politics of revolution. Is our hope to be in such a people, whose presence in such churches has the condemnation of Scripture?

True, the American people are capable of getting angry now and then at election time. They don't like riots, obvious corruption, and other things, but a protest vote is not a reviving power. Even the criminal syndicates resent corruption in their own ranks and liquidate thieves. Victory at election time is *very* important but it is not the answer. Good plumbing is necessary in any building at any time, but it cannot take the place of a reservoir. We need both the reservoir and the right kind of plumbing, religious, political, and educational. To place our hope in plumbing alone is both foolish and disastrous.

The basic error of liberalism and socialism is *environmentalism*. Environmentalism holds that it is not man who is responsible for evil but his environment, his family, school, culture, and economic condition. Change the environment and you will change man. As a result, environmentalists are very eager to win elections, change laws, and thereby remake man. To try to answer environmentalism by changing the environment is a surrender to their position. To believe that this can be done means that we belong in the environmentalist camp.

Our problem is this: the plumbing is in *very* bad shape. We do need new plumbing, i.e., new politics, new churches, new schools, and so on, and we need these things urgently. But all these things are useless without the reservoir, the triune God. We need more faith, and real faith, not the compromising position of men like Billy Graham, nor the wicked stand-pattism of people who feel that if they grumble occasionally God will bless their membership in apostate churches. Real faith makes a stand first and foremost in terms of the faith.

Is there much of this? On the contrary, there is very little real faith. Even in the few separated and faithful churches, members move in terms of trifles, not in terms of faith. They leave because of a spat with Mrs. Jones, or because they have found a church with a better choir, or a better youth group. They move in terms of everything except faith. And they too shall be judged.

The prospect then is one of judgment. But is that all? On the contrary, every time of judgment is also one of salvation, because when God judges the ungodly, He also moves to deliver His faithful saints.

But, most of all, the future is a glorious one because it is in the hands of God, *not* in the hands of men. Man proposes, but God disposes. As far back as the days of the flood, and then the Tower of Babel, man planned a world of tyranny under man's humanistic world order. But God has confounded every plan of man to establish his humanistic world order, and His power is unchanged still.

In this blessed season, therefore, as we look forward to the celebration of our Lord's nativity, we can rejoice that the government of the universe is upon His shoulder Who is the "Wonderful Counsellor, The mighty God, The everlasting Father, The Prince of Peace" (Isaiah 9:6). Let us stand in confidence, because it is He who governs us and is our Lord.

CHALCEDON REPORT NO. 16
January 1, 1967

No better means of understanding the purpose or goal of modern education, and especially of colleges and universities, has been offered us by the opposition than a statement by Dr. Franklin Murphy, chancellor of the University of California at Los Angeles. This statement appeared in the *California Living* section of the Los Angeles *Herald-Examiner*, Sunday, December 11,1966, in an article by John Bryan, "Franklin Murphy on The Return of Renaissance Man."

What we are rapidly moving into, according to Dr. Murphy, is a renaissance, i.e., a rebirth of man, but it is unlike the Italian Renaissance because "It has few historical benchmarks"; in fact, "I think it's more of a revolution than a renaissance because it has very few roots in the past." This revolutionary change "is especially evident in the arts."

> What are the sources of this glorious "cultural awakening?" reporter Bryan asked. "I'll list three major inputs," Dr. Murphy replied quickly. "First is the death of Calvinism, that set of traditions which said that to live richly in one's emotional life is a dishonorable thing for a man to do.
>
> "Secondly...the impact of the scientific revolution. It's shaking up everybody's confidence that there are any timeless verities. It's leading to an acceptance of experimentation. That's almost the name of the current game.

> "The third input is the growth of a new open-endedness, a willingness to look candidly at the old prejudices, which we find today in our entire society. "All of this is producing what you may call a Renaissance man...what some have called a 'man for many seasons.' "Of course, he is not being born without a certain amount of friction. "People are having a hard time understanding, for instance, the reluctance of the Supreme Court to restrict freedom of expression by rigid definitions of what is 'obscenity'." (p. 6)

Dr. Murphy felt that the Supreme Court justices actually "are a bit behind the times." For him, the purpose of the university is to create this Renaissance man.

Now all three of Dr. Murphy's "inputs" add up to one thing alone: the Death of God, of morality, of truth. There must be no "timeless verities" or absolute truths, no absolute right and wrong --- only "experimentation", total moral relativism. It is significant that Dr. Murphy called this "new man" *Renaissance Man*, because the Renaissance was dedicated to moral relativism. It held, according to John S. White, in *Renaissance Cavalier*, that "Good and bad are not absolute concepts, but products of their time... Good is what conforms to its time, what corresponds to actual society --- in other words, good usage. Bad is what is out of date --- the antiquated" (p. 13).

This moral relativism, or moral anarchism, went hand in hand with statism and totalitarianism in the Renaissance, and the same is true today. Because moral relativism denies that there is an absolute right and wrong, it puts no moral limits on the powers of the state. Also, it does not allow any moral grounds for criticizing the state. If nothing is really evil; then nothing is really morally wrong with anything the state does. Wherever and whenever moral relativism flourishes, then and there totalitarian statism also flourishes. Dr. Murphy and other modern educators are thus educating for totalitarianism.

The Death of God movement which is at the heart of all this, is one of the most deeply rooted and most basic movements of our time. It states openly what is prevalent secretly.

One of the social effects of this decline of Biblical faith is the operation of the principle of Gresham's law in every realm. As the *Santa Ana Register* editorial of Monday, December 19, 1966, (p. B 8), observed: "Gresham's law states that bad money drives out good money. The same principle appears to apply to people." Isaiah observed long ago that a religious and moral breakdown meant also a breakdown of authority: "As for My people, children are their oppressors, and rule over them" (Isaiah 3:12). In such an age, there is not only a desire to make the bad rulers, but the good see the futility of the situation and say, "Make me not a ruler of the people" (Isaiah 3:7), because they recognize that the people cannot be led except into evil and slavery. It is a dangerous education we are giving in our colleges and universities. It is education for slavery. We should not be surprised at the results.

CHALCEDON REPORT NO. 17
February 1, 1967

"The Plague - An Ultimate Arm of War?" So reads the title of a front-page news story by William Hines, *Washington Star Service*, in the Thursday, January 19, 1967, Oakland California, *Tribune*. The article reviews a two-part report in the magazine, *Science*.

Chemical and biological warfare (CBW) is today extensively studied and planned. Hines writes:

> It is already possible to make some dreadful conjectures on the basis of things presently on the record. The possibility of a militarily instigated outbreak of plague is one.
> We know that plague ("the Black Death") is one of the munitions of war being worked on in the CBW program. We know this because a soldier named Ralph Powell fell ill of pneumonic plague in 1959 working at Fort Detrick, Md., where CBW research is centered.
> Pneumonic plague is one of two forms of the worst scourge ever visited on mankind. From a military point of view the pneumonic variety is preferable to the bubonic because bubonic plague requires the cooperation of a rat and a flea in the cycle of epidemic infection. Pneumonic plague can be distributed more effectively by aerosol sprays from airplanes or fog from smoke-type artillery shells.

Because of quick diagnosis, Hines reports, Powell was cured, but the intensive care with quick diagnosis and strict isolation are essentials which would not be available should an epidemic strike a large city". Although estimates vary, Hines states that "Twenty-five million of the 75 million people then living in Europe died in the first great Black Death between 1347 and 1350. More than one-seventh of London's population of nearly 500,000 perished in the Great Plague of 1655, and other areas were subsequently hit when Charles II and his court fled, taking the scourge along with them" (p. 4).

Other aspects of CBW include "war against food. A woman scientist was awarded the Army's highest civilian service medal for her work on a fungus particularly effective on rice." Hines concludes, "For 20 years man has been juggling the nuclear tools of his own destruction. Now he may be on the verge of acquiring a new and equally 'unthinkable' tool. Carried to its logical conclusion, CBW could provide a solution to the population problem --- the 'final solution', as Adolf Hitler so felicitously put it" (p. 4).

Man proposes, but God disposes. The nations of the world are busily engaging in chemical and biological warfare studies as the next step beyond atomic warfare. It is regarded as a superior method because it offers opportunities to capture an area with the people unharmed, or with the resources unharmed and the people eliminated.

But, meanwhile, an unplanned, non-socialistic plague is getting under way in Asia. In Santa Ana, California, *The Register* for Monday morning, November 21, 1966 reported on page one, "20th Century Man Menaced by Revival of 'Black Death'". The article stated that, for the first time in 42 years a case was brought into the United States by a soldier returning to Dallas, Texas, from Vietnam. "In one year 11 nations in the Southeast Asia-Pacific region reported the number of plague cases had almost tripled." But these statistics do not tell the story, because few deaths in that area pass through medical and statistical hands." The report concludes (P. A2):

> Recent checks showed that fleas in the port areas of Vietnam are now immune to DDT and every ship or plane leaving the war zone could carry plague-ridden fleas.
> "The world today faces a growing menace of the outbreak of human plague." World Health Organization scientists said.
> The main reasons are rapid urbanization and lack of appreciation of the danger."

The most important developments, however, are in Communist China. Within that nation, three diseases are spreading: Asian Flu, pneumatic plague and cholera. According to Robert S. Allen and Paul Scott, in their "Washington Report" (Oakland, California, *Tribune*, Friday, January 27, 1967, p. 30):

> With these deadly diseases appearing in epidemic proportions in several northern and western provinces, U. S. and Russian officials are gravely concerned that the spreading civil disorder in China may turn that country into a massive incubator of epidemics.

As a result, the United States, through Secretary Dean Rusk, and the Soviet Union, through Ambassador Dobrynin, are discussing common action against the threat of plague. It is one thing for nations to plan to unleash plague against mankind; it is another for God's judgment to unleash it against man. Then all good nations are called to work together through the United Nations to stop the plague. Man's biological and chemical warfare is good socialist planning: God's judgment simply cannot be permitted by the United Nations and the World Health Organization! This is good humanism but not good sense.

Allen and Scott report that the epidemics in Red China are potentially a far graver threat to our troops than the Viet Cong and North Vietnamese. They are an even greater threat to the Soviet Union. A Red Guard defector has reported that the flu epidemic has already entered Soviet areas. The fear is that the other epidemics, the plagues, will follow.

Plagues are a common occurrence at the end of an age, whether of the Roman Empire, the medieval era, or any other culture. The end of an age is marked by a general breakdown of morality, law and order, money, soil, morale, the will to live, and of all things, because the basic faith which has undergirded the culture is either gone or abandoned. When man lays waste his spiritual resources, he also lays waste all other resources, natural, economic, political, agricultural, and all things else. When men are without faith and cannot say why they are alive, their will to live is weakened. Men with strong faith and a sense of calling have the strongest resistance to death. The forces of life are in them stronger than the forces for death around them. In an age when men cannot say why they are alive, or what life's purpose is, the survival ability is on the whole poor. Men live, not because of a zest for life, but in fear of death. Men with a zest for life under God and a joy in their work tend to have a long and vigorous life.

Today men are spiritually sick, more than that, spiritually dead, because of their apostasy from God. As a result, they have a poor survival ability. It is significant that it is in Communist China that the plague is beginning, for life has become most meaningless there. But life is basically meaningless everywhere if man's chief end is not to glorify God and to enjoy Him forever.

Jesus Christ speaking as Wisdom ages ago through Solomon, declared, "But he that sinneth against me wrongeth his own soul: *all they that hate me love death*" (Prov. 8:36). Men may hate the thought of plague, but if they hate God more, it is the plague they will inherit and unconsciously choose. And this is their judgment.

In our world today, we are seeing the spread of socialism, which is a man-made sociological plague. We shall soon see the plague of socialism itself plagued with all kinds of plagues, in every area of its existence. Significantly, *Revelation* speaks of God's judgments on Babylon the Great, the one-world humanistic order, as a series of "plagues" which destroy its planning in every area. Against all man's planning, God's plan stands secure.

CHALCEDON REPORT NO. 18
March 1, 1967

Few things are more readily and easily subverted than *words*: the subversion of words is accordingly a major factor in all subversive activity. The word "republic" has an important meaning for conservative Americans, and as a hope for many peoples of the world; the communists adopted it for their order, U.S.S.R., Union of Soviet Socialist Republics. The word *love* has been re-interpreted to mean revolutionary action and the subsidizing of all kinds of evil, and Christians are told they are not showing Biblical love if they fail to support Marxist social action.

But perhaps the most subverted word of all is *God*. One of the first things we need to recognize when we talk about God is that virtually all religions are atheistic. As Christians, for us religion means God, but this is true of very little else than Christianity, if of any other religion. Humanism is the religion of humanity, the worship of man. Animism, the worship of primitive peoples, has no God. Shintoism has a multitude of *Kamis*, divine ancestors, but no God. Buddhism is an atheistic religion; for it nothingness is ultimate. Hinduism also sees nothingness as ultimate, and the goal of reincarnation is to escape karma into eternal nothingness. Confucianism, a philosophy which became a religion, has no God. Taoism holds to an ultimate relativism; nothing is absolutely right or wrong since all things are relative. Greek religion, and Roman religion, had no God; their many "gods" were, like men, creatures born of chaos and destined to pass away. Greek philosophy talked of a first cause or God, but this was not a person but an original source, whether atoms or something else, none could say. The religion of the Germanic peoples again was Godless; the "gods" they talked about were creatures out of chaos who were simply ahead of man in their development. Apart from Biblical religion, the religion whose faith includes a God is Mohammedanism, but its concept, borrowed from the Bible, quickly was dissolved into an idea of Fate on the one hand, and mystical pantheism on the other. Mormonism does not hold to the God of Scripture; instead, it holds to many gods who are all men who have graduated in rank, and Mormonism is a form of ancestor worship under its superficially Biblical language. Judaism grew out of the rejection of Jesus Christ and steadily became humanism, and the Talmud is essentially the exposition of humanism under the facade of Scripture. There is thus actually no true theism, or worship of the absolute God, apart from orthodox Christianity.

The word *God*, however, is widely used in order to nullify the gap between Biblical and non-Biblical religions, between Christianity and humanism. The churches today are quite vocal about the believer's duty to God, but they clearly take the name of God in vain, because it is humanism (and revolution) which they proclaim, not the gospel.

The Death of God school of thought is perhaps the most honest group on the religious scene today. They honestly declare that they have a double purpose: *First*, they want to destroy all faith in the God of the Bible, the triune God, and to destroy with this faith the whole structure of moral law which comes from God. If there is no God, then there is no law, and anything goes. Man is his own god and his own law. Therefore, the Death of God thinkers want to "*liberate*" man from God and morality by declaring that God is dead and man is "free." *Second*, by their own statements, they look forward to a "rebirth" of "God", this time as a united world order. The one world order of brotherhood and socialism is this new god waiting to be born, and the Death of God thinkers want to stimulate this birth by furthering revolutionary thought and action.

By and large, the established religious leaders and churches are equally radical but less honest. They try to delude people into believing that it is still Christianity they preach by using all the old language with a new revolutionary meaning. One of the major forms of this deception is neo-orthodoxy, i.e., a seeming orthodoxy. But the churches of today are promoting revolution and calling it Christianity. It is the purpose of the church of today to murder God and the church in the name of fulfilling their Christian calling.

The support given to revolutionary activity is heavily borne by the churches. Saul Alinsky is one among many who depends on the churches for his support. The graduates of seminaries become revolutionists both in and out of the churches. At the University of California at Berkeley, Mario Savio originally was destined for the Jesuit order; Steward Albert planned to be a rabbi. Steve Hamilton went from Wheaton College to Bishop Pike to civil-rights protests and U.C. activities. He represented the University Church Council in 1964 in the Free Speech Movement. Patrick Taggart led in Youth for Christ activities and was a counsellor in Billy Graham's last Los Angeles Crusade. With Lois Murgenstrumm, who became the nude "living altar" in a satanist wedding in San Francisco, Tuesday, January 31, 1967, Taggart is a leader in the Satan-worship cult there and in the propagation of "liberal" ideas.

Many groups use the name of God, but, for all except those who hold to orthodox Christianity, God is the enemy who must be destroyed. These revolutionists hate God, because God means that there is an ultimate Judge over all men, and an ultimate right and wrong in the universe, an inescapable truth, apart from which all else is a lie. These revolutionists are out to destroy not only God but all language, since language still reflects the idea of a right and wrong. Friedrich Nietzsche called for a "new language" to express this new faith, a mode of communication in which "The falseness of an opinion is not for us any objection to it." Man must live "beyond good and evil", beyond all law, and deny that there are any "thou shalt nots." "Love" as self-indulgence is his only law. In this new order, Nietzsche said, it is necessary "To recognize untruth as a condition of life", having as much "right" as the truth and perhaps more necessary. This philosophy undergirds both church and state today: churchmen and politicians lie to us "for our good" and with no sense of wrong-doing apparent. The "god" of these men is the state. George William Friedrich Hegel (1770-1831), the spiritual father of Marx, Kierkegaard, Dewey, Sartre, and others, and the grandfather of Marxism, pragmatism, Fabianism, existentialism, and much else, said, "The state in and by itself is the ethical whole, the actualization of freedom." This means that the state is god and is the source of all law and morality. Hegel said, "The march of God in the world, that is what the state is." The state is thus god walking on earth, and men must bow down to statism or be punished as evildoers, because the state is the fulfillment of man and of man's law.

This is the issue then, the state versus God, Christ versus Caesar. Every man who supports a church which is not proclaiming orthodox Christianity is supporting antichrist and is in the camp of statism. These churches talk about God, but they mean the state. They speak of Christ as savior, but by salvation they mean socialism. Language has been subverted, and first of all the word God. We cannot counteract the subversion of our day without beginning at its root cause. We need to be "honest to God." And, as Dr. J. I. Packer, an Anglican scholar, remarked, in criticizing the book *Honest to God* by John A. T. Robinson, Bishop of Woolwich, "The man who is 'honest to God' is the man who listens to God's Word and lets it have its way with him, not evading its substance, nor deflecting its application one iota." The Bishop of Woolwich has another god and another savior than the Bible offers.

As against these false definitions of God, the Bible reveals the true God to us. Long ago, the Larger Catechism summarized the Biblical statements thus:

> What is God?
>
> God is a Spirit, in and of himself infinite in being, glory, blessedness, and perfection; all-sufficient, eternal, unchangeable, incomprehensible, everywhere present, almighty, knowing all things, most wise, most holy, most just, most merciful and gracious, long-suffering, and abundant in goodness and truth.
>
> Are there more Gods than one?
>
> There is but one only, the living and true God.
>
> How many persons are there in the Godhead?
>
> There be three persons in the Godhead, the Father, the Son, and the Holy Ghost: and these three are one true, eternal God, the same in substance, equal in power and glory although distinguished by their personal properties.

CHALCEDON REPORT NO. 19
April 1, 1967

Since we are in the midst of inflation, it is important for us to realize what inflation does. One of the central results of inflation is *decapitalization*.

Decapitalization means the progressive destruction of capital, so that a society has progressively less productive ability. Capitalization is the accumulation of wealth through work and thrift, and decapitalization is the dissipation of accumulated wealth. A free economy, capitalism, is an impossibility without capitalization. Some of the potentially wealthiest agricultural countries are importers of agricultural produce, such as Venezuela and Chile. The fishing-grounds off the Pacific coast of South America are some of the richest known to the world, rich enough to feed the countries of that area. Chilean fishermen cannot market fish properly, and dump marvelous catches of fish into the sea, because they have neither storage nor transport facilities to take their fish to the markets. Thus, there is neither a lack of labor nor a lack of markets for the fish, but the necessary capitalization to provide the facilities for bringing labor, produce, and market together is lacking. Much of the world is in the same predicament: it has the labor, the natural resources, and the hungry markets for its produce, but it lacks the necessary capital to make the flow of goods possible. Socialism tries to solve this problem but only aggravates it, because it furthers the poverty of all concerned. Socialism and inflation both accomplish the same purpose: they decapitalize an economy.

Capitalization is the product of work *and thrift*, the accumulation of wealth and the wise use of accumulated wealth. This accumulated wealth is invested in effect in progress, because it is made available for the development of natural resources and the marketing of goods and produce. The thrift which leads to the savings or accumulation of wealth, to capitalization, is a product of *character*. Capitalization is a product in every era of the Puritan disposition, of the willingness to forego present pleasures to accumulate some wealth for future purposes. Without character, there is no capitalization but rather decapitalization, the steady depletion of wealth. As a result, capitalism is supremely a product of Christianity, and, in particular, of Puritanism, which, more than any other faith, has furthered capitalization.

This means that, before decapitalization, either in the form of socialism or inflation, can occur, there must be a breakdown of faith and character. Before the United States began its course of socialism and inflation, it had abandoned its historic Christian position. The people had come to see more advantage in wasting capital than in accumulating it, in enjoying superficial pleasures than living in terms of the lasting pleasures of the family, faith, and character. Inflation succeeds when people have larceny in their hearts, and the same is true of socialism. Socialism is organized larceny; like inflation, it takes from the haves to give to the have-nots. By destroying capital, it destroys progress and pushes society into disaster. As the products of capitalization begin to wear out, new capital is lacking to replace them, and the state has no capital of its own: it only impoverishes the people further and therefore itself by trying to create capital by taxation. Every socialist state decapitalizes itself progressively.

When inflation and socialism get under way, having begun in the decline of faith and character, they see as their common enemy precisely those people who still have faith and character. In 1937, Roger Babson, in *If Inflation Comes*, wrote, "Only righteousness exalteth a nation today, as it did 3000 years ago. Hence, speaking strictly as a statistician, I say that the safest hedge against inflation is the development of character" (p. 178). We can add that the greatest enemy of inflation is faith and character. Inflation and socialism attack as the enemy Biblical Christianity, because it is their common purpose to destroy the roots of capitalization. By taxation and inflation, thrift is made both difficult and economically unsound, since money ceases to be gold and silver and becomes counterfeit, unredeemable paper. People are barred from possessing gold and silver in some countries; inheritance taxes work to destroy capital, as do income taxes. Education, television, the press, and all other media foster relativism and humanism; they promote *the decapitalization of character*. We have seen the progressive decline of public and private morality. Missionaries on furlough who return home every seventh year, have commented on the sharp erosion they witness with each return. Things which were once intolerable and forbidden are now openly promoted and sponsored.

We who stand for Biblical Christianity thus face a steadily more hostile world. We are everything which socialism and inflation hate most.

How are we to defend ourselves? And how can we have a return to capitalism? Capitalism can only revive if capitalization revives, and capitalization depends, in its best and clearest form, on that character produced by Biblical Christianity, by the regeneration of man through Jesus Christ. This means that we must begin afresh to establish truly Christian churches, to establish Christian schools and colleges, to promote Christian learning as the foundation of Christian character. Capitalization does not depend on winning elections, important as elections are. No election has yet really reversed decapitalization. The demand is for increasing decapitalization in the form of more welfare, more social security, more medicare, and the like. For the past generation, no office-holder has done more than to slow down this process very slightly. An election does not produce character, which is the foundation of capitalization.

Socialism and inflation work to create a depletion of spiritual resources as a necessary step towards their success. No counter-movement can succeed if the depleted spiritual resources are not replenished. When modern capitalism began, its critics love to point out, every capitalist was a Bible-toting, Bible-quoting man. He knew the Good Book from end to end far better than most clergymen do today. The Fabian Socialist, R. H. Tawney, in *Religion and the Rise of Capitalism* saw modern capitalism as substantially a product of Calvin and Puritanism. Calvinism, he said, produced "a race of iron" because of its "insistence on personal responsibility, discipline and asceticism (i. e., self-denial), and the call to fashion for the Christian character an objective embodiment in social institutions." In England, as capitalism began to develop as the new power in the state, Tawney said "the business classes were...conscious of themselves as something like a separate order, with an outlook on religion and politics peculiarly their own, distinguished not merely by birth and breeding, but by their social habits, their business discipline, the whole bracing atmosphere of their moral life, from a Court which they believed to be godless and an aristocracy which they knew to be spendthrift." Instead of holding that "business is business", these men held instead that business is a calling under God to be discharged in terms of His word and law. It was held that it was the *first* duty of man to know and believe in God. A Scottish divine of 1709 wrote of Glasgow, "I am sure the Lord is remarkably frowning upon our trade...since it was put in the room of religion." Priority in every man's life belongs to God alone. The *second* duty of man is to fulfil God's calling in his chosen vocation. A Puritan divine, wrote, "God doth call every man and woman...to serve Him in some peculiar employment in this world, both for their own and the common good...The Great Governor of the world both appointed to every man his proper post and province, and let him be never so active out of his sphere, he will be at a great loss, if he do not keep his own vineyard and mind his own business..."

It is a liberal and romantic myth that America and the frontier was colonized by people who had nothing. Men came here with capital, or worked to accumulate it, but their basic capital was *spiritual*: it was their Christian faith, and this led to economic capitalization. Far more actual capital migrated to Latin America than to North America, but it was an accumulated aristocratic wealth which either barely sustained itself on landed estates or else rapidly decapitalized because it had little spiritual capital.

This letter is written by one who believes intensely in orthodox Christianity and in our historic Christian American liberties and heritage. It is my purpose to promote the basic capitalization of society, out of which all else flows, *spiritual capital*. Without the spiritual capital of a God-centered and Biblical faith, we are spiritually and materially bankrupt. We will only succumb to the inflated and false values which govern men today and which are leading them to destruction. Where do you stand?

CHALCEDON REPORT NO. 20
May 1, 1967

A very basic fact hides behind a rather difficult philosophical term, *epistemological self-consciousness*. What does this mean?

Two simple illustrations will help us grasp its meaning. An artist with marked epistemological self-consciousness is Willem de Kooning. De Kooning paints in terms of Nietzsche's statement, "The will to a system is a lack of integrity." For de Kooning, no system of thought or of art is possible, because there is no meaning. As a result, his painting is simply meaningless daubs and blotches, a defiance of meaning and pure self-expression, expressive of the moment and its impulses. According to Hess, de Kooning paints in terms of "No-Environment," and this concept Hess defines for us:

> NO-ENVIRONMENT --- the metaphysical and social alienation of man from society and the nightmare of urbanization have been a preoccupation of modern writers from Marx and Dostoievski to Heidegger and Celine. For de Kooning, however, "no-environment" is a metaphysical concept with physical materiality -- with flesh and cement. In the Renaissance, he has pointed out, the painter located a Christ and a Roman soldier in their appropriate "places". What is a "place" today? (Thomas B. Hess: *Willem de Kooning*, p. 18. New York: George Braziller, 1959.)

For de Kooning, man has no "place", and the very idea of "place" is meaningless. There is "no-environment", because there is no framework of meaning for anything. As a result, de Kooning paints nothingness, because there is really nothing else to paint. The world is a world of nothingness, and, for many artists, art to be realistic must portray nothingness. Modern art is not photographic, but it is realistic. For modern art, reality is brute factuality, it is meaninglessness. The interest of modern artists in Buddhism is because of this agreement with Buddha that not God but nothingness is ultimate. As a result, these men are at war with the world of God and law, the world of meaning; for them, the true faith is in nothingness. Their nihilism calls for the destruction of the "pretense" of meaning. Of such men we can say that they have a high degree of epistemological self-consciousness. They know that on their atheistic premises a man can know nothing, and some of them, the "hippies" in particular, try to live in terms of their faith.

For a second illustration, take any modern, atheistic scientist. The scientist denies that there is a God who has created all things and whose predetermined plan governs all things. Like de Kooning, the scientist believes in a meaningless, "no-environment" world where nothing has a "place", because the very idea of a "place" for things means an absolute law and plan. But the scientist still works in his laboratory as though a plan existed; his scientific theories assume a plan and a place for all things, and he operates in his science on the assumption that there is a meaning and a direction in the universe. If he allowed his atheism to govern his science, the scientist would have to deny his science as surely as de Kooning has denied everything that art once meant.

De Kooning, of course, does not have full epistemological self-consciousness. This full self-knowledge would be suicidal for unbelieving man, and he fights against it. Without God there is neither meaning nor life. Every non-Christian presupposes at some points the existence of God, even as he consciously denies Him, because without Him all knowledge and meaning would be impossible. But God steadily moves all men and history to epistemological self-consciousness. He forces men to know that without Him they have no foundation, that their lives are built on sand.

Men want the world of law and order which God created, but they want it without God. They complain because all respect for authority is disappearing, and their children fail to give them the honor and obedience which is their due. But if God's absolute law and plan are withdrawn from education and denied, a child and an adult is given then the right to think that *his* plan is just as good as anyone else's plan. If there is no God, then there is no authority. A very brilliant college student, who headed a criminal gang, told me that there was no such thing as crime, because there was no absolute law. His very fine parents were deeply hurt and shaken by his criminality and his arrest and trial, but the young man was not. His education had told him that man was merely a product of chance evolution, and he believed therefore that all the old standards were false. By the age of 20, he had already lived more luxuriously than his well-to-do parents ever had, and enjoyed more of the "best" pleasures of life than they ever could; a year in prison was a cheap price, and a kind of vacation.

This young man had more epistemological self-consciousness than his parents. He knew at least the basic choices: God and moral law, versus no God, no law, no meaning. The trouble with most men today is that they want the "best" of two worlds, the moral order and meaning of God's world, and the freedom from God of atheism. The liberals, as a result, dream of a new world order in which all men will be well-behaved brothers, as good as the best Sunday School children, having full freedom from God's moral law without misbehaving or becoming socially destructive. The non-Christian conservative thinks that by winning some elections he can restore the old godly law order and authority, and have a free country again, when most men are drifting into de Kooning's world and have no use for the ideals he espouses. Man cannot re-establish true authority and law-order without first acknowledging and obeying the true authority, the triune God.

As a result, as history moves ahead, because epistemological self-consciousness increases, sinful man's rebellion against authority increases, because he progressively denies all authority and all meaning. Once non-Christian man was held in line by some of the God-given institutions, established at creation. The family in particular long functioned as man's basic policing power and source of order. But as men developed the principles of their unbelief, of their rebellion against God, they progressively rebelled against every authority God set up, in family, state, school, society, and everywhere else. Their only authority has become steadily their own will. Atheism itself is destroying the family, whether under communism, socialism, or democracy. Atheism is destroying authority in every area. College students are taught disrespect even for their teachers by their teachers, because the corrosive face of atheism destroys all authority. Instead of community, there is only a mob. Students were once self-reliant, individualistic, capable gentlemen who were taught how to exercise authority and also submit to authority. Today they are only members of a mob, meaningless blobs because for them there is no meaning apart from their momentary impulses.

It is therefore of the utmost importance for Christians to develop epistemological self-consciousness. This means Christian education. It means a Christian philosophy for every sphere of human endeavor. It means recognizing that *every* issue is basically a religious one. As Stacey Hebden-Taylor has written, in a very important study, "He who rejects one religion or god can only do so in the name of another." (E. L. Hebden-Taylor: *The Christian Philosophy of Law, Politics and the State*, p. 22. Nutley, New Jersey: The Craig Press, 1967.) The humanists religiously deny every authority other than man, and their totalitarian state is a deliberately conceived man-god defying the order of God with man's own order. The intensely powerful religious force of humanism, with all its hatred of God and God's world of law and order, can never be defeated by people whose ground of operation is vaguely Christian and largely humanistic. The lack of Christian epistemological self-consciousness is one of the major reasons, if not perhaps the major, for the growing victory of the enemy. Christians are too often trying to defend their realm on humanistic grounds, with Saul's armor, and as a result, they are steadily in retreat. Often, they are actually fighting for the enemy without knowing it

But victory should be ours. The more the enemy becomes what he is, the more his epistemological self-consciousness matures, the more impotent he becomes. What competition is a "hippie" for a truly Christian man? What competition is a de Kooning or a Bob Dylan for a Johann Sebastian Bach? But if we rear up a generation on humanistic premises, they will follow humanistic leaders. Humanism is progressively decaying; the more it becomes itself, the more repulsive and impotent it becomes. Nothing is more deadly for tares than maturity: they are then openly identified as tares, as worthless and poisonous, as definitely not wheat.

Today the impotence and confusion of humanism is marked. It is wallowing in failure all over the world, in failure, but not in defeat, because there is no consistent Christian force to challenge and overthrow it.

Nietzsche said, "The will to a system is a lack of integrity," that is, to believe in a system of truth is to submit oneself to a higher law, to God. The strength of the humanists is their denial of a system: it is their lawlessness. They have been successful destroyers, but they cannot build. The strength of the Christian can only be a "system", i. e., systematic theology, a knowing, intelligent, and systematic obedience to the triune God, and a faithful application of God's law order to every sphere of life. If the Christian operates without this system, he is a humanist without knowing it. And this is the reason for the very great impotence of conservative, evangelical Christianity: it is neither fish nor fowl.

God cannot bless a cause which does not honor Him. As Dr. Cornelius Van Til has said, "The Holy Spirit cannot be asked to honor a method that does not honor God as God." (Cornelius Van Til: *A Christian Theory of Knowledge*, p. 9. Craig Press, 1954.) Let us honor God, that He may honor us and our cause.

CHALCEDON REPORT NO. 21
June 19, 1967

A subject of growing importance and urgency today is *devaluation*. According to the dictionary, "devaluate" means "to fix the value of the currency to a low level to which an emergency has driven it." In its simplest form, devaluation occurs when the value of the gold backing of a paper currency is raised, and the paper money is accordingly lowered in value. Thus, if the gold is worth $35 an ounce, or is held at $35 an ounce, and is then raised in price to $70 an ounce, the paper money goes down in value and is now worth proportionately less. Previously, paper money was redeemable (as U.S. paper money is today by foreign countries) at 35 paper dollars for an ounce of gold; if gold goes to $70, then it takes 70 paper dollars to buy an ounce. The purchasing power of the paper has decreased in the same ratio that the gold has increased.

Devaluation is not the same as *debasement*, although the two often go together. In debasement, the weight or standard of the gold or silver in coins is reduced without reducing the face value of the coin. Thus, the silver quarter had $.23 in silver in it, at $1.29 an ounce, the old price; the new quarter has only 2 or 3 cents of materials in it but passes for $.25; the Mint makes a sizable profit on it. Debasement affects coinage, and this is a limited part of our money today. Devaluation affects most of our money.

Devaluation is a product of controls and of socialism; it follows the expansion of paper money and credit. The vast increase in money supply with paper money does not change the fact that the basic money is gold. Those who say there is not enough gold in the world to be our monetary unit forget that gold is already our monetary unit all over the world. Our trouble comes from the fact that we are trying to substitute a counterfeit, paper money, for it. The paper inflates because it is counterfeit; gold is going up in price, not because gold is changing in value, but simply because the inflated paper is worth less. Before 1913, gold had changed very little in price for 85 years. It has changed since then because gold is now traded, not for real wealth, but for inflated paper money. The more inflation increases, the more gold will demand a higher price. Only gold backed currencies flow in international trade; no foreign country is interested in irredeemable paper money.

Devaluation thus is a product of irresponsibility. The more paper money a state prints, the more a civil government goes into debt, the more the demand mounts for gold as a protection against increasingly worthless paper. The printing press treasury wants to say that its money is still "as good as gold", but people begin to show their fears and prefer gold. To devalue is to confess that the paper money is failing, and this treasuries hesitate to do. On the other hand, once they devalue, the treasuries double the value of the gold they possess, if they double the price of gold, and this gives visions of instant wealth and frees them for more inflation. Devaluation is like a partial bankruptcy; it frees a country from some of its debts and gives it power to incur far greater debts. It prepares the way for total bankruptcy.

We have scarcely touched the economics of devaluation, but our concern is with its morality, its ethics. Devaluation of money is simply one of the consequences of moral devaluation. Moral devaluation is the erosion of moral standards and of godly law and order. It comes when people pay lip service to God but re-interpret God's law to suit their tastes. Moral devaluation is present when people are against immorality generally, but feel that there is no point in being a "blue -nose" about it. They are against perversions, but they do not favor the severity of God's law concerning it. They disapprove of stealing, but hotel "souvenirs" are another matter. Moral devaluation produces a world in which people want the law and order of morality but not its responsibility. We are thus against abortion, but with increasing qualifications. We are against murder, but we enforce capital punishment less and less, although it is required by God. We want other people to be responsible so that we will have less troubles and problems ourselves.

Moral devaluation always precedes monetary devaluation. The first and foremost step in monetary devaluation is *inflation*, and, in 1936, Freeman Tilden, in *A World in Debt* (p. 279), observed that there were two facts which preceded inflation. *First*, there "is the intent to falsify the true economic position of a nation, or to relieve the debtor at the expense of the creditor." *Second*, "Inflation, whether of bank credit or of paper currency, cannot be effective until the larcenous purpose is generally comprehended." Both these facts represent moral devaluation, moral collapse. It is absurd to try to tell socialistic legislators and voters that their course of action is immoral from a Christian perspective: this is why they chose it! Larceny in the heart precedes inflation and is necessary before inflation can work. Moral devaluation is thus the source and cause of monetary devaluation.

A minor but vivid sidelight on our moral devaluation has been cited by Charles H. Brower. The word "square" was once a symbol of perfection in Bible times. More recently, it has been a term indicating integrity, honesty, dependability and character. Now the word "square" is used by our youth and by radicals as a term of contempt; it means that people who are honest and moral are ridiculous and foolish.

Monetary devaluation is the progressive destruction of money, often ending in economic collapse and anarchy. But before that stage sets in, moral anarchy begins to prevail. Moral anarchy precedes economic anarchy and is furthered by it. The world of monetary devaluation is a world which prefers and encourages more moral devaluation.

What to do about it? A man does not become moral merely by being against sin. No one hates stealing more than the gambling house operators of Las Vegas, and they take stern measures against it. Morality believes that the universe is governed by God's absolute law, and that the wages of sin are death, but the gift of God, eternal life. Morality moves positively to bring the world under God's law, and to establish the dominion of God's law over man and his society. As Moses said long ago, "Who is on the Lord's side? let him come unto me" (Exodus 32: 26). The test, Moses declared, was an open stand and warfare in God's name to establish God's order. Nothing less than faith and the obedient works of faith are acceptable.

CHALCEDON REPORT NO. 22
July 1, 1967

Syncretism is an unfamiliar word for a very familiar and dangerous reality. The first definition in the second edition of Merriam-Webster's Dictionary calls it "The reconciliation or union of conflicting beliefs", and the second definition defines it as "egregious compromise in religion or philosophy."

If a man believes that God and Satan, good and evil, can be reconciled and united, he is a syncretist. If a man holds that we can remain true to the U.S. Constitution and have a welfare state, that man is a syncretist. If a man believes that orthodox Christianity can be reconciled and united, or live in peace with, modernism, humanism, Mohammedanism or Buddhism, that man is a syncretist, not a Christian. A syncretist has always abandoned his original position, even though he refuses to acknowledge this fact,

Syncretism has a very long history, and a very honorable one, on the whole, unfortunately. Most cultures have been essentially syncretistic. The hostility to syncretism was born with the Biblical revelation and is inseparable from it. The intellectual attitude of antiquity was geared to the absorption of rival doctrines and religions, and syncretism was a matter of basic policy in many cases. In the Biblical revelation, God repeatedly identified Himself, not only as the only true God, but as a "jealous God" (Exodus 20:5), i. e., totally exclusive in His jurisdiction, truth, revelation and government. Therefore man can have no other gods before Him; there can be no syncretism. Biblical revelation cannot be mixed with anything else.

Israel, however, was inclined towards syncretism, especially the northern kingdom, Israel, which gave itself more consistently to syncretism, whereas Judah, sometimes faithful, sometimes apostate, was less inclined to attempts at uniting Biblical religion with Canaanite cults. The ministry of the prophets was largely a denunciation of syncretism and a pronouncement of judgment against it. Ahab has gained particular eminence in history as a great syncretist, but every monarch of the northern kingdom from Jeroboam to the end held the same position. Hence the destruction by God of the northern kingdom in their separate existence.

Now syncretism is destructive of the human mind, of rationality. To recall earlier illustrations, a man who wants to unite good and evil, Christianity and Buddhism, the U. S. Constitution and socialism, has lost the capacity for clear thinking. His mind is darkened, clouded, fuzzed over, and incompetent. And, apart from the history of the Biblical faith and its cultures, the intellectual history of the world is a sorry one. The one clear period of eminence, Greek philosophy, perished because of its reconciliation of unreconcilable ideas, i.e., form and matter, change and permanence, etc. The same is true of Chinese, Indian, and Arabic (Moslem) philosophies. Their years of eminence were relatively brief, and their collapse notable. As syncretists, they themselves destroyed the minds of men by attempting to reconcile what they themselves saw as antinomies of reason. Their bent to syncretism, bent on uniting all anti-God aspects into a system, made them finally immune to clear thinking. All non-Biblical thought is essentially humanistic; it is guilty of the basic, the original sin, the attempt to be a god, determining for one's self what constitutes good and evil in relation to purely personal or humanistic standards. Man, by presuming to be god, has by that act destroyed the possibility of true thinking; from so radically false a premise, no valid conclusion can follow.

Syncretism is thus one aspect of the destruction of the mind and evidence of it. Syncretism blinds the mind to the most obvious facts. To cite a painfully obvious example, on Friday, June 23, 1967, President Lyndon B. Johnson and the Soviet dictator, Premier Alexei N. Kosygin, met at Glassboro, New Jersey. The President of the United States happily reported of Kosygin, "He has been a grandfather longer than I have --- and he an I agreed that we wanted a world of peace for our grandchildren." (*Oakland Tribune*, Saturday, June 24, 1967, p. EB, "Grandfather Summit.") For

Johnson, peace is peace; as a consummate syncretist, bent on integrating everything (which is what syncretism does to all things), Johnson fails to recognize that there are different kinds of peace. Soviet peace is for a Christian both war and slavery. To negotiate peace with Marxism is to negotiate for war and slavery. As a good humanist, Johnson believes that all men and all religions really want the same thing, and, each in their own way, are all working towards the same goal. Johnson's course, which is America's course, offers no hope whatsoever.

But Kosygin is a syncretist also, not as muddled a one as Johnson, but still a syncretist. Like all Marxists, he assumes that the dictatorship of the proletariat (himself and his associates) is the only god history knows. He assumes that Marxist politics, like God, can *create*; therefore, he believes that politics can legislate economic production. As a result, Marxism pushes its people nearer to famine continually. The Marxist tries to reconcile economic prosperity with a war on economics: this is syncretistic thinking, an attempt to reconcile conflicting things. The Marxist tries also to reconcile the total enslavement of man with the total liberation of man. His thinking is too muddled for him to recognize the chaos he creates.

A central goal of modern syncretists is the union of all religions into a one world religion as a companion to a one world state. Some authorities say that the June, 1966, 18th National Convention of the Communist Party in New York City, in promulgating its "Operation '76," placed high on the list of goals the union of all organized religious bodies in the early 1970s as a universal "Church of World Brotherhood." But this goal is more than a Marxist hope: it is a devout hope with all syncretists, who see man's greatest freedom and peace in the total integration of all religions.

Other syncretists call for racial integration as a means of breaking down "divisive barriers" and "freeing" man. Still others demand a new morality geared to man, one which will bring men together in terms of "peace" and "unity" rather than dividing them in terms of Jesus Christ and His absolute law and His exclusive salvation. Christian chastity and morality will be assaulted by such men, and is being sharply attacked, as neurotic and unhealthy. All who do not unite in the "health" of the world syncretistic order will be treated as mentally disturbed and sick. Already in the name of Christ man is being worshipped and the Bible denied by the religious leaders of this syncretistic world. The Bible itself is already a banned book in some parts of the world, forbidden as "hate" literature and as subversive to the unity of the syncretistic order.

In the face of this, some humanistic conservatives want us to be syncretistic also, to forget our religious differences and to give priority to a particular project or election, as though the world's salvation rested on the candidacy of Joe Doaks. Elections are important, but truth is more important, and the root reason for the syncretism of our age is that Biblical

Christianity has been abandoned by most Americans in favor of humanism.

Make no mistake about it: the American people *want* syncretism, and they are paying good money to get it. They may complain sometimes because of certain aspects of its program, but they are basically committed to it. Syncretism, remember, tries to reconcile two irreconcilable things, and this is what people want. A prominent, wealthy, conservative and very influential woman told me, more graciously than it sounds in print, that my religious faith is "barbarous." The only kind of God she stated that she can believe in is one who saves everyone from every kind of problem and never sends anyone to hell; in other words, religiously she wanted to eat her cake and have it too. She was insistent that she is "as good a Christian as anybody", and "a good humanist too". She believed that Buddhists, atheists, Moslems, and others *all* went to heaven also, like herself on their own terms. She is only unhappy at the socialism she gets from the pulpit, not the humanism, and basically she is content with her church. And there are more than a hundred and fifty million like her. They are syncretists. For them, God's only purpose is to ensure man, the true sovereign, of the best of all possible worlds! They *complain* about some things in their syncretistic churches, but they *hate* Biblical Christianity. They are buying the kind of religion they want in preference to bowing down before the sovereign and triune God. They have cast their vote and their dollar, against the God of Scripture --- but the power of God is not dependent on their vote or their dollar. "The word of God is not bound" (II Timothy 2:3). And their syncretism will have results: it will lead to their integration into death and judgment. God still remains a "jealous" or exclusive God, and truth will forever be exclusive of error, and right will be exclusive of wrong, for "The earth is the LORD'S, and the fullness thereof; the world, and they that dwell therein." (Psalm 24:1).

CHALCEDON REPORT NO. 23
August 1, 1967

The evidences of anarchy are increasing on all sides. Criminality rioting, looting, burning, and general lawlessness are becoming 'normal' in our society, and law and order unusual and 'abnormal'. Who, in 1964, would have believed that in 1967 over 80 cities would see racial violence, and the violence has only begun. The anarchism of existentialism is apparent in radical student movements, in popular music, and in the "hippies". The churches are proclaiming this gospel of anarchism: one recent sermon in a prominent church was on "the Advantages of Adultery". The world of business and civil government is also saturated with dishonesty and immorality, as Fred J. Cook has shown in *The Corrupted Land, The Social Morality of Modern America* (1966).

But what we have seen is only the beginning. The worst is still ahead of us, and people may soon recall 1967 as "the good old days" of peace and quiet.

We have no right to be surprised at all this. Basic to all social order is *authority*, religious authority. The authority undergirding Western civilization has been the authority of the triune God. Christian authority led, *first*, to godly peace and to law and order. In other cultures, order is imposed by force and by a pagan religious faith which induces subjection. Christian law and order, instead of stifling man and society, liberated it. *Second*, this liberation of the Christian was twofold. Man was freed from the burden of sin and guilt, thereby gaining *inner* liberty, and man was freed from subjection to a divine state or ruler, thereby gaining *outer* liberty. *Third*, the free Christian man was able then to capitalize, to work productively and to save for the future. The modern world of technology has only arisen as a result to this Christian heritage.

Now, however, Christian authority is denied. All godly authority is overthrown in church, state, school, home, business, and private associations. And when men deny and despise God's authority, it is then nothing for them to deny and flout all human authority. Freedom from God's authority means finally freedom from all authority, and the result is that man moves steadily and rapidly into the abyss of chaos and anarchy.

Having denied God, man makes himself a god and insists on equality, since all men are gods. The basic principle in law today is *equality*, so that it is now predicted that law-suits will demand equality of income as the next step in the "civil rights" revolution. Richard M. Elman, in *The Poorhouse State* (1966), favors a high "guaranteed annual income" for all on welfare and an end to "doctrines of individual achievement" as means of victimizing the poor (p. 299).

In the name of equality, we are being led into socialism and communism. Even the "right to privacy" is being steadily attacked. Thus, a psychologist has attacked the concept as a front for evil and deviation and has written, "An honest mind should be an open window," i.e., should withhold nothing. Moreover, "The closed door, in most households, is not so much a guardian of privacy, as a symptom of prudery; a barrier between the generations, an obstacle to fluent sex education, a reinforcement of guilt and repression." (Chester C. Bennett, "What Price Privacy?" in the *American Psychologist*, Journal of the American Psychological Association, Inc., vol. 22, no. 5, May, 1967, pp. 371-376).

Equality is the basic principle of anarchy. It levels all things and denies authority, that is, any authority other than the anarchic individual. Where God's supreme and absolute authority is recognized, then equality is automatically denied, because all things then are good or evil, better or worse, higher or lower, as they fulfil God's moral law or represent His legitimate authority. In the history of socialism, over and over again its basic premise is cited: "If there is no God, then all things are equal." All men are then equal, all ideas are equal; good and evil are equal, right and wrong are equal. The only difference in things, as John Dewey pointed out, is then pragmatic; all things are equal, but some are more useful at the moment.

The destruction of authority in our Western civilization and all over the world, is now far gone. The result will increasingly be anarchy.

Historically, collectivism has succeeded best where it has had a background of authoritarianism. Marxism has succeeded most, as in Russia and China, where it can utilize a strong tradition of authority, of church and state in Russia, of family and state in China. In every area, however, Marxism itself creates anarchy and moves towards anarchy and collapse; without outside help, every Marxist economy and state would collapse.

Western civilization, by denying the sovereign authority of God is moving steadily into anarchy. It is destroying its foundations. Christian law and order are disappearing, and evil is being rewarded. The rioters are given federal subsidies, and the godly are taxed to provide the millions of dollars given to these anarchistic revolutionists. Liberty is disappearing rapidly, and not a week passes but someone in our circle reports on a further intrusion of statist power. Moreover, capitalization is being destroyed, as confiscatory taxation makes it increasingly impossible. Also, the products of our statist schools increasingly lack the capacity to capitalize. They share, in varying degrees, the ideology of the "hippies." They have "dropped out": they will only coast, not build.

Thus, we are seeing the basic products of Christian authority, 1) law and order, 2) Christian liberty, spiritual and material, and 3) capitalization, rapidly disappear from our civilization. They cannot be restored by a gimmick. No political candidate or officeholder can re-create this sequence or re-establish a spiritual condition. The mob, the majority, governs the politicians today, and the forces of anarchism are growing.

We have anarchy because we do not have godly authority. To re-establish law and order, and liberty, and to capitalize our culture, we must again have godly authority. The sovereignty of God must become our basic concern: "Man's chief end is to glorify God and to enjoy Him forever." In terms of this, we must also "teach" or "make disciples" of all nations" (Matt. 28:19), and this requires self-discipline. The weakness of much of evangelical Christianity is a moralistic reduction of the faith to a few "thou shalt not's", but the alternative is not license, but, as Christian athletes (I Cor. 9:27), to commit our entire being to the cause of Christ and His sovereign authority.

Anarchy is the end product of the denial of God's authority. Armed officers can and must quell revolutionary anarchy, but they cannot destroy the anarchy in the hearts of men. That inner anarchy, like a cancer, is destroying the life of Western civilization. Instead of declining, each year the forces of anarchism in church, state, school, business, society, and home are growing. They will not disappear until anarchy is replaced by God's authority. Until men seek that remedy, the anarchy will increase, and will steadily strike closer to home. And when it strikes, it will not come knocking politely.

How can we have God's blessing in the face of all these things? We must render to God what belongs to God, His due. Men must become godly men, heads of their households, spiritually and materially. We must render to God the faith and obedience which is His due spiritually and materially, the tithe which He requires (Mal. 3:8-10). The tithe belongs to God, not to the church, which is often at odds with God, and must be administered for godly causes. We must recognize that the future is in God's hands, not in the hands of godless conspiracies (Psalm 2) and we can have no part in God's future apart from God's terms.

As Joshua said, "Choose ye this day whom ye will serve...but as for me and my house, we will serve the LORD (Joshua 24:15).

CHALCEDON REPORT NO. 24
September 1, 1967

It is urgently important that we think now of *Christian reconstruction*, but our thinking cannot be idle talk: it must be both Biblical and also practically applied in our daily life. There are many people ready to eliminate statism, but they have nothing but wishing to replace it. How then will independent schools, private welfare, and individual initiative deal with the vast complex of our social problems? Already most of our Christian conservative causes, and Christian schools, are continually short of funds. What is the answer?

In any advanced social order, social financing is a major public necessity. The social order cannot exist without a vast network of social institutions which require financing and support. If a Christian concept of social financing is lacking, then the state moves in quickly to supply the lack and gain the social control which results. Social financing means social power.

The Bible provides, as the foundation law, in the practical realm, of a godly social order, the law of the *tithe*. To understand the tithe, it is important to know that Biblical law has *no property tax*; the right to tax real property is implicitly denied to the state, because the state has no title to the earth. Repeatedly, the Bible declares, "The earth is the LORD'S (Exodus 9: 29, Deut. 10: 14, Ps. 24: 1, I Cor. 10: 26, etc.); therefore, only God can tax the earth. For the state to claim the right to tax the earth is for the state to make itself the god and creator of the earth, whereas the state is instead God's ministry of justice (Romans 13: 1-8).

The immunity of land from taxation by the state meant liberty. A man could not be dispossessed of his land: every man had a basic security in his property. As H. B. Rand, in his *Digest of Biblical Law* pointed out, "It was impossible to dispossess men of their inheritance under the law of the Lord as no taxes were levied against land. Regardless of a man's personal commitments he could not disinherit his family by being dispossessed of his land forever." The land is not the property of the state, and no state therefore has the right under God to levy taxes against God's possessions. The Bible cites it as a sign of tyranny when the state claims the right to take as much as God, i.e., a tithe, or ten percent of one's increase. Thus, Samuel said of the tyrant, "He will, besides, take a tenth of your grain crop and of your vineyards and give it to his officers and to his servants...He will appropriate a tenth of your flocks, too, and you yourselves will become his servants" (I Samuel 8:15,17, Berkeley Version). Today, civil government takes more than a tenth of our income: it takes about 45 percent!

When America was colonized, the settlers in every colony made Biblical law their basic law. There was no tax on property: this was basic to Biblical liberty. The inscription on the Liberty Bell is taken from the Biblical land law: "proclaim liberty throughout all the land unto all the inhabitants thereof" (Lev. 25:10). In the first session of the Continental Congress in 1774, Congress denied that Parliament could tax real property. Gottfried Dietze has summarized the American opinion then: "As to property, the delegates felt it should be free from seizure and taxation." The property tax came in very slowly, and it appeared first in New England, coinciding with the spread of Deism and Unitarianism, as well as atheism. Such anti-Christian men saw the state as man's savior, and as a result they favored placing more and more in the hands of the state. The South was the last area to accept the property tax, and it was largely forced on the South by post-Civil War Reconstruction. Moreover, as far as possible, when the property tax was adopted in the pre-Civil War era, conservative elements limited it to the county and retained the legal requirement that only owners of real property could vote on the county level.

Today, the property tax is in effect a rent for the use of our own land; the state has the power of confiscation for non-payment, and also the "right" of eminent domain. This is, in terms of the Bible, a mark of tyranny, as both the law, and the story of Naboth's vineyard, makes clear.

The tithe is God's tax for the use of the earth; it is *not* a gift to God. Only when the giving exceeds ten percent is it called a gift and a "freewill offering" (Deut. 16:10,11; Ex. 36:7, Lev. 22:21, etc.). The tithe is required of *all* men by God. Failure to pay the tithe brings on God's curse; yielding God His due results in so great "a blessing, that there shall not be room enough to receive it" (Malachi 3:8-10).

The tithe was used for a variety of purposes. It supported the religious and educational institutions of Israel, and also of colonial and early America. In fact, in the United States the tithe was for many years legally binding on all men, and failure to pay it was a civil offense. The tithe supported the churches, Christian schools, and colleges. When Virginia repealed such a law, which made payment of the tithe mandatory, George Washington expressed his disapproval in a letter to George Mason, October 3, 1785. He believed he said, in "making people pay toward the support of that which they profess." The position Washington took was one which the early church had established as soon as any country became Christian. State laws began to require tithes from the 4th century on, because it was believed that a country could only deny God His tax at its peril, and therefore the various civil governments required all their citizens to pay tithes, not to the state but to the church. From the end of the 18th century, and especially in the last century, such laws have steadily disappeared as a result of the atheistic and revolutionary movements of our times.

In the early years of this country, virtually the only taxing power of the federal government was duties and excise taxes; the taxing powers of the states and counties were also exceedingly small. The total take in taxes was originally scarcely more than one percent. The functions of civil government were very limited: justice and defense, mainly, plus the mails. The tithe and giving took care of most religious and social needs, voluntarily and economically.

Before going further, let us examine the Biblical law concerning the tithe. The tithe is described in Leviticus 27:30-33. A tenth of all produce or production was claimed by God as His due and was holy or set apart for Him. If the owner wanted to retain this tenth in its original form, i. e., as fruit or grain, he could do so by paying its value plus a fifth.

This tithe belongs to God, not to the church, nor to the producer. It cannot be given to an apostate church without being given thereby *against* God, not to Him. It must be given therefore to godly causes. The Priests and Levites, to whom it was originally given, had charge of religion, education, and various other functions. The tithe was paid six years in seven, the seventh being a rest for the land and the people.

But there was a second tithe, called also the festival tithe (Deut. 14:22-27, 16:3,13,16). The purpose of this tithe was to rejoice before the Lord, "and thou shalt bestow the money for whatsoever thy soul desireth" in order to "rejoice, thou and thy household: and the Levite that is within thy gates." This second tax required by God was thus for the family's pleasure.

There was also a third tithe (Deut. 14:28f.), every third year, or twice in seven years. Some scholars feel that the correct reading makes this a substitute for the second tithe in the appointed year. Henry Lansdell, in *The Tithe in Scripture* called attention to I Tobit 1: 6-8 (in the Apocrypha), and to Josephus (Antiquities, bk. IV as well as to Jerome (*Commentary on Ezekiel*, XIV, i, 565) and Chrysostom (*Homily* lxiv on Matt. xx. 27), to hold that a tithe in addition to the first two was meant. Maimonides in the 12th century held that this third tithe was the second tithe shared, but Aben Ezra disagreed. This tithe was a kind of social welfare tithe, to be shared with lowly foreigners, not as a hand-out, but in common feasting and rejoicing before the Lord. As Lansdell pointed out, Christ did not repeal the law of tithing (pp. 117-126). Jesus did not condemn the Pharisees for tithings: "these ought ye to have done, and not to leave the other undone", that is, "the weightier matters of the law, judgment (justice), mercy, and faith" (Matthew 23: 23). Chrysostom declared, "If under the law it were dangerous to neglect tithes, consider how great a danger there is now" (*Hom.* iv, in *Eph.* ii). Joseph Bingham, in *The Antiquities of the Church*, wrote of the early church that "the ancients believed the law about tithes not to be merely a ceremonial or political command, but of moral and perpetual obligation" (v,1).

Now, what did the tithe do? *First* of all, the tithe was an admission that the earth is the Lord's not the state's, and the only legitimate tax on land is by Almighty God. The tithe established property as a right and privilege under God. As Rand noted, "Nowhere in the Bible is there any indication that property rights are to ever be abolished. On the contrary, such rights are emphasized and safeguards are placed around that property to protect a man and his possessions. Liberty for the individual is non-existent apart from freedom of possession and the protection of personal holdings and property, with adequate compensation for its loss or destruction."

Second, when men forsake God's law and His sovereign claim as Lord of the earth, they are cursed by Him and sold into bondage (I Samuel 8, Malachi 3:8-10). What belongs to God must be rendered to God. We cannot have God's blessing if we deny Him His due, the first tithe in particular. To be blessed by God, we must obey God.

Third, the tithe made a free society possible. If every true Christian tithed today, we could build vast numbers of new and truly Christian churches, Christian schools and colleges, and we could counteract socialism by Christian reconstruction, by creating Christian institutions and a growing area of Christian independence. Consider the resources for Christian reconstruction if only 25 families tithed faithfully! Socialism grows as Christian independence declines. As long as people are slaves within, they will demand slavery in their social order. The alternative to a godly society, as God made clear to Samuel, is one in which men, having forsaken God make man their lord. And, when their decision finally comes home to them, and they cry out to God, God refuses at that late date to hear them (I Sam. 8:18). The time for repentance and reconstruction is before judgment strikes. Conscientious and intelligently administered tithing by even a small minority can do much to reconstruct a land.

Fourth, the tithe is thus the financial basis of reconstruction. Good wishes, votes, letter-writing, attendance at meetings, all have their place, but they are not enough. Reconstruction requires a financial foundation, and this the tithe provides. The tithe can recreate the necessary Christian institutions.

Fifth, the tithe restores the necessary economic basis to society: it asserts the absolute lordship and ownership of God over the earth, and the God-given nature of private ownership under God. To pay the tithe is to deny the foundations of statism. To pay the tithe means therefore also, not only the practical steps possible towards Christian reconstruction, but also the sure blessing of God in our battle against socialism. Having now sided with God, we have sided with victory.

Sixth, the tithe restores the necessary spiritual basis to Christian action. Today, many people do give generously to various causes, but their giving is impulsive and emotional. They like to give to a church or program which provides excitement and glamour, and the result is irresponsible stewardship. The person who provides the best Hollywoodish production, and the best press-agentry, gets the money. When people are disillusioned with such a project, they move on to look for another exciting and glamorous action. But the law of the tithe makes clear it is God's money and must go to God's causes, to Christian worship, education, outreach, and reconstruction. The tithe cannot be channeled to "exciting" causes but to godly causes, to solid, steady, consistently Biblical causes. And the tithe must bear the whole burden of Christian reconstruction. Conservative giving goes much of the time to fighting against the inroads of the enemy, which is of course necessary; the tithe goes for reconstruction.

Seventh, the tithe restores power to the little man. Today, it is the rich man who dominates most causes, his money counts; he can donate a hundred thousand or a million and make his influence felt. But a thousand little men who tithe can far outweigh the rich man. They can keep a Christian cause from being dominated by a handful. Tithing is the way for the little man to have power with God's blessing. A hundred men paying an average tithe of $100 a month means $10,000 monthly, which means that a relatively small group is capable of great things and will gain God's blessing in the process. Socialism has filled a void vacated by Christians. The spread of Unitarianism and atheism in the United States was closely followed by the spread of socialism. It was not by accident that the early American socialists of 1800-1860 attacked the tithe. To break down tithing meant that another source of social financing had to be forthcoming, the central civil government. And it was the total social impact of the little man's tithe that was so over-powering: the millionaires were few, but the little people were many. Make no mistake about it: social financing is a social necessity. It will either be done by an irresponsible and godless state, subsidizing irresponsibility and godlessness and penalizing the godly, or it will be done by godly men, who, through Biblically grounded administration and godly wisdom, will further social order, true churches, Christian education, and a society flourishing in liberty under God.

You vote here with your pocketbook. Take your choice: or have you already made it?

CHALCEDON REPORT NO. 25
October 1, 1967

Why pray, when you can worry? Some years ago, Dr. 0. Hallesby told the amusing story of a not too bright old woman in his rural Norway. She trudged to and from town with her sack of groceries. When a neighboring farmer offered her a lift home one day in his wagon, Mary climbed up beside the farmer, but she still clutched her heavy bag over her shoulder. "Put your bag down in the back, Mary," suggested the farmer. But Mary refused: "The least I can do to help, when you've been so good to me, is to carry my own load." As Hallesby pointed out, most of us are like old Mary in relation to God: we clutch our own load, as though He were not carrying us and all that we have.

In the days ahead, we must be prompt to act, and prompt to pray. But how do we pray?

First of all, as St. Paul made clear, "he that cometh to God must believe that he is, and that he is a rewarder of them that diligently seek him" (Heb. 11:6). It is useless to pray if we do not believe that God is the absolute sovereign, able to answer our prayers, and in His righteousness, given to a strict accounting, yet loving and gracious to His own. The first premise of successful prayer is thus faith, and the obedience of faith.

Second, prayer is simply talking with God. Theologians have defined the forms of prayer, and the ingredients of prayer (confession, praise, thanksgiving, petition, etc.), but our concern here is elementary, and not liturgical. Prayer then is our conversation with God. But conversation dies when it is one-sided. Nothing is more trying than to maintain a formal, polite attitude of conversation with persons we dislike or cannot talk to. On the other hand, two very good friends can spend hours together and talk freely and endlessly and with pleasure. It is impossible for us to talk freely and easily with God if we are not listening to Him and have very little idea of what He has to say. God's side of the conversation is the Bible. To speak with God freely and successfully, it is important first of all to hear Him. Regular, daily Bible reading is the best and surest stimulus to prayer, and also a necessity for our spiritual and moral growth. Family Bible reading, a chapter after dinner with prayer, is an excellent and much needed practice.

Third, the manner of prayer is a question in the minds of many. When our prayers are more deliberate, or with the family, we need to remember all God's mercies and blessings and to express our gratitude as well as our needs. But another type of prayer needs to have a major part in our lives also; brief, silent, sentence prayers throughout the day. If you must deal with a difficult problem, pray quickly first, "Lord, I don't know how to handle this situation. Give me wisdom to cope with it. In Jesus' Name, Amen." If a trying person must be met during the day, pray, "Lord, give me patience, firmness, or whatever I need to face this person." And so on. These sentence prayers, by the dozen, should dot our day, and they will make it an easier day for us.

With respect to table graces, there are many forms, but I like in particular the Anglican form:

> Father: The eyes of all wait upon Thee, 0 Lord.
> Family: And Thou givest them their meat in due season.
> Father: Thou openest Thy hand,
> Family: And fillest all things living with plenteousness.
> Father: Glory be to the Father, and to the Son, and to the Holy Ghost,
>
> All: As it was in the beginning, is now, and ever shall be, world without end, Amen.
> Father: Bless, 0 Father, this food to strengthen our bodies. Bless us to Thy loving service. In Jesus' name. Amen.

Instead of the concluding formal prayer by the father, I prefer an informal, spontaneous prayer in terms of daily needs.

Fourth, prayer should be "in Jesus' name". We approach God, not in our righteousness, but in His righteousness as declared unto us in Jesus Christ. As members of Jesus Christ, we have access to God through His person. Hence, we pray in His name, because we stand in His righteousness and in His grace. Because our salvation is the work of Christ, our merit and standing in God's sight are also of Christ.

Fifth, we must remember that God is absolute Lord over all things. The tendency to limit God's power to things spiritual is a Manichean heresy. God is able to give us things material and spiritual. The Bible is very plain-spoken in its promises: Jesus said, "Therefore I say unto you what things soever ye desire, when ye pray, believe that ye receive them, and ye shall have them" (Mark 11:24). "And whatsoever ye shall ask in my name, that will I do; that the Father may be glorified in the Son" (John 14:13). "Verily, verily I say unto you, Whatsoever ye shall ask the Father in My name, He will give it to you" (John 16:23). "Ye have not chosen me, but I have chosen you...that ye should go and bring forth fruit, and that your fruit should remain; that whatsoever ye shall ask of the Father in My name, He may give it you" (John 15:16). St. John wrote, "And whatsoever we ask, we receive of Him, because we keep His commandments, and do those things that are pleasing in His sight" (I John 3:22). "And if we know that He hears us, whatsoever we ask, we know that we have the petitions that we desired of Him" (I John 5:15).

These verses make it clear that prayers which are full of vague statements are meaningless. God has given every man a calling, responsibilities and duties under Him in Christ, and He expects us to discharge those duties and challenges. And, in the process of meeting our responsibilities, we must rely on His help by prayer. I have heard prayers by ministers which are really an insult to God: these so-called prayers are full of flowery compliments but say nothing and ask nothing. The man is apparently too sure of his own ability to handle every problem to ask God's help specifically and concretely. But if God is sovereign, we cannot function without Him. "In Him we live, and move and have our being" (Acts 17:28). If we have nothing to ask of the absolute Sovereign, it is because we feel ourselves to be sovereign. We ask, because we cannot live without Him and His help, because God's grace, mercy, blessing, and providential care are the ground of our being and the safety and prosperity of our lives. We ask "in Jesus' Name", in terms of His person and our godly responsibilities and fulfillment in Him.

Sixth, our prayers must be concerned about our own real needs, as well as the needs of the church as a whole, or of the world. Prayer must be personal, but there is a difference between personal petition and greedy petition. We can ask for much without being greedy, and ask for little and be greedy. As St. James said, "Ye ask, and receive not, because ye ask amiss" (James 4:3). We cannot treat the world and God as though all things exist for our sake, as though all things have to justify themselves by serving our goals and purposes, our own desires. The first petition of the Lord's prayer says, "Thy kingdom come. Thy will be done in earth, as it is in heaven" (Matt. 6:10). Our Lord said, concerning all the necessities and normal hopes of this life, "Seek ye first the kingdom of God, and His righteousness, and all these things shall be added unto you" (Matt. 6:33). Prayer must be personal, but it must be in Christ and in terms of the calling of God, and our responsibilities, needs, and hopes in Him.

Seventh, some writers have much to say about the "mistakes" in praying, but, very simply, the biggest mistake is not praying. We need not trouble ourselves about mistakes in praying. If we read the Bible and persevere in prayer, the mistakes take care of themselves, even as a child's language grows in maturity with schooling. I like the story of the small boy who wrote his first letter, to his father who was away on business: "Dear Daddy, I luv you and mis you. When are you comeing hom. Are you bringing me a pressent. Your luving son." The letter was faulty, but it was still perfect: it expressed a love and dependence which delighted the father. Our prayers are often like that. God views the prayer of faith with grace, righteousness, and love, not with the human nit-picking attitude.

Eighth, central to our Lord's teaching on prayer was the emphasis on perseverance: "Men ought always to pray, and not to faint" (Luke 18:1). "With God all things are possible" (Matt. 19:26), and whatever our petitions are, if they can be prayed "in Jesus' Name" we are encouraged to persevere in prayer.

Ninth, all our petitions save one are conditional upon God's grace, but one petition has as its only condition *faith*. We can, if we have faith, ask God for wisdom, "and it shall be given" (James 1:5,6). Wisdom we all need in these days, and we need to pray for it. Obviously, not many are praying for it.

Prayer is inescapable. Man is not omnipotent, nor is man self-sufficient. For a man to feel self-sufficient means that he is self-deluded and insane; life has a bitter disillusionment in store for him. Men with any sense of reality *know* their limitations, sins, and shortcomings as they face the problems of this world and of their own being. They will look to a higher power. Most men make the state that higher power, and their prayer, in effect is that "The socialist kingdom come, and the will of the state be done" so that they may have this day their socialist security and bread. In this respect, the socialists have more common sense than the anarchistic libertarians who dispense with God and the state. We are all familiar with the emotional instabilities and problems of these deluded peoples. But the socialists, in trusting in the state, are only trusting in man magnified; the state has vastly more power than themselves, but also less wisdom. Take your choice: pray to yourself as your own god, pray to the state as most men are now doing, or pray to God. Your life and your future depend on your answer.

CHALCEDON REPORT NO. 26
November 1, 1967

Most people today believe in fairy tales. Jesus said, "Do men gather grapes of thorns, or figs of thistles?" (Matt. 7:16). As St. Paul stated it, "Whatsoever a man soweth, that shall he also reap" (Gal. 6:7). People who believe in fairy tales deny this. A student can neglect his studies and somehow get a good grade. A man or nation can spend more than they take in and somehow remain solvent. The believer in fairy tales expects reality to match his dreams without any effort or work on his part.

As a nation, we have been subsidizing evil, improvidence, criminality, and anti-Christian and anti-American thinking and activity for a generation. We have been sowing a storm: can we reap anything but a storm? We have been subsidizing evil and penalizing good: can we expect anything but evil to result?

In his study, *Grover Cleveland* (1948), Allan Nevins observed, "Character is not made overnight. When it appears in transcendent degree it is usually the product of generations of disciplined ancestry, or a stern environment, or both." The old Puritan discipline left a long and powerful influence on the American character. The humanistic discipline of state-supported education is now making itself felt in American life. Our politics, the hippies, the erosion of character and morality, all these things and more we are reaping because we sowed for it. In brief, we have been sowing for revolution and for economic disaster, and we are on the verge of reaping both.

In the economic sphere, we are asking for disaster. A hard-money policy has been abandoned, and inflation is increasing. There is no likelihood that the paper-money policy will be altered by anything save disaster. The socialist answer to every problem is appropriations and controls. The appropriations buy votes and increasingly make more and more of the people parasites living off the rest. Don Bell, in his excellent newsletter (Oct. 20, 1967) calls attention to the fact that "the number of persons drawing pay or benefits of some kind from the federal government (state, local and private assistance not included)...is...102,900,000", but, "Granted that in many cases the benefits may be small, and millions of people are actually earning what they get (as the military on active duty) but the figures remain: over half the people in the United States are drawing pay or benefits from the Federal Government...About 40 million persons receive *regular* monthly payments from federal funds. This figure does not include businesses, farmers and others receiving checks on an irregular or occasional basis." Most of these people will not vote an end to their pay-checks. They will only vote more socialism. Economically, our future offers us basically two choices. First, we can have a depression, but only accidentally, because, while a depression is the easier way out, it is politically suicidal, in that it loses votes. If we fall into a depression, the political answer to it will be more controls. Second, we can have a runaway inflation, which means runaway controls also, culminating in social chaos and anarchy.

Religiously, we see the churches today serving the cause of revolution. The gospel they preach is anti-Christian and their morality is deliberate immorality. Christ came to free men from guilt, but the "now" gospel is designed to make us feel guilty for the sins of others, and for the backwardness of other peoples and races. Thus, Harvey G. Cox of the Harvard Divinity School wrote in the June, 1967 *renewal* Magazine on "Penance, From Piety to Politics. Reparations as a Religious and Political Issue." According to Cox, we must pay reparations to the Negro people, among others: "This debt is not a charitable contribution, but an honest debt, and the majority group in America remain the debtor group. Only when the relationships between the two groups are put on this basis of legal right and wrong, and of just reparation do we escape the unconscious condescension which so often distorts even the most well-intentioned individual in this delicate area." In other words, white America must pay a heavy tax penalty for some time to come because of its initiative and superiority. Earlier this year, the Stanford Presbyterian theologian, Dr. Robert MacFee Brown declared: "Not only is Christendom gone, but in its place is revolution. The question is not whether the revolution will succeed, but how much bloodshed there will have to be before a more equitable balance has been reached between rich and poor..." (*Presbyterian Journal*, June 7, 1967). Brown is for revolution, and his gospel is revolution, The Jesuit president of the University of Santa Clara, the Very Rev. Patrick A. Donahue, has expressed his hatred of the John Birch Society, which has killed no one and works to restore constitutionalism, and his preference for Marxism, which has killed millions of Christians: "For myself, Birchism and its multiple variants are more destructive to human freedom than the crudest form of Marxism." (Oakland, California, *Tribune* Wed., Oct. 25, 1967, P. 2, "A Jesuit's Barrage at Alumni.") If these men are clearly wrong, then how much more wrong are those who stay in these churches and help subsidize and support anti-Christianity by their presence and their gifts?

In education, the situation is no better. When an anti-war teach-in at U.C.L.A. was poorly attended, with only 20 students turning out to hear four Negro speakers, Prof. Donald Kalish, chairman of the sponsoring University Committee on Vietnam at U.C.L.A declared: "When the intellectual and middle class community refuse to even listen to spokesmen from our ghettos, I think that is sufficient grounds to burn our city down and I might even join them" (Los Angeles *Times*. "Anti-Vietnam War Teaching Called Failure." Part III, p. 18 Thursday, Oct. 12, 1967). Both here and abroad student groups call for guerrilla warfare (John Chamberlain, "SDS Impulses Span the Sea," Los Angeles *Herald-Examiner*, Friday, Sept. 22, 1967, p. B2). At Berkeley High School a patriotic program, "Up With People", was banned because "it deals with images rather than realities and...sets standards of morality, of right and wrong, good and bad", according to a faculty-student committee (Oakland *Tribune*, Wed., Sept. 27, 1967, p. 1, Noel Lieberman "High School at Berkeley Bars Singers"). Nothing indicates more clearly what our statist education has become than this: "Standards of morality of right and wrong, good and bad", are subversive to it! Meanwhile, sex education is becoming increasingly important to schools whose pupils are less and less able to read well. A popular teaching aid "is a series of 35 slides dealing with the reproduction of flowers, chickens, dogs and human beings. The anatomy and physiology of reproductive organs are shown in brightly colored representation designed to capture children's attention. A simply written text labels everything with its proper name as chickens and dogs are shown copulating. An 'optional' slide shows a man and woman in bed covered, to illustrate human intercourse." (*The Wall Street Journal*, Tuesday,

Sept. 19, 1967, p. 1, Neil Ulman, "The facts of Life"). We are told that "very shortly" special private classes will be established to relieve parents of the responsibility of instructing their own children. "Initially, there will be the usual outraged hue and cry when movies are used to demonstrate positions," but the courts will vindicate "academic freedom" and 'enlarge' our freedom (H.S. Kahm, "had any lately?" in *Cavalcade*, Nov., 1967, p. 17). This is, of course, part and parcel of the attack on privacy. A psychologist has said, "The closed door, in most households, is not so much a guardian of privacy, as a symptom of prudery; a barrier between the generations, an obstacle to fluent sex education, a reinforcement of guilt and repression"...(Chester C. Bennett, Boston University, "What Price Privacy?" in *American Psychologist*, vol. 22, no. 5. Is it any wonder that the very halls of many schools today must be patrolled not only by teachers but sometimes by the police as well?

Meanwhile, the police are under attack. A testing program has been set up to cull out undesired persons. "Typical questions" include statements like this: "I believe in the second coming of Christ." (Guy Halvorson, "Culling All Police, *Wall Street Journal*, Wed., Oct. 18, 1967, p. 16). In many cities, police are forbidden to fire on looters or rioters (Santa Ana, California *The Register*, Monday (m) Aug. 21, 1967, p. C 5, "My Cops Forbidden to Fire at Looters; see also L.A. *Times*, pt. 1, p. 12, Sat., August 26. 1967, "Winced at Riot Order, Guard Chief Recalls," by George Lardner, Jr.). A bill proposed in California would limit the right of the police to use their weapons even further (Santa Ana, *The Register*, Friday (m) Oct. 20, 1967, p. A8, "Solons disagree on When Cop can use Gun"). Similar legislation is proposed elsewhere.

When we turn to the political sphere, the picture is no less grim. *Barron's Weekly*, on August 28, 1967, wrote on "Guerilla Politics", an apt title, in that contemporary politics, like guerrilla warfare, is action aimed at the destruction of the existing social order. On July 31, 1967, the leading article in *Barron's* told its story in the title: "Poverty Warriors. The Riots are Subsidized as Well As Organized." Story after story reports on the subsidies to criminal and hoodlums ("Negro Gang Leaders To Get Federal Jobs." in *Washington Report*, Robert S. Allen and Paul Scott, in the *Oakland Tribune* Friday, August 11, 1967, p. 22), as well as subsidies to revolutionists (Santa Ana, *The Register*, Thursday (m) August 24, 1967, p. B7, "Violence Pays, 'Liberation' School Told"). The federal government today is actively and deliberately subsidizing revolutionists in the name of alleviating social distress. Some of this is clearly due to liberal soft-headedness, to the belief that money will save men. But not all the bureaucrats involved are fuzzy-minded liberals; many are dedicated socialists and social revolutionaries. We *cannot* understand what is happening around us unless we see the Negro revolutionists, the Hippies, the student radicals, and others who receive federal aid in one form or another as the *Red Guards* of the Establishment, called upon to break down the freedom of the people. Mao Tse-Tung called on the Red Guard to break down all opposition in supposedly spontaneous demonstrations. It is easy to understand the Chinese Red Guards from a distance but we cannot understand our American subsidized revolutionists as another *Red Guard* until we see them as an instrument being used to destroy the old free America. The American Red Guard will be used to destroy the cities, cripple the police, infringe on our liberties, and then, in the name of controlling the Red Guard, the Establishment will pass legislation to control its subsidized rioters and agitators, and to control us. An angry populace will demand "riot control", and, although existing laws provide more than enough means for the police to control riots, the riots will be permitted to continue until "emergency" legislation can be rushed through on demand and all our liberties be confiscated in order to "control" the American Red Guard. The Red Guard will be ruthlessly killed off, if need be, to please the people, but their liberties will also be killed off.

In all of this, the major enemy is Christianity, and Christian law and order, Christian faith and Christian morality. As Dr. Lars Ullerstam, M.D., has written in *The Erotic Minorities*, "To be chaste is no longer praiseworthy; rather, it is something *unnatural*, and therefore almost intolerable" (p. 24). For Dr. Ullerstam, we need "a sexual bill of rights" which will not only permit liberty to homosexuality, incest, exhibitionism, pedophilia, saliromania, algolagnia, scopophilia, and every other kind of perversion and pervert, but will also provide state subsidies for these people to compensate for their 'persecution' by Christians. Here again, the issue is the same: *a subsidy for evil*. Having subsidized evil so long, how can we help but reap a harvest of evil?

It would be possible to write several volumes on the evidences of subsidies to evil, to revolution, to anti-American activities, to laziness, to a variety of persons and activities which need legal control rather than legal subsidization. The important question is this: *why is evil subsidized*? The answer to this question is the great dividing line. The Greek and pagan view, the anti-Christian view, is that man's problem is a failure of knowledge. If man does wrong, it is because of inadequate, insufficient, or incorrect *knowledge*. The answer therefore is *re-education*. This is, of course, the answer of Marxism and Fabian Socialism. Re-education of people out of Christianity, or, if they are too old for re-education, "purge" them or kill them off. The anti-Christian puts his hope therefore in knowledge, in education, and, whether he be of the radical or of the conservative variety, he plans to save mankind by education.

The Christian view is that man's problem is not a lack of facts but a hatred of godly knowledge. Man's problem is *sin*, a corrupt and depraved will and mind, a total unwillingness to do other than suppress the truth. Knowledge cannot save man; only Christ can. The redeemed man will then grow in grace and therefore seek knowledge in order to serve and glorify God more ably.

In terms of this, let us examine the question *why is evil subsidized*? It is not subsidized out of ignorance, out of any lack of knowledge as to its meaning. President Johnson and Vice-President Humphrey have both sounded the call to world revolution in full knowledge of what revolution means. *Evil is subsidized to destroy the good, to destroy Christianity and its law order*. The kind of planning for destruction varies from group to group. Some revolutionists plan in terms of mass burning, looting, raping, killing, and total destruction. Some plan in terms of totalitarian controls and ruthlessness only towards trouble-makers. In either case, the goal is, whether directly or slowly, *total destruction of Christian civilization*. Some have called for, as I pointed out in *This Independent Republic* (chapter 9), a long period of chaos and revolution, of anarchy, racial amalgamation, and the total destruction of civilization.

In times like these it is well to remember the words of an ancient Hebrew, Jesus (or Joshua) ben Sirach, who wrote:

> "They that fear the Lord will not disobey his word; and they that love him will keep his ways. They that fear the Lord will seek that which is well-pleasing unto him; and they that love him shall be filled with the law. They that fear the Lord will prepare their hearts and humble their souls in his sight, Saying, *We will fall into the hands of the Lord, and not into the hands of men: for as his majesty is, so is his mercy*."

Don Bell Reports, for October 27, 1967, stated briefly what this writer has said repeatedly at great length: "As a nation we have become too filthy to recover; we must reconstruct."

Our tax dollars are subsidizing evil. While there is still time, our free dollars had better subsidize Christian reconstruction. Rebuild or perish. Lot's wife turned back longingly to the old familiar places and perished with Sodom. Those who try to save the old forms, the old churches, the public schools, the old and captured citadels, will go down with them. The days ahead are days of death, and of reconstruction. Our tax dollars are already subsidizing revolution and an American Red Guard, and we are getting our money's worth there. As Clark H. Pinnock observed, in *Set Forth Your Case* (1967). "One of the best kept secrets from the public at large in the twentieth century has been the death of hope and the loss of the human." We are all involved, by compulsory taxation, in the subsidy of evil and the death of hope, as well as the loss of the human. But the question remains: to what extent are we using our remaining freedom for the Lord?

CHALCEDON REPORT NO. 28
December 1, 1967

In our April, 1966, Newsletter 7, the *progressive confiscation* of private property and of constitutional safeguards was discussed briefly. This Newsletter will deal with *economic confiscation.*

As we survey the economic crisis, it is easy for us, from a Christian perspective to see the present course of action as stupidity. For the federal government to attempt to control the price of silver is foolishness, and it has been costly foolishness, and the unrealistic price of gold is equally costly to us. The question is very often raised, "Don't they see what they are doing?", and the answer is, clearly yes. What we are experiencing is planned stupidity, and it's goal is confiscation.

Marxist economics clearly aims at confiscation: its goal is a communist economics and the destruction of free, private capital. But this is *equally* the goal of Keynsian, neo-Keynsian, and welfare state economics. (John Maynard Keynes, incidently was described as a homosexual by Walter Scott in "Personality Parade", in *Parade*, November 12, 1967, p. 2, citing as reference for this fact Michael Holroyd's *Lytton Strachey, The Unknown Years*, published by Holt, Rinehart, Winston.) Keynes' very influential book, the *General Theory of Employment, Interest, and Money* (1936) had as one of its central points the hostility to savings as a "vice." (Attention has been called to this aspect of Keynes by Henry Hazlitt: *The Failure of the "New Economics"*, Princeton: Van Nostrand, 1959; and Theodore Macklin: *Gold - Key to Confidence*, published in September, 1967, by the Economists' National Committee on Monetary Policy, 79 Madison Avenue, New York, N. Y. 10016.) Keynsian economics works to destroy savings *and* to make savings impossible; it does this, not with an open policy of confiscation, but with a humanitarian concern for the general welfare, but, under any name, it is a policy of confiscation.

Now it is important to define the savings which are attacked by Keynsian economics: this involves more than savings accounts in banks and savings and loan associations. It involves pension and insurance funds, private property, inheritances, and every other evidence of thrift and providence.

This confiscation is done by means of "doctored" money, counterfeit money. Lenin plainly said that a central banking system and paper money are nine-tenths of socialism; our welfare state knows this and operates on the same premise.

Gold and silver are real money, an economy geared to real money always has a healthy check on unsound economic practices. In such an economy, because both money and banking rest on a gold basis, credit cannot expand indefinitely. As bank loans increase to the limit of gold reserves, interest rates rise, credit is cut off, and a short, quick depression results. Before

World War I, U.S. depressions were short, a matter of weeks and months only and not as total in their effects. Unsound business practices are a condition of man: there is no fool-proof protection against them. But a free economy limits credit because it has a hard-money basis, and a credit expansion which is foolish and unsound is curtailed by hard-money requirements. If a bank is too free with credit, depositors can withdraw their money in gold and break the bank. If a civil government becomes unsound in policy, the people can vote against it also simply by withdrawing and hoarding gold, or demanding gold for their paper notes.

But socialism wants to penalize the hard-working, the wise, and the thrifty, to protect the fools and to subsidize them. Its answer to depression is to manage money and credit. Increase the credit: this is the socialist answer, a social credit scheme. As Alan Greenspan wrote, in "Gold and Economic Freedom" (in Ayn Rand, editor: *Capitalism: The Unknown Ideal*, 1967, p. 99), "if shortage of bank reserves was causing a business decline --- argued economic interventionists --- why not find a way of supplying increased reserves to the banks so they never need be short! If banks can continue to loan indefinitely --- it was claimed --- there need never be any slumps in business." As a result, a federal agency was created, The Federal Reserve System, to maintain a flow of credit and money.

Now if an economy works to insure fools against failure, it will be progressively advantageous to be a fool or a parasite. The successful businessman is no longer the man who follows sound practices and holds to the Christian virtues; such a man is increasingly penalized in order to subsidize the fools, knaves, and parasites. Debt is made into a business asset, and a private asset, by means of tax write-offs for interest and other advantages. Living on credit becomes a way of life, and also a steady confiscation of real wealth to provide for the rascals.

Today most big business and labor are socialistic simply because their profit comes from the inflationary, confiscatory policies of federally created credit. In Newsletter 27, Gary North pointed out "IBM needs $600 million a year in credit." IBM is not unusual in this respect by any means. What does this mean? It means that, because the federal government, big and small business, and private citizens everywhere are deeply in debt and living on credit, they will demand more easy money, more inflation. They will want to pay off good debts with bad money. As a result, all the pressure will be for more easy money, more counterfeit money to be exact, for more inflation. To stop now is to court disaster. As a result, the total disaster of runaway inflation is invited.

In order to avert the disaster of *runaway* inflation, *controlled* inflation will be the policy. This means progressive controls and "credit crunches" to keep the inflation from getting out of hand. The attempt is ultimately doomed to fail, but it will still be pursued.

In the free banking system of pre-Civil War days in particular, the failures of judgment affected individuals, banks, and business firms. The affect was essentially local, not national. Under a nationally controlled economy, every mistake is a national disaster.

Credit under free banking was dependent on available gold; without it, a bank too easy on credit failed: depositors lost confidence in a speculative bank policy. Under socialistic banking, such as the Federal Reserve System, continued easy credit requires continued confiscation of someone's wealth. The credit has to come from available wealth. The welfare state makes this fresh credit available through heavy taxation, bond issues, and other means of confiscation, direct or indirect. The wealth of the thrifty, productive, and conservative people is steadily confiscated in order to provide for the fools, knaves, and parasites. Don Bell has pointed out (see Newsletter No. 26) that the number of people who receive federal pay or benefits numbers 102,900,000, over half the population of the United States. Of this number, about 40 million receive regular monthly payments, the rest seasonal checks. It becomes profitable to be a rascal, and the result is a population-explosion among welfare recipients, easy-money business firms, and scoundrels in every field. These people now can outvote the rest of the people. And these people know only one way to prosperity: rob the thrifty, hard-working people. The new-rich of America have gained their wealth by soaking the old-rich, i.e., those rich in character, hard work, thrift, and ability.

They will continue to do this until everything is confiscated and destroyed. The end result of socialism is total poverty. Some kind of disaster is inescapable.

In this situation, the disaster devoutly to be wished for is God's judgment on these knaves and parasites as well as fools. The present order will not change unless it is shattered, and it is God's shattering we need. God, who governs all things, is never absent from history. He created and ordained it. He demonstrated His intervening power and concern in the incarnation of our Lord Jesus Christ. "For unto us a child is born, unto us a son is given: and the government shall be upon his shoulder: and his name shall be called Wonderful Counsellor, The mighty God, The everlasting Father, The Prince of Peace. Of the increase of his government and peace here shall be no end" (Isaiah 9:6,7). Christ shall confiscate the power of the confiscators. All laws, including economic law, are a part of His creation and ordination: defeat is written into the nature of the universe for all who transgress His laws. Both naturally and supernaturally, Christ's government works to punish evil. They who live by easy credit will die by easy credit. They who steal shall be robbed of all they have. "But they that wait upon the LORD shall renew their strength" (Isaiah 40:31).

We face perilous times. But we do not face them alone.

Make no mistake about it: the issues are religious. All socialists oppose gold because they believe in neither God nor in freedom. Gold and silver represent independent wealth, wealth which is natural, God-created wealth. Paper money is state-created "wealth", and it can be destroyed by the state. A government decree can and often has changed the value of paper money, or abolished one paper currency to replace it with another. As Lenin clearly saw, there can be no total control of society without total paper money, i.e., fiat money. Wealth in gold represents independent and uncontrolled wealth, and therefore socialism tries to abolish it. Man's only "freedom" must be what the state permits, and this is like the freedom of a prisoner to move around in his cell.

Recently, U.S. Treasury officials denied that gold has any real value apart from the price the U.S. gives it. They threatened to "bankrupt" hoarders by lowering the price of U.S. gold from $35 to $6 an ounce --- an act which would only raise the price of gold all the more rapidly, because it would only mean the bankruptcy of the U.S. dollar! The U.S. Treasury officials do not believe in gold because they do not believe in freedom. Such men believe themselves to be wiser than God: they do not believe that freedom can work. Only that which they themselves create and totally control, a paper "gold", can work, because only humanistic controls are for them man's hope.

The issues are thus religious: man's order or God's order. The outcome in such a struggle is certain. We have therefore this assurance in the days ahead: The battle is the Lord's.

CHALCEDON REPORT NO. 29
January 1, 1968

Samuel Pepys (1633-1703), an important figure in the history of the British admiralty, left a secret diary which is one of the most entertaining and revealing documents. Pepys, who was quite congenial to a consistently adulterous life, was also a very self-righteous and moralistic man. He was ready to take and to create any opportunity for adultery, but he also wanted to be morally clean. As a result, Pepys worked out a system of moral book-keeping. In one way or another, he fined himself or made amends to his wife for his sins. Also, he regularly "reformed" immediately after an act of adultery, when his desires were at a low ebb. One set of rules he made to keep himself "moral" even included rules about kissing women other than his wife: The first kiss would be free, but every additional kiss would cost him twelve-pence to the poor. (John Harold Wilson: *The Private Life of Mr. Pepys*, p. 134f.) Mr. Pepys was a very charitable man. Mrs. Pepys herself in various ways regularly cashed in on her husband's sinning.

What Samuel Pepys represented is moralism. The dictionary definition of moralism is that it is the practice of morality without religion; that is, it is a humanistic and man-centered morality. This definition is not entirely accurate, because moralism has a religious faith, and that religion is humanism. Pepys, for example, wanted to maintain appearances before man and society, and, since he believed he was basically sinning against man, he as man could also make atonement for his sins. Briefly, moralism is man-centered, not God-centered in its conception of sin.

In Pepys we have seen the *negative* side of moralism. Negatively, moralism believes that man can make atonement for his sin, cleanse himself from evil, and right the balance of good and evil. Negatively, the moralist indulges in all kinds of works of atonement as the means of ridding himself from guilt. This is very different from the Biblical law of restitution. For the Bible, sin is, first of all, against God, in every case. Thus, David, in repenting of his adultery with Bathsheba, said to God, "Against Thee, Thee only, have I sinned, and done this evil in Thy sight" (Psalm 51:4). It was God's law David had violated, and second, God was also his only savior: "Create in me a clean heart, O God; and renew a right spirit within me" (Psalm 51:10). Man is neither creator, law-giver, nor Savior.

Positively, moralism believes that man can save himself and remake himself and the world he lives in. God, if He is acknowledged, is at best a senior partner in this endeavor. Man saves himself and re-creates the world. Socialism is a conspicuous form of moralism, or humanism. It is a religion of salvation by the works of man, the works of the humanistic state. Marxism is thus moralism compounded. And too many "ex-Marxists" are simply rebelling against a particular manifestation of moralism in the name of a purer moralism. A telling example of moralism is a book by Stalin's daughter, Svetlana Alliluyeva: *Twenty Letters to a Friend* (1967). The religion she advocates is a one-world religion; in other words, humanism. She reduces Christianity to total love and total forgiveness. She wants us all to "have faith in the power of decency and goodwill" which is "the same thing" as faith in God (p. 72). In other words, man is the true god, and we must believe in man's essential goodness. Her picture of the Communist leaders is along these lines; all of them, including her father, Joseph Stalin, were good men, filled with zeal and good-will towards men. The only evil man was Beria, who somehow exploited these simple, decent souls and brought about so much evil. "What sterling, full-blooded people they were, these early knights of the Revolution who carried so much romantic idealism with them to the grave!" (p. 234).

Before we laugh this off, let us remember that Stalin and many others like him saw themselves in these same terms. They were the pure "knights" waging war against the monsters of capitalism and Christianity, and any who opposed them, including their nearest and dearest friends and relatives, immediately became evil. This is *logical*: humanism makes man his own god, and if man is god, then his enemies are devils. And Karl Marx made clear, in an early writing, that the enemies of the revolution must be seen as devils:

it is liberators versus oppressors. All dissent is evil, and opposition must be destroyed.

The religious fanaticism of socialism rests on this faith. It is moralism, and moralism makes man his own god and his own savior. When such a man sins, he can also, like Pepys right the balances according to his own tastes, twelve-pence a kiss, four shillings for adultery, or what have you. The socialist makes easy amends for his sins according to his own law; and, according to his own law, whoever sins against him must die. He is the law.

The social gospel, modernism, and Arminianism are all moralisms. They believe that man is his own savior by works of law, man's law. The humanism may be dressed up in seemingly Christian language, but its end purpose is the same, to supplant the sovereignty of God with the sovereignty of man.

Liberal politics too is simply moralism. Its anti-Christianity is apparent at a number of points. *First*, liberalism holds to the sovereignty of man rather than the sovereignty of God. There can be no reconciliation between these two points of view. Sovereignty is a theological concept: it is an attribute of God alone. For this reason, the word "sovereignty" was strictly avoided in the U.S. Constitution. The entrance of the word came with the rise of Arminianism and Unitarianism.

Second, the characteristic doctrine of liberalism is equality. The Bible is anti-equalitarian. The doctrine of predestination is a total negation of the concept of equality. Modernists often cite Gal. 3:28 as "proof" of equality: "There is neither Jew nor Greek, there is neither bond nor free, there is neither male nor female: for ye are all one in Christ Jesus." Now the point of this verse, and the entire passage, is simply that, with respect to God, not with respect to human society, all distinctions are equally worthless before God's sovereignty and electing grace. We stand before God in Christ's work, not in terms of human status. In terms of society, we *are* male and female, and many things more, but in terms of God, nothing we are gives us any credit before God, we are saved by grace. This verse, instead of asserting equality, asserts God's sovereign and electing grace.

Third, liberalism tries to build the civil government and the social order on humanism rather than on Scripture. Every civil government is a religious establishment. All civil law rests on moral law and all moral law presupposes a religion. When a state begins to alter its laws and constitution, it is because it has altered or changed its religion.

Moralism is thus the morality of humanism. It is a works-religion and a works-morality. When such a faith appears within the church, it is not to be regarded as a variation of Christianity but as anti-Christianity. Its goal is always the same: to enthrone man as his own god and savior. It may have a facade and form of Christianity, as Samuel Pepys did, but moralism is always anti-Christian. It tries to set the world right by man-made gimmicks, but, from the Christian perspective, the end of moralism is always immoralism.

The only hope of men and nations is therefore in Christ. "Except the Lord build the house, they labor in vain that build it" (Psalm 127:1).

CHALCEDON REPORT NO. 30
February 1, 1968

Want to subvert a social order and sound noble and beautiful doing it? It's easy: demand love and forgiveness for everybody and everything. With "love and forgiveness" on a total basis you can destroy all laws, empty prisons, handcuff justice, and make evil triumphant.

Unconditional love is a more revolutionary concept than any other doctrine of revolution. Unconditional love means the end of all discrimination between good and evil, right and wrong, better and worse, friend and enemy, and all things else. Whenever anyone asks you to love unconditionally, they are asking you to surrender unconditionally to the enemy.

Unconditional love is contrary to the Bible. The charge of the young prophet Jehu, the son of Hanani, to King Jehoshaphat was blunt: "Shouldest thou help the ungodly, and love them that hate the LORD? therefore is wrath upon thee from before the LORD" (II Chronicles 19:2). The commandment is, "Ye that love the LORD, hate evil" (Psalm 97:10), and the prophet Amos repeated it: "Hate the evil, and love the good, and establish judgment in the gate (i.e., in the city council)" (Amos 5:15). David could therefore say of himself, in speaking of his obedience, "Do not I hate them, O LORD, that hate thee? and am not I grieved with those that rise up against thee? I hate them with a perfect hatred: I count them mine enemies" (Psalm 139:21,22).

We are told to love *our* enemies, that is, those who offend us personally on non-religious and non-moral issues. When the cause of division is petty and personal, we must rise above it with an attitude of law and justice; we must continue to extend to all such persons the full protection of the law from injustice, malice, and false witness. But the enemies of God's justice and God's law, of fundamental law and order, must not be loved. To love them in to condone their evil. The accusation of the psalmist is to the point: "When you see a thief, you delight to associate with him, and you take part with adulterers" (Psalm 5O:18, Berkeley Version). What we condone morally, we also approve of or delight in. St. John forbad hospitality to those who were trying to subvert the faith: "If there come any unto you, and bring not this doctrine, receive him not into your house, neither bid him God speed: For he that biddeth him God speed is partaker of his evil deeds" (II John 10,11).

Those who preach unconditional love are simply trying to disarm godly people in order that evil may triumph.

The same is true of the idea of unconditional forgiveness. Forgiveness in the Bible is always conditional upon true repentance. Unconditional forgiveness is simply the total, unconditional toleration of and acceptance of evil. It demands that we accept the criminal, the pervert, the degenerate, the subversive *as they are*. But to do so means that *we must change*. We must surrender our laws, faith, religious standards, and all godly order. The demands for unconditional love and unconditional forgiveness are demands for total change on our part, total revolution in society. They are in reality demands that we commit suicide in order that evil may live.

Anyone who subscribes to the doctrines of unconditional love and unconditional forgiveness is either a fool or a knave and very probably both. These doctrines demand a love of evil and a hatred of good, and they are aimed at the destruction of godly law and order.

This anarchistic, anti-christian doctrine of love erodes law and brings in a breed of sentimental, antinomian (i.e., anti-law) preachers, and a breed of lawless rulers, politicians, and bureaucrats who have no regard for law and cater to feelings, and mob feelings increasingly govern them.

There are basically four kinds of politicians. *First*, there are the professional, practical politicians who are men without principles and who are basically interested in staying in office. There are many such men today. They respond basically to pressure and to money. Principles do not move them: self-interest does. The less godly law and order there is in an age, the more these practical politicians respond like weathervanes to pressure. They are the creatures of the establishment, of the mob, and of any and every force that blows their way: they are weathervanes.

Second, there are the idealists in politics, and I here use the word idea and idealist in its original meaning. An idealist is a man who has an idea, ideal, pattern, or goal to which he tries to push humanity. The ancient Greeks, especially Plato, were great idealists, and their legends also contain the best satire on idealism in the myth of the robber Procrustes, who either stretched his victims to fit his standard bed, or else amputated them if they were too long. This is the technique of the idealist, whether he be Marxist, Fabian, or democratic; the idealist will sacrifice man and God to achieve his ideal communist, socialist, or democratic order. The idealist, whether Plato, Rousseau, Marx, or a contemporary liberal, believes that it is the environment which is evil and man who is good. Since man is good, who is better and more trustworthy than the elite man, namely, himself, the idealist? The idealist is thus a moral monster who confuses himself with God and seeks to destroy the world in order to remake it in terms of his ideal. Since he sees no evil in himself, he is intensely dangerous. And the first step towards remaking the world is for him the destruction of God's world, which means a dedication to revolution. Our politics today is saturated with idealism.

Third, some men enter politics in anger at the knaves who predominate in it, at the weathervanes and at the Procrustean idealists. These men lack faith; they are governed by nostalgia for the past, or love of the past, *not* by a systematic body of principles, by a religious philosophy and faith, which guides their whole being. The longer they remain in politics, the more they become *cynics*. They begin with a love of country and a love of their follow citizens; they end with a contempt for their stupid fellow men. The *cynic* thinks of man as a pig and a dog, a fool to be conned. The next step, which he often takes unconsciously, is to become himself the con man who takes the greedy fools for everything they have. The purpose of the cynic in politics becomes then, *power*, naked power, although in the early stages he does not always recognize it. Abe Ruef, the most notorious politician in California history, began as an idealist bent on reforming society and ended as a cynic who organized his powerful "System" to control the state. Napoleon too began as an idealist, an earnest believer in the revolution, but he changed his mind during the Egyptian campaign. He decided that men were little better than dogs, governed basically by lust, hunger, and greed, and he began to move in terms of exploiting that situation. The *cynic* in politics is thus a dangerous man also, and we have them with us.

Fourth, the Christian in politics is governed not by his dreams or by man's sin, but by God's law. His perspective is not man but God. He moves in terms of objective law, in terms of fundamental justice. His purpose is to place himself, man, and society under God, and under godly law and order. Because he believes in the sovereignty of God, he refuses to accept the sovereignty of either man or the state. He believes in limited powers and limited liberties for both man and the state, a principle early established in America by the Rev. John Cotton and basic to American constitutionalism. This then is the Christian in politics, a rare man these days.

In the churches, we have similar men, and the Christian is almost as rare as in politics. Some years ago I heard a churchman, holding now one of the highest positions in a major branch of the church, describe in my presence the ideal symbol of a true church: a weathervane! (There was one on top of the very large church where he was speaking.) The weathervane, he said, meant *sensitivity*, and a church should be sensitive to the people and to "revolutionary ferment." I asked him later if the weathervane did not suggest to him a symbol of spinelessness and no personal standards, no caliber of resistance to evil. He answered that he had never thought of it in that way.

But to return to love. Modern doctrines of love are simply doctrines of anarchism, of total receptivity to evil. Their purpose is to break down the differentiation between good and evil and to produce lawlessness. Modern sensitivity training has this function. It is a part of the love religion: it demands total receptivity to the world and a submission to it rather than a resistance to evil in terms of God's law. Its goal is to teach a love of evil and a hatred of good.

The love religionists and love politicians are also strong advocates of equalitarianism and of equal rights causes. Total equality means that good and evil are on the same level and without differentiation. Evil must then have equal rights with good, and the criminal must have equal rights with the good citizen. This means that the criminal must have the same freedom to rob and kill that you want in order to support your family and worship God. Strict champions of equal rights like the Marquis de Sade (whose works are now being translated and published) demand precisely this, equal rights for the criminal, which means simply that the criminal has a right to rob and kill you, and you have a duty to submit to him, or else you will violate his rights.

The goal is total revolution. The language is love, forgiveness, and sensitivity: its function is subversion and destruction.

Solomon said it wisely long ago: "To every thing there is a season...A time to love, and a time to hate; a time of war, and a time of peace" (Ecclesiastes 3:1,8). We had better know it.

CHALCEDON REPORT NO. 31
March 1, 1968

In our last Newsletter, our subject was anarchistic love as a revolutionary concept and an erosive force. To continue our analysis, it must be pointed out next that the total impact and purpose of all such thinking is *moral disarmament.*

Moral disarmament always precedes the economic, political, and military disarmament and dismemberment of a people. Disarmament begins first in the mind and soul of man, and it proceeds then to affect his every activity.

The forces of moral disarmament have always been present in history, but, in recent years, they have become progressively more vocal. The nature of their attack, if anyone had missed it previously, became obvious in 1928 when Ernest Sutherland Bates published his book, *The Friends of Jesus.* In many respects, Judas came out as Jesus' best friend! In fact, one could say Judas came out better than Jesus at Bates' hands. But the book attracted only minor notice: moral disarmament had already reached the point where Bates' book was not startling.

Evil was now getting more sympathy than good; a betrayer had become a tragic and noble figure, and treason was thus somehow a higher loyalty. Instead of a clear-cut stand by people for truth and against error, for God against Satan, for right against wrong, and for law against crime, there was now a growing and serious moral confusion.

The next decade saw gangsters extensively glorified in motion pictures, and the films made money simply because they met a growing popular demand. Sympathy was now with the rebel, the criminal, and the pervert. Captain Bligh, who was actually a man of calibre, became a symbol of evil, and the degenerate lot of mutineers in the *Bounty* became popular heroes.

Moral disarmament makes us sympathetic with evil in order to make us hostile to good. If we are made to feel for Judas, to that extent we are separated from Christ. The end result is that we are asked to be friendly with hell itself, to approve of co-existence with everything evil, religious, moral, political and economic.

The next step is to call the good evil. Thus, an Episcopal scholar, Marshall W. Fishwick, in *Faust Revisited, Some Thoughts on Satan* (1963), sends Christian conservatives readily to hell. Thus, Fishwick writes on one man:

> Descended from a Good Family,this public-spirited fellow made a Good Thing out of cleanliness.
> He ran for public office on a ticket of clean government, clean elections, and clean towels in City Hall. Campaigning in immaculately white collars, he won easily, and self-righteously crowed proudly from the Church steeples.
> He was very busy up until the day he died. There were so many meetings of the Children's Welfare Bureau that he neglected his own children, one of whom ran off with the trombonist in a jazz combo. He was too clean to allow his city to go in debt, so it built no new schools. He also refused to take federal funds to provide free lunches, since he thought that was dirty politics. He erred in the name of High Principles. He went to hell. (p. 39f.)

Fishwick also declares, "There is something satanic about suburbia" (p. 80), and he hopes that someone will "burst our ideas of good and evil all to hell" and free theology (p. 128).

Notice Fishwick's association of ideas: clean government, clean elections, clean towels, and clean collars are all somehow marks of self-righteousness and evil. They lead to a neglect of one's children. If you do not go into debt, you are against progress ("new schools") and are a Pharisee. Taking federal funds is good, refusing them is bad. High Principles will send you to hell.

After a couple of generations and more of such teaching and preaching, is it any wonder that the people are morally disarmed? In the name of the modernist "Christ" they are now for evil and against good. In the name of Americanism, they tolerate Communists and oppose anti-Communists. In the name of morality, they invite perverts into their fellowship, and exclude Christians because they refuse to tolerate evil. Pastor Richard Wurmbrand has written that many Western Christian Church leaders defended their associations with Communist leaders, saying, "As Christians, we have to be friendly with everybody, you know, even the Communists." Why, then, were they not friendly to those who had suffered? Why did they not ask one word about the priests and pastors who had died in prison or under torture? Or leave a little money for the families that remained. These church leaders were either morally disarmed, or were busy disarming the churches morally. Their sympathy is with evil, not good, with antichrist, not Christ.

Of course, these churchmen assure us that their hearts are full of love for everyone, and they are burning with a passion to "save" mankind. A very prominent and able English Congregational theologian, John S. Whale, in *Victor and Victim* (1960), assures us that "The goal of the universe is the end of all estrangement, the fullness of reconciliation in Christ," and this means "that Satan himself is finally saved" (p. 41). Now if Satan himself is going to be saved and spend eternity with us, why should we, and how can we, be too hostile to him now? If Stalin and Kosygin are going to be our brothers in heaven, can we deny them love and brotherhood now? If coexistence is our destiny in heaven, why not begin practicing it now?

Whale said, "The goal of the universe is the end of all estrangement." This means the end of all discrimination and division. But the Biblical doctrine of heaven and hell is a denial of coexistence in time and eternity. It means that the *goal* of the universe is actually the final estrangement of good and evil, of the saints and the sinners; it means that a separation in terms of the righteousness of God in Christ is basic to the historical process. Take away this doctrine, and you deny that there is an ultimate distinction between good and evil. Coexistence then becomes a religious and political necessity. Emory Storrs once said, "When hell drops out of religion, justice drops out of politics." (Cited by Harry Buis: *The Doctrine of Eternal Punishment*, p. 122. Philadelphia: Presbyterian and Reformed Publishing Co., 1957.)

The coexistence preachers tell us that hell is a horrible doctrine, but is there any hell to equal the horror of co-existence between God and Satan, good and evil, Christ and antichrist? Religious and political coexistence has created more misery and horror than we can begin to imagine. Justice and hell bring law, order, and sanity to life.

But moral disarmament wants to destroy all the God-given distinctions. Its hope is that problems disappear if we say they are non-existent. Its moral disarmament is the necessary step for a surrender to evil. Some of the disarmers talk about moral re-armament. But is it moral re-armament to blur the distinctions between religions, to work for the unity of things which are by nature contrary, and to assume that God will ratify man's open contempt for His call to separateness?

Any honest survey of the world scene indicates that we have been morally disarmed. The churches on the whole are in the enemy's camp, actively engaged in moral disarmament. The Bible is neither believed nor taught, and an alien religion is preached from the pulpits. We are also politically disarmed. We treat our enemies as friends, and our friends as enemies. We are soft on Communism and hard on Christianity, orthodox Christianity. The unpopular man is he who demands a moral stand in any area, in religion, politics, economics, education, or anywhere else.

Moral disarmament is the prelude to collapse and ruin, to captivity and slavery. The reason we are not already enslaved is simply that our enemy is still weaker than we are, and we still have a saving remnant.

To counteract the prevailing moral disarmament more than pietism is needed. Christian maturity, Christian growth, is necessary. Reconstruction requires first of all sound doctrine, Biblical faith, and second, the development of Christian thinking in every area, in economics, politics, education, science, and all things else.

The Reign of Terror in the French Revolution was directed, quite openly, against three groups: *First*, the political counter-revolutionaries were to be liquidated. *Second*, the economic aspect, all who "hoarded" food or money to protect themselves, were marked for execution. *Third*, organized, faithful Christians were marked for beheading on the guillotine also.

The last target, Christianity, was the central one, the nerve of hostility to revolution. By November, 1793, the Marquis de Sade and other revolutionists were ready to propose a new religion of Reason, Humanism.

The goal was moral-disarmament; the *purpose* was to create a humanistic paradise on earth. The *result* was hell on earth. As a loyal biographer of Sade admits:

> Reason had been exalted to the status of a god, and committees, assemblies and communes deliberated on concepts of law, order and justice; but it was Madame Guillotine who ruled, without Reason, without Justice. She served all men with equal candor as they knelt at her feet, and blessed them with the benediction of her weighted blade. (Norman Gear: *The Divine Demon, a Portrait of the Marquis de Sade*, p. 131)

The goal of the revolution, of moral disarmament then, was liberty, fraternity, and equality: liberty from God, fraternity in sin, equality of all moral, economic and religious distinctions. But the end was liberty from life, fraternity in death, and equality in hell. This is always the conclusion of moral disarmament.

Let us heed St. Paul's words: "Finally, my brethren, be strong in the Lord, and in the power of his might. Put on the whole armor of God, that ye may be able to stand against the wiles of the devil. For we wrestle not against flesh and blood, but against principalities, against powers, against the rulers of the darkness of this world, against spiritual wickedness in high places. Wherefore take unto you the whole armor of God, that ye may be able to withstand in the evil day, and, having done all, to stand" (Ephesians 6: 10-13).

CHALCEDON REPORT NO. 32
April 10, 1968

The economics of the world are *out of control.* The various civil governments, all socialist in varying degrees, have long experimented with controlled economics, that is, with socialism in its various forms. They have favored a controlled economics over a free economy because it means more power to the state. But now, with the inevitable economic chaos of socialism beginning to appear, both power and economic productivity are going down the drain. The *immediate* result will be *more* controls.

How can two such assertions be made: "out of control" and "more controls?" Simply this: the reaction to the loss of power and control over the economy is to grab for more power and more control, as though this were the answer. The controls put the economy into a disastrous course; more controls will only increase the disaster. But frightened men react dangerously and hysterically. When a man's car begins to go out of control, the reaction is to grab the wheel more tightly, not to act sensibly. I have seen men, sliding on an icy road, do the very worst possible things; hit the brakes hard and grab the wheel sharply, and only *increase* the loss of control by their actions.

Thus, we shall have controls, but the controls will aggravate the disaster. The controls are already there, all over the world. Some in use. Some ready to use. Consider, for example, some of the controls which exist, ready for use, in the United States. First, the federal government has the legal right now to enter all safety deposit boxes when it deems that an emergency warrants it. Second, *all* checks are subject to and routinely processed by microphotographing so that a complete file of every check written is available for federal inspection. Third, all large withdrawals of cash must be recorded for reporting. Fourth, all money sent abroad by check is carefully recorded, and so on. The vast data files accumulate, to give us as nearly total a picture of every man's economic life as possible. Banks are a key to this information, and, through the Federal Reserve System, banking is today virtually socialized.

This all sounds frightening, and, in one sense, it is. But let's examine it from another perspective. The federal government, like all civil governments virtually, is drowning in an ocean of data. The more the data accumulates, the less manageable it becomes, and the less usable it becomes, because there is too much to handle, assimilate, and use. You can find a needle in a pin-tray, but not very readily in a haystack.

Take, for example, the Internal Revenue Service, one of the most efficient and best managed branches of the Federal Government. Criticize Internal Revenue as much as you will on other grounds, but grant this fact: it has to collect and deliver funds to the federal government regularly. It has to produce, in other words, something not required of most federal agencies. It functions successfully because it has a core of able and effective administrators, officers, clerks, and workers. But Internal Revenue is increasingly plagued with internal problems: lost files, misplaced records of receipts, and so on: problems connected with missing data. The reason is twofold: massive volumes of data, and the human factor, i.e., inefficient help. One man who misplaces data can create months and years of work for efficient men, and considerable trouble for the citizens whose files are missing. Increase the number of inefficient workers, and the situation is out of hand, and an agency breaks down.

In some countries, this break-down is appearing. Luigi Barzini has written: "The late Luigi Einaudi, Italy's foremost economist and ex-president of the Republic, calculated that, if every tax on the statute books was fully collected, the State would absorb 110 per cent of the national income." (Luigi Barzine: *The Italians*, p. 108). In many countries, there is a growing inability to collect taxes because of the breakdown of a huge bureaucracy which is drowning in its own files and processes.

But this is only a small part of the breakdown which controls bring on. The attempt at total control is essentially religious: the state usurps the prerogative of God. It plays at being god, and like God, it aims at total knowledge. God, having created and determined all things, knows all things. The aim of the state is total knowledge for total controls. The state cannot possibly attain either, and the result is a collapse.

In the Soviet Union, the failure of data came early, and it came thoroughly. The result was a loss of control over the economic facts of the country. Practically, this meant famine in the early twenties, again in the thirties, and a continuing economic and agricultural crisis. The Soviet Union's planning is a radical failure, because its knowledge is ignorance, and its controls are a joke: it cannot control the economy. Without foreign aid in the form of credit, and without imperialism, it could not survive. For knowledge and controls, the Soviet Union substitutes *force and brutality*. Its data is a mess, and its controls a jumble of ineffective contradiction. Its answer to its self-created crisis from the beginning has been to seek control by brutal force.

But brutal force is not an instrument so much of control as it is of open warfare. The first and last war of Communism is against its own people, because they are really out of control. The state's planning cannot move the people; it only cripples them. And the socialist state reacts with savage hatred: it wages war against the people.

How far will we go in a world out of control, a world reverting to jungle warfare in the streets of America, South America, Africa, Asia, Europe, and behind the Iron and Bamboo Curtains? Much of the jungle warfare, if not almost all, in the United States is subsidized by a federal government *already at war with the people*.

But a socialist world is an impossibility, It is a consumption-economy, not a production-economy. Without outside help,it quickly perishes. That death is in the offing, and it will be an ugly, hard death, but die it will. The economic tailspin, devaluation followed by devaluation, inflation and more inflation, all this and more, followed by and accompanied by plague and epidemic, will mark the end of an age. The era of the Enlightenment, the age of humanism, will perish. In its place will come a Christian reconstruction, a free economy and true law and order. "It shall come to pass, that at evening time it shall be light" (Zechariah 14:7). At the moment when total darkness seems about to overwhelm, the light of God's liberty shall blaze forth afresh.

CHALCEDON REPORT NO. 33
May 9, 1968

A false perspective leads quickly to moral disarmament. If a man sincerely believes in the brotherhood of man, he is morally disarmed as he meets the reality of man's enmities. If a man believes that Martin Luther King, Jr. was a basically good man but sometimes misguided, he is morally disarmed in coping with the evil begotten by King.

It is important, therefore, to analyze some of the broad outlines of perspectives. *What are the basic perspectives* which a man can have with respect to our world crisis?

The *first* perspective is that of the *drop-outs*. The hippies, of course, come to mind first of all. The hippie holds that all of modern civilization and religion is hypocrisy and fraud; only a fool becomes involved in it and a part of it. The basic act of virtue and of wisdom for the hippie is, therefore, to drop out. The glow of self-righteousness which characterizes all hippies comes from this fact of dropping out: it is a sign of superior wisdom and virtue, and, accordingly, the hippie despises all those who do not share his superior wisdom. The hippie talks about love, but he seethes with hatred for everything in the "square" world; he feels no compunction about exploiting it, defiling it, or destroying it.

A second element in the drop-out movement is the Negro "civil rights" champion and revolutionist. The readiness of these people to burn and destroy comes from their hatred of the existing order. But this is not all. The civil rights movement is first and last an anti-Negro movement, seething with hatred not only for the white man but for the black also. The first targets of burning are usually Negroes who are law-abiding and hard-working. In one city, when King was murdered, many Negroes sat on their roofs with guns to protect their homes from black revolutionists, while their wives met in payer meetings, beseeching God's mercy and protection. The Negro civil righters have dropped out of American life, white and black; they hate and despise the liberals who aid them, and they spit out contempt for the good men of their own race. They are drop-outs: they despise the achievements and morality of Western Christian culture, and their one target is to destroy: "burn, baby, burn."

There are many other varieties of drop-outs, but a third will suffice to illustrate the nature of the drop-out. The leading drop-outs are the Marxists. Marx's basic philosophy was a faith in the regenerative power of destruction, the religion of revolution. Marxists are thus dedicated above all else to destruction. The appeal of Marxism to all kinds of drop-outs is thus very great. This means, too, that Marxists can exploit drop-outs easily because it offers organization to their urge to mass destruction. The hippies, the student rebels (who are drop-outs in their own way), and the various radical groups are all easily used by the Marxists to further their drop-out goal, the total destruction of the past and of all godly law and order.

The Negro "civil rights" movement is made to order for the Marxists. In Russia, the Bolsheviks were too few and too "intellectual" to fight a revolution themselves. They had to use dupes to do the job for them. Basic to the revolution was the naval mutiny of the sailors of the Kronstadt fleet. This was the beginning of the collapse of Russia into lawlessness, anarchy, and revolution. The sailors had their grievances; but when it was all over, the settlement the sailors of the Kronstadt fleet received was death for all. February 23 - March 17, 1921, marked the mutiny of these sailors against the Bolsheviks; instead of getting their original demands, the sailors were worse off. Their pay-off now was death.

The Negroes are the modern Kronstadt fleet. They are encouraged and subsidized for violence; and, at the same time, local law enforcement agencies are progressively hamstrung to lead to a federal power over all people in order to "cope" with rioting. The Negro is made increasingly the object of hatred by the subsidized rioting of some so that the majority of whites will later welcome a socialist power which suppresses the disorders.

The Marxists, as the strongest and most systematic drop-outs, cash in on every drop-out effort: it all contributes to their ultimate goal of destruction. But many who do not consider themselves Marxists or who are anti-Marxist actually contribute to the Marxists' success. This is done by accepting the basic Marxist premise: environmentalism. The *Report of the National Advisory Commission on Civil Disorders* (March, 1968) blamed the riots, not on hoodlums and revolutionists; but placed the guilt on the law-abiding white population, i.e., on the environment. Now, there are two steps in settling any problem: *first*, find out what is wrong and who is responsible; *second* remove the conditions and persons which are responsible. At this point, the Commission was not honest. It blamed the white environment. It called for certain corrective actions. But it did not openly state that it was in effect calling for the punishment of the law-abiding white population. By calling for more taxes and more laws it was instituting repressive measures against those who must pay the taxes and whose freedom of association is limited by the laws.

Now, environmentalism places the blame, not on the guilty parties, but on the human environment and the cultural environment. It condemns that environment and calls for a drop-out from it and then, logically, the destruction of it. The Marxists are the leaders in the world of drop-outs: they see the implications most clearly.

The *second* basic perspective can be called that of the *drop-ins*. The drop-in declares that everything is basically fine: all that is needed is a little tinkering, some neat changes here and there, and all will be well.

In analyzing drop-outs, we began with the hippies, an adolescent phenomenon. In dealing with the drop-ins, let us begin with another adolescent phenomenon, the great drop-in voice of youth, *Playboy* magazine. The gospel according to *Playboy* is total humanism. Accordingly, *Playboy* is strongly hostile to orthodox Christian faith and morality and wages unceasing warfare against it. For *Playboy* the glory of life is our humanistic culture; get rid of the Christian hang-over, get rid of Internal Revenue and the income tax, and get rid of federal snoopers which invade our privacy, and all will be well. Even as Marxism represents a radical humanism, *Playboy* represents a conservative humanism. For both, Biblical Christianity is the enemy. *Playboy's* philosophy presents "the good life" for those who believe in dropping in, in creaming our heritage without any responsibility to it, who want to live well rather than to live responsibly under God.

Another kind of drop-in is to be found among the political liberals and conservatives who believe that with a little tinkering, an election or two, the world will be well. This position is basically rationalistic. It has no sense of roots or life. Some political cure all is the answer. H. du Berrier has again and again called attention to the fallacy of the liberal rationalists (and radicals) whose cure for Vietnam was to remove the emperor and institute "democracy." But their action has effectively destroyed Vietnam and left it without a principle of authority. We may not like it, but in terms of the religion of these people, the emperor is a divine-human figure and is the source of authority. Take away the emperor, and you take away authority and introduce anarchy. Now, we may prefer a Christian Vietnam, or a "democratic" and liberal Vietnam, or a conservative republic there: but the reality of Vietnam is that such things cannot have roots there; in the future, perhaps, but not now. Remove the principle of authority, and what are your choices? Anarchy or totalitarian coercion. There is nothing left to hold society together.

Rationalists, conservative and liberal, are ready to dream up ideal schemes to build a new world: a little tinkering or a great tinkering, but always some addition or subtraction, and paradise will come. It's a fine world, say these men: we want it to realize its possibilities. But does paradise come? Unfortunately, the Marxists arrive instead, to cash in on the anarchy.

But these drop-ins refuse to learn. One more tinker, one more election, one more something, and all will be well. The election of Eisenhower, I was told some years ago, would "turn the tide." And not too long ago some people refused to speak to me because I saw no gain in electing Reagan.

The drop-ins refuse to face up to the fact of evil, its deep and religious roots, and its power. Pass a good law or win an election, and does evil go away or does it not rather move more savagely against you? We are at war, and the basic war is between the Kingdom of God and the Kingdom of Man; and there is no coexistence in that war.

The drop-ins believe that everything is basically well with us, except for their little or big gimmicks. They want to cure cancer with nose drops, whereas the drop-outs want to "cure" it with a gun.

How can you deal with the world of the drop-outs without seeing its deep roots? Darwin, Marx, and Freud are the shapers of the modern mind and of environmentalism in its present form. Their influence saturates state, church, school, home, society, and both work and play. No law or election can change that fact overnight. It takes the grace of God (conversion) and the response of man (education, instruction, application).

This points us to a *third* perspective, one to counteract moral disarmament: *Christian reconstruction*. This means facing up to the facts of the situation and recognizing how far gone we are, and it means driving that fact home to people. It means then re-educating and reconstructing society from the ground up. This means Christian schools instead of statist education. It means new and truly Christian churches instead of humanistic ones. It means building from the ground up in politics in terms of Biblical perspectives. It means a Christian economics, godly science, agriculture, and so on. It means the centrality of the family, and it also means a Christian principle of authority as against a humanistic doctrine of authority.

When the drop-outs say of our culture that it is sick, they are right; but their answer is to kill the patient. When the drop-ins say they love our culture and want to improve or heal it, we can commend their wishes but not their common sense because cancer is not cured by nose drops, nor glaucoma by eye drops. Whether sincerely held or not, a false perspective leads to moral disarmament. But moral disarmament is a major step towards suicide.

CHALCEDON REPORT NO. 34
June 17, 1968

One of America's original and greatest bleeding heart liberals was Horace Greeley, famous editor and socialist of Lincoln's day. Greeley was not a Christian but a humanist. Of him, President Andrew Jackson wrote, "Greeley is all heart and no head. He is the most vacillating man in the country. He runs to goodness of heart so much as to produce infirmity of mind." Greeley's religion, by his own words, was simply this: "my affirmation creed is mainly summed up in the belief that God is infinitely wise and good, and that all evil is temporary and finite and to be swallowed up in the end by Universal Good." Greeley's "God" was a vague Universal Good.

As a result, it always bothered me to read that this agnostic and bleeding-heart liberal supposedly had a death-bed conversion and died murmuring, "It is done! I have fought the good fight. I know that My Redeemer Liveth." Various church papers, preachers, and writers have made much of that statement, but it never rang true to me, no more than did other "last words" of some famous old reprobates. But Henry Luther Stoddard quotes it in his book, *Horace Greeley*, as do others. Lucius Beebe, in *The Big Spenders*, gives us another version. Whitelaw Reid, editor of the *Tribune*, who gradually took over ownership from Greeley, was at Greeley's bedside with Greeley's daughters. Greeley, at the end, opened his eyes, saw Reid, and muttered, "You s.o.b., you stole my newspaper." When Reid rejoined the others who were awaiting the end, he was asked by Tom Rooker, "What were his last words, Mr. Reid? Give us his last message." It was then that Reid said, "His last words were, 'I know that my redeemer liveth!'" It made a prettier story, and it stuck.

Why am I quoting this story? Because it illustrates so well the desire of many people for a happy ending, for fairy tales. A few years ago, when I spoke in one city, a woman told me (the entire group knew the story from her) that Charles Darwin had renounced evolution in his old age and died a Christian. Also, she claimed, this could be found in a book she had seen of Darwin's letters, and that the book had since "disappeared" from the public library. I stated that I owned that book, and it contained no such statement. The result: no one in that group wanted to hear me again! Or take another case. Martin Luther King has been compared to Christ by the pope, by many ministers, and by many lecturers. But King denied the Bible and Christ and worked in association with a pervert and with communists. How do some of these people square their church's stand with their conscience? Well, the story is making the rounds that a day or so before he was killed, King told a friend that he had been very wrong that the Bible was true, and Jesus indeed was the incarnate Second Person of the Trinity! The story is not only false, it is wicked. The people who believe it are trying to run away from reality and from responsibility. Their position is one of escapism, of moral irresponsibility.

One such group of people is today urging Christians to do nothing about our world problems: instead, they should separate themselves from every political, social, and religious controversy and problem and simply await the "rapture." Indeed, this group is preparing for that "event" by equipping itself with rapture suits!

I have not taken time heretofore to criticize various other theological viewpoints. I only do so now because repeatedly various persons have raised the question of the "rapture". It has been repeatedly said that because I and others do not hold to this view, we are either defective Christians or are not preaching the Gospel, or are even enemies of the Gospel. Several friends have been told that they are not Christians and that they must submit to truly "fundamental" teaching or be lost.

Before going any further, let me state that not all who hold to a belief in the rapture are so arrogant, nor are all so given to escapism. Indeed, at one meeting, where one such believer attacked my concern with social problems, another stood up to say that the Lord's command is "Occupy till I come, and no one, whatever their doctrine of the last things, could afford to neglect this order."

The main source of these escapist doctrines is in the Scofield Bible notes. Scofieldism is a system of doctrine which sees the fulfillment of Biblical prophecy in national Israel. (It is a kind of Christian Zionism.)

Related to this teaching is the school known as Dispensationalism. Dispensationalism holds to three major intervals or "parenthesis" in history: 1) between the first two verses of Genesis 1: 2) The Church or Mystery parenthesis between Pentecost and the Rapture; and 3) the Jewish Remnant parenthesis, a seven year interval between the rapture and the appearing. Scofield basically accepted this system. Dispensationalism is essentially evolutionary, while claiming to be fundamental; instead of a God who is unchanging, it gives us a changing God; it makes room for modern geological theories. It becomes antinomian or anti-law. A major dispensationalist group, the Plymouth Brethren, emphasize other-worldliness and a surrender of this world and its problems. Some have refused to hold public office, to take daily papers, to vote, or to become involved in the world's activities by trying to establish Christian law and order.

In its extremes, Dispensationalism becomes anti-Christian. S.D. Gordon rejected the cross of Christ and held that the Mosaic sacrifices saved men in and of themselves. He wrote, of the cross, "It can be said at once that His dying was not God's own plan. It was a plan conceived somewhere else and yielded to by God. God had a plan of atonement by which men who were willing could be saved from sin and its effects." This plan was the Mosaic sacrificial system. Scofield held to a similar belief to a great degree, and he looked for the restoration of the temple and of sacrifice. Those who want a detailed examination of the heresies of Dispensationalism and Scofieldism can find it in O.T. Allis: *Prophecy and the Church* (Presbyterian and Reformed Publishing Co.)

Mysticism too leads to similar viewpoints, that is, a denial of the importance of this world and an attempt to escape from history and its problems and responsibilities. The roots of all such thinking are neoplatonic or else Manichaean.

Neoplatonism held (it stemmed from Greek philosophy) that only spirit or mind is real, and that matter is not equal to spirit, nor as real. This belief Horace Greeley echoed, and its culmination is in Mary Baker Eddy.

Manichaeanism held to two kinds of reality, matter, which is evil, and spirit, which is good. (In some versions, such as Marxism, matter is good, and spirit is evil, or, in an inverted neoplatonism, non-existent). The spiritual Manichaean forsakes the world of matter, of history, politics, and problems to concentrate on the world of spirit. The "higher" Manichaeans said marriage was evil, and put marriage on the same moral level as rape and incest.

The Biblical position is that body and soul are alike created wholly good, alike fallen, and alike redeemed in Christ. The Christian's duty and responsibility is to bring all the world into subjection to the rule of Christ, in whom alone is our true and perfect freedom. To deny either our material or spiritual responsibilities is to deny God. The Christian must seek to bring all things into captivity to Christ.

Those who expect to be "raptured" out of their problems are not Christian. This is paganism: it is a *deus ex machina* belief, that is, the Greek belief that salvation means being rescued from our problems. Biblical faith holds that salvation means that, now, having been justified by God's grace, we are empowered to overcome our problems, to do battle unto victory.

I have had some of these escapists tell me that if the Lord will not rapture them out of the "tribulation," they see no point in being a Christian! This is not faith: it is blasphemy. (The "rapture," incidentally, is not to be confused with the doctrine of the second coming, which is different.) I do not find this escapist doctrine of the rapture taught in the Bible. I do find a commandment which declares that the church must "teach all nations" (Matt. 28:19). Men and nations are to be brought into subjection to Christ the King and His law-word. We have been saved, not to run from the world, but "That the righteousness of the law might be fulfilled in us" (Romans 8:4). The world must therefore be brought under God's law. This is not escapism: it is a marching order.

CHALCEDON REPORT NO. 37
September 2, 1968

After World War II, an American in Shanghai, the Rev. D. R. Lindberg (one of our Newsletter family) walked downtown one morning and witnessed an amazing sight. Wealthy Chinese sat on the sidewalks and even in the streets, weeping and sobbing uncontrollably. Scattered around them were large piles of paper money, in denominations up to $5,000. A government order, in view of rapidly growing inflation, had declared all bills of $5,000 and under to be invalid, and their wealth and life savings had just been abolished. They had gone from store to store, bank to bank, hoping to realize something, and they had failed. However the money, if accepted, would have done them little good. A little later, this American paid $25 million for a new suit; exactly a week to the day later, a small dime store mouth organ for his son cost $50 million, and such was the distrust of all paper money that it took two American paper dollars to buy one Chinese silver dollar. This is inflation, the breakdown of paper money. Millionaires find themselves unable to buy a slice of bread with their millions, and, in some instances, have starved to death.

Inflation is one of the results of managed money, and managed money is the cornerstone of socialism. In fact, socialism is impossible without managed money. Managed money is the deliberate, state-controlled debasing or counterfeiting of money as the basic form of social planning. Paper money, and coins of baser metals passing in the place of silver or gold, is managed money, whereas gold and silver coinage, which constitutes real wealth, is valid money. For money is not merely a medium of exchange: it is a form of wealth, and if the medium of exchange is a controlled and counterfeit one, wealth is progressively confiscated and destroyed. As a result, the first and basic step in any socialism, in any statist confiscation of private wealth, is to require people to accept a counterfeit or debased money, a mere representation of wealth, in exchange for their very real wealth, their labor, goods, and properties. Managed money is the basic form of socialist planning. The state produces the managed money and begins to spend it for social planning. With this managed money, the state can further its welfare programs, its progressive controls and expropriations, and its total programs of planning and socialization, because, as the producer of managed money, it is the biggest buyer on the market. The state buys real wealth in the form of labor, goods, and properties and gives managed money, counterfeit wealth, in exchange. The paper value of the people's wealth increases for a time, and prosperity seems to prevail, until the process reaches the point of increasing confiscation as the money rapidly inflates and becomes worthless.

But a runaway inflation not only destroys the creditors, the middle classes, and all with savings, it also destroys the state which permits it. It leads to a collapse of the civil government which promoted it. Previously, runaway inflation has repeatedly occurred. Will it again be the route to disaster?

Managed money, or socialism, is a parasitic economy. The state feeds on the people's wealth, and the people eat up their own future, and their country's future, with a debt economy and growing areas of socialization. Socialization produces temporary benefits to some, but socialization, as a parasite economy, must rob and confiscate in order to give. Instead of creating new wealth, it destroys existing wealth.

As a result of this progressive confiscation and destruction of wealth, the country begins to falter and to move towards economic collapse and catastrophe. A savage struggle for survival then begins. The socialist, interventionist, or welfare economy then faces a grim choice: who shall survive, the people or the state? Increasingly, in the modern world, the socialist answer is that the people must be sacrificed to preserve the state. To stop deficit spending and return to hard money would create a depression, which would hurt but would save both the state and the people, although at a cost, but this would involve abandoning socialism. This the state will not do, because to sacrifice socialism now means to sacrifice the state, which now sees itself as identical with socialism.

As a result, the state turns to what Wilhelm Roepke and Hans Sennholz have described as repressed inflation. Repressed inflation, according to Roepke in *Economics of the Free Society*, "consists, fundamentally, in the fact that a government first promotes inflation but then seeks to interdict its influence on prices and rates of exchange by imposing the now familiar war-time devices of rationing and fixed prices, together with the requisite enforcement measures." In other words, the cure for the disaster bred by the growing controls of money, men, and property is total controls! This is like saying that the cure for tuberculosis in one lung is its presence everywhere in both lungs.

Roepke noted that repressed inflation is more deadly than open inflation and "ends inevitably in chaos and paralysis." And it is repressed inflation which we are steadily getting, as the federal government moves to control steel, copper, and aluminum prices, and to limit private spending by taxation, while continuing and increasing its own deficit spending. On May 9, 1959, Arthur Upgren, in the Minneapolis *Star*, stated that the U.S. would "go bust" by 1970 because of the breakdown of money. In a paper on the subject, "Why the United States is Most Likely to Have a Financial Collapse in 1970", Upgren offered as his answer to the pending crisis more money management. But more money management means simply more socialism. Briefly, such answers in effect declare that the only way to escape economic law is by means of the totalitarian law of the state.

This is then the course being progressively taken, more money management, which means more socialism, and thus progressive confiscation. This means chaos and disaster. It means the breakdown of money also. But, most of all, it means the end of socialism. The socialist states of the world are all parasites. As parasites, they have lived off their people first, and then off the United States. Now, as repressed inflation begins to work to gut the American social order, the socialisms of the world will collapse with this breakdown of American free enterprise. When the host body dies, the parasite also dies. The desperate attempt of socialism to survive by sacrificing its people fails to work; without outside help, socialism dies. A socialist world cannot exist.

Thoughtful men will naturally seek to protect themselves by investing in land, gold, silver, and other historic hedges against inflation, but the counter-hedges of socialism against self-protection are greater than ever before. And, while survival is important, it is not enough. Socialism is finished: it is destroying itself, and, although the worst lies ahead, the certainty of socialism's collapse is nonetheless inescapable, and it must be a basic premise of all thinking concerning the future. The central concern even now must be reconstruction, the creation of new institutions dedicated to liberty, education to that end, and the assurance that the fresh air of liberty is ahead, past the days of chaos. The wise, therefore will recognize that the breakdown of money, socialist money, is overtaking us, and that there is no security in counterfeit currency. Before they sit weeping, like the Chinese of Shanghai, surrounded with their worthless money, they had better dedicate themselves and their wealth to the cause of liberty before it is too late. As Sennholz has pointed out, our managed money today is the poorest form of investment for the future. In the long run, an investment in liberty offers better returns.

The above was written two and a half years ago and filed away. Today, there is no reason to change a word of it.

The news accentuates our crisis. For some years now, people have profited by inflation. They are now geared to what Gary North calls "the economics of addiction."

A news report of Saturday, August 24, 1968, is headed "Brink of Credit Disaster" (Oakland, CA, *Tribune*, p. 1) states that "Over one-third of all American families are on the brink of serious financial trouble" because of heavy indebtedness. And most other Americans are also very much in debt and cannot take a real crisis. The reason is that "a consumption ethic has replaced the work ethic."

The demand by all these people in debt will be for more easy money, more paper, in order to pay off good debts with bad money. The people have a vested interest in more inflation; their prosperity depends on it. The federal government also has a vested interest in more inflation; its power depends on it.

When *over* one-third of all American families face financial disaster or very serious trouble, according to the American Association of Credit Counselors, can anyone imagine an administration doing anything but inflating? Virtually all the politicians of these days seem primarily interested in power, not the future, and the road to political power is now inflation. After them, the flood.

The foundations are being destroyed. It is high time to rebuild, to rebuild on a solidly Christian foundation.

CHALCEDON REPORT NO. 38
October 1, 1968

One of the deadliest errors of our day is the failure of political science. In the teaching of political science, there is no true doctrine of the state; indeed, we can say that there is no theology of the state, but only a pretended science.

In the ancient world, the state was regarded as a divine-human order, and the ruler or his office was divine. The true religion of pagan society was the religion of the state. The word "liturgy" comes from a Greek word meaning "public work", religion in Greek society was a part of the state's public works to ensure morale. Not the Biblical God, but the state was the sovereign lord over man, and his "true" god. Man, the Greeks held, was a political animal, a creature of the state, not a creature of God.

When Christianity began to spread throughout the Roman Empire, and beyond it, the Biblical doctrine of the state under God went with it. The result was a life and death struggle between the church and the state, between two rival theologies. Christ or Caesar? Who was man's true lord and master?

As the persecutions of the church ended, and the state had to abandon open paganism, they adopted a pseudo-Christian guise to reassert their pagan doctrine of the state: Arianism, and especially Pelagianism. Our concern here is with this Pelagian doctrine of the state, or the politics of Pelagianism.

According to Benjamin Breckinridge Warfield, "the central and formative principle of Pelagianism is the assumption of the plenary ability of man." (B.B. Warfield: *Studies in Tertullian and Augustine*, p. 291. New York: Oxford University Press, 1930) Pelagianism believes in the natural goodness of man; it is not man who is evil but his environment. The state also is naturally good and is therefore to be trusted with all the powers necessary in order to cope with an evil environment.

The Pelagian state believes in a state-created paper money rather than the intrinsic value of precious metals, of gold and silver. The Pelagian state sees itself in every realm as the source of standards and values.

The real and major revolution of the modern age is the revolution from a Biblical to a Pelagian doctrine of the state. This revolution began in the "medieval" period; such figures as Frederick II represented the growing Pelagian doctrine; it flourished in the Renaissance, and it triumphed with the Enlightenment.

The faith of modern man is Pelagianism. As a result, literature abundantly reflects this faith. It shows us the hero as one who stands "for truth or Edenic innocence" and is victimized by society (as in Truman Capote. Jean Stafford, James Purdy, and others). The hero is a lonely youth "exposing the corrupt adult world" (Salinger's *The Catcher in the Rye*). The hero is a well-meaning lover (in Nemerou, Bulchner, and Macauley), or a homosexual (in Vidal and Baldwin) whom evil institutions condemn. "In time of organization, Eros is utterly disorganized." The Negro especially is seen as the poor innocent condemned by an evil society, and so on. (See Joseph J. Waldmeier, editor: *Recent American Fiction, Some Critical Views*, p. 31. Boston: Houghton, Mifflin, 1963.) In brief, the more evil, or the lower society deems a man to be, the better he must be in the eyes of the Pelagian! It is the debased, the pervert, the criminal, and the shiftless who ipso facto represent the most oppressed and down-trodden, the most naturally good of society. As a result, the hero for modern fiction, and, increasingly, the hero for modern life and politics, is increasingly the lowest kind of man. The worst elements are subsidized, lionized, and catered to, because, in the eyes of Pelagians, they are really the best. The law-abiding and orderly people become a part of the evil environment; if they were good, they would revolt. To revolt is a sign of natural goodness. Thus, the more Negroes riot and revolt, the better they are in the eyes of the Pelagians; if they are godly, they are overlooked.

Pelagian churches hold to a similar anthropology or doctrine of man, and, because virtually all churches are Pelagian today, they attack God (the Supreme Environment), and glorify revolutionary man, the innocent and holy victim.

For the Pelagians the "normal" man, i.e., the godly, law-abiding citizen, is vicious, perverted, and insane. This is the thesis of the student revolutionists, and of Herbert Marcuse. Ronald D. Laing, a British physician and psychiatrist, in a book highly praised by the Los Angeles *Free Press*, writes:

> The condition of alienation, of being asleep, of being unconscious, of being out of one's mind, is the condition of the normal man.
> Society highly values its normal man. It educates children to lose themselves and to become absurd, and thus to be normal.
> Normal men have killed perhaps 100,000,000 of their fellow normal men in the last fifty years.
> (Dr. R. D. Laing: *The Politics of Experience*, p. 28. New York: Ballantine Books, 1967.)

If you are a Pelagian and believe this, you will then believe that it is the duty of all good men to revolt against the society of normal man and to work for its destruction. This is the faith of the New Left as well as the Old Left. Staughton Lynd, in the *Intellectual Origins of American Radicalism*, makes it clear that he has an unqualified trust in the natural goodness and perfectibility of man.

This same Pelagian faith governs present political action. The rioters are subsidized and catered to; the welfare recipients are treated with increasing favor. Welfare recipients are encouraged to act as though the state owes them a living. In New York City, one out of seven receive welfare, and one out of six babies born are illegitimate. The law-abiding are penalized; they are taxed heavily to subsidize all this.

Pelagianism, being sympathetic with evil, cannot cope with violence, because it provides a justification for violence. Abbie Hoffman, 31, a Yippie leader in the Chicago disturbances, declared to the liberal New York *Post*, "They call us hard-core anarchists with plots to overthrow the government. Well, that's not a secret. That's always been the case, so what's the big deal? So far as I'm concerned we totally won the Battle of Chicago. I have just written a book about it. It's title is 'Revolution for the Hell of It.'" ("Meet Abbie Hoffman", Los Angeles *Herald-Examiner*, Tuesday, September 10, 1968, p. B-2.) How can a Pelagian cope with an attitude which he creates and justifies?

In foreign affairs, a Pelagian state will believe that, because men and nations are naturally good, the response to goodness will be goodness also. Include the enemy as a friend and a co-worker, and all will ultimately be well, because he is not really evil. Thus, on Monday, September 9, 1968, a 31 - nation committee of the United Nations convened to draft a new international agreement aimed at defining principles for "friendly relations and cooperation" among U.N. member countries. Committee members included the Soviet Union and Czechoslovakia! ("Ultimate Irony", L.A. *Herald-Examiner*, Monday September 9, 1968, p. A-17)

Meanwhile, a Pelagian, a retired Supreme Court Justice, Tom C. Clark, insists that society is to be blamed for the increasing crime rate. (*Parade*, June 2, 1968, p. 4, "Why the Crime Rise?")

This Pelagian trust in the goodness of man goes deeply into our culture, into the modern mind everywhere. Police report that a sizable proportion of rape victims invited trouble by being too trusting. One of the most startling things I ever encountered was the report of a woman in the rape of Shanghai in the 1930s. Her reaction was almost beyond belief. Repeatedly raped by the soldiers, her one thought was that she could hardly believe it was really happening, and that men could actually act that way!

A generation so blind, so deeply devoted to a Pelagian faith, is incapable of coping with evil, because it cannot recognize evil in itself or in other men.

Its inability to see evil leads to a radical trust in man and in the state. Evil is continually projected on the environment. If the state becomes so evil that its evil must be cited, then somehow the state has become a part of the corrupt environment; it is the establishment, and it must be overthrown and replaced with a pure regime.

The New Left regards the Establishment as a part of the evil, oppressing order of the past, of priestcraft and religion. It insists that we have evil rulers but a good, misguided people. Many pseudo-conservatives share this opinion, and they tell us also that the church has evil leaders but good, misguided members. This is the Pelagian theme of moral man and immoral society.

On the contrary, however, it can with justice be said that our leaders in church and state are better than we deserve. In neither church nor state do we find men of moral courage, that is, the courage of their convictions. They are pushed by the mob rather than leaders of it, whatever their position. We have today the fruit of generations of statist education, arrogant Pelagian man.

The statistics of our world and of the United States, are interesting. *All* elements, i.e., the various age groups, are Pelagian on the whole; they differ only in their intensity and dedication. In the closing years of the last century, and the early years of this century, there was a high birth rate: there is thus today a sizable element of the population of retirement age. The generation between the wars represents a lower birth rate. From World War II to the later 1950s, there was again a high birth rate. In terms of the death rate, by 1970, the great majority of Americans (and this will be true in other countries also) will be under 25. The erosion into permissiveness and radical Pelagianism has meanwhile been rapid. Our more astute politicians, the Kennedys, McCarthy, and others, have had their eye on this rising power, and they are more governed by it than able to govern it.

The Pelagian state, by its philosophy and education, creates a mass man, a mob. It begets the new barbarians and scientists. The new barbarians assume that all the heritage of the past is simply a natural resource which simply exists: what is not desired can be destroyed, and the rest will remain. The new barbarian refuses to believe that each generation must accept and develop a tradition to retain it.

Recently, I have encountered a number of cases of hippies from excellent families who despised and rejected the Establishment, including education. Apart from reading revolutionary writings and demonstrating, their education gave them no competence whatsoever. (Many received good grades also from sympathetic professors.) Faced suddenly with a girl and a baby to provide for, a licit or illicit family, they found themselves incompetent for any kind of work. The reaction is either a mental tailspin, or wilder revolutionary involvement. And why not? More and more have come to believe that *work* is obsolete, that man can now provide total security and welfare by means of a truly human social order. Failure to do so is an ugly plot by reactionaries.

The Pelagian mentality is a departure from reality, and the Pelagian state inescapably pursues a suicidal course.

The desperate need is for Christian, for Biblical, statecraft. This means establishing our concept of the state, among other things, on the Biblical anthropology, on the doctrine of the fall. Neither man nor the state is to be trusted. Sovereignty is essentially an attribute of God alone. The state and man can only handle limited power and limited liberty. The supremacy of law, God's law, must govern every sphere of human activity, nor can any sphere be divorced from God. Church, state, school, work, art, science, agriculture, society, and all things else must be under God, or else they are under judgment.

This then is obviously a time of judgment. Equally obviously, we must make it a time for reconstruction.

CHALCEDON REPORT NO. 39
November 1, 1968

Foundations are one of the most important, abused, and misunderstood aspects of our contemporary scene. Most large foundations are strongly oriented to statism, and virtually all the rest are too afraid of losing their tax-exemption to do more than drift with the current. But foundations have a central and basic place in Christian history. To understand them, let us examine briefly the ancient pagan state.

The pagan state was a totalitarian divine-human order: the state was a god walking on earth. Its divinity might be manifested in the person of the ruler, or his office, or the state or people as a whole, but this divinity was believed to be there. There was no freedom from the state: everything was absolutely under state control, whether in China, India, Babylon, Egypt, Greece, or Rome. Religion was merely a department of state.

The one exception was the Commonwealth of God's people, Israel. God and His law-order were accorded sovereignty over all things by all true believers. God's prophets could rebuke kings, because even apostate men were aware of the sovereign word and its power. The tyrant Ahab had to be nagged by his foreign wife, Jezebel, to act against the prophets.

The church in the Roman Empire could have readily become a recognized and legal religion by offering incense to Caesar and acknowledging his sovereignty. This the church refused to do. The Christians *as citizens* were ready to submit to Caesar in all matters of civil justice, but in those areas where God gave the state no jurisdiction they obeyed God. The Biblical faith is not in the state as an over-arching, all-governing institution which takes all others under its wings, but in God's sovereign and over-arching law-order, under which church, state, school, family, vocation, and all things else exist as separate yet interdependent spheres of life. The state has no more legitimate right to govern the church and school than it has to govern the laws of mathematics and physics, and the realm of the church is similarly restricted. The realm of the state is justice and order under God; the realm of the church is the ministry of the word and the sacraments and the discipline of its body; the realm of the school is the development of learning and knowledge under God; and so on.

The triumph of Christianity meant the death of totalitarianism, and, as a result, the state at first tried ruthlessly to exterminate all Christians. For a time, the swords and axes of executioners worked from morning to dark to kill the lines of condemned Christians. Later, when extermination failed, infiltration and subversion became the strategy.

But Christianity began to create a new society, a decentralized and free society. And *foundations* very, very early were basic to that society. These foundations were free and independent agencies, free of church and state, dedicated to specific purposes: charity and welfare, hospitals and medicine, education, orphanages, missions, and so on. These foundations began to accumulate wealth to fulfil these purposes. The history books tell us that, by the end of the so-called "middle ages" much of the wealth of Europe was in the hands of the church. They lie. There was considerable wealth in the hands of foundations, Christian orders and foundations, who were doing a great work for rich and poor alike. A greedy church and greedy states were trying to seize and often succeeding in taking over these foundations for their own unchristian purposes. In this imperialism by both church and state, the state finally won.

But let us examine those foundations again. The church very early expressed its disapproval of the neoplatonic pagan flight of the hermits from the world. In fact, in 819, the Council of Aix made it plain that the Christian duty of monastery communities or foundations was to care for the poor, or, in one way or another, minister to Christian society. Some of these foundations were monastic and clerical; others were lay foundations. All were responsible for great progress.

To cite one group, established by rich merchants with their poor tithes and other gifts, the Order of St. John of Jerusalem (also known as the Knights of Malta) was by the end of the 11th century famous for its hospital work. We have an excellent description of one of their hospitals, built in Valetta, Malta, in 1575, for 800 patients, in a recent study of hospitals and their history:

> The equipment and service in the Malta hospital were the finest of their day. "In regard to the dignity of the Infirmary", the patients' meals

> were served on silver plates and in covered bowls; pewter dishes were allotted to the slaves in attendance. The three hundred and seventy beds were curtained, and fresh white linen curtains were used during the summer. All beds and bedding used by consumptives were burned, and sheets were ordered changed several times daily if necessary. The hospital was fortunate in having vast endowments, which permitted this comfortable equipment.
>
> The medical staff included a physician who gave students daily lectures in anatomy. Two practitioners supervised the carrying-out of the surgeon's orders, and about a dozen other men were assigned various medical duties.
>
> The wards were separated: one was for the aged pilgrims or religious, a small ward for the dying, one for hemorrhage cases, and a separate ward for the insane and their warden. As for food: herbs, all sorts of meats, pigeons, fowls, beef, veal, game, fresh eggs, almonds, raisins, sweet biscuits, apples, pomegranates with sugar "according to the wants of each" made up a partial list of the hospital's elaborate selection of foods for the patients.
>
> (Mary Risley: *House of Healing, The Story of the Hospital*, p. 107. Garden City, New York: Doubleday & Co., 1961.)

The Knights of Malta are still active, and it is possible that their greatest work is ahead of them. This brief citation does serve to illustrate the fact that hospitals were once almost entirely a domain of foundation work, serving all people in Christian charity and with real ability. In the modern age, the hospital has become "independent" of Christian foundations; it has not been successful as an economic unit, that is, it has trouble breaking even financially and it has provided the state an excuse for stepping in with socialized medicine.

The point is clear: certain social functions must be provided: hospitals, schools, welfare agencies, and so on. When Christian foundations establish and control them, they serve the purposes of Christian concern and love.

It is not enough to "vote the rascals out", although this surely needs doing. What will be done about the basic social functions, health, education, and welfare? When the state handles these, it ladles out benefits with politics in mind, and the results are social decay and anarchy. When Christian foundations assume the responsibility, the results further godly law and order.

Before Horace Mann began the state school movement in the United States in the 1830s, all children were educated by the Christian schools of the day, which were independent and self-governing. The slum children, children of newly arrived immigrants, and others as well were educated by educational missionary societies or foundations, and the work they did was excellent. (One such still existing school was recently the target of Supreme Court interference and forced integration, in violation of the founder's wishes. Whether the founder wished integration or segregation was none of the Court's business.)

As late as 1907, all welfare needs in the depression of that year were met by Christian churches and foundations. The foundation was once an independent agency whose inception, purpose, and reason for being was to manifest Christian faith and concern for all manners of men and needs. They were a basic aspect of Christian society and important and central to the cause of freedom. The plan to remove tax-exemption from churches and Christian agencies is an attempt to destroy Christian civilization.

The lingering echoes of the old liberty remain in the confused statements of university students and professors. When the University of California professors and students protest *any* control by the state, we can agree with them, *provided* they renounce *any and all* support by the state and the federal government. Any other course is irresponsibility and immorality: they are seeking the best of both worlds, Christian and statist, and the responsibilities of neither. As such, they are a force for anarchy, not freedom. For liberty's death-knell is always sounded by irresponsibility and license.

The forces of Christian reconstruction are already in evidence, most notably in the Christian school movement. Today 25-30% of all grade school children are not in the public schools, and 10% of all high school children are in non-statist schools. And this is merely the beginning.

As many of you already know, our purpose, as a small group of Christian scholars and Christian men and women dedicated to Christian reconstruction, is to establish a center of study and learning for this cause. A new order of foundations is central to this purpose as well as a center of Biblical learning dedicated to total Christian reconstruction.

CHALCEDON REPORT NO. 40
December 1, 1968

In order to understand the direction of history, it is necessary to understand the meaning of *the city*. The city has a long and strange history and has at various time been regarded as a man's ideal society, and, at other times, as a thing to flee from. The countryside similarly has been viewed sometimes as a wilderness and at other times a refuge, an idyllic haven from the city. The reasons for this are important for us to know.

Too many people in modern times have seen the origin of the city in Cain, who built a city and called it Enoch (Gen. 4:17). The Hebrew word for city probably means in origin "to rouse", or "to raise an alarm", according to H. C. Leupold, and Enoch means "Beginner"; the city of Cain was thus both a new beginning, and a place of refuge when an alarm was raised. But Cain's "beginning" had reference to an earlier beginning, Eden. We are accustomed to thinking of the Garden of Eden exclusively as a "garden"; but Revelation 21 and 22 make it clear that Eden is both garden and city, "The New Jerusalem", the Kingdom or City of God. The common characteristic of ancient cities was a wall; Eden was walled *after* the Fall to keep sinful man out, the wall being "Cherubims and flaming sword" (Gen. 3:24).

In terms of this, we must say that the city is intended to represent *community* and *a common life and refuge*. The two basic aspects thus of the city are (1) a common faith, and (2) a common defense. But today the city has no common faith, and it is a place of increasing lawlessness and terror. Somehow, the city has failed; the city has failed to be a city. Instead of walling out the enemy, it has walled in the enemy. It is important for us to know why.

Let us analyze briefly the two basic aspects of the city in its origin, first, a common faith. Originally, a city represented a common faith, and citizenship rested on atonement. In ancient Rome, for example, a man lost his citizenship, except for soldiers on duty, if he were absent from the annual lustrations, the annual rites of atonement. Citizenship meant adherence to a common religious faith and a common doctrine of law. To be a citizen once meant something more than a vote, it meant a covenant of faith. Citizenship was a religious fact.

Second, the common defense aspect of a city meant the defense of the citizenry from enemy attack. That enemy was not only a foreign invader but also lawbreakers and unbelievers within. The law-order of the city could be overthrown by unbelief, because every law-order represents a religious faith. The criminal and the unbeliever are thus equally subverters of a law-order, although for different reasons. The city therefore walled itself with stone walls against foreign invaders, and, by temple, ritual, and law against the enemy within.

In ancient Israel, the true concept of the city was clearly maintained, not only in that a common faith, the covenant God, and a common defense, the covenant law and national defense, were maintained, but that a *common justice* was accorded to non-citizens: "Ye shall have one manner of law, as well for the stranger, as for one of your own country: for I am the LORD your God" (Lev. 24:22). The stranger or alien could not become a citizen unless he became a member of the covenant, citizenship being religious, not racial, but in any case he was under law, under a common justice.

But certain changes began to occur in the life of the city. The New Testament era, like our own, was the urban age, the era of great cities. But the concept of citizenship was changing. The Christians were persecuted in terms of an older standard: because they denied the religion of the state, they were enemies of the state, and war was waged against them. This war was logical and inevitable, because two mutually contradictory religions and standards of citizenship were involved.

But, meanwhile, Rome was destroying its own standard of citizenship. Citizenship came to have a negative meaning: a citizen was not a Christian, or should not be a Christian, because a Christian by definition was an enemy of the state. But citizenship at first could be bought, at a great price, then a cheap one, and, finally, it was being granted to everyone and had no meaning, dignity or responsibility.

Meanwhile, welfarism, combined with the ruin of the farmers, created a welfare mob in Rome which increasingly dominated the city and made for lawlessness. Instead of the city being a refuge from the world, it was increasingly the hell-hole of the world. Instead of the emperor ruling Rome, increasingly the emperor was ruled by fear of the mob. In 274 A.D., the concessions to the welfare mobs reached the point under Aurelian that bread was substituted for wheat in the welfare grants (to make baking unnecessary for welfare families), with free pork, olive oil, and salt added, *and*, more important, the right to relief was made hereditary. Welfare children no longer had to undergo the trauma of applying for relief, when they came of age; it was their birthright! The increase in taxes, and in inflation, virtually wiped out the middle classes. Aurelian, a brilliant general, tried to restore Rome to order; he tried to replace bad coinage with good. A new coin proclaimed him "Deus et Dominus Matus", God and lord from birth. The coin showed Aurelian as the sun-god arising to bless the whole earth. But in 274 A.D Aurelian was assassinated by the very corrupt officials he planned to expose. An able general, he had done brilliantly against the outside enemies; the enemies within, he tried to overcome, but his efforts were futile: he removed a few officials, but he created a greater welfare mob.

By the time Rome fell, the city was radically sick. Emperors no longer ruled from Rome; they had moved from city to city, but cities were increasingly unsafe, and, when Rome fell, the actual capitol was a minor city, Ravenna. Moreover, plague, flight from the city, lawlessness, and welfarism had progressively made the city a poor place to live and had depopulated the cities.

Earlier, the city had represented civilization, religion, and safety as against the countryside, which was seen as a wilderness, pagan, dangerous, and lawless. But men now fled to the wilderness for safety. The all-inclusive city had walled in anarchy and lawlessness, so that men of law and religion sought shelter in the wilderness.

There are, as St. Augustine said, two cities, the City of God versus the City of Man. The more openly and clearly Rome became the City of Man, the more clearly its inherent ruin and collapse began to govern its history.

The concern of the succeeding centuries was the city, to establish the rule of the City of God. Space does not permit an analysis of its history. It was an important and central part of the Christian message. St. Patrick, for example, in the *Book of the Three Habitations*, taught concerning the City of God that it is the goal of history. Much later, Otto, Bishop of Freising, in *The Two Cities*, grieved because the two cities had become one in the church. The various reform movements, and the Reformation, were aimed at separating the two cities.

An important stage in the development of the city was the Enlightenment, which concerned itself with the City of Man. The City of Man was to be an open city, open to all men, *and* open to the rulers. City planning began in the 18th century, and it called for straight streets, so that the state could send its cavalry charging down the streets and dominate the city. With straight streets, guns could be mounted at strategic intersections to command every approach. All men were to be citizens, because all men were to be ruled by the philosopher-kings.

For Jeremy Bentham, political power was necessarily unlimited and undefined. His concept of the state, the City of Man, was perhaps the best description of a total prison we have had.

This *open* city of the humanists was supposedly an ideal concept of brotherhood; in practice, it meant the opportunity for total control of all men. It led to totalitarianism and tyranny.

But another important step in the history of the city was the colonization of North America. The Puritans in particular were concerned with the City of God. They settled, not as lone individuals, but as cities and towns. When they migrated westward, they migrated in companies, not as lone individuals, and they established towns every few miles. The farmer out in the country saw himself in relationship to his township.

The town was the City of God, the countryside was the wilderness, outside of God but to be brought under the sway of the City of God. Laws, including the so-called "Blue Laws", had as their purpose the conquest of the wilderness outside of the city and inside man. The purpose of law is to bring God's order to the world within and the world without. The city had, i.e., every state in the union had originally, religious and moral tests of citizenship.

But humanism has gradually extended the boundaries of citizenship. Attempts are under way to restore citizenship automatically to all criminals. Citizenship is increasingly defined, in the 20th century, in a physical sense, by race, or by membership in humanity as such, or by birth. It no longer has reference to faith, law, and defense. The more inclusive the city becomes, the more demonic it becomes, because it denies that faith and law are governing principles, and it makes the fact of being a man, a human being, the governing principle. Citizenship is then beyond law, beyond good and evil: it is amoral and demonic.

The City of Man is beginning to rule the earth. In Marxism, it has perpetrated greater evils and more mass murders than history has ever seen, tortures and cruelties beyond all past conceptions.

In the democracies, lawlessness is increasingly the rule in the cities. Signs of this were apparent early in the last century in America. New York City, under Tammany, began to propagate democracy, rule in the name of the people, and the result was tyranny, massive fraud, the enforced prostitution of helpless women, and, a steady perversion of justice. (See Alfred Connable and Edward Silberfarb, *Tigers of Tammany*. New York: Holt, Rinehart and Winston, 1967.) As the city decayed, what men had once regarded as the wilderness, the rural areas, came to be a paradise by contrast.

Today, all over the world, the philosophies of the Enlightenment govern, especially in the cities, and the result is what a November, 1968, newspaper article described as the "Exodus From The Cities." The cities now lack community. Many live in distrust of providing protection for the citizens; the city is increasingly unable to protect even its police and firemen, and the death-toll of the police increases annually. The city is dying, and the vultures are gathering to feast on its corpse. The city has become the ideal arena for guerrilla warfare, and again civilization is witnessing a turning to the wilderness as a stage in the rebuilding of civilization.

The purpose of the City of God is that covenant man subdue the earth and exercise dominion over it. Both town and country must be brought under the sway of God's law.

Humanism cannot contain the flames of anarchy: it feeds them. It replaces God's law by man's law, an absolute order by a relative order, and it gives ultimate authority, not to God, but to elite, planning, scientific man. Men are reduced from creatures created in the image of God to laboratory animals who are used in social experiments. Humanism cannot be fought on humanistic premises. The humanist believes, not in an absolute God and an absolute law, but in a pragmatic, relative standard. In politics, he grounds sovereignty in man and the state, not in God. In economics, he denies the validity of any economic law and an objective monetary standard, gold, and grounds his economics and money on "character" and "integrity", forgetting that man is a sinner. In education today the humanist denies that the student must conform to an ultimate moral, intellectual, and scientific standard of scholarship but progressively asserts man and his existential need as his only law. In religion, man is the new god of the humanists, and the new commandments are read out of man's biology, not from Scripture. It is no wonder then that humanism cannot contain the flames of anarchy, since its very nature feeds the flames. The flames will devour the existing humanistic order, because all the remedies of state only pour gasoline on the flames, and the mobs in the street shout, "Burn, baby, burn!"

That which is for burning shall be burned, and those who are destined for the fire shall go into the fire, but we who are the Lord's people look "for a city which hath foundations, whose builder and maker is God" (Hebrews

11:10). In terms of this expectation, we begin now the work of reconstruction.

CHALCEDON REPORT NO. 41
January 1, 1969

The death-of-God movement is one of the deepest and most powerful forces in the modern world. The mistake most people make in trying to understand it is that they only see its most obvious manifestation in men like Altizer. But the death-of-God movement is everywhere, and it is extremely powerful in conservative and evangelical circles.

This point is important, very important. Let us examine it briefly but carefully. If a man professes to be a Christian and yet is guilty of sexual offenses against God's law, he is in effect saying, by his persistent contempt of the law, that for him God is dead in the area of sexual morality. He is denying, to all practical intent, that God and His law govern the sphere of sexual activity, and he must therefore be classified, whatever his religious profession, as a member of the God-is-dead school.

Now the same reasoning applies to every other sphere of life. If a man professes to be a Christian and yet favors the public (or statist) schools, and sends his children to them, he is declaring that God is dead in at least the sphere of education. He is denying the sovereignty and the existence of God for educational life. No less than the sexual offender, he is saying that God is dead and can be safely disregarded in the area of education.

To speak even more plainly: some who find fault with my emphasis on free schools as against state schools, and Christian education as against statist, humanistic education, tell me that we should concentrate on "realistic" objectives, like keeping the public schools in line, or getting prayer back into the public schools. But trying to make socialistic education work for freedom, or humanistic education serve God, is like trying to make adultery a respectable part of marriage. Education is either under God, or it is under man and man's authority. The purpose of education cannot be the service of the state (public schools), or the service of the church (parochial schools), but the service and glory of God. No school can serve two masters: ultimately, it will serve the church or the state rather than God, and our public schools and church schools are steadily revealing their true nature.

But to go a step further: some very devout ministers have taken exception to my emphasis on economics and the gold standard; they feel I should be "preaching the gospel" instead. And, of course, I am. I am declaring the good news that God is alive and governs not only the church but the state, school, science, economics, agriculture, art, and every other sphere. Our modern economics is the death-of-God economics: it denies that God exists and governs the sphere of economics by His law. The statist economics of our day holds that economic truths are relative truths, that the state can determine economic policy in terms of its needs and without reference to objective law. But "conservative" or "libertarian" economics has become no less relativistic. Its position is anarchistic. Since there is no truth, no absolute truth, then let a free market exist for *all* ideas. As a result, some prominent "libertarian" economists have become strong friends of radical causes and bitter enemies of Christianity. One professor told me of his "libertarian" economist colleague who regards, as the great enemy of libertarianism, Christianity because, with its authoritative and infallible Bible its doctrine of an absolute God and His absolute truth, it denies a free market-place for all ideas.

As against all this, we must affirm that God's law is alive and operative in economics as in every sphere. We must affirm that economic disaster looms ahead for our relativistic economics because it denies God's absolute laws.

And that disaster draws daily closer. Federal Reserve statistics indicate that by November, 1968, the money supply for 1968 had been increased by 23%: that spells approaching runaway inflation. But, even more serious, all this new paper money pumped into the economy failed to give the demanded inflationary prosperity, and federal income via taxes was definitely lower. Now, even greater inflation is planned for 1969, and Washington, D.C., expects the paper dollar to be worth radically less. Accordingly, almost certainly, before Nixon takes office, President Johnson will institute large pay raises which take effect within 90 days unless killed by Congress. Congress will see its salaries go from $30,000 a year to $50,000; the chief justice, from $40,000 to $75,000, and associate justices from $39,000 to $65,000, and so on. These salary increases are based on anticipated inflation, so that we have here a vivid illustration of what the Kappel Commission expects to happen to the dollar.

If a man denies God's existence in the economic sphere and fails to prepare for the future in terms of godly economics, he will fall under the same judgment as all other profligates and unbelievers.

But, to continue, a man may claim to believe in God when he is actually an atheist to all practical intent if he tries to separate religion and the state, if he denies God His sovereignty over the state. It is impossible to separate religion and state. All law is enacted morality, and all morality rests on religious foundations, and is the expression of religion. Thus, every legal system, i.e., every state represents a religious order and is a religious institution. The state cannot be neutral to religion. It is either Christian or anti-Christian. A state may be neutral with respect to churches, i.e., the particular institutional forms of Christianity, but it cannot be neutral with respect to Christianity. Today, Christianity is in the process of being disestablished as the religion of Western states and Humanism is rapidly being established as the official religion of church, state, and school. The decisions of the courts increasingly have little reference to Christianity and older legislation: they are religious decisions which promulgate the faith of Humanism.

It is amusing, and not at all surprising, that some humanists, like Erich Fromm, are proposing a humanistic vatican, to be called the "National Voice of the American Conscience" to "make technology subservient to humane ideals." (Erich Fromm: *The Revolution of Hope*; see Kimmis Hendrick, "Fromm proposes volunteer group to "humanize technology", in *The Christian Science Monitor*, Saturday, December 7, 1968, p. 21.)

In every area, all authority is in essence religious authority. The religions vary from country to country, but authority is in essence religious. When men deny the ultimate and absolute authority of God, they do so in the name of another ultimate authority, the autonomous consciousness of man. Where authority is broken, either chaos and anarchy will reign after a time, or brutal coercion will prevail. As Hilaire du Berrier, in his superb reports has pointed out, the tragedy of Vietnam is due to the destruction of the emperor's authority. The Emperor's authority has politico-religious roots which went deep into the life of Vietnam. As Christians, we may rightly hold that a Christian-theistic doctrine of authority should prevail, but we may not destroy institutions by revolutionary activity: we must create new institutions by means of new (converted) men. But, to return to *H du B Reports*, the weakness of South Vietnam is the inability of any of the successive governments to command authority in a situation where every man now feels, with the Emperor gone, that he is as much an authority as the head of the state. In North Vietnam, legitimate authority has been replaced by brutal coercion and this coercion seeks to replace the old authority with a new and Marxist concept.

Science too must be under authority, or it will make itself the authority. We should not be surprised at the article written by the British anthropologist, Edmund R. Leach, "We Scientists Have the Right to Play God." (in the *Saturday Evening Post*, November 16, 1968, pp. 16, 20.) And why not? Leach's point is logical: a god is needed, and, if God-is-dead, as Leach believes, then the scientists, as the new authorities, must play god and have a right to do so, if not a duty. We have no right to be surprised at this: we have so long been a part of the God-is-dead movement (dead in education, in economics, in the state, in science, art, and all things else) that we should at least recognize that our chickens are coming home to roost. And, when we have claimed God is dead everywhere else, should we be surprised that His death is being proclaimed in the churches? In short, Altizer and his cohorts who proclaim the God-is-dead theology are more logical than the conservatives and evangelicals who are shocked by this but fail to see their part in this movement.

The truth is, our finest people have become sadly schizophrenic. They believe in God, and they live sober, godly, and productive lives, but they have not and do not wage war against the God-is-dead movement as it takes over one domain of life after another. Outside the church and their personal lives, they have joined the death-of-God movement. But a man cannot serve two masters; sooner or later, he will hate the one and serve the other.

The same is true of the unbeliever who tries to cling to aspects of the Christian world-view. Mark Twain was a sad case in point. He was a professed agnostic who still retained a Biblical frame of reference. For example, he saw man as a sinner, thoroughly depraved and fallen, and at this point Mark Twain was at war with his age. In 1884 he decided to satirize the already growing romantic view of the American Indian, and so he started to write a *Huck Finn and Tom Sawyer Among the Indians*. He used some actual historical narratives as his basic story. Tom Sawyer, believing in the noble savage, the marvelous natural man, was to have his faith destroyed. The book is very amusing as it begins, as Tom spouts the liberal view of man, the noble savage as against the polluted white man. But Peggy Mills is taken captive, and Twain recorded this, and he knew what it meant: Richard Dodge had described it in a book "how Indians customarily treated a recalcitrant female captive, tying her to pegs in the ground and then abusing her until not infrequently death releases her." *Life Magazine* says that Twain stopped writing and left the book unfinished because he "was by modern standards a hopelessly prudish Victorian." (*Life*, vol. 65, no. 25, December 20, 1968, "Huck Finn & Tom Sawyer Among the Indians," p. 504.) But this is grossly unfair to Twain; the truth is, the book had ceased to be funny. It was no longer a Tom Sawyer book but a grim encounter with human depravity, with fallen man. The answer was beyond laughter, beyond satire: it was a grim, religious issue, and Twain dropped it. He was unwilling to push his view of man to its logical end, but he was equally unwilling to push his unbelief to its logical end. As Dr. Van Til has often written, man fights epistemological self-consciousness; man refuses to know the truth about himself and about his knowledge. When faced with the ultimate issues, he drops them and turns to trifling things. As Douglas M. Scott observed of Goethe's *Faust*, "we see a scholar who has exhausted the resources of study and bursts out to experience what holds the world together, to learn the inmost secrets of creation and what does he experience? A student brawl in a tavern and a love affair in which he plays an inglorious part." (Douglas M. Scott: *Goethe's Urfaust*, A Translation, (p. xxiv) Woodbury, NY: Barron's Educational Series, 1958.)

Faust in effect proclaimed the death of God when he turned to Mephistopheles for power and wisdom. But the end result was that Faust became a trifler and a seducer, and he died. The real proclamation of Faust from the onset was the death of Faust: he died to the real world for the imagined world of Satan and Satan's false authority. Marlowes *Faustus*, as he turned to the black arts, declared,

> O, what a world of profit and delight,
> Of power, of honour, of omnipotence,
> Is promised to the studious artisan!
> All things that move between the quiet poles
> Shall be at my command...

He dreamed of becoming "a mighty god" and ended a frightened, crying man. Not God, but Faustus ended dead.

And so it is today: either we become alive to God in *every* sphere of life, or we become to that extent dead to Him. But God remains alive.

CHALCEDON REPORT NO. 42
February 1, 1969

G. William Domhoff, associate professor of Psychology of the University of California at Santa Cruz, has written a very interesting study of *Who Rules America*? (Prentice-Hall, Inc., Englewood Cliffs, New Jersey. 1967) The book is extensively researched; Domhoff goes to conservative sources, such as Dan Smoot, as well as to very liberal writers. But he could not be more wrong in his conclusions. Domhoff finds that "the American upper class" controls the executive branch of the U.S. government, controls foundations, education, the C.I.A., most important corporations, mass media, and much more. There is a "governing class" in America, he believes, and he lumps together such families as the Rockefellers, the Pews, and the Lillys as a more or less working team in this "governing class."

How does he define this "governing class"? Here Domhoff is a faithful scholar: he gives us his premise:

> A "governing class" is a social upper class which owns a disproportionate amount of a country's wealth, receives a disproportionate amount of a country's yearly income, and contributes a disproportionate number of its members to the controlling institutions and key decision-making groups of the country. (p. 5)

The key word here is "disproportionate": it can mean whatever we want to make it mean. If the governing class *earned* their income and power, is it disproportionate? If they exercise their income and power in the name of the people or as the dictatorship of the proletariat, does it cease to be disproportionate?

The plain fact is that any and every society has its "governing class" in Domhoff's sense. Does a group represent a conspiracy simply because they govern? There has never been a society without a "governing class." Sometimes that governing class has gained power fraudulently, but, all the same, in every society it is there, for better or worse.

Domhoff's thesis is not unlike C. Wright Mill's *The Power Elite*. And there are many such studies written, from both the right and the left.

Let us examine this idea from the perspective of an old American belief, in the natural aristocracy of talent. The founders of the United States believed in an aristocracy, but not an hereditary one but in the natural aristocracy of ability and talent. Such an aristocracy always rises to the top: the best attitude of a country should be to further its progress to the top rather than to impede it. In other words, *superiority asserts itself and governs*. If the moral character, if the faith of a people is defective, then the superiority which prevails is of an evil sort, but, if the character be godly, then a godly superiority prevails.

This does *not* eliminate the fact of conspiracies. Any group of people who take counsel together to gain an end or goal are conspiring, whether for good or evil. If the times are evil, then the superior men of evil will prevail. If it be an age of sound faith and character, then superior men of righteousness will prevail.

With this in mind, let us examine some of the conspiracy ideas which are commonly bandied about in some circles. Some maintain that a Jewish conspiracy secretly governs the world; what they are actually saying then is that the Jews are the world's true elite and that a handful of them can govern the vast masses of the world. Others hold that the real conspiracy is a German one, and everything is viewed in terms of a new German threat; again, these people are declaring implicitly the superiority of Germans and their belief that only a world anti-German policy can save us from the German menace. Still others see the threat as an English one, involving the Rhodes funds and much more; again, this is a confession of English superiority.

But there *are* conspiracies, and they *are* a threat, some will protest, and they are right --- up to a point. Let us examine one of them, where court and federal records document the conspiracy: communism. In the hands of Karl Marx, a sorry, disorganized bumbler, Marxism was simply wild, confused hatred. But superior men, but evil men, took over, and they made Marxism an instrument of *power* and *superiority*. Take Lenin: vicious, depraved, ruthless, all that and more, but also very intelligent, clearly *superior*. His writings are still amazing reading, and they explain why, in an evil age, he could ride that tide to power. For example, he saw clearly that any abandonment of gold as money, and the adoption of a central banking system, was *nine-tenths* of socialism, so that the logic of economics would drive a world going off gold and into central banking into communism in time. We are busy today proving Lenin was right here and elsewhere. When Khrushchev said, "We will bury you" he had in mind the inevitability of the forces at work in the free world. Get rid of every communist in the United States, sever relations with the Soviet Union, and defeat communists in Vietnam and elsewhere, and the U.S. will still go communist because of its present monetary policy, one in operation for a generation and more. The worst "communism" in the U.S. is that which is written into our monetary policy, and there is no sign of a change.

Am I suggesting that we stop fighting communism? Far from it. But you can't fight atom bombs with pop guns.

Let us examine the basic issue: *First*, a natural aristocracy of talent always rises to the top in a society congenial to its moral bent. This is true even where a hereditary caste exists. Over the centuries, many of the nobility, and royalty, rose and fell in terms of their ability or inability to rule. We may sometimes regret the passing of a good line, but if it fell, it was *either* through inability to rule, *or*, if they were still able, because the moral foundations of their rule were destroyed. In old Russia, the schools and universities created a generation of men whose moral foundations were anarchistic and anti-Christian: this new breed represented tremendous but evil ability, and the war enabled them to capture power. The moral foundations were at the same time destroyed in a number of countries: the difference in the time of collapse was made by the crisis of the war and the blockade of Russia. Today, those same moral foundations are virtually gone everywhere.

Second, because there will *always* be a governing class, and that governing class will reflect the good or evil directions and impulses dominant in society, it is important therefore to do things, *one* to produce and train a superior class, and *two*, to produce and train a vast body of people who will want the leadership that new superior class can provide.

It is most certainly necessary to fight against subversion and against heresy, but something more is needed, a new faith and character in society at large, and a new leadership, a new governing class in terms of that faith and character.

Today, the liberal and leftist establishments or governing classes prevail in virtually every area of the world. They are powerful, but they are sterile. They have promised the humanistic masses they rule a paradise on earth, and increasing disillusion with their promises and abilities is leading to a generation of drop-outs, people who believe the liberal myth but disbelieve increasingly in its leaders. These revolting youths are themselves sterile: they share the same myth and lack the capacity to communicate it or realize it.

What needs to be done is, *first*, to bring forth a new people. This is the basic task of evangelism. Moral dry-rot has not only destroyed the older

Christendom but the newer humanistic world order. There can be no new class as long as we remain tied to the forms of the old, such as statist schools. Truly Christian schools must be established, and both old and young re-educated in terms of a total faith. Every sphere of life must be viewed in terms of the whole counsel of God.

Second, new leadership must be trained, a new aristocracy of talent in terms of the new humanity of Christ. This leadership must re-think every discipline in terms of Biblical thought: theology, philosophy, science, economics, statecraft or political science, law, and all things else must be re-thought and re-established in terms of Biblical premises.

Remember, there will *always* be a governing class. Our present schools, colleges, universities, churches, and foundations are essentially geared to producing a humanistic leadership. Fight this order all you will, but as long is it shapes the minds of the leaders and the followers, it will continue to prevail. Document its evils and chronicle its corruptions all you want, and you will not change it unless at the same time you work to establish a new people, and a new leadership.

This is our purpose. Are you with us?

CHALCEDON REPORT NO. 43
March 1, 1969

In an earlier newsletter (no. 24, September, 1967) the subject of Christian reconstruction was discussed. It was pointed out that, in any advanced social order, social financing is a major public necessity in order to maintain a vast network of social institutions which require financing and support.

Historically, there have been in the main two means of social financing: *first*, by state taxation and then state control and maintenance of the various social institutions which must be maintained, and, *second*, by the law of the tithe, whereby the tithe, as God's tax, is used to maintain education, welfare, religious institutions, and a variety of social functions.

Earlier, the tithe barn was a familiar aspect of the Western world. Religious foundations (lay and religious orders) ministered to a variety of needs, providing welfare, education, hospitals, orphanages, grants to the arts, and much more. Until World War II, gleaning was a familiar part of American rural life in some areas. Organizations like Goodwill Industries had applied the gleaning principle to urban life. Education as a state function is a relatively modern concept. Through the depression of 1907, welfare in the U.S. was taken care of by churches, foundations, and various similar agencies; it was Pendergast, in Kansas City, who saw the political potentialities of welfare as an instrument of political power and instituted the first tax-supported welfare program. Other civil units saw the possibilities of political power in welfare and quickly followed suit.

The law of the tithe was gradually eliminated in America (over Washington's disagreement), and gradually replaced by state taxes, in particular the previously unknown property tax. The revolutionary ferment from Europe was largely behind the desire for state action. After 1860, this revolutionary influence merged with still another influence, Darwin's doctrine of evolution.

Social Darwinism led to the application of ruthless egoism (as against Christian individualism) to the economic world, and the "robber barons" emerged. In a congressional investigation during President Buchanan's term, members of Congress referred to Vanderbilt, *not* as a capitalist, in fact, they denied him that title: he was a government manipulator, i.e., his wealth came from government contracts gained by manipulating politicians. But with social Darwinism, the new breed began to deny all social responsibility and formed a working alliance with the state in order to exploit the people and all natural resources. Since then, this socialistic alliance of big business with big government has added to itself big labor, big foundations, and statist education to make up our modern establishment, with the big churches as the chaplains of this new order. We are dealing with amoral power today, power which allies itself with power against the weak. As a result, socialism is the best means ever devised to give more power to the powerful, and to make the rich richer. There are, incidentally, more millionaires in the Soviet Union today than in Russia under the czars, but the middle class is gone, and the workers are far poorer.

Social Darwinism meant a denial of social responsibilities by the socialistic industrialists. When the demand for these social functions became too great, the answer of social Darwinism was to tax the middle classes and the poor to maintain education, welfare, and all things else. The middle classes are being now steadily expropriated in their possessions on the plea that the needs of the people require it.

True. The needs of the people do require something, but the statist "something" is the destruction, first, of the middle classes to provide for the lower classes, second the destruction of the lower classes to provide for the state, and, third, civil war within the establishment as social cannibalism sets in. Socialism, moreover, because it is by nature a parasitic economy, is also imperialistic. It exercises an imperial confiscation towards its people, and it must also expand and gut fresh territories in order to gain fresh resources. The Soviet Union has been and must continue to be a ruthlessly imperialistic power to survive. Moreover, the more the U.S. becomes socialistic, the more it will require imperialism to survive. A parasite, when it destroys one host body, requires another to survive.

The social functions of statism, of socialism are thus aspects of its imperialism and parasitism. When the state assumes social functions, its purpose is statist; the state is more concerned with its survival than with the survival of some people, or a class of people. The statist assumption of social functions removes responsibility from the people and promotes social isolation. The statist talks largely about loving mankind but acts in actual contempt of man. He accuses the orthodox Christian of holding to a low view of man, because the Christian believes man is a sinner, but Christians hold that man is a *responsible* sinner, not a conditioned reflex. It is the Christian who requires man to be responsible, whereas the statist makes the state responsible.

The tithe has a major social function which needs restoring. It is futile to rail against statism if we have no alternative to the state assumption of social responsibilities. The Christian who tithes, and sees that his tithe goes to godly causes, is engaged in true social reconstruction. By his tithe money and its activity he makes possible the development of Christian churches, schools, colleges, welfare agencies, and other necessary social functions. The negativists, who have merely campaigned against statism, have steadily lost ground since 1950. Those Christians who have concerned themselves with Christian reconstruction have since 1950 established a vast number of Christian schools as well as other agencies. Within fifteen years, almost 30% of America's grade school children were no longer in the statist schools.

What we must do is, *first*, to tithe, and, *second*, to allocate our tithe to godly agencies. Godly agencies means far more than the church. In the Old Testament tithe went to the priests and Levites. The priests and Levites had a variety of functions in Israel: religious in the sense of ministering in the sanctuary, and religious in the sense of providing godly education, music, welfare, and necessary godly assistance to civil authorities. The realm of the godly, of the Christian, is broader than the church. To limit Christ's realm to the church is not Biblical; it is pietism, a surrender of Christ's kingship over the world. The purpose of the tithe must be to establish that kingship.

This means stewardship. We are not our own: we belong to God, and all our possessions and wealth are a trust from Him.

This trust means, *first*, a responsibility to care for our own, our families. We have a responsibility under God to care for our parents, and for our children. The family is the world's greatest welfare agency, and the most successful. What the federal government has done in welfare is small and trifling compared to what the families of America do daily, caring for their own, relieving family distresses, providing mental care and education for one another, and so on. No civil government could begin to finance what the families underwrite daily. The family's welfare program, for all its failures from time to time, is proportionately the world's most successful operation by an incomparable margin.

Beyond a certain point, however, the family cannot care for its own without sin. If children are delinquent and reject authority, or if they grow up and depart from the faith, we cannot subsidize them in their sin without sharing in their guilt. They cannot be partakers or heirs of what is the Lord's inheritance. But, within the circle of faith, the family must care for its own.

Second, as we go outside the family, the *minimum* requirement of God's law is the tithe, God's tax on man. The tithe can be used as we, under God, feel led to use it, provided always the receiving agencies are doing the Lord's work in their areas. We need to assess the need for Christian reconstruction and then conscientiously support those agencies which we believe best further it: a church, an organization dedicated to creationism, or the cause of Christian education, missions, Christian scholarship, and so on.

In all this, we must be mindful that the cause is reconstruction. We have an obligation under God to bring all things into captivity to Christ, and under His dominion, to establish Christian order. Too many Christians are engaged in fighting a local, small battle, if they are fighting at all. But we are in the midst of total war and must be engaged with total dedication and a total plan. Without this perspective, we waste much of our time, activity, and money.

There are many who say, how can I pay my taxes and still tithe? (Incidentally, many who are rich and many who are poor *are* tithing and still paying their taxes.) But you have *no* other alternative. Are you going to wait for the state to lower its taxes? The state will never lower its taxes, nor will the people permit it to, as long as the necessary social functions are left in the hands of the state. We have higher taxes because most people demand them, and they demand the services the taxes provide. People only oppose higher taxes for themselves; they favor "soaking the rich", soaking the unions, the railroads, the gas companies, the telephone company, anyone and everyone except themselves. The problem most legislators face is the unrelenting pressure for higher taxes from people who are demanding new services for themselves at public expense, and this always means taxes.

We cannot wait for taxes to be lowered. We must begin now, *not* merely to tithe but to begin Christian reconstruction with our tithe, to re-establish the necessary social functions as Christian action.

We need to do this in delight and anticipation of a godly order; we also need to do it in fear of the consequences if we do not. Either we work to establish a godly order, or we go down into the hell of total statism. We need, moreover, to fear God. Most people are afraid of prison if they fall to pay their taxes, or of confiscation of property at the least. They need to fear God also for all their sins of commission and omission. The God of love has been preached so long that we have forgotten the sovereign and almighty God whom we must fear as well as love. Shall we rob this God of His tithe, the tithe which is His ordinance for our own prosperity in terms of godly order? Yet we rob Him when we deny Him the tithe (Malachi 3:8-12). Let us therefore serve God in that true love which fears to offend His love, and let us work for Christian reconstruction in every sphere of our lives and our world.

CHALCEDON REPORT NO. 44
April 2, 1969

The question of conspiracies is often discussed and seldom understood. Usually, the term "conspiracy" is reserved for the hated opposition. Communists refuse to regard their movement as a conspiracy because they believe in its historical inevitability; only the enemies of the proletariat are conspirators. Similarly, in the 1880's, the bomb-throwing anarchists of the day actually held that "Anarchy is the negation of force;" their reasoning was that capitalism was using violence (the police power) to block the historically inevitable death of the state, so that anarchist action was simply an attempt to nullify force. Again, South American military regimes hold that they seized power to block radical conspiracies: they themselves were not conspirators but patriots. While one of the dictionary definitions of conspiracy is that it is a "combination of men for an evil purpose," another meaning is a "combination of men for a single end." Conspiracies thus are more than enemy action: they are any and all plans to gain a particular goal through more or less covert action.

The important question to ask is this: What makes a conspiracy work? Let us suppose that a number of us conspired together to turn the United States into a monarchy, and ourselves into its nobility; let us further suppose that we could command millions from our own circle to achieve this goal. Or, let us suppose that, with equal numbers and money we conspired to enforce Hindu vegetarianism on the country. In either case, we would have then, not a conspiracy, but a joke. A successful conspiracy is one which is so in tune with the faith and aspirations of its day that it offers to men the fulfillment of the ideals of the age. It is an illusion to believe that dangerous or successful conspiracies represent no more than a small, hidden circle of diabolical men who are manipulating the world into ruin. Such groups often exist, but they only exist and succeed because their plan and hope is closely tied to the public dream and the faith of the age. If the threat were only from small circles of hidden men, then our problem would be easy. Then, as Burton Blumert has observed, "if we only unmasked the conspiracy, all our problems would be solved, but if the trouble is in all of us, then we really are in trouble."

He is right: we really are in trouble. The Enlightenment dream, as Louis I. Bredvold pointed out in *The Brave New World of the Enlightenment*, has five basic tenets in its faith: 1) there is a rejection of the past and of history; man makes himself and his world, and the past is a hindrance; 2) there is a rejection of institutions and "customs", in particular, Christian institutions and standards; 3) evil is not in man but in his environment; 4) "by changing human institutions human nature itself will be born again;" and 5) those who should manage human affairs are the scientific planners, the educators, and the statesmen. These are the men who best represent the will of man in terms of man's potential and future.

Man today believes this with all his heart. All over the world, the reigning faith is in this democratic, humanistic faith in the scientifically guided order. The Communists affirm democracy and the ballot box: they hold elections even though there is no choice on the ballot. Men who have started private or Christian schools all too often subscribe to democracy to the point that they insist on giving teachers and parents a voice in a school which represents only their funds and planning; the result is democratic chaos or failure.

The myths of the Enlightenment infect all of us. In church, state, school, press, in every area, the myths are held with earnest faith and zealous endeavor. The conservative in most cases simply holds to an earlier version of the myth.

Recently, I heard a number of conservative candidates for a city school board speak and almost all simply repeated the basic humanistic faith. Within the first few minutes, I jotted down these sentences: "The proper education can cure all our ills." "The right to vote is the most precious right man has won." "We need representation from every ethnic group in order to be just." "You can do without everything else in the world, but you can't do without an education." And so on.

If tomorrow the secrecy were stripped from all conspiracies, and their goals revealed, most people would merely say, "Well, isn't that what we all believe?" and go on with their dally lives.

A conspiracy has power to the degree that it speaks to the prevailing beliefs and hopes of the day. And our age, as a humanistic one, dedicated to "man's fulfillment" in a humanistic sense, is ripe for every conspiracy which promises to deliver on those dreams. Man believes that he can make a new start, create a paradise on earth, without God and without regeneration. We have for some time been in process of revolution against Christianity, and we have been moving towards this "Great Community" of Man. Our establishment, political and educational, represents the older phase of the revolution, and youth is in part in rebellion against the older phase of the revolution in favor of a faster fulfillment of the dream. The more radical the conspiracy, the greater its appeal, because it is then all the closer to the dream.

The basic myths of the day are so much a part of the age that most conservatives simply want to return to an earlier phase of humanism; they believe in statist schools, in the priority of politics to religion, economics, the family, and all things else.

But, meanwhile, some people are losing faith in the dream: they are *dropping out*. They are dropping out, because the humanistic dream has failed them. No new faith has taken its place. As a result, their attitude is one of total negation. They hate the dreamers of the dream, the men who make promises, and they hate the society and social order which surrounds them. As drop-outs, whose faith is negation, their only action is to destroy, to burn, loot, kill, and bring down the old order.

There is thus a double revolution and conspiracy at work today. *First*, there is the humanistic revolution against the whole world of Christian order; this revolution is well entrenched and nearly successful. *Second*, there is the revolt against the new humanistic establishment by its own sons, who are bent on destroying everything in sight. This is a revolt within the revolution and against the revolution, and it is present in the Marxist states as well as in the West.

Thus, we are in trouble. As Arnold Rosin observed, in *The Age of Crisis* (1962) "Only dreamers believe there is a peaceful way out." Communism is dedicated to the total destruction of Christian order and the conquest of the Western and Eastern non-Marxist states. The democracies are steadily moving into dictatorships. The student generation is disillusioned with the whole of the present era and is readily led into hostile and destructive action. And the economic crisis is steadily pushing the world towards a total monetary collapse.

Our crisis goes deeper than a circle of conspirators. The conspirators themselves are creations of our faith, called in part into being by our own apostasy. When men forsake God's law-order, they must inescapably resort to a man-made order, and this is what men have done. The answer is not simply to unmask the conspirators but to unmask ourselves, to know that we are sinners in rebellion against God and His law-order. Our's is a total problem, a religious problem. It cannot be solved on any other level.

It is thus distressing to see a man who denounces Marx turn then to Emerson and write glowingly of him: he has not gone far from Marx! After all, before Marx, Emerson had renounced Christianity: he was a high-level leader of the Secret Six conspiracy which worked to bring about the Civil War and financed John Brown. Members of the Secret Six helped Horace Mann bring in the state school system. One of Emerson's closest associates and a top Six leader, Thomas Wentworth Higginson, founded the L.I.D. and the Intercollegiate Society of Socialists. The distance between Marx, Comte, Emerson, Stalin, Whitman, Hitler, F. D. Roosevelt, John Dewey and others is a short one: they were all humanists who offered variations of a humanistic dream.

Their dreams and their world are under God's judgment and shall perish. If we are not to perish with them, we must move in terms of another order and rebuild in terms of it. The duties are ours; the results are in God's hands.

CHALCEDON REPORT NO. 45
May 1, 1969

As was pointed out in our last Report, working conspiracies are more than a small circle of hidden men. The conspiratorial men are there, but they are able to work successfully because they bring to focus the basic trends of their day.

As a classic example of a conspirator who was also the man who brought to focus the currents of his age we cited Ralph Waldo Emerson. Ralph Waldo Emerson was a member of the "Secret Six", a powerful group of men who conspired to bring about civil war, and financed John Brown, a hoodlum pretending to be a religious prophet, to incite that war. The men of the Secret Six were "no muttering little clique of non-entities". They were Theodore Parker, Dr. Samuel Gridley Howe, Gerrit Smith, Thomas Wentworth Higginson, George Luther Stearns, and Franklin Benjamin Sanborn. The second echelon, or second six, included Emerson, Henry David Thoreau, John Murray Forbes, Thaddeus Hyatt, and, briefly, Amos A. Lawrence. (See J. C. Furnas: *The Road to Harper's Ferry*. New York: William Sloane Associates, 1959.) Earlier, some of these men had worked to bring about state control of education. Higginson, who had been a zealous supporter of Horace Mann, and of course of John Brown (Higginson once wrote Brown, "I am always ready to invest money in treason" but regretted he was out of funds at the moment), lived long enough to join Clarence S. Darrow, Jack London, Upton Sinclair, and others in issuing the Sept. 12, 1905 "Call" which started the Intercollegiate Socialist Society! Are you interested in conspiracies? Then why "patronize" foreign groups? Emerson and his circle accomplished as much in American history as any!

When I was a university student, one of my professors was a brilliant but unstable man who was romantically inclined towards anything subversive. The list of subversive "front" organizations which carried his name on their letter-heads was over a page long. He was a nudist, a champion of every rebellious cause, *and* a great admirer of Emerson. Emerson, he declared, was America's great social revolutionary leader. He led the way in denouncing Christianity and shifting issues from a theological to a sociological orientation. He replaced communion with God with communion with one's own soul. He shifted the interest of Unitarianism from church reform to social reform. After Emerson, American society lost its orientation to the Kingdom of God and moved towards the Kingdom of Man. And, most of all, Emerson made his revolution popular because he restated all the old truisms of Puritan morality in a humanistic framework. People could now read Emerson's replay of good, old-fashioned Christian moralisms without any tie to the triune God: it was now good humanism, ready to give man a moral glow without God. With Emerson, the revolution became respectable.

All this is true, too true. Emerson shifted society from a God-centered to a man-centered orientation, from the conversion of men by God's grace to the conversion of the state and society by laws. But Emerson was only able to succeed in this task because the older God-centered orientation had lost its vigor and vitality, and a creeping humanism had already infected much of American life. Emerson and the Secret Six were thus logical developments of American intellectual history. Just as the earlier tradition had its evangelical fervor, its movements to establish schools, seminaries, and missionary societies, so the new tradition had a like evangelical fervor to change the social order by statist action. As a result, it organized to promote that action.

Let us suppose now that we, stepping back in time, uncovered and exposed the conspiratorial work of the Secret Six. What would have happened? Some would have been alerted and forewarned, but as many others would have hailed Emerson and his associates as forward-looking and thinking men and mailed their checks to indicate their support.

Our present-day conspiracies have been exposed again and again and again. If people do not know, it is because they do not want to know. As religious humanists, the people of today are far more congenial to socialism in its every form than they are to Biblical faith. The Bible today is accepted by many only if they can re-interpret it in terms of their humanistic presuppositions. At the root of our impotence in stemming the present tide of evil is a spiritual impotence.

Under normal circumstances, a political revolution is long preceded by a moral revolution. Before the Red Reign of Terror in Hungary in 1918 and 1919, there was a moral collapse. The sense of property, for example, had eroded, and soldiers were casually seizing what they wanted from their own people. From such a working attitude, it was a short step to a theoretical and political faith which said, "Now that there is a republic, everything belongs to everybody." As Cecile Tormay, an eye-witness, reported, "well-to-do farmers go with their carts to the manors to carry off other people's property." These farmers were not communists, but they made communism possible. The general moral collapse meant that law in its historic Christian sense had at least temporarily disappeared.

Let us turn to the present. Man today is creating a world ruled by violence because of his false premises. Consider the Harvard faculty statement of April, 1969, which read in part, "As members of a community committed to rationality and freedom, we also deplore the entry of the police into any university. Some of us believe the decision to use force to vacate the building was wrong. Some of us believe it was unwise. Some of us consider it unavoidable though regrettable." (*Los Angeles Times*, Sunday, April 13, 1969, p. 1, "Harvard Faculty Rebukes Both Sides.") This is clearly a schizophrenic view of man. The whole man goes to Harvard, with his reason as well as his will to violence. To assume at any point or in any area of life that one is coping only with a fragment of man is a dangerous illusion. But the humanist dream of rational man leads to a progressive inability to cope with reality. Like the Marxist dreamers, the liberal humanists will turn to total terror and violence to cope with the monsters they unleash. From the Christian perspective, man at every point is the whole man, and unredeemed man is a sinner whose reason and every other aspect is governed by violence and hatred against God and His law-order. Man's only freedom is under law; his only possible power and liberty are limited liberty and limited power. At every point we deal with man's reason, man's love, man's violence, man's total being, and to assume that a particular sphere has a monopoly on reason is to neglect the whole man and find to one's destruction that man is more than reason.

Because of the university's anarchistic concepts of reason and freedom, it cannot cope with lawless man except schizophrenically, by finally abandoning reason in favor of violence. Cornell's pathetic incompetence in coping with revolutionary students who gave the university only three hours to live ended in a surrender. When the liberal god, reason, fails, another humanistic god, man's revolutionary violence, takes over. Violence is the order of the day. The only question is: who will exercise it, the establishment or the rebels? Neither has any alternative to violence, since both have abandoned transcendental law, *God's law*. The new god is man, and, in the war of gods, the rational man-god loses to the violent man-god.

Concerning the new god, listen to Ann Landers (*Los Angeles Herald-Examiner*, Thursday, April 24, 1969, p. C5):

> Dear Ann Landers: Your cavalier treatment of the question from "that nut" who asked if it was true that God is a Catholic, a Negro and a Democrat, was, in my opinion, undeserved.
> You should have told the inquirer that God is indeed a Catholic, a Negro and a Democrat. He is also a Hindu, a Jew, a Protestant, Chinese, Japanese and Indian --- a Republican, a Socialist and an Independent. He speaks Spanish, Portuguese, Swahili, Russian, German, French, Italian and Thai. God is a priest, a rabbi, a minister, a merchant, a miner, a farmer, a truck driver, a physician, a lawyer, an architect, an engineer, a musician, a bootblack and a bank president. He is Everyman.
>
> ONE WHO READS OFTEN
>
> Dear One: I'm pleased that you read me often. I wish you'd write often. Thanks for a superb letter.

Most people find this very beautiful. As humanists they worship his new god, "Everyman", and deny the triune God of Scripture. As a result, they believe in a totally man-made order, in the Kingdom of Man. And Fabianism and

Marxism are classic examples of the Kingdom of Man. Exposing their conspirators means also exposing the seeds of humanism in modern man's heart. Modern man is not greatly concerned about the conspiracy. After all, he is a part of it. If the threat is only from a small circle of hidden men (and such circles did and do exist, before and after Emerson), then, to quote Burton Blumert again, "If we only unmask the conspiracy, all our problems would be solved, but if the trouble is in all of us, then we really are in trouble."

Well, we really are in trouble. And our problem is educational, political, economic, scientific, and much, much more. Above all, it is religious. If God be God, then serve Him. But if man is your god, then this is your revolution, mister, and you are a real "soul-brother."

CHALCEDON REPORT NO. 47
July 1, 1969

In Reports 44 and 45, we discussed the fact of working conspiracies as expressions of a moral and spiritual failure in a people. Wherever there is a decline and shift in the basic faith of a culture, there various conspiratorial groups can and do develop the implications of the changing standards into a new social order.

The case of Emerson and the "Secret Six" was cited, as significant a group as any in American history. Certain facts characterized this group: They were Unitarians; they hated the old New England Calvinism and its social order, and they hated the newer Calvinism of the South; their answers to man's problems were statist and sociological not Christian and theological. The responsibility of these men was very real: they wanted armed conflict as the means of changing the Union and the entire social order.

But, lest we make the mistake of seeing the South only as a victim, let us remember that the South succumbed to the tactics because it too was in moral and spiritual decline. A generation earlier, every Southern State save South Carolina had been against slavery; the one question had been, what to do with the slaves after liberation. After all, only a very small minority of Southerners owned slaves, and the others were especially hostile to the institution of slavery. Why then did the South allow itself to be pushed into a stand alien to its best interests? Why did the Southern states secede when its best men opposed secession? The Senate debates of the era reveal the radical Unitarian self-righteousness of Sumner, but they also reveal the failure of the Southerners (except Andrew Johnson) to do more than react: they too often lacked a moral perspective to assess their situation. When South Carolina seceded and proclaimed itself a sovereign and independent nation, a very prominent citizen of Charleston, James Louis Petigru said sadly: "It won't work. South Carolina is too small for a nation and too large for a lunatic asylum."

The "Reconstruction" which followed the War was a vicious and unconstitutional order, and E. Merton Coulter's *The South During Reconstruction, 1865-1877* (a book disliked by our liberals today), is a good account of those ugly years. The liberals, in their moral bankruptcy, try to justify reconstruction, and the conservatives condemn it. Both tend to overlook the fact that Reconstruction was first applied by the Confederacy to Tennessee at the beginning of the War, and with all the ugliness which later marked, over a longer span of time, the Southern Reconstruction. Neither one justifies the other. Both indicate the moral climate of the day. A change in the religious and moral climate had made both possible.

Ideas not only have consequences, they have roots. The roots of ideas that govern an age are deeply imbedded in the faith of that age.

To cite another example, in recent years the U.S. Supreme Court has radically altered the Constitution by legislative interpretations. Certainly the judges have exceeded their authority, but their actions have deep roots in the popular mind. Recently, one of our Chalcedon Report family reported a statement made in Southern California, by a teacher of a large, ultra-fundamentalistic women's Bible Class: "Human needs come before God's law." She was almost alone in her protest. If fundamentalist Bible teachers hold this position, need we be surprised that the Supreme Court holds that human needs come before man's law? Remember, the Constitution forbad the use of militia, i.e., drafted men, for any purposes save (1) to repel invasion, (2) suppress insurrection, and (3) enforce the laws of the Union. President Wilson set this aside, and the Court backed him. Two World Wars, the Korean War, and the Vietnam War are clearly illegal in terms of Article 1, Section 8, para. 6. If this provision of the Constitution is bad, it should be amended, but, if it is not (and I believe it to be one of the best safeguards of the Constitution), then why not work to re-establish it? If we let it stand as a dead letter, then nothing in the Constitution can stand against "need" and expediency.

Because there is now no sense of, or respect for, higher law, God's law, how can men be expected to respect man's law? A generation which treats God's law-word lightly will most certainly treat man's law even more lightly.

The roots of our problem, and our vulnerability to subversion, are in our moral and religious decay. Nothing is more foolish than the attempt by many to say that only a small minority of people are involved in the violence and disorder of our day, and that "the silent majority" is against all this disorder. The reality is otherwise. Some polls show very happy results: almost everyone is against higher taxes, violence, riots, etc.; well, everyone, or almost everyone, may be against sin, but they are still sinners. Most people, as one legislator has remarked, ask for lower taxes in theory but in practice call for measure after measure which will only raise taxes.

The fact is that most colleges see radical students voted into student body offices. The fact is that, according to a variety of authorities, from one third to two thirds of all college students experiment with drugs and narcotics. The fact is that, with each year, our situation grows worse, and even now high school students reveal a greater degree of lawlessness than do college students. Moreover it is feared that soon junior high schools will reveal still worse anarchy and contempt of law. The moral collapse grows deeper yearly.

Are the big cities the only trouble spots? Recently, *Life* called attention to the problem at Fort Bragg, California, where perhaps three out of four high school students were on narcotics. And a recent news note stated that, in Greenland, 6,191 out of its 40,000 inhabitants contracted gonorrhea *last year alone*. The moral collapse is world-wide, on every side of the Iron and Bamboo curtains.

Everywhere, the sources of legitimacy, of the right to govern and command, are under challenge and attack. The ideas of legitimacy and authority are basically religious ideas. When the faith behind the idea is gone, the idea is soon gone. Today, the orthodox Christian faith which undergirded our doctrines of authority is being fast replaced with humanism, the religion of humanity, and, as a result, the old authority is rapidly disappearing. It cannot be preserved by a rootless conservatism which wants to preserve the fruits without the roots. Every rootless tree is soon dead. The result is lawlessness, anarchy, and violence.

But the humanism which is replacing orthodox Christianity is unable to formulate a doctrine of authority which can give order and stability to society. Recently, the head of a major university, shown on television addressing a convocation, deplored the use of force on his campus by both police and students. The university, he said, is a place for reason, and coercion has no place in the academic community. Everyone applauded; in fact, it was a standing ovation at this point. No place for coercion? Today, taxes are basic to "private" and state colleges and universities. (Private universities and colleges are *virtually all* heavily subsidized by federal funds.) Taxes represent an aspect of coercion; without this coercion, the schools would soon close. Compulsory education into the teens in every state is a form of coercion, as is testing. Without police protection around the borders of our colleges and universities, the existence of these schools would soon cease.

Because the humanist has no valid doctrine of authority, he creates a world of anarchy and coercion and soon must invoke total coercion as his only answer. Marxism proclaimed a world without tyranny, without oppression, and without coercion (not even a state, finally), and it instituted the world's most oppressive coercion. Its doctrine was pure reason, and the inevitability of those forces established by pure reason, but it made brutal coercion inevitable, because man is not pure reason but rather a sinner who needs not only grace but God's law-order. *At every point, man is and must be under God's law-order, and he is either under it by grace or by judgment.* To dream of a domain of reason removed from authority and coercion is to be living in terms of an illusion. The whole man meets us at every point, whether in the academy, the market-place, the church, or the street, and to reckon without that reality is to court suicide.

But we are asking for trouble. We are denying doctrines of responsibility. Dr. Efren E. Ramirez, M.D., in *Science Digest* ("Drug Addiction is not physiologic", May, 1969), states that the typical drug addict "has a weak sense of responsibility, little commitment to anyone or anything. His life is dismally disorganized and he can't seem to learn from his failures. He shows poor motivation to be cured, and the current belief that addiction is physiologic just gives the drug addict another excuse for saying, 'I can't help myself.'" This is not only a good description of the addict but of most people in varying degrees. In varying degrees, all, like the addict, want to blame their problems on someone else, their biology, their inheritance, the capitalistic system, the leftist conspiracy, and so on. There may be elements of truth in some of these things, but the basic problem is man's moral and religious failure.

No addict cures himself with excuses, or by documenting his problem. No society heals itself of subversion by blaming anyone or by documenting its problems, but only by changing its ways. Our revolution today is everyman's revolution; in country after country, the people are voting in favor of it, at the ballot box and in their everyday lives. The world's vote is for man and revolution, not for Christ and God's law-order. People are getting what they asked for. And, in the sight of God, they have no right to complain at what they shall get. And, brother, they *will* get it. By the way, according to the daily papers, they are already beginning to get it.

CHALCEDON REPORT NO. 48
August 1, 1969

Our subject this month is *authority*; let us begin with *police authority.*

In the early 1920's, in Detroit, my father went one day to meet a newly-arriving immigrant, an elderly priest. The old man's life had been spent in the Near East and Europe; he came directly from the continent. After their greeting, my father asked certain plain questions about conditions in the Old World, and the priest hastily shushed him, indicating the presence of a policeman nearby. My father laughed with delight and explained that, in America the police are our friends and protectors. The old man could not have been more emphatic in his disbelief. On their way home, my father stopped at a home near a school for a few minutes. The school was letting out, and children ran happily to the crossing. The patrolman was a favorite of all the children, and the children competed happily to hold his hand. At this, the old priest broke down and wept openly. This, he said, was the difference between America and the old world; here, the police were loved by the children and regarded by the people as their protectors; there, the police were feared as political agents.

What has happened since then? If the police have changed, it is generally very much for the better: better trained, more courteous, more honest, and better informed on the law. That old priest, who died in the 1940's, always spoke of the authority and honor of the policeman's position in America. Things have changed since then. What is the reason? And what has changed?

Very clearly, the police have been the target of a subversive attack; there has been a systematic attempt to discredit the police. Granted, but an attack is a failure unless it finds a receptive people. Why have people been so ready to accept anti-police propaganda? Faults are there in the police as in every group in society, but why this demand for perfection? Why the total hostility to law and order? Some insist that anyone who uses the term "law and order" favorably belongs to the enemy, i.e., is a part of a hated establishment. Why?

Let us examine briefly the mainsprings of the modem or humanistic era in order to know the answer. *Education* has been the basic faith and hope of modern man. "Knowledge is power", and education is man's salvation. Added to this is humanistic man's denial, first, that man is a sinner, and, second, that even in his sin man has an inescapable knowledge of God and of God's law (Romans 1:18-20). Instead, humanistic man, after John Locke, held to the belief that man's mind is a blank piece of paper awaiting the work of the teacher. The child, therefore, could be, it was held, totally reconditioned by the right kind of education. If only the church and family could be prevented from polluting the child's mind before the school reached it, utopia would speedily arrive. The school and university have, over the generations, worked successfully to undercut the authority of the home and of Christianity.

This has meant replacing the authority of God with the authority of man. But, if man is his own authority, who can be an authority over man, except many men, many gods outvoting one god? Moreover then, there can be no over-all law binding either individual man or mass man. Law and authority thus become enemies to humanistic man and his schools.

Numerous college and university students have reported to me their experiences, all very much alike. Education professors commonly begin a course by saying, "How can we educate for the future, when we do not know what the future is? There is no truth for today and tomorrow alike. We cannot teach a body of knowledge as valid for tomorrow. The one reality is *change*, and we must *educate* for change, for continuous revolution." An historian began a course by denying that there is such a thing as history, a law professor by attacking the idea of law, and so on. Only in the sciences is there much educational discipline left, and only because without it, their field would collapse; even here, engineers and others report a growing decline.

If man is his own authority, then there is no authority over man, and God, parents, and police become symbols of tyranny and oppression, because authority other than anarchistic man's is intolerable. The New Left is the logical and inescapable product of modern education because it is anarchistic and statist to the core. Anarchism and statism are different aspects of the same humanistic creed. The anarchist denies the state: man is his only god, law and authority. The statist (Marxist, Fabian, Fascist, or democratic) says, true, but many men have more authority than one man. In ether case, there is an erosion of authority, a break-down of law and order. We are getting today what we have paid for: our public schools are delivering precisely the product of humanistic education that they have been asked to deliver. To deny Christian faith a place in education, to convert schools into statist agencies, and then to expect anything other than what we have is the mark of a fool. And fools can be more dangerous than knaves, because the fool is on every side of the field.

Every society, whether a backward tribe or a highly advanced nation, represents a law-order. Every law-order is an expression of a moral and religious faith. Change the faith and morality which undergird that law-order, and its authority and its ability to maintain itself begins to collapse.

This is our problem. Our Christian foundations have been destroyed. We now have *humanism* as the established religion of church, state, school, and society. This new religion is denying and shattering the old authority with only anarchism and statism as its alternatives. The result is growing chaos.

This is not all. Because humanism makes a man his own authority, it enthrones childishness, self-indulgence, and tantrums over maturity, self-discipline, and reason. Much of the protests have been marked by more emphasis on childishness than on issues. Observers have noted the high glee and immense self-satisfaction many of these demonstrators show on urinating and even defecating in public. The glow of childish delight in these acts was the most startling aspect of the performance, the sheer joy in a baby's act.

This impulse is deeply imbedded in our humanistic age. Not too long ago, a television interviewer asked a group of guests, kindergarten children all, what they would most like to be. The answers were the same: they all wanted to be babies! Why? because, they answered, babies have nothing to do, and they are cared for! There was a time when kindergarten children wanted to be grownups; this was the social ideal, maturity. Now it is babyhood. Elderly women dress like little girls, and old men like small boys, and they try to act as though perpetual youth was their hope. Is it any wonder that high school and college youth act like babies, and that kindergarten children want to be babies, when the adults of our time are themselves at war with mature responsibility? Is it any wonder that authority is gone? A baby has to be trained into respect for authority, but grownup babies are at war against authority, and therefore at war against life as God ordained it.

Authority is an inescapable necessity. It is authority which binds man to man in society. This binding is only secondarily by force; the essential and primary power of authority rests in a common faith and a general assent to certain religious presuppositions. Humanism denies the principle of transcendental authority. It affirms the satanic principle that every man is his own god, knowing or deciding for himself what constitutes good and evil (Gen. 3:5). The world of autonomous, humanistic man is a world of lawlessness in which every man asserts his independence of all laws not of his own making or choosing. Humanism leads to self-righteousness, since every man is right in his own eyes, and there is no other law. The war of the humanist against law and order is *an immoral, self-righteous protest*, in that he begins by assuming religiously that righteousness was born with him and that all law and order is by definition evil. The total humanist will, if logical, become the total criminal, totally at war against all law and order. And this is precisely the goal of the "new intellectuals." The police have been able in the past to cope with ordinary criminals, but the total criminal works to subvert every basis of authority and law, in church, state, and school, in the courts and in the legislative chambers. His warfare is more nearly total war than anything else we have yet seen. But it is also destructive of himself. Man needs air for his physical life, and law is the air of his social life. Unless that law is true law, God's law, society dies of strangulation.

We are thus in the last days of a humanistic era. Man's attempt to return to the womb is a fast trip to the tomb. The world of humanism is sick; let it die. Its spoiled brats are bent on suicidal destruction. Mature man will work for Christian reconstruction.

CHALCEDON REPORT NO. 49
September, 1969

On July 26, 1969, it was my privilege to attend Dr. Hans Sennholz' seminar on "The Dollar Crisis." As Dr. Sennholz concluded his very able and intensely interesting account of our monetary problem, he analyzed the decline of the paper dollar and the grim future and then concluded thus (to cite my summary notes): The people are to blame; the government is their tool. People make demands on the government for a growing list of services, demanding aids, services, grants, which create an inflationary economy. Peter has been taxed to pay Paul. The end of the road is in sight, but the pressures on the government by the people continue. Price controls and a dictator loom ahead on this road, and economic destruction. The people must change, before the trend can change.

These admirable words reflect a Christian perspective; they echo the faith in personal responsibility which is basic to Christian western civilization.

Yet within a week, as I reported these words to a number of Christian and conservative ministers and laymen, I received a large number of objections. I was told: Not true, the people have been misled. Not true, it has been a conspiracy against the innocent public. Wrong, let me give you a book proving who has fooled the public...and so on. During the same time I also saw a leftist analysis of the tight money situation: it was described as a capitalistic conspiracy against the people!

The leftist analysis alone was logical, although wrong. The Marxist perspective is that not individual responsibility but environment is the source of sin, wrong, and evil. Men are victims, not sinners. Change the environment, and you change man. Dr. Sennholz had echoed the Christian presupposition: change the man, and you change the environment. These "Christians" and "conservatives" who criticized Dr. Sennholz were revealing the extent to which they had absorbed Marxist premises; they were carrying the old banners but marching in an alien army.

Let us analyze the matter more carefully, *first*, the matter of *conspiracy*. Most simply defined by the dictionary, a conspiracy is a "Combination of men for a single end"; in law, it is a combination for either unlawful ends or to use unlawful means towards an end in view. The Christian must take the conspiracy view of history seriously, because Scripture teaches throughout that history is a struggle, with the forces of evil conspiring against God and His anointed (Ps. 2). History is not a blind, impersonal force, as for the Marxists, but a very personal work of God primarily and secondarily of men. Thus, conspiracies are real, because men are very real forces in history.

But, *second*, because the Bible denies that history is the product of unconscious, impersonal forces and drives, it asserts *individual responsibility*. In Genesis 3, it made clear that the essence of sin is to blame other persons or the environment for one's own guilt. Adam, by blaming his environment (God), and his wife (Eve), for his sin only aggravated his guilt.

It follows, therefore, that we can alert people to what various conspiracies are doing to undermine or subvert a nation, but we cannot as Christians blame any conspiracy for our weakness or fall. Men stand or fall in terms of their faith and character. True, man's faith and character is subjected to attack, but so was Adam's; in this world, there is *always* testing, temptation, and trial. The question is, Do we submit to it or overcome it? Dr. Sennholz was right; The people must change, before the trend can change. Any conclusion other than individual responsibility is a denial of Christianity and is an implicit Marxism.

Because so many ostensible Christians and conservatives lack a Biblically grounded faith, their actions and statements often end up in an unconscious anti-Christianity. As a result, some so-called conservative movements are moving into strange waters and revealing anti-Christian and anti-conservative tendencies.

Take, for example, an article in the Summer, 1969, issue of *American Mercury*, by Revelo P. Oliver, Ph.D., "Christianity - Religion of The West." The editorial heading indicates that the editors regard the article to be very good and of "major importance." The thesis of the article is that only Western (or European) man is congenial to Christianity. (The Bible says no man naturally is congenial to it, whatever his race, only God's supernatural grace conforms him to it, but, for Oliver, the natural Christian, and only real one, is the Western, racial man.) According to Oliver, missionaries only succeeded where imperialistic guns backed them, and failed where there was no backing. (This is, of course, the Marxist line on the relationship of imperialism and missions. This does not mean that Oliver is a Marxist, but his non-Biblical thought places him in a common camp at this point.) Oliver chooses to ignore the vast evidences of native faith in Asia and Africa in the face of persecutions, nor does he acknowledge the frequent opposition of imperial agents to missionaries as "meddlers." His evidence is negligible and his total picture anti-Christian. True, in recent years Christianity has had serious set-backs in many parts of Asia and Africa, but not because imperialism has waned. The decline has been due to the same reasons for the decline of Christianity in Europe and America: men have turned to alien and humanistic faiths.

Oliver, *The American Mercury*, W. A. Carto, and others who are regarded as strong conservatives are also great admirers of the late Francis Parker Yockey and his work, *Imperium, The Philosophy of History and Politics* (1948). Yockey's position is atheistic and anti-Christian. Yockey was also a strong champion of race, and especially of what he called "Ethical Socialism" (p. 617). (Ethical Socialism is the socialism you operate; the other man's socialism is always unethical!) Yockey's work has overtones of Nietzsche and an inferior echo of Spengler. Incidentally, his complaint against Marxism is not that it is socialistic but that "the ethical and social foundations of Marxism are capitalistic" (p. 80). Yockey's book is a pompous, turgid restatement of every kind of immoralistic philosophy of the last century which said, "Somebody did this to us, not we ourselves." Like Adam, who said, "The woman whom thou gavest to be with me, she gave me of the tree, and I did eat" (Gen. 3:12), so Yockey worked to absolve Western man of guilt, even as he compounded it with unbelief and moral irresponsibility.

The people must change, before the trend can change. This is not a popular program. People want an enemy to blame, not themselves. How much easier to expose and blame than to reconstruct! Marxism has a simple, sure appeal: "The bad guys did it to us." People, as sinners, love this. Biblical faith has an unpopular message: Whatever anyone else has done, and as sinners they will sin, what about your responsibility and your guilt? The greatness of David was that he did not blame Bathsheba or anyone else; he acknowledged that it was his guilt, his act, his sin.

But most people today will not acknowledge their guilt. They attend churches which preach another gospel, and they will not break with them. They claim that they are trying to reform the church from within, but each year these churches become more openly anti-Christian, and they still remain. These people profess loyalty to Christ, but the only loyalty they manifest is to an anti-Christian church. Are they not guilty?

We can go on indefinitely. Suffice it to say that most people find it convenient to turn to the Marxist, environmentalist answer and say, "The bad guys are responsible for all our problems." And they continue to believe that they can redeem the public schools, a socialistic agency! They turn their children over to a non-Christian, socialistic school and then ask God to bless them. And they wonder why their children turn into rebels.

(Appended to this report is a graduation address by Gaye Patapoff, valedictorian, San Jose Christian School, 8th grade, June 13, 1969. Gaye reflects her Christian home and school in her address, and she has a maturity lacking in the 8th graders of our socialistic schools.)

But to return to our point: The trend will not change until the people change. We have too many people who want to change the world, too few who admit that man needs changing--and that only the grace of God can accomplish this. God's appointed means are Christian institutions. We must therefore begin reconstruction now, prayerfully and hopefully. We must stand on individual responsibility as against environmentalism. We cannot excuse ourselves by saying, "The woman gave me...and I did eat", or by saying, the Communists are to blame, or the Democrats, or the capitalistic warmongers. That excuse did not work when it was first tried by Adam. What makes us think it will work with God now? Adam to Marx to men today, it has been a ticket to judgment. Dr. Sennholz is right: The people must change, before the trend can change. Do you agree? Or do you prefer to line up with Marx and blame the system?

In case you missed it in your newspaper, a major university last June granted a master's degree to a student whose thesis was simply eight pages of lines of typed periods. The university accepted the thesis, and the vice-president defended the action, although the library decided against filing it (National Observer, June 30, 1969). Now read the address of an 8th grade student in a Christian School by way of contrast.

Valedictory Address, by Gaye Patapoff, 8th grade.

Distinguished members of the Board, our devoted Principal, dedicated teachers, loving parents, most welcome guests, and fellow students:

It is with great joy that I am able to speak to you tonight in an effort to express the gratitude and thankfulness of my classmates and myself for being able to attend and graduate from the San Jose Christian School.

As we all know, there are many philosophies and ideologies striving to win the minds and hearts of the youth today. Christianity, in our Reformed Churches, is being challenged by the theory that a sovereign God is no longer necessary when we have a "sovereign" federal government that will provide everything God can from the cradle to grave.

Communism is winning the minds of the youth in our country and throughout the world on the theory that when the youth become adults the world will be theirs. This godless form of government denies the very existence of God. It bases its hopes for success on man being perfect and sinless, which we know is impossible, since man is totally depraved, sinful, and selfish.

Our world is in a state of turmoil and confusion. Wars which were once considered infrequent catastrophes are now every day current events. Students in high schools in large numbers are taking drugs as a rebellion against authority. Students in colleges and universities almost daily practice violence and defiance of authority as an expression of independence.

We, who are graduating, are thankful that we have learned not only English, history, mathematics, and science, but that God is the source of all truth, the Creator of order in the world, and the author of all history, past and future. Our devoted teachers have taught us God's part and place in every subject. We have daily studied the written Word, and learned His instructions on how we must live to please our great Creator, thus insuring true happiness as we grow into adulthood.

Our greatest wish is that all the children in the world, could attend schools such as this, with devoted teachers by whom we learn about God, His Word, and the peace that comes only through Jesus Christ our Savior.

I thank you again on behalf of the eighth grade graduating class for building a firm foundation on solid rock rather than sinking sand. I would like to close with our class theme, Romans 8:38,39: "For I am persuaded that neither death, nor life, nor angels, nor principalities, nor powers, nor things present, nor things to come, nor height, nor depth, nor any other creature, shall be able to separate us from the love of God which is in Christ Jesus our Lord."

CHALCEDON REPORT NO. 50
October 1, 1969

A friend recently reported his experience to me. He was debating with a Marxist at a major university campus, and he recognized, in the course of the debate, that both of them were championing "peace and freedom", but with very different meanings. Underlying the words were radically different presuppositions.

Before any of us line up with "freedom fighters", "libertarians", liberty leaguers, lobbies, defenders, or what have you, it is important for us to know what these words mean to those who use them.

One of the key words of the modem era is freedom. The Renaissance and the Enlightenment laid great stress on freedom (and yet produced tyranny), and basic to the dialectics of the modern world are the notions of freedom and nature. This new doctrine of freedom came into its open philosophical expression, in Kant and Hegel, and its political expression in revolutionary movements from the French Revolution to the present.

Someone once remarked, after listening to a variety of Marxist, existentialist, New Leftist, and Fabian speakers, that they were nothing but hypocrites, because they championed freedom while promoting statism and totalitarianism. This charge could not be more unjust; these men (and student speakers) were not hypocrites; they were intensely sincere and passionately convinced of the rightness of their position, however wrong from our view.

We cannot understand the movements of our time if we fail to understand what freedom means in the modern age. In Hegel's philosophy, this doctrine found powerful expression, and it has since influenced most modern thinkers: Stirner, Marx, J.S. Mill, Spencer, Nietzsche, Emerson, Dewey, Sartre, Marcuse, and others. Hegel was intensely concerned with freedom, and he traced its history carefully in several studies. For Hegel and the modern mind, the essential meaning of freedom is man's liberation from and independence of God; freedom from God, this is what liberty means in the modern age.

In America, from the colonials through the founding fathers, it was repeatedly affirmed that freedom from God is slavery to man; after 1860, the modern concept of freedom was clearly dominant in the United States also.

This new freedom was sometimes anarchistic and sometimes totalitarian. ("Anarchism" is a word coming from the Greek, and meaning, "without authority"; "tyranny" means confusion, having no divine law.) In either case, its basic idea of liberty is freedom from God. As a result, anarchists and socialists have never been too far apart. Anarchism replaces the authority of God with the authority of the individual man; socialism, democracy, fascism, and other forms of collectivism replace the authority of God with the authority of collective man. Many of the leading figures of both sides have often moved back and forth between anarchism and socialism. Marx incorporated both into his system. John Stuart Mill moved from a semi-anarchism to socialism. Thoreau advocated anarchism; Emerson held to a semi-anarchistic position but was also congenial to socialism; (Emerson's influence on Nietzsche has not been fully appreciated, Nietzsche spoke of him as "my beloved Emerson"); abolitionists like William Lloyd Garrison have aspects of both positions in their thinking, and so on.

The liberal, conservative, and radical traditions of our day have all been profoundly influenced by Hegel and the post-Hegelian thinkers, and their ideas have a common secularism, that is, they think of freedom and social order without God. The liberals and the radicals are usually self-consciously atheistic; they knowingly advocate a doctrine of freedom from God as true liberty. The conservative is usually unconsciously atheistic: he denies that he is anti-God, but he by-passes the whole matter because he claims that he wants to avoid "sectarianism".

But if God is not our sovereign source of authority and freedom in every area, then we are to that extent atheistic. The state should not be under the church, nor the church under the state, nor the school under either. Each are under God and positively required to serve Him or else they are atheistic. Church, state, school, family, and every other sphere of life are either under God, or they are under men as their sovereign power. Freedom from God means servitude to man; freedom under God means freedom from man.

Revolutions in the modern age are essentially revolutions against God. Several of the "new libertarians" have lately stated that it is not necessary to have a purpose *for* revolution; what is necessary is to have a revolution *against* the idea of a God-given order. In other words, their goal is freedom from God, and to gain this, all existing institutions, because they represent a hang-over from a Christian society, *must be destroyed*. The result is total warfare.

When a social order begins to break down, and the end of an age appears, man begins to feel uncertain of his ground because his basic premises are being destroyed. Although the days prior to the Reformation saw less social and economic changes than the 17th century witnessed, the lack of faith led men to despair, so that they felt, in the-words of historian A. G. Dickens, in *Reformation and Society*, "a dread of universal dissolution." This same dread obsesses men today who live in greater prosperity than their forefathers.

Having no faith to live by but a crumbling humanism, they live in "a dread of universal dissolution."

But, even worse, too many of them, as a matter of humanistic principle, are waging a revolutionary war designed to bring about universal dissolution. To gain freedom from God, they seek the destruction of all existing social order.

This is not a limited war. It cannot be fought with a limited faith. More than the church is at stake, and more than a political election and control of the state, schools, or any other sphere. Elections are regularly being won, and the war lost, because every side has the same anti-God doctrine of freedom. And it will not do to talk about "God and America" and feel that words are the answer.

If we are for freedom *under* God rather than *from* God, we must re-establish our institutions, and our society on that basis. We must begin now the task of Christian reconstruction, establishing Christian homes, Christian schools and institutions, Christian scholarship, a Christian civil order, a social order in its every aspect grounded on the Biblical law-word. And we cannot do that without knowing the Bible. The tragedy of our age is that the church has reduced the Bible to an ecclesiastical or church book, whereas it is God's word for the *whole* of life, and for every institution.

In 1925, T. S. Eliot wrote a telling poem on "The Hollow Men." The Hollow Men are the men of this generation, men without faith; they are "the stuffed men", full of facts and data, ready with words, but basically meaningless, so that their heads are really "filled with straw." Having no faith, they have no direction; they move, but go nowhere:

> Shape without form, shade without color,
> Paralyzed force, gesture without motion.

They have eyes, but cannot see; they are acted upon, rather than acting. They are hollow of meaning but stuffed with straw, meaningless pretenses at meaning. They can only produce a "Wasteland" out of life.

Hollow men cannot create a social order; they can only destroy it. Hollow men can defend nothing, because they themselves are nothing. We live in a day of hollow men who blame everyone for their predicament except themselves. When they declared their freedom from God, they became hollow men, whatever their politics, conservative or radical.

Sartre defined freedom as man's freedom from God, and its goal or "project is to be God." Man declares his independence from God in order to be his own god. The goal is a futile one, however, and Sartre concluded, "Man is a useless passion." Not surprisingly, humanists who have been proclaiming the death of God are in some cases now going a step beyond. In France a new and influential philosophy whose spokesman is Michel

Foucault is now proclaiming the death of man. Man, as a useless passion and a futile being, must soon disappear, we are told. The Hollow Men are bent on suicide and destruction.

More than that, they have what Albert William Levi so aptly termed Nietzsche's "will to illusion", a love of a lie and a preference for it, a delight in illusions rather than reality, a preference for grand gestures rather than meaningful acts. The result of freedom from God is a generation of Hollow Men.

What do *you* want, Hollow Men, or God's men? If you want Hollow Men, well and good: our schools, universities, churches, and families are all doing an excellent job of producing a generation for whom liberty means freedom from God. They may call themselves leftists, conservatives, libertarians, churchmen, and whatever else they will, but unless they recognize the sovereignty of God over *every* sphere of life and *every* area of thought, they are practical atheists. If what you want is freedom from God, then congratulations! You are doing your job effectively in every area. But if not, "How long halt ye between two opinions? if the LORD be God, follow Him" (I Kings 18:21).

CHALCEDON REPORT NO. 52
November 20, 1969

Over the years, I have, on several occasions, talked with some evangelists, and members of "revival teams." The experience has been uniformly the same. Their position has been one of a lowest common denominator theology. They have been vague and general on doctrines such as the sovereignty of God, His eternal decree, creationism, and much more. Moreover, the more concern I showed for Biblical knowledge, the more irritable they became. The discussion was usually terminated by their objection to "fine points of doctrine", and a charge that I lacked "a passion for souls." My feeling in return was that they lacked any concern or passion for God and His word. The important thing for them was *man*, the conversion of man and the cause of man.

Their position was and is *humanism*. Because of their concern for men, and for "saving" men, they are to that degree unconcerned about God and His word as far as priority is concerned.

The roots of this humanism go deep in every branch of the church. Pietism in the 18th century was humanistic to the core. Its concern was religious experience, the personal experience of the believer rather than God's order and His word. Pietists like Madame Guyon placed their feelings ahead of all godly authority.

In Protestant circles, humanism led to revivalism, to an insistence that true faith was identical with a form of man's experience rather than a

God-given grace which led to an assent to God's word and authority.

The end result of this humanism in religion is a radical erosion of standards and law, and a progressive insistence that the true test of religion is not the word of God but service to man. One radio priest has declared that God must be identified with our neighbor. At one Protestant Bible Conference in the summer of 1969, high school youth were taught songs of civil revolution in the name of evangelism. The goal of Christian activity, according to one chorus, was human unity, and the test of Christianity, "love", all men walking together. In France, Father Cardonnel has written, "From now on, God exists only in downtrodden people; that is what God's transcendence amounts to." For Father Maillard, a French Franciscan and director of *Freres du Monde*, revolution is an absolute value in itself. He has declared, "If I noticed that my faith separated me by however little from other men and diminished my revolutionary violence, I would not hesitate to sacrifice my faith." In the U.S., at Notre Dame, a non-Christian layman, Bayard Rustin, has been added to the board of trustees.

The Protestant churches have extensively identified true Christianity with the love of man, and the true Christian tradition with revolution. The church, according to a National Council study guide of 1966 must overcome all "dividing walls" between men in order to create a truly human community. "The church does not exist for itself. It exists for the world, as the part for the whole." But, according to Scripture, the church exists for Christ, *not* the world. The gospel presented by one Protestant church after another is the gospel of the Kingdom of Man, not the Kingdom of God.

Radical humanism commands every area of the church today. Man is so important, that the supreme offense is any kind of resistance or opposition to man. Jacques Ellul says of America, "Why, in the face of the black violence they provoked, do they not seek peace *at any price*?" He calls for a humanistic "love that is total, without defense, without reservation," as the answer. (Jacques Ellul: *Violence* p. 174.) For Ellul, the Christian is not God's man, but man's spokesman: "The Christian must be the spokesman for those who are *really* poor and forgotten" (p. 53). And why not? For Ellul, "Values have no meaning except as they are lived by man! We always come back to man. Everything depends on how man relates to man" (p. 113).

Humanism is the basic revolutionary force of our age. It is not surprising at all that the average European, Canadian, and American is indifferent to the Marxist threat. By his humanism, amoralism, and implicit anti-Christianity, the average man is only removed from Marxism by degree, but alien in kind to Christianity. To condemn Marxism, he must condemn himself. Marxism makes man the absolute; so does humanistic man today. Marxism is environmentalistic; it believes that evil is in the environment, in society, not in man. Again, most people today would agree. Marxism believes that a new politically ordered arrangement of society is the answer to all man's problems. This is precisely the faith of most people today. Marxism looks to man for salvation, and again most people agree. Is it any wonder that they refuse to see Marxism as a threat? To condemn Marxism, most people must then logically condemn themselves. Instead, they join the humanistic revolution. Billy Graham has said "Amen" to revolutionary oriented evangelism, and why not? His basic humanism requires that he move in the direction of a more systematic humanism.

Humanism today governs virtually every country, and it is triumphant in virtually every church. Only small pockets of resistance to humanism remain in Christendom. The triumph of humanism seems virtually complete.

But humanism can no more bring about a successful social order than suicide can offer a better life. Humanism is suicidal. It erodes every form of social and religious tie and creates an atomistic man. This atomistic man boasts of his god-like status and yet lives in radical alienation from all other men. "Communication", the most elementary and basic reality of every normal society, becomes a major problem when humanism infects a people. Men lose the ability to communicate, because they have nothing to communicate. In my study of *Intellectual Schizophrenia* I cited the witness of Georges Simenon's novel, *The Man Who Watched the Trains Go By* (1946). Simenon portrays an empty man in an empty world of meaningless men and events, where "Nobody obeys the laws if he can help it." The main figure, Kees Popinga, tries to explain the series of events which lands him in trouble, to tell the *truth* about himself. He begins writing an explanation, "The Truth about the Kees Popinga Case", but he can write nothing, because, in a meaningless world, nothing has a truth which can be communicated. Humanism can only corrode and destroy; it is a disintegrating force. Some humanists even boast of it. I have heard some point to the radical disorders of our time as proud evidence that humanism is on the march. An old rabbinic saying stated, "Without law, civilization perishes." Without God's law, civilization dissolves into anarchism.

In the face of all these things, the command of St. Paul remains, "Rejoice evermore" (I Thess. 5:16). This seems like a strange word from a persecuted saint, but it rests on a basic premise that, "in all these things we are more than conquerors through him that loved us" (Rom. 8:37). Since God is on the throne, the inescapable victory is our's in Christ. Life is indeed a battlefield, but a triumphant one for the believer. The faith set forth in all Scripture is a victorious one. Again, an old rabbinic proverb sums up this aspect of Scripture: "The world is a wedding", i.e., a place of rejoicing. Because Jesus Christ is the Bridegroom, all friends of the Bridegroom rejoice (John 3:29), because they hear His voice.

We are summoned by Scripture to join in God's laughter. The ungodly nations conspire and take counsel together against God and His anointed; their world-wide conspiracy seeks to overthrow God's law-order. But "He that sitteth in the heavens shall laugh: the Lord shall have them in derision" (Ps 2:4). The triumphant laughter of God resounds over the fall of Babel, Assyria, Babylon, Rome, and all other empires of the past, and it shall resound over the humanistic tyrannies of today.

We live therefore in the last days of humanism. Its suicidal nature brings it to ruin as a result of its very triumph. Our problem today is not the strength of the humanists, for they are weak. It is the absence, laziness, and weakness of Christians.

Meanwhile, God's calling remains. Man was called by God to exercise dominion and to subdue the earth (Gen. 1:26-28). Man fell from his calling in his sin. He was restored into the image of God and his calling by the saving power of Jesus Christ. It is therefore man's duty now as ever to exercise dominion. The duty of godly reconstruction is an inescapable one. Nothing else can be a substitute for it.

CHALCEDON REPORT NO. 54
February 1, 1970

When a religion begins to die, the people begin to turn against it. Mobs ransack and burn the temples, mock, defy, and express contempt for its priests, and hurl stones and abuse at its defenders. Religions die hard: their hold on people is profound and far-reaching; when disillusionment sets in, and the once faithful believers suspect that the god is dead and the priests are deceivers, their bitterness is intense. They may be better off materially than ever before, but, because man does not live by bread alone, the death of man's gods is always a painful thing.

We are living now in the last days of a powerful religion, Humanism, and we are experiencing the bitterness of its disillusionment. We are witnessing the death of its god, man as god, and this god dies with real blood.

Horace Mann, the founder of the state-supported public school movement in the United States, saw the public school (and university) as man's true church and his great hope of salvation. As I pointed out, in *The Messianic Character of American Education*, Mann saw the school as "the agency which can change society and create a true Utopia, paradise on earth." In Mann's own words, "Let the Common School be expanded to its capabilities, let it be worked with the efficiency of which it is susceptible, and nine-tenths of all the crimes in the penal code would become obsolete; the long catalogue of human ills would be abridged; men would walk more safely by day; every pillow would be more inviolable by night; property, life, and character held by a stronger tenure; all rational hopes respecting the future brightened." This was in the early 1830s; by 1886, Zach Montgomery, prominent attorney and assistant attorney general of the U.S., had pointed out, in *The School Question*, that a rising crime rate followed the introduction of the public schools in every state. Even the conservative statist education of that day could not give the moral discipline and the faith undergirding that discipline which Christian schools had given.

Not too many years ago, criticism of the public schools and universities was tantamount to blasphemy, and indeed it was blasphemy to the humanists. Anyone criticizing these "sacred halls of learning" was regarded as either dangerous or stupid. Ironically, today it is the children of Humanism who are destroying their own temples. The *Los Angeles Herald-Examiner* (Sunday, January 25, 1970, p. A-8, Robert Knowles, "School Vandals Cost Whopping $2.4 Million") gives us a sorry picture of the cost of vandalism in Los Angeles County's 86 elementary and high school districts in fiscal 1968-69: $2.4 million. At that Los Angeles County got off lightly when compared to other major urban schools. The attacks are largely motivated by sheer hatred, by a desire to destroy a symbol of a failing faith, the public school.

The same is true in our colleges and universities, virtually all of which are controlled either by state or by federal funds. The "private" university has virtually ceased to exist. Stanford, for example, recently had between $40-42 million per year in federal funds, as against $29 million from private sources. Since much of the $29 million represented endowed funds, the actual amount from living donors was very much less. Stanford thus is better described as a federal university than a private one, and the same is true of all our major older universities of supposedly "private" character.

In these colleges and universities, the hatred and contempt for administration and faculty is often intense. It is a hatred shared even by those who do not demonstrate and riot. The faculty, bewildered priests of an old and fading cult, cannot understand why they are hated and despised. Their hope is that somehow the mood will change, and the rites of the temples of learning will return to their old established authority.

But Humanism has on its hands a dead god who cannot be resurrected, and it has bitter worshippers whose hopes have been confounded. Humanism has not brought in an age of peace but rather the era of total war. It has not made man more peaceful but rather more radically at war with all things and with himself. It has not solved man's basic problems but rather aggravated them. Malaria and smallpox have been largely eliminated in its central areas, but ulcers and heart attacks have replaced them. Man's growing inner pollution has been progressively matched by a radical pollution of his world. Now the grim fact has been discovered that the plankton of the ocean, source of 70% of the earth's oxygen, are being killed by pesticides, and humanistic man is afraid and angry. Like the angry and disillusioned believers of old, he turns on his priests, the educators, and on his temples, the schools. He turns on the world of Humanism, and its great cities, and cries, "Burn, baby, burn!" Men of faith build; men whose faith is dying, and they dying with it, have instead an urge to destroy. The vandals now destroying the Rome of Humanism are its own sons.

Men of faith build. The era of Humanism culminated in a time of dissection; scholarship came to mean endless analysis of a dissecting variety. Psychology replaced faith, and self-analysis, action. Ulcers became the hallmark of a humanistic culture, man destroying himself. Then came the days of burning, when schools, state buildings, and cities became the targets of destruction.

In a time of destruction, growth is not too conspicuous. In a forest being cut down or newly burnt over, the little sprouts of fresh growth do not loom too large, but they are there.

The new growth is definitely all around us. The Christian school movement is the most conspicuous example. Since covenant children belong in covenant schools, Christians are steadily creating a new society by means of Christian education. A highly disciplined, better trained, and truly educated youth is in the making.

The Christian school is based on the logical premise that, while the gods of Humanism are dead, the Christian God is not dead. Our choice of schools indicates our faith. If our God is left out of every area of life, or virtually every area, then we subscribe to the death of our God, or at least His basic irrelevance to our world. The growth and popularity of Christian schools means that, for more and more people, the God of Scripture is alive. Even as the growing collapse of statist education signals the death of the religion of Humanism, so the growing strength of the Christian school movement heralds the fact that God is alive and strong. By faith in Him, a generation is growing strong and holds a promise of reconstruction.

But the death of Humanism in the days ahead will take down with it all those institutions associated with Humanism, and today that includes virtually every church. Humanism has deeply infected and captured Eastern Orthodox Churches, the Roman Catholic Church, and Protestant churches, including "evangelical" churches, and they will pay the penalty for their infection and surrender.

Men of faith build: their eyes are on the future, not on a return to the past.

One of the tragic examples of a man looking backward was the great Roman general, Stilicho. He was born a Vandal, became the highest officer under the emperor in Rome, and married into the imperial family. Stilicho was deeply moved and impressed by the past glory of Rome: it was his life's hope to restore and strengthen Rome's glory. Again and again Stilicho, a Vandal of humble birth, saved Rome and stopped the invading Visigoths under Alaric. But within Rome the decay was deep in men's hearts, and as a result Stilicho was hated for his barbarian origin and his power. As a result, the emperor was prevailed upon to sentence Stilicho to death for high treason. Although innocent, according to Giorgio Falco, he did not resist. He could have counted on the soldiers to defend him, but, in loyalty to Rome, he refused to start a civil war and obediently bent his head to the executioner's axe. As a result, Alaric, on August 24, 410 A.D., entered Rome and sacked it.

Stilicho was a very great man, but he could build nothing, because his vision was geared to the past, to a dying order, not to the future.

Somewhat later, Theodoric the Great (455-526) failed for the same reason. His very able mind and his exceptional powers made him a remarkable monarch of an Ostrogoth kingdom in Italy. Few men have seen the issue with respect to law more clearly than Theodoric. He wrote to the Provencals, when he annexed them to his kingdom, "Here you are then by the grace of Providence back in the Roman society and restored to your ancient liberty. Take back then also customs worthy of the people who wear the toga; strip yourselves of barbarity and ferocity. What could be more beautiful than to live under the rule of the right, to be under the protection of the laws and have nothing to fear? Law is the guarantee against all weakness, and the fount of civilization; individual caprice belongs to barbarity." Few men have equalled that insight, but it was misdirected in Theodoric. Although he gave Italy in his thirty years reign a peace and prosperity it had not enjoyed for centuries, his life was a failure, because his vision was directed also to Rome's past glory, and the old Romans rejected him. Even more, Rome was dead. The future belonged to Christ.

The future always belongs to Christ, because He is always Lord of history, the maker and sustainer of all things, and their absolute Judge. Christ's words to us in a time of burning, and of dying gods, is still this, "Follow me; and let the dead bury their dead" (Matt. 8:22). Nehemiah, when he began a work of reconstruction among the ruins, wasted no time in negotiations with the men of the past. He continued working on the walls, declaring, "I am doing a great work so that I cannot come down" (Nehemiah 6:3). The schools, churches, and institutions of the dead must not hold us: we have a great work to do, reconstruction under the mandate of the sovereign and living God. Certainly there is destruction and burning all around us: the modern Baal worshippers are turning on their gods.

And their gods are destroying them. Isaiah long ago warned his generation, saying, "Cease ye from man, whose breath is in his nostrils: for wherein is he to be accounted of?" (Isa. 2:22). But faith in man is the essence of humanism, and it is the foundation of modern politics and economics. God as sovereign Lord is able to create out of nothing. In Humanism, statist man is given credit for the same power, the ability to create out of nothing, or so the Humanist believes. *John Law*, the father of the economics of virtually every civil government in the modern world, believed that money and wealth can be created out of nothing. "I have invented a new kind of currency," John Law wrote. "What is this coin you are holding in your hand at this moment? It is a piece of metal which bears an impression. What are you now in need of? Cash. I cannot create metal, but I am able to multiply the impression by having it put upon paper. And for my own part I maintain that it is the impression that is the cash. Just reflect! Yesterday, when the last of the cash in the Bank of Scotland was paid out, there were people who said 'but the bills are still in circulation.' I pledge my paper money on land, and I might pledge it upon the wealth contained in the ocean. The ideal method would be to pledge it upon nothing at all...But human beings have not yet reached such an advanced stage that they can accept *confidence* as their only guarantee. You are poor because you have no cash. I am giving you some. My paper-currency can and must be always equal to the demand made for it. Thanks to it the inhabitants of this country will have employment, manufactures will be greatly improved, home and foreign trade will be extended, and power and riches will be gained."

Law stated it honestly, this modern faith. Man the creator can create instant money and virtually instant wealth. The basis of this money is "confidence", trust in man, trust in the state. But Isaiah warned against trusting in man, and he called attention to the debased coinage of his day as an offense against God's order (Isa. 1:22).

Paper money is a fitting symbol for the dying world of Humanism; like the temples of Humanism, it too is being burned, in this case by inflation.

Wise men will keep the smoke out of their eyes and build. The whole world is ours to conquer in Christ. This is our duty and our calling, and we shall do it.

CHALCEDON REPORT NO. 55
March 2, 1970

One of the more delightful comic strips, "Eb and Flo", in its February 6, 1970, number has a very telling point. When Mabel comes to visit Flo, she learns that Flo's husband, Eb, has gone to a big youth rally in town. Mabel asks: "Youth Rally? You mean all those hippies, Hell's Angels and skinheads? Why? Is he thinking of joining them?! Flo answers: "Never! He just goes to their meetings to keep his disgust fresh!" Here the humorist has put his finger on the essence of much religion and morality today: it lacks any real faith; it is essentially negative, and its main impetus is disgust.

More than a few prominent religious figures who present themselves as bold warriors of the Lord have really only one essential purpose: to keep disgust fresh. They publish by press, books, radio, and sometimes television, as well as in person, a stream of exposures about the menaces to church and state. Their purpose is essentially to freshen disgust. Beyond that, they have little in the way of a gospel to present, and their morality is often suspect.

The same is true of many political commentators of the right and the left. There is a continual turn-over of periodicals, newsletters, and radio programs as both sides trot out their horror stories and then give way to someone else who is better at keeping disgust fresh.

Take away fresh disgust, and you rob a vast number of people of the most important part of their intellectual, religious, and moral diet. With many, it becomes their whole life. In one so-called "evangelical" church, one of the largest, movie attendance is forbidden to members; a prominent woman in the church regularly sees and reviews all the worst films before a large church mid-week gathering to freshen their sanctimonious disgust. A man now in his fifties, to cite another case, is still busy, when last heard from, collecting clippings and data to prove to his comrades that a fascist revolution is about to capture America; he began his task in the 1940s. He feels it is his duty to keep the faith by freshening disgust.

What lies behind this kind of mentality? It is certainly very prevalent on all sides and is a basic motive with many people. Many members who stay in churches riddled with modernism, the new morality, and revolutionary doctrines, will not leave, nor can they be interested in sound theology; their sorry churches are a delight to them, because their disgust is kept continually fresh. Similarly, many who have left the modernist churches make it their life to review the horrors of the old church: their gospel is fresh disgust.

What lies behind this kind of mentality is phariseeism. A Catholic woman, no better than she had to be, loved calling attention to her priest's flagrant sins. Her attitude was this: "If he's a Christian, I'm a saint." A Presbyterian layman, of sorry character, delighted secretly in the bad character of his pastor: "I'm a lot better Christian than he is." Neither one was ever happy with a good pastor: the bad ones pleased them, the bad pastors gave them grounds for fresh disgust. Their mentality was exactly that of the Pharisee of whom Christ spoke, whose prayer was in essence simply this: "God, I thank thee, that I am not as other men are, extortioners, unjust, adulterers, or even as this publican" (Luke 18:11).

Here is the heart of the matter. The Pharisee needs a continual tale of evil, a steady recital of the depravity of men and movements around him in order to feel a moral glow. His self-justification is the sight of fresh evil in others. Hence, such people need and demand fresh evil. Is the new movie worse than any before, a fresh departure in evil? They attend it to freshen their disgust and keep their moral glow. Are their new exposures of corruption in politics? Millions of voters find it a wonderful means of self-justification: the nasty, evil men are plotting them into evil and corruption; it is not their own corruption writ large.

One brilliant professor at a major university spent an evening reciting the tales of perversion and degeneracy within his circles, amazing accounts of the moral bankruptcy of a group of scholars. His stories were true, but, subsequent events proved, his own activities were equally degenerate and brought about his own destruction. His self-justification had been to freshen his disgust at his colleagues' similar degeneracy. Much historical "debunking" has rested on shaky moral foundations.

Is the answer positive thinking? God forbid. Man cannot live by bread alone, nor by fresh disgust, nor by positive thinking. "I think only positive thoughts", a woman told me: "anything negative mars life and ages a person." Her husband had to do the negative thinking with respect to the children and every other family responsibility. Every positive thinker is a parasite and requires some family member or associate to do the negative thinking which is inescapable in life. Progress requires its "nay" as well as its "yea".

Am I suggesting that we refuse to expose evil, or to examine it? On the contrary, the only valid ground for examining evil is that positive action be taken, and this involves more than mere negation. Mere counter-action leaves the initiative to evil. A pharisaic "tut, tut", is not improved if millions of people are organized to say "tut, tut", together.

Our Lord declared, "Man shall not live by bread alone, but by every word that proceedeth out of the mouth of God" (Matt. 4:4). Now the word of God is not a sterile word, most churches to the contrary: it is a creative word. When man lives by every word of God, he begins to remake the world around him in terms of that creative word.

Is a man living by that creative word? Then he is at work establishing godly institutions, not in looking for fresh disgust. Those who have no creative word hate those who live by it. One man who has established three new churches in a few years, and a truly great Christian school, was recently the target of trouble from these living dead men. They tried vainly to freshen their disgust by finding fault with him. The Pharisee must be able to say, "God, I thank thee, that I am not as other men are." He needs the scoundrels to keep his disgust fresh and his self-righteousness flourishing. His greatest enemy, a constant affront to him, is the godly man who, in terms of the creative word, is actively engaged in godly reconstruction. Against all such the hand of the Pharisee is forever raised.

The Pharisee claims to be the only true believer, the only activist, and the only person "alive to the issues." Can anyone else compile a like record for "exposing" evil, for nosing out the living men and demanding they be disciplined for accomplishing something, and for getting ever greater responses of fresh disgust? The Pharisee needs evil: it is the air he breaths.

Men who live by the creative word of God know the reality of evil all around: it was there when they were born, and it will be there when they die. For them, the important question is this: will they have extended the boundaries of the Kingdom of God a little further before they die? Will they have exercised dominion under God and subdued the earth in terms of His creation mandate? The world was not empty when we came in to it; we must add more than a pharisaic "tut, tut", to it before we leave.

The church in the apostolic and post-apostolic age was not a great force numerically, it did not even possess a church building for probably two centuries. Yet Rome felt it necessary to wage a war unto death against these "followers of the way." By their family life and their sexual morality, by their quiet stand against things like abortion, by their strict obedience to the law of God, and by their strong sense of charity and mutual care of one another, these "followers of the way", members of Jesus Christ, were creating a new social order in the midst of an old one.

Let the dead bury the dead. The living must follow their King in the task of making all things new. But if you want to keep your disgust fresh move over into Sodom, and take out your citizenship papers. You'll be happy there.

CHALCEDON REPORT NO. 56
April 2, 1970

The death of an age is a bloody business. Men, disillusioned with the promises of their faith, yet unwilling to surrender them, strike out at everything in rage and in frustration. Like a rudderless ship, the civilization loses its direction and is driven by events instead of driving through them. Today, in the last days of humanism, as men steadily destroy their world, it is important for us to understand the meaning of the times and act in terms of that knowledge. The humanists in their blindness celebrate "the death of God" when it is in fact the death of humanism and their own funeral; they are racing to in their heedless course.

Humanism is dying because its faith is false, and its promises bankrupt. Let us examine that faith in order to understand more clearly its failure. *First* of all, humanism presupposes a faith in man, even to insisting on the basic goodness of man. This idealistic affirmation comes with it the assumption that evil is not in man but rather in his environment. Change the environment, and you thereby change man, it is held. As a result, humanistic sociology and politics are rigorously environmental: every effort is made to provide better housing, better education, every kind of environmental control, but, in all of this, man's evil only seems to proliferate.

As a result, many humanists have themselves abandoned their faith in man. Nietzsche, ahead of most, proclaimed the need of superman to replace man, and evolutionists and socialists have dedicated themselves to working towards the creation of a new man. Man as he now is, in terms of this hope, is expendable: he is merely the ape who shall produce the man of the future.

Lenin who held this view, could therefore treat with ruthless contempt the apes beneath him as he worked to bring the new man out of them. In every version, this belief is a break with the humanistic faith in man.

A *second* basic concept of the humanistic faith is its affirmation that man is his own god. As I have pointed out, in several of my books (e.g., *This Independent Republic*, p. 142f.), basic to every sound theology is the doctrine of the unity of the godhead. A schizophrenic god is no god at all. Mankind, humanity, being made up of gods, must be united to avoid a division in this new godhead, man. This means world unity, a one-world order; it means world peace, for the godhead must not be at war with itself.

Ironically, this faith has led to what has been called "perpetual war for perpetual peace." To demand the unity of all men is the essence of total imperialism. The result is total warfare. The peace lovers are history's greatest warmongers. Worldwide interventionism to effect world peace has characterized the policies of late of the U.S.S.R., the U.S., the U.N., and others. Granted their presuppositions, all are "sincere", but sincerity does not mean either truth or justice.

Moreover, man without God ends up as man without man, unable and unwilling to live at peace with anyone, and unable to live at peace with himself. The existentialist Sartre has stated the modern mood bluntly: "Hell is other people." If every man is his own god, knowing or determining for himself what constitutes good and evil, then every man is at war with any limitation upon himself imposed by other men or by a state. Hell then is logically "other people", and the humanistic faith in man as his own god becomes history's major impulse towards suicide. The Satanic temptation (Genesis 3:5) thus becomes the counsel of death to men and nations.

The *third* basic doctrine of the religion of humanism is the belief in equality (see again *This Independent Republic*, p. 140). Equality is a concept of the age of humanism, with its respect for the authority of science, transferred from the realm of mathematics and applied to man. The results have been devastating. Two plus two equals four is a valid concept, and a necessary abstraction. Such abstractions are important tools. In dealing with board feet of lumber, all cut to size, and graded, such abstractions work. But the richness and variety of man cannot be expressed by abstractions. Two Africans and two Englishmen do not equal four Americans, or vice versa: the equation mark now becomes an absurdity. Who are these eight men, and what are their talents? Are they saints of God or are they apostates, criminals or good citizens? One may be a plumber, and the other a concert violinist; the plumber may be more important to you today, and the violinist tonight. Each have their place, their function, and the term equality is irrelevant to it: it imposes an abstract mathematical judgment in an area where a vast variety of considerations must govern.

But we are governed today by the politics of equality. To challenge the doctrine is in bad form, although everyone is troubled, and society in an uproar, over the unrealistic attempts to enforce an abstraction onto the concrete facts of life.

The doctrine is honored in principle and denied in practice. The Marxist world affirms, "From each according to his abilities, to each according to his needs", but this is not an equality of work but of wealth. In practice, even this is abandoned by the Marxists in favor of a variety of rewards and a radically unequal society, one with greater variations of social status than the old Russia had. Both Fabian and Marxist socialisms now favor Meritocracy, rigid examinations, state control of all jobs, and positions being assigned (and power) in terms of examinations. The result is the rise of a new privileged class. In Britain, the House of Lords is steadily packed with Labor politicians, who have been made peers, and there are signs that its power may be revived under the leadership of this new elite. The equalitarians end up by asserting, as in Orwell's *Animal Farm*, that some animals are more "equal" than others! Whether it is the peasants of Russia, or the Negroes of America, the most rebellious and angry people, the most disillusioned members of equalitarian society, are those who have been "made equal" by acts of state. They know that they have been defrauded, and their impulse becomes revolutionary.

The *fourth* basic concept of the religion of humanism is its belief in the inevitability of progress. This is a secularized version of the belief in Providence. Humanism, by denying God, has depersonalized history. The world and its events are no longer the plan and handiwork of a personal, sovereign God; they are the product of anonymous, impersonal social forces. These impersonal forces, with planning man now guiding his own evolution, are supposed to ensure, not only progress, but more rapid progress. The result is, as Robert L. Heilbroner, in *The Future as History*, has termed it, a "philosophy of expectations." In terms of humanism, mankind should now be moving rapidly into a paradise on earth. In the 1920s and 1930s, teachers and professors often waxed lyrical in portraying the golden age which scientific planning would usher in. Today, the most intelligent of humanism's children are most in revolt against its failure to deliver on its promises. According to Kenneth Keniston, in the November, 1969, *Yale Alumni Magazine*, the students involved in campus protests are usually the most intelligent on the campus. "One study finds that the best way to predict whether a college will have anti-war protests is to count the number of National Merit Scholars in the freshman class...Furthermore, protesting students have been shown again and again to be an elite within each college and university more privileged in background, more academically successful, more socially concerned than their less active classmates...It is partly for this reason that student unrest concerns us profoundly. To be sure, if we consider white students (and I will not discuss black militants here), only a minority of America's almost 7,000,000 college students are vocally disaffected. Yet if this minority is selectively drawn from the future leaders of our society, does this fact not threaten the continuity of our culture?" It does indeed, and the continuity of humanistic culture is being destroyed by its own bitter and disillusioned sons.

The destruction is also written into humanistic culture at every turn. Because of this belief in the inevitability of progress, men can believe that progress will come inevitably after destruction. Destroy the past, clear the ground, and progress is inevitable. This is basic to the revolutionary mentality. This scientism is described by Ortega y Gasset In *The Revolt of the Masses*, as a new form of barbarism. Such a barbarian "believes that civilization is *there* in just the same way as the earth's crust and the forest primeval." As a result, this barbarian destroys in order to advance, because the destruction supposedly speeds up progress. The more revolutionary humanism becomes, the more it is suicidal.

Fifth, the basic saving institutions of humanism, i.e., its church or temple, are state and school. Both today are morally bankrupt. The implicit anarchism in all humanism makes man hostile to the state: it is always a hated establishment to him, a restraint on his freedom to be his own god. Whatever form the state takes, it displeases humanistic man. Very consistently, some leaders on the new left now call for perpetual revolution as the only answer.

The school is also bankrupt. The mathematical dream of equality is especially absurd when applied to education, which is the process of differentiation, analysis, and understanding, not a massive levelling, of ideas and facts. Education is thus in growing chaos, and it cannot improve on humanistic terms. Nothing is more ridiculous than a "save our public schools" movement. In its origin, the public school movement was socialistic and humanistic, and it cannot be otherwise. It is a state agency for state purposes, and its basic premise is the state's right to control and educate the child. The public school movement is bankrupt, and it is dying.

Humanism is dying, if not dead. Living with a corpse is no pleasant matter. It does not require documentation to tell us that a corpse is far gone. The answer to our problem lies elsewhere, not in documentation on death, but in reconstruction for life.

Humanism is dead, but the triune God lives and rules, sovereign over all. There must be reconstruction, godly reconstruction. Let the dead bury the dead. The living have work to do. All things shall be made new; new schools, new social orders, new institutions, renewed family life, in every area the principle of godly reconstruction must be applied.

Defensive warfare is a mistake: it leaves the initiative to the enemy. Those who are content to protect the past die with it. Our calling is to offensive warfare to subdue the earth and to exercise dominion over it (Gen. 1:26-28). This is what it means to be a man, created in the image of God. Remember: dominion does not belong to a mouse.

Some years ago, J. Allen Smith, by no means a conservative, wrote as follows in *The Growth and Decadence of Constitutional Government* (1939): "The basic conception of the old political order was not the divine right of kings, but the sovereignty of God. The assumed divine right of the temporal ruler was not an essential part of this doctrine. Divine sovereignty, as envisaged in the Christian theory of the world, was simply a conception of God as the ultimate source of authority. Direct human intermediaries, such as pope or king, were purely adventitious features of this belief." This belief in God's sovereignty meant also the rule of law. As Smith continued, "Supreme unlimited power had no place in the political thought of the early constitutionalists. All human authority was conceived to be limited." The "ultimate sovereignty of God precluded the idea that any human authority could be unlimited."

Precisely. And because today the sovereignty of God is denied, the sovereignty of man and the state is affirmed. It is useless to rail against the present trend if we are a part of it, and unless we affirm the sovereignty of God in its every aspect, we are to all practical intent affirming man and his humanistic order. In other words, you have already taken sides, and you had better know it. You are either working for the "Crown Rights of King Jesus" or for the crown claims of humanistic man. You cannot logically affirm "the rule of law", "moral principles", and "old-fashioned virtues" without affirming the sovereignty of God. The Marxists are right in recognizing God as the basic and ultimate enemy. Unless you stand in terms of the sovereignty of God as your strength, your first and last line of defense, and the ground of all advance, move over and join the enemy: you are a humanist.

CHALCEDON REPORT NO. 57
May 1, 1970

One of the most logical expressions of the modern mentality is *anarchism*. In anarchism, the basic premises of the Renaissance, the Enlightenment, Kant, and religious modernism come to maturity and their logical conclusion. Not only is anarchism the most logical expression of the modern mind, but it is also its most psychopathic manifestation. In anarchism, the radical evil and sickness of the modern mind comes to focus.

Let us examine some of the basic presuppositions of anarchism, which simply pushes the modern faith to its logical conclusion. *First* of all, anarchism denies the doctrine of original sin and holds to the natural goodness, or at the least, moral neutrality of man. The sin in the world is therefore not a product of man's fallen nature but rather a product of an evil environment. If there is evil in man, the environment is responsible. As Herbert S. Gershman observed (in *The Surrealist Revolution in France*, p. 189), "For Rousseau man's desires (which are wicked) were instilled in him by society; for the surrealists, man's desires (which are good, in that their satisfaction will presumably make him happy) are regularly thwarted by society." In either case, society, the environment, or the state, is guilty, not man; therefore, make war on society and the state. The premise of all modern revolutions is here. The anarchists are most logical in their application of it: since evil is in the environment, and man's strongest environment seems to be the state, free man totally by destroying the state totally. The logic of this position is so compelling to the modern, humanistic mentality, that even the total statists, the Marxists, justify their totalitarian state as the necessary means for eliminating the state.

The *second* main premise of anarchism is its belief in the autonomy of man, his total independence of God and man. It is the heresy of absolute self-government. There must be no God, no church, no state, no family, no institution with any authority over man, because man is his own god, his own law and state. An interesting early expression of the anarchistic ideal is to be found in an early and seminal book, Daniel Defoe's *Robinson Crusoe*, still excellent reading. We are often told that Crusoe represented the expression of the spirit of private enterprise, of capitalism, turning a desolate island into an ordered world. There is more than a little truth to this opinion, but another strand of thought is also apparent. The most compelling fact about Defoe's day was the great wealth capitalism was bringing to the cities. One reason for the growth of and poverty in cities was the influx of the poor to the cities to get jobs in this area of wealth. A continual influx meant a continual new class of poor as the earlier arrivals gained status in the growing middle class. The slums, in brief, were a first station on the road up, and people crowded into them readily in hopes that their ride would be upwards. The city was thus a focal point of the new world of capitalism; out of the confusion, crowding, and poverty of the city, capitalism was shaping an amazing new world. But Defoe chose a deserted island, a primitive and savage one, a condition of radical autonomy rather than the intense community of the city of his day. The element of anarchism was thus strongly present. The only other man in Crusoe's world was not a capitalist competitor, but a savage to emphasize his autonomy and dominion.

This is the world of the anarchist, a world in effect without other people. The problem of philosophy for the existentialist Sartre is not God, but other people. In *No Exit*, Sartre has Garcin declare, "Hell is...other people!" Levi, in *Philosophy and the Modern World* (p. 420), observed that "Hell is other people for Sartre because in his quaint universe of appropriation and domination (a kind of Hobbesian state of nature where the stakes are not the externals of wealth and deference but purely internal states of consciousness like nausea, shame, pride, and alienation) all contact with the Other implies a latent contest."

Crusoe at least had a real island, the modern anarchist increasingly flies to a new island, his own inner world, one, he trusts, no man can invade. According to Gershman, "Liberty, to the surrealist, has a pronounced negative aspect -- or perhaps it would be more accurate to say that it recalls the principles and goals of Riesman's inner-directed man. If it seeks martyrdom and oracular revelation, at the same time it denies the world and man's flesh and blood existence" (p. 12). The real world is, after Kant, to be found in the mind and imagination of man and his autonomous reason. Living with the reality of the outer world is seen as compromise. The new absolute is "the individual man" (p. 132).

For this autonomous man it is a moral necessity to deny not only the claims of God but the claims of law, society, the state, and the family. The attitude is, "I am god: don't fence me in." With many hippies, there is a denial of cleanliness and of social graces as a means of denying any interdependence with other people. The family, because of its strong and God-given ties, is especially warred against, and a major hallmark of the anarchistic mentality is rebellion against the family.

To cite a typical instance of this: a young man infected by the anarchistic mentality went out of his way to be offensive to his parents in appearance. Were they going to an important social function? He refused to cut his hair, wear clean clothes, or be other than a boor in his manners. Requests for compliance were treated as attempts to control him, but he felt entitled to take whatever he needed from them as his right. He married a girl of like anarchistic tendencies: on one occasion, his deliberately bad manners upset her and she remarked about it. He turned on her in a screaming rage and slugged her. He was logical at last: his rights were total in his eyes, his freedom absolute, and the rights of the world to "invade" his absolute freedom were non-existent: he was "resisting" an invasion. Precisely because he loved his wife as much as he was capable of loving anything, he resented her attempt to presume on that tie. He was, he declared, captain of his own soul, lord and general of his life, and no one had better try to "dictate" to him. In brief, like a good anarchist, he believed in autonomy: "I am god, don't fence me in."

Autonomous man indeed finds life with other people, and especially life with a loving family, to be "hell." How can a man be his own god and his own world, if other people make claims on him? People who have never heard the word "anarchism" today are deeply infected by it. A young father brutally beat his infant because she was crying; his excuse: "she was bothering me with her crying." How dare anyone disturb our little gods. Another young man, whose mother had long walked in fear of his tantrums, turned on her when she asked when he would come home that night and slugged her: his excuse, "she was always bugging me." How dare anyone limit his independence with a suggestion or even a question? "I am god: don't fence me in."

A *third* basic premise of anarchism is closely related to the second. It is the belief that the rational is the real. After Hegel, modern man has progressively remade the world after his own image, in terms of his concepts of rationality. People well beyond the borders of formal Hegelianism are infected by this belief. To cite an example of this, a best-seller widely read by conservatives and liberals is *The Peter Principle* by Dr. Laurence J. Peter and Raymond Hull. The Peter Principle is simply this: "In a Hierarchy Every Employee Tends to Rise to His Level of Incompetence." In other words, every bureaucracy promotes a man until he reaches a point where he is no longer competent, and there he remains, so that all jobs are potentially held by incompetents. The "beauty" of this "principle" is that it is so "rational", and therefore the appeal of the principle and the book.

But is it true? Some years ago, on an isolated Indian reservation, I saw in practice a decidedly different principle. The Indian agency superintendents gave their most competent employees poor or average ratings: this prevented promotion to another, higher agency and kept them there and enabled the superintendent to build up a better rating for himself. The incompetent men were given the highest ratings and promptly moved upward and out to another agency. Eventually, some of the competent men became discouraged and quit.

The same is true of several corporations I checked on. Incompetent executives, who know only management and nothing about engineering, transfer men from plant to plant to prevent anyone from being around long enough to spot their ignorance. These executives regularly move from company to company to prevent anyone from detecting that they are, as executives, mainly paper-shufflers and buck-passers.

The Peter Principle, however, appeals more to people than does the truth: it is more "rational." Much of modern politics and economics rests on the same premise, that the rational is the real. In other words, man remakes the world in terms of his own supposedly creative word.

A *fourth* premise of anarchism is its relativism. Since all objective law is denied, and God is rejected, every man is his own god and law, and no one law is binding on all men. Outside of man, no absolutes exist. The "purpose" of art and music then becomes a desire to prove that it makes no difference what note is sounded, which color or line is used, or which word follows another. Anarchism prevails in art and in science. The result then is the death of science, because objective meaning and purpose are dead. Gunther S. Stent, in *The Coming of the Golden Age: A View of the End of Progress*, believes it is not only the death of science which lies ahead, but the gradual decay and death of mankind. Jerome Lettvin, reviewing Stent's book in the

March, 1970, *Natural History*, praised it but added, "However, I am not convinced by his optimism." Sudden, rather than gradual death, is more likely for an anarchistic world.

The denial of law is the affirmation of death. The dead are insensitive to law. Maturity is not anarchism, the ability to live in independence from man and God, but rather to live in interdependence with others under God. Without God, men are soon dead, their culture and civilization in ruins. "He that sinneth against me wrongeth his own soul: all they that hate me love death" (Proverbs 8:36). The love of death is deeply rooted in our age.

Earlier, we cited the childish tantrums of the anarchistic mentality in reaction to normal claims on their lives. Not surprisingly, *hysteria* has been a major concern of psychology in the modern era. Dr. Ernst Kretschmer, in his study of *Hysteria, Reflex and Instinct* (p. 132), observed, "We can therefore sum up the situation in these words: *such hysterical persons are not weak-willed but weak of purpose*."

Without God, meaning and purpose wane and disappear; anarchistic man can only lash out hysterically at a world he never made and therefore hates. He destroys civilization, as though civilization were the sinner rather than himself. Anarchistic man has no future: he cannot construct; he can only kill, and die.

Let the dead therefore bury the dead. The world is ours under God, to exercise dominion over it and to subdue it. Because God is sovereign, every day is the day of the Lord, and every year is Anno Domini, the year of our Lord. God only and always reigns.

CHALCEDON REPORT NO. 58
June 1, 1970

War against "the Establishment" is a basic fact of our time. This in itself is a significant fact, in that, not too long ago, it was a basic hope of most college youth to become a part of the Establishment.

In the late 1930s, I recall my first day in a required course I had long postponed taking. An auditorium was required to accommodate the large enrollment. When the professor entered, there was a round of applause; when he finished his first, introductory lecture with some general remarks on the current scene, there was a standing ovation. Even in those days, professors were not usually well received, but this man carried weight with most students: he had, for two years or more, been a fifth echelon "Brain Truster" in Franklin Delano Roosevelt's administration. He had the prestige of the powers that be, plus the "independence" to be critical at points, and as a result this mild non-entity was a "somebody" to the students.

There are still some lingering echoes of this attitude, but now, on the whole, students are at war with the Establishment, which represents to them everything which is evil and hateful: the entrenched and established men and institutions of the past and the present. For these rebels, the Establishment is the state, the church, and the school. It is the family and their parents. It is the world of the police and the law, of professors and parents, of the military forces, and everything which seeks to perpetuate the present order.

Students are not alone in being anti-Establishment. Many radical groups, as well as conservative organizations, are, each from their own perspective, anti-Establishment. More than that, many members of the hated Establishment seek favor from the mob by taking an anti-Establishment stance. Some politicians succeed momentarily, as do some professors and clergymen, as long as they run with the mob. Many only gain contempt for their efforts. Thus when a mob of students, some 2000, "liberated" the faculty club at a Canadian university, seizing liquor and money and celebrating with various antics, the head of the faculty club, according to Jerry Rubin, "tried to co-opt the orgy. He stood on top of a chair and thanked everyone for coming."

The reasons for this deeply rooted hatred of the Establishment deserve attention. Only a few aspects can be touched on. *First*, a dramatic aspect of this protest is the increasing involvement of the U.S. in southeast Asia. Protests range from the total hostility of the radical left to the "win and get out" stand of many conservatives. There are good grounds for the protest. The U.S. Constitution does not permit the use of drafted men in wars outside the boundaries of the U.S. The Spanish-American War, and the Pershing campaign against Villa, were fought with volunteers and a professional army. Two World Wars, the Korean War, and now the Vietnam-Cambodian War have been waged in violation of the Constitution. Moreover, the war is fought in a strange way: perhaps more harm has been done to the cause of our allies than to our communist enemies. The distrust and resentment of both right and left have good grounds and much justification.

Second, a major target has been "the law", i.e., the courts and the police. The Police have been the unhappy targets of much of this, although the basic resentment is against the "system." The radical hostility to the courts is the basic aspect of this protest. This hostility has been apparent in a variety of movements, from the conservative "impeach Earl Warren" movement to the revolutionary antics of the Chicago conspirators when on trial. Again we must say that there are good reasons for this protest. A study of Chicago, Ovid Demaris' *Captive City* (1969), makes clear the connection between organized crime, politics, and the courts. The author is emphatic, as are many other students of the subject, that organized crime cannot exist without a working alliance with politics and the courts. The criminal world today is a part of the Establishment, and its power is manifest in the highest places of the country.

The radical relativism of the courts is apparent in Supreme Court William O. Douglas' book, *Points of Rebellion* (1969), as well as in many other judges' statements. Chief Justice Burger holds to ideas alien to justice. *The Chicago Daily News* of June 3, 1969, reported that "Among the 'techniques, devices and mechanisms' Burger questioned were: The jury system, the presumption that a defendant is innocent until proven guilty, the right of a defendant to remain silent and putting the burden of proof on the prosecution...Burger suggested that defendants ought to be required to testify in a courtroom. And, he said: 'If we eliminate the jury we would save a lot of time.'" (*The Review of the News*, April 22, 1970, p. 23) There is no lack of reason for rage and protest: the courts today do all too often present a spectacle of studied injustice.

Third, the church is despised and with reason. Where the church today is not captured by modernistic relativism, it shows instead a pious irrelevance, antinomianism, phariseeism, and a general immoralism. Consider, for example, the comment of Billy Graham in Hamburg, Germany, as reported by Robert Davis ("News Briefs", *Chicago Tribune*, April 7, 1970, from an interview in *Der Spiegel*). Graham "refused to discuss communism, although he had once been known as a great foe of that system. 'For years I have not spoken about that,' he said. 'I cannot go around the world and say who is right and who is wrong.'" If a minister is unable to say whether or not communism is morally wrong, who can? If a minister finds no ground to call communism wrong, what ground can he claim to say anything? The church today is so radically irrelevant, whether it represents the modernist or evangelical branches, that it is scarcely worth attacking. But it is a cause for deep grief.

Fourth in every area, there is a radical impersonalism. Students have protested against being a mere cipher in the university. They have satirized the computer-like mechanistic operations by wearing badges reading, "Do not fold, staple, or mutilate," because they insist on being persons. A classic example of this impersonalism is Dr. Arnold Hutschnecker, a Nixon associate, who proposed that all children between 6 and 8 years of age be tested for possible criminal tendencies; all those whom the tests ruled to be potentially criminal should then be subjected to special psychological training. (Psychiatrists disowned the plan.) Dr. Hutschneker declared that he was "shocked" and upset at reactions: "I was bewildered as I could be." (Jack Nelson, "Ex. Nixon Doctor Upset Over Reaction to Plan," *Los Angeles Times*, Section E, p. 1, Sunday, May 3, 1970.) Well, bless his little pin head: he plans to play god in the lives of all children, and he fails to understand why people are upset. After all, he said, it was merely preventive medicine! This total unawareness that people are persons, not social fodder for the future, is increasingly characteristic of the modern mentality, and

Establishment planning usually reveals this impersonalism in varying degrees.

It would be possible to discuss at great length the various areas of protest, but the foregoing is sufficient for our purposes. The modern Establishment is basically humanistic and relativistic: it recognizes no law save man. It despises God's law and therefore it cannot admit that there is a law order in any realm. Hence, whether in politics, economics, or religion, the modern mentality believes in a do-it-yourself law: set aside the old laws, and write your own, in terms of your planning.

Having no law to judge by, the Establishment pays lip service to man. Thus, when Commissioner Otto N. Larsen, a University of Washington professor of sociology and a member of a federal commission, received a pie in the face from Thomas Forcade of the Underground Press Syndicate, Larsen did not protest: "What he wanted was outrage. I refused to engage in physical interaction...I've had classroom confrontations with militants before. I try to engage all kinds of people in serious dialogue. These people have something important to tell us." (*Los Angeles Herald-Examiner*, Thursday, May 14, 1970, p. A-11.) This statement reveals a radical moral bankruptcy. The facade of receptivity covers a radical emptiness. What is the something important to be told? The modern intellectual has no principle of truth, no concept of real transcendence. As a result, he is formally open to everything, because all things are equally important, but actually open to nothing, because nothing is really of value. In consequence, his own will to power is his only truth.

The Establishment today is radically relativistic. This is the cause of its deep immoralism, its opportunism, and its contempt for all law, economic, constitutional, religious, or otherwise.

The forces of student protest, however, are not better and actually worse. The students are the true sons of the Establishment: they reflect the relativistic philosophy of state, school, and church; if anything, they apply it more honestly and systematically. The students have simply learned their lessons well.

Recently, some rather conservative doctors, when questioned about abortion, responded usually with surprising uniform answers. One said, "I don't like it, but who is to say what's right and wrong?" Another declared, "I'm personally against it, but who am I to inflict my morality on others?", and so on. We should not be surprised at the results. Relativism today breeds a radical and total lawlessness.

An episode was reported to me on one of my trips. During a demonstration and protest march, one hippy marcher stopped to urinate openly and defiantly in the street. Thirty years ago, the reaction would have been swift: arrest, public disapproval, and a general feeling that the young man was a "nut", a mental case. Now it was different: students quickly and gleefully imitated him. Young men from the "best of families" took a defiant pride in following suit. They professed that they were symbolically urinating on the Establishment, and, no doubt they were, but even more they were demonstrating that a civilization and its discipline had died.

To cite another example: a quiet, stable city in 1950 had 22,000 people; a ranking police officer told me then that it had perhaps 100 adults who were petty, small-time criminals, 300 juveniles who had at some time been in trouble, of whom 150 would probably, as adults, be in and out of trouble. The work of the police was light; crimes were few and minor, and traffic problems their main concern.

By 1970, this same city, now with 27,000, has a major problem: its juvenile offenders are more than the officer could readily cite, and they are out of hand. Their offenses are all more serious, and drugs and robbery are common problems. The increase of adult irresponsibility and crime is also marked, and the police feel the situation is out of hand.

In a major city, an officer stated that the day may not be too far distant when the law-breakers outnumber the law-keepers, and the result will be radical lawlessness and anarchy.

Protests against the Establishment are justified, in that the Establishment reveals a moral relativism which is destroying the country, but the protesters themselves in most cases reveal an even more radical relativism themselves. The evil they protest against is most fully present in themselves. As a result, the protests against the Establishment are sterile and morally bankrupt. They only compound and aggravate the evils they complain about. The protesters are merely revealing that they are indeed sons of the Establishment.

This moral bankruptcy is also true of too many conservative. Those who truly believe in the triune God see His handiwork in all things: they believe that God's absolute decree and law govern every area of life, that men either obey God's law-word or they are shattered by it.

Too many conservatives, many of whom claim to be Christians, are in reality Satanists. They see all things controlled by satanic conspirators: every event is read as the careful development of a satanic plan. They see, not God in control, but the powers of darkness. The world for them is governed, not by God's law and decree, but by dark and hidden evil conspirators. They fear, not God, but these evil powers. Whatever their profession, they are in practice Satanists, Satan worshippers.

But the world is only and always governed by God and His law. Progress and reconstruction are only possible under God and His law. The world is not changed by futile rage nor by protests, but only as men, by the grace of God, reconstruct their lives, their calling, and the world around them in terms of God's law-word. It is time to rebuild.

CHALCEDON REPORT NO. 59
July 1, 1970

Among the earliest battle-lines between the early Christians and the Roman Empire was the matter of *abortion*. Greek and Roman laws had at times forbidden abortion, even as they had also permitted it. The matter was regarded by these pagan cultures as a question of state policy: if the state wanted births, abortion was a crime against the state; if the state had no desire for the birth of certain children, abortion was either permissible or even required. Because the state represented ultimate order, morality was what the state decreed. To abort or not to abort was thus a question of politics, not of God's law. Plato, for example, held that the state could compel abortion where unapproved parents proceeded without the approval of the state.

Very early, the Christians accused the heathen of murder, holding that abortion is a violation of God's law, "Thou shalt not murder." It was also a violation of the law of Exodus 21:22-25, which held that even accidental abortion was a criminal offense. If a woman with child were accidentally aborted, but no harm followed to either mother or child, even then a fine was mandatory. If the foetus dies, then the death penalty was mandatory.

Because the law of the Roman Empire did not regard abortion as a crime, the early church imposed a life sentence as a substitute: penance for life, to indicate that it was a capital offense. The Council of Ancyra, 314 A.D., while making note of this earlier practice, limited the penance to ten years. There were often reversions to the earlier severity, and for a time, in later years, the administration of any draught for purposes of causing an abortion was punishable by death. The Greek and Roman influence tended to weaken the Christian stand by sophisticating the question, by trying to establish when the child or foetus could be considered a living soul. The Biblical law does not raise such questions: at any point, abortion requires the death penalty.

(Incidentally, the old question as to whether the foetus is "a living soul" has been given an answer by research, according to William P. O'Connell, who declares: "Many feel that the choice is the woman's. I would agree if it were clear that the fetus is part of the woman and thus hers to dispose of. The evidence, however, is to the contrary. Microbiology has established that the zygote is human and an autonomous, if dependent, organism from conception. Once fertilized, the cell is no longer latent life. It has its full and human allotment of chromosomes. It is uniquely human, like no other living thing or part of a thing, anywhere along the evolutionary chain." (*Los Altos Town Crier*, Wednesday, April 22, 1970, p. 1.)

The *Didache*, an early Christian document, called all abortion murder, and a love of death, whereas Christians are called to a love of God and of life.

Wisdom declared of old, "all they that hate me love death" (Proverbs 8:36). Here is an important key to the problem of abortion. We shall return to it later.

The debate and discussion of the subject of abortion is very extensive today, quite academic, and unrelated to reality. Thus, the *American Medical News*, June 8, 1970, p. 7, has in article by Dr. Charles A. Dafoe, M.D., entitled, "Thoughtful Action Needed to Find Middle Ground on Abortion." Dr. Dafoe is an obstetrician-gynecologist in Denver, and chairman of the Therapeutic Abortion Committee of the Presbyterian Medical Center there. Dr. Dafoe wants a "middle ground" between a total ban on abortion and total permissiveness. Is this possible? Is there a middle ground between murder and the protection of life, between adultery and chastity?

The reality of the situation has been reported to me by two doctors as well as by other persons. Supposedly, therapeutic abortions are permitted only after approval by a psychiatrist, or two psychiatrists, and review by a board of doctors. In reality, in those states where abortion can be authorized, psychiatrists often sign the requests without bothering to see or interview the applicants, and the review boards are not consulted. One doctor, on a review board, but never consulted, stated that he walked into his hospital one morning to learn that ten abortions had already been performed. His hospital performs very few abortions as compared to others. University and county hospitals are often chief offenders and are becoming "abortion mills;" some religious hospitals perform a large number of abortions also. The invention of suction machines, which are quite cheap, have made mass abortions a reality.

According to Governor Reagan of California, under the mental health section of the new law in California, "Our Public Health Department has told us its projections that if the present rate of increase continues in California, a year from now there will be more abortions than there will be live births in this state. And a great proportion of them will be financed by Medi-Cal." He said "under a technicality" a "young, unmarried girl" can become pregnant, go on welfare 'and she is automatically eligible for abortion if she wants it, under Medi-Cal. And all she has to do is get a psychiatrist - and they're finding that easy to do - who will walk by the bed and say she has suicidal tendencies.' Reagan said that in Sacramento 'a 15-year-old girl has just had her third abortion, with the same psychiatrist each time saying she has suicidal tendencies. I don't think the state should be in that kind of business.'" ("Reagan Sees Abortions Topping Births", Santa Ana, California *The Register*, Friday (m) April 24, 1970, p. D 5.)

According to the *American Medical News* for May 25, 1970, the Board of Trustees of the American Medical Association has urged a "new abortion policy to permit the decision to be made by the woman and her physician."

This is a return to paganism, to the belief that no sovereign and transcendental God governs man and the universe; it is a pagan belief that the control of life is essentially and finally in the hands of man, or of man's agency, the state.

This total control of life by human agencies is a part of the plan of the predestination of man by man. Predestination is an inescapable concept. If we deny that God predestines, we will assert ultimately that man or the state predestines. Whenever belief in God's predestination declines, planning or predestination by the state rapidly takes its place. There is no lack of belief in predestination today, but it is belief in statist predestination, in planning and control by statist agencies.

We should not be surprised, therefore, at a report from Paris of a UNESCO meeting on the problems of aggressiveness:

> A U.S. scientist told an international scientific meeting here Tuesday that therapeutic abortions might prevent future Hitlers from being born. Dr. David A. Hamburg, of the psychiatry department of the Stanford University medical school, told the meeting that research had linked the presence in mothers of abnormally high amounts of testosterone, the male sex hormone, with aggressiveness in their children. While there was not enough knowledge at present to apply these findings practically, Hamburg foresaw that decades from now a doctor and his patient might choose a therapeutic abortion to prevent the birth of an extremely aggressive individual. The U.N. Educational, Scientific and Cultural Organization (UNESCO), where the meeting was held, mentioned a future Hitler or Chenghis Khan as people who might be eliminated in this way...("Abortions Held Way to Avoid Tyrants", *Los Angeles Times*, Wednesday, May 20, 1970, part I, p. 9.)

It is clear that abortions are, *first* of all, an attempt by man to play god. The widespread approval of abortions by churches reveals that these churches are anti-Christian and are in fact humanistic churches. When man plays god, he seeks first of all to control life, to grant or to take life on his own terms rather than God's. God, as the creator of all things, has given mankind His law in Scripture whereby we are to govern all things under God. Not man's but God's will is the concern of God's law. It is precisely this power which humanism grasps at by law, to take or to spare life in terms of its own decree. Does God require capital punishment for certain offenses? Very well then, will the humanist, being against capital punishment, deny the "right" to abortion? No, the humanist will establish a "right" to abortion on his own terms and execute capital punishment on the fetus.

Not surprisingly, there is an increase in assassinations and in murder. Men resort to their own will and their own plan and set aside God's law, which is God's declared plan. They seek to control life apart from God.

Man has made himself the arbiter and god of life, and he decides quite readily, in terms of his own logic, who shall live. Thus, in Colorado, the question of euthanasia, so-called mercy killings, was put to a vote by the Colorado Nursing Association. "Voting in favor of euthanasia, only a third of the nurses favored the idea. After hearing arguments in favor, a majority voted for what only a third had accepted before." ("Eliminating the Old", *Twin Circle*, June 14, 1970, p. 6.) More significant than the vote was the attitude of these nurses that euthanasia is an open question, one for man to decide or to vote upon. Today they vote in favor of killing the aged and the infirm; will they vote to kill doctors tomorrow? Or will the doctors vote to kill all nurses?

If men can decide who shall live, whom will they kill? Unwanted children can be aborted, the aged put to sleep, all priests and ministers killed, all Communists, Nazis, or conservatives executed, the Jews sentenced to death, or the Germans eliminated, all blacks wiped out, or all whites: all of these are open questions if man can decide who shall live. All of these *have* become open questions as humanism has developed in the 20th century. Either God's law prevails, or man's law. If man's law is accepted, everything is an open question. When man plays God, man himself is the victim.

Under God, the doctor is a minister of life, of healing. His profession has had a long and necessary connection with a priestly calling. Under humanism and with abortion, the doctor ceases to be a healer and a protector of life and becomes a murderer. (Statute law may permit abortion, but it is still murder, not only under God's law, but under common law, as doctors may sometime find out.) Under the influence of humanism, a radical change is taking place in the medical profession. Instead of being a man who regards life as sacrosanct, as wholly governed by God and beyond his province to destroy, the doctor is playing god in most cases. But, because the doctor is not god, he becomes a murderer. The majority of people may favor abortion, but they will still not respect an abortionist. Man, created in God's image, will, even when fallen, reflect to some degree the judgment and law of God. With the increase of abortion, the medical profession will rapidly decline in prestige. As a hated and despised group of murderers, even the women who use them will welcome the total control of doctors by the state. Few will wish them well.

Second, as we have noted, abortion represents a hatred of life. This hatred of life manifests itself in a number of ways, from outright suicide to suicidal activities. It is estimated that 250,000 will commit suicide in the 1970s, and another two million will try and fail. ("250,000 U.S. Suicides Predicted During 70's" *Los Angeles Times*, Sunday, June 7, 1970, Sec A, p. 21.) The use of drugs represents a form of suicide and a hatred of life. Hardin Jones of the University of California has stated that in the U.S. "over 100,000 young people (2.5 times U.S. war deaths in Vietnam) have been killed by drugs and far more hare been converted into mental cripples." ("Drug Toll", *Twin Circle*, May 17, 1970, p. 12) A wide variety of suicidal activities are common today, The hatred of God is also the hatred of life.

In his novel, the *Death of Ivan Ilich*, Tolstoy tells the story of the death of Ivan Ilich, a conscientious official but a man without faith. As his fatal illness progresses, he begins to hate all people in good health. He hates his wife and children for being so strong, clean, and healthy "with all the loathing of a diseased body or all cool, white, sweet-smelling flesh." (Henri Troyat: *Tolstoy*, p. 559) Tolstoy's Ivan Ilich can serve as a symbol of humanistic mankind and his culture. As it faces death, humanism turns on life with hatred; it pursues a suicidal course of action in every realm and strikes at life with savage and murderous intent: It professes to reverence and affirm life even as it murders it. The drive for legalized abortion is a world-wide manifestation of this hatred of life. Pompously, the legal and medical authorities write in various restrictions on abortion even as they approve it. All is supposedly wisely governed and therapeutic. But in actual practice the decision is a thumbs down on life; abort, abort; no restrictions in actual practice. Their love of death and hatred of life manifests itself in an increasing abortion rate. With some girls and women, it has become a kind of status symbol of "liberation" to have secured an abortion; they have proven their freedom from God and their dedication to ecology, to preventing a supposed over-population.

On every level it is a mark of a dying culture, a hatred of life, and a desire to play god. Indeed, all they that hate God love death. And death shall be their destiny. But we are called life.

CHALCEDON REPORT NO. 60
August 1, 1970

Our concern this month is with two supposedly dissimilar subjects, the myth of the silent majority, and decapitalization; the two are actually very closely related.

The myth of the silent majority is not a new one; it has been widely used for almost two centuries by right, left, and center politicians. The basic feature of this myth is that all our problems are created by a small, evil minority, whereas the majority are good people and are simply misled. All the publicity and press is controlled or filled by news of this evil minority, and the good majority are silent. Who this evil minority is depends on the person propagating this myth: it can be a group of revolutionists, radical students, or a race; it can be capitalists or communists. It can be also a conservative organization, or a church.

The myth works all the better if some evidence exists that there are some communists, or nasty capitalists, or any other element which is clearly engaged in subversive activities, rioting, or lawless stands.

But the myth is anti-Christian to the core, in that it denies the fact of sin. According to the Bible, man's problem is sin, and, in every race, class, and group, sin is the central problem. Our problem today is that the vocal minorities and the silent majorities all over the world are rebellious against God and His laws, so that we need to pray, from our hearts, in the words of the general confession: "We have followed too much the devices and desires of our own hearts. We have offended against thy holy laws. We have left undone those things which we ought to have done; and we have done those things we ought not to have done; and there is no health in us." There is neither absolution nor grace in confessing other people's sins, and yet this is the essence of the myth of the silent majority.

Our bodies are always exposed to a variety of diseases; we fall prey to them when our general resistance is weak. Similarly, every body politic has always been exposed to a wide variety of subversions; it never succumbs to them as long as its general health remains. If the infection, the subversive minority, gains a foothold, it is because the body, the silent majority, is weak and unhealthy.

With this in mind, let us examine the class structure of society. Here, one of the most important studies is by Dr. Edward C. Banfield of Harvard, *The Un-heavenly City, The Nature and Future of Our Urban Crisis* (Boston: Little, Brown, 1970.) Banfield sees classes as an inescapable aspect of every society, and he divides society into four classes: upper class, middle class, working class, and lower class. The important thing about Banfield's work is the way class status is identified: "the individual's orientation toward the future will be regarded as a function of two factors: (1) ability to imagine a future, and (2) ability to discipline oneself to sacrifice present for future satisfaction" (p. 47). As Banfield observes, "It must again be strongly emphasized that this use of the term *class* is different from the ordinary one. As the term is used here, a person who is poor, unschooled, and of low status may be upper class; indeed he *is* upper class if he is psychologically capable of providing for a distant future." (p. 47f). Many man of great wealth are basically lower class; they have no orientation to the future. The upper class has a personal and broadly social future orientation. The middle class is similar, but of more restricted vision. The working class's future orientation is limited to very personal factors; a comfortable home, a new car, or the like. The lower class has no future orientation; he does not plan. "Things happen *to* him, he does not *make* them happen" (p. 53). Outside the lower classes when poverty occurs, it is "the result of external circumstances; death of the breadwinner, illness, involuntary unemployment, or the like." Even when severe, such poverty is not squalid or degrading, because standards are maintained. On the other hand, "Lower-class poverty, by contrast, is 'inwardly' caused (by psychological inability to provide for the future, and all that this inability implies)" (p. 126).

Let us now analyze the implications of this analysis of class structure. Very obviously, the old monarchies and nobilities fell because they had ceased to be a true upper class and had become lower class in mentality, geared only to the moment and its pleasures. The entrepreneurs who gained the ascendancy in the new society were thus not "middle class" but a true upper class, men with a future oriented vision for themselves and society.

The United States was settled by men, who, however humble their English origins, were upper class by virtue of their vision of the future. Many of the immigrants who arrived were similarly upper class in vision: they left their native lands in terms of a future oriented vision. The United States, usually cited as the great example of a middle class culture, probably had, from the colonial period well through much of the 19th century, an upper class orientation perhaps unequalled in history.

A Christian faith which is geared to victory and the establishment of a Christian law order is future oriented. No other religion has been capable of creating a like progress, because none other has the future orientation of Biblical faith.

A future oriented people capitalize a civilization; they work in terms of a goal. They forgo present pleasures for future gains. Their entire life and activity is geared to capitalization, and the family becomes a major instrument for capitalizing society.

Today, however, the mood of modern man can best be described as existentialist. It subscribes to a philosophy in which the "moment" is decisive. It is not future oriented in that it does not plan, save, and act with the future in mind. The existentialist demands that future now. Some of the causes which concern student rebels may be valid, but their existentialist demand that the future arrive today makes them incapable of capitalizing and planning; they are instead capable only of decapitalizing a culture. Existentialism requires that a man act undetermined by standards from the past or plans for the future; the biology of the moment must determine man's acts.

Very briefly stated, existentialism is basically lower class living converted into a philosophy. It is, moreover, the philosophy which governs church, state, school, and society today. The "silent majority", has perhaps never heard of existentialism, but it has been thoroughly bred into it by the American pragmatic tradition of the "public" or private schools.

Our basic problem today, all over the Western world, is that Western civilization no longer has a true upper class at the helm. Future-oriented men no longer dominate society, politically, economically, religiously, educationally, or in any other way. Instead, dreamers who are basically lower class; who believe that political power can convert today into tomorrow, are in charge. The result is the domination of our politics by an economic policy which is the essence of the lower class mind and which leads to radical inflation. Spending today with no thought of tomorrow is a lower class standard, and this is the essence of our modern scene. The vocal minority and the silent majority are both deeply in debt, and they create national economies which are deeply in debt. The growing anarchism of our social life is a product of this same lower class mentality. This popular anarchism is a refusal to submit to law and discipline, an unwillingness to accept any postponement of hopes and dreams. It is closely related to the tantrum of a child who demands that his will be done now. Every major social agency today, church, state, school, and home is dedicated to creating this anarchistic, lower class mentality.

The need thus is for a new upper class, a segment of society dedicated to a future orientation governed by Biblical faith. This means establishing new schools, free Christian schools, new churches, a new society in terms of our own readiness to live in terms of a broadly future oriented purpose. The "public" or state schools are shaping a large new lower class, and the universities are finishing schools for this new lower class. The Christian schools are shaping a new upper and a new middle class.

The purpose of Chalcedon is to further the thinking and scholarship of a new upper class, of people geared to the future and dedicated to godly reconstruction.

To return to Banfield's book, Banfield cites two groups in American history which have had the strongest future orientation, the Puritans and the Jews, and both had it as long as their perspective was still colored with the belief that God summons man to work for "the realization of God's plan for the future" (p. 57). Biblical faith has been basic to American progress, to future orientation.

On the other hand, a characteristic of a decaying social order is that men decline and become more and more lower class in character. The women then provide whatever future orientation the society has. Among American Indians, too commonly, whatever stability a home has is provided by the woman. Among Negroes, the woman again is usually the member of that family who does whatever planning and saving there is. In American society at large, the same fact is increasingly the reality; the woman is provident, plans for the future, is politically, economically, and religiously concerned, whereas the man has a rather lower class absorption with the moment. A society in which men surrender leadership and lack a practical vision of the future is in serious decline.

Thus, the new barbarian is not merely in the slums; he is in the schools and universities, in business houses and factories, in church, and home.

In their study of *The Lonely Crowd* (1953), Riesman, Glazer, and Denny showed that man today has become consumption-centered rather than production-centered. The group is now the source of morality and the framework of reference. The emphasis is thus more on morale than on morality. Man is other-directed rather than inner-directed, and the group has taken the place of God as the authority. What these men were describing was simply the development of the lower class mind, and we are beginning to see the shape of a world dominated by such a mentality. This lower class mind has been some years in the making; it will take time and effort to shape a new mentality. It is necessary to work, therefore, while there is still time. The cause is recapitalization and reconstruction.

These are frustrating times for any man with a practical future-oriented character. Our world is geared to the present. When Lord Keynes was asked about the long range consequences of his economic policy, he gave as his answer, "In the long run, we are all dead." This is a classic expression of a lower class perspective. How then can a man plan for the future in a world that insists on living only for the present? How, when our politics, economics, religion, education, and all else expresses a lower class world view, can we assert again the priority of God's law and the future?

We begin by planning our own lives and assets in terms of the certainty of the collapse of any order that denies law and the future. We establish new institutions, churches, schools, and agencies. There are beginnings of new medical associations, standing in terms of principles. We need new associations of professional men to oppose the present link between humanism, the state, and the professions. There is a need for new insurance companies that will insure doctors who break with the A.M.A. and stand in terms of Biblical morality.

From where you stand, what can you do? You can join the lower class, and eat, drink, and try to be merry, for tomorrow you may die. Or you can plan for yourself, assist others in their planning, and work to create again a future oriented society. If a future oriented, upper class society is to be established, *you* will have to do it. The federal government *never* will. To look to politics for the answer is a mark of the inferior mind. It is time to upgrade ourselves, before the judgment of God flunks us out of history.

CHALCEDON REPORT NO. 61
September 1, 1970

The city has a very important and central role in the history of civilization and human progress. We fail to appreciate this nowadays because the romantics have greatly obscured the role of the city. Some Christians condemn the city, because Cain built the first city (Genesis 4:17). They fail to reckon with the fact that *Revelation* gives as the goal of God's movement in history and beyond history, a city, the New Jerusalem in which garden (or country) and city are combined.

The city represents a common life. From the earliest days, the function of the city has been to provide men with community, to bring like-minded men together in terms of a common purpose and life. The city served as an expanded family. Men felt "at home" in their city, because it represented a larger family and a closely knit sense of community.

This aspect of the city is now gone. Instead of a sense of belonging, the city gives a sense of isolation. The word "citizenship" comes from the word "city"; citizenship was originally membership in the common life and faith of a city. Instead of "citizenship", modern man finds instead "alienation" in the city. The modern poet, Jack Fulbeck, in 1951, wrote of life in the city with words which eloquently expressed the fact that modern man is a stranger in the modern city:

> Not in the jungled city can I find
> That vagrant tribe my memory pursues.
> Here are fidelities I did not choose...
> I sleep with strangers, crying for my people.

Another important aspect of the city in history has been a common faith. In ancient times, a city always represented a common faith. To be a citizen meant to share in the same religious faith as all other members of the city. The law of the city was derived from that religion, as well as all other standards. No one could share in the life of the city if he denied its faith. To do so made him an alien, if not an enemy. This is why it was necessary for the Christian to face persecution once they denied the city's faith, and this is why, when they conquered, the reorganized city or country had to have a religious unity. Every law and standard which binds man to man, in state, school, church, commerce, and society is a product of religion. When that common faith is denied, the people of the city become strangers to one another.

Next, the city was man's greatest source of material protection. The city provided walls, a watch, and other men as a means of mutual defense against enemies. From ancient times, men have fled to the city in times of catastrophe as their best and surest defense. A dramatic example of this deeply rooted feeling is the eruption of Mount Pelee, a long dormant volcano, in 1902. Some time passed after Mount Pelee became active again. Rivers of lava flowed daily down the mountain side; homes and business places were destroyed day after day; the cable to the outside world was cut by the shifting of the ocean bed. Finally, when Mount Pelee climaxed its eruptions on May 8, 1902, 8:02 a.m., 30,000 people died. The two survivors were a prisoner sentenced to death and a madman. Why didn't the people leave? As a matter of fact, people fled from farms and villages *into the city*, although conditions were no better in the city. Professor Roger Bordier of the Lycee of St. Pierre summed it up thus in describing the people's attitude: "They had a blind faith in the protection of the town." When the press assured them that all was well, the people were ready to believe the word of the newspaper against the sight of their eyes, because their faith in the protecting power of the city was so great. It had almost become instinctive with men to believe in the city as protection.

The twentieth century has rapidly changed that ancient role of the city. Air war has made the city the most vulnerable area, and the most practical place to attack. As a result, in World War II, Britain sent many children out of London into the country for their protection. The city, in modern warfare, had ceased to be the place of refuge and had become the most exposed arena of warfare.

But this was not all. The new religion of the city, humanism, cannot bind man to man, and, as a result, the city has become a house increasingly divided against itself. Race and class warfare have become a part of the life of the city. Warfare has thus been introduced into the heart of the metropolis. Urban sprawl is in part due to this fact. Men of the city flee from the city to its borders in order to escape the city's newer citizens and their warfare. Man now feels nowhere less protected than in the city. More and more city dwellers arm themselves with guns, watch-dogs, barred windows and an alarm system. The city has become the battlefield of the twentieth century.

Pollution has also altered the life of the city. When, in the mid-thirties, this writer had a physical examination at the university, the examining doctor said, "You're from the country." Why? The dust of the farm showed on my lungs, whereas city dwellers had cleaner lungs. This, of course, is no longer true. Today, in many areas, it is the city dweller whose lungs show the effects of city life and smog.

The city is also being destroyed by modern money. The stability and growth of the city and its economic life depends on good money, hard money, gold and silver. Modern paper money inflation works harm in every area of life but especially to the city, because the life of the city is so intensely dependent upon the flow of sound money. When inflation finally debauches the paper currency (or radically adulterates the coinage), the city suffers a massive heart attack, because money is its life blood. Continuing inflation finally helped destroy urban life in the Roman Empire, so that, when the City of Rome fell, it was a shadow of its former self. It had ceased to be the place of imperial residence, and its population had declined greatly. When the end of an age witnesses also the breakdown of money, it means also the death of the city.

The problem of the city is not "congestion." This is its advantage. It puts us close to other men, to opportunities, advantages, and instruments of progress. Congestion can mean more stimulating ideas, more possibilities of progress, but *only* if some kind of community is maintained. A good religion unites people in terms of a common faith and purpose. Good money also unites people, in that it makes economic community and progress possible.

Remove good religion and good money, and the situation moves toward anarchy. The very advantages of the city become its disadvantages.

The city is today being destroyed. But the city must be rebuilt if civilization is to continue. The city represents life in community, it represents industry and commerce, progress and achievement. There is no progress without community action, and, in the city, community action is giving way to statist action, and there is a growing paralysis of the spirit of enterprise.

The true life of the city is a continuous rebuilding in terms of a continuously improving perspective on the goals of godly society. It is a life of change because it has goals. Where men believe only in change, all things are equal, and therefore there is no value in change. Chinese philosophy very early accepted the ultimacy of chance and change, and as a result Chinese civilization stagnated. It constantly required outside conquerors to revivify it, before they too succumbed to its stagnation. Change should be a product of a faith which is discontented with the present and continually reshapes the present in terms of a future-oriented goal. Thus, Biblical religion rather than Chinese philosophy has produced progress and advance. It will do so again.

Briefly, a good city is an upper-class product. It is future oriented, and, as such, it is a religious, cultural, and economic center. The city represents the free planning of many men of enterprise who chart the future in religion, economics, education, science, and other areas. When the city becomes lower class oriented, it also becomes entertainment oriented. Not planning for the future but enjoying the moment becomes all important. Instead of a concern for the future, people become concerned with the present, and with status. In a class structured society, governed by an upper class, men are important to the degree that they command the future by their enterprise. In a lower class society, the present is all important; and caste prevails; lines are hardened in terms of birth and color, because almost all being lower class, men feel threatened by one another. Instead of groupings in terms of degrees of superiority, men seek to maintain their groupings artificially. On some levels, it may mean a social register; on another level, it is neighborhood hostility to an outsider. Thus, the more "equal" men become because of their present oriented, lower class inferiority, the more they divide one from another. Then caste lines are resorted to in order to freeze society; socialistic legislation is used to freeze the economy; the church tightens its laws and works for unity in order to constrict and limit the power of truth; the schools tolerate everything except a Christian upper-class, future orientation. Then the city, the focal point of progress, becomes the focal point of decay and death.

But the power and the word of God cannot be bound. God requires change because He requires progress, sanctification, development, and growth. His people are called to be "pilgrims and sojourners" here, because they are forbidden to absolutize the moment or the present, but must move forward as citizens of that city whose builder and maker is God. The present must be reshaped in terms of the future. The hymn writer, Henry F. Lyte (1847), in "Abide With Me", reflected a Greek, not a Christian perspective, when he wrote of "change and decay" as though they were two things of a kind. Decay must be coupled with death; in this world, change is essential to life and growth, basic to a future-oriented and Biblical faith. The lower class mentality and its cities have a destiny of decay and death. Is that your choice?

CHALCEDON REPORT NO. 62
October 1, 1970

We have in the last two Reports, been analyzing the significance of an upper class and its decline, and the growing victory of the lower class mentality. Our concern now, as we study the lower class mind, is to examine the popularity of two very different peoples, the American cowboy and the Polynesian.

In America today, the cowboy is a popular television hero, and a national symbol of sorts. The sheepherder, on the other hand, has no like prestige, nor does the farmer. We must remember too that the cowboy's prestige does not include the cattleman, except to a minor degree. The cattleman, the ranch owner, is a responsible, independent man. The farmer too is a man who must exercise foresight, patience, and diligence to survive and prosper. The despised sheepherder is actually only a hired hand, like the cowboy, but with a difference. The sheepherder must live with the sheep in a sheep-wagon, doctor and care for them, living alone continuously. He must thus be a responsible, patient, and future-oriented man. Significantly, few young Americans ever become sheepherders today. The pay is good, and, after ten or more years of such work, a herder who has saved his money can go into some enterprise of his own. Few Americans are so future oriented or patient. Most sheepherders must be imported: Basques, Greeks, and some Mexicans. After a period of time, these herders retire to their homeland as well-to-do citizens, or they go into ranching or business in America. Many of the most important citizens of the Western inter-mountain areas of the U.S. are ex-sheepherders, or their sons.

On the other hand, it is rarely ever the case that a cowboy saves up his money to go into his own enterprise. Many cowhands have only the clothes on their back; they are drifters, gamblers, and present-oriented spendthrifts. But it is the cowboy's very lack of foresight and law, his heedlessness of responsibility, which makes him a folk hero today.

The modern mind is existentialist. It is concerned with the moment, not the future. It despises thrift, patience, and enterprise. John Cage has recommended to other musicians and composers that the proper approach to writing must be a "purposeful purposelessness". The arts work towards a breakdown of rational control, purpose, and meaning. Robbe-Grillet has called for the end of the "universe of signification" i.e., the world of meaning, in the arts, so that we have, according to Erich Kahler, the jeopardy of language itself and the triumph of incoherence. We have, he states, "the outspoken attempt to produce incoherence...What these movements ultimately arrive at, what in the end they want to accomplish is the total destruction of coherence, and with it the deliberate, and that means, the conscious destruction of consciousness." (Erich Kahler: *The Disintegration of Form in the Arts*, p. 95f. New York: Braziller, 1967.)

Returning to the cowboy, he is a natural rather than a philosophical existentialist, and as a result he is a television hero. On television, the cowboy is, naturally, not a married man; marriage means responsibility; it means the necessity of thinking about someone other than yourself. Moreover, the television and movie cowboy rarely solves problems: his answer is the gun. Thus his "solution" is in effect war and revolution, not a constructive development. The cowboy hero wipes out problems: he does not solve them. Having left death and destruction in his wake, dead men, rooms turned into a shambles, and grieving people he gets on his horse and rides on. There is no thought of reconstruction.

The future-oriented, upper class man knows that every act today has implications for tomorrow. His actions are aspects of a planned life, and he is highly conscious of what the future may bring. As a result, his actions are responsible and future-oriented. He "counts the cost" as a religious duty, because Jesus Christ requires it of His followers (Luke 14:27-33). To count the cost means to recognize that we live in God's universe of law, and that ideas and actions alike have consequences. Any man who fails to count the cost is a fool, and a lower-class mind, whatever his wealth or social position.

A generation which is lower class in outlook will seek lower class heroes, and, as a result, the cowboy is its folk hero. Another kind of person widely idealized in our time is the Polynesian. From Melville's day to the present, the Polynesian has been to many people a citizen of paradise, a person living in a beautiful sexual heaven where there is neither work, responsibility, nor consequence, only erotic and dream-like native girls to titillate their idiot imagination.

Dr Robert C. Suggs, anthropologist, has recorded some data about Polynesian orgies (he regards them as a wonderful people): "Much of the really heavy drinking done by the adults was done in the spirit of contest to see who could manage to drink under the table the husbands of the most accessible females and still remain conscious enough to possess the victor's prize. Many such contests soon became sexual orgies, with discretion and custom thrown completely to the winds; wives took lovers right beside their dead-drunk husbands, young boys lured women of their mother's generation into the bush, and even incest prohibitions were transgressed." (Robert C. Suggs: *The Hidden World of Polynesia*, p. 110. New York: Mentor, 1962, 1965.) This is the appeal of Polynesia to the lower-class mind, and not only hippies but young executives are busy trying to turn the Western world into a new Polynesia.

The lower class mind is not future oriented because it does not recognize that it lives in a world of law. To the extent that any culture departs from Biblical faith, to that extent it becomes lower class, because it denies God's sovereign counsel and law, and it is therefore not future oriented. Only to the extent that man recognizes that the world is under God's law does he at every point then plan and act in terms of that law. Lower class religion, economics, politics, and all things else deny that any absolute law exists which can bind man. Man must move in terms of the moment and human need, according to these humanists. Instead of a future conditioned by God's law-word, by supply and demand, by economic realities and basic laws, the future is seen as entirely made by man. Man makes his own law, his own future, and his own consequences, according to humanists, in radical contempt of any law alien to man.

But when man strips the world of meaning, he also strips himself of meaning. This is very sharply apparent in the writing of archeologist Geoffrey Bibby, *Looking for Dilmun* (New York: Knopf, 1969). Bibby gives an interesting account of a great ancient civilization, beginning about 3000 B.C. and dying about 1000 B.C., whose name was even unknown to us for 2400 years. In conclusion, after describing his work, Bibby wrote:

> And when, one day, it will all have been said and done, when the last basketful of earth has been carried up from the diggings, and the last word of the last report written---what will it all have mattered? That Dilmun has emerged once more from the mists of oblivion, that we can cross the threshold which Uperi, king of Dilmun, trod, look up at the fortress walls that guarded the emporium of all the Indies---what does it matter? Does it matter who the people were who, in the dawn of our time, opened up the trade routes from Meluhha to Makan, from Makan to Dilmun, from Dilmun to Sumer? For two and a half millennia even the fact that they had been was forgotten, and the world went on happily enough, unaware that it was unaware. Among all the lost volumes of human history, what is one lost chapter more or less?
>
> They are dead and gone, these merchant adventurers of another age; and neither the archaeologist's trowel nor the pen of the chronicler can bring back the argosies that once sailed the blue waters of the Arabian Gulf. It can matter as little to them as it does to us, that now once more we know a little of their doings, a few of their names. (p. 383)

How long can research and science endure when the work men do has no meaning because the universe is for them meaningless? The sickness of the world of science and learning is this sickness of meaninglessness.

Men whose lives are meaningless are incapable of making sound decisions. In fact, they postpone decision-making. Intelligent men make decisions because their future-oriented thinking calls for responsible actions. A crisis confronts them with live options, and they decide in terms of a planned evaluation of alternatives. The lower-class reaction to a crisis is to postpone decision in the hopes that the crisis will go away: he wants "time" to solve what he is morally required to solve. (The September 1970, IMF meeting's answer to the world's economic and monetary crisis was to "mark time".) The lower-class man floats with the current because he will not look beyond the moment. According to Solomon in Proverbs 16:22 (Berkeley Version) "Prudence is a fountain of life to its possessor, but folly is the chastisement of fools." The fool is the man who does not consider consequences; his mentality is lower class.

Class is thus not a social issue, nor is it related to a social register. All too many whose names are in a social register are lower class descendents of upper class ancestors, who now coast on an inherited name and wealth.

Class is ultimately a religious matter. It is the recognition that the world is God's world and therefore under God's law. At every point we must therefore count the cost; we must be future-oriented, otherwise we are trash, "neither fit for the land, nor yet fit for the dunghill; but men cast it out. He that hath ears to hear, let him hear" (Luke 14:35).

History is God's handiwork. If man and nations do not reckon with the future under God, religiously, politically, economically, ecologically, and in every other way, they will wind up on the manure pile of history. Is that your destiny?

"Awake thou that sleepest, and arise from the dead, and Christ shall give thee light. See that ye walk circumspectly, not as fools, but as wise, redeeming the time, because the days are evil" (Eph. 5:14-16).

CHALCEDON REPORT NO. 63
November 1, 1970

We have been analyzing in our recent Reports the meaning of upper class culture. An upper class is the future-oriented element in a society; the term upper class does not mean members of a social register; such people are all too often lower class and present-oriented today. An upper class is made up of those who have a realistic and future-oriented perspective; such people forego present pleasures in terms of future goals and plans. They plan and execute their affairs in terms of providing for a future for themselves and for society under God. An upper class provides the spiritual and material capitalization of a society; a lower class decapitalizes a culture. Because a lower class is present-oriented, it uses up inherited spiritual, intellectual, and economic capital without any realistic planning for tomorrow. The lower class man dreams about the future; the upper class man works to bring it into being.

The relationship of agriculture to class is a very important one. Farming and ranching require a certain amount of foresight in order to operate at least passably. Historically, the fact that the suppliers of food have been lower class has meant that food has been a chronic problem in world history, and most people have lived at the bare subsistence level.

In England, under George III, an important change took place in agriculture. Britain, defeated by the American colonies and while apparently declining into insignificance as a power, actually began to revive and moved ahead to its greatest strength. The agricultural revolution was a basic aspect of this change. Agriculture had been a meager way of life for many people. Now lords and gentlemen saw their lands as fields of investment and as areas for skill and scientific management. The sandy soils of eastern England were made highly productive. Robert Bakewell defined a sheep as "a machine for turning grass into mutton." As White notes, "Nothing less than aristocratic patronage and resources could have achieved the transformation of agricultural organization and technique within the intensely conservative society of rural England at that time." Even King George III began to patronize agricultural reform and to be proud of the title, "Farmer George." (R.J. White: *The Age of George III*, p. 10f. New York, Walker, 1968.)

Some have bewailed this agricultural revolution: it forced many poor tenants off the land, into the cities or to America. The half-starved tenants found work in the cities, and the Industrial Revolution had the man-power to move ahead. Those who bewail the conditions of the working class then forget that it was a major step upward for them, economically.

This continuing agricultural revolution has taken a major step forward in recent years, especially since World War I. It is a fallacy of the lower class mind to see things in terms of numbers, by counting noses. We are told by such people that half the labor force was on the farm in 1900; as recently as 1945, one third of the U.S. population was on the farm; now it is less than ten percent, and, especially with the move of the Southern Negro into cities, it is dropping even lower. But does this mean the decline of agriculture in importance to the economy? In reality fewer men are producing more food than ever before. According to Drucker, "The main engine of economic growth in the developed countries during the last twenty years has been agriculture. In all these countries (excepting only Russia and her European satellites), productivity on the farm has been increasing faster than in the manufacturing industries." (Peter F. Drucker: *The Age of Discontinuity* (p. 5) New York: Harper & Row, 1969.) The steel industry is second to agriculture "as a moving force behind our recent economic expansion," and steel faces problems because of obsolete methods. Railroads, electronics, plastics, and other areas of industry all lag behind agriculture, where a smaller labor force has steadily increased its productivity. The American expansion, as well as the Japanese, has been possible because agricultural progress has supplied the country both with food and a released labor force to make industrial growth possible. Japan, with 60% of its population in farming at the end of World War II, now has barely 20% on the farm. Drucker feels that "a period of very fast increase in farm productivity for the developed countries may be just ahead" (p. 14). Agriculture has become in these countries "the most technologically advanced and the most industrialized of basic industries" (p. 111).

The results of this development are important. In America it has meant that less and less of a man's income has had to go for food, since food has been produced more cheaply. In lower class cultures, a major portion of a man's income has to go for enough food to survive. Today the percentage of income spent for food is at an all time low in the U.S., but with a larger consumption per person. This releases more money for other expenditures, or for capitalization. As the *Farm Journal* has observed, "Our amazing farm productivity is a chief reason for our national affluence. Americans can spend 86 cents out of every dollar of personal income for things other than food. "In India where they have only 40 cents left per dollar after buying food, the economy can't get off its back. Russia has a third of her work force tied up producing food --- she can marshal resources to go to the moon, but it's a disappointing trip to the Russian food store." Moreover, "Farmers are industry's best customer, using each year 1/2 as much steel as the automobile industry; enough rubber to put tires on 85% of the new cars; and more petroleum than any other industry. Farming employs more people than any other industry and is the biggest customer for the products of the nation's workers. In 1970, farmers' production expenditures will reach $40 billion --- with another $32 billion of family spending." (*Farm Journal*, October, 1970, p. 62) One reason why many businessmen who try to enter into agriculture lose heavily is because they are not accustomed to operating as carefully and narrowly as farmers and ranchers.

What does all this mean? It means that, while the urban culture of the cities of the Western world has declined from its status as the vanguard of civilization and become steadily an area of lower class culture, the country-side, once a lower class area, has become progressively middle and upper class in character. There is a significant trend of once great industrial families to the land, to successfully operating farms and ranches. The fact that agriculture has had proportionately fewer federal controls has stimulated its growth as an area of freedom and enterprise.

This does not mean that the future of agriculture is assured. The

California grape strike and the lettuce strike represents an important indicator. California wages are higher than those of other states. The strikers have asked for much more per hour than grape pickers of any calibre regularly make. The key lies elsewhere. The productivity of California has made it America's chief supplier of foods; in some products, 90-100% comes from California; in very many, over 50% of the nation's supply is California grown. Control of California farm labor, and the ability to strike and to stop the flow of that produce to market, could, in a general strike, produce food rationing across the United States in a fairly short time.

There is much more that can be said. The 1970 corn blight is straw in the wind. Abuse of the soil and its micro-organisms, plus hybrid plants (more productive sometimes but also more vulnerable), has been a part of a growing present-oriented perspective which mines the soil rather than developing it. Oil companies and their subsidiaries are now major advertisers in farm periodicals (in one case, an owner apparently) and their products have been heavily promoted. Short-term gains have been real; long-term consequences are probably equally real and a potential threat.

Rural conservatism has also eroded. The county and small town church long remained Christian when its city branches were captured. Today the dry rot of unbelief has infected the countryside.

The man firmly grounded in Scripture is future-oriented; he is required by God to be responsible in all things, redeeming the very time of day as a religious duty. For many generations, Puritan children and many Americans were brought up on Isaac Watts' *Divine and Moral Songs for Children*. The first, third, and fourth stanzas of one of the best known read:

How doth the little busy bee
Improve each shining hour,
And gather honey all the day
From every opening flower!

In works of labor or of skill
I would be busy too;
For Satan finds some mischief still
For idle hands to do.

In books, or work, or healthful play,
Let my first years be past;
That I may give for every day
Some good account at last.

I can recall, while a student at the University of California at Berkeley, hearing a degenerate professor of English read this poem as a prize joke, and the large class roared with laughter. A new generation, a lower class, had been born and was being bred to despise work, thrift, and responsibility.

We should not be surprised at what has happened in recent years. Each area of the upper class mentality is being overwhelmed and destroyed by the lower class, of which the modern university is a major representative.

A recent murder of an entire family had as its excuse only one fact: they were rich, and the murderer hated them for it. (The murdered man had begun in very poor circumstances, unlike the murderer.) The lower class mentality is given to envy; its action is basically twofold, to spend and to destroy. A lower class culture is thus easily led into revolution as its solution to problems.

Our need today is for a new upper class. It cannot be created without a thorough and systematically Biblical faith. Christian reconstruction begins with man, regenerated in Christ and then proceeds to re-ordering the world.

CHALCEDON REPORT NO. 64
December, 1970

When Louis XIV came to the throne, he felt that the monarchy was threatened by France's powerful nobility. One of his central policies thus was to undercut the power of the nobility. He attached the nobility to his court and gave them a great variety of functions which seemed to confer favors on them. As Dr. Wolf remarks, "It became important who 'gave the King his shirt,' who 'held his candle at night,' the service of his table; even the bringing of the 'pierced chair' took on solemn overtones." What Louis did was to separate "the reality and the *mystique* of power and position" so that finally, in the next century, the nobility had become of a parasitical class without meaning to the real life of the nation." (John B. Wolf: *Louis XIV* (p. 270f). New York: W.W. Norton, 1968.) From powerful lords who managed vast estates and helped govern France, the nobility was reduced to social butterflies who gambled, danced, and drifted from one sexual escapade into another. What Louis XIV had done was to destroy the nobility as an upper-class and reduce them to a lower-class mentality. From being a future-oriented group of leaders whose planning might run counter to the wishes of the crown, the nobility was reduced to a group of ineffectual, present-oriented incompetents who were a hindrance to the life of the nation.

This process was furthered by two things: *first*, the association of work with something beneath the dignity of a gentleman, and *second*, the secularization of society.

To consider the first, a gentlemen came to mean a man who did not work but lived off an estate. This meant, practically, that he lived off the past accomplishments and work of his family, and the present work of underlings. This meant that a gentleman was clearly lower-class, that is, not future oriented; rather, he was intensely present-oriented, sensitive to matters of dress, appearance, and impressions made on others. The gentleman lived for the moment, and to be heedless of the future was made into a virtue. As early as in the days of Louis XIV, fortunes were gambled away carelessly at the tables of Versailles. Earlier, in the Renaissance, Castiglione had set forth the standard for the courtier, a relativistic standard. The important thing was not a faith, but an impression made on others, not meaning but the impact of selling one's self, salesmanship on a courtly level. In the 18th century, the expression of this faith was the "dandy", and in the 20th century, it is the existentialist, who has formulated the same faith into a philosophy. Thus the French novelist Alain Robbe-Grillet "feels that nothing is so fatal to literature as a concern with 'saying something.'" According to Robbe-Grillet, "The world is neither significant nor absurd. It *is* --- quite simply." (*Time* December 2, 1966, p. 419.)

This ties in with the second aspect, the secularization of society by humanism. If God is denied, then man lives in a world without meaning, a world without law, without standards, and without purpose and direction. The future offers no grand design unfolded by God. The culmination of humanism is relativism: since every man is his own god and law, then no one law is truth, since every man is his own private truth and law. The only thing that matters is the moment, since *existence* is all that man has in a world without meaning. In a relativistic world, where absolute standards and law are denied, men look at the world through out of focus binoculars; everything is blurred or unseeable. Relativism destroys vision and standards; it produces a present-oriented, lower-class mind.

A lower-class society becomes a *political society*. Because the majority of men have become lower class and are incompetent in the basic task of social planning, the state is given the functions of individuals, and state planning replaces individual and social planning. Where people are unwilling or incapable of planning for the future, this task is handed over to the state. But statist planning is *political planning* and is thus present-oriented and lower-class. The purpose of statist planning, whatever its declared goals, is to gain votes and assure political power. The state therefore aggravates the already existing evil: it adds to the incompetence of a lower-class people the burden of a radically lower-class national policy. How extensive this deterioration of functioning power is on the statist level was indicated by statistics issued by the vice-president emeritus and former business manager of a middle western University, according to which "$1.00 of relief to a needy individual through a private volunteer agency costs seven cents; through a Municipal Welfare, twenty-seven cents; through a State Welfare Agency, one dollar; and through a Federal Welfare Agency, two dollars" (*The Review of the News*, Nov. 4, 1970, p. 20). Statist planning, (or welfare) being always primarily political planning, the political cost is high, whether it be welfare or road construction. The more society is politically governed, the more incompetent it becomes in coping with its problems.

The lower class mentality also dominates education, and to the degree that education is state controlled, to that degree it represents education into a lower-class world and mind. The academic community today is an example of the lower-class mind; it is relativistic, existential, and politically oriented in its problem solving. The academic community has steadily withdrawn from the world with contempt. All too often, where men cannot compete successfully, there they run down the competition by contempt. The academic community thus approaches the world only with revolutionary contempt and hatred. A century ago, scholars wrote for the world; thus, the great historians expected to be read by literate men everywhere. Since then, the academician has progressively written for other scholars, not for the public; he has written to gain academic approval, not to apply knowledge to problems. The scholar is usually so busy protecting his statements from possible criticisms by other scholars, that all too often he says little or nothing. The Marxists have at least had the courage of their convictions and have sought to be relevant; much of their influence on students has been due to the fact that they have at least been plain spoken.

Education as a whole, however, because it has become relativistic, existentialist, and state controlled, has been the major means of creating a lower-class society.

A society can drift into a lower-class culture and, in pride, maintain that it is on the high road to greatness. Spain gives us a classic example of this. Ferdinand and Isabella united their kingdoms and sought to make Spain "Spanish" and Catholic (Ferdinand almost certainly was in part Jewish.) The "Moors" were expelled; the number of Moslem conquerors who came to Spain much earlier numbered only 25,000 at the most; by 1311, of the 200,000 Moslems in Granada, only 500 were of Arabic descent, according to an Arabic document. Powerful Moslem, Jewish, and Christian families regularly inter-married to consolidate their power and alliances; all were equally "Spanish." But, in the name of "purity", the Moors were expelled, then the Jews, and finally the Germans (who had helped Charles V bring Spain to greatness), and only "Spaniards" were left, of supposedly pure blood. (The question of pure blood could never be asked of the royal family!) In brief, only "gentlemen" were left. The businessmen and the farmers of calibre had been run out. As the Catholic historian, Heer, has pointed out, the results were disastrous: "The Spanish did not cultivate the land. Agriculture in Spanish hands declined catastrophically. Until the nineteenth century there was no such thing, strictly speaking, as an economy. In the fourteenth and fifteenth century the Spanish left this to the Germans, the Revensburg Trading Society and the Foggers, and then to the Flemish. Later they had to leave it to the French, the Dutch, the English, and the Americans. The Spanish built cities, monasteries, and palaces, as settings in the world theater and as suitable trappings for its world-spectacle."

(Friedrich Heer: *The Intellectual History of Europe*, (p. 255) Cleveland: World Publishing Co., 1966.) Spain lived parasitically off its colonies. Its standards became those of the picaresque novel they produced, the clever opportunist who lives without work.

This same prolonged drifting cannot occur now. Every modern country, virtually, is a modern "Spain"; it is substituting grandiose ideas and plans for production, and the result is a steady decline everywhere into socialism. But socialism is by nature imperialistic; since socialism cannot produce goods successfully and economically, it must expropriate. Expropriation at home is followed by expropriation abroad. The imperialism of the Soviet Union is a necessity: it is its means of gaining fresh capital. As the other powers move deeper into socialism, they too will extend their area of expropriation. Just as the lower-class man steals casually to make ends meet, so too does the lower-class state.

Our answer to this problem cannot be political: that is the lower-class answer. This does not mean that we abandon politics, but that we recognize that politics is a reflection of the life of the people. The answer is essentially religious and moral. No election can make men future-oriented; only a living faith in the sovereign God can do this. A scholar, in analyzing the thinking of colonial Americans, has remarked on their amazing confidence. Whatever their problems, they were confident that men who moved in obedient faith to the sovereign God would triumph, that neither the hostile forces of nature, Indians, nor a tyranny in England could long survive in a battle with God's freemen. Very simply, they believed that victory is built into the universe for God's people. They were thus future-oriented: they built for the future. They kept diaries and records faithfully for unborn generations. Rev. Samuel Hopkins dedicated his "Treatise on the Millennium", i.e., on the era of the triumph of the Gospel, to the people who should be living then; he expected that golden era to come not too long after the year 2000.

In 1930, in *The Book of Journeyman*, Albert Jay Nock said "We have hopefully been trying to live by mechanics alone, the mechanics of pedagogy, of politics, of industry, and commerce; and when we find that it cannot be done and that we are making a mess of it, instead of experiencing a change of heart, we bend our wits to devise a change in mechanics, and then another change, and then another." Men are trying to enter the Kingdom of God by manipulation rather than regeneration.

Men have moved in fear rather than in faith, and the courage of faith. In II Peter 2:5 we are told that God "spared not the old world (before the Flood) but *saved* Noah." The word translated "saved" can be better rendered "guarded." In the face of all the hostility of that world, we are told that Noah was guarded or preserved, because he had been called to a new world, and to rebuild in that world, and Noah was faithful to that call.

Men who seek to survive are doomed; their interest is in their own skin, and they are a form of lower-class mentality. Men whose desire is to rethink and to rebuild under God are men geared to life and faithful to the Lord of life.

Whatever men may do, God cannot be dislodged from the throne of the universe. If God is our Savior, then He is also our sustainer and vindicator. We can face the future in the confidence of His government, and we must at all times, think, act, and rebuild in terms of that certainty. "If God be for us, who can be against us?" (Rom. 8:31).

CHALCEDON REPORT NO. 65
January 1, 1971

A lower class culture is generally politically oriented; its major concern is with the state, and it sees the state as man's instrument for regaining paradise. The state is given a paternal role: as father, the state provides cradle to grave security for its children. A statist culture is thus a lower class culture, childish and present oriented.

This does not mean that politics and the state are not important, nor does it mean that we should neglect them. The fact that sound nutrition and good eating habits are important does not mean that we should become gluttons and live to eat. Similarly, the importance of politics by no means can be made a justification for statism.

A political society is one in which politics takes precedence over all things and governs all things. This is exactly what Lenin required, declaring, "Politics cannot but have precedence over economics. To argue differently means forgetting an ABC of Marxism." (Cited by Liu Piao: *Report to the Ninth National Congress of the Communist Party of China*, Delivered on April 1 and adopted on April 14, 1969, p. 60. Peking: Foreign Language Press, 1969.) In a political society, politics governs economics.

It also governs education. Just as economics is made to serve political goals, so is education. The school becomes an instrument for the control of the people, or, as James G. Carter, co-founder with Horace Mann of statist education in America, stated it, "an engine to sway the public sentiment, the public morals, and the public religion, more powerful than any other in the possession of government." (Carter: *Essays Upon Popular Education*, p. 49f. 1826. See R. J. Rushdoony: *The Messianic Character of American Education*.) The purpose of controlling education becomes, not to further education, but primarily to increase the control by the state over the people.

A political society also seeks to control religion, and a major target of dictatorships is always the church, which is either suppressed or controlled. Man's religious independence from man, his allegiance to God, and his strength from God, are challenges to the state's claim to be man's only lord and savior.

Similarly, the family is controlled, and the independence of the godly family is viewed with distrust.

A political society inevitably moves towards totalitarianism. Before World War I, an Englishman, A. G. Gardner, in *The Pillars of Society*, described Theodore Roosevelt as the consummate politician. He quoted Roosevelt as follows: "The most successful politician is he who says what everybody is thinking most often and in the loudest voice." In a *godly* society, a politician moves in terms of higher law and his conscience, with a sense of responsibility to God and to man. In a *political* society, Roosevelt's definition holds true: the politician is the voice of the crowd.

When the United States was founded, its leaders feared the crowd mentality. Thus Mason, Jefferson, and others feared the growth of cities because they feared a crowd culture, a lower class society. Others like Hamilton felt rightly that cities were not the problem but the minds and hearts of men; as a result, Hamilton began to work towards a Christian Constitutionalist party to develop a godly and responsible electorate. His death cut short his efforts. The rise of humanism and the erosion of Biblical faith destroyed both upper and middle class culture in city and country alike, and the entire country began to develop into a politically oriented society and a lower class culture.

Where there is no restraint of a higher law, politics soon becomes the art of people pleasing. Instead of statesmanship, politicians manifest only a desire to gain votes by pleasing the crowds. The upper class mind is future oriented; it plans practically in terms of long range goals. The lower class mind is present oriented; it thinks primarily in terms of the satisfaction of present needs.

Today we have no lack of intelligent politicians, but they are almost all present oriented because little else gains votes. Politicians and people, priests, pastors, and teachers, are alike present oriented and lower class in mentality. The socialite and the welfare recipient differ only in wealth; they are alike in thinking essentially of today as the truly lower class people they are.

A lower class society is like a ship without a rudder; being geared only to the existentialist moment, it is driven by every wind. It does not give direction to life but takes direction from the weather. As a result, it is catastrophe bound.

The lower class mind, moreover, does more than drift into catastrophe: it provokes and invites disaster. The man who plans practically, with religious vision and hard-headed economic knowledge, knows that it takes *time and work* to realize a dream. The lower class mind, being politically oriented, despises both time and work. If it wants something, it seeks to realize its utopia by political action. The only major result of such political action is more taxes. The result; disillusionment and despair, and then a revolutionary rage. If the television set does not work, kick or smash it; if the political order does not produce on demand, burn and destroy it. If the old order is destroyed, then, miraculously, a new paradise will emerge from the ruins.

The lower class mind, the political mentality, is a gambler's mind. The key to the future lies in a gambler's hope, a miraculous break which will reward the gambler. Work is thus avoided to play the political slot machine. Let us finance John Doe, who will save our country if elected. The fact that John Jones, John Johnson, and every other financed hope has failed them does not register with them. Can a lower class electorate elect anyone but a lower class politician? But the gambler does not believe in logic or the odds: his hope is in miracles, godless miracles. Thus, he pins his hope, come every election, on another great "white hope."

Feeling and fantasy begin to govern such a nation. To be reasonable is regarded as the epitome of sterility and reaction. People begin to cultivate experience for experience's sake. Perversions, pornography, new taste sensations, more and more flamboyant dress, an emphasis on the perpetually new, these and like emphases mark the lust for experience, for satiation in terms of the present.

A present oriented people grows heedless of the consequences. We are safe today: why worry about national defense tomorrow? We eat today: why bother about planning ahead? A present oriented economy is thus of necessity inflationary: it burns up past, present, and future assets in terms of its demands now.

One of the chronic problems of mankind is that it has usually been dominated by a lower class mentality, whether ruled by kings, oligarchs, dictators, or democrats. The lower class mind is ultimately the mind of Satan, a denial of causality, a declaration that man is his own god, and an insistence on the existential moment. An upper class society can only develop where a truly Biblical faith governs men, where the absolute lordship and saving power of the triune God is recognized, and His sovereign law acknowledged. Where there is no respect for, obedience to, and delight in God's higher law, there can be no upper class mind or vision. Where men acknowledge with pleasure that the world of men, of physics, economics, biology, politics, and all things else are governed by God's law, there men will be future oriented and will be upper and/or middle class in outlook.

The significance of God's absolute law is that it requires a future orientation. Law speaks of consequences, of penalties, of rewards for obedience, of life and death, success and failure. Because law indicates causality, it requires that men who respect law analyze cause and effect and be governed by that knowledge. To reject law is to reject the past and the future.

A purely experiential religion thus stresses the mystical or emotional feelings of the moment; it derides time and history. An experiential economics is only or largely concerned with needs, not with the practical matters of supply and demand.

The politics of the new left and of the old left is an ugly expression of romanticism and the romantic depreciation and denial of time, history, and, above all, law in favor of experience and the moment.

Preaching in the church has long been aimed largely at generating experience, too little towards teaching God's law. Many evangelicals cite Joseph A. Seiss as their mentor, but Seiss, in his lectures of 1859, declared there could be no preaching of grace without a teaching also of the law. The goal of Christian redemption and action he held, is "Restoration" (Joseph A. Seiss: *Holy Types; or, The Gospel in Leviticus*.)

Restoration or reconstruction requires the law, for law is the instrument, in every area, of planning for the future practically. We cannot expect to live long by taking poison, nor to prosper economically by denying sound economics. The redeemed man therefore plans to structure his life and future and that of his society by means of God's law.

Earl Warren recently called for a "new civilization". He asked for a new law order in which men "become truly partners in a new creation --- creation of a new heaven and a new earth---better than any which preceded it." ("Earl Warren Asks 'New Civilization'," Los Angeles *Herald-Examiner*, Monday, December 14, 1970 p A-10) Warren has for years worked to use the courts to further that "new civilization" of humanism. Warren's new heaven looks, unfortunately, more and more like the old hell.

The most beautiful cathedrals and building always represent not only beauty, but planning, work, and dedication. To expect a happy future by electing John Doe is to court disaster, a habit with the lower class, political mind. To work, slowly, patiently, and under law to establish godly order and justice, to maintain and develop all things under law and with patience, is to assure, not paradise today or tomorrow, but progress steadily towards a world under God's law. This our purpose. Is it yours?

CHALCEDON REPORT NO. 66
February 1, 1971

No society has yet existed without its share of lower class people, that is, persons who are incapable of a future-oriented life and who are often parasitic in their living. Very often, the number of upper and middle class minds in a culture has been very limited, a thin strata of future oriented and planning minds governing and directing the vast majority of men. The remarkable progress of Western civilization in the 19th century was due to the fact that great numbers of people moved into the ranks of the middle and upper classes. Society was radically altered; instead of a limited number of men governing a culture, an increasing number of self-governing and foresighted men were rapidly expanding the potentialities of man and society in every area of life. The result was a great era of progress. The ranks of the lower classes of Western countries shrank markedly, especially in the United States, where society, as the community of men whose vision was of a prosperous, developing, and expanding future, came close to including most men, and, in some areas, almost all. The American mission of "manifest destiny" was to spread civilization, religion, and liberty to every corner of the continent, if not the whole world. (See Frederick Merk: *Manifest Destiny and Mission In American History*. New York: Knopf, 1963)

The school was a very important aspect of this vision. A future oriented people believed emphatically that education was basic to a people with a mission. The purpose of the schools, from grammar school on through the university, was to educate for leadership, to prepare the man of the future for his responsibilities. Schooling meant dignity and a status. Commencement exercises were a great joy to parents, especially of immigrant children: the student had now advanced a step towards the upper class, into the ranks of those who govern rather than are governed.

Men shared a vision of a world transformed by religion, education, and free enterprise into a realm of liberty and progress in which all men dwelled together in contentment and prosperity. It is easy to criticize various aspects of this vision today, but the fact remains that the 19th century did witness vast strides in conquering age-old problems of human society. There was not only a very extensive material progress but one of the greatest advances in Christian missions in history.

Today, however, a very real cultural counter-force is in operation. The ranks of the lower classes are again growing because of the collapse of the upper and middle classes. Civilizations decay when the leadership falters and fails, when its upper class abdicates its responsibilities or abandons its character.

The school as the agency of creating the upper and middle classes of the modern era has become the great mass producer of a lower class mentality, of a present-oriented generation. The modern academic community presents an ironic picture. On the one hand, there are monumental buildings and beautiful grounds which echo the old vision of planning and order. On the other hand, there are the unkempt minds and bodies of the faculty and student body to set forth the new contempt for the old order. It is as if a barbarian horde has captured the temples of an ancient faith. Some curious facts confirm the change. The intellectual today is more susceptible to propaganda than are other people. There is also a correlation between vulnerability to hypnosis and education. Instead of strengthening the mind for leadership, education today weakens it and makes a man a better follower. Occultism, astrology, and other forms of ancient superstitions have had a ready receptivity among educated peoples. Whereas once the educated man derided these things, today he tends to show interest in them and promote them. More and more universities are adding courses on magic, astrology, and other superstitions to their curriculum.

What has happened? Why have the schools created to educate an upper and middle class become the great creators of new barbarians, of the most powerful lower class in history?

The reason lies in the studied rootlessness of modern education. Because the intellectual is at war with Biblical faith, he is at war with the past; he rejects it as lacking his own enlightenment. In terms of modern thought, enlightenment begins by a denial of God. This denial of God is accompanied by an assertion of the autonomy of man and his reason, his mind, and this autonomy means a deliberate rootlessness, a calculated severing of ties with the past. In other cultures, the lower class mind was rootless because it was too poorly educated to have root in the past, and too indifferent religiously to think and plan in terms of a religious faith. As a result, such a lower class mind cuts itself off from the past and from the future by default. The new lower class of the modern intellectuals cuts itself off from the past by choice, by a revolutionary choice and act, and is more rootless than any previous lower class. This rootlessness is reinforced by its philosophical existentialism, its exaltation of the moment, of the present, and its attempts to cut off that existential moment from any influence from the past and from any fear of future event. As a result, the intellectuals are rapidly becoming the most truly lower class element civilization has yet seen.

Not only is there a rootlessness grounded in philosophical principle but also in emotional hatred. The intellectual refuses to see himself as a true child of his past. As Molnar has pointed out, with reference to Sartre, he sees himself as a "bastard", an outcast and an enemy to the past. The bastard mentality, anti-bourgeois, revolutionary, non-conformist, and perpetually at war, is made into the modern hero by the intellectuals. More than a hero, he is also seen as the new prophet. "The new philosopher abandons the traditional role of the *teacher* and assumes that of the *prophet*." Instead of investigating and communicating immutable truths, this bastard-prophet gives a vision of a new world which depends on the ruin of the present order. (Thomas Molnar: *Sartre: Ideologue of Our Time*. New York: Funk & Wagnalls, 1968.) This vision is a vision of hate, and even love is defined as hate by Sartre. In *Le Diable et le bon Dieu*, Sartre defined love as the "hatred of the same enemy." To love is simply to be united in hatred of God and His order.

Not surprisingly, the new barbarians, like Lenin, Trotsky, Stalin, Hitler, Mao, Castro, and others, emphasize, not truth and justice in establishing a new order, but the power of "charisma" (miraculous power) by commanding personalities. (See L. Clark Stevens: *est, The Steersman Handbook*, p. 130. Santa Barbara: Capricorn Press, 1970.)

The goal is *freedom*, but freedom as defined by Hitler and Stalin is not freedom as defined by Christ. Almost 30 years ago, de Rougemont saw clearly what freedom had become for modern man: "For most of my contemporaries, Liberty is the right not to obey. When they are given this right they are bored and clamor for a tyrant." (Denis de Rougemont: *The Devil's Share*, p. 97. New York: Pantheon Books, 1944.) This is it exactly. For an upper class mind, freedom is the opportunity to plan and work realistically for future goals and to create a personal and a social order in terms of those goals. Freedom becomes the condition for work and planning: it has a function in terms of the present and the future. For the lower class mind, freedom is "the right not to obey", and the right to disrupt and destroy an order that requires obedience.

Obedience is a future oriented virtue. Children are taught obedience because they must be schooled into living with reality and mastering it. Dictatorships require obedience from their subjects in order to further their plans for the present and the future. Obedience comes into its own in a free society, where men by an inner discipline commit themselves to practical work and planning for the future. Such men maintain this discipline in the face of disappointments and frustrations, because the ability to use failures and setbacks profitably is an aspect of their future oriented nature.

Philosophically, therefore, our schools today are grave diggers, committed by principle to destroying the past and to denying that God's absolute laws govern man's past, present, and future. Dr. Timothy Leary is a true product of the modern university and has a natural appeal to a generation educated into the rootlessness he represents. In a New York meeting, Leary once declared, "We do not pray to anyone up there but to what is inside ourselves...Let us go back and free the world from good and evil...Then we are all through with the good-evil thing and you will be reborn." (Diana Trilling, "Celebrating with Dr. Leary," *Encounter*, June, 1967.) This is the dream: dispense with good and evil, with all absolute law, and live as "free" men in a world where moral law, economic law, all law is destroyed in favor of "free" man, man with a total right not to obey.

As men face a world collapsing around them because the lower class mind, like a plague, is infecting old and young, they have two ways out. *First*, they can retreat into pessimism and despair. They can recognize the hopelessness of dealing with lower class minds and surrender. This is easy to do. A particularly vicious young hoodlum was killed by police recently in a gun battle. The record of violence by this teen-aged criminal was a serious one. The mother, with no criminal record, is proving herself even more depraved than her son. She is demanding action against the police, who fought in self-defense, for killing her murderous son. Her son could rob, maim, and murder as a part of his right not to obey, but she refuses to recognize the right of the police to require obedience to the law and to use force to protect the law, innocent victims, and themselves. Such an attitude becomes daily more prevalent. It is easy to become discouraged. But to surrender is in effect to deny God; it is to deny that He is on the throne, and that "Of the increase of his government and peace there shall be no end" (Isa. 9:7).

The *second* course is the realistic one: to rebuild. Are the schools our grave diggers? Then we must build new schools. Already, every year, more and more children and youth are being educated in Christian schools and into a Biblical perspective. The future belongs to those who prepare for it, not to those who destroy it, or who fear it.

Only as future oriented men, men of God, begin each in their calling, to rebuild all things in terms of their faith, can there be any restoration or direction to history. We will never regain that direction if we wait for the majority to join us; we are then only weathervane men, incapable of doing more than responding to the winds of history. We shall be driven instead of driving. We will then, whatever our professed faith, have joined the lower class. The reconstruction of schools, families, churches, civil governments, and vocations will be accomplished only as men under God feel that they have no other alternative but to act. Then, by faith, as free men whose calling it is to command the future for God, they will, a step at a time, accomplish His purposes in history.

CHALCEDON REPORT NO. 67
March 1, 1971

American Indians are the subject of much romance as well as much prejudice, so that it is often difficult to make a realistic appraisal of their cultures. So much in Indian history suggests remarkable abilities: men like Joseph Brant, Tecumseh, Chief Joseph and others were clearly men of rare abilities. Or the other hand, despite evidences of a superior genetic inheritance, Indians are on the lowest level of American society all too often. Very early, Indians showed an amazing ease of adaptability; they recognized the horror Europeans in America felt towards their cannibalism and torture, and they readily took on the mores of their surrounding settlers. They usually showed, however, an inability to unite; they were divided into hostile and warring tribes, and within each tribe the various bands were often more uncongenial to one another than to the European settlers. Then too, despite their intelligence and ease at adaptation, they failed to develop beyond a certain point, and, in all too many cases, became a part of the lowest class in American life.

It is important for us to understand a central cause of this failure, because it is very closely related to the rapid slide of all America (and Western civilization) into a lower class status.

Indian cultures had a fairly uniform concept of child rearing. As Wallace has noted of the Seneca Indians of the colonial era, early observers noted that "Parental Tenderness" was carried to a "dangerous Indulgence."

Punishment was lacking, and "Mothers were quick to express resentment of any constraint or injury or insult offered to the child by an outsider." Moreover, "such control as the child obtained over its excretory functions was achieved voluntarily, not as a result of consistent punishment for mistakes. Early sexual curiosity and experimentation were regarded as a natural childish way of behaving, out of which it would, in due time, grow." (p. 35). Freedom was important to the Senecas and other Iroquois. "The intolerance of externally imposed restraints, the principle of individual independence and autonomy, the maintenance of an air of indifference to pain, hardship, and loneliness --- all these were the negative expression, as it were, of the positive assertion that *wishes must be satisfied, that frustration of desire is the root of all evil.*" (Anthony F. C. Wallace: *The Death and Rebirth of the Seneca*, p. 74. Italics added. New York: Knopf, 1970.)

The situation has not greatly changed since then, as I can witness, having spent eight and a half years on an Indian Reservation among two Western tribes. I never saw a frustrated Indian child; perhaps an Indian baby cried at some time, but I cannot recall it. The baby or child was fed when it wanted to be fed; it was not denied but was rather indulged at every turn. The love for and delight in children was real and sometimes moving, although it was obvious how unhappy the consequences of that indulgent love were. I found the Indians a lovable people, of real ability and more than a little charm, but the *permissiveness* of their society guaranteed their continuing unhappy and low estate.

An unfrustrated child is inescapably in for trouble. It is impossible to live in a fallen world where conflict of wills is a daily problem, and a minor one in the face of our major world and local problems, without having frustrations. Discipline in childhood is a schooling in frustration and a training in patience and work. Discipline not only prepares us for frustration but gives us the character to work towards overcoming frustration. Permissiveness in child rearing thus avoids frustrating the child only to insure continual frustration for the adult.

The reaction of the Indian to frustration from very early times was escapism, and alcoholism was a major form of such a retreat. The more the Indian met frustration, the more readily he became an alcoholic. It was at the request of Indian leaders, who were aware of their people's weakness, that prohibition of liquor for Indians (now repealed) was legislated at the beginning of the last century.

In American society at large today, the same permissiveness in child rearing prevails. Earlier, alcoholism was more often linked, among white Americans, to an intense perfectionism. Such alcoholics were or are very capable, hard-working men frustrated because they make too great a demand of themselves and life. Now, increasingly, the alcoholic is a product of permissiveness, of his or her inability to accept a world of frustration and overcome it. Instead of too much drive, it reveals a lack of drive.

Similarly, sexual immorality was and is a serious problem in Indian life. Indians who deplore it are often guilty of it, but they find themselves too weak of will to maintain the standard of fidelity they admit is best. As a result, Indian family life is regularly shattered by dissension and conflict. The inability to deny themselves leads to greater unhappiness and frustration.

Increasingly too American life as a whole sees a like pattern. Permissiveness in the home, church, and school has created an undisciplined people who feel that freedom is license and that degeneracy is health. A popular singer expressed the feeling of the age in a half-sobbing song which said at one point, "Don't deny me."

A common consequence of permissive societies is a high suicide rate. Suicide is the ultimate in self-frustration. Anyone who has talked with would-be suicides knows how intense their self-pity is. Sometimes their problems are very real, and at other times appallingly trivial. In either case, there is an inability to accept frustration and an overwhelming self-pity that life should bring them to such a pass.

Suicide is historically very common among American Indians, and some have seen this as evidence that their origin is in the Orient. Rather it is a mark of their permissive culture, and, as religious faith has declined in Western civilization, and as a permissive, humanistic society has grown, suicide has increased.

A permissive society lacks the capacity to overcome problems, because it retreats into liquor, narcotics (peyote among the Indians), sexual immorality, and a criminal and revolutionary rage whenever frustrated. Dr. Nathan Ackerman (whose viewpoint is not ours), in commenting on the great depression, remarked, "In those days, regardless of impoverishment, there was more constraint of behavior. I cannot imagine looting thirty-five years ago. Despite want, the patterns of authority prevailed. Today, those standards have exploded. Looting and rioting have become sanctioned behavior in many communities." (Studs Terkel: *Hard Times, An Oral History of the Great Depression*. p. 219. New York: Pantheon Books, 1970.)

We thus have today a more affluent society than ever before, yet less capable of accepting frustration than ever before. As a result we now have what Dr. Gunther Stent has called "a view of the end of progress." Progress is an impossibility where there is no patient work to overcome obstacles and to improve on things. Both revolutionary rage and narcotics represent forms of escapism, of a refusal to cope with problems constructively, and both are evidences of a lower class mentality.

One of the problems facing anyone who works with people today, young and old, is this radical lack of discipline and the lack of ability to meet frustrations realistically and to overcome them. The desire of most people is to walk away from problems. But nothing does more to increase the problems inherent in a society and constant to a man's life than the refusal to meet them head-on and then work patiently to overcome them. To ask for a trouble-free, unfrustrated life is to ask finally for death, and, before death, a lower class, slave status.

Slavery has been a constant problem in history. Many slaves have been victims of kidnapping and war, but many more have been victims of their own demand for security. As Sir William M. Ramsay long ago pointed out, the Romans wanted slavery; serfdom began on the imperial estates. "The paternal government was 'Salvation'." In fact, the entire concept of salvation was in essence a form of slavery to the emperor. "The 'Salvation' of Jesus and Paul was freedom: the 'Salvation' of the Imperial system was serfdom." (Sir W. M. Ramsay: *The Bearing of Recent Discovery on the Trustworthiness of the New Testament*, pp. 191-198. London: Hodder and Stoughton, 1920.)

This is no less true today. The salvation of modern man is some form of socialism, some form of slavery to the state. The state is asked to guarantee man against frustrations and is given increasing powers for that purpose. The more the state does, however, the deeper the discontent grows, because a permissive culture intensifies frustration as it increases gratification, because it thereby decreases man's ability to bear up under any kind of inhibition or trouble. Today people increasingly "fall apart" under less and less tension and trouble. Like the Senecas, they see frustration of desire as the root of all evil, and, short of becoming themselves God, they are inescapably doomed to frustration by their human estate.

Christian reconstruction thus begins in the home with godly discipline. The influence of Biblical law on Hebrew life and society was an important factor in their society, and the lingering respect for and obedience to that law has given Jews an advantage in Western history. The advantage of that law-discipline was once basic to all Western civilization, but it is now being rapidly eroded. An upper class is the product of a law and discipline which gives it a practical future oriented perspective. Too often, however, such a class, having arrived at power, seeks "liberation" from discipline by living for the moment, by treating immorality as a prerogative of wealth and power. As a result, it cuts the vital nerve of its power and rapidly declines into a lower class mentality which is easily toppled by any serious challenge.

Wallace reports that, in 1657 the Jesuit chronicler of the Iroquois mission wrote, "There is nothing for which these peoples have a greater terror than restraint." (p. 38). Much the same can be said of modern man today. Freedom is seen as freedom *from* law, not freedom *under* law. Man's life then becomes a study in irrelevance, in an evasion of reality, because his concept of freedom is destructive and negative, not positive and constructive. Not truth but satisfaction then concerns man. Edward Dahlberg, in *The*

Carnal Myth (1968), wrote, "Ultimately, it is only style that is important." This is a concept of writing with Dahlberg; with many it is the program for life. Thus, in fine style, they march towards death and the ultimate frustration.

Let the dead bury the dead. Those who self-consciously make themselves a lower class encumber the earth; they are suicidal, and they shall perish.

Meanwhile, there is a social order to be reconstructed, frustrations to overcome, troubles ahead to be met and solved, and much hard work to do. This is the way of life, and of true joys also. Those who run out on problems have abandoned life. Have you?

The implications of this came to focus not too long ago on a television program. The master of ceremonies was talking to young school children, asking each in turn what they considered the best age to be. When he came to one little girl and asked, "And what age would you like to be?", she answered, "A baby." The surprised master of ceremonies asked, "Why?" "Because then people do everything for you." This is the modern dream, and even little children have caught it, to be an unfrustrated modern baby in a totally permissive world.

A neighbor of an internationally famous film director, currently in America, reported that it was not the nude sun-bathing or strolling which surprised her at this beach colony. The surprise was in other areas. The totally nude young mistress of the film director sun-bathes with a pacifier in her mouth.

At least the builders of Babel said, "Go to, let us build us a city and a tower" (Gen. 11:4), the City of Man. The builders of the modern Babel are working instead to build the City of the Baby, the Kingdom of the Child. They are working to create a social order which will serve as a grand pacifier for all our self-made babies.

So you don't like problems, troubles, and frustrations? Join the babies; you will have lots of company. And buy yourself a pacifier and go to bed. Get out of the way. The rest of us have work to do.

CHALCEDON REPORT NO. 68
April 2, 1971

A lower class society is one in which the spirit and will of the lower class predominates. Practically, this means that the society becomes present oriented and is governed by envy and class hatred. The lower class mind does not respond to excellence with respect or a desire to excel. Its reaction instead is to hate and to tear down, to level all things to its own status instead of seeking its own advancement by work and emulation. Instead of having working goals, either independent or imitative, the lower class mind responds with envy and hatred. Whenever a society sees the rise to power of a lower class, it also sees the growth of class conflict and social warfare.

When this happens, it is also a part of a parallel development on the upper levels of society, the breakdown of the upper classes. Power is turned into license, and responsibility is abdicated. The monarchies of old Europe, for example, had become thoroughly lower class; they were pleasure and present oriented, contemptuous of moral responsibility, exploitive of the poor, and heedless of the future. Instead of respect, they excited envy. The wealthy and the poor increasingly had a common social goal, to 'live it up', and to exploit the opportunities of the present without regard for the future. The poor envied the nobility, because they shared a common present-oriented goal.

Society was given a new leadership by the rise of a class of merchantmen, entrepreneurs, who were future-oriented, and social renewal and progress followed. Now, however, the decay of that class is again creating a growing mood of envy and class conflict. The basic answer to social problems is again the revolutionary and lower class alternative of levelling. But where class conflict begins to govern, progress wanes proportionately.

Some years ago, as a student, I recall hearing the passionate defense of his country by a foreign student. Someone had questioned the native ability of his people by calling attention to their lack of progress. His answer was in essence this: "We have a large number of brilliant men, many educated in America, but we do not have your religious situation nor your freedom. Certainly, we do not have your moral stature, so that credit and honesty in transactions is impossible. Policing is largely a personal matter; there is so much lawlessness, that a fair share of our income goes for bribery and protection. Survival and self-protection take up so much of our time and income, that too little is left for capitalizing society. We have the intelligence and resources, but we do not have the background of America's Puritan self-discipline, and so our capital and energies are dissipated and progress is difficult." He could have added that most of their energy also went into class warfare.

Consider the plight of North Ireland and of England today. Religious warfare in the one and class war in the other are destroying these countries. Industry is leaving; superior men are beginning to migrate elsewhere, and social energy goes into conflict rather than into progress. Where the commitment to social conflict is deep or total, peace and progress become difficult or impossible,

In the Soviet Union, class warfare is a matter of religious and philosophical principle. The ills of society are always ascribed to a hostile class. This means that there is a built-in inability to cope with problems, because the principle of responsibility is denied in favor of environmentalism. An evil, hostile class is always responsible. The bourgeois mentality is credited with pervasive powers and conspiratorial activities against the regime, and therefore unrelenting warfare is the answer. This warfare continues from year to year, but the inner problems are not resolved. Instead, they are aggravated.

In Western nations, class conflict is deepening. It is the lower class answer to problems. Instead of developing spiritual, moral, economic, and social capital, the people increasingly want to blame their ills on a clique, class, or cabal. Such groups exist, and a lower class society makes their spectacular rise to power possible. In a class warfare society, conspiracies and revolutionary disturbances proliferate, because every faction begins to see them as both the answer and the threat.

A society which assumes that class conflict is a natural and permanent state of affairs is doomed. It has lost the capacity to be a society or a community. Instead, it is now a battlefield in which all peoples are the potential victims. To demand class warfare is to commit social suicide.

There can only be a *society* where there is a harmony of interests. The word *society* in Old English meant what we now call *communion*. The Apostles' Creed before the Norman Conquest, read, instead of the modern "I believe...in the communion of saints," "And of the saintes the societie." Without either the saints (the believers) or the communion, there is no society.

The modern liberal is well aware of the need for communion; his goal is a society living in peace. His answer, however, is to ignore the fact of sin and conflict, and to insist on peace by enforced legislation. By neglecting sin, he neglects the roots of conflict, and by trying to legislate peace, he aggravates the conflict. As a result, the nation drifts deeper into class conflict.

Let us consider one aspect of that conflict, the racial situation. The attempts to force integration and to force segregation by law are very old. With Assyria, forcible integration was a policy of state. All these attempts failed when the social conditions militated against them. If two peoples were relatively equal and religiously congenial, integration quickly followed, despite all legal obstacles. Where the differences were marked, neither opportunity nor law was able to bridge the gap. Neither legalized integration nor segregation accomplish anything more than to aggravate a situation. To introduce the state into an area of personal, religious, and moral decision is to abdicate the harmony of classes for a statist imposition. If a person or if a people are inferior, nothing can compel their rise; if they have a potential, why prevent their development? Where there are religious and social reasons against mixed marriages, nothing can further such marriages as long as the faith and the society are strong. If these factors are invalid or disappear through disbelief, nothing can prevent integration in the short or long run. The energy expended on both sides to force by law what is an act of principle and based on a way of life is a waste of energy. To rebuild or to build a society, develop your faith. The modern answers are statist. The state takes over, for example, education, and then the factions struggle to control the state in order to impose their concepts by force. The result is class warfare. Where people are free to establish their own schools and do so, the decision is then their own. In statism, men try to decide for others, rather than for themselves.

A harmony of interests is not the same as an identity of interests. The goal of class warfare is to create an identity of interests, to level society to one status and a common interest. Such a society is of necessity totalitarian and equalitarian. A harmony of interests assumes a diversity of interests. This the totalitarian mind opposes. I recall, not too many years ago, at a symphony concert, listening to the many foreign tongues spoken in the lobby. A fair percentage of the music lovers were of foreign backgrounds. The resentful reaction of one person was "They're in America. Why don't they speak English?" Of such stupidity is class warfare begotten. Is there an obligation to hate their homeland in loving their new country? Must we have an identity of interests in order to be unified as a people? An identity of interests is not compatible with freedom, nor is it possible. A harmony of interests allows for the free, independent, parallel and unified development of classes and races according to their progress and achievement.

The *consequences* of a harmony of interests are social, economic, and political. Its *roots* are religious. Only when men share a common faith in the sovereign and almighty God and His government can they recognize a common law and destiny. Amos rightly asked, "Can two walk together, except they be agreed?" (Amos 3:3). One of the first steps towards a harmony of interests is for man to recognize that the government of all things is not upon his shoulders, but the Lord's (Isa. 9:6). This means that he cannot absolutize his thinking nor project his own will against history. God always remains the Lord. God having made all men, all races and all classes, has His purpose and His judgment in mind for all. Our duty is to fulfil our calling in our place and to uphold God's law-order in all things. The force of God's law must be maintained against all men, including ourselves. Our relationship towards other classes and other races cannot be essentially one of warfare, integration, or segregation, but basically one of a) requiring all to obey God's sovereign law, and b) proclaiming the saving power of the gospel to all men. Neither church nor state can require more than that legitimately. In class and race warfare, the warfare is first of all against God and His law-order. Victory in warfare can impose a truce, a cessation of formal warfare; it cannot bring in either peace or a solution. Nothing was settled by World War I, except to lay the foundations for World War II, which in turn has even deadlier consequences in store for the world. The drift is steadily into a more radical conflict and a greater loss of freedom.

We must therefore rebuild the foundations. We cannot assume, with the foolish liberals, that the response to their peace-making is peace. Their concept of peace is not God's peace, and it does not have His blessing. Neither can we assume, with many foolish conservatives, that the answer is in making war victoriously. To win a war no more eliminates our moral crisis than losing a war; it only eliminates an enemy outside, when the greatest enemy is within. Short term gains cannot eradicate major and abiding losses. A dying man who becomes conscious and talks briefly has not thereby escaped death. Our real sickness is moral and spiritual, and our real solution rests in a religious renewal, in personal and societal regeneration.

Envy, hatred, and warfare offer easy and ready answers to the lower class mind, but the results are short-term answers and long-term disasters. For the upper class mind, the answer is not warfare but reconstruction in terms of Him who said, "Behold, I make all things new" (Rev. 21:5).

The grace of God can keep us from envy and hatred. His grace can make us proud and content with the gifts and calling which is our inheritance from Him. We are what we are by the grace of God, and our being is His gift to us. "Thou shalt love thy neighbor as thyself" (Matt. 23:37-39) has four conditions, all of which are inseparably related. First, "Thou shalt love the Lord thy God with all thy heart, and with all thy soul, and with all thy mind. " Second, "Thou shalt love thy neighbor," and third, "Thou shalt love thy neighbor *as thyself*," meaning that you shall love yourself and be content and happy with what God made you to be. If a man hates God, he will also then hate himself and his neighbor, whatever his class or color. If a man loves himself, he will respect and develop his own abilities instead of envying another man his abilities. Fourth, "love is the fulfilling of the law" (Rom. 13:10), so that to love God and our neighbor means to obey God's law and to work 'no ill' to our neighbor. Deep and radical divisions exist in our world today; they will not disappear either by talk of peace or acts of war. The only remedy is the sovereign grace of God and man's response of love and obedience to God's law.

Envy is a form of hatred, and our world talks at length, and hypocritically, of love while it fosters and cultivates hatred.

Peace and love are by-products of our relationship with God; when these are made primary and are divorced from God, then they become a dangerous mask for a multitude of evils. We cannot have the gifts of God without the Giver. The lower class mind is very different from a working class mind. The lower class mind has appeared in kings and bishops, rich men and poor men, and it is essentially an existentialist mentality, living for the present and governed by the biology of man's moment rather than by the word of God. The peace and the harmony of interests the lower class mind aims at is a graveyard peace and harmony.

Before it is too late, we must examine our institutions and ourselves. Have we been contributing to class conflict and warfare, or are we working for a harmony of interests?

CHALCEDON REPORT NO. 69
May 1, 1971

An age without faith and the leadership of faith is like a rudderless ship. It will be driven by every current and is destined for shipwreck, unless it is repaired and given direction.

The central failure of the modern age has been the failure of the churches. In the United States, as nowhere else in the world, the culture should be dominated by the churches. The majority of Americans are church members. If we eliminate those who are modernists, we must still recognize that thirty to forty million Protestants claim to be evangelicals who believe that the Bible is the infallible word of God. No other group in America, however, has less impact on the national life. The communists, who are less than one percent of the population, exercise a deeper influence. But this is not all. The more this Protestant evangelicalism is "revived", the more irrelevant it becomes. The deeply rooted antinomianism of its pietism (and the same antinomianism or anti-law temper is apparent in Roman Catholic pietism, as witness St. Alphonse de Ligouri) has made it unable to work effectively in society. It has become present oriented and experiential. Its answer to problems is not the application of God's law-word to man and society but instead a yearning for more emotional experiences and supposedly charismatic manifestations. Such experiences have been pursued to the point of the demonic.

Jesus Christ required His followers to be good fruit-pickers "by their fruits ye shall know them" (Matt. 7:20). He came as the great redeemer to save His people by grace, in order to restore them to the way of sanctification, the law (Rom. 8:4; Matt. 5:17-18; Luke 16:17). The law of God is His future-oriented program for man and society; it is the means of warfare and conquest which God has ordained. The emphasis on experience as a substitute for law is antinomian and anti-Christian. The "Jesus freaks" who want to repeat with God what they experienced with narcotics ("Freak out with Jesus") are guilty of blasphemy as well as irrelevance. Their concern is not with God but with themselves. Quite rightly, the reviewer of one such leader's book commented, "after all the shouting and talking about God, it is Mr. B. (the hippy pastor-author), not our Lord who is the hero of the book." What people seek in pietist experiences is themselves and their satisfaction or fulfillment; what they seek in obeying the law-word of God by faith is His Kingdom and righteousness.

Pietism is a form of modernism. The open modernist finds his truth in the world, not in God's inscriptured word. The pietist formally retains that word but practically denies it. When science began to dominate the minds of men in the eighteenth century, it emphasized *experimentalism* as the main and even only source of truth. This idea infiltrated the churches, and "experimental religion" or revivalism was born. To "prove" his conversion, many American churches demanded experimental or experiential evidence in the form of a revival experience. Godly faith and law-abiding living were not accepted as proof. Christian schools were regarded with hostility as a breeding ground of formal or "head" religion as against "heart" religion, and the result was that the churches began their decline from relevance. From men who worked to bring every area of life and thought into captivity to Christ, churchmen became men who sought an emotional experience within and retreated from the world into the cell of their withdrawn souls. To such people, Christian schools and post-millennial thinking became horrors to be decried. From being the dominating and future-oriented leaders of society, the churches began their retreat to a lower class, present and experience oriented status. Even the Calvinistic, Presbyterians were conquered by the new trend. Faith was not enough for church membership; they began to require an "experience."

Not surprisingly, the whole tradition of pietism has been readily infected by existentialism (Kierkegaard and others among Protestants, Gabriel Marcel among Roman Catholics), and with good reason. Existentialism is simply a more honest and rigorous form of experimentalism and pietism. It emphasizes the moment, and the experience of the moment, in divorce from the past, all law, and all schooling and morality. Logically, Sartre and others divorce that experience even from God to bring about the total self-concern of the questing, experiencing soul.

Because of this emphasis on experience, increasingly the churches seek new dimensions of experience for their members, new forms of worship, "Jesus rock", participation in demonstrations, the experience of peoples of other colors, sensitivity training, and so on. "Social relevance" is to be found, they insist, in experience. A hard, systematic study of Scripture, the application of this knowledge of Scripture to the problem of communism, economics, race, political society, and family order is avoided. Not study, not an understanding in the light of Scripture of our world and problems, but an existential experience is held to be the answer. With amazing callousness and brutality, people are used to provide these experiences. Import some black children, they insist, into your Christian school or church, and give your children and adults a new dimension of experience. Trot out some minority groups into our groups, so that we can revel in our growing social experience. Like dolls that are moved at will by little girls in their play, so these churchmen want to treat people, as lifeless dolls to dance to their tune, so that their social experience may be enriched and fulfilled. Not surprisingly, the black response to this unfeeling integration game has been black nationalism and an ugly, hostile segregationism.

Into this world of a decaying church, Marxism made an easy headway. The conquests of Marxism have been largely violent and brutal. They have been grounded on conspiratorial and revolutionary action. This action has been made possible, however, by the default of all other leadership. The growing bankruptcy of the modern world made it susceptible to overthrow by any well organized group, because the real revolution had already occurred. That real revolution was the progressive abandonment and overthrow of orthodox Christianity by leaders and people. The forms of faith were retained, but the power was gone, and the collapse of the churches was rapid.

Marxism, despite its evils, was at least future-oriented. It had a plan and vision for man's future. As a result, it was able to capitalize on the spiritual vacuum of the twentieth century and to capture many superior minds.

The shallowness of its future-orientation became very quickly apparent wherever Marxism gained power, and the disillusionment of its followers has been very real. Moreover, Marxism has become, in every country where it has gained power, very rapidly and inescapably bureaucratic, a super-establishment. It moves in terms of power, not faith.

The results have been gradually apparent. The brutality of Marxist states has not abated and has in some areas increased. The hostility to Christianity has often been intensified. But a bureaucracy is not adventurous; it is usually concerned with protecting and perpetuating itself. It can be exceedingly brutal in its self-protection, but it lacks initiative, although it has momentum. Thus, the bureaucratic momentum carries world Marxism along the same lines established by Lenin and Stalin, but the bureaucratic self-protection makes it both resistant to charge and unwilling to risk defeat. A bureaucracy is thus present-oriented; as a result it can blunder into serious disaster because of its inflexibility and its inability to see consequences beyond self-perpetuation.

What happens in a world of present-oriented people? A basic lawlessness sets in. No law is recognized as valid if it does not suit the person or people. The situation becomes comparable to a busy intersection, where traffic lights are suddenly removed, together with policemen, and every driver races to the intersection as though he alone existed. The wise driver thinks ahead; the fool tramps on the gas pedal.

The failure of the churches, and the inner decay of Marxism, is matched by the decay of capitalism. As Irving Kristol and Daniel Bell have shown (in *The Public Interest*, no. 21, Fall, 1970), capitalism has declined because it has lost its basic faith.

We can add that most capitalists (like labor) are not libertarians. They do not believe in free enterprise but are instead champions of protectionism and subsidies. The rise of capitalism was an aspect of the development of Christian faith. Without agreeing with much or all that Weber and Tawney have written on the subject, it must still be granted that the development of capitalism had deep roots in Christian theology. Those roots are now largely gone, and with them the faith and the rationale that made for a society of dedicated entrepreneurs. Too often today, when a businessman talks about freedom, he is not too different in his basic premises from the new leftist student. His concept of freedom is not too closely tied to responsibility; it is merely a desire to be free from the state's regulation while reaping the benefits of the state's subsidies. When freedom as an ideal is divorced from independence and responsibility, it is not truly freedom but welfarism disguised.

Meanwhile, in this context of civil, economic, and religious irresponsibility, hatred flourishes as one group after another tries to push all the blame on a particular class, race, or group. That tensions and hostilities are a part of life, every wise man will readily acknowledge. That conflict is sometimes unavoidable is all too true. Under normal circumstances, law is the means whereby society controls hostilities and wages war against its enemies. Those who work to aggravate hostilities are fools. As Solomon observed, "He that passeth by, and meddleth with strife not belonging to him, is like one that taketh a dog by the ears" (Prov. 26:7). When you declare war, you had better be prepared to wage it. This is a lesson that many blacks and whites, and many working men and many employers, have failed to learn. It is an aspect of the lower class mind that it does not count the cost nor think ahead.

A future oriented man recognizes that, while many problems have easy and simple answers, few problems have agreeable people involved. "Your problem is very simple," said a simple-minded pastor once to a husband and wife who could not get along with each other; "you've got to learn to live with each other." How true, and how absurd! Men are not angels, and, sometimes, their problems will not disappear until they disappear, because they will not change. Even simple problems thus are often not simply solved. Passing a law, or making an obvious statement as that pastor did, is no answer.

Our progress in the past usually came slowly, and our recovery will come slowly. It will come as men, each in their sphere of action, begin the task of reconstruction. Reconstruction begins with our lives and God's grace; it extends to our vocations, our institutions, homes, and society. Life and progress are made up of a great number of little things; we cover a mile by small steps, and the surest move forward is that small step rather than a giant day dream.

Remember, a shovel turns over more earth than a wrecked tractor. Our religious, civil, and educational institutions are largely like wrecked tractors today. It is time then for shovel work, a great and exciting time when new foundations shall be laid, a world recaptured, and a future established by those who will work for it.

CHALCEDON REPORT NO. 70
June 1, 1971

Early in this century, an English scholar began to study the relationship between sexual regulations and cultural behavior. He was skeptical of the idea that there is a direct consequence, that chastity and monogamy produce a high culture and a superior class. As J. D. Unwin wrote, "Frankly, I hoped to dispel the idea, but I had not proceeded far before I was forced to conclude that the brave hypothesis probably contained an awkward and perplexing truth." Unwin was compelled by the data to revise his personal philosophy.

It is not our purpose to go into a detailed analysis of Unwin's study of *Sex and Culture* (Oxford Press, 1934). Very briefly, a society which permits its youth to be "sexually free" produces a low culture; where prenuptial and post-nuptial chastity are absent, the culture is on an exceedingly primitive level and manifests little intelligence, production, or foresight. As the level of sexual regulations increase towards a Biblical standard (although Unwin would not use that term), the level of culture improves. Where virginity before marriage and chastity after marriage becomes the standard, a high level of intelligence, culture, science, and religion appears. Unwin's conclusions were based on a study of every society for which sufficient data is available. The cultures studied included ancient civilizations as well as the American Indian tribes, African, South American, and Asiatic tribes and societies. Unwin also held that "The amount of energy that uncivilized people could display is the same as that of any other society; the amount they do display depends on the degree in which they have satisfied the necessary conditions." Moreover, "In human records there is no case of an absolutely monogamous society failing to display great energy." In fact, Unwin found "The relation between compulsory continence and cultural behavior...exact enough to be expressed by means of mathematical symbols." In three generations, by sexual license, an upper class can reduce itself to the lowest class level. Moreover, "if I am right in concluding that these potential powers can only be displayed under conditions of compulsory continence, such conditions cannot be unnatural."

Writing again in 1935, in a summary address on his work, Unwin, in *Sexual Regulations and Cultural Behavior*, saw a growing rebellion against the morality which alone produces an upper class culture. There was a possibility, if men retained their moral standards, of great cultural advance and a major scientific era. He added, however, "Soon there will be born into a new tradition a new generation that will probably submit to almost any external conditions so long as it is permitted to eat, drink, dance, copulate, and sleep as it desires. I hold no brief for social energy, which may or may not be desirable, but there can be no doubt that a study of human records reveals the fact that a group in such a psychological condition has never displayed a great energy, and that such ambitions are typical of societies in a state of little or no energy." Unwin's predictions were certainly to the point: we now have indeed a generation that does "submit to almost any external conditions" of filth and disorder as long as it is free "to eat, drink, copulate, and sleep as it desires."

The cultural changes Unwin describes were not the product of any rational decisions. No lower class culture suddenly decided to raise its status and then proceeded rationally to implement that change. Instead, the changes were products of religious conversion, a new religious faith, which introduced a new motivation and force into society.

Unwin, saw cultural energy as a direct product of moral standards and laws. It must be added that moral law is in turn a direct product of religion. As George Washington saw so clearly in his Farewell Address of 1796, every moral order presupposes a theological order. He wrote, "Let it simply be asked, Where is the security for property, for reputation, for life, if the sense of religious obligation desert the oaths, which are the instruments of investigation in courts of justice? And let us with caution indulge the supposition, that morality can be maintained without religion. Whatever may be conceded to the influence of refined education on minds of peculiar structure, reason and experience both forbid us to expect, that national morality can prevail in exclusion of religious principle." To deny this, Washington felt, was an attempt "to shake the foundations of the fabric," which he could not look upon with indifference.

Since Washington was making a political address, his argument was practical rather than philosophical, but it was still true; the basic faith of a culture determines its morality and character.

C. G. Jung, in the epilogue to *Modern Man in Search of a Soul*, wrote that "It is becoming more and more obvious that it is not starvation, not microbes, not cancer, but man himself who is mankind's greatest danger, because he has no adequate protection against psychic epidemics, which are infinitely more devastating in their effect than the greatest natural catastrophes." The "psychic epidemic" of our time is a lower class mentality, a rejection of work and discipline, and above all, a rejection of the sovereignty of God.

In the 1920s, Ortega y Gasset foresaw the rise of this new mentality, and, in 1930, set forth his earlier thesis in *The Revolt of the Masses*. He held that "the type of man dominant today is a primitive one, a *Naturmensch* rising up in the midst of a civilized world. The world is a civilized one, its inhabitant is not: he does not see the civilization of the world around him, but he uses it as if it were a natural force. The new man wants his motor-car, and enjoys it, but he believes that it is the spontaneous fruit of an Edenic tree. In the depths of his soul he is unaware of the artificial, almost incredible, character of civilization, and does not extend his enthusiasm for the instruments to the principle which made them possible." The scientific specialist of our day is also a barbarian: "He also believes that civilization is *there* in just the same way as the earth's crust and the forest primeval." As a result of this abandonment of "principle", Ortega said that "Europe has been left without a moral code." Of the talk then of a "new morality", Ortega said, "When people talk of the 'new morality' they are merely committing a new immorality and looking for a way of introducing contraband goods."

Ortega, Unwin, and others have seen the issue, but they have not looked to the answer. The morality or immorality of our day is a lower class phenomenon; it is a present oriented perspective which considers the future irrelevant and the present all important. John Lukacs, in *The Passing of the Modern Age*, has made an important point with respect to property. Ownership, or property, has lost its importance in modern society, and consumption has replaced ownership as a goal, but consumption itself has failed to satisfy modern man. We can add that consumption is a lower class goal; it is present oriented entirely, whereas ownership or property is a future oriented and upper and middle class goal; it represents work, planning, and capitalization.

This lower class morality cannot be replaced by a lower class religion. Even at its best, the "Jesus movement" is almost entirely lower class in nature because it substitutes emotionalism and enthusiasm for discipline and work. A man's religion can be defined as what he has when he is tired, discouraged, and disappointed; when hope and success are stripped from him, then his spiritual capital, or lack of it, is in evidence.

The average so-called Christian today has little or no spiritual capital when his happy-happy meetings, his lovely choirs, his beautiful churches, and his robed clergy are taken away from him. Not surprisingly, in his religion he is consumption oriented and lower class. Just as in the realm of politics, he wants the state to provide him with cradle to grave security, so in the realm of the church he wants similar provision. He wants to remain a babe in Christ, endlessly fed pious pap and given a religion, whether "evangelical" or "liberal", which satisfies his appetites as a consumer. The fallacy of socialism is that it assumes that society's problem is essentially one of distribution and consumption; it fails to recognize the priority of production, and, as a result, every socialist society is beset by problems it cannot solve. The *future* has a habit of becoming *today*, and the consumption oriented man eats up his inheritance from the past and sells out his future in order to "enjoy, enjoy," today.

Thus, much more than a religious revival is needed; what is required is a serious application of fundamental faith to every area of life; thought, work, and discipline are required, and the patient work of reconstruction. The smorgasbord principle is good eating at times, but, applied to religion, is false. Man is not sovereign: he cannot pick and choose what he wants to use in religion. God is absolute lord and sovereign, and man must obey Him whether it pleases man or not, and He must obey in everything God requires of him. Because of this smorgasbord principle in religion, a systematic theology is denied today, because it requires assent to the sovereign God.

A good way to see what modern thought means is to listen to Negro leaders: they echo, simply, directly, and bluntly, the basic faith and morality of modern man. John R. Coyne, Jr., in *The Kumquat Statement* (1970), cites a Negro student who was involved in serious acts of violence at San Francisco State as saying, "I've been denied so long that anything I take is right." This is a familiar and old refrain, heard by many pastors and counsellors as they deal with men and women seeking self-justification. The most affluent people of all history reek with self-pity. This cancer of self-pity is today apparent in the Negroes, the hippies, parents and children and in virtually all peoples in our society.

Not surprisingly, with a lower class generation, we are in difficult times, and many hold it against God that all is not sweetness and light. They want to walk by sight and have all problems eliminated in advance. Spurgeon wisely observed, "If we cannot believe God when our circumstances appear to be against us we do not believe Him at all. We trust a thief as far as we see him; shall we dare to treat our God in that fashion?"

Reconstruction must begin with our faith; it must continue into our institutions, Christian schools, homes, churches, vocations.

In 1940, Unwin, in *Hopousia, or the Sexual and Economic Foundations of a New Society*, saw less hope for civilization than in 1934. Writing in Hitler's and Stalin's day, he saw America as "the most degenerate of the white nations." While few Americans would agree with that judgment, his comment on the world scene is of interest: "The power of thought has diminished. The Press dictates, suggests, insinuates. A collection of highly selected data masquerades as news, giving a false impression of events. There is little real mental activity although there is a great deal of talk. The mob falls a ready prey to the oratory of demagogues who, in their will to power, create dissension in order to secure their ends. Numbers, that is quantitative criteria, rule everywhere; and since the rule by numbers always implies a rule by force, force is the weapon the governments use more and more. In international relations the rule of force is covered by words of idealism, but it is there." Unwin's only answer was a plea for a return to moral discipline, a futile plea to men without faith and without moral principles. Unwin's plea was pragmatic, not principled.

Because reconstruction must be principled, it must begin with God as man's priority: "Thou shalt love the LORD they God with all thine heart, and with all thy soul, and with all they might" (Deut. 6:5; Luke 10:27). It must then apply God's priorities to man's life and world, to his institutions and his practices. The goal Unwin desired comes not by pragmatic calculation but by moral discipline and religious force.

CHALCEDON REPORT NO. 71
July 1, 1971

Because more than a few have become aware of the growing decay of our world-wide humanistic culture, the concern for answers is extensive and intense. Some of the most anti-Christian leaders have expressed strongly religious hopes and answers. As Theodore Roszak, in *The Making of a Counter Culture* (p. 126), says of one degenerate writer's emphasis, "The cry is not for a revolution, but for an apocalypse: a descent of divine fire." The humanists need miracles and demand them, they want a radical change in everything except themselves. Even here, however, some humanists see the problem also. The young leaders of the May, 1968 Paris insurrection, Daniel and Gabriel Cohn-Bendit, in *Obsolete Communism: The Left-Wing Alternative*, write that "The real meaning of revolution is not a change in management, but a change in man." True enough, but who shall bring about that change in man? God is rejected, so this leaves man in control. Experiments using man as the test animal are already in progress. Is this what the Cohn-Bendits want? If man is to change man, some kind of coercion and inhumanity becomes inescapable. Man as he is becomes then only a raw material, a resource for the future, and is thus expendable.

Such an answer only enforces the call for more statism. Whether proposed by statists or anarchists, the insistence that man must change man is a requirement for statist coercion and control. Having abandoned God, the humanist has not thereby rid himself of his need for God. As a result, he makes the state into his new god. The state is a Moloch demanding the sacrifice of youth in every age, demanding that the priorities of the state become sacrosanct in the eyes of its citizens. The humanists may rail against the Establishment, but their only alternative is to become themselves the Establishment. In the new states of Asia and Africa, revolutions come and go. Each new set of leaders vow idealistically to institute a new order and soon reproduce the old evils. Nat Hentoff, who earlier wrote an idealizing campaign book about New York's Mayor John V. Lindsay, now finds Lindsay practicing all the tricks of the "power brokers" whom he once fought against. Men have a habit of remaining sinners, and neither state office nor state coercion can usher men into a state of grace. The statist answer is a moral and social dead end.

When God changes man by His sovereign grace, He then commissions man to change society by means of God's law. The rebirth or regeneration of man is God's task; the application of God's law-word to all of life is man's task.

There are today many earnest champions of reconstruction, concerned humanists who recognize that civilization is in decay. Because their answers are humanistic and/or statist, they inescapably fail, because they simply reproduce the existing evils. The answer is well stated in the title of T. Robert Ingram's excellent study, *The World Under God's Law*.

The financing of godly reconstruction is by means of the tithe (see Report no. 43). Social financing is an inescapable necessity. It will not do to rail against the state, welfarism, public schools, and other forms of socialism if we do not have a legitimate alternative. In every era in Western civilization when tithing declined, social financing was instituted by coercive and statist means.

During much of the medieval era, health, education and much more were all financed by means of the tithe. Later, under Puritanism, all these things and newer institutions, such as work-houses for job training, were products of the tithe. When state financing returned with the decline of Puritanism, the evangelical re-awakening led, in the early part of the 19th century, to an abandonment again of statist answers. W. K. Jordan, *Philanthropy in England, 1480-1660*, (1959) has given us an account of the English scene in that era. In the U.S., in the first half of the 19th century, voluntary societies, products of tithe funds, were formed to deal with every kind of social problem, provide Christian schools for immigrants, care for orphans, seamen, servants, and others, and to work to further the "Moral Government of God" in every sphere.

Whatever its faults, America then was a very free society, and its people were truly upper and middle class because of their emphasis on certain principles. *First*, they were future oriented as Christians who saw history in terms of God and a glorious and manifest destiny in terms of Him. *Second*, this purpose was to be unfolded by means of the voluntary principle, and those who believed in that future gave their money and their efforts to furthering it.

Social financing cannot be avoided. The state is ready to assume it as a means of power (as is the church); the tithe places the power and decision in the hands of the believer. State financing cannot be "abolished" unless it is replaced. The answer is therefore not legislation but Christian reconstruction. We cannot wait for people to vote the abolition of welfarism and the public schools; we must construct our own schools and our own more godly welfare agencies. Quietly and steadily, these things are being done.

Many of the older agencies, schools, and colleges have been captured by the humanists and statists. The best way to honor the memory of their founders is to carry on in their spirit by establishing new agencies, churches, schools and colleges. The lower class concentrates on the present and blames "the world" or the "Establishment" for all its problems. An upper class is too busy with the problems of reconstruction and the duties of every-day life to have much time for tut-tutting over the world. Every man who builds has his eye on the future, and he is busy making it for when tomorrow comes, it is his work that stands in it, whereas all the whining and complaining of the bewailers is gone with the wind. The world was not empty when we came into it. Other men have labored, and we have entered into their labors. Now, in a time of cultural decay, the need to rebuild is especially urgent, and, as always, it takes time, money, and work. Those unwilling to pay the price, and those who discourage easily, have no future. Let them eat, drink, and be merry, for tomorrow they die. Of such men Solomon said, "Give strong drink unto him that is ready to perish, and wine unto those that be heavy of heart" (Prov. 31:6). Nowadays, those who are "ready to perish" want marijuana as well!

Meanwhile, the work of reconstruction goes on all around you. True, new foundations do not loom as large as old structures, but they are there. But where are you? In the old structures, or building on the new foundations?

CHALCEDON REPORT NO. 72
August 4, 1971

Western civilization today is approaching the last days of the age of the state. This does not mean that the state will soon disappear, or disappear at all, nor does it mean that there is likely to be an immediate decline in the power of the state. On the contrary, the short run prospect is for vastly increased powers concentrated in the state, in the hands of civil government.

What it does mean is that the religious expectancy that the state can provide man with the saving power and answers to human needs and problems is waning. For some time now, humanistic man has looked to the state in the same way that Christian men once looked to God. Man's hopes have had a political answer. Political campaigns have had a religious overtone, and politicians and voters have talked about "saving" the country. That hope and expectancy is now waning.

Not too long ago, I had an opportunity to hear a discussion among business executives, only one of whom, an older man, was a conservative, of the injustices of various federal regulations. One man suddenly raised a hypothetical question: what would you do if a confiscatory regulation affected you? The immediate response was: conceal and lie; the general attitude was that the state is a potential enemy and an unscrupulous ally at best. The old man, a board chairman, quite emotionally disagreed. I was brought up, he said, to respect my country and to obey it, and, however wrong their action, I could not be disloyal or treat it as an enemy. To the others, the old man was a pathetic voice out of the past; they themselves voted to the left, but cynically. Their expectations of the state were cynical, short-run gains, nothing else.

Political power in the ancient world was religious power. The state was man's true church and even his god in some cases. Man's hopes could only be realized through the state. The ruler was in many cases believed to be a god, or else his office was divine, or the state was a divine order. In any case, man's savior was the state. When St. Peter declared, "Neither is there salvation in any other; for there is none other name under heaven given among men, whereby we must be saved" (Acts 4:12), he was not only affirming Christ as lord and savior, but denying at the same time that any ruler or caesar was man's redeemer. For Rome, the name of the caesar or emperor was the saving name, the name of power and redemption.

The collapse of Rome was twofold. There was, first, the collapse of belief in the saving power of Rome; the more power became centralized in Rome, the more its failure to cope with man's problems became manifest. The same is true today. The state increases its power, claiming that more power will enable it to solve man's pressing problems, but the increased powers only lead to more aggravated problems, and more cynicism and resentment among the people. The concentration of power in the state leads to the inner collapse of the state's authority. This same development occurred within the medieval church: the more powerful it became, the less it could solve its problems, and the greater the hostility it aroused. Finally, even the renaissance popes and their associates viewed their offices with cynicism and expediency. This inner collapse of imperial Rome was very vividly described by the Presbyter Salvian. Second, Rome fell physically because, as William Carrol Bark has pointed out, the millions of Rome did not feel it was worth defending against the tens of thousands of barbarians.

Today the state is again facing an inner collapse, a decay of authority. There was a time when young men were ready to die for their country, "right or wrong." The nation could command a religious sacrifice such as the Christian martyrs of the early church gave to Christ as they went to death in the arena. It is now becoming difficult for a nation to command loyalty even when it is in the right. The bitterness manifested by youth towards the state is often a religious bitterness, an iconoclastic desire to destroy a false god.

In the middle ages, the church at one time could bring forth a children's crusade. In more recent times, boys lied about their age to enlist in the armed forces. Now, they even maim themselves to avoid service. The causes lie deeper than the unpopularity of the Vietnam War, or leftist agitation, although both are important. The last "children's crusade" commanded by any state was in Red China, the use of the Red Guard, and it ended in disillusionment and serious trouble.

The authority of the state is everywhere in decay, but everywhere the state is grasping for more power as the cure-all for man's problems. The powers of the state are thus likely to increase markedly in the years ahead, but that increase is the forerunner of the state's collapse as man's saving agency.

The Roman Empire offered the masses "land and employment, food and money." According to Levi, this was a Roman application of an idea borrowed from Athens of the fifth century B.C., namely, "that the rulers of the state had a duty to help support the citizens." The function of the state's officers came to be "the collection and redistribution of money and property." (Mario Attillo Levi: *Political Power in the Ancient World*, p. 174f. London: Weidenfeld and Nicolson, 1965.) What men once looked to the gods for, the state now offered to provide. The popularity of such measures was enormous, and the benefits to the Empire very great, in that its authority was greatly advanced by the increased scope of its provisions.

The fallacy, of course, was a very simple one, and its effect was inevitable. The state is not god: it cannot create. To provide land and employment, food and money, the state had to tax and confiscate. It provided resources to the masses at the price of destroying the sources. The masses grew, and the producers declined. Faith in the Empire also declined and turned gradually into cynicism and contempt.

In every era, cynicism and contempt can lead to lawlessness, and disorder, never to reformation or reconstruction. Revolution and destruction can be spawned by bitterness and a loss of faith, but not progress. When an era has lost its faith, it seeks to find a substitute for faith in charismatic leaders, and political figures come to the fore whose only asset is their appearance, voice, or glamour. The political leader becomes essentially an actor playing an expected role. The commanding person becomes the substitute for a commanding faith.

Moreover, the more man becomes empty spiritually, the more he intensifies his demands materially. What was already impossible for the state to deliver becomes all the more so as men come to imagine that nothing should be withheld from them. Students in an elementary public school in Los Angeles told their teacher that they were "entitled" to the best homes in Beverly Hills and had a right to take them. After all, that was what democracy was all about.

To the man without faith, all things that are logically impossible to others become possible, because the discipline of faith is gone. The man who believes in the sovereignty of God and the godly uses of reason under God knows the possibilities as well as the limitations of human action. A madman often does not. Similarly, the man without faith has destroyed the old boundaries and landmarks, and his thinking has no discipline to it.

A telling cartoon recently depicted the irrationality of the Keynisian economics. A man, depicting the economy, was standing on the ledge of a very tall building. Behind him the fire of inflation promised death, and before him, the long leap down ensured death. A modern economist was calling out his advice to the harried man: "Jump slowly." Modern relativism, by denying the absoluteness of truth, has made it possible for people to believe that a man can "jump slowly." Relativism destroys the old distinctions and restores a belief in magic to an equal footing with long developed and tested knowledge.

Relativism also undercuts all loyalties. Not surprisingly, the state has been a major victim of the erosions of relativistic philosophies. When, early in the 1960s, a college president included, in a plea to dissident students, a call for "loyalty" to school and country, the only response was snickers. Few would now dare to make such an appeal. None of the old virtues can be invoked, and no new virtues have replaced them. Instead, a deep resentment and disillusionment prevails, and, whether it be the right, left, or center, various groups thrive today by capitalizing on resentment.

Resentment against what? It to hard to get a concrete answer out of many students. The resentment is against the "hypocrisy of the Establishment", the fraud of the social order, the stagnation of leadership, and so on. Issues may be cited, notably the war, but the resentment goes deeper than issues. According to Hebrews 12: 15, the alternative to faith is a "root of bitterness", a deeply rooted disposition which sours and pollutes the whole of a man's life. That root of bitterness is deeply imbedded in the mind of modern man. His hope, the state, is failing him. The Negroes and the students have demonstrated their bitterness by violence. Their only practical results have been to increase the powers of the state. At Berkeley, the effect of all the student violence has been to increase professors' pay and decrease their working hours, as a university bribe to retain their services under such adverse circumstances.

We are indeed in the last days of the age of the state; men are losing their hope in the power of the state to redeem and regenerate man and society. This disillusionment will grow deeper, but at the same time the power of the state will grow stronger. There will be no change until men change, until faith in the state is replaced with faith in the sovereign God, not until the law-order of God is recognized as man's only true environment.

The problem thus, while apparent in the political sphere most dramatically, is essentially a religious problem. It cannot be reduced to a church problem. To replace the state as man's savior with the church is surely no progress. The urge for institutional salvation and saviors is a desire to have gods that can be pressured, manipulated, and controlled. This is in essence paganism.

As we analyze the crisis of our age, it is well to remember that the contributions of the state have been real ones, as have been those of the church, Both have an important and continuing function, and a necessary one. The end of the age of the state will not mean the end of civilization but rather its revitalization. The greatest threat to civilization would be the continued power of the state a man's saving agency.

New foundations are being laid, and the future is as bright as the promises of God. God the Lord reigns, and He alone is sovereign. History is in His hands, not in the hands of the state and its charismatic leaders. To be without God is to be without hope: to believe and obey Him is to be certain of His victory.

CHALCEDON REPORT NO. 73
September 1, 1971

A great American business leader and philanthropist, William Volker, observed in 1918 that "Government must be restricted to those activities which can be entrusted to the worst citizens, not the best." These words ran counter to the developing statism of American life, but they reflected the historic American distrust of man and the state. America's Puritan heritage had left its mark on political life; Washington saw the state as a dangerous fire, useful if tamed and guarded, dangerous if unchecked. The purpose of the constitution of 1787 had been to chain down the federal government in order to free the people while having enough federal civil government for purposes of union and development.

The developing theology of the state in Western civilization gradually and steadily eroded the premises of American politics. In its place came the state as "the fatherland." The word "fatherland" does not appear in Noah Webster's 1828 dictionary; it came later from the Dutch and German, although like terms existed in French and other languages. In medieval and Reformation eras, if men spoke of anything like this, it was of God's eternal Kingdom. "Jerusalem the golden" (Bernard of Cluny), or "O Mother dear, Jerusalem." For the Christian, God was his Father by grace, and the term "mother" could at best be given to his homeland, which was first of all the Jerusalem from above. In pagan antiquity, the ruler was commonly man's god, father, and shepherd. Biblical faith warred against this religion of the state, and a new civilization emerged out of its victory, the "West." Anton Hilckman, in describing the ideas of Feliks Koneczny, contrasted the West and Asia, or Turanian civilization, stating, "The West and Turan are absolute, contrary poles. The deepest root of this opposition is a fundamentally different attitude towards man and towards the position of an individual in the human group. Turan does not know man as a person; it does not know any dignity of a person; the individual has value and importance only in his role of a component part of the State's organization. In Turanian civilization...there is, legally, no such thing as a society in existence; the State is everything. The European lives *also* in the State, the Turanian lives exclusively in it." (Introduction to Feliks Koneczny: *On the Plurality of Civilizations*, p. 27. London: Polonica Publications, 1962.) This difference, however, is not one of race or geography but of religion: Biblical faith gave the West presuppositions which undercut the ancient religion of the state. However, as that faith has waned in the West, the old pagan political theologies have returned. Rulers began to talk of the divine right of kings; their successors asserted the divine right of democracy and the masses: "the voice of the people is the voice of God." For Marxism, the voice of the divine masses is incarnated in the dictatorship of the proletariat and speaks infallibly through them alone. Thus, in place of God the Father of an elect people, the doctrine of the Fatherland and an elect party ruling it emerged. The powers of God and of man under God are being progressively transferred to the new god, the state.

In the process, God was ridiculed and denied. God's government was held to be unjust and partisan, because some were predestined to salvation and others to reprobation. Earlier, an Oriental story had made the same point. Some children were given a bag of walnuts, and they disagreed as to how to divide it, and the town sage was asked to do it. His response was, "How do you wish me to divide these walnuts among you? Shall I do it according to principles of divine or of human justice?" The children asked for divine justice. The old man then gave one walnut to one boy, two to another, a dozen to the next one, and then the whole bag to another. When the boys protested, the old man answered, "Did you not ask me to divide your walnuts according to divine Justice? And does not Providence always proceed in this manner when dividing her favors among mankind?"

The state offered a "better" answer. The state steadily gained increasing power in its effort to bring "true justice" to the human scene, and this true justice increasingly came to mean equality. Walnuts for all in abundance was the state's professed goal. Increasingly, the walnuts have ended in the state's coffers, and, instead of justice, the state has been seen as the source of increasing injustice. As Galore observed of the paternal state in 1898, it leads progressively to social hatred and dissatisfaction among the people, and insecurity for the state; everybody always is expecting from omnipotent managers virtues which nobody possesses." (Henry Galore: *The Paternal State in France and Germany*, p. 223. New York: Harper, 1898.)

The irresponsibility of the state is a product, not only of man's sinful nature, but of his humanism. The humanist faith is ably summed up in the motto of a publication by "Marxist Humanists," *News & Letters*: "Human Power is its own end." There is no god or law beyond man: therefore human power is its own end, its own law. Justice, as George Orwell saw, quickly disappears from such a faith, and all that remains is human power expressing itself as naked power, a boot stomping on a human face forever.

Humanism has not only worked to destroy religious authority of the older Biblical form, but it has undercut its own "rational-legal" authority. Henry Adams, early in the century, wrote that "it will not need another century or half a century to tip thought upside down. Law, in that case, would disappear as theory or *a priori* principle, and give place to force. Morality would become police. Explosives would reach cosmic violence. Disintegration would overcome integration. According to Schaar, the ethical relativism of the modern era is destroying it: "the modern man, having now reached nearly full development, is turning back upon itself and undermining the very principles that once sustained order and obedience in the modern state." Moreover, Schaar holds that "contemporary social science has failed to appreciate the precariousness of legitimate authority in the modern states because it is largely a product of the same phenomena it seeks to describe and therefore suffers the blindness of the eye examining itself." Justice in the modern state has come to mean material abundance for all and security for all in spite of their improvidence. Both states and people have become relativistic in their morality. Practically, moral relativism means, "What's in it for me?" Authority has been attacked as an enemy of liberty, but, as Schaar asks, "Can anyone today still believe that liberty expands as authority contracts?" With the breakdown of authority, civilization is itself breaking down, and liberty is waning. Schaar, whose viewpoint differs from ours very ably raises the fundamental question: "But it is clear for our time, as Philip Rieff has written, the question is no longer as Dostoevski put it: "Can civilized men believe?" Rather: "Can unbelieving men be civilized?" (John H. Schaar, "Reflections on Authority," in *New American Review*, no. 8, pp. 44-80. New York: New American Library, 1970.)

The state appeared on the scene in the medieval era as the unifier of civilization and as its defender and champion. The more the state has gained its goals and separated itself from Biblical faith and law, the more it has become the destroyer of civilization. Statist man, who sees the state as his father and shepherd, under whose care man shall not want, is progressively a new barbarian, welcoming statist measures which destroy his liberties and seeing these measures as great blessings.

Imperial salvation in Rome meant cradle to grave security on the imperial estates, where serfdom was born. For the imperial serfs, "salvation means to be delivered from the uncertainties of freedom into the blessed assurance of a welfare government which provided for their entire lifetime." As Ramsay pointed out, "The paternal government was 'Salvation' in the estimate of the cultivators on the estates...The 'Salvation' of Jesus and of Paul was freedom: the 'Salvation' of the Imperial system was serfdom." (Sir W. M. Ramsay: *The Bearing of Recent Discovery on the Trustworthiness of the New Testament*, p. 197f. Fourth edition. London: Hodder and Stoughton, 1920.)

As the state gains power to "save" man, it distrusts power in all other hands with increasing fervor. It is a serious offense, in the Soviet Union, to give private charity, because such gifts establish a bond between people which is a power outside the state.

An American historian, writing in 1944, satirized the new philosophy of work emerging among statist social scientists. According to Andrews, such men believe that:

> We must have an entirely new philosophy of work. Work must be recognized not as a virtue or a blessing but as an intrinsic evil.

> Work is power, and the modern trend is of necessity to subject power to increased social regulation and supervision.
>
> An automobile, a revolver, a medical or legal education, a fishing rod, are all embodiments of power of one sort or another. As such, society requires their possessors to secure a license or permit of some kind as a guarantee that the power will not be used to social detriment.
>
> When mechanization has been carried to its ultimate perfection, there will be so little of routine production left for human hands and minds to do that in all probability there will be actual competition for the doing of it for its own sake.
> (Matthew Page Andrews: *Social Planning By Frontier Thinkers*, pp. 56ff. New York: Richard R. Smith, 1944.)

Andrews foresaw a day when work would be distrusted and regulated by the state as an alien power, and attempts made by automation to "free" man from work in order to give the state unhindered control of power. His book today reads less like a satire and more like a report.

As the state has gained power, it has also lost authority. Heads of state are less and less revered figures held in respect and awe by the citizenry. More and more, as the modern era has advanced towards its logical end, the protection of heads of state from their own peoples becomes an increasingly more urgent problem. Security measures grow more and more severe in order to protect rulers, and, on both sides of the iron curtain, the state sees the people as an enemy and a threat.

The state everywhere now has power, in fact, steadily increasing power, with steadily diminishing authority. The state's power is like the gold of Toulouse: it brings shame, dishonor, evil and disaster, and calamity upon calamity. The state, like Oscar Wilde (*De Profundis*), has denied God and His law to hold that "the false and the true are merely forms of intellectual existence," and it has thereby made its own authority another myth as well. As a result, it has produced the new barbarian, who believes nothing, respects nothing, and works to destroy everything, especially the State and its "Establishment."

The state thus, while more powerful than before, and likely to increase very markedly in power in the immediate future, is increasingly in a state of siege. As it moves toward total power, it also incurs total guilt and total attack. To meet attack from its own "sons", the state has only an intellectual void and the power of the gun. In 1960, Daniel Bell wrote on *The End of Ideology*, and President John F. Kennedy, at the Yale Commencement, declared that man's problems were no longer ideological, religious, or philosophical, but technological. After Comte, he held that man had passed the age of religion or mythology, and the age of philosophy or speculation, during which times *meaning* was basic to man. In the age of science, technology or method is everything supposedly.

Against this emptiness, college students and others, themselves empty, have rebelled. The fatherland should provide life and meaning, but instead it offers death (or war) and a denial of meaning. Earlier marches and demonstrations were in effect cries of, "O Baal, hear us!" Now Baal is hated and bombed by a generation as blind and empty as Baal.

Men can kill and destroy out of hatred; they can only build in faith. Our statist age will continue to flounder in its meaningless and downward course, hating its false god while believing in nothing else. It will, like the Baal worshippers of old, mutilate itself while it assails also its false god, because it knows no other hope.

A Biblical faith, to offer man hope, must restore the dimensions of victory and insist on the radical responsibility of the believer to work in Christ to make all things new.

David Little has shown that, for the Anglicans of the 17th century, the Word of God and the Christian faith meant that which is "old"; to *conform* rather than *reform* was their concern. The Puritans, on the other hand, saw the word of God as ever fresh and new and as the continually reforming force in society. (David Little: *Religion, Order, and Law, A Study in Pre-Revolutionary England*. New York: Harper, 1969.) Not surprisingly, Puritanism triumphed as long as it maintained this faith.

A faith which hopes for escape from the world is doomed neither to escape nor to triumph. Those who, under God, are confident that the sovereign and omnipotent God has called His people to victory will experience both battle and victory.

History is not a spectator sport. There are no sidelines. It is a battle, and it results either in victory or defeat. Those who expect to escape, or to sit on the sidelines, will be the first victims. Why bewail the battle? Get off your duff and work for victory.

CHALCEDON REPORT NO. 74
October 1, 1971

When words, inappropriate for political application, become political slogans, they create impossible problems. One such word is *equality*. That word has had many meanings. Several Greek words are translated as *equal* in the New Testament. One of these, in Galatians 1:14, means "one of the same age", and others also have meanings very different from modern usage. The word *isos*, however, which appears in Matthew 20:12, John 5:18, Phil. 2:6, and Rev. 21:16, and *isotes* (equality) in II Cor. 8:14 and Col. 4:1, means the same in size, number, quality, and so on. It is in essence a mathematical term, and this is its meaning in Matthew 20:12 and Rev. 21:16, as well as II

Cor. 8:14 and Col. 4:1. The other usages indicate the identity of the persons of the Godhead.

But it was in the modern era that *equality*, a mathematical concept, became a political slogan. With the Enlightenment, mathematics became very influential as a standard for man's thinking. Some philosophers felt that thinking, like geometry, should proceed from axioms and theorems to inescapable conclusions. In mathematics, the equal sign shows a balance on both sides of a problem, and the problem is solved if it is proven that they balance. The idea of equality thus came to be an attractive idea for politics: solve the political problem by introducing the solving balance of equality.

The idea of equality, once introduced into politics, created a false dilemma and offered false alternatives. Men who opposed the idea of equality began to argue that inequality was the truth of the matter.

But the idea of equality applies best to a mathematical problem; it is an abstraction. Two plus two equals four; true. But do two Englishmen plus two Frenchmen equal four Japanese? Immediately the problem becomes absurd. Who are these eight men? Some may be criminals, others great men. In any case, how can they be equated? How can the diversity of talents, character, and usefulness be reduced to an abstraction? Can two trees plus two clouds equal four birds? If we are dealing with lumber, steel, and other standardized and manufactured items, the equal sign is a very important and necessary tool of science and business. Applied to people, it is meaningless. To talk about either equality or inequality is to reduce the human situation to a level of abstraction. Even more, it introduces a false perspective which can only damage society. Men will try to promote their ideas of equality and inequality with passionate intensity, and political discourse and action will be geared to myths.

What is the answer? Is Willie Mays equal to Richard Nixon? Is a plumber equal to a councilman? The question must be ruled out as meaningless. It obscures the basic fact, first, that God's law declares that rulers and judges must be no respecters of persons: their judgment must be in terms of the law, not in term of the wealth, poverty, or color of a man (Deut. 1:17, Lev. 19:15, etc.); in this respect, justice is blind to the status but clear-eyed with respect to the law. These human factors may or may not be important; they are, however, irrelevant to the law. Second, men are ultimately judged in terms of their relationship to God and His law-word, not in terms of their relationship to man's standards. Faith and character are thus central to a man and his society in any godly order; there is then a natural aristocracy of talent and character.

In a statist order, however, neither an organized majority or minority, nor any kind of independent aristocracy, are tolerable. In a statist order, lower must be concentrated in the state in clear-cut fashion. The facade may be "power to the people", but the reality is *power to the state*.

Since the Crusades, the state has worked to eliminate all other contenders in its quest for power. It has worked to level and cut down any group within the state that might be a rival to its ambitions, or which possesses independent powers.

Three early enemies were thus the feudal lords, the Jews, and the church. Feudalism meant localism and decentralization, and, to create the centralized power of the state, feudal power was steadily undercut. The Jews, as the builders of urban pre-Crusade Europe, represented too great a power, and thus the state worked to destroy the Jews. The church too represented a threat to the state because of its refusal to accept a subordinate and controlled status, and it too had to be undercut and brought under control.

The rise of nationalism, a by-product, furthered the unity of the state, and therefore minority groups and their 'ghettos', which were self-governing and independent areas, had to go. Cities were planned with straight streets so that cavalry charges could sweep them free of revolutionists, and guns mounted at intersection could cut down people from all sides. The state was religiously concerned with protecting and increasing its power.

Equality came to be a valuable tool on the part of the state in eliminating diversity within the state, and in undercutting areas of separatism. Thus, in the U.S., in the name of equality, the New Deal began to break up the Old South and its regional loyalties. A Negro voting bloc was created which, after World War I, began to grow in power. A statist order, however, can no more tolerate a Negro bloc than a white Southern bloc, and, as a result, integration became, not an idealist but a political step to break up bloc solidarity.

The effects of integration have too often been studied only by proponents and opponents of integration. Unfortunately, both believe that enforced integration is possible. From the days of the Assyrians, who moved nations and peoples about to homogenize their empire, to the 20th century, such attempts have been failures. People do not inter-marry unless a common faith, culture, and standard brings them together. Then, they cannot be kept apart. The Basques have not been independent for 14 centuries, but they refuse to surrender their separateness and their desires for independence. The Soviet Empire has regularly liquidated both people and party members for favoring their local national groups, but without success. The Ukrainians, Georgians, Armenians, and others still retain their separateness and their dreams of freedom.

In the U.S., a Negro leader who favors racial intermarriage stated that integration laws decreased the number of such unions and drove blacks and whites apart. Integration has not integrated. What has it done? It has introduced class divisions into the black bloc. By requiring a percentage employment of blacks, the civil rights laws have given a large number of blacks a middle class status and middle class aspirations. From a number of sources the reports have come of the results: a large percentage of these middle class blacks refuse to identify themselves with specifically black causes. They still go to black churches, visit with black friends, and create social organizations of their own, but these are essentially black *class* organizations. The reaction of many black political leaders has been resentment. The Black Panthers, Muslims, and others have reacted by calling for a black nation, black separation, and so on. They have rightly seen the statist course of action as more politics, than benevolent. Blacks scattered throughout a white culture are finished as a political force. If black so-called ghettos are broken up, then black revolutionary action is less likely also.

But these black revolutionists are themselves being destroyed by the state. Either by direct subsidies or through foundations, they are made dependent on the state, so that every black leader eyes all others with suspicion as a paid hireling. The black revolutionary leaders thus have a short-term popularity before they lose their following.

The black revolution is a hopeless, bought-out failure, but it is still a very important and weather-vane movement. The statist dream of instant paradise for all true believers when the right set of laws is passed has been broken. The bitter black disillusionment with the promises of the state has shattered the myth of a new Garden of Eden by statist measures. This disillusionment with politics is growing one. As a state senator, a Christian, remarked to me, of his fellow legislators, "Very few of these men believe any more in what they are doing." Their belief that politics is the way to the good society is dying or dead.

For more and more of the people, on both sides of the iron curtain, all over the world, the state is the enemy. It is the god that failed, and men are increasingly ready to smash their false gods.

The advanced stage of the statist dream has been of a scientific state. When Marx spoke of scientific socialism, the word "scientific" still had magic to it. But now, like the word "equality" and even more so, the word "scientific" has come to represent a myth and not reality.

The ideal of a scientific state is of a planned social order conducted like a scientific experiment. In an experiment, all factors are controlled there is no place for freedom. Thus Dr. Marvin Karlins and Dr. Lewis Andrews, authors of *Requiem for Democracy? An Inquiry in the Limits of Behavior Control*, believe in controlling man scientifically, because "the real problem is the threat of freedom." Dr. B. F. Skinner of Harvard, in *Beyond Freedom and Dignity*, also believes that freedom must be replaced by controls over man. When the behaviorist J. B. Watson talked along similar lines a generation or so ago, only reactionaries on the whole, were distressed; most people saw in Watson the promises of a glorious future through science. The reaction now is hostility on all fronts. The scientific-educational-statist Establishment is viewed with radical suspicion and fear.

Much is said nowadays about "the credibility gap." Pronouncements by the U.S. Federal Government are viewed with distrust as politically motivated lies. There are good reasons for this suspicion. However, the political lies of Wilson's era, by all the nations, far exceeded those of today. When they were exposed, there was a period of shock, and then a quick return of confidence. At that time, men were more ready to trust the state and thus to believe that some officials were guilty that their "government" was still benevolent and sound. That belief is largely gone now, and thus "the credibility gap" has grown and exists even when the truth is told. As a businessman said of a prominent politician: "I'm suspicious even when he tells the truth. I start figuring, what's his angle?"

The state is no longer seen as the potential Garden of Eden: it is the world after the fall. For many bitter, revolutionary youth, the state has in fact become the Serpent! This radical distrust of the state is the most ominous fact of our time. It spells the end of the age of the state.

To avoid statist answers, men, as before, prior to the fall of Rome, and the collapse of the Middle Ages, resort to all kinds of wild alternatives: astrology, witchcraft, healing cults, magic, anything that offers a rival power to the omnipresent state. In reaction against science, many youths today adopt primitive dress patterns, advocate a return to primitive farming, and generally yearn for a pre-scientific, pre-statist order. Such movements are futile and pathetic. Their value is simply as weather vanes of popular sentiment and disillusionment.

Neither negation nor protest have ever built a social order. The Weathermen, Black Panthers, and others are simply dangerous backlashes of the past; they represent anger and rage, not a new order. People who give dramatic interviews do not make revolutions! They are self-conscious actors: they want a stage more than a battle.

The future always begins yesterday and today. It is an act of faith, and it is an act of recapitalization of spiritual and material capital. The state everywhere has become the destroyer of spiritual and material capital, not its protector. The church has largely joined the humanists and statists and is bankrupt. The state school, as the tool of the state, is facing the collapse which is threatening the state.

Only in a Biblical faith and a reconstruction of church, school, and state, family, economics and all of life in terms of God's law order is there any hope. This reconstruction is under way.

Homesick for Sodom, Lot's wife turned back, choosing life in a perishing city to freedom and a new beginning. Those who life Lot's wife have a backward look are doomed. The future lies ahead, and it is in the hands of our sovereign God, not the enemy.

The state is not god, not is it the lord of life. To be alive is a marvelous thing, and to have the privilege of reconstructing a world by means of our own recapitalization is a pleasurable duty. To allow the state to sour our lives is to do violence to ourselves and to make ourselves into children of the state. Our problems are small compared to those of others in the communist world, and in past eras. If life is a burden for you, perhaps you are the real burden, a drag on time and progress. This is indeed a difficult era, but it is a time of great change and opportunity, and, under God a glorious time to be alive.

CHALCEDON REPORT NO. 75
November 1, 1971

The age of the state is not only creating serious problems for man and society by its belief in the applicability of the idea of equality to man, but also because of its trust in the fallacy of simplicity.

Men yearn for simplicity, and, especially when their problems are complex and overwhelming, they hunger most for a quick and simple answer. The yearning for simplicity is especially prominent among youth in every generation, and rarely more so than now. Youth, as it wakes up to the immensity of the world's problems, wants a quick answer, a simple solution, in order to cope with an overwhelming problem. The less equipped we are to cope with a problem the more prone we are to want a simple answer, one we can understand, and one we can apply. The deliberate primitivism of modern youth is an aspect of this yearning for simplicity. Faced with problems of war and peace, economics and politics, and theological and philosophical questions, the answer of many youth is simplicity and primitivism: bare feet, love as a panacea, old, ragged clothes and an abandonment of careful dress and grooming, and a denouncement of technology. But such demands for simple answers are usually flights from real answers, not solutions.

William Carroll Bark, in *Origins of the Medieval World* (Garden City, New York: Doubleday Anchor Books, 1960) has called attention to a central aspect of the failure of Rome. As Rome grew into an empire, her problems became more complex, but the Roman mind began to resist complexity. As Bark points out, "they confused simplicity with strength, as if one could not exist without the other" (p. 144).

The same fallacy of simplicity governs the state, and its logical conclusion is some form of socialism. As society grows more complex, it grows complex because specialization and decentralization increase. The more specialization and decentralization increase, the greater is the complexity and the advance in a society. Moreover freedom increases with specialization. When a man no longer has to build his own house, grow his own food, and protect his own family, his ability to be free and productive increases. Similarly, if a woman has to weave her family's cloth and make their garments, make soap, kindle fires, and hand-wash clothes, her freedom is lessened, and her life is more complex. Thus, a person's life becomes progressively more free and simple as complexity, specialization and decentralization increase in productive society.

These things, which are the marks of progress and advance, are seen as dangerous social facts to the statist mind, whose constant urge is to simplify. Thus, B. F. Skinner, whose behavioristic thinking is the psychological companion of statism, sees our freedom as a threat to man's welfare. In *Beyond Freedom and Dignity* (New York: Knopf, 1971), he argues for the end of traditional concepts of human freedom and dignity, as well as of moral values in any Christian sense. His case was better stated some years ago by John Broadus Watson (1878-1958). (On Watson, see R. J. Rushdoony *Messianic Character of American Education*, pp. 162-169.) Skinner's position is pure environmentalism. In the old view, he points out, people were blamed for their failures; liberals then blamed bad parents, teachers, and communities. "The mistake...is to put the responsibility anywhere, to suppose that somewhere a causal sequence is initiated" (p. 76). The answer is conditioning, the control of all men to create a society beyond freedom and dignity for mankind's best welfare.

Skinner's answer is not too different from that of the rebellious youth of our time. Both are guilty of the fallacy of simplicity. The young rebels want simplicity by a return to primitivism, whereas Skinner wants simplicity by means of the scientific, statist control of men.

The fallacy of simplicity is a humanistic, rationalistic fallacy. It rests ultimately in the belief that some few men have the answers whereby all men can be saved, all society ordered, and man's future assured. The fallacy of simplicity is an easy one for the statist mind to accept, because it usually concentrates power into a few hands. If all problems are to be answered by eliminating freedom, decentralization, and independent specialization, then an elite will have awesome and godlike powers. (If *Time Magazine's* article on Skinner in its September 20, 1971, issue, pp. 47-53, is to be believed, then Skinner too is marked by a "desire to dominate.")

Consider the vast powers concentrated into statist hands by the departures from the gold standard. By creating a paper-money basis for economics, and by making money a creation of the state rather than a commonly accepted standard of value, the state has given itself virtually total powers over the wealth of all its citizens. It can confiscate the wealth of the people at will. As Leonard Read has observed, in his essay, "Little Lessons Along the Road", "Inflation is a device for syphoning private property into the coffers of government. Successful hedging would require finding a form of property that cannot be syphoned off or confiscated. It does not exist!"

The state, however, can offer simple answers like economic controls, paper money, centralized planning, and so on, *only* when people themselves are guilty of the fallacy of simplicity. What breeds that fallacy?

Examining the matter closely, it will become apparent to us that, if power were concentrated in the wisest hands of the world, they would still make mistakes and their errors would have deadly consequences for all of us. Thus, no group of men is wise enough to rule for all of us. The best we can hope for is that men will rule themselves wisely by God's grace and word. For any group of men to seek power over all other men is to play god. This, clearly, is the key to the matter, and it is man's original sin, to try to be as god, determining for himself what constitutes good and evil (Gen. 3:5).

Only God can give simple answers, because only God is totally omniscient and omnipotent. Only God can simplify because, by virtue of His omniscience and omnipotence, He is, to use humanistic terms, the only universal specialist with a full grasp of the total complexity of things. Moreover, because all things originate in His sovereign purpose and will, His purpose and word provide the only possible ground for a simple answer, since He is the only lord and maker of all things.

Thus, when men claim to have a simple, centralized answer, they are claiming to be god, and they are demanding the allegiance that only God can rightfully claim.

Every effort therefore to give a statist, simplified, centralized answer, is not only a move which works to level and destroy civilization, but also a move against God. The fallacy of simplicity is thus an aspect of original sin, man's attempt to be god and to order all things by his own will. Man's fiat will then requires fiat law, fiat money, and fiat morality. The word fiat is the Latin for "let it be done"; just as God said, "Let there be light: and there was light" (Gen. 1:3), so man's fiat is an attempt to create something out of nothing. The dictionary defines "fiat money" as "irredeemable paper money made legal tender by law." Because man is not God, his fiat money always erodes and finally becomes worthless. Because man is not God, his fiat law also fails to provide order and becomes instead the cause of disorder. Likewise, man's fiat morality leads to the collapse of society and to moral anarchy.

God's commands, His fiat declarations as stated in Genesis 1, brought all creation into being by means of simple commands. Genesis tells us, "God said and it was so." Here is true simplicity, because here is true deity. The compromising theologians who want to extend Genesis 1 and creation over millions and millions of years, and to convert a simple act to an involved and complex process, are thereby denying God's sovereignty. Not surprisingly, these theologians are usually strong advocates of simplicity on the human scene: they believe in fiat money, and in a fiat state, which, by simplifying and centralizing, will solve man's social problems. Their god has obviously migrated from the heavens to their national capitol.

The fallacy of simplicity is thus at heart a theological issue. The remedy for man's attempts to play god is for man to see himself as a creature, a sinning creature, who must submit to and live under God and His law. The fiat will of the state, and the fiat will of anarchistic individuals, can only destroy social order, undercut civilization, and hamper technology.

It is very popular these days to regard technology as an enemy. Men who are guilty of the fallacy of simplicity want to downgrade technology because it so clearly requires specialization. Karl Marx, in *The German Ideology*, and Engels in *Anti-Duhring*, declared that, when communism is fully realized, all experts and specialists would be unnecessary. Clark quite aptly asked, "I wonder who will perform brain surgery?" (Gordon H. Clark: *Historiography, Secular and Religious*. p. 86. Nutley, New Jersey: The Craig Press, 1971.)

Let us see how this fiat mind works. Some years ago, as a student at a major city, I saw this fiat mind, the mind of the humanist, at work. Hegel long ago stated the case for such men with his assertion that "the rational is the real." The mind creates and then incarnates true reality. Thus, one professor once put on the blackboard the x number of acres in America capable of farm use, the x number of bushels of wheat, corn, and so on that could be produced, and then the x number of people in the U.S. and in all the world who could be fed *if* someone (presumably with his intelligence) organized and centralized all this and gave the right orders. At that time, in the 1930s, a similar plan in the Soviet Union had destroyed production and led to famine; he refused to believe that this was anything but propaganda. If proven to him, he would no doubt have said that the peasants were resisting progress when they resisted collectivization. In any case, he was guilty of the fallacy of simplicity. He actually believed that all problems are solved in life as easily as, theoretically, and with no contradictions permitted, they are "solved" on the blackboard.

Such "blackboard solutions" are increasingly the rule today as international economic conferences of the major nations "settle" monetary problems. As senates, parliaments, and other legislative bodies ponder problems of politics, economics, education, and agriculture, they look for "blackboard solutions" and "blackboard experts." Then, if things go wrong, it is the people's fault for failing to become robots to the central plan.

The problem, of course, is that all men are inescapably creatures of God. They can deny God, but they cannot escape Him. At every point in life, and in every fiber of his being, man is inescapably and totally tied to God's law order and sovereign power. Those who are guilty of the fallacy of simplicity believe that man's fiat will can somehow change all this and make the masses of mankind move totally in terms of man's fiat will. This is Skinner's thesis no less than Marx's. It is the thesis of London, Washington D. C., Paris, Rome, Peking, and Moscow, in varying degrees. It is the faith of man when he separates himself from God and tries to play god.

Thus, the closer the age of the state comes to realizing its dream of centralization and simplification, the greater the potential for misery and disaster increases, and the closer the age of the state draws to suicide. Our Lord declared that "Man shall not live by bread alone, but by every word that proceedeth out of the mouth of God" (Matt. 4:4). The humanistic state sees man as a politico-economic animal and declares that man shall not live by the word of God but rather by the fiat word of the state and the fiat bread of the state. However, the closer the state comes to realizing its dream, and the nearer it comes to having the power to issue a simple fiat word, the more it faces economic collapse. Its fiat money buys less and less, and often nothing, and there is also finally no bread to eat, and the state is dead.

Our Lord said, "all they that take the sword shall perish with the sword" (Matt. 26:52), i. e., all who make the sword, force, their answer and their mainstay, rather than making it subordinate, shall perish by the same meaningless exercise of force. Likewise, all who make the state, which, in its subordinate place is necessary, their mainstay, and its fiat will their law and hope, shall perish with the state.

It is time therefore to rebuild apart from the state, to establish independent Christian schools and institutions under God and His fiat word and dedicated to His glory. It means establishing marriages and homes grounded, not on romantic love, but a common obedience to God. It means establishing new businesses, relying not on a federal subsidy, but providing goods and services for free men. It means exploring the world of things and ideas to develop our knowledge and technology under God. We cannot be guilty of the clean-slate idea of the Enlightenment, of waiting for a clean-slate before we begin. We begin now, because our duty is a constant one, and the opportunity a very present one. It is a time for building, because the old structures are coming down. This, like every year, is the year of our Lord, and man's fiat word shall be shattered by the word of His power. It is therefore a glorious time to be alive, a time to work, and a time to rejoice.

CHALCEDON REPORT NO. 76
December 1, 1971

A few years ago, a writer described the modern American order as "the warfare state." His argument was a faulty one, but his term was a very apt one. The age of the state has led inescapably to the warfare state. An important and central aspect of the life of the state has been war.

Now St. James makes clear in his epistle (4:1-3) that the source of conflict and war is in the heart of man; it is a product of his sin, and he cannot therefore blame war on the capitalists, a military-industrial complex, other nations, the communists, or anything else. The basic and essential cause of war is the sin of man. This does not rule out secondary causes; it does make it morally necessary to avoid giving primacy to secondary causes, for then we absolutize circumstances over man and man's freedom and responsibility. We must also hold that the secondary cause always rests in the primary cause, sin.

A theorist of the last century said that war is the continuation and extension of diplomacy into military action. A state is continually seeking its advantage by one means or another, so that diplomacy and war are alike instruments to a continuing evil.

The fact of warfare gained prestige when Darwin set forth his theory of evolution. The struggle for survival was widely assumed to mean warfare in one form or another, economic and class warfare, warfare for resources, warfare in every area. When Darwin published his *Origin of Species* on November 24, 1859, a waiting world was delighted with his thesis and the entire edition sold out on the day of publication. Two of the happiest of the earliest readers were Marx and Engels, who rightly saw in Darwin the confirmation of their beliefs: they correctly held that Darwin's success would ensure the triumph of socialism. The reason is an obvious one. If evolution rather than creation by God is true, then two things follow: first, life is a struggle for survival, and a theory of class warfare is simply a sociological application of evolution, and, second, if God is eliminated, nothing morally binding remains to ensure private property, Christian marriage, and religious authority in any realm. Life is then an amoral struggle for survival, and in that amoral struggle mass man has the best chances for victory, supposedly.

The age of the state, already firmly geared to warfare as an instrument of politics, thus turned warfare, with Darwin and Marx, into the holy crusade of humanism on its march to utopia. Much is said about "holy wars" in past history, and most of it is nonsense. The true holy wars in the fullest sense of the word are after Darwin and Marx. World Wars I and II were holy crusades "to make the world safe for democracy", and to "end war and ensure peace", and so on. The terminology of communist warfare is the most intense example of holy warfare in all history.

Since accepting the necessity of struggle for survival, our humanism of today has in it the grounds for the holy war of our evolutionary faith. The established humanistic religion of modern states sees conflict as always the means of progress; every struggle against a reactionary, racist, or fascist enemy is by definition an act of faith and a step towards peace and freedom. The evil is war by the enemies of a particular socialist state, or by any who oppose the religion of statism.

Thus, despite all the pious bleatings about a love of peace, ours is an age of warfare, and of holy wars. These wars serve two purposes: first, a war always consolidates greater power over the citizenry in the hands of the state, so that a victorious state emerges not only victorious over its enemies but over its people as well. Thus, whatever losses the Germans, Japanese, North Koreans, and Vietcong or North Vietnamese may have suffered at American hands, this much is certain, that, since 1917, the major and consistent losers have been the American people. By their sinful propensity for the cult of the state, they have seen their freedom diminished and economic slavery emerge: the state has been the consistent winner. A huge bureaucracy has developed in Washington and in every city and state; from a standing army of a few thousand, we now have an army of millions; from almost inconsequential taxes, the citizens now pay taxes which are almost equal to a rent on their property and a permit to live. Second, warfare is more and more a way of life, and a basic philosophy of progress. The result is class warfare.

How does labor see progress for itself? The answer is clearly by means of warfare, war against management, and against the consumer. It is unthinkable for labor negotiators to assume that anything but conflict can assure progress, and benefits for the working man. As a result, labor is committed, by virtue of its religious faith in the evolutionary humanism of our day, to a warfare philosophy.

This is no less true of capital. Very early, in men like Carnegie, industry committed itself to social Darwiniianism, and the result was a growing breach between capital and labor. In this grim warfare, having a religion of conflict, concession is sin, and even elementary decencies must be fought for by both sides, since both maintain a hostility to concessions. There have been notable exceptions on both sides, but, basically, the philosophy of warfare governs them. We have thus, in every area, a warfare state.

In all this, of course, the state is the gainer. Warfare works to the disadvantage of industry and labor; it is destructive of the economy and of society, since progress rests on a harmony of interests. For the state, however, progress in its march to power rests on warfare, which greatly increases its power. The greater the hostility between capital and labor, the more both will turn to the state for an ally, so that the real victor in all cases is the state, which gains steadily in its power over both capital and labor. The state emerges as the victor, and capital and labor as the chained and controlled servants of the state.

The state thus has an advantage in promoting class warfare, and statism inevitably promotes it, because its interference furthers conflict. Progress in race relations in America was real, until statist legislation turned it into class warfare and riots in the streets. Neither blacks nor whites have been the gainers, but the state's powers over both, and over labor and industry, are greatly increased.

But the state cannot profit by its victories. When the state steps beyond its God-appointed realm as the ministry of justice, the state begins to fail in its ability to function effectively. The state is not a producer. For the state to gain vast powers over society is about as fruitful of good as for a mule to gain power over a corral full of mares: it is a sterile victory which can only embarrass the victor. The result is even greater tension and conflict.

The greatest powers for the state are just ahead of us, and its greatest defeats, its inability to keep its promises and a consequent disillusionment of peoples. Already, everywhere, the state is failing in its ability to maintain an elementary and basic need of the people, security in their homes and safety in the streets; failure here will only increase in the days ahead. Already, a sum equal to 50% of all federal, state, county, and local police costs is spent for varying forms of private protection, and this sum will only increase. As controls over the police increase, and public morality declines, lawlessness will become more open and extensive.

The more power and money an individual or an enterprise gains, the more effectively it functions, because, normally, people and businesses have a productive function which thrives on further capitalization. However, this is not true of the state. The more power and money a state gains, the less effectively it functions, because it feeds on power and money, not to function in terms of a productive end but to enhance its power and wealth. Power and money give muscles to men, businesses, and organizations, but they feed a cancer in the state.

The modern state is thus a sick enterprise which resents health in its midst and penalizes it. It grows in wealth, but regards wealth in others as an evil. Its senators vote for busing for the masses and send their own children to private schools to avoid busing. The state has a double standard of morality, one for itself, and another for the people.

A deepening disillusionment with the state is ahead of us, and a growing decline in its authority. However, because the warfare state rests firmly on the foundation of the warfaring man, *disillusionment will not change the world.* As long as men believe, after Darwin and Marx, in a warfare world as the way for progress, they will create and perpetuate a warfare state. A man spent some time recently telling me how bad socialism, controls, and statism generally are. Then he concluded his random remarks by saying, "Well, its a dog-eat-dog world." His perspective ensures precisely the kind of world he has. It is not a dog-eat-dog world: it is God's world, and His law prevails. All who violate it will sooner or later suffer the consequences. Those who insist that it is a dog-eat-dog world are debasing life, the world, and themselves, and they are the losers. *To live on the foundation that this is God's world* may not give us as many bones as this man has, but, instead of a dog's life, *we live a rich life under God.*

Jesus Christ is declared to be "the Prince of Peace" (Isa. 9:6), but this does not mean surrender. He came to bring a sword (Matt. 10:25ff.) of moral division in terms of Himself and His law-word, but an offer of peace to all men of all classes. His peace is more than a cessation of warfare: it is a way of life and a relationship to Himself. Progress is not through a struggle for survival or warfare but by means of obedience to His law-word and its application to every sphere of life.

The warfare state sees progress through the destruction of its enemies or their subjection to the state; it sees conflict as the essence of progress. The Biblical perspective is radically different: there is no progress unless there is, first of all, *regeneration, a change of heart, life, and nature through Jesus Christ, and then obedience to His law-word*. Men may hope for peace through other means, but they will instead feed the forces of war.

Conflict, instead of being a force for progress, is an aspect of man's fall and a product of his sin. It is unfortunately sometimes necessary in a fallen world, but it is not the norm, nor is it the means of progress. Sometimes good very definitely does come out of conflict, and sometimes conflict is morally necessary, but this still does not mean that conflict is the way to progress. A man who lost his sight in an accident was led, step by step, to a forsaking of a reprobate way of life and to a useful and godly existence. This does not mean that we should all blind ourselves in order to make progress! Neither the source of change, nor the thing changed, are in the environment or in accidents, but in the relationship of God and man. Man's basic war is with God and God's law-order, and man's true peace begins with peace with God.

In all of this, the state is futile. To hope for political salvation is like hoping for a colt from a mule. The state will change when men change. The warfare state will give way to a godly state when men are godly men, not the warfaring men St. James described (James 4:1-3). Meanwhile, the age of the state is what we deserve. In fact, it is better than this generation deserves.

CHALCEDON REPORT NO. 77
January 1, 1972

According to Scripture, the state is the ministry of justice, whose duty it is to administer God's law as "the minister of God" in its realm (Rom. 13:1-4). The church is the ministry of grace, and the state the ministry of justice, each in its appointed realm to serve God. Only by such a service can society flourish and prosper.

Much of the struggle between church and state in the medieval era was a dispute over priority; was the emperor or the pope God's chief minister? Pope Gregory VII, in his letter to the Bishop of Metz, 1081, referring to his struggle with Emperor Henry IV, spoke of "kings and emperors who, too much puffed up by worldly glory, rule not for God but for themselves." The point was well made, but it was all too often a valid charge against both church and state, that their concern for power and priority supplanted the proper administration of their ministry.

In the modern era, this old battle was supposedly by-passed and a new order instituted by the progressive separation of church and state. Both church and state were now supposedly free to pursue their respective callings without interference and with greater faithfulness. The result has been, within the state, a graceless law, and, within the church, a lawless grace, pietism and antinomianism.

The state, however, has become intensely concerned with justice, now usually termed social justice. Rarely in history has the state expressed more concern with human welfare, with problems of health, education, and welfare, war and peace, environment and ecology, science and research, as well as agriculture and a variety of other spheres of interest. The state in effect has embarked on a zealous search for justice in every realm of life. Minority groups have been systematically studied and courted, and their claims to justice strongly championed, by state after state. All over the world, the modern states justify their existence by their zealous quest for social justice. Old wrongs and injustices are to be righted, human brotherhood instituted, and a reign of world peace insured. It was believed that the twentieth century was to see many of these goals realized; instead, it has seen the progressive disintegration of world order and a growing resentment against the state. The effort has been a notable one, but the results have been disastrous. It is important to understand why.

Perhaps an illustration from two countries may help us to understand the problem. The tsarist order of old Russia had more than a little popular hostility to the Jews, and some legal discrimination. Many Jews left Russia for this reason, and a few of the wealthier American Jews helped finance Russian revolutionary parties in order to bring in justice. The results are now even less satisfactory, and the freedom of Soviet Jews is greatly reduced, so that the tsarist days seem like a dream of freedom by comparison. Various Jewish groups all over the world demand freedom for Soviet Jews and insist that they are the targets of discrimination and repression. The Soviet Union very indignantly denies these charges and affirms that its order is without prejudice and is indeed dedicated to brotherhood. The Soviet Union is in fact an empire of many minority groups. It must avoid a charge of discrimination and favoritism, lest it be a target of a dreaded, revolutionary liberation movement. Earlier in its history, the Soviet Union faced a charge within the country of favoritism to the Jews.

How has the present problem developed? The problem has arisen out of the attempt to avoid all favoritism and discrimination. The Soviet hierarchy is well aware of the deeply rooted prejudices which divide its many racial groups. (See Paul Lendvai: *Anti-Semitism Without Jews: Communist Eastern Europe*. Garden City, New York: Doubleday, 1971.) To maintain its power, it must keep peace internally. As a result, to maintain justice and equal representation, it has instituted a quota system. The various graduate schools and professions must maintain a fair balance of all groups so that equal representation and justice prevail. The result has been instant injustice. Some of the minority groups, such as the Jews, normally have a high percentage in higher education and the professions, whereas some of the backward peoples of central Asia have a very low representation. If the two are put on the same basis of representation, the result is a discrimination in favor of the backward group and against the advanced group. Moreover, the state receives a civil servant of lesser calibre. Thus, the steps taken to eliminate discrimination have given Russia its most repressive order in history.

Let us turn to the United States for a similar development. There was a time when some medical schools limited the number of Jews who were accepted for admission. This was discrimination clearly. All the same, the percentage of Jewish doctors was quite high in ratio to the population, as was the percentage of Italian and Jewish musicians, and so on. Certain minority groups did gravitate to certain professions and sometimes dominated them. Steps are now being taken to "correct" this situation. Medical schools must now accept a percentage of Negro students equivalent to the Negro population. This means, however, that the number of Jewish, German, Anglo-Saxon, and other students who can enter medical school is proportionately reduced. If we continue to try to "correct" the situation by applying the quota system across the boards, we will very quickly lower, as we have begun to do, the calibre of medical education by introducing an alien factor. Instead of ability, race will govern. Apply the matter to every field, and the injustices increase. If opera must have an equal representation (in the pit and on stage) of all races and Italian eminence broken, then opera ceases to be a musical feast and becomes an arena of racial tension.

Such a policy will only increase racial hostility and aggravate existing problems. It will also mean that positions which should be granted in terms of merit are instead granted in terms of race. Every society already has its inner workings which favor some against others. Very often, getting a job depends on knowing the right people. Such favoritism is inescapable in any society, but, in a free society, there is always room for ability to assert itself and advance in spite of such problems. In a quota system, besides having more scope for "pull" with insiders, those of lesser abilities are consistently favored in order to equalize the situation. The state's concern with social justice has thus led to systematic and planned injustice. Why?

The framework of reference in social justice is man, not God. The attempt to gain social justice is humanistic to the core, and it lacks an objective frame of reference as its standard. The matter has been very powerfully summed up by the historian John Lukacs (*The Passing of the Modern Age*

New York: Harper and Row, 1970) who writes: "Our world has come to the edge of disaster precisely because of its preoccupation with justice, indeed, often at the expense of truth. It is arguable, reasonably arguable, that there is less injustice in this world than a century ago. Only a vile idiot would argue that there is less untruth. We are threatened not by the absence of justice, we are threatened by the fantastic prevalence of untruth. Our main task ought to be the reduction of untruth, first of all --- a task which should have been congenial to intellectuals, who, however, failed in this even more than the worst of corrupt clerics. Of justice and truth the second is of the higher order. Truth responds to a deeper human need than does justice. A man can live with injustice a long time, indeed, that is the human condition: but he cannot long live with untruth. The pursuit of justice can be a terrible thing, it can lay the world to waste - which is perhaps the deepest predicament of American history" (p. 166).

In a chapter on "Truth and Liberty" in my study of the *Politics of Guilt and Pity*, I showed how truth has been denied by our courts in favor of liberty and justice. Justice Douglas has declared that "Truth is not the goal, for in most areas no one knows what truth is." To search for truth is to construct "totalitarianism", according to Douglas, by imposing a right and wrong on society, when the duty of men "is not to discover 'truth' but to accommodate conflicting views of 'truth' and the common good or conflicting needs." By abandoning truth, men have thus also abandoned justice, and the "justice" of the courts today is becoming steadily a new form of injustice. Truth and justice are indivisible although different, and their separation has led to an age of statist tyranny and injustice.

Under the guise of a separation of church and state what has actually taken place is a separation of Christianity and the state (and, one might add, a separation of Christianity and the church). The state is inescapably a religious establishment, because justice, law, and social order are inescapably religious questions. What the modern state has done is to disestablish Christianity as well as the church, and to establish humanism as its religion. The speeches of heads of states and the decisions of modern courts are exercises and proclamations of the religion of humanism. In this religion, there is no truth beyond man; truth is thus relative to man and is not an objective, absolute, and transcendent order created by God's eternal decree. Where truth disappears, justice soon disappears also. China was a most progressive and advanced civilization, as was India, until relativistic and pragmatic philosophies commanded the minds of people; then, instead of advance, stagnation set in, because, truth having lost its meaning, justice and life also declined in meaning. This same decay is now infecting Western cultures.

The impact of this down-grading or by-passing of truth is apparent in many areas. In the church, it has led to an emphasis on unity above truth in the ecumenical movement. The early councils of the church (Nicea, Ephesus, Chalcedon, Constantinople) emphasized truth and waged war against heresies, holding that the only ground of unity is the truth of God. In the ecumenical movement today, unity has priority, and truth is by-passed or neglected. In fact, this emphasis on unity has gone so far that unity is popularly equated with grace, and nothing is more frequently used as a modern anathema than to pronounce a movement as "divisive" and potentially or actually "schismatic." To oppose unity for unity's sake is regarded as being opposed to grace.

In the realm of the so-called social sciences and of education, the perspective of Comte prevails: meaning is derided, and the concern for truth is declared to be a mark of a more primitive society, whereas modern scientific man concerns himself, not with meaning, but with methodology and technology.

The neglect of truth has led to the progressive destruction of the church as a power in society, and to the decay of education. This neglect of truth is now destroying the life of the state and reducing it to a naked and empty display of force against which its own youth rebels. Even more, the neglect of truth has led to the erosion of the individual's strength to resist the growing tyranny of the state. Man is never more defenseless than when he is without the truth. Modern man is especially vulnerable because he is a man without truth, and, even more, a man denying the possibility of truth. Impotence is thus deeply imbedded in his will and present in his every act.

As against this prevailing darkness, the light of Scripture reveals the incarnation of truth in the person of Jesus Christ. The truth of God, His absolute law, decree, and person, is unchanged and unchanging. Men are judged by that truth. "Whosoever shall fall upon that stone shall be broken; but on whomsoever it shall fall, it will grind him to powder" (Luke 20:18). The truth is either our foundation, the Rock on which we build, or it is our destruction, grinding us to powder.

The days of the age of the state are thus numbered. Its temples of humanism, its schools, are regularly being bombed and burned by its own sons. Its chief officers are despised and regarded with contempt. Even as the state increases its power it also increases disrespect and disobedience.

Wise men will spend little time weeping over the past: they prepare for the future.

CHALCEDON REPORT NO. 78
February 1, 1972

The idea of Genius is an important but too little studied aspect of Western history; it is an important pagan concept which still governs our thinking. We can begin to understand what *genius* means if we recognize that it is basically the same word as the Arabic *jinn* or *genie*. The word *genius* comes from the Latin, and the idea is Roman, but it is hard to distinguish it at times from the Arabic idea, because the two are so similar.

The idea of *genius* comes out of pagan animism and ancestor worship. The *genius* of a family, house, group, or state was the protecting, guiding, inspiring supernatural spirit which took care of it and was also the object of its worship. All good Romans therefore worshipped "the genius of Rome." "The genius of Rome" was the divine power protecting Rome, the Roman mission, Rome itself ("divine Rome"), and its heroic leaders and emperors. Godlike men were believed to receive from the gods a special destiny above that of ordinary mortals. These men became the *Lares* or *genius* for their time.

With the coming of Christianity, the idea of *genius* receded, as did the related Greek idea of the hero. The hero was a great protector of men who was descended from the gods, or born of a god, and he was worshipped as a god after His death. Because Biblical faith makes a sharp and clear distinction between God and man, between the uncreated and divine Being of God, and the created and creaturely being of men, the idea of the *genius* (and of the *hero*) was for some time in the background. With the revival of Greek philosophy, of Aristotle and of Plato, the idea of the genius again came to the fore, especially with the Renaissance. The *hero* or divine leader of men came to be a leader of the state. The Leader or Hero now became a commanding and totalitarian figure. The Genius, the man with divine powers of insight and guidance, came to be the artist. Previously, in Christian Europe, the artist was *not* an artist in the modern sense. He was a craftsman, an artisan, and a businessman who was a specialist in his field. (In recent years, one composer, Igor Stravinsky, specifically denied being an artist in the modern sense and saw himself as an old-fashioned semi-Christian artisan, an opinion for which he was widely attacked.) The Christian artisan did his work like any other skilled specialist, without any pretensions. With the Renaissance, the artist was not only regarded as a man of genius, but also called by extravagant names, "the divine Aretino", "the divine Michelangelo", and so on.

But this was not all. In paganism, the genius had been essentially a political figure in the developed form of the idea of genius. The medieval artisan was essentially related to the faith, and his greatest work was in the church. After the Renaissance, the artist associated himself increasingly with the state. The church continued to be a great patron of art, and, in the following eras, such creations as baroque church art certainly represented very great outlays of money, but artists found their *chief* voice and their *best* self-expression in works done for the royalty and the nobility, for the state. The neo-pagan genius and hero were working together.

The artist, and especially the writer, began to see himself as a genius, producing for the ages. He was thus an *elite* man, but he was more than merely an elite man; the elite are the pick of society, the choicest part. The genius is much more than that: he is a supernormal and somewhat supernatural break-through into society and thus above even the elite.

The literary elite at first identified themselves with the nobility and with royalty, with the great heroes of the arena of politics. With the Enlightenment, however, the artists, especially the literary and pseudo-philosophical ones, began to turn against the nobility and royalty even while often fawning on them.

The French Revolution was preceded by a long war by men like Voltaire, Diderot, and others on church and state alike, with a new concept of society vaguely imagined as the true and coming order. In the French Revolution, men who believed in their genius overthrew a social order and began the ruthless destruction of all things which ran counter to their "inspiration". Because the middle class had been held back and hindered by the monarchy, the literary elite briefly championed the middle class cause as a useful weapon towards overthrowing the old regime. Very quickly, however, they turned on the middle classes with venom.

In the 19th century, the idea of the hero as the organizing principle of society (together with his instructor, the artistic genius) became very common. It was widely taught by such men as Carlyle, Nietzsche, and Wagner, and, in the 20th century, by Spengler, Stefan George, D. H. Lawrence, and others. The world, they held, cannot be understood by the faith and creeds of Christianity but only by intuition, history, and the hero. The evolution of things in history is in terms of the hero, who acts without being hindered by old moralities and creeds. He incarnates the true evolution of the world and brings in a new order as the next step of evolution. His attitude is pragmatic, not dogmatic. He has his roots in the folk or people, and he moves them into the future and progress by his ruthless, powerful drive. The hero is a realist who is not afraid to kill or to sin in order to further his cause. As Bentley summarized Carlyle's view, "The man who is undefiled by pitch...must be in the wrong, for he has not been willing to sin and compromise. He has not seized reality by its filthy hand." (Eric Bentley: *A Century of Hero-Worship*, p. 56. Boston: Beacon Press, 1957, second edition.) The ideas of the men of "genius" of the 19th and 20th centuries helped produce the "heroes" they imagined, men like Lenin, Stalin, Hitler, and Mao.

Moreover, the genius, having broken quickly with the middle class, then turned against the middle class savagely for failing to bow down to him and to recognize his genius. He called therefore for the liquidation of these insensitive clods who could not appreciate genius and were too much concerned about business and profits. The "genius" class or elite turned now to the working class, the proletariat, as a new hope for society, as a people who would follow the leadership of genius into a brave new world. The Russian Revolution was the longed-for proletarian revolution. The workers, however, failed the artists and writers: they did not appreciate genius. Only by a dictatorship could the state proceed with its plan for a new society. In the 20th century, and especially with the 1960s, the men of "genius" began to look for a new class to overthrow workers and the middle class alike, the *outlaw*. The existentialist genius in particular began to see the criminal as the true hero (and this criminal-hero definitely includes the homosexual in the forefront), and prison riots became revolutionary events in which men of genius located new heroes. (Remember too that the prison days of Lenin and Hitler were widely hailed as a part of their heroic history.)

For some time now, the men of genius have been in search of a society to lead. Some have dreamed of a society of programmed men, as in B. F. Skinner's intellectual nightmare, men with electrodes in their brains to obey the commandments of heroes and geniuses. The Genius has been increasingly a man with a pathological hatred of society, of normality (of the "squares"), of a world which rejects his privileged and superior wisdom. He has not found that world in the nobility and royalty, nor in the middle and working classes, nor will he find it among the outlaws, who, like him, are incapable of true loyalty and allegiance, let alone subservience. The genius believes that he is beyond the law, that he should, in fact, be the organizing force in society today, even as in ancient Rome the genius was worshipped, and, in the person of the emperor, ruled. By the 1830's, the writers of France had come to a logical conclusion of the doctrine of genius: "everything is permitted to men of intelligence." (Cesar Grana: *Bohemian versus Bourgeois*, p. 42. New York: Basic Books, 1964.) Their hatred of the normal world was so great that one writer of that era said, "I would give half my talents to be a bastard." (*Ibid.*, p. 145.) In his excellent study of Sartre, Molnar has shown how the idea of bastard and intellectual came to be identified; the bastard-intellectual is a heroic outlaw at war with middle class society and culture, deliberately at odds with normal, well-integrated people. (Thomas Molnar: *Sartre: Ideologue of Our Times*, pp. 5ff. New York: Funk & Wagnalls, 1968.)

The bastard-intellectual-genius is in search of a society to lead, but he can only disintegrate society: he can neither create nor lead one, because the essence of his inspiration is destruction. He no longer looks for a hero, because, in his pretensions he no longer needs the hero, but only followers. Such ideas were prominent in Nietzsche, who wrote to his sister in December, 1888: "You have not the slightest idea what it means to be next-of-kin to the man and destiny in whom the question of epochs has been settled. Quite literally speaking: I hold the future of mankind in the palm of my hand." Everything was settled, if only the world would recognize it! But what the world recognized and learned from each bastard-intellectual-genius was the corrosive, burning hatred of man and society, the radical contempt of all things save its own superiority and genius. Carlyle said, "There is nothing else but revolution and mutation, the former merely speedier change." The goal thus is perpetual revolution for perpetual destruction. The state must obey genius and must liquidate all things in terms of a gospel of perpetual revolution or destruction.

The idea of genius in the modern world gained much from Rousseau. Among other things, Rousseau, in his *Social Contract*, held that "Whoever refuses to obey the general will shall be compelled to do so by the whole body. This means nothing less than that he will be forced to be free." As Andelson has pointed out, this is echoed in the slogan of Orwell's *1984*, "Freedom is Slavery." The general will is not merely the democratic majority, it is the genius-intellectual's interpretation of what the general will of the whole body or country should be. Robespierre, as spokesman for the Jacobins, said bluntly, "Our will is the general will." (Robert V. Andelson: *Imputed Rights*, p. 8. Athens: University of Georgia Press, 1971.) The old Latin expression, vox populi, vox dei, the voice of the people is the voice of God, now had a new development: the voice of the genius-intellectual is the voice of the people and of the gods.

As against the idea of the genius, Biblical faith offered and offers to men the idea and office of prophet. Most people make central a secondary aspect of the office of prophet, namely, one who foretells the future. The primary function and office of a prophet is to speak for God and to represent Him in total faithfulness to His law-word. This is the duty of *every* man in whatever calling he has. His reliance must not be on his word, or his idea of truth, or his concept of good and evil, but on the absolute and unchanging word of God. That word must be applied to church, state, school, science, all society and all learning, and its implications faithfully developed. The Christian must work for the liquidation of the idea of genius and its replacement by the calling of the prophet.

But this is not all. The believer has a priestly office. In his priestly office, the believer must dedicate himself, his social order and institutions, his family, work, and all things to the glory and service of God. "Man's chief end is to glorify God and to enjoy Him forever," the Westminster Catechism tells us; this is a priestly calling and task, and its emphasis is on joy. The priesthood of Israel was radically separated from death and mourning; it could not indulge in grief as could other men, because the priesthood set forth not only the triumph of God but joy in Him. Nehemiah told a sorrowful people, "This day is holy unto the LORD your God; mourn not, nor weep...for this day is holy unto our Lord: neither be ye sorry; for the joy of the LORD is your strength" (Neh. 8:9,10). The priestly calling of man brings him joy and peace.

Man also has a royal calling in Christ, to be a king under God and to exercise dominion over the earth, by knowledge, authority, science, invention, farming, and in every other way. As kings under God and His law, we must oppose the lawless idea of the hero, the fuhrer, the dictatorship of the proletariat, and all like variations of the pagan faith. This dominion under God means the development of all things under His law, and it is a mandate for orderly progress and advancement. It means culture. The word culture is related to cultivate and agriculture, it means tillage, development, improvement. Culture requires time, capitalization, and work. The bastard-intellectual-genius program of revolution is also a war against culture and calls for the destruction of culture, which can only thrive with time, capitalization, and cultivation. Culture cannot be limited to the arts; it is a myth propagated by the artists of the modern era that culture means what they do. Culture, however, is the faith or religion of a people externalized in their total activities. True culture is today being warred on, and many people travel widely to see the relics of culture which are surviving our age of revolution.

The state as the apotheosis and incarnation of genius is proving to be an anti-cultural, anti-human ideal, a destroyer of man and society. When the Bolsheviks were accused of being anti-culture, they answered the charge by turning to the past: they revived the tsar's ballet! This is the way of the Yahoo, on both sides of the iron curtain.

If our hope is in a hero or in genius, we will wait for such a leader, and we will get a fuhrer or dictator, and we will deserve him. If, however, we see our calling as prophets, priests, and kings under God and in Christ, we will begin the task of reconstruction wherever we are, because we are the future. The Christians of the Roman Empire were ready to swear allegiance to the emperor, but they refused to swear by the genius of the emperor, and for this they were persecuted (Tertullian: *Apologeticus*, 32.) Under God, they could not surrender their own calling under God to the will of a man, nor commit their future to the will of man.

The culture of tomorrow will not come from the state and the bastard-intellectual-genius elite of the state. It will come from us who are prophets, priests, and kings under God, who are doing our duty under God and to His glory. St. Paul's counsel still stands: "Therefore, my beloved brethren, be ye steadfast, unmovable, always abounding in the work of the Lord, forasmuch as ye know that your labour is not in vain in the Lord" (I Cor. 15:58). The world of the hero and the genius will disappear. Good riddance.

CHALCEDON REPORT NO. 79
March 1, 1972

One of the persistent problems facing the state in every age has been the question of *authority*. How can the state justify its claim to power over the people? By what right does the state claim its jurisdiction and its authority?

The basic argument has usually been historical, an appeal to tradition, inheritance, and long possession. Kings have justified their rule by appealing to the fact that they inherited the throne, all the while conveniently forgetting that someone in their family's past once seized the throne. Similarly, civil governments which once gained power by revolution piously condemn all new revolutions and declare that they are the only legitimate authority. A painfully pathetic example of this tired argument appears in Vine Deloria Jr., "An Indian's Plea to the Churches" (*Los Angeles Times*, Sunday, February 6, 1972, p. G-1, 2.) Deloria, an Indian, says to white Americans, that, before their coming, "we inhabited and owned the continent upon which you now live." The heart of his argument is that the Indian has a prior right to America and thus a moral claim against the rest of us. The fact is that there were no such "people" as "the American Indian" prior to Columbus, but many warring peoples, often culturally and perhaps racially diverse, each supplanting others before them and seeking ascendancy over one another. Shall we acknowledge the Indian's "right" to America, and must then the Indian relinquish it to a tribe which can prove it was the original, displaced "owner" of America?

Shall we say also that England must be dispossessed of all who are of Norman blood, and returned to Anglo-Saxons? Must the Anglo-Saxons return it to the Britons, and the Britons to those whom they displaced? And must France be returned to the Celts or Gauls (Galatians) in its midst, and they in turn restore it to the Basques whom they displaced? The historical argument leads to moral insanity. The authority of a state cannot depend on an original historical claim, although possession has an element of authority to it.

Another answer to the problem of authority is the democratic one. It was raised in an English rebellion of 1381, when the popular cry was,

> When Adam delved, and Eve span,
> Who was then the gentleman?

Authority rests in the people, supposedly, and the only moral ground of authority is the will of the people, in this view. In effect, the voice of the people is the voice of God. This view again breaks down in practice. Must the civil government be changed or overthrown whenever the people change their mind? Is man, any more than the state, the source of authority?

This is the heart of the issue: is authority derived from man, from history, from the state, or from tradition, or is it derived from God? On the other hand, is it derived from *force*? Very clearly, force and the state are inseparable. The state has the power of the sword, the power of coercion, and it can compel men and take life. Is its only authority simply power, naked force? More than a few people have held this to be the case. Some of these have been radical statists and others anarchists. In either case, the state is not much more than a gangster who rules with a gun in his hand and only by force.

This is a view which appeals most to the intellectually simple-minded and morally derelict. It denies that the governing force in history is moral and religious. Men allow power to that which, rightly or wrongly, they hold to be morally legitimate and right. When men ceased to believe in kings as the repository of divine right and authority, then kings quickly gave way to "the people" as the source of right. Today "the democratic state" has moral authority in the eyes of the people, and they will endure more at its hands than men earlier endured from kings.

Men at one time believed in the "King's Touch", the healing power of the king. This faith was mild compared to the faith of contemporary man in the power of the state. The state is looked to for every kind of answer, the solution to problems of poverty, health, war, natural disasters, and even death itself is supposedly going to be overcome by the state's power to apply science and solutions to every realm. Recently, someone in California filed suit against the federal government for damages in the 1971 earthquake! The state has become god for modern man, and therefore the state is responsible and accountable for all things. Perhaps someone will next accuse the state because natural death overcomes man.

The state is powerful today, because the state has a religious and moral force in the lives of people. The "common man" has not heard of Hegel, but he is a Hegelian, and the state is for him a god walking on the earth, whose duty it is to provide him with cradle to grave security. A state senator from a very conservative district recently told me that, in answer to a questionnaire geared to revealing the implicit socialism and statism of people, 75% of the people in his district were shown to be statist to the core while formally conservative. He added that, however socialistic many legislators are, the pressure from their districts is even more to the left in terms of practical demands. Even people who cry for lower taxes demand more benefits and subsidies, all of which means more statism. Statism is thus the religion and the morality of most men.

The state, however, is also very weak today in that it is a god that fails people, and its more brilliant sons are savagely at war with it because of its failures. They demand all things from the state and then turn on it savagely as a Baal that has failed them. Their morality and faith is still statist, but it is deeply infected with bitterness and despair.

Force rules history, but that ruling force is moral and religious force and conviction. *The Letters of Junius* held otherwise. *The Letters* spoke of "the first original right of he people, from which all laws derive their authority", and also of tradition as authority: "One precedent creates another. They soon accumulate and constitute a law. What yesterday was fact, today is doctrine." But men overthrow both precedent and "original right" when it violates their moral convictions, so this view is superficial. Men find their basic and ultimate authority in what they hold to be *truth*. The modern age being a humanistic one, men have sought for truth on the human and temporal level, and the state has thus come to be the basic institution for them. Humanistic man believes that the state is the way to the good life; the state is the final authority over men, and the state is the supreme court in all things. Not surprisingly, the courts of the state have increasingly become law-makers, because the standard for legality is man and the fullness of life for man. If capital punishment limits man's life, then capital punishment must be ruled unlawful. If war limits man's life, then war must be challenged in the courts. If men have a "right" to good food, housing, clothing, and all things else, whether or not they work for them, then the courts must and will establish men's "rights" to these things. The courts are keeping pace with the religious beliefs of modern man.

In view of our humanism, it is not surprising that constitutionalism is virtually dead. Even the conservative defenders of the constitution want the results of it without the Christian presuppositions and faith which undergird it. As Drucker points out, "Constitutionalism is much more than a respect for law...It is a belief that power, to be beneficial, must be subject to general and unchangeable rules. It is an assertion that ends and means cannot be meaningfully separated or considered apart from each other." (Peter F. Drucker: *Men, Ideas and Politics*, p. 175. New York: Harper & Row, 1971) Constitutionalism rests on a belief that the sovereign God has an absolute law order to which every human order must relate itself. (See Edward S. Corwin: *The "Higher Law" Background of American Constitutional Law*. Ithaca: Cornell, 1955.) The essence of humanistic law is that, instead of relating social order to God's absolute law, society must relate law to human needs. This belief is the moral force behind the modern state and the source of its authority.

The failure of humanistic authority is that it is essentially totalitarian and/or anarchistic. If the people are the source of authority, then we must either wind up in a dictatorship, in which the general will or the consensus finds its incarnation in a leader, an elite, or a party, or in anarchism, in which all men as gods do each their "own thing." There is a drift in both directions today.

The basic decisions by states in the second half of the 20th century have been made outside the normal legislative channels. Thus, in the United States, the basic and most important decisions have not been made by Congress and the normal political process, as Drucker has pointed out. In domestic politics, the basic decisions, with respect to school segregation and reapportionment, were not made by Congress but by the Supreme Court. These decisions, while opposed by many, met favor with many, and they were in line with the basic liberal, humanistic faith of church, school, and people. The opposition to these measures has also depended largely on non-political protest: the legislative branches of "democratic" civil government have not been the primary means of opposition.

Again, in foreign affairs, the U.S. committed itself to two major wars, in Korea and then in Vietnam, without any legislative action. These commitments were aspects of a humanistic and messianic save-the-world faith, and they were made by Truman and Kennedy, heroes of liberal humanism. The opposition, however, which has developed towards the Vietnam war is also grounded in humanism, and this opposition has bypassed state means increasingly for direct action and pressure.

Thus, while faith in the state remains, there is an increasing break-down in the authority of the state, because its moral foundations are crumbling. The decline in law enforcement and the rise of lawlessness is a symptom of the breakdown. What many people forget is that law enforcement is not basically a police and court affair but a moral concern. Most laws cannot be enforced unless they are first of all enforced by the moral conscience of the people. No state, however dictatorial, can enforce a law which is radically at odds with the conscience of its people. Before a revolution can occur in the political realm, it must be preceded by a revolution in the religious and moral sphere. Before the French Revolution could occur, a religious and moral decline and collapse had sapped the life of France. The Russian Revolution was preceded by a widespread decline of vital faith and a growing humanism. The people in the Soviet Union have widespread discontents, but most of them are morally in agreement with their regime and thus lack the moral force which is the forerunner and mainspring of change.

The modern state thus has great power but a declining authority. In this it resembles the regimes of kings like Charles I and James II of England, power without moral authority, in each case a prelude to ruin. In William Langland's poem, *Piers Plowman*, the angel declares to clergy and king of the late 14th century: "King and a Prince art thou, Tomorrow nothing." The moral force was gone from the social order, and the result was a long era of revolution and civil war, when men who had power today, tomorrow had nothing.

Langland's answers were unfortunately too much like those of the royalty and nobility of his day, and his earnest hope for a new order was frustrated. His answer was "charity" and a bold and heedless following of Christ. In this he echoed the "virtues" prized by the upper-class of his day, the very men who were destroying England. For them, virtue means "a prodigal generosity ('largesse') and the quality of being physically rash ('outrageous')." (Gervase Mathew: *The Court of Richard II*, p. 22 New York: Norton, 1968.) In this impotence Langland is followed by the youth of our day, who echo the statist principles and humanism they are supposedly rebelling against.

The only moral force which can undercut the power of statism is a Biblical faith in the sovereign and triune God and His absolute law-word. God said of all the nations of Isaiah's day, and of all history, that they are "nothing" in His sight (Isa. 40:23-24). "Behold, the nations are as a drop of a bucket, and are counted as the small dust of the balance: behold, he taketh up the isles as a very little thing" (Isa. 40:15). As long as men believe that salvation comes by the state, its politicians and leaders, and by the laws of the state, they will give the power of a god to the state, and the moral force of a god as well. In our day, both conservatives and leftists are at odds with the state, and often at war with it, but both are agreed in seeing it as their savior, and they concentrate their energies on statist action and control as the key to salvation. They want to capture the state machinery, such as its socialistic schools, rather than to establish independent and Christian schools. However angry they may be at the state, and rebellious against its authority, they will bow down before the state as their god and savior until they turn to their true Lord and God and serve Him only. The state will shrink to its proper place *only* when men give God His due priority and authority. There is no other way.

The power of the state will not be broken by lawless rebellion but by godly faith. As Sister M. Margaret P. McCarran observed recently, "Christ came into a world that was exactly the same kind of mess. He honored legitimate authority no matter how evil its bearer. He lived peaceably in the world of real people for thirty years in spite of revolutions, over-taxation, aggressor nations, and surrounding paganism...Our era is not a mere repetition of a historical pattern, it is the same pattern. However, our Lord said, 'I have overcome the world.' He is still saying it, it is still the same world." (Letter, December 7, 1971.)

The world has always been ruled by religious and moral force. The issue is between the moral forces of humanism and Christianity. You have your choice: are you a part of the problem, or a part in the victory?

CHALCEDON REPORT NO. 80
April 1, 1972

The sustaining force behind all authority and power is moral force. When the moral force decays, the social order decays. Men are governed by brute force only when they are ready to believe in the ideas governing that force.

More than a few men regard any reliance on moral force with cynicism. It was Stalin who said with contempt, "How many divisions has the pope?" Guns alone spelled power to him. Many leftists as well as conservatives nowadays believe that force and brute power will govern men, and they alike despise religious faith as an evasion of the issues. Political pressure and military power are their essential trust. The new left today, and such groups as the Weathermen, have a similar belief. "Direct action" really means that legal process and the battle of ideas are treated with contempt and brute force is alone trusted to change things. In this they are true sons of the current Establishment, in that the political order relies increasingly on pressure, coercion, and direct action instead of ideas, due process, and legislation. Executive orders, a moratorium on legal process, and the by-passing of law constitute forms of direct action, as do bombs and assassination.

Direct action techniques are admissions of moral bankruptcy. The old saying that the thing to do, when you run out of ideas, is to shout louder, has more than a little truth to it.

Stalin's direct action, as also Lenin's, was a result of moral bankruptcy. The Marxist dream called for the destruction of capitalism so that communism might flower. Instead, famine was the immediate result of collectivization. The greedy masses who had cooperated with revolution now found themselves the victims of it. Every kind of intellectual gymnastic was performed to rationalize the failure of the ideal order to materialize. War was declared against "counter-revolution" and a blood-bath was stepped up, with the revolution devouring its own fathers and sons. By the time Stalin died, the belief in the Marxist hope was all but dead, and cynicism had replaced it. Anatoli Kuznetsov, in his forward to *Octobriana and the Russian Underground*, declares that, "Hidden behind the official fine words, cynicism -- both political and moral -- has become the dominant feature of the average Soviet man, who no longer believes either in God, or the devil, or Lenin, or Communism, or in anything at all: his heart holds nothing but smoldering ruins." The result, Kuznetsov points out, is a radical moral collapse among the people, in high places and low.

Attempts to offer political salvation always lead to a decay of moral force, because the state cannot provide men with a faith for living, nor with moral character. The state itself must rely on the people for these things; the state is a mirror of the faith and hopes of the people, and it cannot generate in and of itself what its members lack. As a result, the religious and moral collapse of a people creates a crisis for the state. The moral emptiness of a people becomes the moral emptiness of the state.

Most politics have become pragmatic and relativistic. Thus, in the United States, the solution to problems is increasingly based on such premises. As a result, its "best" answer is always to buy off the trouble-maker. There is no belief in a harmony of interests. The reverse of this is a philosophy of a conflict of interests; this often appears in speeches, but, in practice, it is all too often neither the free market harmony of interests, nor the Marxist conflict of interests, which prevails. Rather, it is the philosophy of the bribe and pay-off. Pay-off foreign powers and give them what they want to win their support. Grant subsidies, favorable legislation, and pay-offs to minority groups, capital, labor, agriculture, college students, senior citizens, and every strong protesting groups as a means of quietening protests. The answer is thus not a principle but a pay-off. In this, the state mirrors its people who are themselves unprincipled. Parents "buy-off" their children instead of disciplining them; money is spent as a means of winning the child's love and allegiance. The methodology of Dr. Spock's baby-care has become the politics of a nation.

This is not new, of course. It has happened again and again in civilization. When nations lose their moral force, they substitute for it something else as the rationale of their civilization, because man in no age has been able to live by bread alone. Very commonly, such a decaying civilization, having lost all faith in moral absolutes, turns to a non-religious source for its justification. Aesthetics becomes a substitute for ethics, beauty the replacement for morality. The classic example of this, under the influence of Buddhism, was ancient China; in the thirteenth century, Japan also turned to aesthetics for its faith.

In such a culture, moral character is replaced by a subtle and refined appreciation for every nuance of beauty and taste. Men may be butchers and sadists, but they can talk learnedly of the finest details of aesthetics, of gourmet experiences, and of delicate variations of aesthetic taste. The Renaissance gives us many examples of such people. John Tiptoft, Earl of Worcester and Constable of England earned the title of "Butcher of England" in the fifteenth century; at the same time, he was a world traveler, a scholar, and a cultivated gentleman; he could weep over a torn manuscript and yet view cruelty and murder coldly. Significantly, at the same time, the belief in sorcery and magic was strong. Men looked for power, and the occult thus attracted them. Since they sought unprincipled power, the occult was to their taste. Since aesthetics was concerned with good taste, not good morals, they could readily combine perversity and perversion with an emphasis on good taste.

Aesthetics, however, when separated from ethics and theology, ceases to become a delight in beauty and becomes a refinement in bad taste, then perverted taste. Any analysis of avant garde art, of pop art, primitivism, and every major movement of recent years makes clear very quickly that art is now a pursuit in large part of ugliness, but, even more, of shock and impact, an attempt at power through continually heightened perversity. Originally, this turning to the primitive had been based on a philosophy derived from Rousseau, a trust in the primitive as the simple, virtuous, and healthy; as faith in the masses declined, this return to the primitive became perverse: it became a philosophy of negation, and art and politics became a negation of principle, law, morality, and, above all else, God. Alfred Jarry, in *Ubu Roi - Ubu Enchaine'*, has his actors appear on "The Field of Mars" and say: "We are free men and here is our corporal. Hurrah for liberty, liberty, liberty. We are free. Never forget that our duty is to be free. Walk a little slower or we'll arrive on time. Liberty is never arriving on time - never, never! Let us have our liberty drill. Let's disobey all together, one, two, three, you first, you second, you third. There's the difference. Every one of us marches in a different rhythm, even though it's more tiring. Let us disobey individually our freeman's corporal. The Corporal: Riot!" Mehring commented on this: "Collective disobedience under orders from the corporal of liberty in the 'riot camp' - that would be total freedom for humanity, the freedom of all with respect to each. The next step after that kind of freedom was to press the muzzle of a revolver to one's temple -- and that was the step Alfred Jarry took." (Walter Mehring: *The Lost Library*, p. 94f. London: Secker & Warbuly, 1951.)

The aesthetics which develops in a world of relativism is an aesthetics of destruction. In 1856, Walt Whitman gave the philosophy of an aesthetics of destruction in his poem "Respondez!", declaring,

> Respondez! Respondez!...
> Must we still go on with our affectations and sneaking!
> Let me bring this to a close - I pronounce openly for a new distribution of roles;
> Let that which stood in front go behind! and let that which was behind advance to the front and speak;
> Let murders, bigots, fools, unclean persons offer new propositions!
> Let the old propositions be postponed!
> Let faces and theories be turn'd inside out! Let meanings be freely criminal, as well as results!...
> Let us all, without missing one, be exposed in public, naked, monthly, at the peril of our lives! let our bodies be freely handled and examined by whoever chooses!
> Let nothing but copies at second hand be permitted to exist upon the earth!
> Let the earth desert God, nor let there ever henceforth be mention'd the name of God!
> Let there be no God!
> Let the reformers descend from the stands where they are forever bawling! let an idiot or an insane person appear on each of the stands!...
> Let shadows be furnish'd with genitals! let substances be deprived of their genitals!

This description of total revolution is a description of our times. The aesthetics of violence believes in the cleansing power of violence and force. Thus, a culture which denies faith and moral force turns to aesthetics and finally a justification of violence as a new moral force.

Violence as the new moral force is then directed against other men. Leon Trotsky, in *Literature and Revolution*, declared that "Our goal is the total recasting of man." This total recasting requires total coercion and total power, because man wants his world to change, not himself. Man wants the world to meet his needs, not he the standards or needs of the world. Man then becomes the subject of coercive action to recast him in terms of the state's plan for man. Andre Malraux, in *Man's Fate*, wrote that "It is very rare for man to be able to endure...his human condition...It is always necessary for men to intoxicate themselves." Marx said that men found refuge in the opium of religion; Malraux called it intoxication. As Mehring sarcastically observed, "It is obvious that so marvelously complicated a life factory as the modern state has become must naturally seize completely not only the means of production, but the means for intoxication as well." In terms of Malraux, man is deprived of his means of intoxication; in Whittman's language, he is stripped naked in order to be recast.

In 1944, Werfel wrote, "Everyone of us needs a re-connection, a *'re-ligio'* - in its etymological sense - with an established entity." He saw the coming bankruptcy of modern man: "Modern man is loth to accept the truth that certain creative forces in him are bankrupt, that this great loss has left him a shivering beggar in spite of his strenuously built-up physique. On the contrary, he believes himself to be the possessor of a promissory note on happiness which one day will be redeemed when his political Ersatz religion will have created the material prerequisites for it." (Franz Werfel: *Between Heaven and Earth*, pp. ix, 21f. New York Philosophical Library, 1944.) Men are now finding that they have no "promissory note on happiness" and no political paradise around the corner of history. Instead, they are beginning to realize that their contempt of religious and moral force is leading them into the most fearful of all bondage, slavery to the state. Man has become the property of the state, the sheep of the state's pasture, kept for shearing and given no right of appeal against the supremacy of the state. By believing in nothing, man is becoming nothing. By granting creation no creator and no direction and no transcendental meaning, man has deprived himself of meaning. By denying God and the moral force of God's word, man has left himself a world in which apparently only brute force and coercion rule. But man cannot live by bread alone, and he cannot live under coercion alone. Man having been created in God's image requires meaning and purpose to live, and this meaning can only truly come from God. Werfel observed, "As intellectual beings we can as little conceive meaninglessness as a square circle or a bent straight line. Without an over-meaning, i.e. without world-conception, world-creation, world-direction, the universe would be meaningless and therefore inconceivable" (p. 126).

The coercive power of statism is very much with us. It will become much worse before there is a change. The hollow men of humanism can protest, riot, and destroy, but they cannot supply that moral force which alone can restore meaning and direction to man and history. T. S. Eliot was right: the hollow men and their world can only end, and "Not with a bang but a whimper."

This is not so with men of faith. W. Haller, in *The Rise of Puritanism*, observed that "Men who have assurance that they are to inherit heaven, have a way of presently taking possession of earth" (p. 162). In one of his letters, Samuel Rutherford (1600-1661) declared, "Duties are ours, events are the Lord's." Men who have God for their sovereign can neither believe that evil shall triumph nor can they tolerate it. Their lives are governed by moral force, and they govern everything they can control with that same moral force.

The world is full of wailing men who see the enormity of evil but not the sovereignty of God over all things. It is impossible for man to triumph against God. The purpose of God is not the enthronement of evil, nor is it the counsel of the ungodly which shall prevail. The triumph of God and His cause is inescapable, and, whether we see that triumph or not, we must never doubt that it will prevail. Samuel Rutherford wrote, "The thing which we mistake is the want of victory. We hold that to be the mark of one that hath no grace. Nay, say I, the want of *fighting* were a mark of no grace." All too many who call themselves Christian lack this mark: there is no fight in them as they face evils and troubles, only a long whine. In 1641, Hansard Knollys, in the midst of troubles and war, summoned men to struggle unremittingly for God's New Jerusalem and to beseech God concerning it: "It is the work of the day to give God no rest till He sets up Jerusalem as the praise of the whole world." This is religious conviction and moral force. Man was called to rule, not to be ruled, to have dominion, not to be a subject (Gen. 1:26-28). Apart from God, this is impossible. Under God, man has a mandate to reconstruct all things, and the power of God to do it.

CHALCEDON REPORT NO. 81
May 1, 1972

Predestination is very much a political issue today, and a very central one. The churches have little to say on the subject these days; they either do not believe in it, or are often embarrassed by the entire question. Predestination is simply the doctrine of total law, total government, and total planning. The important question is not, do we believe in it, but rather, whose predestination do we believe in? The alternative to predestination is a universe of meaningless and brute factuality, a world of chance.

Predestination goes by a number of other terms in its humanistic and antichristian versions. It is called scientific determinism, dialectical materialism, scientific socialist planning, and a number of other names. Modern humanistic predestination is total planning and control by the state and its elite planners; it has a concept of an electing decree, but not by God, but rather by man, statist man. Moreover, because predestination is an inescapable concept, as men have denied predestination by God, they have affirmed predestination by the state. Predestination is an unavoidable concept, not only because it is a God-ordained category of thought, but also because the alternative to a purpose and plan is chance and meaninglessness, and man requires meaning. Without meaning and direction to life, man perishes. Today, in our existentialist age, even seven year old boys are committing suicide. Man requires a meaning and a plan to life, an assured and certain direction. The problem enters in when he chooses to find that meaning and plan in man or the state rather than in God. Man is then courting the world of George Orwell's *1984*; he is asking for a totalitarian humanistic order as his preferred alternative to a totalitarian government by the sovereign God.

The origins of our present crisis are important to understand. In pagan antiquity, religion was an aspect of political order. Man's basic hope was in political salvation. Man was regarded as a political animal, the creature of the state and therefore entirely subject to the government and power of the state.

With the coming of Christianity, a long battle began between statism and Biblical faith. (See R. J. Rushdoony: *The Foundations of Social Order*, Presbyterian & Reformed Publ. Co., Nutley, New Jersey, 1968.) Throughout the centuries, the predominance has gone back and forth, but, in the now dying modern era, the age of the state, men have looked to the state rather than to God for their salvation. Previously, in Christian eras, men looked to the sovereign God for government and law. With the Enlightenment, however, predestination by God was replaced with predestination by "Nature". The idea that such a thing as "Nature" exists is, of course, a myth; *nature* is a collective noun for a universe of particular facts. It is not nominalism to deny the reality of nature as a governing being or entity. Enlightenment thinkers, however, saw "Nature" as a governing, predestinating entity which so perfectly ordained all things that, in the words of Alexander Pope, in his *Essay on Man*,

> All nature is but art, unknown to thee;
> All chance, direction, which thou canst not see;
> All discord, harmony not understood;
> A partial evil, universal good:
> And, spite of pride, in erring reason's spite,
> One truth is clear, WHATEVER IS, IS RIGHT.

Pope and other Enlightenment thinkers clearly held to a doctrine of infallibility by "Nature" and the predestination of all things in terms of "Nature's" perfect and "universal good." At the same time, they denied vehemently the sovereignty and predestination of God.

When Darwin published his *Origin of Species in 1859*, this Enlightenment doctrine of Nature rapidly crumbled. Darwin himself showed traces of the old belief, but the new view of nature which appeared in Darwin was one of blind, meaningless, directionless chance. Moreover, as Darwinism developed, more than a few thinkers drew the logical conclusion. Not only was life without meaning and purpose, but man and the universe were only accidents in a meaningless ocean of being. They were products, as Lucretius had ages before held, of the fortuitous concourse of atoms, arising out of emptiness and destined to return to nothingness.

Another logical conclusion followed. Since God was supposedly dead, and since the old idea of Nature was a myth, if meaning and direction exist at all, man must supply them. Man must take control and issue his own law and predestinating plan against the hovering darkness of chaos. Man must make his future, creating, planning, and governing it as surely as he controls and governs a machine. Predestination by man was the answer to the now obsolete predestination by Nature.

The perverse and twisted mind of Karl Marx here revealed its calibre. Marx had earlier grasped, together with others, that the next step in humanism was predestination by man. He read that step back into nature, after Hegel, seeing man and in particular scientific planning man as the incarnation of a struggling mind in the universe, as man's elite mind working out a plan of predestination to impose upon history and nature. The emerging force would incarnate itself in the communist world order.

Marx realized that Darwin, by destroying the Enlightenment view of Nature, had made scientific socialist predestination the next step in history. The publication and immediate acceptance of Darwin's thesis was thus hailed by both Marx and Engels as the assurance of their victory.

Since their day, a third of the world has become Marxist and subscribes to their version of predestinarianism, or, at least, bows down before it. The rest of the world almost entirely follows other versions of the same humanistic predestinarianism, Fabian Socialism, democratic socialism, fascism and like faiths.

Predestination is thus very much a live issue. More than that, it is now a politico-religious issue. Men daily look to the predestination of the state. An unplanned life is to them anathema; the gods of the state must govern all things.

Two very popular and best-selling books have set forth this doctrine of radical humanistic predestination, Alvin Toffler's *Future Shock* (1970), and John McHale's *The Future of the Future* (1971). Both portray a future in which a scientific elite predestines all things: the future of the future is to be made by man. Man shall predestine all our tomorrows.

An ominous cloud, however, appears in both books. Planners are always having trouble with man. A machine can be totally controlled: it is man's creation. A computer can be programmed to do exactly what the programmer requires, within the limitations of the computer's ability. But man is God's creature, not man's. Man cannot be programmed in the radical and total way man wants. In every society, man is the stumbling block towards realizing the plan. Man still moves in terms of God's plan and purpose, not man's.

In this respect, as far as humanistic planners go, B. F. Skinner, in *Beyond Freedom and Dignity* (1971), is still a conservative one. He still believes that by conditioning and/or controls (whether by brain implants or other means is for the moment immaterial) man can be controlled. Others are less hopeful, and they look for an artificial man to replace God's man in their humanistic earth or hell. Toffler tells us that humanoids ("carefully wired" robots) will begin to replace people, and we will be unable to "determine whether the smiling, assured humanoid behind the airline reservation counter is a pretty girl or a carefully wired robot." He reports also that "Professor Block at Cornell speculates that man-machine sexual relationships may not be too far distant." (p. 211). President Nixon has established a National Goals Research Staff of scientific and other experts to plan "the projection of social trends." All of this is a modern jargon for predestination.

In this humanistic plan, man is increasingly obsolete. In God's plan man is either a God-ordained heir of all creation, created to exercise dominion under God, or a reprobate and rebel. His every act is a part of a cosmic meaning. In man's idea of predestination, only a robot or an artificial man can meet the specifications.

In various ways, man is beginning to recognize this. Among the first to see it were the disillusioned, humanistic, and rebellious students of the early 1960s. The motto of one of the earliest student demonstrations, carried on badges and banners, was "Do not fold, staple, or mutilate." This was a bitter resentment against a controlled humanism which was trying to turn man himself into a machine. The revolt declined into sullen and meaningless protest and violence, because the students had no answer to the question, "What is man?" Their only answer to statist predestination was to demand either more action from the state or to turn to a sterile anarchism. The students had sensed the issue, but they had not answered it. The liberals, conservatives, and Marxists still looked to the state, and to control of the state and its machinery, for their answer.

A great hero of the Enlightenment radicals, as well as of the 20th century conservatives, was Cicero, a champion of salvation by the state. Cicero regarded religion as a convenient means of keeping the masses obedient; for him, salvation was political and statist. He championed racial levelling, especially in his oration defending Lucius Balbus, as a means of strengthening the power of the state. He spoke of Rome in religious terms and furthered the cult of the City of Rome. He called Rome "the light of the world", but within a century, Jesus Christ answered Cicero and Rome, declaring, "I am the light of the world" (John 8:12). Cicero saw the philosopher-king as the earthly incarnation of the divine mind; he hailed Augustus as savior, saying, "In him we place our hopes of liberty; from him we have already received salvation." In 61 B.C., Cicero, who knew more than a little about the God of Israel and the Old Testament Scriptures, rejected all of it as "barbarian superstition"; his hope was in politics and in political leaders, and he was glad to see Israel conquered and its ideas ostensibly defeated. But Cicero died at the hands of his political leaders, and Rome became not a savior but a corrupt empire. The Ciceros of our day may not do as well, and they have less excuse than Cicero to hope in political salvation and political predestination.

In 1959, the late Wilhelm Ropke wrote, "The ultimate source of all mistakes in our dealings with communism is intellectual and moral. In fact, it is our inability or unwillingness to comprehend the full substance and nature of this conflict between communism and the free world, its tremendous implacability and deeply moral and intellectual implications. Again and again, we fall into the error of conceiving this conflict to be an old-fashioned diplomatic power struggle. In reality it is a collision of two irreconcilable systems that are intellectually and morally diametrically opposed." (Wilhelm Ropke, "How to Deal with the Communists" in *The Individualist*, Jan. - Feb., 1963.) Since then, the free world has moved closer to communism, and the basic cause of its decline has been its growing humanism, its preference for the predestination of man rather than of God.

But here we can borrow the language of an eloquent champion of humanistic and statist predestination, Chairman Mao Tse-tung. Mao is confident that all his enemies, domestic and foreign, are "merely paper tigers." He is not impressed by the power of any nation in the world, because, in terms of Marxist predestination, they are doomed, and they are therefore ultimately only "paper tigers." But Mao is wrong: it is not Marx's plan which governs all men, nations, and history, but God's plan, for God only is absolute Lord and Sovereign of the universe. Thus, for all their momentary power, it is Marx and Mao who are "paper tigers" before God.

We must see ourselves and all things as God ordains it. We are told emphatically, "Behold, the nations are as a drop of a bucket, and are counted as the small dust of the balance: behold, he taketh up the isles as a very little thing" (Isa. 40:15). It is God whom we must fear and revere, not man. It is God who shall create the future, and already has, and it is His purpose and plan we must serve, not His enemy's. The Scriptures are an announcement to men on a battlefield of the certainty of God's victory, and it is a summons to prepare for victory and to act on it.

Those whom you fear, you will bend before and serve. "The fear of man bringeth a snare: but whoso putteth his trust in the LORD shall be safe"

(Prov. 29:25). We have been called to victory: we must expect it, fight for it, and act on it. It is God's purpose for us.

CHALCEDON REPORT NO. 82
June 1, 1972

Despite their differences, which are very real, our political left and right have much in common: they are concerned, in varying ways, with peace, and with law and order. The left, militant in its hostility to the war in Vietnam, has international law and order in mind. Granted that many of the recent demonstrations against the war have been communist-controlled (as Mayor Yorty of Los Angeles proved), they clearly have a popular following because the hostility to the war is very deep. The hostility has good constitutional grounds, moreover. According to the U.S. Constitution, a drafted army, or militia, can *only* be used to repel invasion, suppress insurrection, and enforce the laws of the Union, *not* for a foreign war. Those conservatives who favor the war are thus as lax in their use of the Constitution as the U.S. Supreme Court, and they contribute to the erosion of the law.

The conservatives, on the other hand, also want peace, and law and order. They maintain that international law and order depend on defeating communism. Nationally, it means strict law enforcement, and here they are able to score against the left for its lax use of the law and the attendant erosion of the vitality of the law. They can point to the steady disintegration of social order, the increase of crime, and the widely prevalent disrespect for law.

The reigning liberals are no less concerned with peace, and with law and order, although their definitions would not agree with those of the left and right. Their involvement in Vietnam, according to every President from Kennedy to Nixon, has been a peace-making involvement. Their attempts to gain internal peace are very prominent, although they are in effect the same as their international efforts, namely, to gain peace by buying peace. Concessions are made to the communists, to minority groups, to capital and to labor, both to buy support and also to buy peace. The principle is simply the old idea that a tiger with a full stomach is safer to live with than a hungry one. The hope, in fact, is that the satiated tiger can be turned into a pussy-cat with constant stuffing.

But peace on all sides is a common goal, however differently sought. Men are weary with trouble, tension, and the growing lack of safety for man in his own home or on his own street.

This situation is not new. Mattingly gives us a telling insight into the attitude of the people of the Roman Empire:

> Peace is the boon that is most steadily and fervently desired, for on it depend such possibilities of the good life as the Empire can still offer.

> Liberty is still valued, but no longer as the supreme good; it is never for long in the foreground...The Empire gave stability and rest to a weary and aging world.
> (Harold Mattingly: *The Man in the Roman Street*, p. 111. New York: W.W. Norton 1966.)

The Romans, Mattingly points out, had "a great absorption in the present with a vast respect for the past." They had less interest in the future. "'The rapture of the forward view' is very hard to find in any corner of the Roman Empire." The Roman concern was to maintain what they had, not to work and plan for a greater future. (*Ibid.*, pp. 137, 141f., 149.) As a result, despite the lack of any real enemy other than itself, Rome fell. It had only one future-oriented element, the Christians, who then built a new civilization.

The people of Rome wanted peace with law and order, and Rome was less and less able to deliver it. Today, the failure of the state to give peace is everywhere apparent. The goals of most people are limited ones, simply to be given enough law and order to enjoy what they have in peace. If they could turn the clock back twenty years, they would be very happy. But people whose goal is peace rarely enjoy it. Peace is a product of true victory, and law and order cannot flourish unless first of all there is theological law and philosophical order. People today want the fruits of peace, not the roots.

Where people long for peace rather than victory and progress, there also a distorted vision prevails. This distorted vision governed many American writers of the 19th century. They had broken with the Puritan faith of their fathers and were hostile to the America it had produced. As a result, many of them could see little good in the United States and everything evil. Still surrounded by forests, streams, and a continent of rich resources, they looked all the same to other shores for their paradise and hope. Herman Melville, in *Clarel*, spoke of Tahiti as the only fit place on earth for the advent of Christ. But both the authorities Melville used and his own knowledge confirmed the fact that the South Sea islands were no paradise, less so then than now: the islands were marked, Baird tells us, "by filth and disease, idiocy and cruelty. They had plagues of stinging flies, fetid heat, ordure around the dwelling places, filth and vermin over the food, and so on." William Ellis reported that on an island near Tahiti he had seen a hungry child given a piece of her own father's flesh for nourishment. Lt. Wise, following Melville on Nukuhiva, saw the chief's brother, drunk with *ava*, coiled upon a bed of filthy mats, 'half dead with some loathsome disease'." (James Baird: *Ishmael, A Study of the Symbolic Mode in Primitivism*, p. 120f. New York: Harper Torchbooks, 1960.) Somewhat later, Gauguin, while admitting that Tahitian women were "not beautiful, properly speaking," still held that they had an indefinable quality "of penetrating the mysteries of the infinite" (p. 149). Both Melville and Gauguin failed to see the potentialities of their respective countries and looked for the impossible in the South Seas and imposed their imagination on a world they would not face realistically. This same imposition of dreams on to an ugly reality has been common among travellers to the communist countries: they see no good in their country and see the Marxist states in the light of their imagination.

When men place peace above other considerations, they are unwilling to face up to anything which tells them that their dream is a futile one. They are ready then to compromise truth in order to gain peace, because they are weary of the struggle.

But peace like happiness always eludes men when they make it a goal of human endeavor. Peace and happiness are by-products of other goals. We cannot make ourselves truly happy by deciding we need to be happy. Happiness is a product of work well done, of a life lived in successful community, of peace with God, and of much more. Men make happiness a goal when they have failed miserably in all other objectives, and what they then mean by happiness is really a narcotized state wherein they feel no griefs and can enjoy some very limited pleasures of play. Similarly, peace is a by-product of a general success in one's relationships to God and man, in one's calling, and in a confident prospect concerning the future. Peace implies a harmony of affairs and a general harmony of personal and social interests. What most people mean by peace is an attitude of, 'Leave me alone, and don't bother me with the problems of the world,' or, 'Do anything, but get rid of all these problems, and leave me to enjoy myself.' Peace in this sense is a retreat. It is more than that: it is a form of suicide, a surrender of life for a retirement to the sidelines of life.

Unfortunately for these people, the world is now moving towards a radical confrontation of man by the basic issues and problems of life. All the postponed problems, the deferred and pressing debts of life, are beginning to fall due and are demanding attention. The luxury of indifference is fast waning. Church members who left the defense of the faith to their clergy are now finding that God is requiring them to defend their faith or to surrender it. The state, which has been promising man more and more cradle to grave (or womb to tomb) security is less and less able to delivery any kind of security. A radio announcement today by a presidential candidate asked, 'Are you tired of phonies in political office? Then vote for me...' The appeal of this approach has been great, and the reason is an obvious one. *Any* politician who offers man peace and security will offer thereby a fraudulent claim, so that a contender can always impugn his integrity in order to gain office. He in turn will be regarded as equally a fraud, because no politician can deliver what God Himself alone can give, and does not give more than a limited amount of in this world. Psalm 24:2 tells us something about the world, and our life in it, which men prefer to forget: "For he hath founded it upon the seas, and established it upon the floods." This is a very precarious foundation for life! The seas and the floods are places for alert and steady movement, not a peaceful standing still. History is a battlefield, and it calls for action to victory. There is peace and order in the graveyard, not on the firing line. A culture or civilization which thinks first of peace is most certain to have war and death, because it has lost its will to live.

In the midst of a Roman Empire dedicated to peace and security, oblivious of the future and trying to hold on to the remnants of the past, one element was future-oriented and able to command the day, the Christians. For long years now, the church has been asleep, clergy and laity alike. The widespread apostasy of the clergy is forcing many of the laity out of their slumbers. If the faith is to be defended, they must do it. The result is a spreading revival of doctrinal concern, a re-awakening of faith, prayer, and action, and a readiness to stand for the faith which did not exist twenty years ago, The old forms are crumbling, perhaps because they must. Old wineskins cannot contain new wine. The oldest and most worn of the old wineskins is the humanistic state. The state as man's savior has tried desperately to give man that peace and security which its political lullabies have promised; however, even its pampered brats of the academic community are awake and squalling. The things the modern state least provides are those it most promises, peace and security, and, in the growing monetary crisis, its ability to give even a measure of these is limited.

We live in a momentous and exciting era, a turning point in history. Before the healing rains come, the sky always darkens, and the thunder and lightning are very much in evidence. We are not in the winter-time of the world, but in its spring. Wise men will plant for the future.

CHALCEDON REPORT NO. 83
July 1, 1972

Webster's New International Dictionary, in its supposedly conservative second edition, defined totalitarian thus: "Of or pertaining to a highly centralized government under the control of a political group which allows no recognition of or representation to other political parties, as in Fascist Italy or in Germany under the Nazi regime." Several things are wrong with this definition, which is a good example of the fact that even good dictionaries do not always define either too honestly or too well. First of all, the definition is slanted when it comes to citing examples, in that it omits the major totalitarian state, the Soviet Union. Second, and more important, the definition is purely political. Is it of the essence of totalitarianism that it allows no representation or freedom for other political parties, or is it not rather that it allows no freedom for any element of society at all? Third, and closely related to this, the definition simply ignores the word defined:

totalitarian. The word means that the totality of life, men, property, religion, education, and all else, are controlled by the state. Just as God as sovereign lord and creator absolutely governs and ordains all things by His omnipotent counsel and decree, so the totalitarian state plays god, and by its total plan seeks to govern every aspect of life and to conform it to its purposes.

Totalitarianism is not new in history. What is new is the added potential for total power which modern communications and transportation media give to the totalitarian state. Ancient Egypt and many states since have been totalitarian. The sovereign and absolute government of God over all things is one that institutions and aspects of the created order have again and again claimed and sought to arrogate to themselves. It is important to analyze some of these totalitarian claims and attempts in order to understand the issue more clearly. Very clearly, the church in the "medieval" era did declare itself to be the Kingdom of God and the umbrella over all society and all things therein, so that some have referred to the church then as having been totalitarian. It is easy to see the faults of another era, less easy sometimes to see our own in perspective. The 20th century has already seen, it is said, the death of 100 million people by torture, famine, war, and forced labor. The "medieval" church at its worst was not totalitarian in the strict sense of the word because its faith required a denial of any such claim, in that God alone is sovereign lord and governor of all things. The creed of the church was a witness against every false churchman. It asserted the transcendental, super-natural nature and origin of God's absolute government, so that there was always a built-in judgment against false churchmen.

This is very important. True totalitarianism must deny God's transcendental government, law, and counsel. The origin of all things must be here and now, in the universe, within the grasp of man. Totalitarianism and immanence go hand in hand. A philosophy of immanence holds that all essence, being, and power are fully present in the world, and exclusively in the world, so that the world is fully governed by its own inherent nature and potentiality. From Hegel through Marx and Darwin, the modern philosophy of immanence received its great expression and made possible modern, totalitarianism.

Earlier, many areas of science had been totalitarian in their philosophies. Thus, physicists sought and some still seek to reduce all reality to physics. Mathematicians of an earlier day would only allow a God who was the Great Mathematician, that is, the built-in cosmic computer of the universe. Reality, in brief, was reduced to a particular institution or discipline of which men were the governors or interpreters.

This same fallacy has marked economics, in that all too many free market advocates under the influence of a philosophy of immanentism, have taken this one sphere of law and absolutized it as the *only* law. We do agree with classical economics as *economics*, but not as a religious philosophy. When it is converted into a religious philosophy of immanence, it denies validity to any transcendental law of God and to all other institutions and orders of life unless they pass the test of the free market. Free market economics then becomes totalitarian and absolutist: it becomes idolatry. Some hold that the family and prostitution, and normal and perverted sexuality, must compete on a free market basis. Narcotics and good food are reduced to the same free market test. In brief, anything and everything goes, because there is only one law, the free market, and only one value, the free market. (One person contends that there should be no title to property, but only the right of access by everyone who is able to command the power and money to take the property, in other words, a free market for power and violence as well.) Any value derived from any other sphere, or any principled judgment derived from a transcendental order, from God, must compete on a free market basis, it is held. This is simply saying that the free market is god, and that it is the absolute and sole value in the universe. It assumes that there is no God beyond the market, no other law, no other value, than the free market. Moreover, because the free market has its truth in the economic sphere, they sit back smugly, satisfied that they have the key to life. The Marxists no less than other totalitarians stress one or two partial "truths", which they use to exclude all truth and God, and the same is true of those who reduce the world to matter. *The free market religionists* are really great enemies of free market economics, in that they pervert an instrument of freedom into a form of totalitarianism. It is not surprising that many free market religionists have in recent years been very congenial to the New Left: both are alike in their strident totalitarianism.

The political religionists, however, are far more numerous. They believe in salvation by the state, and, even when democratic or republican in their governmental forms, they are essentially totalitarian. Contrary to Webster's Dictionary, a state can have many political parties and still be totalitarian. Let us examine how this is possible. First, a totalitarian state either denies God or ignores Him because it is, to all practical intent, the ultimate power in its universe. By denying or ignoring the transcendental and sovereign God, a state makes a major and decisive step into totalitarianism. It says in effect, "I am god, and beside me there is no other power in my realm." Second, a totalitarian state, having denied God, assumes the role of God by taking control over every area of life, education, health, welfare, the family, the church, private associations, and all things else. As the predestinating god, the state insists on working out a plan for every area of life, and it progressively requires strict obedience to that plan. The plan represents the god-like wisdom of the state in its concern for its creatures, and to oppose the plan is to be seen as a devil and an enemy of the state.

Third, this means, of course, that for political religionists all the problems of life can be solved by political action, by and through the state. This requires the control of science, medicine, property, money, education, and everything so that the state can marshal all its powers to overcome the obstacle at hand. Not surprisingly, politicians speak of the conquest of war, ignorance, poverty, disease, and even death as legitimate objects of statist action. If all power is of this world, not of God, then all answers are of this world and from man organized as the state. Because it is believed that total power is in man, total power is sought in and through man's great agency, the state.

Fourth, as long as the people of the state are largely political religionists, people who believe in salvation by politics, all their political parties will share this faith. In virtually every country today, political parties, whatever their differences on methods and measures, do believe in salvation by politics. Theirs is a statist totalitarianism (as against the free market religionists' totalitarianism of the market-place). Quite rightly, therefore, Huntford speaks of Sweden, which has more than one political party, as totalitarian, and he sees the same elements of totalitarianism in varying degrees in other Western nations. In his very important study, he sees Sweden as an approximation of Aldous Huxley's *Brave New World*, and the rest of the West as nations in quest of the same goal. (Roland Huntford: *The New Totalitarians*. New York: Stein and Day, 1972.)

The only valid answer to totalitarianism of every variety is a Biblical faith which denies all philosophies of immanence and holds to the sovereignty of the triune God. The ultimate standard, power, and authority in the universe resides, not in the state, nor the market-place, nor in physics, mathematics, nor in anything else which pertains to the created order. To God alone belongs dominion, power, and authority. There is no ultimacy in the created universe, only change, the possibilities of change, either to grow or to decline, and sin, a transgression of God's law and order. There is also obedience, the possibility of progress towards God's purpose for us, purposeful growth toward an established goal. There is moreover freedom; since ultimacy belongs to God, only God can bind man by His decree. Man has no right to bind his fellow man by any man-made concept or law. Only God's law is binding. Man is thus freed from his worst oppressor, man.

A philosophy of immanence leads to totalitarianism, because it places all power and authority in the present order of things, and it gives man no supreme court of appeals in God against the world. Wherever and whenever a philosophy of immanence has governed men to any degree, to that degree totalitarian tyranny has also governed men.

The power of the modern state is very great, and it is totalitarian, but it rests on a false faith. That faith is crumbling now, but it is not enough for men to become bitter at a particular form of totalitarianism. They must reject the faith which undergirds it, which means that they must reject it first in themselves.

It also means more than a humanistic and pietistic return to religion. Men have often looked to God as a life-raft, a spare tire and an insurance policy in case of trouble, or as an aid to life. In a very humanistic bit of advertising, we are told that "The family that prays together stays together." True enough, but is that the purpose of praying? And is it not an offense to the sovereign God to see the purpose of prayer merely as family togetherness? The triune God must above all else be for us the sovereign lord, authority, and power, whom we serve and obey because it is the essence and requirement of life to do so. "Man's chief end is to glorify God and to enjoy Him forever."

The power of the God with whom we have to do is not the blundering, brutal power of man and the state but an all-wise, all-holy government which is mindful of every hair of our head (Matt. 10:30), and whose victory and purpose are assured.

Life has always been a time of testing, and it is no less so now. It is also a time of choosing, a time when men choose and are chosen, when men reveal what they are and then move in terms of it. If we are governed by our fears of men, then we are governed by men, and if we are governed by our humanistic love of man, then we are governed by man. "The fear of man bringeth a snare: but whoso putteth his trust in the LORD shall be safe" (Prov. 29:25). How safe are you?

There is nothing in our creeds about defeat. Rather, in the glorious words of the Benedictus, God "hath raised up an horn of salvation for us in the house of his servant David;...that we should be saved from our enemies, and from the hand of all that hate us...that we being delivered out of the hand of our enemies *might serve him without fear, in holiness and righteousness before him*, **all** the days of our life" (Luke 1:71,74,75). Having this assurance, St. Paul declared, "Rejoice in the Lord alway: and again I say, Rejoice" (Phil. 4:4).

CHALCEDON REPORT NO. 84
August 1, 1972

One of the telling aspects of life and thought in Old Russia was the rise and prevalence of Nihilism. The history of Nihilism as a movement and a philosophy competing with Populism, Marxism, and other movements, is an important one, but, even more important, nihilism was a mood and an outlook which infected more than those who called themselves Nihilists. The philosophical Nihilists bowed to no authority and accepted no doctrine unless proven to their satisfaction; they were the fathers of anarchism. Bakunin, the great Nihilist, was an atheist who called for the abolition of church, state, marriage and the family, and private property. His thesis was, "Be ready to die and ready to kill any one who opposes the triumph of your revolt."

Very quickly, however, it became apparent that the Nihilist-Anarchist youth were persons, as one of their number frankly stated, who had a "psychological unfitness for any peaceful work." As a matter of fact, the anarchist Boris Savinkov made it as a test of membership "that only those psychologically unable to engage in peaceful work should enter the terrorist field and that, in general, one should not make the decision hastily." (Boris Savinkov: *Memoirs of a Terrorist*, pp. 13, 77, 85. New York: Albert & Charles Boni, 1931.) The nihilistic temperament was thus one of an apocalyptic love of destruction and an inability to work. It was a hatred of everything in the world at hand, and a lust to kill, maim, and destroy as the means to peace and freedom. The only joy was in cynicism and destruction, and activities were strongly suicidal. No law was recognized beyond their own will and desires. As Lida, by no means a philosophical anarchist, observed to herself in Michael Artzibashev's novel of the early 20th century Russia, *Sanine*, "she had a right to do whatever she chose with her strong, beautiful body that belonged to her alone." The contemporary advocates of abortion hold to a similar faith; without being philosophically self-conscious, they have absorbed the same nihilism with the same corrosive effects. Earlier than in Artzibashev, who favored the new mood, Dostoyevsky had bitterly attacked the same temper, and its socialistic-anarchistic expressions, especially in his novel *The Possessed* (or, the devils).

This nihilistic mood in the people at large made the Russian Revolution possible. The socialists and communists were a very small minority; success would have been impossible had not the widespread popular nihilism made for a ready acceptance of destruction.

Today, a similar mood infects Soviet Russia's intellectuals and students. Petr Sadecky's *Octobriana and the Russian Underground* (New York: Harper & Row, 1971) gives us a vivid and documented glimpse of this present-day nihilism. The communist leaders fear and hate this temper and recognize its danger. They maintain the false face of a happy puritanism in their empire, when the reality is a bitter and unhappy nihilism. Sadecky quotes one youth as saying that they indulge in no assassinations and no revolutions: "We're even milder than Ghandi ---- we don't even indulge in passive resistance." The words of Lermontov are again the words of youth: "All are alien to me and I to all." They believe "in nothing, past, present or future." Immorality, perversion, orgies, and insanity are their protest. As one girl remarked, "Life is an absurd torment anyway. We must simply get to the end of it, as pleasantly as possible. Whatever it costs. There's nothing to be done about it." There is a suicidal retreat from and hatred of reality. The idea that communism is the savior of mankind and the architect of a better world, one from which oppression, exploitation, and misery are forever excluded, is viewed with contempt and cynicism. The new nihilists of the Russian empire are the children of communism, and the true underground movement is the underground church, of which the Rev. Richard Wurmbrand has kept the Western world informed. The new nihilists are sufficiently numerous so that production lags in the Soviet Union, because nihilists are not psychologically suited for peaceful, productive work. The new nihilists make the older nihilists look like optimists by comparison. Artzibashev's hero Sanine did believe that a revolution offered hope. The modern nihilist has no hope.

Throughout the world, in varying degrees, the nihilistic temper is widely present. It is not as hopeless as the Russian variety, and is more destructive, as was the pre-1917 temper, but it is still nihilism. In travelling to many colleges and universities, I have found in secular and religious schools alike, a widespread belief that mankind has no hope unless a total destruction works a clean sweep. More than a few students from good middle-class conservative homes have assured me that in 20 years people will be dropping dead everywhere from pollution and over-population, and the only hope is massive revolutionary violence to stop the Establishment in its tracks. After that, what? Here they grow vague: the basic impetus is a lust for nihilistic violence and destruction.

But there is a difference. Increasingly, the new nihilism is directed against the doctrine of salvation by the state. The older nihilism was directed against Christendom. Now the bastions of liberalism and socialism are attacked. Why, ask bewildered adults, do they attack the liberal Bank of America, the leftist universities, and a socialistic establishment? They attack it because it represents failure, frustration, and evil to them. Their contempt for Christendom is real, but the great enemy for nihilism today is the state and its gospel of salvation. They despair of and despise parliamentary government, but they also are cynical of Russia's dictatorship of the proletariat. There was a time when, under the influence of the Enlightenment, the words "priest" and "pastor" meant "deceiver"; man's hope was in the state and its plan of salvation by the rational actions of political man. Now the word "politician" gets the same unreasoning hatred that the word "priest" and "preacher" once aroused, and the same slander is applied to the new scapegoats of society.

The nihilists believe in nothing except destruction and the apocalyptic value of destruction. By destroying, they hope somehow to bring in a paradise in which all dreams are suddenly realized. The new nihilists of Soviet Russia, despite all their nihilistic passivism and contempt for life, still can write about the "One Salvation --- the horizon. The longing for the horizon and what is waiting beyond it" (*Octobriana*, p. 75.) This is a fantasy-oriented perspective, as is all nihilism. The nihilist denies reality and seeks to destroy it in the name of fantasy.

For youth today the hated reality is the state, the state and its allies who together make up the "Establishment." The state drafts youth into warfare; the state is the new god whose "Thou shalt nots" confront rebellious youth at every turn. The state and the family represent authority, and nihilistic youth is at war with authority. An air force officer has reported to us that one of the principal manifestations of psychological disorders encountered in the service is father-hatred. To be under authority, to be indebted to any man or institution, is, for would-be gods, the ultimate in indignity. The state has become the target of most of this hostility, and the state has only succeeded, with all its efforts, in creating more hostility. Never before has the state subsidized more people with more benefits, benefits for child care, education, health, welfare, and much more, and never before has the state been more resented and hated.

The state requires recognition of its authority to survive, but, by undercutting Biblical faith by means of a humanistic and statist education, the state has undercut not only the authority of the family and the church, but also and most of all its own authority. The more the state increases its power and services, the more it diminishes its authority. The age of the state is climaxing in the crisis of the state and its authority.

The only valid alternative to nihilism is a Biblical faith. The Westminster Confession defines faith thus: "The grace of faith, whereby the elect are enabled to believe to the saving of their souls, is the work of the Spirit of Christ in their hearts; and is ordinarily wrought by the ministry of the Word: by which also, and by the administration of the Sacraments, and prayer, it is increased and strengthened." Without faith, man lives in a flat, one-surface world, the world of time. Because in such a world time itself is meaningless, and a nihilistic cynicism reduces the world to change alone, even that world is lost to man: he despises the reality around him. The man of faith lives in a world of time, against the background of eternity. Time rests in a cosmos of meaning and has implications in and from eternity. There is thus depth and perspective in such a world, and, above all, meaning. Humanism (existentialist, rationalist, empiricist, etc.) always ends in a nihilistic denial of and hatred for reality. It believes in "nothing, past, present or future." It holds that "Life is an absurd torment", and the beginning of wisdom is to believe in no truth or wisdom. Sadecky observed, of the girl in the communist youth underground who held life to be absurd and pushed the idea to the limits, that this "brought her to the edge of insanity and finally to the psychiatric hospital" (*Octobriana*, p. 30.) Men cannot live without faith, and the collapse of false faiths is productive of strongly suicidal tendencies in modern man.

The communist world is aware of this suicidal loss of faith in communism; it does everything possible to disguise and to conceal it. It cannot overcome it. The hatred for Christians, who are too helpless to be a revolutionary threat, is governed by a fanatical and vicious hatred for the hope, love, and faith which marks the believer. The most unspeakable tortures and indignities are perpetrated on Christian prisoners, as Wurmbrand and others have reported. How dare the Christians have faith when others have none? How dare the Christians hope in God rather than the dictatorship of the proletariat, and how dare they seek to bind man to man in the love of grace and the grace of godly love, when only the state should provide social cement?

Here is the irony of the Soviet empire: the well-paid nihilistic youth and intellectuals, who are the elite of the regime and live in material comfort, are going out of their minds, or, are living in nihilistic despair and helplessness, whereas the brutally tortured and persecuted Christians live and pray in the assurance of God's victory.

Here in the West prayer can be backed by work, by Christian reconstruction. In every area of life, there is an urgent need to rebuild all things in terms of Biblical faith. Humanists gravitate to statist action because they can only believe in "starting big", big expenditures, big schools, big organizations. We have a generation of men who fall under God's judgment: "For who hath despised the day of small things?" (Zech. 4:10). Only as men value, honor, and work to establish small beginnings will great results ensue. The idiots of our day waste their time and money on beginning big, a national impact, a demonstration of epic proportions, and so on. They have the statist mentality even in their hostility to the state. God's people work in terms of small beginnings and great results under God.

They work in terms of reality because they work by faith. The nihilists, who believe in nothing, also believe in everything. By reducing all reality to nothingness by cynicism and doubt, they make all things equally meaningless, and therefore equally valuable. The door is then opened to superstition, magic, occultism, and witchcraft as in every era of nihilism. People who believe in nothing make all allegiance a matter of taste, and their taste runs to the occult and demonic. Those whose faith is in the God of Scripture have a standard and a grasp of reality to preserve them from the superstitions of nihilism. They look "for a city which hath foundations, whose builder and maker is God" (Heb. 11:10). Men of faith cannot tell what the future will bring to them, but they know Who brings it, and they know that God makes all things work together for good to them that love Him, to them who are called according to His purpose (Rom. 8:28).

The nihilists are all around us, and they are dangerous, as are all suicidal people, but they are also futile, because they have lost their hold on reality. They are in flight from life. As against them, the people of God must stand, not in terms of the past or present, not in terms of what they like, nor in terms of conventions, but in terms of the Truth, Jesus Christ. As Tertullian wrote in *On the Veiling of Virgins*, "Christ did not call himself the conventions, but the truth." The conventions will go: the Truth will endure and prevail.

CHALCEDON REPORT NO. 85
September, 1972

Lurking in the background of every system of thought is an implicit doctrine of infallibility. Men require, in their philosophies and faiths, an assurance that their way to truth is actually, potentially, or ultimately the true and certain guide. Various concepts of infallibility have been offered, although the word "infallibility" has usually been avoided. The infallibility of the aesthetic experience was thus the implicit faith of the philosopher Croce. The Enlightenment saw *criticism* as that sure guide, the intellectual critique of the philosophes. "The organized habit of criticism" would eliminate superstition and religion and bring forth the pure light of truth. Hume, in his *Enquiry Concerning Human Understanding*, called for a grand book-burning of all works not ruled by "criticism." These men believed, as Peter Gay points out (Peter Gay: *The Enlightenment*, vol. I, p. 141, 145. New York: Knopf, 1967) in "the omni-competence of criticism." They held that "All things are equally subject to criticism" (p. 150), because "criticism" by the autonomous mind of man is the sure guide to truth. Other concepts of infallibility (the scientific method, etc.) can be cited.

When the state began to claim priority over man, like the philosophes, the scientists, and the aesthetes who were to follow, it too claimed to be infallible. Such claims by the state were not uncommon in antiquity. In Frederick II (1194-1250), the medieval church faced a great antagonist who boldly claimed infallibility.

Kantorowicz wrote of him, "His knowledge of natural law now reinforces his unity with God and further established his infallibility; for he goes on to say 'therefore we scorn to err'. The Pope under the inspiration of the Holy Ghost may be infallible in matters of faith, similarly the Emperor 'overfilled by *Justitia*' is infallible in matters of law. In accordance with this imperial infallibility, Frederick adopted, as the Norman Kings before him had done, the sentence of Roman law: 'to discuss the Emperor's judgments, decrees, and statues is sacrilege', a sentence that was so vital to the constitution of the whole state that Frederick boldly quoted it to the Pope when he ventured to criticize some measure of the Emperor's." (Ernst Kantorowicz: *Frederick the Second 1194-1250*, p. 232. New York: Ungar 1957.) Frederick saw himself as "Law incarnate upon earth" (p. 233). He held also that "It is sacrilege to debate whether that man is worthy whom the Emperor has chosen and appointed" (p. 235).

The doctrine of the divine right of kings was a form of this doctrine of the infallibility of the state. In 1660, in the trial of the men who had executed Charles I of England for his treason to the state, the presiding judge, Sir Orlando Bridgeman, asserted this doctrine bluntly: "The trial opened on Tuesday (October 9, 1660) with the presiding judge's charge to the jury.

Bridgeman traced the legal position of the monarchy from the earliest times, showing that no single person or community of persons had any coercive power over the King of England; that the King was supreme Governor, subject to none but God, and could do no wrong, and that if he can do no wrong he could not be punished for any wrong." (Patrick Morrah: *1660, The Year of Restoration*, p 184. Boston: Beacon Press, 1960.)

This idea of infallibility did not disappear with kings; instead, it was transferred to democracies and to socialism. The dictatorship of the proletariat is the infallible voice of history for Marxists. In democracy, the old pagan principle prevails, vox populi, vox dei, the voice of the people is the voice of God.

Politics thus has become a major area of messianic and infallible activities. Frances Stevenson, Lloyd George's secretary, recorded at the 1919 peace conference a suppressed paragraph of Woodrow Wilson's opening speech, in which Wilson explained "how Christianity had failed in its purpose after two thousand years, but the League of Nations was going to go one better than Christianity and would supply all defects." (A. J. P. Taylor, editor: *Lloyd George: A Diary by Frances Stevenson*, New York: Harper.) The modern state increasingly sees itself as man's savior and as the infallible voice of man and history; it seeks progressively to eliminate criticism and to become the effectual god of the world.

When humanism began to divorce the idea of infallibility from God and His word, and to attach it to men and institutions, one of the immediate results was that a variety of claims to infallibility resulted. This power and authority, having been separated from God, was thus "up for grabs" by men. The medieval university was one such claimant, and it sought to instruct kings and popes as the voice of infallible reason. The doctrine of academic freedom is an aspect of this claim to infallibility. The academy is beyond control by men because it is in its freedom the infallible source of truth.

The artist was another claimant to infallibility. Previously, he had been an artisan, a businessman whose activity was the arts. Whether an architect, sculptor, painter, or writer, he was a working man of practical status and function. With the rise of humanistic versions of infallibility, the artist developed. He became self-consciously a new kind of prophet, outside the normal affairs of men and beyond the control of law. The Bohemian idea of the artist developed. Instead of being a skilled and disciplined artisan, he was now supposedly an inspired man. The artistic frenzy and studied irresponsibility were systematically cultivated. The less normal and the less sane an artist acted, it came to be held, the more he was inspired. As men denied the super-natural, inspiration was sought, not from above, but from below. It was necessary to break laws, to cultivate chaos and primitivism, in order to reach the fountains of the new inspiration and the new infallibility. This meant the end of disciplined art and the rapid development of "spontaneous" and unthinking art. It meant too that a premium was placed on being more and more irresponsible, lawless, and primitive as evidence of inspiration.

All this was not unrelated to the development in politics. When inspiration and infallibility were transferred from God to man, it was at first kings who exercised this power, then parliaments and assemblies. But as the source of power moved from above (God) to below (evolution, chaos, and the primitive), authority also moved downward. It moved from kings to the aristocracy, from the aristocracy to the middle classes, from the middle classes to the lower classes, and now from the lower classes to the criminals and psychopaths. It is not the Negro as such who is favored in this new mood but the lawless Negro. It is not the working man who is now the hero of the left but the criminal and the welfare recipient. Power and authority have moved downward.

As a result, the children of the upper, middle, and lower classes increasingly ape the hoodlum and the psychopath. They imitate the new prophets of history by wearing their hair long, by being lawless, and by despising authority, because they have come to believe in the infallibility of the existential moment and its experience.

Moreover, as men look for the infallible word and experience downward, they will soon look beyond the criminal and the psychopath to the demonic and occult. As a result, there is already a widespread interest in magic and witchcraft, and various forms of satanism flourish and abound. Those who are busily, and religiously, seeking the newest inspired voice are in eager pursuit of the newest and most extreme form of occult authority.

The morality of God's infallible word, it is held, must give way to the new morality of the new infallibility of existential experience. Not too long ago, a prominent Hollywood actress committed suicide because she was pregnant by a prominent actor who refused to marry her. Today, some young actresses are deliberately giving birth to children out of wedlock, with as much publicity as possible, in order to gain the approval of the "now generation", those to whom the existential moment is the infallible and inspired word. Immoralism is now a matter of boasting. In many circles among youth, there is a new phariseeism pretending to be sexually profligate even when one is not, in order to gain acceptance as intelligent and modern.

The voice of the people is the voice of God, in terms of democratic thinking, but increasingly "the people" are defined in terms of the lowest common denominator, so that the standards are brought down to the level of the lowest of the low. Men worship the fountain of this new infallibility, the primitive and the outlaw. Some years ago, I sat next to an anthropologist who spoke with strong emotion about the nobility and beauty of a backward people whose habits under discussion hardly bear repeating even today. He despised our middle class culture; although personally very neat and clean, he rhapsodized over the filth of his "unspoiled" tribe. Such attitudes are routine now. A few days ago, in a television film of a native culture, natives were shown picking and eating lice and fleas out of each other's hair. Meanwhile, the narrator with reverent tones, spoke of how wonderfully these unspoiled people lived! I recall the wry comment of a very able Christian Negro that he faced the ultimate in disadvantages in America: racists disliked him for his color, and liberals and radicals disliked him for being Christian, peaceful, and prosperous!

As a result, the state, which once gained great power as it claimed infallibility for itself, now finds that its source of inspiration, the people, is its major problem. A disintegrating force has been unleashed by the belief that power and authority lie downward, so that the state is faced with the corrosive pressures of anarchy. Its response is a suppressing coercion, but coercion does not answer the problem of authority. The new nihilism in the Soviet Union is a major threat, as is the same mood in the United States. Men who have become their own gods and their own infallible oracles will not submit to any authority.

There can be no return to legitimate authority until men return to the faith that establishes that authority. The infallible power is not man but God; the infallible word is not in or from man but in and from God alone. The greater man's pretensions, the greater his emptiness becomes. As E. E. Cummings expressed this emptiness after World War I,

> i am a birdcage without any bird,
> a collar looking for a dog, a kiss
> without lips; a prayer lacking any knees.

In Cummings' poetry, man was empty; his "I" had become an insignificant "i", not deserving a capital letter, because man and life had become meaningless. In the poetry of Wallace Stevens, death also became meaningless; modern man has no hope or dreams, only nightmares: "And that's life, then: things as they are." When man looks within for his inspiration, when he seeks it in man as such, the more faithfully he looks the closer he comes to the grim fact that man is nothing apart from God. Man is a creature who can only be known, understood, and interpreted in terms of God's infallible word. The institutions of man, church, state, school, family, and all things else are only to be known and understood in terms of God's word. To attempt the understanding and development of anything apart from God is to take a toboggan ride to meaninglessness, despair, and anarchy.

CHALCEDON REPORT NO. 86
October, 1972

Herman Kahn, director of the Hudson Institute, recently predicted that the counter-counterculture will dominate the next decade. There is, he holds, a growing reaction against the moods and ideas which dominated the 1960s. "The pendulum has swung too far. We've abandoned too many traditional values and we haven't replaced them with satisfactory new values." He believes that the upper middle class, the communications people, educators and students, and city planners "are all basically out of touch with reality." Crime in the streets has aroused anger in the great majority of Americans. He holds that 67% of America is "quite square and getting squarer" and that this is "the biggest thing going in America today and it will either dominate or heavily influence the next decade or two." Kahn favors this trend and adds "I have a strong desire to give life a kind of meaning and purpose that can only come out of revealed religion." He regrets that he cannot believe in a revealed truth, but he insists that there is meaning to life. Kahn criticizes the claims that the United States is a racist society and adds, "No one has ever shown any good results from busing." ("Herman Kahn: The Squaring of America," an interview by Jonathan Ward in *Intellectual Digest*, vol. III, no. 1, Sept., 1972, pp. 16-19.) Kahn's opinions usually carry weight, and, without agreeing with him, we should give attention to his statements.

Others have given similar reports. Furlong has called attention to the fact that, whereas in the 1960s it was the alienated students on college campuses who dominated the scene, today it is increasingly the alienated working man and middle class citizen of our cities. These people are angry at what has happened to their neighborhoods. They resent higher taxes, busing, corrupt politics, crime, and senseless change for change's sake. They are ready to make peace with law-abiding blacks (and are doing so) to fight against politicians and bureaucrats. Such people "are not trying to change the system so much as they are trying to change the politicians who exploit it." These people are the "non-mobiles", the people who do not move but remain in a fixed neighborhood. "The white-ethnic, blue-collar workers generally, remained non-mobile through these years (after World War II), often living in well-defined pockets of the inner city." (William Barry Furlong, "Profile of an Alienated Voter," in *Saturday Review*, vol. LV, no. 31, July 29, 1972, pp. 48-51.)

A similar protest has developed to a degree among many middle-class and upper middle class men. Companies who used to move men freely across country, and to promote only by moving, are now beginning to cut down on this process: too many good men now refuse to move and resent the rootlessness which has marked executive and professional life since World War II.

There is thus a markedly different mood now than that which marked the years from World War II to c. 1970. It is conservatism of a sort, and more than a few have welcomed it as a sign of great changes ahead of a happier kind than those of recent years. Are they right?

But, before answering that question, let us examine a very important area of the new conservatism, one which is intense in its criticism of "big government", of ideas of a scientific elite controlling man and society, of a growing bureaucracy, and much more. This sector of the new conservatism is the growing number of "men's magazines" which emphasize nudity, free love, and a laissez-faire attitude towards sexuality, i.e., the abolition of all laws governing sexual conduct. Less well known to many is the fact that these publications carry this laissez-faire attitude into other areas. Joe Goldberg, in his study *Big Bunny, The Inside Story of Playboy* (New York: Ballantine, 1967), called attention to the fact that one of Hugh M. Hefner's favorite authors is Ayn Rand (p. 64). *Playboy* accordingly manifests a continuing critique of strong civil government and a hostility to statism. Other magazines of the same general nature are equally vocal in their critique of statism and scientism. Thus, Al Goldstein has called various federal acts, and B.F. Skinner's book, *Beyond Freedom and Dignity*, an "Outrage Against the Soul." Goldstein sees *1984* and Orwell's nightmare looming ahead and speaks of the "outrage" of statist controls over man: "the Senate Finance Committee voted to require that all children entering the first grade after January 1, 1974, be assigned social security numbers. The rationale for this dictator's dream is that of combatting welfare cheaters, since duplicating numbers would be ended. Under the present law, a person normally obtains a number when he is first employed. Since FBI dossiers are increasing in number and scope for each and every American, it seems only reasonable that Big Brother now wants to poke his nose into the kindergartens and diapers of our youth." (Al Goldstein, "The Garbage Pail: Outrage Against the Soul," in *Cavalier*, vol. 22, no. 10, August, 1972, pp. 6-10) This is not an isolated example. The hostility to and sense of outrage over statism and scientism is very strong in such circles, and it appears on both sides of the Iron Curtain.

A "fantastic tale" by "Vlas Tenin", *Moscow Nights*, a product of Russian underground literature, reflects the feeling of pornographic bitterness in intellectual circles in the Soviet Union for statism and scientism. A song sung by the youth of the underground is savage in its hatred of scientific socialist planning, which aims at playing god, seeking to make figs grow among Eskimos, and snow to fall in the Sahara, according to the song. The song also says,

> Those bastard scientists, just for a bet,
> Have turned the whole world on its head...
> Whether it's rabbits they deal with, or man ---
> The scientists couldn't give a damn!
> (Vlas Tenin: *Moscow Nights*, p. 80. New York: Olympia, 1971.)

It would be easy to pile up data and make a case for Herman Kahn's belief that we are moving into a counter-counterculture. In fact, some might call it a counter-revolutionary mood. Even some of the Black Panther leaders have of late rejected revolutionary action in favor of legal process. The important point is this: is there anything in this new conservatism which offers hope for the future? We must remember that, the closer Rome drew to its collapse, the more it railed against the tightening noose of statist power, looked nostalgically to the past, and blundered ahead to its death.

The new conservatism is very heavily marked by a neo-anarchism, so that its very conservatism is in essence a radicalism. The new conservatism wants all the benefits which the state provides but not the state itself, an impossible picture. It wants a strong state to enforce its particular interests, such as ecological controls, welfarism, anti-racist legislation, and much more, but it wants a laissez-faire attitude with respect to sexual regulations, neighborhood schools and busing, privacy, and much more. To create a powerful state in certain areas of life means to create a powerful state which will not stay out of other areas. A power state which has the power of life and death over industry will exercise the same power over the little people of the country, whose ability to withstand civil power is much less than that of "big business." The stronger man makes the state, the weaker he makes himself. Thus the new conservatism is very much a meaningless protest. Lacking a consistent philosophy, it can only win battles, never a war. It may succeed, in its middle class and workingman's forms, in stopping busing, although even this is dubious, and it may stop a few other things, but it will not check the growth of statist power. In its neo-anarchistic forms, this neo-conservatism may gain far more drastic abolition of sexual regulations, and it may win some victories for personal privacy, but it is also increasing statist controls by some of its other demands.

An even more serious weakness marks the new conservatism. The older conservatism, still present in the middle class, was marked by serious weaknesses and a divorce from its Christian roots. It had, however, this virtue: it was still production oriented. The very deadly flaw of the new conservatism is that it is consumption oriented. A fact seldom appreciated is that in most decadent and dying societies there is a strong nostalgia for the past and a rootless and sentimental conservatism. The *faith* that made the longed-for past is dead, but the longing for its *fruits* is widespread. Today, for example, the Puritanism of early America, its strong belief in the sovereignty of God, its emphasis on God's law, and its insistence on godly order are all gone, but the antiquarian interest in early America is at an all-time high. Antiques command a growing price; early Americana of all kinds is prized; books on Americana sell at a rapid pace, and interest in the past has spread to Indian culture, early French-American culture, and early Spanish-American culture. A similar nostalgia for and interest in the past is common in Europe. This interest, however, is a part of the problem: it is a part of the consumption-oriented mentality which wants to enjoy the best of the past, present, and future, to consume and to enjoy, rather than to produce.

Friedrich Heer, in *The Medieval World* (1962), writes of the "open Europe" of 1100; men travelled freely from England through Russia, from Europe to Byzantium, and from Europe to the Islamic world. Trade routes were well travelled, and inter-marriages were common. Even in Spain, despite the combat, marriages between Islamic, Jewish, and Hispano-Christian families, especially among the aristocracy and merchant classes, were common. In addition to the commercial travel, there was a great deal of movement across frontiers by pilgrims. Commercial travel is still very much with us, but pilgrims have been replaced by tourists, a significant fact. The pilgrim was moved by a strong faith and a vision of the Kingdom of God on earth; the tourist is concerned with seeing the past before it disappears. The tourist sees greatness in the past; the pilgrim sees it in the past in order to establish it in the present and the future.

A consumption oriented conservatism thus looks to the past, builds museums, establishes national forests, and works to conserve a heritage in its outward forms. It often accomplishes worth-while goals in its nostalgia. Winning some battles, it loses the war, because it sees no greatness ahead for man, only disaster. A production oriented conservatism will not neglect the past, but it will regard today and tomorrow as man's best opportunity and his truest hope.

The older middle class conservatism is still with us, and it is still production oriented, but, having lost its Christian moorings, it has become rootless, and it has drifted into alien waters. Moreover, as a result of its humanism, it has picked up three ideas which are the essence of socialism in its every form. Increasingly, conservatives are ready to accept one or more of these premises, and, in all too many cases, all three. These three ideas are: *First*, a belief in the conflict of interests. Instead of holding that, basic to reality is God's sovereign government and law and an over-riding, governing, and ultimate harmony of all interests, most conservatives accept dialectical, existential, pragmatic, or Hegelian philosophies with their principle of a conflict of interests. The theory of evolution makes conflict, and the struggle for survival, the basic aspect of biological reality. As a result, the philosophy of a conflict of interests, the economic form of which is the doctrine of class struggle, saturates both left and right. *Second*, both Marxists and many "conservatives" are agreed on the belief in a capitalist conspiracy behind all events, and some leftist periodicals are beginning to praise "conservative" literature on this subject. *Third*, Lenin called the acceptance of statist central banking and a paper currency "nine-tenths" of socialism; all too many "conservatives" are ready to demand both of these things as their hope. The "funny money" advocates are as "conservative" as

Lenin! Philosophically and religiously, most conservatism is bankrupt and intellectually in contradiction to itself.

Morally too there is a bleak outlook for the "counter-counterculture." The amount of shop-lifting today is an important factor in the price of many items, but great as this shop-lifting is, the amount of theft by officials and employees in any business or shop is far greater. In many areas, theft adds more to the price of goods than do taxes. The most difficult part of any business today is very often the finding of honest employees. There is nothing modest about the stealing. One businessman recently stated that he discovered, in tracing only a portion of his losses by theft, that the daily profit to only a few employees was far greater than that of himself and his partner. Thefts, in fact, were endangering his survival, and his situation was no worse than that of many other businessmen, and even better. The moral collapse apparent in all classes is very grave, and very deep.

Robert N. Winter-Berger, in *The Washington Pay-Off* (1972), gives a telling account, as a former lobbyist, of corruption in Washington, D.C. He is naive in believing that knowledge of these facts will arouse the country and save the nation. The corruption in Washington (and in capitols all over the world) is a corruption which reflects the life and morality of the people.

Knowledge of these facts has no long-term effect. Men are not saved by knowledge but by the grace of God. It is not knowledge of corruption, or of conspiracies, or of evil, which will revitalize man and society, but a knowledge of God's grace and His law-word. The "counter-counterculture" is a futile thing: it longs for the past when it should be building for the future. Man is in trouble, and the humanistic state is in trouble also. God is not in trouble, nor are we, if we stand in terms of His government and law-word. "Choose ye this day whom ye will serve" (Josh. 24:15). Your life depends on it.

CHALCEDON REPORT NO. 87
November 1, 1972

An idea very heavily promoted by humanists in recent years, and, unfortunately, picked up by all too many Christians, is that we are moving into a post-Christian era. According to this belief, the Christian centuries have come to an end, and we are now moving into a new age. Some call it the era of scientific humanism, others of scientific socialism, and still others call it the age of aquarius. For the occultists, as of old, this is the "third age" or third world era. The occultist, Foster Bailey, in *The Spirit of Masonry* (1957), wrote that "the Jewish dispensation came to an end, and the Christian dispensation began with the passing of our sun into the sign Pisces, the Fishes...Today,...we are passing rapidly into another sign, the sign Aquarius." The theologians who get their doctrine from the popular press and the streets have echoed this humanistic chorus, and they tell us we are in a post-Christian era. Is this true?

With the waning of the "middle" ages, Europe moved into an anti-Christian era which culminated in the Renaissance. The church was largely captured by cynical humanists who treated it as a prize to be exploited. The Reformation and the Counter-Reformation were reactions against this, and they strove to recapture church, state, school, and society for Christian faith. In varying degrees this was done. Humanism, however, was revived in the Enlightenment; it began its conquest of Christendom; it embarked on a deliberate and determined anti-Christian and post-Christian era. Historians have long masked and under-played the militant anti-Christianity of the Enlightenment thinkers and their successors; it is to the credit of Peter Gay's work, *The Enlightenment* (2 vols), that he develops this aspect of their thought. It was clearly central.

With the 18th century, Europe moved steadily into a post-Christian era. Every area of life was steadily divorced from Christianity and re-interpreted in humanistic terms. True, there were Christian counter-movements against the humanistic culture, but, because these were largely pietistic, they did not challenge humanism as such. In fact, because pietism came to emphasize soul-saving above all else, it became thereby humanistic also: it put man at the center of its gospel, whereas Christ said, "seek ye *first* the kingdom of God, and his righteousness; and all these things shall be added unto you" (Matt. 6:33). The Shorter Catechism had taught, "Man's chief end is to glorify God and to enjoy Him forever." Now humanism and religion had come to agree that the glory of man is the end and purpose of all things.

The 18th and 19th centuries were humanistic and anti-Christian in their *basic* motives, and yet they were very largely influenced by still powerful Christian standards also. In the sciences and in various other areas of study not only did Christian scholars predominate but the idea of an ultimate and God-created order still governed men's minds. In philosophy, God had been abandoned; in every-day life as well as the sciences He was still the ultimate power, although receding in centrality. With Darwin and Freud, humanism abandoned the God-concept and at the same time committed suicide. For Darwin, not God but chance is essentially ultimate, although traces of providence still are strong in his system. The basic emphasis, however, was away from God's design to chance variations and natural selection. Instead of an ultimate mind, man lived against the background of an ultimate meaninglessness, and man was depreciated. If all the area surrounding a man's house is suddenly turned into a dump, then that man's house is not only depreciated but possibly rendered untenable as rodents take over the area. Similarly, humanism, as it dispensed with God dispensed also with the meaning, purpose, and dignity of life. Freud furthered this process, knowing full well what he was doing to humanism thereby. However, holding to an evolutionary position, he reduced mind to a frail late-comer whose every working was an outcropping of primitive motives from the unconscious. Philosophy could not very well survive under this premise. Darwin himself wrote in 1881 that "with me the horrid doubt always arises whether the convictions of man's mind, which has been developed from the mind of the lower animals, are of any value or at all trustworthy. Would any one trust in the convictions of a monkey's mind, if there are any convictions in such a mind?" (Francis Darwin, editor: *The Life and Letters of Charles Darwin*, vol. II, p. 285. New York: Basic Books, 1959.) The effect of this collapse of humanism was apparent in every area of life. Prideaux has observed, of Delacroix, "He was the last painter in whom the humanist Renaissance conception as a totality manifested itself with poetic fervor." (Tom Prideaux: *The World of Delacroix*, p. 12. New York: Silver Burdett, 1966.) Since Delacroix, humanists have presented us with a limited world, then a fragmented world, and now an exploded and dying world. Suicidism has possessed the humanists. Fiedler has cited this weariness with life which marks humanistic writers. "There *is* a weariness in the West which undercuts the struggle between socialism and capitalism, democracy and autocracy; a weariness with humanism itself which underlies all the movements of our world, a weariness with the striving to be men. It is the end of man which the school of Burroughs foretells, not in terms of doom but of triumph." The writer William Burroughs, to whom Fiedler refers, gives us a "vision of the end of man, total death." (Leslie Fiedler: *Waiting for the End*, p. 168. New York; Stein & Day, 1964.) Fiedler is right: modern humanistic man is "waiting for the end."

The end of every age is marked by certain recurring interests. As meaning from God is abandoned, meaning is sought by man from below, in occultism, satanism, magic, and witchcraft. Rome in its decline was marked by such interests. As Christendom collapsed after the 13th century, these same movements revived and with intensity possessed the minds of despairing men. The same interests are again with us, not as signs of the birth of the age of aquarius, but as evidences of the dying agony of humanism.

Are we facing a post-Christian era? The men who so declare are as blind as that false messiah, Woodrow Wilson, who believed that he had a better way than Christ, who held that a war could be fought to end all wars and to make the world safe for democracy, and who felt that paper documents could harness and control the evil goals of men and nations. Wilson's great crusade did not usher in a new world order of peace and prosperity; rather, it inaugurated the armaggedon of humanism. Franklin Delano Roosevelt embarked on a similar crusade in Europe, and the breakdown of humanism was only hastened.

It is not a post-Christian era that we face but a post-humanistic world. Every thinker who evades that fact is past-oriented and blind; he is incapable of preparing anyone for the realities of our present situation. Humanism on all sides is busy committing hara-kiri; it is disembowelling itself with passion and fervor; it needs no enemies, because humanism is now its own worst enemy. We have lived thus far in a post-Christian era, and it is dying. The important question is, what shall we do?

We must recognize that this is one of the greatest if not the greatest opportunity yet to come to Christianity. This is a time of glorious opportunity, a turning point in history, and the wise will prepare for it. True, the church is remarkably incompetent and sterile in the face of this crisis. It has very largely joined the enemy. This, however, has happened before. In the fourth century, the church repeatedly condemned St. Athanasius, as the state listed him as a wanted outlaw. He was accused (by churchmen) of trying to stop the food supply to the capitol. He was accused of murder (but the dead man was proven to be alive). He was charged with magic and sorcery, and much else, and his life was lived in flight, with five periods of exile. All the same, it was Athanasius and not his enemies, nor the powerful churchmen of his day, who shaped the future. History then as now is not shaped by majorities but by men who provide the faith and the ideas for living.

Smith has said of modern man, "How may we describe the present situation? Man is his own master, and thus aware that there are no bounds to his powers. He can do anything that he wishes to do...He is free, and come of age, but he is also the slave of ideologies. He recognizes that his existence as a man carries with it the demand to be himself, as a single personal being (in Kierkegaard's phrase), and at the same time he finds himself continually threatened with immersion in the life of the collective --- and he even desires this, in order that he may evade the hard demand to be a single person." (Ronald Gregor Smith, "Post-Renaissance Man", in William Nicholls, editor: *Conflicting Images of Man*, p. 32 New York: Seabury Press, 1966.) This is an interesting admission, coming as it does from a modernist position. It is an indication of the paralysis and helplessness of humanistic man. Men who are at war with themselves, and resentful of life and its requirements, are not able to command the future: they cannot even command themselves.

Every day our problem is less and less humanism and more and more ourselves. Is our life and action productive of a new social order? Are we governed by principles and ideas which will help determine the new direction of history? Is our thinking still directed by sterile statism, and do we believe that the answer to man's problems is to capture the machinery of the state, or do we recognize that we must first of all be commanded by God before we can effectively command ourselves and our futures?

Leslie Fiedler aptly titled his study of the modern mood as reflected in literature *Waiting For the End*. We can add that it also involves waiting for a ready-made answer. The temper of our radicals is a demand for total solutions *now*; quite aptly, they call themselves the "now generation." Quite logically, magic and witchcraft are very closely tied to the "now generation." Magic and witchcraft offer a mythical alternative to patient work and reconstruction. A few words and formulae, and, presto, the desired thing supposedly appears. In the politics of magic, a few catch-phrases are endlessly repeated, some laws passed or some revolutionary action paraded, and, presto, paradise should suddenly come, but for the nasty work of the vile reactionaries. Push the right revolutionary button, such is the faith of the "now generation", and the dream world will emerge: no sweat, only revolutionary heroics in terms of the late, late movies our radicals and their baby-sitters grew up with.

This generation would do well to remember the words of Christ concerning the Kingdom of God, words too rarely if ever preached on: "For the earth bringeth forth fruit of herself; first the blade, then the ear, after that the full corn in the ear" (Mark 4:28). There is a spontaneity of growth which is not dependent upon man: the earth brings forth growth. But man must sow the seed, till the field, and work to bring forth the harvest. There must be, first, faith that results will come, and, second, work to plant and till for that harvest. Men doubt today that God brings forth His purposed results, and they refuse to work for any goals. We live in an age when men want to harvest corn before they have planted it. We live, briefly, in a political or statist era, a day when men believe in the ability of the state and its politicians to solve problems by means of their legislative hocus-pocus, when the desperate need instead is for faith and work. The important question for a "now generation" becomes the search for a politician with the right hocus-pocus.

But "first the blade", and the blade cannot appear without a planting. This is the time to create new and free schools, Christian hospitals, independent professional societies, Biblically principled, and new enterprises of every kind. The time is now. I recall the words of a supposedly intelligent man, speaking in 1939, holding that it was "too late." No doubt those words are as old as man, and still a mark of defeatism and stupidity, still a mark of waiting for ready-made, push-button answers. I recall vividly as a school-boy being told of automatic, thermostat-controlled heating systems, then a new thing, as the forerunner, it was held, of a push-button, automatic world, in which all answers came freely. Nothing was said about the work that went into producing the thermostat, nor the new industries it furthered, nor the new kinds of work it made possible. It was seen only as a step forward towards the dream of instant paradise in a ready-made world. I did not know it then, but those teachers were preparing the way for the return of a faith in magic and witchcraft.

But, our Lord said, "first the blade"! Done any planting lately? Or are you waiting for someone with the right hocus-pocus? If so, you will die with this dying non-Christian era. Don't count on us sending flowers.

CHALCEDON REPORT NO. 88
December 1972

A persistent myth cherished by humanistic man is to locate sin and the responsibility for it not in himself but in his environment, and in the ruling class. In every era, men have blamed their griefs and sins on the existing establishment or power structure. To cite a few examples, during the "medieval" era, men found it easy to see evil as the monopoly of rapacious churchmen, and the myth of the greedy, lustful priest was fostered. True, some priests were evil, but, to this day, we hear much about the sins of the priests and too little about the sins of the people. No class has a monopoly on sin or virtue. There were many sensual priests, but only rarely are we told of the many women whose delight and game was to seduce sexually innocent and dedicated priests. At a later date, we hear of the debauched royalty and nobility, who bled a people of their meager means and dishonored their wives and daughters. Again it must be pointed out that the royalty and nobility were freely robbed by those under them, and women thrust themselves at them as a means to personal advancement. In the last century, when a young king went to a spa, the place was crowded by mothers and daughters anxious to advance themselves as royal mistresses. The bourgeois also, on attaining power, became the targets of the same mythical thinking. The brutal factory owners seduced working girls and cast them aside, according to the myth. Certainly, this happened, but as often as not every attempt was made to gain advancement by seducing the factory owner, or his sons. The same was true of slavery; slaves as often seduced and exploited their owners, as the owners their slaves. Vice and virtue have never been the monopoly of a class, and it is only mythological thinking that makes it so. In fact, a sure road to disintegration and decline is for a ruling class to become sufficiently immoral to feed the myth with a semblance of confirmation and thereby inflame reaction.

The myth of the monopoly of evil by the power structure is best promoted when the intellectuals and artists of a society become hostile to the rulers and then promote hostility in their culture. Intellectuals and artists have been essentially a subsidized group in most societies. At first, the clergy supported them, and there are Biblical grounds for a close tie between the church and the arts. However, as both intellectuals and artists saw themselves as the true elite of a society, they then became of necessity the enemy of their rival, the current ruling class. Today, it is increasingly the state that subsidizes them, so that every "Establishment" is becoming the enemy of its intellectuals.

In the modern era, the monarchy and nobility were both excellent patrons and easy targets. The evil of monarchy was not that its taxation was so great but that its rule was so selectively restrictive. The monarchs taxed far less than modern democracies do, and they generally ruled much less restrictively; their failing was that their governments were restrictive of production and trade, and economic progress was stifled thereby. The decline of monarchy was essentially an internal decline. Courts became no longer a place of justice, i.e., the nation's supreme court, but a place of social events. Louis XIV created the first "pentagon" and bureaucracy of power, while turning his palace into a pleasure area to seduce the nobility away from power. Middle class men were used to rule, while Louis XIV gave the forms of power to the nobility. The old upper class was turned into a show piece, irrelevant progressively to the nation and to its power.

Even more serious, royalty had begun to commit suicide by both unwise unions for political purposes and excessive inbreeding. To cite examples from England, there was a "taint of madness" in the Tudors, which showed up in Henry VII and Henry VIII. (Paul Murray Kendall: *Richard III*, p. 186. New York: W.W. Norton, 1955.) Even the respectful biographer of Mary, Queen of Scots, admits to the weaknesses inherited by that queen. (Antonia Fraser: *Mary Queen of Scots*, p. 12. New York: Delacorte Press 1970.) Catherine of Aragon brought a questionable heredity to her union with Henry VIII, and their child was Mary. Some of these, and others, were rulers of faith and dedication, but at critical points their judgment was faulty. George III and George IV suffered the consequences of excessive inbreeding, and porphyria as well as leukemia became "royal" diseases. Of Princess Alexandra of Bavaria (in the 19th century) it was unhappily true that her "whole life was clouded and confused by an unshakable conviction that she had once swallowed a grand piano made of glass." King Ludwig II of Bavaria had impaired judgment, which led to disaster, and his brother Otto was pronounced "incurably insane." (Wilfred Blunt: *The Dream King, Ludwig II of Bavaria*, pp. 16, 159. New York: Viking Press, 1970.)

The monarchs and nobility made themselves irrelevant to their times by their pursuit of pleasure. Being themselves empty, they came to see life as empty. Voltaire himself, both a critic and very much a part of this culture, said, "Trifle with life; that is all it is good for." (Pierre Schneider: *The World of Watteau, 1684-1721*, p. 60. New York: Time, 1967.)

Long before the monarchs and the nobility either disappeared or were relegated to ceremonial functions, in Western Europe effective power had been assumed by the middle class. Commerce and industry came to the forefront, and the new power structure began to remake Western civilization, rapidly and efficiently.

Unfortunately, however, the new ruling class began to imitate the old ruling class. It became fashionable for artists, intellectuals, and businessmen to imitate the vices of monarchs of an earlier era, or the surviving ones. Had women like Madame Pompadour ruled kings once? The new elite made courtesans into rulers, and their salons into palaces and places of judgment. By the 1860s, Theophile Gantier wrote, "the religion of money is today the only one which has no unbelievers." The courtesans of Europe rose to great power and wealth. According to Richardson, "Sexual license had always been a privilege of the aristocracy, an element in their education; but now it was claimed by the middle classes who had risen to wealth and power." Rather, the middle class equated the degeneracy of royalty as the mark of its power, and it imitated those same vices with relish. The courtesans were made rich and famous, because they "symbolized frivolity and irresponsibility." (Joanna Richardson: *The Courtesans*. pp. 2, 221, 230. London: Weidenfeld and Nicolson, 1967.)

Meanwhile, the same bitterness men had once felt for the royalty they felt now for the middle class and for the intellectuals and artists. Marie Antoinette had earlier been blamed even for bad weather; the new power structure was now the target of like unreasoning hatred. It first became vocal, after the French Revolution, when it was only partially expressed, in the revolutionary movements of 1848. The moral scandals of industrialists and the poverty of the working class were widely discussed. Moreover, the intellectuals and artists were also debauching the wives and daughters of the citizenry! As Tom Prideaux observed, "An outbreak of personal scandals - among them a jealous husband's discovery of his spouse in a hideaway with Victor Hugo - convinced the man in the street that the morals of the dominant bourgeoisie were no better than those of the decadent aristocrats they had supplanted." (T. Prideaux: *The World of Delacroix 1798-1863*, p. 166. New York: Time, 1966.)

The poor, down-trodden people, and the torch-bearers, the intellectuals favoring socialist revolutions, became now the new bearers of innocence, and all other classes were seen as evil exploiters. Everything was done to develop and perpetuate this myth, and to suppress evidence to the contrary. Thus, on June 23, 1851, Helene Demuth, the Karl Marx family servant, gave birth to a son. Marx had either seduced or raped her, and Payne feels the slim evidence suggests that "it was rape rather than seduction." (Robert Payne: *Marx*, p. 260. New York: Simon and Schuster, 1968.) The Communists, having made much of the bloated capitalists ravishing working girls, worked to suppress the fact that their great theoretician is the best example of this kind of exploitation, as have been most other Communists. Peter Stafford, in *Sexual Behavior in the Communist World*, has made clear that communists are as ready to exploit people as any other class, and, because of their totalitarian powers and goals, more able to do so than any class heretofore. Moreover, the lives of intellectuals and artists have been no more re-assuring that they represent any power to reform society, let alone themselves.

In recent years, therefore, the position of the self-styled intellectual and artist has been to favor perpetual opposition and perpetual revolution. Having been burned by favoring various alternatives to the church from monarchy, through the bourgeoisie, the working class, the Communist movement, and the new left (which turned on it's teachers), the intellectuals favor now the "adversary role." Their own political action has revealed their failings too well. If anyone adopts a position defensive of a faith or tradition, he is called a "counterintellectual", and some who are described this way include Edmund Burke, Alexis De Tocqueville, August Comte, Harold Lasswell, George Orwell, Raymond Aron, Eric Hoffer, Daniel Bell, Nathan Glazer, Daniel Moynihan, Irving Kristol, and others. (Peter Steinfels, "The Counterintellectuals", in *New American Review*, no. 14, pp. 115-138. New York: Simon and Schuster, 1972.) The intellectual stance now is a radical cynicism and relativism, "the adversary role", but every critique is in terms of a criterion, and the criterion of the intellectuals is a deep faith in the reason of autonomous intellectual man. The absence of a social program is, however, a major retreat from responsibility; whatever is offered is done in the spirit of relativism and cynicism. Not surprisingly, the word to intellectuals in Washington politics from their universities has been a demand to "come home" and be again the critic on the side-lines.

The humanistic myth is playing out. Sin has become a chronic factor on the political scene as elsewhere, and no power structure has been immune to it. No class or power structure has had a monopoly on virtue or on sin, and sin has become a dark cloud on the humanist horizon, a forerunner of a destroying storm. Reinhold Niebuhr, to whom sin was a sociological reality and grace a religious myth, taught the intellectuals well. The lesson has come home to them in varying degrees: man's efforts to reconstruct society are always limited, frustrated, and defeated by the fact of sin. Men like Robert Ardrey have since been documenting man's rapacious and quarrelsome nature. The modern world was fashioned by thinkers whose faith came into focus in Rousseau; now it is kicking against the pricks of a self-knowledge which smacks more of Calvin's doctrine of man. In fact, whether it be Orwell, Golding, or any other contemporary writer, the emphasis on man's depravity in some respects goes beyond Calvin's imagination.

The emphasis on sin, evil, and depravity is all around us. Pornography, once a vice of a degenerate and declining royalty and nobility, is now mass produced for mass consumption. The world of humanism is everywhere in decay, and the humanists themselves acknowledge that this age is in serious trouble. Leslie Fiedler has described this mood as "waiting for the end" (see Report no. 87).

The alternative to waiting for the end to come is to wait on God's grace, and this too many refuse to do. Milton's Satan held that it was better to reign in hell than serve in heaven, and this is the mood of many. The end, however, does not come, only progressive slavery.

The alternative is the freedom of grace. It means a distrust of man, and of man's agencies. It means a strict limitation of power for man, and for church, state, school, and all other institutions. It means that, instead of submitting to man-made controls, man submits to divine controls, the sovereign sway of God's law in every area of life. Trust in God requires a distrust of man, man as monarch, industrialist, worker, intellectual, and clergyman. To be truly dependent on God we must be independent of man except and insofar as God, within very narrow limits, requires it in His word.

Sin is not abolished by the abolition of monarchy, democracy, or oligarchy, nor by abolishing the state, the church, or anything else. The problem is in man, and the answer is in God. The age of the state has seen the answer in a reformed state, a state purged of an evil, oppressing class, but humanism is running out of classes to abolish! Isaiah, in speaking to the humanists of his day, who had debauched the country, and its money (Isa. 1:22), said, "Cease depending on man, whose breath is in his nostrils; for at what should he be valued?" (Isa. 2:22). This means us, first of all. The world is too full of people like us, "good people", who trust in our own righteousness too often more than we trust in God. No state can supply to its people that character which the people lack. The need for grace begins with everyone of us.

CHALCEDON REPORT NO. 89
January, 1973

Desperate men take desperate measures. Very often, the most bitter and costly battles of a war are fought when the end is in sight, and the losing side is aware of its impending defeat. Then men often take reckless and extreme measures, gambling on a break-through to victory.

The end of an era sees a similar desperation. Men work intensely and savagely to destroy everything in sight, hating the culture which had promised so much and delivered so little, according to their judgment. Similarly, men who value the good in the dying culture fight with intense zeal to preserve it at all costs. There is a polarization of ideas and issues, and an intensification of ideas. As a result, in these last days of the age of the state, a humanistic culture in which the state has replaced the church as the key institution and has presented itself as man's savior, there is a fanatical will to believe in man. Not surprisingly, in the 1972 U.S. presidential election, there was on all sides an intense populism in evidence. Eric F. Goldman saw this as the triumph of populism. (Eric F. Goldman,

"Just Plain Folks", in *American Heritage*, June, 1972, vol. XXIII, no. 4, pp. 4-8, 90f.) It could also be called its last stand before its collapse into disaster.

Every U.S. political party of 1972 was in varying degrees populist. John Lindsay, George McGovern, George Wallace, Richard M. Nixon, Frank Rizzo, John D. Rockefeller IV, and many, many others made a populist appeal. Goldman reports that McGovern, in the primary, denounced Lindsay as a "Park Avenue populist" (i.e., not the real thing), and Lindsay denounced Wallace as a "phony populist", and so on.

The term "populist" comes from the old People's Party of the last century. According to Goldman, "The heart of populism has been a glorification of 'the people', defined in a way that permitted them to also be called 'ordinary folks' or 'the average man'." A study of the old People's Party platforms reveals the strong faith that salvation for society means a 'people's state' in which the state controls "big business", agriculture, and also issues money in quantities sufficient to supply the needs of the people. The state is seen as the controlling power to aid the working man; it has a duty to maintain full employment with public works projects, and the state should own and control the railroads and most public utilities. The populist movement has infiltrated into and captured the thinking of all political parties. Its triumph was correctly predicted in 1901 by the *Harper's Encyclopedia of United States History*.

It has triumphed indeed, but it has also gone to seed. The "reform" measures advocated in the 1890s are now law, and, instead of furthering the power and freedom of "the common man" or "the people", they have steadily whittled away at his liberties. Moreover, instead of seeing the evil in the statist repressions they advocated, the populists, unwilling to see the sin of the people, have insisted instead that the problem is not sin (the people are good at heart, only misled, the populists hold,) but conspiracy. The conspirators have robbed them, the innocent and pure people, of their victory. This is the thesis of the new leftist underground press and some conservatives.

Let us examine the triumph of Hitler and National socialism in Germany in terms of this thesis. Supposedly, the people were betrayed by the wealthy capitalists, who ostensibly financed Hitler's rise to power. Of course, the common people who followed Hitler did so because they had been supposedly betrayed in 1918 by the Jews and others. Did the German industrialists finance Hitler? In reality, the attitude of German Industrialists was pragmatic. According to Pritchard, "most industrialists preferred pragmatism to ideological doctrine." The same pragmatic self-interest marked the military and the great estate-owners. "The contributions of German industry to the Nazi Party equalled only a small percentage of the amount they gave to Hitler's opponents until he became chancellor. There is no basis for the fiction that the industrial cartels financed Hitler's way to power." The Nazis were chronically short of funds until they took power. The majority of the people, high and low, were motivated by pragmatic self-interest, and their political voice was diffused, whereas the Nazi voice was organized and united. (R. John Pritchard: *Reichstag Fire: Ashes of Democracy*. New York: Ballantine, 1972.)

Some German industrialists did give to Hitler as a part of a policy of giving to all major parties as a matter of political pragmatism. The same is true in the U.S. and elsewhere: play safe, and contribute to all possible winners. One reporter has remarked that sometimes the same faces appear at $100 a plate-dinners for rival candidates. Both industrialists and workers were pragmatic; but why are the industrialists alone made the scapegoats and conspirators? The reason is that the workers are the innocent and heroic victims in this myth, and politicians, industrialists, churchmen, large land-owners and others are the oppressors by definition. Every gnat must be strained and every camel swallowed in order to sustain the thesis that the innocent people were misled and betrayed.

The problem is instead sin. Humanism in all its forms, from monarchism to democracy, has refused to admit this fact. They have readily seen the mote in another person's eye and failed to admit the mote in their own. Thomas Babington Macaulay had some telling comments to make on the future of the United States. Writing, in a letter of May 23, 1857, Macaulay said, "The day will come when in the State of New York a multitude of people, none of whom has had more than half a breakfast, or expects to have more than half a dinner, will choose a Legislature. Is it possible to doubt what sort of a Legislature will be chosen? On one side is a statesman preaching patience, respect for vested rights, strict observance of public faith. On the other is a demagogue ranting about the tyranny of capitalists and usurers, and asking why any body should be permitted to drink Champagne and ride in a carriage, while thousands of honest folks are in want of necessaries. Which of the two candidates is likely to be preferred by a working-man who hears his children cry for more bread? I seriously apprehend that you (Americans) will, in some such season of adversity as I have described, do things which will prevent prosperity from returning; that you will act like people who should in a year of scarcity devour all the seed-corn, and thus make the next a year not of scarcity, but of absolute famine. There will be, I fear, spoliation. The spoliation will increase the distress. The distress will produce fresh spoliation. There is nothing to stop you. Your Constitution is all sail and no anchor. As I said before, when a society has entered on this downward progress, either civilization or liberty must perish. Either some Caesar or Napoleon will seize the reins of government with a strong hand, or your republic will be as fearfully plundered and laid waste by barbarians in the twentieth century as the

Roman Empire was in the fifth; with this difference, that the Huns and Vandals who ravaged the Roman Empire came from without, and that your Huns and Vandals will have been engendered within your own country by your own institutions." (G. Otto Trevelyan: *The Life and Letters of Lord Macaulay*, vol. II, p. 409f. New York: Harper, 1875.)

What Macaulay failed to see was that the leaven of humanism worked to the same end in the monarchies, autocracies, and principalities of Europe as in America, and often more rapidly. Faith in man and the savior state, "the people's state", leads to the same goal everywhere, to the destruction of freedom, the rise of statism, and the progressive enslavement of man. The problem for Macaulay was the common man; the problem for the populists, then and now, was and is the evil big people who oppress the little people. Both are right about each other: neither are to be trusted, because man is a sinner.

Man is free to the proportion that he sees himself as the problem and takes steps to remedy himself by the grace of God. Man is doomed to slavery if he insists on projecting the sin of man on to a particular class or group of men, as though the world's evils come from a special group rather than a general condition of sin and apostasy.

In 1791, Edmund Burke observed, "Men are qualified for civil liberty in exact proportion to their disposition to put moral chains upon their own appetites...society cannot exist unless a controlling power upon will and appetite be placed somewhere, and the less of it there is within, the more there is without. It is ordained in the eternal constitution of things that men of intemperate minds cannot be free. Their passions forge their fetters." The usually astute Macaulay was wrong: it has not been the Constitution and the "institutions" of the United States which have been at fault, whatever their imperfections, but the people of the United States, as well as the peoples of Europe and the world over. The problem is man: he is a sinner who will not admit to the nature of his problem, nor recognize his remedy. The result is a desperation of action, a readiness to try every extreme measure to demonstrate that sinful man can build a good society if only he has time and power enough to do so. Has the state failed in some measure aimed at changing man and society? It will try a more extreme measure next. The results are always assured failure and less freedom.

"But we *must* believe in man," someone insisted to me after a lecture; by man, he meant statist man, working with sovereign power in and through the state to remake man and society. Why *must* we believe in man, I objected. "Because there is nothing else to believe in." That was a few years ago, a very short time ago. Now, more often, I encounter another attitude, "there is *nothing* to believe in." The false gods go, and they leave behind them shattered youth and a divided culture. The will to destroy everything is very great in these bitter and disillusioned youth. The children of the age of the state are increasingly the self-appointed grave-diggers of the state, determined to bury the present order and bitter with hatred against it.

The will to rebuild is basic to those who see sin as the problem, and God and His law-word as the answer. They are concerned with rebuilding in their own lives, to exercise dominion over themselves and the earth, and they are thus the forerunners of reconstruction in every realm. To them all things are possible under God. Thus, William Carey and his associates were not discouraged by the bleak prospects of missionary work in India, declaring almost two centuries ago, "He who raised the Scottish and brutalized Britons to sit in heavenly places in Christ Jesus, can raise these slaves of superstition, purify their hearts by faith, and make them worshippers of the one God in spirit and in truth. The promises are fully sufficient to remove our doubts, and make us anticipate that not very distant period when He will famish all the gods of India, and cause these very idolaters to cast their idols to the moles and to the bats, and renounce for ever the work of their own hands."

More such men are needed now, in every sphere of endeavor, who will, under God, work to further His Kingdom, establish His law-order, and bring all things under the dominion of man as God's vice-gerunt.

The basic problem is in man, not in his environment. Man's freedom begins within, and man's dominion begins within. We are not in the twilight of man and his history, but rather closer to the dawn. This is still God's world; He has not abdicated. Have you?

CHALCEDON REPORT NO. 90
February, 1973

A particular type of literature marked the beginning of the modern age, Utopianism. One writer and scholar after another gave his version of the City of Man, the man-created and man-planned society of the future. Thomas More, Francis Bacon, Campanella, Harrington, and many others wrote their accounts of how the world could be remade by man into a paradise. (See R. J. Rushdoony: *The One and the Many*, pp. 266-276. Nutley, New Jersey: Craig Press, 1971.)

There had been no need for utopias in preceding centuries. Christian man already had his blue-print for the future in Scripture, and the way thereto, by faith and by obedience to God's law-word, was clearly set forth. The utopias of the Renaissance expressed a new hope, and they looked to another god, the state. By capturing the state, philosopher-kings could remake man and society into a happy and perfect order of life. The utopias were in part tracts aimed at persuading rulers and statesmen to allow their humanist scholars to guide them and the nations into the promised land.

Van Riessen, in an excellent chapter on "Utopias", commented, "The

Utopians are driven by homesickness for the lost paradise, and long for the new earth. Their dreams are utopias, 'never to be realized', because they seek a road to such a paradise that does not pass along the station of the fall into sin." (H. Van Riessen: *The Society of the Future*, p. 38. Philadelphia: Presbyterian & Reformed Publishing Co., 1957, 1972.) Man is not seen as a sinner, nor does man need a Savior; man's need is for the expert, the elite mind, to take over man's life and all society and to reorganize all things in terms of his wisdom. Man, especially elite man, is beyond good and evil. Man must become his own maker, and, in terms of the thinking of his philosophical and scientific elite, rethink all things and redefine the public good, happiness, profit, and justice. Van Riessen observed of Plato's *Republic*, the model of all utopias: "The argument of the 'Republic' boils down to the contention that an ideal just communal life can be obtained, and existing deficiencies and injustices can be corrected simply by permitting the state to *organize* society in terms of its own *conception of justice*. This is the key to *Plato's* reasoning; it is the basis of all utopias, including present day socialistic proposals. *Sin* in society is to be overcome, paradise regained, an ideal state established, simply by employing *human power*, in the *central organization of society*. Life is not to be redeemed by the Messiah but by man!" (*Ibid*., p. 39.)

For utopian thinkers, the problems of man can all be solved by a different arrangement of things. Thomas More was close to the heart of all such utopianism when he located sin in the private ownership of property; abolish private ownership, and man's problems and misery will disappear. Bacon added another central theme to the utopian myth: the scientific elite as the central planning agency to ensure a perfect society. The way was prepared by More, Bacon and others for the communist theoreticians, for Proudhon, who held that "ownership is theft", and Karl Marx, who made 'science' basic to his utopianism.

At the same time, however, other humanists were beginning to torpedo their own hope. Nietzsche, as utopian as any, in his disillusionment and bitterness wrote the finish to utopianism by admitting that man is a beast of prey ruled by the will to power. He tried vainly to use this fact constructively but could not: it led only to nihilism. H. G. Wells, in *The Time Machine*, saw the future as a perverted one, with security destroying most men, and the will to power destroying their rulers. Forster's *Celestial Omnibus* foresaw man's doom as scientific socialist man became the slave of his own creation, the machine.

Even more devastating a picture was Aldous Huxley's *Brave New World* (1932) which saw a statist future in which man surrendered his freedom for a drug-controlled euphoria. Man in his brave new world lives only for today as a total existentialist. His slogans include, with regard to sex, "Do not put off till tomorrow the fun you can have today"; "Civilization is sterilization";

"Everyone belongs to everyone else", and so on. A ruler in this world is of the opinion that God exists (the people are kept from all knowledge of God), but God is not to be spoken of in a statist society: "God is not compatible with machinery, scientific medicine and universal happiness." God is therefore replaced with Henry Ford as the originator of the assembly line.

George Orwell, in *1984* (1948), saw the future in terms of Nietzsche's will to power. The goal of the state is not man's happiness but power. Power means "inflicting pain and humiliation. Power is in tearing human minds to pieces and putting them together again in new shapes of your own choosing...If you want a picture of the future, imagine a boot stamping on a human face --- forever." (p. 203).

According to Roland Huntford, in *The New Totalitarians*, we have the *Brave New World* in Sweden, and *1984* in the Soviet Union.

Other writers continued in the same vein, seeing only disaster ahead as a result of utopianism. Thus, Constantine Fitz Gibbon, in *When the Kissing Had to Stop*, gives a chilling picture of the hypocrisy and inability to face reality on the part of the utopians. (Constantine Fitz Gibbon: *When the Kissing Had to Stop*. New Rochelle, N.Y.: Arlington House, 1960, 1973.) The more deeply men commit themselves to the utopian dream, the less able are they to recognize their own depravity. The equation is a simple-minded and pharisaic one: I want what is best for humanity, and my idea of a peace-loving socialist state is the best and most moral order; therefore, I am the best and most moral of men.

Elliott Baker, in *A Fine Madness* (1964) gives us another glimpse of the uses of power: a psychiatrist uses his position to perform a lobotomy on his wife's lover. This kind of tale right-wingers were discussing as a possibility; now a writer from another camp saw it as a logical aspect of the developing social order. The future was no longer seen as a new paradise, but as a nightmare.

A telling account of the future as nightmare is a tale written not too long before the Russian Revolution of 1917 by Valery Brussof, *The Republic of the Southern Cross*. The setting is an ideal socialistic republic, built some time in the future at the South Pole. Star City, the capitol, is exactly at the Pole, but no star is visible, because it is covered by an immense opaque roof. Everything works to perfection in terms of democratic socialist planning; everything is uniform (clothing, buildings) and standard in construction, but all are happy, since all their wants are met. The secret police were a real force, but men were gently conditioned into the right paths. The Republic of the Southern Cross was the dream utopia realized. Suddenly it collapses into anarchy as a mental malady overcomes everyone, *mania contradicens*, with people contradicting themselves. The stricken, instead of saying "yes" say "no"; wishing to say caressing words, they splutter hate and abuse. Nurses cut the throats of children. A concert violinist begins to scratch out dissonance. People abandon their homes in fear of the mobs. Youth runs wild, and their mothers do the same. "The moral sense of the people declined with astonishing rapidity. Culture slipped from off these people like a delicate bark, and revealed man, wild and naked, the man-beast as he was. All sense of right was lost, force alone was acknowledged. For women, the only law became that of desire and indulgence." In the anarchy, "cannibalism took place." (Valery Brussof: *The Republic of the Southern Cross*, p. 25. New York: Robert M. McBride, 1919.) A socialist society which ruled in terms of power (the Republic began as a large steel plant) and by-passes morality soon finds itself faced, Brussof showed, with an amoral people who become the voice of raw, anarchistic power, and the result is a vast and nightmarish blood-hunt. Organized power is contradicted by anarchistic power. The only reality recognized by the socialist state is power: it finally leaves nothing in the minds and lives of the people but the lust for contradicting power.

Brussof wrote his tale in the form of a news report by a writer piecing together stray pieces of information from the outside, and the picture which emerges is of startling depravity. The fiction writers, champions of man's goodness have turned into reporters of his depravity and sin!

Now, from the world of reality comes another telling report, J.A. Parker's *Angela Davis, The Making of a Revolutionary.* (New Rochelle, N.Y.: Arlington House, 1973.) Parker writes as a Christian, one who cites the works of J. Gresham Machen as the great influence in his life. He cites evidence for the fact that revolutionists like the Jackson brothers were from a comfortable and good background, if anything, over-protected and over-indulged. The problem is not one of injustice but a contempt of truth and a search for power, which, according to Mao Tse-tung comes "out of the barrel of a gun" (p. 104). Language is used as a tool for power (p. 150). The appeal of the left, of Marxism and its examples in China and Russia, is not primarily for the dream of justice, but far more plainly in terms of the lust for power. This lust for power is motivated by a radical hatred and a contempt rather than a love of either the truth or of people. The only proper goal as held and visualized by these people is a revolution, "completely destroying the American social, political and economic fabric and replacing it with one designed by the Communist Party" (p. 77).

The modern humanistic state has abandoned Christianity; it believes in a planning economy, *in technological rather than moral answers*. It thus operates on a power basis, very rigorously under Marxism and less rigorously by far in the democracies, but, as the socialism of the democracies increases, the rigor and the control increases. On both sides of the Iron Curtain, the *mania contradicens*, the contradiction of amoral power by amoral power, is increasing.

The humanists everywhere, *in* the establishments and at war with the establishments have denied the doctrine of original sin, but they have become prime examples of it! Their own literature testifies to this fact. They refuse, however, to take the logical step and to declare that this is sin, and it is exactly what Scripture says it is. To say so would require them logically to add that man needs the Savior. This they cannot and will not say, because for them, their savior is the State, and the State is already on the scene. Their alternative to the State is anarchistic man, but Nietzsche has already described him as a beast of prey, driven by the will to power. Dostovevsky saw it clearly in his novel, *The Possessed*, a biting indictment of revolutionary socialism. The gods of modern man are really devils.

Van Riessen, in criticizing Orwell's thesis in *1984*, saw the issue clearly. However idealistic Orwell was, "His conception is that of a negative freedom, a freedom from tyranny...Orwell can oppose a nihilism of power by substituting for it the nihilism of freedom, the nihilism of Sartre. Therefore he cannot 'stand firm' in his freedom (Galatians 5:1)." (*Society of the Future*, p. 66.) Utopianism is dying, and its hopes and dreams have turned into a nightmare. But the dreamers of Utopia can only awaken from that nightmare through Christ.

When a man awakens from a bad dream, it is often more real to him for a brief while than the reality around him, his home, familiar room, the slumbering dog at the side of his bed, and the familiar sound of the clock. Then, after a few minutes or more, the nightmare has so faded that by morning he cannot even recall what it was. So it is with a culture. When men break with a culture, when its dream world of ideas suddenly loses all hold on them, its reality rapidly fades away.

St. Paul summoned men to break with the dream world of their day, saying, "Awake thou that sleepest, and arise from the dead, and Christ shall give thee light" (Eph. 5:14). This is our task: scatter the nightmare, and bring in the Light.

CHALCEDON REPORT NO. 91
March, 1973

One of the key factors in any era is the attitude of the people. Men have often put up with great evils because they have been loyal to the system, and yet at other times men have resented trifles because of their hostility to the order, or because of their own inner restlessness.

An interesting example of this is England after the Black Death. An intense discontent followed as the old order disintegrated and men felt out of place in the new. According to Sir Arthur Bryant, "Everyone tended to blame someone else for his sufferings." A vivid expression of this discontent was William Langland's *Piers Plowman*, often called "The Vision of a People's Christ." *Piers Plowman* depicts corruption in church and state and contrasted undeserved wealth with undeserved destitution. Langland's poem presented a mild and reforming view which soon gave way to more radical answers. The later defrocked priest, John Ball, declared, "Things will never go well in England so long as goods be not in common and so long as their be villeins (serfs) and gentlemen. By what right are they whom we call lords greater than we?...We are formed in Christ's likeness and they treat us like beasts."

One of the most important ideas in the Western European tradition, one which has been especially important in England, Scotland, and the United States, is the medieval doctrine that "law is not law unless it is the voice of equity." (Gervase Mathew). From John of Salisbury to Langland, this was a powerful concept. It was basic to the outlook of John Knox in Scotland at a later date, and again important in the American colonies. Both a great measure of the vitality and progress of the West has been due to this concept as well as much of its troubles. Our Western liberties are rooted in this concept, and also many civil disobedience movements and revolutionary parties. One of those who misused the doctrine was John Ball. The monastic chronicler Walsingham tells us that Ball preached "those things which he knew would be pleasing to the common people, speaking evil both of ecclesiastical and temporal lords, and won the goodwill of the common people rather than merit in the sight of God. For he taught that tithes ought not to be paid unless he who gave them was richer than the person who received them. He also taught that tithes and oblations should be withheld if the parishioner was known to be a better man than the priest."

The age of Richard II (1367-1400) had real evils and problems to contend with. Du Boulay has declared, however, that the era did see economic and social advances. The problem lay elsewhere. The authorities did not take the dissatisfaction of the people seriously, and the people now did not view matters theologically. The appeal of John Ball was a humanistic one; it was not the relationship of rulers and people to God's law that he stressed, but the questions of wealth and status. The result was a rebellion, and the people, who had begun with *Piers Plowman*, the "People's Christ", chose as their leader Wat Tyler, an ex-soldier who had since then been earning his living by highway robbery.

A contemporary chronicler wrote of John Ball's program for the insurgents: "He strove to prove that from the beginning all men were created equal by nature, and that servitude had been introduced by the unjust oppression of wicked men against God's will, for if it had pleased Him to create serfs, surely in the beginning of the world He would have decreed who was to be a serf and who a lord...Wherefore they should be prudent men, and, with the love of a good husbandman tilling his fields and uprooting and destroying the tares which choke the grain, they should hasten to do the following things. First, they should kill the great lords of the kingdom; second, they should slay lawyers, judges and jurors; finally, they should root out all those whom they knew to be likely to be harmful to the commonwealth in future. Thus they would obtain peace and security, for, when the great ones had been removed, there would be equal liberty and nobility and dignity and power for all." The chronicler added, "When he had preached this and much other madness, the commons held him in such high favor that they acclaimed him the future archbishop and chancellor of the realm."

John Ball's program has a familiar ring. *First*, it was a gospel of salvation by equality. *Second*, evil was seen as the characteristic of a particular class, and a theory of class conflict was preached. *Third*, to solve society's problems, Ball held, eliminate the evil class and all will be well. The call for justice had now become a cry for mass murder as the way of salvation.

The ruling classes responded with no less a fallacious doctrine. *First*, it was progressively held that virtue and power were a class monopoly, and the monarchy claimed more and more of this for itself in the succeeding generations. *Second*, evil was seen as the especial property of the low-born, especially those who might speak of equality in any sense. The word *villein*, meaning serf (and related to village) came to be our modern word *villain*. The common people were villains, thieves, and robbers. In our day, race has intensified this idea. *Third*, to solve society's problem, it was held that it was important for the right people to rule. *Fourth*, as against John Ball's idea of salvation by mass executions, the rulers held to salvation by legislation. In 1349 and 1350 attempts were made to freeze wages and control labor. However, as Du Boulay noted, "solemn laws do not stem such rising tides." (See F. R. H. Du Boulay: *An Age of Ambition*, New York: Viking Press, 1970; Gervase Mathew: *The Court of Richard II*, New York: Norton, 1968; Sir Arthur Bryant: *The Fire and the Rose*, Garden City, N.Y.: Doubleday, 1966.)

Then as now society floundered from crisis to crisis, searching for answers. It looked, however, for both problems and answers in the wrong place, and hence aggravated its problems. Both the rulers and the ruled were clearly a part of the problem rather than the answer. Sir Arthur Bryant called the problem "spiritual" and a "sickness of soul." The peasants resented the controls over them, and yet also demanded that something he done for them, and the same attitude marks our own day, and with far less excuse. Andrews has observed that "The power to do things for you is also the power to do things to you." (p. 33). In every era, to ask for benefits is to ask for bondage. The origin of serfdom was in the Roman Empire. In exchange for cradle to grave security, people surrendered themselves and their possessions to the imperial estates and called it salvation. As Ramsay stated it, "The 'Salvation' of Jesus and Paul was freedom: the 'Salvation' of the Imperial system was serfdom." (Sir W. M. Ramsay, "The Imperial Salvation", in his *The Bearing of Recent Discovery on the Trustworthiness of the New Testament*, p. 198. London: Hodder and Stoughton, 1914, 1920.) Salvation is still seen as serfdom, as cradle to grave security, by all too many people.

The theoreticians of statism do understand one fact, as Andrews noted, and it is this: "Work is Power, and the modern trend is of necessity to subject power to increased social regulation and supervision." (Matthew Page Andrews: *Social Planning by Frontier Thinkers*, p. 57. New York: Richard R. Smith, 1944.) Exactly. Work is power, and, properly understood and directed, is essential and basic to God's Kingdom and man's exercise of dominion under God. The control of the future always depends to a large degree on motivating and governing work. If the state governs work, then we have a statist order and a decline of social energy as men sullenly withhold cooperation from the state, as in the Marxist empires. If man govern their work, then men are as powerful as the motives which provide the fuel for their work.

But men who have the malaise and "sickness of soul" Bryant spoke of are better at sterile protest than at productive work. Moreover, then as now there is a strong correlation between protest, lawlessness, and theft. The connection is a logical and natural one. When a man wants things on demand rather than in return for work, theft is a logical consequence of his demands.

The sins of the rulers are no less, and, in fact, are greater. The prophet Ezekiel gives us God's indictment of the rulers of Israel, saying, "The diseased have ye not strengthened, neither have ye healed that which was sick, neither have ye bound up that which was broken, neither have ye brought again that which was driven away, neither have ye sought that which was lost; but with force and with cruelty have ye ruled them" (Ezek. 34:4). Instead of being shepherds protecting the flock from hostile forces, the rulers have been wolves, preying on them. As in the 14th century, rulers offer laws as the solution to problems they have helped to create.

The great sin of the modern state and its theoreticians is the pretense of moral and religious neutrality, whereby humanism has been introduced as the new value and the new established religion. However, as Orton observed, "It is simply impossible to maintain, in either pure theory, or practice, that the state is by nature amoral -- that is, morally neuter" (p. 24). Moreover, Orton pointed out, "every major political system rests on an act of affirmation as to the nature of man...The affirmation it embodies is therefore by nature moral rather than political or economic" (p. 55). It follows that "The central concern of the state is therefore, in the widest sense, justice; not power; not even prosperity. The state is the social structure through which our sense of right becomes articulate and effective" (p. 59). The state in its law structure is a theological establishment. It represents a doctrine of man, law, and ultimacy. The control of the state today by "organized atheism" is simply a new form of religious establishment. "In the sphere of values it is simply not possible to be neutral -- neither individually nor collectively" (William Aylott Orton: *The Economic Role of the State*, p. 31f. Chicago: U. of Chicago Press, 1950.) One more important comment from Orton: "For it is the essence of the Christian position that there are limits both extensive and intensive to the scope and exercise of secular authority. I do not need to remind the reader of the history of this issue; but I do need to emphasize the fact that it is a uniquely Christian tradition and that, whenever and wherever it is denied, the community ceases in both theory and practice to be Christian. Its values as well as its policies undergo a radical change" (p. 29).

It is this change we have been undergoing since the Enlightenment of the 18th century, and we now are approaching its end results. The future will not be commanded by protest; then, in the 14th century, as now in the 20th, it is sterile and destructive. Similarly, barren statist power is again effective only in controls and destruction. Only as our thinking, our faith, and our values are again informed and governed by the word of God, and only as we recognize again that work is power, and we work productively and effectively in terms of freedom under God will we again have the motive force to redirect men and nations. Sterile men are governed by their fears and hates. Productive men are governed by a faith for living.

CHALCEDON REPORT NO. 92
April, 1973

The failure of statism, whether in ancient Rome or today, usually centers on two areas, religion and economics. The two moreover are very closely related. In fact, economics was once taught as a branch of Christian ethics, because sound economics is simply the application of the principle, "Thou shalt not steal." Monetary policies and welfare economics have historically been very common means of robbing the middle class and redistributing a nation's wealth and resources.

There are two basic premises to a sound social order, both of which, are strongly emphasized in the Bible. *First*, "Man shall not live by bread alone, but by every word that proceedeth out of the mouth of God" (Matt. 4:4; Deut. 8:3). Food alone cannot satisfy man. Man requires a purpose and meaning to life, and the absence of meaning renders life impossible. Wordsworth in October of 1803 did not suffer materially, but, his hopes in the French Revolution having been destroyed, he could, with the rise of Napoleon, feel only despair. He wrote, in "Poems Dedicated to National Independence and Liberty," Part I, No. 22,

> I find nothing great:
> Nothing is left which I can venerate;

So that a doubt almost within me springs
Of Providence, such emptiness at length
Seems at the heart of all things...
I tremble at the sorrow of the time.

A year earlier, Wordsworth wrote (1802, *ibid.*, Part I, No. 15) of man's plight in his day as one of

Perpetual emptiness! unceasing change!
No single volume paramount, no code,
No master spirit, no determined road.

Wordsworth experienced some of the earlier anguish which ushered in the era of revolutions. We are now deeper in that crisis and despair. "What's there to live for?", asked a youth of twenty recently, who had tried every kind of experience, felt burned out, and was seriously considering suicide. Time and again, generations of men who have been materially rich have turned on their culture and destroyed it, because it failed to provide them with a reason for living.

Second, while man cannot live by bread alone, neither can he live without bread. Man can no more neglect the material necessities of life than he can the religious. Food is basic to life, and economics deals with the necessities and the amenities of life, their supply and demand, and their flow. Men require a sense of security with respect to their ultimate goals, with regard to the meaning of life, *and* with respect to the economic realm. A man can take a great deal of hardship and difficulty, if he feels that what he earns is sure, that his work pays off and that his property is not subject to confiscation by decree or by taxation. To feel insecure in one's possessions is unsettling and destructive: it erodes the value of man's work and purpose. As a result, while inflationary economics brings, for a time, more than a little wealth to the debtor classes, they also bring an unsettling fear of confiscation.

Consider, for example, what Orton reported in 1950 concerning Britain. "A steeply graduated income tax has long been the backbone of British fiscal policy. The standard rate is now (1949-50) 45 percent. On this was superimposed, in 1948-49, a special tax on investment income which in effect was, and was acknowledged to be, a capital levy. On higher income brackets the total tax ran well over 100 percent of gross income. A man with wife and two children, getting an investment income of $36,000, was liable for a tax of $37,500. A bachelor with $100,000 of such income had to find $130,000. This of course meant throwing all kinds of property-land, houses, cottages, farms, furniture, books, art collections onto a buyers' market. That was done. But it also meant, as it was intended to mean, the transfer of innumerable personal and private social responsibilities to the state. That was done too.

Now the state has them. The Inland Revenue Commissioners, in their report for the year ended March 31, 1949, officially state that there are only seventy people left in Britain with incomes after taxes of more than $24,000. Quietly as this result has been accomplished, one would have to look back to the French or Russian revolutions for a comparable precedent." (William Aylott Orton: *The Economic Role of the State*, p. 101f. Chicago: University of Chicago Press, 1950.) After such a confiscation, wealth is still possible, but it is at the sufferance of the state and subject to its confiscation.

The modern state is in crisis both religiously and economically, and it has created both crises. Since the French Revolution, the modern state has worked against Biblical religion steadily. This has been under the guise of a separation of church and state, a worthy goal, but in reality what has been done is to disestablish Christianity and to establish humanism as the religion of the state. Every state or political order is a religious establishment. All law is enacted morality or procedural thereto, and morality is the relational aspect of religion. The January 22, 1973 U.S. Supreme Court decision on abortion (*Jane Roe* et al. v. *Henry Wade* 41 LW 4213) specifically cited as precedent and authority for abortion "ancient religion." By this it plainly meant, not the Old Testament faith, but the religion of Greece and Rome, paganism. The court rendered a religious decision in terms of modern and ancient humanism.

The major offensive against Biblical faith began with the statist take-over of education and its conversion from a Biblical to a humanistic orientation. Modern statist education is intensely religious, but its religion is humanism, and its goal is the conversion of youth to the faith of the state and faith in the humanistic state.

The power of the state has been greatly enhanced by the take-over of education. The child was re-shaped in terms of statist premises and statist loyalties and expected to be a ready martyr for the state and its warfare. Nothing has contributed more to the rise of the state and its power than the statist school, and nothing is now more destructive to it. Whether in the Soviet Union or the Western world, the product of the state school is increasingly a lawless moral and political anarchist who is as hostile to his country as to God.

The result is a growth of lawlessness which the state cannot check. Oscar Newman, in *Defensible Space* (New York: Macmillan, 1972), points out that we are witnessing the breakdown of the social mechanisms which once checked crime and supported police activity because few neighbors share beliefs and values. The sense of community is gone, and also the sense of security in one's own home. As Newman points out, "The home and its environs must be felt to be secure or the very fabric of society comes under threat."

In the economic sphere, the policy of theft has led to the progressive decline of economic morale. The attitude is that being economically successful is somehow a sin that must be atoned for by paying off the failures. As a result, the tax structure is designed to redistribute the wealth in terms of this principle. The U.S. foreign aid program a also an application of this same idea, and money has been readily appropriated to the "under-developed" countries as a compensation for their backwardness. In the past year, the same policy has been used by the U.S. in dealing with the European dollar crisis. John Connally, Peter Peterson, Arthur Burns, and President Nixon have all, in various ways, attacked the idea of surpluses as immoral. The establishment economist, Paul Samuelson, stated, "Even if the dollar should turn out to be somewhat overvalued, this primarily puts the onus on the surplus countries to appreciate their currencies unilaterally -- particularly the mark and the yen. Or else they should swallow our dollars of deficit without complaining." (*The Morgan Guaranty Survey*, New York, July, 1972.) Success and enterprise, in other words, must be punished as somehow *immoral*.

Here is the key. Over and over again, it is insinuated that somehow success. enterprise, and profits are per se immoral. The U.S. Supreme Court cites pagan religion for its authority, and statists the world over cite a thief's morality to vindicate their principles. Economics cannot escape from moral fundamentals: either "Thou shalt not steal" is true, or the good society requires that we "Steal from those who have in order to equalize society and reward those who have not." The new religion and morality (with its economics) of statism is the same old sin condemned by Scripture from Moses through St. John.

Bewailing the situation will not alter the matter. The answer lies elsewhere. There is no dramatic road to recovery. Only as men change will society change. Irresponsibility today, whether in the various branches of the state, in the church, in society at large, in schools, unions, corporations, and families, stems from the false faiths and values of the individuals involved. We live in a day when a pornographic film has become the "in-thing" to see, and "porno-chic" is common is prominent circles. In late 1972, in a few weeks, a book, the autobiography of a prostitute and "madam," sold at a record level and was expected to reach five million copies by Spring, 1973, for the U.S. and Canada alone. Very popular also have been two books by a notorious pimp, and pimps have becomes "heroes" to many.

Men live, not by faith today, but by debt and envy, and they look with suspicious eyes on anyone better than themselves. We are told by Plutarch how in ancient Greece the men of Athens banished the honest Aristides. When Aristides the Just, unknown to the man, asked one voter if Aristides had ever done him any injury, the man replied, "None at all, neither know I the man; but I am tired of hearing him everywhere called the Just." The mentality today is not too different. Is a man successful? Then he must be a scoundrel, and, if not, why should he have more than others?

The result is an economic problem, but the cure is not economic. It is moral and religious, and it begins with you. If it does not begin there, then judgment will.

The easiest answer in too many eras has been to point the finger at persons and classes and demand, "Off with their heads!" Such people want the world to be good, but they want to be spared the necessity of being good themselves, a schizophrenic position. They want evil to be punished in others, but not in themselves. They see the mote in another man's eye, but not the beam in their own (Matt. 7:5). But above all else, such people look for a statist answer rather than the personal moral and religious one. If only we can control the state and manipulate people, all will be well, they reason. True order is seen as a man-made order, as some form of humanism. In one of his early writings, Karl Marx summed up the essence of radicalism in religious terms: "To be radical is to grasp things by the root. But for man the root is man himself...the doctrine that man is the supreme being for man." (T. B. Bottomore, editor: *Karl Marx, Early Writings*, p. 52. New York: McGraw-Hill, 1964.) Marx's definition of the radical fits most modern men and almost every state in the world today. Man is the supreme being for modern man. It should not surprise us that the world moves more and more into the jungle of Marx's mind: it begins with the same premise. If man is the supreme being for man, then man makes his own laws as he goes along. As a result, if man says that theft is virtue, then supposedly theft becomes virtue. Our modern economics, and our modern established religion, humanism, are alike consequences of making man his own god.

But our Lord declared. "It is written, Thou shalt worship the Lord thy God, and him only shalt thou serve" (Matt. 4:10). And God has built in a problem which confronts the humanistic state, and will progressively in the days ahead. Man shall not and cannot long live by bread alone, and neither can he live without it. The more the state increases its power, the more it undermines both the religious and economic life of man, and its own life as well.

CHALCEDON REPORT NO. 93
May, 1973

Thomas A. Kempis (1379-1471) wrote a devotional manual entitled *On the Following* (or *Imitation*) *of Christ*, said by some to be, after the Bible, the most widely read book in history. The title sums up the major cultural goal in the history of Western civilization, the attempt to create a social order in terms of Christ and Scripture. With the Renaissance, and then with the Enlightenment and the French Revolution, another cultural goal came into existence, the imitation of the non-working rich, royalty, or nobility. The object of envy and imitation became the idle classes, men beyond work, men who could live in contempt of monetary considerations, morality, and law. The rake and the dandy became heroes; they seemed to live a life without reckoning, and without a day of economic or religious judgment.

The beginning of the era of revolutions did not lead to a proletarianization of culture. Instead, the new classes in power began to imitate the vices of the old aristocracy and to flaunt their contempt of economics and religion as a means of proving that they had arrived. In France, from Louis XIV on, the court was marked by gambling on a massive scale, and sexual immorality. Nineteenth century France saw the new classes imitate royalty, and courtesans triumphed as never before. In Red China, the elite communist cadres put the old war lords to shame with their more systematic exploitation of women, their use of power to promote their idle fancies, and their childish and senseless pride.

Each new generation of leaders has imitated the older idle rich and have built houses, not in terms of convenience and utility, but as imitation palaces, and furnishings still are prized because they echo the ornate vulgarity of the Bourbon styles. The "proletarian art" of Marxist countries is officially required to imitate the older styles of royal Europe in the name of socialist realism, whereas non-Marxist art despises the same tradition in art because the middle classes borrowed and used it for a time. Modern art strives instead for a new elitism which is non-utilitarian in a radical sense.

In education, the goal on the part of the traditional scholar is the training of gentlemen. Witonski thus deplores the instrumentalism of American universities, where, "Instead of studying, say, Latin poetry, a student can study urban race relations, an instrumental course that will be of little use to him in the real world." (Peter Witonski: *What Went Wrong With American Education*, p. 112. New Rochelle, N.Y.: Arlington House, 1973.) But of what "use" is Latin poetry "in the real world"? Witonski's idea of a liberal education is hopelessly obsolete. A liberal education is an education in the art of freedom, of being a free man (*liber* meaning free), and Witonski, as an Oxford and Harvard scholar, has a view of freedom which is irrelevant to our world, and, in its own way, almost as worthless as courses in hotel management. The scholar as a member of the idle clan, a man who *is* rather than *does*, is meaningless increasingly. The scholar who *does* asks to initiate the "social relevancy" of agitators. The academic scholar thus has been unable to define himself in our era because he lacks a faith which makes for valid definition. This underscores his increasing irrelevance to the future in any constructive sense.

The styles of men and women in the age of aristocracy stressed clothing which made people useless for work. Women emphasized this by their hairstyles, shoes, and finger-nails: they were beyond work. The goal of most moderns is the same non-utilitarianism and the same lust for an aristocratic idleness. The hippies have also manifested the same contempt for the world of work: they drop out of study and work. They emphasize hand crafts and aristocratic arts as alone relevant to their cultural goals.

"The Puritan work ethic", as the antithesis of this imitation of the non-working or idle rich, has been especially under attack. In the 1920s, as a boy in Detroit, one of the most remarkable facts was the pride of workers in automobile factories: they urged friends to take the guided tour through, for example, the Ford plant, to see the assembly line. Instead of boredom, there was a delight in the high volume of production and a boastfulness about what their work was doing to change the world. The reason for this attitude was the "Puritan work ethic." The increasing signs of boredom today mark not only the automobile workers but white collar workers, executives, intellectuals, and men in every area of work. The reason is a change of faith, the growth of a delight in idleness rather than work. Increasingly, men no longer live to work, but work in order to be able to play. The *Playboy* dream is to cultivate the appearance of being a member of the idle rich from college days on.

The idle rich were a reality, but always a sign of approaching death and collapse. The nobility of France, for example, became idle and useless when Louis XIV required their presence at court and stripped them of power to prevent revolts. As a growing bureaucracy took over, the monarchs themselves became idle and finally irrelevant. Today, because of the Proletarianization of the dream of idleness, men of all classes are determined to make themselves irrelevant and to commit cultural suicide.

The hatred of capitalism is largely inspired by the old dream of imitating the nobility and royalty, not in their greatness, but in their decadence. The life style of the future requires, we are told, living in terms of fun and games. We are asked to despise mass production in favor of handcrafts, and to love the new morality rather than to obey God.

The rich have always been with us, as have the poor. The lines, historically, have been very sharply drawn. To the horror of the nobility, the Industrial Revolution not only created a new rich class, the industrialists and merchants, but it made good living cheap enough for the middle and lower classes. Capitalism undermined the old aristocracy and dramatically benefitted the masses. As Hazlitt notes, "Before the Industrial Revolution the prevailing trades catered almost exclusively to the wants of the well-to-do. But mass production could succeed only by catering to the needs of the masses." (Henry Hazlitt: *The Conquest of Property*, p. 54. New Rochelle, N.Y. Arlington House, 1973.) The result was the rapid rise in the standard of living among all peoples in Western Europe.

A savage counter-attack came from the two major branches of the old aristocracy, the lords and the intellectuals. A series of "investigations" were launched in England to dredge up every case of capitalistic exploitation in order to build a case against the new class. Since no class is exempt from sin, such examples were found and publicized by both the lords and also by the intellectuals. (See F. A. Hayek, editor: *Capitalism and the Historians*. The University of Chicago Press, 1954.) Socialists and aristocrats made common cause in their hatred of the levelling influence of the free market. Karl Marx, by virtue of being an intellectual, entered the ranks of the aristocracy and married into the nobility. In *The Communist Manifesto*, he echoed the aristocratic hatred of the Industrial Revolution while admitting its revolutionary impact on the world. Marx charged, "The bourgeoisie, wherever it has got the upper hand, has put an end to *all feudal, patriarchal, idyllic relations*. It has pitilessly torn asunder the motley feudal ties that bound man to his 'natural superiors', and has left no other nexus between man and man than naked self-interest, than callous 'cash payment'." The bourgeoisie had replaced the old aristocracy, with its junior members, the intellectuals, with a new upper class, the producers, and Marx could not forgive them for that offense. While ready to admit the remarkable effects of industrialism, he took offense at its by-passing of the intellectual. He countered with an Hegelian dream in which the seduced masses, rejoicing in the new affluence, were offered even more affluence if only they followed the intellectuals as their philosopher-kings. One point Marx saw clearly. Power had belonged to the royalty and landed nobility, because, in the old order, they largely controlled property. This old aristocracy had made room for the intellectual; a Ph.D. had standing as a junior member of the aristocracy, and, if he were a Goethe or a Voltaire, with or without a degree he was an uncrowned king. That eminence had been shattered. Capitalistic production had created new and cheap property, good property, and even landed property was being taken over by the middle and lower classes with their new wealth. In *The Communist Manifesto*, Marx declared, "The distinguishing feature of Communism is not the abolition of property generally, but the abolition of bourgeois property...In this sense, the theory of Communism may be summed up in the single sentence: Abolition of private property...Capital is therefore not a personal, it is a social power." Once a feudal aristocracy had controlled this social power, property. Marx now proposed that a new feudal aristocracy, the dictatorship of the proletariat, the intellectual elite, control this social power. The Marxist "revolution" was the ultimate in counter-revolutionary thinking: it was aimed at undoing the effects of the Industrial Revolution.

In a variety of ways, the New Left continues in this reactionary, counter-revolutionary tradition. "Detroit" is a symbol of the hated mass producer. Production has polluted the world, the ecology people hold, ignorant of the greater pollution which preceded the Industrial Revolution, or of the times when the rivers of Europe were dead streams in a way beyond our present knowledge. The goal of the New Left is to sabotage the great seducer of the common man, production. Instead of realistic attempts at dealing with pollution, the "eco-freaks", the New Leftist exploiters of ecology and conservation, concentrate instead on *destroying production*. Through legislation and sabotage, production is hampered. Oil shortages are one result. The oil reserves in America alone are enormous, despite the statements to the contrary, but drilling is restricted, and new refineries are not built because of restrictions. Off-shore drilling has a remarkable record of safety: the Santa Barbara incident had overtones of sabotage. Today, guards are necessary on off-shore installations to prevent sabotage by groups who want to create destruction in order to make production anathema. It is the mark of the New Leftist aristocracy to despise mass production in the name of the masses, to hate an abundance which enables "the common man" to have as much as an intellectual. One well-paid university professor climaxed and concluded a long tirade against capitalism by declaring, "Do you realize that my plumber makes more money than I do?" This was the ultimate insult: the free market economy had given a plumber more money than a professor! The professor's contempt of capitalistic materialism had a materialistic ring. In every age, disproportions have existed such as the professor cited, and in every society. They are not corrected by envy and mass suicide.

We see also a horror of abundance in the New Left and a desire to *destroy abundance*. The delight of the New Left in handcrafts is revealing. What they produce is sometimes good, sometimes crude and childish, but, in either case, it has for them the virtue of being a scarce product. Scarcity is prized and abundance is despised. There is a contempt in every area of the common and the abundant. For example, to have a lovely flower or shrub in one's garden which grows and blooms readily is somehow despised and frowned upon. The idea is to coax growth out of something which does *not* do well in that locale. Achievement is not seen as beauty but as scarcity and exclusiveness. For many, a flower is not beautiful if it is common. In my university days, I heard professors on a few occasions ridicule the Californian's affection for his state flower, the poppy. In those days, tens of thousands of acres were covered with poppies every spring. Since then, cultivation and the extension of farming into new areas has caused the poppy to recede. A student has told me that he has heard professors denounce the destruction of the California poppy by the extension of farming. This is typical: abundance is despised, and scarcity is prized, because only the elite can afford the scarce item.

To cite one more example among many, *styles* reflect the same hatred of that which all men can enjoy and the same lust for the aristocratic. The aristocratic in this definition is not the superior but rather the exclusive and the scarce. Whether the style is in dress or in a fad, as long as it is the mark of the avant garde, everybody is ready to imitate and adopt it. The imitation of the idle rich, the jet set or any other group, is a major passion. Is it chic to see a certain pornographic film, to favor homosexuals, or to adopt a style? Then all climb aboard the bandwagon of liberal or radical chic, hippie chic, or what have you. However, when it becomes popular, it perishes. Is everybody doing it? Then forget it.

The imitation or the following of Christ had as its goal life. The imitation of the ideal of the idle rich, or aristocracy as imagined in the modern era, has as its goal *irrelevance*.

The *privileged* groups of the monarchist era in France had as their social goals and principles four things. First, they believed in inequality, however much they idolized Rousseau and his gospel of equality. It was an article of faith with them that some men are more equal than others. Second, they believed in the autonomy of the aristocracy; they were exempt, or should be, from the laws which bind common men. Third, they were "different" and hence could not be included in the body politic in the same way as other men. Fourth, even though they had little power, they regarded the exercise of state power as their natural right. It is this heritage which the intellectuals and the New Left (as well as the Old Left) have largely adopted. It is a policy of studied irrelevance, and its only real power is, not to produce, but to destroy.

Another factor which has since been added is *madness*. The extent to which madness is a theme of importance in modern culture is rarely appreciated. Before Freud, the cultivation of new and aristocratic mental illnesses was already prominent. Psychoanalysis became an "in thing" for a time for the self-style elite. In fiction, television, and motion pictures, the subject of madness is a common one, and an appealing one to many. Mental illness is in fact systematically courted as a liberating process by sensitivity and encounter groups, and industry for a time recently worked to cultivate mental illness as though it offered a way to a higher status and health. This cultivation of mental illness is still a "growth industry", typical of the new, non-productive growth "industries" of our time. Gene Church and Conrad D. Carnes, in *The Pit, A Group Encounter Defiled* (New York: Outerbridge & Laynard, 1972), gives us an account of the kinds of depravity cultivated in the attempts to gain leadership and aristocracy through induced madness.

An age which despises production and abundance and pursues scarcity, idleness, and irrelevance will certainly gain all these things, and will destroy itself in the process. Scarcity is ahead, and irrelevance, and death as well. The age of the state, the world of humanistic man, is committing suicide. We will be hurt in that process, but it is also a forerunner of our deliverance. More than ever, we must work to re-establish our roots in the Biblical faith and order, to establish new schools and institutions to rebuild society.

In 1961, in the concluding paragraph of my book, *Intellectual*

Schizophrenia, Culture and Education, I wrote: "The end of an age is always a time of turmoil, war, economic catastrophe, cynicism, lawlessness, and distress. But it is also an era of heightened challenge, and creativity, and of intense vitality. And because of the intensification of issues, and their world-wide scope, never has an era faced a more demanding and exciting crisis. This then above all else is the great and glorious era to live in, a time of opportunity, one requiring fresh and vigorous thinking, indeed a glorious time to be alive." More than ever, this is true today.

CHALCEDON REPORT NO. 94
June, 1973

One of the by-products of the ecology movement is a slogan which often appears as a bumper sticker: "Fight smog. Get a horse." Supposedly horses provided a cleaner atmosphere than automobiles do. Behind that assumption lie some very interesting philosophical and religious beliefs. However, before commenting on them, let us look first at the day of the horse.

Joel A. Tarr, in "Urban Pollution-Many Long Years Ago" (*American Heritage*, October, 1971, vol XXII, no. 6). gives a vivid picture of how much pollution horses created. Milwaukee, in 1907, had a population of 350,000 people, and a horse population of 12,500. It had a daily problem of 133 tons of manure. It should be noted that every city, apart from its own horses had a daily influx of wagons and teams from farms, with produce, and from small towns nearby, so that at all times, and especially in the early 1800s, the horses which daily entered a city were very numerous. In 1908, when New York's population was 4,777,000, it had 120,000 horses. Chicago in 1900 had 83,330 horses. Remember too that by this time the street car and some automobiles had alleviated the need for horses to a great degree; there were, however, still three and a half million horses in American cities and seventeen million in the countryside.

Consider the implications of this. In the winter or spring, the manure turned to slush, and it meant walking (and slipping and falling) into liquefied manure in bad weather. Americans then were not as calm and sedate as romantics would believe. The weather then led to more bad tempers than we can imagine today. What the well-dressed man and woman said on being splattered by liquefied manure by a passing carriage, or on slipping and failing into the foul slush, is best left to the imagination. It was not a pretty picture.

Summer weather did not improve matters. The summer sun dried the manure, and the carriage and wagon wheels soon turned it into a floating dust to be breathed by all, and to coat clothing and furniture with a foul covering. People complained about breathing "pulverized horse dung," and a summer breeze was a disaster. Summer rains only brought back a manure mush.

The wind blown particles were a reservoir for disease spores, such as tetanus. Because of a variety of other forms of pollution, in those days, epidemics of cholera, dysentery, infant diarrhea, small pox, yellow fever, and typhoid were common.

The manure, of course, bred flies by the billions, and they were everywhere. It was impossible to keep swarms of flies out of the houses, and a common gesture at the dinner table was to keep waving your free hand to keep the flies off the food. The sparrows were also a major problem. They fed on the grain particles in the manure and they multiplied astronomically. A very common complaint in those days was the sparrow problem. Sparrows could make it difficult to sit under the shade of that old apple tree, and housewives found that their clothes on the clothesline often bore evidences of sparrow droppings.

But this is not all. Freighters, junk men, delivery men, and cabbies were commonly brutal in their treatment of horses. This led to the founding in 1866 of the American Society for the Prevention of Cruelty to Animals. In spite of their efforts, men still killed an animal which dropped in its tracks or broke a leg, and left him dead on the city street. In 1880, there were 15,000 dead horses left on New York streets; as late as 1912, Chicago had 10,000 dead horses left on its streets, although by then street cars and automobiles were lessening the horse population. One of the first things that happened to a dead horse, before any disposal agency could get to it, was that dogs, by nature scavengers, were quickly busy tearing it to shreds and carting hunks of meat into nooks and alleys.

Much more can be said. For example, the noise pollution was very great. Iron horse shoes on cobblestone pavements, four shoes to a horse, and sometimes two and four horses to a wagon, made a tremendous racket, night and day. Automobiles and trucks are silent by comparison. The noise also involved the shouts and profanity of teamsters trying to get the maximum effort out of their over-worked animals.

But we have barely touched the surface of urban pollution. Cooking and heating by wood and coal stoves meant that, winter and summer, coal soot was a part of urban life. In heating with coal, faulty flues often led to carbon monoxide poisoning. (In 1902, Emile Zola lost his life in France through charcoal fumes.) Faulty flues often led to serious fires. On winter days, the balls of greasy soot would form and drift in the wind and on the streets. With smog at its worst, cities are today far cleaner. With coal as fuel, housewives could not allow curtains to go unwashed more than six weeks: they would disintegrate if not washed very regularly. This meant too that painted walls were regularly washed down by tidy housewives as a routine in housecleaning. Housewives aged more rapidly in those days, not because they did not know how to take care of themselves, but because severe pollution, and constant heavy work in combating it, aged them rapidly.

Remember too that, without the automobile, urban sprawl was not nearly as possible then as now, and cities were more compact and concentrated. This meant that every form of pollution was also more concentrated and had a corresponding effect on city dwellers.

Other forms of pollution then common can be cited, but the picture is by now clear. The coming of the twentieth century technology and the automobile did not increase pollution. Rather, it helped limit it severely. Bad as smog is, a very strong case exists for the very important fact that the air over cities is now definitely cleaner.

Moreover, more power to the agencies of civil government is not the answer. The worst pollution today is probably in the Soviet Union. (See Marshall I. Goldman: *The Spoils of Progress: Environmental Pollution in the Soviet Union*. Cambridge, Mass.: The MIT Press, 1972.) Most pollution today is created by statist agencies, or, as Dr. Hans Sennholz has shown in a recent study in *The Freeman* (Foundation for Economic Education, Irvington, N.Y.), by those sectors of industry which have some form of statist subsidy.

People, however, are very ready to believe that technology and progress are responsible for pollution. In fact, with very many it is a truism that progress means pollution, and the only way to restore the earth is to return to a more primitive way of life.

So-called primitive man was and is a great polluter. One reason why such "primitive" tribes have not done more damage to the earth is that their way of life leads to so much pollution and disease that it limits their population, and their ability to damage is thereby restricted. Many such tribes would set grass and forest fires in order to drive game to them. (This was common among some American Indian tribes.) Others would spread nets across a river to trap all spawning fish. A tribe would stay in one place until all the fish and game were too scarce, or until it was too filthy from human pollution to be tolerable, and then move on. This myth of "primitive" man as a conserver is a part of the broader myth which is so deeply rooted in the very unhealthy and twisted aspects of the ecology movement.

The roots are in Rousseau and Rousseau's idealization of "primitive," natural man as against civilized and Christian man. Rousseau's thesis was essentially this, as he himself described it: "man is by nature good, and...only our institutions made him bad." The way to the future was for Rousseau a return to man's barbaric and primitive past.

Last month, a woman interviewed on television described in glowing terms her visit to a backward tribe. One of the most "wonderful" things about them was their total disregard for time. She found it "beautiful" that someone who promises to do something tomorrow morning might decide to do it only days later. The woman conducting the interview also rhapsodized over this and declared that we are all too much ruled by the clock, and how wonderful it would be if we could all get rid of living by the clock.

This, of course, is pure Rousseau. Rousseau gave away his watch and declared that time-watching was an evil manifestation of civilization and a mark of decadence. Civilization, the church. private property, technology (as much as then existed), and much more were all damned by Rousseau as aspects of degeneracy. Man's hope was in a return to primitivism, to a Golden Age of unspoiled, non-Christian man.

The philosophy of Rousseau meant thus a negation of Christian civilization. It meant, to use Methvin's apt phrase, the development of "the technology of social demolition." (Eugene H. Methvin: *The Rise of Radicalism*, p. 99. New Rochelle, N.Y.: Arlington House, 1973.) It meant also the birth of revolution as man's hope of salvation, of salvation by mass destruction. The philosophy of Rousseau is basic to modern education, politics, and religion. It means that the modern world pins its hopes on destruction, and it has a hatred of progress and civilization, of technology, religious and philosophical principle. The more deeply all these agencies succeed, the more deeply suicidal destruction becomes a way of life. Increasingly, militant sons of Rousseau work to bring technology to a halt out of a radical hatred of technology and progress. A gasoline shortage is developing in the U.S., because no new refineries can be built due to opposition on the grounds of a Rousseau-inspired ecology movement. New oil fields cannot be developed for the same reason, and so on and on. Add to this statist controls which are restricting industry, and the picture is one of a man-created crisis caused by a serious shortage of common sense.

In a very important book, *Out of Revolution*, Eugene Rosenstock-Huessy (New York: William Morrow, 1938) pointed out that the basic movement of the modern world is from Christ to Adam, from redeemed and supernatural man to natural man, from Christian civilization to an anti-Christian world. Goethe's formulation of this new gospel was to the point: "Allah need create no longer. We instead create his world." As Rosenstock-Huessy observed, the word "creation" was transferred from God to the man of genius. The new world imagined by the followers of Rousseau is the world of post-historical man because primitives know no history. "Books like James Henry Breasted, *Dawn of Conscience*, with its ardor for an age preceding the despicable age of revelation, or like Frazer's *Golden Bough*, pave the road for an age when Jerusalem, Athens and Rome can be eradicated from our children's textbooks, and where the life of Indians, negroes, Egyptians, Sumerians, Teutons, and Celts will seem much more attractive than the so-called classics of Greece and Rome" (p. 118). The hero of James Joyce's *Ulysses* says, "History is the nightmare from which I will awake."

To say that we are developing a post-Christian civilization is absurd. It misses the whole point of the revolution of our times. What humanistic men are trying to do is to *destroy* Christianity *and* civilization, not to create a new civilization. Seidenberg's *Post-Historical Man* is also post-civilization man, man beyond and without civilization.

This dream is both insane and impossible, because it reckons without God, but it is no less destructive. There can be no compromise with it, no catering to it, and no collaborating with it. If you are busy bemoaning or apologizing for technology and the machine, either wake up, or get over into the ranks of the barbarians. And leave all your clothes behind as you go: if you are logical and true to your faith, you will not need them. They interfere with your "natural" environment. Take your picket signs with you as you go: you may need them for firewood when your bare butt gets cold, if you believe in fire, that is.

Meanwhile, the rest of us had better realize that it is *Christian* civilization that we must reconstruct, one systematically and faithfully established on Biblical premises. We must have a healthy regard for the world God has given us, *and* for the things He has given us the power to develop and to use in the exercise of our dominion under God.

We do not despise the "primitive" or the past, and we recognize that what we have developed today is "primitive" compared to what is to come. We owe much to the men of the last century, and their horse drawn carriages, but respect for their accomplishments requires that we build further in terms of them.

Remember at all times that God who made all things has also ordained all things in terms of His sovereign will. The future belongs, not to the sons of Rousseau and their "technology of social demolition," but to God, and to the people of God. We must remind ourselves, as courageous men of past ages have done, that the results are in the hands of God, but the duties are ours. It is time we met them.

CHALCEDON REPORT NO. 95
July, 1973

When Colin M. Turnbull's *The Mountain People* (New York: Simon and Schuster, 1972) was first published a year ago, at least one reviewer felt that the book should not have been written, and more than a few were disturbed. None came to grips with the book's central point. Turnbull, in spite of himself, has written an epitaph on humanism. Turnbull is by no stretch of the imagination Christian. He tries to derive a humanistic moral from his experience as an anthropologist among the Ik people in Africa. He says, in fact, "Although the experience was far from pleasant, and involved both physical and mental suffering, I am grateful for it. In spite of it all, and contrary to the first tidal wave of disillusionment, it has added to my respect for humanity and my hope that we who have been civilized into such empty beliefs as the essential beauty and goodness of humanity may discover ourselves before it is too late" (p. 12). His book tells a different story.

The Ik are a small group of Africans in the mountains between Uganda, the Sudan, and Kenya. They were moved out of their homes, when a National Games Reserve was created, into a barren area. In this new area, they now live without their old faith and tradition. They are a "modern" people, i.e., rootless, without any ties to the past or the future. They are truly "existential" in their outlook. The result is a world of total isolation, total egoism, and a radical immoralism. The family has ceased to exist. Turnbull, an honest reporter, saw no evidence of family life, no affection, no tears of sorrow, nothing except the rule of "the immediate moment, and with relation to one standard value, the good of self" (p. 129). The mother "throws her child out at three years old." The child must then provide for itself or die. This means eating what the baboons leave, berries, bark, grub, insects and the like (p. 133ff.). Turnbull speaks of "the almost universal practice of adultery" (p. 181). Marriage is losing all appeal. Since either marriage or fornication require some kind of gift to the girl, young men have come to believe it is cheaper and simpler to masturbate (p. 258). The girls sell themselves to outsiders. The Ik have, however, attained the goal of modern libertarians: theirs is a society without any coercion, and also without either law or responsibility. Turnbull, as a liberal and an anthropologist, approves of this, stating, "The Ik, however, have learned to do without coercion, either spiritual or physical. It seems that they have come to a recognition of what they accept as man's basic selfishness, his natural determination to survive as an individual before all else. This they consider to be man's basic right and at least they have the decency to allow others to pursue that right to the best of their ability without recrimination and blame" (p. 182).

Turnbull is not quite accurate, however. Where food is concerned, coercion exists. The Ik can and do steal food out of the very mouths of infirm parents, and they regard it as a joke to do so, as hilarious fun. The weak are ridiculed, tormented, and cast out to die. There is no sense of any moral responsibility to one another. "It was rather commonplace, during the second year's drought, to see the very young prying open the mouths of the very old and pulling out food they had been chewing and had not had time to swallow" (p. 261).

As a humanist, Turnbull reacted both with horror to what he saw, by trying to preserve life and offer help, and also with intellectual assent: he had no moral grounds to condemn what the Ik did: "I wonder if their way was not right" (p. 228).

When a good harvest came, Ik life did not improve. When welfarism by the state came to the Ik's aid, they did not improve. It only heightened their isolation and egoism, their anarchism. "If they had been mean and greedy and selfish before with nothing to be mean and greedy and selfish over, now that they had something they really excelled themselves, in what would be an insult to animals to call bestiality" (p. 280). The degeneration of society became even greater. "The surface looked bad enough, the hunger could be seen and the trickery perceived, and the political games were well enough known, but one had to live among the Ik and see them day in and day out and watch them defecating on each other's doorsteps, and taking food out of each other's mouths, and vomiting so as to finish what belonged to the starving, to begin to know what had happened to them" (p. 283).

The point which concerns Turnbull is the Ik in all of us. Modern culture has abandoned its ancient religious faith which bound man to God and man to man. The Ik have developed the implications of no faith more logically than the rest of the world. Modern man looks to the state; the Ik looks only to himself for answers. The Ik have become parasites through welfarism; apart from that, they were still radically contemptuous of all standards and law other than the will of the individual. The moral values we have historically prized turn out to be, Turnbull sees, not a part of human nature at all, nor is man "the social animal" scholars have deemed him to be. The Ik have abandoned morality and religion, and they have renounced society as well, for survival "values" alone. For them, it is enough to survive and to have your own way. According to Turnbull, "The Ik teaches us that our much vaunted human values are not inherent in humanity at all, but are associated only with a particular form of survival called society, and that all, even society itself, are luxuries that can be dispensed with" (p. 27).

This latter point is of especial importance. The humanist has long held that moral values are "inherent in humanity" itself, and now humanistic anthropology has itself denied the validity of this faith. Man is *not* the source of moral law and order: God is. Law and value are inherent in God: they are aspects of His being. God does not do or conform to values: He is Himself the sum total of all values, in that they are simply manifestations of His nature. Man is required to conform to God's law; apart from God, man is lawless and value-less, in that he can only affirm, as do the existentialists, his own being. In such a world without God, as Sartre rightly recognized, man has being (he *is*) but not essence (i.e., man has no pre-established nature, law, or standards). Man must them become his own god in order to establish any values, and this quest, as Sartre concluded in *Being and Nothingness* (1959), is a futile one. In the humanistic world view, the Iks are the best existentialists of all, and we are all destined to become Iks. The Marquis de Sade saw and welcomed this almost two centuries ago.

"The Ik in all of us" is a matter of growing concern. In the prologue to *The Mugging* (New York: Signet Books, 1972), Morton Hunt writes of the rapid growth of crimes of violence against persons. Their growth has changed the nature of American life, and life within the cities in much of the world. The result is, as Hunt points out, a very real threat to civilization. "For when unpredictable violent attacks upon one's person become an ever present and uncontrollable danger, the great mass of citizens lose their faith in the integrity and viability of their society; they cease seeing themselves as members of a cooperating community of fellow creatures and no longer come to each other's aid or band together to seek broad solutions to the problem, but look individually for some private *modus vivendi*, some form of survival through retreat or escape. With this loss of belief and this erosion of the spirit of communality goes society's only change of survival" (p. viii).

Hunt's point deserves more attention on all sides. Both liberals and conservatives have persisted in failing to see the issue. Radicals and liberals want to change man by re-arranging society: they fail to see that society is a social product, an expression of the faith and character of a people. Experiments in new housing in slum areas have shown that the changed environment is speedily reduced to the level of the people in it. The fallacy of radicals and liberals is to see sin in the environment rather than in man.

The non-Christian conservative's answer is similar: he sees the need as "law and order." Law and order are profoundly important and necessary, but they cannot supply faith and character. When the number of law-breakers in a society, and the number of disbelievers in the religious foundations of a society, reach a level of determinance, then the society will be governed by its unbelief and its lawlessness, not by its past faith. No law and order crusade today can restore what only Biblical faith can give. It is suicidal to look for law and order, the fruit of the tree of Biblical faith, and to reject the tree itself.

Thus, the answers proposed by both the left and the right are no answers at all: they are a part of the problem. The beatniks, the hippies, the dropouts, the careless parents, the faithless churches, the humanistic schools, *the people*, these are the Ik in our midst. In talking today to a young man who works at an open-all-night store from midnight to eight in the morning, I learned that the great majority of customers are teenagers, many just barely teens. Many of these are on narcotics. This is in a good, suburban neighborhood, with a high percentage of engineers and research men in the sciences. The key question is, why do these parents permit their 14-year-old sons to drift around all night? Summer vacation is not excuse enough. For some of these boys, drifting is "better than being home," which is the worst alternative. The radical rot in the parents is the most appalling fact. There are only limited number of Iks in the mountains of Africa; there are millions throughout the rest of the world. More than a few scholars are fearful that the world will soon belong to the Iks.

We can be grateful to Turnbull and the Iks for spelling out so plainly the collapse of humanism. The death of humanism will be the triumph, however, of the ultimate barbarian, the sophisticated, existentialist Ik, unless we work for the reconstruction of faith and society.

Godly reconstruction must thus be the order of the day, the rethinking of every area of life and thought in terms of Biblical faith. (This is the function of Chalcedon, and the studies we are sponsoring at present.) The collapse of values apart from that faith has been inevitable. Only by reconstruction in terms of the foundations of that faith is any on-going civilization possible. The implicit humanism in all other cultures is carrying them down the road of the Iks (pronounced Eeks).

In terms of godly reconstruction, the future is a most promising one. The progressive failure of laws and controls to solve man's economic, cultural, and political crises only underscore the failure of humanism and its age of the state. The times are strongly clouded with threats and storms, and disasters are clearly ahead, world-wide in their scope as never before. These future events also mean the collapse of the statist hope and the humanistic world of values. They offer the promise, if we but use the opportunity and build in terms of our faith, of a more free society and a richer one. This is a time of unequalled opportunity, the greatest age of the frontier man has yet seen. The new frontier is the challenge of a new civilization, of the most sophisticated and intensive pioneering the world has yet seen. It is a time of times, an exciting time to be alive, a time to build and a time for advance. To be most alive is to be alive when and where it counts most, and this is the day. Get with it!

CHALCEDON REPORT NO. 96
August, 1973

Almost every week, by letter, person, or telephone, a number of reports come to me which indicate a common malady, moral paralysis. A state senator reported that most of his colleagues were less and less sure of their liberal and radical doctrines; they saw events confounding their faith, and their old, easy assurances were giving way to a fearful and bitter uncertainty and uneasiness, and an inability to act with their old vigor.

A meeting of prominent "conservatives" turned up a wide variety of ideas. More than a few were pro-abortion, and a variety of other radical ideas were present in virtually all, so that a visitor remarked that a conservative is an unawares liberal. The meeting got nowhere, in that nothing could be agreed upon, except to be anti-radical, whatever that might mean.

Still another example: a doctor of considerable ability and influence is unable to act to check the rapid moral deterioration of his own children, or of his medical society. He dislikes the "new" morality, and he does not believe in abortion, but he is unable to oppose either. "After all," he says, "who am I to force my ideas on anyone else? I have no way of knowing what is right and wrong, and my ideas may simply reflect the mores and customs of my youth. All I can say is that I have my principles, and they are mine, but I can't say they are good for everybody."

To a limited degree, the doctor is right. If a man's principles are merely his own, then he has no right to impose them on anyone else, nor can he logically do so. The result is a moral paralysis: Even what he holds to be good for himself is then meaningless, because it has no roots in reality for him. As long as the Marxists believed in dialectical materialism and the "inevitability" of the triumph of the proletariat, they had vitality and drive: they believed that history made their victory inescapable. The growing disillusionment of Marxists, and the growth of awareness of the basic relativism of their premises, have led to a decline of power and a creeping moral paralysis.

Moreover, the followers of the left have become increasingly aware that pragmatism, not principles, governs their leaders. However pragmatic people may be in their personal lives, they want their leaders to be guided by principles. This is a moral contradiction, but all the same true. In the 1930s, dedicated young liberals read *The Nation* as the voice of idealism. Now, aging and pragmatic liberals read *The Nation* and agree with writers like Hans Koningsberger when he denies that Juan Domingo Peron was ever a "Fascist dictator." Koningsberger solemnly declares that the Fascist and Nazi labels were tied to Peron by the U.S. State Department and a section of the press. Peron is now the champion of the Argentine Left, and we are reminded that he was never in favor of free enterprise and free trade. Koningsberger gives us a lyrical portrait of Peron and "Saint" Eva, including an account of a mass for Eva on the 20th anniversary of her death. The old magic is gone, however, and the report reads better as humor and caricature rather than political fervor. (Hans Koningsberger, "Argentina Joins the Third World," *The Nation*, July 2, 1973, vol. 217, no. 1, pp. 17-20.) It is, however, typical. Pragmatism and partisanship have displaced principles to a very great degree.

The 1960s saw world-wide student action, followed by student inertia. For many, the student movements of that decade were the beginning of a new world order, but their only consequence has been a deeper descent into cynicism and moral paralysis. The flaw of these movements was a very obvious one. Moral strength and advantage was associated, not with character and principles, but rather with holding that things are wrong. Youth held itself to be morally superior because it was declaring the world and its parents to be in the wrong. This was true enough at many times, but it meant nothing, because these young critics were no better and sometimes worse than the things they criticized. Recognizing theft when one sees it does not make one an honest man. After all thieves are best at recognizing theft! Moral reform does not mean the ability to recognize evil but the power to do good and to rebuild in terms of righteousness and justice. A major fallacy of our time is that righteousness is equated with denunciations of evil, which means that those with the best nose for dirt gain the best reputation for character. Not surprisingly, moral reform in the 20th century generally begins and ends with investigating committees and groups, and a report on evil is equated with moral strength.

The result is a growing moral paralysis, and, increasingly, a world scene in which every pot is calling every kettle black, and they are all right! Let us repeat it: there is no moral advantage in detecting evil, only in doing good. At this point, our world is seriously derelict and ineffectual. Its moral paralysis runs deep, and its roots are in the inability of men to declare what is right for all men at all times. Let us turn again to the doctor who does not want to impose his ideas on his family and his profession. If we are moral, and if we refuse to practice abortion, only because we do not like the alternatives, then we can neither claim righteousness for our position nor impose it on anyone else. We have no reason for holding our position to be true other than our own prejudices. Logically. we can then only say, "Let every man do that which is right in his own eyes."

But if we hold that a sovereign God governs things and holds all to be accountable to Him and His absolute law, we have no right to condone in ourselves or in anyone else a denial of that moral order. We then do not stand on our own options but on ultimate and unchanging law. Instead of moral paralysis, we then have moral vitality.

The modern state has shifted its legal foundations from Christianity to humanism, from a belief in ultimate law to an affirmation of ultimate relativism. The modern state has taken over education in order to organize mankind in terms of statist humanism, and the result has been the rise of totalitarianism and moral paralysis. The fundamental principle of legal positivism or relativism is that the state declares that the good is what the state does and just law is whatever the state decrees. There is then no god but the state, and the party in power is its prophet.

But man is still God's creature, created in His image, and, no matter how much the state seeks to remake man, man's thoughts inescapably witness to his true Maker. Man may hold to moral relativism, but his being is governed by moral absolutes. A few years ago, a professor who insisted that there is no good and evil, and that all things are relative, insisted also that the Vietnam War was absolutely wrong morally. When I asked him how he could say *anything* is morally wrong in terms of his premises, or say more than, *for me* it is wrong, he became angry. Some things have to be wrong, he insisted. This was illogical, but it reflected his basic schizophrenia. He was denying the God who created him, and he was still affirming that somehow moral judgment could transcend man. If there is nothing beyond man other than more people, then every man's judgment has equal validity, and the "law" of society becomes the hippie slogan of the 1960s: do your own thing. The result is anarchy and moral paralysis.

Men wish the world to be just and moral while denying moral law. Selwyn Raab, writing in the same issue of *The Nation* as Hans Koningsberger, speaks with intensity of justice and cites a case of serious injustice. Clearly, justice in society is desired. Yet in the next article Alan Wolfe criticizes Irving Kristol's analysis of our contemporary situation by saying, "like all historical conservatives, Kristol attributes the problem to a moral crisis." If there is no moral crisis, then why are there serious problems of injustice? And if there is no absolute right and wrong, why be concerned about purely relative matters? The fact is that people in growing numbers are unconcerned. Truth and justice mean less and less to them.

In a relativistic perspective, the only legitimate personal "moral" goal can be self-realization. Nothing counts save the absolute individual, who can realize himself only at the expense of others. If we try to replace this with a social realization for humanity, then we say that the state has the right to realize itself at the expense of the individual. In either case, we have no valid ground for moral action.

A man cannot climb up a ladder unless that ladder can be given a base on hard and solid ground. A ladder cannot be planted on air or on clouds. To climb, a man must first have a valid base to start from. Similarly, men and society require a valid base for moral action and progress. That foundation is the God of Scripture. As the Psalmist observed long ago, "Except the LORD build the house, they labour in vain that build it: Except the LORD keep the city, the watchman waketh but in vain" (Ps. 127:1).

Moral paralysis affects different men in different ways. Some years ago, Gosse commented on the deep melancholy of the poet Thomas Gray and others, who showed clearly the decay of the will to live which was an aspect of the Enlightenment. Of Gray he wrote, "He never...habitually rose above this deadly dulness of the spirits...Nothing was more frequent than for men, in apparently robust health, to break down suddenly, at all points, in early middle life. People were not in the least surprised when men like Garth and Fenton died of mere indolence, because they became prematurely corpulent and could not be persuaded to get out of bed." (Edmund W. Gosse: *Gray*, p. 13f).

Not all men show their moral collapse by means of physical or mental inertia. With some it manifests itself in a savage hostility to moral order, in attempts to smash and obliterate everything which reminds them of a world they refuse to recognize. In either case, there is a moral paralysis insofar as any effective command of the future is concerned, and there is a loss of the ability to rebuild or even to perpetuate an order.

For this reason, although moral paralysis is always a dangerous phenomenon, it is also a suicidal one: it has no future. Today, we have a phenomenal interest in the future, a vast curiosity about it, and futurology has become a "science." A curiosity about the future is however definitely not the same as the ability to command it. There is a difference between idle curiosity and dominion.

The calling of man under God is to dominion, and, wherever there is true faith, there is an extension of God's power and of dominion in, through, and under Him. Moral action means dominion, in the family and in all society. It means dominion over ourselves and over all the world, in every area of science, art, industry, agriculture, society and life.

Western civilization was not lost by the church to its enemies: it was surrendered by default, by the inner decay of Christian theology and philosophy, and humanistic statism readily occupied the territory which the churches defaulted by their apostasy and waywardness. Today, the same process of default is in operation, this time by the humanists and statists. One report after another cites the growing cynicism and contempt of people for their political leaders and their growing disillusionment with the political hope, as well as the moral decay and paralysis which runs deeply in all classes. This being so, this is a time of great opportunity.

The future belongs to men who can exercise dominion and who are under the dominion of Almighty God. The mind of the dying turns over the good and bad in his doctors and nurses. The living are at work, because the present and the future are theirs to redeem. For the living, the time of opportunity is a time of promise. There is no clearer way to view our time.

CHALCEDON REPORT NO. 97
September, 1973

A very popular myth, first propagated by the Romans, is that the early Christians were recruited from the dregs of society and from slaves. While the early church won converts from all classes, it very clearly appealed most to thoughtful and educated men, who saw the decay of civilization. Pliny the Younger (c. 112 A.D.) referred to Christianity as "a depraved and extravagant superstition," in his report to the Emperor Trajan, but Pliny also admitted the high moral character of the Christians and the fact that a number of them were Roman citizens. In those days, citizenship was reserved for the elite. (Many slaves, however, were highly educated people.)

The myth tells us also that the disciples were ignorant fishermen. The high level of education in Israel in that era rules out ignorance. Moreover, fishermen are not necessarily or by any means poor or backward. We know that John and James were the sons of Zebedee, a wealthy fisherman, and either related or a family friend to the high priest (John 18:15f.). St. Paul was a man of education and importance, as was his family, in the Roman Empire.

The New Testament gives many evidences of the importance of many of the early converts. St Luke addressed his Gospel and Acts to Theophilus, a man of high official rank. In the very earliest days of the church in Jerusalem, "a great company of the priests were obedient to the faith" (Acts 6:7). The converts included the officers of Caesar's court (Phil. 4:22), prominent merchants like Priscilla and Aquila, and many other persons of note.

The first eye-witness account we have of the execution of Christians, on March 7, 203 A.D. at Roman Carthage, is an especially revealing account. *The Passion of St. Perpetua* gives us an eye-witness narration of the arrest, trial, and death in the arena of a group of Christians of various strata of society, from slaves to Vibia Perpetua, who was a young wife and mother of noble birth. Like all converts, they had not only their faith in common but also an awareness of the decay of the civilization around them. The anonymous author of the account writes to give his readers "modern instances" of faith and martyrdom. Perpetua's stand was especially offensive to Hilarian the procurator, because he was a family friend. The young woman, however, could not be shaken from her faith and was thrown to the wild animals. (R. Waterville Muncey editor: *The Passion of St. Perpetua*. London: Dent, 1927.)

The reason for such incidents was an obvious one. Young mothers like Perpetua, concerned about the decay of culture and the future of their families, were drawn to study groups and accepted the new faith. The same was true of many intellectuals of the day. This, in fact, was a major problem to the church. So many intellectuals were drawn to the faith but brought with them the framework of their old philosophies that the early church had a major battle continually against the syncretistic heresies created by philosophers who fused old philosophies with the new faith.

The humanism of Greece and Rome had decayed into superstitions. Astrology, occultism, magic, pornography, perverse sexuality, and much more, had become the working faith of many. Because of their extensive adoption of astrology and occultism, these humanists had lost increasingly the idea of causality, and, with it, science. The cult of Fortune, according to Cochrane, led to "the deification of chance itself. To make the course of history turn on such a principle is fatal to intellectual integrity and moral responsibility alike." (Charles N. Cochrane: *Christianity and Classical Culture*, p. 479. New York: Oxford, 1944.) All that Rome had was the power of the state, an increasingly brutal power: it was increasingly bankrupt, intellectually and spiritually. The more Rome became bankrupt, the more it depended on brute force.

For a thoughtful minority, the Christian faith offered a solution, the only possible solution. As Cochrane noted, the central theme of early Christian thinkers was one of "emancipation" (p. 221), as witness Justin Martyr's joyful summation of the difference in his *Apology*, i. 14. Joy, meaning, and direction had been restored to life.

Much of the savage hatred and slander of the early church by Romans was based on the fact that they resented the drain of great minds to the opposition, and their answer was to call them "superstitious" and "slaves."

The same situation prevails today. An undergraduate student declared that no scientist could believe the Bible. When he was told of the distinguished men of science who did, and of the number of important men in space research who did, his answer was simply, "No one can believe that God literally made the earth and be a scientist."

The fact is, however, that, for the past decade, many of the best students from the camps of statism have "freaked out" and have become irrelevant freaks. By default, more and more positions of authority are being lost to the statists and quietly occupied by Christians. As Wheeler has so plainly stated it, "The secular thrust is toward the creation of natural man, i.e., men who do not have a strong internalized sense of guilt and whose interest is to do pretty much as they please." This "new" man of secularism sees the enemy as the repressive past. (Richard S. Wheeler: *The Children of Darkness*, p. 11. New Rochelle, N.Y.: Arlington House, 1973.) As a result, he wages war on the "past," on tradition, institutions, laws, and, above all else, the church. His vision is past-bound, and his answer is essentially to destroy, so that, whether it is Marcuse or unthinking hippies, the result is a belief in salvation by destruction. In any other era, if as many persons were involved in anti-social warfare as the 1960s saw, it would have meant revolution. The undisciplined "natural man" of the secular world was not able to function well even in his rebellion.

The modern state is bankrupt, and its children are bankrupt. There is no future with them. In all the world today, there is not a single head of state with any intellectual calibre and direction, or with great moral force. One nation after another is faced with internal corruption and moral decay. Many of these rulers have great power, but they are incompetent in the exercise of power in any form other than repression. Their answer to problems is to control and repress, not to solve them. More than in the days of the early church, an intellectually alert Christianity is needed to provide the answer. The world is up for grabs, but only by the men of faith and ideas to command it.

CHALCEDON REPORT NO. 98
October, 1973

St. Paul declared that "after the flesh" ("that is, judged by human standards," as Moffatt renders I Cor. 1:26), not many elite men were in the ranks of the church. To become a Christian in the early centuries was to be disqualified from consideration as a gentleman and a scholar. The Romans regarded membership in this new faith as disgraceful. However, as time passed, it became more and more apparent that what Rome had was totalitarian and repressive power, and what the church had was the thinkers of the day. Charles Norris Cochrane's study of *Christianity and Classical Culture* (New York: Oxford University Press, 1944) makes clear how bankrupt Roman thought had become. Rome had no real argument against Christianity and substituted brutal force for intelligence. It reached the point where Constantine recognized that the empire was suicidal in waging war against its best element, a point his successors usually failed to realize, for they favored humanistic doctrines thinly disguised as Christianity. The intellectual leadership had passed into the hands of the Christians, in spite of all persecution, because they alone provided a faith for the future. Not all Rome's power, nor its attempts first to eliminate the new faith and, second, to use it as social cement, succeeded in deferring the day of bankruptcy and collapse. Rome had attempted to substitute power for faith, and it finally had few who trusted in or believed in the ability of Rome's power to save them. Rome was not so much overthrown but, rather, it crumbled away.

The Christendom which arose out of the ruins of the empire and on barbarian soil had a major task, in that it had great handicaps to overcome in the new Europe, barbarians who practiced human sacrifice, social and moral anarchy, and an extensive absence of continuing authority. The new order, however, was marked by an emphasis on youth. It is startling to see how, from Boethius to Calvin, youth marked the thinkers of the new era. Whether orthodox or heterodox, men of intellect came to the fore in their early years. Boethius wrote his first work at twenty years of age. Anselm of Canterbury was prior in Le Bec at thirty; Bonadventura was a university teacher at twenty-seven, at thirty-six the General of the Franciscan order. Many others can be cited who gained eminence in their youth. John Calvin, born in 1509, wrote his *Institutes* in 1536, and it was not his first work. Men found themselves quickly, gained eminence early, and found that ideas readily had consequences because however much denied at times in practice, men recognized the priority of faith and intelligence.

Christian thinkers ceased to be the elite men of Western culture with the Enlightenment. (There had been a blackout previously with the Renaissance.) It is not an accident that Pietism and the Enlightenment arose at the same time. As Christian thinkers retreated from the world and regarded the inner, spiritual realm as the only valid sphere for the faith, so the vacuum which remained was occupied by the new humanists, the men of the Enlightenment.

Society is an act of faith. Power cannot bind men together. At best, it can compel a sullen submission, but, even then, a serious problem remains. Without a faith to give meaning and direction to the power structure, not only is it impossible to convince the men who are herded into submission by guns to have any hope in the power structure, but it also becomes progressively difficult to convince the men who hold the guns that there is any sense to what they are doing. The Red Army under Trotsky was motivated by a savage zeal for their cause. Today, the new tsars of Russia do not trust their own army. Soldiers, whether on patrol or on the rifle range, are given a numbered amount of ammunition and must return the same number of empty or full shells each day: there is a fear of what the men might do if free access to the power of bullets were to exist.

At the beginning of the 17th century, Protestant, Catholic, and Jewish thinkers were agreed on one thing, the necessity for godly rule and for a godly concept of society: they disagreed on what the specific nature of that rule should be. By the end of the 17th century, men in all three groups had come to accept the idea of secular, humanistic rule, of a society built on a social contract, with, not faith but self-preservation as the key. The purpose of religion was now seen as a duty to convert men and make them moral, but to leave the rest of life to secular man. The inner world belonged to God, it was held, but the outer world was a neutral realm at best. The men of the early 17th century saw religion not only as conversion and morality but also as godly rule in every area of life. By the end of the 19th century, the secular world began to feel the necessity of claiming the inner world also. Freud insisted that the whole of the supposedly spiritual realm was a product of the unconscious and within the province of humanistic science. The problem of guilt was also made a scientific rather than a religious concern. (See R. J. Rushdoony: *Freud*. Nutley, New Jersey: The Craig Press, 1965, 1972.) Religion itself began to turn more rapidly into another area of humanistic thought and to surrender its theological character.

Christians had surrendered the world to the enemy willingly. They were busy asserting that it is a virtue to be unconcerned about the problems of this world. As a recent best seller representing this policy of surrender states it, "We should be living like persons who don't expect to be around much longer." (Hal Lindsey: *The Late Great Planet Earth*. p. 145.) What was once said of a famous senator can also be said of these men: theirs is a trumpet that always sounds retreat.

The churchmen have surrendered the world to the enemy, and the humanists, after having tried one remedy after another, now have essentially only one more answer: more power. As in the days of Rome, this is a confession of bankruptcy. It is also a threat to peace, because the man without a philosophy has not answer but brute force. But brute power is impotent as a constructive force; it can only destroy.

The necessity for Christian reconstruction has never been greater.

CHALCEDON REPORT NO. 99
November, 1973

For well over 500 years now, Western civilization has been in a state of civil war, with two aspects thereof in a growing conflict with one another. These two contending forces are humanism and Christianity. Humanism began its rise to power in the medieval era, and its strength was such that it captured the church, much of the academic world, and the state as well. The so-called Renaissance was the victory celebration of the triumphant humanists. While preserving the form of Christendom and the church, the humanists put them to other uses. Lorenzo Valla openly turned to anti-Christian standards as the new yardstick, without bothering to deal with the Bible as a serious source of law. The source of all virtuous action, Lorenzo Valla held, is man's natural bent to pleasure. Ficino held that virtue and love were responses to beauty. However much these and other men disagreed as to the true standards for life, they were agreed that God could not be the source of standards, but, that man and man's reason is the yardstick in terms of which all things must be judged. The standard, it was held, is man, and the moment. Ficino's inscription in the Florentine Academy concluded thus: "Flee excesses, flee business, and rejoice in the present." For these men, the church was to be the instrument for a new kind of salvation, a refined Christianity informed and remade by humanism. As Cronin has pointed out, Botticelli's painting of the *Birth of Venus* was an expression of this faith: the symbolism of Venus in this portrayal means that "Natural love, purified, is about to become Christian love, *eros* to become *agape*." (Vincent Cronin: *The Florentine Renaissance*, p. 211. New York: Dutton, 1967.)

The unnatural union between Biblical faith and humanism was shattered by the Reformation. In the regrouping of forces which followed, it gradually became clear that, more basic than the division between Protestant and Catholic, was the division between Christendom and humanism. Both branches of the church were quickly infiltrated by humanism, and, with the French and Russian Revolutions, two things became clear. First, the old attempts at synthesis and union had been discarded. Humanism was now strong enough to stand on its own, to judge and condemn Biblical religion.

Second, it was also clear that, however much the facade of synthesis has since been offered to Christendom, the real issue is a war to death. In the Marxist world, the persecution of Christians (and orthodox Jews) has not diminished with the years. A very considerable number of the people in the slave labor camps are there for religious reasons, and their persecution is savage and intense. The triumph of statist humanism has been very nearly complete, in that virtually every state in the world is either dominated by or under the influence of this alien faith.

At the same time, however, the growing bankruptcy and imminent collapse of humanism has been increasingly in evidence. By replacing God with man as the new ultimate and absolute, humanism has introduced moral anarchy into the world. If every man is his own god and law, then no order is rationally possible. Humanism, having deified rationality, must now use the irrational and coercive power of the socialist state to hold society together.

Moreover, having denied that there is any truth beyond man, humanism has surrendered the world outside of man to total irrationality. There is no meaning, purpose or truth in the world: it is held to be mindless, meaningless, brute factuality. But man, once seen as the principle of reason in the universe, has since Freud been seen as himself irrational and meaningless, so that man no longer can find truth or meaning anywhere. The world and man are essentially pointless and meaningless. The fact that church, school, and state have all been captured by this bankrupt humanism makes the crisis all the greater.

The bankruptcy of humanism makes all the more urgent a return to a consistent and thorough commitment to Biblical faith, to Biblical law, and to a Biblically governed world and life view. It means too that the opportunity for the resurgence of such a faith has never been greater. As the crisis of the 20th century deepens, the opportunity will become more and more obvious. Men will not long cling to a humanism which cannot provide them with anything to satisfy either their mind or body. One man, speaking of modern humanistic politics, once told me, "Sure, the system is rotten and senseless, but it still gives me a good living." There are millions like him, feeding on the relics of humanistic civilization. Every day, however, the emptiness of humanism becomes more apparent; its money is progressively bankrupt, its politics corruption, and its education mindlessness. As a result, since nothing has any meaning, bad taste, vulgarity, profanity, and insanity are enthroned as "art" to express total contempt for all things. As one very popular modern "musician" said recently, "Sometimes I think I'm playing for the lunatic fringe. Luckily, it is widening. In fact, I think it is outdistancing the mainstream." ("Kinky and Country Music," *LA Times Calendar*, p. 68, Sunday, Sept. 30, 1973.) But the cultivation of insanity is the cultivation of irrelevance and death. Such people will not be with us long. The question of importance is, will we stand and move in terms of God's word and law?

CHALCEDON REPORT NO. 100
December, 1973

Bertrand Russell, when asked about the future of religion, answered, "I think it depends upon whether people solve their social problems or not. I think that if there go on being wars and great oppressions and many people leading very unhappy lives, probably religion will go on...I think that if people solve their social problems religion will die out." (*Bertrand Russell Speaks His Mind*, p. 25. New York: Avon Books, 1960.) This idea was not original with Russell. A similar belief was basic to Freud's psychology. Freud believed that religion would survive as long as the sense of guilt existed *and* was treated as a religious concern. Freud's psychology had as a central concern a desire to convert guilt into a medical problem, explain it in terms of social evolution, and thereby eliminate religion. (R. J. Rushdoony: *Freud*, Philadelphia: Presbyterian & Reformed Publishing Co., 1965, 1968.)

Other social philosophers have held that the elimination of religion will come as man is led into the great society or community, into a world beyond good and evil, and a world without problems and without a law structure derived from God. As a result, the drive to establish that perfect world order has had a double impetus for humanists. For them it means, *first*, the elimination of God and of religion. Where man has all that he wants, and problems of guilt and death have been overcome and peace and plenty prevail, who needs God? Hence the frantic and urgent drive to eliminate all of man's problems through the scientific socialist state, to bring in a humanistic paradise, and to forget forever the very idea of God. Hence too the readiness of scientists and people to delude themselves and to believe always that they are on the verge of a great breakthrough to the creation of life, its control, and its endless extension. All too many are ready to believe, as the world stumbles into hell, that paradise is just a few years or a generation away. *Second*, with the God of the Bible eliminated by man's victory, man can then comfortably declare himself to be the new god of creation, and the elite planners can operate freely as the gods of a new world.

However, the more earnestly this hope is pursued, the more desperate man's plight becomes. Technology has supposedly brought man closer to the solution of his problem: in reality, it has only intensified and aggravated man's long existing problem. The problem is not technological; it is not a question of a breakthrough in biology, politics, futurology, economics, or anything else. The problem is man: he is a sinner, and nothing can alter that fact save the grace of God.

The humanistic myth of human perfection is thus a dangerous one. It rests on an illusion of human autonomy and ultimacy, on the belief that man is his own god, can make his own laws, and can re-order reality in terms of his imagination. It leads man to that fundamental error which, for example, is at the heart of the new economics: if men determine that certain goals are to be desired, then nothing prevents their realization except the absence of power and technology. Given enough statist power and technology, socialism, it is held, will work. Given enough money and power, the state schools believe that they can produce the ideal socialist child of the ideal socialist state. Given the power and the technology, the new world order will begin to emerge, and then religion, the state, inequalities, sexual differences, and all like "evils" will gradually wither away.

The Biblical answer to this is to call attention to the real problem: man himself, and man's relationship to God. The next step is to recognize that God has His determined plan for man's progress, peace, and prosperity: His law. The law specifies what constitutes a good society, how to attain it, and how to suppress its enemies. The world under God's law, to use T.R. Ingram's great phrase, is a world in which there is a realistic achievement of the great goals of history. It is also a world in which the magnificent promises of Deuteronomy 28 are the natural consequences of faith and obedience.

The humanistic approach to life's problems is suicidal. The word of Wisdom, ages ago, stated this clearly: "He that sinneth against me wrongeth his own soul: all they hate me love death" (Prov. 8:36).

In 1966, more than 100,000 college students, ostensibly the future of America, threatened suicide; more than 10,000 actually attempted it, and 1,000 or more succeeded. The future leaders of the technological humanistic paradise saw no future. They were sick at heart, involved in sexual delinquency, drugs, and the "accepted forms" of student violence. Finding meaning in nothing, some finally sought escape into what was for them total meaninglessness, death. In 1973, even kindergarten and primary grade teachers report amazing acts of lawlessness and anarchy in their pupils. The heirs of Russell and Freud are destroying themselves, or their future.

Meanwhile, a growing number of students are in Christian schools, being trained for responsibility and leadership. The futurologists, who try to read the 21st century in terms of their technology, grind out their pipe dreams, unaware of the new power growing up all around them.

Proverbs 29:18 tells us that where there is no vision (in terms of God's word) the people run wild and perish, but happy is he who keeps the law.

CHALCEDON REPORT NO. 101
January, 1974

The denial of God has meant the denial of any meaning beyond man. The universe is held to be a product of meaninglessness and chance accidents, and the attempt of any to find purpose or mind behind the universe is ridiculed as wishful thinking.

The social consequences of such a belief are rarely admitted by atheists or agnostics. Among the few who have been a little consistent with their unbelief was John Rutledge, the Southern leader and one of the first associate justices of the United States. (A little later, the Senate refused to confirm him as chief justice.) Rutledge rejected every argument drawn from "religion and humanity" to apply to social and political issues. His principle was plainly stated: "Interest alone is the governing principle with nations." Under the facade of laissez-faire, Rutledge in fact affirmed moral relativism and a statist economic order.

It was with the 20th century that the politics of relativism began to flower into totalitarianism and slavery. Moral and religious values having been denied, there were now no restraints on the power of the state.

The December, 1973, *Harper's Magazine* carries an interesting example of this relativism, Frank Herbert's article, "Listening to the Left Hand," subtitled "The dangerous business of wishing for absolutes in a relativistic universe." Herbert gives us an illustration to "prove" relativity. If three bowls of water are lined up, one with ice water, another with lukewarm water, and the third with hot water, if we soak our left hand in the ice water, and our right hand in the hot water, and then plunge both hands into the lukewarm water, our left hand will report the middle bowl to be warm, and the right hand will report it cold. Herbert calls this "a small experiment in relativity" and adds, "We live in a universe dominated by relativity and change, but our intellects keep demanding fixed absolutes. We make our most strident demands for absolutes that contain comforting assurance. We will misread and/or misunderstand almost anything that challenges our favorite illusions." It is amazing that a man could come to such a conclusion, and a periodical print it! Where is the relativity *except* in naive experience? In reality, is there not a difference between hot and cold water, and is there not an observable temperature to the three bowls, one which can be registered, apart from Herbert's childish game?

Herbert, however, wants to destroy differences by means of relativism, which is his private god. He posits that the human world or species is a "single organism" and must be understood as such. Herbert continues to make a number of conclusions in terms of his faith. There are no absolutes, and to try to think in terms of them is to rule out "an answer with a sensible meaning." After all, Herbert asks (apparently ignorant of thermometers or that a man can put both hands into all three bowls in turn), "Which hand will you believe, the 'cold' hand or the 'warm' one? It serves no purpose to ask whether absolutes exist. Such questions are constructed so as to have no answer *in principle*." Herbert concludes, "Accordingly, both Pakistan and

India could be equally *right* and equally *wrong*. This applies also to Democrats and Republicans, to Left and Right, to Israel and the United Arab Republic, to Irish Protestants and Irish Catholics."

Practically, this means that there is no right or wrong, and, short of total knowledge about all of reality, no conclusions can be drawn, for "we do not like unproven propositions." Herbert's proposition is not only unproven, however, but it represents a very great act of self-blinded faith.

If there is no right nor wrong, and humanity is one organism, then there is no warrant whatsoever for any resistance to enslavement, or for any independence from the mob, or from a slave state. The rapid spread of statist slavery in the 20th century has coincided with the spread of relativism and unbelief. Politics is thus far more than a political affair: it is a moral and a religious concern. Like all of life, it has deep roots in man's faith, in the basic presuppositions of his life and outlook. As long as relativism spreads, so long will slavery increase and the polities of slavery will dominate us. Education for slavery is the daily routine of modern, statist education, both in the Marxist states and in the Western democracies and republics. The continued decline in the learning ability of youth is a natural one: if all things are relative and in essence meaningless, then why should education, discipline, and a job have any meaning? Why bother with marriage, if marriage has no meaning because all is meaningless?

We should not be surprised at the social anarchy of recent years: we have been schooling our youth for it. To school youth into a belief in relativism and the essential meaninglessness of life is at best to educate them for irrelevance, but, even more, for death and final oblivion. Any culture which negates its heritage by its education has no future: it will be supplanted by those with a faith for living. Over and over again, this era is underscoring the truth of Wisdom's declaration: "But he that sinneth against me wrongeth his own soul: all they that hate me love death" (Prov. 8:36). "Therefore choose life, that both thou and thy seed may live" (Deut. 30:19). If our foundation is not the Rock, it will be the sands of relativism.

CHALCEDON REPORT NO. 102
February, 1974

In the early 1850s, Unitarian Boston was horrified and alarmed because of the great influx of Irish Catholic immigrants, and the result was the triumph of the anti-Catholic, anti-foreigner political group, the Know-Nothing Party. In 1854 J. V. C. Smith was the Know-Nothing mayor of Boston. Yet Smith continued to maintain close business relations with Irish Catholic friends, including the bishop, John Bernard Fitzpatrick, a close personal friend. As an able amateur sculptor, Smith executed a fine bust of the bishop. Such a relationship between an anti-Catholic mayor and a bishop bothered neither the mayor nor the bishop: the mayor's position was political pragmatism, a belief that success is more important than truth. The Know-Nothing Party was simply a popular tool to be used to disrupt the Whig and the Democratic parties. The same motive led some leaders of the Anti-Masonic Party to join the Masons secretly, and it led some liberals in the 1920's to join the Ku Klux Klan.

It has been said that politics is the art of compromise, of working out a practical means of cooperation between conflicting groups. A principled pragmatism has its place and is by no means immoral. It is simply a recognition that goals can be attained usually only by degrees. The problem in politics is unprincipled pragmatism, the insistence not only that success is more important than truth but that success is truth. For modern pragmatism, truth is what works, that which succeeds.

Moreover. as the statist schools of the country have steadily trained each generation in turn with a humanistic, relativistic pragmatism, the United States has seen the growth of a purely opportunistic politics to a position of dominance. In virtually every modern state around the world, the same development has taken place in varying degrees. In many European states, for example, lacking the Puritan background of Americans, the development is much further along. After all, the disciples of Machiavelli very early converted European diplomacy and politics into an unprincipled pragmatism.

In America, it was the philosopher Charles S. Pierce who, between the Grant and Wilson years, formulated the new American faith and defined it as pragmatism. Pierce defined pragmatism thus: "In order to ascertain the meaning of an intellectual conception one should consider what practical consequences might conceivably result by necessity from the truth of that conception; and the sum of these consequences will constitute the entire meaning of the conception." The meaning is the result. Those who followed Pierce pushed the idea much further. For William James and especially for John Dewey, truth became instrumental. In *Reconstruction in Philosophy* (1920), Dewey wrote: "The hypothesis that works is the *true* one; and *truth* is an abstract noun applied to a collection of cases, actual, foreseen and desired, that receive confirmation in their work and consequences." Dewey defined social progress as growth towards the desired community or Great Society, but he had no standard in terms of which growth could be defined. There was also no objective criterion whereby the Great Society could be defined to distinguish it from the Great Tyranny. Truth being what works, anything that succeeds is therefore the truth. Logically, the historically elect people for these pragmatists are those who succeed. Attempts to define this Great Society in terms of traditional liberalism have failed: no principle of definition other than the pragmatic one is logically tenable.

Thus, humanism, by developing pragmatism, has created an

anti-humanistic doctrine. If man does not "work," if he becomes a polluter and a social roadblock, then away with man. The modern humanistic and pragmatic state has thus become, in the name of man, history's greatest killer of man, by means of wars, slave labor camps, mass murders, and purges.

Pragmatism has led also to a new isolationism. In the older America, isolationism meant a respect for the self-determination of other states: people were free to contribute to the cause of freedom anywhere, but the function of the state had to be non-interventionism. Now the interventionism is pragmatic and Machiavellian, based on the balance of power politics, and the isolationism is personal and immoral. It means "doing your own thing" and rejecting all moral norms which would bind all men and nations.

Unprincipled pragmatism, philosophical pragmatism, erodes the power of judgment. If the truth is what works, everything that works is true, and thus, why get excited about anything? Why condemn anything, or defend anything? Where the power of judgment is eroded, the ability to act is also eroded, and a moral paralysis results.

No era of history has ever been free of problems, and no era of history has ever been governed by majorities, but only by dedicated minorities who have provided the direction to others. The modern state everywhere has a crisis of authority: its ability to command the people apart from brute force is severely limited. It can at times unite the people in hatred, hatred of an enemy, but this does not eliminate the underlying disunity.

Thus, in a time of great material progress when men should feel most hopeful, hopelessness is very common, for man does not live by bread alone. In a world without truth or meaning, how can a man define hope? This bankruptcy is most apparent where power is the greatest. From *Foreign Affairs* and the CFR to the local supervisors, the pragmatic philosophy of retreat is to vote more money to satisfy the trouble-makers in the name of social peace and harmony.

But "man does not live by bread alone, but by every word that proceedeth out of the mouth of God" (Matt. 4:4). Apart from that King and His *every word* we end up with *no word* at all. The future can have no other foundation than Christ, because there is none.

CHALCEDON REPORT NO. 103
March, 1974

A pilgrim is one who journeys to a destination from a religious motive. Thus, we are all pilgrims in that our lives are a quest for those goals which are to us most desirable, goals which our faith makes us live for. There was a time when pilgrimages were exclusively religious, as with medieval man, and with the Puritans who became pilgrims by their journey to America, to establish a godly church and society.

With the Enlightenment, however, pilgrimage took on a new dimension, the Grand Tour of Europe in quest of experience. To become a gentleman, it was necessary for an English youth to go to Paris and Rome and to enjoy the pleasures thereof. The goal of pilgrimages had become, not Christian experience, but humanistic experiences, esthetics, intellectual, or sensual, depending on one's desires.

The Romantic movement added a new dimension, the pilgrimage into the bizarre, the perverse, and the insane, as Mario Praz documents so well in *The Romantic Agony*. The lust for experience meant a quest for the abnormal and for the perverted.

In the 20th century, this quest has been greatly developed. Both in vicarious and in actual experience, the lust for the abnormal and perverted, and the delight in being shocked, has led modern culture into strange by-ways. Culture has become pathology. In recent years, entertainment has been heavily dominated by the pathological, and the film industry increasingly caters to an almost entirely voyeuristic sado-masochistic audience. The vast appeal of a stupid and tasteless film like *The Exorcist* is simply its appeal to this mentality: lines of people have waited by the hour to see it, and newspaper reports that some viewers had fainted and vomited only increased its appeal.

Thus, a fine symbolic note was struck when a major airline advertised a 1974 travel pilgrimage, "Spotlight on Dracula," a guided "totally unique travel experience which involves you in an adventure combining present-day reality with medieval history and ancient folk beliefs. You participate in a re-creation of the Dracula legend, completely immersed in the original environment in which it flourished" with re-enactments "for your exclusive benefits."

Of the historical Dracula, the papal nuncio reported in 1475 that he had by that date personally authorized the killing of 100,000 people, usually by torture and impalement. Contrary to the travel guide brochure, Dracula was not a medieval but a Renaissance figure. The Renaissance, which proclaimed the love of man and his rebirth, set a precedent for the 20th century by its lust for torture and murder. It was the era of men like Ludovico Sforza, the Borgia pope Alexander VI, Sigismondo Malatesta, Caesar Borgia, John Tiptoft, and others.

It is fitting therefore that the 20th century pilgrim pay his money for a pilgrimage to Dracula's palace and realm: he is closer to Dracula than to God. Dracula's world is the world of his heart. The newspaper head-line reads, "600 Serious Crimes Reported in City Schools for 7 Month Period," and it tells of murders, rapes, robberies, assaults, and other crimes committed in "public" schools despite the presence of security guards. In spite of this, a prominent man objected heatedly when I suggested Christian schools as the alternative. Dracula is better than God, in the eyes of millions.

By their pilgrimages you shall know them, pilgrimages to Dracula's castle, to *The Exorcist*, to schools that educate for ignorance and godlessness, to entertainment geared to shock, violence, and horror, to blasphemy and immorality, this is the love of modern man. A new bumper sticker perhaps is needed, which will simply read, "Dracula lives again." In the age of communism, Naziism, and mass violence in the name of "rights," perhaps Dracula is too mild a figure; the 20th century has surpassed him.

Ironically, Dracula was killed in 1476 by his own men, as a result of his own folly. In this, he is a fitting symbol of our time. Our Lord declared, "all they that take the sword, shall perish with the sword" (Matt. 26:52). Again, we are told, "he that killeth with the sword must be killed with the sword" (Rev. 13:10). The meaning here is not the use of force in the execution of justice, but the denial of justice in the name of power. All who set aside God's law shall fall under its judgment. Those whose pilgrimage of life is a quest for experience and power outside of God will pay the penalty thereof.

The goals of the pilgrimage of modern man, both in his own person and by means of the statist orders he creates, are quests for Dracula, for experience in the perverted and demonic, and for an order created through total tyranny. Dracula instituted so rigid a control over his people that he placed a golden cup near the fountain of a public square in his capital, and no man ever stole it: they did not dare. This did not mean that Wallachia was crime-free: the biggest thief and murderer was Dracula's tyrant state, and it tolerated no petty criminal to interfere with its life of crime.

Today, lawless as our cities are, the worst crime is committed by the state, the theft of freedom. Moreover, a people who themselves have a perverted pilgrimage, conspire to help the state destroy them.

But a more important fact remains: the Draculas of history are historical curiosities, they pass, but God remains, and His purpose prevails. The false pilgrims of our day can only build ruins, but we "know that (our) labour is not in vain in the Lord" (I Cor. 15:58). The future is ours under God, and it is a time for strengthening the foundations, and for preparing to take over and govern. The Lord's order is very clear: "Occupy till I come" (Luke 19:13), and He does not issue impossible orders.

CHALCEDON REPORT NO. 104
April, 1974

It was around 1660 that the structure of Western civilization began its shift from a Christian to a humanistic basis. In England, this meant the accession of Charles II; in France, Louis XIV was soon to begin changing the country; Germany, recuperating from the Thirty Years' War, was no longer determined by religion but by the balance of power. Spain was lacking in the religious fervor of Philip II of some years previously, and Russia was beginning its westernization in terms of humanism.

Earlier, the goal of all Christians had been godly rule in every area of life: in the individual by means of regeneration and sanctification, in the state by means of obedience to God's law in education by the government of all disciplines in terms of Christian premises, and in every area of life by the Scriptures. But, as Lamont pointed out, "By 1660 these assumptions are no longer widely tenable...Virtue was now an end in itself, not a means to an end" (i.e., the world under God's law), and the province of religion was reduced to the inner life alone. (William M. Lamont: *Godly Rule, Politics and Religion, 1603-60*. pp. 163, 166. London: Macmillan, 1969.) The older dream persisted longer in America and was revived by some theologians after 1740, but in the mid-1800s, it too had faded.

Increasingly, the church saw itself in terms of a new calling. Previously, it had declared the requirements of the word of God for every area of life. It had required the state to be specifically Christian, the schools to educate in terms of the word of God, callings and vocations to be governed by Biblical premises, and every area of life to be under the dominion of God. The requirement to be Christian was not limited to the church: it was mandatory for the whole world and for every aspect and sphere thereof. After 1660, and especially with the rise of pietism, the role of the church (and the Christian) was limited to *piety and worship*. Previously, this limited concern had been the characteristic of mystics and some (but by no means all) cloistered persons, monks and nuns. Now, the entire church began to remake itself into a cloister. "Every man a priest" had become "every man a monk."

As the church began its slow retreat from the world, the humanists began their conquest of it. The state was first of all captured, and, especially after the French Revolution, became more and more openly humanistic in one country after another. Schools were also captured, turned into state institutions, and made the voices of the new established religion, humanism. Law was steadily changed from a Biblical to a humanistic basis and one area after another captured for the new religion. This conquest was capped by the possession of the churches by the new religion. Priest and pastor began to proclaim, not the word of God, but the word of man, not regeneration by the sovereign and saving grace of God, but revolution by the supposedly sovereign power of man. Not the Kingdom of God but the Kingdom of Man was the gospel of the new order in the churches. The new pilgrimage of man was not to Bethlehem or Golgotha, but to Dracula's Castle (see Report 103).

This was not the first time humanism had captured the church, nor the first time the church had been irrelevant to its purpose and hostile to it. Barraclough has written, of the Renaissance popes, that "the popes of the first half of the fifteenth century, from Martin V to Nicholas V, gave way again both to fiscalism on a scale unthought of earlier (for example, the wholesale creation of new offices for the sole purpose of selling them), and to nepotism so unashamed (for example, the placing of the pope's illegitimate offspring in the college of Cardinals) that it might be thought that Christendom would have revolted in scandal. What is astounding is that it did not: and the fact that it did not is the best evidence that people had, so to say, already 'written off' the papacy; it no longer had any hold over men's minds -- not even enough to provoke angry hostility." (Geoffrey Barraclough: *The Medieval Papacy*, p. 192. Harcourt, Brace, & World, 1968.) Once again, the church does not matter much, because it has ceased to be relevant: its gospel is the state. It has confused godly rule with statist rule, and its answer to most problems is the capture and control of the state.

What marvelous wisdom churchmen have shown in recent years: now that the ship of state is sinking, they clamber aboard! The gospel of statism is creating a world crisis for civilization, and the churches have found it to be the hope of man, not his problem. Apparently in the belief that a drowning man needs more water, churchmen are giving a world sickened by means of humanism even more humanism.

But the irrelevance of churchmen does not mean the irrelevance of God, who is the only ground of all relevance. All things have their being and their meaning in His creative act, and no reconstruction, progress, or hope is tenable or possible apart from Him.

The crisis of our time is a hopeful and heartening fact: it means emphatically that the world is under God's law, that what a man sows that shall he also reap. True, it means times of crisis and judgment, but how else is history cleared of the debris of man's sin and folly? What takes place on television is pale and lifeless when compared to the excitement and development of the world around us. History is the work of God, and it has a good beginning and ending.

CHALCEDON REPORT NO. 105
May, 1974

On the last page of *The Cantos of Ezra Pound*, we have a sharp and clear statement:

> I lost my center fighting the world.
> The dreams clash and are shattered
> ...I tried to make a paradiso terrestre.

The last line of all expresses the forlorn hope: "To be men not destroyers." The *Cantos* were written in the bloodiest years of world history, when men were destroyers. Between 1911 and 1945 at least seventy million died in two wars, massacres, famines, and executions. After 1945, in Red China and Africa, as well as elsewhere, the slaughter continued. Men had become destroyers in their attempts to create an earthly paradise.

Earlier, in Canto LXXIV, Pound's massive frustration is expressed in these lines:

> I don't know how humanity stands it
> with a painted paradise at the end of it
> without a painted paradise at the end of it.
> (p. 136).

Mankind has a dream, derived from Scripture, of a world of peace, in which wars cease, men beat their swords into plowshares, and their spears into pruninghooks, and all men live in peace one with another (Isa. 2:1-4, etc.). Wherever this dream goes, men begin to change and to work frantically for the new world order, but, apart from faith, the dream is a frustration and a troubler of man. Life is impossible with this dream, and impossible without it, as Pound saw.

Some, of course, have tried to escape from the dream by a return to primitivism as they imagine it. Walt Whitman, in his well-known lines expressed this hope of escape:

> I think I could turn and live with animals, they
> are so placid and self-contain'd;
> I stand and look at them long and long.
> They do not sweat and whine about their
> condition;
> They do not lie awake in the dark and weep
> for their sins;
> They do not make me sick discussing their
> duty to God;
> Not one is dissatisfied -- not one is demented
> with the mania of owning things;
> Not one kneels to another, nor to his kind that
> lived thousands of years ago;
> Not one is respectable or industrious over the
> whole earth.

Whitman, however, was less than honest. He had not surrendered by any means the dream of an earthly paradise. Not only in "Passage to India," but in poem after poem he celebrated this soon to be realized future. Whitman's hope of realizing an earthly paradise depended on man, more specifically, on awakened man. Man must realize, he believed, that he is an unfallen creature, and man must rouse himself out of the sickness of Christianity into the health of free, natural, uninhibited man. Then, man will enter into perfection. In "A Song," Whitman wrote,

Come, I will make the continent indissoluble;
I will make the most splendid race the sun ever
    yet shone upon;
I will make divine magnetic lands,
    With the love of comrades,
    With the life-long love of comrades.

Abolish Christianity and the idea of sin, and the natural goodness of men will flower and will create heaven on earth.

In France, George Sand in 1869 wrote, "If one does ill, it is because one is not aware of doing it. Better enlightened, one would never do it again...I don't believe it is due to wickedness but to ignorance."

Modern man bought this argument. How easy it was going to be to create an earthly paradise! Simply abandon orthodox Christianity, and educate people out of their erroneous ways. Sin is ignorance, it was held, a lack of proper knowledge and instruction, rather than an evil character and a wilful commission of acts of lawlessness.

The great instrument in this mighty transformation would be the state by means of its control of education. The statist schools, as Horace Mann, James G. Carter, and others, following the example of Prussia, envisioned, would gradually reduce and eliminate the role of Christianity and stress education as the means of salvation. The problem being ignorance rather than sin, the cure to social problems would be education.

When the products of statist schools have revealed themselves to be barbarians, the answer of the statist educators has been faithful to their presuppositions: they have demanded more money for more education. While the *content* of education has been steadily lowered, the *extent* of education in terms of years in school has been extended. Now many educators believe that every child should have a college education. If the answer to "doing ill" is education, this is a sensible answer, and statist educators are faithful to their humanistic faith. Events, however, have demonstrated that they are disastrously wrong, and the results of their work are the rise of a new barbarism and widespread social disorders.

Walt Whitman's new Adam, who denies the fall and the possibility of sin, is very much with us, and his good news is animalism. A pornographic "underground" paper, which espouses freedom for any and all kinds of voluntary and consenting acts of sex, was attacked recently for being too "puritan." Why? The young man declared, after espousing "free natural animal sex" without any formalities of courtesy or attraction. "You are still imbedded with old wives tales, Mrs. Robinson. You can't have sex without bringing into play fantasy, affection, mother protection, quasi-prostitution (men spending money on dates) and personality and 'in-crowd' cults." Eliminate all attention to personality, and rut in animal fashion, he demanded.

In brief, let there be no principles, and the sexual utopia will arrive. Abolish God and His law from the universe, and men will be at peace. Instead of sin, our problem is ignorance, it is held, ignorance of the fact that there is no sin, no law, no absolutes to limit or govern man. The modern state denies that there is any higher law. A former chief justice of the U.S. Supreme Court asserted, "Nothing is more certain in modern society than the principle that there are no absolutes." These words of Frederick Moore Vinson sum up the credo of the modern state: beyond the state, there is neither a god nor a law.

A problem remains, however, and it is a problem in every modern state, the U.S.S.R., the U.S.A., and others. The state has denied all absolutes; it has denied God, and it has sought to make itself the new god, and its purposes the new absolutes. Statist trained youth have learned their lesson well, however, and the result is that they are as rebellious against the state as against God, and even more so! By destroying the principle of authority, the state and its schools have destroyed their own authority. By exalting rebellion and revolution into the only virtues, the state and its schools have created a world programmed for perpetual revolution. The earthly paradise has in fact come to mean total civil war by mankind. The world thus drifts towards a third world war while caught up within by an even deeper war, the isolation of man from man, and the warfare of man against man because no common faith binds them to a higher law, and to each other in terms of the God of that law. The earthly paradise is fast becoming an earthly hell.

St. James declared, "There is one law giver, who is able to save and to destroy: who art thou that judgest another?" (James 4:12). All men's attempts to create a law apart from God, or to make judgments apart from Him, are doomed. The only possible order is from God and His law. He alone can destroy evil by His sovereign grace. He is the only lawgiver. Apart from Him, men lose their center: they have no valid principle of judgment, and their efforts collapse finally into anarchy. They may dream, with Ezra Pound, of being "men, not destroyers," but they only become destroyers and ravagers of mankind.

It is only God's grace and God's law which can reconstruct and restore a world ravaged by sin, by man's attempt to be his own god, determining for himself what constitutes good and evil (Gen. 3:5). Erik von Kuehnelt-Leddihn, echoing Proudhon, has pointed out that "at the bottom of politics one always finds theology," (Erik von Kuehnelt-Leddihn: *Leftism*, p. 54. New Rochelle, N.Y.: Arlington House, 1974.) The theology at the bottom of our contemporary politics is the theology of humanism, the worship of man.

We cannot have a new politics without a new theology, and the only theology which can provide the needed justice and order is Biblical theology. Our present politics is a product of a bankrupt humanism. Bad as that politics is, men will continue to flounder in the morass of its decay and corruption until they surrender their faith in man for faith in the living and triune God. The renewal of politics is urgently and desperately needed, but it must be preceded by the renewal of Christian faith. This will not come from waiting on the churches but only from the Lord.

CHALCEDON REPORT NO. 106
June, 1974

In 1923, the lawyer and writer, Henry Dwight Sedgwick, wrote *Pro Vita Monastica*, in defense of the contemplative virtues and to a degree a defense of monasticism. Sedgwick did not write as a Christian, but as a concerned modern man fearful of the collapse of our humanistic culture. Something like the ancient monastic groups was needed, without the old faith, to preserve civilization in isolated pockets. In his last sentence, however, his despair at the possibility of a humanistic holiness and reconstruction was openly stated: "The sun is set, the moon no longer shines, no stars twinkle in the sky; we must light our candles, or we shall be in utter darkness."

Fifty years later, in 1973, another book with a similar plan appeared, but one which made Sedgwick look optimistic by comparison. Roberto Vacca, in *The Coming Dark Age* (Garden City, New York: Doubleday, 1973) devotes his last chapter to a proposal that a new kind of monastic order is necessary to conserve civilization from the collapse just ahead. "The new monks" would have to preserve and transmit scientific knowledge in order to make rebuilding possible some day. *Things* rather than *values* are to be conserved: tools, implements, motor-generators, and things of a like character. For Vacca, hope is not great, but "in certain cases at least -- making more information available can bring salvation" (p. 221).

The "monastic" refuges imagined by Sedgwick and Vacca are very much like the world they see near ruin. The humanistic sinner carries his sin with him into his retreat, and there is no reason to suppose that his retreat will be any the less disastrous than the culture he flees from.

The problem, of course, is that the disaster is within modern man, and he is determined to project it onto the world around him. Because humanistic man is sick, he is determined that the whole world must sicken and die with him. As a result, he cries doom and disaster wherever he turns.

Two able books have recently exposed the irrationality of this modern mood: Melvin J. Grayson and Thomas R. Shepard Jr., in *The Disaster Lobby, Prophets of Ecological Doom and Other Absurdities* (Chicago: Follett Publ. Co., 1973), and John Maddox in *The Doomsday Syndrome* (New York: McGraw Hill 1973). Behind this urge to condemn man as the polluter and destroyer is a radical hatred of man, a self-hatred, and a will to death. Modern man finds it difficult to say almost anything too bad about himself.

Almost. He will not call himself a sinner against God. The pride of modern man is in his supposed wisdom in seeing all the evils in the world around him. The humanistic doctrine of holiness is one in which the more a man exposes the real or imagined sins of the state, the establishment, the left or the right, and of other men, the greater his status. Since the days of Theodore Roosevelt, "the muckraker" has been the virtuous man for humanists, and men as stupid as Lincoln Steffens became heroes because they acquired a skill in denunciation.

Just as in films and fiction, each new work must out-shock the old, so in scandals, charges, and in crime, the urge to surpass previous horrors is in evidence. Revolutionary groups change their strategies regularly, not to out-fox the police, but to increase their shock value. Part of this shock requires an intensifying of destruction. Thus, the predictions of the modern humanists are self-fulfilling prophecies: destruction is predicted, and everything is then done to heighten chaos, ruin, and anarchy.

As men once emulated one another in righteousness and holiness, in the new mood men emulate one another in anarchism and destruction. I recall vividly the admiration in the voice of a student I overheard in the 1960's: hearing of a radically immoral and anarchistic act, he glowingly declared, "Far out, man!"

Modern man is suicidal, and his goal is death. The world, however, is vastly bigger than modern man. A new culture is in process of formation, neither statist nor humanist, nor church-oriented. In many cases, Christians are leaving their impotent churches, sometimes to build new ones, often to find in associations, fellowships, and in their homes, the new foundations for a renewed Christendom.

An old expression speaks of "the country of the soul." Modern man's soul is homeless and has only death ahead of it. Those who have the assurance that in Christ they have a citizenship in heaven and a lordship over the world have a very different "country of the soul" than the lonely soul who denies all ties and asserts his existential isolation. The "country of the soul" of modern man has become limited to the dimensions of his own inner being, and this he finds to be, not an empire, but a hell. He cannot look at the world and sing, as does the Christian, "This is my Father's world." It is for him a dead, cold, and alien world, and his constant theme is of alienation and isolation.

In the early church, we find a new system of dating appeared early: we have it today in A.D., in the year of our Lord. When the martyr Polycarp was burned at Smyrna on Caesar's festival, February 23, 155, the church recorded it "in the consulship of Statius Quadratus, but in the reign of the Eternal King." This phrase occurs often: "in the reign of the Eternal King." It expressed the confidence of the early Christians in victory over Caesar. Because the Eternal King ruled the country of their soul and the universe, they knew that in time they would triumph.

In whose reign are you living?

CHALCEDON REPORT NO. 107
July, 1974

Among the cultural motives which dominated Western man when, after 1660, the structure of Western civilization began to shift from a Christian to a humanistic basis was *experience*. A new idea began to emerge, *the truth of experience*, which was to supplant progressively the idea of objective and absolute truth. In the church this meant experiential religion, priority given to experience rather than to the facts of doctrine, priority to the individual and his experience rather than to God. A modern evangelical has summed it up thus: "The most important thing in the world is to experience Christ as your Savior." Clearly, any experience cannot be more important than, for example, the incarnation, not even *for me* can it be more important without turning a cosmic religion into an egocentric concern. However wonderful or necessary my salvation may be, it cannot take priority over God and His total purpose even in my own mind without sin.

To cite another example: in speaking a few years ago of the consequences of inflation, I cited the German monetary collapse of 1923 as one possible consequence. One man immediately objected: "That's impossible. The German experience cannot be the American experience, because the Germans believed in gold and distrusted paper. Americans do not believe in gold and there can therefore be no bad results with our currency." In such thinking, the truth of experience has replaced objective reality.

To cite still another example, last night an outstanding and superior Christian layman told me of a sermon he heard preached by an evangelical pastor. Experience was made so basic that the experience of love made the objective facts of a marriage license and ceremony unnecessary and superficial. This is not a new attitude: the stress on experience has made the church, modernist and evangelical alike, antinomian, anti-law. With this stress on experience rather than God and His law-word, it should not surprise us that mass evangelism, by its own statistics, leaves 95% of its supposed converts unchanged in their lives. Its audiences are largely experience-mongers.

This stress on experience has a related motive, a stress *on quantity, on numbers*. Experience is a visible thing; so is quantity. I have often heard it said that criticism of this or that mass evangelist is wrong: "Think of the numbers of people he reaches." Such people assess any and all things by this same quantitative approach: How many people read him? How many people hear him? How much press does he get? By their logic, these people should have been pro-Hitler and pro-Stalin, and today should be pro-Mao and pro-Brezhnev. To stress quantity, numbers, is evidence of radical humanism (and of stupidity as well). If our faith is in man, it will show. Our criterion will be, how much appeal does one have with man? For the orthodox Christian, the criterion of judgment is faithfulness to God.

One consequence of this emphasis on quantity and experience has been the debasement of the pulpit. From 1660 to the present, the calibre of preaching has declined in content, and the emphasis has shifted from solid thought to popular appeal and entertainment. With a few exceptions, the larger the church, the weaker the content of the preaching.

In politics, the consequence has been crowd-pleasing of the most blatant sort. Justice has come to mean giving the most hand-outs to the most people by robbing those who are the targets of envy. The logic of the emphasis on experience and quantity makes socialism or communism the natural and inevitable faith of a culture which stresses their centrality.

Basic to this stress on experience and quantity or numbers is *relativism*. All things are made relative to man, to mass man. Truth is made relative to man, not to God. Things are important if man so regards them, not because God has established a priority.

Because all things are made relative to man and man's experience, things are unimportant unless they command masses of men. God's warning against despising "the day of small things," i.e., small beginnings (Zech. 4:10), is regularly despised by modern fools. They see a thing as good only as mass man takes to it, not because it is good in terms of God and His word.

The implications of all this is that the supreme good is man, and the more men who approve of something and experience it favorably, the closer that thing or cause is to the supreme good. The logic of total democracy is that man is the ultimate standard, law, and good, and the more men there are who approve of anything, the better it must be.

Humanistic culture is collapsing, however, and its elite now have turned on man. The fewer there are who appreciate an avant-garde art form, the better it must be! If the crowd-man takes to it, that art form is dropped for another. The fewer people there are who go to a resort, the better it is, and, however bad the food and beds, and however flea-ridden, that inn is "quaint" and "unspoiled." The humanistic mass-man stupidly follows the crowd, and the crowd is his standard of judgment. The humanistic elitist avoids the crowd and stupidly assumes that what the crowd ignores must be good: his standard, as against mass-man's judgment, is private judgment and is humanism still. God's truth is not in the picture for either as they blindly stumble towards the collapse of their culture.

I may believe without any doubt that the lights will go on when I flip the switch, but the lights only go on when all is well with the power. Modern man assumes that he is the power-plant. Reality, however, is not a product of man's faith in himself.

CHALCEDON REPORT NO. 108
August, 1974

A partial definition of history is that it is the remembered past. Whereas heredity is genetic, history is cultural, religious, and emotional: its roots are in memory, meanings, and faiths. A Tatar child adopted at birth by an English family will show Tatar features, but his history will be English. History thus is a road-block to those who wish to remake man. Historical memories and meanings are not rational, i.e., they are not products of logical thought but of acts of good and bad faiths. Hence it is that, in the age of statism, educators and political theorists have been hostile to history and have replaced it with "the social sciences," whose purpose is to study the control of man by man. Not surprisingly, some thinkers have dreamed of some means of electro-shock "therapy" to destroy history in the individual. More practically, modern education has dedicated itself to the clean-slate theory of the mind: the child can be best educated if his mind is swept free of the influences of home, church, community, nation, and faith. As a result, statist education is anti-historical and alienates children and youth from their past, from *roots*. The goal is to produce a rootless person who will then see issues in terms of science and reason.

Existentialism and pragmatism have been logical philosophies in terms of this trend, in that they require a separation from all past influences and history and see freedom as a conditioning in which man is determined solely by the biology of his being without reference to the complex of history. The demand is for rootlessness as freedom.

As a result, roots are seen as slavery. As a university student, I recall how professors regularly denied value to any pro-Southern points of view in historical research, making it the butt of jokes, and concluding with the remark, "They're still fighting the Civil War." Any anti-Communist books or articles by refugee scholars were similarly discounted: these men were involved and had historical memories. All primary sources thus, while basic to research, had to be treated with a radical suspicion.

Clearly, it is true that involvement in history can lead to distortions. I recall vividly an old Paiute Indian talking about the Padicap War (so "minor" that many specialists in Western American history are unaware of it) as though world history had to be understood in terms of it: for him, it had to be. I have had the same experience with Central Europeans, Near Easterners, Basques, and others. I have heard scholars dismiss such historical memories as "living in the past." Some people do live in the past too much, some live only for the moment, and some, most foolish of all, think they live only by reason.

The fact is that peoples with long memories have long lives, as witness the Jews, Armenians, and others. Basic to that long memory is a hard core of faith. Moreover, justice and memory have a necessary relationship. Men to whom past evils are nothing, and present rational considerations everything, will do evil to eliminate the present non-rational problems. For the social scientists, the non-scientific and the non-rational are virtually identical with evil. After World Wars I and II, the peace treaties re-aligned the world in terms of political, statist considerations, and ensured injustice and war. Had they been more scientific, the evil would have been greater, because history would have been even more flagrantly denied.

Such a destructive course would logically follow from the premises inherent in the modern perspective. For Karl Popper, for example (in *The Open Society and its Enemies*), "History has no meaning." There are interpretations of history, and they vary from group to group, but history as such has no objective meaning. There is no predestinating God to give an established meaning to history. Only man can do that. For Popper, "although history has no meaning, we can give it a meaning." This is the key to humanism and the age of the state. God's meaning is denied, and the meaning of the scientific planners is progressively asserted. This requires the denial of God's history, and the suppression of historical memory, so that a new history, a social science, can be created. As a result, the modern state is progressively perverse, to anyone with an historical and Christian perspective. It denies Gresham's law, and it denies the faith and tradition of peoples. These are all irrelevant considerations to scientific reason.

The meaning of history, as created by such thinkers, is known only to them, because *they* "give it a meaning." State schools and massive brain-washing are necessary to convince the people of this meaning. God's meaning, however, is known to all men, although they suppress it in unrighteousness (Rom. 1:17-21). It is the meaning in terms of which we were created, and apart from which our lives disintegrate into meaninglessness.

The more nearly the age of the state comes to realizing its meaning, the more radical the revolt against it grows. Men are not yet turning in great numbers to Christian faith, but they are turning against the bankrupt modern establishment: it has bred emptiness, not meaning, the experience of nothingness rather than faith. Its new order is turning out to be death.

CHALCEDON REPORT NO. 109
September, 1974

According to Norman Zacour, in *An Introduction to Medieval Institutions*, "The idea that where there is no justice there is no authority was firmly entrenched in feudalism." Thus, despite the common violations of law, there was a principle of justice in terms of which judgment and progress were possible. With Niccolo Machiavelli and then Thomas Hobbes, a new idea began to develop, one which John P. Roche, in *Courts and Rights*, summed up as holding in effect that "Law is the command of the sovereign," whether the sovereign be the ruler, parliament, or, later, the people.

For some time, these two ideas, however contradictory, co-existed. Rulers and people were, in varying degrees, Christian. They believed in common ideas of right and wrong, and they were agreed as to what justice means. As a result, the sovereign's law was still to a large degree tied to an essentially Biblical framework. This framework was entirely subject at first to the ruler's choice. The people were Lutheran, Catholic, Episcopal, or Reformed in terms of the ruler's choice: his word was law, and his religious preference was the people's church, and no other legal choice was possible.

The result was the development of *civic religion*, a religious foundation for a purely national state, or for the ruler's state. The God of the state was the ruler's choice, and the ruler's supposed ally. The belief of the rulers was that God should be grateful to the king for keeping the realm in the camp of the church, whatever the true church was held by the king to be. Thus, in 1706, after the defeat of the Battle of Ramillies, Louis XIV said, "God seems to have forgotten all I have done for Him."

As time passed, however, this civic religion became less and less concerned with theology and church and more and more concerned with maintaining the bare bones of Biblical morality. A nation was held to be God-fearing if it had an occasional prayer and Bible reading at official (and educational) functions and vaguely upheld a minimal view of the Ten Commandments and a few other things. Even this minimal civic religion declined to the point where the Regents of New York composed, as Roche noted, "a non-partisan prayer essentially addressed 'To Whom it May Concern' for daily recitation in the public schools;" then this prayer was invalidated in 1962.

Since then, civic religion has become even broader. In 1965, unbelievers who were pacifists gained the right to affirm and maintain with civil sanctions a totally private religion as the basis of their morality.

Meanwhile, the old feudal idea that, where there is no justice, there is no authority, was revived in terms of Thoreau and Bakunin to give a moral basis to civil disobedience. A key problem of the modern era was thus brought into sharp focus. The foundations of all law are in essence religious and theological: they are questions of ultimacy and moral necessity. Law without faith is an impossibility. Every law order is a moral and a theological order, a structuring of society in terms of a fundamental faith. If the faith dies, the law order dies also.

Earlier centuries had insisted, erroneously, on identifying faith and the church, limiting the faith to a particular form of the church. Later, the faith was identified with the state, and now, with the purely personal tastes of the individual, for whom the faith is existential, not something beyond man but totally of man. The consequences of all three positions have been destructive of social order and of Christian faith. To make either the church, the state, or the individual the voice of God is to limit God and absolutize the human order.

The old pagan Roman maxim was, "What pleases the prince has the force of law." To reduce the law to an institution or person is destructive of law, in that law then is tyranny. If ultimate law comes from man, or an agency or institution of men, then I have no appeal against its arbitrariness except my personal dislike and dissent. I have no religious or moral stand against the law. If I have an appeal to supernatural and ultimate law against all that man may do, then I have a basis for resistance and for reconstruction.

Because relativism has so long prevailed, men no longer affirm as a society any faith in an absolute right and wrong. The result is an erosion of the idea of the rule of law, and the normality now of the rule of political pressure.

Kant reduced law to a humanistic moral imperative: "Every formula which expresses the necessity of an action is called a law." But where is necessity in the modern point of view? It was clearly formulated in the 1960s, by the hippies, thus: "Do your own thing." Necessity is no longer cosmic; it is no longer a part of the essence or nature of reality: it is entirely personal and anarchistic. The result is a break-down of the very idea of law. Increasingly, there is neither justice nor authority.

When such a situation prevails, darkness settles in, because there is no light of justice to illuminate society and to give authority. The psalmist's words stand confirmed: "Except the LORD build the house, they labour in vain that build it: except the LORD keep the city, the watchman waketh but in vain" (Ps. 127:1).

CHALCEDON REPORT NO. 110
October, 1974

One reason why man has rarely been free in his long history is his fear and hatred of freedom. Over and over again, men have paid lip service to freedom while constructing instead social orders which allowed no room for freedom.

Historically, one of the major functions of the state has been to protect man and society from the dangers of freedom. In the ancient world, stateless man was regarded as worse off than the dead. Egyptians, Sumerians, Babylonians and others regarded the state as the true life of man.

The Greeks, who despite modern mythology, had no love of freedom, defined man as a political animal. Man could not be truly man apart from the state. Plato's *Republic* is a blueprint for totalitarian communism, and Aristotle's *Politics* saw man as the property of the state. Aristotle espoused state control of education, because "The citizen should be molded to suit the form of government under which he lives." Moreover, "Neither must we suppose that any one of the citizens belongs to himself, for they all belong to the state, and are each of them a part of the state" (*Politics*, Bk. VIII, ch. 1). He held also that "the state is by nature clearly prior to the family and to the individual, since the whole is of necessity prior to the parts" (Bk. I, ch 2).

For most of history this pagan view of the state has governed men. Men have found freedom to be a threat, and they have readily turned over their lives to the claims of the state.

But this is not all. Salvation has been defined in terms of the state, and the state seen as man's savior. For the Romans, salvation was security under Caesar. According to the archaeologist, Sir William M. Ramsay, "The paternal government was 'salvation'" for those who live on imperial estates. Ramsay concluded, "The 'Salvation' of Jesus and Paul was freedom: the 'Salvation' of the Imperial system was serfdom" (Sir W. M. Ramsay: *The Bearing of Recent Discovery on the Trustworthiness of the New Testament*. p. 197f. London: Hodder & Stroughton, 1920).

This faith in salvation by the state was basic to the Renaissance and is essential to an understanding of modern man. Except for the partial but profound counter-movement of early American developments, especially between 1750 and 1850, the basic belief of modern man is that the good life and salvation can only be attained by means of the state. This means increasing state powers, because, in order to save man, the state must be stronger. Thus, the more serious man's plight, the more the state must increase its power in order to save men.

The Biblical doctrine of salvation holds that because the triune God is the sovereign and omnipotent lord, salvation is possible. Only a sovereign God can save, because He alone determines all things, and He alone cannot be overthrown in all His ways. Man's salvation is only assured where his savior is omnipotent and his salvation cannot be annulled or overruled by any other force. Man in relation to God cannot have a primary freedom; man has only a secondary freedom, the freedom of a creature, to be what God has ordained him to be.

Quite logically, the salvation of the state mimics this pattern. In order to give man an assured salvation, one which cannot be set aside, the state must set aside man's freedom and work towards its own omnipotence. The state must be sovereign, and it must be beyond challenge. Man must be simply what the state ordains him to be, and nothing more. For the state to plan or predestinate man's salvation requires totalitarian powers for the state, and this the state constantly aspires to gain.

In this quest, the state has the active support of modern man. Having turned away from the triune God, he looks religiously to the modern state for salvation, for womb to tomb security, and for the fatherhood he once attributed to God. Thus, although at times the modern state has gained its powers by legal usurpation, it has generally been with the active or passive consent of the people.

Man, said Jesus Christ, is by virtue of the fall a slave, a slave to sin, and therefore partial to slavery, until He makes man free by His grace (John 8:33-36). Modern man has still enough of the trappings of his religious and cultural past, so that he feels that lip service must be paid to freedom. He honors it at every turn, and every day works to diminish it. The one assured fact today about any convening legislative body is that it sits, not to increase man's freedom, but to limit it. Freedom to slaves is a dangerous thing, and, in the heart of his being, modern man is a slave. He has converted church, state, and school into schools for slavery. He has waged war against the threat of freedom at every turn in order to assure the free flow of statist salvation. Men who are by nature slaves will only tolerate slavery, and, as a result, freedom is under fire and on the wane.

The battle-ground is not the state. The state is the echo chamber, reflecting man's real desires. The problem is in the minds and hearts of men. "If the Son therefore shall make you free, ye shall be free indeed" (John 8:36). There is no other way.

CHALCEDON REPORT NO. 112
December, 1974

Not only has man, during his long history, distrusted freedom and feared it, but he has also distrusted righteousness. As a powerful American monopolist said of a politician, at the beginning of the 20th century: I like a man who, when you buy him, stays bought. Evil can be depended on to be for sale.

This preference for evil has been basic to the diplomacies of states in the modern era. The more evil a state becomes, the more readily it is trusted by the various international powers. A classic example of this is Turkey. By the mid-seventeenth century, over 300 years ago, it was apparent that the Turkish Empire was corrupt and ready to fall if attacked by any major power. Its collapse would have freed the Christians of central Europe, the near East, and North Africa. When the powers of Europe realized this weakness of Turkey, they immediately came to its defense. Control of the Dardanelles means control of the Black Sea, the Danube, central Europe, and the Near East. More shipping and commerce then and now is controlled by this key area than any other point in the world. None were willing to place this power in the hands of even slightly principled power: Turkey alone was "dependable," because, by its very corruption, it could clearly be bought and controlled.

When the Hungarians, under Prince Eugene of Savoy, shattered Turkey at Zenton in a battle in which 3,000 Turks perished, including the Grand Vizier and four other viziers. Europe sprang to Turkey's defense. The result was a treaty hammered out at Carlowitz in 1699. Austria was able to keep two thirds of Hungary, and the Russians gained Azov and the area north of the Sea of Azov. The peace conference, led by Britain and Holland, made Turkey the concern and in a sense ward of all Europe. In the Congress of Vienna in 1815, this principle was more bluntly formulated: Turkey must never pass into the hands of any one power. However, earlier, in 1774, in the Treaty of Kainardji, Russia had been able to wrest a concession from Turkey: "Turkey promises to protect constantly the Christian religion and churches and allow the ministers of Russia at Constantinople to make representation on their behalf." A check was to be placed on the Turkish savagery towards Christians. This was too much for Europe. In the Crimean War, Europeans, led by Britain, treated the Turks as great and heroic men and fought with them against Russia, and, in 1856, in the Treaty of Paris, Russia was compelled to abandon her religious concern for Christians in Turkey. (One result was that Turkey now had a free hand to plan the total extermination of Armenians and other Christians, culminating in the massacre of nearly 2 million Armenians alone in World War I and after.) Queen Victoria's hatred of Russia was so intense that she despised Gladstone, the champion of Christian minorities, and was ready to listen to the Sultan as a brother-ruler. Earlier, before Britain's entry into the Crimean War, she had issued an ultimatum in writing to the prime minister: "If England is to kiss Russia's feet the Queen will not be a party to the humiliation of England and would lay down her crown."

After World War I, except for Britain this time, the powers conspired to revive Turkey as against Greece, leading to the massacres at Smyrna. The full story of the massacres was suppressed everywhere, and the American High Commissioner at Constantinople, Admiral Mark L. Bristol, sent out anti-Christian reports. (Standard Oil, American Tobacco, and Chester Concessions had large commitments in Turkey.)

In World War II (and thereafter) Turkey received huge sums in aid from various powers, on both sides, and its role as a necessary power was strengthened. In fact, the break between Stalin and Hitler was the result of their conflict over Turkey: both wanted it for themselves. In the 1970s, Cyprus or any other area is readily sacrificed rather than allow anyone to touch Turkey. If any power, no matter how slightly principled, should take over Turkey, every modern (and Machiavellian) state would feel threatened.

The thesis is simple: evil is trustworthy and can be bought and controlled. Better a Turkey, and better a Marxist Russia and a Red China than freedom there or elsewhere. This is power politics, with its balance of powers ploy, its readiness to deal with corrupt regimes and to treat them with dignity, with its collectivism, its humanism, and anti-Christianity. It governs the modern age and is destroying it. It is becoming its own judgment and nemesis. All its efforts to patch and prop up the decaying international order only aggravate the problem.

The shattering of that order will come as the new wine of Christian faith returns, shattering the old bottles (Matt. 9:17). The word of God stands: "Except the LORD build the house, they labour in vain that build it: except the LORD keep the city, the watchman waketh but in vain" (Ps. 127:1).

The rebuilding of Christendom can only come as men are regenerated and are faithful to the law-word of God, only as once again men put their trust in God's law rather than man's evil. The modern motto seems to be, "In evil we trust"; men being themselves evil can better understand and trust in evil, and will continue to do so, as long as they continue in their own depravity. The Psalmist said of idolaters, who worshipped the evil they imagined and fashioned, "They that make them are like unto them: so is every one that trusteth in them" (Ps 115:8).

Where is your trust? What Power do you believe dominates the world, God or Satan, righteousness or evil? You will stand or fall in terms of your answer.

CHALCEDON REPORT NO. 113
January, 1975

When Pilate asked Jesus, "What is truth?" (John 18:38), he spoke as a Roman. Guilt or innocence of the charge at hand, he could understand, but the idea of truth was beyond him as too abstract and irrelevant. One of the most ancient premises of Roman law was the declaration, "The health (or welfare) of the people is the highest law." Expediency and pragmatism took priority over all other considerations. The premise of success and advancement in Rome, for individuals and for the state, was threefold: survival, self-gratification, and opportunism.

With the Renaissance and the Enlightenment, the European states began to operate with progressively easier consciences on the classical Roman model. One of the abler statesmen, Lord Palmerston, British Foreign Secretary, was a student of things Roman, and he applied the Roman premise in his famous aphorism: "We have no perpetual allies and we have no perpetual enemies. Our interests are perpetual." Self-interest had become the new law for men and nations, the "higher" law.

This shift from the higher law of God to the higher law of man is a significant one. It comes to focus in part in the idea of laissez-faire. The background of this doctrine is theological: it rests on a belief in the higher law of God. Non-intervention by the state in economics and in other areas rests in origin in a belief that the sovereign and absolute God governs all things by His law. For man to legislate where God has already legislated is not only irrelevant and foolish but also potentially dangerous. After all, one does not legislate laws of physics, biology, or mathematics. To do so is dangerous, as the Soviet Union found out with Lysenko: it can mean disastrous failures in the agricultural realm, or in some other practical realm. Such laws of God await man's discovery, not man's legislation.

This older view led to a secularized version: "Nature" is the source of this higher law, it was held, and interference with natural harmony makes matters worse. The laws of nature govern all things, and statist tampering with natural harmony leads only to disaster.

The next step was to secularize the matter further: the source of natural harmony is the individual and his self-interest. The best working of society thus rests on the radical self-interest of the individual. Thus, the source of freedom and law shifted from God to nature to man, and then, finally, to the state, the humanistic state, in the twentieth century.

In Adam Smith's *Wealth of Nations* (1776), the first three factors, God, Nature and man were blended and identified. Smith wrote that the individual "generally neither intends to promote the public interest nor knows how much he is promoting it. He intends only his own security, and by directing that industry in such a manner as its produce may be of the greatest value, he intends only his own gain, and he is in this, as in many other cases, led by an invisible hand to promote an end which was no part of his intention." As a defense of the free market, this was hardly accurate. Self-interest then and now leads many industrialists and labor unions to prefer the security of subsidies to the free market and to connive against both freedom and law. Moreover, no sooner were freedom and law clearly grounded in man than man shifted it to his agency, the state. John Stuart Mill began by championing a radical concept of liberty for man and concluded by transferring liberty and law to the socialist state.

Not principles but self-interests are perpetual, modern man has held, together with Palmerston, and to maintain the autonomy of man in his self-interest, man has been ready to scrap freedom and law. For the new existentialists, true autonomy means only existence, not essence, not a pattern, purpose, or law, inner or outer, to limit man's autonomy.

The older cry of humanistic man was "I want to be free," but this has given way, in terms of existentialism, to a new creed, well expressed in the theme of a popular song, "I Wanta Be ME." This ME does not want to be anything except itself: it denies the validity of any objective norm, law or standard. This ME is in fact at war with all standards: it hates slavery and freedom alike; it hates justice and injustice, and it has only one goal, the destruction of all norms.

The modern state, as it increasingly reflects this existentialist man, also lives for its own sake. Its purpose in politics and economics is meaningless except in terms of its only motive, survival on its own lawless terms. Thus, from a world of natural harmony we have come to a world of total and natural disharmony and war.

The warning of Isaiah 2:22 still stands: "Cease ye from man, whose breath is in his nostrils: for wherein is he to be accounted of?" Men and nations who build upon man make their foundation sand. In the storms ahead, they cannot stand (Matt. 7:24-27). Look to your own foundations: do they rest upon sand, upon your own being, or are they established on the Rock?

CHALCEDON REPORT NO. 114
February, 1975

The modern state, having divorced itself from Biblical faith, has not only lost the criterion for truth, but it has also lost the ability to create a working society. Work in the Bible is God's ordained means whereby man gains dominion. Work for modern man is an ugly necessity which takes away time from the pursuit of pleasure. In turning from work to pleasure, modern man has chosen the pleasure principle over the reality principle as the operating standard for life.

The inability of most cultures to advance beyond a limited degree is due to their distaste for work. Work is regarded in most of history, as well as in much of the modern world, as a degrading and distasteful necessity, to be required by force of the lower classes.

A college girl, a relative, shared an apartment with three other girls, one of them from Latin America. Although the Latin American girl came from a family of somewhat less means than the other three, who were of the American middle class, in terms of her country she belonged to the upper class. She never picked up a dish. In the bathroom or bedroom, she dropped her clothing to the floor in the expectation that someone should pick them up for her. She obviously expected a full-time servant to feed her, pick up after her, and be at her beck and call. Work was something which should not be expected of her: her dignity placed her beyond work.

This attitude with respect to work is in increasing evidence. In the Soviet Union, the first generation had the background of disciplined work because of their upbringing in old Russia. With a third generation, this discipline is waning, and work is regarded with contempt and production suffers. All over the world, a growing element, products of the humanistic state and its culture, regard work as an evil. Significant sectors of the New Left believe that machines and automation can eliminate work and "free" man, and only the evil conspiracies of the capitalists prevent this.

This is their goal, to be "free" from work. But, first of all, freedom from work is a surrender of dominion. Work was and is the God-ordained means to dominion. In spite of all its political stupidities, the United States remains the world leader because of its still remarkable productive abilities, a continuing consequence of the Puritan work ethic. Man cannot escape work. He will either work as a man gaining and exercising dominion, or he will work as a whipped slave, but he will work.

Second, a godly work ethic is time conscious and respects time. Much contempt is expressed today for people who are clock-conscious, as though freedom means despising time. But time is life; it is man's most precious commodity. Time lost cannot be recovered, nor can time be boarded up. To despise time and clocks is to be suicidal. A godly work ethic practices the most basic conservation of all, the conservation of time and life.

Third, work is a theological fact: it is God-ordained for the creature who alone is created in God's image, man. It is God's appointed way for man to realize the implications of that image, namely, righteousness, holiness, knowledge, and dominion. By means of work man is able to fulfil God's creation mandate and calling, and to become a ruler over himself, his calling, his household, and the world around him.

Basic to the dream of the humanistic state is the creation of a new world order, one in which man supposedly "finds" himself without God's help. The realization of man and history is seen as the rebirth of man as the new god and the death of the God of Scripture. This is to be the freedom of man.

This statist dream is not only antinomian, i.e., hostile to God's law, but also anti-work. Man's liberation is seen as freedom from God, law, and work. But life cannot be redefined. The conditions of life are given by God, life is God's creation, and its conditions are also totally God created. No more than man can live without breathing and eating can he live without law and work, nor can he live without God, without thereby choosing death. As Wisdom declared, ages ago, "all they that hate me love death" (Prov. 8:36). The conditions of life require the fountain of life.

The modern state, however, has by its humanism cut itself off from the fountain of life. It no longer has the ability to provide meaning to life, nor can it give work any enduring meaning. Social cohesiveness is waning, and the city becomes less and less a community and more and more a battleground between classes, races, and gangs. Modern man is rootless and cynical; he has trouble living with himself, and to live and work with others is for him a great burden.

A few generations ago, one of the most popular and common proverbs of the Western world held that "Every man is the son of his own works," i.e., a man could not blame others for his own failures. Increasingly, however, this belief has given way to the approach or classical Greek tragedy, namely, that man is a prisoner of his past. Classical and modern humanism are agreed on this radical environmentalist position: work is futile, for the past has doomed us. Humanism then and now ends up hostile to life and to man.

The future like the past will be dominated by those cultures which can work with purpose, ability, and zeal. Oratory can command votes, but purposive work commands history.

CHALCEDON REPORT NO. 115
March, 1975

Institutions, as they lose their function and purpose, forfeit also their lives, or, at least, their necessary role in society.

For example, the modern image of a knight or a lord is of a hand-kissing fashion plate and snob; for medieval man, he was a necessary source of law and order and a capable protector. However unjust and arbitrary he might be at times, he was still so valuable that his uses outweighed his faults. Medieval man knew that his lord had a poor life expectancy because of his military and protective function: as late as 1330-1479, about one in two of every English duke's sons died a violent death, and, as a class, their life expectancy was only 24 years.

Only later, when knights and lords lost their necessary function to medieval man, and begin to work for their self-perpetuation and advancement in relation to the monarch, did they become irrelevant to those who once found them necessary to society. The peers of the realm became intolerable to European man, not because they had become worse in character, because it can be argued that their character commonly improved, but because they became irrelevant and therefore a burden.

The same point can be made with reference to monarchy, and also the church. For most of European history, the church was the most necessary institution, and, even in some eras of very real corruption, the church was not only tolerated but its reform urgently sought on all sides. As the institution most basic to the structuring and development of society, life without the church was to most men unthinkable. Thus, even as they damned the evils in the church, they sought with intensity its reform and renewal.

However, where the church made itself irrelevant, men gradually by-passed it, and, from a necessary institution, the church became an optional one. Once as necessary as daily bread, it became a luxury or an extra item for those with a taste for it. Then and now, the church has done this to itself. In the medieval era, the concern of the church for self-perpetuation, the development of naturalistic theologies and philosophies, and the growth of mysticism and pietism, made the church progressively an irrelevant luxury. The Reformation and Counter-Reformation for a time restored relevancy, but the same old tendencies soon rendered the church irrelevant, an optional rather than a necessary institution.

In the modern era, the state and the state school have been the necessary institutions, and man's hopes have been closely tied to the state and the state school. The same irrelevance, however, is again setting in. The state school in Europe is mainly geared to preparation for civil service, in the United States, to the democratic life. In either case, it is less and less relevant to man's basic problems and needs. As a result, in the United States especially, statist education is dying, and independent Christian schools are growing very rapidly.

Indicative of the irrelevance of the state is the fact that, in the United States, as much money is spent for private policing and protective devices as for statist policing. The state has so hampered its police that one of the most basic functions of the state, protection from criminals, is passing into private hands.

Similarly, courts are increasingly geared to adjudicating equality rather than justice, and, as a result, the very central function of justice is less and less expected from the state.

As a result, both the right and the left are agreed that the state as it exists, the Establishment, is the enemy. Both seek to capture the state and reform it, but, increasingly, most people expect less and less good from the state in any hands, and more and more evil and corruption. The modern humanistic state, once religiously revered, is increasingly distrusted and feared.

While the final break is not yet here, and the modern state is not yet regarded as irrelevant, there is a tendency in that direction. Associations, contracts, business arrangements, and prices are set with an eye to avoiding statist controls and intervention. Instead of utilizing the state, a growing segment of the population work to avoid the state, a most telling indicator of approaching irrelevance. Add to this the fact that, in the United States and elsewhere, recent elections saw a remarkably low percentage of people voting, and a trend towards irrelevance becomes clear. The state was once universally regarded as a necessary good; now it is seen by its very defenders as simply a necessary evil. The modern humanistic idea of the state is thus in transition to irrelevance.

This means, of course, very dangerous and trying years ahead. It means major dislocations and upheavals in what is already the most bloody and revolutionary of centuries. But it also means a time of opportunity without equal to present the whole counsel of God, and His law as the only tenable basis for men and nations. There is no other alternative to tyranny and anarchy. Humanistic man's order is coming to its necessary conclusion. Unless the Lord's people set forth His answers, the enemy will provide his alternative.

CHALCEDON REPORT NO. 116
April, 1975

As we have seen, institutions can lose their necessary place in society as they decline from their function and purpose. Knights and kings once necessary to man, became irrelevant and were cast aside as impediments to society, and the church, once the key institution, became a peripheral one, membership in which was optional and whose social role was increasingly minor.

One such key era of transition, when institutions began to fail men, and men began to turn against them, was the 1400s. Long before the Reformation, men were feeling the shock of a world out of joint. The basic twin ideas of estate and calling governed men's minds, and, under different terms, they still do. It was assumed that men are sinners, but it was still held that, in a working society, men acted in some degree in conformity with their position and calling: An old man did not try to act like a youngster, a rich man made a point of being charitable, and a judge remembered that justice had to be his primary concern. Whatever their failings, men had to fulfil the requirements of their office or estate and calling.

Men did not suddenly become worse in the 1400s, any more than they have in the 1900s; evil tendencies were always there. What happened rather was the decline of strength of purpose and calling among the godly, so that society passed into ungodly hands by default. Thus, as men of the day looked at church, state, and law, they felt that the sense of estate and calling were gone, and that, without them, their clergy and rulers had turned into enemies. The *Reformatio Sigismundi* (c. 1438) declared, "Obedience is dead. Justice is grievously abused. Nothing stands in its proper order. Therefore God has withdrawn His grace from us. We ignore His commandments." Johann Geiler in 1498 preached on the consequences of the loss of estate and calling: "power-mad fools" now ruled everywhere. Indignant clergymen cried out that the church itself led in the violations of God's laws, and in 1498 in *Reynard the Fox*, it was charged, "Little crooks are hanged; Big crooks govern our lands and cities."

A common complaint was that the law had become an instrument of injustice. One pamphleteer of c. 1500 wrote, "Adultery is licit, blasphemers are respected, the usurer has the law on his side, murderers sit in the judgment seat, and the plunderer of the church has become the very shepherd of the house of worship." As early as 1493 desperate German peasants began to plan revolt under the banner, "God's Justice Alone," a movement which led soon to disaster. More than a few had come to agree with a proverb of the day, "The devil is master of the world."

In spite of all this, it could well be argued that men were economically and materially better off than they had been a century or more earlier. The marks of progress were alive in one area after another. It was in 1492 that Columbus discovered America, and this was not an isolated event but part of a pattern of aggressive and inquiring advance, scientifically, geographically, and commercially. More people had full stomachs to complain on than people in earlier eras had.

It can be argued that it was the very rapidity of change and progress which left people restless and unhappy. The tempo of history had become too rapid, and the movement of things too complex for many, who yearned for the imagined simplicity and peace of the past.

All this is clearly true, and more, but it ignores a central fact: the marks of progress were there, but not of justice, nor of faith. Western man in 1500 found his society meaningless in terms of the requirements of faith and justice. To the movers of society, in increasing numbers, talk of God and justice had become irrelevant. It was a later age which affected dismay at Machiavelli (1469-1527) and his writings, not his own era. Machiavelli had simply expressed the philosophy of his century: man should be governed by, and should govern in terms of, *what is*, not what ought to be, in terms of pragmatism, not religion.

It was not until the 20th century that man again affirmed openly the same philosophy, and the results, are again the same: the loss of estate and calling, the loss of meaning. Even though the man on the street is by and large a pragmatist himself, he hates, fears, and distrusts politicians as pragmatists, and he has contempt for a pragmatic clergy. The writers of our times are again full of self-pity for their plight, and, while themselves unjust, cry out for justice. Man cannot live long without justice; a world without justice soon quenches the spirit of man, or moves him to savage rebellion. But, without the foundation of faith in the triune God, man's ideas of justice turn out only to be injustice. Isaiah declared (59:14f), "And judgment is turned away backward, and justice standeth afar off: for truth is fallen in the streets, and equity cannot enter. Yea, truth faileth; and he that departeth from evil maketh himself a prey." Because the primacy of *truth*, absolute transcendental truth, had departed from society, justice and integrity were gone, and men were governed by and governed in terms of their evil.

Rome had world power in its hands when, in the person of Pilate, it pronounced truth irrelevant. "What is truth?" (John 18:38) said Pilate, finding truth irrelevant even as he faced it in Jesus Christ. Without truth, Rome decayed and finally collapsed. It was not really overthrown: it fell apart. Today, without truth, the modern world, with its pragmatism, is decaying from within. There can be no regeneration and reconstruction apart from Him who is the way, the truth, and the life (John 14:6).

CHALCEDON REPORT NO. 117
May, 1975

One of the basic premises of Christian culture, as taught and developed very early by the church, is the insistence that the world and all men therein are under God's law. Power and authority are derived from God's law, and this is true of every area of life, the family, church, state, school, and all vocations. As a result, a fundamental principle of the medieval period was the doctrine that the king, and all others in authority, must rule according to law, God's law.

The too common backward look of medieval philosophers and their readiness to follow Greek and Roman thinkers, led to the adoption of a Roman premise, common also to the Germanic tribes and to all pagan antiquity, that "necessity knows no law." The forms of this proverb vary: some read, instead of necessity, "the public" or "common utility," "public welfare," "emergency," or "reasons of state," but the idea in all is the same. Necessity became the governing *public* principle, so that, as Post has pointed out, it came to mean "necessity knows no *private* law." (Gaines Post: *Studies in Medieval Legal Thought, Public and the State, 1100-1322*, pp. 8ff., 22. Princeton, New Jersey: Princeton University Press, 1964.)

In time, this came to mean that God's law was a private concern of religious man, and thus it could be over-ruled by the state. Instead of God's law as the higher and ultimate law, *necessity* came to be the new higher and ultimate law. Even churchmen began, to see necessity as the higher law, and one result was the justification of theft in cases of necessity, i.e., to forestall hunger in some cases, or to alleviate extreme distress. Man's necessity was given priority over God's requirements, a logical result of the return to the humanism of antiquity and of the barbarian kingdoms.

The belief that "necessity knows no law" meant the breakdown of "private" law as well, and thus of morality, because a higher law always supplants and negates all lower law. One result was a growing moral anarchism and the brutalization of the law, the courts, and public life, culminating in the Renaissance. The individual began to govern his own life in terms of his own priorities or necessities, and, the more widely men came to believe that "necessity knows no law," the more widely they defined necessity. Every desire and whim of man began to pass for necessity and thus was exempt from the governance of law.

The state was the biggest gainer from this new principle. Having used the idea of necessity to increase its power, the state began to define itself as the realm of necessity and therefore beyond all law. The state thus began to claim jurisdiction over every area of life, including the church.

Although the Reformation and Counter-Reformation for a time pushed back the pagan principle of necessity, it soon returned with the Enlightenment, and, since then, has become the governing principle of virtually all civil governments. *Reasons of state*, or necessities, are deemed sufficient to justify all policies and courses of action. In terms of the state as the necessary principle of life and law, the state has taken over education and is beginning to look towards more and more control of the churches. The state, claiming to be the new god of creation, claims jurisdiction over every area of life. State law is held to govern all of life, but the state is itself under no higher law.

The state cannot be neutral towards God. When it denies God's law as binding over itself, it affirms thereby that the law of the state is ultimate and binding over all things and bound by none. Its basic premise then is that the world is under the state's law, not God's.

The end result of the premise that "necessity knows no law" is total tyranny and terror under a totalitarian state determined to permit no independent existence to any man or institution. Such a consequence cannot be prevented merely by fighting totalitarianism but only by undercutting its basic premise. The priority of God and His law must be asserted, maintained, and acknowledged in faith and life.

The "death of God" school of thought was a logical result of the belief that necessity can be separated from God and His law. By declaring that "necessity knows no law," men in effect declared that God is dead and man reigns. By affirming and applying the principle that the only necessity is God and His law, men in effect declare that the totalitarian state is dead and God reigns.

Fear and hatred for, and opposition to, the totalitarian state are ineffectual and generally futile as long as men see it as the necessary order: they cannot by hatred nullify its power. Only as they by faith recognize the absolute necessity of God's law, and the absolute sovereignty of God himself, will they cease, whether in love or in hate, to bow before that modern Baal, the sovereign state. Until then, men are impotent, and they continue to bow before the gigantic eunuch, the sovereign state, which claims all potency but can only kill, never make alive. Only then can men declare. "The Lord reigneth; let the earth rejoice; let the multitude of isles be glad thereof" (Ps. 97:1).

CHALCEDON REPORT NO. 118
June, 1975

The old Christian doctrines of *estate* and *calling* were often violated in earlier centuries, but their importance was nevertheless very great. Even in violating them, men knew that their office or position, and their calling made certain duties mandatory, and that both God and man expected their fulfillment from them. The common acceptance of the doctrines of *estate* and *calling* compelled men to assess themselves and other men in terms of a God-centered standard.

With humanism, a steady decline and then a disappearance of the ideas of estate and calling began. How extensive the loss is will appear in the fact that the once-common saying, "Act your age," a relic of the idea of the dignity of *estate*, is now almost gone. Thus, I have a picture of a woman in her eighties sun-bathing in a flimsy bikini at Nice, France, a fitting symbol of the disappearance of the old doctrine. People who try to act their age are now often ridiculed, because "You're only as old as you feel" (or pretend you feel). The *mind*, not objective reality such as age, God's law, and other people, now governs.

With the loss of all strong and theological ideas of estate and calling, men now live for themselves, and they make their own needs and whims their end or goal. The purpose of life is sought in man's own desires, not in God's sovereign purpose and order.

This raises a very significant fact: the criminal is the man who lives for himself, makes his wishes and needs his law, and disregards the law structure of God and man. He seeks his purpose and goal within himself, in his own fallen nature, not outside himself or in reference to anything higher than himself.

Thus, the man of today and the criminal are essentially in agreement on their philosophy of life. Each makes himself the measure of reality and the source of his own law or standards. What then separates the law-abiding citizen from the criminal? Both alike seek their own fulfillment without regard for God's law and order. Both are alike man-centered to the core of their being.

Their only essential difference is that the man of today tries to realize himself within the law, whereas the criminal operates outside the law. Both, however, have abandoned the idea of objective law and the sovereignty of God over all things. Law as something other than a convenience or their own desire is an exploded idea for both of them.

As a result, the children and youth of today show that the distinction between the man of today and the criminal is being blurred. A U.S. Senate sub-committee has estimated, in April, 1975, that vandalism in state schools now costs about half a billion dollars a year; the murder of a hundred students, and rape, robbery, and assault on school premises are a part of an accelerating rate of school crime. As more than one teacher has reported to me of late, the line between a hoodlum and a state school pupil is becoming more and more vague and blurred.

Of course, their elders are busy blurring the lines also. A UPI news item from Olympia, Washington, reads, "Proposed legislation before the Washington House of Representatives to legalize prostitution provides that licenses be given 'only upon satisfactory proof that the applicant is of good moral character'." (Santa Maria, California, *Times*, Thursday, February 20, 1975, p. 11.)

Humanistic scientists who were earlier predicting a new paradise when man became "liberated" from Christianity, are now busy predicting the end of the world and man with pompous solemnity and no sense of their own guilt. Having "liberated" man from God's law, they are amazed at his supposed irrationalism, refusing to see it as the logic and reason of man-centered unbelief. Loren Eisely, in the April, 1975, *Science Digest*, writes of man, "His mounting numbers and ideological fanaticism may force his disappearance into ice and darkness just as he arose from those same natural forces he has threatened to outwit."

Men who have proclaimed the death of God have not realized that they thereby proclaim the death of man, of godless man. The judgment of the living God is clearly in evidence on them, and an age without God's law is an age of death, because the condition of life is law, God's law (Deut. 28).

The future is thus a very good one for those who are the redeemed in Christ and who, in terms of God's law, move in terms of recognition of their *estate* and *calling*. The rest will perish, because, with their every action, political, economic, educational, familial, and personal, they invite death. As Wisdom declares from of old, "He that sinneth against me wrongeth his own soul: all they that hate me love death" (Prov. 8:36).

In terms of God's law we have a plan of action for dominion over all things, a guide to knowing our estate and calling, and the means of the fulfilling thereof. In terms of God's law, we live, not unto ourselves or for our own wishes, but in terms of His calling and purpose, knowing that only in this way can we ourselves be fulfilled. As our Lord declared, "Seek ye first the kingdom of God, and his righteousness; and all these things shall be added unto you" (Matt. 6:33). He having made us can alone be our fulfillment. The necessary condition of our life is the sovereign God: without Him, we have no estate and calling, and, finally, no life, society, or culture. In the graveyard, there is no estate and calling.

CHALCEDON REPORT NO. 119
July, 1975

Marxism succeeded in spite of Karl Marx. A man of remarkable stupidity, he had an annual income of a very well to do gentleman, but he consistently lost a large portion of it on get-rich-quick schemes. His economic and political ideas were as bad as his investments. Incidentally, one of his absurd ideas for instant revolution in 1849 is still with us, now used by unknowing conservatives: the tax revolt.

Marxism succeeded because it ceased to be merely a politico-economic theory and became a religious faith. It offered a total faith, an explanation for all of life, and it succeeded because the world was busy becoming relativistic and pragmatic and uninterested in truth. Theologians became less and less concerned with God and more and more pragmatic and existential. Meanwhile, Marxist theologians, who call themselves theoreticians, have provided a total philosophy of life for a world hungry for a faith. Khrushchev saw the weakness of the purely pragmatic interests of the West. True, he recognized, "theory must be tied to life. Theory, my friends, is gray, but the eternal tree of life is evergreen." However, he pointed out, practice without theory is "doomed to wander in the dark." This was his ground for believing "we will bury you." Western man moved purely in terms of self-interest and practical concerns, not in terms of principle, or faith.

While Khrushchev did not see any strength in the Christian West, he saw the weakness of the humanistic West clearly. Its pragmatism and its contempt of principles ran deep. Palmerston, Bismarck and others had governed in terms of it. In the U.S., it was adopted tardily and with fervor by President Theodore Roosevelt, whose unprincipled foreign policy was based on the premise "Speak softly and carry a big stick." Since World War II, the U.S. has apparently, as Griffith noted, rephrased Roosevelt's maxim into "Speak loudly and carry a big wallet." (Thomas Griffith: *The Waist-High Culture*. p. 114. New York: Harper, 1959.) The belief that dollars will save the world is now perishing in an international glut of Euro-dollars.

Our Lord declared, "Man shall not live by bread alone, but by every word that proceedeth out of the mouth of God" (Matt. 4:4). The heart of modern humanistic politics is the belief that man can live by bread alone, that the religious issues, and God Himself, are irrelevant, and that bread and security are alone essential. The Marxists are in agreement, but they have made the "bread alone" idea into a world and life philosophy and faith. They are thus more consistent in their materialism and as a result more successful to a degree.

Everywhere, however, humanism is collapsing; Marxism promises bread and delivers hunger: inflation in the Marxist world has led to unrest and riots. The West gives bread but with it spiritual hunger, and Western man is also discontented and rebellious. Man cannot live by bread alone, and every attempt to reduce man to a bread-consuming animal, to an economic creature, is doomed to fail.

Man is a religious creature, inescapably so, created in the image of God, and having no peace apart from the service of the Lord. Sooner or later, every society which denies man's essentially religious being, and his theological *estate* and *calling*, is doomed to collapse. The modern humanistic state, both Marxist and democratic, denies its own theological estate and calling, and it denies the theological estate and calling of man. It is thus making itself more and more irrelevant to God and to man, more and more irrelevant to life's basic problems.

In a time of crisis, irrelevant institutions, no matter how powerful outwardly, begin to crumble, because they are unable to cope with life's basic problems. Even more, they have *become* the problem. The medieval order collapsed when the church became the problem instead of a channel for the answer. The modern order, the state, everywhere is creaking and faltering with decay, and it too has become the problem, not a channel for answers. As a result, the modern state and its world are headed for dissolution.

This then is a time of decay and dissolution, but also a time of reconstruction. Only as men regain a theological sense of *estate* and *calling* will they regain a command of their world and its problems, because they will then, under God, have a command of themselves. Under God, the good life does mean material progress, but when it is reduced to that it ceases to be a good life and becomes frustration and emptiness. Because man cannot live by bread alone, the destruction of all "bread only" societies is inescapable, and because the world is God's creation and totally governed by His word and law, the triumph of God's purposes is also inevitable.

One meaning of the Lord's Supper is that Christ our Passover, having been sacrificed for our redemption, is now our Lord who feeds our total being. As we walk in faith and obedience, all the material things which men seek after are given to us. "Seek ye first the kingdom of God, and his righteousness; and all these things shall be added unto you" (Matt. 6:33). This requires more than merely saying, Lord, Lord. It means knowing our estate and calling in Him and under Him.

CHALCEDON REPORT NO. 120
August, 1975

One of the more important people in medieval life was the miller. Then, far more than now, bread was basic to man's diet and life. In terms of estate and calling, the miller should have been one of the more highly esteemed men in the community, because his was a most necessary function. In reality, he was one of the most hated of men.

Chaucer's Canterbury pilgrims delighted in hearing a ribald story about a miller, because all shared the common dislike for millers. A medieval riddle asked, "What is the boldest thing in the world?" Answer: "A miller's shirt, for it clasps a thief by the throat daily." All kinds of laws were passed to try to control millers, but they failed, because the heart of the problem was not dealt with.

The problem was monopoly. The millers, working under a lord, an abbot or bishop, or the Knights Templars, were granted a monopoly on all milling in their area. No man could go to another miller, or use a hand mill, except on severe penalty and serious trouble. This monopoly, very profitable to the miller and his over-lord, also meant no competition and, as a result, high and exorbitant profits as well as great inefficiency. The fee for milling was more than a fee: it was a harsh and brutal tax on the people. Chaucer said of his miller that the man knew how to steal grain and to charge thrice over for milling it, and yet was reasonably honest as millers go!

The miller was a necessary member of society, but, because his position had been used to gain a strangle-hold over the people, men did everything possible to avoid using his services, to gain other means of food, and to undercut the prestige and position of the miller. From a social necessity, the miller had descended to the level of a social plague.

There was nothing in milling as such to make millers evil men, any more than there is anything in church or state as such to make either by nature and necessity evil. In fact, millers despite their disrepute in medieval England, were obviously superior people, because their descendants, who today bear the name Miller, have a long and demonstrable record of superiority. Criminals and welfare recipients bearing that name are uncommon.

The problem was that, what should have been an honorable estate and calling was turned into a vicious monopoly and a social plague. Millers were problems, not mainstays, to medieval man.

The analogy to the modern state is an obvious one. Instead of confining itself to the realm of civil justice, the modern humanistic state has extended a monopolistic power over one area of life after another. As the central means of protection against criminals and against foreign invaders, it has a necessary function, and the loyalty and patriotism it once inspired was great. As the monopolistic oppressor, it has become a feared and hated enemy, an oppressive taxing power whose exactions are beginning to destroy society. The most elementary function of the state is policing, but Americans are now spending more money on private forms of policing than the state does. This is a clear indication that the state, in its quest for power, is failing to discharge its most elementary and basic service. The failure of the modern state is thus far greater than the failure of the medieval miller, or, for that matter, the medieval church. The monopoly enjoyed by church and miller led to their rejection, and today there are on all sides signs of a growing disillusionment and incipient rejection of the modern humanistic state.

The matter has been very aptly summed up in the title of an excellent article in the February, 1975, number of the *California Real Estate Magazine*, written by a friend of Chalcedon, Frank J. Walton, "Government: It's the Problem, Not the Solution." Men have been asking the problem to give the answers.

It has been man's faith in the state, his humanism, which has led him into his present crisis, and disillusionment is not enough to take him out of it.

Some of the best analyses of the decay of Rome, written by Romans of the day, were also the most impotent of statements. Problems do grow so great that awareness of them is finally inescapable for most men, but we have too long labored under the silly idea that knowing the problem is half the answer. Knowing the problem is simply knowing the problem.

The Bible gives us God's answer. It rests first of all in His regenerating power, and, second, in the application of His law to the problems of life. The answer is not in man's hatred, nor in man's love, nor is it a new combination of men and organizations. Scripture gives us God's plan of action for victory, for the godly reconstruction of all things according to His law and under the authority of His Son.

There is no greater sign of hope today than our world crises: they witness to the collapse of the enemy's power and the impossibility of his world-plan. If all were going well today, then we would indeed have cause to tremble and to be afraid, because it would mean the decay of justice, judgment, and mercy. It would mean that God's mercy had been withdrawn from us. But our crises are evidences of God's judgment against the present world order, and we had better see them as such; they are evidences of the decay and approaching collapse of world humanism and its dreams.

Look to your foundations: if they are being shaken, you are in the wrong camp, or else you are placing your trust in what must pass away.

CHALCEDON REPORT NO. 121
September, 1975

Communism does not need to defend itself militarily in the same way as do other forms of politics, because it is usually on both sides of every border. It is on the march in enemy territory as a militant faith. Its real strength is its religious appeal. However, as a false religion, unable to deliver on its promises, its defeat begins wherever it is victorious, in that a disillusioned people then must be kept in suppression by force. It is thus destined to become one of the biggest failures of the twentieth century.

Wherever a people rely on the military as their first line of defense, they are lost. Military strength is a necessity, but a reliance on it for security is a disaster. If men rely on the sword for their defense, our Lord made clear, they shall perish by the sword (Matt. 26:52), because "Man shall not live by bread alone, but by every word that proceedeth out of the mouth of God" (Matt. 4:4).

The first line of defense is a true and living faith. In the nineteenth century, when the U.S. had little military power except in wartime, U.S. power moved men all over the world, and America was the dream and ideal of millions. In those years, the U.S. peace-time army numbered from 200 to a maximum of 20,000 shortly before World War I, yet its influence made

European and Asian autocracies afraid because of the "subversive" infiltration of American beliefs and practices. In every situation of need, American aid, not from the federal government but from the people, was a decisive factor in every area of the world. As against defense by military power, the American strength then was a strong offensive by means of a sense of Christian mission. Earlier, Christian Europe had commanded the world with that sense of mission and power, then America.

A primary reliance on military (or police) defense is the last resort of impotent men. Where men's minds and passions see force as the essential answer, it means that faith, while professed, is lost. The cry of, "*kill the* (black, white, yellow, Communist, Fascist, or what-have-you) *bastards*," is the mark of impotent men, with no sense of mission and no faith to command themselves or others.

When a century ago, Sir Samuel Baker took his beautiful and protected bride into the heart of Africa to search for the sources of the Nile, his companions were all pagan and murderous Arabs and blacks who determined to rob and kill the Bakers at the first opportunity. They never did. Baker's sublime sense of mission and command held them in awe. At the least sign of trouble, he lectured them like an earnest Sunday School teacher putting a disorderly class in its place. His aura of power was enough to command them.

Western man now has instead an aura of fear and of greed. He thinks of himself only, and his only mission is self-security. He wants to be left alone, to have privacy, his pleasures, and his own way. He cannot command himself, let alone a world. He can be in the majority in a country and still lose. Before he acts to defend anything, he asks himself, "Will they come after me if I lose?" When this is true, a man is already dead within, and already a prisoner.

The Puritans, as against the usurping power of the king, Charles I, made their standard, "The crown rights of King Jesus." The Puritans at their maximum strength were four percent of England, but the crown rights of the monarchy fell before them. When they began to think more of the rights of their church and their interests than of Christ the King, the Puritans also failed.

The key thus is return to a sense of Christian mission and to a faithful application of God's law to every area of life. St. Patrick's greatness was that, in an age when the enemy was over-running the land, St. Patrick over-ran the enemy. He set out to convert his enslavers and enemies, and he made of pagan Ireland one of the greatest Christian cultures the world has known and the great missionary force on the continent. More able men than St. Patrick failed because they hated and bewailed the savage enemy. St. Patrick converted and commanded them.

Impotent men give impotent answers. Leave them alone and pass them by.

God's regenerating power and His law give man power, estate, and calling. To be a redeemed man and to have God's law is to have the plan of conquest and dominion and the power to execute it.

Remember too before you call yourself a Christian that *God has no impotent sons*. He has suffering and sometimes martyred sons, but never impotent, and ultimately always victorious sons.

There are hundreds of millions of peoples in Communist countries who hate Marxists and wish them dead: such people, impotent and self-destructive in their hatred, are easily cowed and controlled. The underground church is a far greater problem: it is busy trying to convert its oppressors, and often succeeding. The Communists realize that they have little to fear from hatred: it is too deeply grounded in fear to be other than impotent. It is Christian faith which is for them the menace. "Holy fools" are aggressive and confident, and everywhere at work.

Well, where do you stand in all of this? Have you made it your mission to fear and to hate? (We may hear from you then, an angry, hateful, and of course, anonymous note!) Or is it your estate and calling to believe and obey the Lord, and to exercise dominion in His name?

CHALCEDON REPORT NO. 122
October, 1975

Modern man has often little pleasure in *work* because he has no sense of *estate* and *calling*. Without this, work for him is meaningless, and simply a chore to be performed.

The changed view of work was rather sharply manifested in Massachusetts, once the home of the Puritans and their dedication to work, in a senatorial election of the 1960s. One candidate was Edward Moore (Ted) Kennedy. An opponent charged that Kennedy had never worked a day in his life, an accurate statement and one which he felt would disqualify Kennedy in the minds of voters. The next day, an Irish working-man expressed a popular sentiment to Kennedy: "Teddy, me boy, you haven't missed a thing." As Olsen reports, "The election was a runaway. The opponent learned too late that Edward Moore Kennedy's appeal was *precisely* that he had never worked a day in his life." This placed him on a higher and princely plane. (Jack Olsen: *The Bridge at Chappaquiddick*, p. 9. New York: Ace Books, 1970.)

In 19th century America, men who retired in good health or lived off inherited income often left the United States, because the contempt for non-working able-bodied men was very great. In 20th century America, such men became presidents and presidential candidates. The change is indeed a dramatic one.

It is also an evidence of a radically different religious situation. The reality principle has given way to a pleasure principle. Men live to enjoy themselves, and work is an ugly necessity which, hopefully, civilization will eliminate. Remember, all over the world during the 1960s, rioting students charged that work was unnecessary and constituted a form of conspiracy to keep man enslaved.

The lack of Christian faith has meant not only a decline in purposive activity or work, but also a radical lack of elementary standards. James Bacon commented this year in his column on the insanity resulting from a lack of standards, as it appears in "sex magazines", heavily produced now in Europe and America. An advertisement in the "personals" column of one such periodical read: "Couple who dig whips, branding irons, handcuffs and snakes wants to meet new friends. No weirdos, please." (*Los Angeles Herald-Examiner*, Monday, June 9, 1975, p. A-10.)

Where standards are gone, meaning is gone, and, without meaning, work is pointless. Not surprisingly, the ancient proverb, "It is better to work for nothing than to sit idle," is very much forgotten today. Such a statement has meaning only in a world where purpose and activity can have meaning.

All of this means that people find a candidate who does not need to work very appealing, having all the romance of Camelot and story-book princes, as Olsen noted of Kennedy. It means that work begins to loom in their minds as a form of oppression. For the early socialists, such as Marx and Engels, the working man was by definition an oppressed man because he had to work for his living. This attitude has since become commonplace.

Such an attitude towards work leads to a decline in productivity. It also leads to an evasion of work, to welfarism and drifting. In the United States, in 1974 and 1975, the number of Americans supported by taxes (government employees, the disabled, servicemen, the unemployed, those on welfare, and those on social security) comes to 80.65 million. Workers in the private sector number 71.65 million, and many of these are in services rather than production.

As work declines in importance, and the workers decline in numbers, society has two alternatives. The first, already in operation, is to compel, by taxation and sometimes by totalitarian measures as well, the minority to support the majority, or to put the non-working majority to work by compulsion. In the Soviet Union, the latter course prevails: there is, technically, no unemployment, but there is not much production either. Without the help of the West, the Soviet Union would collapse. The second possibility is radical collapse, as the whole society falls apart because it is both ungovernable and non-working. Both alternatives are ugly ones. The first is now operative, and the second a growing possibility.

Neither offers any solution. Only by a return to a theology of work, i.e., of estate and calling, and a theology of rest, or of the Sabbath, can man be both productive and relaxed. This makes all the more urgent the reconstruction of all things in terms of a Biblical faith, with a restored doctrine of estate and calling.

Work is the key to dominion, and, ultimately, the productive and competent will survive and command. The modern perspective, which lionizes the non-working (F. D. Roosevelt, the Kennedys, Rockefeller, etc.), is without a future. Its menace is that it can command people and their allegiance. Its failure is that it destroys productivity.

To believe that the immediate future is a troubled one is common sense; to believe that the future is a doomed one for man is practical atheism: it is a denial that God's order governs creation and makes, in the long run, any condition of life untenable other than that which conforms to the law of God. We have been called, not to defeat nor to slavery, but to victory and dominion.

CHALCEDON REPORT NO. 123
November, 1975

The origins of socialism in the modern world are deeply rooted in oriental thought, in Hinduism and Buddhism in particular. With the Enlightenment, modern man began to show great interest in Far Eastern thought, because he believed that he found therein the "natural" religion he felt was basic to all men. Few people today appreciate the extent to which 18th century man was interested in India and especially China. This interest led to the very extensive work in the 19th century, by Friedrich Max Muller and others, in translating and interpreting the philosophies of the Far Fast.

The idea of "natural" religion died, but what remained from these studies was the essential relativism of Far Eastern philosophy. Because of the despair of truth, these philosophies insisted on the meaninglessness of standards and values, discriminations and distinctions, and the ultimate oneness of all things. Whereas Christianity established distinctions and requires a division between God and sin, good and evil, the saved and the lost (Matt. 10:34-35), Buddhism, for example, works to overcome divisions. Kwan-yin, the Chinese goddess of mercy, was held to affirm that she could not enter paradise as long as any human beings were excluded. "Never will I receive individual salvation," she is supposed to affirm, and stands outside the gates of heaven waiting for the last man to come in. Kwan-yin was very popular with Western liberals, and Unitarian leaders like M. D. Conway, in the 19th century, made much of her equalitarian creed.

Their point was well taken. If Biblical faith is not true, then the total inclusiveness and equalitarianism of Kwan-yin is the logical faith. All things being relative and equally meaningless, they are also equally meaningful if we give them any relative meaning or value.

It is thus easy to see why, in their rebellion against Christianity, modern men, from the 18th century to the present, have been so intensely interested in Oriental religions and philosophies. Some of them have sounded like children of Kwan-yin, so faithfully have they reproduced her philosophy. Thus the Socialist leader of U.S. World War I days, Eugene Debs, thrilled the American gurus and faithful with his passionate equalitarianism. Called the "Billy Sunday of Socialism," Debs would affirm his faith with intense fervor: "While there is a lower class, I am of it. While there is a soul in prison I am not free." This is a denial of the validity of criminal law; it means all men and all acts are equal. Debs did not go that far, but men since then have done so, and the result is the progressive defense and "vindication" of the criminal, and the reduction and disarming of the law-abiding.

In July, 1975, Doris L. Dolan, founder and president of Citizens for Law Enforcement Needs, a California based organization, declared, "Crime is caused by criminals, and we, as law-abiding citizens, have the absolute right to be free of the criminal element - I am brokenhearted about the things I have witnessed and learned over these past 10 years of citizen involvement in the workings of the judiciary system. Our organization has files bulging with statistics on criminal activities and reasons why crime has reached epidemic proportions as recorded today. We have determined that a majority of the United States Supreme Court members, as well as a California Supreme Court majority, and some legislators, do not understand the right of the citizen to be free of the criminal element. They understand nothing but the right of the criminal." (*The News*, Van Nuys, Calif., Sunday, July 25, 1975, p. 25A.)

This situation should not surprise us. Because Biblical faith and law have been undermined, modern man tends increasingly to view things with the eyes of Kwan-yin rather than Christ, equalizing good and evil rather than establishing justice and stamping out evil. Meanwhile, as socialism is imported into the Far East, it is readily accepted, because, however much Westernized, it is simply the logical development of Far Eastern philosophies. Socialism will prevail in the East and West alike until its underlying relativism is rejected in favor of Biblical faith.

The answers thus are not to be found in the ballot-box. Ballots simply express the minds and faiths of men. The problem is in essence religious. We can summarize it as Kwan-yin, or Christ. Are all things relative, or is there an absolute God with an unchanging word? How we answer this question will determine our lives and our politics. If we deny God's justice and law, we must eventually accept Kwan-yin's democracy of good and evil.

Kwan-yin supposedly cannot and will not enter paradise until every last man is included. How beautiful this sounds to our modern sentimental relativists. However, when every last man enters, it will not be paradise but hell! Meanwhile, the application of this Kwan-yin principle is turning earth into hell. It denies justice, demolishes law, and, by mercy to the vicious, is merciless to the law-abiding. The rot of relativism cannot be eliminated by ballots and laws: it requires a return to Biblical faith, regeneration in Christ, and a society established on God's law. There is no substitute for the Truth.

CHALCEDON REPORT NO. 124
December, 1975

Alexander Dolgun's Story, *An American in the Gulag*, (New York: Knopf, 1975), reports a fact referred to by many prisoners of Marxist regimes. On trying to correct blatant misrepresentations by his inquisitor, Dolgun was told, "You say we have made a mistake. I tell you we never make mistakes" (p. 18). We cannot grasp the direction of modern statism unless we recognize that this declaration, openly stated by Marxism, is basic to all humanistic statism.

Humanistic sociology since Comte has denied the validity to modern man of the idea of *meaning*. *Meaning* belongs, it is held, to the old world of religion and myth, and to the more recent but now dead world of philosophy and the metaphysical quest for understanding. In the new era, there must be no concern with meaning; man's society must not be religious but technological; things must be judged, not in terms of good and evil but in terms of utility and pragmatism. All things are relative to the purposes of "society." If society, re-defined as the state, says that you and I are better off, for the general welfare, in a prison camp, there is then no mistake, because there can be no standard or criterion above the actions of the state to judge it. *Meaning* is declared dead, and therefore good and evil are non-existent as anything beyond and over the state.

Modern art has adopted this same faith. As a result, it renounces all objective meaning and protests against it. We are told that we must not ask of any work of art, "What does this mean?", but, rather, "What personal or social experience does it evoke in me?" There can thus be no lasting works of art, in terms of this theory, but purely contemporary ones. The art world is thus moving towards a theory of disposable art, which, like paper tissue, is to be used when needed, and then discarded.

But, in such a world, all meaning is denied, and therefore man too is disposable; man is there to be used by the state when needed, and then promptly discarded. Alexandr I. Solzhenitsyn, in *The Gulag Archipelago 1918-1956* (New York: Harper & Row, 1973), is really telling us about the Marxist application of this modern theory, *The Doctrine of Disposable Man*. If people were needed for a new construction plan in Siberia or elsewhere, as much as one fourth of Leningrad was arrested and transported to the slave labor camps (pp. 13, 58). The people were impotent in the face of this: they tried to find the meaning of their arrests, but there was no meaning! There was only pragmatism, utility, and terror.

Since Darwin, meaning is dead in the modern world, and with it, all ideas of good and evil. This is the same as proclaiming *the death of man*, because man cannot live without meaning. All attempts to cope with the growing collapse of the modern age are futile, because there is nothing in humanism and the doctrine of evolution which makes possible a restoration of cosmic meaning. As a result, man becomes more lawless, anarchistic, and senseless as he accepts the modern world view's picture of himself. He becomes in his own eyes only a meaningless bundle of urges and drives seeking existential satisfaction. Disposable Man then lashes out at the world and civilization around him: if man is disposable, then all things else must be made disposable, and must be smashed.

As against all this, St. John declares of Christ, "All things were made by him; and without him was not any thing made that was made. In him was life; and the life was the light of man" (John 1:3-4). Not Disposable Man, but Religious Man, not a meaningless world, but a universe of total meaning, this is the teaching of Scripture and the reality of the cosmos. Because *all* things were made by Him, all things, being totally the handiwork of an absolute and perfect purpose and decree, have a total meaning. There is not a meaningless nor a disposable fact in the universe. Everything has meaning, God's meaning, and the direction of all things is neither death nor meaninglessness, but the triumph of God's glorious purpose and plan.

The doctrine of Disposable Man is suicidal, and the art and culture of such a doctrine races into disaster and death. It has no future. The idea of a future belongs to the world of meaning, purpose, and direction. For this reason, humanism, and its age of the state, is doomed. It builds on sand, and creating its own storms of judgment, collapses under the storms. Only men and civilizations which build on the Rock, Jesus Christ, can endure (Matt. 7:24-29). As men become more epistemologically self-conscious, the only possible post-Christian "culture" is the graveyard, because culture is a religious fact and presupposes faith, meaning, purpose, and direction. Thus, as the old pagan forms of humanism erode, the only possible form of civilization and culture is increasingly manifest: it can only be a Christian culture, one firmly rooted in the whole counsel of God and His law-word. If you are not working to reconstruct all things in terms of the word of God, you are headed for the graveyard of history and God's judgement.

CHALCEDON REPORT NO. 125
January, 1976

The struggle to command history is an intense one in our day, with a variety of groups contending for mastery, some essentially political in organization and others religious. This struggle for power in history is the attempt by men to impose their ideas and plans on to history and to re-direct the world in terms of their purposes.

There are two aspects to history that men can neglect only at the risk of becoming a failure in history. These are *permanence* and *change*. By *permanence* we mean those standards and values which are eternal in nature and absolute, God-given and unchanging. Direction and meaning are given to history by the absolutes which govern it. God as the Lord of history and the maker of all things alone can give an unchanging and absolute law to it. *Change* has reference to development and program within history. Change is possible because permanence is basic to it, i.e., there are standards and absolutes which require that men and nations repent, grow, develop, and mature. To deny either permanence or change is to become eventually irrelevant to history. Old China once was ahead of the West, but its acceptance of total relativism meant a denial that absolutes exist; Taoism and Confucianism, and, later, Buddhism, denied absolutes and all permanence. In so doing, they made change meaningless, because there was then no standard which required change. As a result, Chinese civilization stagnated, except where conquerors briefly imposed their will on it. Relativism destroyed the meaning of both permanence and change.

In the Western world, the church has too often been infected by neoplatonism and has not seen the necessity of change and has stressed essentially permanence. The result of such faith has been to make the church irrelevant. The same has been true too often of political conservatives. They have stressed permanence and resisted change. Moreover, their idea of permanence has been commonly defective, humanistic rather than godly. By permanence they have been prone to mean simply the world up to yesterday, not the Lord and His word.

Liberals and radicals, political and religious, have stressed change, and this has given them a great advantage in capturing the mind and imagination of youth. The idealism of youth and its dissatisfaction with accepted evils leads it to an uncritical demand for change, and the result is a boon to the prophets of change. Since change is inevitable, the champions of change come to believe in the inevitability of their doctrine of change, an entirely different matter. Moreover, change is mistakenly identified with progress, whereas some changes are an obstacle to progress. Furthermore, faith in change breaks down when a society loses its trust in absolutes. Nothing then has meaning, and change and permanence are alike meaningless and empty concepts.

Biblical faith alone does justice to both permanence and change. It declares the triune God to be the sole and absolute source of all true law, interpretation, and meaning. It is He who creates, predestines, and governs all creation and history. Change is required by His word. *First*, man must subdue the earth and exercise dominion over it under God and in terms of His word (Gen. 1:26-28). This requires change, development, and growth. *Second*, His word requires change within ourselves, since we are fallen creatures and cannot put our creation mandate properly into force apart from His regenerating power. Change is thus required of both man and his world in terms of God's law and calling. Only Biblical faith does justice to history's requirements for permanence and change.

The duty of the Christian is thus to know and understand the word of permanence, God's word, and to apply its requirements of change to himself and the world, and to every area and aspect thereof. This means godly reconstruction.

Non-Christian thought cannot do justice to history. It can only prevail for a time where the church defaults and defects from Biblical faith. In our time in particular, political and religious groups are increasingly incompetent in their grasp of history, in their defective views of permanence, and change. Having forsaken God, they have forsaken the command of history, and the result is our growing collapse and the rudderless drift of the nations from one crisis into another. Men do not command history now but are more and more commanded by it. The mood of men becomes one of irrelevance and impotence. Instead of God's Dominion Man, we have instead our modern Disposable Man, whose function is trifling and whose life is readily dispensable.

God did not make man to be disposable. The idea of Disposable Man is a human creation, and a deadly one. God created man in His own image to be the lord of creation under God, to exercise dominion. Man was given estate and calling and made the crown of creation. God made man the necessary point in history, the bearer of God's plan, and He made the incarnation a means of recalling and regenerating man in terms of His purpose and plan.

The future then cannot be in doubt. Dominion Man will prevail over Disposable Man. The issue then is us: which man are we? Disposable Man, or Dominion Man?

CHALCEDON REPORT NO. 126
February, 1976

In recent years, there has been a parallel growth of the idea of human rights and bureaucracy. This common growth has been a closely related fact, so much so that Peter Berger, Brigitte Berger and Hansfried Kellner, in *The Homeless Mind* (1973), speak of "bureaucratically identifiable rights." There must, they point out, be some bureaucracy to complain to (the humanist version of prayer), and bureaucratic procedures to enforce rights. "Thus there is a progression from the notion of universal human rights to the notion of a necessary universal bureaucracy. The United Nations may be seen as a somewhat ironic anticipation of this cosmological vision of bureaucracy" (p. 115). In brief, humanism's emphasis on human rights leads to the nightmare world of a totalitarian bureaucracy and George Orwell's 1984. Why? It is important for us to understand this relationship, because our future depends on it.

There must be, and is, in every system of thought and social order, a sovereign power, a determiner, a central, controlling agency. or else there is no cosmos, unity, or order possible, only chaos and confusion. If that power is the triune God, then, while man can flounder in evil, confusion, and disorder because of his sin, he is still able, on the human level, in history, to assert himself against all other powers. The history of Christendom has often been marred by great evils, but it has been, to a degree unequalled elsewhere, volatile, rich in struggle, contention, and growth. It has resisted stratification and petrifaction. We can disagree strongly with the medieval English rebels, and still must recognize the intensely Christian framework of their revolt, when they opposed the lords of the realm with their battle-cry,

> When Adam delved, and Eve span,
> Who was then the gentleman?

To defend themselves against tyranny, they had God's yardstick to apply to all man-made orders. Moreover, even in defeat they had the assurance of faith that, since God is the Lord of history, in time their cause would triumph. God's word and law gave them a court of appeals against man, and a freedom from any total claim by man.

In humanism, man is his own god, and the state exercises the deity as the general will of man. Therefore, human rights require man, i.e., collective man as the state, to assure them. God is omnipotent, and, in time, His purposes shall prevail in history. The state as the new god, in order to assure the triumph of the human rights it proclaims, must gain greater power over man, it must become omnipotent. As a result, in the name of human rights, man is obliterated. The more fully the state and its bureaucracy become man's champion, as in Marxism, the greater the oppression of man.

In the Christian scheme of things, man's progress depends on his struggle with sin, in himself and in the world, so that, by the grace of God, he grows in freedom and dominion and his ability to exercise knowledge, righteousness, and holiness. In the humanistic scheme of things, human rights requires that a bureaucracy control man for his welfare and "freedom", so that, as Orwell saw, slavery becomes freedom.

We may therefore rail as much as we choose against the growth of bureaucracy. But it will only continue to grow as long as man remains a humanist. There must be a center to and a governing power in life, and, for humanism, the choice is between anarchism, every man is his own god, and the bureaucratic state. Human rights require the state as god to assure them.

As a result, complaints against the inefficiency of the bureaucracy usually lead to the creation of more bureaucracy, because more power must be handed to this new god to make him function. But this is not all. Just as the God of Scripture is all-knowing, so the new god must have a total knowledge of his subjects, and must build up a data bank on all of them. The kind of bureaucracy envisioned by some would require the state to expand more than is humanly possible in order to have the knowledge for full planning power. The future of all bureaucracies headed in that direction is a growing incompetence rather than power.

The Biblical answer is not bureaucracy but God, man under God, stumbling, growing, developing in history, knowing that his essential bill of rights is the word of God. It is not the state but the word of God which has the binding word. The purpose of the stumbling, painful growth which freedom under God makes possible is the development of Dominion Man. A bureaucracy reduces man to the status of Disposable Man, something to be used to create the supposedly glorious future. Stalin callously held that it was necessary to scramble some eggs, i.e., liquidate millions, in order to make an omelet, to create the socialist paradise. This is the grim irony of humanism: its doctrine of human rights becomes an instrument for the destruction of man. The more vocal the cry for human rights becomes in our day, the more fearful modern man rightly is, because each legal "gain" in his battle increases the powers of the bureaucracy over him. The bureaucracy grows, but not his freedom, his safety, or his "rights." Disposable Man has no rights.

CHALCEDON REPORT NO. 127
March, 1976

In the modern era, reform has very often been a prelude to revolution, not because the reforms have not been needed, but because they have been stiffly rational in conception rather than realistic. The humanistic reformers have erred badly, *first*, in developing rational programs for reform which are rootless and unrelated to the content of men's lives. Thus, instead of satisfying those whom they were intended to help, the reforms have only left them more disgruntled. The advances have often been very real, but they have not been welcome. *Second*, the humanist has concluded that the life of reason and of rational freedom is the most desirable life, but, unhappily, most people have preferred bondage, and their dream, like that of all slaves, is of bondage with plenty.

An example of a reform which aggravated discontent was the abolition of serfdom in tsarist Russia. It was a triumph of liberalism, but it created conditions which became a breeding ground for disaster. Serfdom in Russia was a modern product, only a couple of centuries old. Some serfs lived better than others, but most would have envied the life of an American slave. Their huts were without windows or chimneys, and without any artificial light, except for the limited use of bits of wood and tallow candles. The freezing cold outside made it necessary to keep new-born calves indoors. The serf, however wretched, had some security. Also, he regarded all of the lord's land as in some sense his also. "Freedom" handed him over to the world of modern statism and taxation. He was at once taxed, and, if he lacked the income to pay his taxes, he was imprisoned for at least two weeks, and then, if no funds were forthcoming, everything he had was sold, down to the family milk-cow and chickens. If he had nothing, or if the sale failed to produce enough, he worked off the taxes in forced labor wherever the state officials chose to send him.

In 1856, Alexander II told the aristocracy of Moscow, in preparing them for the emancipation of the serfs, "Reforms must come from above unless one wishes them to come from below." Unfortunately, the reforms from above came as disruptions and further tyranny to the serfs, and a distrust of everyone above developed.

Reforms rationally conceived at the top are too often seen as disruptive and threatening to those below, and the result is the creation of a rootless mob below, whose life-style has been broken, their loyalties shattered, and their conditions all too little improved. Statistically, the ex-serfs were in a much better condition. Realistically, they were discontented and felt cheated, and their discontent made it possible later for professional revolutionists to take over the country.

Humanism has all too often failed to distinguish between reason and rationalism. Reason is a necessary tool in man's exercise of dominion, and it is basic to knowledge, and is inseparable from righteousness, which requires, among other things, the intelligent understanding of and commitment to God's law. Rationalism is the rigid application of man's idea of reason to reality as the ultimate yardstick and criterion, whereas godly reason recognizes that it is the mind and reason of God which is ultimate. Rationalism thus tries to remake the world in its own image, after its own reason, and its end result is a collapse into irrationalism. It forces a product of man's mind onto reality in order to make reality man's creation; in the insane this is unreason, whereas in humanistic planners it is irrationalism.

Rationalism once believed that the universe to some degree corresponded to man's reason, but now, with pragmatism and existentialism, it no longer believes this. The only area of rationality is in the mind of man, but, in the light of Freud and Skinner, modern humanism cannot place much trust in even that faint glimmer of rationality. It is held, however, that by some miracle, rationality will prevail in an elite group of scientific planners and through them conquer humanity and the universe. As the new gods of creation, by whose fiat word the world is to be remade, they logically regard humanity as it is, as the realm of chaos. Out of this chaos, light and order are to be brought forth by their supposedly sovereign word.

But will it? The new proverbs of humanism are marked by a wry and radical pessimism. "If anything can go wrong, it will." "If you see light at the end of the tunnel, it's not the sun but a train coming." "In the long run, we are all dead." "A fool and his hope are soon parted." There is an increasing cynicism about all humanistic reform plans, and modern man is more and more concerned with only enough peace to enjoy himself. The philosophy is close to that of ancient Rome: "let us eat, drink, and be merry, for tomorrow we die." Give us, more and more men say, not reform and change, but a respite.

But history requires change; it requires movement. Time does not recess so that an era can take time for play. Humanism is in power, but it cannot function as the motive force for action, production, and change. Its troops are no longer eager for orders, but rather eager for discharge.

The time is ripe for a strong and virile Christianity, one firmly committed to Biblical law, to command the day. Nothing else can provide a comparable motive force for the reconstruction of all things. Change is certain, but whether or not it will be progress depends on who controls it.

THE SEARCH FOR A HUMANISTIC EDEN

Almost weekly, we read of a delegation of congressmen, congresswomen, diplomats, actors, actresses, professors and others who have made a trip to Red China speak glowingly of the great accomplishments of this ostensible paradise. The real horror of Red China was effectively set forth by Tung Chi-Ping and Humphrey Evans a few short years ago in *The Thought Revolution*. Why the insistence that a new world order exists in that nightmare world? And why the shift of liberal hope from the Soviet Union to Red China?

Only lately have the illusions concerning the Soviet Union begun to wane. Alexander Sozhenitsyn's *Gulag Archipelago*, Vols. I and II, have contributed greatly to that end. But the facts were well known long before his day. They were described amply in the 1920's and 30's and thereafter. Why the rejection of those facts? In the 1930's, I heard professors repeatedly describe Stalin as a stable, conservative and humane force as against Trotsky. Then in the late 1950's and the 1960's, the successors of Stalin were presented as less repressive and more humane than Stalin. In both cases, they were wrong.

The humanistic presupposition is this: what man decrees *must* be, *will* be. The Marxists in Russia, as true humanists, decreed the birth of a new world order, a humanistic order. True, Stalin said, and the humanists everywhere echoed, you can't make an omelet without breaking the eggs, so the breaking of the eggs, tens of millions of men, was casually accepted as the road to the perfect omelet, the humanist paradise.

But by the 1970's, it was beginning to be obvious that the omelet smelled badly. The trouble with the Soviet Union, the humanists apologized, is too much bureaucracy. This evades, of course, the heart of the matter, the evil of the humanist dream. The hope was retained; it was simply transferred to Red China, always with a hope that the Soviet Union will get back on the track again.

The roots of this insanity are in Hegel, with his great humanistic first principle: the rational is the real. What man decrees is logically necessary will become reality. On this principle, men everywhere are being murdered to make the humanistic illusion a reality. The collapse of this fantasy, this insanity, is inevitable. Only what God decrees stands. There is no other reality. The grandiose and murderous fantasies of humanism are doomed.

THE FAILURES OF HUMANISTIC SALVATION

Instead of being depressed by current events, we have every reason as Christians to feel vindicated. On all sides we see the failures of humanistic plans of salvation.

Let us glance at a few examples of such failures. The idea that dollars can save the world is dying a grim and painful death. Billions of dollars have been poured out as a salve for all human ills, and, instead of a grateful and redeemed world, we see in 1976 a far more critical world problem that in 1946. Salvation by military power and interventionism has been tried by most of the great powers with little success as far as man's basic problems are concerned, and with much loss of life and ill-will. Both the U.S.A. and the U.S.S.R. are now the objects of ill-will and the subjects of self-doubt because of their costly interventionism.

Salvation by psychiatric and psychological rehabilitation has not solved the problem of crime but only aggravated it. Salvation by education, that most popular doctrine, has created instead a generation and more of new barbarians. Salvation by statist law, applied by messianic legislators and judges, is shattering the fabric of society. Salvation by monetary manipulation is destroying money and with it sound economic wealth.

Seeing these things and more should encourage and strengthen our hearts, because they demonstrate the growing decay and collapse of humanism. They stress all the more the need to return to God's plan, redemption through His Son, and then the application of His law, as the ordained plan of conquest whereby covenant man, as God's king, priest, and prophet in Christ, will exercise dominion over every area of life and thought to the glory of the triune God. There is no other valid answer, and current events are a dramatic demonstration of this. If we are too distressed over these events, we need to ask ourselves the question: Are we pulling for the wrong side?

CHALCEDON REPORT NO. 128
April, 1976

In 1943, a novel, bitterly fought against by Western pro-communists, saw the crisis of civilization in the fact that its first faith, Christianity, was virtually gone, and the second, free-thought or humanism, was also fading. "Nothing exists that can fill the chasm: there is no third faith!" wrote Mark Aldanov in *The Fifth Seal*. His character, Vermandois observed, "Humanity is marching toward a dumping ground." Men could resign themselves to it, or choose a fairy tale pleasing to themselves and use it to proclaim "that the dumping ground is in reality a crystal palace." In any case, the future meant the dumping ground.

Now a dumping ground, like every trash pile, has a characteristic feature: nothing has any relationship to anything around it. Things are simply dumped there, whether worthless or still usable, without any rule or any meaningful relationship to things next to them. Philosophically speaking, we can say that every dumping ground or trash pile gives us an excellent example of Existentialism. Nothing derives meaning or significance from anything around it. There are no rules governing relationships or imposing an order. There is no philosophy governing all the facts in the dump. Each piece of junk must develop its own philosophy of existence or else have none.

A plain-spoken expression of this philosophy came to light in 1975 through a follower of Charles Manson. Lynette "Squeaky" Fromme, the 27 year old girl who tied to assassinate President Ford, declared to her captors, "If you have no philosophy, you don't have any rules." By philosophy Lynette Fromme meant a faith which prescribes rules binding on all people, a universal morality and law. Existentialism is a philosophy which denies this emphatically, and existentialism, whether held formally or informally, is the refining faith of the 20th century.

In *Defiance, A Radical Review #1* (1970), one of the key declarations was simply this: "Good News! 2 and 2 no longer make 4." The Revolution, one writer held, had already occurred. He was right, of course. The principles of relativism, of existentialism, i.e., the philosophies of the dumping ground, have triumphed. When I cite the *Defiance* gospel to some, they are shocked: 2 and 2 do make 4, they insist. However, when pressed about God's law, it is clear that they are existentialists about everything except a few practical items like arithmetic. Most 20th century men are to some degree existentialists; they object only when younger existentialists go a little further than they themselves are prepared to go.

The dumping ground future predicted by Aldanov's Vermandois is increasingly apparent to more and more intellectuals and youths. Their answer is to look for that third faith. Hence the deep interest in Oriental religions, primitive faiths, magic, witchcraft, occultism, and much else. On all fronts, the religious interest is intense, but it is futile. All the "new" third faiths are simply variations on a common theme, humanism. I know very casually one such seeker, a brilliant and attractive woman, who regularly finds the great answer in some new form of this old faith, and then, before finding another, is suicidally pessimistic. For her, the one alternative never to be considered in her quest is Biblical faith. Not surprisingly, each new collapse drives her closer to suicide, to her own dumping ground.

Now more than once civilization has turned itself into a dump-heap by its adoption of some form of moral relativism, although never so drastically as in the 20th century. There is a common consequence to every such event in history. Our Lord expressed it thus: "For wheresoever the carcass is, there will the eagles be gathered together" (Matt. 24:28). When civilization turns itself into a garbage dump, there the vultures will gather, and then too the vulture nations have an opportunity to gain ascendancy.

Certainly in our time men seem determined to turn history into a dumping ground, and the vultures are not lacking on the scene. The second faith, humanism, is morally bankrupt: existentialism is simply its logical conclusion. There is no third faith, and there is too little left of the first faith to be a factor in the minds of vultures. The churches have virtually all succumbed to the influences of the second faith, humanism. But the first faith, Christianity, alone offers hope. Humanism has failed, because it has been applied and developed. Christianity has not failed; rather, it has been abandoned for humanism disguised sometimes as Christianity.

If the dumping ground and the vultures, both products of humanism, are to be avoided, it will only be in terms of Biblical faith. Existentialism can only destroy and negate: it must deny all meanings and relationships in order to affirm the autonomy and the ultimacy of humanistic man. Dotson Rader, writing also in *Defiance*, stated it clearly: "to destroy all limits is, in a perverse sense, to be truly free. To destroy is to *feel* free."

Reconstruction is only possible on radically alien terms, terms which make basic not man's feelings or experience, but God's atonement and God's law. Churchmen who deny the validity of God's law are humanists: they make man's feelings and experience basic to the faith rather that Christ's work and man's required response of faith and obedience.

The only way that the vultures can be exorcised from civilization is by the road away from the dumping ground, from humanism or existentialism, to a full-orbed and militant Biblical faith.

Existentialist man can never be Dominion Man on his own terms. He has no world except himself, no meaning except his will, and no arena of operation except a vacuum. The will of existentialist man is to be god, but even Sartre, the foremost existentialist, saw this goal and man himself as a "futile passion."

Godly reconstruction by Dominion Man has as its instrument Biblical law. God's plan of conquest. It provides for the re-ordering of every area of life in terms of God's sovereign word and purpose, and for the establishment of man as king, priest, and prophet in Christ over the earth.

Man has a "choice": to be a pretended god and sovereign on a dump-heap, surrounded by waiting vultures, or a Dominion Man in Christ over the earth. In either case, there is only one sovereign, God. That can never change: it is man who must.

CHALCEDON REPORT NO. 129
May, 1976

It amazes me, as I travel, how many people who are Christians will attack the idea of laissez-faire as though it represents some pagan abomination. Not only that, but they mistakenly assume that modern corporate structures are dedicated to laissez-faire, when in fact, with a very few exceptions, most are intensely hostile to it.

What is involved in the doctrine of laissez-faire, the idea of built-in laws which ensure that freedom will produce the best results? What lies behind the "Invisible Hand" doctrine? Laissez-faire is a secularized form of the Biblical doctrine of Providence. The Bible makes clear that God is sovereign Lord and Creator, and that His law and predestinating counsel absolutely govern all things, so that all creation moves, not in terms of chance or chaos, but in terms of God's master plan. Faith in this plan and purpose means that it is not man's plan but God's which must govern reality. The consequences of such a faith, as developed by such a medieval thinker as Bishop Oresme, were the theoretical foundations of classical economics.

Modern man, however, wanted the consequences of God's being and government, but not God Himself. As a result, the modern era shifted the emphasis from Biblical law to natural law, and from Providence to laissez-faire. In writing about laissez-faire, 18th century thinkers were in essence re-formulating the doctrine of Providence to gain the full effect of God without acknowledging God openly. Their adoption of this doctrine of Providence, and their emphasis on it made for a tremendous input of social energy and vitality, as men proceeded to act, in the economic realm and elsewhere, in the assurance of an Invisible Hand which provided a total and absolutely providential government. However secular their interest, their work was a major theological development in Western thought. Its ties to the Reformation doctrine of God's sovereignty and decree were very strong, however humanistic the framework of their concern.

Laissez-faire gave men a freedom from church and state, and from the law of institutions, in the name of a higher law. It thus developed to an unprecedented degree the implications of the doctrine of creation. The church had too often sought to act as the visible hand of God in a presumptuous manner, and the state had surpassed the church in playing the role of manifest providence. Laissez-faire placed the institutions in the background and gave the ultimate and active workings of Providence priority. The social implications of this were far-reaching, and the growth created thereby dramatic in its historical consequences.

Laissez-faire, however, collapsed because of its humanistic framework. The logic of humanism continued to develop the implications of its separation from the doctrine of God. This meant that the doctrine of creation had to be dropped. Hegel developed the concept of social evolution, and Darwin applied it to biology and the sciences. With Darwin's acceptance, laissez-faire became an obsolete doctrine. The world of Darwin is a world of chance, a world of meaningless and brute factuality in which whatever develops does so accidentally rather than in terms of a cosmic plan. Social Darwinism could mean a ruthless economic individualism (not laissez-faire), as in Andrew Carnegie, but there is no law beyond man to govern him. It can lead to economic interventionism and socialism, as in the Rockefellers and others, but again it is a human decision, not an aspect of a cosmic plan.

In a meaningless universe, there is no Invisible Hand, and laissez-faire means a senseless chaos. The implications of Darwinism were quickly grasped. Men like John Stuart Mill moved from laissez-faire into socialism, because no doctrine of Providence was possible in a Darwinian world view.

But man cannot live without a doctrine of Providence. The idea of predestination is an intellectual necessity, because the alternative is a world of total chance and meaninglessness. The doctrine of laissez-faire had shifted the government and decree from God to Nature, while tacitly retaining all the forms of the theological formulation of the doctrine. With Darwin, a further transfer took place. Now the state (or, with libertarians, anarchistic man) became the source of providence and predestination.

The result has been the rise of socialism and economic interventionism. Social planning and control mean that the state now issues the decree of predestination. The providential government of all things has become a function of state, and churchmen solemnly approve of this blasphemy and condemn the mild departures which laissez-faire represented. Not surprisingly, we are in the midst of a major theological decline and collapse, because the heart of the doctrine of God has been transferred to the state. Sovereignty and control now belong to an institution of man, and scientific socialism logically calls for the total control of man. This includes not only economic control but genetic control and engineering.

Even as Scripture, because of the Fall, calls for the re-creation of man in Jesus Christ, so too the modern sovereign, the state, calls for the remaking of man by scientific engineering. Man must be changed from God's creation into the state's creation, and this change is necessary in order to establish the state's sovereignty, so that we can expect more and more emphasis on the re-making of man by science and the state.

Despite its serious defects, laissez-faire had as its great virtue the fact that it did concentrate on the doctrine of Providence. Its failure was that it could not maintain the doctrine of Providence without the Sovereign and absolute God. On the other hand, the church has not been able to defend its doctrine of God when it has abandoned implicitly the doctrine of Providence. As a result, the church condemns itself to impotence. It clings formally to doctrines it castrates in fact. It affirms predestination by God and bows down to predestination by Caesar, by the state.

Where are the theologians who are discussing the implications of the doctrines of creation and providence in terms of the realities of every-day life, in terms of economics, politics, and all things else? The answer is that, outside of Chalcedon, they are almost non-existent. Is it any wonder that we are in trouble? Can we affirm Providence without far-reaching personal, social economic and political consequences? Can we believe in the God of Scripture without such consequences?

The consequences of our day are those of humanism in church and state, in economics, politics, education, and theology. Until we begin to think theologically, the consequences will not change. Are you with us?

CHALCEDON REPORT NO. 130
June, 1976

In 1951, a group of prominent Americans wrote on *The Fabulous Future, America in 1980*. The writers included David Sarnoff, George Meany, Nathan M. Pusey, Earl Warren, Adlai Stevenson, Charles P. Taft, Henry R. Luce, and others of note. They saw as likely by 1980 the global control of climate, a sharing of wealth, and George M. Humphrey, then Secretary of the Treasury, wrote of things to come under the title, "The Future: Sound as a Dollar." This glorious future is possible because "the management of government is in the hands of men of integrity and high moral purpose." Henry R. Luce said that by 1980 World War III "will have happened or been bypassed," but, if it had happened, men would have moved ahead into greater progress.

Luce saw a great change coming in man himself. He saw a "new human nature" ahead, a "new mutation," in man's evolution. This great change would be engineered by man himself. Man would control his own evolution in collaboration with God. The key word for Luce was "evolution." As he pointed out, "The American word, before evolution, was Providence." Precisely. Now, however, a new word, a new gospel, had replaced the old. While man was now a "collaborator" with God, to all practical intent, the new man and his new world would be the handiwork of man.

Earlier, the Providence of God had been naturalized into laissez-faire; Providence had been retained in its workings, but had been disassociated from God. God remained in the system of Adam Smith as the very necessary insurance agency and foundation, indispensable but best left invisible and unmentioned. Darwin's faith in the omnipotence of chance left God unnecessary. In this new world view, all things are held possible, given enough time, for chance to accomplish, and nothing is impossible for chance. Now omnipotence was taken from God and given to chance, or to whatever person or agency could control chance. Man immediately set out, by means of the scientific socialist state, to be that agency, and the result in the 20th century has been the epiphany of the new god, statist man.

With this in mind, it is easy to understand the confidence of the authors of *The Fabulous Future*. They knew the new god well, meeting him as they did daily in their mirrors. They had unlimited confidence in him. The new god has all the benefits the old God lacks, i.e., science, sociology, state-controlled education, and much, much more. The new god is not afraid to intervene directly and thoroughly into human affairs, into every sphere of life by means of a super-imposed controls. Slow, painful trial and error ways are thus obsolete, as well as the necessity for moral decision; a superior agency provides man with the government he needs. The only question in the minds of these new gods is with respect to the people: will they become "a new man...a new mutation," soon enough?

The target date, 1980, is approaching, but the hope set forth gets dimmer. [John von Neumann of the Atomic Energy Commission had predicted in 1955 that in "a few decades hence energy may be free - just like the unmetered air - with coal and oil used mainly as raw materials for organic chemical synthesis."] The new gods have not lacked power: they have governed in almost every nation on earth; they have applied their plan, or their decree of predestination, to one sphere after another. Instead of being content with a mere tithe, as the old God is, the gods have taxed from 40-110% of a man's income, and their paradise only becomes more remote, rather than nearer.

Man's Plan has replaced God's Providence as the governing principle of men and nations, and it is Man's Plan that is failing. Surprisingly, however, the very eloquent praise-singers of Man's Plan come from the churches. Man's Plan seems to all such to be humane; it shows "concern" for humanity and is a logical outgrowth of their "Christian" faith, and so on. Laissez-faire is a dirty word to them and its root doctrine, Providence, a forgotten faith. A city in colonial America was named "Providence," and men once felt secure, not because tax money was available to them, but because Providence under-girded their total being. Now the word is rarely heard, in or out of church. When the church ceases to speak of Providence, it ceases to speak of God.

Why? Providence is the superintendence and care which God exercises over creation; it is God's continuous government over all things in terms of His sovereign lordship, decree, and purpose. Where men trust instead in Man's Plan rather than God's Providence, they are of necessity antinomian: they substitute Man's Law for God's Law. The government is then upon man's shoulders and in man's hands.

In almost all churches today, God is God Emeritus, while Man reigns instead. God is honored by lip service even as He is relegated to the oblivion of retirement. After all, why should the old God interfere with things, when the new god is doing so well. If the new god is failing, it is because the people are not yet new mutations, or are clinging too much to their remnants of the old faith. Besides, the new god has only been at the job for a short time; give me more time, he says, and I will remake all things.

In brief, the new god has his own doctrine of laissez-faire. Leave me alone, he says to the old God and His people. Do not interfere with or sabotage my Plan. To work, it must have no extraneous impediments. Given that freedom from "outside" control (anything from God and man which might distress the Planners), and Paradise will surely come on schedule.

In fact, the authors of *The Fabulous Future* could all but hear the footsteps of Paradise approaching. Now, of course, their spiritual sons hear them too, but they suspect that it is the Beast and Hell which approaches. And, as long a Man's Plan operates, nothing else can result.

Providence, anyone?

CHALCEDON REPORT NO. 131
JULY, 1976

As was pointed out earlier (Report 123), Christianity establishes distinctions and requires a division in terms of God between sin and righteousness, good and evil, and between the saved and the lost (Matt. 10:34-35). There is a required line of separation, but the line must be God's, not man's. As humanism flourishes, however, the exaltation of man leads to a progressive equalization of all men, the criminal and the law-abiding, the rich and the poor, the intelligent and the dull-witted, and all others are levelled into one common status in the name of democracy and equality. For humanism, all things are relative to man, so that no standard can be allowed to judge man, who is himself the only standard.

Whenever man is affirmed as the standard, life and the world (as well as God) are negated. If man is his own god and law, no outside standard or law can judge him. The result is the collapse of all standards and of society's ability to progress. If man is his own god, then, because there is no need for a god to improve, progress, or be educated, there is no need for man to change or improve himself.

Early in man's history, the Far East developed the great civilizations, reached a high estate, and then stagnated or collapsed. Why did Asia lose its eminence? From an area of growth and vitality, it turned into an area of decay and of defeatism. Its philosophies uniformly came to a position of world and life negation. The reason for this decay was the triumph of humanism and the negation of all absolutes other than man. Kwan-yin, the Chinese goddess of mercy, typified this triumphant humanism: she refused to enter heaven, supposedly declaring, "Never will I receive individual salvation" until every last man born or to be born is received into heaven. This equalitarian creed means no heaven, and no peace on earth. Heaven can only be heaven if all are saved, and earth can be good only if all are held to be equally good and equally deserving of the best. But this is impossible, and the result is cynicism, despair, and pessimism. Without standards and with only a total democracy of all men and values, not only are good and evil equal, but all men, and life and death are also equal. Nothing has meaning, and the result of all this democratic faith and love of all things was the equal hatred of all things, and, in the end, a belief only in nothingness. As a result, Asiatic thought and life decayed: its basic premise was in effect the exaltation of nothingness.

This strain of thought invaded Greece and contributed to its decay. This same nihilism was a factor in the fall of Rome. The Middle Ages decayed as the same humanistic relativism became again prominent and wandering folk singers and student-rebels propagated the faith from place to place, and churchmen echoed it from the pulpit.

Today, the same situation confronts us. The logic of modern humanism has led to the same collapse of values. As a result, modern men find the old faiths of Asia, a while ago rapidly being tossed onto the garbage piles of civilization, suddenly very attractive. Their nothingness finds an echo in modern man's emptiness. Zen Buddhism, Taoism, Hinduism (Transcendental Meditation), and much more are being dragged out, dusted off, and pressed into re-use for the funeral of modern man.

In these faiths, there is no Providence, only nothingness and the lonely thoughts of man projected against an ocean of meaninglessness. Love is affirmed, and a vague hope that there is some kind of impersonal tendency in the universe which is congenial to man's ideas, but this is only a profession of desires, not a description of reality. How long can a man under pressure be sustained by a vague belief in a mindless "goodness" of sorts?

A universe stripped of Providence is a universe stripped of God and meaning. Love and hate, good and evil, and life and death are then equally meaningless. When man makes himself god, he not only robs the universe of meaning, but also himself. The line between man and the animals is broken down, and the line between organic and inorganic becomes also vague and indistinct.

When God declares, "Ye shall be holy: for I the LORD your God am holy" (Lev. 19:2). He is declaring himself to be separate and calling upon us to be separated in terms of His law, calling, and covenant. The principle of His creation and re-creation is holiness, the separation of all things in terms of His creative purpose and calling. Man is called to understand the meaning of God's holiness and to develop that line of division in all creation. A line must be drawn between the holy and profane, that which is brought under the dominion of God's Kingdom (or Temple) and that which is outside of it. Because of the Fall, the world and its peoples are profane. First. they must be made holy by God's grace, which we must proclaim. Second, in terms of His law all things and men must be developed in terms of their potential and dedicated to the purposes of God's Kingdom. *Holiness requires dominion*: no dominion means no holiness, which indicates a profane estate.

The modern forms of the Kwan-yin philosophy indicate that ultimate profanity is exalted into ultimate bliss and salvation. All things must be separated from God, according to this faith, in terms of the equality of nothingness. The Kwan-yin faith is hostile to separation and to progress: the idea of "advance" it promotes is a levelling of all things to the lowest common denominator. As a result, the modern devotees of Kwan-yinism are hostile to Christianity, progress, technology, freedom, all things else which further the line of divisions among men and nations. All must be levelled.

Let us remember, as we see this exaltation of levelling, that, for the Middle Ages, quite rightly the great symbol and illustration of equality and democracy was death.

CHALCEDON REPORT NO. 132
AUGUST, 1976

To all practical intent, there are three basic doctrines of the nature of man, although numerous variations of each exists. The *first* is *the doctrine of man's natural goodness*. This is more often affirmed in theory than in fact.

To affirm that man is naturally good means sometimes that man as he is needs no improving. Everything that is, some in more than one age have affirmed, is holy. Evil is a myth, and every person, thing, or act is holy. There is then no such thing as an evil person or an evil or perverted act. The logic of the doctrine tends to this position. Others, however, affirm the goodness of man but the evil of the environment, and the environment can be defined almost in any way possible. The problem then becomes this: if man is naturally good, why is he so readily prone to evil influences? The doctrine of the natural goodness of all men is more logical, but then no change or progress is necessary. A good humanity in a good environment means that all things as is are as they should be.

Humanism. however, has usually preferred a *second* doctrine, *the doctrine of selective depravity*, one of the most pernicious ideas ever propagated by man. According to the doctrine of selective depravity, most men are naturally good, but some men are diabolically evil. These depraved men have been variously defined in various eras: priests, pastors, communists, fascists, capitalists. bankers, the masses, the blacks, the whites, the Jews, Germans, Japanese, the Americans, and so on. The doctrine of selective depravity, whether in the hands of radicals, conservatives, or liberals, leads always to Phariseeism. Depravity is limited to a class or group. Instead of seeing the problem as sin, and sin as pandemic to all men in Adam, it sees sin as limited to a segment of humanity. Instead of fighting against sin, it calls upon us to fight against a particular group of men. This means a radically different plan of salvation than that which is set forth in Scripture. Instead of Jesus Christ as the Savior of all men, of every race, color, and class, it sees one segment of humanity, the "good guys," as the world's hope. The problem then is to exorcise the "bad guys."

Because of the prevalence of the doctrine of selective depravity, the modern era, and especially the 20th century, has become a time of especially bloody warfare, torture, and persecution. On all sides, men seek a solution by going after their scapegoats. The present hue and cry everywhere about "corrupt politicians" is an example of this idea of selective depravity. There is no reason to believe that the people are any better than their politicians, and they are probably not as good, but there is a widespread Pharisaic moral self-satisfaction today in exposing the sins of politicians. The politicians themselves, of course, have often gained power by using the idea of selective depravity to damn a class or group and appeal thereby to the Pharisaic greed and self-satisfaction of the electorate.

Marxism thrives on the doctrine of selective depravity. Having carried the doctrine to its logical conclusion, the Marxists find that every use of the idea favors their position and finally leaves them the winners.

The doctrine of selective depravity ensures conflict, not against sin, but between man and man, class and class. It has made humanism the most divisive creed ever to exist, and it-leads to the isolation and "alienation" of man. In terms of this doctrine, no solutions are possible. A whole segment of mankind must be exterminated, if this doctrine be held, or at the very least brain-washed into submission. However, as new problems arise, a new group will be classified as the depraved class, because no other explanation for evil is possible.

The doctrine of selective depravity is basic to modern politics, education, sociology, and, too often, our religions. As long as this doctrine prevails, and it is deeply imbedded into modern man's being, no solutions are possible. In fact, every "solution" only aggravates the problem.

The *third* doctrine is the Biblical doctrine of *total depravity*. By total is meant that all men are involved in it, and that the total life of man is involved in his depravity. It does not mean that the totally depraved man is not capable of some good. It does mean that the depravity is total in its extent in all of mankind and in all of a man.

In such a situation, it will not do to limit depravity to a class, race, or group. All men in Adam have a common nature. The problem is thus not limited to some men, nor is the answer in any man. As St. Paul declares, in his great theological, social, and political statement, "There is none righteous, no, not one" (Romans 3:10). The answer is in God incarnate, Jesus Christ, who redeems man from his plight, gives him a new nature, and enables him to walk, not in the spirit of disobedience, but in the spirit of obedience to God and His law.

Man is removed from the bondage of his depravity into the status of a covenant man. Once a covenant-breaker, he now becomes a covenant-keeper. No longer an outlaw, he becomes God's law man. He is now on the road to dominion as God's dominion man.

There is thus no solution to our social crises as long as the humanistic doctrines of man's natural goodness, or of the selective depravity of man, prevail.

CHALCEDON REPORT NO. 133
September, 1976

The doctrine of selective depravity is a doctrine of radical phariseeism. By isolating depravity in a particular class, race, or group, it implicitly locates virtue in all others, particularly in the defining group. If evil is a national or racial trait, then membership in the other group, whether black, white, red or yellow, Anglo-Saxon, Arab, Japanese, or whatever it may be, constitutes virtue. All "facts" are collected to prove the point: we are the good guys, they are the bad guys. This is a very widespread and common practice, but it is no less evil and pharisaic for that.

(As a boy, I picked up an interesting form of this doctrine of selective depravity. My father went to Scotland for his advanced degrees and fell in love with the people and country. His Scottish friends kept me well supplied with books and magazines full of Scottish tales. Sir William Wallace was an early hero. The English were the villains, foul despoilers of all things good and pure. My American history confirmed that! I have since learned differently, but *not* because my wife is of Scottish ancestry! At any rate, Scottish nationalism is *no* surprise to me. I am only amazed that it took so long to develop.)

But, to return to the very aspects of the doctrine of selective depravity, it is inevitably a doctrine of murder. Sin must be destroyed. If sin is in us, we must through Christ destroy the principle of sin in order to be redeemed and to redeem history. However, if sin is incarnate in a race or class, it is then logical to destroy that race or class. Capital punishment is basic to human action, whether admittedly so or not. Marx placed virtue in the workers and evil in the middle (and upper) class. Hence, Marxism works to execute and eradicate the incarnations of evil in its midst. Hitler defined the evil class as the Jews: hence, the Jews had to be destroyed. Hitler himself had no anti-Jewish beliefs: his action was pragmatic. However, the logic of his position required, in a time of emergency, the elimination of evil. The result was the gas chamber. In the latter days of the war, he believed that the Germans were unworthy of him and betraying him, so he set the stage for the destruction and partition of Germany.

Whatever form the doctrine of selective depravity takes, it is a call, logically, for murder, and it begins to express itself accordingly. It declares: The only good Indian is a dead Indian. The only good Jap is a dead Jap. The only good nigger is a dead nigger. The only good honky is a dead honky (or white). The only good cop is a dead cop. The only good lawyer is a dead lawyer (according to something passed on to me today). And so on and on.

The doctrine of selective depravity leads not only to phariseeism, and murder, but to a pharisaic self-righteousness about the most vicious murders. It closes the door to Christ's salvation, because it defines sins, not in terms of every man's apostasy from God, and the fall of man in Adam, the federal head of *all* men without any exception save the second Adam, Jesus Christ, but it defines sin in terms of some men, other people. Salvation then means the elimination of these other people. On all sides of the political scene, the answer to problems is in terms of the doctrine of selective depravity. Who is to blame? Why, the Communists, the conservatives, the whites, blacks, Jews, capitalists, workers, or what have you. The result is a radical incapacity to deal with the problem. Every "answer" only aggravates it.

In terms of Scripture, *every man* is created in God's image, to be God's covenant keeper, and to be a Dominion Man, subduing the earth under God's law to be God's Kingdom. *No* man is exempt from this calling. It is *not* enough to profess faith and to be moral: we are called upon to develop God's dominion requirements and to make every area we live and work in an outpost of His Kingdom. Otherwise, we are called "unprofitable servants," and are cast into the "outer darkness" (Matt. 25:30).

The means to dominion is the law of God, the means to sanctification. God's covenant people live in terms of God's covenant law. This means tithing, restitution, responsibility, the family as the basic governmental and social unit, and much, much more.

There are different kinds of outlaws and prisoners in a jail. Some are there for major offenses like murder, rape, and kidnapping: others are petty criminals, with a string of small crimes. *But all are outlaws.*

Similarly, if we feel that we have not committed any "major" sins against God and are therefore still a part of His family, we must remember that all sin has as its principle the belief that "my will, not God's be done, unless it is to my advantage and convenience to obey God." *The principle of selective obedience* is as offensive to God as the principle of selective depravity.

The covenant man knows that his problem was total depravity: in every area of his life he served himself rather than God. By God's grace, he is now a redeemed man, a Dominion Man, and therefore a law-man, not an outlaw. Christ's declaration becomes his also: "Lo, I come to do thy will, O God" (Heb. 19:9). Salvation for him is not the elimination or murder of a social class, race, or group, but the atoning death and the resurrection of Jesus Christ. The mark of salvation and the way of sanctification is the delight in God's law-word, and his desire to place his whole life and world under God's law. His calling becomes, in the words of T. Robert Ingram, "The world under God's law," beginning with himself. This is not a doctrine of salvation by murder: it is a calling to regeneration and life in and through Christ.

CHALCEDON REPORT NO. 134
October, 1976

The doctrine of selective depravity creates a political order and a law structure after its own image.

In an earlier era, when kings and noblemen ruled, and again in the age of aristocracy, it was a common conviction that the "rabble" were incapable of morality and order unless kept firmly in check by a powerful force. Intelligence, virtue, responsibility, and the ability to rule were powers communicated by blood and rank.

Later, this idea of a ruling elite took various other forms: the Germans, Anglo-Saxons, the whites, the workers, the freemasons, and so on, and now it is gaining modern forms in Asia and Africa, where such ideas have long existed. Marxism, of course, holds militantly to one version of this faith.

We have seen that the final implication of the doctrine of selective depravity is salvation by murder. Eliminate the evil group. Of course, re-education is often attempted first, but, in a society of failures, as in

Marxism and Fascism, there must be a sacrificial victim for the continued failures. The evil class or race must therefore be "purged."

In the meantime, however, the people are told that their political order is their savior, and that salvation is a matter of law, and, in democracies, this also means elections. Elect the right people, who will pass the right laws, and salvation will arrive or be accomplished. More social security, medicare, more taxes on the rich (or middle classes, or poor), more this and that kind of legislation, and paradise will begin.

This program of salvation by law means legislating against certain people in favor of other people. It means legislating against the rich, the poor, the middle classes, this or that race or class, or whatever group is defined as evil.

It is easy, of course, for the devout believers in the doctrine of selective depravity to catalogue the sins of the evil class. We all have our share of sins. On one trip, a man tried hard to convince me of the special depravity of the oil companies and the international bankers. All our problems and evils he traced to them. When I tried to present a Biblical doctrine of sin, he was rude, arrogant, and hostile. I had a duty to keep quiet and listen to him, or else I would lead people astray with my ignorance! Later, his wife apologized for what I learned was his chronic behavior and added, "I don't know anything about the oil companies and bankers, but I do know from living with my husband that they have no monopoly on sin!" Exactly. There is no monopoly on sin. No class, race, or group has a corner on the sin market (although all nowadays seem to be trying!).

Legislation as well as thinking which has as its premise the doctrine of selective depravity not only denies the facts about all men, but it denies the very idea of justice. True justice, God's justice, requires that we be blind to the people involved but alive to God's requirements. It is in this sense that justice is blind, blind to human prejudices, partisanships, and claims, but alive to the law of God. God declares, "Ye shall do no unrighteousness in judgment: thou shalt not respect the person of the poor, nor honour the person of the mighty; but in righteousness shalt thou judge thy neighbour" (Lev. 19:15). We are not justified before God's law by our estate: rich or poor, believer or unbeliever, clergyman or layman, our estate is not a determining factor, but God's law is at all times to govern all men. At the same time, we cannot, in rigorously applying God's law, forget that we are also under it, and that the person on trial is our "neighbour." We cannot treat him as a different kind of humanity in whom selective depravity is operative. As the old expression has it, we are to remember, "There, but for the grace of God, go I."

The doctrine of selective depravity overthrows justice because it legislates in terms of class, race, or group. It declares a segment of humanity to be the depraved element by nature, because of their membership in a class, race, or group. Injustice then becomes a way of life, as it is now, in varying degrees, all over the earth.

Moreover, if we believe that some other group is the selectively depraved group, then it easily follows that they will decide that we are the selectively depraved blight upon the earth. Present-day economic and political thought begins and ends, on the whole, in terms of the doctrine of selective depravity.

The returns are now coming in. Politics has long operated on this premise of selective depravity. Now more and more people are concluding that the depraved class is the political one, politicians and bureaucrats. Terrorists are increasingly in evidence everywhere, and political assassinations are becoming common, because the true believer in selective depravity believes finally in salvation by murder. The solution is then simple: Kill the men of the Establishment, and freedom and paradise will be born. Hence, "death to the pigs," or death to the Establishment in its every form. Salvation by murder becomes a passionate faith and hope. And I do mean passionate, as I have often seen. For example, on one occasion, I argued with a university student, who believed in selective depravity. He lost his temper, and began to shout that all the pigs in power should be killed, and I should be "prevented" from going around the country corrupting people. It does not take too much pressure for such people, whatever their politics, to express their demands for murder.

Consider then what hard times will do to many of them. It will push them over the edge in demands for revolutionary or for repressive, reactionary actions. Salvation by murder will become a faith in action. Reasoning with such will not work. The premise of their thinking, whatever their professed politics of religion, is a false doctrine of man, a doctrine of selective depravity. Nothing short of a return to the total word of God can give men and nations a new direction.

CHALCEDON REPORT NO. 135
November, 1976

In recent months, I have bought and read four new books on Mary, Queen of Scots. My reason for this is that Mary is a symbolic figure, one who epitomizes much of the modern world and who accordingly has a passionately loyal following to our own day, I find, in fact, at times an intense feeling about Mary among a wide variety of peoples.

Perhaps Madeleine Bingham is right (*Mary Queen of Scots*, p. 1): "Those who die well attract the courtesies of history." The Christian martyrs then and now, however, have attracted no such loyalty. Perhaps Antonia Fraser is right that Mary was more sinned against than sinning. But Mary began early what one biographer has politely termed a course of "prevarication."

She continued her course with adulteries and murder, while maintaining a amazing self-righteousness through it all. In marrying the Dauphin of France, Francois, she lied to the Scottish delegates and signed away the Scottish succession to the French. Bingham sees this as contributing to her troubles and death in a central way. She tried to apply the divine right of kings to Scotland, which was alien to the dogma. She was so foolish in her speech that she spoke of her mother-in-law, Catherine de Medici, as a woman descended from shopkeepers, a slur that queen took action against when Francois died. Mary had a gift for making enemies and assuming that charm and tears could remedy the matter. An English ambassador saw her rule in Scotland as suicidal to Mary's interests. Her two marriages there were, to be kindly, very foolish blunders. Having lost her kingdom in battle finally, she sought refuge where all her friends advised her not to go, in England. She had made herself a rival claimant to the throne of England, and then a focal point of continuing conspiracy and rebellion, and yet Mary foolishly placed her hopes on charming Elizabeth's just fears away by a personal confrontation. That her execution was so many years in coming was due to Queen Elizabeth's horror of shedding royal blood. Mary's dying words showed self-righteousness, and also courage.

On the other hand, her appeal is understandable. She had beauty, charm and remarkable courage. Although years before her death both the Vatican and the Scottish Kirk had given her up as incorrigible, she died confident in her faith, and with an amazing physical and spiritual fortitude. It is easy to understand why the Romantic revival made so great a heroine out of Mary.

But my interest in Mary is because of her modernity, because she exemplifies an aspect of sin in every age, and an aspect of modern man in particular.

Bingham, who dislikes Knox and likes Mary, says all the same, "Mary was constitutionally devoid of either fundamental sincerity or natural prudence" (p. 69). The problem lies deeper, and Bingham's judgment must be held in abeyance until we can recognize that Mary saw herself as outside the law, and openly said so. In part, she based this on the divine right of kings, but in part also she based it on her renaissance humanism. Her view of life, law, politics, and people was totally personal. Her interest was not in a cause but in herself. The kind of humanism she manifested came to focus finally in Max Stirner's *The Ego and His Own*, the classic statement of total anarchism. Roy Strong explains Mary thus: "Her behavior was always conditioned by her upbringing and she thought of government and policy in terms of the personal intrigues and amours which motivated politics at the Valois court: (*Mary Queen of Scots*, p. 72). Not law but an anarchic personal concern governed her every action; Strong is right: this was the reason for all her disasters.

But what about her faith, to which she witnessed so eloquently before being beheaded? One pope renounced her, and Knox denounced her; some in her day, at her death, saw her as a saint, others as a devil. The truth is, Mary was very much like all of us. Where her faith was concerned, she practiced *the principle of selective obedience*. She was obedient to God, and true to her faith, when it suited her to be so. At such a time, she was more zealous in her defense of it than most of us ever are. But we have this in common with her, for the most part; we in our time practice a very selective obedience. We, of course, cannot put people to death as she did, for example the poet Chastelard, but we are no less hostile to those who cross us, and as ready to regard our sins and lusts as somehow excusable ones.

Mary's principle of selective obedience made her faith inoperative in the rule of her kingdom; it was her passions which ruled her and the kingdom and brought disasters to both. It is also the modern Christian's selective obedience which makes his faith inoperative and ineffectual in our world today. Such a professing believer may claim to believe the Bible from cover to cover, but his selective obedience makes him a practical and practicing humanist. If we are honest with ourselves, we would have to say that Mary is the real patron saint of today's Catholics and Protestants alike, because we are so radically selective in our faithfulness to God and our obedience to His law. Even more, to denounce Mary we must first denounce ourselves and our flagrant practice of selective obedience.

It is childish to blame various persons for Mary's disaster. Her biographers at this point are more or less agreed: she did it to herself. The same is true of us: whatever enemies we or our cause may have, we have our selective obedience to thank for our plight. We are doing it to ourselves.

After all, the principle of selective obedience means also selective disobedience to God. Even more, it has implicit in it the principle of total disobedience and revolt: it says in effect, "Not Thy will, O Lord, but mine be done."

The Prince de Ligne is said to have replied, when his wife asked if he had been faithful to her, "Frequently." She was hardly likely to be happy with that answer. If we can give no better answer to God, He is hardly likely to be any more pleased with us than the princess was with the Prince de Ligne. We are then humanists not Christians. Our condition is more than sin: it is lawlessness.

CHALCEDON REPORT NO. 136
December, 1976

The principle of selective obedience to God means finally no obedience at all. It means that, whether we obey God's word or not, in either case it is our will that is done, because we insist on being in the driver's seat. We pass judgment on God's requirements and pick and choose what suits us. In such a world, every man is his own god, determining for himself what constitutes good and evil. In such a world, anarchism rapidly takes over.

Hand in hand with anarchism we have terrorism. Where man takes control, he assumes the right, whether through the state or as an individual, to enforce his own will. No law then exists outside of man, and this comes down basically to the individual.

Terrorism is very much with us today, all over the world. In a few countries, stern measures control it to a degree, but they do not eliminate it, as witness the riots and murders in Communist countries, nor do they remedy the causes.

Although only a very small minority in any country are terrorists, the seeds of it are in most of us. Terrorism believes that no progress is possible through the normal processes of law, civil government, and society. The situation is seen as hopeless: it requires violence to clear away the road-blocks. Therefore, the answer is in disruptive acts of murder and terrorism. The idea is to disrupt and break down all normal processes, because they are seen as evil beyond redemption.

In one country after another, the popular mentality is congenial to terrorism. More and more people on the left, right, and middle insist that things are hopeless. The aphorisms expressing this feeling are many. To cite a few: "You can't fight city hall." "This country needs a few good funerals." "Why bother to vote? It all adds up to the same thing." "All politicians are crooked," and so on. These attitudes are very common, and they are the philosophy of terrorism. During the student riots of the 1960s, I met an anguished father whose son had gone "underground" to "fight the Establishment." The father shared all these opinions we have just cited, but he held a fine position and functioned as an upper-middle-class leader. His son was simply applying his father's (and professors') logic: if the Establishment is hopelessly rotten, then knock it over. All counsels of despair logically require us either to withdraw from the world and retreat into the desert, as some did before Rome fell, or to overthrow the supposedly hopelessly evil order.

I find it significant that so many people are more and more indifferent to voting. They regard it as useless to vote for anyone: they claim that there is no man on any ballot worth voting for, and that voting is useless anyway. "It's all been decided." Such people are the parents of terrorism.

The terrorist and the indifferentist are agreed: the "Establishment" is hopeless. All too many who vote share their despair concerning change.

The problem, of course, is that all these people confuse the "Establishment" with God: they ascribe omnipotence and/or eternity to it. Moreover, they see the "Establishment" as the great cause, the great determiner, rather than an effect, an effect of man's sin.

The locale of sin is not the "Establishment" but in the heart of man, all men. The false principle of selective depravity leads men to localize sin in a race, group, class, or "Establishment." The answer then is to destroy that element in society. Such a course only increases the corruption of society.

All counsels of despair are denials of the lordship of Jesus Christ. They deny His sovereignty and His government of all things.

The terrorists are very much the children of our times, the apt pupils of their parents, teachers, professors, pastors, and elders. They are conscientiously applying the lessons they have been years in learning. The "drop-out" mentality in all its forms, terrorism, drugs, liquor, the sexual revolution, hedonism, and more is a product of these counsels of cynicism and despair. In Rome, this "drop-out" mentality led to a common reaction, "let us eat and drink: for tomorrow we die" (I Cor. 15:32). Some people commit suicide; others plant bombs; both have a common despair of life and a cynicism regarding progress.

The faithful Christian knows, however, that he has a duty to "occupy" (Luke 19:13) every area of life and thought for His Lord. He knows that the very "gates of hell" cannot "prevail" (i.e., hold out) against Christ's Kingdom (Matt. 16:18; the word *ecclesia*, translated as *church*, means the assembly or congregation, the entire people, with its institutions and armies). To this Lord he must render, not selective, but *unqualified* obedience. Anything short of this makes man the lord, not Christ. The Lord says to all who render Him selective obedience, "And why call ye me, Lord, Lord, and do not the things which I say?" (Luke 6:46).

Terrorism? Most of us don't like it, but most of us help create it. We sometimes talk like Christians, but we act otherwise. We sometimes talk like terrorists with our cynicism and despair, but we are horrified at the idea of terrorism. Somebody has been taking us seriously, and it is not the Lord.

CHALCEDON REPORT NO. 137
January, 1977

We have seen that the doctrine of selective depravity is very dangerous because, while having a seemingly Biblical doctrine of sin, it shifts the area of sin from all men to some men. Sin is localized in a class or race.

We must now turn to another form of this same pernicious and dangerous doctrine, one inherited from the Enlightenment. Enlightenment thinkers believed in the natural goodness of man, provided the man was a *philosophe* like themselves, a rationalist and a skeptic. Religion meant for them superstition and evil. For most men, their natural goodness was only *potential*, because they were influenced by religion. For the intellectual and scientific elite, the *philosophes*, natural goodness was *actual*, because they had abandoned the superstition of the Christian religion.

This doctrine has been, in various forms, a persistent factor in modern history. Marxism, with its dictatorship of the proletariat, Fabian Socialism and democracy, with its guidance by scientific planners, and National Socialism with its leadership principle, are forms of this belief in selective depravity. If we believe in selective depravity, we then believe also in selective leadership by an elite class, race, or group.

In neo-orthodox thought, there was a supposed revival of the Biblical doctrine of original sin. Karl Barth and Reinhold Niebuhr, for example, seemed to echo the orthodox doctrine of man and his sin. Their doctrine of sin, however, was only formally theological but actually sociological. An example of this was Reinhold Niebuhr's *The Illusion of World Government* (1949), which first appeared in the April 1949, issue of *Foreign Affairs*. Men assume, Niebuhr held, that because world order is desirable, it is therefore attainable. There is no proof, he held, that there is "either the moral ability of mankind to create a world government by an act of will, nor of the political ability of such a government to integrate a world community in advance of a more gradual growth of the 'social tissue' which every community requires more than government." The underlying presupposition and faith of Niebuhr are here revealed. There is no *theological* moral inability, but only an *historical* inability. Given enough time, an international community and government will develop. (There are echoes of Edmund Burke here.) The disability of sin is not theological and does not require regeneration. It is sociological and requires simply the passing of time.

Of course, Niebuhr and Barth had no real answer to break-downs of national and local communities because of sin. For them, an historical development became a natural asset, because there was for them no truly supernatural grace in history. The centuries of Christian grace and development were for them a natural asset, a product of an evolving history, which would grow a new social tissue, the world community. Of course, some of them, as superior men, had already developed that social tissue and could therefore guide the world into the new order!

Because for them creation by God's supernatural act is a myth, theological concepts of sin and grace are all mythical. Sin is sociological, and grace and power come from the context of history. Adolph Hitler, that clear-cut theologian of Humanism, stated the implications of historical rather than supernatural grace. As a super-democrat, he told Chancellor Bruning at the end of 1931, "the fundamental thesis of democracy runs, 'All Power issues from the People.'" There can be no law or right beyond the will of the People. The majority will of the People can thus abolish any constitution, previously granted rights, or laws and do no wrong, because there is no power, right, or grace, Hitler held, beyond the People.

It is not enough to hold to the possible or actual depravity of all men, as some neo-orthodox thinkers have done. Is man's sin theological, i.e., against the sovereign and living God, or is it sociological, against human society?

Sin is against law, against ultimate power and authority. If that ultimate creating power is society, then salvation is social salvation, and it involves, as it did for Niebuhr, a world community. If that ultimacy is in society, then grace, saving grace, can only come from society, and hence the importance to Barth and Niebuhr of creating a new world order. We can then understand why, for political (rather than theological) man the problem of social salvation by a social gospel becomes so urgent. For them it is man's only hope.

This doctrine of selective depravity thus has two or three important presuppositions. *First*, it holds that all sin is in essence sociological, against society, rather than theological, against God. *Second*, it holds that some enlightened ones are aware of this fact and are living in terms of a world community which is to be beyond sin, beyond good and evil, and they are thus empowered to deal with those who are less enlightened. This can lead to a *third* presupposition, and usually does, that "power to the people" means power to the *philosophes*, the enlightened ones.

David, however, saw the meaning of sin more clearly: it is in essence always theological, because the law broken is God's law. Therefore, of his sin of adultery with Bathsheba, and his murder of Uriah, he declared to God, "Against thee, thee only, have I sinned, and done this evil in thy sight" (Ps. 51:4). It was because it was God's law he had broken that David knew the enormity of his offense against Uriah and Bathsheba.

The only true doctrine of depravity is thus theological. Only when we face up to the meaning of sin can we also know what grace is, and whence it comes. The harvest of the Enlightenment and neo-orthodox doctrine of sin, which now prevails everywhere in the councils of state, is an evil harvest, and a bloody one.

CHALCEDON REPORT NO. 138
February, 1977

When the first academician, Satan, confronted Eve, he challenged her to abandon her naive faith and to subject the word of God to critical analysis. He raised the question, "Yea, hath God said?" (Gen. 3:1). Every word of God, he held, was a partisan and subjective word and should be given the careful scrutiny of critical analysis. Only then, he held, can man determine what the objective content of any word from God can amount to. And so was born modern education.

I recall during my university days one elderly professor who held that poetry was to be enjoyed, and any study of poetry should have as its purpose our greater appreciation of it. He was regarded with amusement by the other faculty members who were busy training us all to sit in judgment as little gods on Shakespeare, Milton, Donne, and others. The more apt we were in critical analysis, the better our grades, and the faculty's opinion of us.

Our seminaries today do not really train pastors, although this is their formal function, and even though they do include a number of trash courses which are supposed to fulfil that purpose. What they do educate for is the production of an effectively trained group of critical analysts who can dissect Scripture but never or rarely see its relevancy to the real world.

Thus, all too often churchmen not only are deeply imbued with an apologetics which has as its first principle autonomous man, but they also apply that autonomous man's basic tool, the idea of critical analysis. Critical analysis brings all things before the bar of man's autonomous mind as judge and arbiter of all things. Christian analysis subjects all things to the judgment of God's enscriptured word as the standard. The distance between the two cannot be bridged.

Critical analysis is a weapon of impotence. It engenders nothing: it can only dissect. I am regularly told that, while Chalcedon is doing some very important thinking, in order to gain more academic attention, we should do something in the area of critical analyses. My answer is that we are in principle opposed to such thinking, and we gladly leave that domain to the intellectual eunuchs of our time. We are interested in thinking for action. St. Paul had this in mind: "Study to show thyself approved unto God, a *workman* that needeth not to be ashamed, rightly dividing the word of truth" (II Tim. 2:15).

This is not all. Critical analysis is a form of retreat from the world. Man is not autonomous, nor is he God. All thinking which presupposes man as the basic judge and arbiter involves a flight from reality. It is no wonder that the world of autonomous intellectualism, the modern university, has had an ivory tower reputation. Critical analysis makes one remote from reality.

This remoteness is never more apparent than when the critical analyst tries to desert the ivory tower. Karl Marx was savagely critical of the ivory tower mentality and the world of critical analysis. In his *Theses on Feuerbach*, Marx attacked the abstractness of critical analysis and called for its replacement by the revolutionary or practical-critical activity he favored. In this scheme of things, autonomous man still remains. However, the critique is now no longer abstract and intellectual but intellectually and actively destructive and revolutionary. Autonomous man must smash and remake the world after his own image, analysis, and imagination.

These two concepts, on the one hand critical analysis, and, on the other, critical-practical revolutionary action, are basic to modern education. At every turn, the student is prepared to judge the world, and to require the world to meet his standards. Naturally, this involves judging his parents, teachers, and society. It also means passing judgment on the world, life, and God.

The implication of Christian faith and analysis is that it is man who much change and be conformed to the will of God, and then to bring all things under the dominion of his Lord and Christ. The implication of critical analysis is that God, man, and the world must be conformed to our will, because we are the center, judge, and standard.

It should not surprise us therefore that the major area of struggle in the United States today is between statist, humanistic schools, and the truly Christian schools. This battle is not a dramatic, front-page story in most cases, although it has such moments. It is being fought in the minds and hearts of men, and in the courts of law. Too long a compromise with humanistic education has given the church weak men, double-minded, unstable in all their ways, incapable of receiving anything from the Lord (James 1:7-8), let alone acting ably for Him. Only as an education which assumes that every child is an autonomous mind, independent from God, and to be trained in a critical analysis, is replaced by an education which is in root and branch Christian, training and educating youth in the truly liberal arts, (the arts of liberty or freedom in Christ, and dominion under His royal law), can we have an education which has a grasp on reality and trains men of power rather than eunuchs.

A society of eunuchs has no future, unless it makes eunuchs out of youth. A Christian society alone has an assured future: it has the certainty of the sovereign and omnipotent God who cannot fail, and whose every word and purpose shall be fulfilled or put into force.

Our interest is thus not in critical analysis but in preparing men for dominion.

CHALCEDON REPORT NO. 139
March, 1977

One of the key myths governing our age we owe to John Locke (1632-1704). This is the myth of consent. Locke held that all legitimate governments rest on consent: society is not natural to man, but rather conventional.

With this myth, Locke laid down the foundations for civil disobedience and revolution. It was this myth of consent which governed the student movements of the 1960s, the revolutionary movements of the past two centuries, and is the basis of every protest movement of our time.

According to this myth, the most basic right of man is this act of consent. Locke held, in his *Second Treatise of Government*, that all men are in the state of nature and remain therein "till by their own consents they make themselves members of some politick Society." Autonomy (or anarchy) is thus the natural and basic state of man. This autonomy or independence nothing can alter, diminish, or take away from, except by the free consent of man. While Locke added that men have a natural inclination to society, he made it clear that it is their autonomy which is basic and which is the fundamental source of right.

Consent was thus exalted to a higher place of authority than any word or law of God and man. True, Locke, because of his Christian rearing, assumed that these autonomous men would more or less act like Christians, but he reduced the actual role of Christianity to a very minor one. Locke held that religion (meaning Christianity) is essentially a private affair, and that churches must be private associations only. The ultimate consequence of his views has been to reduce the faith to a domain within man's heart and mind only, not of concern to his social life and world. The essence of Biblical faith, however, is that Christianity is the most public of faiths, and that church, state, school, family, the arts, sciences, vocations, and all things else must be governed first and foremost by the faith, not by either an institution or individual man. Lordship belongs to God, not to man nor to the state or the church. To restrict Biblical faith to the private realm is to deny it and to deny the God of Scripture.

The myth of consent, however, transfers lordship to individual man; it makes man autonomous of man, society, and God. The ultimate sin and depravity then becomes any act which deprives a man of consent. Consent takes priority over God's law. It takes priority over other men, and man's law, over property rights, over justice, over everything. It means that the whole world and everything in it must pass the bar of man's judgment. (It was Margaret Fuller, in the last century, who, after much deliberation, said, "I accept the universe." After great thought, she gave her consent to reality! Today, many refuse to do as much.)

This myth of consent has infected all levels of humanistic education and the children themselves. The final word, as boldly pronounced by many children, and accepted by too many parents, is, "I Don't like it." The child quickly learns the myth of consent. In dealing with children, mothers have moved through several states, from 1) eat it, or I'll slap you: 2) eat it, it's good for you: 3) see what I'll give you, if you eat it: to 4) if you don't like it, don't eat it.

In the face of this myth of consent, any effort to restore Biblical authority is regarded as a monstrous act of oppression. One gentle and goodly pastor, who established a Christian School on the premise of God's word, was pictured, in a caricature by a national magazine, as brandishing a bullwhip over cowering children. The fact that the pastor has never owned a bullwhip and is a kindly man meant nothing: for those who hold to the Lockean mythology, any denial of this ultimate power of consent is depravity personified.

In terms of Biblical faith, however, it is not man's consent but God's word which is authoritative. The Biblical pattern of government by councils of elders involves mature consent, but it is always subject to God's word.

Government ultimately and essentially rests on the absolute and autonomous God, not on man's pretended claim to autonomy. It is God's word, not man's consent, which is authoritative.

The myth of consent thus redefines depravity as anything which withholds the power of consent from man. The myth, moreover, has redefined consent. After Rousseau, Hegel, and Marx, the general will, the consent of all men, is mystically incarnated in a self-designated elite who embody that total consent in their will. Thus, whatever happens to any victim of Red China, the Soviet Union, the new African Socialist states, or to any Cuban, is mystically his own consent judging him! The heirs of Locke and Rousseau find it a greater privilege and a higher freedom for a man to be a victim of a socialist tyranny than to be prosperous or reasonably free in a society which limits his consent.

The myth of consent, however, destroys its adherents. I once asked an ex-student about a reformed professor of liberal beliefs who taught at his mid-western university. The printable part of his verdict was, "An opinionated bastard." Why? consent to the student's own more radical ideas, and opinions about class conduct, had been denied: the ultimate sin had been committed, because consent had been denied.

The myth of consent presupposes autonomous man. This myth of autonomy is only attained by man in the graveyard. A graveyard man has no problems with others: he is a logical existentialist, but he has ceased to exist, and therefore consents to nothing.

CHALCEDON REPORT NO. 140
April, 1977

John Locke's basic political principle was the myth of consent: "Man being...by nature all free, equal, and independent, no one can be put out of this estate, and subjected to the political power of another, without his own consent." For Locke, this universal consent took place in early time, when all men were in the state of nature. (Now, some revolutionists invoke revolution to create a new state of nature, and a new beginning.) Normally, in history, Locke held that the majority represented the whole body politic. Locke was a majoritarian to the core, as Willmoore Kendall pointed out a few years ago.

Locke's humanism placed right in man. Humanistic monarchism had located divine right in the King; Locke now re-located it in the majority. After Rousseau, this majority found its general will expressed by the actions of an elite minority who know best what the majority should want. Dante Germino, in *Modern Political Thought: Machiavelli to Marx*, holds, for example, "It is possible that today a minority of the people could prove to be the most authentic and effective exponents of substantive democracy" (p.

137). Frank L. Field proposes re-educational centers to re-mold dissidents, but claims these are, not "full-blown concentration camps" because their purpose is benevolent (F. L. Field: *Current Bases for Educational Practice*, p. 46ff.). The myth of consent leads to "benevolent" concentration camps, where consent must be extracted.

Locke began by denying implicitly the sovereignty of God and His word in favor of the sovereignty of Right Reason. True and valid government was for him, as Germino perceptively notes, "government of rational man, by rational men, for rational man." The champions of Right Reason soon find, however, that most men, including certainly the orthodox Christian, are not "rational." Thus civil government cannot be of or by them but over them for their welfare.

Locke rightly saw the tyranny of rule by one man, a monarch, ruling by his will. The will of one man expresses the greed and sin of that one man. His alternative, however, was the will and word, not of God, but of the majority. The majority, however, is no less sinful and greedy for being a majority. The rise of majoritarianism has given us a greater tyranny at times than the old monarchism in that the greed of the majority is potentially greater than the greed of one man and his circle of courtiers. Socialism and fascism give us the civil government of envy and greed, and hence they decapitalize and destroy society.

The power to rule, whether by one man, a minority, or a majority is a menace to society whenever and wherever it is separated from the objective and absolute law of God. It then becomes, not a government of justice, but of envy, greed, class conflict, and class and race hatred. The basic faith in all forms of humanistic political theory is that a selective rationality exists. This doctrine can hold that one man, a monarch, has divine rights and a rationality sufficient for his task. In other forms, minority and majority rule theories insist that this power of rational rule is compassed by their elite groups or numbers. For Marxism, rational rule is selectively incarnate in the dictatorship of the proletariat. For fascism, rational rule is the province of the elite party and its leader.

Hitler, for example, believed in neither God nor in conscience, which he called "a Jewish invention, a blemish like circumcision." Man's hope was for him in scientific reason. During the war, he stated, "The dogma of Christianity gets worn away before the advances of science...Gradually the myths crumble. All that is left is to prove that in nature there is no frontier between the organic and the inorganic. When understanding of the universe has become widespread, when the majority of men know that the stars are not sources of light, but worlds, perhaps inhabited worlds like ours, then the Christian doctrine will be convicted of absurdity...The man who lives in communion with nature necessarily finds himself in opposition to the Churches, and that's why they're heading for ruin - for science is bound to win." *Science is bound to win*! We cannot understand why the German universities so extensively supported Hitler if we fail to grasp this central aspect of Hitler's faith. Hitler's war time plans for rebuilding Linz included a great observatory and planetarium as its centerpiece. It would become the center of a religion of science, and Hitler said, "Thousands of excursionists will make a pilgrimage there every Sunday...It will be our way of giving man a religious spirit" (Alan Bullock: *Hitler, A Study in Tyranny*, p. 389 f.). There is no reason to believe that our universities will not be equally ready, throughout the Western world, to receive another Hitler or Stalin.

Having denied the sovereign God, men will locate sovereignty somewhere on the human scene, and close to themselves. Having transferred justice and righteousness from God to man, men will confuse their will with justice, and other men will be less than men in their sight.

If man is defined in terms of God and His word, all men are created in His image; all men are alike sinners, and the call to redemption is extended to all men. If man is defined as a rational animal, then man is defined by his rationality. In campus discussions, I have been told by some who oppose me that my Christian position is totally irrational; for me, their unbelief (or, sometimes, heresy) is "totally irrational." We have here a flexible yardstick which depends on our presuppositions. Thus, whenever we begin with a humanistic definition of man, we dehumanize most men. They are then sub-human, and their consent is unnecessary, because they lack mental competence supposedly. The myth of consent is leading increasingly to no consent, and in socialism and fascism it redefines consent to make it a farce.

God having made us, defined us, and established us in our world and circumstances, reserves unto Himself the right to remake us. Any attempt by man to remake man in terms of a humanistic righteousness is usurpation.

CHALCEDON REPORT NO. 141
May, 1977

The myth of consent, so basic to the modern age, rests on the doctrine of the sovereignty of man. Because man is sovereign, nothing is valid unless man gives his free assent to it. Where man's assent is not secured, civil disobedience, it is held, is not only justifiable but sometimes a moral necessity.

This doctrine of the sovereignty of man began, of course, as a doctrine of the sovereignty of some men. With Plato, it meant the sovereignty of the philosopher-kings, the elite planners of society and the rulers of the state. This form of the doctrine is still very much with us and takes a variety of forms: the dictatorship of the proletariat, the Fuhrer principle, the brain trust concept, and so on. A major and early form of this belief in the modern era was the doctrine of the divine right of kings. Although it pretended to Biblical roots, its origins were in ancient paganism.

The divine right of kings gave way to the sovereignty of the aristocracy in many areas, and the aristocracy treated the right to rule as their own special privilege, a right of birth and inheritance.

The next to claim the right to rule were the middle classes. The Industrial Revolution was their handiwork; they were responsible for the great and important changes in society, and progress had been made dramatically under their leadership. The aristocracy bitterly opposed this rise of the middle classes, and it saw only disaster ahead in this shift of power. The shift occurred all the same, and the aristocracy went into eclipse.

Almost at once, however, the middle classes were challenged everywhere. Their own advances had sufficiently improved the lot of the lower middle classes to make them highly articulate and vocal. The lower classes ceased to be the silent, servile, and unknown sector of society and became highly vocal. It was because this new power in society was becoming no longer invisible but visible that the aristocracy and intellectuals began to make themselves self-appointed voices of the lower classes. After some time, they gained an appreciative response, and such men as Lenin and F.D. Roosevelt became possible, in person very alien to the lower classes, but in action idolized by them and made their voices. The intellectuals and aristocrats did not create the new locale of sovereignty: they saw it coming and attached their own ideas and goals to it.

The sovereignty of man had begun with kings and concluded with "Power to the People," a faith used by Hitler, Stalin, and democratic leaders to gain and retain power. The logic of the sovereignty of man had come to mean the sovereignty of man in the mass, and it became necessary for other classes to ally themselves with the masses.

When John Locke formulated the doctrine of consent, by consenting man he meant a very limited class of man. The logic of his myth, however, meant the extension of that consent to all men. If all men are sovereigns, then no man can be compelled, and nothing is valid for any man without his consent.

Max Stirner, the great thinker of anarchism, saw this clearly. Granted man's sovereignty, no man could be compelled; all men are bound only by their own will. The state is then only a substitute god, and man cannot allow himself to be coerced by any god.

Karl Marx recognized the danger in Stirner's thought. In perhaps his most violent work, he attacked Stirner savagely. Marx realized that the logic of humanism requires that every man be his own god and that no man be compelled. Anarchism, however, for Marx meant the collapse of humanism into disorder and defeat. The way out was socialism, the sovereignty of the scientific socialist order and its freedom to remake man into that "free" condition where he would naturally function in terms of an over-riding humanistic plan.

Thus, in one form or another, the sovereignty of man has led to the enslavement of man, the breakdown of social order, and what Dr. Cornelius

Van Til has in another context called integration downward into the void.

Apart from the sovereignty of God, society has no real principle of law and order. The logic of Stirner is the logic of humanism, of the sovereignty of man. Stirner argued that all men who have any moral hesitation about incest are still Christians, because they are governed by something other than their will. The truly sovereign man knows no law except his own will and desire. Because the truly sovereign man can tolerate no other sovereign, it is a moral necessity for him to defy every law of God and man. As Sartre recognized, freedom then becomes negation. The result, whether in politics or art, is a program of rebellion, revolution, and negation.

This then is the necessary course of the modern world, rebellion, revolution, and negation, as long as it remains faithful to its humanistic faith.

The alternative, the sovereignty of God, declares that there is a mandatory law and order. This mandatory law and order is not the expression of man's sovereignty or of a class interest but of God's infallible word. Whereas the sovereignty of man leads to a world of conflicting interests, man against God, man against man, class against class, and race against race, the sovereignty of God leads to a total harmony of interests. The universe is totally God's creation and absolutely serves and fulfills His purpose, which includes the fall and sin of man, and uses it to further His perfect decree.

The myth of consent supposedly stresses man's responsibility; in actuality, it destroys it, because it makes an untenable claim of sovereignty for man. Under God's sovereignty, man's creaturely freedom and consent have their place, because man has found his place. The logic of the modern age is leading to attempts at dictatorship almost everywhere, but at the same time a growing threat of anarchy. Because man is a creature, only when he submits to God's sovereignty can man know freedom as a man, a creature.

CHALCEDON REPORT NO. 142
June, 1977

Humanism exalts man as sovereign, but, in practice, this means that it is some men, an elite group, who rule as sovereign, as the working god of the social order. Most humanists are unwilling to state their case so baldly. Nietzsche, however, did. Among his manuscripts collected after his death was a piece of paper stating simply, "Since the old God has been abolished, I am prepared to rule the world." Nietzsche recognized that the growth towards democracy in his day was also the denial of God and the exaltation of man, which meant the great opportunity for the elite man, the tyrant. He held, "The democratization of Europe is at the same time an involuntary preparation for the rearing of tyrants taking the word in all its meanings, even in its most spiritual sense." Of men in general, he held, "One has no right to existence or to work, to say nothing of a right to 'happiness.' The individual human being is in precisely the same case as the lowest worm." If there is no God, then there is no absolute law protecting any man or anything from any use demanded by any power. As Dostoyevsky saw, if there is no God, then everything is permitted.

Earlier, the same point had been made in the 1760s by Diderot in *Rameau's Nephew*. In this dialogue, the nephew, a Nihilist, gives us the thesis of the book: there is no difference between a gardener who prunes the garden and the worms who perform the same task by feeding on the leaves. The philosopher cannot say that the worm is not equal to the gardener. This short novel was translated from the French by Goethe. Hegel was delighted with it, and Marx found it a joy. Why? After all, these men were, in a sense, gardeners, philosophical gardeners. Were they demoting themselves? On the contrary, they were demoting God and absolute law, moral standards and human integrity. By calling the worm equal to the gardener, the worm was not exalted; rather, all moral standards were subverted. The worm and the gardener were made equally meaningless and equally free from God's law. When a gardener and a worm are both cut lose from all restraints, considerations, laws, and standards, it is not the worms who win but the gardeners. This was clearly demonstrated by Robespierre and other "gardeners" in the French Revolution. Otto J. Scott, in *Robespierre, The Voice of Virtue*, has shown how the revolutionary gardeners treated their human worms. Humanistic democracy has moved very rapidly into fascist and socialist statism, with the masses of men being called sovereigns while disposed of as worms.

But this is not all. *Rameau's Nephew*, Nietzsche, and others, the Marquis de Sade included, all argued that, because there is no God, there is no law. This is not altogether an honest argument. What they meant rather was that, because there was for them no God, this meant that God's law was invalid. This cleared the ground for a new lawgiver, man. The "gardener" now made the laws, and the chief gardener, the dictator, legislator, president, prime minister, or chairman declared what law should be, and how his law would create a new Garden of Eden.

According to the Bible, the world is God's creation and totally under His law. The Garden of Eden was to be tended entirely in terms of His purpose and law and made the exemplar and testing area in terms of which the whole world was to be brought under dominion by man in terms of God's rule and law. The Head Gardener was thus declared to be God. In this Garden, man is not a worm but a creature made in the image of God, created for knowledge, righteousness, holiness, and dominion.

Diderot's garden abolished God and instituted a democracy, but a meaningless one. Since gardener and worm are alike meaningless and the same, and no objective values exist, the only functioning and pragmatic value is power. The goal of Diderot's disciples thus became power, and the test of power was the ability to control and prune the garden and the worms, and to kill all who resisted. The original and full slogan of the French Revolution was thus almost honest: "Liberty. Fraternity, Equality -- or Death." It should have read, "Liberty, Fraternity, Equality, and Death." When all values are reduced to nothing, then only power establishes value, and death is the means whereby this new value is applied.

Prospective gardeners over the planned humanistic Garden of Eden have since been busy defining who the worms are, depending on their particular humanistic starting point. For some, the human worms are the capitalists, for others, the lower classes. Others define the human worms as a particular race, nationality, or color, a religious group, or a vocation (i.e., bankers. lawyers, doctors, or what have you). In any case, it is some men who become expendable in the name of freedom and equality.

Rameau's Nephew saw the whole world and life as absurd and meaningless. Nothing is more absurd in such a world as any attempt to maintain moral standards and values. Freedom means freedom from God's law. Camus, in *The Rebel*, drew the logical conclusion in the 20th century. Freedom for atheistic, existential man is from God and from God's law, from righteousness and the idea of the good. It thus means freedom to do evil, freedom to create a demonic world. The "free" spirits of the modern world thus delight in evil, pornography, occultism, and Satanism.

For us, however, there can be no freedom except under God and His law. Life apart from God is hell, and man's pretensions to be god are insanity. Nietzsche was prepared to be god and to rule the world, regarding other men as equal to "the lowest worm." Nietzsche ended in a mental institution, hopelessly insane and under the jurisdiction of custodians with a better philosophy than Nietzsche's.

Because God reigns, His law governs, and His Kingdom shall prevail. If you live apart from God and His law, you will be living in Nietzsche's world. "Wherefore come out from among them, and be ye separate, saith the Lord" (II Cor. 6:17).

CHALCEDON REPORT NO. 143
July, 1977

One of the most confused ideas in the history of Western thought is the concept of natural law. Because of their Christian faith or background, most men assume that it means that, because God created the world, His laws are basic to the constitution of all created being. Whether we deal with matters of physics or biology, psychology or chemistry, we deal with God's creation and therefore God's law. Both Catholics and Protestants have commonly understood natural law in this sense.

The concept of natural law, however, is essentially Greek in origin, and its Hellenic and naturalistic meaning has again and again dominated the doctrine to give it a radically anti-Christian meaning and use. The French Revolution was based on this doctrine, as was the Russian Revolution, which gave it a different name.

In terms of the Greek mind-body dualism, natural law could mean two things. First, it could be a universal, an idea, and the imposition of that idea onto history. The idea was known through reason, and Right Reason became an equation for natural law. Plato's *Republic*, a blueprint for a communist society, was intended as a statement of what constitutes pure reason (or natural law) and therefore necessary order for man and the state. The philosopher-kings are therefore the voice of natural and the elite minority is the voice of true law.

Aristotle associated natural law with matter, not mind, as an expression of mind's universal expressed in nature. This expression of the material world is the state, and man is a political animal. The life of the state is law, and law expresses nature (and justice) when it gives every man his due. This meant treating equals equally and unequals unequally. Men have tried to derive a workable system of justice out of Aristotle but have only succeeded when they have imported Biblical law into it. The reason is that, for Aristotle, as he stated at the beginning of his *Politics*, "the state or political community, which is the highest good of all, and which embraces all the rest, aims at good in a greater degree than any other, and at the highest good." The state is thus the voice of justice and of natural law. For Aristotle, therefore, ethics is a branch of politics, not of theology. It is thus impossible to fit either Aristotle or Plato into a Christian view of things. Biblical law declares that God is the author of all things and the only valid source of law. The repeated preface to law in Scripture is the declaration, "I am the Lord."

After the Enlightenment began to rethink natural law, there was a steady separation from the concept of the Christian additions to it, and the result was that natural law became the source of the theory of natural rights, i.e., rights that are inherent to man and in man. Just as law is now identified with nature as separated from God, so right was identified with man apart from God.

The logic of this view came into focus with the French Revolution. The Revolution and its regime became the triumph of natural law and the rights of man. In the "Declaration of the Rights of Man and of Citizens, by the National Assembly of France," it was held that "The nation is essentially the source of all sovereignty; nor can any individual, or any body of men, be entitled to any authority which is not expressly derived from it." Right Reason was now the revolutionary regime, and natural law was whatever the state declared it to be. In Marxism, new terminology replaced the old, but the ideas remained the same: the dictatorship of the proletariat is the rule of Right Reason and Natural law.

It should be obvious why the church's use of the term natural law has been so troublesome. It has incorporated into it too many anti-Christian premises. What a consistent Christian means by it is creation law, laws governing the universe because God is its maker and sovereign. He knows, moreover, that creation is the handiwork and law sphere of the triune God because Scripture, God's revealed law, so declares it. Man can understand and validly approach creation law when he is first of all under Biblical law by God's grace. Only as we stand in terms of God's law can we contend with the dangerous legal heresies and paganisms which surround us.

Because of the prevalence of the idea that Right Reason is the voice of law, we have the increasing arrogance of modern science. Rebecca West, in *The New Meaning of Treason*, cited the belief of many scientists in their sinlessness. As on angry scientist told her, "Science is reason. Why should people who live by reason suddenly become its enemies?" (p.173). As Rebecca West observes, this is simply "a new door into the old world of fanaticism."

For us, it must be a closed door. We have the sovereign and triune God, and we have His enscriptured law. He is the maker of heaven and earth and all things therein. "All things were made by him; and without him was not anything made that was made" (John 1:3). The doctrine of creation is the starting point for valid sciences.

As we deal with the problems of man and society, we have the clear guide of God's law, a surer foundation than fallen man's unregenerate reason. For us, neither the reason of an intellectual elite of would-be philosopher kings nor the law of the state give valid law. Only God can legislate, and only God's law is true law. Man's administration of law must express God's law, not man's reason or the state's will. On any other basis we have injustice and a world in chronic crisis. Isaiah (8:20) states it very plainly and clearly: "To the law and to the testimony (of the prophets to the law): if they speak not according to this word, it is because there is no light in them."

CHALCEDON REPORT NO. 144
August, 1977

A number of confused ideas have met repeatedly in history to create a false idea of sin, one which has again and again been destructive of civilization. In the Western world, neoplatonism, Manicheanism, and various ideas about nature and the natural life have fed this dangerous notion, and, in the Far East, similar tendencies have also prevailed. Rome was dominated by this error, and the hippies of the 1960s believed in it also, as do many radicals, liberals, conservatives, and ecology advocates. This great error involves a false idea of both sin and virtue. Not only humanistic groups and movements, but also the church repeatedly over the centuries, have been dominated by this error.

Very briefly, to cite the Roman statement of it, sin is luxury, and virtue is the simple life.

For Scripture, sin is the desire of man to be his own god, knowing or determining for himself what constitutes good and evil (Gen. 3:5). Man can express this will to autonomy or independence from God, to be his own god, in many ways. He may choose the way of wealth and power, but he can be as guilty as an Alexander the Great or a Stalin and Hitler while seeking his autonomy in a very simple life. The key to sin is not in the outward forms of life but in the nature of the man, in his heart.

In Rome, as in other cultures, this false idea of sin and virtue was suicidal. It meant that every real advance was seen as an evil, and that virtue meant a return to primitivism and poverty. In the modern world, the revival of this doctrine in many quarters has meant that a marked hostility to progress and technology is seen as a sign of virtue. Countless people will argue that the automobile is a disaster to culture, and electricity also. Such people work for Zero Economic growth, but they actually mean a minus economic "growth," a return to a supposedly ideal primitive past. Such "moralists" teach people to have a bad conscience about progress, comfort, and wealth. One of our finest Chalcedon friends left an executive position with a small company he led from losses to profits because the new owner regarded the profits he brought about as "obscene." Another such "moralist," a wealthy liberal, was hurt when I reminded him of the luxury he lived in and replied, "Yes, but I don't enjoy it!" He went on to claim that he used his wealth as a trust to help reform society. Because of his false idea of sin, his ideas on reform were false and dangerous.

The founding fathers of socialism were all children of Rousseau in this respect. They looked to the masses for revolutionary fervor and hope because they led "the simple life" and were hence naturally virtuous. In the 19th century, a major socialistic movement in Russia was based on this faith: students went to the peasant masses convinced that in them lay the hope of reform, of social salvation.

The Roman historian Tacitus, faced with the problems of Rome, saw the sin as luxury and then idealized a people he knew nothing of, the German tribes, and created the myth of the simple, primitive Teuton and his virtues which Hitler drew upon centuries later. The American Indian is similarly viewed, not as a decadent people, but as an example of primitive virtue. Many ethnologists and anthropologists are guilty of such thinking. The ecology movement rests on primitivism, on the idea that virtue means the simple life.

Romans like Tacitus could give no answers to the problems of their day, because they misread the problems due to their false doctrines of sin and virtue. The same situation exists today. Virtually all politicians, parties, and reforms are carried on, not in the name of God, but in the name of the people. All political parties make a common claim, namely, that they best represent the people, and therefore they best represent virtue. "The common man," whoever he is, is supposedly the repository and source of virtue because his limited means requires that he live a relatively simple life.

However, in terms of Scripture, no more than wealth can create virtue can poverty or the simple life create virtue. To say that economic want creates virtue is to sentence civilization to death. From the standpoint of Scripture, the rich and the poor are alike sinners. Virtue is not a product of wealth nor of poverty but of grace, the grace of God through Jesus Christ. Now to say this is not merely to make a theological statement but also a statement of great importance for economics, politics, law and education. It tells us at once that all currently reigning theorists are wrong, and that their ideas that economic arrangements are responsible for sin and virtue are very dangerous notions. On the one hand, we have those who believe that appropriations of money, taxation and public or federal grants, i.e., wealth applied to problems can save society. For us, wealth itself is no evil, but as a savior, it can be made into an evil. On the other hand, others believe that man's salvation requires a return to the simple life, and a casting away of our technological civilization; salvation is in a return, really, to poverty. For us as Christians, poverty in itself is no evil, although any view of it as man's salvation is again ludicrous.

Clearly, the urgent crises of our times cannot be solved as long as men have false and dangerous ideas about sin and virtue. By beginning with false religion, they end in suicidal ideas about the future. Failing to see what the real problem is, they work desperately on answers which are destroying civilization. If wealth is the answer, then attempts at "sharing the wealth" decapitalize society and create conflicts. If poverty is the answer, then society is attempting to liquidate itself and calls suicide life.

Theology is everything, and a false religion is a prescription for suicide and a very present danger.

CHALCEDON REPORT NO. 145
September, 1977

We are very often told that men everywhere have a natural love of freedom and justice. Again, it is held by many that no slave really loves slavery. I have read several savage attacks on a liberal historian's study of slavery which upset critics greatly, because it seemed to imply that many slaves in the Old South were content with slavery; I have heard scholars say flatly that this is impossible and contrary to human nature.

This is the key: are slavery, tyranny and injustice contrary to human nature? To believe that they are is to believe that men are naturally good and naturally just and free. This is, of course, at the heart of the liberal faith, but it is contrary to the Biblical view of man's sin and depravity. Men have rarely loved freedom and justice, and, very often, when claiming to love freedom and justice, they are in fact working against it. Many slaves were very content with slavery, while objecting to some aspects of it. Most people in the Soviet Union, while ready to grumble about various particular conditions, are, according to some observers, very much content with the basic aspects of life under socialism. In the Western democracies, we have the steady loss of freedom because people prefer other things to freedom. True, here as elsewhere, people would best like to have their cake and to eat it too. They would like the advantages of both freedom and slavery, of both justice and injustice, but in the final analysis, they talk of freedom and justice and choose the opposite.

In fact, as George Orwell saw, the new slavery comes in the name of freedom. People talk of freedom, equality, social justice, and brotherhood while busily voting in their opposites.

I have known some scholars who became irate at the suggestion that slaves could love their masters, and yet these same men could idolize some of our recent presidents, who have been ushering in the new slavery. For more than a generation at least, U.S. presidents, all put into office by a majority vote, have been actively furthering the new slavery to the usual applause of the majority. The New Master gains more adulation at times than the Old Massa ever did! When a president asks the people to tighten their belts, it is in order to enable the federal government to untighten its belt and get fatter, but the slaves, despite regular grumblings, basically ask for more slavery.

As Christians, we cannot begin to cope with the problems of our time unless we recognize that man as a fallen creature is, whatever his profession outwardly, a person who prefers slavery and injustice. He is more at home in such a world. Freedom means responsibility, and the sinner is in flight from his basic responsibility, to the sovereign God. Justice means our own condemnation, and what sinner wants that? As a result, men, in the name of freedom and justice, work to suppress the substance of these things.

The impotence of modern politics rests on the inability of so many liberals and conservatives to recognize the nature of the problem. The success of one great humanist, Napoleon, was based on his recognition that his earlier views of man as naturally good, just, and free were false. The Reign of Terror and the Egyptian campaign brought home to Napoleon the depravity of man. Accordingly, he did what others have since done; he used the facade of the revolutionary movement as a means to power.

Freedom and justice will rise and fall in terms of man's faith. Where men are regenerate and live in terms of God's law, freedom and justice quickly become imperatives. Where men are reprobate, the facade of freedom and justice becomes basic to the New Slavery. A faith without consequences is no faith at all.

The prevalence today of myths of consent and equality provides a facade for less and less consent and more and more inequality. This should not surprise us. The remedies men seek, political and social action, organization, legal battles, and more are all impotent unless at the same time we recognize that the basic problem, the sin of man, must be also and first dealt with. The foundation is the sovereign and regenerating grace of God. Man is the problem, not his circumstances. Man's circumstances are a consequence and product of his slavery and injustice.

The redemptive purpose of God is a total one, and all our activities must be seen in the perspective of God's purpose. As Dr. Cornelius Van Til has pointed out, the redemptive revelation of God had to be as comprehensive as the sweep of sin. Redemption must, in the nature of the case, be for the whole world. This does not mean that it must save every individual sinner in the world. It does mean, however, that "the created universe which has been created as a unit must also be saved as a unit" (C. Van Til: *An Introduction to Systematic Theology*, p. 133).

Our faith thus gets to the root of the problem, the nature of man, and it has a total solution for man and the world. It does not declare that men are free, but rather that they are slaves, and that only the truth can make them free (John 8:31-34), and the truth is Jesus Christ (John 14:6). Only then are men turned from loving and believing a lie (Rom. 1:25; Rev. 22:15) into men whose lives are founded upon the truth. All our problems, political, personal, or otherwise, are at their root theological. Until we recognize the essential problem, man's revolt against God, and the answer, faith, and obedience to God's law, we will be providing only facades for the New Slavery. And we will ourselves be whited sepulchres.

CHALCEDON REPORT NO. 146
October, 1977

In a very interesting article in the September, 1955, *Encounter*, Hugh Seton-Watson, writing on "The Russian Intellectuals" of the pre-revolutionary era, pointed out that these men adopted Western humanistic and secular ideas wholesale. One might add that they adopted them more intensely and faithfully than did Western humanists at times. As a result, "The notion of law had little meaning for them. They could not conceive that the principle of the rule of law could be important." Their idea was "the reign of virtue on earth," and this reign meant the triumph of the intellectual and his ideas.

In the West, the facade of the rule of law was maintained, but a new content was given to it. In Biblical thought, law is the expression of the nature, holiness, and mind of God. God's law is repeatedly prefaced by the declaration: "I am the LORD," because God's law is an expression of the being of God and sets forth His ultimacy and lordship.

The same principle is true of humanistic law. The mind of the intellectual is seen as ultimate. Autonomous man and his reason constitute the final judge and standard of all things. As a result, the intellectual, whether Russian, Asiatic, African, or Western, sees his thinking as basic to the idea of law. Law is what humanistic man determines it when he thinks in purely autonomous terms, without reference to God. For the Russian, this has meant direct rule and power; for the Western intellectual, it means the facade of legal tradition. In either case, law is what the autonomous mind of intellectual man says it is. As a result, the modern intellectual has applied his faith to the world as a new revelation of law with all the fervor of a god who knows he is right. It was for this reason that Otto J. Scott titled his book *Robespierre, The Voice of Virtue* (1974). Not only Robespierre, but all the revolutionaries saw and see themselves as virtue incarnate, and their enemies as demonic. Marx was insistent in his early writings that the imagery of hell and the demonic be retained and applied to the enemies of socialism. Such thinking is logical: if the elite intellectual is the new god, then his opponent is the new model of the devil. As Scott points out, the Jacobin edict which called for the confiscation of churches and church properties and the destruction of all Christian objects and symbols began, "All is permitted those who act in the Revolutionary direction."

The new gods ruled *divine justice*, *God's law*, out of court. Henceforth, a new doctrine of justice came into being from the new gods of creation, *social justice*. This was social in that it was the voice and justice of man and society as incarnated in the humanistic elite, the intellectuals.

This doctrine of social justice became a declaration of war against God, the church, the family, humanity, capitalism, and much more. Efforts to counteract it have been miserable failures. How can capitalists fight a humanistic concept of justice which means injustice to them and which robs them, when they themselves are humanistic and have no regard for God's law? They lack all moral, religious, and intellectual bases for any intelligent counteraction. The church is in even worse straits: it tries hard to prove that it is the best champion of social justice. It cannot challenge the humanism of that doctrine, because its own faith is humanistic. Man and man's salvation and welfare take priority in the churches, whether modernist, Reformed, or fundamentalist, Catholic or Protestant, over God and His glory. When the prophet Amos speaks of justice, it is *God's* justice, not *social* justice. His law comes from God, not man, and his grief and anger are due to man's contempt for God's law and justice.

Social justice reduces a large segment of humanity to a less than human status in the name of justice. For Scripture, men, however sinful, are God's creation and their need is regeneration. For Robespierre, the critics are less than man, and Robespierre demanded their purge. *Purge* was then a medical term, Otto J. Scott has pointed out, "meaning the forced expulsion of feces." Since Robespierre, the word has become political: it now means the forced expulsion and usually destruction of human beings as wastes. Thus, the enemies of humanism are not men: they are feces.

There were divisions in humanity in the days of kings and commoners, deep and important ones. In economic terms, men are closer together now, because of the industrial revolution. The gaps between rich and poor in Western society are the narrowest in history, as far as economics is concerned.

The cleavage between men, however, is greater than ever before in every other way. The conflict of interests idea is basic to modern society, and the goal of politics is to purge society in the name of social justice. The doctrine of social justice has thus become a mighty instrument for the degradation of man.

CHALCEDON REPORT NO. 147
November, 1977

One of the consequences of the Enlightenment was the legal and social down-grading of women. Because the Enlightenment exalted Reason to the place of God, it also exalted man as against woman. Man was seen as the vessel and voice of pure reason. Woman at best was practical reason, or, more commonly, emotion (or unreason). Legal discriminations aimed at enforcing the supposed incapacity of women to manage property began to proliferate. Because religion was seen by the men of the Enlightenment as emotionalism, religion was made the province of women, and philosophy the realm of males. These concepts, which began in Europe after 1660, reached America in the early 1800s.

The result was the deformation of both men and women. The sexes, instead of being complementary, were now seen as opposite, and the old pagan idea of conflict again predominated.

Man saw himself as reason, and woman as a grown-up child, because she represented unreason. In some areas, as in England, "privileged" boys were early separated from their mothers for their better schooling, with unhappy consequences. In France, Bodin, with others, saw woman as closer to the animals.

A woman, if beautiful and witty, could be treated as a goddess, or a plaything, but her status was at all times made dependent upon a man's judgment, not God's ordination. Reason had become incarnate, and its name was Man, and woman had better bow down to the new god of creation.

The Romantic Movement exalted emotions, without surrendering man's priority and man's claim to be Reason incarnate. All the same,the Romantic Movement did give birth, by this emphasis on feeling, to feminism. In fact, in the 19th century, many women, imbued with the philosophy of Romanticism, saw woman as a higher and purer being, because she was more emotional. The men of the Romantic Movement, however, saw only one kind of relationship with woman as "exalted," safe, and Romantic, the adulterous relationship. The free expression of Romantic emotionalism meant a separation from the family and from responsibility. To be responsible was to be unfree. As a result, the feminist leaders, whether Mary Wollstonecraft or Victoria Woodhull, were "liberated" women, liberated from family ties and from responsibility. If any of these women began to make demands for responsibility from the male Romantics, they were dropped as goddesses who had fallen from grace.

The "freedom" of man which marks the modern age is freedom essentially and primarily from God. This also requires freedom from all forms of responsibility. The family is especially hated. In Nietzsche, this Enlightenment principle meant a ridicule of the idea that a philosopher could be married.

Instead of attacking modern man as insane and irresponsible, the feminists began to hunger for the same irresponsibilities, forgetting that it would only increase their vulnerability and victimization. This particular emphasis came to the forefront, although long present, in the 1960s, in the renewed feminist movement. Women too have to become Reason incarnate; women too have the right to "freedom" or irresponsibility. If men can be playboys, women can be playgirls. So went the demands.

Liberation meant the same thing, freedom from God, and therefore freedom from all God-ordained responsibilities. It means antinomianism and unbelief.

St. Paul declares, "where the Spirit of the Lord is, there is liberty" (II Cor. 3:17). The modern faith is, where the spirit of unbelief and lawlessness is, there is liberty. The result is social suicide.

The rapid erosion of responsibility has meant an increasing social atomism and the stress on the radical autonomy of the individual. Classes now exist for women, to teach masturbation, so that they can dispense with men. Similar emphases are made for men, at home and abroad. Not only is God dead for these people, but all other men and women.

The insane can only exist in their withdrawal from reality if someone supports them in their flight. Without that support, they either perish or return to functioning. The modern state everywhere is attempting the impossible, to create a state which will permit all men the security of retreat from reality into cradle to grave security. The end of such an attempt is either disaster, or return to sanity.

The premises of modern man involve a flight from reality and delusions of deity. With his women and children now joining him in his heedless course, modern man's days are numbered. His support from the stable elements of society is being endangered and progressively destroyed by his actions, and the time of collapse approaches.

What modern man forgets is that this is God's world. Because it is God's world, these are good days and good times. God's blessings and His judgments are alike good, and righteous altogether. Let us look forward to them.

CHALCEDON REPORT NO. 148
December, 1977

The modern era has seen man, not as a religious creature made in the image of God, but as a rational and political animal. This has meant a warping of man, who is viewed, not in terms of the wholeness of his being and in terms of God's image, but rather in terms of reason. Moreover, reason took on a new meaning; it now meant an autonomous and final judge over all things, so that man became the working god of the world. Moreover, because man has been seen, not only in terms of this new view of reason, but as a political animal, man's answers and salvation take a political form.

Because of this new definition of man, the modern age began by excluding women from their newly defined "real" world. Man, the male, was defined as a rational and political animal; the rational and political aspects were man's male prerogatives because woman was essentially seen as irrational and hence basically as a human animal. She was thus in essence a household pet to be kept in captivity as a tamed animal. An untamed woman could be a social problem.

Biblical law had restricted woman's governmental role, not because of any incompetence, because Proverbs 31:10-31 makes clear her high potential, but because of a division of labor ordained by God. Moreover, the male spheres of church and state are in Scripture clearly subordinate to the female sphere of the family. The "limitation" thus has as its goal the maintenance of the priority of the family in society and in the woman's attention.

Now, however, new priorities prevailed. Earlier, the church had claimed priority. Now, the state made the claim, with far greater intolerance and insistence, and the new view of man meant the radical down-grading of woman. Moreover, the exaltation of reason and politics limited the male priority to certain men alone, the man of Reason and politics. This meant that Plato's philosopher-kings were the true humanity, because they represented Reason and politics, and other men and all women were social cattle, animals. Not surprisingly, the modern age saw the worst development of serfdom since the fall of Rome. Serfdom became more oppressive, and the serfs of Europe more and more beaten down and treated as an almost sub-human species. When radicals began to champion "the common man," they did so with the basic assumption that these human cattle could only become "authentically human" under the guidance of the philosopher-kings. Basic to this conveyance of the gift of humanity to the peasant and working classes was the politicizing of man. This meant two things. *First*, man had to be separated from Christianity, "the opium of the masses." Since to be a man requires the conversion of man to Reason and to politics, no poor peasant or worker could become "authentically human," to use a phrase dear to modern theologians, without a separation from his old-fashioned Christian faith. Hence, the de-humanizing "shame" of Christianity had to be wiped out. *Second*, the means whereby this fallen man was to be remade and rescued was seen as education. The move of the state therefore into education was a rapid one. To modern men everywhere, it had the force of an inevitable and necessary truth. It was seen as the mission of the state to re-create man by means of statist education.

Meanwhile, the life of Reason was expanded to include Science, and Science became a great potential instrument in the remaking of man and society. In the theory of scientific socialism, all the basic elements of the new view of man were put together: the politicizing of man, man as Reason, and Science as the great instrument of Reason in the new plan of salvation. The "real" world was now the world of science, politics, and autonomous Reason.

Through these new instruments forged by Reason, Science, and Politics, the excluded human "cattle" could now be let in, after being remade, "born again" by statist education, controls, and science. Peasants and workers were gradually separated from their old faith. Women were made to think that the once-prior world of the family was now a prison, or, at best, a stultifying and irrelevant domain. The goal of the obliteration of Christian faith and the family seemed closer to realization.

In the United States, where the roots of the past seemed least deep, the sharpest reaction began after World War II, the Christian School movement. The next decade will see bitter warfare between the modern establishment and the Christian School, a war to death. Similarly, the Christian family regained unexpected strength and priority with increasing numbers, and modern youth, in considerable numbers, began to forsake the statism of their fathers for Christian roots.

All of this is a threat to the life of the modern establishment, and the battle is and will be a bitterly sharp one. The instruments of political and social power are almost all in the hands of the enemy, but it is in his camp too that disintegration is most dramatically at work. Moreover, in this battle, there is more involved than the two protagonists. The triune God is never absent from history: it serves His purpose, moves to His goal, and is absolutely governed by His sovereign power. The battle is the Lord's.

CHALCEDON REPORT NO. 149
January, 1978

The essence of original sin is its declaration of independence from God and its claim to autonomy (Gen. 3:5). Man denies all superior authority and declares that, as his own god and final court of appeal, he will decide or "know" what constitutes good and evil.

However, because man is a creature, his life is one of radical dependence,

dependence on the physical world and air, on his family and friends, his social environment, on institutions and society, and much, much more, but, supremely, he is dependent upon the God who creates and orders all things. In particular, the family and marriage are strong areas of dependence and interdependence. For this reason, the family and marriage are savagely attacked by humanists, because they so eloquently witness to this fact. Modern philosophy has a long history of hostility to marriage and women, of which Schopenhauer, Nietzsche, and Sartre are only more conspicuous examples. Men may dominate their wives unjustly, but even in their sin they cannot hide from themselves their deep dependence upon them. As a result, sinful men have always either ridiculed marriage, or sought to suppress their natural dependence on their wives by an unwarranted domination to conceal their dependence and need.

In the Biblical sense, authority does not diminish dependence. The greater a person's authority, the greater his dependence upon all who are under that authority. The increase of human authority and power means an increase of dependence; the refusal of man to face that fact means tyranny. The dependence of a head of state on those around and under him is a very great one, whereas the dependence of a minor clerk on others is not as critical or extensive. Both the growth of civilization and of authority increase dependency and interdependency.

Humanism, however, has sought autonomy together with power and authority, an impossible union for the creature. One aspect of this quest is the steady assault on women and marriage in the thought of ancient and modern humanism. How can a man safely assert his autonomy when he needs a woman as his helpmeet? One way of "resolving" this problem has been prostitution: the man "satisfies" a physical need without any responsibility; promiscuity has the same appeal. It meets the need for autonomy, which, practically, means irresponsibility. The prostitute and the promiscuous girl or woman seek the same goal, a sense of power in exploiting a person without any responsibility towards that person. Another "resolution" has been to turn marriage into an arena for the fiat will of man without allowing the woman any voice or authority.

First, man declared himself autonomous from God and man. *Second*, he declared that the universe is autonomous from God also and represents merely the blind product of evolutionary chance. This view made autonomy a constituent and basic aspect of reality. Newtonian science began the enthronement of a cosmos on its own. Later, the very idea of a first cause, long held as a limiting concept, was dropped. The universe needs no cause in the newer view: it is itself whatever cause may be. *Third*, this doctrine of cosmic autonomy began to affect all men, not philosophers only. It became the doctrine of revolution, and, finally, the doctrine of women's rights, children's rights, homosexual rights, and more. Every segment of society began to claim "rights" divorced from all responsibility and from God's law.

The philosophy of humanism came home to the bedroom; original sin, with its claim to total autonomy, became the justification for every group and class in its revolt against all moral authority.

Thus, the various "rights" movements represent no new social order: they are humanism come to flower. Some of them call attention to legitimate claims and to actual wrongs; they fail to see that these are the products of the very humanism they themselves are embracing. Modern man has been irresponsible; all that the liberation movements usually say is, we too want the privilege or irresponsibility.

The idea of autonomy begins with the revolution of irresponsibility from God; it ends with a world of warring and irresponsible peoples, each of whom is god in his own eyes and seeks his or her own advantage in contempt of all others. Humanism becomes logically the philosophy of a well-educated prostitute, who has declared; "I don't believe in having a relationship with expectations and requirements...Anything that breaks down inhibitions is good...I've experienced myself as infinite, and as God, and as the universe" (Peter Whittaker: *The American Way of Sex*, pp. 156, 153, 147. New York: Putnam, 1974). Not surprisingly, best-selling books now regularly promote, in fiction and non-fiction, this whorish faith of looking after Number One, and Number One is not God but the individual. A world of millions of Number Ones is a world of lawlessness and total warfare.

And why should not women and children buy this faith when schools, pulpits, politicians, courts, films, and television promote it? Autonomous man is the man of the fall. He will only change when he is regenerated by the power of God through Christ. Either every man is king, or Christ is King. These are the two logical alternatives. The end result of autonomy is hell, the realm of total isolation and of no communication, where every person is his own universe, and man is in everlasting self-communion; the borders of his life are forever closed to God and to other men. The end result of the life of faith in God and obedience to Christ the king is full communion with God and man, the perfection of interdependence and love.

The borders of the lives of men and nations are closing, and all hell rejoices as more men embrace the prisonhouse of autonomy. But we need not "fear, though the earth be removed, and though the mountains be carried into the midst of the sea" (Ps. 46:1). Not even the gates of hell can stand against our conquering King (Matt. 16:18). This is a time of decay and defeat for the enemy, but a time of opportunity and conquest for us through Christ our King.

THE NEW WAR OF RELIGION

Alan N. Grover; *Ohio, Trojan Horse*. Greenville, South Carolina: Bob Jones University Press, 1977; xv, 154 pp. Also obtainable from Christian Schools of Ohio; 6929 W. 130th Street, Suite 600; Cleveland, Ohio 44130.

The publication of this book is an important fact. It is the account of the attempt in Ohio by the statist educators to control Christian Schools, and of the resistance to that attempt. It is, however, much more. What the Christian Schools of Ohio came to realize, in their resistance, was that they were engaged in a major battle of an emerging war of religion, Humanism versus Christianity. In that battle, the major agencies of church, school, and state are in the hands of the enemy, so that the battle lines, while clear-cut, give a confused picture insofar as the forces of Christianity are concerned.

The state or "public" schools are religious schools, earnestly dedicated to the teaching of the religion of humanism. In their minimum standards, their curriculum, their accreditation, standards and policies for teachers and schools, and their stated purposes they represent a faith alien to Scripture. Even more, they represent that faith which Scripture declares was first set forth by the tempter and which constitutes original sin: every man as his own god, knowing or determining for himself what constitutes good and evil (Gen. 3:5). It is indicative of the extent to which the churches have gone over to the enemy that CSO (Christian Schools of Ohio) had criticism in its stand from pastors and "Christian" schoolmen.

One of the opening guns of the assault on Christian Schools was the case of the Rev. Levi W. Whisner, (to whom this book was dedicated), who was ably defended by Attorney William Ball, already an established and great champion of Christian conscience. In the Canal Winchester case, Attorney David C. Gibbs, Jr., began his active and extensive involvement.

At issue has been the claim of the state to virtually universal jurisdiction. In opposition to this has been the declaration of the embattled Christians that Christ's Kingdom (*ecclesia*, or church) cannot be under anyone or anything, that the state, like the church and school, must obey Jesus Christ. What the state demanded in Ohio, and is now demanding in other states is a single culture, a humanistic one. It became apparent in Ohio that even small and struggling Christian Schools educated their pupils more ably than the state schools. Where the basic skills are involved, the Christian Schools are clearly superior. The demand for controls and for accreditation is a first step towards creating a single and humanistic culture. In Ohio, the state's minimum standards require the promotion and teaching of humanism in every aspect of the curriculum.

As against this, the Rev. Levi Whisner held that a Christian School cannot compromise and must be independent. The regenerate man cannot place his school or children under the control of an unregenerate school system which promotes an alien faith.

What came clearly into focus in the Ohio battles was the recognition by the men of CSO that all education is inescapably religious, and a religious neutrality is impossible in education. Every school will implicitly or explicitly witness to and indoctrinate its pupils in one religion or another. The rise of humanism and anti-Christianity in the U.S.A. and throughout the world has been a result of state control of education, and the use of that control to promote humanism.

Moreover, although many churchmen have refused to face up to this fact, the courts have recognized and stated that secular humanism is indeed a religion, and Alan Grover develops the implications of this fact. What we have thus in public education is a state religion, the religious establishment of humanism. (To restore Bible-reading and prayer to such schools would be simply to white-wash sepulchres. We do have, however, a considerable number of churchmen representing a major denomination of our time, the Church of the Whited Sepulchres.)

Grover analyzes the religion of humanism in all its forms, its two Humanist Manifestoes, in the state schools, and in general thought. Its presuppositions are those of the tempter; its faith is anti-Christian, and its plan of salvation involves, among other things, the deliverance of man from Biblical faith. It is a religion of the "now," of enjoying life in terms of self-realization rather than in terms of faith in and obedience to the triune God. Humanism is hostile to all godly authority. As Alan Grover summarizes it, it is man-centered; it is "now-oriented;" and it teaches faith in a world government as basic to man's hope. The Christian must not be "conformed to this world" (Rom. 12:2), and all state controls on Christian Schools, minimum standards, accreditation requirements, and other controls have at root an implicit requirement and goal of conformity to humanism. (One of the most pernicious of illusions is the faith that bumbling, corrupt and inefficient civil bureaucracies can set and maintain better standards for schools, medicine, businesses, or anything else than can anyone else. This view does not represent experience but rather a blind faith in the state as the omnicompetent agency.)

The issue, as Grover states it clearly, is *not quality but control.* State intervention or control does not produce quality; quite the contrary. Educators themselves view education as a means of social control. Grover quotes John Dewey to this effect again and again. The goal of the school, Dewey held, is "the formation of the proper social life,...the securing of the right social growth..." and "the teacher is always the prophet of the true God and the usherer in of the true kingdom of God." Dewey's "God" is really humanity.

Education in origin was a church function; in essence, it has always been inescapably a religious function. The Christian School is a Christian ministry, and it cannot be made subject to statist controls without a denial of the faith. As Grover points out, "Professional educators have endorsed control of society through education, and they have sought to control all of education to implement their goal. They have been sought to control religion in their grasp for power" (p. 115).

In this battle between Christians and humanists, the courts have closely examined the faith of the Christian defendants. At stake has been the issue of motivation and faith. Are the defendants motivated by a preference, or by a conviction? If the decision is a matter of preference, the court refuses to honor the defendant's position. A man may prefer one course above another, but the alternative is then not an impossible one for him but simply lower in acceptance. Conviction is another matter: it is faith, and the conscience of faith. Conviction is grounded in the mandate and law of God, which gives us no alternative but to obey. Is the independence of the Christian ministry in church and school grounded on a total dependence on and an obedience to Christ as Lord? If so, it is conviction, when a man's faith and a life in conformity to that faith are in evidence. (It was clear to the Ohio Supreme Court that the Rev. Levi Whisner is a man of conviction, and hence his vindication.)

It is the expectation of major federal judges that one of the most common kind of cases appearing on appeal during the next decade will involve Christian Schools. A battle is under way which will not disappear simply because men choose to ignore it. The importance of this book is that it sets forth the basic geography of that battle, and, as a result, is necessary reading.

It will be a major, if not the central, battleground because it will govern the future. If Christian Schools continue to grow at their present rate, they will, in 20 years or less, have created a different kind of United States, one in which trained and informed Christians predominate, and one in which leadership will pass into the hands of Christians. The humanists recognize this clearly. This is the reason for their full-scale offensive in state after state to control and thereby suppress and destroy this strong and resurgent Biblical faith. What is at stake is, *first*, the life or death of Christianity or humanism. Whichever triumphs educationally will prevail. The humanistic state schools are a growing disaster. The only way that disaster can be prevented from bringing on the death of humanism and its culture is to kill off the opposition, the Christian School movement, through controls. This is a fight for life for both parties. If the state schools prevail, then the destruction of our children will be effected. *Second*, the future of the United States is at stake. Humanism spells the degeneration and collapse of any country it commands. The Christian School movement is America's best hope for a Christian future.

In this developing war of religion, there is no neutrality. The delusions of neutrality are ably exposed by the Rev. Alan N. Grover.

THE MEANING OF ACCREDITATION

A growing and central issue of our time is accreditation. The central area of conflict is with schools; in the background lurks another issue, the accreditation of churches (by welfare agencies, because of their nurseries; by councils of churches for their legitimacy, etc.)

Accreditation is an act of faith. We express our faith in someone when we go to them for accreditation, for approval. Paul speaks of accreditation when he tells Timothy, "Study to show thyself approved unto God, a workman that needeth not to be ashamed, rightly dividing the word of truth" (II Tim. 2:15).

The root meaning of accreditation is credo, I believe. When a school goes to an accreditation council, it declares, I believe in you and in your word, and I present myself as one who seeks to be approved by you. If you approve of me, then I need not be ashamed, for then I teach the word of truth and respectability.

Again and again, we have seen seminaries established in order to reform the church. The new seminary wants to teach the true word, it claims, but one of its first steps is to seek accreditation. Very quickly, the new seminary begins to resemble the old, and, in all its ways, it seeks the approval of the very world of humanistic scholarship it abandoned. As a result, the new reform begins to resemble more and more the old sin.

This is no less true of Christian Schools. Parents rebel against the corruptions produced by the humanistic state schools. Christian Schools are started and flourish, but soon evil voices begin to promote the need for accreditation, and they seek the approval of the same corrupt system they abandoned. Such men are no different than the Israelites in the wilderness journey who said, "Let us make us a captain, and let us return to Egypt" (Numbers 14:4). Such men are governed by the principle of reprobation.

Whose approval do you seek? Where your faith is, there too is your source of accreditation. Those who seek accreditation from humanistic agencies carry within their heart the principle of captivity and sin. They feel naked if they stand in terms of the Lord and His word, and they demand of the enemy, come and clothe us with the rags of your accreditation.

Accreditation is the humanistic form of circumcision or baptism. It summons the faithful humanists to show the marks of their faith and to witness to it. Accreditation councils simply require the faithful to stand up and be counted in terms of their faith in humanism and its agencies.

The real cause for the persecution of the Christian Church by Rome was the refusal of the church to submit to licensure and taxation by Rome, i.e., to submit to state approval and accreditation. Rome promised to leave the church more or less alone if only Christian leaders would offer a little incense before Caesar's image and say, "Caesar is lord." They would then be licensed or accredited and free to go their way. Instead, Christians confessed, "Jesus is Lord" and resisted; the apostates were accredited. The same issue is with us today, and, again, the apostate cry is, what harm is there in licensure, in accreditation? The harm is still the same: another lord is confessed, another creed is affirmed, and another faith is put into practice.

CHALCEDON REPORT NO. 150
February, 1978

Autonomous man wants an autonomous universe: the goal is the independence of all things from God, and from one another. Of the renaissance mind of Francis Bacon, Judah Stampfer writes, "When his negotiations are finished, the universe - the world of things - is in business for itself. We will shape, experience, and know it at out pleasure - let God be circumspect in His complaints." Later, Hobbes and Isaac Newton reduced reality to matter, to "eternally bouncing mini-marbles." (Judah Stampfer: *Face and Shadow*, p. 61f. 1971.)

In this materialistic realm, God had no real place. Man and the universe were in business for themselves. Instead of God's law, man's law (first of all royal law, later democratic law) is operative. Instead of all life and society under covenant with God, all things were seen instead as a contract between men. The covenant of God with man was set aside and denied in favor of a social contract, the contract of free agents with one another. As a result, civil government and law were grounded on a social basis; they were determined by men, not by God. The social contract led to social justice. Because the foundations of the state and of law are of human ordination, it was logically held that justice also must be of human or social origin; hence, true justice is seen in this tradition as social justice, socially determined.

When in the first half of the 1970's then Senator John Tunney of California was confronted by pro-life advocates, he defended abortion as moral *because* it was legal and the will of the people. He was then asked if theft would be moral if the majority of the people voted its legalization; the senator felt that then theft would be moral.

This is the logic of the doctrine of social justice. Justice is what man says it is. Man may be variously defined: as elite man, as the dictatorship of the proletariat, as the democratic consensus, or as the majority, or as individual, anarchistic man. In any case, justice is what man says it is. As a result, we have Marxist justice, National Socialist justice, democratic justice, white justice, red justice, black justice, and so on, all forms of the humanistic definition of righteousness.

But this is not all. If justice is social, then injustice and evil are all things which are anti-social. Again, we have a term which can mean anything. Everything from communist propaganda to Christian missions can be called anti-social, depending on who does the defining. I recently heard opposition to abortion and homosexuality described as injustice and as anti-social activity.

How far gone this erosion of the doctrine of God's law and justice is appears clearly in the fact that so many churchmen speak of social justice and call any appeal to God's law legalism. Their doctrines of good and evil, and justice and injustice, are derived, not from God's law, but from man's law and man's doctrines of social justice and anti-social activities. Men may name God and Christ when they talk of social justice, but in reality they worship at alien altars and another god whose name is man.

But here is the irony and the built-in disaster of the social contract and its children. When man rejects God in favor of autonomy, he cannot arrest the principle of autonomy. Independence from God is followed by the independence of man from man. Humanism may seek a *social* order, but it creates an *anarchistic* state instead. The demand for autonomy from God is followed by a demand for a demand for an autonomy from all law and morality, and from all men. Everyone has "rights" to autonomy and to a judgment-free world: men, women, children, criminals, perverts, all are to be autonomous, free from all controls and judgment. Some have even proposed the autonomous nature and "rights" of trees and wild-life.

But autonomy is an illusory dream for the creature. He is absolutely the creature of God, and his life is one of dependence and inter-dependence. The fulfillment of man's dream of autonomy is death and hell. The dead in a cemetery are the only people who are in any sense autonomous, and independent from the world around them. Social justice finally means anarchism and death. The only alternative to social justice is God's justice, or, in brief, God's law. In Scripture, righteousness and justice are the same word and meaning. God's law is true justice or righteousness. If men will not build on faith and on the obedience of faith to the law of God, they build only for disaster.

Social justice holds that man the sinner can define right and wrong and can set forth the meaning of justice. This is like asking a mule to be fertile, or appointing a prostitute to be the guardian of virtue. Every doctrine of justice set forth by man the sinner will be an attempt to present sin as a virtue, and lawlessness as law.

Social justice does not exist. It is a myth. Every effort to achieve social justice instead increases injustice, because it enacts an illusion and an evil.

God's law, however, works to effect restitution and restoration, and it stresses responsibility. It does not express man; rather, it governs, guides, and protects man in terms of God's calling and purpose.

Men who move in terms of God's law are not guided by the social consensus nor by the majority. For them, God, not man, is the author of possibilities and they move in terms of God's calling. Stampfer tells a delightful story of a relative, an immigrant fresh from Poland, who was at once employed in his first sweat-shop job in the garment industry. After half an hour, he asked the next stitcher in Yiddish, "Please, exactly how much money will buy this entire establishment?" We need Christians with the same sense of confidence in God's possibilities. What God commands and requires is much more easily attained than that immigrant's dream. All things shall be brought into captivity to Jesus Christ, men and nations, the arts and the sciences. The only question we face is this: will we be a part of that victorious army, or one of the defeated?

WHAT IS THE CHURCH?

One of the central problems plaguing the history of Christianity has been the definition of the church. Part of the problem is that the word *church* comes from *Kyriakos*, as used in phrases such as *Kyriakon doma*, meaning the Christian place of worship, but it is also used for *ecclesia*. The deeper problem is the claim of the worshipping body to be more than it is.

The Old Testament has two words for the covenant people: *edah* (congregation) and *qahal* (assembly). *Ecclesia* covers both meanings. These terms cover the same ground: a single community of believers, or all communities; the covenant people as a worshipping group, or as an army, or as a nation, or in all their capacities. This point is not new; in the past century, such Biblical dictionaries as those of James Hastings and J.O. Douglas have cited it, as has the *Encyclopaedia Judaica* in its article on "Congregation."

In brief, the *church* in the New Testament means God's Kingdom and its constituent parts. The church *in* or *at* Corinth or Philippi meant the covenant people of Kingdom outpost at that point, including the ecclesiastical.

To limit the meaning of the church to the Christian synagogue or chapel is thus to distort radically the meaning of Scripture. It reduces the redemptive scope and function of Christ's work and of His church from a universal and cosmic scale to a limited and institutional one. Jesus Christ declared that, "All power...in heaven and in earth" (Matt. 28:18) is given to Him as Lord and King; the false definition of the church, which limits it to the Christian institution for worship, limits Christ's Kingship to the institution's borders and limits the scope of redemption and government.

As a result, the institution for worship takes two courses. First, it has often become an imperial church, claiming sovereignty over state, school, and every other area as itself the Kingdom. Second, it denies the imperial claim and becomes a withdrawn and monastic group isolated from the world around it, and denying Christ's claims over it.

Both courses are untenable, and they result in a false view of the Kingdom, of eschatology, and of redemption. The Christian synagogue is a part of the church or Kingdom, a necessary and central part, but never itself the church in its entirety or its essence. The Kingdom is in and of the King, and He is more than the sum total of the parts thereof, and is beyond them all. The true church or Kingdom includes the full concourse or general assembly of the firstborn, the entire assembly (Heb. 12:22-24), and is thus inclusive of all men and angels and all their realms. The continuity of the *church* with the Old Testament *theocracy* is repeatedly stressed in the use of such terms as Zion and Jerusalem (Heb. 12:22-24). What the old was, the new now is. Christ declares Himself to be the glorious Lord of the theocracy in its world-wide scope in the Great Commission (Matt. 28:18-20).

The church thus cannot be defined except in terms of Christ as King, and His whole realm in heaven and on earth, and all men and things brought into captivity to and under the dominion of our Redeemer Lord. It is His realm and His new creation.

CHALCEDON REPORT NO. 151
March, 1978

Disasters are often the works of able men who, seeing a problem more clearly than others, try to solve it dramatically, but with the wrong answers. In the 20th century, we have seen the damage done by such solutions as World War I and the Versailles Treaty, the League of Nations, World War II and its treaties, the United Nations, Korea, Vietnam, Keynesianism, and much more. It is not enough to condemn sins and errors: it is necessary to understand what wrong religious premises went into them.

One of the ablest men of history was Innocent III, who in 1198 became pope. He was faced with a serious problem: Europe was nominally Christian, but in reality had relegated Christian faith to a formal and irrelevant position in political and social life. In Frederick II (1194-1250), the Holy Roman emperor, this indifference to the faith was more openly expressed, because Frederick's power gave him the freedom to do it. Frederick ruled more like a Moslem sultan than a Germanic king. He kept a harem, guarded by eunuchs, a troupe of Muslim dancing girls, and was generally skeptical about religion. Frederick spoke fluently in German, French, Italian, and Arabic, read both Greek and Latin, and was widely read in ancient and current works of scholarship. He moved with an indifference to moral and religious considerations and held to a humanistic perspective.

Most Europeans were either not as "advanced" in their skepticism, as was Frederick II, or not as vocal, but most churchmen and laymen shared Frederick's indifference to Christian faith. Innocent III thus was the spiritual head of a Christendom seriously adrift in its moral and religious foundations. Innocent had the power to assert authority in one realm after another, enough to break rulers, and he had the power to institute reforms. Both answers he felt were insufficient, however necessary, and not to be neglected. What was needed above all, he felt, was a revival of religious fervor. This he believed could best be generated by a crusade, and the result was the preaching of the Fourth Crusade. This was begun in 1199, and every effort was made to keep this Crusade under control and strictly Christian in purpose. The result was one moral disaster after another. One of the worst consequences was the sack of Zara and then of Constantinople in 1202 and 1204, and, in 1212, the horrors of the Children's Crusade. What was begun as a means of reviving Christian faith and fervor became a powerful instrument for unleashing evil and destructive forces on all of Europe and the Byzantine Empire. The Albigensian Crusade in 1208 plunged southern France into blood, and Innocent's dream began to unravel.

Innocent was an Italian patrician of Germanic blood; eight popes came from his family. He sought to make Europe a single moral and religious community under his spiritual leadership. An able administrator, his reforms and re-organization of the papal chancery greatly improved and strengthened papal government. His idea of reviving faith in Europe, however, led only to disasters and griefs. Reform by new action is not reform when the old man is still involved; all of Innocent's efforts only gave morally indifferent and evil men new scopes for the enactment of their greed and evil.

Innocent's program, which has roots in old Rome, is still very much with us. From Woodrow Wilson to the present, the Innocentine idea of moral revival and accomplishment has led the United States into one crusade after another, with results even more deadly than those of Innocent's crusade. All over the world, indeed, men share this same faith: institute a good program of moral action to save the world. From wars, to leagues and unions of nations, from army corps to peace corps, the plan is put into action, and things somehow grow worse. No moral cause can survive immoral men, nor can the world and history be regenerated by unregenerate men.

The difference between Innocent's day and ours is that then the crusades were launched in the name of Christianity; now they are launched in the name of Humanity and the religion of humanism. In either case, the implications are not Christian.

Crusades now are as religious as ever, but they are proclaimed by politicians, not by popes. Men run for political office, and gain control of nations, by promises of another crusade, this time, the candidate in effect declares, with the right spirit. A new and "innocent" group of men will supposedly lead us into a true crusade.

The Children's Crusade, in which tens of thousands of children ended as slaves, prostitutes, or dead, began with such a faith. The average age of the children was twelve; their belief was that their "innocence" would lead to miracles and deliver the Holy Land to them. Many ended in massive corruption, cannibalism, and horrors, only a minority retaining their faith.

Other and minor child pilgrimages occurred later, all evidences of the humanistic faith in the natural innocence of children, and the power of that innocence. This same faith in the untainted innocence of youth marked the student movements of the 1960s: like the pretentious youth of the Children's Crusade, the Youth's Crusade of the 1960s pitted its ostensibly holy innocence against the corruption of the Establishment; the confrontation showed the prevalence of sin on all sides. Another crusade failed, but not man's faith in crusades.

For us as Christians the crusade offers no hope. It is a costly evil. The crusade puts its hope in some men's innocence and action, and it leads to phariseeism, hypocrisy, and the brutalities of self-righteousness.

For the Christian, the answer begins with regeneration, and it continues with obedience to God's law. It means restitution, Christian education, the increase of godly knowledge and dominion, and the centrality of the family as a unit under God and to His purposes.

When Innocent came to office, indifference and hostility to the church were common among lay people, and prevalent in all circles. During his eighteen year pontificate, Innocent punished two emperors and seven kings; he acted with vigor, and fearlessly. All the same, he left the situation worse than he found it: power had been countered with power, sometimes wisely, sometimes wrongly, but the faith was not advanced, and indifference only grew. The crisis was not resolved but only aggravated.

Men can be indifferent to problems; they can aggravate them; or, by the obedience of faith to the law of God, they can take steps to resolve them as He requires it.

CHALCEDON REPORT NO. 152
April, 1978

Because of his humanism, modern man believes strongly in the innocence of children and their natural goodness. It is the world, the environment, which is sinful, whereas, as Wordsworth wrote, in his "Ode on Intimations of Immortality," of children it must be said that "trailing clouds of glory do we come" into this world; unhappily, "Shades of the prison-house begin to close upon the growing boy." These ideas were not new with Wordsworth; in the modern era, they went back to at least John Locke, who borrowed them from Aristotle and the Scholastics.

The medieval version had led to the Gospel of the Child, a heresy culminating in the disaster of the Children's Crusade in 1212. Adults believed in the child and the power of the child's purity, and children learned this new faith from their parents and fervently preached it. The children actually believed that their "innocence" would result in miracles to transport them over the sea to the Holy Land. "Who would remain here, when there lies a path in the sea, between emerald walls, to the land where glory waits us? They declared, "Between waters, which are to be to us as a wall on the right hand and the left, are we to cross the untrodden bed of the sea, and, with dry feet will we stand on the distant beach by the walls of Acre of Tripoli. We bear no weapons and we wear no armor! The pathway of other Crusaders may be marked by the stain of blood and the glitter of steel, and martial music may have timed their many steps, but our pilgrim's robes are our armor, our Crosses are our swords, and our hymns shall time our march!" (J.Z. Gray: *The Children's Crusade*, pp. 86, 108, 1870, 1972). What the children gained was either death, slavery, venereal diseases, or, at the least, disillusionment. Of nearly 100,000 children, one third never returned home.

The Student Crusade of the 1960s was another like movement. The students began with a belief in their holiness and the evil of the world. It was their mission to bring the world to peace by imposing their holiness upon it. One scholar dates the origin of the movement in October, 1955, when Allen Ginsberg read his poem, "How!" at the San Francisco's Six Gallery. Its message was simplicity itself: the world is like a mad-house because of the evil Establishment, whereas everything is in and of itself HOLY; it is the duty of Youth, before all are driven mad like young Carl Solomon, to redeem the world. Ginsberg said, "I'm putting my queer shoulder to the wheel." Soon many more young shoulders, queer and unqueer, were being put to the wheel.

The results were even more disastrous than in 1212. In the conflict with ancient evils, the Youth Crusade invented its own variations. It raged with Phariseeism against all evil outside itself and failed to see that, in the process, it was compounding evil with evil. For most, the movement ended with disillusionment, narcotics, disease, or a retreat into the pleasure principle of the sexual revolution. Others, more hardened in their self-righteousness, went underground to make up various world-wide terrorist groups. Its gospel of love, innocence, and change had hardened into murder.

The above-ground movement is even more ominous. It has taken a new form, the Children's Bill of Rights movement, an effort in varying degrees all over the world, to "free" the child from parental and church controls and give him the right to govern himself as he pleases. The child, it is believed, will somehow still save us.

What is surprising is that these movements did not come sooner, and more drastically. Their basic principles have been taught for generations, (as I pointed out in *The Messianic Character of American Education*). Most graduation speakers, from grade school through the university, have been preaching the Gospel of the Child for generations. Sooner or later, this was bound to produce action and results.

Rousseau, of course, was one of the great earlier preachers of this faith, and we have a series of revolutions to thank him for! Friedrich Froebel (1782 - 1852), an educational philosopher of very great influence, had warbled, "Dear little children, we will learn from you." If children feel they know better than their parents, and are rebellious, they do so with good reason: our humanistic schools have taught them to think so. Nora Smith, a theorist of the Kindergarten, wrote in a *Ladies Home Journal* book, *The Kindergarten in a Nutshell* (1907), that mothers had a rare honor in carrying their children: "like St. Christopher, we have borne the Christ upon our Shoulders." When the educator and Kindergarten theorist Emma Marwedel lay dying in 1893, she said, "I believe in the power of the Kindergarten to reform the world." Since 1893, we have been seeing more and more of the meaning of that "reform."

The spirit of crusades is to locate the holy, good, innocent, or pure class in society, or age group. This pure group has been variously identified as the upper class, the middle class, the lower class, the workers, the capitalists, the intellectuals, the children, women, and so on. The quest goes on. It has also been sought in various nations and races. Where is the Sir Galahad to find the Holy Grail and change the world and re-charge it with his purity?

All such crusading is an implicit or explicit denial of Jesus Christ and His word. It looks for a redeemer other than Christ, and a plan other than God's law and Kingdom. Such quests and crusades glorify self-righteousness and phariseeism, and they are uniformly blind to their own sinfulness. Their failures are always blamed on an evil world and an evil Establishment. The world was not ready for their purity and wisdom!

The disillusioned ranks of the crusaders keep looking for another leader, another charismatic figure, one who can charm the snakes of evil out of their fangs and poisons, part the waters or walk on water, and somehow deliver mankind. The enthusiasm and fervor of political campaigns tell us that men are looking, not for sound and godly administration, but for miracles and miracle-workers. It is their passionate hope that this new man might be the real one.

Meanwhile, they turn their backs on God the Savior, and the only means for man's redemption, Jesus Christ.

THE RETREAT OF THEOLOGY

One of the disasters of the modern age is the retreat of theology into a narrow discipline having to do with very limited doctrines relative to the Christian synagogue or church. The roots of this retreat are very old, and evidences of it appear from the early days of church history, but never has it been more radical and thorough than now.

What is theology? Perhaps the simplest way to define it is to go to a dictionary definition. Noah Webster, in the 1828 first edition, defined theology as that form of knowledge "which teaches the existence, character and attributes of God, his laws and government, the doctrines we are to believe, and the duties we are to practice." Now, since God is Creator of all things, and governs all things, and since there is no area of life outside of God and outside our duty to Him, it is clear that theology, the declaration of the word of God and its meaning, must govern every area of life and thought. Our Biblical and systematic theology must set forth the requirements and implications of Scripture for the total life of man and for all of creation.

Theology is thus more than an ecclesiastical discipline. It is basic to all of life and learning. It was theology which began the university by setting forth the fact of the one (and triune) God, one universe of law and meaning, and the one faith as the key to its meaning. Paganism had usually a polytheistic faith and believed in a multiverse: no development of science was possible without a belief in the unity of creation and common laws. Some forms of paganism held to a unity of the cosmos, but their lack of a Biblical theism led them to view that cosmos as blind necessity and meaningless. Biblical theology made knowledge flourish because it held to a unified and cosmic field of meaning; as a result, the university was born.

With the rise of humanism, this faith has faltered and is waning. Clark Kerr, then president of the University of California, in the 1950s called for a change of the university into a multiversity. In such a cosmos, all things are possible except God, truth, and meaning. As a result of such thinking, the academic community has become less and less relevant to life as man must live it and more and more productive of chaos.

Theology must speak to the whole of life. A theology which becomes an ecclesiastical discipline, and no more, denies the doctrine of creation and God's sovereignty. It treats the God of Scripture as no more than a Greek god, governing a limited community and territory, and a small cult. The theologies of the churches today are thus implicitly polytheistic and anti-Biblical.

Theology must speak to the whole of life, because God is the Creator and Lord of all things. The theology of politics must be developed, or we will have anti-Christian politics. Law has to do with good and evil, right and wrong, and nothing can be more essentially theological than this. For a theology to neglect law means to neglect the Bible and the God of the Bible.

Education means indoctrination into a way of life and the skills thereof. This means religion, and this means that, unless Christian theology governs education, our education will teach humanism or some other religion. We are today under God's curse and judgement, because we have treasonably given our children over to another faith and school. We are, together with our children, God's property, and we dare not make ourselves the possession of humanism and its schools. To do so is treason, and it is sin.

The arts and sciences are all to be under God's word and informed by God's interpretations of all things as set forth in His word. We cannot have, in any area, any ultimate or basic authority other than God. If the world is not God's creation, then it is ultimately meaningless, and all our learning, our arts and sciences, are a veneer on the cosmic surd. But if God is God, Creator and Lord, we cannot begin on any other foundation than that faith without ending in contradictions and absurdity.

Our vocations must be theologically governed; we must be concerned with exercising dominion, extending knowledge, righteousness, and holiness, and acting as God's priests, prophets, and kings over every area of life and thought. A theology silent about such things will be in due time silenced and judged by God.

Theology thus must assert the Crown Rights of Christ the King over every area of life and thought. It must set forth and clarify God's command word, the Bible, in order to arm men for action. The Bible is not a devotional manual nor an inspirational book, but a command word for the army of God. To reduce theology to an academic or an ecclesiastical matter is to deny the God of Scripture.

If the God of our theology is merely the God of our imagination, we can confine him within the walls of the classroom and the church building, and have all kinds of room left over. But, if He be the living God, then our theology will burst at the seams as it sets forth the universal commands and demands of God the Lord.

Moreover, a theology of the living God will be a theology of joy, victory, and confidence. Our Lord declares, "*All power*, is given unto me in heaven and in earth. Go ye therefore, and teach all nations, baptizing them in the name of the Father, and of the Son, and of the Holy Ghost: Teaching them to observe all things whatsoever I have commanded you: and, lo, I am with you alway, even unto the end of the world. Amen." (Matt. 28:18-20).

Christ is both born and risen from the dead as victor over sin and death, King of Kings, and Lord of Lords. He is our Immanuel, God with us. Let His enemies tremble.

This is theology, to be taught, proclaimed, and the ground of action to victory.

RELIGION AND THE STATE

One of the key points of confusion in the modern mind, an error doing great damage to the cause of Christ, is the failure to distinguish between the separation of *church* and state, and the separation of *religion* and the state. *Church* and state can be separated; they are two different institutions. They can be subordinate one to the other, interdependent, or separate; or, in the case of anti-Christian states, the church can be denied a legal existence.

Religion and the state is another matter entirely. It is impossible to separate the two, and the idea of a non-religious or religiously neutral state is a myth, and a very dangerous myth. A state cannot exist without laws, and all laws are expressions of one or another religious faith. Laws are enacted morality, and procedures for the enforcement of that morality. Laws and morality in general are expressions of religion, of ultimate concern, of a faith in what constitutes true and ultimate order. Every legal system is inescapably an establishment of religion. There can thus be no separation of religion and the state.

The important question is this: since every state or civil government is an establishment of religion, what will the religion of the state be? The laws of all civil governments represent a doctrine of religious order, a faith in moral government and truth. If a state is not Christian, it will be an expression of humanistic, Buddhist, Islamic, Shinto, Hindu, or some other religious system of order, morality, or law.

To talk thus of the separation of religion and the state is clearly wrong: it is impossible. People who indulge in such talk are, *first*, clearly ignorant of the basic facts of the matter and the nature of law. *Second*, if they are not ignorant, they are then working quietly to supplant one kind of religion with another, to replace one doctrine of law and morality with another doctrine derived from an alien religion.

One of the problems of Western history has long been the mixture of conflicting laws and religions in its political order. The Christian foundations of law have had many admixtures of ancient forms of pagan law. Now, more than ever before, the pagan element is militant and is self-conscious in its desire to purge civil government from all traces of Christian law and morality. Humanism, the religion of man, seeks to destroy Christian doctrines of law in favor of humanistic doctrines. Humanism is increasingly the religion of our laws and of our courts. It is clearly the established religion in all state schools, from kindergarten through the university.

The triumph of humanism will mean the suppression and persecution of Christianity. Signs are not lacking that this is already in progress. No Christian can be indifferent to this struggle and retain the name and blessing of the lord. Either Christianity becomes the source of law, or humanism will be. The humanists are right in seeing the need for a religiously consistent system of laws. All law is an expression of a religious faith. Before this century is over, it will be apparent whether churchmen are humanists or Christians. This is a time for decision. Just as there can be no separation of religion and the state, so there can be no evasion of the necessity to stand.

The challenge of Elijah is again before us: "How long halt ye between two opinions? if the LORD be God, follow him: but if Baal, then follow him" (I Kings 18:21).

CHALCEDON REPORT NO. 153
May, 1978

One of the marks of the crusading temperament is the desire to reform everyone except one's self. The crusader has a simple solution: to remake the world after his own image. Crusading thus fosters self-righteousness, and self-righteousness promotes and feeds on hypocrisy.

Modern warfare is a form of crusading, and hence its particularly intense form of horror. It is total war, because the more clearly it becomes a crusade, the more it works for obliteration. At its worst, we see this total warfare in the various forms of international and national socialism, but it is present in all modern states.

The first great rehearsal of total war was the American conflict, 1860-1864. Before the U.S.A. and the Confederate States joined battle, both had developed a crusading fervor and a radical blindness to evil on their part. The horrors of the battle for Kansas by slave and anti-slave forces begat moral monsters like John Brown and William Clarke Quantrill. The war itself led to insanities of men like Major General David Hunter, a Virginian who fought for the North. Like Quantrill, Hunter majored in terrorism, although the regular army exercised some restraint on him, whereas Quantrill, as a guerrilla, had none. In Virginia, Hunter burned his own cousin's home, and he refused to allow Mrs. Hunter or her daughter to save their clothes and family pictures; Andrew Hunter, named after Major General Hunter's father, and a civilian, was imprisoned.

Quantrill, a twisted mind, criminal, suspicious of all kindness shown to him, took no prisoners, waged total war and often used the war as an excuse to settle personal hatreds.

Northern troops, under the vicious Col. Strachan, executed ten men as a gesture of revenge against Quantrill. The response of "Bloody Bill" Anderson and Quantrill was the slaughter of Centralia and the sacking of Lawrence.

Early in the war, Confederate authorities praised Quantrill, while Northerners condemned Strachan. By the end of the war, the North chose under Sherman to wage total war, and men like Lee and Jackson seem remote and alien in their Christian standards amidst the prevailing horrors. Each side saw evil in the other as justification for an evil crusade, and self-righteousness became a governing temper.

Since then, two world wars, several smaller wars, and many revolutions have developed and refined the crusading temper, and the world has gone from horror to horror as total war has become a principle of action in both war and peace, in politics and in life.

The crusader does not build: he wars. The crusader does not seek to convert but to destroy. His answer to problems is militancy, suppression, chains, hatred, and obliteration. In the mouth of the crusader, the word "love" becomes a self-righteous weapon. The crusader says in effect, I am love, truth, and goodness, and all you say and represent is hatred and hate-mongering, a lie, and evil. The crusader hopes for a better world through a better organized suppression of all opposition, through gaining political power, control of wealth, and of peoples, and through a domination of society in the name of his "good."

Crusaders can be found on most sides of every issue, and it is their activities which reduce their cause to impotence and the world to a shambles. Crusaders want to accomplish great things with other people's lives and money, and control of the machinery of state is a constant goal of all crusaders. They do not see politics as a question of good government but as a means of power, the power to compel people.

For crusaders of all kinds, good and evil are in essence humanistically defined, or else, if they appeal to a Biblical basis, it is an appeal to a limited segment of Scripture. The Bible, in its totality, takes both authority and justice out of the hands of crusaders and places them in God's law. Whereas the crusader indicts a segment of humanity, God's law indicts all men, everywhere, every man without exception. God's law-word requires the condemnation of all, and it provides also for redemption and regeneration through Jesus Christ and His atonement. It then requires the redeemed man to believe and obey by bringing every area of life and thought under Christ as Lord. This means the reconstruction of all things in terms of the law-word of God.

Deuteronomy 28 makes clear that irresistible blessings follow obedience, and irresistible curses follow disobedience.

Our Lord indicts the whole crusading mentality as one of hypocrisy and blindness, because it seeks an outward conformity and cleanliness rather than true justice and faith (Matt. 23:13-33).

Total war presupposes the validity of this emphasis on externals. As Tung Chi-Ping, in his very telling account of Red China, *The Thought Revolution*, points out, hypocrisy succeeds best in such a regime. Because humanism in all its forms, as well as the crusading mentality, sets a priority on outer controls, a premium is placed on surfaces rather than meaning. Communist ideology, says Tung Chi-Ping, believes "that human nature can be changed by changing the environment." Conformity is thus rewarded, and thinking distrusted. The answer to each crisis is another planned crusade, massive demonstrations, testimonial meetings, and dramatic gestures. Faith and work are replaced by power and appearance, and so, the more the society crumbles, the greater the monuments to itself that it raises.

Where environmentalism replaces regeneration as the salvation of man and society, there power must prevail as the saving agency. In regeneration, God's power is at work, to create a new man who is then commissioned to exercise dominion in terms of God's law by rebuilding all things on the foundation of Jesus Christ. The key power agency is in God and His Spirit. Where environmental faiths govern, a human power agency must do all the changing, and the means is not by an inner conversion but by an outer coercion. The "tactic" then is not faith and obedience but power and coercion.

Because we live in a crusading era, we live therefore in a highly coercive era, one in which compulsion replaces freedom, and power replaces the Spirit. Men may regret the consequences of our present course, but they will not change them until they themselves are changed.

CHALCEDON REPORT NO. 154
June, 1978

The historian, Sylvia L. Thrupp, in *Society and History* (1977), wrote on "The City as the Idea of Social Order." For her, the idea of order was an invention of man early in history, and the city became the expression of *cosmological order*. The city represented the fact of order, authority, and purpose which was inherent in the universe. Order was thus seen as basic to the nature of the universe, and, for man to live in terms of reality, meant that man had to be in line with ultimate order. The city was thus a religious entity.

Then cities developed another concept of their being: they were expressions of *social order*, of the proper relationship between man and man, between ruler and ruled. Some forms of urban planning, as with Plato's *Republic*, combined the ideas of cosmological with social order to set forth an opinion concerning *perfect order*, the just or moral order in terms not of God, but an idea. The doctrine of progress and/or evolution was added to this by some thinkers to set forth the doctrine of the city as basic to the future and its perfection.

With the Enlightenment, another concept began to appear, and, in Montesquieu, became vocal, the city as a product of *economic order*. Some added to this their belief in the city as the home of Deism and enlightenment. Voltaire saw the city as *the home of pleasure*, a concept very powerful since his day.

The 19th century saw still further concepts set forth, the city as the center of a racial culture, or of a bureaucracy, or of culture conceived as the arts (the city then becoming an aesthetic experience). Romanticism arose about the same time and, very powerful in the 20th century, has been in revolt against the idea of the city. Romanticism has influenced many sociologists to view the city as *pathological.*

With this brief survey in mind, let us examine the implications of our present situation. What has happened? At the beginning, the city represented religious order. Later, it came to represent various ideas of social order, political, economic, cultural, experiential, and so on. Modern man, however, tends to be, even when he is agreeable to the city, *anti-order.* The intellectuals have become hostile to law and order; both words together or singly are anathema to them. The existentialist impulse is against a prescribed law or order, and, as a result, is an enemy to the city even when most a part of it.

The result is a basic conflict. Some doctrine of order is essential to the life of a city, but the intellectual, the urban man par excellence, is hostile to the very foundation of urban existence, a doctrine of order.

The modern city is totally indifferent to any concept of religious order as basic to its life. It regards industry as a necessary evil to be controlled and taxed as much as possible. Social order is gone, because, without a common faith and goal, next door neighbors are usually strangers. Such order as the city may have is political power and police authority. The politician is increasingly distrusted, and the police are out-manned by the lawless and criminal element. The police power can give good and clear order when the majority of people subscribe to a doctrine of order, but, when most are at heart orderless and lawless the police power begins to lose efficacy.

In brief, modern man complains bitterly about the growing disorder and lawlessness of urban life but fails to recognize that his own life and faith are in essence antinomian and lawless. Modern man is getting the kind of society and city he believes in.

No idea of order can long survive unless it is grounded in a doctrine of theological order. If God and His decree, His order, are not basic to all reality, then all doctrines of order are empty and rootless. If chaos and disorder are ultimate in the universe, or if man believes that they are, they will be basic to his life and action.

Some years ago, I visited in prison a brilliant young thief, head of a criminal gang of thieves; all were college men. His rationale was simple; everything in his education made clear that no God exists, and that all religion and morality were myths. Hence, he held, the sensible man will establish his own life-style and try to get all he can for himself. Next time, he added, he would be wiser in the conduct of his faith. His logic was sound, but his premise was false. His logic had been the logic of countless persons in this existentialist generation. It has turned the city into a place of disorder. Once the city walls kept out disorder. Now men hope that the walls of their house will keep out disorder.

As the psalmist said, "Except the LORD build the house, they labour in vain that built it; except the LORD keep the city, the watchman waketh but in vain" (Ps. 127:1). The restoration of the city requires more than urban renewal and money. It requires a faith in the triune God as the source of order, and in the New Jerusalem as the goal of society. It requires theological foundations for urban life and for the doctrine of society. Law must become Biblical; humanistic law hastens decay and collapse. Education is a religious fact; it must become Biblical in nature. The family is not simply a cultural and biological entity; it is a religious order, established by God. Unless in *every* area of life and thought we see the Biblical foundations and the prescribed order, we will soon see them in none. If we view all order simply as a human invention, then we have made disorder ultimate, and it will prevail in our lives. Theology is still queen of the sciences; it is not dethroned by men's rebellion. Rather, by their rebellion, men sentence themselves to death. Wisdom is God and His order, and declares from of old: "He that sinneth against me wrongeth his own soul: all they that hate me love death" (Prov. 8:36).

THE CHURCH AND THE SCHOOL

The meaning of the word *church* in Scripture is essentially congregation or assembly, i.e., the Kingdom of God in all its functions. As we analyze the meaning of the church in the Old Testament, the pattern for the New, we find that basic to the functioning of God's congregation is the work of the Levite. Tithes were paid to the Levite; the Levite apportioned them to the priests, to the musicians, to health, education, and welfare. The three basic responsibilities of the Levites were, *first*, the management of the tithe and tithe agencies, and *second*, instruction in God's law-word (Deut. 33:10), and, *third*, supervision of sacrifices. Christ's atonement replaces this third function. It is clear, however, that education remains as central to the Levitical function, and the Levitical calling is instruction, not the direct ministry of the preaching of the word, and administration of the sacraments. It is even more clear that this teaching function is basic to the life of Christ's church, so that Christian Schools are not peripheral but central. Where this function is denied or controlled, as in the Soviet Union, the church declines dramatically. Where this function is revived, the life of the church flourishes. In the life of the church, the great leaders have been teachers, and the life of the church has been governed by this teaching function, as witness Anselm, Aquinas, Luther, and Calvin.

The modern state is at war with the church, and most directly with its teaching ministry, with its life-blood. State after state seeks to control this Levitical function and to deny its centrality in the life of Christ's church. For the church to surrender this area to the state is to deny Jesus as Lord. For churchmen to submit the Levitical ministry into Caesar's hands and control is to forsake the faith.

CHALCEDON REPORT NO. 155
July, 1978

As Otto J. Scott has pointed out, in *Robespierre, The Voice of Virtue*, the abolition of Christianity was a goal of the French Revolution. With the Russian Revolution it was again a major objective.

However, what is too seldom recognized is that the abolition of Christianity was an Enlightenment goal which was quietly being made a policy of state well before the outbreak of the French Revolution. The revolutionary regime in France made public and open what had long been held in private, namely, that the "superstition" of Christianity needed to be eliminated from civilization.

In some events, this hostility was openly manifested. One of the very much neglected aspects of the War for American Independence was the British war against the churches. This savage assault is excused, when mentioned, on the grounds that the involvement of the Puritan clergy in the American cause angered the British. True, the British resented the stand of the clergy, but, even more, they were represented by officers and men who represented the European spirit of contempt for Christianity. Their hostility was manifested against the Bible itself. Churches were turned into stables, a prison, or into fire-wood. Desecration of churches was so routine that in some cases townspeople burned their own churches to prevent blasphemous usage and desecration by the British. Bibles were systematically destroyed. Pastors were sometimes murdered. On Sundays, British regimental bands played outside existing churches to disrupt the services.

Little of all of this is mentioned by historians, who, being "freethinkers," see no harm in the destruction of Christianity. (Most people in England had little or no knowledge then of what was going on. Over half of parliament then was elected by less than six thousand voters, and the war lacked popular support.)

The bias of historians is obvious in the treatments of Major Andre and Nathan Hale. John Andre, despite a godly rearing, was a humanist and an unbeliever. He took part in the Paoli Massacre, and, as John R. Terry noted, in *America's Revolutionary Spirit*, "he was convinced that if a few more Yankees were stuck like pigs, they would surrender quickly." Before his execution as a spy, the Americans offered to provide a chaplain; but Andre rejected this as a freethinker. Historians still regard Andre as a noble soul, failing to add that it is his lack of faith that ennobles him in their eyes. Had he as a Christian been involved in the Paoli Massacre, it would be a different story!

Nathan Hale, the American spy, gets less favorable treatment. We are not told of his strong faith, nor is it mentioned that the British rejected his request for a pastor, or a Bible to read before his execution. In this refusal of the British to allow a condemned man to have a Bible we see the intensity of this hatred of Christianity.

Was it then only, or does it exist now? Roland Huntsford, in *The New Totalitarians*, sees two kinds of totalitarianism in power today. The older form is embodied in Marxism, in Russia, and its method is open hostility and terrorism. It is, however, the new totalitarians who are increasingly dominant all over the world, and their social order is best epitomized in Sweden. (Even the U.S.S.R. is beginning to imitate this new model tyranny.) Instead of terrorism, education is used, and the radical state control of all education. Instead of open hostility to Christianity, there is rather a multitude of regulations designed to strangle it slowly to death. On the one hand, there are state churches, and, on the other, a government legal expert says plainly, "our aim is to remove all traces of Church morality from legislation" (Alvar Nelson). The Swedish state is not against the church; it is against Christianity.

In the rest of the world, the same process is under way in varying degrees. One nation after another would profess shock if charged with being anti-Christian, but one after another is stripping its laws of all traces of Biblical law and also introducing a multitude of rules, regulations, and licenses designed to make the Christian community, church and school, a puppet and a pawn of the state.

Crudities such as burning churches and Bibles are part of a less enlightened era, or a more backward part of humanity. The enlightened anti-Christians profess to believe in religious liberty: their self-professed noble concern is to prevent irregularities and to establish "reasonable" rules and boundaries for Christian functions.

This strategy of the new totalitarians is a very shrewd one. It enables them to wage total war against Christianity in the name of peace, friendship, and legal concern. It enables them to declare the supposed lordship of Caesar over Christ in the name of legal order and common sense. The argument carries weight, except with those who know Christ as Lord.

Because Jesus Christ is Lord, His sovereignty cannot be infringed nor usurped by any man or institution. He alone is Lord over all things, and church, state, school, family, vocations, the arts and the sciences, and all things else, are under His dominion and subject to His law-word. God's warning from of old still stands: "Be wise now therefore, O ye Kings: be instructed, ye judges of the earth. Serve the LORD with fear, and rejoice with trembling. Kiss the Son, lest he be angry, and ye perish from the way, when his wrath is kindled but a little. Blessed are all they that put their trust in him" (Ps. 2:10-12).

WHO IS THE LORD? CONFLICT WITH CAESAR

In order to understand the origins of the church and state conflict, it is important to recognize the roots of the problem in pagan faith and practice. In paganism, the state saw itself as the sovereign, and, as the sovereign, its life and power constituted an umbrella under which all things existed. To have a legitimate function, all things had to be licensed, controlled, and taxed by the state, and the state was seen as that power in whom and under whom all peoples and institutions had their life and being. The function of religion under that umbrella was to assist the state by providing social cement. The very word *liturgy* in origin means *public work*; religion and its rites were among the public works of the state. Rome thus did not want to persecute any religion: it only sought to bring them all under control as licensed practices. Rome persecuted the church, not because of religious hostility, but because the church refused to become a licensed religion, and Rome regarded this as a *political*, not a religious offense. Legge observed, "The officials of the Roman Empire in times of persecution sought to force the Christians to sacrifice, not to any heathen gods, but to the Genius of the Emperor and the Fortune of the City of Rome; and at all times the Christian's refusal was looked upon not as a religious but as a political offense." (Francis Legge: *Forerunners and Rivals of Christianity from 330 B.C. to 330 A.D.*, vol. I, p. xxiv. New York, NY: University Books, (1915) 1964.)

The sacrifice to the imperial image meant that the Christian acknowledged the sovereignty or lordship of Caesar and Caesar's right to license, control, or tax the church. This the Christians refused to do. Those who submitted were regarded as apostates and not Christian. Why?

The Bible makes clear in all its aspects that God alone is Sovereign. "The earth is the LORD's" (Ps. 24:1, etc.). He is the law-maker, and His law is set forth in the Scripture. The basic and original Christian baptismal confession was and is, "Jesus is Lord" (Phil. 2:11, Eph. 4:5; I Tim. 6:5, etc.), the most common New Testament designation of Jesus is *Lord*, in the Greek, *kurios*. The word *kurios* means both *God* and *absolute property owner* or sovereign.

In the Old Testament as in the New the state is kept strictly out of any levitical or ecclesiastical function. Both church and state, like all things else, are equally under God, and equally duty-bound to obey Him, but only God can exercise sovereignty. No one sphere of life can rule over others, i.e., the state over the church, or the church over the state, but each must fulfill its duty to the Lord.

The nature of the church or Christian synagogue has firm roots in the Old Testament: its offices, law, and practice are derived therefrom. It is important therefore to examine the levitical functions and place in the Bible. The Levites were the tribe from whence the priests were derived, but their functions, broader and more basic, survive in Christendom. The levitical functions include:

1) The Levites received and managed the tithes (Num. 18:21ff.; Heb 7:50)
2) The Levites were custodians of the place of worship (Num. 1:47-54, etc.)
3) Most important, the Levites were responsible for instruction: they were the teachers of old and young, and this was the heart of their work (Deut. 33:10).

This central emphasis on instruction has been the particular mark of Christianity. It is an emphasis absent in other religions. When interest or emphasis on education declines in Christendom, either from indifference or by reason of statist intervention, Christianity quickly wanes and grows weak. Basic to any renewal of faith is a renewal of the centrality of education.

With respect to the U.S., it should be remembered that, in the colonial era, all schooling was Christian, and, until 1833-34, in Massachusetts, there was no system of state control of education in the young republic. The great floods of immigration which doubled the U.S. population every few years in those days were met and educated by Christian Schools. The state control cause, headed by James G. Carter, Horace Mann, and others, was anti-Christian, Unitarian, and centralist.

In one of the key areas of recent conflict, the very issue manifests the essentially religious nature of the problem, *accreditation*. The word *accreditation* comes from *credo*, I believe. Accreditation is an act of faith. It looks to an authority regarded as sovereign, i.e., God, the state, Reason, etc., as the approving agency and authority. To seek state accreditation, or to submit to it, is to affirm faith in the lordship of the state and to recognize the over-all sovereignty of the state as the "umbrella" under which all things reside.

The Bible, on the other hand, affirms the function of the state, and the duty of obedience to the state, as a ministry of justice, or, literally in the Greek, a diaconate of justice (Rom. 13:1-8). Its domain or sphere of operation is to be a "terror...to the evil" (Rom. 13:3). The state is not, Hegel to the contrary, God walking on earth: it is a ministry, diaconate, or service under God. Thus, the Bible accredits the state and requires obedience to it "for conscience sake" (Rom. 13:5), i.e., as a matter of conscience towards God, as long as the state is faithful to its calling. In the ultimate nature of things, we must, with St. Peter, declare, "We ought to obey God rather than men" (Acts 5:29).

The modern state has revived the old pagan doctrine of state sovereignty. The word sovereignty is absent from the U.S. Constitution. Washington called the idea a monster, and, as late as the Versailles Peace Conference, U.S. Secretary of State Lansing was critical of the concept. (A. F. Pollard: *Factors in American History*, p. 31f, New York: Macmillans 1935). Murray commented:

> Nowhere in the American structure is there accumulated the plenitude of legal sovereignty possessed in England by the Queen in Parliament. In fact, the term "legal sovereignty" makes no sense in America, where sovereignty (if the alien term must be used) is purely political. The United States has a government, or better, a structure of government operating on different levels. The American state has no sovereignty in the classic Continental sense. (John Courtney Murray, S.J.: *We Hold These Truths*, p. 70. New York: Sheed and Ward, 1960.)

The modern state everywhere is claiming sovereignty: as the supposed sovereign and lord, it demands that all peoples and institutions live under its shade or umbrella and submit to its licensure, controls, and taxation. The same issue faced by the early church in Rome is again with us. There is no escaping the necessity to stand. The issue is still the same: Who is the Lord? Christ or Caesar? For the Christian, the answer is, now as then, Jesus Christ is Lord.

CHALCEDON REPORT NO. 156
August, 1978

The two great motive forces of the modern age are equality and freedom. The two contradict each other, in that a demand for equality means a radical curtailment of freedom. Few moderns see any contradiction, however, because the meaning of freedom has been re-defined.

Very simply defined, freedom means an absence of constraint, or deliverance from the restraint of another person or power. But such a definition makes clear that freedom is relative to our basic faith and standards. For me, to be married is freedom; for another man, it may mean slavery. For me, a family and children mean freedom and godly wealth; for another, it may mean bondage and a financial liability. The serfs of the Roman emperors regarded their status as salvation because it gave them security, and freedom, because as serfs they were no longer faced with the problems of personal responsibility and self-government. Thus, talk about freedom is meaningless, unless we understand what is meant by freedom. Freedom from what, and for what? The communists believe that what they offer is true freedom; Socialist Sweden believes the same of itself, as does Britain and the U.S.

Moreover, all of them give us definitions of freedom, which, while often in bitter contradiction, are in some essentials agreed. They are modern, humanistic, and statist definitions of freedom.

For statism, freedom means above all else freedom from God. However important the French and Russian Revolutions are, they are also only the more dramatic moments of a long, and now modern revolution against God. Above all else, for man the sinner, freedom means freedom from God. The fall of man is from freedom under God into the quest for freedom from God. The Christian prays, "Deliver us from evil," or, from the evil one; the implicit prayer of fallen man is, "Deliver us from God the Lord." For fallen man, God is the Great Oppressor, and His law is the great shackle on man's freedom. As a dedicated antinomian, the fallen man is emphatic that God's law is slavery and tyranny. Thus, he wants freedom from God, from God's law, and from Christ and His church.

But this is not all. Fallen man wants freedom also from the family. We are seeing a flood of propaganda concerning "children's rights," the essence of which is to free the child from the family. Humanistic man has long since regarded the family and strict familial responsibility as nonsense. Women have been working for "liberation" from the family, and the goal is now to "liberate" the children also. Some have proposed state subsidies and independent incomes for every child in order to separate the child from the family.

In numerous other ways, modern man seeks liberation from a variety of things, from work, responsibility, society, duty, and even from death itself. But this is not all. He seeks freedom from these things through statist action, so that for him the state is the agency of liberation. This is the heart of the state's claims and power over man: the state presents itself as the savior of man, as the agency of liberation. The state, however, has a better record throughout history as the oppressor and enslaver of man. It is easy for men to laugh at the idea of Stalin or Hitler as liberators, but they are no less gullible than those enslaved by Stalin and Hitler when it comes to their own state. Each preserves the illusion that their state, whatever its faults, is different and is the source of their freedoms. They are thus faithful followers of the cult of Molech, of state worship.

For the Christian, however, trust cannot be in the state but in the Lord. Freedom is from sin to Christ and to self-government under God and His law.

Freedom is a theological concept. It is concerned with liberation, or salvation. The great religious battle of history, and especially of our time, is thus: Does salvation mean freedom from God, or freedom through God's grace and to God's purposes? Freedom from God, or under God? Our politics is thus theological. Our education is also, and education either sets forth salvation or liberation from God, or under God.

We cannot separate salvation off to a narrow corner of our neighborhood, or of the universe, labelled the church. Salvation, whether called by its more secular names of freedom and liberation, still is a total thing. It involves all of our lives, our church, school, family, politics, economics, arts, sciences, and all things else. Christ being totally Lord, King over all kings and Lord over all lords, is totally our Savior, redeemer of our whole lives and of the whole of our world and activities.

Thus, when the statist (or humanist) and the faithful Christian talk of freedom, they are talking of two radically different things, and there can be no reconciliation between the two: they are rival plans of salvation. The modern state sees the issue: if its plan of salvation or liberation is to prevail, then the Christian plan must be suppressed. Christian churches, schools, and agencies which refuse to compromise must be suppressed. No man can serve two masters or have two lords. This is the issue of our time, and all men will be pushed to a decision by God's providential government of history. Who is the Savior, Christ or the State?

WHO IS THE LORD?

The July, 1978, edition of *Yankee Magazine* carries a very interesting article about one of the last Connecticut small farmers, John Ludorf. The author, Georgia Seron, a neighbor, describes Ludorf at work, as he cuts timber for firewood: "The final log, weighing 150 pounds, resists splitting completely and he lifts it in one swift, clean swing to lay atop the waiting pile. John Ludorf is 81 years old today."

Ludorf has a problem. His family cannot afford to inherit his farm: "I never made more than $3,800 a year in my life from my farm but by my dying on it the government gets to make $70,000!" The inheritance tax will wipe out the family farm.

If this sounds familiar, it is, *first*, because it is happening to 75% of all farms, businesses and properties in the United States. The inheritance tax wipes out the family. Scripture repeatedly speaks of the treatment of widows and orphans as revelatory of a people's righteousness. Today, virtually all nations are found wanting in this respect; widows lose their homes, and young men find they are working for a new owner of the family business.

Second, there is a clear echo here of the Naboth story. Ahab, however, was crude. The modern state confiscates by means of taxation and disinherits widows and children.

Such a condition is a product of our contempt for God's law. Men refuse to believe that God's righteousness or law is an unchanging one, like the Lord, the same in every age. They turn away from God's righteousness for a self-generated holiness which is no holiness at all.

In the Christian Schools trials, the church trials, we see these self-holy men turn savagely against persecuted pastors, schoolmen, and parents, because the stand of these men against humanistic statism troubles their conscience. These compromisers seem to feel that holiness comes, not by faith with works, but by faith with criticism, and they thereby manifest their faithfulness to Phariseeism.

On almost any given day, Monday through Friday, somewhere in the U.S. Christians are in court for their faith. Our Lord makes clear that He is there also: "Inasmuch as ye have done it unto one of the least of these my brethren, ye have done it unto me" (Matt. 25:40). What is our Lord's word to you?

Where the freedom of the faith to be under Christ's Lordship alone is gone, then the basic theft has taken place. Then too our inheritance in faith, land, and goods is also gone.

Either Jesus Christ is Lord, or the state is. The question of our time is this: Who is your Lord, Christ, or Caesar? Will you say, with the false priests of old, "We have no king but Caesar?" (John 19:15).

CHALCEDON REPORT NO. 157
September, 1978

The Russian 19th century novelist, Dostoyevsky, in *The Brothers Karamazov*, had an important section often printed separately as *The Grand Inquisitor*. Dostoyevsky portrayed powerfully the dereliction of the church when it sees itself as man's hope rather than Christ Himself. His account is both sympathetic and devastating. The church begins by becoming more the friend of man than the servant of the Lord. Its tender concern for man leads to a more "humane" application of Scripture. The "hard" laws and sayings of Scripture, and its heavy requirement of responsibility, impose too great a burden on men. The church thus begins with a benevolent concern for human welfare and ends up as the Grand Inquisitor, all the while still professing to be Christian and to be truly concerned about human welfare. The reason for the transition from disciple to Grand Inquisitor is that the church has moved from God's way for God's goals to man's way as wiser and more expedient.

In all sectors of the church, the mentality of the Grand Inquisitor still remains, dedicated, earnest, and hard-working, but still ready to burn Christ at the stake in the name of Christ. But, to all practical intent, the church is the discredited Grand Inquisitor, and its efforts are futile and by-passed.

A new and successful Grand Inquisitor is now on the scene, not the church but the modern state. The goal of the state is the salvation of man, not in God's declared way, but in man's wiser and more scientific manner. The modern state is Messianic in all its being. It wants man saved, paradise restored, sin and death abolished, and its own New Jerusalem, the Great Community, established from pole to pole. We cannot begin to understand the grand missionary passion of the modern state if we fail to see its zeal to save man. Man must be saved from God and from himself. Man must be born again, remade, into a new humanity of his own creation. Through its great missionary agency, the state schools, "the children of the state" are to be given the new life of freedom from God and the past into self-realization. The rebirth of humanity is from God into an existentialist, lawless freedom wherein man is his own god and his own law.

Obviously, many do not agree. They continue to believe in the old God and His Bible, and they form Christian Schools and churches to perpetuate their out-moded and unmodern faith. They resist attempts by the state to control what belongs to Christ and must be governed by God's law, not man's.

The state views these efforts with dismay. As the great, modern Grand Inquisitor, the state regards all doubts about itself as misguided. To believe that the state and its controls are evil is for the state the modern form of blasphemy. How can there be a good society, when the working god of that society is resisted, blasphemed, and rejected?

Remember, the essence of the Grand Inquisitor is his belief that his actions are for the true welfare of mankind. To fight against him is to wage war against truth and man's best welfare, and against man's hope and future. For the Grand Inquisitor, false religions bring salvation to the elect alone, whereas the Grand Inquisitor brings it to all men, it is held. The state affirms total democracy increasingly, and world brotherhood. All men everywhere will be saved, because all men will be declared acceptable as is.

The modern Grand Inquisitor is the most powerful oppressor in all history, because he has the powers of state in his hand. He holds the knife and the gun, the courts, and the funds. Law is what he declares it to be.

The Grand Inquisitor emerges in history in one form or another. and in one institution after another, whenever and wherever men deny God's law-word. Man cannot live without law. If, as antinomians, they deny God's law, they do not thereby live without law: rather, they substitute man's law for God's law. It is then that the Grand Inquisitor emerges. If law and a truly moral concern for human welfare are defined by man, then the defining man or institution emerges as the god of that social order. Men will have a law; it may be their own law, in which case they deny God the King, and every man does that which is right in his own eyes (Judges 21:25). It may be statist law, in which case the state is God walking on earth. If it is any kind of law other than God's law, then that law-making body has usurped God's prerogative and is declaring itself to be man's Lord and Savior.

The Grand Inquisitor cannot be voted out; he re-appears in the new rulers in a new guise. He can only be destroyed by the only wise God, our Savior, whose grace redeems us, and whose law is our way of sanctification in His Spirit.

CHALCEDON REPORT NO. 158
October, 1978

A question often raised by many people is this: why did not God so create man and the world that sin and evil would be unnecessary or impossible? This question exposes the heart of humanistic statism, because it reveals its doctrine of ideal order. The essence of original sin is man's desire to be his own god, determining for himself what constitutes good and evil (Gen. 3:5). Man's idea of good means in part to prevent the possibility of evil. Man seeks to spare himself and his children the necessity of moral testing. One of the great evils perpetrated by parents in the name of doing good is the attempt to spare their children from the hardships, testings, and decisions they themselves faced. As a result, they help destroy their children.

Biblical law deals with actual sins. The adulterous, covetous, or envious *thought* is sin, but God's law calls for the punishment by men of the actual act. It is punishment after the fact, not before. God requires the courts of men which He ordains to deal with actual transgression, not potential sins. God Himself can alone deal with the heart and mind of man, with intentions. Thus, the courts of law are strictly limited: their jurisdiction, and the state's coercive power, extends to lawless actions, and not over godly men.

When the state begins to play god, it seeks to make men good by legislation which seeks to prevent, not punish sin. The state as god on earth seeks to make sin impossible to commit. It therefore punishes any intention, situation, or organization which may transgress its doctrine of brotherhood, health, order, or society. It begins when, for example, the state's surgeon-general or some agency determines that smoking, drinking, breathing, or living may be hazardous to a man's health, and then continues by denying man the right to do what the state feels it is wrong for man to do.

The result is that the state moves from government by God's law to rule by agencies, committees, and departments of state. It moves from rule by law to rule by bureaucracy. Instead of punishment and control over the fact of crime, we have punishment and control before the fact. Instead of a small criminal element being the controlled segment of society, all of society is then controlled. To be uncontrolled, or to seek to be uncontrolled, is to be therefore criminal.

One of the most revealing aspects of the current investigations and trials of Christian schools and churches has been the attitude of state officials, both in court, in the hall-way, and in more private conversations. Like parents who seek to prevent their children from the testings of moral decision, these bureaucrats believe that the good state is the controlling state. For any segment of society to be uncontrolled is plainly evil in their eyes. In terms of their doctrine of righteousness, a thing is good or potentially good only if it is in the safe-keeping of the state, and a thing is holy if it is separated from freedom under God to "freedom" under state rules and policies.

This means, of course, that the state is usurping God's place and prerogatives. It is functioning as the visible god on earth, and it does not lack for worshippers (Rev. 13:4). It seeks by total controls to make sin and evil impossible (Rev. 13:16-17). It sees itself as superior to the godly state and to Biblical law, because it does not merely punish sin but instead by controls works to prevent all forms of transgressions. It fails miserably in this task, but it succeeds in making itself the great transgressor, and the enemy of God (Rev. 13:6).

Neither man nor the state has any legal rights or powers apart from God. God alone is the source of all law. A significant biblical fact witnesses eloquently to this. To put off one's shoe was to surrender a legal right and duty in relationship to another person (Deut. 25:9,10). In relation to God putting off one's shoe meant to be totally without rights. As a result, when men were in God's presence, they had no rights or claims against Him: they could only be commanded. God commanded Moses out of the burning bush, saying, "put off thy shoes from off thy feet, for the place whereon thou standest is holy ground" (Ex. 3:5; cf. Josh. 5:15). Shoeless before God, man's status was like that of a slave to be absolutely commanded by God. (Shoeless before men, a man had surrendered his duty and place.) Man before God had God's word alone; man before men again must be governed by God's word alone. To depart from God's word is to be shoeless, i.e., a slave.

The choice before men today is a question of rulers. Will men be ruled by God or by the state? Will they stand in terms of God's sovereign law word, or in terms of man's word, the state's law? Shall the law punish the ungodly, the criminals, or shall it enslave all men? To whom do you answer, "Speak: for thy servant heareth" (I Sam. 3:10), to God or to the state?

CHALCEDON REPORT NO. 159
November, 1978

Aleksandr I. Solzhenitsyn has distressed many segments of Western society since coming to the West. The liberals had mistakenly assumed the Solzhenitsyn was one the them. To their shock, they found him speaking from a Christian perspective. Others had become upset at his criticism of the West, of democracy, capitalism, the press, and more. What is an anti-communist doing, criticizing democracy and its press, capitalism and socialism, and more?

This misunderstanding of Solzhenitsyn is part and parcel of our misunderstanding of the problem of our time. Moreover, the cause of this misunderstanding is a religious and moral failure, not an intellectual problem.

All too much anti-communism is not only shallow but also involves a surrender to the basic evil. If we agree with our enemy on six to nine points out of ten, our quarrel is a family fight for power, not a principled conflict. Most Westerners agree with most of the Communist Manifesto, and much of it is now law.

This still does not get to the root of the matter, however. The root cause and foundation of Marxism is humanism, and humanism is also basic now to most of the politics, economics, capital and labor, education, churches, and press of the West. As a result, the disagreements between the Communist and the democratic powers are in essence a family fight, because both are agreed on the ultimacy of man. In practical terms, this means the sovereignty, not of God, but the state.

Franklin L. Baumer, in *Modern European Thought, Continuity and Change in Ideas, 1600-1905* (Macmillian, 1977), has a chapter on modern man's faith in the state as lord or sovereign. The title of the chapter is very apt: "The Mortal God." As faith in God gave way to the Enlightenment, faith in the state replaced it. The state was seen as the lord over every area of life, including religion, and hence the state as lord and sovereign has the supposed right and duty to control every area.

Solzhenitsyn, in *The Gulag Archipelago Three* (Harper & Row, 1978), speaks with intense feeling of the Soviet tyranny. One of the moving charges of his narrative is the horror of Baptist children being separated from their parents because their parents had given them religious instruction, i.e., Christian teaching.

But consider this fact: in state after state in the U.S., Baptist parents have been hauled into court and threatened with the loss of their children because their children were in schools which refused to submit to statist and humanistic controls. The charge against these parents? Contributing to the delinquency of their minor children! It has been demonstrated repeatedly that the results of standard testing show that the children in Christian Schools are markedly in advance of children in state schools. The state is not impressed: the children are "deprived" of humanistic religious teaching, a "democratic" environment, and so on.

Why do the Soviet citizens do nothing about the persecutions there? Most know little about them, and it is safer to know nothing. The Soviet regime does not publicize its evils.

Why do U.S. Citizens for the most part do nothing? Most know little about the persecutions and prefer to know less. Others, evangelical, Lutheran, Reformed, and modernist, will even appear in the court-room or elsewhere to oppose those of us who make a stand. The press gives little publicity to these trials, on the whole.

Where humanism prevails, whether in the pulpit, classroom, or court, God will be denied, and Jesus Christ despised. They will say, like the men of old, "We will not have this man to reign over us" (Luke 19:14).

The issue in the Christian School trials, in the various church battles, with respect to Biblical law, in the church and state conflicts, is the reign of Christ. Humanism in its every form requires the reign of man and battles against the freedom of true faith.

Solzhenitsyn speaks of the ruthlessness at the heart of the Soviet authority. What it does not create and rule, it works to destroy. This should not surprise us: the lords of humanism cannot bear to see or tolerate the work of an alien God. Only that which they create and govern can thus be tolerated. As a result, isolated groups in the Siberian forests are hunted down and destroyed.

Humanism everywhere works toward the same goal. Only that which it creates and controls must be allowed to exist. All who do not conform are deformed in their eyes and must be controlled, re-made, or punished. This means that Christ's redeemed people are the enemy, and it means that we are at war. In that war, there are no neutrals. The power of humanistic statism looms very large and dangerously, but only Jesus Christ is the Lord, King of Kings and Lord of Lords. He alone shall prevail, and we only in and through Him. The tombs of His enemies are all over the world, and death and hell await the current crop. His is the empty tomb, and the victory. As for us, "whatsoever is born of God overcometh the world, and this is the victory that overcometh the world, even our faith" (I John 5:4).

WE ARE AT WAR

Although done without publicity and fanfare, a war against Biblical faith is under way all over the world, in varying degrees. The civil governments are in the main in the hands of humanists, whose passionate hatred of Christianity is intense.

This, however, is a disguised war. The Soviet Union, as a leader in the humanistic vanguard, began its history with a brutal and open assault on Christianity. Later, for strategic reasons, this gave way to another approach, attack by indirection, a method adopted from Nazi and Swedish practices. The Soviet Constitution guaranteed freedom of religion to allay fears and criticisms, but it made this "freedom" totally subject to licensure, permits, regulations, controls, etc. In other words, the state supposedly granted a right while at the same time ensuring that it would be non-existent. In practice thus, there is no freedom of religion in the U.S.S.R.

In the U.S., there is a concerted effort to accomplish the same goal by the same means. The First Amendment guarantees freedom of religion. While the U.S. has no church establishment, Christianity has been from the earliest days the religious establishment, i.e., the determiner of law and morality in the U.S. But, as John W. Whitehead points out in *The Separation Illusion, A Lawyer Examines the First Amendment* (Mott Media, Box 236, Milford, Michigan 48042, $4.25), the U.S. Supreme Court decided by 1952 that "God was dead, and His church was dead." The remaining task was to dismantle the church and Christianity and to make way for the new established religion, humanism. Now that war against Biblical faith, designed to control, dismantle, and eliminate it, is under way.

It is a well-planned war. When virtually all 50 states embark on a common program, in unison, and appear with federal directives in hand, it is no accident. Of course, they declare themselves innocent of any attempt to control a Christian School, church, missions agency, or organization, but this is the practical results of their requirements. These efforts are directed at present mainly against small or independent groups, those least able to defend themselves. Meanwhile, major church groups are not disturbed or upset. Legal precedents established against these smaller groups can later be applied against all others.

These demands take a multitude of forms: attempts to control church nurseries, the various religious uses of church buildings, zoning regulations, etc. Christian Schools are told that they must pay unemployment compensation, seek accreditation by the state, use state textbooks, teach humanism, and so on. Catholic orders and Protestant missionary agencies are told that they must pay unemployment compensation also. The National Labor Relations Board seeks to unionize parochial and Christian School teachers, and so on and on. Now too there is a demand that Christian Schools be integrated at a percentage set by the Internal Revenue Service, this despite the fact that such schools have not been involved in segregation. In another case, a church is being taken to court for firing a homosexual organist. In one way or another, all are being told that they must wear the mark of the beast (Rev. 13:16-18).

Fighting this battle is not easy nor cheap. The great pioneer and leader, whose victories in the Yoder and Whisner cases represent legal landmarks, has been and is Attorney William B. Ball, of Ball and Skelly, P.O. Box 1108, Harrisburg, Penn. 17108. Mr. Ball is active in a number of cases currently, and during the summer of 1978, for example, was involved in cases in Kentucky and North Carolina. Attorney David Gibbs has formed the Christian Law Association (P.O. Box 30290, Cleveland, Ohio 44130) and is also actively involved in cases in many states. The *C.L.A. Defender* is a magazine which reports on some of these cases and is available to supporters of the C.L.A. But all these men cannot continue without support. They are working long hours, and often sacrificially. Numerous new cases are arising weekly. Attorney John Whitehead of the C.L.A. estimates that in a very few years, perhaps two or three, $500,000 monthly will be required to fight these cases!

The price of resistance is high, not only in money, effort, and abuse, but in many other ways. One pastor, facing the possibility of jail, spoke of the very real threat of gang rape by homosexual prisoners who looked forward to assaulting a preacher. It also means the animosity of the compromising churchmen whose conscience disturbs them and who therefore lash out against the courageous men who make a stand. I know that, when I support any who resist, I am usually given "friendly" warnings by these compromisers that it would be inadvisable for a man of my stature to associate with such men, and I have no doubt that these resisting Christians are warned against associating with the likes of R.J. Rushdoony!

But "the battle is the LORD'S" (I Sam. 17:47), and those who are the Lord's will fight in His camp: they will not seek terms with His enemies.

One reason for the intensity of the battle is this: the growth of the Christian School movement is far greater than most people realize. If it continues at its present rate, the humanists fear that, by the end of this century, (not too far away), the U.S. will have a radically different population, one made up of faithful and zealous Christians. Humanism will then perish. Moreover, the birthrate for humanists has been low for some years now, and the birthrate for various minority groups, even with the "benefits" of welfarism, is beginning to drop markedly from its earlier high ratio. But the people involved in the Christian School movement have a high birthrate. The Christian Schools are producing the better scholars, who are going to be the leaders twenty and forty years from now. This is for them a threat, and a crisis situation.

But this is not all. Humanism is failing all over the world. The politics of humanism is the politics of disaster. Because humanism is failing, it is all the more ready to attack and suppress every threat to its power. The issue is clear enough: humanism and Christianity cannot co-exist. Theirs is a life and death struggle. Unfortunately, too few churchmen will even admit the fact of the battle.

The battle is more than political or legal: it is theological. The issue is lordship: Who is the Lord, Christ or the state, Christ or Caesar? It is thus a repetition of an age-old battle which began, in the Christian era, between the church and Rome. *Lord* means sovereign, God, absolute property owner. For us, "Jesus Christ is Lord" (Phil. 2:11): this was the original confession of faith and the baptismal confession of the Christian Church. Now, too often the confession, whatever its wording, seems to be a pledge of allegiance to a church or denomination, not to the sovereign Lord, Jesus Christ. Thus, our great need is to confess Jesus Christ as Lord, our Lord and Savior, Lord over the church, state, school, family, the arts and sciences, and all things else. If we deny Him as Lord, He will deny us. "Whosoever therefore shall confess me before men, him will I confess also before my Father which is in heaven. But whosoever shall deny me before men, him will I also deny before my Father which is in heaven" (Matt. 10:32-33). To confess means to acknowledge and to be in covenant with, to stand for in a position of testing or trial. The question thus is, Will the church of the 20th century confess Jesus Christ? Will it be His church, or the state's church? And whom will you and I confess?

The issue is lordship. Because we are not our own, but have been bought with a price of Christ's blood, we must serve, obey, and glorify God in all our being and our actions (I Cor. 6:20). We cannot live for ourselves: we are God's property, and we must be used by Him and for His Kingdom. All too many churchmen are like the likeable and earnest young man, very active in a sound church, who insisted that he was "entitled" to enjoy life. A power-boat and water-skiing were his goals, and, in view of his support of, and faithfulness to the church, he felt "entitled" to enjoy these in due time without having his conscience troubled by the Christian School battles, and tales of persecutions at home and abroad. In brief, he wanted Christ as Savior but not as Lord. He wanted Christ to provide fire and life insurance, so that he could live his life in peace. But if Jesus is not our Lord, He is not our Savior. If we are not His property and possession, He is not our shield and defender (Ps. 5:12; 59:9,16; etc.).

The philosopher Hegel, the spiritual father of Marx, John Dewey, and almost all modern humanists, saw the state as god walking on earth. The humanist is a very dedicated and religious man: he cannot be countered by lukewarmness. (Our Lord's indictment of the lukewarm is especially severe in Rev. 3:14-16.) The humanist's church, his lord and savior, is the state. The salvation of man requires that all things be brought under the lordship of the state. Hence, the current moves against churches, Christian Schools, and Christian organizations is a religious move, designed to further the humanistic salvation of man and society.

Because these attacks on Christianity are religiously motivated and are religiously grounded, they cannot be met by merely defensive action, or simply by legal action, although defensive legal action is urgently necessary. Our Lord is greater than Caesar: He is King of Kings, Lord of Lords (Rev. 19:16), and the Creator and governor of all things visible and invisible (Col. 1:16). We must take the offensive as His ambassadors, His army, and His bringers of great and glorious tidings of salvation, to bring every area of life and thought into captivity to Christ the Lord. Of Christ's victory, and of the defeat of His enemies, there can be no question. What is at issue is which camp we will be in.

We are at war, and there are no neutrals in this struggle. The roots of humanism are in the tempter's program of Gen. 3:1-5, man as his own god, knowing or determining good and evil for himself. Those who claim, in the name of a false and neoplatonic spirituality, that they want to rise "above" the battle, are also trying to rise above Christ and the meaning of His incarnation. To stand for the Lord is somehow unspiritual and unloving in their eyes. They are like the 14th century monks of Athos, who "rose above" the problems of their day and found spiritual ecstasy and visions of God in contemplating their navels. When Barlaam condemned this practice, these loving, spiritual, navel-watchers arose in a fury (of love, no doubt), called a Synod, and cited and condemned Barlaam and his party as heretics! So much for being loving and spiritual! We still have, in other forms, our navel-contemplators all around us, very much around us, but not with us. All well and good: let us donate them to the enemy. "If God be for us, who can be against us?" (Rom. 8:31).

CHALCEDON REPORT NO. 160
December, 1978

Basic to Biblical law is the fact of restitution. God's law requires restitution and sets it forth as the essence of justice or righteousness. Between man and man, restitution is required, as such laws as Exodus 22:1-6, etc., make clear, and this restitution must be at least double and can be as much as four-fold or five-fold (Ex. 22:1; Luke 19:8). Between man and God, restitution is also basic to justice, and Christ's perfect obedience to the law, and His atonement on the cross, assuming the death penalty passed upon us, constitute Christ's work of restitution for His people.

Wherever the law of restitution prevails, it follows that crime does not pay. If the minimum restitution for a crime is the restoration of full value, plus the same, (i.e., for a theft of $100, $200 is restored), it follows that crime, and sin in any fashion, is highly unprofitable. The ultimate penalty of restitution can include death ("then thou shalt give life for life," Ex. 21:23).

Although there were periods of apostasy, and also the common rebellion of civil governments against God's law, the usual practice of the Christian community over the centuries has been to require restitution as God's mandate. This meant too that the habitual criminal, in terms of the case law of the incorrigible son (Deut. 21:18-21), was to be executed. The execution of habitual criminals was once common in the United States; later, third or fourth offenders were given life imprisonment, and then even this disappeared.

Biblical law has no prison system. A criminal was held in prison only pending a trial, and then either made restitution, or was a bond-servant until he worked out his restitution, or was executed.

As late as 1918, the United States echoed this principle of restitution in its foreign policy. In a report on "Armenia and her Claims to Freedom and National independence," it was stated: "According to the law of all civilized people, including the Sheri law, no murderer can inherit the property of the victim of his crime. That inheritance or estate must pass not to the murderer but to the next of kin of the victim" (U.S. Statutes at Large, 65th Congress 1917-1918, 3rd Session, Senate Document No. 316). This statement, while not specifically Christian did all the same set forth restitution.

In recent years, the erosion has been rapid. Instead of seeing love as the fulfilling or keeping of the law (Rom. 13:8), modern churchmen have seen love as replacing law. Judges have readily picked up this doctrine. I recall the shock of a small businessman, in the late 1950s. A man with a record of passing bad checks had bilked him also. When he went to court, the businessman saw the guilty man given a suspended sentence and placed on probation. He himself was savagely lectured by the judge for demanding restitution and treated as unloving and unchristian.

Since then, of course, this evil has proliferated, and law has decayed because of this hostility to restitution. Crime is now highly profitable, and injustice prevalent.

But the fact remains that restitution is God's law, and it is God's law not only for all relationships between man and man, but also between man and the earth, and man and God. Remember, God required the land to have seventy years of Sabbaths by sending the people into captivity "until the land had enjoyed her sabbaths" (II Chron. 36:21). In one way or another, in His own time and way, God requires and effects restitution. At the end, the final accounting is rendered.

Restitution thus can no more be abolished than God can be abolished. When men sidestep or by-pass restitution, God exacts a penalty. We can evade and play games with man's law, but never with God's law.

Without restitution, man's idea of law loses its center and becomes erratic and unstable. Among the more common eccentricities of law have been emphases on class, caste, race, or status, whereby the law becomes an instrument for inequality. A related eccentricity is the emphasis on equality, so that law and justice are separate from justice as restitution and made the instruments of a drastic levelling of men, circumstances, and institutions. Eccentric law loses its orientation towards righteousness or justice and becomes governed by social standards, mores, and pressures. Law then becomes the product of pressure politics, not of a principle of justice.

But restitution cannot flourish on the social and civil scene if it is weak or absent on the theological level. Where the legal aspect of Christ's atonement as His work of satisfaction or restitution for the sins of His people is weakened or denied, there too all of the foundations of law are affected. The cross of Christ sets forth restitution as the essence or nature of God's law. It makes clear that there is no reconciliation between God and man apart from Christ's satisfaction for our sins and the imputation of His work to us. The heart of the gospel is this legal fact of the atonement. Regeneration and conversion, basic as they are, still rest on Christ's work of atonement. Justification by faith in and through Christ's work of satisfaction is the foundation of our standing before God.

The cross requires us to see the centrality of restitution in our standing before God and in our world of law and human affairs. If we do not require restitution of ourselves and all men, God will require it of us.

CHALCEDON REPORT NO. 161
January, 1979

Restitution is basic to Biblical law. For all offenses, man must make restitution to man. For offenses against God, only Jesus Christ can make restitution, and basic to the doctrine of the cross is the fact of restitution, the satisfaction of God's justice. Thus, the principle of restitution goes hand in hand with justification by faith in Christ's atoning work.

Humanism, however, has other doctrines of law, all of which stress man's salvation by works of law. Whenever in the civil order men adopt a humanistic doctrine of law, they undermine Biblical theology because humanistic law requires another doctrine of salvation.

First among the humanistic doctrines of law is the doctrine of law as a means of reformation, i.e., the salvation of man by legal reformation. A leading figure in this faith was the Quaker, William Penn. Although it was about a century and a half before his ideas were adopted, it was Penn's thinking which gave the rationale.

Penn, as a Quaker, believed that every man has within him an inner light, a spark of divinity, and, by heeding that inner light, a man can be saved. The solution therefore to all problems of crime is simple, from this perspective. Give the criminal an opportunity to develop his inner light and become a new man. This, of course, was not anything but heresy but, with the development of the Enlightenment, and then Romanticism, this doctrine caught on. As Roger Campbell, in *Justice Through Restitution* (Mott Media, Box 236, Milford, Mich. 48042, 1977) points out, the Quakers became leaders in "prison reform".

How was the criminal's inner light to save him? The humanistic reformers, in England, Europe, and America, saw salvation in isolation from corrupting influences. Let the criminal be placed in a new kind of monastic cell in order to meditate on his sins and become a new man through the inner light. As Michel Foucault, in *Discipline and Punish, The Birth of the Prison* (Pantheon Books, N. Y., 1977), has pointed out, prisons began to be built as a new kind of monastery for a new kind of monk.

Prisons, moreover, began to gain new names to fit their new functions. The term "penitentiary" recalls medieval penitential exercises. "Reformatory" spells out the humanistic doctrine of reform or salvation by law. "Correctional facility" is again a term which witnesses to the salvific purpose of the law as reformation, as does "reform school."

Conservatives and churchmen who advocate "stiffer" applications of the prison system had better re-assess their efforts. They are demanding a humanistic plan of salvation. Biblical law requires restitution, not imprisonment, and with habitual criminals, the death penalty; only such a system means that crime does not pay. The prison system does not solve the problem of crime, and prisons are not reformatories but schools for crime. Men come out worse than they went in.

Of course, the means of reformation by law have changed in recent years. A variety of more modern means of salvation have been proposed and tried. One is work therapy, prison shops, work farms, and the like. Another is psychological and psychiatric help, a very popular but highly ineffective practice. Still another is education, so that both in and out of prison, in dealing with all men, many humanists see the hope of the salvation of man and the reform of society in education. (It was for this reason that I titled my study of the philosophies of statist education, *The Messianic Character of American Education.*) All of these efforts have one thing in common, failure.

But the idea of law as a means of reformation has not been limited to the theory of penology: it has been applied to all of civil society. Statist legislation has today as basic to its motivation the faith that man and society can be saved by works of law. Every time a legislature, parliament, or congress meets, it works to save man by law. Moreover, now, as humanism is in its death-throes all over the world, it works more furiously to legislate salvation and to stifle dissent.

What happens to churchmen who live at peace with a civil government whose life and purpose are governed by a humanistic plan of salvation by law rather than by Biblical law? *First*, it is clear that they have failed to understand Scripture or to apply it. They have not seen the ramifications of the atonement, nor that Scripture is a total word for all of life. They try to serve two masters, two plans of salvation (Matt. 6:24), with sorry results. How can men advocate one plan of salvation in the church and another through civil government without schizophrenia and moral paralysis?

Second, the church then recedes from most of the world, which is thus surrendered to another plan of salvation. It limits its concern to man's soul and to heaven, and it surrenders God's word to the devil. Theology becomes irrelevant to life, and is no longer the queen of the sciences. The Bible becomes a devotional manual, not God's command-word for the whole of life and the world.

Clearly, for the church to live at peace with the doctrine of salvation by law in the state means to compromise justification by faith everywhere. Is it any wonder that the church has long been in retreat? This retreat cannot he reversed until the church stands clearly against all doctrines of salvation by works of law and declares that God's word is the sufficient word for man, in church and state. Only Biblical law is in harmony with the Biblical doctrine of salvation.

(In subsequent months, other humanistic doctrines of salvation by law will be discussed.)

CHALCEDON REPORT NO. 162
February, 1979

Biblical law requires restitution; humanistic law has some man-conceived alternatives to God's law. *First*, as we have seen, law is held to be a means of reformation. Man is to be saved by legally compelled reformation.

Second, another humanistic approach to the problem of law is salvation by regulation. The purpose of the state and of law is seen as prevention. By means of a multitude of rules and regulations, the humanistic state proposes to control man so thoroughly that sin will become impossible. Men will be good, because no other option will be open to them.

Superficially, this principle has been with us for centuries, and some aspects of it have been adopted by many Christians. To go beyond God's law is to play god, and to hope for salvation by man-made means. Thus, temperance is clearly required by God's law; law-enforced prohibition is another matter. It is not liquor which turns men into drunkards, in the moral sense, but intemperate men who use liquor to become drunkards. Guns do kill, but gun control does not alter the murderous heart of man. When we stress the legal solution, we under-rate or by-pass the religious answer. We then give ourselves and society a false emphasis.

But such regulations are superficial when compared with the current trend in legislation. The citizen, the laborer, the industrialist, the farmer, and every producer is surrounded by a vast network of rules and regulations. Moreover, we cannot understand the meaning of this plan of salvation by regulatory laws unless we recognize its religious nature. These humanistic law-makers believe themselves to be the very soul of benevolence and nobility. They want a good world for all of us, and it pains them that we misunderstand their motives. They are religiously governed, and their faith rests, *first*, on a belief that man can be saved. Bad as man's plight may be, man can be salvaged, and, even more, perfected. With this salvation and perfection, man can enjoy life and this earth as never before, and a world order with world peace is a very real possibility and a necessary goal. *Second*, the salvation of man can be best or only accomplished by man, and the human agency best suited for this function is the state. The state is thus modern man's true church and savior. Politics becomes dominant in human interest and action whenever men see salvation in humanistic terms. Then the cry is, O Baal, save us. We fail to comprehend the direction of modern politics if we do not see that the state is humanistic man's agency for self-salvation.

Third, for the state to become an effectual savior, it must control every area of life and thought. This means that laws must regulate all human activities and direct them into approved and salvific channels only. Accordingly, regulatory laws govern education, economics, agriculture, production and consumption, health, welfare, and all things else. This means too the progressive regulation of the press and of religion. Increasing statist efforts whittle away by regulation at every freedom of the press and of religion, because humanistic salvation by regulation leads step by step to total regulation for total salvation.

In the earlier form of humanistic law, law as the means of reformation, prisons were made into the new monastery for the reformation of law-breakers. Like the monk, the prisoner faced a totally prescribed life as the regimen of his salvation and sanctification. This concept of law as reformation has been expanded to circumscribe all men: law, salvific law, is now the salvation of man by the total regulation of all men. The monastery was and is a voluntary place, and its roots are in self-regulation, something the humanists forgot. In the Great Society of humanistic man, all the world will be turned into a prison, with total regulation by total law. Of course, the humanistic reformer believes that our current protests against these regulations is evidence of sin on our part, but time, and humanistic law, will change us all, and we will rejoice, each of us in our well-regulated nook or cell.

As a result, all over the world, the humanistic legal reformers are working busily for our salvation. Every day, a multitude of new regulatory laws surrounds us to hem us in from sin. In the U.S.A., the Federal Register is evidence of this. Not content with the slow-moving pace of Congress with its hundreds of new laws, the administration and the bureaucracy issue new regulations by the thousands through the Federal Register. How great is their concern for us! They plan to save us, come what may.

Like it or not, men will get humanistic salvation unless they find theocentric salvation through Jesus Christ. Our option is not between God's salvation or none, but between God's plan and man's plan. The fall originated in the creature's plan for his own salvation (Gen. 3:5), and the pages of history give us the grim struggle between various man-made plans, and also and supremely, the struggle between man-made plans, and God's eternal plan through Jesus Christ. Man, in rejecting God's plan, issued his own. By means of his own law-decree, man plans to save himself. If the state is anything but Christian, it will seek to impose on all men a man-made system of law and salvation. The choice is between God's law and man's law; it is between Christ and Caesar.

CHALCEDON REPORT NO. 163
March, 1979

Biblical law requires restitution and restoration. Humanistic law begins by seeking the reformation of man by law. In *reformatory legislation*, the law-breaker is the goal of controls. The next step in humanistic law is *regulatory legislation*. Regulations seek to control all men to make crime impossible, or nearly so.

But humanistic law does not stop there. The third step is *redistribution*. The control of all men goes hand in hand with the control of all property. Men, land, and money are redistributed. Law becomes a total plan for the total salvation of men and society by means of total control.

In education, the goal becomes the equalization of all children in every way, so that grading is seen as an evil to be overcome or eliminated. Schooling stresses, instead of the acquisition of knowledge, the acquisition of social attitudes which will enable the child to belong to a levelled, redistributive society. Instead of an emphasis on excellence and individual achievement, there is instead an emphatic demand for socialization and group dynamics.

In religion, humanism seeks by law to eliminate or bring into conformity those churches which deny the Great Community as ultimate. All appeals must be to Caesar rather than to God. Ultimacy is held to be in the state, not in God, so that the state is viewed as god walking on earth and as the agency of social salvation. The Christian School is thus seen as a dangerous agency, because it teaches a higher allegiance and trains youth in terms of another faith.

In economics, redistributive legislation in Marxist countries means the open transfer of land and wealth from private ownership to the state as the trustee of all the people. In the democratic nations, the same redistributive goal is achieved by a variety of means, most notably the inheritance tax and the income tax. In the United States, 75% of all farms, businesses, and activities are wiped out by the death of the owner because of the confiscatory nature of the inheritance tax. The income tax works annually to redistribute wealth, as does the property tax, and a variety of other taxes. In fact, the goal of taxation can no longer be said to be the maintenance of civil order and justice; rather, its goal is social revolution by means of taxation. Taxation has indeed become the new and most effective method of revolution; it is the reactionary redistributionists who still think in terms of the armed overthrow of existing orders. The more liberal ones know that taxation is the more efficient means of revolution.

In politics, the redistributive state works to equalize and scatter all independent sectors, whether religious, racial, or economic, which can form pockets of strength and resistance to the saving power of the state. The redistributive state wants no dissident minorities, only an undifferentiated and submissive majority.

In brief, the redistributive state wants a world beyond good and evil. Where there is no good nor evil, there can be no criticism, and no judgment. Doris and David Jonas, an anthropologist-psychiatrist couple, declared, in *Sex and Status* (1975), after discussing a number of obviously warped and sinning relationships, "What, then, constitutes a basis for an harmonious male-female relationship? We are forced to the conclusion that this is not determinable from the outside" (p. 102f.). For them, there being no good and evil, no God, sin and perversion are merely matters of taste and choice. In a world beyond good and evil, there is no standard for condemning a civil government, and the civil law is thus beyond criticism. Moral judgment disappears, and coercion replaces it. In fact, where there is no moral law, and no God whose court is the source of all law and judgment, then the only binding force in any social order is coercion.

Thus, the more humanistic a state becomes, the more coercive it becomes. The brutal slave labor camps of the Marxist states are not aberrations nor errors of principle on their part: they are the logical outcome of their humanism. The humanistic state replaces God's predestination with man's plan of predestination by total coercion, and it replaces God's moral law with a purely coercive law whose purpose is alien to man's being and destructive to it.

All three forms or stages of humanistic law are very much with us all over the world. The Christian cannot be indifferent to law without denying his faith. Humanistic law is a plan of salvation in terms of Genesis 3:5; its goal is to make man his own god, determining good and evil for himself. However, when man seeks to affirm himself in defiance of and apart from the triune God, what he actually does is to destroy himself. By his sin, he brings in death; by his rebellion in the name of freedom, he assures his slavery.

God's law, in its every aspect, requires restitution and restoration. "God is not mocked: for whatsoever a man soweth, that shall he also reap" (Gal. 6:7; cf. II Cor. 9:6). What shall *this* generation reap, when churchmen count it a virtue to be hostile to restitution and to God's law?

Law can never be neutral. Law always condemns one kind of practice and protects another. The law can be fair, and in its procedures conscientious, but it is never neutral. Law is always religious: it is an expression of faith concerning the nature of things and a statement of what constitutes righteousness or justice. Historically, and in essence always, law is a theological concern. For churchmen to be indifferent to the triumph of humanistic law means that they are indifferent to the claims and demands of the triune God. Such an indifference is suicidal, and it is sin.

IS GOD NOW SHRIVELLED AND GROWN OLD?

Blasphemy often loves to present itself as a new and higher truth and therefore the true way. Certainly this is true of many today who tell us that God, Who declares, "I and the LORD, I change not" (Malachi 3:6), has indeed changed. Apparently, with age and a new "dispensation" of declining powers, their god now confines himself to purely "spiritual" concerns. Once, in his younger and cruder days, he may have spoken about weights and measures, diet, money, sanitation, politics, economics, education, and more, but, now that man and science have supposedly caught up with him in these spheres, and passed him, this god is silent, and he deals only with spiritual matters as befits an aged and declining person. The laws of this old and shrivelled god are now primitive and obsolete, and man can now do, we are assured, a much better job in all these areas.

This is the plain meaning of dispensationalism and antinomianism. It limits God. It declares that God is now not sovereign and therefore has no word for every area of life and thought. These people in effect believe in an aged and old god who is for old or retreating people whose only thought is to leave the world, not to exercise dominion under God over it as their necessary service.

The recent conflicts with state and federal agencies over Christian Schools have brought forth a coast to coast chorus of protests from these champions of retreat and flight. The schooling of our children, they declare, is not a Christian concern but a secular and humanistic one. The concerns of our faith are to be purely spiritual and ecclesiastical, they declare.

This very clearly denies God's sovereignty. It implies and declares that most of the world is *secular*, which the dictionary defines as "pertaining to this world or the present life, worldly as contrasted with religious or spiritual." If this be true, then it is a serious error for the church to regulate sex and marriage and to condemn adultery, because our Lord makes clear that sex and marriage are for this life only (Mark 12:25). One of the most influential dispensationalists perhaps holds to this view, because he is currently adulterous and yet widely honored. Nonetheless, God does ordain and regulate sex and marriage strictly, because His law and government are total, not merely spiritual and ecclesiastical.

God's sovereignty, law, power, authority, and government cannot be limited. He is Lord and Savior of all things, their total creator and governor. Hence, in every area of life and thought, we must be under His law-word and jurisdiction. There is no sphere of life, nor any area of activity, which is outside God's jurisdiction. Man can never step outside of God's government and law to create a purely humanistic area of government and law wherein man is sovereign. At no point in man's life or in all creation can we say, "Here God's government and sovereignty stop, or abate, and here man's word, sovereignty, and government take over." All such thinking, however spiritual it professes to be, is a radical compromise with humanism. It is an assertion of the tempter's principle that man is somehow, somewhere and in some way entitled to be his own god, knowing, or determining for himself, what constitutes good and evil (Gen. 3:5). Such a view is original sin, whether in the mouth of Satan or in the mouth of a spiritual pastor. God is alone the Lord, in all things, over all things, and everywhere.

CHALCEDON REPORT NO. 164
April, 1979

One of the fundamental beliefs of the Enlightenment was in what Peter Gay termed "the omnipotence of criticism." Few doctrines have been more influential on the modern mind; we are all, to some degree, infected by it. Belief in the omnipotence of criticism means a belief in the power of criticism, the critical word; it means that the solution to problems is seen as a judgment or a law.

This belief rests on original sin, man's belief that he can be and is his own god, able to determine and create good and evil for himself (Gen. 3:5; cf. Isa. 45:7). God's word is omnipotent: He says the word, and creation appears; He passes the word of judgment, and heaven and earth pass away, His word declares. God's word is law: when He says, Thou shalt not steal, all theft is judged with an eternal judgment. Hell is a witness to the omnipotence of God's critical word.

With the Enlightenment, and with existentialism today, man's belief in the omnipotence of criticism has developed rapidly. The impotence of the modern intellectual and of his community (the college, university, and seminary) is due to his illusion that his criticism is potentially or actually omnipotent. The "solution" to problems is thus critical analysis. (Perhaps no other Chalcedon Report has stirred more hostility than No. 138, wherein I discussed critical analysis; the anger of many academicians was intense.) This belief in the omnipotence of criticism has led to an age of judgmental churchmen, whose solution to problems is not Christian reconstruction but critical analysis.

Politics has been the art of criticism by law-making. Hearings are held, legislation framed and passed embodying a series of judgments, and the problem is supposedly on its way to solution. After one major piece of restrictive legislation was passed several years ago, a legislator, interviewed briefly on television, declared that a major step had been taken towards solving a serious problem. The problem has not been solved; it has become more pressing since then, because man's fiat word has no creative power; man's criticisms, his laws, have no omnipotence. Instead of producing or bringing forth something new and better, they inhibit, alienate or destroy.

The growing curse of the modern world is the belief that criticism and fiat legislation can be creative and productive. Criticism and judgment are replacing thought and work as the supposed means of productivity. God's word and judgments are creative and productive because He is the almighty and omnipotent one. His laws have behind them His power and government. When man stands in terms of God's law-word, he stands within the power and government of the Almighty. When man trusts in the omnipotence of his word, he commits suicide.

But this trust in the omnipotence of criticism is basic to our culture and to our time. When I speak, I find that the commonest type of question rests on a faith that criticism is the answer. Many of the letters which come to us daily rest on the same faith. Depending on whether they are liberal or conservative, questioners will demand that I criticize colonialism, racism, democracy, the illuminati, the communists, the fascists, the military-industrial complex, and so on and on. Again, I will be asked to pass judgment on this or that sentence that one of my associates has written. The "test" is not faithful Christian action but criticism. This demand, however, is an invitation to impotence, to sit on the sidelines as a perpetual judge.

I recall, as a university student, the tremendous pride of the Trotskyites; they were the critics of Stalin, of fascism, of capitalism, and of everything else. This made them, in their own eyes, the purest of the pure, because they were the super-critics! All too many liberal, conservative, Christian, and non-Christian persons and groups today (i.e., all of us, to some degree) are victims of the same sin in us, a faith in the omnipotence and virtue of criticism.

God's command to Adam was not to critique the Garden of Eden but to exercise dominion and to subdue the earth, to dress the Garden and to keep it, to care for it (Gen. 1:26-28; 2:15). Man fell when he turned from his calling to subject God to criticism (Gen. 3:1-6). One immediate consequence of the fall was that Adam then subjected both God and Eve to his criticism (Gen. 3:12), a sure mark of sin.

Since the death of Trotsky, the world of the Trotskyites has been a very revealing one. Only in one country, Ceylon, have they had any important role. The Trotskyites began as the purest of the pure, judging everyone else, and, step by step, they so refined their criticism, that they were soon criticizing one another. This, of course, is not an unusual course of events. Wherever the Enlightenment doctrine of the omnipotence of criticism takes hold, virtue becomes a matter of judging others and isolating yourself from their corruption. The result is the fragmentation and atomization of every cause; it is the collapse of movements into cannibalism, mutual self-destruction.

Our calling in Jesus Christ is not to critical analysis, to a seat of judgment from whence to judge all others, but to serve and obey the Lord in faith. He is the Lord, the only wise judge, and it is His word that must govern us. It is sin in all of us, and we are all prone to it, to sit in judgment. Nothing creates more havoc on the mission field, among hard-working and able men, than this proneness to pass sentence on one another. Similarly, nothing creates more tensions in churches and other groups than this same fact. In the world of nations, it makes us prone to see lawmaking as the solution to our problems. But humanistic laws rest in a trust in the omnipotence of criticism, in man's law-word, a judgmental, critical word, as the problem-solving word. However, in all of history since man submitted to the critical, "problem-solving" word of the tempter (Gen. 3:1-5), man's problems have only increased. There's no omnipotence in criticism, only impotence.

CHALCEDON REPORT NO. 165
May, 1979

For over a century and a half, Rome was in the midst of a civil conflict and class struggle, a battle fought in a variety of ways, over, among other matters, the issue of law. The plebians claimed the right to know the laws and the rules of court. This right was first claimed by the plebians in 462 B.C.; it was conceded to a degree in 45O, but it was not really assured until 304 B.C. The victory, however, was in reality a defeat, because the result was the Twelve Tables, the fountainhead of all law, public and private, in Rome. The fundamental principle of Roman law came to be the summary statement: "The health (or, welfare) of the people is the highest law." Here was a good legal principle to satisfy the people! However, instead of satisfying the plebians, and bringing peace to class conflict, this principle prepared the way for the later civil war and for Roman totalitarianism. Yet, to its very last day, Rome and its tyrants ruled in the name of public health or welfare!

The lesson of Rome is an urgent one for us today. Beginning with the French Revolution, we have had a like demand in the Western world for "People's rights." This demand has now become world-wide. At the same time, the growth of totalitarian slavery has become world-wide also. Clearly, the old order had its grievous evils, but the new order only compounds these. In the name of rights, modern man is getting slavery.

The plebians were clearly right in demanding that law cease to be arbitrary. Men must know the law. Law is simply enacted morality and is an establishment of religion. How can men do right and avoid evil if there is no law which all can know?

All over the world, men face this same problem today. What taxpayer can really know the law of the Internal Revenue Service when it means whatever the IRS chooses to make it mean? And who knows all the multitude of bureaucratic rules, regulations, and laws? It has often been observed that any citizen can be found to be a law-breaker at some point or another, so many and so detailed are all the statutes and rules. Our knowledge of the law is very limited, and inescapably so, given our present legal system. It was only when our law was Biblical law that it could be said, ignorance of the law is no excuse, because God's law is the law of creation, and of every man's being.

Whenever the humanistic state makes the health or welfare of the people the highest law, then the state itself becomes law, justice, and righteousness incarnate. The state then determines what that welfare is, or a majority vote of the people determines it, so that there is no fixed law, and no unchanging justice. Law and justice become what the state or the majority choose to make it, and all who differ are suddenly illegal and unjust. In the U.S.S.R., the slave labor camps are an aspect of Soviet justice; in the U.S.A., the persecution of churches and Christian Schools is beginning in the name of the public welfare or health, and public prosecutors and attorney generals invoke the public welfare against Christian pastors, school leaders, and parents.

Thus, the victory of the Roman plebian destroyed them, and the victory of the peoples of the modern world is enslaving them. Where God's infallible law and word are denied, the variable law and the word of man replaces it. The law then becomes whatever man, playing god, believes will best effect his own humanistic plan of salvation.

This is why all piece-meal legal reforms are failures in the final analysis. Unless God's law be the foundation of a civil order and a society, its legal basis will be some variation of the Roman principle. Instead of the infallible word of God, the health or welfare of the people, as interpreted by fallen man, becomes the foundation of law and the fountainhead of tyranny. The triumph of the people becomes their downfall and the victory of the Fall of man.

"Except the LORD build the house, they labour in vain that build it" (Ps. 127:1). The Hebrew word for *house* has a broadly inclusive meaning and here embraces every institution man builds, including the state, as the rest of the verse makes clear: "except the LORD keep the city, the watchman waketh but in vain." Our legal foundations, like those of Rome, are built on sand and cannot withstand the storms of judgment (Matt. 7:24-27).

Law-making is an attribute of deity. The issue in law is simply this: who is the Lord? As Harold J. Brokke wrote, in *The Law is Holy* (1963), "*God* has revealed His will; *man* must decide who shall be God." Man's decision does not change God nor His law, but it can destroy man and his society.

CHALCEDON REPORT NO. 166
June 1979

To understand the modern age it is important to understand the case of the mired horse. In 1825, Robert Owen came to the United States "like a god from a machine," according to one scholar, to recruit converts to form his first socialist community, the Community of Equality at New Harmony, Indiana. His was the humanistic gospel of salvation. Children were to be taken at birth and trained as "blank paper" into the true way of life. The colony began with a Declaration of Mental Independence from the "social evils" which plagued mankind: "*Private, or Individual Property* - absurd and irrational *Systems of Religion* - and *Marriage*, founded on individual property combined with some of these irrational systems of religion."

In 1826, a visiting Frenchman, Gabriel Rey, interested in joining the colony, found some discouraging signs of trouble and left later. He arrived on April 5 at supper time but had to go to bed supperless, on a short, creaking bed. At dawn, Rey took a walk to see this humanistic paradise at first hand. He found a mired horse, groaning, with none to help him. Nine days later, when Rey left, the horse was still mired and helpless, with none making any effort to rescue it. While Rey was there, necessary work went undone, *but a new constitution was announced.*

Here we have in classic form, in the case of the mired horse, a telling aspect of the modern age insofar as its intellectuals and leaders are concerned. Hegel declared, in a sentence which sums up modern thought from Descartes to the present, that "the rational is the real." Reality being equated with thought, the key to the future became, not the worker or the producer, the laborer or the capitalist, but the intellectual. The key to dominating the world and creating a new reality became the intellectual. Biblical faith, by setting forth the absolute sovereignty of God, and the necessary response of faith on the part of man, was the great enemy of the intellectuals, because it denied their version of reality. Biblical faith sets forth the sovereign God whose government is total. Because God is the creator of all things, His eternal decree establishes the necessary bounds and framework of all life and thought. Predestination, that is, total planning and control, is thus an inescapable concept and fact. If it be denied to God, it accrues to man. As a result, the intellectuals have seen a new locale for sovereignty and predestination, in either the "autonomous" intellectual, or in the scientific socialist state. In man's hands, this means confusion. If the rational is the real, if what the intellectual determines is a necessary "fact," then it is either ipso facto reality, or some hostile force is frustrating and destroying the coming into being of reality.

This leads, *first*, to the case of the mired horse. Whenever any congress, parliament, politburo, or like agency meets, it majestically outlaws the possibility of mired horses. This is the nature of modern politics, the abolition by fiat decree of mired horses. Man's problems are legislated out of existence whenever such bodies meet.

Second, because these mired horses do not disappear, we then see attacks launched against the evil element which destroys the rational order. In the Soviet Union, this means slave labor camps. In the United States, for example, the economy is a mired horse, mired by the Federal Government itself, and by its monetary and fiscal policies. However, war is waged by the Federal Government against capital and labor, and also against consumers - against everyone else as the real offenders. Stern warnings are issued, and speculators attacked. All the while, more horses are mired by the Federal Government, and more people are blamed for it.

The men of New Harmony framed a new constitution while the mired horse remained mired and died apparently. The apostles of the new world order are killing more than mired horses. The key for them is not faith and work but more noble pronouncements and laws.

As long as men in high places and low have the same outlook and hope as the men of New Harmony, we will continue to have mired horses. At New Harmony, all men were required to put all their capital into the colony, except the leaders, Robert Owen, his son Robert Dale Owen, William Maclure, William S. Phiquepal d'Arusmont, Marie Duclos Fretageot, and other leaders. Apparently contributing their presence and "ideas" was more than enough capital!

Now, if we put any faith or hope in men who mire horses, we ourselves will be mired at the very least. We and our society will perish most assuredly. Yet modern man's hope has been in men who mire horses!

Even worse, the church too often denies the lordship of Jesus Christ by limiting His kingship to the church only, or to the future, and thereby turns the world over to men who mire horses. Some will even argue that to assert the crown rights of Christ over every realm is "the social gospel"! But the social gospel is humanism: it asserts human autonomy and sovereignty and the satisfaction of human needs as the gospel. It is an appalling blindness to confuse Christ's Kingship over all things with its opposite, and it is an open invitation for the judgment of God. Such men are fools who say in their hearts, There is no god outside the church. And this is a greater evil than miring horses.

CHALCEDON REPORT NO. 167
July, 1979

In the world of Biblical faith, because all things are created by the triune God, all things work in terms of His will and decree. There is thus a total harmony of interests. Love and justice, grace and law, faith and works, and all things else have a common purpose and goal. In all non-Biblical faiths, a conflict of interests prevails, and the result is a radical conflict, for example, between love, law, justice, and grace, or a false peace between them.

Because this conflict of interests was basic to pagan antiquity, every revival of pagan thought was a revival of conflict. This conflict could be in any and every area, i.e., between mind and body, or between love and justice, because where God's eternal decree is denied, the unity is gone.

With Abelard, a major revival of Hellenic philosophy took place in medieval thought. The results were radically destructive, in the long run, to Christendom, because the doctrine of law was eroded. In Abelard, we see hints of the modern dialectic of nature and freedom, with nature being the realm of the law and of necessity, and the heart the domain of love, freedom, and morality. As John Gillingham, in *Richard the Lionheart* (1978), observed: "Peter Abelard could argue that those who crucified Christ had not sinned because they genuinely believed that they were acting rightly" (p. 43).

The implications of this position are far-reaching. First, the unity of man is denied. A man's acts and a man's heart are divided. If the heart be right, the consequences do not count for Abelard. Second, sin is no longer a matter of a violation of the law of God but rather of the subjective will and intent of man. If a person can plead, "I meant no harm," any man is justified in such thinking. God's law is not the standard by which man is then to be judged, but the condition of a man's heart is the final test. Sovereignty has been transferred from God and His law-word to the subjective heart of man. Third, the implication is clear that man's heart is good, and that man's problem is not a fallen and depraved nature but inadequate or faulty knowledge. Abelard's presupposition is that the men who crucified Christ were naturally good men with defective information. Such a position assumes that men will act justly and wisely if they are provided with correct information; this view is in contradiction to all of Scripture.

Abelard's perspective is an honest statement of a position widely prevalent in the modern world, among unbelievers and churchmen alike. His view is basic to antinomianism and to antichristian faiths. It destroys the wholeness and unity of life and leads to defective and one-sided judgments in every realm. To illustrate, increasingly King John of England is regarded as an able and competent king, because his reign coincides with the beginning of bureaucratic record-keeping on a larger scale. If we consider record-keeping in abstraction from life, we can call King John a great king, and American presidents all great men, and we will thereby prepare ourselves for our own destruction by a totalitarian bureaucracy.

Very plainly, the doctrine of law has been undermined in the modern world, because law is seen as something lesser than the heart of man rather than as an expression of God's righteousness. For the law to regain its due place in society, it must be seen as a theological concern. Law is not a statist product in Biblical thought: it is the revelation of God's holiness and righteousness. It is the canon or rule of life. Every word of God is a law-word, a command word from the Almighty.

Law is either revealed or made; it is either God's word or man's word. In any system of thought or faith, the source of law is the sovereign, lord, or god of that system. If the source be man or the state, then we have either anarchic, autonomous man, or the totalitarian state. If it be God the Lord, then God is the sovereign, the law-giver. The basic step in humanism is the usurpation of law-making. This usurpation begins with the tempter, who, in

Genesis 3:5, summoned man to be his own god, law-maker, or legislator, knowing or deciding for himself what constitutes good and evil. The tempter was thus the first antinomian.

A professor of law, J. H. Merryman, in *The Civil Law Tradition* (1969), stated that "the age of absolute sovereignty began" when the state claimed that "the ultimate law-making power lay in the state" (p. 20f). There was then no law to control the state, because the state was now the author of all law. "The legislative act was subject to no authority, temporal or spiritual, superior to the state, nor was it subject to any limitation from within the state (such as local or customary law)" (p. 22). The state became, after Hegel, a god walking on earth.

Where the heart of man takes priority over God's law, then finally statist law rules absolutely over man to the obliteration of man, his heart, property, and family. The result is a conflict society, and the antinomian becomes the victim of the tyrant state.

CHALCEDON REPORT NO. 168
August, 1979

Law-making is an attribute of sovereignty; the source of law in any system of thought is the god of that system. Modern man, however, has become so used to the claims of the humanistic power state to be god walking on earth that he takes for granted the state's claims to be sovereign and to be the law-source.

Combined with this claim to be the source of law, the modern state claims to be man incarnate. Louis XIV stated this in an earlier form, when he said, "In France the nation is not a separate body, it dwells entirely within the person of the King." A century later, Louis XV told the Parliament of Paris, "The rights and interests of the Nation, which you dare to make into a body apart from the Monarch, are of necessity one with my own, and lie in my hands only." The man within the state found his incarnation or corporation in the person of the king. With the French Revolution, the Nation-State claimed to be the locale of the embodiment of man. Article Three of the Declaration of the Rights of Man and of the Citizen (August 26, 1789), reads: "The essential principle of all sovereignty lies in the Nation. No body and no individual can exercise any authority not expressly derived therefrom." As this doctrine developed, in terms of Rousseau's general will, the state became the incarnation of man's general will and the federal head over man.

At this point, the Christian begins to see clear parallels to the doctrine of Christ. He is the last Adam, the federal Head over the new humanity He creates, and its king. The old Adam brought sin and death for all who are members of him, whereas the new Adam brings forth righteousness and the resurrection (I Cor. 15:21ff.). All men are members of Adam; the redeemed become members of Jesus Christ. In His deity, Jesus Christ is one with the Father; in His humanity, He is one with the new mankind, the new Israel of God. He is their Savior, their King, Priest, Prophet, and Law-giver.

The modern state says that it is the true Adam and therefore represents all men in the totality of all their lives. It is their law-giver and therefore the source of morality. We cannot begin to understand the great revolution of the modern age unless we see that for man today the state, not God and His word, is the source of morality.

But this should not surprise us. The state sees itself as the moral arbiter because it is the source of law now. All law is simply enacted morality. Whoever or whatever is the source of law is thus thereby the source of morality. As a result, we see those moral zealots, the men of the U.S. Internal Revenue Service, laying down the moral law for Christian Schools, colleges, churches, and organizations. In the modern world, and for humanism, the I.R.S. is closer to the new Holy of Holies than the church!

The legislative program of the modern state is humanistic moral reform in terms of the gospel according to the new god, the state. Not the God of Scriptures but the state sets forth the moral law and path for modern man.

The modern state thus sees itself (1) as the true Adam, as corporate man, and as (2) sovereign, and hence (3) the source of law and morality.

Institutions arise to meet functions, real or imagined which are neglected by other agencies. Modern man saw the state as the sound and safe substitute for the church, and as an agency capable of giving freedom and security to society. Men turned to the state with a religious trust, and the state at first seemed to be an answer to man's hopes.

The state, however, is increasingly an obstacle to man, the creator rather than the solver of problems. At every turn, man finds the state a threat to his freedom and security, in family, religion, work, school, business, medicine, and everywhere else. The benefits of the state are being dwarfed by its threats and evils.

There is still another factor: the state grows increasingly irrelevant where it should be most useful. Thus, most crime protection is now in private hands, where it is clearly more effective.

Pierre Goubert, in *The Ancien Regime, French Society, 1600-1750*, calls attention to an important aspect of the French Revolution. The old order disintegrated at an alarming rate. The revolutionaries should not have been able to topple France as quickly and easily as they did. But the old order was in too many areas obsolete, useless, or a roadblock. It was, Goubert points out, "deeply stained with the seigniorial dye," and, "noble or otherwise, the seigniors *qua* seigniors had long since given up protecting anybody against anything" (p.87). The old order was serving itself far more than it served

France. Where it was better than what followed, the merit was accidental.

The modern state is, like the France of Louis XVI, an obsolete ancien regime, an old order serving itself rather than its people. The only growth it produces is of its own power. It seeks total power, because without total power it cannot forestall the forces of erosion it has itself created. In spite of this, its days are numbered.

The key question thus is, not, when will the humanistic state collapse, but, when will Christian reconstruction establish forces sufficient to create a new and godly order? When will the change occur? The forces for change are already at work, and Christian Schools and renewed Christian scholarship are basic to them.

"LET MY PEOPLE GO!"

An ancient antichrist, Pharaoh, ordered the murder of all the sons of old Israel, seeking thereby the destruction of God's covenant people and his own triumph. He was a tyrant, and the original meaning of tyrant is one who rules without God. The tyrants and antichrists are very much with us now: they rule in the state house and White House, in the courts, and on the school boards, but more subtly than old Pharaoh. But again the goal is the destruction of God's covenant children, this time by forcing them into humanistic schools, or by imposing humanistic, statist controls over schools and children which belong to the Lord.

And again the word of the Lord comes through His faithful servants to the tyrants of our time: "Thus saith the LORD God of Israel, Let my people go!" (Ex. 5:1). It is never easy to serve the Lord, but it is much harder not to, for those who refuse to obey His voice are under the plagues of Egypt. "Come out of her, my people, that ye be not partakers of her sins, and that ye receive not of her plagues" (Rev. 18:4).

Because we are not our own, but have been bought with the price of Christ's blood (I Cor. 6:19f), the choice as to whether or not we will work out a bargain or compromise with the Pharaohs and Caesars of this world is not our own. We are God's property, and we cannot dispose of ourselves, our children, our churches, and our schools according to our word but must keep all things entirely under His word. He is the Lord. He declares, "I am the LORD, and there is none else, there is no God beside me: I girded thee, though thou hast not known me" (Isa. 45:5). God has girded or armed us before we knew Him, and He girds us to stand in His Name against all enemies of His Kingdom.

The enemy we face is the oldest and the basic enemy of God and His people. It is humanism, the worship of the creature, of man. The first humanistic manifesto was issued in the Garden of Eden by the tempter. Its affirmation is that every man must be his own god, knowing or determining for himself what constitutes good and evil (Gen. 3:5). Humanism's war against God is the oldest and most central of all wars, but the least recognized. If we know the Lord, we know who His enemies are.

God's word to His enemies remains the same: "Let my people go!"

CHALCEDON REPORT NO. 169
September, 1979

I was on the stand in a church and Christian School trial, and the church's attorney, Charles Craze, was questioning me about the Biblical doctrine of church and state, and its relationship to the First Amendment. The state attorney objected to the line of questioning and testimony as "irrelevant;" he remarked that it was interesting, but had no bearing on the case.

I suddenly realized how familiar this kind of objection had become to me, and how, in various conversations with civil authorities, the same point had been made. First Amendment questions were called "historical" rather than "legal."

One of our failures as Christians is to assume that the humanists think exactly as we do on everything except the Lord. However, the essence of unbelief is that the whole of life, the world, and history are viewed very differently. As practicing existentialists, these civil officials see the First Amendment as a part of the dead past: it must not bind them. Truth springs out of the existential moment, not from God. The past has meaning only for the past, not for the present. Hence, an argument which rests on a faith and on history, i.e., the accumulated victories of the faith in history, is to them irrelevant. The existentialist uses the past: he sees no binding force coming from above nor behind in time. Thus, in one ugly case, in California, the state has gone past the First Amendment to appeal to seven hundred years of precedent in English law, i.e., to tyrants like Henry II and Henry VIII and their controls over the church.

Where there is existentialism, there is no law, only the arbitrary acts of the moment. The existential moment makes its laws in terms of its present demands.

The nature of law has changed over the centuries, as faith has changed. In Western civilization, under Christian influence, the source of law was God and His word, the Bible. God being sovereign, He alone could be the source of law, because law-making is an attribute of sovereignty. This faith has never been more than partially prevalent, because, with the surviving paganisms, many held that the king was the lord or sovereign, and hence the source of law. Not the canon (or rule) of Scripture, but the canon of the king or state was held to be law.

With the Enlightenment, this faith triumphed, first, as the divine right of kings, and then as the divine right of parliaments, or of the peoples: "Vox populi vox dei," the voice of the people is the voice of God, and hence the source of law. The result was civil law replacing Biblical law. The state or civil order was seen as the lord, as sovereign. The French Revolution simply stated openly what had become an implicit fact.

Then, however, the socialists began to attack civil law as class law, as a means of war by one class (the capitalists) against another (the workers). Socialism openly calls for class law, and therefore class warfare. Civil law renounces God and God's jurisdiction. Class law renounces God and all men who are not of the "working class," and it reserves the right to define by death anyone who does not belong to that class.

The existentialists have had close affinities to Marxism, as well as family quarrels. Both are militant humanists, and the existentialists (or pragmatists, who are a branch of existentialism) are the more radical. The Marxists have been more brutal, but the existentialists have been more radical. The stronghold of existentialism or pragmatism has been the democratic Western nations. In the U.S., John Dewey and all philosophers of state education after him have been existentialists or pragmatists.

The Marxist believes in a planned society; the existentialist believes in a planning society. For the Marxist, a plan exists, which must be enforced. For the existentialist, no plan exists; the moment and its needs determines the plan and its controls, but tomorrow another concept of planning must or may prevail. However, at all times, planning is an attribute of man. The Marxist believes in a fixed plan of humanistic predestination by law, whereas the existentialist believes in a moment by moment, pragmatic and instrumental planning or humanistic predestination. The result of existentialist planning and law is a destructive drift.

The Marxists thus usually gain the upper hand against the existentialists, who have disarmed themselves of anything which God, man, or history can teach them. But the logic of Marxism points towards existentialism and its anarchic world. Marx recognized this, and his most passionate and illogical work was his attack, in two volumes, on the anarchist, Max Stirner. He saw Stirner's logic as leading to the death of humanism. Stirner limited meaning to man's arbitrary will; Marx wanted to retain enough meaning in history, but without God, to vindicate socialism and the dialectical process in history. Like King Canute, he tried to order the waves of an ocean of meaninglessness to stop short of engulfing Marxism and its world. His effort was futile. Without God, man is lost in a shoreless ocean of emptiness and meaninglessness.

Logically, Christians are, and always will be, "more than conquerors" in Jesus Christ (Romans 8:37). Practically, most churchmen preach impotence by limiting God and His meaning to a single vessel on the ocean of history, the church. Recently, one very able European theologian sharply criticized all views of the Book of Revelation which saw a meaning for all of history therein. It is a covenant book, he held, meaning a church book, speaking only about the life of the church, not the world! But the covenant of God in Adam is with all men, all men are thus covenant-breakers or law-breakers. The covenant renewed in Christ requires all men to confess God, in every state and institution, or else be judged and broken by the King. When we limit the covenant to the church, we have no law and no gospel.

The word gospel, after all, was an imperial-political word, meaning that the Savior-King his ascended to the throne, and He reigns. If Christ does not reign, we are without gospel, law, or hope. But He reigns, and shall prevail, and the gates of hell shall not be able to hold out against His ecclesia or Kingdom (Matt. 16:18).

CHALCEDON REPORT NO. 170
October, 1979

One of the central failures of the church in our age is its retreat from the historic Christian faith in and reliance on God's law in favor of humanistic law. All forms of humanistic law, such as civil law and class (or Marxist) law, presuppose man's autonomy from God. Autonomy means literally self-law, i.e., man as his own god, determining for himself what constitutes good and evil (Gen. 3:5), as against theonomy, God's law. Humanistic law is leading to the suicide of civilization.

Basic to the church's error is its failure to understand the relationship of law and grace, and behind that failure is its neglect of the doctrine of the covenant. Covenants are treaties, literally, and they are of two kinds. *First*, treaties can be made between equals, or between two powers of varying strength, who agree on a mutual faith and law. Every covenant requires a common faith and law, and hence Scripture forbids covenants or treaties with unbelieving nations and peoples, or a covenant of marriage with an unbeliever (Ex. 34:12-16). To make a covenant with an unbeliever is to concede the validity of his faith and law, and to practice polytheism, to say that religions are equally good.

Second, covenants or treaties can be acts of sovereign grace by a supremely greater power to an insignificant one, and the covenant law is an act of grace from the sovereign to one whom he receives into fellowship by grace. The law then sets forth the life of grace. Such is God's covenant with man. God the Lord, as the total and absolute creator and sovereign, needs no alliance or treaty with His creatures. Such a covenant is an act of pure sovereign grace on God's part. Now, without law there is no covenant. The law sets forth the sovereign's requirements for the recipients of His grace, so that, instead of being in opposition to grace, law is concomitant to grace. When the Lord in His grace made a covenant, He also gave His law.

All too many churchmen in the past century have seen it as virtue to reject God's law in favor of man's law. Even so important a man as Abraham Kuyper, while waging a major battle against the forces of revolution, undermined the permanence of his own work by undermining the historic Netherlands's belief in Biblical law. He refused to ground civil government in God's revealed law. Instead, he held that civil government is an agent of "common grace" empowered with the coercion of the sword against law-breakers. Thus, Kuyper sought the authority of the state in God's law-word, but he then turned loose an authorized state to make law by the democratic process. The authority of God's word was thereby attached to the humanistic law-making of the modern state. Not surprisingly, covenantalism, with its law and grace was soon in disarray and retreat, and the Netherlands became precisely the kind of revolutionary society Kuyper had opposed. The covenant was undermined by "common grace."

Throughout the Western World, in varying degrees and ways, the modern state was freed by churchmen and theologians from any accountability to God's law while at the same time increasingly stronger doctrines of submission to civil authorities were preached. At the same time, higher criticism began to challenge the authority and infallibility of God's enscriptured word. Positivism in civil law began also to deny that any law exists beyond the law of the state, so that the "right" of the state became the final and only "right."

In 1943, John H. Hallowell's very telling work appeared, *The Decline of Liberalism as an Ideology, With Particular Reference to German Politico-Legal Thought*. Liberalism had replaced God with the state as the source of law. Then, by affirming materialism, liberalism placed the world, man, and law beyond good and evil, and all ultimate and absolute values were rejected. Truth and value then became relative to man, and thus to collective man in the state. A form of this materialism is pragmatism, which is basic to John Dewey's world, to modern education everywhere, and to politics. In Hallowell's words, "Pragmatism, like materialism, rejects absolute values, but it goes beyond materialism by saying that individuals are justified in acting as if certain things are true and good" (p. 89). Liberal or modern Phariseeism thus claims over all men a "right" which it denies in essence. The result was a "liberalism" which in practice became a despotism in Nazi Germany and is in the process of becoming the same thing throughout the world. National Socialist Germany was not an aberration: it was the advance guard of the Western liberal humanism. World War II was largely a family quarrel between competing versions of the humanist faith.

In all of this, the critical battle of the centuries, the church has in the main been studiously irrelevant. Instead of opposing autonomy with theonomy, it has hailed autonomy as the true light. (A telephone call yesterday from a very faithful adult teacher in a church reported a split and departure. A leader of the dissident group, attacking his teachings on election, declared, "You can take everything else away from my faith, but you can never take away my free will." In other words, Christ is expendable, but not my free will, my autonomy!)

Statist slavery thus advances in the name of man's autonomy. It will not be reversed by humanism nor by pietism. Only by a return to covenantalism, to God's covenant in Christ, and to the grace and law of covenantalism, will man be free. "If the Son (not "free" will, nor the state) shall make you free, ye shall be free indeed" (John 8:36).

CHALCEDON REPORT NO. 171
November, 1979

Two or three years ago, in response to numerous requests, I passed on to our *Journal of Christian Reconstruction* editor, Gary North, the suggestion that an issue be devoted to the menace of liberation theology, and the Biblical answer to it. Soon thereafter, he reported that liberation theology is so prevalent in all segments of the church that we would virtually have to write such an issue ourselves.

But the requests have continued, especially from foreign students, coming from Asia and Africa, and studying in the U.S. Their statements can be summarized thus: American missionaries and theologians, Catholic and Protestant, Reformed, Arminian, or modernist, are almost all teaching envy and greed as well as class hatred, to our peoples. If we try to tell the truth about these things, our American teachers, in colleges, universities, and seminaries, accuse us falsely of representing the rich of our country, although most of us never met a rich man at home, nor until we came to America, where all seem rich to us. (To this can be added the fact that any American, like myself, who attacks liberation theology is accused of being the friend or champion of the wealthy.)

What is liberation theology? *First* of all, it is Marxism transported into theology and missions. It preaches revolution not regeneration. Some of the milder champions want a peaceful social revolution, but, in all cases, regeneration is set aside as a goal, or as a primary goal.

Second, it is held that it is both wrong and even impossible to preach the gospel to hungry peoples. Somehow, all our missionary efforts over the centuries are held to be invalid, because the "central" problem has not been dealt with. That problem is hunger and poverty, not sin. Sin is held to be a class trait, a property of the wealthy and of capitalists, not the poor, the middle classes, and the rich alike. But sin is no respecter of persons!

Third, although poverty is seen as the great and ultimate evil, somehow there is virtue in poverty! Ronald J. Sider, in *Rich Christians in an Age of*

Hunger: A Biblical Study (Intervarsity Press, 1977), a book praised by Frank E. Gabelein and others, asks, "Is God a Marxist?", and the essence of his answer is, "The rich may prosper for a time but eventually God will destroy them; the poor on the other hand, God will exalt" (p. 72). Again and again, this is set forth by Sider as the gospel. If this be true, God is a Marxist!

But Scripture is clear that it is not poverty which is the central problem of mankind and the key evil, but sin, which is "any want of conformity unto, or transgression of, any law of God" (Shorter Catechism, no. 14). Sider thus gives us an alien gospel, one we meet in the devil's demand of our Lord: "If thou be the Son of God, command that these stones be made bread," i.e., minister first to people's poverty, a temptation our Lord rejected, but Sider accepts for Him.

Sider finds "the Jerusalem model" of voluntary sharing, the sale of properties to supply needs, as the Christian ideal. He fails to point out that this was limited to Jerusalem because it was a unique situation, a doomed city. The remaining believers there believed our Lord's prediction of the total destruction of Jerusalem in their lifetime (Matt. 24). They either sold out to move away, or to remain as witnessing missionaries to their own people.

Sider gives promise of treating God's law seriously, only to dismiss it. His treatments of the tithe, gleaning, jubilee, etc., have only one purpose, to develop his concern for the relief of poverty as the heart of salvation, not to point us to obedience to the Lord. Rather, he replaces God's law with his own law, "The graduated tithe and other less modest proposals." He wants us all to be poor, to abandon church buildings, and so on. (His proposals do have some resemblance to the demands made on the church by Red China in the 1950s.)

Sider's proposals are indeed less than modest. When God, who declares that He does not change (Mal. 3:6), gives us His law, it is blasphemy and arrogance for man to set it aside in favor of his own law. Sider defines sin humanistically, in terms of specific outworkings of sin, such as covetousness and greed. But the heart of sin is to be as God, the desire of man to replace God as the determiner of good and evil (Gen. 3:5). To play God, to issue our own moral laws, and to redefine sin humanistically, is lawlessness and sin, however "noble" and humanitarian our purposes may be.

Moreover, Sider's book, and like works, are becoming manuals for a new Phariseeism, a new and high-minded covetousness. As I travel, I encounter the Siderian commune cultists: young peoples who share housing (a Christian commune), strum a guitar for entertainment and singing, and speak with Pharisaic contempt for the lesser breed who live suburban lives of capitalistic greed. (Some of the better meals I have had in the past few years were with such groups; there was no sin in living together and eating well; their sin was their spiritual pride and Phariseeism.)

What are we to seek first, the welfare of the poor, or the Kingdom of God and His righteousness (Mat. 6:33)? The Great Commission does not promise the exaltation of the poor, nor command it, nor does Scripture ever teach us that sin is a class factor. Rather, we are told that "all have sinned, and come short of the glory of God" (Rom. 3:23). It was the habit of the Pharisees to define sin as the mark of a class or a race. At the very least, the new Phariseeism, like the old, rejects Christ for its own wisdom, and, in place of the grace of God, it offers its own plan of salvation. Its end and condemnation are the same.

CHALCEDON REPORT NO. 172
December, 1979

William J. Brandt, in *The Shape of Medieval History* (1966), wrote of the new sense of meaning which marked the passing of the medieval era. In such men as Shakespeare and Marlowe, a new view of man and history was apparent. The older view (often marked by Hellenic influences) gave way to "the conviction that meaning lies within the relationship of events." Such an understanding is so natural to modern man that it requires some reflection to see the error in it.

For Biblical faith the source of all meaning is God the Lord; because He is the Creator of all things in heaven and on earth, all things have their being and meaning only through His eternal counsel and decree. The true meaning of all things is the God-ordained meaning. Moreover, because God is totally God and totally self-conscious, there are no gaps in His world of meaning. In other words, there is not a meaningless moment in our lives or experiences, nor a meaningless, purposeless atom or second in all of creation. In Him there is no darkness at all, and we live in a universe of total purpose and meaning. Thus, while there is a meaning in all events, and no event is empty or purposeless, the meaning thereof lies, not within the relationship of the events, but in God the Lord.

The modern age, by shifting the locale of meaning from God to the events, also thereby shifted the determination of events from God to nature and man. If God establishes the meaning of my life, it is because He creates and determines it; if I establish the meaning of my life, then I declare that I make and determine my life. If I am a Christian, I develop the meaning of my life under God and in terms of His word; if I am a humanist, I claim to develop the meaning of my life in terms of my word.

This same principle applies in the area of law. Humanism seeks to develop law within the relationship of events, and in terms of them. Law is then a product of man's history, not God's revelation. Law then can be, as some once commonly held, a product of man's logic. Law as logic is man's analysis of the meaning of events in terms of his autonomous reason. From

Plato on, we have had a very widespread emphasis on law as logic, the product of man's critical analysis and summation.

In this century, the stress has been on law as experience. Man's social experience enables him to see what his problems are and then how to answer them. Laws are then framed to give authoritative expression to the wisdom of experience.

Other relational views of law are possible. The Marxists see law as the instrument of class power and an expression of class-created meanings. One way or another, humanism sees law and meaning as forthcoming from the relationship of events.

This is, of course, a clear-cut manifestation of humanism. For man to admit that meaning and law are alike derived from the God of Scripture, and only derived from Him, is to admit that he must believe in the God of Scripture, and he must obey Him. Such a confession is anathema to the humanist, and he will not make it.

Rather, the implicit humanist confession is that I, man as god, make all meaning, and I create law. This is a logical confession for humanism. It is, however, no confession for a Christian. Unhappily, too many churchmen make it. They go to the Bible for salvation, to the sociologist for meaning, and to the state for law. Not surprisingly, their doctrine of salvation is soon compromised, weakened, and broken. A god who is a god over only a sliver of life, the salvation realm, cannot save and really has no realm.

The modern age, both in and out of the church, sees man as god and law-maker, man as the determiner of meaning. Of course, this doctrine had deep roots in the medieval era. The game of chess was very popular with the aristocracy then, because it allows the human will to plan beforehand the sequence of events as against other wills. In effect, the appeal to the medieval aristocracy was the hope that, by his own determination, man could say, "I prevail." On the other hand, autonomous man, then and now, does not like our Lord's words in Matthew 6:34; "Take therefore (by seeking first the Kingdom of God) no thought for the morrow: for the morrow shall take thought for the things of itself. Sufficient unto the day is the evil thereof." God determines all history; His law decrees the future of our events and relationships. If we believe and obey the Lord, and walk in his laws, we are blessed, and our future is as God has declared it (Deut. 28); if we sin, the wages thereof are death (Rom. 6:23). God's law-word sets forth the meaning of all events.

CHALCEDON REPORT NO. 173
January, 1980

While at the University of Colorado recently, I picked up a copy of the independent Colorado Daily because a front-page article caught my eye. Its title is one which reflects a now common opinion: "The wolf: a victim of bad publicity." More than a few naturalists assure us that the wolf does not attack human beings, and they cite their work with wolves as an example. (Of course, they work with well-fed wolves.) A few days previously, I had finished reading a very interesting family history of Michael Charnofsky, *Jewish Life in the Ukraine, A Family Saga* (1965). The book describes an experience, on a cold night, driving home with horses and sleigh, of an attack by a wolf-pack; escape came at the price of tossing overboard, one by one, the load of prepared geese for Passover.

Again, the October 10, 1979, *Time* reported on a book by anthropologist William Arens, *The Man-Eating Myth*, which states that cannibalism may never have existed anywhere as a regular custom. Of course, many explorers and missionaries have given eye-witness accounts of cannibalism as a regular practice, but they were not anthropologists! The October, 1979, *American History Illustrated* carries a letter of August 5, 1782, by Louisa Cheval, describing her experience with Indians, cannibals, in Spanish Louisiana. The poor women lacked the insight of modern anthropologists and thus, did not assess her experience properly!

Why such skepticism about well documented events and practices? Some years ago, one man, an anthropologist, remarked by way of rebuke to me for an observation I made, that all our records of past human experiences are distorted and false. The reason for this, he held, is that so much of all our historical data came to us through the filter of religion. Christianity in particular, he said, has distorted all data by seeing man in terms of "the myth" of the Fall, and Calvinism especially, with its doctrine of total depravity, has led to falsification of all records concerning man. The great task of "science" in the next generation, he held, would be to undo that false picture of man and history, and especially of "primitive" man and nature.

Well, the revisionism is now under way, and wolves are very dear, loving creatures; cannibals are really vegetarians; and criminals are really abused and misunderstood peoples, hurt and in need of love! The law still believes in punishment, but now it seeks to punish Christian Schools, godly men, Christian families, and the like. A new doctrine of man is the presupposition of our laws now, and nothing is more reprehensible to the new law-maker than Christianity.

It is not surprising that a growing but largely unpublicized problem in the national parks and forests of the American West is the attack on and maiming of human beings by animals. A generation reared to think of bears as sweet, cuddly animals acts with a foolishness around bears (and other animals) which makes it very susceptible to serious injury. (On top of all this, we have evidences of a vocal minority who are ready to defend the rattlesnake, but not, of course, these horrid Christians!) A generation brought up on television cartoons in which animals are fine, sensitive souls has little sense of reality. It leads to the kind of insanity which led an army officer to express shock to a rancher who spoke of shooting and poisoning squirrels and other varmints. (What kind of an army can we have, when an officer bleeds for a rodent pest?) And what kind of laws and society can we have when men hold such opinions?

The answer is that we will have the kind of society we are steadily getting, from San Francisco to New York, and around the world. Man's vision of life is a false, distorted one, and, "Where there is no vision, the people perish: but he that keepeth the law (of God), happy is he" (Prov. 21:18). A man's ways are now right in his own eyes, and men insist that man's will must replace God's law. Nothing is sacred, and everything is permitted, in this new faith (which is like the faith of the Assassins of old). Reality now comes, for more and more people, from drugs, hashish, marijuana, opium, heroin, and the like, all of which are used to blot out God's world and "free" man's mind to remake reality in the dreams of drugs.

But the issue is not drugs: it is false religion. Humanism requires a drug culture. A world under God's law does not need it. Which world do you live in?

CHALCEDON REPORT NO. 174
February, 1980

The purpose of all law is to set forth the doctrine of justice or righteousness and to punish injustice or sin. When a society's doctrine of righteousness and sin changes, its laws also change. Every social order has a doctrine of law, of justice and injustice, and the source of that doctrine is in its religion.

In our day, because humanism is the established religion of the modern state, our law is in process of change, because we have a new definition of the meaning of righteousness and of sin. The Biblical doctrine of sin holds that all men are sinners by virtue of their birth into the humanity of Adam. Only by rebirth into the new humanity of Jesus Christ are they transferred to a life of righteousness, although not perfectly sanctified in this lifetime. Thus, sin and righteousness are attributes of birth and rebirth.

Humanism too have doctrines of sin by birth. To cite some examples of this, many hold that it is a sin to be born rich, and to remain rich; richness is seen as a form of depravity. The same doctrine holds that to be born into the middle class involves a similar taint which only mass destruction or perhaps re-education can remove. Likewise, to be born poor is to be born deprived, tainted, and by definition oppressed. It is a taint which for many only revolution or great social upheavals can remove.

But this is not all. There is also added to this burden of guilt a racial guilt. To be born white is held to be an example of sin; it means an immediate inheritance of centuries of supposed guilt, expletive propensities, and assumed arrogance. The white man is told he should feel guilty. The black man has a similar guilt trip laid on him. He is told that he is by nature inferior, or that the white man has made him inferior and exploited him, and that he is a betrayer of his race and destiny if he works, minds his business, and enjoys life. Wherever he turns, a guilt trip is laid on him. The same is true of every racial and national group; false pride and false guilt are posited, and a false doctrine of sin which blames others for their past, and then for failure to become engines of revolution.

The same is true of the sexes. One feminist leader has written a book on the supposed fact that all men are by nature rapists, and the idiot clergy have given favorable reviews to the book, thereby telling more about themselves than about reality in general. The feminists tell men they are by nature and history guilty, and the women that they are guilty for being women in the Biblical sense. Humanistic male supremists work to make women feel inferior and guilty, and godly men to feel weak and foolish.

The point is sufficiently clear. All men have a doctrine of sin or injustice. The Bible declares, "sin is the transgression of the law", God's law (I John 3:4). For the humanist, sin is not an offense against God's unchanging law, but against man's changing standards.

The relief of sin is by law. For the Christian, salvation as received by man is by God's sovereign grace alone, but it is all the same an act of law. The atonement of Jesus Christ is our salvation and justification, and it is the satisfaction of God's unchanging law, of God's death penalty against man. Thus, in the economy of the Trinity, our salvation is an act of law, a fact set forth in the doctrines of atonement and justification. In the experience and life of man, salvation is an act of sovereign grace. Thus, salvation is both an act of law and an act of grace: to deny one part of this fact is to undermine the other.

For humanism too salvation is an act of law, but statist law, and it is also an act of grace. The law of the state is a changing law, however. Daily, thousands of pages of new laws are added to city, county, state, and congressional codes, and to the federal register. As against one unchanging Book which all can read and understand, we have with humanism a jungle of laws, volume upon volume by the tens of thousands, which none can read in full or understand; courts and commissions regularly alter their meaning, and no man can escape being in violation of many of them. Moreover, the grace of the state is purely external. It grants funds, subsidies, and privileges, but it does not touch the nature of man. By its externalism, it aggravates and feeds man's sin and increases social decadence and disintegration. The humanistic doctrine of law becomes a form of social suicide.

When God declares, "Wherefore come out from among them, and be ye separate" (II Cor. 6:17), He did not mean a merely ecclesiastical separation but one governing our total life. Having given us His law, He certainly does not countenance our "concord" with humanistic law.

CHALCEDON REPORT NO. 175
March, 1980

One of the things about the early church which upsets some people and puzzles others is the fact that, as soon as churches were built, whether small or large, they were built with a magnificence which goes against certain opinions men hold about early Christianity. Under the influence of evolutionary mythology, men speak of the early church as "primitive Christianity." In its architecture, it should thus represent a "simple" faith and give us no more than a meeting house.

In actuality, the first churches not only reflected self-consciously the splendors of the Old Testament temple but sought to surpass it. We cannot begin to understand the faith of the early church without understanding its architecture. The early church had theological problems and conflicts, but it had certain presuppositions reflected in its architecture, which were very important, and which we need to return to.

From the very beginning, churches were built of the finest materials and on a pattern of magnificence. Later, in the middle ages, churches became much larger, as time passed, but they were no more splendid. Churches were built to surpass other structures and to reveal a particularly impressive appearance to one and all.

The reason for this was the nature of the church: it was the palace of God the Son, Jesus Christ, and a palace must be a place of splendor. The church did not belong to the congregation: it belonged to the Lord, Christ the King.

Thus, in the years 401 to 404 A.D., Paulinus of Nola, of Aquitane, built a church at Cimitile. In a letter, *Epistola 32*, he described this church. On either side of the nave of the church were four rooms (*cubiculi*) "for those who prayed secretly or meditated on the law of God." (Paolo Verzone: *The Art of Europe, The Dark Ages from Theodoric to Charlemagne*, p. 15, 1968.) The King's Palace was the place for prayer or petition, and also for the study of the law of the King.

The churches also had mosaics and paintings. The early church saw in Scripture the fact that the Temple and Tabernacle had carved items ordained by God, and it held that, unless abused and worshipped, such objects were permissible. Their purpose was to emphasize that the believer was in the King's palace: they depicted the King, the apostles, angels, and saints, and often throngs of humble believers, in brief, the royal family and servants. These were not realistic works of art; they did not depict personalities, nor action. The eye was emphasized to show the clear gaze of the eternal King on His earthly family.

One may agree or disagree with various aspects of this architecture. It is clear also that some aspects of the mosaics and paintings were more neoplatonic than Hebraic. However, one aspect of the theology of this architecture rang true: the church is Christ's palace and court, not man's meeting-house. It is the place for the proclamation of the King of Kings, and for the declaration of His grace.

It is this emphasis which the church later lost. In the later middle ages, the church began to stress, not God's presence in Christ, but man's soaring aspirations. With the Counter-Reformation and baroque art, the effort was made to impress and please man. The vault of the church seemed to open into heaven, so that man had the illusion of looking up into heaven at will.

Protestantism began its long journey towards the emphasis on the church as man's meeting-place, a meetinghouse, where many could feel at home. The same became true of the 'worship' of the church: it was governed progressively by a desire to please the people rather than to glorify God. This same impulse has increasingly governed Roman Catholic and other liturgical churches: the satisfaction of the people has become paramount.

This, of course, is humanism. The architecture of the modern church, whether great or small, imposing or simple, is man-centered. The church is no longer seen as the palace of the King of Kings, nor as the world's law-center and mercy seat. It is a social center instead, ministering to human needs by a variety of sociological and psychological means. The church works to make people feel "at home" rather than in the presence of the King by His grace. Esther 4:11 tells us that, even for a queen, to go into the presence of a king without his consent was death. The church once held this to be true of Christ's palace: to be within His gates was a tremendous privilege, a fact of royal grace; therefore, "Enter into his gates with thanksgiving, and into his courts with praise: be thankful unto him, and bless his name" (Ps. 100:4).

Let us bring back the King, to rejoice again in His law and grace. Let us make of the church again a palace.

CHALCEDON REPORT NO. 176
April 1980

The Biblical word perfect (*teleios*) normally means fully grown, mature. Unfortunately, too often modern man, in reading Scripture, misunderstands it to mean sinless, thus giving it a different meaning. In politics too the word has been misunderstood. When the Preamble to the U.S. Constitution speaks of "a more perfect union," it refers to a more mature union, not a flawless, sinless estate.

This false demand for perfection is a product of sin. In the Garden of Eden, a sinless place, there was no perfection in the sense of a mature and fully developed order. On the contrary, Adam and Eve faced daily the necessity for hard work in caring for the trees, vines, and vegetables, in developing tools to enable them to do their work, in providing themselves with housing, and so on. Eden was a pilot project: what they learned there was to be applied later to the development of a vast world of wilderness. The world of Eden was sinless, but it was not perfect in the sense of being fully developed. The world was at its beginning, not its end.

Their temptation, and their sin, was to reach out to gain a final result without the intervening work, planning, capitalization, and trial and error learning which was required of them as two novices at every task. The tempter's program was simplicity itself: God is preventing you from realizing your true goals; you can yourselves be gods, knowing or determining good and evil for yourselves (Gen. 3:1-5). Man could become his own lord and creator; he could abolish all evil at will and he could remake the world into a better place for mankind.

Man's solution to his problems was thus not growth and maturation, not work and planning, but rather the attempt as his own god to re-order reality in terms of his own will.

Since then, history has been the repeated attempts of man to legislate reality into conformity to his will. Problems are not to be dealt with in terms of Eden's "primitive" way but by fiat legislation. The state becomes the great agency whereby man as god seeks to hurl his fiats against the world, demanding that the world be transformed by the will of the state.

As a result, fallen man seeks for the abolition of all evil by means of law. Are there problems sometimes with parents, and in a number of families? Abolish the family. Are there problems in industry, and in the operation of the free market? Control industry, and abolish the free market. The logic leads to a final conclusion: is life a continual problem? Abolish life: suicide answers all questions!

The world, and all things therein, as God created it, was "very good" (Gen. 1:31). Disorder and chaos are products of sin. The very demand for perfection is a creation of chaos and confusion.

Men, however, are now accustomed to regarding their desires for perfection as legitimate demands to make on God, man, and society. What do I need, they ask, to enrich my life and give me what I believe is necessary for self-realization? Is it more money, a new home, husband, wife, children, or another job? Then God and life must supply it, or else we will "punish" God and man by being miserable, sulky, and petty!

This is clearly the attitude of all too many people. A very large percentage of all pastoral, psychological, and personnel problems have their roots in such demands. All too many people throw a tantrum and expect the world to come to a halt with an awed hush, and them jump to do their will! Even worse, such people, with their demands for perfection, do more than mess up their own lives and the lives of all who are near them. They are all too often effective in other arenas as well. They are citizens, church members, workers, executives, union-members, corporation council members, and more. The demand for perfection now is carried into one sphere after another.

The result is tantrum legislation to satisfy those who scream the loudest. Tantrum legislation seeks to by-pass human factors and relationships, as well as work and forethought, to give man instant utopia. The result instead is the march of hell, which, like the Sahara and its winds, erodes everything it touches.

Perfection, as maturity, is not a product of legislation but of growth, faith, and work. Humanistic law has too long been loaded with all kinds of utopian expectations and has been a fertile source of increasing disorder. Laws whose premise is a radical immaturity as well as a sinful rebellion against God can contribute nothing to society except more erosion.

The very ancient definition of *tyrant* in Greek was one who rules without God. Humanistic law is tyranny.

CHALCEDON REPORT NO. 177
May, 1980

A very common remark made by an angry or distressed husband or wife is this: A man (or, a woman) has a *right* to some peace in his home. This is a routine reaction to marital problems, and also a typically modern one. We would have to call it, in fact, a Kantian reaction.

In 1795, Immanuel Kant wrote on *Perpetual Peace, A Philosophical Essay*. The essay is a classic of humanistic reasoning. Kant began with the admission that war is the natural condition of man, not peace. Step by step, however, he led his readers to the conclusion that peace is a basic human right. Kant was a leader in the shift of Western culture from the emphasis on God's law to human rights. Peace now became a human and public right. With that transition, Western civilization moved into an era of total warfare, perpetual war for perpetual peace, as someone termed it.

Why? What was it in the Kantian perspective which has proven so deadly to peace? The reason is a very simple one. Peace is unattainable when it is regarded as a right rather than a duty, as something which should come to us out of necessity, rather than something we must work for.

Let us return to the illustration we began with, marital discord. Marital problems are built into the modern view of marriage, the expectation that marriage will give us love as our right, and more. People marry expecting to be loved, rather than to love, and, as a result, both are disappointed. Like all things, marriage requires work to further and enhance the relationship. Without work, we are sure only of troubles.

The same is true of social problems. To assume certain things as our human rights ensures that we will demand them rather than work for them. The doctrine of rights thus becomes a major focus for social discontent, warfare, anarchism, and dissolution. Society is then faced with the maximization of demands and the minimization of work. It becomes a conflict society, and the harmony of interests is ridiculed.

Law and politics are radically deformed by the emphasis on rights. Everything which men must of necessity work for is politicized: the assumption is that rights can be legislated into existence. A tragic and insane example of this mentality was the Kellogg-Briand Pact of Paris, 1928, which outlawed war and proclaimed peace. By August, 1932, sixty-two of the sixty-seven nations of the world had signed it. Only Argentina, Bolivia, El Salvador, Uruguay, and Yemen failed to sign it. The spirit of this pact was revived by the United Nations: it was held that the problem had been a lack of instruments for the enforcement of this great human right, world peace. In every country since World War II, political and economic legislation has furthered the abolition of peace by creating massive conflict. We are told by these humanists of human rights at the same time that we are assured that a conflict of interests is basic to human society. This means that only the state can "enforce" the rights! The modern humanistic state, however, is the great enemy of man, and the great disturber of the peace.

Law in the process is made the instrument of rights. Fiat legislation replaces work as the means to legitimate goals, and men who suffer the consequences of the power drives, their hostilities to God and to man, and their wilful lawlessness, cry out that they have been deprived of their rights.

Peace as a right? No, peace is a moral duty (Heb. 12:14). Brotherhood a right? No, brotherly love is a moral duty (II Peter 1:7; Rom 12:10; I Thess. 4:9; Heb. 13:1). The language of rights is alien to Scripture; the language of God's law, and our religious duty to hear and obey, is basic to it. No man has a right to peace or brotherly love, but every man has a duty under God to work towards these things, and to live in terms of them.

The doctrine of rights presupposes man as sovereign, and the world and God duty-bound to give "every man" his rights. In a world where every man is demanding his rights from every other man, peace is lost and unattainable, and conflict is inescapable. At the core of humanism is this false doctrine of sovereignty and lordship. Ours is an age of warfare between the humanistic gods, and it has no possible solution other than a different doctrine of sovereignty.

Before God, all men have duties, none have rights, and all have His law to obey.

"I AM THE DOOR"

One of our Chalcedon friends remarked, not too long ago, that Jesus said, "I am the door" (John 10:9); He did not say, "I am the doormat!" All too many churchmen seem to believe that what Jesus actually said was, Father, I am the doormat. They further assume that true piety means making ourselves into doormats. As a result, they counsel an implicit pacifism, surrender, and a continual subservience to every evil that comes along.

As a result, we see today persecuted pastors, Christian School teachers, and parents facing a double assault, from humanistic statists on the one hand, and compromising churchmen on the other. These churchmen who counsel meek submission to statism and humanism are anything but meek in facing their persecuted brethren! Then they are indeed bold and vocal.

If Christ is indeed the door, as we believe He is, He is the door to salvation, to freedom, to power over the forces of darkness (including humanism and statism), and to victory. Doormat Churchianity is not Christianity. John says emphatically, "For whatsoever is born of God overcometh the world: and this is the victory that overcometh the world, even our faith" (I John 5:4). Victory is a condition of our new creation. To counsel surrender and defeat is to counsel a form of unbelief.

CHALCEDON REPORT NO. 178
June, 1980

The writer, Frank Harris (1856 - 1931), had a number of great passions which commanded his time and energies. One was a continuing desire to enslave women sexually; another was the right to insult and cut down men, especially all waiters. A third was his concern over what he called "The Crucifixion of the Guilty." In his prospectus on his biography of Oscar Wilde, he wrote in part, "The Crucifixion of the guilty is still more awe-inspiring than the crucifixion of the innocent. What do we know of innocence?" Life for Harris was the perpetual crucifixion of the guilty because they were more honest than the supposedly innocent. As a result, Harris was determined to be "honestly" guilty: in his often fictional autobiography, the impotent old man happily and romantically confessed to endless adulteries which were at best greatly romanticized and extensively fictional. Because he believed that Jesus was a guilty lecher like himself, he identified himself with Jesus, whom he believed to have been crucified by the same "hypocrites" who assailed Harris. As biographer Philippa Pullar states it, in *Frank Harris, A Biography* (1976), when Harris, at the age of 71, married his mistress Nellie, "The belief that he was Jesus was by now so embedded that he recorded in the register that his mother's name was Mary Vernon, confused no doubt with Mary the Virgin" (p. 395f).

Frank Harris, editor, writer, and member of Parliament, was a noisy but minor figure in his day, but he did give focus more clearly than others to certain major strands of thought, one of which was the vindication of the guilty. With far more sophistication, Emile Durkheim had developed the same philosophy. Durkheim (1858-1917), in *The Rules of Sociological Method* (1895), saw crime as a normal part of society, because no society is exempt from it: "it is to affirm that it is a factor in public health, an integral part of all healthy societies." The criminal is a necessary part of social evolution: his lawlessness may be social pioneering; it may indicate the next step in social development. "Crime is, then, necessary; it is bound up with the fundamental conditions of all social life, and by that very fact it is useful, because these conditions of which it is a part are themselves indispensable to the normal evolution of morality and law" (p. 70; 1938 edition).

With such thinking, guilt began to appear as a social asset. True, the influence of Christian thought continued to weigh guilt as a liability, but "liberal" thought saw guilt as a cause to champion. About ten years ago, a student reported to me that a speaker had declared that it was the presence of lesbians in the women's liberation movement which made it a worthy cause; feminism in itself he saw as a middle class matter and nothing to get excited about.

As Harris saw it, innocence is a myth. All men are guilty (Freud would have agreed), but not because of the Biblical doctrine of sin. Guilt was a product of social hostility by the social cowards against all free spirits. Hence, the crucifixion of the guilty.

Clearly, this concept has had a very powerful and pervasive influence on contemporary law. The protection of the guilty is a major cause, whereas the growing persecution of Christian Schools and churches gets almost no attention from the press. The "rights" of parents are diminished, and the "rights" of the guilty are stressed and broadened. Going back at least to Lord Byron, literature has shown a morbid interest in the guilty, and an impassioned defense of all such.

It is a serious mistake to content ourselves with bewailing this doctrine of "the crucifixion of the guilty." It is a product of the loss of faith. If Nietzsche is right, and God is dead, then good and evil are both myths, and "the guilty" are wrongfully "crucified." Nietzsche, Freud, Dewey, Holmes, and others have acted as though God were dead. The same is true of the church: it has acted as though God were dead in relation to education, economics, politics, law, and more. As a result, the word of God has been "dead" to these areas.

If Harris was right, then the so-called guilty are wrongfully "crucified," and the rightfully guilty are those who apply the outmoded Biblical doctrines of good and evil to man.

But God is not dead, and the world of Frank Harris, and the derelict churches, is becoming a growing nightmare. Unless men repent, the Lord who declares, "it is easier for heaven and earth to pass, than one tittle of the law to fail" (Luke 16:17), will have His time of judgment come upon us.

CHALCEDON REPORT NO. 179
July, 1980

The police rarely have much to laugh about these days, but one of them did recently. A big and heavy-set purse snatcher grabbed my daughter Rebecca's handbag. Her instinctive reaction was to double up her fist and hit him in the stomach with all her might. Shocked, and almost doubled-up by the unexpected pain, the thief immediately screamed for the police! One was unexpectedly near, and hence his laughter, as he saw the thief, with my daughter's handbag on his shoulder, demanding protection from the "assault!"

No doubt the thief was outraged at what the world is coming to: first, civilian "brutality," i.e., resistance to theft, and, second, police "brutality," an arrest!

This arrogance of evil should not surprise us. It is a lesson well learned from much of the press, from many newscasters, and from some judges. While there are many fine and conscientious judges on the bench, we have all too many who are very protective of criminal rights, and indifferent to the courtroom harassment of police and witnesses.

The result is the growing arrogance of evil. Thus, more than a few cases exist where homosexuals are demanding that churches and Christian Schools be denied the right to pass moral judgment on them, or to refuse them employment. Such demands ask for the "right" to deny freedom of judgment and action to all who disagree with them. When law concerns itself with "human rights" rather than God's law, it soon seeks to defend all human practices in the name of man's freedom or autonomy from God's law.

We then have not only the arrogance of evil but the new phariseeism, the phariseeism of evil. The reasoning behind it is simple: there is no God, and hence God's law is obsolete and evil. All human practices are therefore to be permitted. The cause of freedom is best represented by those who practice the once condemned things. Therefore, the true heroes and social pioneers are the practitioners of homosexuality, bestiality, and incest. This then makes them the new moral elite.

An example of this sense of a new moral destiny is Hefner, of *Playboy*. His phariseeism is notable: he is filled with a sense of self-righteousness, and a feeling that the trivia of his mind and life are important. A few years ago, there were one or more *Playboy* television shows. They were largely empty of content other than a parade of self-importance and self-righteousness.

In this they mirrored our times, and were somewhat in advance of it. The watchwords of the new consciousness from the 1960s on have been "Do your own thing." "Find yourself," and "I want to be ME." This quest for self-realization means a contempt for others, for the family, for unborn babies, and for God's law. Not surprisingly, even a purse-snatcher's reaction to resistance is to demand police help: his "right" to self-fulfillment has been denied.

Men approach the church with the same self-centered and pharisaic concern. It was with some dismay that I came to realize that for many people involved in some of the recent church divisions and formations of new church bodies the real problem with the "old" church was not wrong belief but too much belief. These people want no commitment either to modernism or to orthodoxy: they want a church which does not "rock the boat" nor make any moral and theological demands of them. Instead of representing a revival of faith, too many represent a preference for a studied lukewarmness. Modernism and orthodoxy are zealous faiths; the lukewarm want neither. Instead, with the new phariseeism, they want the right to be indifferent and lukewarm in the name of Christ. Our Lord makes clear in Revelation 3:17 that it is the lukewarm who have a pharisaic self-righteousness and confidence.

All self-righteousness has self-defined moral goals. George Sarton, in *The History of Science and the New Humanism* (1931), said that survival and hope require that "we must anchor ourselves to some great purpose" (p. 190). All this sounds noble, but, when the "great purpose" is self-defined, we identify our thinking and purpose with greatness and true morality. Wherever men define the "great purpose" apart from God's declared law-word, they quickly fall into self-righteousness and phariseeism. The definition of law and purpose is not a right nor a prerogative of man, but of God only.

"To the law and to the testimony: if they speak not according to this word, it is because there is no light in them" (Isa. 8:20).

CHALCEDON REPORT NO. 180
August, 1980

One of the most dangerous, of ideas that have dominated men's minds is the dream of total justice. This is a humanistic dream. The humanist has only one world, this present life, and he is determined to make a heaven out of earth. The result is consistently hell on earth.

The menace of the dream of total justice is that it requires perfect people and a perfect social order and state to establish itself. The fact is that man is a sinner; he is also unwilling to change, content with himself although discontented with the world, and, by virtue of his fallen nature, a slave to sin and hence a slave by design (John 8:31-36). As result, every dreamer of a world of perfect justice, a habitation for supermen, and a realm of triumph for humanistic dogmas of justice, must begin to eliminate men as they are to make way for men as they should be. The French Revolution planned the reduction of France's population to a malleable fraction of what it was; Nietzsche called for the death of man to prepare the world for superman; the Russian Revolution and its exported revolutions have meant the planned murder of all who represent the old order. In Cambodia, since 1975, half the nation has been killed to eliminate all who cannot be reshaped in terms of the Marxist dream of a perfect order. The Cambodian Khmer Rouge leaders have killed off all who worked for the old order, all Christians, all who were educated, all who lived an urban life, all who had been abroad, and all who had worked for foreigners.

No more murderous force has ever been unleashed by man against man than the humanistic dream of justice. Tyranny and evil have governed most of history, but never more rigidly and thoroughly than by those who bring in totalitarian controls in the name of total justice. In 1931, Charles Pettit's *The Impotent General*, a brief and light novel, was translated into English. When the old war lord is replaced by an ideologue, the peasants are unhappy. A peasant is asked if it is because of affection. "By no means...Tan Pan-tze was an infamous robber, who shamefully harassed the countryside, thrashing inoffensive folk and raping women of all ages and conditions..." "Then may I ask why you appear to mourn him?"...The peasant replied: "Simply because his successor, General Pou, is very much worse than he was...he extorts his tribute methodically, which is even harder to endure... and, moreover, he now exacts the death penalty for non-payment and he does so in a legalized manner which has multiplied the executions" (p. 171).

It is not surprising that, in the quest for total justice, the humanistic regimes have instituted total terror. The people are whipped into line "for their own good." They are ruthlessly subjected to savage repressions and forcible changes, all designed to make them conform to the new model man for the new model society.

All this is logical. A better world does require better men! The question is, how to get better men, how to produce them? In the final analysis, two choices appear before men as the instruments whereby men can be changed: revolution or regeneration.

If men deny the possibility of regeneration then their only logical option is revolution. Since 1660, and the birth of the Enlightenment, the logic of humanism has moved the world steadily and more deeply into revolution. Every continent is now in the grips of a faith which demands the coercive remaking of men.

But total justice on earth is an impossible dream. Man does not have God's omnipotence nor omniscience: he cannot control nor see all things. Lacking total knowledge, his institution of justice, even in godly hands, is at best partial and incomplete. Not every wrong can be righted, nor every balance restored. Men can live, under God, in a just society, but never in this world in a totally just society. For the humanistic state to seek total justice means claiming God's omnipotence: the state must exercise total power for total justice. Likewise, it must claim God's omniscience: it must have total knowledge of all people, institutions, and things. A bureaucracy is created to exercise these "divine" powers.

In the Biblical perspective, man as sinner needs regeneration. As a sinner, he cannot establish a just order, only an evil one. By the regenerating power of God in Christ, he is a new creation. He is now able to serve God, to institute an order in terms of God's law, and to know what godly justice is, and to pursue it. He knows that only in God's eternal Kingdom is total justice attainable, so that, even as he strives to obey God in all things, he knows that he cannot expect of imperfect men and societies a perfect and total justice. All the same, only a new creature can make for a new creation.

A law order and state dedicated to a humanistic faith in total justice will create total revolution. An order dedicated to the whole word of God and Christ's regenerating power can give justice, because it rests on a new man of God's making, not man's.

CHALCEDON REPORT NO. 181
September, 1980

Otto J. Scott, in *The Secret Six*, a study of John Brown of Harper's Ferry, calls attention to a group of Unitarian leaders whose answer to the problem of slavery was apocalyptic warfare. Their answer, in fact, to all problems was conflict and terrorism, not peaceful solutions. Scott has seen a fact which other scholars and historians prefer to ignore. The nineteenth century saw the abolition of private slavery in all the areas under Western control. Except for the United States, the abolition was everywhere peaceful. Autocratic Russia freed its serfs without conflict. Latin American countries with a higher ratio of slaves than the United States also abolished slavery, legally and peacefully. Only the United States chose war.

The founding fathers, at the time of the Constitutional Convention, foresaw the essential disappearance of slavery as inevitable. In the early 1800s, in every Southern state save South Carolina, a majority favored the end of slavery; the only question was, how? Instead of a concern for the practical mechanics of such a step, a growing minority chose an all-out assault on the South. Conflict, not solution, was their goal. As a result, the nation was divided over the issue. In his Fourth Annual Message, December 2, 1856, President Franklin Pierce challenged this view of conflict as solution. It presupposed a belief that slave labor is superior to free labor, and that free labor cannot compete with it; it assumed an "irresistibly superior vitality" to slavery which was false. Implicitly, he believed that the means of eliminating slavery was already at hand: freedom. Slavery could not compete with free labor, and would disappear in time.

This was, of course, the problem. Then as now, those who call for conflict (and assume a conflict view of society) may oppose private slavery, but they believe in slavery to the state. The early opponents of serfdom in Russia were socialists: they wanted all men under the power of the state, with themselves as the elite managers. They did not believe in freedom for any but the power state.

Not surprisingly, the heirs of the abolitionists in the United States (and a few of the original ones in their later years) became strong advocates of centralized and statist power as the solution to all problems. Despite all their talk about liberty, they distrusted freedom - freedom of the individual, or the non-statist institution, that is. They wanted unlimited freedom for the state.

Their "solution" to problems is still conflict. In the name of peace, they demand war. There is a logic to this. Crises and wars are the best tools of revolution. In the modern age, every war becomes an instrument for enlarging state powers and creating a social revolution. Every modern state is prepared for a national crisis: a series of emergency executive orders are readied long in advance. The effect of these is not to aid the country and economy in a crisis but to control and paralyze it, and to enlarge the powers of the state. In every modern war and crisis, the winner has been statism: the powers of virtually every state are increased, and those of the people decreased.

This means that the modern state has a vested interest in wars and crises. Nothing does more to further its accretion of power: this is the grand solution by the state to all its people's problems, more power to the state.

In *The Journal of the Absurd* (1980), Jules Siegel and Bernard Garfinkel characterize the statist or "official mind" thus: "It hates logic, simplicity, spontaneity, common sense, and people as individuals. It loves power, regulations, duplication, complexity, titles, penalties, and people as categories. Its philosophy: More is better, even if it's worse. Its program: There are no solutions, there are only bigger problems" (p. 113).

As long as men expect statist solutions, they will get bigger problems, more wars, and more crises, as surely as the sun rises and sets. The only valid alternative to this is Jesus Christ. If men are truly Christian, if Christ be their King, they cannot look to Caesar for solutions, hope, or salvation. When we speak of the modern era as the era of humanistic statism (or, statist humanism), we are saying that the world has been in a post-Christian age. That age is now perishing. The Christian must separate himself from it. Alan Stang's book title puts the matter tellingly: God's law is, "Thou shalt have no other gods before Me - including the state."

We Americans are obviously slow learners. For a century and a half, our leaders have been giving us conflict as the solution to problems. Many countries have an even longer history of failure to learn. As a result the powers of the state increase, and man's freedom wanes. The conflict society is assumed by some to be a fact of nature, and inevitable. They look to the state and its men, where corruption and venality are at their highest pitch, for solutions to moral problems. All this constitutes moral idiocy.

The God who has turned us over to destruction for our apostasy and rebellion, summons us to faith and obedience: "Return, ye children of men" (Ps. 90:3). In no other way can we enter into a post-statist and a Christian era.

DEBT

Men can disobey or disregard God's laws, but they cannot set them aside nor eliminate them. God's law forbids debts by believers for more than six years. The seventh year must be a sabbath (Deut. 15:1-6). As a general rule, debt must be avoided. Paul says, "Owe no man anything, but to love one another" (Rom. 8:13). Solomon says, "The borrower is servant (or, slave) to the lender" (Prov. 22:7). Thus, debt is permitted for necessary purposes on a short-term basis but is to be seen as something to be avoided. Debts to the unbeliever have not the same meaning. Since they are already slaves (John 8:31-36), long-term debt is no problem to them. The believer, however, having been bought with a price, is not to be the slave of men (I Cor. 7:23).

We live, however, in an age when men believe that it is no longer necessary to obey the law of God, *which is another and implicit way of saying that God is dead*. Whereas earlier in the century, Christians, in the United States at least, restricted debt to one thing only, the purchase of a house or a farm with at least one-fourth down payment, and a short-term debt, now long-term debt, and debt-living for furnishings, clothing, vacations, and so on is commonplace.

One result is inflation. Inflation is the expansion by statist fiat of money and credit. We have today the world-wide and massive debt-living of civil governments and their peoples. Basic to debt living is theft. In 1935, Freeman Tilden, in *A World in Debt*, observed, "Inflation, whether of bank credit or of paper currency, cannot be effective until *the larcenous purpose is generally comprehended*." In an inflationary economy, there is behind the inflationary economics, a "new" morality which demands that envy and theft become legal and profitable. Everyone becomes a thief. In a world of big and little thieves, the biggest thief, the state, finally destroys the little thieves before God's law finally brings destruction to the state also.

The prelude to such a "new" morality is the decay of humanism. The earlier phases of humanism are marked by idealism, and belief in a set of humanistic principles. From 1660 to the early 1900s, humanism struggled to apply its principles, belief in the goodness (or, at least, moral neutrality) of man, in some kind of "natural" law, in the messianic nature of the state (except among anarchists) and its humanistic schools, and so on. However, as humanism eroded into cynicism, its one prevailing belief came to be in the over-riding reality of evil: it's a dog eat dog world; anything goes; get it while you can, and other like comments. When the late medieval humanism eroded into the "renaissance" mind, men made a show of their vices, even to claiming vices they did not possess. Machiavelli boasted, "In hypocrisy, I have long since received baptism, confirmation, and communion. In lying I even possess a doctor's degree. Life has taught me to temper falsehood with truth and truth with falsehood" (Valeriu Marcu: *Accent on Power: The Life and Times of Machiavelli*, p. 281f., 1939). Today, a like temper prevails. At the beginning of the 1970s I heard a university campus comment of like character, which included the counsel, "If you're still a virgin, keep it a secret."

All over the world today, nations have not only debauched their money but even claim that there are virtues in devaluation, which is like treating cancer as a sign of health. In the United States, the dollar remained constant (with minor fluctuations) from the early 1800s to the time of World War I. Now, with inflation, the dollar has eroded. Because inflation is a form of taxation, industry is suffering. Detroit's automobile manufacturers have not advanced the assembly line much over the days of Henry Ford and have grown weaker and fewer. American steel companies have facilities not even equal to Mexico's. The economy is near bankruptcy, in the U.S. and all the world. On June 27, 1980, R.E. McMaster, Jr. (a friend of Chalcedon), devoted his economic weekly letter, *The Reaper*, to a study of "The Fifty-Year Debt Cycle." One could say, by way of summary, that men either take God's sabbaths from debt or face disaster, either the jubilee or judgment: take your choice. McMaster noted, "In April, one-third of the U.S.

taxpayers were so illiquid that they couldn't pay their taxes. They couldn't even borrow to pay them. They filed returns, but enclosed no money" (*The Reaper*, P.O. Box 39026, Phoenix, Arizona 85069; $225 a year).

As Tilden noted in 1935, evil develops delicate sensitivities to justify itself. Behind all its sinning is a supposedly good purpose and a noble cause. Judgment is treated as an insult. "'If you had let me alone, I would probably have paid,' says the defaulter, with an injured air, 'But now that you are trying to badger me, you won't get it.' There is no sensibility so delicate and easily wounded as that of a person or a nation that knows it is in the wrong" (Tilden, p. 250).

Meanwhile, the state's power increases, and so does its greed. The degenerate Stuart rulers of England, before their fall, had so over-taxed and over-spent England, that under William and Mary it reached the stage of confiscation. Tax-collectors entered forcibly into the dwellings of cottagers to seize anything, including bread-boards and pillows to satisfy their exactions. Having chosen the monarchy over the Puritan commonwealth, the English were now paying the price of their choice.

We are now beginning, only beginning, to pay the price of our choices. No amount of bewailing will alter the matter, nor another set of lying politicians. A root and branch faith is required. We must say with Joshua, "Choose ye this day whom ye will serve...but as for me and my house, we will serve the LORD" (Joshua 24:15).

CHALCEDON REPORT NO. 182
October, 1980

An urgently important fact, too seldom appreciated by reformers is that power aligns itself with power, not weakness. Attempts thus to counteract a prevailing power by creating another power therefore aggravate existing problems instead of alleviating them. A more powerful evil confronts the reformer, who then seeks remedy in the creation of still another power bloc, only to see a union of powers now facing him.

The same is true in personal relationships. Peer group pressures govern most people. The reforming politician, once elected to office (and power), becomes usually less sensitive to the will of those who elected him, and more sensitive to the will of those around and above him.

Thus, big civil government, big labor, and big business (and big agriculture as well), may often be in conflict, but they are more often working together to the detriment of smaller groups and persons. Subsidies go to a great extent to power blocs. If a big businessman is independent of this union of powers, he is more than an outsider; he is a threat, and he may find himself before a congressional committee before long.

When Adam Smith wrote against mercantilism and in favor of the free market, he was opposing an economy and social order in which all major powers were linked together in the state, to the detriment of freedom and the people. So distrustful was he of the association of power blocs, that he opposed even an association of manufacturers or businessmen.

Since those years, we have seen the rise of neo-mercantilism, and the steady accumulation of power in the state. Statist controls and laws have promoted and fostered the growth of corporate trusts and large unions whose existence rests extensively on subsidies and legal immunities. The same has been true of banking. Not only so, but big education, being statist, is a part of the power circle. Even major private universities are recipients of large federal grants and subsidies. These power blocs become a working directorate to govern and control society.

Moreover, power in a society will collect around the central source of power and control in a society. If men believe that the chief power in life is the state, i.e., if they believe that the state is god walking on earth, they will draw near to that power. The more their own power grows, the more they will seek to be close to, and in a good relationship with, the power center, the god of that system. If that god is the state, then all social forces will seek to work with and through the state. Society becomes statist, and the goal of man becomes the gaining of grace and power from the state.

However, if man's religion, instead of being humanistic, is Biblical, then his power center will be neither man nor the state. If the Lord be his God, then the sun and center of man's life will be the Lord God. Man and his society will then gravitate around God and His word. Man's law will then be, not statist, but Biblical. Power will be defined accordingly in terms of righteousness or justice, not the manipulation of the state.

Man having been created in God's image has an inescapable urge to order. Faced with chaos or power, he will, as Adolf A. Berle noted in *Power*, choose power. However, because man is fallen, and his decisions governed by his fallen nature, his definition of power is likewise evil. The more clear his departure from God, the more clearly is his idea of order evil, and actually a form of organized disorder. The Soviet Union, Red China, and other like regimes are examples of this. Corrupt power seeks to corrupt every institution and agency it can touch. Statism thus seeks the control and corruption of every segment of society as a necessity.

The promise of Scripture is power from on high (Joel 2:28-29; Luke 24:49); etc.), power from the triune God. This gift of power is not to an institution but to the covenant people. It comes from the Person of God to persons. It creates an alliance of power for the sake of the Kingdom of God, and God's righteousness or justice (Matt. 6:33). Men who are aliens to this power seek power in collectivity and institutions, and in this way make themselves, whether of high or low degree, into mass men.

Power aligns itself with power; so too does weakness: it seeks the protection of power. We will seek to align ourselves with the power in our lives and faith. Will it be God or the state?

DARKNESS AND NEED?

A distinguished writer, in a very undistinguished book setting forth his humanistic faith, concluded thus: "the more darkness the future casts across our past, the more we need each other." This was his hope for the future! Because people "need" each other in a world disaster, the closer they will therefore become, supposedly, and the more moral.

Unfortunately for him, past disasters have only manifested the fallen nature of man. The growing darkness he describes is a product of man's sin and apostasy, and the problems of that darkness will only aggravate and expand the scope of man's sin. Darkness and need will not make things better, and especially not man.

Need and crisis can save no man. Man, created in the image of God, is a religious creature, and the only solution to his moral crisis is God's appointed one, Jesus Christ. Regeneration, not need, can alone change man.

This humanistic writer was using fresh and more liberal language to set forth an old faith in "the school of hard knocks." The idea was a fallacy in the last century, and it still is. Schooling, experience, and time can only teach the teachable, not the outlaw nor the rebel. If we are made teachable by regeneration, we will learn and grow in every context; if not regenerate our essential growth is in rebellion.

CHALCEDON REPORT NO. 184
December, 1980

A major area of revolution in law has been family law. The family has been re-defined to eliminate the Biblical meaning of the family by degrees, and the process is well under way. We are told that the family in law must include the voluntary family, and sociologists are among those promoting this new definition. The voluntary "family" can be homosexuals or lesbians living together, or a group of runaway youths sharing quarters, or a sexual commune. By being voluntary, such a "family" is held to be morally superior to the Biblical family, which is "coercive."

The "coercive" family is the target of more and more abuse, legislation, and regulation, whereas the "voluntary" family is quietly being accorded status.

For years now, we have been told of the need for legislation to control child abuse. Child abuse is an ugly fact, and a symptom of a lawless and godless society and a people without love or faith. However, we have long had more than enough laws to cover cases of child abuse. The problem has not been a lack of legislation. In fact, the proposed laws move rather in the direction of statist controls over all families, not the correction of an evil, but the imposition of a greater one.

Moreover, in all the newspaper and political talk about child abuse, the central and growing term thereof is rarely ever mentioned, discussed or condemned. The traditional family is the target, whereas this new, deadly, and rapidly growing form of child abuse is outside the family. It is the sexual exploitation of young boys and girls by homosexuals and lesbians. This practice is in fact being promoted as a sexual right by many and is called "intergenerational sex." One advocate is a nationally known writer. Child abuse of the worst and most prevalent sort is thus being made a right and a needed freedom.

On occasion, some macabre murder cases have come to light, the murder of a number of boys by some homosexual. We then see a glimpse of the sordid world of homosexual child abuse. What we do not see on the part of these humanistic reformers is any concern about this particularly vicious form of child abuse, the sexual exploitation of children by homosexuals.

There is a reason for this unconcern. Humanism has no desire to uphold, defend, or maintain the Biblical standard of law and morality. The world it envisions is free from God and His law, and from the Christian family.

The present direction of statist "concern" for the family should arouse Christians to action. Our faith, after all, sees the family as God's basic form of government, not the church nor the state. Moreover, the Bible is most revealing as an anti-statist document in these and other matters. It tells us, for example, of Pharaoh and the Egyptian state, and their planned extermination of the Hebrew children. The greatest condemnation is reserved for Molech worship (king or state worship), which required the dedication of all children to the state, and their possible sacrifice to the state's welfare. We see Babylon seizing all superior children, such as Daniel, separating them from their families to rear them as civil servants. Supremely, of course, we see Herod slaughtering all the children of Bethlehem up to two years of age, in his effort to kill the Christ child. The Bible gives us every reason to be suspicious of the state, especially when it professes a concern for our children. Add to that "concern" a humanism which is antichristian through and through, and it becomes sinful to he indifferent to Caesar's usurpations.

The tragic fact is that many families are not only unbelieving but evil in their care and rearing of children. The state is no better, and its record of custodial care is even worse, so that the failures of bad parents are compounded by a supposedly beneficent state. It is a very serious error to believe that problems have solutions outside of Christ. All around us, we see statist and humanistic solutions routinely aggravating problems.

I once heard a humanistic high school teacher say to a student who intended to leave a blank space for a question he could not answer, "Come up with some kind of answer. At least it will show you are thinking." On all sides today, people are demanding "some kind of answer," any answer, to problems. They then wonder why evils are compounded.

The family is God's first and basic area of government. It rests on the self-government of the Christian man under God. If we do not have such self-government, we will not have valid government in any area of life, including the state. Again and again, we have seen in history that declining and corrupt civil governments, as they decay, increase in their insistence on omnicompetence. The statists see themselves and their ideas as the solution to all problems. Men find such a view agreeable, because they like to believe that they can sin and then eliminate the consequences of sin by a legislative or administrative act. Sin is a moral fact; it is not solved by bureaucratic fiats.

We have a crisis in family life; this is a moral fact. We will continue to have a crisis in family life until there is a moral renewal, regeneration, among men. Moral facts have moral answers, not bureaucratic ones. This is the requirement and fact of Biblical faith.

CHALCEDON REPORT NO. 185
January, 1981

A law can come to have a radically different content and consequence without a word thereof being changed. All that is needed s a change in the faith which interprets the law. All law is simply an enactment of morality, or the procedural principles of a moral system, and every moral code is an expression of religion. If the religion of a culture changes, either the law changes, or its meaning changes.

Both kinds of change are apparent today, both changes in the meaning of existing laws, and new laws. The faith behind these changes is humanism.

The approach of humanism, as it approaches crime, social disorder, or deviant behavior is governed by *the medical model.* Such aberrations as are illegal are regarded, not as immoral or sinful, but as a sickness. The problem of criminality thus becomes either a psychiatric or medical problem. We are given endless analyses as to the social causes of theft, rape, murder, alcoholism, drug addiction, and more. The medical model constantly increases the number of "criminal" or deviant offenses. Instead of the limited and fixed number of offenses stated in Biblical law, the medical model has an ever-expanding number of offenses. It becomes a mark of expanding knowledge to identify, catalogue, and legislate about these new social offenses, sicknesses, or diseases.

The medical model governs virtually all statist agencies. The state schools promote the medical model and apply it to student counselling; their teachings on the subject color the thinking of all their students in varying degrees. Prison psychologists and psychiatrists are very much dedicated to the same faith, as are other public agencies, such as welfare or "human resources" departments.

This medical model is no less pervasive in films, television, and fiction (not to mention non-fiction). Newspaper columnists like Ann Landers apply it wholesale. Unhappily, it is also all too common among certain segments of the clergy.

The menace of the medical model is its destruction of responsibility. If my criminal behavior is not a moral fault in me but a social disease for which a disorderly society is to blame, I am then a victim, not an offender. It is not surprising that, in a generation reared on such a faith, even our criminals write essays indicting society for their crimes!

In terms of Christian faith, however, not only is the medical model wrong but it is in itself evidence of sin. Scripture sets forth *the moral model*. God's law having been broken, man fell into sin; his problem is not sickness or disease but sin, his moral or ethical rebellion against God and His law. Man's irresponsibility is not due to an immaturity or to sickness but to a moral choice, a decision to be his own god and to determine good and evil for himself (Gen. 3:5).

The medical model sees the problem as a lack, an imbalance, a disease or sickness, or some like problem. The environment of the deviant needs to be made new, not the deviant. The lack must be supplied, i.e., love, learning, housing, and so on. Only so will the deviant be healed and made new. Of course, instead of healing, we have a subsidy to evil, and its proliferation.

The moral model, as set forth in Scripture, calls for moral solutions: regeneration, restitution, chastisement, and so on. The individual is held to be responsible and accountable, not sick nor immature.

The medical model implicitly calls for the elimination of law, and all instruments of law enforcement, and their replacement by the psychologist, sociologist, and their cohorts. The individual at most needs reconditioning in a better environment, not a moral change.

The medical model seeks to get the individual to abandon guilt or condemnation in favor of seeing his problem as purely medical. (Some have inveighed against implying to any degree that venereal diseases can involve immorality; they must be viewed as a sickness purely. In one clinic, a doctor was regarded as having erred very seriously because he said to a girl in for a V.D. test, "Be good." Ann Landers tells a girl with a serious moral problem, "There are many excellent mental health facilities in your city. I urge you to make an appointment at once.")

Our laws today are under the influence of the medical model to an extensive degree. As a result, we are in the midst, not only of a moral crisis, but a legal crisis. In the medical model, the lawyer and judge must give way to the psychologist and psychiatrist. Lawyers who promote this medical model, and clergymen as well, are furthering this cultural decay and collapse. (We need to remember that for the past generation pastoral psychology books, almost all of which promote the medical model, have been the most popular reading with the clergy. Is it any wonder that their parishioners spout humanism without knowing it?)

It must he said that, without a concept of personal responsibility, a culture and civilization will collapse. A moral model is a social necessity, and a moral necessity. The deepening decay of our culture has basic to it the medical model. Men find it easier to claim a sickness, for which society is held responsible, than to affirm a moral model, which requires them to confess, "I acknowledge my transgressions: and my sin is ever before me. Against thee, thee only, have I sinned, and done this evil in thy sight" (Ps. 51:3-4).

CHALCEDON REPORT NO. 189
May, 1981
PASSIVE "CHRISTIANITY"

The March, 1981, issue of *Moody Monthly* has a page of letters from church members with a very common complaint: one person has been a member of a particular church for sixteen months, and, until the past Christmas, no one visited her or invited her into their home, except apparently the pastor and his wife. Another, a member for six years, feels left out because her husband does not attend with her; although people are kind to her, she feels hurt because other members go to one another's homes, and she is not asked. Another visited a new church and felt totally ignored, and so on and on.

This is a familiar complaint one can hear from coast to coast, year in and year out. It is always evil, and the complainers are clearly in sin. No one is called to be a passive Christian, to be courted, waited upon, or soothed by the pastor and church. Passive Christianity is a contradiction in terms.

I have heard young people in their twenties, and retired people, make like complaints of being ignored in church. In two years, the pastor never called on me," said a husky man in his late twenties; it did not matter to him that the pastor had been in and out of surgery for two years and had sometimes been in the pulpit laboring under some pain; it did not occur to him to call on the pastor!

Passive Christianity is an offense to Almighty God. If a member is at all able-bodied, let him or her volunteer to call on the shut-ins, the sick, and the visitors. If a newcomers wants friends, let them be friendly, let them volunteer to help, and they will soon have friends enough.

The church is Christ's army. Its purpose is not to provide breakfast in bed for all members, and a social lift for the unsocial, but a faith for life, preparation for battle against the powers of darkness, and a strategy of life for victory. The ineffectiveness of the modern church is partially due to this passivity.

Our Lord makes it very clear that He had no use for passive church members; in fact, He sends them to Hell! He demands that they visit Him in the person of the stranger or alien, the naked and the needy, the sick, and the persecuted and imprisoned Christian. "Verily I say unto you, inasmuch as ye have done it unto one of the least of these my brethren, ye have done it unto me" (Matt. 25:40). Of the passive, complaining church members who want the church to wait on them, our Lord says, "And these shall go away into everlasting punishment: but the righteous into life eternal" (Matt. 25:46).

This is strong language from Our Lord, but our Lord did not establish the church to be a pampering agency but a mighty army which shall overthrow the very gates of hell (Matt. 16:18). The church is not our property; we cannot ask it to serve us. Rather, we are called to serve the Lord, and, clearly, the Kingdom of God cometh not by egocentricity and whining.

CHALCEDON REPORT NO. 192
August, 1981
The Economics of Death

The Bible is full of economic wisdom which often goes neglected in our day because the Bible, the book for all of life, is too commonly reduced to a devotional manual and all " non-spiritual" truth is discarded. Solomon, for example, tells us, "Cast thy bread upon the waters; for thou shalt find it after many days" (Eccles. 11:1). The reference here is to rice planting. The rice is broadcast into water paddies, as it were; the family's "bread" or food is thrown away, in a sense, but only thereby is a harvest possible in the days to come. In Psalm 126:5,6, the same fact is stated even more vividly: "They that sow in tears shall reap in joy. He that goeth forth and weepeth, bearing precious seed, shall doubtless come again with rejoicing, bringing his sheaves with him." Here we have a famine in view; the precious grain is sown with tears, because life depends upon its harvest. In both texts, the *first* emphasis is that present advantages must be sacrificed for future benefits; there is no harvest tomorrow without a sowing today. Sowing seed constitutes an investment in the future.

Second, very obviously, the man who sows seed has, on the most basic and elementary level, some hope for the future. A society without hope is present-oriented. It is a consumer society; it eats up its seed grain rather than planning for a future harvest. It becomes therefore something that God condemns, a debt-oriented society rather than a saving and sowing one. It pays no heed to the six-year limitation on debt, nor to the principal that the godly goal is to owe no man anything save to love one another (Rom. 13:8). A debt society is death oriented; it makes saving, thrift, and future-oriented planning difficult or unprofitable, because it encourages consumption but not production. A "tax-break" is offered to debtors on their interest payments; savings are taxed (for accrued interest) as well as production and profit (or harvest). The tax structures of our time are anti-Scriptural with a vengeance. Moreover, the moral order is reversed; debt becomes an asset to these statist humanists, and wealth a liability and an evil. Money today does not have gold or silver behind it, but debt. The Monetary Control Act of 1980, which went into effect on June 1, 1981, allows the U.S. to monetize debts other than those of the Federal Government, debts both domestic and foreign. This is eating our bread or grain, not casting it upon the waters!

The power of a popular existentialism on the 20th century mind is apparent in its present-oriented economics. For existentialism, the moment, stripped of all morality and religion, and all considerations from the past or about the future, is everything. This too is the essence of all the varieties of Keynsian economics. Keynes despised the future; his premise was, "In the long run, we are all dead." This death orientation marks modern economics, and it marks the reprobate. As Proverbs 8:36 declares, "But he that sinneth against me wrongeth his own soul: all they that hate me love death."

The Bible requires a future orientation of us, but, not in terms of ourselves, but in terms of Christ, the gospel, and the Kingdom of God. Our Lord says, "For whosoever will save his life shall lose it; but whosoever shall lose his life for my sake and the gospel's, the same shall save it" (Mark 8:35; cf. Matt. 10:39, 16:25; Luke 9:24; Matt. 6:33). Our Lord here, in speaking of "losing" out lives, is not talking about martyrdom, but about "sowing," casting our lives by faith on the waters of the future, to yield a harvest to Him, and ourselves in Him.

Third, we are told that our godly investment in the future, God's future, shall certainly bear fruit: "Cast thy bread upon the waters; *for thou shalt find it after many days*." Again, "He that goeth forth and weepeth, bearing precious seed, *shall doubtless come again with rejoicing, bringing his sheaves with him*." Humanly speaking, while there is no harvest without sowing, there is still then no certainty of a harvest. Drought, blights, floods, insects, war, and other disasters can wipe out a potential harvest. We are, however, promised a certain and inescapable harvest if we, in all our ways, seek to serve and glorify God: "And we know that all things work together for good to them that love God, to them who are the called according to his purpose" (Rom. 8:28). This same fact is set forth powerfully and in detail in Deuteronomy 28.

Deuteronomy 28 emphasizes beyond any possibility of misunderstanding the moral and economic consequences of faithlessness to God. Inescapable curses and blessings are set forth: the religious, political, economic, personal, and agricultural consequences of denying God's law (and becoming present- and man-oriented) are clearly spelled out.

The economic world of humanism is a world of present possibilities and no future certainties. Hence, existential economic experimentation is held to be both possible and necessary. We have then fiat money and economics, with man playing God and seeking to determine all possibilities by his fiat will. The world of causality is replaced by a world of non-consequential possibilities. Such a perspective leads to the economics of death: a thousand and one ways of economic death are experimented with rather than to pursue an economics of life, because only the economics of death reserves determination to man. The world of law is replaced by the fiat word of man.

As a result, by March 31, 1980, what Martin D. Weiss, in *The Great Money Panic* (1981; Arlington House) calls "The Debt Monster," meant a $1.5 trillion debt for the nation's corporations; a $949 billion Federal debt; and, for homes, office buildings, and shopping centers, a $1,362 billion mortgage debt. At the same time, cash liquidity is at an all-time low; unemployment in the United States and aboard is increasing, and the "solution" more and more in view is increased inflation. This is like prescribing more liquor to an alcoholic!

With all this, we have seen a reversal in moral order. As even one "Reverend Doctor" wrote me recently, "gay" is good, and heterosexual is evil (and all "straights" should be put into concentration camps, he held!) Abortion is good, and pro-life is fascistic, it is also held. Such moral disorder is to be expected in an era which sees debt as an investment in the future and an economic asset.

One of the great evils of modern economics is its purported scientific basis. Mathematics of a sort, and science of a sort, are substituted for morality. It will not do to tell our statists that their economics is a form of theft by law; their graphs and statistics are designed to replace economic morality with economic "science."

Economics was once taught as a branch of "moral philosophy." Adam Smith himself was a Professor of Moral Philosophy (although his ethics followed Hume, unhappily, but his economics presupposed an "Invisible Hand"). Today, moral considerations are banished from economics in favor of pseudo-science.

As a result, economic issues are seen, not in terms of moral considerations, which require character, work, and a future orientation, but in terms of "needs" and "lacks." Because of this, we speak of "underdeveloped" nations, which Peter F. Drucker, in *Toward The Next Economics, and Other Essays* (1981; Harper and Row; p. 64) calls an error: no country, he holds, is underdeveloped because it lacks resources; rather, it does not utilize its resources; its capital in such forms is not productively employed. Neither its human resources nor its physical resources are put to productive use.

We must add that productive use requires a faith and character geared to the future, and to a vision of a growing and dominion-oriented society. Unless such a faith revives, all nations will soon be "underdeveloped." As Proverbs 29:18 summarizes it, "Where there is no vision, the people perish; but he that keepeth the law, happy is he."

To abandon moral and theological considerations in any area, including economics, is to abandon reality and meaning. It is to deny knowledge. Drucker cites the shift to a new definition of knowledge as "whatever has no utility and is unlikely to be applied." p. 49). We can add that such "knowledge" cannot successfully be applied. This certainly would cover the contemporary economics of death and suicide.

When a civil government rules by fiat, and when its economics is a violation of moral order, the result is either anarchy, or a return to or a revival of, the most conservative forms of moral order, or, usually, both of these at the same time. The U.S.S.R. has no lack of anarchy; it is a way of life for many. For many others, very ancient forms of family life and order are providing a close world of meaning. As a result, even the levirate continues within the U.S.S.R. (Helene Carrere d'Encausse: *Decline of an Empire, The Soviet Socialist Republics in Revolt*; Newsweek Books, 1979; p. 256).

The pre-occupation of contemporary national economic policies is with "the problems of unemployment and inflation," as Lewis E. Lehrman has pointed out ("The Creation of International Monetary Order," in David P. Calleo, editor: *Money and the Coming World Order*, p. 71; N.Y.U. Press, 1976.) Economic order having been violated, the consequences of national economic policies are disorders and increasing problems.

In the face of all this, the silence of the church on economic evils is amazing. Not only so, too often it manifests hostility to any mention of the critical issue of debt. In the past decade, my own comments and those of Gary North on unbiblical debt policies have brought forth some outraged responses. Just recently, because of references to the question of debt in some Chalcedon Position Papers, some highly emotional and angry letters have come in from people who have been handed copies of these Papers. This is not surprising. We have in such cases a very obvious fact. The person of the church is heavily in debt, and in debt for many, many years to come. They are also in a serious economic "bind." Instead of confessing to the Lord that their debts are violations of His law, and seeking His help to re-order their lives, they pray for "blessings," i.e., to be relieved of their debt situation by some miracle, and without penalties. To be told that they are in sin, and that the wages of sin are always death (Romans 6:23), triggers in them an angry hysteria. They want a god who will let them eat their cake and have it too.

There is a *fourth* aspect to the religious, moral, and economic implications of Psalm 126:5,6: He who is future oriented and sows with hope in the Lord, "shall doubtless come again *with rejoicing, bearing his sheaves with him*." The result is not only productivity, but joy. David, in Psalm 144:12-15 prays for an obedient people, a faithful people, faithful to their covenant God and His law, "That our sons may be as plants grown up in their youth; that our daughters may be as corner stones, polished after the similitude of a palace; That our garners may be full, affording all manner of store that our sheep may bring forth thousands and ten thousands in our streets; That our oxen may be strong to labour; that there be no breaking in, nor going out; that there be no complaining in our streets. Happy is that people, that is in such a case: yea, happy is that people, whose God is the LORD."

Such a society begins with your faithfulness and mine. It is time to say, "as for me and my house, we will serve the LORD" (Joshua 24:15).

TAXATION AS REVOLUTION

With the wrong kind of instruction, a university education can be a deadly thing, if it links us to the dead rather than the living past. The student movements of the 1960s witness to this fact. A variety of factors in the present aroused student indignation, some justifiably so, and others definitely not so. Our concern is with the element of revolutionary fervor in some quarters of the movement.

The religious faith in revolution is an important aspect of the modern age. Revolution is seen as the way to change the world; it functions in many modern circles to replace the Biblical doctrine of regeneration. Conversion is to occur, not by the grace of God through Christ, but by revolution.

This faith has been subjected to searching and telling analysis. Jacques Ellul, for example, has shown that the results of revolution are consistently reactionary rather than progressive. The faith, all the same, remains.

This is ironic, because the modern world is increasingly making armed revolution obsolete and unnecessary. Such revolutions now occur in the more backward areas, whereas in theory the more advanced capitalistic areas should be the revolutionary centers.

In the centers of advanced humanistic culture, it is increasingly only the minority of a minority of radicalized youth who are revolutionary. Even here, the revolutionary activity has become a militant terrorism rather than a program of revolution. Instead of commending them to the workers, it disaffects them. Not many workers appreciate losing a few days wages because their plant was bombed! Bomb the revenue service, the city hall, maybe, but not my job! Revolutionary movements alienate themselves from the workers whom they profess to champion. They are out of touch with reality.

Even more, they are out of touch with the realities of revolution today. The *first* and foremost fact today is that revolution is a state monopoly. Even the terrorists are a part of this monopoly, being subsidized and controlled by one or another Marxist regime. (The U.S. State Department, and other foreign agencies of states abroad, also subsidize various groups for their own purposes). An independent and popular revolutionary group does not exist in our day; they are instruments and puppets of state. The modern state has a monopoly on revolution.

Second, the major form of revolution in the modern world is taxation. Such taxes as the income tax, the property tax, especially the inheritance tax, and many more serve to effect a state-controlled and state-directed revolution. Armed revolutions are inefficient and alarming: they create a strong resistance, and they alarm the people. Taxation effects a more thorough revolution, and it can be sold to the people as a humanitarian measure. The purpose of taxation is said to be the relief of the poor, jobs, relief of the sick, the aged, and more. To oppose this revolution leaves one open to charges of inhumanity and unconcern. Few dare oppose such a revolution by taxation; it is a means of being marked as evil.

Third, the main purpose of taxation thus becomes, not the support of civil government in its necessary functions, but the creation of a power state in the name of social justice. Modern totalitarianism comes in the guise of social welfare and humanitarianism. Today, if the funds allocated for welfare went to each recipient without intermediaries, the amount per receiving person of family would be $40,000 a year; what they receive is dramatically less. The difference creates a bureaucracy dedicated to its own welfare and growth. The end of civil government is more government; its use of power is to gain more power. Dedicated to its omnicompetence, the modern state sees it as a social necessity that it gain more power.

Fourth, a major function of modern taxation is destruction. Since World

War II, some civil governments have raised the income tax to over 100% in order to force the wealthy into liquidating their assets. Others, whose taxes are a "modest" 50%, are less open in their revolutionary and destructive goals, but are still dedicated to the same ends. In the United States, for example, over 75% of all families face the loss of their business or farm at the death of one of the owners. Few may recognize the inheritance tax as a radical form of revolution, but it is, all the same.

Fifth, taxation thus works to dissolve the past more drastically than have armed revolutions. Few more corrosive social forces exist than taxation. Holdings, both small and great, which have been in the same families for generations, and even centuries, are dissolved. The stability of town and countryside is broken. Taxation is revolution at work.

Modern taxation is a humanistic and anti-Christian form of revolution. It must be fought by a renewed and dedicated faith, and by tithing. The Lord's goals are furthered by the Lord's tax. It is futile and immoral to rage against taxation and then refuse to manifest the faith and the tithing which can alone establish God's order.

It is equally wrong to demand a cheap faith, one that asks no price of us in commitment nor in tithing. One of the greatest indictments of the church members of our day is their unwillingness to support financially their church and all Christian agencies except on the most meager terms. They want Christ's all, but their response to the needs of Christ's Kingdom is miserly and niggardly. They want every guarantee from the Lord of a blessed life, and then give the Lord a lesser percent than to a waitress! Should the Lord be grateful for this, or angry?

Taxation is a form, the major form of revolution. The faithful can, with God's tax, turn the world upside down. They can reconstruct one area of life after another. If they wait for the state to stop taxing them before they begin to obey the Lord, they will wait their way into judgment. Taxation is revolution; use God's tax to establish God's reign and Kingdom.

One of the goals of taxation is economic redistribution. Statist redistribution does not work to eliminate great wealth but rather to create a new wealthy class made up of bureaucrats, Party bosses, and those whom they subsidize. The new wealthy class of the Soviet Union, for example, is more arrogant and deadly than any czarist lords ever dared to be. The "haves" in economic redistribution in the modern world are the friends of the state and the state's ruling hierarchy; all of the rest become "have-nots." Socialism does not equalize wealth: it concentrates it rigidly. The most powerful instrument in this redistribution of wealth is taxation.

Taxation serves another purpose, namely, to provide funds for the state's self-justification. The modern state is history's most powerful advertising and propaganda agency. First, as state-paid projects increase, so too does the state's control over the economy, capital, and labor. The freedom of every sector is diminished.

Second, the state controls education and uses the school to teach statism at the taxpayer's expense. Neither the cause of Christianity nor of freedom from statist controls gain much place in state schools. Rather, the state school teaches that freedom means deliverance from Christianity, and from the independence of the church, man, and the market-place.

Third, taxation enables the state to revolutionize other areas, most notably law, to justify its radical departures from morality and justice. The law, divorced from God, becomes an instrument to further statist coercion.

Fourth, the press is subsidized. Probably no news agency can equal the power and funds of the federal "news" dispensing agencies. When I testified at the Internal Revenue Service hearings in December, 1978 (against the proposed regulation to control Christian Schools), I was interested to see, after the initial testimonies (mainly by the IRS) on the first of the four days of hearings, how reporters simply walked in to pick up the IRS "news" releases from the "Press Table." No non-federal news agency can afford to give the thorough coverage which the modern scene requires. Thus, a large amount of our "news" is the product of statist handouts to the press, or press conferences designed to create news in terms of statist goals.

This revolution by taxation will not be defeated merely by votes. There is often little relationship between campaign pledges and performance in office, as recent presidential elections have shown.

The key is the reconquest of government by Christians through God's tax, the tithe. It means the creation of schools, hospitals, welfare agencies, and more which are Biblical in character, not statist. The early church, weak in numbers by comparison, defeated Rome in this way. We must do no less with statism now. This revolution by taxation must be countered by a Christian revolution financed by tithing, the creation of new institutions and agencies which are governmental in character and faithful to the Lord.

CHALCEDON REPORT NO. 193
September, 1981
GOD, THE DEVIL, AND LEGAL TENDER

To view the idea of legal tender theologically seems strange to the modern (and humanistic) mind, but it was once an important issue in the United States. The legal tender doctrine holds that the power to define legal money belongs to the state, and the state can therefore declare what constitutes legal money for the payment of all debts, public and private.

The Rev. John Witherspoon attacked the idea very early. It was unnecessary for any state to require people to accept good money. Gold and silver were always acceptable. A legal tender law simply requires people to accept bad money, and it does take civil coercion to make bad money acceptable.

The U.S. Constitution, Article I, Section 10, states that no state can make "anything but gold and silver coin a tender in payment of debts." *The Federalist*, no. 44, gives us Madison's opposition to paper money. Patrick Henry opposed paper money, and Daniel Webster argued that a legal tender law is unconstitutional.

It was the lexicographer and Calvinist Noah Webster who spoke most bluntly. In 1790, Webster called a tender law "the devil." He warned, "My countrymen, the devil is among you." Of legislators who favored legal tender laws, he said that honest men should exclaim, "You are rogues, and the devil is in you!" Legal tender laws, he pointed out, were the preliminary to adulterated money, and all those who favored them were counterfeiters, deserving of the gallows, or at least the whipping post!

Legal tender laws allow good debts to be paid with bad money, so that a debt is paid with only a fraction of the value it was contracted for. The result is a form of legalized theft, Webster held. He declared in part,

> "Remember that past contracts are sacred things; that legislatures have no right to interfere with them; they have no right to say that a debt shall be paid at a discount, or in any manner which the parties never intended. It is the business of justice to fulfill the intentions of parties in contracts, not to defeat them. To pay bona fide contracts for cash, in paper of little value, or in old horses, would be a dishonest attempt in an individual; but for legislatures to frame laws to support and encourage such detestable villainy is like a judge who should inscribe the arms of a rogue over the seat of justice."

Why did Webster see legal tender laws as the devil manifested in law? We cannot understand the legal revolution wrought by humanism unless we understand that fact.

For Webster and others, gold and silver represented natural and hence a God-given order of things, whereas legal tender creates an arbitrary value which can only stand with coercion. Values are God-created, not man or state created. The temptation of Satan in the beginning was to doubt God's order: "Yea, hath God said?" (Gen. 3:1). Rather, the tempter suggested a new order in which man creates his own laws, values, and morality: every man shall be his own god, determining or knowing good and evil for himself (Gen. 3:5). In such a society, the state as man incarnate can set aside God's laws and make its own laws. It can issue a legal tender law and require obedience to it. (In God's natural order, there is no need to require the use of gold and silver; they commend themselves and are in demand.)

The essence of the theocracy as Scripture's law presents it is that the state is at best minimal. A.J. Nock saw the Old Testament design as one for government, not a state. Repeatedly, God declares, This do, and live (Deut. 5:33, etc.). God's law is the way of faith and life, whereas "he that sinneth against me wrongeth his own soul: all they that hate me love death" (Prov. 8:36).

Legal tender laws are thus the tip of an iceberg. They represent a man-made world, one in which the state, by total coercion, seeks to overthrow God's order and to replace it with a humanistic one. In this new order of things, the state is the new god walking on earth, and demanding totalitarian powers and command. There is a symbolic significance that, not too many years after taking a deliberately statist course with respect to money and banking, the United States, on its dollar bills, featured a new symbol and the Latin words proclaiming the new order of the ages. That order is statist tyranny.

Legal tender laws thus cannot be viewed in isolation. Churchmen show no interest in them, although they are a clear manifestation of humanism in economics. On the other hand, economists see legal tender laws in isolation from theology, although they are a clear expression of the new established religion, humanism. Both are manifesting tunnel vision and are failing to recognize the roots of the problem.

Noah Webster saw the issue; it is a moral and theological issue. Webster saw, and again and again called, legal tender laws "the devil." He saw what these laws represented, "a deliberate act of villainy," a contempt for God's justice, the legislation of theft into law, and the deliberate conversion of the state into an instrument for theft and evil. He was right.

AMATEUR CHRISTIANITY

I was once going by a tennis court I passed from time to time, and I overheard an argument. One young man was objecting to a too faithful following of the rules, which meant that he had lost a game. "Look," he protested, "we don't have to be that particular! We're not pros!" On another occasion as I walked by, one young man made an especially bad play, and his friends on the sidelines teased him. He called back, "I'm just protecting my amateur status!"

I thought of these incidents today when I received a long letter from someone who is not on our mailing list. A friend had given him one or two Chalcedon Reports to read, hoping to interest him. He was writing to me to tell me why he could not be interested. We were not "relevant." What did he mean by relevant? We were asking too much of people. He said he had seen one of my books previously, so he know whereof he spoke. You must talk, he advised, to people on their level and not expect too much of them. He was as good a Christian as any, better, to judge by his bragging, and he knew that maybe in heaven everybody would be totally faithful, but, in this life, getting them saved, and getting a trifle more out of them, was enough. Relevant Christian work has to begin where people are and move them an inch or two ahead. After all, he said, progress in history is by inches.

This man was trying to protect his amateur status as a Christian! He was saying, in effect, don't expect too much out of me, or anyone else. We can't be proficient, professional, full-time Christians, only amateur part-time "Christians," (if such is possible).

The trouble with that argument is that God does not "buy" it. From beginning to end, the Bible makes clear that the Lord requires a total obedience, and that, having given us His covenant grace and law, and climaxed it with the gift of the Spirit, He expects great things from us. The Lord does not call amateur Christians, only full-time professional ones. Nothing is more ridiculous than the idea of many that "full-time Christian service" means the mission field, a pastorate, or some like calling. We are all, whatever we are or wherever we are, called to a full-time Christian life and service.

Trying to protect our amateur status as Christians is like trying to protect our reprobation.

All the same, many churchmen have tried to make "amateur Christianity" into a standard. One leader of a generation ago, and the founder of a seminary, wrote: "To impose a need to surrender the life to God as an added condition of salvation is most unreasonable." Another man has gone even further, stating that, once you say "Yes" to Jesus, He is bound eternally by a contract to save you: you can "commit every sin in the Bible, plus all the others, but there is just NO WAY you can go to Hell!" (See A. ten Pas: *The Lordship of Christ*, pp. 13, 19f, for a critique of these and many more like statements. Ross House Books, P.O. Box 67, Vallecito, California 95251.)

Man is created in the image of God, in knowledge, righteousness, holiness, and with dominion (Gen. 1:26; Col. 3:10; Eph. 4:24). Our standard of relevancy cannot be man as he makes himself, but man as God made him. Man is "fearfully and wonderfully made" (Ps. 139:14). He was created to be God's Dominion Man over all the world, and to rule it according to God's law. To diminish man's responsibility and calling, to reduce God's law to a few vague moral precepts, and to set a minimum standard of faithfulness is evil. We cannot minimize God's law and calling. The one thing we cannot be as Christians is amateurs: it is a total calling.

However, nothing more clearly marks the modern church than a reduction of faith from God's supernatural act in us to our easy believism and casual disobedience. Early in the last century, one famous man, on his death-bed, remarked easily, when asked to repent for his many sins, "God will forgive me: That's His business."

Protestants, quick to criticize the sorry medieval doctrine of indulgences, have fashioned their own doctrine of indulgences: Accept Christ, and then you are safe; if you sin, He'll have to forgive you. Easy believism offers great benefits if you buy the policy, but it delivers nothing but reprobation.

Amateur Christianity is not Christianity but a modern version of Phariseeism. Paul well describes it as "Having a form of godliness, but denying the power thereof: from such turn away" (II Tim. 3:5). The road to Hell is lined with amateur Christians.

Pick up your Bible, and take a good, studied look at the road signs!

CHALCEDON REPORT NO. 194
October, 1981
OUTLAW SOCIAL GOALS

One of the most important aspects of the modern age has been the triumph of what Dostoyevsky called underground man. Underground man is not necessarily a lower or middle class man: he can be very wealthy, or a member of the nobility and even royalty. What all such people have in common is their hostility to and resentment of the established social order. It is the passion of their life to see the faults and evils of that order, and to feel a great sympathy for all who are condemned by that society. Is the establishment hostile to criminals, homosexuals, abortion, the sexual revolution, or whatever else it may regard as lawless? Then the outlaw favors all those things. If, as with Henry Miller, who disliked homosexuality apparently and apologized for his disinterest, the outlaw is not in sympathy with one of the forbidden groups, he is unhappy about it.

The result of all of this is a powerful social force for a variety of causes, a force based on a common hostility to the existing order, whatever it is. (The Marxist countries have their own hostile, outlaw element.)

A telling example of this was Nancy Cunard, daughter of a titled English family. She loathed life; she was in rebellion all her life against her mother, Lady Cunard. Lady Cunard was a poor mother; she disliked motherhood and called it "a low thing - the lowest." Nancy set out to shame and disgrace her mother. For her mother's cautious adulteries, she substituted flagrant and open ones. She early had a hysterectomy, to give herself more "sexual freedom." Every cause which would be offensive to her mother's social set, Nancy Cunard espoused: she was friendly to the cause of lesbians and homosexuals, anti-Francoism, communism, modern trends in the literary world, and more. She took a Negro lover to hurt her mother even more, and did her best to indict her mother publicly, because her mother was ready to entertain wealthy rajahs, but not lesser men of another color. Nancy Cunard became a patron of the arts, a champion of liberal and radical causes, and also an alcoholic and a mental derelict. (See Ann Chisholm: *Nancy Cunard*,

1979). By her own statement, she was at enmity with life, in fulfillment of Proverbs 8:36, "all they that hate Me love death."

Much of the social impetus and action of the modern age has come out of this same outlaw temper. Persons at war with the establishment feel a kinship to every banned or disapproved cause, and they work for the overthrow of the existing order, even to their own destruction.

Having said this, we need to recognize a much more ugly fact. The social goals of the outlaw have at times overthrown existing customs, laws, and practices, some of which needed overthrowing. Social initiative in the modern age has too often belonged to underground man and his outlaw mentality. It has belonged to him by default, because the Christian Church has either withdrawn from the world into a pietistic retreat into the inner world, or else has, with a guilty conscience and an awareness of its irrelevance, made common cause with the outlaws. In either case, it has been faithless to its Lord and the mandate of Scripture.

God's law-word is a plan of action for the remaking of all things in conformity to God's righteousness or justice. When John tells us that we are given "power to become the sons of God" (John 1:12), we must appreciate what these words meant in his day. In the religious mythology of the Roman Empire, the gods (Jupiter and others) often mated with human beings. The results were godlike men of superhuman powers, and with divine protection. These sons of gods were the earth's greatest heroes, the men of action, power, and dominion. It was the greatest compliment to be paid to any man, to compare him to the sons of gods, or god. Thus, when the centurion at the crucifixion said, literally, "Truly this man was son of god" (Mark 15:39; there is no "the" in the original), he spoke out of the context of the Roman world and life view. Jesus, the miracle-worker, was in his eyes so super-human a man that He had to be in the Roman sense an offspring of some god.

Now, when John, inspired of God, declares that we are given by God's adoption of grace the power to be the sons of God, he meant even more than the Romans imagined by that phrase. We become God's dominion men, the people of power, called to occupy till He come (Luke 19:13). Instead of the ineffectual spirit of negation which marks all outlaw social goals, we have God's law-word as our plan for dominion. The most that Roman demi-gods could be was a conqueror, one to whom a triumphal arch was raised. Paul, however, tells us that in Jesus Christ "we are more than conquerors" (Rom. 8:37); we are more than any Roman emperor could dream of being.

To return again to the outlaws. The 1960s saw the great American manifestation of a war against the establishment. Clearly, there was much that needed changing, but the rebellious youth was less interested in change that in negation and destruction. Their power to challenge and shake the status quo and the establishment was clearly very, very great, but the youth preferred hostility to constructive action, and their impetus was wasted. A goal of negation winds up being no goal at all. Their stands were a mixture of very conservative and very radical causes, not principles. For example, in World War I, constitutionalists rightly protested the use of drafted troops in foreign wars, since the U.S. Constitution allows only three uses for a militia (a drafted military force): 1) to suppress insurrection, 2) repel invasion, and 3) enforce the laws of the Union. The Wilson regime subverted the Constitution. The youth of the 60s had a great opportunity here, but they were not interested in it. At one university after another, I asked the question: Are you against the use of draftees in foreign wars as a constitutional principle? Would you oppose using them in both Vietnam and South Africa? Their lack of principles was quickly apparent.

A second area of failure was a lack of commitment. Milton Viorst, in his thoughtful view (with empathy) of the 60s, sees the end of the movement at Kent State. The issue then became this: were they ready to die for their practices? "On these terms, radicalism turned out to have a less committed following than had once been believed. Few were ready to die, and so the decade reached its end." (Milton Viorst: *Fire in the Streets*, p. 543. New York: Simon and Schuster, 1979).

The disaster of our time is that Christians are about as uncommitted as the youth of the 60s. There are signs of a change. Men like Pastor Levi Whisner in Ohio, Dr. Lester Roloff in Texas, and Pastor E. Sileven in Nebraska have been ready to go to jail for their faith. (As I wrote this, Pastor Sileven was expecting arrest for re-opening the Christian School in the Louisville church; instead, the church has been padlocked). A growing resistance indicates that God is raising up Dominion Men who will not surrender Christ's domain to the enemy, and who are extending the frontiers of His Kingdom. The outlaw social goals are failures. Where the Lord's people move out in His Name and power, the gates of hell cannot prevail (or, hold out) against them.

CHALCEDON REPORT NO. 195
November, 1981
HUMANISM AND CHANGE

In the modern age, humanism has been the major driving force in social change. With a missionary fervor rivalling Christianity and Islam, humanism has captured men and institutions all over the world, and much in our world today is a product of humanism.

In a study of *The Renaissance in Perspective*, Philip Lee Ralph (St. Martin's Press, 1973), commented on the humanists' hope: "Together with other thinkers of the age, Erasmus, More, and Machiavelli shared a conviction that, without any change in human nature or any drastic altering of institutions, the political order could be made to serve desirable human ends." Ralph rightly calls attention to Machiavelli's "most remarkable quality," his belief that "splendid opportunities lie at hand, waiting to be seized upon" (p. 75f.).

Ralph is right, of course. The basic Christian premise is that man has a critical fault which is ineradicable by man, original sin. Only God's regenerating grace can change man and thereby alter the human prospect. The impediment of man's sin colors his life and institutions, so that death and corruption haunts all man's efforts outside of the triune God.

As a humanist, Machiavelli held high hopes for man. He rejected any form or return to the medieval theocratic ideal, or to any other theocratic goal. His perspective was humanistic and pragmatic. Like Stalin much later, he believed that a man cannot make an omelette without breaking and scrambling the eggs. As man was "freed" from the Christian world-view, his pragmatism would have a clearer humanistic goal. Thus, Machiavelli was ready to allow to rulers a broad spectrum of moral freedom and power. As Ralph stated it, "Machiavelli exalted power - even naked brutal power, uninhibited by religious dictates or moral scruples - because this was the only reality that seemed to him effective" (p. 63). Machiavelli had high hopes for man by means of the humanistic state.

Erasmus was the same. In February, 1517, he wrote a letter to a friend, expressing his belief in "the approach of a golden age: so clearly do we see the minds of princes, as if changed by inspiration, devoting all their energies to the pursuit of peace" (p. 74). Man was coming into his own; the state was emerging from the custodial eyes of the church, and man would soon be free: this was the humanist hope.

It is no less so today. Human solutions are sought to all human problems. Man's freedom is sought without God, and changes in man and the world are sought without reference to God. Where humanism recognizes faults in man, these are environmentally explained - in terms of society, religion, the family, and so on. Man has been victimized, and he must be freed.

As a result, the humanist reacts intensely to any Christian concern for political order. Since the Spring of 1980, and the participation of evangelicals in politics, much has been written against this ostensible threat of fascism, censorship, tyranny, and so on. Every name anathema to the humanist is hurled against these men, against all reason. Thus although the Rev. Jerry Falwell is well-known for his eschatalogically governed pro-Jewish outlook, and friendship with M. Begin, he is irrationally called an anti-Semite! In other words, if you are against the humanists, you must conform to their stereotype.

At least in Humanist Manifestos I and II, the humanists stated certain religious presuppositions which should have made them aware that the differences are religious, and that strong faith exists on both sides. *First*, humanism rejects the idea that man needs regenerating by God; any changes necessary to man can be made by man. Humanistic and Christian views each necessitate radically different concepts of education. Both have fought for control of the state schools; both need to drop their efforts to force their educational faith on others and create independent schools to propagate their position. Until then, they are advocating coercion and imperialism.

Second, the humanist believes in a self-generated universe whereas the Christian believes in its creation by God. Each position has far-reaching implications for life, ethics, and the sciences. Each rests on a faith assumption rather than verification.

Third, the humanist denies God's government and predestination in favor of man's controls, planning, and predestination. For anarchism, this means man is in total control; for other humanists, it is the state. The rise of humanism has made the state the agency and ultimate power, replacing God.

Fourth, man, not God is seen by humanism as the source of law. This means that law is the expression of man's will or mind, either of individual man, or statist man (the democratic consensus concept). It follows that ethics or morality is also man-made, and we are told that man should have the moral freedom to do as he pleases, provided that he does not injure others. This seems to be a simple and fool-proof doctrine, but it poses serious problems. Incest with minors is now defended by some in terms of this doctrine, (although such a practice is not a general tenet of humanism). What constitutes injury? What constitutes coercion? Is injury to others merely physical? Anti-Semitism may be purely verbal, but is can do injury to a person, can it not? Them why is this not true of anti-Christianity? Or, of anti-humanism, for that matter? The law codes and moral codes of humanism prove to be rubber yardsticks which can cover anything, and also justify anything.

Fifth, humanism does more than reject God. It affirms that man's hope must be in man, that "In man we trust;" it is an ethical faith and process that sees progress only in terms of a confidence in man and in man's reason, agencies, and activities.

The sad fact is that humanism is very much a part of the church scene, not only amongst modernists but evangelicals as well. The application of the Bible is limited to the church and to "private" life by all too many, and most spheres of life are viewed humanistically. It did, after all, take the gross and abysmal failure of the state schools to wake up Christians to their educational mandate. Only now is the corruption of modern humanistic politics compelling Christians to look to God's law and mandate. The churches are weak because they are only occasionally Christian.

C.R. Morey, in *Christian Art* (1935) said, of contemporary architecture,

"The academic styles that have succeeded each other since the seventeenth century, as a consequence of this curious divorce of beauty from truth, can hardly be classified as Christian art, since they recognize no inspiration higher than the human mind" (p. 67). Exactly. Today, "Christian" action simply lines up with a humanistic alternative, not in terms of Scripture. Dominion man must apply God's dominion word to the problems of this world.

THE PRINCIPLE OF CHANGE

Change is a necessity in a fallen, sinful world, but the principle behind change determines the value of change. Is it the sovereignty of man, or is it the sovereignty of God?

The U.S. Constitution deliberately omits all reference to sovereignty, because the framers regarded it as a theological, not a political, attribute. Having just waged war against one sovereign power, they were not about to create another.

Very early, however, the concept of sovereignty was reintroduced, and, significantly, with respect to money and banking. The constitutional limitation of money to gold and/or silver barred the Federal Government, and all branches of the United States, from claiming any sovereign power to create arbitrary monetary values. However, in the U.S. Bank controversy under Washington, Hamilton argued that "every power vested in a Government is in its nature *sovereign*, and includes by *force* of the *term*, a right to employ all the *means* requisite, and fairly *applicable* to the attainment of the *ends* of such power; and which are not precluded by restrictions and exceptions specified in the constitution; or not immoral, or not contrary to the essential ends of political society." These last three restraining clauses proved to be meaningless: where sovereignty exists, there can be no restraint upon it. A sovereign is a lord: he restrains and is not restrained.

This doctrine of sovereignty was made law by Chief Justice John Marshall in *McCulloch v. Maryland*; the United States and its member states were all held to be sovereign. In the years that followed from the early 1800s to 1935, the concept of sovereignty was amplified, and legal tender established, so that the Constitution became a pretext and a facade. In court decisions, the governing principle became and is the doctrine of statist sovereignty. The Constitution was dead, and no one knew it, since sovereignty operated behind the facade of constitutionalism. (Henry Mark Holzer, in *Government's Money Monopoly*, 1981; Books in Focus, 160 E. 38th St., New York, N.Y. 10016; $19.95; as a lawyer, very ably traces the development of this monetary sovereignty through various court decisions.)

The implications of this are far-reaching. A humanistic doctrine of sovereignty is now the governing principle. No law nor any moral restraint can bind a sovereign power: it defines all things. Hence, only to the unchanging God, who alone is truly sovereign, can we ascribe such power. In the hands of any other agency, it is the principle of tyranny.

Not surprisingly, in *Times*, October 5, 1981, "All That Talk About Gold," the objection to gold is that it imposes, according to Ernst Schneider of Switzerland, a "discipline" the world does not want. According to Charles Schultze, Carter's chief economic adviser, gold operates in a "fixed mechanical way" rather than by "trusting human beings." Exactly. Humanism wants no external order to discipline in any sphere. It is making a new Tower of Babel of the whole world; confusion and destruction are ahead of us. We must, in every sphere of life, political, economic, educational, ecclesiastical, and all things else, acknowledge always and only the sovereignty of the triune God.

CHALCEDON REPORT NO. 196
December, 1981
DETENTE

One of the central aspects of the modern age is the politics of detente. Detente represents a development with deep roots in modern philosophy and a close relationship to the popular culture of our time. In the 1960's, one expression of this faith was summarized in the maxim, "Better Red than dead."

It is important for us to recognize that this is a very logical, not an illogical, faith. It is grounded, not in cowardice, treason, or an evil design, but a humanistic religious presupposition. One of our key problems today is our unwillingness to face up to the basic premises of our position, and the positions held by others.

A humanistic faith sees the world as having evolved out of nothing, a product of chance development, and as having only those values imputed to it by man. There is no inherent or created value in life and the universe. Man creates values and imputes them at will to whatever he chooses. Man can thus give central value to progress and technology in one era and despise it in another, favoring instead of progress and technology zero economic growth and the environment. The closest the humanist comes to an unchanging value is himself, and even here we have seen humanistic social orders sacrifice present man to future and ideal man.

In brief, humanism has no fixed and unchanging principles. It has no Jesus Christ, nor a Ten Commandments. Its standards are situation ethics; they are variable in terms of circumstances and human needs. Law too becomes variable: it is a product of man's experience and is thus a changing product of change. Over ten years ago, a frustrated lawyer remarked to me: The law books only tell me what the law was yesterday; the judge decides what it is today.

When we turn to Biblical faith, we are in a very different world. We are here in the world of God's fiats and His unchanging word. Biblical faith requires confrontation. In a meaningless world, nothing is worth dying for, and detente makes very obvious sense. If there is no God to declare that things are clearly good or evil, and that blessings and curses, heaven and hell, follow our moral decisions, then nothing is really worth living for or dying for.

In a meaningless world where nothing is worth living or dying for, men will be ready to do anything if the price is right. The presupposition then is this: the other side believes as little as we do in an absolute meaning, and thus they too will believe in compromise as a way of life. Both sides then enter into detente, each seeking to gain the utmost advantage from the situation. Both operate in terms of advantage, not principle. Without principles, detente is inevitable and necessary. It is a religious requirement of humanism. Wars do result, not because of principled opposition, but because of lost or imperiled advantages.

Biblical faith, on the other hand, requires confrontation. This confrontation can take two forms. The first, basic, and necessary one is evangelism, with conversion as the goal. To men without hope, it offers hope. Its power is the obvious witness to a life with meaning, or freedom, to a world of order under the triune God. This witness is both a personal missionary endeavor and a political witness as well. The dream of America once dominated the world and is still not entirely lost, despite our humanistic politics. The American Christian missionary presence is still a potent world force for Christ and His Kingdom. The evangelical impact on American politics in 1980 and 1981 stirs up daily wrath in the press and from politicians, because it re-introduces into politics a dimension which politicians largely have sought to avoid, moral confrontation. The hatred for all such evangelical groups is not because of their real or fancied blunders but because they have re-introduced biblical morality into politics. Since 1960, politicians have congratulated themselves on eliminating the moral dimension. John F. Kennedy saw future problems as simply technical ones. Richard M. Nixon, with his China policy, made central to American foreign policy the ancient and evil balance of power politics of Europe. The Monroe Doctrine, and, even more, the important but now forgotten Polk Doctrine, were aimed against the introduction of power politics into the Americas. All this was now forgotten. The United States abandoned moral considerations from politics. The age of detente had supposedly begun.

At the same time, however, Christian reconstructionism was infiltrating one area after another. The Biblical mandate for every area of life and thought has been increasingly apparent to people, not only in the church, but in politics, education, the sciences, and more.

As we have noted, the first and primary mandate of Biblical faith is evangelism, with conversion as the goal. The second requirement is battle against evil. Battle takes various forms. A significant aspect of this battle on the current scene is in the church and state conflict, especially with respect to the resistance of Christian Schools. The growing anger of the humanists against Christians has as its basis their inability to understand why these people will not compromise. For the humanists, the course of reason requires compromise. In a meaningless world, reason has no grounds for intransigence. How can there be irreconcilable differences in Darwin's universe?

True, there are humanists, usually conservatives, who take a hard line on things, but they do so on borrowed premises. There is no valid ground for a principled and unwavering stand on non-biblical grounds; only traditionalism and nostalgia inform such behavior.

Ironically, this century of relativism and compromise is the bloodiest century in all of history. Humanism in essence has one "virtue," compromise, a coming together to bury ostensibly superficial differences. It also has one "sin," coercion, but it does love to sin! The spirit of compromise and detente is the desire to gain an advantage over the other party; it denies absolutes. Self-interest governs the coming together, and when the self-interest is violated or outraged beyond a point, self-interest demands coercion. The politics of compromise becomes the politics of coercion, because if nothing is worth living or dying for, then submission is the "reasonable" course for the opposition. The century of relativism and compromise has become the century of coercion.

The implications for law are great. If law ceases to be the instrument of principled morality, of good against evil, it becomes an instrument then of power, and the end it serves is power. Accordingly, law is less and less today a protection of our persons and freedom from evil, and more and more an instrument of statist power. The modern state abandoned God's covenant law to establish itself on the myth of the social contract, a detente between men to create a state ostensibly, but more a detente between men and the state. In that detente, man has been the loser. Only the return of Christian covenant man to the political scene will make the state the loser. Christ calls us to be dominion men.

CHALCEDON REPORT NO. 198
February, 1982
INFLATION

A news item recently called attention to the fact that Israel in 1981 had an inflation rate of 101.5%, down 30% from 1980, but not down to the 98% the state had sought to attain. Very obviously, the worst enemy Israel faces is its own inflation, not external enemies. In any country, inflation destroys values and penalizes the thrifty, hard-working and solvent in favor of debtors. Moreover, wages never keep pace with inflation (How many, I wonder, in Israel received a pay increase of 101.5% in 1981? The difference between the increase in income and inflation spells disaster everywhere.)

However, there is an even more serious aspect. inflation means that no true standard exists, every day the monetary "standard" is variable. But this points to a lack of standards in the people themselves. Instead of holding to a faith and moral law which is unchanging, a changing and unstable yardstick exists.

In the past two decades, we have seen changes in the prevailing judgment concerning abortion, homosexuality, and much, much more. These changes rest in the same perspective which produces inflation: the validity of all standards external to the will of man is denied. Man as his own god determines whatever he deems is good or evil.

Inflation does not stop because men deplore it, no more than crime ends because people are weary of its threat. A change in monetary policy is necessary, and the change in policy presupposes a change in perspective. In the early years after World War II, Richard Weaver wrote a book with a telling title: *Ideas Have Consequences* Even more, we can say that a man's faith has consequences.

That humanism should lead us to the present crisis should not surprise us; humanists are true to their faith. The sad fact is that, with evangelicals so numerous in the United States, their fruits are so few. Our Lord says, "By their fruits ye shall know them." (Matt. 7:20). If our faith is inflated with pious fluff, empty professions, and an unwillingness to obey the Lord, the churches will be as solvent as Israel, the U.S.S.R., the United States, Britain, and all other inflation-sick nations.

Is the Church its own worst enemy?

CHALCEDON REPORT NO. 199
March, 1982
EXECUTIVE PRIVILEGE, or THE RIGHT TO STEAL

One of the acts of the Puritan Commonwealth in England was to try and to behead King Charles I. For this act, many historians to this day seem to bear a grudge against Cromwell and the Puritans. With the Restoration in 1660, and the reign of Charles II, the men associated with Charles I's trial were themselves tried and executed. The presiding judge at this trial was Sir Orlando Bridgeman, who, in his charge to the jury, declared that kings were subject to none but God, and could do no wrong; even of they could do wrong, they were beyond punishment. This "legal" position made a guilty verdict inescapable. The Church of England added to its liturgy a service for that noble "martyr" of the faith, Charles I, a liturgy used for generations.

The fact is that, apart from being a stupid and very unconstitutional monarch, King Charles I was also a thief. At one point, Charles marched off with 130,000 English pounds of other people's money, expropriated from London's goldsmiths, who stored their deposits in the Tower of London. It was a theft that failed, like everything Charles did, but at least he tried! Somehow, historians often gloss over this aspect of Charles' reign. This is not unusual. When Otto J. Scott, in *James I*, noted in passing that monarch's homosexuality, one historical journal disapproved and spoke of that vice as a royal privilege!

Such thinking is all too prevalent. In the 1960s, a prominent pastor, deeply involved in sin, was confronted with the facts thereof by a church officer. The pastor defended himself, by holding that, as "the Lord's anointed", he was above criticism. More than a few people agreed; all that man's numerous congregation did. And everywhere people will say that we are only to pray for, never to criticize, those in authority over us. Somehow, the prophets of Scripture missed that doctrine when they listened to God!

We have a modern name for King Charles' "right to steal." It is called executive privilege. It means that we can supposedly be legally robbed of money, information, and self-government in the name of executive privilege. Make no mistake about it: theft can be of more than money. The courts have in fact held that certain types of exclusive and "inside" information about a company and its stocks can constitute a form of theft and a means of gaining an unfair advantage in the market. In the Old West, people paid a price for dishonest means of knowing what another man's poker hand was, such as by means of marked cards. Federal regulations which legislate and limit our freedom outside the elective and representative process are certainly forms of theft. Then too inflation is a form of theft, a means of counterfeiting available only to civil government.

Charles I thus should be the patron saint of the modern state, but, of course, he was an amateur, and he paid the price for his bungling. But the modern state too will pay the price; God's day of reckoning awaits all sinners. The "right to steal" becomes the right to perish.

CHALCEDON REPORT NO. 200
April, 1982
TIPPING

Tipping is a form of rewarding service. If a waiter serves us well, we give him a generous tip; if his service is indifferent or poor, we either do not tip him, or we give him a very trifling tip. A tip is from a superior to an inferior. It is normally to someone who is poorly paid and must depend on tips to make a reasonable salary.

Most tipping is perfunctory; we do it because it is expected of us, not because we are strongly motivated to do so. It is a social form we abide by, whether we like it or not.

Most giving to God is simply a form of tipping, a perfunctory act we feel obligated to perform. We are more often motivated by what others expect of us than what God requires. Too few tithe to God. A tithe is a tax paid to the sovereign God: it is His due. We cannot give a gift to God unless it is above and over the tithe, because anything other than that is simply a debt and an obligation.

If we try to tip God, we incur His wrath and judgment because we treat Him then as in underling, not as the Sovereign. We are then thieves, trying to rob God of His due tax, and Malachi 3:8-12 makes clear the kind of judgment God brings upon all such thieves. Men know that the state takes very seriously any tax evasion; can they imagine that God is any the less angry when men evade His due tax?

Our giving puts a price on God's government. We say in effect, when we refuse God His tax, that the government is much better left on our shoulders. We say that we can put the money to better use than God can, and that our rule is the primary and essential one. We make clear, by our refusal to tithe, that we are humanists.

We also deny God's power and word. We say in effect that the promises of blessings and curses pronounced in Malachi 3:8-12 and Deuteronomy 28 are not to be taken seriously, and that God's word is not as important in our lives as our own word and will. We doubt God's statement too that our disobedience can carry us to a point where He will not hear us (I Samuel 8:18).

How we give makes clear who is the Lord in our lives, the triune God, or ourselves. It manifests whether we are idolaters or believers.

CHALCEDON REPORT NO. 201
May, 1982
WHY WE AID RUSSIA

The major recipient of U.S. foreign aid, credit, loans, and technology in the 20th century has been the Soviet Union. It is very likely the most massive assistance ever rendered by one state to another in all of history. The nearest rival to this condition of aid is possibly Turkey, which for a few centuries has been propped up and maintained by world powers, because none will trust the Dardanelles to any but a totally unprincipled state, one without any loyalties except to itself. Without U.S. aid, the U.S.S.R. could neither feed itself nor maintain any technology. Dr. Antony C. Sutton, while at the Hoover Institution, documented the technological factor in the three volumes of *Western Technology and Soviet Economic Development.*

The Soviet Empire, the United States, and the European states have at times had their differences, and they will have more. On the whole, however, they have been working allies, and with good reason. All have a common goal, the control of man by means of humanistic statism. All are agreed, in varying degrees of openness, in their contempt for God and His law.

Their essential differences are not with respect to principles, but methodology. The U.S.S.R. seeks the total control of man directly and openly, using terror readily, from its earliest years, to compel conformity. The U.S., the U.K., Sweden, and the other Western powers use education, humanistic education, as the primary means to a goal shared with the U.S.S.R. Of course, if Christians, as in the U.S., seek to establish Christian Schools uncontrolled by humanistic statism, the iron fist of statism moves against them. Pastors like Levi Whisner, Lester Roloff, and Everett Siliven have gone to jail because of this.

All these states, Western, East European, African, and Asiatic, have a common enemy, God and His rule of the people. Modern statism is a war against the God of Scripture, and against man, Christian man. In the 20th century, the various powers have at times had their differences, and even gone to war against one another, but they have in the main been allies against God and man. Through taxation, legislation, and controls, the modern state wages unceasing war against its own people. It regards its citizenry as the major enemy to the state apparatus. In the United States, we see presidents keeping their word to the U.S.S.R. (in detente, etc.), but not to the American people. Promises are made to gain votes, only to be broken with impunity upon election.

Psalm 2 is right: the nations take counsel or conspire together against the LORD, and against His Anointed, saying, Let us break their bands or laws asunder, and cast away their cords or restraints from us. Still, as of old, "He that sitteth in the heavens shall laugh: the LORD shall have them in derision." Either the nations will serve the LORD, or they shall be broken with a rod of iron. Unless we now stand with the LORD, we too shall be broken. God allows no neutrality.

DO WE NEED A LICENSE TO DIE?

It is not as easy to die these days as it once was. I can remember when dying-time meant that family and friends stopped by to say their farewells. On the day of the funeral, friends came from miles around, and everybody brought food for a big pot-luck banquet. Enough was left over to keep the family from having to cook for days after. It was a big reunion. At the cemetery some folks would show me their own grave-sites and headstones, with everything chiselled in except their death-date. Dying was easy then.

What happens now? Well, all kinds of certificates have to be filed, and they cost money. State and federal taxes on the house, farm, or business, can tie up a family for almost a year, and they also very often wipe them out financially. It's getting so bad that almost nobody can afford to die these days.

But this is not all. One law, which is catching on in state after state, requires that an autopsy be performed on the deceased if he or she had not been to a doctor within three weeks prior to death. Think of the implications of that. If you and I or anyone else is old and ailing, we must see a doctor, every month approximately, whether it does any good or not, or else an autopsy must be performed.

This means a tidy and steady income for the doctor, or else an income for the coroner. Much of this is taken care of by Medicare, but, or course, our tax money pays for that.

Now we have all heard of ghoulish people who try to cash in on death. They come around, on reading a death notice, and claim that the deceased ordered something and then try to collect on it. Fortunately, there are not too many such people.

However, what can we say about our ghoulish federal and state governments which make death a time to gouge and rob widows and orphans? This subject is not a pleasant one, but I submit that any civil government that deliberately plans to make money out of death and the griefs of people has sunk as low as anyone can.

The Bible tells us over and over again that God regards the treatment of widows and orphans as a key test to the character of a people and a nation. God promised judgment on those who exploit widows and orphans.

In other words, God sees it as thoroughly rotten and contemptible for a nation to use the time of bereavement and grief to rob and impoverish a people. We have, however, made this policy into law. One estate planner says that about 75% of all families are economically wiped out by the death of a husband or wife.

People sometimes talk about the high price of funerals, but such costs are a trifle compared to the toll exacted by the federal and by many state governments.

It is time we told the ghouls in Washington that we have had enough of this. The taxation of death is the ultimate insult a civil government can impose upon a people. It is a degrading and an evil tax. The rich can utilize some provisions of the law to protect themselves to a degree, but most of us are the victims of the Washington ghouls.

CHALCEDON REPORT NO. 203
July, 1982
POWER OVER THE PEOPLE

In a recent (May, 1982) trial of a church (in Texas), a four-page complaint was filed against the church by the Dept. of Human Resources (or welfare dept.). One of the charges or complaints was with respect to a goldfish bowl in the nursery:

"If there are animals on the premises the facility shall have a licensed veterinarian evaluate animals annually to determine which ones need to be examined and vaccinated. Examinations, vaccinations, and treatment shall be given as the veterinarian recommends.

"Non-Compliance: It was observed that the veterinarian's statement for the fish was not on file."

Another item: a retired army colonel, a good friend of Chalcedon, reported on a problem faced by one of his sons. A young photographer, he is currently working supermarket and shopping center parking lots. He photographs children mounted on his pony. He was arrested for operating without a license. Since he covers 82 different city jurisdictions in a metropolitan area, 82 licenses would put him out of business. All that a license does is to provide each city with revenue. When arrested, he was called "worse than a criminal" by the judge, fined $350, given a suspended sentence of one year, and told that he would get a year in jail if picked up again. (Many rapists are less severely treated.) The state is more a threat to this young photographer than it is to most criminals.

The modern state is failing to provide justice. Its main goal is increasing *power over the people*. The cry of our statists is "power to the people," but their goal is the tyranny of power over the people.

Rome fell, not because of the barbarians, but because of its own evils. The tens of thousands of barbarians could not have defeated the millions of Romans, if the Romans had defended Rome. After generations of tyranny and oppressive taxation, the people of Rome no longer felt Rome was worth fighting for, and they simply refused to defend it.

As the power of the modern state increases all over the world, we are approaching a similar disillusionment. The patriots of Rome loved Rome for its past glories, not for its then current tyrannies. Similarly, the patriots of various modern states are often patriots because they value their past, their heritage and traditions. As the modern state lays waste that inherited capital, it invites on itself the whirlwind of judgment.

FREEDOM OR SLAVERY?

One of the interesting facts about the United States is the amount of land owned by the Federal Government. In Alaska, 90% of the state is federally owned; in Nevada, it is 87%, Utah, 65%; Idaho, 64%; Oregon, 52%; Arizona, 45%; California, 44%, and so on down the line. Supposedly, these lands are kept in trust for the people, but in reality private conservation groups and corporations have done and can do a better job of it.

But this is not all. We need to ask the question, how much of us do the Federal, state, and local agencies of civil government own? About five to ten years ago, we were told that between 40% to 45% of our income went for direct of hidden taxes; some now place that estimate at 50% to 60%. Whichever figure is right, it constitutes a very big share of our income.

Slavery is defined as a property right in the labor of other men. If you own a slave, it means that he must work for you. Very obviously, through taxation, civil government now owns about half of us, and this means that we are half slaves, whatever else we may call ourselves.

When the federal government, more than a century ago, abolished slavery, it abolished only the private ownership of slaves, not public ownership. If fact, all over the world, slavery is more common than ever before. In the communist bloc, all the people are slaves of the state. In the democracies, we are half slaves and half free.

What we need is an emancipation proclamation from slavery to the modern state. You can be sure that neither Washington, D.C., nor the state house will issue any such charter of freedom on its own. Only if we, the people, compel them to do so will the various branches of civil government disgorge their powers over us.

We may think we belong to ourselves, our family, our church, or our community, but, with every pay-check, we are reminded that we belong to Washington, D.C., and, before we see our pay-check, Big Brother has put the bite on us.

The plain fact is that the modern state owns too much of us. Instead of being our servant, it has become our master, and we have steadily been stripped of our assets and our freedom. Very definitely, it is time for a change.

To gain that change, we must be changed. As Paul says, "where the Spirit of the Lord is, there is liberty" (II Cor. 3:17).

CHALCEDON REPORT NO. 204
August, 1982
ARE WE USING LANGUAGE TO CONFUSE OURSELVES?

Too often in our time, the terms we use to organize our thinking are created by statist agencies and serve to mislead us. One such set of terms, created by the Internal Revenue Service, is profit versus non-profit. Profit-making activities are taxed; non-profit enterprises and agencies are not. People have come to classify activities in terms of these two terms, as though they described reality instead of a statist taxing category. Would it not be much more realistic to classify things without reference to I.R.S.? If the I.R.S. were to disappear in the next decade, how useful would these terms be? After all, they have reference only to tax status.

I submit that the terms productive versus non-productive are much more useful. Churches, schools, and libraries are "non-profit", but they are at the same time among the most productive agencies civilization has ever known. To eliminate them would be to eliminate civilization. Civil government is emphatically non-profit; often it is not productive of too much good, but, when kept within its limits, can be productive of social order. The family is a non-profit community, but it is a most emphatically productive agency, and its decay is the decay of society and civilization.

Because we have emphasized the profit versus non-profit perspective, we have tended to falsify our view of life. In every area, intellectual, industrial, and personal, we have down-graded the productive man in favor of the profiting man. Production has thus been displaced by administration, i.e., the visible symbols of profitable power in church, university, state, and business, have gained ascendancy over the productive mind and hand.

Religiously speaking, this means that form has become more important than substance, and pragmatism has replaced theology. When we look at the world through categories governed by the I.R.S., we have beggared ourselves intellectually, and we have allowed the tax-man rather than the Lord God to frame our thinking.

We need to remind ourselves of St. Paul's words: "Study to shew thyself approved unto God, a workman that needeth not to be ashamed, rightly dividing the word of truth" (II Tim. 2:15).

WHATEVER HAPPENED TO DEATHBED SCENES?

When I began my ministry at the end of the 1930s, the world was a dramatically different one. Aspects of that world survived until the late 1950s, and then disappeared. One common fact of that and earlier eras which has since become a rarity is the deathbed scene, the family coming in to say goodbye or to be blessed, the last words, and then the end.

Philippe Aries in *The Hour of Our Death* (1981), studied the changing attitude towards death from the earliest Christian times to the present day. As faith and culture have changed, so too men's basic attitudes towards death. For example, during the middle ages, the ideal was a death in bed, surrounded by family and friends. As a result, what developed was a kind of ritual of dying, because, from start to finish, it was known to be a religious act and a stage in the development of life and faith. In the later medieval era, people came to desire a sudden death; there was less faith, and also a lessened sense of community with the world of the living on earth and those in the world to come. Instead of a rite of passage, there was a desire for an unexpected and sudden passage.

After 1500, the deathbed scene, with ups and downs of popularity, was again an important fact, a kind of liturgical act. (In fact, in Catholic circles, extreme unction made it so. In Protestant circles, the pastor was a necessary part of the deathbed scene. Over forty years ago, an elderly Scot recited to me some verses he had been taught as a child, to recite on his deathbed.)

The Romantic Movement was greatly attracted to the liturgy of the deathbed because of its potential emotional content, and, in non-Christian circles, the deathbed now gained a new and romantic content. It became the occasion for the manifestation of greatness, a new-found purity, and a cleansing of the pollutions of life. The high (or low) point of this tendency came somewhat later, in Charles Dickens' famous deathbed scene of little Nell. Readers on both sides of the Atlantic shed an abundance of tears over it.

Within the circle of Protestant orthodoxy, the approach of faith to life and death was very well expressed by John Newton, author of "Amazing Grace", in his great hymn, "Come, my soul, thy suit prepare" (1779). The last verse reads,

> Show me what I have to do, / Ev'ry hour my strength renew; / Let me live a life of faith. / Let me die thy people's death: / Let me die thy people's death.

Children were taught in their earliest years a simple prayer:

> Now I lay me down to sleep. / I pray Thee, Lord, my soul to keep; / And if I die before I wake, / I pray Thee, Lord, my soul to take. Amen.

In more recent years, the last two lines have been changed to read:

> In peace and safety 'till I wake, / And this I ask for Jesus' sake. Amen.

In recent years, what has happened to deathbed scenes? For the most part, they have been drugged out of existence. This has been done, because most people want it so, both the dying and their families. For the smallest complaint or pain, let alone dying, people demand of a doctor, "Can't you give me something for it?" We have a drug culture because we are unwilling to face either life or death. We prefer drink or drugs to reality, because we do not want reality impinging upon our dream world. Man's original sin, his desire to be his own god and his own universe, finds pain and death shattering realities. Hence, all frustration and suffering must be made the targets of legislation and of the therapy of drugs. We have a world-wide drug culture because the Spirit of our age is hostile to God and His real world. Drugs are the stuff of dreams and illusions, and hence their appeal.

I mentioned earlier an old Scot, a quiet and rock-like Calvinist. He died of cancer; he was a year in dying. His children and grand-children urged him to take some medicines (drugs), and to give up his solitary life for a "rest home," or to move in with a widowed daughter. He refused, saying he enjoyed his house and garden, liked his own cooking, and could take care of himself. He took care of his flowers with especial pleasure, talked matter-of-factly about the progress of the cancer. He was a vigorous and hardy man who had never paid too much attention to pain. I visited him very frequently, to read Scripture and to pray. He was active in his garden until the day before his death and made a good witness to his daughter, who was present at the end. He had lived with a clear mind and died with a clear mind. He died with dignity and grace.

Death has no dignity for us now, because life is for us without dignity, and we fail to see life as a grace (I Peter 3:7), and thus cannot end it with grace. We prefer to be drugged, if not by narcotics or liquor, then by entertainment, and unthinking routine, or a life of escapism.

What we have "gained" is one of the horrors of history, the hospital death, with drugs, tubes connected to the failing body, and strangers called nurses, nurse's aids, and orderlies, going and coming all around us. Death is pushed out of sight, and the deathbed has lost its dignity. Drugs have reduced or eliminated pain, but they have also eliminated feeling and consciousness. Because for the modern age, death is a dirty fact, we have sanitized it and made it anonymous. From a time of communion, it has become a time of final loneliness. This should not surprise us. A dying culture, and the world of humanism is dying, cannot give dignity to either life or death.

CHALCEDON REPORT NO. 206
October, 1982
ARE WE ROBBING WIDOWS?

When is your property not your property? The answer to that question is that, any time the federal and state governments choose to claim, tie up, or regulate your property, they feel free to do so.

The Farm Journal (April, 1982, p.10) cited the case of a Missouri farm wife whose husband died. It was harvest-time, but she could not use the farm machinery to proceed with harvesting. For her to have done so was held to be illegal, since they were in her husband's name, and tied up in the estate. With all her grief and the cares of widowhood, there was now added another. She had to hire men and machines for the harvest.

Now I know that lawyers can give me long reasons why this was so, citing laws, cases, and precedents. The fact remains that the whole thing stinks. Our lawmakers seem to feel that widows are chickens to be plucked, not human beings. I wonder haw state and federal legislators can look at the estate, death, and inheritance taxes and regulations they have passed and still look in the mirror without throwing up.

A woman can work alongside her husband to develop a farm or a business. She can be as much a part of it as her husband, and sometimes more so. However, unless they have seen a lawyer or accountant and prepared for death, she is likely to see the tax man rob her of much that she spent years working for. Even seeing a lawyer or accountant is not enough. The laws are changed almost every year, so that a good legal provision of last year may be no safeguard this year.

Isn't anyone ashamed or angry about all this? Are we living in a society where the state and federal governments are so much at was with us that we must retain a lawyer to protect ourselves?

Our Washington politicians scream, every time there is talk of a tax-cut, about the harm it will do to the poor. Has it never occurred to them that maybe taxes are making us all poor? Does it never bother them that they pass laws aimed at robbing widows?

We have several organizations of senior citizens in this country. Why are they not doing more to protect widows and survivors? Death is a sufficiently sad time without being made more so by acts of Congress.

It is high time we told our state and federal representatives to show more consideration for widows and orphans. We have many ugly taxes on the books, but perhaps none of them half so bad as those which tax death. Something is seriously wrong with a society which tolerates such a tax.

Our Lord says, "Woe unto you, scribes and Pharisees, hypocrites! for ye devour widows' houses, and for a pretense make long prayer: therefore ye shall receive the greater damnation" (Matt. 23:14).

CHALCEDON REPORT NO. 207
November, 1982
JUSTICE AND THE LAW

One of the most disastrous facts of the modern age is the separation of justice from the law. Such a separation has existed before in history, usually as a product of moral corruption, sometimes as a result of cynicism. The modern separation is a product of philosophical and religious skepticism.

Perhaps no other man in this century has had an influence on American law equal to that of Oliver Wendell Holmes, Jr. (1841 - 1935). A 1944 biography of Holmes, *Yankee from Olympus*, by Catherine Drinker Bowen in effect placed him among the American gods by its title. Holmes' grandfather, Abiel, was a Calvinist, his father Oliver Wendell Holmes a Unitarian, and the man from America's Olympus saw life simply as "action and passion." Like proper Bostonians, he held that men could make their own rules out of human experience and abide by them. As an associate justice of the U.S. Supreme Court, 1902 - 1932, he held, "I am not here to do justice. I am here to play the game according to the rules."

It was precisely this same separation of justice from the law, and the reduction of law to the will of the state, that created the legal climate which led to German National Socialism and Hitler, as John H. Hallowell demonstrated so ably in *The Decline of Liberalism as an Ideology, with Particular Reference to German Politico-Legal Thought* (1943). More recently the late Princeton philosopher Walter Kaufmann, in Without Guilt and Justice (1973), held that guilt and justice are theological concepts and have reference to accountability to God (and rightly so); hence, a humanistic society should, Kaufmann logically insisted, abandon all concepts of guilt and justice. A more radical legal revolution is impossible to imagine. The fact is, that revolution is now in process. This is the reality of modern statist law in virtually every modern state. It is also the reality (implicit in most cases) of virtually every law school; the exceptions are there, but they are few in numbers.

As a result, justice has been separated from the state. The people, for the most part, are not aware of this philosophical fact of the separation of justice from law and the state. The appeals of politicians for votes still contain vague references to justice, and then stress mainly special interests. The people go to court expecting justice and are bewildered by the results. As a result, a growing cynicism is in evidence. Ominous too is the rise of violence against judges.

The rationale of the state and its reason for being is justice. For the state to forsake justice is to forsake its reason for existing. We have seen, in recent years, the steady decline of all churches which abandon their reason for being. If the church does not proclaim the gospel of salvation and history through Jesus Christ it is like a father who, when his son asks for bread, gives him a stone; or, when the son asks for fish, the father gives him a serpent (Matt. 7:9-10). Those churches which feed men stones and serpents are seeing the departure of their flocks. The bankruptcy of the modern state is similar and perhaps greater.

The modern state replaced the church as man's central institution. Even more, it became a saving institution, offering men the ostensible way to the good life, to brotherhood, peace, and plenty. A religious fervor accrued to patriotism as a result, and flags replaced the cross as the symbol around which men rallied. Man's sense of corporate membership in a mystical body was for many most readily aroused by the sight of the flag than the sight of the cross.

However, as humanism developed its legal rationale, justice had to go. The fundamental premise of humanism is Genesis 3:5, "Ye shall be as God (i.e., every man his own god), knowing (determining or, establishing for yourselves) good and evil." In one country after another, the foundations of the state and of the law were shifted from justice to the will of the state, or the will of the people, or the will of the dictatorship of the proletariat, and so on. The law of the state began to represent less and less justice and more and more a power bloc. The goal of men became the capture of the state machinery to control power in their own behalf, and justice became a facade.

The facade, however, is cracking and crumbling. One result is a growing hostility to politicians, lawyers, and judges. Nothing the state can ever do can educate men out of the expectation of justice from the law, and when men become convinced that there is a radical difference between justice and the state and law, it will be the state and law that will pay the price.

Just as the separation of gold and silver from money is destroying money by inflation, even more so does the separation of justice from the law destroy the state.

In this development, the churches have been asleep to the revolution under way around them. They have failed to see what Kaufmann saw clearly (and Nietzsche, Stirner, and others before him), that, where the God of Scripture is denied, guilt and justice cannot exist. They are theocentric or God-centered facts and are theological through and through. No "return to the Constitution" can restore justice; only a truly Biblical faith can make justice again a reality.

Justice is not a vague idea; it is the righteousness of God expressed in His law-word. If we separate justice from the law of God, we are then left with saying that men as gods issue the articles of justice. The words "justice" and "righteousness" are one and the same; they express the meaning of the Hebrew word "tsdak." If justice and law are not from the God who created all things, they are then from men who claim to be god, because justice and law declare the basic and inescapable accountability. To whom are we accountable, to God, or to man and the state?

The Bible is emphatic that "the judgment is God's (Deut. 1:17), because God is the Creator, the Lawgiver, and the All-Righteous or All-Just-One. There can be no justice apart from Him and His law-word. Justice is inescapably a theological fact.

For Kaufmann, the goal of this legal revolution is "Liberation", a word used by a variety of movements in our time. In virtually every case, it means most of all liberation from God. Kaufmann said, "Liberation is a movement toward a goal: autonomy." The word "autonomy" tells it all: auto, self, and nomos, law; man becomes his own law. Kaufmann held, "Being autonomous and being liberated is the same thing." The classic statement of autonomy and liberation, according to Kaufmann, was Genesis 3:1-5, "The Serpent's Promise." It means that "nobody knows what is good. There is no such knowledge." Therefore humanity should "leave behind guilt and fear" and "be autonomous."

Kaufmann saw the issue clearly. Our problem is that churchmen refuse to do so. They prefer to halt between to opinions. Elijah, faced with a Baal-state like our own, said to the people, "How long halt ye between two opinions? if the LORD be God, follow him: but if Baal, then follow him" (I Kings 18:21).

The sad fact is that of the too many people, who, as they see the law reduced to a game without justice, are ready to express anger, too few are ready to take the logical step and see that without God, there can be no justice. Paul Hoffman's study of a criminal lawyer sums up that lawyer's premise in its title, "*What the Hell is Justice?*" (1974). The man was logical. Without God, there can be neither truth nor justice, not good and evil.

Until men return to the living and triune God, justice will continue to be separated from law and the state, and from everyday life as well.

WHAT IS CIVIL RELIGION?

Among the dishonest charges levelled against Christian orthodoxy is the assertion that it has been and is guilty of "civil religion." Even reputable historians are assuming as fact this very dishonest claim; one such scholar speaks of John Foxe as a leader in the movement in which "the saga of the chosen people of the Old Testament" was identified with "the elect people of England." One evangelical "Amen Charlie" to the liberal establishment has written against the idea of a Christian state and "the notion that God has been at work" through the history of the American people and nation.

The fact is that the New Testament declares the continuity of the chosen people through the Christian community, which can include its churches, states, families, and more. The twelve apostles succeed the twelve patriarchs. The church is the true Israel of God, and believers are the sons of Abraham in Christ. The New Testament identifies the believer and the community of believers with the chosen people of the Old Testament.

This means that "the elect people of England", the United States, Canada, Japan, Chad, and all the world, and their institutions when brought under the dominion of Christ, are to be seen as in continuity with ancient Israel as God's chosen people. To deny this is to deny the Bible.

A civil religion is one in which the state is man's savior. This describes the modern state. A civil religion has no transcendence beyond the state; this is the faith of modernists and political liberals on the whole, and of non-Christian conservatives. In a civil religion, there is no power over the national or world state, and this again describes the faith of those who charge orthodoxy with "civil religion."

To deny the continuity of Christians with the chosen people of the Old Testament is to deny their salvation; it means that they are not the chosen of God in Jesus Christ. It means that we are outside of Christ, David's greater Son, and that we have no part in the election of grace. For a man, a Church, school, family, state, or any other institution to be a part of the chosen people means that it is an instrument whereby God manifests His grace, law, order, and covenant to this world. Election means the sovereignty of grace.

Civil religion means the sovereignty of the state, never the sovereignty of God. It is civil religion which we see all around us in liberal religion and humanistic politics. E. Stanton Evans recently commented, with respect to our liberal churches, that they do not believe in mixing Christianity and politics, so they avoid Christianity altogether. This is civil religion!

CHALCEDON REPORT NO. 208
December, 1982
JUSTICE AND THE STATE

The modern state is profoundly religious; in every continent states pursue their religious goal with dedication and fervor. The problem, however, is that virtually all modern states are, in varying degrees humanistic. Instead of acknowledging that the God of Scripture is above and over them, they see man as ultimate, and the state as the expression of the collective or general will of man. This means that ultimacy is ascribed to the state, which, since Hegel, has been modern man's god walking on earth.

The implications of this shift from Christianity to humanism are far-reaching. Humanistic statism has evangelized the world for its cause, and, in every continent, salvation is earnestly sought on humanist and statist terms.

Salvation and the triumph of the state have, however, become identical, as they were in Rome. God having been denied, there is now no law nor justice that transcends the state. Since there is no God beyond the state, there is no justice beyond the state either. Justice is what the state does. This identification of justice with the state has been basic to Marxist civil governments and to National Socialism. For the Marxists, the dictatorship of the proletariat incarnates the general will of the workers and is infallibly just. For National Socialism, a similar equation prevailed.

If the state is justice, and there is no higher God nor law to give an assessment of the state and its law, then no one can legitimately judge the state. This equation has already been made. In *Institutes of Biblical Law II, Law and Society*, I cited the 1975 statements of the then Senator John V. Tunney. Tunney equated morality with legality. Whatever the state legislates against is immoral, but, if the state legalizes something, it is moral. Asked about theft, he answered, "If you repeal the law it would not be a crime" (p. 372). Tunney's thinking was logical and consistent humanism. He made an equation which is increasingly common everywhere. In Nebraska, Christians in Louisville insisted on keeping open a Christian School closed by the state (and Pastor E. Sileven was jailed); their actions were non-violent. State newspapers condemned the Christian resistance as illegal and immoral. (It was once a truism of Christian thinkers and civil courts that resistance to evil legislation is not illegal.) Two other Christian Schools in Nebraska were also closed. In the second of these cases, all the parents will be tried for contributing to the delinquency of their minor children; if the state wins, the children will be taken from their parents and placed in foster homes. These children are receiving a superior education; the state, however, does not regard quality education as important as state control; this is totalitarianism, state power as the ultimate value.

But this is not all. In various states, pro-life picketers of abortion clinics are being sued for libel or slander. The premise is that abortion is now legal; because it is legal, it is therefore moral, and to declare by picket signs that abortion is murder, and that abortionists are murders, is to defame a moral man engaged in legal activities. Sadly, the first of these cases has been won by the abortionists.

Consider the implications of this fact. If what is legal is moral, and to speak of it as immoral is actionable, then free speech and freedom of religion are finished. Once a law is passed, attacks on it are attacks against law, morality, and justice. The great function (now much neglected) of the church has been, over the centuries, to uncover sin and to indite it. Men like Nathan, Elijah, and other prophets of old confronted kings and all sinners with the accusation, "Thou art the man." The early church fathers like Chrysostom, Ambrose, and others did not spare rulers nor commoners; in the name of God, they set forth the sins of all; they declared the law of God, and they set forth God's Savior, Jesus Christ. What the courts are now saying is that this prophetic task is illegal and immoral.

Because the state now recognizes no higher law, it therefore absolutizes its own will and law. The law-maker and the court (with the bureaucracies) then replace God. Moreover, because the state identifies its will and law with justice, to gain total justice means to gain total power. Marxism and Fascism thus begin with the premise that total power is necessary to attain the good or just society. The democracies are no less dedicated to the same goal, total power, but by means of democratic persuasion. Roland Huntsford, in *The New Totalitarians* (1972), documented the "democratic" road to totalitarianism. Whereas the older totalitarians (Marxist and Fascist) use terror, the new totalitarians use education. By controlling education, the new totalitarians control the minds of children, the future. The goal is to gain a voluntary acquiescence to slavery, which, of course, these men view as salvation, the elite planners in control of the masses.

This makes understandable the savage hostility of the new totalitarians to the Christian School movement. In this growing movement they see the destruction of their control over the future. The Christian School movement is indeed growing rapidly, and its enrollment now in the United States is a major threat to humanistic statism. One has only to be in the courtrooms regularly, as I am, as a witness for the churches, to realize the extent of the hostility. The statists see this as a life and death battle obviously.

The new totalitarians are resentful and hostile to the introduction of any higher law concept. The testimonies of the persecuted Christians is that they must obey God rather than men; they take the stand to cite Scripture as their law and mandate. (One judge, earlier this year, spoke out against this use of Scripture texts; he saw clearly that the witnesses were citing God's word as law against the laws of his state). These Christians have become aware that a state which does not subordinate itself to God and His law will demand that all things be subordinated to the state; the result is tyranny. The true freedom fighters of the twentieth century are the Christian School peoples who are resisting state controls. The future generations will be deeply in their debt.

The sad fact is that most churches are indifferent to this battle. In the days of Athanasius, that saint stood almost alone against the forces of the Roman state and the heresies and cowardice of churchmen. Today, the resistance is far more widespread.

However, the death-like sleep of the churches is appalling, but not surprising. The source of law in any society is the god of that society. If our source of law is the state, then the state is our god. If our source of law is God and His word, then God is our Lord and Sovereign. The modern church is antinomian. Because it sees man and the state as the source of law, it in effect abandons the God of Scripture for the modern Moloch. By viewing the state as the source of law, it surrenders man to statist law. Salvation then becomes either the social gospel of statism, or a rapture out of this world.

Justice, God's justice or righteousness, then ceases to be a concern for the Christian. For the statist, justice is whatever the state does. There is no escape from this impasse other than the Lordship of Christ as Savior, Law-giver, and Ruler. Christ is King, and "of the increase of His government and peace there shall be no end," for the government is upon His shoulders (Isa. 9:6-7).

CHALCEDON REPORT NO. 209
January, 1983
INJUSTICE IN THE NAME OF JUSTICE

The modern age talks much about justice while denying its existence. Walter Kaufmann, in *Without Guilt and Justice* (1973), held that guilt and justice are theological concepts and hence no longer valid; if there be no God, there is neither good nor evil, nor guilt and innocence, and the idea of justice is a myth. Not all humanists are as honest as Kaufmann was, and, as a result, the concept of justice has been retained as a facade for the perspectives of humanism.

The humanistic state, as its own god and law, thus identifies its will with justice. This identification is increasingly ruthless. In Red China, legal restrictions have been placed upon birth. Guandong Province, for example, sets an annual quota for births, and prospective parents must apply for an allotment. When in one area two women urged pregnant women to hide from the family planning workers, they were imprisoned for 15 days; all but 9 of the 325 women with unlicensed pregnancies were given forcible abortions and fitted with IUD's; forcible abortions in this province numbered into the thousands.

In this country some schools supply children with contraceptives (*Review of the News*, November 3, 1982, p. 76). A part-time English professor, Suzanne Clarke of Bristol, Tennessee, has been sued for calling contemporary public education humanistic (*Bristol Herald Courier*, January 24, 1982). Recently, some writers, besides calling Christians neo-fascists, have called for the limitation of civil liberties to Christians. It is obvious, in reading and hearing some of these people, that the only freedom of religion they will allow us is one confined to the area between our two ears.

Anyone who opposes the growing trend to control the churches and to destroy our freedom of religion is likely to be subjected to slander, hate mail, and even worse. The Rev. Jerry Falwell, whose stance is a mild and gracious one, is subjected to about 200 death threats monthly, and his ministry has been the target of vandalism. This should not surprise us. Scripture tells us that the ungodly have always raged and taken counsel together against the Lord, and therefore against His people (Ps. 2).

What is distressing is that so many who call themselves Christians take part in this attack. In the past few weeks, three "Christian" periodicals have attacked and misrepresented a Christian leader of another country, whose main offense is that he is a Christian and not a Marxist. Such periodicals are equally hostile to Pastor Falwell. (Does this mean that I agree with Falwell? For starters, he is premillennial and Arminian, and I am postmillennial and reformed. We are, however, in the same battle and the same army, whose commander is not I but Jesus Christ. I prefer as a general principle to critique ideas, not men. I believe that, if a man spends much of his time shooting at his fellow-soldiers, he is in the wrong army.)

Why do these churchmen do it? The answer takes us back to the question of justice. Justice and righteousness are one and the same word in the Bible. If we are dedicated and true antinomians, there is then for us no law of justice from God. Several articles of late in "Christian" periodicals have attacked the idea of a Christian society and state; the faith is something to be *confined* to a closet, and one person wrote me recently that praying should be confined to a closet also! Some, in writing to me, have insisted that the state is "safer" for all if left in the hands of humanists! The humanists who, like Kaufmann, are logical, deny that justice can exist. All too many churchmen are ready to agree; the law and justice are done away with, and we are in an era of grace only (or, the modernists would say, love only). The result is a license to and freedom for injustice.

Moreover, these men in effect deny the sovereignty of lordship of Jesus Christ. The lordship of Christ is not restricted to the church or to the soul of man but is total. It extends to the whole universe, to church, state, school, every institution and calling, to the arts and sciences, and to all things else. God the father, with Christ's resurrection and ascension, has made Him sovereign over all creation and has put all things under His feet (Eph. 1:19-31). It is civil religion to allow the state's claim to sovereignty to stand. It is a return to Caesar worship to give in to the age-old claim to license and accredit the church and to allow Caesar's claim to be lord to stand.

Moreover, the state cannot be the source of law nor of justice. Law is a theological concept; justice has to do with ultimate right and wrong. If we see the sources of law and justice in anything other than the God of Scripture, we thereby confess another god, usually man or the state. The result then is injustice in the sight of God.

When Paul says "there is none righteous, no, not one" (Rom. 3:10) before God, the word *righteous* is in the Greek, *dikaios*, just (before God). Because we are not righteous or just before God, Paul does not thereby abolish justice of the law. Rather, God through Christ by His grace makes us justified before His court and then gives us a new heart to serve Him in righteousness or justice, and holiness. Paul concludes, "Do we then make void the law through faith? God forbid; yea, we establish the law" (Rom. 3:31). Men now love the law (Ps. 119), because it is the law of their Lord and King, His way of life and therefore our own in Him.

When men disregard God's law, they turn their back on justice. All too many who profess to believe the Bible are critical of and hostile to those who fight against abortion. The "pro-life" movement is called by all such persons a "social gospel" effort. The result is an unconcern with God's justice and a preference for the dictates of a humanistic state. Injustice is "vindicated" and defended in the name of the Gospel! Civil religion then triumphs, and it goes under the names of humanism, modernism, and evangelicalism as well as Calvinism. The adherents of civil religion are agreed on the sovereignty or lordship of the state. Injustice for them becomes any insistence on the crown rights of Christ the King as Lord over all men, nations, and the universe. Unless we insist on the priority and sovereignty of Christ as King over every area of life and thought, we enthrone injustice and deny Christ.

The psalmist asks, "Shall the throne of iniquity have fellowship with thee, which frameth mischief by a law?" (Ps. 94:20). The word "mischief" can also be translated as misery. The throne of God cannot be in fellowship with ungodly or non-theistic doctrines of so-called justice. Justice or righteousness is an attribute of God and is revealed in His law-word. When man seeks to establish his own doctrines of justice or of good and evil (Gen. 3:5), he sins, and he produces injustice. He frames, as the psalmist declares, mischief or misery by law. Our present law structure is producing a growing misery and injustice. The more it departs from God's law-word, the more deeply it moves into misery and injustice. "Except the LORD build the house, they labour in vain that build it" (Ps. 127:1).

CHALCEDON REPORT NO. 211
February, 1983
GRAMMAR AND FAITH

In an interesting report on Shammon's theory of information, Jeremy Campbell: *Grammatical Man: Information Entropy, Language and Life*, 1982), we have a return to a medieval definition of the word "Information." In terms of this, information is the form, meaning, or instructive force or character within all things. In terms of this, "nature" is not only matter and energy but also information.

One of the first points of attack this perspective takes is against *Darwinian* evolution (without abandoning evolution), because *information* is an anti-chance concept which recognizes a pattern in all things. It is not our concern here to dwell on the fact that there are very obvious connections between information theory and the ancient Greek doctrine of the idea or form. The theory re-establishes the place of meaning in the world in a particular form but is not thereby Christian.

The theory is important to Christians, however, because of its clear recognition of the place of law and meaning in all things. Of particular importance are the implications of the theory for man and for speech. As Campbell says, "Grammar is an anti-chance device, keeping sentences regular and law-abiding. It is a systematic code applied at the message source" (p. 165). Underneath all languages lie universal abstract principles and rules, and these are "unconscious systems of rules" (p. 172). "Universal grammar is the innate, anti-chance device in the brain which restricts syntax in this way" (p. 177), and "Grammar can be thought of being like Kepler's laws of planetary motion," setting down the constraints which govern language (p. 179).

Let us briefly examine some of the implications of this for Christian thought. In our day, the teaching of grammar is at a low ebb, and we have a nation of functionally illiterate youth. These are products of statist schools which are governed by a humanistic faith and the Darwinian world view. They are thus reared systematically into a religion of chance.

There is, in the faith taught by the state schools, a denial of God and meaning, and an affirmation of chance. The validity of rules is denied, and grammar with it. In fact, the most recent dictionaries in many cases affirm this rejection of grammar and rules. The result has been a growing breakdown of language.

The Christian Schools, on the other hand, begin with a Biblical faith, the triune God as Creator, and a universe of total meaning. They are thus by faith committed to a rejection of meaninglessness. It is natural and necessary for them to stress grammar, because by faith they are dedicated to a world of meaning. We should thus expect that, as their understanding of a faithfulness of the faith grows, Christian Schools will increasingly excel in grammar and all things else. It is the Christian who through Scripture is informed by the word of God, re-formed by Christ, confirmed by the Holy Spirit, and daily formed by the knowledge that this is a universe of total meaning whose Creator and meaning is His Lord. His faith is anti-chance, whereas the faith of the state schools is in chance and meaninglessness.

CHALCEDON REPORT NO. 212
March, 1983
THE FEAR OF FREEDOM

One of the great fears of the twentieth century is of freedom. Freedom is honored in name but not in fact. Modern man today wants what Dr. Elgin Groseclose has so aptly termed the *riskless society*, a society in which failure is impossible, poverty and problems are abolished, and causality and consequences never prevail.

In the trials of Christian Schools and churches at which I am regularly a court witness, I find that implicit in the position of state and federal officials is the belief that the unregulated society is capable of producing only chaos. An imaginary scenario is often cited in conversation about the abuses which could ensue.

What is the answer to that question? Very simply, it is true that abuses can ensue. In one state, where a large number of home schools exist, one family has done little to educate their two children. However, all other home schools are producing superior to very superior students, whereas, given the same number of children in a public school sampling, the results are usually very bad, and the illiteracy rate growing. Likewise, I have encountered weak Christian schools, but, compared to the state schools, the Christian schools are dramatically superior.

Clearly, educational freedom has produced superiority in the Christian schools, whereas regulation has led to inferiority and incompetence in the state schools. Moreover, as the regulations have increased, the quality has decreased.

In striving for a problem-free answer, the statists have relied on regulations, and these have only increased the problems. The same applies to other realms, including the economic.

Recently, as oil prices began to fall, alarm was expressed by one scholar in the press. Failing oil prices would create serious dangers. Automobile manufacturers have borrowed billions of dollars from the banks to retool their plants to produce small, fuel-efficient cars. Now that investment is threatened; it may spell trouble for both the banks and the automobile manufacturers. New companies have arisen to make coal and wood stoves for homes; their future may now be uncertain. Our foreign policy will be affected if, for example, Mexico and Saudi Arabia, to name only two countries, find their oil income cut. The fear was expressed in America's major daily paper that widespread bankruptcies could follow our oil glut and a collapsing oil price, not a stimulus to the economy.

The regulators thus see disaster when prices go up, and disaster when prices go down. In fact, they see only disaster where the free market prevails. Their only confidence is in their own regulations.

They have a religious fear of freedom. A philosophy or faith which sees the state as god will fear any and all diminutions of the state's controlling and regulating power. It will fear freedom as the obvious road to hell.

Those, however, who believe that this is God's creation, and that freedom allows God's ordained laws for every realm to prevail more readily, will welcome freedom and change as necessary to progress and as the surest defense against the tyranny of man.

Where man plays god and seeks to predestine each and every realm in terms of his own counsel and plan, disaster ensues. Man's plan runs counter to God's plan, and only God's order can prevail.

The world is moving into the greatest economic crisis of history. It is a religious crisis, the product of man's efforts to play god and to control all things. For humanistic man, freedom is anathema, because it runs counter to scientific planning and control. The growing crisis is thus a religious one, and we must see it as God's judgment on a false and rival order. The crisis must be seen as good news, as evidence that God is at war, that the wages of sin in any sphere are always death, and that every tower of Babel man erects has a common destiny, disaster and confusion. The Lord is at work; let the people rejoice.

CHALCEDON REPORT NO. 215
June, 1983
SHOULD WE CLEAN UP TELEVISION?

One of the things most of us can agree on is that television is full of programming which is aesthetically and morally on a very low level. The usual targets of the critics of television is the strong emphasis on sex and violence. (One can add to that the increasing vulgarity of television, so that it is painful to watch even momentarily so cheap and degrading a view of man.)

But are the critics right? Is "cleaning up" what television needs? Will we have better television if we eliminate the offensive sex and violence, the profanity, and the vulgarity, or will it not in fact be worse?

Our Lord issued a warning against a false and empty cleansing. To expel one demon without remaking the man means to lay him wide open to seven worse demons (Matt. 12:43-45). Such a false reform leads to turning men into "whited sepulchers" which are the epitome of uncleanness (Matt. 23:27).

If all we do is to "clean up" television and the films, will we not be creating whited sepulchers? This is in fact what will result. We will give a facade to humanism to make it resemble Christian morality. Most television programming and film productions as well give us the "gospel" of humanism. Do we want to put a Christian face on that? Humanism with a facade of Christian morality will be the greatest deception and evil imaginable. Apparently this is what such churchmen want? What we need instead is programming which reveals a Christian world and life view. This means a work of affirmation and reconstruction, an entrance into the arts, not a retreat from them. The image of the Christian as critic is a false one. The true Christian is a builder and a re-creator in Christ our Lord; the Christian's calling is to bring every area of life and thought under the reign of Christ the King.

Should we "clean up" television? Rather, should we not make it our own? Should we not move into it and make it a Christian domain?

CHALCEDON REPORT NO. 216
July, 1983
THE NEW INQUISITION

Our history books are quite extensively the product of humanistic scholarship and reflect an anti-Christian bias. As these historians view the past, they see it as a struggle out of the darkness of Christianity into the light of humanism. Their version of the past is governed by this premise. As a result, we get a twisted version of history.

One example of this is with reference to the Inquisition. We are rarely told that the Inquisition was begun by the Hohenstaufen emperor, Frederick II. While Pope Innocent III played his part in the matter, the legal revolution was Frederick's. The premise of law in Christendom had been that a criminal prosecution required or implied a plaintiff. Without an accuser, there was no trial or judgement. Frederick II introduced the new element: the state as the plaintiff as well as the prosecutor and the judge. By this means, Frederick II moved against dissent.

One civil government after another adopted this procedure and the Inquisition. An advantage to the state in condemning dissenters was that their properties were then seized by the state, which gave incentive to finding men guilty of treason and heresy. To a degree, the church was bribed to be silent or to cooperate in the process by being given something like a tithe of the seized properties. In spite of this, the church often opposed the process. Richard Kieckhefer, in *Repression of Heresy in Medieval Germany* (University of Pennsylvania Press, 1979), showed that Germany had no true Inquisition, and the bishops tended to oppose such activities. The work of the French crown in furthering the Inquisition of the Knights of Templars was in spite of the pope. In Spain, no victim of the Inquisition was allowed to appeal to the pope; the Spanish Inquisition was fully a state operation.

What then was the purpose of the medieval Inquisition? The answer is an obvious and simple one; to stifle dissent and to create a unified and totalitarian civil order. Because most subjects were Catholic, the unity was framed in Catholic terms, but the goal was a unified state in which no dissent could exist. We should remember that sometimes high-ranking and independent-minded churchmen were targets of the Inquisition.

It is important for us to understand this, because we live in the century of the most evil uses of the theory and practice of inquisitions. Frederick II's legal revolution is now a part of the law of all modern states. Agencies of the state now act as the plaintiff against the people, their prosecutors, and their judges. The goal more than ever is uniformity, now in terms of humanism.

The doctrine of public policy holds that nothing contrary to the policy of the state has a right to exist. The U.S. Supreme Court, in the Bob Jones University case, has plainly affirmed this evil doctrine. Step by step, this doctrine will be used to eliminate all right of dissent. Uniformity will be the law.

The legal revolution begun by Frederick II (not a Christian, and probably a secret Moslem, although his ideas were his own) have resulted in Marxist law, National Socialist and Fascist law, and in totalitarian democracy. The difference between the Soviet Union, Nazi Germany, and the United States has been reduced by the U.S. Supreme Court to one of degree, not of kind. Unless Christians work quickly to change this situation by legislation, the days of freedom are numbered.

The New Inquisition of the state and federal governments is now in power. The question which will determine our future is which government we will serve and obey with all our heart, mind, and being, the governments of men who seek to cast off all the restraints of God's rule (Ps. 2), or the government of Jesus Christ, who is King of Kings and Lord of Lords? Only the Lord controls all things, and we have no future apart from Him.

WHAT IS LAW?

Not too many years ago, an American scholar who in his day was regarded as a very great legal mind and authority, wrote an influential book entitled, *The Sanctity of Law: Wherein Does it Consist?* (1972). The author, John W. Burgess, very soon was set aside as a conservative and then as a reactionary, and his once widespread influence faded. In retrospect, perhaps we had better re-classify Burgess as a radical of sorts.

Burgess began his study by citing and then objecting to Sir William Blackstone's definition of law. For Blackstone, law was "the rules of civil conduct prescribed by the supreme power in a state *commanding what is right and prohibiting what is wrong*." For Burgess, this definition "confused" morality (and religion) with law, and "to rid the definition of this embarrassment", he eliminated the last nine words "as not belonging to the etymology of the law." His definition read: "Law is a rule of civil conduct prescribed by the supreme power of a state." It is an exercise of sovereignty. Burgess turned away from a religious, i.e., for him Christian, definition of law to define it historically. Blackstone still saw law as essentially related to revelation, God's law. Subsequently, law was viewed as logic, but Oliver Wendell Holmes, Jr., in *The Common Law* (1881), held, "The life of the law has not been logic: it has been experience." Both Burgess and Holmes were by choice limiting the concept of law to the written laws of nations. The ground of the law could not be moral or religious validity but political legitimacy. The law was valid if it was the instrument of a legitimate sovereign state and enforced by a physical penalty when necessary. Man in his social infancy looked to God for law, but he must now look to his social experience. The triumph of Christianity was for Burgess "a black pall over the entire Content" of Europe. The only advantage of the medieval order was that it prevented anarchy and gave sanctity to law. With the twentieth century, the outworn creeds gave way to a new answer: "It was that the national consciousness of truth and right was the source of law - of sovereignty - in the modern state, and that a genuine *national* consciousness, from the point of view of the sanctity of law, was produced by a conjunction of the geographic and economic entities with the ethical and the political." The one higher step in the growth and the sanctity of the law would be the rise of an international order. The League of Nations did not impress Burgess as that hoped for order.

Thus, for Burgess the voice of the people had become the voice of law and of true sanctity. For him, God was replaced by man and by the state as the true sovereign and the valid source of morality and the law.

Holmes, in an 1885 speech before the Suffolk Bar Association, had seen the law also as the reflection of the people. "What a subject is this in which we are united - this abstraction called the Law, wherein, as a magic mirror, we see reflected, not only our own lives, but the lives of all men that have been! When I think on this majestic theme, my eyes dazzle." In 1897, in a speech at the Boston University School of Law, Holmes called attention to the fact that "The law talks about rights, and duties, and malice, and intent, and negligence, and so forth, and nothing is easier, or, I may say, more common in logical reasoning, than to take these words in their moral sense, at some stage of the argument, and so to drip into fallacy." The language of the law is radically moral; there is more morality in the pages of the law, whether good or bad morality, than in most sermons, but Holmes saw this as a fallacy. He spoke sharply against "the confusion between legal and moral ideas." The forces for him which determine the law are not religion nor logic, but, rightly, social experience and this should not be confused with morality. Laws are historical, not moral, facts, and this for Holmes was as it should be. This represented an evolutionary view of law, an Heglian concept in part, and the religious (i.e., Biblical) aspect was treated as an archaic relic. This was "legal realism." It was in reality a humanistic religious faith which Holmes at times expressed with lyric power and hope, as in his speech to the Harvard Law School Association of New York, February 15, 1913. This strong affirmation of a Darwinian humanism was reprinted by the U.S. Senate, 62nd Congress, 3rd session, as deserving of wider attention.

In such a social order, what does the law then become? If it is separated from justice, what is the function of the law? The term *justice* continues to be used, but the concept has been separated from God and humanized, i.e., made humanistic. It is now *social justice*.

But what then does social justice mean? It means a social order in which the state gives protection and material aid to "the common man," Law and justice thus are separated from God and His revealed law-word and become aspects of the life of the state. Justice is by some scholars related to "human dignity." Man's sense of injustice is "an active, spontaneous source of law," according to Edmond Cahn. Justice is thus related to a sense of security in one's human dignity and status. Law, justice, and power are harnessed to broad social purposes and concerns in order to create a better commonwealth.

Given these humanistic definitions of law and justice, it is not surprising that social orders based on these dogmas, such as Soviet Russia, Red China, and Sweden, have many apologists and defenders in humanistic circles. These social orders exemplify various facets of the humanistic dream.

The God-centered nature of law and justice has ostensibly been eliminated and relegated to the museum of history. The modern state is a humanistic state, and the law is its creation, and justice is what the state does. "Justice" is also the title, although not the nature, of U.S. Supreme Court judges, and other judges in other countries.

This humanistic justice, however, satisfies very few, certainly not those who receive the protection and material aid called "social justice." The major consequence is the corruption of the recipients, their loss of responsibility, and the massive cultivation of envy. Envy is as corrosive a social force as man has ever known. It does to the societal sphere what earthquakes do to the physical. Envy fractures a society and turns it steadily into a hostile and even armed camp. Social classes, races, minorities, and other groups view one another with hatred and suspicion. Envy solves no problems and creates new ones.

The modern state, however, is increasingly prone to legislating envy. Since it derives its law from man, not God, its law and "social justice" become revelations of the nature of man, not God. The law of God is a revelation of the righteousness or justice of God. The Ten Commandments give us in summary form not only God's covenant law for man but a revelation of the righteousness and holiness of God. The law is often prefixed with the words, "Sanctify yourselves therefore, and be ye holy: for I am the LORD your God" (Lev. 20:7). The law governs man, and it reveals God. The law gives to man the way of holiness, because God is holy, and His law is holy. It separates good and evil, and the just and the unjust.

Man, like God, legislates his nature, but man's nature is not justice but sin, a fallen nature, and he legislates his sin. The law thus, as man becomes more and more humanistic, becomes more and more evil. It vindicates homosexuality, and it kills millions of unborn babies. It legislates covetousness, and it enforces legalized theft against every social class. The end of sin is death, and so too the humanistic state is suicidal. In every age, the word of Wisdom stands: "But he that sinneth against me wrongeth his own soul: all they that hate me love death: (Prov. 8:36).

The future of humanistic laws and states is death. "Except the LORD build the house, they labour in vain that build it" (Ps. 127:1).

CHALCEDON REPORT NO. 219
October, 1983
SECULARISM

Discussions of secularism are complicated by the fact that the word has two major meanings. *First*, secular means *lay* as opposed to the *clergy*.

Secular humanism is the religious practice of humanism by laymen. The application of humanism by school teachers, legislators, and judges is secular humanism. Its application in churches by the clergy is clerical humanism.

Our conflict in the courts and in the world at large is with secular humanism. It is the religious force present in newspapers, television, the world of labor and capital, the arts and sciences, and elsewhere as well. Secular humanism is a major and powerful force on every continent and in virtually every nation in the world.

But, *second*, secular means of the world, profane, and not sacred or religious. Secularism in this sense is a matter of recent history, although it has deep roots; only in the modern era has this kind of secularism commanded society.

In earlier eras, all things were seen as religious by Biblical and non-Biblical faiths. The sacred governs the totality of life, and to regard any area of life as secular was profane and evil. St. Paul is clear on this point: "whatsoever is not of faith is sin" (Rom. 14:23). In this sense, to make anything secular is to diminish our view of God and to sin. Since God created all things, governs all things, and sustains all things, to regard anything or any area of life as outside His law-word and government is to be guilty of profanity and to sin. God's rule is total, and to declare anything or any area of life and thought *secular* means that men claim that area as one reserved to human sovereignty and law.

The roots of secularism in this sense go back to neoplatonism at least. Elements of this entered into the church and colored the monastic movement. Successive reforms within the monastic movement placed the monks into the context of the world, however. Late medieval reform movements and mysticism stressed a withdrawal from the world as secular, as did some major strands of Anabaptism.

However, it was only after 1660 and with the rise of Pietism that this movement into secularism began to command Christendom, Catholic and Protestant. The pietists began to withdraw from politics, economics, the arts and sciences, education, intellectual pursuits (even rejecting an emphasis on doctrine as "arid" intellectualism) and to stress pious gush and "spiritual exercises" as the essence as well as the fullness of the faith.

All concerns over political order, social problems, and intellectual pursuits were seen as worldly; all were declared secular by deliberate choice. God was limited to the narrow world of inner experience. As a result, antinomianism triumphed. In the first half of the 18th century, the pastor of the French Church at the Hague, Jacques (or James) Saurin preached powerfully against this trend. By 1800, however, the pietists had so triumphed that Saurin's name in religious encyclopedias is still blackened by their hostility and one of the great theologians of the pulpit goes neglected.

The doctrine of sin was thus radically altered. William Wilberforce, in *A Practical View of the Prevailing Religious System of Professed Christians...*

Contrasted with Real Christianity (1797), wrote: "Sin is considered in Scripture as rebellion against the sovereignty of God, and every different act of it equally violates his law, and if persevered in, disclaims his supremacy" (p. 223). Sin now came to be defined in terms of pietistic spirituality, not the Lord and His word.

Secularism in this second sense limits the realm of God and of the sacred. It surrenders most of the world and life to the devil and reserves only a small corner for God. This kind of secularism began in the church and still prevails in much of the church. The church found the world happy to receive this release from the government of God.

The devotees of this perversion of the faith actually warn Christians against "worldliness", i.e., involvement in politics, art, intellectual and scientific disciplines, and so on. *One* natural consequence of this is antinomianism: God's law *requires* us to act in relationship to the world in terms of God's holy purposes. The law is thus discarded as a lesser and worldly matter. A *second* consequence is a disregard for the Old Testament and a misreading of the New. The prophets are read in abstraction from the controversy with the state or civil government of their day, and in abstraction from the false concepts of economics and justice which the prophets attacked.

To be *profane* is literally to be outside the temple, or outside the faith. Secularism in this second sense places most of the world outside of God's province. We must add, however, that nothing can be nor is more secular, or, *more profane*, than a church or churchmen who places most of the world outside of Christian faith and concern, and outside of the government of God and His World. This is the ultimate profanity, and it is all too common.

CHALCEDON REPORT NO. 220
November, 1983
RELIGION AND CULTURE

In 1959, in *The Calvinistic Concept of Culture*, Henry R. Van Til pointed out that culture is religion externalized. In recent years this fact, once a commonplace recognition of the nature of reality, has given way to a variety of newer doctrines. Marxists have held that economics determines culture; others have located its source in the unconscious, and so on. The Nazis saw the source of culture as race, and, in recent years, liberals have tended to agree. Ethnocentric studies, emphasis on "black" consciousness and black culture, and so on have been forms of genteel racism.

At the same time, a racist denigration of supposedly "white" culture has occurred, as witness the common term WASP, i.e., White Anglo-Saxon Protestant. To begin with, this term shows ignorance of the fact that, the world over, most Protestants are not Anglo-Saxon; they include a few million blacks in the United States, for example, a growing number of

Latins, Orientals, and others, and the world figures are even more impressive.

We can grant that what is called a WASP culture does exist: many who reflect it are Catholics, blacks, and others, and some reflect it better than the old-line so-called WASPS! (Recently, one "WASP" who went to one of the city's best restaurants commented that most of the well-dressed and mannerly people present were blacks!)

Culture is not a product of race, the unconscious, economics, or any such thing. Culture is religion externalized. A vast number of peoples today, black and white, reflect the culture of humanism. Judith Moore, in the September 4, 1983 *Review*, in discussing Rosemary Radford Reuther's *Sexism and God-talk: Toward a Feminist Theology*, gives us an excellent statement of the humanistic faith: "Except in seminaries of Fundamentalist denominations, sin has become synonymous with racism, sexism, elitism, colonialism, ethnocentrism, pollution, violence - every dualism and division. Salvation has become just another way to say 'Freedom Now!' And what is meant by freedom is a cutting loose in the real world, not some transcendent 'up-there' headtrip spiraling out of the here-and-now." This is humanism, a religious faith, and it is one of the two cultural forces at work in the United States and the Western world of our time.

The other is Christianity. If Christianity is not the determiner of culture, then its churches are dead; they are as salt that has lost its savor: "It is thenceforth good for nothing, but to be cast out, and to be trodden under foot of men" (Matt. 5:13). It is horrifying to see great segments of the church insisting that there is no relationship between Christianity and culture. They hold that we must go to the humanists for our culture (and then sit back and criticize it as it pollutes our homes), and to the humanists for our laws. This is worse than surrender: it is suicide.

Henry Van Til said of God that because, "For of Him and through Him and unto Him are all things," God is sovereign in His being and in all His works. It follows thus, "Religion based on divine sovereignty is religion for God's sake. Such a religion is direct, putting man into immediate fellowship with God. It is all-embracing, extending to every phase of human life, not merely to external worship and personal piety" (p. 52). As a result, "a people's religion comes to expression in its culture, and Christians can be satisfied with nothing less than a Christian organization of society" (p. 245).

Beware of those who are satisfied with less!

CHALCEDON REPORT NO. 222
January, 1984
THE NEW IDOLATRY

At the heart of every evil and all sin is false religion. The original and continuing sin of man is set forth in Genesis 3:5, man's desire to be his own god, knowing or determining for himself all good and evil, all law and morality. Because sin has a religious root or foundation, it is especially urgent that we be more alert to false thinking on the religious root or foundation, it is especially urgent that we be more alert to false thinking on the religious scene than anywhere else.

Two areas of such false thinking which are very influential today are current ideas about truth and history which have a strong following in theological circles. The first of these is the concept of history as myth. The adherents of this view see the universe as essentially meaningless and history therefore as devoid of meaning. If meaning exists, it is man-made; man's faith, ultimate concern, or first principles constitutes his myth. Event and interpretation are one, because nothing with meaning exists apart from man. Nietzsche said, "There are no facts, only interpretations," and this is basic to this contemporary theological perspective. The language of Scripture is used, but God is quietly held to be a limiting concept, not a real Person who is Lord over all. Man's "only hope" of freedom for such thinkers is to "recognize ourselves as standing within the myth of history" (W. Taylor Stevenson: *History as Myth*, p. 122, 1969). The goal of such thinkers is to demythologize the Bible and to free man from the idolatry of a mythological objectification of God and history. Such a position is logical if humanism is true, for, if man is god, to believe in the God of Scripture is idolatry.

The second variety of false thinking, very popular in liberal circles of Dutch religious thought, is the hostility to "propositional thinking." Propositional truth is simply the view that God so created the universe that reality can be, within limits, understood by reason under God. Granted that there are non-Christian views of propositional truth and of reason, the fact remains that this concept affirms that reality is not meaningless, lawless, disjointed, and absurd, but rather that it is created by God's design and purpose and is a realm of total meaning. Opposition to rationalism, which exalts man's autonomous mind over God, is necessary, but opposition to reason or to propositional truth is not. Language is propositional, as are words themselves. The attempt of Marcel Duchamp to create a God-free, propositional truth cannot be equated with positivism, as these thinkers claim. Such men deny that what they call a "gaze-on-God" revelation of truth can be found in Scripture; they do insist on presenting a clear vision of God in their theology! This is idolatry. Supposedly, to insist on propositional truth is to turn the church from a convicted, heartfelt knowledge of Jesus Christ to an intellectual assent. By seeing a distinction between heart-knowledge and head-knowledge, these men are falling into an ancient and Greek mode of dialectical thought.

By separating propositional truth from the Bible and limiting it to a heart-knowledge, they are also limiting God and His word. The Bible is clear that it is not Scripture which is clouded and limited, but our understanding, our being. Sin clouds and blinds us so that the perspicuity of Scripture eludes us. The answer is not to limit God in His word but to limit our sin and pride by repentance. To call the "theory of knowledge and truth yoked to the Word of God" unchristian and pharisaic is amazing blindness. It says, let God and His word be limited, and man free!

Not surprisingly, these enemies of propositional truth are hostile to theonomy, but not to man's word and law. They construct authoritative theological edifices on the basis of some special word which God has communicated to them through a Bible that speaks a la Barth apart from its plainly written text. The result is idolatry.

Given these and other like evils in theological circles, should we be surprised at what nonsense politics, economics, and science produce?

CHALCEDON REPORT NO. 223
February, 1984
COVERT THEONOMISTS

One of the amusing facts I frequently encounter is the fact that many who are very much opposed to theonomy are in fact ready to insist on the validity of God's law -- when it suits them!

Thus, a law I find strictly enforced in many churches where the pastor rails against theonomy is Deuteronomy 22:5. "The woman shall not wear that which pertaineth unto a man, neither shall a man put on a woman's garment: for all that do are abomination unto the LORD thy God." The law is not repeated in the New Testament and thus it does not meet the "test" of the antinomians that only laws repeated in the New Testament are binding on Christians.

The law against bestiality (Ex. 22:19, Lev. 18:23) is not repeated in the New Testament. Why then is it observed? It is clearly a "civil" as well as "moral" law. For that matter, if any civil law is immoral, it surely cannot be law in God's sight. The distinction between civil and moral law is not Biblical.

Homosexuality is clearly condemned in both Old and New Testaments. Homosexuals declare that such texts are now invalid because grace supposedly invalidates the law.

The point by now is clear. The opponents of theonomy affirm law after law in the Old Testament. They are at a hundred and one points covert theonomists. Their position is an awkward and untenable one, because, having rejected the law in principle, they sneak it back in piecemeal.

There is, however, another and more serious consideration. Dr. Cornelius Van Til has stated it very simply in declaring that the choice is between theonomy and autonomy. *Theonomy* (*theos*, God; *nomos*, law, the belief in and submission to God's law) cannot be reconciled with *autonomy*, (*auto*, self; *nomos*, law, self-law). Autonomy is the logical development of Genesis 3:5, every man as his own god, choosing, determining or making his own law and deciding what is good and evil for himself. Theonomy and autonomy cannot be reconciled: they represent Christianity versus humanism.

The covert theonomists are actual humanists, because they sit in judgment on God's law and decide which laws are right in their own eyes. Such a position is a surrender of the sovereignty of the triune God.

CHALCEDON REPORT NO. 224
March, 1984
THE MYTH OF NEUTRALITY

One of the most pernicious and evil myths to plague the human race is the myth of neutrality. It is a product of atheism and anti-Christianity, because it presupposes a cosmos of uncreated and meaningless factuality, of brute or meaningless facts. Because every atom and fact of the cosmos is then meaningless and also unrelated to every other fact, all facts are neutral.

The word "neutral" is a curious one. It comes from the Latin "neuter", meaning neither the one nor the other and has original reference to gender, i.e., neither male nor female. It still has that meaning: a neutered man is a eunuch, a castrate.

It now has also the meaning of not taking sides, and, supposedly, the law and the courts are "neutral." This in itself is nonsense. No law is ever neutral. The law is not neutral about theft, assault, murder, rape, or perjury: it is emphatically against these things, or should be. Again, no good court or judge can be neutral about these things without destroying justice.

Moreover, neither the law nor the courts can be neutral with respect to a man charged with any of these crimes, or others. Rather, a good court "suspends judgment" pending the testimony. Neutrality posits an indifference; a suspended judgment means that any conclusion must be preceded by a rigorous examination of evidence.

The myth of neutrality prevents justice because it ascribes to the law and to the courts a character very much in conflict with their very natures. Moreover, it gives to the courts the power to falsify issues, as the United States Supreme Court habitually does. For example, in dealing with educational issues, the Court, which has declared humanism to be a religion, will not acknowledge that humanistic education, i.e., our state educational systems today, is not neutral religiously. Christian Schools are held to be "religious" and "non-neutral," but the humanistic state schools are seen as "neutral."

There is a reason for this willful blindness. To admit that education is inescapably a religious task and is always non-neutral means that state schools violate the First Amendment. They are religious establishments which teach a religion alien to most citizens, and they do so with public funds. Few things in the United States are more in violation of the First Amendment than the public schools. From its inception, the public or state school system has been destructive of civil liberty and, increasingly, of Biblical faith.

For the Court to recognize this fact would require a radical re-direction of life in America. It would, moreover, require a radical change in the Court. The U.S. Supreme Court has become the Sanhedrin, Vatican, or National Council of humanism in America. It is a militant and fanatical agency of humanistic religion, and it uses its power to suppress and punish the rivals of the Federal religion. The sessions of the Court constitute a modern version of "the holy war" against Christendom.

At the same time, the myth of neutrality has been used to castrate theology and the churches. The American Educational Trust of Washington, D.C. recently published an atlas and almanac by John C. Kimball, *The Arabs* 1983. Kimball writes: "Muslims have always believed strongly that religion concerns not only what a person believes but what he does and the interrelationships of society. Unlike Christian thought that sees a clear distinction between the secular and religious dimensions of life, Muslim thought holds that ideally the secular and spiritual belong to the same sphere." (p. 5) This, of course, is the Biblical position, that all things are under God's law and rule, and any division of life between the religious and the non-religious is false. Because God is the Lord and Creator of all things, there is no sphere of life and thought outside his jurisdiction, government, and law. To hold that there is means to deny God and to affirm polytheism. And this is precisely what all too many theologians have done. The resurgence of Islam is due to the revival of this premise.

The myth of neutrality is most congenial to man's fallen nature. Dr. Cornelius Van Til has pointed out that, if there were one button in all the universe, which, if man pushed, would give him a small realm of experience outside of God and in freedom from God, fallen man would always have his finger on that button.

The tragic fact is that all too many churchmen assume the existence of such a button! They hold that most of life is outside God's law, and even deny the validity of God's law. They believe in effect that man must be saved in the church but can be unsaved outside of the church, in education, politics, economics, and all things else. They literally posit that most of the world is by nature to be and to remain a godless realm.

The Gilgamesh epic of the Babylonians held that only a small area of life is the concern of men, who are inescapably ignorant of good and evil because the gods "withheld in their own hands "knowledge of most things. This was clearly an expression of religious cynicism. Modern theology goes further: it sees God as unconcerned about most of life, and limits the province of the sacred to a small realm. In Babylon, the laws of "justice" came from the king, not the gods. In modern Western civilization, the laws of "justice" come from man, from the state: Babylon the Great is in process of construction.

Philip Lee Ralph, in *The Renaissance in Perspective* (1973), said: "Together with other thinkers of the age, Erasmus, More, and Machiavelli shared a conviction that, without any change in human nature or any drastic altering of institutions, the political order could be made to serve desirable human ends" (p. 75f.). In other words, the whole world is outside of God and neutral to Him, and therefore the good society can be created outside of God's salvation and His law-word and in indifference to Him. In the United States, this is the assumption of every State of the Union presidential address, and it is everywhere the premise of modern politics. By beginning with the premise that there are neutral spheres outside of God, man ends up by declaring God out of bounds as a concern to men. We are told that it is a matter of neutrality whether or not men believe or disbelieve in God and His law. In all such thinking, man is operating on the assumption that, by pushing this intellectual button of neutrality, the claims of God are eliminated and disappear.

The fact is, however, that God controls all the buttons! And His verdict on the myth of neutrality and all its adherents can only be judgment.

CHALCEDON REPORT NO. 225
April, 1984
A CHRISTIAN MANIFESTO

1. Sovereignty is an attribute of God alone, not of man nor the state. God alone is Lord or Sovereign over all things; over state, school, family, vocations, society and all things else.
2. The Bible is given as the common law of men and nations and was for most of U.S. history the common law, as Justice Story declared.
3. Salvation is not by politics, education, the church, or any agency or person other than Jesus Christ our Lord.
4. The myth of Machiavelli, that, by state control at the top, bad men can make a good society is at the root of our cultural crisis and growing collapse. A good omelet cannot be made with bad eggs. Truly redeemed men are necessary for a good society.
5. Civil rulers who rule without the Lord and His law word are, as Augustine said, no different than a mafia, only more powerful.
6. The state is not the government, but one form of government among many, others being the self-government of the Christian man, the family, the school, the church, vocations and society. The state is civil government, a ministry of justice.

7. For the state to equate itself with government is tyranny and evil.
8. The Christian man is the only truly free man in all the world, and he is called to exercise dominion over all the earth.
9. Humanism is the way of death and is the essence of original sin, or man trying to be his own god.
10. All men, things, and institutions must serve God, or be judged by Him.

IS WEALTH MORAL?

Much current writing infers that Jesus and the bible speak against wealth as immoral. It is true that the Parable of the Rich Man (Luke 16:19-31) shows us the rich man in hell and poor Lazarus in heaven, *but* the condemnation of the unjust rich man comes from rich Abraham in heaven. Again, while Jesus said, "It is easier for a camel to go through a needle's eye than for a rich man to enter the kingdom of heaven" (Mark 10:25; Matthew 19:24), the same chapter makes clear that Jesus meant that no man, rich or poor, can save himself: "With men this is impossible, but with God all things are possible" (Matt. 19:26). In other words, salvation is not a do-it-yourself job for anyone, rich or poor; it is God's work and gift. Many rich men and women were among the saved ones close to Jesus (Luke 8:2-3; 19:1-9; 23:50-53).

The Bible condemns fraudulently gained wealth but declares honest wealth a blessing. First, therefore, honest wealth is to be desired or *a blessing from God*. "The blessing of the LORD, it maketh rich (i.e., materially wealthy) and he addeth no sorrow to it" (Proverbs 10:22). The possession of wealth is *lawful* and is *protected* in the Ten Commandments by two commandments: "Thou shalt not steal" and "Thou shalt not covet" (Ex. 20:15,17; Deut. 5:19, 21). Jesus confirmed this, and assumed the lawfulness of wealth as a godly principle (Matt. 25:14-30; Luke 19:12-27; 16:1-8). Jesus made clear that morally acquired wealth is a blessing from and under God. "*Seek ye first the kingdom of heaven and all these things shall be added unto you*" (Matt. 6:32f., Luke 12:30f.), and there is no wrong in desiring it, if we move in terms of the priority of faith in, and obedience to, God.

Second, wealth is morally good, but it is a subordinate good, a means to a better life and not an end. It is too uncertain to be the goal of life (Matt. 6:19f.), and wealth can co-exist with poverty of soul (Luke 12:16-21; 14:18f.; Matt 22:6f.). Thus wealth has moral perils when it becomes primary rather than secondary in a man's life. It is not money which is the root of all evil, but "the love of money", and the coveting after money with this perverted love is cited as a sin by Paul (I Timothy 6:10). Socialists can be as guilty of this "love of money" as anyone else. Thus, riches, wealth, can be dangerous *if* men make them the goal of life, if they idolize wealth.

The evil, then, is not in wealth as such, but in the hearts of men, and to speak of wealth as immoral is a false *logic*, an insistence that things are immoral rather than man. But, as Paul wrote Titus: "Unto the pure all things are pure: but unto them that are defiled and unbelieving is nothing pure; but even their mind and conscience is defiled" (Titus 1:15). Thus, although immoral men can acquire and misuse wealth, it is their hearts and actions which are immoral, not wealth in itself. In its proper place, therefore, wealth is not only moral but also blessed, and it can be honestly desired, gained and held, and is a benefit to all of society.

CHALCEDON REPORT NO. 227
June, 1984
POSTMILLENNIALISM VERSUS EVOLUTION

Recently a very fine television preacher who should know better dismissed postmillennialism as a product of a Darwinian and evolutionary perspective, and he also equated it with the social gospel. This falsehood has been so often repeated that few stop to consider how obviously false it is.

First of all, postmillennialism long pre-dates Darwin and was an important force in the age of discovery and exploration. Hakluyt's *Voyages* tell us plainly how many of the navigators and explorers were governed by this faith. It was also a part of the Reformation, was shared by many of the Westminister Assembly divines, and it appears in the Larger Catechism. Darwinism came very much later, and, in fact, undermined the post-millennial position.

Second, the reason why evolution undermined the prevailing post-millennial perspective was because it replaced the world of God's total providence with Darwin's world of total chance. Postmillennialism stresses the reality of Romans 8:28 that God makes all things work together for good for them who love Him, for all who are called according to His purpose. The world is God's creation and moves to fulfill His goals. Evolution sees the universe as "red in tooth and claw;" if anything develops, it is by chance or accident. Chance replaces predestination, and total meaninglessness replaces God's total meaning. The churches which accepted Darwin dropped postmillennialism.

Third, because with Darwin the world was now without meaning, and because there was no God with His government and meaning, the believers in evolution replaced God and His providence with the state and the social gospel. The social gospel is the antithesis of postmillennialism. It sees the state as the only true providence of man, whereas the rise of postmillennialism in every era has meant a renewed awareness of the providence of God.

To equate evolutionary faith with postmillennialism is like identifying good and evil. It involves a radical confusion of meaning, and it reduces history and logic to nonsense.

As creationism has revived, so too has postmillennialism because the more closely God's creating hand and government are linked to this world, the more men will understand the force of Romans 8:28, and the more literally they will take such promises as Isaiah 60:12, "For the nation and kingdom that will not serve thee shall perish; yea, those nations shall be utterly wasted." The Scripture declares of our Lord, "He shall have dominion also from sea to sea, and from the river unto the ends of the earth" (Ps. 72:8). This is postmillennialism, not Darwinism!

Postmillennialism believes that the God who created heaven and earth cannot be defeated, either by man or by Satan. His declared purpose from the beginning to the end shall be accomplished, and nothing can stay His hand. "All the ends of the world shall remember and turn unto the LORD; and all the kindreds of the nations shall worship before Thee. For the kingdom is the LORD's and he is the governor among the nations" (Ps. 22:27-28). "Yea, all kings shall fall down before Him; all nations shall serve Him" (Ps. 72:11). Can a Christian believe anything less? Ours is the God of victory and salvation.

THE MARXIST SEPARATION OF CHURCH AND STATE

An understanding of the Marxist doctrine of the separation of church and state is urgently necessary, because there is a growing confusion between the Marxist view and the earlier American position.

In the Marxist world, as in the Soviet Union, the separation of church and state means that the church must be totally separated from every area of life and thought. It cannot be allowed to educate or to influence education, let alone the state. Because children are seen as the property of the state, the church cannot influence or teach children. In all spheres, the church is isolated from the world and life of its times and is required to be irrelevant and impotent. In the Marxist view, the separation of church and state is a major legal handicap and penalty imposed upon the church. It is in effect a separation from relevance, the power to influence, and the freedom to function.

In the historic American view, the First Amendment places all the restrictions upon the federal government, which is barred from establishing, governing, controlling, or regulating the church. The Marxist view handcuffs the church; the American view handcuffs the state.

In recent years, the states, Congress, the courts, and the various presidents have in varying degrees manifested an adherence to the Marxist view. Even as the statist power has encroached on every other sphere of society, so now it is encroaching on the church. It is assured that the state has total jurisdiction over every sphere, and the courts in recent years have ruled on such absurdities as school dress codes, and the length of a boy's hair. No concern is too trifling to be overlooked by the courts in their zeal for totalitarian jurisdiction. Without being Marxist, they share in the Marxist belief in total state jurisdiction. Predictably, they are moving in the same direction.

This should not surprise us. Given the humanistic belief in man or the state as ultimate, any freedom or power claimed by the church is seen as irrelevant or wrong. The humanist is being faithful to his faith, to his presuppositions.

The sad fact is that too many churchmen share the Marxist view. For them, the separation of church and state means that the church must never involve itself with anything which is of political concern. I am regularly told by readers of pastors and church leaders who will not permit mention of abortion, homosexuality, euthanasia, or any like subject from the pulpit or even on church premises. Such matters, they insist are now "political" and "violate" the separation of church and state. They claim the name of orthodoxy for their confusion, cowardice and heresy.

The prophets, God's preachers of old, were commanded by the Lord to make God's law-word concerning all things and to correct and rebuke kings and governors. When our Lord promises His disciples that they shall be brought before governors and kings for His sake, and "for a testimony against them" (Matt. 10:18), He did not mean that they were then to forswear the faith, wink at abortion and homosexuality, and be silent about the sins of the state!

There are no limits to the area of God's government, law, and sovereign sway. There can then be no limits to the areas of the church's witness, its preaching, and its commanded concern.

CHALCEDON REPORT NO. 228
July, 1984
THE "RIGHT" TO ABORTION

In recent years, in one country after another, state courts have granted to individuals so desiring it the "right" to practice abortion medically or to abort one's own child. The rhetoric of pro-abortion forces has strongly emphasized the aspect of personal choice and personal liberty. This note has greatly appealed to libertarians also, who have therefore readily echoed the pro-abortion language of "liberals" and leftists. Some conservatives too have been agreeable to abortion on the same premise, that personal choice is the higher good, whatever else may be in consideration.

Ironically, this assumption is a particularly vulnerable one. Abortion strikes at the Christian premise that God's law-word alone sets the rules whereby life can be taken, and abortion has no place in the law of God. The most obvious fact about abortion is that it is a "personal choice and freedom" established by statist courts or by acts of statist legislators.

The state, by granting to individuals the "right" of abortion, and the "right" to euthanasia or "mercy killings," is thereby asserting the prior "right" of the state over both God and man to take human life. Instead of conferring a new freedom on man, the state is taking away freedom from man. The life of man under God is sacrosanct from conception until death. Man can only take human life under very restricted circumstances, essentially for capital crimes as specified by God's law, in self-defense, and in warfare. Wherever the state or man goes beyond God's law, it establishes a man or the state as lord or sovereign over life. The right to exist then becomes a grant from the state, which has then also the "right" to kill man at will.

Marxist states have been ready to grant the "right" to abortion *when they choose*, but all the while have maintained for themselves the "right" to take human life whenever it serves the purposes of the state. Socialism and slave labor and death camps have become synonymous.

To allow to the state one iota of power not permitted by God's law is to diminish man's freedom under God. To permit the state to legitimate abortion is to grant to the state the power to take over lives at the will of the state. Abortion decisions and laws have done two things: *first*, they have made legal the "right" of persons to kill human life. *Second*, the state now has a freedom from God's law to take human life at will.

Every power the state gains it uses. As a result, we have now a *third* factor, as Dr. Charles Rice, a professor of law, has pointed out: the state now, according to the courts, can define what constitutes a person. The definition of a person is no longer theological or even medical: it is civil and legal. We can be declared non-persons by the state or its courts and denied life.

The "right" of abortion thus does not expand personal choice or freedom: it severely restricts it because it establishes the prior "right" of the state to permit or to deny the right to life at will. Such a step, the legalization of abortion, is the beginning of the death of freedom and of man.

CHALCEDON REPORT NO. 229
August, 1984
THE LUST FOR INSTANT GRATIFICATION

Forty years ago, as a missionary on an isolated Indian Reservation, I was quickly impressed by two things. *First*, the Indians had a high order of intelligence and ability; in aptitudes, they had a superior potential. *Second*, in performance, they were inferior, and, in fact, at the bottom level economically in the U.S., and also in other areas ranked very low.

I noticed too that I never heard a crying Indian baby or child. Whatever sign the baby made of unhappiness led to immediate gratification. In talking with missionaries from a variety of foreign fields, among so-called primitives, a like pattern was presented in these places also, I was told.

I recognized soon that Biblical faith creates a radically different pattern of life. *First*, our lives must then be God-centered: "Man's chief end is to glorify God, and to enjoy Him forever," as the Shorter Catechism declares. This militates against self-gratification. *Second*, to affirm that the final and full reckoning for all men is beyond time and history in heaven and hell is to declare that our hunger for righteousness or justice, as well as for blessings and rewards, can never have its fullness in this world. It will, however, finally have perfect fulfillment. This postponement of gratification imposes a discipline upon all of us. It also creates a different frame of reference for child-rearing.

What once marked the so-called primitive cultures now marks the Western World. We have seen the child-centered society create a student generation in revolt, demanding instant gratification in politics, economics, sex, and in drugs. That temper has also created an aborting society: no problems or inconvenience now, only sudden death for the disruptive unborn child.

In a generation which lusts for instant gratification, there are no solutions to problems, only executions. The demand for gratification now denies the validity of time and growth, and therefore of history. It copes with problems by revolution, by the mass murders of all whom it blames for the problems. The doctrine of heaven and hell affirms the reality of history and development.

The lust for instant gratification is a child of Rousseau and a father to revolution. It is ultimately an indictment of God for requiring man to suffer and to grow. More than two centuries ago, Thomas Boston, in *Human Nature in its Fourfold State*, called attention to the foolish belief of some that they could "leap out of Delilah's lap into Abraham's bosom." The premise behind this, he held, was "a shelter to wickedness of heart and life."

The only real fulfillment of the lust for instant gratification is in personal and social suicide, because it is in its essence sin from start to finish.

CHALCEDON REPORT NO. 230
September, 1984
THE "RIGHT TO PRIVACY" AND THE "RIGHT" TO SIN

In an excellent study, Prof. Charles Rice analyzes *Legalizing Homosexual Conduct: The Role of the Supreme Court in the Gay Rights Movement* (Center for Judicial Studies, Cumberland, Virginia 23040). The U.S. Supreme Court has been using the Bill of Rights to accomplish what it was designed to prevent by reading, as Justice Douglas insisted, "penumbras, formed by emanations," into its guarantees. Among other things, these "penumbras" and "emanations" limit the freedom of Christians while increasing that of homosexuals.

In everyday thought, "the right of privacy" has become the freedom to sin.

Although in every other area, federal power has become more intrusive into the life of the churches, all kinds of schools, the family, business, and more; the courts have been drawing a strict wall of separation and protection around sin.

Ideas formulated at the top have a habit of percolating into the streets, closets, and bedrooms. As Richard Weaver insisted, ideas have consequences.

To illustrate: an attractive young woman, in her early twenties, was in bed with her lover when her husband came home unexpectedly. Since the couple was engaged in something other than spiritual exercises, the angry husband, made stronger by righteous wrath, beat up on the adulterer and threw him out of the house, tossing his clothes after him.

Meanwhile, the young wife called the police. When they arrived, she demanded that her husband be arrested, on the ground that he had violated her "right to privacy." The laughing policeman told her that no such charge could be filed, and they left, to her indignation. What, she asked her sister later, is this world coming to?

Strange or unusual? No. The high priests of humanism, the justices of the U.S. Supreme Court, are making new laws based upon their own religion, humanism. The angry young wife was simply anticipating the logical development of her "right to privacy."

This same "right" is invoked to defend abortion, homosexuality, and more. It is the key point in the breaching of the Bill of Rights to replace it with the freedom for men to sin, while the Federal Government assumes vast controls over every other area of life.

The "right to privacy" is thus the basic premise of the freedom to sin, and of our growing totalitarianism. For the substantive freedoms of the Bill of Rights, the degenerative freedom to disrupt the family and sexual order has been substituted.

CHALCEDON REPORT NO. 234
January, 1985
THE NEW POWER IN THE "CHRISTIAN RIGHT"

The most important and virtually unknown story behind the U.S. presidential election of 1984 has not been told. According to one pollster, the Moral Majority was responsible for 20% of the vote. The pollsters, however, lump a variety of Christian groups, some almost unknown but powerful, under the name of the Moral Majority. That organization has served an invaluable purpose, among other things, in drawing the fire of the liberals, and Falwell has been able to defuse the attacks with wit and grace. But Moral Majority has no grass roots, precinct-walking organization, but rather a national voice.

The unknown power was made up of great numbers of young men in their late thirties and early forties, and some younger. These men were campus radicals and leaders in the 1960s and early 1970s, ex-feminists and ex-Trotskyites. They learned political action in confrontations, demonstrations, riots, flag burnings, and more. In the process, they came to realize that the humanistic state, instead of being the voice of Reason and the Good, is an evil monster. Out of this disillusionment, many became Christians: fundamentalists, charismatics in great number, Calvinists, reconstructionists, and so on. With the 1984 election, they returned to political activism as Christians.

In 1976, about 20% of the electorate called itself conservative. The number of dedicated liberals were far fewer. Elections were won or lost in one campaign after another by the ability of one group or another to command the pragmatic majority. This pragmatic majority has voted in terms of their pocketbook: does the economy "feel good," and will a particular party do the least to rock the boat? In 1984, about 40% of the electorate, on pragmatic grounds, spoke of themselves as "conservative," still not enough to elect a man. However, between 15 to 20 million voters were brought into the picture by the so-called "Christian Right." This was apparently the margin of victory.

In this victory, these young ex-Marxists turned Christian played a major role. They had previously scored on the congressional level. In 1984, many of the new congressional victors campaigned as Christians.

Since the election, these young activists have been meeting all over the United States to organize for 1986, as well as to work on the state and local levels at once.

Add to this another factor, the pro-life people, who worked hard on the precinct level, wore out shoe leather, and came to the conviction that education and protests are not enough. Organized political action is necessary.

The president's re-election was thus the surface froth on a new and strong movement which is determined to re-shape the United States on Christian premises. It is principled, and it is future and action oriented. It has escaped notice because of its elusive nature. These ex-campus radicals turned Christians are no longer amateurs!

CHALCEDON REPORT NO. 237
April, 1985
THE TEN FUNDAMENTALS OF MODERN STATISM

1. The first duty of every state is to protect the state, not the people.
2. Other states are occasional enemies; the people are the continual enemies.
3. The purpose of taxation is confiscation, control, the redistribution of wealth, control, the support of civil government, and control.
4. All steps to increase state power must be done in the name of The

People, but the people are to used and stripped of freedom in the process.
5. Freedom is dangerous, controls are good.
6. Freedom must be redefined; it is the right to be morally loose and irresponsible, but Christian morality is social slavery.
7. Children are the property of the state.
8. The two great sources of evil are the church and the family.
9. The only world is the world; there is no God, no heaven, nor hell.
10. Anything the state operates or does is good, in any and all spheres, education, war, peace, spending, and so on. What is "public" or statist is good; what is "private" is bad.

TRUSTING GOD

One of the amazing facts about most church members is their implicit atheism. They believe that all things in this world are stronger than God, and that God's word is least to be trusted. For example, God says, in Isaiah 41:10, "Fear thou not, for I am with thee: be not dismayed: for I am thy God: I will strengthen thee; yea, I will help thee; yea, I will uphold thee with the right hand of my righteousness." We are plainly told that God is our defender, and that He will never leave us nor forsake us (Heb. 12:5-6). God does not promise us an easy life, but He does assure us of a justified and victorious life. He upholds us with His "righteousness." The word in Hebrew is *tsedeq*: it means justice, and it has a legal connotation, but most translations give us a watered down reading.

We trust so many idiocies, including ourselves. Why not take God at His word and trust Him? If we do not believe that God is true to His word, how can we believe that God will be true to us who distrust Him? One of the church's greatest sins is its refusal to trust in the Lord. How can God honor such a people?

CHALCEDON REPORT NO. 241
August, 1985
COMMUNITY AND STRENGTH

Because man is a creature, he cannot stand alone. Neither economically nor socially, can man be a hermit without a serious loss of his function and development. Communion and community are essential to man's growth. It is thus all important to make sure that our community is not a harmful or empty one, and that our communion is not in trifles.

Man's being requires communion and community with the Creator, the triune God. As St. Augustine said, "Our hearts are restless till they rest in Thee." Man's strength is a result of his relationship to God.

Modern man, however, has only a slight relationship to God. His "Christianity" is by and large a matter of fire and life insurance, not a community of life with God. Men today relate more readily to their fellow men, and they are far more dependent on this community than on God. They are more concerned about what other people think of them that what God thinks of them.

All this has consequences. We have seen, in many hijackings and kidnappings, the victims identify with their captors against their own family or country. They may be brutalized by their captors, in one case raped, and yet they will side with them in all too many cases.

This should not surprise us. If men do not have an overruling and governing communion with God, they must have, and will have, such a relationship with men. In our humanistic age, men draw their standards and laws from men, and therefore their basic community and communion is with men. It is only such people who can be "brainwashed;" in truth, "brainwashing" is a myth. It simply means that men without faith are dependent on and vulnerable to men and will be shaped by them. If the Lord does not mold us, then men will.

Communion and community with the triune God is established through Jesus Christ and His atonement. The day by day means of community is maintained by obedience to God's law word, His way for our life in communion. If we follow man's law as our way of life, it is because our community is with men.

This is not to deny for a moment that community with our fellow men is essential, but not on humanistic grounds. We have today a major communications gap among peoples, problems between the generations, the social classes, within the family, between employers and employees, and so on. If men are not at peace with God, they cannot be at peace with one another. The loss of faith in the triune God is followed by a loss of community among men. The rise of antinomianism is a symptom of a changed centrality in the lives of men: man's word and law have replaced God's. The "virtues" of too many churchmen are what James Saurin two centuries or more ago called negative virtues, i.e., abstaining from evil, when we are required also to manifest positive virtues. Moreover, Saurin spoke out against "mutilated virtues." ie., a selective obedience to God and His law where we think He is 'worth obeying' and a neglect of other commandments. True virtue he saw as "connected by the bonds of obedience to the will of God."

Our Lord said, "My meat (i.e., my strength) is to do the will of Him that sent me, and to finish His work" (John 4:34). If Christ's strength came from full obedience, will not our strength and communion come the same way also?